SEVENTH EDITION

HUMAN RESOURCE MANAGEMENT

Gary Dessler

Florida International University

PRENTICE HALL Upper Saddle River, New Jersey 07458

Acquisitions Editor: Natalie Anderson
Development Editor: Elisa Adams
Associate Editor: Lisamarie Brassini
Editorial Assistant: Crissy Statuto
Editor-in-Chief: James Boyd
Director of Development: Steve Deitmer
Marketing Manager: Sandra Steiner
Production Editor: Cynthia Regan
Production Coordinator: David Cotugno
Managing Editor: Carol Burgett
Manufacturing Supervisor: Arnold Vila
Design Director: Patricia Wosczyk
Interior and Cover Design: Ann France
Composition/Illustration: Clarinda Complete Prepress Services
Cover Art/Photo: Susan Le Van

Copyright © 1997, 1994, 1991, 1988, 1984 by Prentice-Hall, Inc.
A Simon & Schuster Company
Upper Saddle River, New Jersey 07458

Library of Congress Cataloging-in-Publication Data

Dessler, Gary.
    Human resource management / Gary Dessler. — 7th ed.
      p. cm.
    Includes bibliographical references and index.
    ISBN 0-13-234352-5
    1. Personnel management. I. Title.
HF5549.D4379 1997
658.3—dc20

96-8622
CIP

Prentice-Hall International (UK) Limited, London
Prentice-Hall of Australia Pty. Limited, Sydney
Prentice-Hall Canada, Inc., Toronto
Prentice-Hall Hispanoamericana, S.A., Mexico
Prentice-Hall of India Private Limited, New Delhi
Prentice-Hall of Japan, Inc., Tokyo
Simon & Schuster Asia Pte. Ltd., Singapore
Editora Prentice-Hall do Brasil, Ltda., Rio de Janeiro

Printed in the United States of America

10 9 8 7 6

Dedicated to my son, Derek

◆

Photo Credits

Brief Contents

Table of Contents

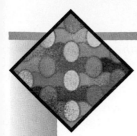

Preface

*H*uman Resource Management provides students in human resource/ personnel management courses and practicing managers with a complete, comprehensive review of essential personnel management concepts and techniques in a highly readable and understandable form.

This Seventh Edition has several distinguishing characteristics. While it again focuses almost entirely on essential personnel management topics like job analysis, testing, compensation, and appraisal, *fostering employee commitment* is used as an integrating theme. Practical applications—such as how to appraise performance, how to establish pay plans, and how to handle grievances—are used throughout to provide students with important personnel management skills. Because all managers have personnel-related responsibilities, *Human Resource Management* is aimed at all students of management, not just those who will some day carry the title Human Resource Manager. The legal environment of personnel management—equal employment, labor relations, and occupational safety—is covered fully. A complete instructor's manual and computerized test bank are available, as is a computer simulation package and several other supplements (described below). A continuing case that runs through each chapter provides vignettes that illustrate the front-line supervisor's role in personnel management.

As this Seventh Edition goes to press, I feel even more strongly than I did when the first edition was published that all managers—not just human resource/personnel managers—need a strong foundation in personnel management concepts and techniques to do their jobs. I have, therefore, increased the practical techniques contained in this book by adding more "how-to" topics such as how to deal with substance abusers and how to avoid wrongful dismissal charges.

The Revision

In revising this textbook, I of course wanted to update the chapters and include the changes emphasized by reviewers while definitely ensuring that the switch by adopters from the 6th to the 7th edition would be virtually seamless and hassle-free.

There are *eight major changes,* and these were made in such a way that adopters will find it very easy to accommodate them:

1. Chapter 1 now contains an *expanded discussion of the strategic role of HRM,* one that builds considerably on the relatively light strategic coverage in the 6th edition's Chapter 1.

2. Instead of a final appendix on International HRM, adopters that want heavier coverage of international HRM will find a *complete new international HR chapter* that builds on that appendix at the end of the book, although most chapters also contain global features that highlight that chapter's applicability in a global arena.

3. I consolidated the 6th edition's Chapters 15 (Labor Relations) and 16 (Collective Bargaining) into *one Labor Relations and Collective Bargaining chapter;* adopters familiar with edition 6 and its predecessors will find the essence of each of the two earlier chapters in the new Labor Relations and Collective Bargaining chapter along with much of the familiar text material and examples.

4. A major addition is the inclusion in most chapters of *"Diversity Counts"* boxes, each of which shows the practical aspects of applying that chapter's material to the issue of managing diversity at work.

5. A new box on *"Information Technology and HR"* emphasizes topics such as using the Internet to recruit employees and using CD-roms in training.

6. A new theme on *"HR and the Responsive Organization"* addresses how today's businesses respond rapidly and effectively to the need for organizational change. For example, see Chapter 12's feature on broadbanding.

7. The new *"Take It to the Net"* Web exercises bring the technology of the 21st century into your classroom today. Each chapter ends with the address of the 7th edition's own Web page—*http://www.prenhall.com/~dessler.* A visit to this address will pull up current examples with the Internet-based exercises and questions.

8. Visit our unique PHLIP (Prentice Hall Learning on the Internet Partnership) Web Site at *http://www.marist.phlip.edu* for links to "Management Web Site of the Week" and other HRM-related materials. This site has been developed by professors, for professors and students.

Several other relatively significant improvements are worth noting:

◆ Each chapter now contains many new end-of-chapter discussion questions and group or individual exercises, at least 8-10 questions and exercises total.

◆ There is now an ABC video case with questions (and accompanying video) at the end of each chapter.

New to This Edition

Here is a brief summary of some of the new or expanded material in each chapter.

Chapter 1: **Introduction:** Expanded emphasis on strategic role of HRM.

Chapter 2: **EEO:** New coverage of diversity management programs, arbitration of EEO claims, and enforcing EEO abroad. Expanded coverage of sexual harassment case law, what is sexual harassment?, ADA, and employer's responsibility for sexual harassment by customers.

Chapter 3: **Job Analysis:** New material on job analysis in a "jobless" world and in "boundaryless" organizations, and new material on job analysis and reengineering and on HR and the responsive organization. Expanded coverage of job descriptions and ADA.

Chapter 4: **Recruitment and Placement:** New material on "diversity counts," recruiting single parents, and using the Internet for recruiting, and for finding a job. Expanded coverage on succession planning, contingency workers, recruiting minorities and women, and computerized data bases and the Internet in recruiting.

Chapter 5: **Testing:** Expanded coverage of negligent hiring, paper-and-pencil honesty tests, drug screening, and reference checking and defamation.

Chapter 6: **Interviewing:** This chapter was substantially reorganized in order to emphasize the interview's important role in selection and in HR in general and to include the latest research findings and thinking regarding selection interviews. New material on computerized selection interviews, and expanded coverage of structured interviews, problems that can undermine selection interviews, and guidelines for conducting good interviews.

Chapter 7: **Training:** New material on using multimedia and CD-roms as well as the Internet for training employees.

Chapter 8: **Development:** New material on building a learning organization and on life-long learning. Expanded coverage of action learning as a development tool.

Chapter 9: **Quality and Productivity:** New material on HR and business process reengineering (how HR makes reengineering successful), on HR's role in winning the Baldrige Award, and on HR and TQM and ISO 9000. New material on HR's role in moving toward empowered jobs. Expanded coverage of extending participative management programs internationally and making self-directed teams more effective.

Chapter 10: **Appraising:** New coverage of computerized performance appraisals, diversity counts in appraisals, bias in appraisals, performance management, 360 degree feedback, TQM-based appraisals, Deming and appraisals, and the legal defensibility of appraisals.

Chapter 11: **Careers:** New coverage of career planning systems, roles in career development, women getting to the top of career ladders, and diversity counts.

Chapter 12: **Pay:** New coverage of broadbanding.

Chapter 13: **Incentives:** Expanded coverage of gainsharing and new coverage of how incentive plans can backfire.

Chapter 14: **Benefits:** New coverage of diversity counts and family-friendly benefits. Expanded coverage of the Family and Medical Leave Act, health care coalitions, and portability.

Chapter 15: **Labor:** This chapter consolidates the essential materials from the 6th edition's Chapters 15 (Labor Relations) and 16 (Collective Bargaining) and adds new coverage of unionizing tactics, unions overseas, and unions' "inside games."

Chapter 16: **Guaranteed Fair Treatment:** New material on electronic eavesdropping and trespassing, employee privacy, and downsizing and morale. Expanded coverage of avoiding wrongful discharge suits and discipline guidelines.

Chapter 17: **Safety:** New coverage of diversity counts, workplace violence and women, and the causes and remedies of violence at work in general. Expanded coverage of OSHA and the small business, of how making firms more flat and responsive impacts safety and health, and of how to reduce job stress. New coverage of gender and job stress, as well.

Chapter 18: **International HR:** New full chapter on international HRM with coverage of the nature of international business, how intercultural differences impact HR, improving international assignments with HR, selecting international managers, adaptability screening, international compensation, and international performance appraisal and labor relations.

HRM Simulation

This end-of-chapter material provides a direct tie-in with Prentice Hall's computerized *HRM Simulation* by Smith and Gorden.

Global HRM

In addition to international applications illustrations in many chapters, there is a comprehensive chapter on HR management in an international business: This covers topics such as international aspects of human resource selection, training, and compensation management, as well as managing intercountry differences in personnel-related laws and requirements.

Small Business Applications

At least two-thirds of the jobs opening up any year in the United States are in small businesses. In addition, many students will end up running their own businesses. A continuing feature of this edition is, therefore, the inclusion of a number of concrete, practical small-business applications that show how smaller businesses with limited resources and limited time can implement improved human resource management procedures. In Chapter 3, for instance, you'll find an example of how to use the widely available *Dictionary of Occupational Titles* to do a job analysis, complete with special client-tested forms. Other examples include procedures for setting up a training program in a small business, incentive hints for smaller employers, and developing a workable pay plan for smaller businesses.

Quality Improvements in Service Organizations

The Seventh Edition contains increased coverage of quality management and total quality management programs, and of the human resource manager's role in setting up and running quality improvement programs.

ABC News/Prentice Hall Videos

To underscore the practical, real-world orientation of this book, we include a customized video library available for class use. Taken from such ABC news shows as *World News Tonight* and *Business World,* and from *Wall Street Week in Review,* these videos deal with relevant topics such as occupational safety, worker pensions, and team training. Each and every chapter has an end-of-chapter case keyed to these videos, which you may use to focus and summarize the chapters in each part of the book.

Acknowledgments

While I am of course solely responsible for the contents in *Human Resource Management,* I want to thank several people for their professional assistance. This includes the following reviewers: Charles Vance, Loyola Marymount University; Kathleen Ganley, Robert Morris College; Fraya Wagner, Eastern Michigan University; Ellen Ernst Kossek, Michigan State University; Kenneth York, Oakland University; and Peggy Anderson, University of Wisconsin—Whitewater.

I would also like to thank Jay Hochstetler, Indiana Wesleyan University; Thomas Lloyd, Westmoreland County Community College; and Lucinda Gatch for their work on the supplementary package under the direction of Lisamarie Brassini.

At Prentice Hall I am very grateful for the support and dedicated efforts of Natalie Anderson, as well as Cynthia Regan, Steven Rigolosi, and Elisa Adams in creating this book.

My son Derek has been an enormous source of pride and useful advice about managing people, and my wife, Claudia, has provided moral support and encouragement.

Chapter 1
The Strategic Role of Human Resource Management

Chapter Outline

- ◆ **Human Resource Management at Work**
- ◆ **The Changing Environment of Human Resource Management**
- ◆ **Tomorrow's HR Today**
- ◆ **Strategic Planning and HR Management**

Behavioral Objectives

When you finish studying this chapter, you should be able to:

Answer the question, "What is Human Resource Management?

Discuss the components of the changing environment of Human Resource Management.

Present examples of the new management practices that are changing Human Resource Management.

Describe the nature of strategic planning.

Give examples of Human Resource Management's role as a strategic partner.

Human Resource Management at Work

What Is Human Resource Management?

To understand what human resource management is, we should first review what managers do. Most experts agree that there are five basic functions all managers perform: planning, organizing, staffing, leading, and controlling. In total, these functions represent the **management process**. Some of the specific activities involved in each function include:

> *Planning:* Establishing goals and standards; developing rules and procedures; developing plans and forecasting—predicting or projecting some future occurrence.
>
> *Organizing:* Giving each subordinate a specific task; establishing departments; delegating authority to subordinates; establishing channels of authority and communication; coordinating the work of subordinates.
>
> *Staffing:* Deciding what type of people should be hired; recruiting prospective employees; selecting employees; setting performance standards; compensating employees; evaluating performance; counseling employees; training and developing employees.
>
> *Leading:* Getting others to get the job done; maintaining morale; motivating subordinates.
>
> *Controlling:* Setting standards such as sales quotas, quality standards, or production levels; checking to see how actual performance compares with these standards; taking corrective action as needed.

In this book, we are going to focus on one of these functions: the *staffing, personnel management,* or (as it's usually called today) *human resource (HR) management* function. **Human resource management** refers to the practices and policies you need to carry out the people or personnel aspects of your management job. These include:

> *Conducting job analyses* (determining the nature of each employee's job)
>
> *Planning labor needs* and *recruiting* job candidates
>
> *Selecting* job candidates
>
> *Orienting* and *training* new employees
>
> *Managing Wages and Salaries* (how to compensate employees)
>
> *Providing incentives and benefits*
>
> *Appraising performance*
>
> *Communicating* (interviewing, counseling, disciplining)
>
> *Training and developing*
>
> *Building employee commitment*
>
> And what a manager should know about:
>
> Equal opportunity and affirmative action
>
> Employee health and safety
>
> Grievances and labor relations

Why Is HR Management Important to All Managers?

Why are these concepts and techniques important to all managers? Perhaps it's easier to answer this by listing some of the personnel mistakes you don't want to make while managing. For example, you don't want:

To hire the wrong person for the job

To experience high turnover

To find your people not doing their best

To waste time with useless interviews

To have your company taken to court because of your discriminatory actions

To have your company cited under federal occupational safety laws for unsafe practices

To have some of your employees think their salaries are unfair and inequitable relative to others in the organization

To allow a lack of training to undermine your department's effectiveness

To commit any unfair labor practices

Many studies have shown that people are more committed to their jobs when their participation is valued and encouraged. Here, a group of assembly-line workers in a Tokyo Nissan factory participate in a worker productivity session attended by managers and supervisors.

Carefully studying this book can help you avoid mistakes like these. More important, it can help ensure that you get results—through others. Remember that you could do everything else right as a manager—lay brilliant plans, draw clear organization charts, set up modern assembly lines, and use sophisticated accounting controls—but still fail as a manager (by hiring the wrong people or by not motivating subordinates, for instance). On the other hand, many managers—whether presidents, generals, governors, or supervisors—have been successful even with inadequate plans, organization, or controls. They were successful because they had the knack for hiring the right people for the right jobs and motivating, appraising, and developing them. Remember as you read this book that getting results is the bottom line of managing and that, as a manager, you will have to get these results through people. As one company president summed up:

> For many years it has been said that capital is the bottleneck for a developing industry. I don't think this any longer holds true. I think it's the work force and the company's inability to recruit and maintain a good work force that does constitute the bottleneck for production. I don't know of any major project backed by good ideas, vigor, and enthusiasm that has been stopped by a shortage of cash. I do know of industries whose growth has been partly stopped or hampered because they can't maintain an efficient and enthusiastic labor force, and I think this will hold true even more in the future. . . .[1]

At no time in our history has that statement been more true than it is today. As we'll see in a moment, intensified global competition, deregulation, and technical advances have triggered an avalanche of change, one that many firms have not survived. In this environment, the future belongs to those managers who can best manage change; but to manage change they must have committed employees who do their jobs as if they own the company. In this book we'll see that human resource management practices and policies can play a crucial role in fostering such employee commitment and in enabling the firm to better respond to change.

Line and Staff Aspects of HRM

All managers are, in a sense, HR managers, since they all get involved in activities like recruiting, interviewing, selecting, and training. Yet most firms also have a human resource department with its own human resource manager. How do the duties of this HR manager and his or her staff relate to "line" managers' human resource duties? Let's answer this question, starting with a short definition of *line* versus *staff* authority.

Line Versus Staff Authority

authority
The right to make decisions, direct others' work, and give orders.

line manager
A manager who is authorized to direct the work of subordinates and responsible for accomplishing the organization's goals.

staff manager
A manager who assists and advises line managers.

Authority is the right to make decisions, to direct the work of others, and to give orders. In management, we usually distinguish between line authority and staff authority.

Line managers are authorized to direct the work of subordinates—they're always someone's boss. In addition, line managers are in charge of accomplishing the organization's basic goals. (Hotel managers and the managers for production and sales are generally *line managers,* for example. They have direct responsibility for accomplishing the organization's basic goals. They also have the authority to direct the work of their subordinates.) **Staff managers**, on the other hand, are authorized to *assist* and *advise* line managers in accomplishing these basic goals. HR managers are generally *staff managers.* They are responsible for advising line managers (like those for production and sales) in areas like recruiting, hiring, and compensation.

Line Managers' Human Resource Management Responsibilities

According to one expert, "The direct handling of people is, and always has been, an integral part of every line manager's responsibility, from president down to the lowest-level supervisor."[2]

For example, one major company outlines its line supervisors' responsibilities for effective human resource management under the following general headings:

1. *Placing* the right person on the right job
2. *Starting* new employees in the organization (orientation)
3. *Training* employees for jobs that are new to them
4. *Improving the job performance* of each person
5. *Gaining creative cooperation* and developing smooth working relationships
6. *Interpreting* the company's policies and procedures
7. *Controlling labor costs*
8. *Developing* the abilities of each person
9. *Creating and maintaining departmental morale*
10. *Protecting* employees' health and physical condition

In small organizations, line managers may carry out all these personnel duties unassisted. But as the organization grows, they need the assistance, specialized knowledge, and advice of a separate human resource staff.[3]

Human Resource Department's HR Management Responsibilities

The human resource department provides this specialized assistance.[4] In doing so, the HR manager carries out three distinct functions:

implied authority
The authority exerted by a personnel manager by virtue of others' knowledge that he or she has access to top management (in areas like testing and affirmative action).

1. *A line function.* First, the HR manager performs a *line* function by directing the activities of the people in his or her own department and in service areas (like the plant cafeteria). In other words, he or she exerts *line authority* within the personnel department. HR managers are also likely to exert **implied authority.** This is so because line managers know the HR manager often has access to top management in personnel areas like testing and affirmative action. As a result, HR managers' "suggestions" are often viewed as "orders from topside." This implied authority carries even more weight with supervisors troubled with human resource/personnel problems.

4

functional control
The authority exerted by an HR manager as coordinator of personnel activities.

staff (service) function
The function of an HR manager in assisting and advising line management.

2. *A coordinative function.* HR managers also function as coordinators of personnel activities, a duty often referred to as **functional control.** Here the HR manager and department act as "the right arm of the top executive to assure him [or her] that HR objectives, policies, and procedures (concerning, for example, occupational safety and health) which have been approved and adopted are being consistently carried out by line managers."[5]

3. *Staff (service) functions.* Serving and assisting line managers is the "bread and butter" of the HR manager's job. For example, HR assists in the hiring, training, evaluating, rewarding, counseling, promoting, and firing of employees. It also administers the various benefit programs (health and accident insurance, retirement, vacation, and so on). It assists line managers in their attempts to comply with equal employment and occupational safety laws. And it plays an important role with respect to grievances and labor relations.[6] As part of these service activities, the HR managers (and department) also carry out an "innovator" role by providing "up to date information on current trends and new methods of solving problems."[7] For example, there is much interest today in instituting reengineering programs and in providing career planning for employees. HR managers stay on top of such trends and help their organizations implement the required programs.

A summary of the HR positions you might find in a large company is presented in the organization chart in Figure 1.1. As you can see, HR positions include compensation and benefits manager, employment and recruiting supervisor, training specialist, employee relations executive, safety supervisor, and industrial nurse. Examples of job duties include:

Recruiters: Maintain contact within the community and perhaps travel extensively to search for qualified job applicants.

Equal Employment Opportunity (EEO) Representatives or Affirmative Action Coordinators: Investigate and resolve EEO grievances, examine organizational practices for potential violations, and compile and submit EEO reports.

Job Analysts: Collect and examine detailed information about job duties to prepare job descriptions.

Compensation Managers: Develop compensation plans and handle the employee benefits program.

Training Specialists: Responsible for planning, organizing, and directing training activities.

Labor Relations Specialists: Advise management on all aspects of union-management relations.[8]

Cooperative Line and Staff Human Resource Management: An Example

Exactly which HR management activities are carried out by line managers and staff managers? There's no single division of line and staff responsibilities that could be applied across the board in all organizations. But to show you what such a division might look like, we've presented an example in Figure 1.2.[9] This shows some HR responsibilities of line managers and staff managers in five areas: *recruitment and selection; training and development; compensation; labor relations;* and *employee security and safety.*

For example, in the area of *recruiting and hiring* it's the line manager's responsibility to specify the qualifications employees need to fill specific positions. Then the HR staff takes over. They develop sources of qualified applicants and conduct initial screening interviews. They administer the appropriate tests. Then they refer the best applicants to the supervisor (line manager), who interviews and selects the ones he or she wants.

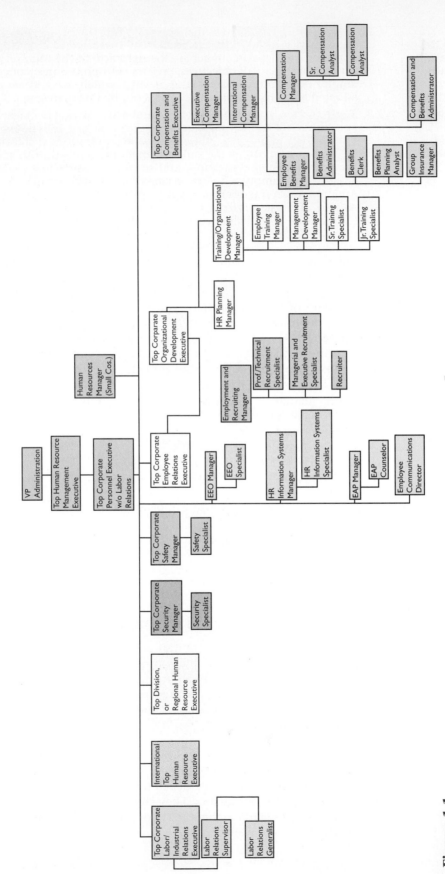

6

Figure 1.1
Positions Often Found Within a Large Personnel/Human Resource Department

Source: Adapted from Bureau of National Affairs, *Datagraph,* July 27, 1995, pp. 236–237.

Figure 1.2
Selected Activities
Illustrating Division of
HR Responsibility
Between Line and
Staff

	DEPARTMENT SUPERVISORS' (LINE) ACTIVITIES	PERSONNEL SPECIALISTS' (STAFF) ACTIVITIES
I Recruitment and Selection	Assist job analyst by listing specific duties and responsibilities of the job in question Explain to HR future staffing needs and sorts of people needed to be hired. Describe "human requirements" of job so HR can develop selection tests. Interview candidates and make final selection decisions.	Write job description and job specification based on input from department supervisor. Develop personnel plans showing promotable employees. Develop sources of qualified applicants and engage in recruiting activities aimed at developing a pool of qualified applicants. Conduct initial screening interviews and refer feasible candidates to department supervisor.
II Training and Development	Orient employees regarding the company and job, and instruct and train new employees. Evaluate and recommend managers for developmental activities. Provide the leadership and empowerment that builds effective work teams. Use the firm's appraisal forms to appraise employee performance. Assess subordinates' career progress and advise them regarding career options.	Prepare training materials and orientation documents and outlines. Advise CEO regarding development plan for managers based on CEO's stated vision of firm's future needs. Serve as resource for providing information regarding how to institute and operate quality improvement programs and team-building efforts. Develop performance appraisal tools and maintain records of appraisals.
III Compensation	Assist HR by providing information regarding the nature and relative worth of each job, to serve as the basis for compensation decisions. Decide on the nature and amounts of incentives to be paid to subordinates. Decide on the package of benefits and services the firm is to pay.	Conduct job evaluation procedures aimed at determining relative worth of each job in the firm. Conduct salary surveys to determine how other firms are paying the same or similar positions. Serve as a resource in advising line management regarding financial incentives and pay plan alternatives.

(continued)

Figure 1.2
(continued)

		Develop, in consultation with line management, the firm's benefits and services packages including health care options and pensions.
IV Labor Relations	Establish the day-to-day climate of mutual respect and trust needed to maintain healthy labor-management relations. Consistently apply the terms of the labor agreement. Ensure that the firm's grievance process is functioning in a manner consistent with the labor agreement and make final decisions on grievances after investigating same. Work with HR in negotiating the collective bargaining agreement.	Diagnose underlying causes of labor discontent with an eye toward anticipating the sorts of morale and other problems that may lead to unionization efforts. Train line managers regarding the interpretation of contract terms and the legal pitfalls to be avoided during the union organizing effort. Advise managers regarding how to handle grievances and assist all parties in reaching agreements regarding grievances.
V Employee Security and Safety	Keep the lines of communication open between employees and managers so employees are kept abreast of important company matters and have a variety of vehicles they can use to express concerns and gripes. Make sure employees are guaranteed fair treatment as it relates to discipline, dismissals, and job security. Continually direct employees in the consistent application of safe work habits. Prepare accident reports promptly and accurately.	Advise line management regarding the communication techniques that can be used to encourage upward and downward communication. Develop a guaranteed fair treatment process and train line managers in its use. Analyze jobs to develop safe practice rules and advise on design of safety apparatus such as machinery guards. Promptly investigate accidents, analyze causes, make recommendations for accident prevention, and submit necessary forms to Occupational Safety and Health Administration.

In summary, HR management is an integral part of every manager's job. Whether you're a first-line supervisor, middle manager, or president, whether you're a production manager, sales manager, office manager, hospital administrator, county manager (or HR manager!), getting results through people is the name of the game. And to do this, you'll need a good working knowledge of the human resource/personnel concepts and techniques in this book.

The Changing Environment of Human Resource Management

Changes are occurring today in the environment of human resource management, changes that are requiring it to play an ever more crucial role in organizations. These trends include work force diversity, technological trends, globalization, and changes in the nature of jobs and work.

Work Force Diversity

The composition of the work force will continue to change dramatically in the next ten years; specifically, it will continue to become more diverse as women, minority-group members, and older workers flood the work force.[10] Diversity has been defined as ". . . any attribute that humans are likely to use to tell themselves, 'that person is different from me' " and thus includes such factors as race, sex, age, values, and cultural norms.[11]

For example, women represented 42.1% of the civilian U.S. labor force in 1979 and 45.5% in 1992, and they should represent 47.7% in the year 2005.[12] This means that in roughly the next ten years the number of women in the labor force will jump by about 24%, while the number of men in the labor force will increase more gradually by a total of about 14%.[13] Related to this, about two-thirds of all single mothers (separated, divorced, widowed, or never married) are in the labor force today, as are almost 45% of mothers with children under three years old. The human resource department will increasingly be called upon to help companies accommodate these employees, with new child care and maternity leave provisions, for example, and with basic skills training where such training is required.

Changes in racial composition will be even more dramatic. For example, between 1992 and 2005 people classified as Asian and other (including Native Americans) in the work force will jump by just over 81%, while the number of employees classified as black will rise 25.2%, and those white 15%. In the same period workers classified as white will have declined as a percentage of the civilian labor force from 87.6% in 1979 to 85.5% in 1992 to a projected 82.9% in 2005. The number of Hispanics in the civilian labor force will jump by almost 64% in the next ten years, so that Hispanics will represent 11% of the civilian labor force in 2005, up from 8% in 1992.[14]

The labor force is also getting older. The median age of the labor force in 1979 was 34.7 years. This has risen continuously since then to 37.8 years in 1995, and a projected 40.5 years in 2005.[15] This is due mostly to the aging of the baby boom generation, those born between 1946 and 1964, since baby boomers now comprise just over half the U.S. labor force.[16]

Increased diversity will place tremendous demands on the HR management function.[17] The large number of baby boom women in the labor force who are having babies has already necessitated the implementation of more flexible work scheduling options and called greater attention to promotional opportunities for women. As the work force ages, employers will have to grapple with greater health care costs and higher pension contributions. There will also be a shortage of workers aged 25 to 34, "while the career opportunities in management for workers in the 35 to 44 age cohort may be constrained by the abundance of more experienced members of the 45 to 54 age cohort."[18] With more females in the work force, an upswing in the number of dual-career couples will force more employers to establish child care facilities on or near company premises and to accommodate the travel, scheduling, and moving needs of dual-career employees.

In some respects these are among the more mundane diversity-related demands that HR will have to cope with. Health care and promotional options are probably relatively manageable compared to the tensions and pressures that cultural, attitudinal, and value-based differences can trigger. Diversity training and similar programs aimed at creating a cohesive and collegial work force out of a group of highly diverse individuals are thus increasingly a necessity.

Creating unanimity from a diverse work force may be more of a challenge for HR than it might at first appear. As several experts recently put it, there are ". . . two fundamental and inconsistent realities operating today with regard to diversity. One is that organizations claim they seek to maximize diversity in the work place, and maximize the capabilities of such a diverse workforce. The other is that traditional human resources systems will not allow diversity, only similarity."[19] These experts specifically refer to the fact that employers traditionally hire, appraise, and promote people who fit a particular employer's image of what employees should believe and act like, and there's a corresponding tendency to screen out those who don't "fit."[20] Establishing HR programs that do more than just pay lip service to the goal of diversity may thus be a considerable challenge for many employers.[21]

Technological Trends   Technological change will continue to shift employment from some occupations to others while contributing to a rise in productivity. For example, telecommunications already makes it relatively easy for many to work at home. Computer-aided design/computer-aided manufacturing systems plus robotics will also increase. Thus, General Motors has over 14,000 robots building automobiles (compared to about 1,000 in 1984), and researchers at Carnegie Mellon University estimated that there were between 100,000 and 200,000 robots in the United States in the early 1990s. Manufacturing advances like these will eliminate many blue-collar jobs, replacing them with fewer but more highly skilled jobs. Similar changes are taking place in office automation, where personal computers, word processing, and management information systems continue to change the nature of office work.

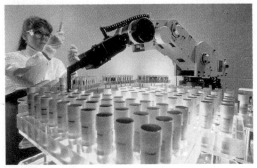

Computer-aided manufacturing processes are revolutionizing work in dozens of industries. These techniques require better trained and more committed employees.

Labor-intensive blue-collar and clerical jobs will decrease while technical, managerial, and professional jobs will increase. Job and organization structures will have to be redesigned, new incentive and compensation plans instituted, new job descriptions written, and new employee selection, evaluation, and training programs instituted—all with the help of HR management.

Technology will also force firms to become more competitive. For example, Inter-Design of Ohio sells plastic clocks, refrigerator magnets, soap dishes, and similar products. Its president explains the impact of information technology—merging communications with computers—this way: "In the seventies we went to the Post Office to pick up our orders. In the early 80s, we put in an 800 number. In the late 80s, we got a fax machine. In 1991, pressured by Target [stores], we added electronic data interchange." Now, just two years later, more than half of Inter-Design's orders arrive via modem, straight into company computers. Errors in order entry and shipping have all but disappeared.[22]

Information technology has also hastened what experts call the "fall of hierarchy;" in other words, managers depend less and less on yesterday's stick-to-the-chain-of-command approach to organizing. For example, with "distributed computing," every employee with a personal computer on his or her desk can tap into the firm's computer network and get needed information. Says one manager at Goodyear Tire and Rubber Company: "It used to be, if you wanted information, you had to go up, over, and down through the organization. Now you just tap in. That's what broke down the hierarchy. It's not why we bought computers, but it's what they did."[23]

HR plays an integral role in any such changes. For example, empowering workers to make more decisions presumes that they are selected, trained, and rewarded to do so.

Globalization

globalization
The tendency of firms to extend their sales or manufacturing to new markets abroad.

Globalization refers to the tendency of firms to extend their sales or manufacturing to new markets abroad, and, for businesses everywhere, the rate of globalization in the past few years has been nothing short of phenomenal.

For U.S. firms, this globalization is manifesting itself in many ways. The value of the U.S. import/export trade grew from 9.4% of the U.S. economy in 1960 to almost 23% in 1991.[24] U.S. exports are reaching new markets, with big gains since 1988 to countries ranging from Uruguay and Mexico to the Netherlands, Hungary, and Kuwait.[25]

Production is becoming globalized, too, as manufacturers around the world put manufacturing facilities where they will be most advantageous. Thus, the Toyota Camry—what many would claim is "obviously" a Japanese car—is produced in Georgetown, Kentucky and contains almost 80% U.S.-made parts. At the same time, the Pontiac LeMans ("obviously" a U.S. car) actually contains almost two-thirds foreign-made parts.[26]

This globalization of markets and manufacturing has vastly increased international competition. Throughout the world, firms that formerly competed only with local firms—from airlines to auto makers to banks—now find that complacency must give way to an onslaught of foreign competitors.

Many firms have responded successfully while others have failed. When Swedish furniture retailer Ikea built its first U.S. furniture superstore in New Jersey, its superior styles and management systems grabbed market share from numerous domestic competitors, driving several out of business.

Such global competition is, of course, a two-way street. Ford and GM have huge market shares in Europe, while IBM, Microsoft, Apple, and countless smaller firms have major market shares around the world. As one international business expert puts it, "the bottom line is that the growing integration of the world economy into a single, huge marketplace is increasing the intensity of competition in a wide range of manufacturing and service industries."[27]

Indeed, more U.S. firms will transfer their operations abroad, not just to seek cheaper labor, but to tap what *Fortune* magazine calls "a vast new supply of skilled labor around the world."[28] Even today, in fact, most multinational firms set up manufacturing plants abroad partly to establish beachheads in promising markets and partly to utilize that country's professionals and engineers. For example, ASEA Brown Boveri (a $30-billion-a-year Swiss/Swedish builder of transportation and electric generation systems) already has 25,000 new employees in former Communist countries and has thus shifted many jobs from Western to Eastern Europe. From tapping the global labor force to formulating selection, training, and compensation policies for expatriate employees, managing globalization will thus be a major HR challenge in the next few years.

Trends in the Nature of Work

Technological and globalization trends are in turn producing changes in the nature of jobs and work. Technological changes including fax machines, information technology, and personal computers have allowed companies to relocate operations to locations with lower wages. For example, Hertz Rent-A-Car's reservation operation is centered in Oklahoma City, while Hyatt Hotel's is in Omaha, Nebraska.[29] There is also a trend toward increased use of part-time and temporary workers. Part-time workers comprised 18.8% of the work force in 1993, up from 15.5% in 1969.[30] However, the most notable trends in the nature of work are the trends to service jobs, and to knowledge work and the stress on human capital.

A Service Society An enormous shift from manufacturing jobs to service jobs is taking place in North America and Western Europe. Today over two-thirds of the U.S. work force is employed in producing and delivering services, not products. In fact, the manufacturing work force declined over 12% during the 1980s. Of the 21 million or so new jobs added to the U.S. economy through the 1990s, virtually all will be in such service industries as fast foods, retailing, consulting, teaching, and legal work. These jobs, in turn, will demand new types of "knowledge" workers and new human resource management methods to manage them.

Knowledge Work and Human Capital Management expert Peter Drucker has said that the typical business will soon bear little resemblance to the typical manufacturing company of 30 years ago. As Drucker predicts it, "the typical business will be knowledge-based, an organization composed largely of specialists who direct and discipline their own performance through organized feedback from colleagues, customers and headquarters. For this reason, it will be what I call an information-based organization."[31] As a result, the distinguishing characteristic of companies today and tomorrow, say many experts, is the growing emphasis on human capital—the knowledge, education, training, skills, and expertise of a firm's workers—at the expense of physical capital like equipment, machinery, and the physical plant.[32]

Fast-food restaurants sell both food and fast service. Because of the intense competition in the fast-food industry, courteous service with a smile is an extremely important ingredient in getting customers to return, and this requires employee commitment.

This growing emphasis on education and human capital reflects several social and economic factors. One is the increase in the service-oriented nature of the U.S. economy. (Service jobs like consulting put a bigger premium on worker education and knowledge than do traditional manufacturing jobs.) Another is the fact that manufacturing jobs are changing, too. Particularly in the United States, manufacturing-intensive jobs in the steel, auto, rubber, and textile industries are being replaced by what one expert calls "knowledge-intensive high tech manufacturing in such industries as aerospace, computers, telecommunications, home electronics, pharmaceuticals, and medical instruments."[33] At the same time, even heavy manufacturing jobs are becoming more high tech: At Alcoa Aluminum's Davenport, Iowa plant, for instance, a computer stands at each workpost to help each employee control his or her machines or communicate data. As *Fortune* magazine recently put it, "practically every package deliverer, bank teller, retail clerk, telephone operator, and bill collector in America works with a computer [today]."[34] Jobs today thus demand a level of expertise far beyond that required of most workers 20 or 30 years ago, so that human capital is quickly replacing machines as the basis for most firms' success.

Furthermore, it is not unusual for more than one-fourth of many firms' sales to come from products less than five years old. As a result, "innovating—creating new products, new services, new ways of turning out goods more cheaply—has become the most urgent concern of corporations everywhere."[35] This means that companies are relying more on employees' creativity and skills, thus placing more stress on the employees' brain power. As *Fortune* magazine recently said:

Brain-Power . . . has never before been so important for business. Every company depends increasingly on knowledge—patents, processes, management skills, technologies, information about customers and suppliers, and old-fashioned experience. Added together, this knowledge is intellectual capital.[36]

For managers, the challenge of fostering intellectual or human capital lies in the fact that such workers must be managed differently than were those of previous generations. As one expert put this, "the center of gravity in employment is moving fast from manual and clerical workers to knowledge workers, who resist the command and control model that business took from the military 100 years ago."[37] Workers like these, in other words, cannot just be ordered around and closely monitored. New human resource management systems and skills will be required to select and train such employees and to win their self-discipline and commitment.

Other Trends Affecting Human Resource Management

Other trends are shaping HR management as well. As we will see in this book, many laws continue to be passed, the effect of which is to limit managers' actions. For example, equal employment opportunity laws bar discrimination on the basis of race, age, disability, religion, sex, or national origin. Virtually all managers are thus now legally bound to uncover and correct instances of discrimination. Mandated health benefits, occupational safety and health requirements, and union-management relations laws are among the other legal constraints managers must deal with, generally with the assistance of HR management.[38]

Similarly, the protection provided by governmental regulation to thousands of businesses in dozens of industries around the world has been stripped away in country after country. In the United States, for instance, a dozen airlines including Eastern, Braniff, and People's Express have either been bought out or gone under as a result of the pressures for better service and lower costs resulting from U.S. airline deregulation in the 1970s. Similarly, bank failures rose from fewer than ten in the 1970s to almost 200 annually in the early 1990s as banking deregulation exposed inefficiencies that less responsive competitors couldn't eliminate in time. The increased competitive intensity puts an added emphasis on the need for human capital and a highly committed work force.

Tomorrow's HR Today

New Management Practices

Trends like globalization and technological innovation are changing the way firms are managed. The basic dimensions of these changes are summarized in Figure 1.3. Organizations today must grapple with revolutionary trends: accelerating product and technological change, globalized competition, deregulation, demographic changes, and trends toward a service society and the information age. These trends have changed the playing field on which firms must compete. In particular, they have dramatically increased the degree of competition in virtually all industries, while forcing firms to cope with unprecedented product innovation and technological change.

In the companies that have successfully responded to these challenges, new modes of organizing and managing have emerged. For example:

The traditional, pyramid-shaped organization is giving way to new organizational forms.[39] At firms like AT&T the new way of organizing stresses cross-functional teams and boosting interdepartmental communications. There is a corresponding

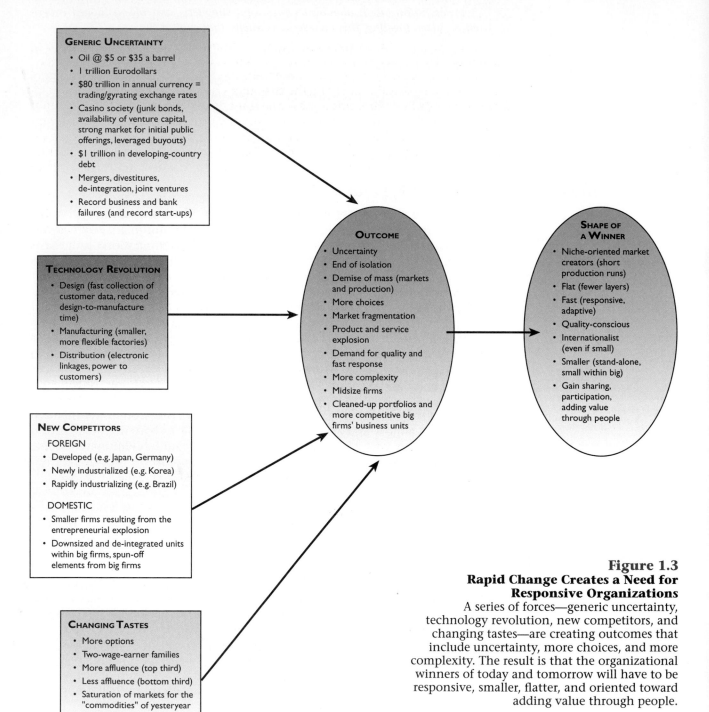

GENERIC UNCERTAINTY

- Oil @ $5 or $35 a barrel
- 1 trillion Eurodollars
- $80 trillion in annual currency = trading/gyrating exchange rates
- Casino society (junk bonds, availability of venture capital, strong market for initial public offerings, leveraged buyouts)
- $1 trillion in developing-country debt
- Mergers, divestitures, de-integration, joint ventures
- Record business and bank failures (and record start-ups)

TECHNOLOGY REVOLUTION

- Design (fast collection of customer data, reduced design-to-manufacture time)
- Manufacturing (smaller, more flexible factories)
- Distribution (electronic linkages, power to customers)

NEW COMPETITORS

FOREIGN

- Developed (e.g. Japan, Germany)
- Newly industrialized (e.g. Korea)
- Rapidly industrializing (e.g. Brazil)

DOMESTIC

- Smaller firms resulting from the entrepreneurial explosion
- Downsized and de-integrated units within big firms, spun-off elements from big firms

CHANGING TASTES

- More options
- Two-wage-earner families
- More affluence (top third)
- Less affluence (bottom third)
- Saturation of markets for the "commodities" of yesteryear
- Demand for superior quality

OUTCOME

- Uncertainty
- End of isolation
- Demise of mass (markets and production)
- More choices
- Market fragmentation
- Product and service explosion
- Demand for quality and fast response
- More complexity
- Midsize firms
- Cleaned-up portfolios and more competitive big firms' business units

SHAPE OF A WINNER

- Niche-oriented market creators (short production runs)
- Flat (fewer layers)
- Fast (responsive, adaptive)
- Quality-conscious
- Internationalist (even if small)
- Smaller (stand-alone, small within big)
- Gain sharing, participation, adding value through people

Figure 1.3
Rapid Change Creates a Need for Responsive Organizations
A series of forces—generic uncertainty, technology revolution, new competitors, and changing tastes—are creating outcomes that include uncertainty, more choices, and more complexity. The result is that the organizational winners of today and tomorrow will have to be responsive, smaller, flatter, and oriented toward adding value through people.

Source: Tom Peters, *Thriving on Chaos* (New York: Harper & Row, 1987), 37.

de-emphasis on "sticking to the chain of command" to get decisions made. At General Electric, Chairman Jack Welch talks of the *boundaryless organization*, in which employees do not identify with separate departments but instead interact with whomever they must to get the job done.

Employees are being empowered to make more and more decisions. Experts argue for *turning the typical organization upside down.* They say today's organization should put the customer on top and emphasize that every move the company makes should be toward satisfying the customer's needs. Management must therefore *empower* its front-line employees—the front desk clerks at the hotel, the cabin attendants on the Delta plane, and the assemblers at Saturn. In other words, employees need the authority to respond quickly to the customer's needs. The main purpose of managers in this "upside down" organization is to serve the front-line employees, to see that they have what they need to do their jobs—and thus to serve the customers.

Flatter organizations are the norm. Instead of the pyramid-shaped organization with its seven to ten or more layers of management, flat organizations with just three or four levels will prevail. Many companies (including AT&T and General Electric) have already cut the management layers from a dozen to six or fewer.[40] As the remaining managers have more people reporting to them, they will be less able to meddle in the work of their subordinates.

Work itself—on the factory floor, in the office, even in the hotel—is increasingly organized around teams and processes rather than specialized functions. On the plant floor, a worker will not just have the job of installing the same door handle over and over again. He or she will belong to a multifunction team, one that manages its own budget and controls the quality of its own work.

The bases of power are changing. In the new organization, says management theorist Rosabeth Moss Kanter, position, title, and authority are no longer adequate tools for managers to rely on to get their jobs done.[41] Instead, "success depends increasingly on tapping into sources of good ideas, on figuring out whose collaboration is needed to act on those ideas, and on working with both to produce results. In short, the new managerial work implies very different ways of obtaining and using power."[42]

Managers will not "manage." Yesterday's manager knew that the president and owners of the firm gave him or her the authority to command and control subordinates. Today most managers realize that reliance on formal authority is increasingly a thing of the past. Peter Drucker says that managers have to learn to manage in situations where they do not have command authority, where "you are neither controlled nor controlling."[43] Yesterday's manager thinks of himself or herself as a "manager" or "boss;" the new manager increasingly thinks of himself or herself as a "sponsor," "team leader," or "internal consultant."

Managers today must build commitment. Building adaptive, customer-responsive organizations means that eliciting employees' commitment and self-control is more important than it has ever been. GE's Jack Welch put it this way: "The only way I see to get more productivity is by getting people involved and excited about their jobs. You can't afford to have anyone walk through a gate of a factory or into an office who is not giving 120%."[44]

The Responsive Organization feature provides an example of how one firm—Asea Brown Boveri—is putting changes like these into practice.

ABB Asea Brown Boveri

Zurich-based electrical equipment maker Asea Brown Boveri (ABB) is one good example of a firm that "dis-organized itself to compete in the fast-moving global market of the next ten years."[45] ABB did four things to make itself superresponsive; it organized around mini-units, empowered its workers; flattened its hierarchy, and eliminated central staff. How did ABB do it?

First, within two years of taking over this $30-billion firm, Chairman Percy Barnevik "de-organized" its 215,000 employees into 5,000 minicompanies, each averaging only about 50 workers each.[46] For example, the ABB hydropower unit in Finland is a highly customer-focused little business, one in which employees' efforts are all centered on its local (Finnish) customers. Each of ABB's 50-person units is run by its own manager and three or four lieutenants. Such small units are very manageable: It's a lot easier to keep track of what everyone is doing when there are only 50 people to keep track of than when there are 1,000, let alone 5,000 or 10,000.

Next, to speed decision making, the 5,000 minicompanies are autonomous and empowered. Their employees have the authority to make most of their own business decisions without checking first with top management.

For example, if a customer has a complaint about a $50,000 machine, a minicompany employee has the authority to approve a replacement on the spot, rather than having to wait for reviews by several levels of management. Giving employees this much authority means, by the way, that ABB's 5,000 businesses must be staffed, as management expert Tom Peters put it, by "high-performance team members," highly skilled employees with the capacity and commitment to make those big decisions.

Next, in a break with most big firms, ABB's 215,000-employee organization has only three management levels (compared to the seven or eight a comparably sized company might have). There is a 13-member top-management executive committee based in Zurich. Below this is a 250-member executive level that includes country managers and executives in charge of groups of businesses. Below this is a third level, consisting of the 5,000 minicompany managers and their management teams. The firm thus flattened the hierarchy or chain of command. By slicing out layers of management and letting lower-level employees make their own on-the-spot decisions, ABB allows its employees to respond more quickly to customers' needs and competitors' moves.

Fourth, since decision making was pushed down to front-line ABB employees, ABB could eliminate most headquarters staff advisers. For example, when Barnevik became CEO in 1980, he found 2,000 people working at headquarters, basically reviewing and analyzing (and slowing down) the decisions of the firm's lower-level employees. Within a few months, Barnevik reduced the staff to 200—and he reduced it even further in later years. As ABB acquired other companies, Barnevik took the same approach. For example, when he acquired Finland's Stromberg Company, he reduced its headquarters staff from 880 to 25. Similarly, he reduced German ABB headquarters in Mannheim from 1,600 to 100.

Responsiveness is the net effect of all this reorganization: a lean, flat organization staffed with highly committed employees who are organized into small, empowered teams, each able to respond quickly to competitors' moves and customers' needs with no need to wait for approval from headquarters. ◆

The Changing Role of HR Management

Not surprisingly, the role of HR management is also changing, to adapt to these trends. In the early 1900s personnel people first took over hiring and firing from supervisors, ran the payroll department, and administered benefit plans. It was a job consisting largely of ensuring that procedures were followed. As technology in such areas as testing and interviewing began to emerge, the personnel department began to play an expanded role in employee selection, training, and promotion.[47]

The continued movement of women into management positions has implications for both career development and recruiting programs.

The emergence of union legislation in the 1930s led to a second phase in personnel management and a new emphasis on protecting the firm in its interaction with unions. The discrimination legislation of the 1960s and 1970s triggered a third phase. Because of the large penalties that lawsuits could bring to a company, effective personnel practices became more important. In this phase (as in phase 2), Personnel continued to provide expertise in areas like recruitment, screening, and training, albeit in a more expanded role. Notice, however, that whether dealing with unions or equal employment, personnel gained status as much for what it could do to protect the organization from problems as for the positive contribution it made to the firm's effectiveness.

Today, personnel is speeding through phase 4, and its role is shifting from protector and screener to planner and change agent. The metamorphosis of *personnel* into *human resource management* reflects the fact that in today's flattened, downsized, and responsive organizations, highly trained and committed employees—not machines—are often a firm's best competitive key.

Examples of HR's new role in these modern organizations abound.

HR and Boosting Productivity   Productivity improvement is crucial in today's globally competitive environment, and HR plays a pivotal role in lowering labor costs. In the U.S. government, for example, researchers found that using a personnel screening test to select high-potential computer programmers could produce savings of millions of dollars per year. For many firms, instituting tough headcount controls is the first line of attack on lowering labor costs; the HR department generally plays the central role in planning and implementing corporate downsizings like those at IBM and Citicorp and then taking steps to maintain the morale of the remaining employees. At employers like pharmaceuticals firm Merck & Company, HR helps employees adapt to the increased pressures in their downsized departments by helping them learn to prioritize tasks and reduce job stress.[48]

HR and Responsiveness   Making the enterprise more responsive to product innovations and technological change is the basic aim of many of the management changes listed previously. Thus, downsizing, flattening the pyramid, empowering employees, and organizing around teams are aimed at facilitating communications and making it easier for decisions to be made and for the company to respond quickly to its customers' needs and its competitors' challenges.

HR plays a crucial role in accomplishing this. At Levi Strauss, HR helped create the firm's new team-based alternative manufacturing system: This ties employees' compensation incentives to team goals and, along with Levi's new flexible-hours program, helps inject more flexibility into the firm's production process.[49] We'll see many other examples throughout this book of how HR practices can help to boost a firm's responsiveness.

HR and Service   Employee behavior is particularly important in service firms like banks and retail establishments. If a customer is confronted by a salesperson who is tactless or unprepared to discuss the pros and cons of the different products or (even worse) downright discourteous, all the firm's other efforts will have been wasted. Service organizations have little to sell but their good service, and that makes them uniquely dependent on their employees' attitudes and motivation—and on HR management.

Therefore, HR plays a crucial role in service companies.[50] It has been noted, for instance, that there are "quite a few [employees] who lack the temperament, maturity, social skills, and tolerance for frequent contact" that customer service jobs require, and that the first step in avoiding this problem is screening and selection.[51] A recent study of service firms illustrates the HR-service link. The researchers found that progressive HR practices such as facilitating employees' career progress, developing orientation/training/socialization programs for new employees, and eliminating conditions on the job that inhibit task performance appear to improve employees' customer service as well as the overall quality of that service from the customers' point of view.[52] The philosophy behind this idea is probably best summed up by Fred Smith, the chairman and founder of Federal Express, whose philosophy is "people–service–profits." In other words, use progressive HR practices to build employee commitment and morale; employees will then provide excellent customer service, which in turn will generate profits.

HR and Employee Commitment   Intense global competition and the need for more responsiveness put a premium on employee commitment. As the vice president of human resources at Toyota Motor Manufacturing in Georgetown, Kentucky put it:

> *People are behind our success. Machines don't have new ideas, solve problems, or grasp opportunities. Only people who are involved and thinking can make a difference. . . Every auto plant in the U.S. has basically the same machinery. But how people are utilized and involved varies widely from one company to another. The workforce gives any company its true competitive edge.*[53]

Building employee commitment—creating a synthesis of employees' and employer's goals so that employees want to do their jobs as if they own the company—takes a multipronged effort, one in which HR plays the central role. For example, two-way communications foster commitment, and firms like Federal Express and Toyota have long had programs that guarantee two-way communications and fair treatment of all employees' grievances and disciplinary matters. High-commitment firms also tend to engage in *actualizing* practices, which aim to ensure their employees have every opportunity to fully use all their skills and gifts at work and become all they can be. HR practices are crucial here, for instance, in establishing career-oriented performance appraisal procedures and open job-posting and job transfer practices. Convincing employees that the company and all its managers care about them is important, too. Therefore high-commitment companies like Federal Express are very careful about whom they promote to manager. All aspiring Fed Ex supervisory candidates must take the firm's multistep leadership evaluation program to prove that they have the values and skills to be Fed Ex managers. About 20% fall out after the first phase ("Is Management for Me?"), a one-day session that familiarizes them with the manager's job. This is followed by about three months of both self-assessments and supervisory evaluations of the candidate's

18

values and skills. Management training courses in the firm's leadership institute then use lectures and exercises to reinforce the firm's people-oriented values and indoctrinate the new managers in the values of the firm. We'll discuss many examples in this book of how HR can foster employee commitment.

HR and Corporate Strategy   But perhaps the most striking change in HR's role is its growing importance in developing and implementing strategy. Traditionally strategy—the company's plan for how it will balance its internal strengths and weaknesses with external opportunities and threats in order to maintain a competitive advantage—was a job primarily for the company's operating (line) managers. Thus, Company X's president might decide to enter new markets, drop product lines, or embark on a five-year cost-cutting plan. Then the president would more or less leave the personnel implications of that plan (hiring or firing new workers, hiring outplacement firms for those fired, and so on) to be carried out by HR management.

Today things are different. Strategies increasingly depend on strengthening organizational responsiveness and on building committed work teams, and these put HR in a central role. In a fast-changing, globally competitive and quality-oriented industrial environment, it's often the firm's employees themselves—its human resources—who provide the competitive key. It is thus now increasingly common to involve HR in the earliest stages of developing and implementing the firm's strategic plan, rather than letting HR just react to it. We thus turn next to strategic planning and HR's strategic role.

Strategic Planning and HR Management

The Nature of Strategic Planning

Managers engage in three types of strategic decision making for their firms. Each represents different levels of strategic decision making in an organization.[54] This is summarized in Figure 1.4. Many companies such as PepsiCo consist of several businesses such as Pepsi, Frito-Lay, and Pizza Hut. These companies, therefore, need a corporate-level strategy. A company's corporate-level strategy identifies the portfolio of businesses that, in total, will comprise the organization and the ways in which these businesses will relate to each other.

At the next level down, each of these businesses (such as Pizza Hut) is then guided by a business-level/competitive strategy. A competitive strategy identifies how to build and strengthen the business's long-term competitive position in the

**Figure 1.4
Relationships among Strategies in Multiple-Business Firms**
Companies typically formulate three types of strategies. Corporate strategies identify the mix of businesses the firm will engage in. The business-level/competitive strategies identify how each of the firm's businesses will compete; and each business then has several functional strategies identifying how the unit's manufacturing, sales, and other functions will contribute to the business strategy.

Source: James M. Higgins and Julian W. Vincze, *Strategic Management Text and Cases,* 5th ed. (Fort Worth: The Dryden Press, 1991), p. 263.

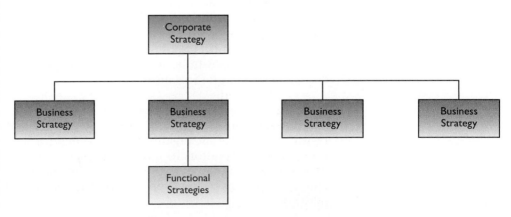

marketplace.[55] It identifies, for instance, how Pizza Hut will compete with Dominos, or how Wal-Mart will compete with K Mart.

Finally, each business will in turn be comprised of departments, such as manufacturing, sales, and human resource management. Functional strategies identify the basic courses of action that each of the business's departments will pursue in order to help the business attain its competitive goals.

While companies pursue three types of strategies, the term *strategic planning* is usually reserved for the company's corporate-level, organizationwide strategic planning process. Specifically, strategic planning outlines the type of business the firm will be, given the firm's external opportunities and threats and its internal threats and weaknesses. Deciding whether Mom and Pop's Supermarket will compete with Enormous Markets head-to-head by building similar superstores or instead will continue with small local gourmet markets is a typical strategic planning problem.

In their strategic planning employers like Burger King and others include close monitoring of trends such as the availability of entry-level labor.

The manager's strategic plan will ideally seek to balance two sets of forces: the firm's external opportunities and threats on the one hand, and its internal strengths and weaknesses on the other. For example, in 1995 IBM bought the Lotus software firm, in part to acquire the Lotus Notes networking programs. Sensing the opportunities and threats presented by the Internet's growing popularity and by IBM's relative lack of expertise in networking software, IBM Chairman Louis Gerstner apparently decided to diversify by buying Lotus to position IBM to compete more effectively with other means of linking or networking companies and individuals.

In any case, the three levels of strategic decision making should be interrelated and mutually supportive. For example, let's consider IBM's Lotus acquisition. At the corporate organizationwide level, the acquisition represents an attempt to reposition the giant corporation to compete more effectively in the coming age of networking computers. However, having decided to acquire Lotus, Gerstner then had to make a business-level strategic decision regarding how to organize IBM's new networking business and in particular how to compete with other firms making similar products. In this case John Manzi, the head of Lotus, proposed to Gerstner the merger of Lotus with IBM's other software divisions with Manzi in charge; Gerstner rejected this suggestion, deciding to keep Lotus and its Lotus Notes software separate, and to let Manzi leave the firm.

Corporate and business-level strategic decisions like these in turn help determine what IBM's functional strategies should be. For example, IBM's push into networking has production strategy implications, since it may require phasing out several hardware manufacturing facilities and consolidating the firm's network program design facilities in fewer locations. Similarly, IBM's marketing and sales efforts may have to be increasingly organized around a networking sales effort. The HR function will also have to accomplish its share: There will be facilities to be closed, new ones to be staffed, and new network program designers to be recruited and hired, for instance.[56]

Building Competitive Advantage A firm tries to achieve a competitive advantage for each business it is in. A competitive advantage can be defined as any factors that allow an organization to differentiate its product or service from those of its competitors to increase market share.[57] Similarly, strategic planning expert Michael Porter says that "competitive strategy aims to establish a profitable and sustainable position against the forces that determine industry competition."[58]

20

There are several ways a firm can achieve a competitive advantage. Cost leadership, one competitive strategy, means that the enterprise aims to become *the* low-cost leader in an industry. For example, Wal-Mart is a typical industry cost leader, a competitive advantage due to its unique satellite-based distribution system, and the fact that it generally keeps store location costs to a minimum by placing stores on low-cost land outside small to medium-sized southern towns.

Differentiation is a second competitive strategy. In a differentiation strategy, a firm seeks to be unique in its industry along dimensions that are widely valued by buyers.[59] Thus, Volvo stresses the safety of its cars, Apple stresses the usability of its computers, and Mercedes Benz emphasizes reliability and quality. Like Mercedes Benz, firms can usually charge a premium price if they successfully stake out their claim to being substantially different from their competitors in some coveted way.

Human Resources as a Competitive Advantage   In today's intensely competitive and globalized marketplace, maintaining a competitive advantage by becoming a low-cost leader or a differentiator puts a heavy premium on having a highly committed and competent work force. Low-cost, high-quality cars like those of Toyota and Saturn aren't just a result of sophisticated automated machines. Instead they're a result of intensely committed employees all working hard and with self-discipline to produce the best cars that they can at the lowest possible cost.

Many experts have emphasized the strategic role that committed workers play in helping their firms achieve competitive advantage. For example, strategic planning experts C. K. Prahalad and Gary Hamel say that competitive advantage lies not just in differentiating a product or service or in becoming the low-cost leader but also in being able to tap the company's special skills or *core competencies* and rapidly respond to customers' needs and competitors' moves. In other words, competitive advantage lies ". . . in management's ability to consolidate corporate-wide technologies and production skills into competencies that empower individual businesses to adapt quickly to changing opportunities."[60] As we've seen in this chapter, building in such responsiveness means depending on the commitment and self-discipline of your employees, since they will have to respond faster with more authority and less supervision than employees had to even five or ten years ago. As a result, today it's most often cadres of committed employees who help to distinguish between those firms that succeed and those that don't. As one expert puts it:

> In a growing number of organizations human resources are now viewed as a source of competitive advantage. There is greater recognition that distinctive competencies are obtained through highly developed employee skills, distinctive organizational cultures, management processes, and systems. This is in contrast to the traditional emphasis on transferable resources such as equipment. . . . Increasingly, it is being recognized that competitive advantage can be obtained with a high quality work force that enables organizations to compete on the basis of market responsiveness, product and service quality, differentiated products, and technological innovation . . . .[61]

Strategic Human Resource Management

The fact that employees today are central to achieving competitive advantage has led to the emergence of the field known as strategic human resource management.[62] Strategic human resource management has been defined as ". . . the linking of HRM with strategic goals and objectives in order to improve business performance and develop organizational cultures that foster innovation and flexibility. . . ."[63] Put another way, it is ". . . the pattern of planned human resource deployments and activities intended to enable an organization to achieve its goals."[64] Strategic HR means accepting the HR function as a strategic partner in the formulation of the company's strategies, as well as in the implementation of those strategies through HR activities such as recruiting, selecting, training, and rewarding personnel.

Whereas strategic HR recognizes HR's partnership role in the strategizing process, the term *HR strategies* refers to the specific HR courses of action the company plans to pursue to achieve its aims. Thus, one of Federal Express's primary aims is to achieve superior levels of customer service and high profitability through a highly committed work force. Its overall HR strategy is thus aimed at building a committed work force, preferably in a nonunion environment.[65] The specific components of Fed Ex's HR strategy follow from that basic aim: to use various mechanisms to build healthy two-way communications; to screen out potential managers whose values are not people oriented; to provide highly competitive salaries and pay-for-performance incentives; to guarantee to the greatest extent possible fair treatment and employee security for all employees; and to institute various promotion-from-within activities aimed at giving employees every opportunity to fully utilize their skills and gifts at work. Let's turn now to a closer look at HR's role as a strategic partner.

HR's Role as a Strategic Partner

Personnel/HR's long history as a staff or advisory function has left it with a somewhat impoverished reputation: Some still tend to view it as less than it is. For example, one view is that HR is strictly operational and that HR activities are not strategic at all.[66] According to this line of reasoning, HR activities simply ". . . involve putting out small fires—ensuring that people are paid on the right day; the job advertisement meets the newspaper deadline; a suitable supervisor is recruited for the night shift by the time it goes ahead; and the same manager remembers to observe due process before sacking the new rep who didn't work out."[67]

A more sophisticated (but perhaps no more accurate) view of HR is that its role is simply to "fit" the company's strategy. In this view HR's strategic role is to adapt individual HR practices (recruiting, rewarding, and so on) to fit specific corporate and competitive strategies. By this view, top management crafts a corporate strategy—such as to buy Lotus—and then HR is told to create the HR programs required to successfully implement that corporate strategy.[68] As two strategic planning experts have argued, "the human resources management system must be tailored to the demands of business strategy."[69] The idea here is that "for any particular organizational strategy, there is purportedly a matching human resource strategy."[70]

A third view of HR management is that it is an equal partner in the strategic planning process. By this view HR management's role is not just to tailor its activities to the demands of business strategy, nor, certainly, just to carry out operational day-to-day tasks like ensuring that employees are paid. Instead, by this third view, the need to forge a company's work force into a competitive advantage means that human resource management must be an equal partner in both the formulation and the implementation of the company's organizationwide and competitive strategies.[71]

HR's Role in Formulating Strategy Formulating a company's overall strategic plan requires identifying, analyzing, and balancing two sets of forces: the company's external opportunities and threats on the one hand, and its internal strengths and weaknesses on the other.

This is where strategic HR management comes in. First, HR management can play a role in what strategic planners call *environmental scanning,* in other words, identifying and analyzing external opportunities and threats that may be crucial to the company's success. For example, in 1995 both United Airlines and American Airlines considered and then rejected the opportunity to acquire US Air, a smaller and relatively weak airline. While both American and United had several reasons for rejecting a bid, HR considerations loomed large. Specifically, both American and United had doubts about their abilities to successfully negotiate new labor agreements with US Air's employees, and both felt the problems of assimilating them might be too great.

Similarly, HR management is in a unique position to supply competitive intelligence that may be useful in the strategic planning process. Details regarding advanced incentive plans being used by competitors, opinion survey data from employees that elicit information about customer complaints, and information about pending legislation like labor laws or mandatory health insurance are some examples. Furthermore,

> From public information and legitimate recruiting and interview activities, you ought to be able to construct organization charts, staffing levels and group missions for the various organizational components of each of your major competitors. Your knowledge of how brands are sorted among sales divisions and who reports to whom can give important clues as to a competitor's strategic priorities. You may even know the track record and characteristic behavior of the executives.[72]

HR also participates in the strategy formulation process by supplying information regarding the company's internal strengths and weaknesses. For example, IBM's decision to buy Lotus was probably prompted in part by IBM's conclusion that its own human resources were inadequate to enable the firm to reposition itself as an industry leader in networking systems, or at least to do so quickly enough. Similarly, about two months after Wells Fargo acquired Crocker National [Bank] Corporation, it surveyed 1500 Crocker employees to ensure that Wells Fargo would discover any problems as quickly as possible.

The strengths and weaknesses of a company's human resources can have a determining effect on the viability of the firm's strategic options. For example, "situations where human resource capabilities serve as a driving force in strategy formulation occur where there are unique [human] capabilities. . . ."[73] Here we often find a company building its new strategy around an HR-based competitive advantage. For example, in the process of automating its factories, farm equipment manufacturer John Deere developed a work force that was exceptionally talented and expert in factory automation. This in turn prompted the firm to establish a new-technology division to offer automation services to other companies.[74] As another example, the accounting and consulting firm Arthur Andersen developed unique human resource capabilities in training. The firm's Illinois training facility is so sophisticated that it provides the firm with a competitive advantage, enabling it to provide fast, uniform training in house and so ". . . react quickly to the changing demands of its clients."[75]

HR's Role in Executing Strategy   We've also seen that HR management can play a pivotal role in the successful execution or implementation of a company's strategic plan. For example, Federal Express's competitive strategy is to differentiate itself from its competitors by offering superior customer service and guaranteed on-time deliveries. Since basically the same technologies are available to UPS, DHL, and Fed Ex's other competitors, it's Fed Ex's work force—its human resource—who necessarily provides Fed Ex with a crucial competitive advantage. This puts a premium on the firm's HR processes, as discussed earlier, and on the firm's ability to create a highly committed, competent, and customer-oriented work force.[76]

HR management supports strategic implementation in numerous other ways. For example, HR is today heavily involved in the execution of most firms' downsizing and restructuring strategies, through outplacing employees, instituting pay-for-performance plans, reducing health care costs, and retraining employees. And in an increasingly competitive global marketplace, instituting HR practices that build employee commitment can help improve a firm's responsiveness, as explained earlier.

Examples of HR's Role as a Strategic Partner Firms like Fed Ex, John Deere, Saturn, and Toyota are not the only ones that rely on HR to perform as a strategic partner in the development and execution of their strategic plans. Here are two others.

Colgate-Palmolive Colgate-Palmolive Company is a global manufacturing company with sales of over $5 billion that recently received new "marching orders." After assuming the presidency several years ago, the new CEO developed and communicated a new strategic direction for the company based on what he

To assess the traits on which job success depends, many firms, such as those that rely on its employees' sales skills, administer a computerized skills assessment before hiring.

called his "corporate initiatives."[77] Among other things, the new strategy emphasized concentrating on new products, being the low-cost producer, simplifying businesses and structures, pushing decision making downward, promoting entrepreneurial action, and improving morale and motivation. The new strategy was aimed at making Colgate a leaner, more responsive competitor in its global markets and in focusing the company more clearly on health-related products.

Consistent with this new strategy, several major steps were taken almost at once. Four major businesses were divested, including two sports and recreation companies. A major reorganization took place that eliminated one level of senior management. Additional resources were diverted to new-product development and research and development. And the human resource programs at Colgate-Palmolive got a new mandate to help Colgate achieve its new goals.

The programs laid out for Colgate HRM provide a glimpse of how HRM today is being pressed to get involved in strategic management. At Colgate-Palmolive, HRM was directed by the president to develop and execute programs designed to create a company culture that would achieve the following:

> Encourage a spirit of teamwork and cooperation within and among business units in working toward common objectives, with an emphasis on identifying, acknowledging, and rewarding individual and unit excellence.
>
> Foster entrepreneurial attitudes among the managers and innovative thinking among all employees.
>
> Emphasize the commonality of interest between the employees and shareholders.[78]

To that end, numerous HRM programs had to be designed. For example, the company's executive incentive compensation plan was redesigned to place more emphasis on individual performance and achieving operating targets. Employee benefits were redesigned to make them more flexible and responsive to employees' needs. At the same time, cost controls and employee pay-for-performance plans were instituted, two changes that were accomplished by effectively communicating both the changes and the reasons for them. The bottom line was that by implementing a number of programs (including those aimed at redesigning compensation and benefits), HRM helped refocus Colgate employees' efforts in a manner that contributed to the execution of Colgate's strategic plan.

Tandy Corporation Tandy Corporation is another example of how HR policies are formulated to support company strategy. In the case of this electronics/computer firm, success depends largely on retail sales profitability. In turn, these sales depend on the ability of retail employees, most of whom are selling items (like computers and electronic instruments) that require solid product knowledge and an intelligent sales effort.

At Tandy, therefore, HR policies (regarding selection and compensation, for instance) are aimed at attracting, hiring, and motivating the people required for Tandy's success. For example, Tandy's selection policy emphasizes identifying candidates who will be successful selling Tandy's products, since 80% of the company's employees are in direct sales. To this end, Tandy developed a computerized program to administer a skill assessment profile. This is aimed at determining a candidate's aptitude for activities like qualifying customers, making sales presentations, closing sales, and providing after-sales customer service. Similarly, its training policies emphasize effective sales training, and its compensation policy puts a heavy premium on sales performance: In fact, 75% of the management compensation plans at Tandy, including that of the vice president of human resources, are tied to the company's profits.[79]

The Plan of This Book

This book is built around two themes. First, we assume that HR management is the responsibility of *every* manager—not just those in the human resource department. Throughout this book, you'll therefore find an emphasis on practical material that you as a manager will need in carrying out your day-to-day management responsibilities. The second theme is that HR programs should contribute to winning employee commitment, given the need to build a self-disciplined work force and responsive organization in these fast-changing times. Therefore, you'll find examples of how HR activities can help foster employee commitment throughout this book. Here is a brief overview of the chapters to come:

> *Chapter 2: Equal Opportunity and the Law* What you'll need to know about equal opportunity laws as they relate to human resource management activities such as interviewing, selecting employees, and evaluating performance appraisal.

Part I: Recruitment and Placement

> *Chapter 3: Job Analysis* How to analyze a job; how to determine the human resource requirements of the job, as well as its specific duties and responsibilities.
>
> *Chapter 4: Personnel Planning and Recruiting* Determining what sorts of people need to be hired; recruiting them.
>
> *Chapter 5: Employee Testing and Selection* Techniques like testing you can use to ensure that you're hiring the right people.
>
> *Chapter 6: Interviewing Job Candidates* How to interview candidates to help ensure that you hire the right person for the right job.

Part II: Training and Development

> *Chapter 7: Orientation and Training* Providing the training necessary to ensure that your employees have the knowledge and skills needed to accomplish their tasks.

Chapter 8: Developing Managers Concepts and techniques for developing more capable employees, managers, and organizations.

Chapter 9: Managing Quality and Productivity Techniques such as quality improvement programs and team building that firms use to help them manage quality and productivity.

Chapter 10: Appraising Performance Techniques for appraising performance.

Chapter 11: Managing Careers Techniques such as career planning and promotion from within that firms use to help ensure that employees can achieve their potential.

Part III: Compensation

Chapter 12: Establishing Pay Plans How to develop equitable pay plans for your employees.

Chapter 13: Pay-for-Performance and Financial Incentives Pay-for-performance plans such as financial incentives, merit pay, and incentives that help tie performance to pay.

Chapter 14: Benefits and Services Providing benefits that make it clear the firm views its employees as long-term investments and is concerned with their welfare—such as stock ownership plans, pensions, and above-average health plans.

Part IV: Employee Security and Safety

Chapter 15: Labor Relations and Collective Bargaining Concepts and techniques concerning the relations between unions and management, including the union-organizing campaign; negotiating and agreeing upon a collective bargaining agreement between unions and management; and then managing the agreement via the grievance process.

Chapter 16: Guaranteed Fair Treatment Ensuring floods of two-way communication within the organization, as well as guaranteed fair treatment as it relates to discipline, dismissals, and employee job security.

Chapter 17: Employee Safety and Health The causes of accidents, how to make the workplace safe, and laws governing your responsibilities in regard to employee safety and health.

Chapter 18: Managing Human Resources in an International Arena The growing importance of international business, and HR's role in managing the personnel side of multinational operations.

Chapter Review

Summary

1. There are basic functions all managers perform: planning, organizing, staffing, leading, and controlling. These represent what is often called the *management process*.

2. Staffing, personnel management, or human resource management is the function focused on in this book. It includes activities like recruiting, selecting, training, compensating, appraising, and developing.

3. HR management is very much a part of *every* line manager's responsibilities. These HR responsibilities include placing the right person in the right job, orienting, training, and compensating to improve his or her job performance.

4. The HR manager and his or her department carry out three main functions. First, the manager exerts *line authority* in his or her unit and implied authority elsewhere in the organization. He or she exerts a *coordinative function* to ensure that the organization's HR objectives and policies are coordinated and implemented. And he or

she provides various *staff services* to line management; for example, the HR manager or department assists in the hiring, training, evaluating, rewarding, promoting, and disciplining of employees at all levels.

5. Changes in the environment of HR management are requiring HR to play a more major role in organizations. These trends include growing work force diversity, rapid technological change, globalization, and changes in the nature of work such as the movement toward a service society and a growing emphasis on education and human capital.

6. Trends like globalization and technological innovation are changing the way firms are managed. For example, the traditional pyramid-shaped organization is giving way to new organizational forms; employees are being empowered to make more decisions; flatter organizations are the norm; work is increasingly organized around teams and processes; the bases of power are changing; managers in the future will not "manage;" and managers today must build commitment. Changes like these mean that organizations must depend more on self-disciplined and highly committed employees.

7. One consequence is that HR management must be involved in both the formulation and the implementation of a company's strategies, given the need for the firm to galvanize employees into a competitive advantage.

8. We defined strategic human resource management as ". . . the linking of HRM with strategic goals and objectives in order to improve business performance and develop organizational cultures that foster innovation and flexibility. . . ." We view HR as a strategic partner in that HRM works with other top managers to formulate the company's strategy as well as to execute it.

Key Terms

management process	line manager	staff (service) function
human resource management	staff manager	globalization
	implied authority	
authority	functional control	

Discussion Questions and Exercises

1. Explain what HR management is and how it relates to the management process.
2. Give several examples of how HR management concepts and techniques can be of use to all managers.
3. Compare and contrast the work of line and staff managers; give examples of each.
4. Working individually or in groups, develop a list showing how trends like work force diversity, technological trends, globalization, and changes in the nature of work have affected the college or university you are attending now.
5. Working individually or in groups, develop a list of examples showing how the new management practices discussed in this chapter (worker empowerment, flatter organizations, and so on) have or have not been implemented to some extent in the college or university you are now attending, or in the organization for which you work.
6. Working individually or in groups, interview an HR manager; based on that interview write a short presentation regarding HR's role today in building a more responsive organization.
7. Why is it important for a company to make its human resources into a competitive advantage? How can HR contribute to doing so?
8. What is meant by strategic human resource management and what exactly is HR's role in the strategic planning process?

Application Exercises

RUNNING CASE: Carter Cleaning Company
Introduction

The main theme of this book is that HR management—activities like recruiting, selecting, training, and rewarding employees—is not just the job of a central personnel group but rather a job in which every manager must engage. Perhaps nowhere is this more apparent than in the typical small service business. Here the owner/manager usually has no HR staff to rely on. However, the success of his or her enterprise (not to mention his or her family's peace of mind) often depends largely on the effectiveness through which workers are recruited, hired, trained, evaluated, and rewarded. Therefore, to help illustrate and emphasize the front-line manager's personnel role, throughout this book we will use a continuing case based on an actual small business in the southeastern United States. Each chapter's segment of the case will illustrate how the case's main player—owner/manager Jennifer Carter—confronts and solves personnel problems each day at work by applying the concepts and techniques of that particular chapter. Here is background information you will need to answer questions that arise in subsequent chapters. (A second, unrelated case incident will also be presented in each chapter.)

Carter Cleaning Centers Jennifer Carter graduated from State University in June 1994, and, after considering several job offers, decided to do what she really always planned to do—go into business with her father, Jack Carter.

Jack Carter opened his first laundromat in 1980 and his second in 1982. The main attraction to him of these coin laundry businesses was that they were capital- rather than labor-intensive. Thus, once the investment in machinery was made, the stores could be run with just one unskilled attendant and none of the labor problems one normally expects from being in the retail service business.

The attractiveness of operating with virtually no skilled labor notwithstanding, Jack had decided by 1986 to expand the services in each of his stores to include the dry cleaning and pressing of clothes. He embarked, in other words, on a strategy of related diversification, by adding new services that were related to and consistent with his existing coin laundry activities. He added these in part because he wanted to better utilize the unused space in the rather large stores he currently had under lease and partly because he was, as he put it, "tired of sending out the dry cleaning and pressing work that came in from our coin laundry clients to a dry cleaner five miles away, who then took most of what should have been our profits." To reflect the new expanded line of services he renamed each of his two stores Carter Cleaning Centers and was sufficiently satisfied with their performance to open four more of the same type of stores over the next five years. Each store had its own on-site manager and, on average, about seven employees and annual revenues of about $400,000. It was this six-store chain of cleaning centers that Jennifer joined upon graduating from State University.

Her understanding with her father was that she would serve as a troubleshooter/consultant to the elder Carter with the aim of both learning the business and bringing to it modern management concepts and techniques for solving the business's problems and facilitating its growth.

Questions
1. What sorts of personnel problems do you think Carter Cleaning will have to grapple with?
2. What would you do first if you were Jennifer?

CASE INCIDENT: Jack Nelson's Problem

As a new member of the board of directors for a local savings and loan association, Jack Nelson was being introduced to all the employees in the home office. When he was introduced to Ruth, he was curious about her work and asked her what her machine did. Ruth replied that she really did not know what the machine was called or what it did. She explained that she had only been working there for two months. She did, however, know precisely how to operate the machine and, according to her supervisor, she was an excellent employee.

At one of the branch offices, the supervisor in charge spoke to Mr. Nelson quite confidentially, telling him that "something was wrong" but she didn't know what. For one thing, she explained, employee turnover was too high, and no sooner had one employee been put on the job than another one resigned. With customers to see and loans to be made, she explained, she had little time to work with the new employees as they came and went.

All branch supervisors hired their own employees without communication with the home office or other branches. When an opening developed, the supervisor tried to find a suitable employee to replace the worker who had quit.

After touring the 22 branches and finding similar problems in many of them, Mr. Nelson wondered what the home office should do or what action he should take. The savings and loan firm was generally regarded as a well-run institution that had grown from 27 to 191 employees during the past eight years. The more he thought about the matter, the more puzzled Mr. Nelson became. He couldn't quite put his finger on the problem, and he didn't know whether or not to report his findings to the president.

Questions

1. What do you think was causing some of the problems in the savings and loan home office and branches?

2. Do you think setting up an HR unit in the main office would help?

3. What specific functions should it carry out? What HR functions would then be carried out by supervisors and other line managers?

Source: Claude S. George, Jr., *Supervision in Action,* 4th ed., pp. 307–308. 1985. Reprinted by permission of Prentice-Hall, Englewood Cliffs, New Jersey.

Human Resource Management Simulation

One of the ancillary manuals available with this text is the *Human Resources Management Simulation* by Smith and Golden. Unlike some exercises, a simulation provides students with the opportunity to practice managing an organization's human resource functions. With a simulation, students have the opportunity to make decisions, see the effects of those decisions, and then try again. In other words, players get hands-on experience with manipulating key human resource variables in a dynamic setting.

Simulation techniques have been used for some time to create business models that can help to explain the real world. Smith and Golden's computer simulation attempts to combine the human resource elements found in the HR world with the business environment found in each situation. Student teams manage the HR department of a medium-sized organization that will be competing with up to 20 other teams and organizations. The program can simulate a profit or nonprofit organization in a manufacturing or service industry. Teams are expected to establish objectives, plan their strategy, and make the decisions dictated by these plans. Decisions are submitted to the instructor periodically. Each decision set represents a quarter of a year (three months). These decisions are entered into the computer, which simulates the reaction of the firm and the labor market and produces a report for each team. This is done for several iterations. All teams will make a few mistakes throughout the simulation, so do not allow a few setbacks to affect your play—mistakes happen in the real world, too. Keep your spirits up and good luck!

Video Case

Revolution at Work—Saturn

Few industrial changes anywhere have been as revolutionary as what GM has tried to do with its new Saturn car-manufacturing facility. As the video explains, the Saturn approach is a "revolution in how workers think about their work." As the employees describe in the video, at Saturn "you call the shots," and it's no longer a case of "management is the enemy." Instead, says one worker, "I feel part of what we did here." One big difference in how Saturn operates, the video points out, is that Saturn employees "use their brains" and work in teams that decide which parts to use and whom to hire. These teams also measure the quality of their products.

Questions

1. How does Saturn's competitive strategy translate into specific HR policies at the Saturn plant?

2. On the basis of the video and the contents of Chapter One, what specific Saturn HR policies do you think will foster employee commitment at Saturn? Why?

3. Why do you think the plant's output is so far below its capacity? Do you think Saturn is emphasizing social skills too much, but productivity not enough?

Source: ABC News, *Revolution at Work: Saturn,* "ABC News Special," August 31, 1991.

Take It to the Net

We invite you to visit the Dessler page on the Prentice Hall Web site at:
http://www.prenhall.com/~dessler
for the monthly Dessler update and for this chapter's World Wide Web exercise.

Notes

1. Quoted in Fred K. Foulkes, "The Expanding Role of the Personnel Function," *Harvard Business Review* (March–April 1975), pp. 71–84. See also Warren Wilhelm, "HR Can Make the U.S. a Global Leader," *Personnel Journal* (May 1993), p. 280.

2. See Robert Saltonstall, "Who's Who in Personnel Administration," *Harvard Business Review,* Vol. 33 (July–August 1955), pp. 75–83, reprinted in Paul Pigors, Charles Meyers, and F. P. Malm, *Management of Human Resources* (New York: McGraw-Hill, 1969), pp. 61–73.

3. Saltonstall, "Who's Who," p. 63.

4. For a detailed discussion of the responsibilities and duties of the human resource department, see Mary Zippo, "Personal Activities: Where the Dollars Went in 1979," *Personnel,* Vol. 57 (March–April 1980), pp. 61–67; and "ASPABNA Survey No. 49, Personnel Activities, Budgets, and Staffs: 1985–1986," *BNA Bulletin to Management,* June 5, 1986.

5. Saltonstall, "Who's Who," p. 65.

6. Fred K. Foulkes and Henry Morgan, "Organizing and Staffing the Personnel Function," *Harvard Business Review,* Vol. 56 (May–June 1977), p. 146.

7. Ibid., p. 149.

8. U.S. Department of Labor, Bureau of Labor Statistics, *Occupational Outlook Handbook,* Bulletin 2250, 1986–1987 Edition, pp. 45–47.

9. Saltonstall, "Who's Who," pp. 68–69.

10. Gerald Ferris, Dwight Frink, and M. Carmen Galang, "Diversity in the Workplace: The Human Resources Management Challenge," *Human Resource Planning,* Vol. 16, no. 1, pp. 41–51.

11. Ibid., p. 42.

12. Howard Fullerton, Jr., "Another Look at the Labor Force," *Monthly Labor Review* (November 1993), pp. 31–40.

13. Ibid., p. 32.

14. Ibid.

15. Ibid., p. 38.

16. Ibid., p. 37.

17. Except as noted, this section is based on Charles Greer, *Strategy and Human Resources* (Englewood Cliffs, NJ: Prentice-Hall, 1995), pp. 49–52.

18. Ibid., p. 50.

19. Ferris, et al., "Diversity in the Workplace: The Human Resources Management Challenge," p. 43.

20. Ibid.

21. For related discussions see, for example, Felice Schwartz, "Women in American Business: The Demographic Imperative," *Business and The Contemporary World* (Summer 1993), pp. 10–19; Karen Stephenson and Valdis Krebs, "A More Accurate Way to Measure Diversity," *Personnel Journal* (October 1993), pp. 66–74.

22. Thomas Stewart, "Welcome to the Revolution," *Fortune,* December 13, 1993, p. 68.

23. Ibid., p. 72.

24. "A Portrait of America: How the Country is Changing," *Business Week,* 1992, p. 51.

25. "Grabbing New World Orders," *Business Week, Reinventing America,* 1992, pp. 110–111.

26. Charles W. Hill, *International Business* (Burr Ridge, IL: Irwin, 1994), p. 6.

27. Ibid., p. 9.

28. Bryan O'Reilly, "Your New Global Workforce," *Fortune,* December 14, 1992, pp. 52–66.

29. See Greer, *Strategy and Human Resources,* pp. 52–53; Brian Stanko and Rebecca Matchette, "Telecommuting: The Future is Now," *B & E Review* (October–December 1994), pp. 8–11.

30

30. "Part-Time Employment," *BNA Datagraph Bulletin to Management,* July 7, 1994, pp. 212–213. For further discussions of how the nature of work is changing, see, for example, Oren Harari, "Back to the Future of Work," *Management Review* (September 1993), pp. 33–35; Julie Cohn Mason, "Workplace 2000: The Death of 9 to 5," *Management Review* (January 1993), pp. 14–18; and Arthur Shostak, "The Nature of Work in the 21st Century: Certain Uncertainties," *Business Horizons* (November–December 1993), pp. 30–34.

31. Peter Drucker, "The Coming of the New Organization," *Harvard Business Review* (January–February 1988), p. 45.

32. Richard Crawford, *In the Era of Human Capital* (New York: Harper, 1991), p. 10.

33. Ibid., p. 26

34. O'Reilly, "Your New Global Workforce," p. 63.

35. Francis Fukuyama, "Are We at the End of History?" *Fortune,* January 15, 1990, pp. 75–78.

36. Thomas Steward, "Brain Power," *Fortune,* June 3, 1991, p. 44.

37. Drucker, "The Coming of the New Organization," p. 45.

38. For a discussion, see "Special Survey Report: Legal Oversight of the HR Department," *BNA Bulletin to Management,* February 2, 1995, pp. 1–12.

39. These are based on Walter Kiechel III, "How We Will Work in the Year 2000," *Fortune,* May 17, 1993, p. 79.

40. Bryan Dumaine, "What the Leaders of Tomorrow See," *Fortune,* July 3, 1989, p. 58.

41. Rosabeth Moss Kanter, "The New Managerial Work," *Harvard Business Review* (November–December 1989), p. 88.

42. Ibid.

43. Drucker, "The coming of The New Organization," p. 45

44. Thomas A. Steward, "How GE Keeps Those Ideas Coming," *Fortune,* August 12, 1991, p. 42.

45. Tom Peters, *Liberation Management* (New York: Alfred Knopf, 1992), p. 9.

46. Ibid.

47. This discussion is based on Gary Dessler, *Management Fundamentals* (Reston, VA: Reston, 1977), p. 2; William Berliner and William McClarney, *Management Practice and Training* (Homewood, IL: Irwin, 1974), p. 11.

48. Charlene Marmer Solomon, "Working Smarter: How HR Can Help," *Personnel Journal* (June 1993), pp. 54–64.

49. Jennifer Laabs, "HR's Vital Role at Levi Strauss," *Personnel Journal* (December 1992), p. 37.

50. See, for example, Benjamin Schneider and David Bowen, "The Service Organization: Human Resources Management Is Crucial," *Organizational Dynamics,* Vol. 21, no. 4 (1993), pp. 39–52.

51. Karl Albrecht and Ron Zemke, *Service America!* (Homewood, IL: Dow Jones-Irwin, 1985), p. 101.

52. Schneider and Bowen, "The Service Organization."

53. Commerce Clearing House, "HR Role: Maximize the Competitive Advantage of People," *Ideas and Trends in Personnel,* August 5, 1992, p. 121.

54. Patrick Gunnigle and Sara Moore, "Linking Business Strategy and Human Resource Management: Issues and Implications," *Personnel Review,* Vol. 23, no. 1 (1994), pp. 63–84.

55. Arthur Thompson and A. J. Strikland, *Strategic Management* (Homewood, IL: Irwin, 1992), p. 38.

56. For a description of the need for an effective and integrated strategy see, for example, Erhard Valentin, "Anatomy of a Fatal Business Strategy," *Journal of Management Studies,* Vol. 31, no. 3 (May 1994), pp. 359–382.

57. Gunnigle and Moore, "Linking Business Strategy and Human Resource Management," p. 64.

58. Michael Porter, *Competitive Strategy* (New York: The Free Press, 1980); and Michael Porter, *Competitive Advantage* (New York: The Free Press, 1985).

59. Porter, *Competitive Strategy,* p. 14.

60. C. K. Prahalad and Gary Hamel, "The Core Competence of a Corporation," *Harvard Business Review* (May–June 1990), p. 82.

61. Charles Greer, *Strategy and Human Resources,* p. 105.

62. For a discussion see, for example, Jay Galbraith, "Positioning Human Resource as a Value-Adding Function: The Case of Rockwell International," *Human Resource Management,* Vol. 31, no. 4 (Winter 1992), pp. 287–300, and Augustine Lado and Mary Wilson, "Human Resource Systems and Sustained Competitive Advantage: A Competency-Based Perspective," *Academy of Management Review,* Vol. 19, no. 4 (1994), pp. 699–727.

63. Catherine Truss and Lynda Gratton, "Strategic Human Resource Management: A Conceptual Approach," *The International Journal of Human Resource Management,* Vol. 5, no. 3 (September 1994), p. 663.

64. P. Wright and G. McMahan, "Theoretical Perspectives for Strategic Human Resource Management," *Journal of Management,* Vol. 18, no. 2 (1992), p. 292.

65. While still largely nonunionized, Fed Ex's pilots did vote to join the Airline Pilots Union and entered into negotiations with Fed Ex management in 1995.

66. For a discussion, see Peter Boxall, "Placing HR Strategy at the Heart of Business Success," *Personnel Management,* Vol. 26, no. 7 (July 1994), pp. 32–34.

67. Ibid., p. 32.

68. Randall Schuler, "Human Resource Management Choices and Organizational Strategy," in Randall Schuler, S. A. Youngblood, and V. L. Huber (editors), *Readings in Personnel and Human Resource Management* (3rd edition) (St. Paul, MN: West, 1988).

69. For a discussion, see Catherine Truss and Lynda Gratton, "Strategic Human Resource Management," pp. 670–671.

70. Ibid., p. 670.

71. For discussions see, for example, Randall Schuler, Peter Dowling, and Helen DeCieri, "An Integrative Framework of Strategic International Human Resource Management," *Journal of Management,* Vol. 19, no. 2 (1993), pp. 419–459; Vida Scarpello, "New Paradigm Approaches in Strategic Human Resource Management," *Group and Organization Management,* Vol. 19, no. 2 (June 1994), pp. 160–164; and Sharon Peck, "Exploring the Link Between Organizational Strategy and the Employment Relationships: The Role of Human Resources Policies," *Journal of Management Studies,* Vol. 31, no. 5 (September 1994), pp. 715–736.

72. William Henn, "What the Strategist Asks from Human Resources," *Human Resource Planning,* Vol. 8, no. 4 (1985), p. 195; quoted in Greer, *Strategy and Human Resources,* pp. 117–118.

73. Greer, *Strategy and Human Resources,* p. 116.

74. Ibid., p. 105.

75. Ibid., p. 117.

76. Schuler and Jackson point out that the competitive strategies of innovation, quality enhancement, and cost reduction suggest different role behaviors and that different human resource practices are, therefore, needed to support these three types of competitive strategies. See Randall Schuler and Susan Jackson, "Linking Competitive Strategies with Human Resource Management Practices," *Academy of Management Executive,* Vol. 1, no. 3 (1987), pp. 207–219.

77. This is based on Robert Burg and Brian Smith, "Restructuring Compensation and Benefits to Support Strategy," Part I, "Executive Compensation," *Compensation and Benefits Review* (November–December 1987), pp. 15–22.

78. Ibid., p. 17.

79. Ibid.

Chapter 2
Equal Opportunity and the Law

Chapter Outline

- ◆ **Introduction**
- ◆ **Equal Employment Opportunity 1964–1991**
- ◆ **Equal Employment Opportunity 1991–present**
- ◆ **Defenses Against Discrimination Allegations**
- ◆ **Illustrative Discriminatory Employment Practices**
- ◆ **The EEOC Enforcement Process**
- ◆ **Diversity Management and Affirmative Action Programs**

Behavioral Objectives

When you finish studying this chapter, you should be able to:

Summarize the basic Equal Employment Opportunity laws regarding age, race, sex, national origin, religion, and handicap discrimination.

Explain the basic defenses against discrimination allegations.

Present a summary of what employers can and cannot do with respect to illegal recruitment, selection, and promotion and layoff practices.

Explain how to set up an affirmative action program.

Introduction

State Farm Insurance Companies recently agreed to pay $157 million to 814 women who were unlawfully denied entry-level sales agents' positions by the company between 1974 and 1987.[1] This was the largest civil rights settlement in history.

State Farm's alleged errors help illustrate the personnel problems equal employment opportunity laws were designed to prevent. The basic problem was that decisions about hiring women as State Farm sales agents were not based on whether they could perform the sales agent jobs; instead, various untested standards were applied. For example, some women were told they needed a four-year degree, although some male agents had no degree. Others were told that it might be unsafe for women to make sales calls at night, although the evidence showed that women could do the job. In other words, the managers doing the hiring were not asking, "Can these women do the job?" Instead, they were applying subjective criteria unrelated to job performance, criteria that let them illegally reject women applicants for jobs for which they were actually qualified. In this chapter we'll look more closely at the equal employment opportunity laws with which employers are required to comply.

Equal Employment Opportunity 1964–1991

Background

Legislation barring discrimination against members of minority groups in the United States is certainly nothing new. For example, the Fifth Amendment to the U.S. Constitution (ratified in 1791) states that "no person shall . . . be deprived of life, liberty, or property, without due process of the law." The Thirteenth Amendment (ratified in 1865) outlawed slavery and has been held by the courts to bar racial discrimination. The Fourteenth Amendment (ratified in 1868) makes it illegal for any state to "make or enforce any law which shall abridge the privileges and immunities of citizens of the United States," and the courts have generally viewed this law as barring discrimination on the basis of sex or national origin, as well as race. Section 1981 of Title 42 of the U.S. Code, passed over 100 years ago as the Civil Rights Act of 1866, gives all persons within the jurisdiction of the United States the same right to make and enforce contracts and benefit from the laws of the land; as we'll see, this has recently become an important legal basis for attacking discrimination.[2] Other laws as well as various court decisions made discrimination against minorities illegal as early as the turn of the century—at least in theory.[3]

But as a practical matter, Congress and various presidents were reluctant to take dramatic action on equal employment issues until the early 1960s. At that point, "they were finally prompted to act primarily as a result of civil unrest among the minorities and women" who eventually became protected by the new equal rights legislation and the agencies created to implement and enforce it.[4]

Title VII of the 1964 Civil Rights Act

What the Law Says **Title VII of the 1964 Civil Rights Act** was one of the first of these new laws. Title VII (as amended by the 1972 Equal Employment Opportunity Act) states that an employer cannot discriminate on the basis of race, color, religion, sex, or national origin. Specifically, it states that it shall be an unlawful employment practice for an employer:[5]

1. *To fail or refuse to hire or to discharge an individual* or otherwise to discriminate against any individual with respect to his/her compensation, terms, conditions, or privileges of employment, because of such individual's race, color, religion, sex, or national origin.
2. *To limit, segregate, or classify his/her employees or applicants for employment* in any way that would deprive or tend to deprive any individual of employment opportunities or otherwise adversely affect his/her status as an employee, because of such individual's race, color, religion, sex, or national origin.[6]

Who Does Title VII Cover? Title VII of the Civil Rights Act bars discrimination on the part of various employers, including all public or private employers of 15 or more persons. In addition, it covers all private and public educational institutions, the federal government, and state and local governments. Public and private employment agencies are also barred from failing or refusing to refer for employment any individual because of race, color, religion, sex, or national origin. Labor unions with 15 or more members are barred from excluding, expelling, or classifying their membership because of race, color, religion, sex, or national origin. Joint labor-management committees established for selecting workers for apprenticeships and training similarly cannot discriminate against individuals.

The EEOC EEOC stands for **Equal Employment Opportunity Commission,** which was instituted by Title VII. The EEOC consists of five members who are appointed by the president with the advice and consent of the Senate; each member serves a term of five years.

Establishing the EEOC greatly enhanced the federal government's ability to enforce equal employment opportunity laws. The EEOC receives and investigates job discrimination complaints from aggrieved individuals. When it finds reasonable cause that the charges are justified, it attempts (through conciliation) to reach an agreement eliminating all aspects of the discrimination. If this conciliation fails, the EEOC has the power to go directly to court to enforce the law. Under the Equal Employment Opportunity Act of 1972, discrimination charges may be filed by the EEOC on behalf of an aggrieved individual, as well as by the individuals themselves. This procedure is explained in more detail later in this chapter.

Executive Orders

Under executive orders issued in the Johnson administration, employers who do business with the U.S. government have an obligation beyond that imposed by Title VII to refrain from employment discrimination. Executive Orders 11246 and 11375 don't just ban discrimination: They require that contractors take **affirmative action** to ensure equal employment opportunity (we will explain affirma-

Office of Federal Contract Compliance Programs (OFCCP)
This office is responsible for implementing the executive orders and ensuring compliance of federal contractors.

tive action later). All firms with contracts over $50,000 and 50 or more employees must develop and implement such programs. The orders also state a policy against employment discrimination based on *age* or *physical handicap,* in addition to race, color, religion, sex, or national origin. These orders also established the **Office of Federal Contract Compliance Programs (OFCCP)**. It is responsible for implementing the executive orders and ensuring the compliance of federal contractors.

Equal Pay Act of 1963

Equal Pay Act of 1963
The act requiring equal pay for equal work, regardless of sex.

The **Equal Pay Act of 1963** (amended in 1972) made it unlawful to discriminate in pay on the basis of sex when jobs involve equal work—equivalent skills, effort, and responsibility—and are performed under similar working conditions. However, differences in pay do not violate the act if the difference is based on a seniority system, a merit system, a system that measures earnings by quantity or quality of production, or a differential based on any factor other than sex.

Age Discrimination in Employment Act of 1967

Age Discrimination in Employment Act of 1967
The act prohibiting arbitrary age discrimination and specifically protecting individuals over 40 years old.

The **Age Discrimination in Employment Act of 1967 (ADEA)** made it unlawful to discriminate against employees or applicants for employment who are between 40 and 65 years of age. As amended by Congress in 1978, the act extended protection to age 70 for most workers and without upper limit for federal government employees.

A 1973 Supreme Court ruling held that most states and local agencies, when acting in the role of employer, must also adhere to provisions of the act that protect workers from age discrimination. Subsequent actions by Congress have eliminated the age cap of 70, effectively ending most mandatory retirement.

One-fifth of the court actions filed by the EEOC recently were ADEA cases. (Another 30% were sex discrimination cases.) This act is a "favored statute" among employees and lawyers because it allows jury trials and double damages to those proving "willful" discrimination.[7]

It is unlawful to discriminate against applicants over 40 years of age.

Vocational Rehabilitation Act of 1973

Vocational Rehabilitation Act of 1973
The act requiring certain federal contractors to take affirmative action for disabled persons.

The **Vocational Rehabilitation Act of 1973** required employers with federal contracts over $2,500 to take affirmative action for the employment of handicapped persons. The act does not require that an unqualified person be hired. It does require that an employer take steps to accommodate a handicapped worker unless doing so imposes an undue hardship on the employer.[8] A federal district court recently held that compensatory damages (a payment for "future pecuniary losses, emotional pain, suffering, inconvenience, mental anguish, loss of enjoyment of life, and other nonpecuniary losses") are available under the 1973 rehabilitation act.[9]

Legal Aspects of AIDS at Work The Vocational Rehabilitation Act took on added prominence because of a ruling that suggested it could be used to prohibit discrimination against people with AIDS. In *School Board of Nassau County* v. *Arline,* the Supreme Court ruled that persons with contagious diseases are covered by the act. In this case a school teacher (Arline) was dismissed because she had tuberculosis, an infectious respiratory disease.[10] In *Arline,* the Supreme Court held that the fact a disease is contagious can place an employee under the protection of the act since mere fear of the disease (rather than its actual likelihood of being transmitted) might cause employers to discriminate against the ailing persons.[11]

School Board of Nassau County v. Arline
U.S. Supreme Court ruling that persons with contagious diseases are covered by the Vocational Rehabilitation Act of 1973.

In any case, the EEOC's position today is that the new Americans with Disabilities Act (discussed later) prohibits discriminating against people with AIDS. Furthermore, numerous state laws now protect people with AIDS from discrimination. The guidelines issued by the Labor Department's Office of Federal Contract Compliance Programs also require that AIDS-type diseases be treated according to the provisions of the Rehabilitation Act.[12] The bottom line is that for most employers discriminating against people with AIDS would be viewed as unlawful.[13] In one recent situation, for instance, Delta Airlines was sued by a former Pan Am worker who said Delta refused to hire him because he was gay and HIV positive. Delta settled the claim, which was brought by New York City's Human Rights Commission.[14]

Vietnam Era Veterans' Readjustment Assistance Act of 1974

Vietnam Era Veterans' Readjustment Act of 1974
An act requiring that employers with government contracts take affirmative action to hire disabled veterans.

The provisions of the **Vietnam Era Veterans' Readjustment Act of 1974** require that employers with government contracts of $10,000 or more take affirmative action to employ and advance disabled veterans and qualified veterans of the Vietnam era. The act is administered by the OFCCP.[15]

Pregnancy Discrimination Act of 1978

Pregnancy Discrimination Act (PDA)
An amendment to Title VII of the Civil Rights Act that prohibits sex discrimination based on "pregnancy, childbirth, or related medical conditions."

Congress passed the **Pregnancy Discrimination Act (PDA)** in 1978 as an amendment to the Civil Rights Act of 1964, Title VII. The act broadened the definition of sex discrimination to encompass pregnancy, childbirth, or related medical conditions. It prohibits using these for discrimination in hiring, promotion, suspension or discharge, or any other term or condition of employment.[16] Basically, the act says that if an employer offers its employees disability coverage, pregnancy and childbirth must be treated like any other disability and must be included in the plan as a covered condition.[17] The U.S. Supreme Court ruled in *California Federal Savings and Loan Association* v. *Guerra* that if an employer offers no disability leave to any of its employees it can (but need not necessarily) grant pregnancy leave to a woman who requests it when disabled for pregnancy, childbirth, or a related medical condition, although men get no comparable benefits.[18]

Federal Agency Guidelines

federal agency guidelines
Guidelines issued by federal agencies charged with ensuring compliance with equal employment federal legislation explaining recommended employer procedures in detail.

The federal agencies charged with ensuring compliance with the aforementioned laws and executive orders issue their own implementing guidelines. The overall purpose of these **federal agency guidelines** is to specify the procedures these agencies recommend employers follow in complying with the equal opportunity laws.

Uniform Guidelines on Employee Selection Procedures Detailed guidelines to be used by employers were approved by the EEOC, Civil Service Commission, Department of Labor, and Department of Justice.[19] These uniform guidelines supersede earlier guidelines developed by the EEOC alone. They set forth "highly recommended" procedures regarding such matters as employee selection, recordkeeping, preemployment inquiries, and affirmative action programs. As an example, the guidelines specify that any employment selection devices (including but not limited to written tests) that screen out disproportionate numbers of women or minorities must be *validated*. The guidelines also explain in detail *how* an employer can validate a selection device. (This procedure will be explained in Chapter 5.) For its part, the OFCCP has its own *Manual of Guidelines*.[20]

The American Psychological Association has published the latest *Standards for Educational and Psychological Testing,* and many experts expect that this document, which represents a consensus among testing authorities, "will be used in court to help judges resolve disagreements about the quality of . . . validity studies that arise during litigation."[21]

EEOC Guidelines   The EEOC and other agencies also periodically issue updated guidelines clarifying and revising their positions on matters such as *national origin discrimination* and *sexual harassment*.[22] For instance, the EEOC issued guidelines on the 1991 Civil Rights Act, the Americans with Disabilities Act, and sexual harassment; the Department of Labor issued guidelines on immigration; and the Office of Federal Contract Compliance Programs issued a compliance manual dealing in part with "glass ceiling" audits—audits of firms that have subtle barriers to promotion for minorities.[23]

Historically, these guidelines have fleshed out the procedures to be used in complying with equal employment laws. For example, the EEOC published guidelines that further explained and revised the agency's position on age discrimination.[24] Recall that the Age Discrimination in Employment Act of 1967 (as amended) prohibited employers from discriminating against persons over 40 years old merely because of age. Subsequent EEOC guidelines stated that it was unlawful to discriminate in hiring (or in any way) by giving preference because of age to individuals within the 40-plus age bracket. Thus, if two people apply for the same job, and one is 45 and the other is 55, you may not lawfully turn down the 55-year-old candidate because of his or her age and expect to defend yourself by saying that you hired someone over 40.[25]

Sexual Harassment

The Judge Clarence Thomas hearings drew wide public attention to the question of sexual harassment; firms are now doubly advised to guard against situations that spawn charges of sexual harassment.[26] In fact, the EEOC recently experienced a 41% increase in sexual harassment claims filed.[27]

sexual harassment
Harassment on the basis of sex that has the purpose or effect of substantially interfering with a person's work performance or creating an intimidating, hostile, or offensive work environment.

The EEOC had earlier issued interpretive guidelines on **sexual harassment.** These guidelines state that employers have an affirmative duty to maintain a workplace free of sexual harassment and intimidation.[28] These and related guidelines state that harassment on the basis of sex is a violation of Title VII when such conduct has the purpose or effect of substantially interfering with a person's work performance or creating an intimidating, hostile, or offensive work environment. The Civil Rights Act of 1991 (discussed later) added teeth to this by permitting victims of intentional discrimination, including sexual harassment, to have jury trials and to collect compensatory damages for pain and suffering and punitive damages in cases in which the employer acted with "malice or reckless indifference" to the individual's rights.[29]

The EEOC guidelines define sexual harassment as "unwelcome sexual advances, requests for sexual favors, and other verbal or physical conduct of a sexual nature that takes place under any of the following conditions":[30]

In the context of sexual harassment, the courts may decide a hostile environment exists even if no direct threats or promises are made in exchange for sexual behavior.

1. Submission to such conduct is made either explicitly or implicitly a term or condition of an individual's employment.
2. Submission to or rejection of such conduct by an individual is used as the basis for employment decisions affecting such individual.
3. Such conduct has the purpose or effect of unreasonably interfering with an individual's work performance or creating an intimidating, hostile, or offensive work environment.

Experts suggest that the EEOC and the courts will ask two basic questions when determining whether or not a company is liable for sexual harassment:

1. Did the company know or should it have known that harassment was taking place?
2. Did the company take any action to stop the harassment?[31]

There are three main ways an employee can prove sexual harassment.

Quid Pro Quo   The most direct is to prove that rejecting a supervisor's advances adversely affected the employee's tangible benefits, like raises or promotions. For example, in one case the employee was able to show that continued job success and advancement were dependent on her agreeing to the sexual demands of her supervisors. And she showed that after an initial complaint to her employer she was subjected to adverse performance evaluations, disciplinary layoffs, and other adverse actions.[32]

Hostile Environment Created by Supervisors   It is not always necessary to show that the harassment had tangible consequences such as a demotion or termination. For example, in one case the court found that a male supervisor's sexual harassment had substantially affected a female employee's emotional and psychological ability to the point that she felt she had to quit her job. Therefore, even though no direct threats or promises were made in exchange for sexual advances, the fact that the advances interfered with the woman's performance and created an offensive work environment were enough to prove that sexual harassment had occurred. On the other hand, the courts will not interpret as sexual harassment any sexual relationships that arise during the course of employment but that do not have substantial effect on that employment.[33]

Hostile Environment Created by Coworkers or Nonemployees   The advances do not have to be made by the person's supervisor to qualify as sexual harassment: An employee's coworkers (or even the employer's customers) can cause the employer to be held responsible for sexual harassment. In one case the court held that a sexually provocative uniform the employer required led to lewd comments and innuendos by customers toward the employee; when she complained that she would no longer wear the uniform, she was fired. Since the employer could not show that there was a job-related necessity for requiring such a uniform (and because the uniform was required only for female employees), the court ruled that the employer, in effect, was responsible for the sexually harassing behavior. The EEOC guidelines also state that an employer is liable for the sexually harassing acts of its nonsupervisory employees if the employer knew or should have known of the harassing conduct.

Case law is quickly accumulating regarding employers' responsibilities for sexual harassment by clients, customers, and suppliers. The gist of these decisions is that employers are increasingly held responsible for sexual harassment by clients, customers, and suppliers if the employers' management employees knew or reasonably should have known about the harassing behavior. Thus, in *Powell* v. *Las Vegas Hilton,* Ms. Powell was terminated after registering several complaints of alleged sexual harassment to her employer. According to Ms. Powell, the worst incident occurred when she was dealing cards to a group of drunken sailors, several of whom allegedly screamed out comments regarding Ms. Powell's anatomy. She became upset and tried to leave the table, but her supervisor would not allow her to do so. The court found that: (1) The harassers' intent is unimportant; (2) terming the remarks "compliments" is not a defense; (3) and Hilton would not have been found liable for failing to remedy or prevent a hostile or offensive work environment if management-level employees did not know (or, in the exercise of reasonable care, would not have known) about it. Since management did at least arguably know about the hostile environment, Hilton was held responsible.[34]

The U.S. Supreme Court's first decision on sexual harassment was *Meritor Savings Bank, FSB v. Vinson,* decided in June 1986. In this case there were three sexual harassment issues before the Court:

> *(1) Whether a hostile work environment (where hostility is due to the victim's sex) in which the victim does not suffer any economic injury violates Title VII, (2) whether an employee's voluntary participation in sexual acts with a manager constitutes a valid defense for an employer to a Title VII complaint, and (3) whether an employer is liable for the conduct of supervisors or coworkers when the employer is unaware of that conduct.[35]*

The Court's ruling broadly endorsed the EEOC guidelines (issues 1 and 2), but the majority on a 5-to-4 split vote declined to issue a definitive ruling on employers' automatic liability (issue 3). However, the clear message of the decision is that employers should establish accessible and meaningful complaint procedures for employee claims of sexual harassment.

What the Employer Should Do Employers can take steps to minimize liability if a sexual harassment claim is filed against the organization and to prevent such claims from arising in the first place:

1. First, take all complaints about harassment seriously. As one sexual harassment manual for managers and supervisors advises, "When confronted with sexual harassment complaints or when sexual conduct is observed in the workplace, the best reaction is to address the complaint or stop the conduct."[36]

2. Issue a strong policy statement condemning such behavior. The policy should include a workable definition of sexual harassment, spell out possible actions against those who harass others, and make it clear that retaliatory action against an employee who makes charges will not be tolerated. An example, presented in Figure 2.1, states, for example, that "such behavior may result in . . . dismissal."

3. Inform all employees about the policy prohibiting sexual harassment and of their rights under the policy.

4. Develop a complaint procedure.

5. Establish a management response system that includes an immediate reaction and investigation by senior management.

6. Begin management training sessions with supervisors and managers to increase their own awareness of the issues.

7. Discipline managers and employees involved in sexual harassment.

Figure 2.1
Sample Sexual
Harassment Policy

Source: Adapted from *Sexual Harassment Manual for Managers and Supervisors,* Commerce Clearing House, Inc., October 1991, p. 46.

The company's position is that sexual harassment is a form of misconduct that undermines the integrity of the employment relationship. No employee—either male or female—should be subject to unsolicited and unwelcome sexual overtures or conduct, either verbal or physical. Sexual harassment does not refer to occasional compliments of a socially accepted nature. It refers to behavior that is not welcome, that is personally offensive, that debilitates morale, and that, therefore, interferes with work effectiveness. Such behavior may result in disciplinary action up to and including dismissal.

8. Keep thorough records of complaints, investigations, and actions taken.
9. Conduct exit interviews that uncover any complaints and that acknowledge by signature the reasons for leaving.
10. Republish the sexual harassment policy periodically.
11. Encourage upward communication through periodic written attitude surveys, hot lines, suggestion boxes, and other feedback procedures to discover employees' feelings concerning any evidence of sexual harassment and to keep management informed.[37]

These steps are consistent with the EEOC's new proposed workplace harassment guidelines. These guidelines state that once the employer knows or should have known of harassing conduct, the employer is expected to take immediate corrective action, even if the offending party is a nonemployee.[38] Steps to prevent harassment should include, at a minimum, an explicit policy against harassment that is clearly and regularly communicated to employees; efforts to sensitize all supervisory and nonsupervisory employees on harassment issues; and an effective internal complaint procedure.[39] See the Diversity Counts box on the next page for another step.

What the Individual Can Do An employee—whether male or female—who believes he or she has been sexually harassed can also take several steps to eliminate the problem. The first step should be a verbal request to the harasser and the harasser's boss that the unwanted overtures cease because the conduct is unwelcome. The next step is for the offended person to write a letter to the accused. This should be a polite, low-key letter written in three parts. The first part should be a detailed statement of facts as the writer sees them: "This is what I think happened . . ." (include all facts and relevant dates). In the second part of the letter, the writer should describe his or her feelings and what damage the writer thinks has been done (e.g., "Your action made me feel terrible"; I'm deeply embarrassed . . ."). Here mention any perceived or actual cost and damages along with feelings of dismay, distrust, and so on. Next the accuser should state what he or she would like to have happen next. For example, "I ask that our relationship from now on be on a purely professional basis." The accuser should, according to one expert, deliver the letter in person if possible to ensure that it arrived and when it arrived; if necessary, a witness should accompany the writer to be present when the letter is delivered. Finally, the individual should report the unwelcome conduct and unsuccessful efforts to get it to stop to the harasser's manager or to the human resource director (or both) verbally and in writing. This will leave no doubt that the employer has notice of the unwelcome nature of the conduct and create an obligation on the part of the employer to investigate and take warranted corrective action. If the letter and appeals to the employer do not suffice, the accuser should turn to the local office of the EEOC to file the necessary claim.[40] The individual can also consult an attorney about suing the harasser for assault and battery, intentional infliction of emotional distress, and injunctive relief and to recover compensatory and punitive damages if the harassment is of a serious nature.

Diversity Counts:
In Sexual Harassment

At this time the appropriate legal standard for determining behaviors that constitute a sexually "hostile working environment" has not been clearly established.[41] The problem is that the behaviors that typically constitute a hostile working environment are subject to individual perceptions and definitions; in other words, behaviors like sexual joking or sexual comments or even touching and patting may mean something different to the various individuals involved. Generally speaking, courts tend to rely on a "reasonable woman" standard when the recipient of the alleged harassment is a woman. This means that the courts' interpretation of whether a specific behavior may be sexually harassing depends on how a "reasonable woman" would perceive the behavior.[42]

There's virtually no doubt about the fact that certain behaviors constitute sexual harassment. For example, behavior of the "quid pro quo" variety (in which, say, a supervisor tells a subordinate that the person either performs a sexual favor or is terminated) is clearly sexual harassment. But where the behaviors are not so blatant but may still contribute to a sexually hostile environment, the question of defining how a reasonable person would interpret the behavior becomes much more important.

One problem is that there are gender-based differences in the way men and women view various behaviors. Based on the literature, for instance, females are much more likely than males to report that they experienced some form of unwelcome sexual attention and to define more social-sexual behaviors as sexual harassment than do males.[43] Similarly, males are less likely to attribute responsibility for sexual harassment to the alleged harasser than are females, and men are more likely to place blame on the female target than are females. Conversely, females have been found to be more likely to assign responsibility for sexual harassment to the harasser.

A study of federal employees illustrates the important role that gender differences play in defining sexual harassment. The survey involved 8,523 respondents employed in 24 governmental agencies. As part of the survey, these employees were asked to assess the following five different behaviors: (1) uninvited letters, telephone calls, or materials of a sexual nature; (2) uninvited and deliberate touching, leaning over, cornering, or pinching; (3) uninvited sexually suggestive looks or gestures; (4) uninvited pressure for dates; and (5) uninvited sexual teasing, jokes, remarks, or questions.

The study's results indicated that males and females did indeed perceive sexual harassment in significantly different ways.[44] As the researchers conclude:

Females are more likely than males to view letters, telephone calls, or materials of a sexual nature, touching, leaning over, cornering, or pinching, sexually suggestive looks or gestures, pressure for dates, sexual teasing, jokes, remarks, or questions as sexually harassing. In addition, females are consistently more likely than males to view the behaviors as sexually harassing regardless of whether the harasser is a supervisor or a co-worker.[45]

One implication of this study is that employers have to do a better job of sensitizing their employees regarding the possibility of such gender-based differences in perceptions. Employees (and supervisors in particular) must understand that it is the target's *perception* of the sexual attention that will be meaningful in a courtroom and that men and women may perceive such behaviors in significantly different ways. A comment that a male supervisor may perceive as merely complimentary might be perceived by a female target as uncomfortable and insulting and create the basis for a sexual harassment charge. Therefore, it is essential to keep in mind the potential for gender-based differences, and more generally the fact that it's the perceptions of the person on the receiving end, not merely the intentions of the sender, that will ultimately determine whether the behavior is unwelcome. ◆

Selected Early Court Decisions Regarding Equal Employment Opportunity

Several early court decisions helped to form the interpretative foundation for EEO laws such as Title VII.

Griggs v. The Duke Power Company
Case heard by the Supreme Court in which the plaintiff argued that his employer's requirement that coal handlers be high school graduates was unfairly discriminatory. In finding for the plaintiff, the Court ruled that discrimination need not be overt to be illegal, that employment practices must be related to job performance, and that the burden of proof is on the employer to show that hiring standards are job related.

protected class
Persons such as minorities and women protected by equal opportunity laws including Title VII.

Griggs v. Duke Power Company   *Griggs* was a landmark case, since the Supreme Court used it to define unfair discrimination. In this case, a suit was brought against the Duke Power Company on behalf of Willie Griggs, an applicant for a job as a coal handler. The company required its coal handlers to be high school graduates. Griggs claimed this requirement was illegally discriminatory because it wasn't related to success on the job and because it resulted in more blacks than whites being rejected for these jobs.

Griggs won the case. The decision of the Court was unanimous, and in his written opinion Chief Justice Burger laid out three crucial guidelines affecting equal employment legislation. First, the Court ruled that discrimination on the part of the employer need not be overt; in other words, the employer does not have to be shown to have intentionally discriminated against the employee or applicant—it need only be shown that discrimination did take place. Second, the court held that an employment practice (in this case requiring the high school degree) must be shown to be *job related* if it has an unequal impact on members of a **protected class.** In the words of Justice Burger,

> *The act proscribes not only overt discrimination but also practices that are fair in form, but discriminatory in operation. The touchstone is business necessity. If an employment practice which operates to exclude Negroes cannot be shown to be related to job performance the practice is prohibited.* [46]

Chief Justice Burger's opinion also *clearly placed the burden of proof on the employer to show that the hiring practice is job related.* Thus, the *employer* must show that the employment practice (in this case, requiring a high school degree) is needed to perform the job satisfactorily if it has disparate impact on (unintentionally discriminates against) members of a protected class.

Albemarle Paper Company v. Moody
Supreme Court case in which it was ruled that the validity of job tests must be documented and that employee performance standards must be unambiguous.

Albemarle Paper Company v. Moody   In the *Griggs* case, the Supreme Court had decided a screening tool (like a test) had to be job related or *valid,* in that performance on the test must be related to performance on the job. The *Albemarle* case is important because here the Court provided more details regarding how an employer should validate its screening tools—in other words, how it should prove that the test or other screening tools are related to or predict performance on the job. [47] In the *Albemarle* case the Court emphasized that if a test is to be used to screen candidates for a job, then the nature of that job—its specific duties and responsibilities—must first be carefully analyzed and documented. Similarly, the Court ruled that the performance standards for employees on the job in question should be clear and unambiguous, so the employer could intelligently identify which employees were performing better than others.

In arriving at its decision, the Court also cited the EEOC guidelines concerning acceptable selection procedures and made these guidelines the "law of the land." [48] Specifically, the Court's ruling had the effect of establishing the detailed EEOC (now federal) guidelines on validation as the procedures for validating employment practices. [49]

Equal Employment Opportunity 1989–1991: A Shifting Supreme Court

Introduction After more or less championing the cause of minorities and women in the workplace for three decades, in a series of decisions in 1989 the Supreme Court signaled a shift toward a narrower scope for civil rights protection. Various factors including the addition of several legal conservatives to the Supreme Court caused the change. But, whatever the factors were, the results were quite dramatic. For example, in one case *(Wards Cove* v. *Atonio)* the Court ruled 5 to 4 that an employer does *not* have to prove that a particular business practice, such as a test, was necessary to run the business, or valid, even if that practice is apparently discriminatory based on statistics. Instead the *plaintiff* (the applicant or employee claiming discrimination) has to prove that only illegal discrimination could have caused the disparity.

Price Waterhouse v. Hopkins The background of this case is as follows:[50] In 1982, the plaintiff, a woman, was proposed for partnership in the Price Waterhouse accounting firm. At the time, the firm had 662 partners, of whom seven were women. In 1982, 88 candidates were proposed for partnership, but only one—the employee who sued—was a woman. Of the 88, 47 became partners, 21 were rejected, and 20 were "held" for further consideration the following year. The employee who sued had brought $25 million in business with the State Department into the firm—but her promotion was held for further consideration. She responded by resigning and bringing suit under Title VII.

At the trial, it was found that both lawful and unlawful factors had contributed to her being passed over. She showed that her sex had been an unlawful factor in her denial of promotion, while the employer showed that "abrasiveness" had been a lawful factor. She won her case and won on appeal, but the U.S. Supreme Court eventually (on May 1, 1989) reversed the U.S. Court of Appeals for the District of Columbia Circuit. The Supreme Court found she would have been passed over anyway due to her "abrasiveness."[51]

Wards Cove v. **Atonio**
U.S. Supreme Court decision that makes it difficult to prove a case of unlawful discrimination against an employer.
disparate impact
Means there is an unintentional disparity between the proportion of a protected group applying for a position and the proportion getting the job.
disparate treatment
Means there is an intentional disparity between the proportion of a protected group and the proportion getting the job.

Wards Cove Packing Company v. Atonio The *Wards Cove* case is important because the Supreme Court's decision made it more difficult to prove a case of unlawful (disparate impact) discrimination against an employer. Disparate impact means there is an unintentional disparity between the proportion of a protected group applying for a position and the proportion getting the job. In disparate treatment, the disparity is allegedly intentional.

The Supreme Court acted in a 15-year-old case of alleged racial discrimination in Alaskan salmon canneries.[52] The facts of the case are as follows: Unskilled jobs in the canneries were held mostly by nonwhite Alaskans of Japanese, Filipino, Chinese, and Alaskan native descent. Higher-paid noncannery jobs (carpenters, accountants, etc.) were mostly held by white employees who were recruited in the Seattle area. Cannery and noncannery workers at Wards Cove Packing Company were housed and fed separately. Predominantly white noncannery workers were assigned to more desirable, better-insulated bunkhouses. The racial minorities at the canneries sued, claiming that the employment practices at the canneries discriminated and also had the effect of blocking them from getting the higher-paying jobs. Decisions at the lower courts were mixed; the U.S. Supreme Court's ruling favored the employer.

We have to step back several years to understand the importance of the Supreme Court's *Wards Cove* decision. In the Civil Rights Act of 1964 Congress had said that an employer may not discriminate on the basis of race, color, religion, sex, or national origin. In *Griggs* v. *Duke Power Company* the Supreme Court had defined what was meant by unfair discrimination and placed the burden of proof on the employer to show that the hiring practice in question is job related *when it has disparate impact on members of a protected class*. In the *Griggs* case the court also defined disparate impact, holding that it occurs when an employer has a policy or practice that appears to be neutral (such as the requirement in *Griggs* that all employees have a high school diploma), but that is, in practice, discriminatory.[53] After the *Griggs* case, proving that you were illegally discriminated against thus often meant just showing statistically that a biased situation existed. For example, the applicant or employee might simply have to show that one classification of jobs was primarily held by whites while a second less attractive classification was held by blacks. With this statistical case made, the burden of proof then shifted to the employer to prove that its employment practices served a necessary business purpose—a defense that became known as the *business necessity defense*. Mounting a defense in such a case was often so expensive that many employers didn't try.

Wards Cove basically changed all that. Under *Griggs,* once bias was shown by the employee, it was up to the employer to demonstrate that its practices were justified by reasonable business necessity.[54] Under *Wards Cove,* statistical imbalances themselves no longer demonstrated disparate impact: Instead the employee/applicant had to prove that the statistical imbalances were caused by an employment policy or practice of the employer.[55]

Patterson v. McLean Credit Union   The Supreme Court's decision in *Patterson* further weakened the rights of minorities and women. The basic facts of the case are as follows: The employee testified that her supervisor periodically stared at her for several minutes at a time, gave her too many tasks, caused her to complain that she was under too much pressure, and gave her tasks that included sweeping and dusting, which were not jobs given to white employees. On one occasion she testified that her supervisor told her that blacks are known to work slower than whites. She also alleged that her supervisor criticized her in staff meetings while not similarly criticizing white employees.

The main issue in *Patterson* involved permissible use of Section 1981 of the Civil Rights Act of 1866. In particular, Section 1981 (rather than the more recent Title VII) was used increasingly in the late 1970s and early 1980s to attack racial discrimination in employment because the section permits the plaintiff to seek compensatory and punitive damages (in addition to back pay), covers all employers regardless of the number of employees they have, and provides for a jury trial which is not available under Title VII.

In *Patterson* the Supreme Court said the plaintiff could not use Section 1981. It held that Section 1981 of the Civil Rights Act of 1866 could be used by minorities and women if their complaint involved either a refusal to make a contract or the impairment of the person's ability to enforce her established contract rights, neither of which, said the Court, applied in this case.[56]

Martin v. Wilks   The *Wilks* case began in 1974 and was decided by the U.S. Supreme Court on June 12, 1989. The case began when the NAACP and seven black firefighters sued the city of Birmingham, Alabama, for practicing racial discrimination. A settlement was worked out in which the city agreed to promote one black for every white it promoted. This resulted in a consent decree in which the courts allowed both parties to settle as they had agreed. A group of white firefighters subsequently sued the city to try and stop the decree from being implemented; they said the decree would have the effect of discriminating against white firefighters. This case involves the issue of affirmative action, which, as we'll see later in this chapter, means efforts made by employers that are designed to eliminate the present effects of past discrimination.

Up until *Wilks*, settlements like the one reached between the NAACP and the black firefighters under the supervision of the court meant that (under a court consent decree) the employer was protected from lawsuits by disgruntled white males. White males, for instance, couldn't sue employers who, when operating under such consent decrees, agreed to promote a certain proportion of blacks. One could reasonably assume that if employers no longer believed they were protected from such suits by white males, they might be very reluctant to enter into such affirmative action settlements. It is exactly this protection that the *Wilks* decision stripped from employers. The court, on a 5-to-4 vote, agreed that one who is not a party to the original court proceedings that led to a consent decree, or who did not agree to the original decree, is not bound by the decree and can sue on a claim of reverse discrimination. The *Wilks* decision is therefore a change in the prevailing law; up until the *Wilks* decision most federal appeals courts had held that consent decrees could not be attacked once they took affect.[57]

Arabian American Oil Company   In the *Arabian American Oil Company* case, the Court held that Title VII protections against discrimination do not extend to the foreign operations of U.S. companies. In this case, the plaintiff Ali Boureslan was a naturalized citizen of the United States who was hired by a Houston subsidiary of Aramco as a cost engineer. A year later he requested a transfer to a position with Aramco in Saudi Arabia, where he remained until his discharge in 1984. He subsequently claimed under Title VII that he was harassed and ultimately discharged on account of his race, religion, and national origin. The U.S. Supreme Court eventually held that Congress has authority to enforce its laws extraterritorially, but that Congress could not have intended Title VII to apply abroad because the statute provides no mechanisms for overseas enforcement. At that point, employees of U.S. firms stationed overseas were no longer covered by Title VII.

Equal Employment Opportunity 1991–Present

The Civil Rights Act of 1991

Civil Rights Act of 1991 (CRA 1991)
It places burden of proof back on employers and permits compensatory and punitive damages.

Supreme Court rulings such as *Wards Cove* and *Patterson* had the effect of limiting the protection of women and minority groups under equal employment laws; this prompted Congress to pass a new Civil Rights Act in 1991. The **Civil Rights Act of 1991 (CRA 1991)** was then signed into law by President Bush in November 1991. The basic effect of CRA 1991 is to reverse several U.S. Supreme Court decisions (including *Wards Cove, Patterson, Price-Waterhouse, Martin* v. *Wilkes*, and *Arabian American Oil Company*). Furthermore, as we'll see, the effect is not just to roll back the clock to where it stood prior to these Supreme Court decisions. The effect is to add additional legislation that makes it even more important that employers and their managers and supervisors adhere to both the spirit and the letter of EEO law. We can summarize the act's main provisions as follows.

***Burden of Proof* (Wards Cove)**   Prior to *Wards Cove* the equal employment litigation process basically went like this: The plaintiff (say, a rejected applicant) had to demonstrate that an employment practice (such as a test) had a disparate impact on a particular group. For example, a requirement that employees be able to lift heavy weights might unintentionally discriminate against women.[58] Then, once the plaintiff showed such disparate impact, the employer had to show that the challenged practice was job related for the position in question. For example, the *employer* had to show that the "lift heavy weights" requirement was actually required for the position in question, and that the business could not run efficiently without the requirement. In *Wards Cove,* the Supreme Court said that the burden of proof was no longer on the employer to prove that the requirement (lifting heavy weights) was a business necessity. The employer just had to show a business justification and then the burden shifted back to the plaintiff. The latter then had to prove that the requirement was put in to intentionally discriminate against the members of his or her minority group. This was difficult for plaintiffs to do.

The Civil Rights Act of 1991 rejects the Court's position and basically turns the EEO clock back to where it was prior to *Wards Cove* with respect to this matter. With the passage of CRA 1991, the burden is once again on the employer to demonstrate business necessity, not merely business justification.

Money Damages Section 102 of the new Civil Rights Act provides that an employee who is claiming *intentional discrimination* can ask for (1) compensatory damages and (2) punitive damages, if it can be shown the employer engaged in discrimination "with malice or reckless indifference to the federally protected rights of an aggrieved individual."[59]

This is a marked change from the conditions that prevailed up until 1991. Victims of intentional discrimination who had not suffered financial loss and who sued under Title VII could not then sue for compensatory or punitive damages. All they could expect was to have their jobs reinstated (or be awarded a particular job). They were also eligible for back pay, attorney's fees, and court costs. Now victims of illegal discrimination including sexual harassment can also sue for compensatory and punitive damages. This of course raises the stakes for employers. It may make it more likely that many employers will be more inclined to settle discrimination claims out of court. And it should certainly make it more likely that employers will be more conscientious about avoiding the conditions that prompt such claims.

Hiring and Promotion Under the Civil Rights Act of 1866 **(Patterson)** As previously explained, there are some advantages to suing under the Civil Rights Act of 1866, Section 1981. In the *Patterson* case, the U.S. Supreme Court held that that law didn't protect employees who, once hired, were discriminated against, for instance, in promotions or discharges. The Civil Rights Act of 1991 reverses the *Patterson* decision and explicitly states that Section 1981 applies to all instances of workplace racial and ethnic discrimination, even if they occur after hiring.[60]

Mixed Motives **(Price-Waterhouse)** In the *Price-Waterhouse* case, the Supreme Court ruled that if a personnel decision would have been taken anyway, based on nondiscriminatory reasons, the fact that there was also a discriminatory reason for the decision was not enough to prove discrimination. The Civil Rights Act of 1991, on the other hand, states that

> *An unlawful employment practice is established when the complaining party demonstrates that race, color, religion, sex, or national origin was a motivating factor for any employment practice, even though other factors also motivated the practice.*[61]

In other words, under the new Civil Rights Act, an employer can no longer avoid liability by proving it would have taken the same action even without the discriminatory motive.[62]

Consent Decrees (Martin v. Wilkes)   The effect of *Martin* was to permit individuals who had not been involved in an affirmative action consent decree to subsequently sue the employer for reverse discrimination. CRA 1991 reverses that decision. Specifically, individuals who had actual notice of the consent decree at the time (or who had a reasonable opportunity to present objections or to be represented by someone whose interests were similar to theirs at the time) cannot come back years later to attack the consent decree. In other words, subsequent objections to consent decrees—decrees often used to institute affirmative action programs—will again be difficult to raise, as they were before *Martin* v. *Wilkes*.

Overseas Employment (Arabian American Oil Company)   Recall that in this case the Supreme Court ruled that the Civil Rights Act of 1964 didn't apply outside the United States. CRA 1991 says that it does. Specifically, it now applies to employees of U.S. firms in foreign countries when such individuals are citizens of the United States.

Other Sections of CRA 1991   This Civil Rights Act contains two more sections that affect employment law. First, Section 107 of this act could actually make it a bit more difficult for minorities to prove discrimination. This section says that test scores cannot be "adjusted" to "alter the results of employment related tests on the basis of race, color, religion, sex, or national origin." Up to now, some employers might have allowed minority applicants who scored, say, 80 on a test to be employed, while nonminority applicants had to score 90. Such adjustments are no longer permitted under CRA 1991.[63]

Finally, CRA 1991 may turn out to be the first big shot in the war to break through the "glass ceiling," the collection of subtle and perhaps unintentional and invisible barriers that often prevent women and minorities from advancing at work. Glass ceiling barriers might include, for example, golf club memberships and trips to football games for male managers from which women and minorities are often unofficially banned. The Civil Rights Act of 1991 does not outlaw such glass ceilings. However, it does set up a commission to study the issue.

Global HRM

Enforcing the 1991 Civil Rights Act Abroad

The 1991 Civil Rights Act marked a substantial change in the geographic applicability of equal rights legislation. Congressional legislation generally only applies within U.S. territorial borders unless specifically stated otherwise.[64] However, CRA 1991 specifically expanded coverage by amending the definition of "employee" in Title VII to mean a U.S. citizen employed in a foreign country by a U.S.-owned or -controlled company.[65] At least theoretically, therefore, U.S. citizens now working overseas for U.S. companies enjoy the same equal employment opportunity protection as those working within U.S. borders.[66]

Two factors limit the wholesale application of CRA 1991 to U.S. employees abroad, however. First, the civil rights protections are not universal or automatic, since there are numerous exclusions. For example, an employer need not comply with Title VII if compliance would cause the employer to violate the law of the host country. (For instance, some foreign countries have statutes prohibiting the employment of women in management positions.)

48

A more vexing problem is the practical difficulty of enforcing CRA 1991 abroad. For example, the EEOC investigator's first duty in an extraterritorial case is to analyze the finances and organizational structure of the respondent, but in practice few, if any investigators are trained for this duty and no precise standards exist for such investigations.[67] Similarly, one expert argues that U.S. courts "will be little help in overseas investigations, because few foreign nations cooperate with the intrusive enforcement of U.S. civil law."[68] It is possible, therefore, that in this case CRA 1991's bark will be considerably worse than its bite and that, as one expert says, "Congress' well-meaning effort to leave no American uncovered by U.S. antidiscrimination law will not have its intended effect."[69] ◆

The Americans with Disabilities Act

Americans with Disabilities Act (ADA)
The act requiring employers to make reasonable accommodations for disabled employees, it prohibits discrimination against disabled persons.

In July 1990 President Bush signed into law the **Americans with Disabilities Act (ADA).** Title I of the act prohibits employment discrimination against the disabled.[70] The employment provisions of the ADA went into effect in July 1992. Since that time employers with 25 or more workers have been prohibited from discriminating against qualified individuals with disabilities with regard to applications, hiring, discharge, compensation, advancement, training, or other terms, conditions, or privileges of employment.[71] As of July 1994, the act covers employers with only 15 or more employees.

The Americans with Disabilities Act was enacted to reduce or eliminate serious problems of discrimination against disabled individuals. The Senate Committee on Labor and Human Resources had estimated that 43 million U.S. workers have some type of disability and that two-thirds of those between the ages of 16 and 64 are unemployed although they want to work. Testimonials like those of a severely arthritic woman who was refused employment by a college because a trustee thought "normal students shouldn't see her" and a blind Harvard law school student who was rejected for employment three different times from each of 600 corporations convinced lawmakers of the need for ADA.[72]

Being disabled does not disqualify a person for a job. Indeed, advantages in technology have enabled many people with disabilities to enter the workforce and work productively. Here, Nancy Thibeault uses specially designed equipment in her job as telephone operator and receptionist at PAC Corporation.

The act prohibits employers from discriminating against qualified disabled individuals. It also says employers must make "reasonable accommodations" for physical or mental limitations unless doing so imposes an "undue hardship" on the business.

The definitions of the act's pivotal terms are important in understanding its impact. For example, specific disabilities aren't listed; instead, the EEOC's implementing regulations regarding ADA provide that an individual is disabled when he or she has a physical or mental impairment that substantially limits one or more major life activities. They also provide that an impairment includes any physiological disorder or condition, cosmetic disfigurement, or anatomical loss affecting one or more of several body systems, or any mental or psychological disorder.[73] On the other hand, the act does set forth certain conditions that are not to be regarded as disabilities, including homosexuality, bisexuality, voyeurism, compulsive gambling, pyromania, and certain disorders resulting from the current illegal use of drugs.[74]

Simply being disabled doesn't qualify someone for a job, of course. Instead, the act prohibits discrimination against qualified individuals, in other words, those who, with (or without) a reasonable accommodation, can carry out the essential functions of the job. That means that the individual must have the requisite skills, educational background, and experience to do the essential functions of the position. A job function is essential when, for instance, it is the reason the position exists, or because the function is so highly specialized that the person doing the job is hired for his or her expertise or ability to perform that particular function.

If the individual can't perform the job as currently structured, the employer is required to make a "reasonable accommodation" unless doing so would present an "undue hardship." Reasonable accommodation might include redesigning the job, modifying work schedules, or modifying or acquiring equipment or other devices to assist the person in performing the job.

ADA's Legal Obligations   The ADA imposes certain legal obligations on employers:[75]

1. An employer must not deny a job to a disabled individual if the person is qualified and able to perform the essential functions of the job; if the person is otherwise qualified but unable to perform an essential function, the employer must make a reasonable accommodation unless doing so would result in undue hardship. One expert says that cases in which handicapped individuals are denied employment because of risk of future injury will represent the largest category of suits under ADA. He says firms must make decisions on a situation-by-situation basis and not make blanket rules excluding all persons with specific disabilities.[76]

2. Employers are not required to lower existing performance standards for a job as long as those standards are job related and uniformly applied to all employees and candidates for that job; tests or other qualification standards that may tend to screen out an individual on the basis of disability must be job related and consistent with business necessity.

3. Employers may not make preemployment inquiries about a person's disability. However, employers may ask questions about the person's ability to perform specific job functions; similarly, preemployment medical exams or medical histories may not be required, but employers may condition job offers on the results of a postoffer medical exam. Under the new EEOC ADA guidelines, "disability-related" questions are illegal and cannot be asked at the initial interview stage, specifically until the employee is actually hired. For example, EEOC says it is illegal to ask: "Do you have AIDS? Have you ever filed for workers' compensation? What prescription drugs are you currently taking? Have you ever been treated for mental health problems? How much alcohol do you drink each week?" On the other hand, an employer *can* legally ask questions such as: "Can you perform the functions of this job with or without reasonable accommodation? Please describe or demonstrate how you would perform these functions. Can you meet the attendance requirements of the job? Do you have the required licenses to perform these jobs?"[77]

4. Employers should review job application forms, interview procedures, and job descriptions. For example, employers may not ask applicants questions about their health, disabilities, medical histories, or previous worker's compensation claims.[78]

5. The ADA does not require employers to have job descriptions but it's probably advisable to do so. As one expert writes: "In virtually any ADA legal action, a critical question will be, what are the essential functions of the position involved? . . . If, for example, a disabled employee is terminated because he or she cannot perform a particular function, in the absence of a job description that includes such function it will be difficult to convince a court that the function truly was an essential part of the job."[79]

ADA in Practice   Several years have passed since the ADA's employment discrimination provisions went into effect in 1992, so we now have some experience regarding how the law is being applied.[80] About half the ADA charges filed so far alleged discriminatory termination, perhaps reflecting the fact that employees are most highly motivated to charge discrimination when they lose their jobs. Another 23% of the ADA charges alleged a failure to provide reasonable accommodations for the charging party's disability. Finally, about 13% of the ADA charges alleged a discriminatory failure to hire the person now suing; 10% raised claims of disability-based harassment at work, and most of the rest alleged claims of disability discrimination in allocation of employee benefits.

The types of disabilities alleged in ADA charges were somewhat surprising. It wasn't common conditions associated with "disability" like vision, hearing, or mobility impairments that represented most of the charges. Instead, back impairments accounted for about 20% of all ADA charges filed. However, what reportedly caught many employers and the EEOC by surprise was the prevalence of charges alleging mental impairments: Such impairments constituted almost 10% of all charges filed during the first 14 months of the act's enforcement, making it the second largest classification of disabilities named in ADA charges.[81] Given the wide range of conditions covered by the term *mental impairments* (including dyslexia, severe depression, brain damage, stress-related disorders, and mental retardation), nonphysical as well as physical job qualifications will have to be considered in drafting or reviewing job descriptions and in identifying "essential job functions" and considering possible reasonable accommodations.[82]

The question has also been raised whether employee appearance may come under the scope of the Americans with Disabilities Act.[83] In some relatively straightforward cases it would seem that the answer is probably "yes." For example, cosmetic disfigurement, anatomical loss, and disfiguring scars are probably to be treated as impairments and the people bearing them regarded as disabled.[84] However, it is not too likely that unattractiveness per se will fall under the ADA, although it may under certain state and local laws. For instance, the District of Columbia explicitly forbids discrimination on the basis of physical appearance.[85] In general the existing court decisions do not suggest that it's very likely appearance per se will emerge as a major discrimination issue over the next few years. However, as several experts have recently noted, ". . . the potential breadth of the ADA, the active scholarly interest in the appearance theme, and the statutes forbidding such discrimination suggest that changes may well be in the offing."[86]

State and Local Equal Employment Opportunity Laws

In addition to the federal laws, all states and many local governments also prohibit employment discrimination.

In most cases the effect of the state and local laws is to further restrict employers regarding their treatment of job applicants and employees. In many cases, state equal employment opportunity laws cover employers (like those with fewer than 15 employees) who are not covered by federal legislation.[87] Similarly, some local governments extend the protection of age discrimination laws to young people as well, barring discrimination not only of those over 40, but those over 17 as well; here, for instance, it would be illegal to advertise for "mature" applicants since that might discourage some teenagers from applying. The point is that a wide range of actions by many employers that might be legal under federal laws are illegal under state and local laws.[88]

State and local equal employment opportunity agencies (often called Human Resources Commissions, Commissions on Human Relations, or Fair Employment Commissions) play a role in the equal employment compliance process. When the EEOC receives a discrimination charge, it usually defers it for a limited time to the state and local agencies that have comparable jurisdiction. Then, if satisfactory remedies are not achieved, the charges are referred back to the EEOC for resolution.

TABLE 2.1 Summary of Important Equal Employment Opportunity Actions

ACTION	WHAT IT DOES
Title VII of 1964 Civil Rights Act, as amended	Bars discrimination because of race, color, religion, sex, or national origin; instituted EEOC
Executive orders	Prohibit employment discrimination by employers with federal contracts of more than $10,000 (and their subcontractors); establish office of federal compliance; require affirmative action programs
Federal agency guidelines	Indicate policy covering discrimination based on sex, national origin, and religion, as well as employee selection procedures; for example, require validation of tests
Supreme court decisions: *Griggs v. Duke Power Co., Albemarle v. Moody*	Rule that job requirements must be related to job success; that discrimination need not be overt to be proved; that the burden of proof is on the employer to prove the qualification is valid
Equal Pay Act of 1963	Requires equal pay for men and women for performing similar work
Age Discrimination in Employment Act of 1967	Prohibits discriminating against a person 40 or over in any area of employment because of age
State and local laws	Often cover organizations too small to be covered by federal laws
Vocational Rehabilitation Act of 1973	Requires affirmative action to employ and promote qualified handicapped persons and prohibits discrimination against handicapped persons
Pregnancy Discrimination Act of 1978	Prohibits discrimination in employment against pregnant women, or related conditions
Vietnam Era Veterans' Readjustment Assistance Act of 1974	Requires affirmative action in employment for veterans of the Vietnam war era
Ward Cove v. Atonio, Patterson v. McLean Credit Union	Made it more difficult to prove a case of unlawful discrimination against an employer
Martin v. Wilks	Allowed consent degrees to be attacked and could have had a chilling effect on certain affirmative action programs
Americans with Disabilities Act of 1990	Strengthens the need for most employers to make reasonable accommodations for disabled employees at work; prohibits discrimination
Civil Rights Act of 1991	Reverses *Wards Cove, Patterson,* and *Martin* decisions; places burden of proof back on employer and permits compensatory and punitive money damages for discrimination

Summary

Selected equal employment opportunity legislation, executive orders, and agency guidelines are summarized in Table 2.1.

Defenses Against Discrimination Allegations

What Is Adverse Impact?

adverse impact
The overall impact of employer practices that result in significantly higher percentages of members of minorities and other protected groups being rejected for employment, placement, or promotion.

Adverse impact plays a central role in discriminatory practice allegations. Under the Civil Rights Act of 1991, a person who believes he or she has been unintentionally discriminated against need only establish a prima facie case of discrimination: This means showing that the employer's selection procedures did have an adverse impact on a protected minority group. Adverse impact "refers to the total employment process that results in a significantly higher percentage of a protected group in the candidate population being rejected for employment, placement, or promotion."[89]

What does this mean? If a minority or other protected group applicant for the job feels he or she has been discriminated against, the applicant need only show that the selection procedures resulted in an adverse impact on his or her minority group. (For example, if 80% of the white applicants passed the test, but only 20% of the black applicants passed, a black applicant has a prima facie case proving adverse impact.) Then, once the employee has proved his or her point, the burden of proof shifts to the employer. It becomes the employer's task to prove that its test, application blank, interview, or the like, is a valid predictor of performance on the job (and that it was applied fairly and equitably to both minorities and nonminorities).

How Can Adverse Impact Be Proved?

It is actually not too difficult for an applicant to show that one of an employer's procedures (such as a selection test) had an adverse impact on a protected group. Four basic approaches can be used.

1. *Disparate Rejection Rates.* This means comparing the rejection rates for a minority group and another group (usually the remaining nonminority applicants). For example, ask "Is there a disparity between the percentage of blacks among those applying for a particular position and the percentage of blacks among those hired for the position?" Or, "Do proportionately more blacks than whites fail the written examination we give to all applicants?" If the answer to either question is yes, you and your firm could be faced with a lawsuit.

disparate rejection rates
One test for adverse impact in which it can be demonstrated that there is a discrepancy between rates of rejection of members of a protected group and of others.

Federal agencies adopted a formula to determine when **disparate rejection rates** actually exist. Their guidelines state that "a selection rate for any racial, ethnic or sex group which is less than 4/5 or 80% of the rate for the group with the highest rate will generally be regarded as evidence of adverse impact, while a greater than 4/5 rate will generally not be regarded as evidence of adverse impact." For example, suppose 90% of male applicants are hired, but only 60% of female applicants are hired. Then, since 60% is less than four-fifths of 90%, adverse impact exists as far as these federal agencies are concerned.[90]

restricted policy
Another test for adverse impact, involving demonstration that an employer's hiring practices exclude a protected group, whether intentionally or not.

2. *Restricted Policy.* The **restricted policy** approach means demonstrating that the employer has intentionally or unintentionally been using a hiring policy to exclude members of a protected group. Here the problem is usually obvious. For example, policies have been unearthed against hiring bartenders under six feet tall. Evidence of restricted policies such as these (against women) is enough to prove adverse impact and expose an employer to litigation.

3. *Population Comparisons.* This approach compares the percentage of a firm's minority-group employees and the percentage of that minority in the general population in the surrounding community.[91] This approach can be complicated to use in practice. For some jobs, such as manual laborer or secretary, it makes sense to compare the percentage of minority employees with the percentage of minorities in the surrounding community, since these employees will in fact be drawn from the surrounding community. However, for some jobs, such as engineers, the surrounding community may not be the relevant labor market, since these people may have to be recruited nationwide. Determining whether an employer has enough black engineers might involve determining the number of black engineers available nationwide rather than just in the surrounding community. Defining the relevant labor market is thus a crucial task here.

4. *McDonnell-Douglas Test.* This approach (which grew out of a case at the McDonnell-Douglas Corporation) shows that the applicant was qualified but was rejected by the employer who continued seeking applicants for the position. It is used in situations of intentional disparate treatment rather than unintentional

disparate impact (for which approaches 1–3 are used). Here the rejected protected-class candidate uses the following guidelines as set forth by the U.S. Supreme Court: (a) that he or she belongs to a protected class; (b) that he or she applied and was qualified for a job in which the employer was seeking applicants; (c) that, despite this qualification, he or she was rejected; and (d) that, after his or her rejection, the position remained open and the employer continued to seek applications from persons of the complainant's qualifications. If all these conditions are met, then a prima facie case of disparate treatment is established. At that point the employer is required to articulate a legitimate nondiscriminatory reason for its action and produce evidence but not prove that it acted on the basis of such a reason. If it meets this relatively easy standard, the plaintiff then has the burden of proving that the employer's articulated reason is merely a pretext for engaging in unlawful discrimination.

Bringing a Case of Discrimination: Summary   Assume that an employer turns down a member of a protected group for a job based on a test score (although it could have been some other employment practice such as interview questions or application blank responses). Further assume that the person believes that he or she was discriminated against due to being in a protected class and decides to sue the employer.

All he or she basically has to do is show that the employer's test had an adverse impact on members of his or her minority group, and there are four approaches that could be used to show that such adverse impact exists: disparate rejection rates, restricted policy, population comparisons, and the McDonnell-Douglas test. Once the person has shown the existence of adverse impact to the satisfaction of the court, the burden of proof shifts to the employer who then has to defend against the charges of discrimination.

There are then basically two defenses that the employer can use: the *bona fide occupational qualification (BFOQ)* defense and the *business necessity* defense. Either can be used to justify an employment practice that has been shown to have an adverse impact on the members of a minority group.[92]

Bona Fide Occupational Qualification

bona fide occupational qualification (BFOQ)
Requirement that an employee be of a certain religion, sex, or national origin where that is reasonably necessary to the organization's normal operation. Specified by the 1964 Civil Rights Act.

One approach an employer can use to defend itself against charges of discrimination is to claim that the employment practice is a **bona fide occupational qualification (BFOQ)** for performing the job. Specifically, Title VII provides that "it should not be an unlawful employment practice for an employer to hire an employee . . . on the basis of religion, sex, or national origin in those certain instances where religion, sex, or national origin is a bona fide occupational qualification reasonably necessary to the normal operation of that particular business or enterprise." BFOQ is a statutory exception to the equal employment opportunity laws that allows employers to discriminate in certain very specific instances. The BFOQ exception is usually interpreted narrowly by the courts. As a practical matter, it is used primarily (but not exclusively) as a defense against charges of intentional discrimination based on age. BFOQ is essentially a defense to a disparate treatment case based upon direct evidence of intentional discrimination and not to disparate impact (unintentional) discrimination.

Age as a BFOQ   The Age Discrimination in Employment Act (ADEA) does permit disparate treatment in those instances when age is a BFOQ. For example, age is a BFOQ when federal requirements impose a compulsory age limit, such as when the Federal Aviation Agency sets a ceiling of age 64 for pilots. Actors required for youthful or elderly roles or persons used to advertise or promote the sales of products designed for youthful or elderly consumers suggest other instances when age may be a BFOQ. As another example, a bus line's maximum-age hiring policy for bus drivers has been held to be a BFOQ by the courts. The court said that the essence of the business was safe transportation of passengers, and given that, the employer could strive to employ the most qualified persons available.[93] Yet Supreme Court decisions such as *Western Airlines, Inc.* v. *Criswell* seem to be narrowing BFOQ exceptions under ADEA. In this case the Court held that the airline could not impose a mandatory retirement age (of 60) for flight engineers, even though they could for pilots. Similarly, in *Johnson* v. *Mayor and City Council of Baltimore,* the Court held that the city of Baltimore could not require its firefighters to retire at age 55.

Some employers historically used "overqualification" as a tactic for rejecting older candidates, but today there is a great risk that a jury will find such an approach to be illegal.[94] In a related case, a radio station changed its format from "beautiful music" featuring violin-driven instrumentals to a more upbeat "easy listening" style and fired all its over-40 DJs on the assumption they didn't fit the new style. The U.S. Court of Appeals in Chicago ruled in the DJs' favor, saying they should have been auditioned and given a chance to change their style.[95]

There has been a dramatic increase in the number of employment-related age discrimination complaints filed with state and federal agencies over the past few years. There are several reasons for this, including increasing numbers of older workers, increasingly militant older workers, corporate downsizings, and the prospect of collecting double damages (as plaintiffs can under the Age Discrimination in Employment Act).[96]

Employer defenses against such ADEA claims usually fall into one of two categories: BFOQ or FOA (factors other than age). Employers using the BFOQ defense admit their personnel decisions were based on age but seek to justify them by showing that the decisions were reasonably necessary to normal business operations. (Here, for example, an airline might insist that a pilot maximum-age requirement is necessary for the safe transportation of its passengers.) An employer who raises the FOA defense generally argues that its actions were "reasonable" based on some business factor other than age, such as the terminated person's poor performance.

Religion as a BFOQ   Religion may be a BFOQ in the case of religious organizations or societies that require employees to share their particular religion. For example, religion may be a BFOQ when hiring persons to teach in a denominational school. Similarly, practices such as Saturday work rules that adversely affect certain religious groups are excusable if the employer "is unable to reasonably accommodate . . . without undue hardship."[97] In this and in all cases, however, the BFOQ defense is construed very narrowly by the courts.

Sex as a BFOQ   It is difficult today to claim that sex is a BFOQ for most jobs for which employers are recruiting. For example, sex is not accepted as a BFOQ for positions just because they require overtime or the lifting of heavy objects. Sex is not a BFOQ for parole and probation officers, nor, of course, is sex a BFOQ for flight attendants.[98] Courts have said that it is illegal to apply a "no marriage" rule to female flight attendants and not to male employees, even though one airline claimed the rule was justified as a BFOQ due to customer preference. On the other hand, sex may be a BFOQ for positions requiring specific physical characteristics necessarily possessed by one sex. These include positions like actor, model, and restroom attendant.

National Origin as a BFOQ   In some cases a person's country of national origin may be a BFOQ. For example, an employer who is running the Chinese pavilion at a fair might claim that Chinese heritage is a BFOQ for persons to be selected as pavilion employees to deal with the public.

Business Necessity

business necessity
Justification for an otherwise discriminatory employment practice, provided there is an overriding legitimate business purpose.

The **business necessity** defense basically requires showing that there is an overriding business purpose for the discriminatory practice and that the practice is therefore acceptable.

It's not easy proving that a practice is required for "business necessity."[99] The Supreme Court has made it clear that business necessity does not encompass such matters as avoiding inconvenience, annoyance, or expense to the employer. The Second Circuit Court of Appeals held that business necessity means an "irresistible demand" and that to be retained the practice "must not only directly foster safety and efficiency" but also be essential to these goals.[100] Similarly, another court held that

> the test is whether there exists an overriding legitimate business purpose such that the practice is necessary to the safe and efficient operation of a business; thus, the business purpose must be sufficiently compelling to override any racial impact; and the challenged practice must effectively carry out the business purpose it is alleged to serve.[101]

Thus, to repeat, it is not easy to prove that a practice is required for business necessity. For example, an employer cannot generally discharge employees whose wages have been garnished merely because garnishment (requiring the employer to divert part of the person's wages to pay his or her debts) creates an inconvenience for the employer. On the other hand, the business necessity defense has been used successfully by many employers. Thus, in *Spurlock* v. *United Airlines,* a minority candidate sued United Airlines, stating that its requirements that pilot candidates have 500 flight hours and college degrees were unfairly discriminatory. The court agreed that these requirements did have an adverse impact on members of the person's minority group. However, the court held that in light of the cost of the training program and the tremendous human and economic risks involved in hiring unqualified candidates, the selection standards were required by business necessity and were job related.[102] In general, when a job requires a small amount of skill and training, the courts scrutinize closely any preemployment standards or criteria that discriminate against minorities. The employer in such instances has a heavy burden to demonstrate that the practices are job related. However, there is a correspondingly lighter burden when the job requires a high degree of skill and when the economic and human risks in hiring an unqualified applicant are great.[103]

Attempts by employers to show that their selection tests or other employment practices are valid represent one example of the business necessity defense. Here the employer is required to show that the test or other practice is job related—in other words, that it is a valid predictor of performance on the job. Where such validity can be established, the courts have often supported the use of the test or other employment practice as a business necessity. Used in this context, the word *validity* basically means the degree to which the test or other employment practice is related to or predicts performance on the job; validation will be discussed in Chapter 5.

Other Considerations in Discriminatory Practice Defenses

There are three other points to stress in regard to defending against charges of discrimination. First, good intentions are no excuse. As the Supreme Court held in the *Griggs* case,

> *Good intent or absence of discriminatory intent does not redeem procedures or testing mechanisms that operate as built-in headwinds for minority groups and are unrelated to measuring job capability.*[104]

Second, employers cannot count on hiding behind collective bargaining agreements (for instance, by claiming that the discriminatory practice is required by a union agreement). Courts have often held that equal employment opportunity laws take precedence over the rights embodied in a labor contract. However, in a related matter, the U.S. Supreme Court, in its *Stotts* decision, did recently hold that a court cannot require retention of black employees hired under a consent decree in preference to white employees with greater seniority who were protected by a bona fide seniority system. There is disagreement regarding whether this decision also extends to hiring, recruitment, promotions, transfers, and layoffs not governed by seniority systems.[105]

Finally, remember that although a defense is often the most sensible response to charges of discrimination, it is not the only response. When confronted with the fact that one or more of your personnel practices is discriminatory, you can react by agreeing to eliminate the illegal practice and (when required) by compensating the people you discriminated against.

Illustrative Discriminatory Employment Practices

A Note on What You Can and Cannot Do

Before proceeding, we should clarify what federal fair employment laws allow (and do not allow) you to say and do. Federal laws like Title VII usually do not expressly ban preemployment questions about an applicant's race, color, religion, sex, or national origin. In other words, "with the exception of personnel policies calling for outright discrimination against the members of some protected group, it is not really the intrinsic nature of an employer's personnel policies or practices that the courts object to. Instead, it is the result of applying a policy or practice in a particular way or in a particular context that leads to an adverse impact on some protected group."[106] For example, it is not illegal to ask a job candidate about her marital status (although at first glance such a question might seem discriminatory). In reality, you can ask such a question as long as you can show either that you do not discriminate or that the practice can be defended as a BFOQ or business necessity.

But, in practice, there are two good reasons why most employers avoid such questionable practices. First, although federal law may not bar asking such questions, many state and local laws do. Second, the EEOC has said that it will disapprove of such practices (as asking women their marital status or applicants their age). Therefore, just asking such questions may raise a red flag that draws the attention of the EEOC and other regulatory agencies. Employers who use such practices will thus increase their chances of having to defend themselves against charges of discriminatory employment practices.

Inquiries and practices like those summarized on the next few pages are not illegal per se. They are "problem questions" because they tend to identify an ap-

Finally, if the EEOC is unable to obtain an acceptable conciliation agreement within 30 days after a finding of reasonable cause to believe that discrimination occurred, it may sue the employer in a federal district court. The EEOC is now also experimenting with using outside mediators to settle claims in selected cities.[117] In a typical recent year about 88,000 charges of alleged discrimination were filed with the EEOC, and the commission had a backlog of close to 85,000 cases.[118] Of discrimination charges filed, about 36% were based on race; 27% on sex; 23% on age; 17% on disability; 8.5% on national origin; 1.6% on religion; and 1.5% on equal pay.[119]

How to Respond to Employment Discrimination Charges

There are several things to keep in mind when confronted by a charge of illegal employment discrimination; some of the more important can be summarized as follows:[120]

Investigating the Charge   First, remember that EEOC investigators are not judges and aren't empowered to act as courts; they cannot make findings of discrimination on their own but can merely make recommendations. If the EEOC eventually determines that an employer may be in violation of a law, its only recourse is to file a suit or issue a Notice of Right to Sue to the person who filed the charge.

As far as documents are concerned, it may often be in the employer's best interests to cooperate (or appear cooperative). However, remember that the EEOC can only ask for, not demand, the submission of documents.[121] The EEOC can ask employers to submit documents and ask for the appearance and testimony of witnesses under oath. However, it cannot compel employers to comply. If an employer feels that the EEOC has overstepped its authority and refuses to cooperate, the commission's only recourse is to obtain a court subpoena.

It may also be in the employer's best interest to give the EEOC a position statement based on its own investigation of the matter. One congressional investigation found, at least in the EEOC's Chicago office, that EEOC investigators were writing up cases based solely on the position statement filed by the employer because the EEOC is under such internal pressure to resolve cases. According to one management attorney, employers' position statements should contain words to the effect that "We understand that a charge of discrimination has been filed against this establishment and this statement is to inform the agency that the company has a policy against discrimination and would not discriminate in the manner charged in the complaint." The statement should be supported by some statistical analysis of the work force, copies of any documents that support the employer's position, or an explanation of any legitimate business justification for the employment decision that is the subject of the complaint.[122]

If a predetermination settlement isn't reached, the EEOC will completely investigate the charge, and here there are three major principles an employer should follow. First, it should ensure that there is information in the EEOC's file demonstrating lack of merit of the charge; often the best way to do that is not by answering the EEOC's questionnaire but by providing a detailed statement describing the firm's defense in its best and most persuasive light.

Second, the employer should limit the information supplied as narrowly as possible to only those issues raised in the charge itself. For example, if the charge only alleges sex discrimination, the firm should not respond unwittingly to the EEOC's request for a breakdown of employees by age and sex. Finally, the employer should seek as much information as possible about the charging party's claim in order to ensure it understands the claim and its ramifications.

Information Technology and HR:
Equal Employment
Utilization Analysis

Companies and universities that have grants or contracts with the federal government are required periodically to complete utilization analyses, which are then submitted to the Department of Labor's Office of Contract Compliance Programs (OFCCP). The basis of comparison may be the most recently completed census on a valid industry survey. The comparison is made between (1) company employees in various EEO categories or subgroups (women, blacks, and so on) and (2) the number of people in the recruitment area who state that they have comparable skills in response to census or employment service requests for information.

A report format called the Availability Analysis, accepted by OFCCP, allows the employer to assign appropriate weights to the following eight factors which are incorporated into the report: (1) general population, but including only those subgroups who are seeking employment; (2) percentage of unemployment; (3) percentage of work force; (4) requisite skills available in the immediate area; (5) requisite skills available in the recruitment area; (6) feeder jobs from which internal employees may be promoted or transferred; (7) training institutions in recruitment area; and (8) internal training available. In other words, this is the employer's opportunity to show the effect on hiring of certain ingredients in the internal and external environments for that specific company. Thus, if there is no adequate training facility for crafts in the area, that factor may have no value (zero) in addressing recruitment needs for Category 5; Skilled Crafts.

On the other hand, the company might hire plumbers' helpers and, over a period of three years, train those helpers both on the job and in the classroom so that the employees can sit for the licensing exam. In this case, internal training would account for a significant portion of individuals placed into the position of plumber. The company could examine the percentage hired versus the percentage promoted over the last few years to appropriately balance the weights.

The usual goal for any given category is for the labor force of the company to approximate the general population's availability of that skill level.

Spreadsheets can easily accommodate these comparisons through user-friendly formulas which calculate weights, percentages, sums, and complicated "if-then" statements. Employees are roughly divided into approximately seven categories which differentiate between sales, clerical, crafts, technical, supervisors, professionals, and executives. These main groups are then subdivided by salary ranges. Within each group, the employees are counted according to race and sex. When a spreadsheet has been established, the count in each category (black male, black female, and so on) may be manually entered along with the number of vacancies that were filled the previous year. All the other data are then completed by the spreadsheet as your formulas pull from the few entries you have made.

The population of the labor area usually changes only with the census. The percentage of unemployment, which is calculated by the state employment service, changes monthly. The weight that you assign each factor should change infrequently unless there has been a significant change in one of the factors, such as the unemployment rate. After the formulas have been established and the raw data entered, the spreadsheet will compare availability with actual current utilization. If underutilization exists, the spreadsheet is able to calculate the percentage of underutilization, how many hires or transfers are needed to overcome the underutilization, and how many need to be hired in the current year. The OFCCP report must be calculated for the major minorities (such as black and Hispanic, or whatever protected groups represent more than 10% to 12% of the labor force in your immediate geographical area) and females.

The reason that this information should be built into a spreadsheet is so that goals for the given year may be available to recruiters and hiring supervisors at the beginning of the measured year. Although affirmative action does not require the company to favor protected groups (assuming there is no court order to require partiality), significant underutilization in a particular group strongly suggests that the recruitment techniques need to be examined. ◆

The Fact-Finding Conference   Problems can arise in the EEOC's *fact-finding conferences*. According to the commission, these conferences are supposed to be informal meetings held early in the investigatory process aimed at defining issues and determining whether there is a basis for negotiation. According to one expert, however, the EEOC's emphasis here is often on settlement. Its investigators therefore use the conferences to find weak spots in each party's respective position so that they can use this information as leverage to push for a settlement.

If an employer wants a settlement, the fact-finding conference can be a good forum at which to negotiate, but there are three big problems to watch out for. First, the only official record maintained is the notes taken by the EEOC investigator, and the parties cannot have access to them to rectify mistakes or clarify facts. Second, the employer can bring an attorney but the EEOC often "seems to go out of its way to tell employers that an attorney's presence is unnecessary."[123] Finally, these conferences are often arranged soon after a charge is filed before the employer has been fully informed of the charges and facts of the case.

An employer should thoroughly prepare witnesses who are going to testify at a fact-finding conference, especially supervisors, because their statements can be considered admissions against the employer's interest. Therefore, before appearing, they need to be aware of the legal significance of the facts they will present and the possible claims that may be made by the charging party and other witnesses.

The EEOC's Determination and the Attempted Conciliation

If the fact-finding conference does not solve the matter, the EEOC's investigator will determine whether there is reason to believe ("cause") or not to believe ("no cause") that discrimination may have taken place, and there are several things to keep in mind here. First, the investigator's recommendation is often the determining factor in whether the EEOC finds cause, so it is usually best to be courteous and cooperative (within limits). Second, if there is a finding of cause, review the finding very carefully; make sure that inaccuracies are pointed out in writing to the EEOC. Use this letter to again try to convince the EEOC, the charging party, and the charging party's attorney that the charge is without merit in spite of the finding. Finally, keep in mind that even with a no-cause finding, the charging party will still be issued a right to sue letter by the EEOC and will then be allowed 90 days from receipt of the letter to bring a private lawsuit.

If the EEOC issues a cause finding, it will ask you to conciliate. However, some experts argue against conciliating at this point for several reasons. First, the EEOC often views conciliation not as a compromise but as complete relief to the charging party. Second, "if you have properly investigated and evaluated the case previously, there may be no real advantage in settling at this stage. It is more than likely (based on the statistics) that no suit will be filed by the EEOC."[124] Furthermore, even if a lawsuit is later filed by either the EEOC or the charging party, the employer can consider settling after receiving the complaint.

Avoiding Discrimination Lawsuits

Employment discrimination claims constitute the largest number of civil suits filed annually in federal courts. As a result, some companies are setting up internal dispute resolution procedures similar to the following one at Aetna Life and Casualty Company:

Step 1   First the employee discusses the problem with a supervisor, who may consult other members of the management team who might have handled similar problems.

Step 2 The employee may contact a divisional personnel consultant for a case review if he or she is dissatisfied with the results of the first step. The employee is then informed and advised on plausible alternatives.

Step 3 If the employee believes that company policy is not being followed, he or she may then request a corporate-level review of the case, and a corporate consultant will review the case with management. The employee is then notified of the decision in writing.

Step 4 Finally, a senior management review committee may be asked to review the case. At Aetna the committee itself comprises the senior vice president of the employees' division as well as the vice presidents of corporate personnel and corporate public involvement.[125]

Compulsory Arbitration of Employment Discrimination Claims

Litigation is not necessarily the only alternative when it comes to resolving employment discrimination claims. The U.S. Supreme Court's decisions in *Gilmer* v. *Interstate/Johnson Lane Corp.* and similar cases ". . . have made it clear that employment discrimination plaintiffs may be compelled to arbitrate their claims under some circumstances."[126] In *Gilmer* the Supreme Court held that an agreement entered into between a stockbroker and the stock exchange providing for mandatory arbitration of all employment-related disputes can require arbitration of claims arising under the Federal Age Discrimination in Employment Act (ADEA).

The Supreme Court's decision helped to clarify a split that had existed among courts. Prior to *Gilmer,* courts had been split over whether plaintiffs who had signed private employment-related arbitration agreements could be compelled to arbitrate statutory employment discrimination claims like those in the various federal equal employment laws described in this chapter. Some courts were willing to compel arbitration of such claims, while others were not. *Gilmer* resolved some of these conflicting views. The court decided that Mr. Gilmer, who had been required by his employer to register as a securities representative with the New York Stock Exchange and thereby sign a registration application containing an arbitration provision, had to arbitrate his age discrimination claim after he was terminated at age 62.

It is still not clear how widely the *Gilmer* decision will affect employment discrimination claims. On the one hand, there seems little doubt that within the securities industry, any employee who executed a similar registration document containing an arbitration agreement may be compelled to arbitrate ADEA claims arising out of his or her employment.[127] The extent of its impact outside the industry is not yet clear.[128]

However, in light of the fact that compulsory arbitration may come to be viewed as an acceptable alternative to litigation by many courts, the following practical suggestions are in order:[129]

> Employers should review immediately all employment discrimination filed against them in state and federal courts to determine whether they involve an employee subject to a registration agreement similar to the one signed by Mr. Gilmer, or some other type of agreement to arbitrate. They should then decide whether to move to compel arbitration of the claim.[130]
>
> Employers "may wish to consider inserting a mandatory arbitration clause in their employment applications or employee handbooks."[131]

5. Broadening the work skills of incumbent employees.
6. Internalizing the equal employment policy to encourage supervisors' support of it.

Some of the possible tactics or actions that the compliance officers felt would reflect a good faith effort on the part of the employer are also summarized in Table 2.2. For example, a good faith effort aimed at increasing the minority female applicant flow might involve actions like "include minority colleges and universities in campus recruitment programs" and "retain applications of unhired minority and female applicants to be reviewed as vacancies occur." Actions like these, this writer concludes, can help to ensure that the employer's good faith effort is an effective one, both in improving the employer's utilization of minorities and women and in convincing the EEOC that a good faith effort to do so was made.

Chapter Review

Summary

1. Legislation barring discrimination is nothing new. For example, the Fifth Amendment to the U.S. Constitution (ratified in 1791) states that no person shall be deprived of life, liberty, or property without due process of law.

2. New legislation barring employment discrimination included Title VII of the 1964 Civil Rights Act (as amended), which bars discrimination because of race, color, religion, sex, or national origin; various executive orders; federal guidelines (covering procedures for validating employee selection tools, etc.); the Equal Pay Act of 1963; and the Age Discrimination in Employment Act of 1967. In addition, various court decisions (such as *Griggs* v. *Duke Power Company*) and state and local laws bar various aspects of discrimination.

3. The EEOC was created by Title VII of the Civil Rights Act. It is empowered to try conciliating discrimination complaints, but if this fails, the EEOC has the power to go directly to court to enforce the law.

4. The Civil Rights Act of 1991 had the effect of revising several Supreme Court equal employment decisions and "rolling back the clock." It placed the burden of proof back on employers, said postemployment decisions were covered by the 1866 Civil Rights Act, held that a nondiscriminatory reason was insufficient to let an employer avoid liability for an action that also had a discriminatory motive, and said that Title VII applied to U.S. employees of U.S. firms overseas. It also now permits compensatory and punitive damages, as well as jury trials.

5. The Americans with Disabilities Act prohibits employment discrimination against the disabled. Specifically, qualified persons cannot be discriminated against if the firm can make reasonable accommodations without undue hardship on the business.

6. A person who feels he or she has been discriminated against by a personnel procedure or decision must prove either that he or she was subjected to unlawful disparate treatment (intentional discrimination) or that the procedure in question has a disparate impact (unintentional discrimination) upon members of his or her protected class. Disparate treatment can be proven under the McDonnell-Douglas standards, while disparate impact proof can involve disparate rejection rates, restrictive policies, or population comparisons. Once a prima facie case of disparate *treatment* is established, an employer must produce evidence that its decision was based upon legitimate nondiscriminatory reasons. If the employer does that, the person claiming discrimination must prove the employer's reasons are just a pretext for letting the company discriminate. Once a prima facie case of disparate *im-*

pact has been established, the employer must produce evidence that the allegedly discriminatory practice or procedure is job related and is based upon a substantial business reason. If it does so, the employee must prove a less discriminatory alternative existed that would have been equally effective in achieving the employer's legitimate objectives or disprove the employer's justification for disparate impact.

7. Various specific discriminatory human resource management practices that an employer should avoid were discussed.

   a. *In recruitment.* An employer usually should not rely on word-of-mouth advertising or give false or misleading information to minority-group members. Also (usually), do not specify the desired sex in advertising or in any way suggest that applicants might be discriminated against.

   b. *In selection.* Avoid using any educational or other requirements where (1) it can be shown that minority-group members are less likely to possess the qualification and (2) such requirement is also not job related. Tests that disproportionately screen out minorities and women *and that are not job related* are deemed unlawful by the courts. Do not give preference to relatives of current employees (when most are nonminority) or specify physical characteristics unless it can be proved they are needed for job performance. Similarly, a person's arrest record should not be used to disqualify him or her automatically for a position, nor should a person be fired whose salary has been garnished. Remember that you can use various tests and standards, but must prove that they are job related or show that they are not used to discriminate against protected groups.

8. In practice, a person's charge to the EEOC is often first referred to a local agency. When it does proceed, and if it finds reasonable cause to believe that discrimination occurred, EEOC has 30 days to try to work out a conciliation. Important points for the employer to remember include (a) EEOC investigators can only make recommendations, (b) you cannot be compelled to submit documents without a court order, and (c) you may limit the information you do submit. Also make sure you clearly document your position (as the employer).

9. There are two basic defenses an employer can use in the event of a discriminatory practice allegation. One is *business necessity.* Attempts to show that tests or other selection standards are valid is one example of this defense. *Bona fide occupational qualification* is the second defense. This is applied when, for example, religion, national origin, or sex is a bona fide requirement of the job (such as for actors or actresses). An employer's "good intentions" and/or a collective bargaining agreement are not defenses. (A third defense is that the decision was made on the basis of legitimate nondiscriminatory reasons [such as poor performance] having nothing to do with the prohibited discrimination alleged.)

10. Eight steps in an affirmative action program (based on suggestions from the EEOC) are (a) issue a written equal employment policy, (b) appoint a top official, (c) publicize policy, (d) survey present minority and female employment, (e) develop goals and timetables, (f) develop and implement specific programs to achieve goals, (g) establish an internal audit and reporting system, and (h) develop support of in-house and community programs.

Key Terms

Title VII of the 1964 Civil Rights Act
Equal Employment Opportunity Commission (EEOC)
affirmative action
Office of Federal Contract Compliance Programs (OFCCP)
Equal Pay Act of 1963
Age Discrimination in Employment Act of 1967

Vocational Rehabilitation Act of 1973
School Board of Nassau County v. *Arline*
Vietnam Era Veterans' Readjustment Act of 1974
Pregnancy Discrimination Act (PDA)
federal agency guidelines
sexual harassment

Meritor Savings Bank, FSB v. *Vinson*
Griggs v. *Duke Power Company*
protected class
Albemarle Paper Company v. *Moody*
Wards Cove v. *Atonio*
disparate impact
disparate treatment
Civil Rights Act of 1991

Americans with Disabilities
  Act (ADA)
adverse impact
disparate rejection rates
restricted policy

bona fide occupational
  qualification (BFOQ)
business necessity
good faith effort strategy

quota strategy
reverse discrimination
*United Steelworkers of
  America* v. *Weber*

Discussion Questions and Exercises

1. What is Title VII? What does it say?
2. What important precedents were set by the *Griggs* v. *Duke Power Company* case? The *Albemarle* v. *Moody* case?
3. What is adverse impact? How can it be proven?
4. Assume you are a supervisor on an assembly line; you are responsible for hiring subordinates, supervising them, and recommending them for promotion. Compile a list of discriminatory management practices you should avoid.
5. Explain the defenses and exceptions to discriminatory practice allegations.
6. What is the difference between affirmative action and equal employment opportunity? Explain how you would set up an affirmative action program.
7. Compare and contrast the issues presented in *Bakke* and *Weber* with new court rulings on affirmative action. What is the current direction of affirmative action as a policy in light of the *Johnson* ruling?
8. Explain how the Civil Rights Act of 1991 "turned back the clock" on equal employment Supreme Court cases decided from 1989 to 1991.

Application Exercises

RUNNING CASE: Carter Cleaning Company
A Question of Discrimination

One of the first problems Jennifer faced at her father's Carter Cleaning Centers concerned the inadequacies of the firm's current HR management practices and procedures.

One problem that particularly concerned her was the lack of attention to equal employment matters. Virtually all hiring was handled independently by each store manager, and the managers themselves had received no training regarding such fundamental matters as the types of questions that should not be asked of job applicants. It was therefore not unusual—in fact, it was routine—for female applicants to be asked questions such as "Who's going to take care of your children while you are at work?" and for minority applicants to be asked questions about arrest records and credit histories. Nonminority applicants—three store managers were white males and three were white females, by the way—were not asked these questions, as Jennifer discerned from her interviews with the managers. Based on discussions with her father, Jennifer deduced that part of the rea-

son for the laid-back attitude toward equal employment stemmed from (1) her father's lack of sophistication regarding the legal requirements and (2) the fact that, as Jack Carter put it, "Virtually all our workers are women or minority members anyway, so no one can really come in here and accuse us of being discriminatory, can they?"

Jennifer decided to mull that question over, but before she could, she was faced with two serious equal rights problems. Two women in one of her stores privately confided to her that their manager was making unwelcome sexual advances toward them, and one claimed he had threatened to fire her unless she "socialized" with him after hours. And during a fact-finding trip to another store, an elderly gentleman—he was 73 years old—complained of the fact that although he had almost 50 years of experience in the business, he was being paid less than people half his age who were doing the very same job. Jennifer's review of the stores resulted in the following questions.

Questions

1. Is it true, as Jack Carter claims, that "we can't be accused of being discriminatory because we hire mostly women and minorities anyway"?

2. How should Jennifer and her company address the sexual harassment charges and problems?

3. How should she and her company address the possible problems of age discrimination?

4. Given the fact that each of its stores has only a handful of employees, is her company in fact covered by equal rights legislation?

5. And finally, aside from the specific problems, what other personnel management matters (application forms, training, and so on) have to be reviewed given the need to bring them into compliance with equal rights laws?

CASE INCIDENT: Eliminating the Effects of Past Discrimination

The Stormsville Company has a job career ladder that starts at job class 1, the lowest paid, and ends at job class 24, the highest. Normally one moves up the ladder, from job class to job class, with the worker who has had the job longest in any one job class being given preference whenever there is a vacancy in the next higher job class. In the past, however, there was one major exception: No African-American could be promoted above job class 5.

Assuming this discriminatory provision is eliminated, what should be the rights of Mr. X, an African-American with 24 years of departmental seniority, who is still in job class 5, while whites with equal seniority are now in job class 15? Three possibilities have been suggested:

1. Mr. X moves immediately to job 15, even though this means displacing someone currently on the job and even though he does not have the training and experience to handle the job.

2. Mr. X will be given special training and he will be moved upward from job to job as fast as his abilities permit him, in each case having first priority for any vacancy, but not displacing anyone from a job.

3. As the longest-service worker in job class 5, Mr. X can move to job class 6 when there is a vacancy, but he can't move to job class 7 until all those currently in job class 6 are promoted.

Questions

1. Which of these alternatives seems most fair? Can you devise a fairer one?

2. Would the nature of the jobs make any difference in your answer?

3. How does the concept of reverse discrimination apply to this situation?

Human Resource Management Simulation

Affirmative action is one of the key elements in the simulation. The firm currently has fewer female and minority workers percentagewise than the local working population. Hiring has been generally done on a "walk-in" basis and there is no formal plan to increase the number of women and minorities in the firm. Your team must decide whether it wants to establish a formal affirmative action program or simply stress hiring more women and minorities in its hiring program. In addition, you will be asked to decide what percentage of women and minorities you want to hire during each decision period. If you do not set a goal that is high enough, you may be charged with discrimination. If the goal is too high, your current work force may conclude there is reverse discrimination. Your status report will indicate the demographic composition of your work force each quarter so you can track your progress.

If your team is to be successful, it is extremely important that you obtain all the information available to you in the simulation. Each decision period you will have the opportunity to purchase industry research that will aid you in the decision-making process. The surveys available are: (1) industry average quality, morale, grievances, and absenteeism; (2) industry average and local comparable wage rates; (3) average industry training, safety, and quality budgets; and (4) the number of firms with employee participation programs.

Video Case

They Need Not Apply

Have we taken equal opportunity too far? That's the question Barbara Walters asks in this video, and the video certainly raises some arguable points. The U.S. Forest Service, in an effort aimed at reducing the effects of past discriminatory practices, agreed to give 43% of its jobs to women. To many women, minority group members, and even some white males, such an agreement is a perfectly reasonable way to remedy past errors. However, to many of the white males who now see Forest Service jobs going not to them but to possibly less qualified women, the agreement and how it is being implemented seems enormously unfair.

Questions

1. What do you think of the Forest Service's notice that, for certain jobs, only "unqualified" people need apply?

2. Do you see any way to reconcile the argument that "past discrimination should be remedied today with affirmative action" with the argument that "it's grossly unfair to discriminate against *anyone* today?"

3. Do you agree or disagree that "Forest Service hiring practices are in full compliance with Equal Opportunity laws?" Why?

4. What do you think of attorney Len Abernethy's idea of posting the "legal assistance available" note on the bulletin board? Do you think he should be penalized by his employer for doing so?

Source: ABC News, *They Need Not Apply,* "20/20," November 18, 1994.

Take It to the Net

We invite you to visit the Dessler page on the Prentice Hall Web site at:
http://www.prenhall.com/~dessler
for the monthly Dessler update, and for this chapter's World Wide Web exercise.

Notes

1. Commerce Clearing House, *Ideas and Trends in Personnel,* May 13, 1992, p. 73.
2. "Section 1981 Covers Racial Discrimination in Hiring and Promotions—But No Other Situations," Commerce Clearing House, *Human Resources Management,* June 28, 1989, p. 116.
3. Portions of this chapter are based on or quoted from *Principles of Employment Discrimination Law,* International Association of Official Human Rights Agencies, Washington, DC. In addition, see W. Clay Hamner and Frank Schmidt, *Contemporary Problems in Personnel,* rev. ed. (Chicago: St. Clair Press, 1977), Chapter 3. Employment discrimination law is a changing field, and the appropriateness of the rules, guidelines, and conclusions in this book may also be affected by factors unique to an employer's operation. They should, therefore, be reviewed by the employer's attorney before implementation.
4. James Higgins, "A Manager's Guide to the Equal Employment Opportunity Laws," *Personnel Journal,* Vol. 55, no. 8 (August 1976), p. 406.
5. The Equal Employment Opportunity Act of 1972, Subcommittee on Labor or the Committee of Labor and Public Welfare, United States Senate (March 1972), p. 3. In general, it is not discrimination but unfair discrimination against a person merely because of that person's race, age, sex, national origin, or religion that is forbidden by federal statutes. In the federal government's *Uniform Employee Selection Guidelines,* "unfair" discrimination

is defined as follows: "unfairness is demonstrated through a showing that members of a particular interest group perform better or poorer on the job than their scores on the selection procedure (test, etc.) would indicate through comparison with how members of the other groups performed. . . ." For a discussion of the meaning of fairness, see James Ledvinka, "The Statistical Definition of Fairness in the Federal Selection Guidelines and Its Implications for Minority Employment," *Personnel Psychology,* Vol. 32 (August 1979), pp. 551–562. In summary, a selection device (like a test) may discriminate— say, between low and high performers. However, it is unfair discrimination that is illegal, discrimination that is based solely on the person's race, age, sex, national origin, or religion.

6. A growing issue today is whether homosexuals are due equal protection from discrimination. Initially, attempts to assert that discrimination based on sexual orientation was illegal were unsuccessful, and even the EEOC was unsympathetic. However, a recent case (*Watkins* v. *U.S. Army,* F.2d 1428, 1429, 9th Cir. 1988) involving an army sergeant forced to resign after 14 years, notable service may possibly open the door to successful suits by identifying homosexuals as a "suspect class that deserves special protection against discrimination." Sabrina Wrenn, "Gay Rights and Workplace Discrimination," *Personnel Journal,* Vol. 67, no. 10 (October 1988), p. 94; "Proposed Bill Would Ban Workplace Discrimination Based on Sexual Orientation," *HR Focus,* October 1994, pp. 1, 8.

7. Bureau of National Affairs, *Fair Employment Practices,* October 8, 1992, p. 117.

8. Note that under the Rehabilitation Act, the law strictly speaking applied only to a particular "program" of the employer. In March 1988 Congress passed the Civil Rights Restoration Act of 1987, overturning this interpretation. Now, with few exceptions, any institution, organization, corporation, state agency, or municipality using federal funding in any of its programs must abide by the section of the act prohibiting discriminating against handicapped individuals. See Bureau of National Affairs, "Federal Law Mandates Affirmative Action for Handicapped," *Fair Employment Practices,* March 30, 1989, p. 42.

9. *Tanberg* v. *Weld County Sheriff,* USDA Colo, No. 91-B-248, 3/18/92.

10. Steven Fox, "Employment Provisions of the Rehabilitation Act," *Personnel Journal,* Vol. 66, no. 10 (October 1987), p. 140.

11. Commerce Clearing House, "Is AIDS a Protected Handicap?" *Human Resource Management Ideas and Trends,* March 20, 1987, p. 46.

12. Bureau of National Affairs, "Guidelines on AIDS," *Fair Employment Practices,* March 30, 1989, p. 39.

13. David B. Ritter and Ronald Turner, "AIDS: Employer Concerns and Options," *Labor Law Journal,* Vol. 38, no. 2 (February 1987), pp. 67–83.

14. Bureau of National Affairs, *Fair Employment Practices,* August 27, 1992, p. 102.

15. Howard J. Anderson and Michael D. Levin-Epstein, *Primer of Equal Employment Opportunity,* 2nd ed. (Washington, DC: Bureau of National Affairs, 1982), pp. 5–7; and Commerce Clearing House, "Federal Contractors Must File VETS-100 by March 31," *Ideas and Trends,* February 23, 1988, p. 32.

16. Ann Harriman, *Women/Men Management* (New York: Praeger, 1985), pp. 66–68.

17. Commerce Clearing House, "Pregnancy Leave," *Ideas and Trends,* January 23, 1987, p. 10.

18. Bureau of National Affairs, "High Court Upholds Pregnancy Law," *Fair Employment Practices,* January 22, 1987, p. 7; Betty Sonthard Murphy, Wayne E. Barlow, and D. Diane Hatch, "Manager's Newsfront: U.S. Supreme Court Approves Preferential Treatment for Pregnancy," *Personnel Journal,* Vol. 66, no. 3 (March 1987), p. 18.

19. Thomas Dhanens, "Implications of the New EEOC Guidelines," *Personnel,* Vol. 56 (September–October 1979), pp. 32 39.

20. Bureau of National Affairs, "First Two Chapters of Long-Awaited Manual Released by OFCCP," *Fair Employment Practices,* January 5, 1989, p. 6.

21. Lawrence S. Kleiman and Robert Faley, "The Applications of Professional and Legal Guidelines for Court Decisions Involving Criterion-Related Validity: A Review and Analysis," *Personnel Psychology,* Vol. 38, no. 4 (Winter 1985), pp. 803–833.

22. Oscar A. Ornati and Margaret J. Eisen, "Are You Complying with EEOC's New Rules on National Origin Discrimination?" *Personnel,* Vol. 58 (March–April 1981), pp. 12–20; Paul S. Greenlaw and John P. Kohl, "National Origin Discrimination and the New EEOC Guidelines," *Personnel Journal,* Vol. 60, no. 8 (August 1981), pp. 634–636.

23. Barbara Berish Brown, "Guidance and Regs from EEOC, OFCCP, and INS," *Employment Relations Today* (Spring 1992), pp. 81–86; Morgan Hodgson and Ronald Cooper, "EEOC Issues Proposed Guidelines and Guidance Memorandum," *Employment Relations Today* (Winter 1993/94), pp. 455–459; "EEOC Issues Disability Guidance," *BNA Fair Employment Pratices,* March 23, 1995, p. 31.

24. Paul S. Greenlaw and John P. Kohl, "Age Discrimination and Employment Guidelines," *Personnel Journal,* Vol. 61, no. 3 (March 1982), pp. 224–228.

25. 29 CFR 1625.2(a) quoted in Greenlaw and Kohl, "Age Discrimination."

26. Charles Mishkind, "Sexual Harassment Hostile Work Environment Class Actions: Is There Cause for Concern?" *Employee Relations Law Journal,* Vol. 18, no. 2 (Summer 1992).

27. Bureau of National Affairs, *Fair Employment Practices,* April 23, 1992, p. 47.

28. Patricia Linenberger and Timothy Keaveny, "Sexual Harassment: The Employer's Legal Obligations," *Personnel,* Vol. 58 (November–December 1981), pp. 60–68.

29. Milton Zall, "What to Expect from the Civil Rights Act," *Personnel Journal,* Vol. 71, no. 3 (March 1992), p. 50.

30. Mary Rowe, "Dealing with Sexual Harassment," *Harvard Business Review,* Vol. 61 (May–June 1981), pp. 42–46.

31. Commerce Clearing House, *Sexual Harassment Manual for Managers and Supervisors* (Chicago, IL: Commerce Clearing House, Inc., 1991), pp. 28–29.

32. Robert H. Faley, "Sexual Harassment: Critical Review of Legal Cases with General Principles and Preventive Measures," *Personnel Psychology,* Vol. 35, no. 3 (Autumn 1982), pp. 590–591; Bureau of National Affairs, "In Terms of Sex-

Chapter 3
Job Analysis

Chapter Outline

♦ **The Nature of Job Analysis**

♦ **Methods of Collecting Job Analysis Information**

♦ **Writing Job Descriptions**

♦ **Writing Job Specifications**

♦ **Job Analysis in a "Jobless" World**

Behavioral Objectives

When you finish studying this chapter, you should be able to:

Describe the basic methods of collecting job analysis information.

Conduct a job analysis.

Write a job description.

Explain the purpose of a job specification and a procedure for developing one.

The Nature of Job Analysis

Job Analysis Defined

job analysis
The procedure for determining the duties and skill requirements of a job and the kind of person who should be hired for it.

job description
A list of a job's duties, responsibilities, reporting relationships, working conditions, and supervisory responsibilities—one product of a job analysis.

job specification
A list of a job's "human requirements," that is, the requisite education, skills, personality, and so on—another product of a job analysis.

Organizations consist of positions that have to be staffed. **Job analysis** is the procedure through which you determine the duties of these positions and the characteristics of the people who should be hired for them.[1] The analysis produces information on job requirements, which is then used for developing **job descriptions** (what the job entails) and **job specifications** (what kind of people to hire for the job).

A supervisor or HR specialist normally aims to collect one or more of the following types of information via the job analysis.[2]

Work activities. Information is usually collected on the actual work activities performed, such as cleaning, selling, teaching, or painting. Such a list may also indicate how, why, and when the worker performs each activity.

Human behaviors. Information on human behaviors like sensing, communicating, decision making, and writing may also be collected. Included here would be information regarding human job demands such as lifting weights, walking long distances, and so on.

Machines, tools, equipment, and work aids used. Included here would be information regarding products made, materials processed, knowledge dealt with or applied (such as finance or law), and services rendered (such as counseling or repairing).

Performance standards. Information is also collected regarding performance standards (in terms of quantity, quality, or speed for each job duty, for instance) by which an employee in this job will be evaluated.

Job context. Included here is information about such matters as physical working conditions, work schedule, and the organizational and social context—for instance, in terms of the number of people with whom the employee would normally have to interact. Also included here might be information regarding incentives for doing the job.

Human requirements. Finally, information is usually compiled regarding human requirements of the job, such as job-related knowledge or skills (education, training, work experience) and required personal attributes (aptitudes, physical characteristics, personality, interests).

Uses of Job Analysis Information

As summarized in Figure 3.1, the information produced by the job analysis is the basis for several interrelated HR management activities.

Recruitment and Selection   Job analysis provides information about what the job entails and what human characteristics are required to carry out these activities. Such job description and job specification information is used to decide what sort of people to recruit and hire.

Compensation   Job analysis information is also essential for estimating the value of and appropriate compensation for each job. This is so because compensation (such as salary and bonus) usually depends on the job's required skill and education level, safety hazards, degree of responsibility, and so on—all factors that are assessed through job analysis. We'll also see that many employers classify jobs into categories (like Secretary III and IV), and job analysis provides the information for determining the relative worth of each job so that each job can be classified.

Figure 3.1
Uses of Job Analysis
Information

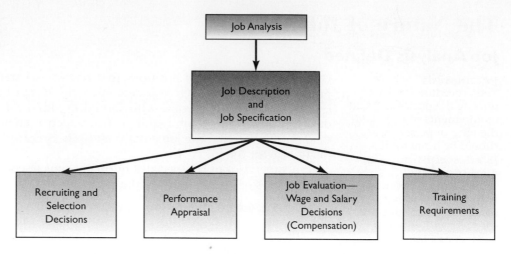

Performance Appraisal   A performance appraisal compares each employee's actual performance with his or her performance standards. It is often through job analysis that experts determine the standards to be achieved and the specific activities to be performed.

Training   Job analysis information is also used for designing training and development programs because the analysis and resulting job description show the skills—and therefore training—that are required.

Ensure Complete Assignment of Duties   The job analysis is also useful for ensuring that all the duties that have to be done are in fact assigned to particular positions. For example, in analyzing the current job of your company's production manager, you may find she reports herself as being responsible for two dozen or so specific duties including planning weekly production schedules, purchasing raw materials, and supervising the daily activities of each of her first-line supervisors. Missing, however, is any reference to managing raw material or finished goods inventories. On further investigation you find that none of the other manufacturing people is responsible for inventory management either. Your job analysis (based not just on what employees report as their duties, but on your knowledge of what these jobs should entail) has identified a missing duty to be assigned. Missing duties like this are often uncovered through job analysis. As a result, job analysis plays a role in remedying problems of the sort that would arise if, for example, there was no one assigned to manage inventories.

Steps in Job Analysis

The six steps in doing a job analysis are as follows.

Step 1   Identify the use to which the information will be put, since this will determine the types of data you collect and how you collect them. Some data collection techniques—like interviewing the employee and asking what the job entails and what his or her responsibilities are—are good for writing job descriptions and selecting employees for the job. Other job analysis techniques (like the position analysis questionnaire described later) do not provide qualitative information for job descriptions, but rather numerical ratings for each job; these can be used to compare jobs to one another for compensation purposes.

**Figure 3.2
Process Chart for
Analyzing a Job's
Work Flow**

Source: Richard I. Henderson,
*Compensation Management:
Rewarding Performance,* 2nd
ed., copyright 1985, p. 158.
Reprinted by permission of
Prentice-Hall, Englewood
Cliffs, NJ.

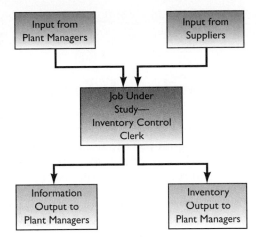

Step 2   Review relevant background information such as organization charts, process charts, and job descriptions.[3] *Organization charts* show how the job in question relates to other jobs and where it fits in the overall organization. The chart should identify the title of each position and, by means of its interconnecting lines, show who reports to whom and with whom the job incumbent is expected to communicate.

A *process chart* provides a more detailed understanding of the work flow than is obtainable from the organization chart alone. In its simplest form, a process chart (like the one in Figure 3.2) shows the flow of inputs to and outputs from the job under study. (In Figure 3.2 the inventory control clerk is expected to receive inventory from suppliers, take requests for inventory from the two plant managers, provide requested inventory to these managers, and give information to these managers on the status of in-stock inventories.) Finally, the existing *job description,* if there is one, can provide a starting point for building the revised job description.

Step 3   Select representative positions to be analyzed. This is done when many similar jobs are to be analyzed, and it is too time-consuming to analyze, say, the jobs of all assembly workers.

Step 4   Next actually analyze the job by collecting data on job activities, required employee behaviors, working conditions, and human traits and abilities needed to perform the job. For this, you would use one or more of the job analysis techniques explained in the remainder of this chapter.

Step 5   Review the information with job incumbents. The job analysis information should be verified with the worker performing the job and with his or her immediate supervisor. This will help to confirm that the information is factually correct and complete. This "review" step can also help gain the employee's acceptance of the job analysis data and conclusions by giving that person a chance to review and modify your description of his or her job activities.

Step 6   Develop a job description and job specification. A job description and a job specification are usually two concrete products of the job analysis. The *job description* (to repeat) is a written statement that describes the activities and responsibilities of the job, as well as important features of the job such as working conditions and safety hazards. The *job specification* summarizes the personal qualities, traits, skills, and background required for getting the job done; it may be either a separate document or on the same document as the job description.

Methods of Collecting Job Analysis Information

Introduction

There are various techniques you can use for collecting information on the duties, responsibilities, and activities of the job, and we'll discuss the most important ones in this section. In practice, you could use any one of them or combine techniques that best fit your purpose. Thus, an interview might be appropriate for creating a job description, whereas the position analysis questionnaire that we'll discuss is more appropriate for determining the worth of a job for compensation purposes.

Who Collects the Job Information? Collecting job analysis data usually involves a joint effort by an HR specialist, the worker, and the worker's supervisor. The HR specialist (perhaps an HR manager, job analyst, or consultant) might observe and analyze the work being done and then develop a job description and specification. The supervisor and worker will also get involved, perhaps by filling out questionnaires listing the subordinate's activities. The supervisor and worker may then review and verify the job analyst's conclusions regarding the job's activities and duties.

Job Analysis and Equal Employment Opportunity Job analysis plays a central role in equal employment law compliance. Federal guidelines and court decisions admonish employers to do thorough job analyses before using screening tools (like tests) for predicting job performance. The main reason is that an employer must be able to show that its screening tools and performance appraisals are actually related to performance on the job in question. To do this requires a competent job analysis describing the nature of the job.[4] Popular methods for collecting job analysis information are discussed next.

The Interview

Three types of interviews are used to collect job analysis data: individual interviews with each employee; group interviews with groups of employees having the same job; and supervisor interviews with one or more supervisors who are thoroughly knowledgeable about the job being analyzed. The group interview is used when a large number of employees are performing similar or identical work, and it can be a quick and inexpensive way of learning about the job. As a rule, the workers' immediate supervisor would attend the group session; if not, you should interview the supervisor separately to get that person's perspective on the duties and responsibilities of the job.

Whichever interview you use, the interviewee should fully understand the reason for the interview, since there's a tendency for such interviews to be misconstrued as "efficiency evaluations." When they are, interviewees may not be willing to describe their jobs or those of their subordinates accurately.

Pros and Cons The interview is probably the most widely used method for determining a job's duties and responsibilities, and its wide use reflects its advantages. Most important, interviewing allows the worker to report activities and behavior that might not otherwise come to light. For example, important activities that occur only occasionally or informal communication (between, say, a production supervisor and the sales manager) that would not be obvious from the organization chart could be unearthed by a skilled interviewer. The interview also provides an opportunity to explain the need for and functions of the job analysis, and it can let the interviewee vent frustrations or views that might otherwise go unnoticed by management. Interviews are also relatively simple and quick ways to collect information.

This technique's major problem is distortion of information, whether due to outright falsification or honest misunderstandings.[5] A job analysis is often used as a prelude to changing a job's pay rate. Employees, therefore, sometimes legitimately view them as efficiency evaluations that may affect their pay. Employees thus tend to exaggerate certain responsibilities while minimizing others. Obtaining valid information can thus be a slow process.

Typical Questions   Despite their drawbacks, interviews are widely used. Some typical interview questions include:

What is the job being performed?

What are the major duties of your position? What exactly do you do?

What physical locations do you work in?

What are the education, experience, skill, and (where applicable) certification and licensing requirements?

What activities do you participate in?

What are the job's responsibilities and duties?

What are the basic accountabilities or performance standards that typify your work?

What are your responsibilities? What are the environmental and working conditions involved?

What are the job's physical demands? The emotional and mental demands?

What are the health and safety conditions?

Are you exposed to any hazards or unusual working conditions?

Most fruitful interviews follow a structured or checklist format. One such *job analysis questionnaire* is presented in Figure 3.3 on pages 88–89. It includes a series of detailed questions regarding such matters as the general purpose of the job; supervisory responsibilities, job duties; and education, experience, and skills required. A list like this can also be used by a job analyst who collects information by personally observing the work being done or by administering it as a questionnaire, two methods that will be explained shortly.[6]

Interview Guidelines   There are several things to keep in mind when conducting a job analysis interview. First, the job analyst and supervisor should work together. Identify the workers who know the most about the job, as well as those who might be expected to be the most objective in describing their duties and responsibilities.

Second, establish rapport quickly with the interviewee, by knowing the person's name, speaking in easily understood language, briefly reviewing the purpose of the interview, and explaining how the person came to be chosen for the interview.

Third, follow a structured guide or checklist, one that lists questions and provides space for answers. This ensures that you'll identify crucial questions

Figure 3.3
Job Analysis Questionnaire for Developing Job Descriptions
A questionnaire like this one can be used to interview job incumbents or may be filled out by them.

Source: Douglas Bartley, *Job Evaluation: Wage and Salary Administration* (Reading, MA: Addison-Wesley Publishing Company, 1981), p. 101–103.

JOB QUESTIONNAIRE
KANE MANUFACTURING COMPANY

NAME _____   JOB TITLE _____

DEPARTMENT _____   JOB NUMBER _____

SUPERVISOR'S NAME _____   SUPERVISOR'S TITLE _____

1. *SUMMARY OF DUTIES:* State in your own words briefly your main duties. If you are responsible for filling out reports/records, also complete Section 8.
_____
_____

2. *SPECIAL QUALIFICATIONS:* List any licenses, permits, certifications, etc. required to perform duties assigned to your position.
_____
_____

3. *EQUIPMENT:* List any equipment, machines, or tools (e.g., typewriter, calculator, motor vehicles, lathes, fork lifts, drill presses, etc.) you normally operate as a part of your position's duties.

  MACHINE   *AVERAGE NO. HOURS PER WEEK*
_____
_____
_____

4. *REGULAR DUTIES:* In general terms, describe duties you regularly perform. Please list these duties in descending order of importance and percent of time spent on them per month. List as many duties as possible and attach additional sheets, if necessary.
_____
_____
_____

5. *CONTACTS:* Does your job require any contacts with other department personnel, other departments, outside companies or agencies? If yes, please define the duties requiring contacts and *how often.*
_____
_____

6. *SUPERVISION:* Does your position have supervisory responsibilities? ( ) Yes ( ) No. If yes, please fill out a *Supplemental Position Description Questionnaire for Supervisors* and attach it to this form. If you have responsibility for the work of others but do not directly supervise them, please explain.
_____
_____

7. *DECISION MAKING:* Please explain the decisions you make while performing the regular duties of your job.
_____
_____
_____

(continued)

Figure 3.3
(continued)

(a) What would be the probable result of your making (a) poor judgment(s) or decision(s), or (b) improper actions?

_____

_____

8. *RESPONSIBILITY FOR RECORDS*: List the reports and files you are required to prepare or maintain. State, in general, for whom each report is intended.

(a)   *REPORT*   *INTENDED FOR*

_____

_____

_____

(b)   *FILES MAINTAINED*

_____

_____

9. *FREQUENCY OF SUPERVISION:* How frequently must you confer with your supervisor or other personnel in making decisions or in determining the proper course of action to be taken?

( ) Frequently   ( ) Occasionally   ( ) Seldom   ( ) Never

10. *WORKING CONDITIONS*: Please describe the conditions under which you work—inside, outside, air conditioned area, etc. Be sure to list any disagreeable or unusual working conditions.

_____

_____

11. *JOB REQUIREMENTS*: Please indicate the minimum requirements you believe are necessary to perform satisfactorily in your position.

(a) Education:
Minimum schooling _____
Number of years _____
Specialization or major _____

(b) Experience:
Type _____
Number of years _____

(c) Special training:
       TYPE   *NUMBER OF YEARS*

_____

_____

(d) Special Skills:
Typing: _____ w.p.m.   Shorthand _____ w.p.m.
Other: _____

12. *ADDITIONAL INFORMATION*: Please provide additional information, not included in any of the previous items, which you feel would be important in a description of your position.

_____

_____

_____

EMPLOYEE'S SIGNATURE _____ DATE: _____

ahead of time and that all interviewers (if there are more than one) cover all the required questions. However, make sure to also give the worker some leeway in answering questions and provide some open-ended questions like "Was there anything we didn't cover with our questions?"

Fourth, when duties are not performed in a regular manner—for instance, when the worker doesn't perform the same job over and over again many times a day—you should ask the worker to list his or her duties *in order of importance* and *frequency* of occurrence. This will ensure that crucial activities that occur infrequently—like a nurse's occasional emergency room duties—aren't overlooked.

Finally, after completing the interview, review and verify the data. This is normally done by reviewing the information with the worker's immediate supervisor and with the interviewee.

Questionnaires

Having employees fill out questionnaires to describe their job-related duties and responsibilities is another good way to obtain job analysis information.

The main thing to decide here is how structured the questionnaire should be and what questions to include. Some questionnaires are very structured checklists. Each employee is presented with an inventory of perhaps hundreds of specific duties or tasks (such as "change and splice wire"). He or she is asked to indicate whether or not he or she performs each task and, if so, how much time is normally spent on each. At the other extreme, the questionnaire can be open ended and simply ask the employee to "describe the major duties of your job." In practice, the best questionnaire often falls between these two extremes. As illustrated in Figure 3.3, a typical job analysis questionnaire might have several open-ended questions (such as "state your main job duties") as well as structured questions (concerning, for instance, previous experience required).

Whether structured or unstructured, questionnaires have advantages and disadvantages. A questionnaire is a quick and efficient way of obtaining information from a large number of employees; it's less costly than interviewing hundreds of workers, for instance. However, developing the questionnaire and testing it (perhaps by making sure the workers understand the questions) can be an expensive and time-consuming process.

Observation

Direct observation is especially useful when jobs consist mainly of observable physical activity. Jobs like those of janitor, assembly-line worker, and accounting clerk are examples. On the other hand, observation is usually not appropriate when the job entails a lot of unmeasurable mental activity (lawyer, design engineer). Nor is it useful if the employee engages in important activities that might occur only occasionally, such as a nurse who handles emergencies.

Direct observation and interviewing are often used together. One approach is to observe the worker on the job during a complete work cycle. (The cycle is the time it takes to complete the job; it could be a minute for an assembly-line worker or an hour, a day, or longer for complex jobs.) Here you take notes of all the job activities you observe. Then, after accumulating as much information as possible, you interview the worker; the person is asked to clarify points not understood and explain what additional activities he or she performs that you didn't observe. You can also observe and interview simultaneously, while the worker performs his or her task.

Participant Diary/Logs

diary/logs
Daily listings made by workers of every activity in which they engage along with the time each activity takes.

Another approach is to ask workers to keep a **diary/log** or list of what they do during the day. For every activity he or she engages in, the employee records the activity (along with the time) in a log. This can produce a very complete picture of the job, especially when supplemented with subsequent interviews with the worker and his or her supervisor. The employee might, of course, try to exaggerate some activities and underplay others. However, the detailed, chronological nature of the log tends to mediate against this.

Interviews, questionnaires, observations, and diary/logs are the most popular methods for gathering job analysis data. They all provide realistic information about what job incumbents actually do. They can thus be used for developing job descriptions and job specifications.

U.S. Civil Service Procedure

The U.S. Civil Service Commission has developed a job analysis technique that aims to provide a standardized procedure by which different jobs can be compared and classified. With this method the information is compiled on a *job analysis record sheet.* Here, as illustrated in Figure 3.4, identifying information (like job title) and a brief summary of the job are listed first. Next the specialist lists the job's specific tasks in order of importance. Then, *for each task,* the analyst specifies the

1. Knowledge required (for example, the facts or principles the worker must be acquainted with to do his or her job).
2. Skills required (for example, the skills needed to operate machines or vehicles).
3. Abilities required (for example, mathematical, reasoning, problem solving, or interpersonal abilities).
4. Physical activities involved (for example, pulling, pushing, or carrying).
5. Any special environmental conditions (cramped quarters, vibration, inadequate ventilation, noise, or moving objects).
6. Typical work incidents (for example, performing under stress in emergencies, working with people beyond giving and receiving instructions, or performing repetitive work).
7. Worker interests areas (the preference the worker should have for activities dealing with things and objects, or the communication of data, or dealing with people, for example).[7]

In Figure 3.4 the first task listed for a "welfare eligibility examiner" is "decide (determine) eligibility of applicant in order to complete client's application for food stamps using regulatory policies as guide." Beneath this task are listed the analyst's conclusions concerning the *knowledge* a welfare eligibility examiner is required to have; any *special skills* or abilities; types of *physical activities* involved in this task; special *environmental conditions;* typical *work incidents;* and the sorts of *interests* that would correspond to this task.

The analyst would typically apply his or her own knowledge of the job as well as information obtained through interviews, observations, logs, or questionnaires in completing the job analysis record sheet. Virtually any job can be broken into its component tasks, each of which is then analyzed in terms of knowledge required, skills required, and so forth. The Civil Service procedure thus provides a standardized method by which different jobs can be compared, contrasted, and classified. (In other words, the knowledge, skills, and abilities required to perform, say, an assistant fire chief's job can be compared with those required to perform a librarian's job. If the requirements are similar, the jobs might be classified together for, say, pay purposes.)

JOB ANALYSIS RECORD SHEET

IDENTIFYING INFORMATION

Name of Incumbent:	A. Adler
Organization/Unit:	Welfare Services
Title:	Welfare Eligibility Examiner
Date:	11/12/97
Interviewer:	E. Jones

BRIEF SUMMARY OF JOB

Conducts interviews, completes applications, determines eligibility, provides information to community sources regarding food stamp program; refers noneligible food stamp applicants to other applicable community resource agencies.

TASKS*

1. Decides (determines) eligibility of applicant in order to complete client's application for food stamps using regulatory policies as guide.

    Knowledge Required
    —Knowledge of contents and meaning of items on standard application form
    —Knowledge of Social-Health Services food stamp regulatory policies
    —Knowledge of statutes relating to Social-Health Services food stamp program

    Skills Required
    —None

    Abilities Required
    —Ability to read and understand complex instructions such as regulatory policies
    —Ability to read and understand a variety of procedural instructions, written and oral, and convert these to proper actions
    —Ability to use simple arithmetic: addition and subtraction
    —Ability to translate requirements into language appropriate to laymen

    Physical Activities
    —Sedentary

    Environmental Conditions
    —None

    Typical Work Incidents
    —Working with people beyond giving and receiving instructions

    Interest Areas
    —Communication of data
    —Business contact with people
    —Working for the presumed good of people

2. Decides upon, describes, and explains other agencies available for client to contact in order to assist and refer client to appropriate community resource using worker's knowledge of resources available and knowledge of client's needs.

    Knowledge Required
    —Knowledge of functions of various assistance agencies
    —Knowledge of community resources available and their locations
    —Knowledge of referral procedures

    Skills Required
    —None

    Abilities Required
    —Ability to extract (discern) persons' needs from oral discussion
    —Ability to give simple oral and written instructions to persons

    Physical Activities
    —Sedentary

    Environmental Conditions
    —None

    Typical Work Incidents
    —Working with people beyond giving and receiving instructions

    Interest Areas
    —Communication of data
    —Business contact with people
    —Abstract and creative problem solving
    —Working for presumed good of people

*This job might typically involve five or six tasks. For *each* task, list the knowledge, skill abilities, physical activities, environmental conditions, typical work incidents, and interest areas.

Quantitative Job Analysis Techniques

Although most employers use interviews, questionnaires, observations, or diary/logs for collecting job analysis data, there are many times when these narrative approaches are not appropriate. For example, when your aim is to assign a quantitative value to each job so the jobs can be compared for pay purposes, a more *quantitative* job analysis approach may be best. The *position analysis questionnaire,* the *Department of Labor approach,* and *functional job analysis* are three popular quantitative methods.

Position Analysis Questionnaire The position analysis questionnaire (PAQ) is a very structured job analysis questionnaire.[8] The PAQ itself is filled in by a job analyst, a person who should already be acquainted with the particular job to be analyzed. The PAQ contains 194 items, each of which (such as "written materials") represents a basic element that may or may not play an important role in the job. The job analyst decides whether each item plays a role on the job and, if so, to what extent. In Figure 3.5, for example, "written materials" received a rating of 4, indicating that written materials (like books, reports, and office notes) play a considerable role in this job.

position analysis questionnaire (PAQ)
A questionnaire used to collect quantifiable data concerning the duties and responsibilities of various jobs.

The advantage of the PAQ is that it provides a quantitative score or profile of any job in terms of how that job rates on five basic job traits: (1) having decision-making/communications/social responsibilities, (2) performing skilled activities, (3) being physically active, (4) operating vehicles/equipment, and (5) processing information. The PAQ's real strength is thus in classifying jobs. In other words, it lets you assign a quantitative score to each job based on its decision-making, skilled activities, physical activity, vehicle/equipment, operation, and information-processing characteristics. You can therefore use the PAQ results to compare jobs relative to one another;[9] this information can then be used to assign pay levels for each job.[10]

Department of Labor (DOL) Procedure The U.S. Department of Labor (DOL) procedure also aims to provide a standardized method by which different jobs can be quantitatively rated, classified, and compared. The heart of this type of analysis is a rating of each job in terms of what an employee does with respect to *data, people,* and *things.*

Department of Labor job analysis
Standardized method for rating, classifying, and comparing virtually every kind of job based on data, people, and things.

The basic procedure is as follows. As illustrated in Table 3.1, a set of basic activities called *worker functions* describes what a worker can do with respect to data, people, and things. With respect to *data,* for instance, the basic functions include synthesizing, coordinating, and copying. With respect to *people,* they include mentoring, negotiating, and supervising. With respect to *things,* the basic functions include manipulating, tending, and handling. Note also that each worker function has been assigned an importance level. Thus, "coordinating" is 1, while "copying" is 5. If you were analyzing the job of a receptionist/clerk, for example, you might label the job 5, 6, 7, which would represent copying data, speaking-signaling people, and handling things. On the other hand, a psychiatric aide in a hospital might be coded 1, 7, 5 in relation to data, people, and things. In practice, each task that the worker performed would be analyzed in terms of data, people, and things. Then the highest combination (say, 4, 6, 5) would be used to identify the job, since this is the highest level that a job incumbent would be expected to attain.

As illustrated in Figure 3.6, the summary produced from the DOL procedure contains several types of information. Listed first is the job title, in this case dough mixer in a bakery. Also listed are the industry in which this job is found and the industry's standard industrial classification code. There is a one- or two-sentence

TABLE 3.1 Basic Department of Labor Worker Functions			
	DATA	**PEOPLE**	**THINGS**
Basic Activities	0 Synthesizing 1 Coordinating 2 Analyzing 3 Compiling 4 Computing 5 Copying 6 Comparing	0 Mentoring 1 Negotiating 2 Instructing 3 Supervising 4 Diverting 5 Persuading 6 Speaking–signaling 7 Serving 8 Taking instructions– helping	0 Setting up 1 Precision working 2 Operating–controlling 3 Driving–operating 4 Manipulating 5 Tending 6 Feeding–offbearing 7 Handling

Note: Determine employee's job "score" on data, people, and things by observing his or her job and determining, for each of the three categories, which of the basic functions illustrates the person's job. "0" is high, "6," "8," and "7" are lows in each column.

jobs with similar scores can thus be grouped together and paid the same, even if one job is dough mixer and another mechanics helper.

Functional Job Analysis This procedure is based on the DOL method but provides additional information regarding the job's tasks, objectives, and training requirements.[11]

functional job analysis
A method for classifying jobs similar to the Department of Labor job analysis but additionally taking into account the extent to which instructions, reasoning, judgment, and verbal facility are necessary for performing job tasks.

Functional job analysis differs from the DOL approach in two ways. First, functional job analysis rates the job not only on data, people, and things, but also on the following four dimensions: the extent to which specific *instructions* are necessary to perform the task; the extent to which *reasoning* and *judgment* are required to perform the task; the *mathematical ability* required to perform the task; and the verbal and *language facilities* required to perform the task. Second, functional job analysis also identifies performance standards and training requirements. Performing a job analysis using functional job analysis, therefore, allows you to answer the question, "To do this task and meet these new standards, what training does the worker require?"

Figure 3.7 illustrates a completed functional job analysis summary sheet. In this case the job is that of grader (a type of heavy-equipment operator employed in road building). As illustrated, the functional job analysis specifies things, data, people, instructions, reasoning, math, and language ratings. The summary sheet also lists the main tasks in the job, performance standards, and training required.

Writing Job Descriptions

A job description is a written statement of *what* the jobholder actually does, *how* he or she does it, and under *what conditions* the job is performed. This information is in turn used to write a *job specification* that lists the knowledge, abilities, and skills needed to perform the job satisfactorily.

There is no standard format you must use in writing a job description, but most descriptions contain sections on:

Sample of the End Result of Using the Department of Labor Job Analysis Technique.

JOB ANALYSIS SCHEDULE

1. Established Job Title — DOUGH MIXER

2. Ind. Assign — (bake prod.)

3. SIC Code(s) and Title(s) — 2051 Bread and other bakery products

4. JOB SUMMARY:

Operates mixing machine to mix ingredients for straight and sponge (yeast) doughs according to established formulas, directs other workers in fermentation of dough, and curls dough into pieces with hand cutter.

5. WORK PERFORMED RATINGS: (From Exhibit 3.9)

	D	P	(T)
Worker Functions	Data	People	Things
	5	6	2

Work Field — Cooking, Food Preparing

6. WORKER TRAITS RATING: (To be filled in by analyst)

Training time required

Aptitudes

Temperaments

Interests

Physical Demands

Environment Conditions

1. Job identification
2. Job summary
3. Relationships, responsibilities, and duties
4. Authority of incumbent
5. Standards of performance
6. Working conditions
7. Job specifications

An example of a job description is presented in Figure 3.8.

Job Identification

As in Figure 3.8, the job identification section contains several types of information.[12] The *job title* specifies the title of the job, such as supervisor of data processing operations, sales manager, or inventory control clerk. (Job titles and

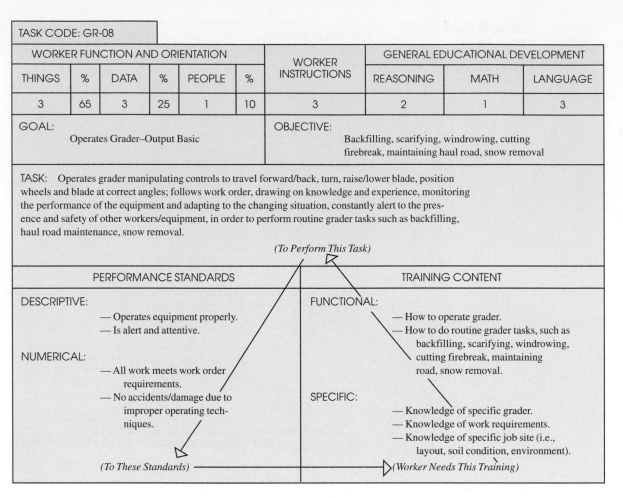

TASK CODE: GR-08										
WORKER FUNCTION AND ORIENTATION						WORKER INSTRUCTIONS	GENERAL EDUCATIONAL DEVELOPMENT			
THINGS	%	DATA	%	PEOPLE	%		REASONING	MATH	LANGUAGE	
3	65	3	25	1	10	3	2	1	3	

GOAL: Operates Grader–Output Basic

OBJECTIVE: Backfilling, scarifying, windrowing, cutting firebreak, maintaining haul road, snow removal

TASK: Operates grader manipulating controls to travel forward/back, turn, raise/lower blade, position wheels and blade at correct angles; follows work order, drawing on knowledge and experience, monitoring the performance of the equipment and adapting to the changing situation, constantly alert to the presence and safety of other workers/equipment, in order to perform routine grader tasks such as backfilling, haul road maintenance, snow removal.

(To Perform This Task)

PERFORMANCE STANDARDS	TRAINING CONTENT
DESCRIPTIVE: — Operates equipment properly. — Is alert and attentive. **NUMERICAL:** — All work meets work order requirements. — No accidents/damage due to improper operating techniques.	**FUNCTIONAL:** — How to operate grader. — How to do routine grader tasks, such as backfilling, scarifying, windrowing, cutting firebreak, maintaining road, snow removal. **SPECIFIC:** — Knowledge of specific grader. — Knowledge of work requirements. — Knowledge of specific job site (i.e., layout, soil condition, environment).
(To These Standards)	*(Worker Needs This Training)*

Figure 3.7
Functional Job Analysis Task Statement

Source: Howard Olson, Sidney A. Fine, David C. Myers, and Margarette C. Jennings, "The Use of Functional Job Analysis in Establishing Performance for Heavy Equipment Operators," *Personnel Psychology,* Summer 1981, p. 354.

descriptions should be kept current, and the Department of Labor's *Dictionary of Occupational Titles* can be useful in this regard. It lists titles for thousands of jobs (as well as lists of job duties for each.) The *job status* section permits quick identification of the exempt or nonexempt status of the job. (Under the Fair Labor Standards Act certain positions, primarily administrative and professional, are exempt from the act's overtime and minimum wage provisions.) The *job code* permits easy referencing of all jobs. Each job in the organization should be identified with a code; these codes represent important characteristics of the job, such as the wage class to which it belongs. The *date* refers to the date the job description was actually written, and *written by* indicates the person who wrote it. There is also space to indicate who *approved* the description and a space that shows the location of the job in terms of its *plant/division* and *department/section*. The *immediate supervisor's title* is also shown in the identification section as is information regarding the job's salary and/or pay scale. The space *grade/level* indicates the grade or level of

Figure 3.8
Sample Job
Description

Source: Richard I. Henderson,
Compensation Management:
Rewarding Performance, 4th
ed., copyright 1985, p. 176.
Reprinted by permission of
Prentice-Hall, Inc., Englewood
Cliffs, N.J.

SAMPLE JOB DESCRIPTION

Supervisor of Data Processing Operations	*Exempt*	*012.168*
Job Title	Status	Job Code

July 3, 1997	*Olympia, Inc.–Main Office*
Date	Plant/Division

	Information
Arthur Allen	*Data Processing–Systems*
Written By	Department/Section

Juanita Montgomery	*12*	*736*
Approved By	Grade/Level	Points

Manager of Information Systems	*14,800 Mid 17,760–20,720*
Title of Immediate Supervisor	Pay Range

SUMMARY

Directs the operation of all data processing, data control, and data preparation requirements.

JOB DUTIES*

1. Follows broadly-based directives.
   (a). Operates independently.
   (b). Informs Manager of Information Systems of activities through weekly, monthly, and/or quarterly schedules.
2. Selects, trains, and develops subordinate personnel.
   (a). Develops spirit of cooperation and understanding among work group members.
   (b). Ensures that work group members receive specialized training as necessary in the proper functioning or execution of machines, equipment, systems, procedures, processes, and/ or methods.
   (c). Directs training involving teaching, demonstrating, and/or advising users in productive work methods and effective communications with data processing.
3. Reads and analyzes wide variety of instructional and training information.
   (a). Applies latest concepts and ideas to changing organizational requirements.
   (b). Assists in developing and/or updating manuals, procedures, specifications, etc., relative to organizational requirements and needs.
   (c). Assists in the preparation of specifications and related evaluations of supporting software and hardware.
4. Plans, directs, and controls a wide variety of operational assignments by 5 to 7 subordinates; works closely with other managers, specialists, and technicians within Information Systems as well as with managers in other departments with data needs and with vendors.
   (a). Receives, interprets, develops, and distributes directives ranging from the very simple to the highly complex and technological in nature.
   (b). Establishes and implements annual budget for department.
5. Interacts and communicates with people representing a wide variety of units and organizations.
   (a). Communicates both personally and impersonally, through oral or written directives and memoranda, with all involved parties.
   (b). Attends local meetings of professional organizations in the field of data processing.
*This section should also include description of uncomfortable, dirty, or dangerous assignments.

the job if there is such a category; for example, a firm may classify programmers as programmer II, programmer III, and so on. Finally, the *pay range* space provides for the specific pay or pay range of the job.

Job Summary

The *job summary* should describe the general nature of the job, listing only its major functions or activities. Thus (as in Figure 3.8), the supervisor of data processing "directs the operation of all data processing, data control, and data preparation requirements." For the job of materials manager, the summary might state that the "materials manager purchases economically, regulates deliveries of, stores, and distributes all material necessary on the production line." For the job of mailroom supervisor, "the mailroom supervisor receives, sorts, and delivers all incoming mail properly, and he or she handles all outgoing mail including the accurate and timely posting of such mail."[13]

Try to avoid including a general statement like "performs other assignments as required." Including such a statement can give supervisors more flexibility in assigning duties. However, some experts state unequivocally that "one item frequently found that should *never* be included in a job description is a 'cop-out clause' like 'other duties, as assigned,'"[14] since this leaves open the nature of the job—and the people needed to staff it.

Relationships

The *relationships* statement shows the jobholder's relationships with others inside and outside the organization, and might look like this for a human resource manager:[15]

Reports to: vice president of employee relations.

Supervises: human resource clerk, test administrator, labor relations director, and one secretary.

Works with: all department managers and executive management.

Outside the company: employment agencies, executive recruiting firms, union representatives, state and federal employment offices, and various vendors.[16]

Responsibilities and Duties

This section presents a detailed list of the job's actual responsibilities and duties. As in Figure 3.8, each of the job's major duties should be listed separately, and described in a few sentences. In the figure, for instance, the duty "selects, trains, and develops subordinate personnel" is further defined as follows: "develops spirit of cooperation and understanding . . .," "ensures that work group members receive specialized training as necessary . . .," and "directs training involving teaching, demonstrating, and/or advising. . . ." Typical duties for other jobs might include maintaining balanced and controlled inventories, making accurate postings to accounts payable, maintaining favorable purchase price variances, and repairing production line tools and equipment.

You can use the Department of Labor's *Dictionary of Occupational Titles* here for itemizing the job's duties and responsibilities. As shown in Figure 3.9, for example, the dictionary lists a human resource manager's specific duties and responsibilities, including "plans and carries out policies relating to all phases of personnel activity," "recruits, interviews, and selects employees to fill vacant positions," and "conducts wage survey within labor market to determine competitive wage rate."

Authority

This section should define the limits of the jobholder's authority, including his or her decision-making authority, direct supervision of other personnel, and budgetary limitations. For example, the jobholder might have authority to approve purchase requests up to $5000, grant time off or leaves of absence, discipline department personnel, recommend salary increases, and interview and hire new employees.[17]

Figure 3.9
"Personnel Manager"
Description from
Dictionary of
Occupational Titles

Source: *Dictionary of Occupational Titles,* 4th ed. (Washington, DC: U.S. Department of Labor, Employment Training Administration, U.S. Employment Service, 1991).

166.117–018   MANAGER, PERSONNEL (profess. & kin.) alternate titles: manager, human resources

Plans and carries out policies relating to all phases of personnel activity: Recruits, interviews, and selects employees to fill vacant positions. Plans and conducts new employee orientation to foster positive attitude toward company goals. Keeps record of insurance coverage, pension plan, and personnel transactions, such as hires, promotions, transfers, and terminations. Investigates accidents and prepares reports for insurance carrier. Conducts wage survey within labor market to determine competitive wage rate. Prepares budget of personnel operations. Meets with shop stewards and supervisors to resolve grievances. Writes separation notices for employees separating with cause and conducts exit interviews to determine reasons behind separations. Prepares reports and recommends procedures to reduce absenteeism and turnover. Represents company at personnel-related hearings and investigations. Contracts with outside suppliers to provide employee services, such as canteen, transportation, or relocation service. May prepare budget of personnel operations, using computer terminal. May administer manual and dexterity tests to applicants. May supervise clerical workers. May keep records of hired employee characteristics for governmental reporting purposes. May negotiate collective bargaining agreement with BUSINESS REPRESENTATIVE, LABOR UNION (profess & kin.) 187.167–018. *GOE: 11.05.02 STRENGTH: S GED: R5 M5 L5 SVP: 8 DLU: 88*

Standards of Performance

Some job descriptions also contain a *standards of performance* section. This states the standards the employee is expected to achieve in each of the job description's main duties and responsibilities.

Setting standards is never an easy matter. However, most managers soon learn that just telling subordinates to "do their best" doesn't provide enough guidance to ensure top performance. One straightforward way of setting standards is to finish the statement: "I will be completely satisfied with your work when. . . ." This sentence, if completed for each duty listed in the job description, should result in a usable set of performance standards.[18] Some examples would include the following:

Duty: Accurately Posting Accounts Payable

1. All invoices received are posted within the same working day.
2. All invoices are routed to proper department managers for approval no later than the day following receipt.
3. An average of no more than three posting errors per month occurs.
4. Posting ledger is balanced by the end of the third working day of each month.

Duty: Meeting Daily Production Schedule

1. Work group produces no less than 426 units per working day.
2. No more than an average of 2% of units is rejected at the next workstation.
3. Work is completed with no more than an average of 5% overtime per week.

Working Conditions and Physical Environment

The job description will also list the general working conditions involved on the job. These might include things like noise level, hazardous conditions, or heat.

Job Description Guidelines

Here are some final guidelines for writing up your job descriptions:[19]

Be clear. The job description should portray the work of the position so well that the duties are clear without reference to other job descriptions.

Indicate scope of authority. In defining the position, be sure to indicate the scope and nature of the work by using phrases such as "for the department" or "as requested by the manager." Include all important relationships.

Be specific. Select the most specific words to show (1) the kind of work, (2) the degree of complexity, (3) the degree of skill required, (4) the extent to which problems are standardized, (5) the extent of the worker's responsibility for each phase of the work, and (6) the degree and type of accountability. Use action words such as *analyze, gather, assemble, plan, devise, infer, deliver, transmit, maintain, supervise,* and *recommend.* Positions at the lower levels of organization generally have the most detailed duties or tasks, while higher-level positions deal with broader aspects.

Be brief. Short, accurate statements usually best accomplish the purpose.

Recheck. Finally, to check whether the description fulfills the basic requirements, ask yourself, "Will a new employee understand the job if he or she reads the job description?"

Writing Job Descriptions that Comply with the ADA As explained in Chapter 2, the Americans with Disabilities Act (ADA) was enacted to reduce or eliminate serious problems of discrimination against disabled individuals. Under the ADA, the individual must have the requisite skills, educational background, and experience to perform the job's essential functions. A job function is essential when it is the reason the position exists, or when the function is so highly specialized that the person doing the job is hired for his or her expertise or ability to perform that particular function. If the disabled individual can't perform the job as currently structured, the employer is required to make a "reasonable accommodation" unless doing so would present an "undue hardship."

As we said earlier, the ADA does not require employers to have job descriptions, but it's probably advisable for them to do so. Virtually all ADA legal actions will revolve around the question, "What are the essential functions of the job?" Without a job description that lists such functions, it will be hard to convince a court that the functions were essential to the job. The corrollary is that the essential functions can't just be listed on the description but should be clearly identified as essential.

Identifying Essential Job Functions *Essential job functions* are those job duties that employees must be able to perform, with or without reasonable accommodation.[20] Questions to be considered in determining whether a function is essential include:

1. Does the position exist to perform that function?[21]
2. Are employees in the position actually required to perform the function?[22]
3. Is there a limited number of other employees available to perform the function, or among whom can the performance of the function be distributed?
4. What is the degree of expertise or skill required to perform the function?

5. What is the actual work experience of present or past employees in the job?
6. What is the amount of time an individual actually spends performing the function?
7. What are the consequences of not requiring the performance of a function?

Small Business Applications

A Practical Approach

Without the benefit of their own job analysts or (in many cases) their own HR managers, many small business owners face two hurdles when conducting job analyses and writing job descriptions. First (given their need to concentrate on other pressing matters), they often need a more streamlined approach than those provided by questionnaires like the one shown in Figure 3.3. Second, there is always the reasonable fear that in writing up their job descriptions they will inadvertently overlook duties that should be assigned to subordinates or assign duties to subordinates that are usually not associated with such positions. What they need here is a sort of encyclopedia listing all the possible positions they might encounter, including a detailed listing of the duties normally assigned to these positions. Such an "encyclopedia" exists, as the *Dictionary of Occupational Titles* briefly mentioned earlier. The *practical approach to job analysis for small-business owners* presented next is built around this invaluable device.

Step 1. Decide on a Plan.
Start by developing at least the broad outlines of a corporate plan. What do you expect your sales revenue to be next year, and in the next few years? What products do you intend to emphasize? What areas or departments in your company do you think will have to be expanded, reduced, or consolidated, given where you plan to go with your firm over the next few years? What kinds of new positions do you think you'll need in order to accomplish your strategic plans?

Step 2. Develop an Organization Chart.
Given your plan, the next step should be to develop an organization chart for your firm. Draw a chart showing who reports to the president and to each of his or her subordinates. Then complete the chart by showing who reports to each of the other managers and supervisors in the firm. Start by drawing up the organization chart as it is now. Then, depending upon how far in advance you're planning, produce a chart showing how you'd like your chart to look in the immediate future (say, in two months) and perhaps two or three other charts showing how you'd like your organization to evolve over the next two or three years.

Step 3. Use a Job Analysis/Description Questionnaire.
Next use a job analysis questionnaire to determine what the job entails. You can use one of the more comprehensive job analysis questionnaires (see Figure 3.3, for instance) to collect job analysis data. A simpler and often satisfactory alternative is to use the job description questionnaire presented in Figure 3.10. Fill in the information called for (using the procedure outlined later) and ask the supervisors or the employees themselves to list their job duties (on the bottom of the page), breaking them into daily duties, periodic duties, and duties performed at irregular intervals. A sample of how one of

Figure 3.10
Job Description
Questionnaire

Background Data for Job Description

Job Title _____   Department _____

Job Number _____   Written by _____

Today's Date _____   Applicable DOT codes _____

I. Applicable DOT Definition(s):

II. Job Summary:
(List the more important or regularly performed tasks)

III. Reports to:

IV. Supervises: _____

V. Job Duties: _____
*(Briefly describe, for each duty, what employee does and, if possible, how
employee does it. Show in parentheses at end of each duty the approximate
percentage of time devoted to duty.)*

A. Daily Duties:

B. Periodic Duties:
(Indicate whether weekly, monthly, quarterly, etc.)

C. Duties Performed at Irregular Intervals:

Figure 3.11
Background Data
For Examples

Example of Job Title: Customer Service Clerk

Example of Job Summary: Answers inquiries and gives directions to customers, authorizes cashing of customers' checks, records and returns lost charge cards, sorts and reviews new credit applications, works at customer-service desk in department store.

Example of One Job Duty: Authorizes cashing of checks: authorizes cashing of personal or payroll checks (up to a specified amount) by customers desiring to make payment by check. Requests identification, such as driver's license, from customers, and examines check to verify date, amount, signature, and endorsement. Initials check and sends customer to cashier.

these duties should be described (Figure 3.11) can be distributed to supervisors and/or employees.

Step 4. *Obtain the* **Dictionary of Occupational Titles.**
Next, obtain standardized examples of the job descriptions you will need from the *Dictionary of Occupational Titles* (DOT).

The best way to learn how to use the *Dictionary of Occupational Titles* is to buy a copy and begin using it. The dictionary is available for about $40.00 from the Superintendent of Documents, Government Printing Office, Washington, DC 20402-9325. (Call the information desk at 202/783-3238 to verify prices and order your manuals).

Step 5. *Choose Appropriate Definitions and Put Them on Index Cards.*
Next, for each of your departments, choose from the DOT job titles and job descriptions that you believe might be appropriate for your own enterprise.

For example, suppose you want to develop job descriptions for the employees in the retail sales department of your store. You leaf through occupational code numbers in the DOT starting with 0, 1, or 2 (since these include all professional, technical, and managerial occupations as well as clerical and sales occupations). On page 134 (see Figure 3.12) you find that category 185 refers to "Wholesale and Retail Trade Managers and Officials," and you find here "Manager, Department Store" (185.117–010) and "Fashion Coordinator" (185.157–010). Moving on, on page 208 you find that category 261 refers to "Sales Occupations—Apparel," and here you find "Salesperson, Children's Wear," (261.357–046), "Salesperson, Men's Clothing" (261.357–050), and "Salesperson, Women's Wear" (261.357–038). On the off chance that you may have inadvertently left out some titles that might be appropriate, you leaf through the alphabetical index of occupational titles under "Retail Trade Industry" occupations toward the back of the manual and stumble across "Assistant Buyer, Retail Trade" (162.157–022). You decide you should pick up several aspects of this job's duties as well. Make copies of each of the pertinent descriptions and glue them to index cards. You now have a comprehensive set of the managementrelated jobs typically found in a retail sales department and can rearrange them on your chart and consolidate positions until you have a division of work that you believe will work for you. This will help to ensure that you've considered the full range of retail sales management jobs that might be pertinent for your enterprise. It also helps to ensure that no important retail–management duties are inadvertently omitted.

Step 6. *Put Appropriate DOT Summaries on the Top of Your Job Description Form.*
Next write a job description for the job you want done. To facilitate this, write the corresponding DOT codes and DOT definitions under "Applicable DOT Definitions" in the Job Description Form in Figure 3.10. Particularly when (as is usually the case) only one or two DOT definitions apply to the job description you are writing, the DOT definition will give your own definition a firm foundation. It will provide a standardized list and constant reminder of the specific duties that should be included in your own definition. Including the DOT codes and definitions will also facilitate your conversations with the state job service, should you use them to help find employees for your open positions.

Step 7. *Complete Your Job Description.*
Finally, in Figure 3.10, write an appropriate job summary for the job under consideration. Then use the job analysis information obtained in step 3 together with the information gleaned from the DOT to create a complete listing of the tasks and duties of each of your jobs.◆

lizing knowledge of railroad maintenance regulations: Analyzes production reports, work schedules, and freight car repair list to determine efficient utilization of human resources, and recommends to superiors increasing, reducing, or shifting human resources as necessary to complete work requirements. Fills out daily worksheets identifying defective freight cars, necessary repairs, and priority of repairs for use of subordinate supervisors. Notifies YARD MANAGER (r.r. trans.) 184.167-278 to close tracks on which freight trains are being inspected to other rail traffic. Coordinates dispatching of wreck crews and heavy equipment to wreck site within yard or assigned geographic area. Contacts private contractors to rent equipment needed at wreck site. Informs consignees of damaged freight cars and obtains permission to transfer loads when necessary. Observes work in yard and repair shop to determine that areas are clean and free of hazards. Serves on committees to investigate causes of wrecks. Conducts investigations to determine cause of accidental worker injuries. Submits written reports of findings to superiors.
GOE: 05.02.02 STRENGTH: L GED: R4 M3 L3 SVP: 7 DLU: 86

184.167-290 SUPERVISOR, COMMUNICATIONS-AND-SIGNALS (r.r. trans.)
Directs and coordinates, through subordinate supervisory personnel, activities of workers engaged in installing, maintaining, and testing communications and signalling equipment within specified jurisdiction of railroad: Reviews reports that describe handling of communications and signal irregularities to discern whether deployment of personnel and maintenance procedures followed administrative and labor regulations. Discusses causes of irregularities with supervisor who directed repairs to suggest changes in inspection or maintenance techniques that would prevent recurrence of irregularities, utilizing knowledge of communication and signal functioning. Writes summary of reports indicating worker overtime involved and nature of equipment malfunctions and routes reports to superior. Confers with company engineers regarding major repairs or installation projects in communication and signal system to stay apprised of changes within system. Confers with supervisors throughout projects to provide technical assistance and to ensure availability of equipment needed to complete project.
GOE: 11.11.03 STRENGTH: L GED: R4 M4 L4 SVP: 8 DLU: 86

184.167-294 SUPERVISOR, TRAIN OPERATIONS (r.r. trans.)
Directs and coordinates activities of personnel engaged in scheduling and routing trains and engines in specified railroad territory: Observes record entries and monitors railroad radio communications and lights on train location panelboard to oversee train and engine movements along specified territory of railroad. Confers with railroad dispatchers to determine scheduling of trains and engines. Directs delays of train departures upon notification of substandard track conditions. Coordinates train movements to utilize train crews efficiently to schedule engines to arrive at service locations when due for maintenance and to maximize use of local trains versus special work trains. Scrutinizes train schedules and advises specified personnel of availability of tracks for scheduled repair and maintenance. Issues directives to subordinates to coordinate movement of expedited, late, or special railroad trains, using information received through railroad information network.
GOE: 05.02.02 STRENGTH: L GED: R4 M3 L4 SVP: 8 DLU: 86

184.267-010 FREIGHT-TRAFFIC CONSULTANT (business ser.) alternate titles: transportation consultant
Advises industries, business firms, and individuals concerning methods of preparation of freight for shipment, rates to be applied, and mode of transportation to be used: Consults with client regarding packing procedures and inspects packed or crated goods for conformance to shipping specifications to prevent damage, delay, or penalties. Selects mode of transportation, such as air, water, railroad, or truck without regard to higher rates when speed is necessary. Confers with shipping brokers concerning export and import papers, docking facilities, or packing and marking procedures. Files claims with insurance company for losses, damages, and overcharges of freight shipments.
GOE: 11.05.02 STRENGTH: S GED: R5 M4 L4 SVP: 8 DLU: 77

184.387-010 WHARFINGER (water trans.)
Compiles reports, such as dockage, demurrage, wharfage, and storage, to ensure that shipping companies are assessed specified harbor fees: Compares information on statements, records, and reports with ship's manifest to determine that weight, measurement, and classification of commodities are in accordance with tariff. Calculates tariff assessment from ship's manifest to ensure that charges are correct. Prepares and submits reports. Inspects sheds and wharves to determine need for repair. Arranges for temporary connection of water and electrical services from wharves. Reads service meters to determine charges to be made.
GOE: 07.02.04 STRENGTH: L GED: R3 M3 L2 SVP: 5 DLU: 77

185 WHOLESALE AND RETAIL TRADE MANAGERS AND OFFICIALS

This group includes managerial occupations concerned with selling merchandise to retailers; to industrial, commercial, institutional or professional users; or to other wholesalers; or acting as agents in buying merchandise for or selling merchandise to such persons or companies.

185.117-010 MANAGER, DEPARTMENT STORE (retail trade)
Directs and coordinates, through subordinate managerial personnel, activities of department store selling lines of merchandise in specialized departments: Formulates pricing policies for sale of merchandise, or implements policies set forth by merchandising board. Coordinates activities of nonmerchandising departments, as purchasing, credit, accounting, and advertising with merchandising departments to obtain optimum efficiency of operations with minimum costs in order to maximize profits. Develops and implements, through subordinate managerial personnel, policies and procedures for store and departmental operations and customer personnel and community relations. Negotiates or approves contracts negotiated with suppliers of merchandise, or with other establishments providing security, maintenance, or cleaning services. Reviews operating and financial statements and departmental sales records to determine merchandising activities that require additional sales promotion, clearance sales, or other sales procedures in order to turn over merchandise and achieve profitability of store operations and merchandising objectives.
GOE: 11.05.02 STRENGTH: S GED: R5 M4 L5 SVP: 8 DLU: 77

185.117-014 AREA SUPERVISOR, RETAIL CHAIN STORE (retail trade) alternate titles: operations manager
Directs and coordinates activities of subordinate managerial personnel involved in operating retail chain stores in assigned area: Interviews and selects individuals to fill managerial vacancies. Maintains employment records for each manager. Terminates employment of store managers whose performance does not meet company standards. Directs, through subordinate managerial personnel, compliance of workers with established company policies, procedures, and standards, such as safekeeping of company funds and property, personnel and grievance practices, and adherence to policies governing acceptance and processing of customer credit card charges. Inspects premises of assigned area stores to ensure that adequate security exists and that physical facilities comply with safety and environmental codes and ordinances. Reviews operational records and reports of store managers to project sales and to determine store profitability. Coordinates sales and promotional activities of store managers. Analyzes marketing potential of new and existing store locations and recommends additional sites or deletion of existing area stores. Negotiates with vendors to enter into contracts for merchandise and determines allocations to each store manager.
GOE: 11.11.05 STRENGTH: L GED: R4 M3 L4 SVP: 7 DLU: 86

185.137-010 MANAGER, FAST FOOD SERVICES (retail trade; wholesale tr.)
Manages franchised or independent fast food or wholesale prepared food establishment: Directs, coordinates, and participates in preparation of, and cooking, wrapping or packing types of food served or prepared by establishment, collecting of monies from in-house or take-out customers, or assembling food orders for wholesale customers. Coordinates activities of workers engaged in keeping business records, collecting and paying accounts, ordering or purchasing supplies, and delivery of foodstuffs to wholesale or retail customers. Interviews, hires, and trains personnel. May contact prospective wholesale customers, such as mobile food vendors, vending machine operators, bar and tavern owners, and institutional personnel, to promote sale of prepared foods, such as doughnuts, sandwiches, and specialty food items. May establish delivery routes and schedules for supplying wholesale customers. Workers may be known according to type or name of franchised establishment or type of prepared foodstuff retailed or wholesaled.
GOE: 11.11.04 STRENGTH: L GED: R4 M4 L4 SVP: 5 DLU: 81

185.157-010 FASHION COORDINATOR (retail trade) alternate titles: fashion stylist
Promotes new fashions and coordinates promotional activities, such as fashion shows, to induce consumer acceptance: Studies fashion and trade journals, travels to garment centers, attends fashion shows, and visits manufacturers and merchandise markets to obtain information on fashion trends. Consults with buying personnel to gain advice regarding type of fashions store will purchase and feature for season. Advises publicity and display departments of merchandise to be publicized. Selects garments and accessories to be shown at fashion shows. Provides information on current fashions, style trends, and use of accessories. May contract with models, musicians, caterers, and other personnel to manage staging of shows. May conduct teenage fashion shows and direct activities of store-sponsored club for teenage girls.
GOE: 11.09.01 STRENGTH: L GED: R5 M4 L5 SVP: 7 DLU: 77

185.157-014 SUPERVISOR OF SALES (business ser.)
Coordinates and publicizes tobacco marketing activities within specified area: Visits tobacco growers, buyers, and auction warehouses to cultivate interest and goodwill. Develops publicity for tobacco industry. Investigates and confirms eligibility of buyers. Collects membership dues for tobacco Board of Trade. Schedules tobacco auction dates. Records quantity and purchase price of tobacco sold daily, and prepares reports specified by board. May prepare report of marketing activities for state and federal agencies. May review and verify reports for individual warehouses. May examine quality and growth of tobacco in fields of individual growers and inform buyers of results.
GOE: 11.09.01 STRENGTH: L GED: R4 M4 L4 SVP: 7 DLU: 77

185.157-018 WHOLESALER II (wholesale tr.)
Exports domestic merchandise to foreign merchants and consumers and imports foreign merchandise for sale to domestic merchants or consumers: Arranges for purchase and transportation of imports through company representatives abroad and sells imports to local customers. Sells domestic goods, materials, or products to representatives of foreign companies. May be required

Figure 3.12
Page from *Dictionary of Occupational Titles*

Source: Dictionary of Occupational Titles (Washington, DC: U.S. Department of Labor, 1991), p. 134.

Writing Job Specifications

The job specification takes the job description and answers the question, "What human traits and experience are required to do this job well?" It shows what kind of person to recruit and for what qualities that person should be tested. The job specification may be a separate section on the job description or a separate document entirely; often it is presented on the back of the job description.[23]

Specifications For Trained Versus Untrained Personnel

DOT job descriptions can help employers specify jobs in enough detail to identify a "salesperson—men's clothing."

Writing job specifications for trained employees is relatively straightforward. For example, suppose you want to fill a position for a trained bookkeeper (or trained counselor or programmer). In cases like these your job specifications might focus mostly on traits like length of previous service, quality of relevant training, and previous job performance. Thus, it's usually not too difficult to determine the human requirements for placing *already trained* people on a job.

But the problems are more complex when you're seeking to fill jobs with *untrained* people (probably with the intention of training them on the job). Here you need to specify qualities such as physical traits, personality, interests, or sensory skills that imply some potential for performing the job or for having the ability to be trained for the job. For example, suppose the job requires detailed manipulation on a circuit board assembly line. Here you might want to ensure the person scores high on a test of finger dexterity. Your goal, in other words, is to identify those personal traits—those human requirements—that validly predict which candidate would do well on the job and which would not. Identifying these human requirements for a job is accomplished either through a subjective, judgmental approach or through statistical analysis.

Job Specifications Based on Judgment

The judgmental approach is based on the educated guesses of people like supervisors and human resource managers. The basic procedure here is to ask: "What does it take in terms of education, intelligence, training, and the like to do this job well?"

The *Dictionary of Occupational Titles* can be useful here. For jobs in the dictionary, job analysts and vocational counselors have made judgments regarding each job's human requirements. Each of these human requirements or traits has been rated and assigned a letter as follows: G (intelligence), V (verbal), N (numerical), S (spatial), P (perception), Q (clerical perception), K (motor coordination), F (finger dexterity), M (manual dexterity), E (eye–hand–foot coordination), and C (color dissemination). The ratings reflect the amount of each trait or ability possessed by people with different performance levels currently working on the job, based on the experts' judgments. Each has also been rated on the extent to which the job involves dealing with Data, People, and Things. Thus an accountant might rate high on Data, while a mechanic rates higher on dealing with things.

Job Specifications Based on Statistical Analysis

The job specification for already-trained candidates, such as the financial analysts here at IBM, should indicate clearly that computer literacy is a requirement.

Basing a job specification on statistical analysis is the most defensible approach, but it is also more difficult. Basically, the aim is to statistically determine the relationship between (1) some *predictor* or human trait such as height, intelligence, or finger dexterity and (2) some indicator or *criterion* of job effectiveness (such as performance as rated by the supervisor). The procedure has five steps: (1) analyze the job and decide how to measure job performance; (2) select personal traits like finger dexterity that you believe should predict successful performance; (3) test job candidates for these traits; (4) measure these candidates' subsequent job performance; and (5) statistically analyze the relationship between the human trait (finger dexterity) and job performance. Your objective is to determine whether the former predicts the latter. In this way the human requirements for performing the job can be statistically ascertained.

This method is more defensible than the judgmental approach, since equal rights legislation forbids using traits that you can't *prove* distinguish between high and low job performers. Remember that hiring standards that discriminate on the basis of sex, race, religion, national origin, or age may have to be shown to predict job performance, and this generally requires a statistical validation study.

Job Analysis in a "Jobless" World

Introduction

A *job* is generally defined as a set of closely related activities carried out for pay, but over the past few years the concept of *job* has been changing quite dramatically. As one observer recently put it:

> The modern world is on the verge of another huge leap in creativity and productivity, but the job is not going to be part of tomorrow's economic reality. There still is and will always be enormous amounts of work to do, but it is not going to be contained in the familiar envelopes we call jobs. In fact, many organizations are today well along the path toward being "de-jobbed."[24]

From Specialized to Enlarged Jobs

The term *job* as we know it today is largely an outgrowth of the industrial revolution's efficiency demands. As the substitution of machine power for people power became more widespread, experts including Adam Smith, Charles Babbage, and Frederick Winslow Taylor wrote glowingly about the positive correlation between (1) job specialization and (2) productivity and efficiency.[25] The popularity of specialized, short-cycle jobs soared—at least among management experts and managers.

By the mid-1900s other writers, reacting to what they viewed as the "dehumanizing" aspects of pigeonholing workers into highly repetitive and specialized jobs, proposed ways of broadening the number of activities employees engaged in. *Job enlargement* is defined as assigning workers additional same-level activities so as to increase the number of activities they have to perform. Thus, if the work was assembling chairs, the worker who previously only bolted the seat to the legs might take on the additional tasks of assembling the legs and attaching the back as well. *Job rotation* means systematically moving workers from one job to another.

Thus, on an assembly line, a worker might spend an hour fitting doors, the next hour installing headlamps, and so on.

More recently, psychologist Frederick Herzberg argued that the best way to motivate workers is to build opportunities for challenge and achievement into their jobs via job enrichment. *Job enrichment* means redesigning jobs in such a way as to increase the opportunities for the worker to experience feelings of responsibility, achievement, growth, and recognition by doing the job well. Five ways to do this are:

1. *Form natural work groups.* Here the job is changed so that each person is responsible for or "owns" an identifiable body of work. For example, instead of doing work for all departments, the typist in a typing pool becomes responsible for doing all the work for one or two departments.
2. *Combine tasks.* For example, one person assembles a product from start to finish, replacing a system in which several separate operations are performed by different people.
3. *Establish client relationships.* Here the worker has contact as often as possible with the consumer of the product.
4. *Vertical loading.* The worker plans and controls his or her own job instead of having it controlled by outsiders. For example, the worker sets his or her own schedule, does his or her own troubleshooting, decides when to start and stop working, and so on.
5. *Open feedback channels.* Finally, the company implements more and better ways for the worker to get quick feedback on his or her performance.[26]

Whether a job was specialized, enlarged, or enriched, however, workers still generally have been assigned to jobs, and these jobs required job descriptions. In many firms today, jobs are becoming more amorphous and more difficult to define: In other words, the trend is toward *de-jobbing* many companies.

Why Companies Are Becoming De-jobbed: The Need for Responsiveness

De-jobbing is ultimately a product of the rapid changes taking place in business today. Organizations need to grapple with a number of revolutionary forces: accelerating product and technological change, globalized competition, deregulation, political instability, demographic changes, and trends toward a service society and the information age. Forces like these have changed the playing field on which firms compete. Specifically, rapid change has dramatically increased the need for firms to be responsive, flexible, and capable of competing in a global marketplace.

The organizational techniques firms have used to foster responsiveness have helped to blur the meaning of *job* as a set of well-defined and clearly delineated set of responsibilities. Here is a sampling of how these techniques have contributed to this blurring:

Flatter Organizations Instead of pyramid-shaped organizations with seven or more management layers, flat organizations with just three or four levels are becoming more prevalent. Many firms (including AT&T, ABB, and General Electric) have already cut their management layers from a dozen to six or fewer. As the remaining managers are left with more people reporting to them, they can supervise them less, so the jobs of subordinates end up bigger in terms of both breadth and depth of responsibilities.

Work Teams   Work itself is increasingly organized around teams and processes rather than around specialized functions. For example, at Chesebrough-Ponds USA, a subsidiary of Unilever United States, Inc., a traditional pyramidal organization was replaced with multiskilled, cross-functional, and self-directed teams that now run the plant's four product areas. Hourly employees make employee assignments, schedule overtime, establish production times and changeovers, and even handle cost control, requisitions, and work orders. They also are solely responsible for quality control under the plant's continuous quality improvement.[27] In an organization like this, employees' jobs change daily; the effort to avoid having employees view their jobs as a limited and specific set of responsibilities is thus intentional.

The Boundaryless Organization   A *boundaryless organization* is one in which widespread use of teams and similar structural mechanisms means that the boundaries that typically separate organizational functions (like sales and production) and hierarchical levels are reduced and made more permeable.[28] Boundaryless organizations foster responsiveness by encouraging employees to rid themselves of the "It's not my job" attitudes that typically create walls between one employee area and another. Instead the focus is on defining the job at hand in terms of the overall best interests of the organization, thereby further de-jobbing the company.

Reengineering   *Reengineering* is defined as "the fundamental rethinking and radical redesign of business processes to achieve dramatic improvements in critical, contemporary measures of performance, such as cost, quality, service, and speed."[29] In their book *Reengineering the Corporation,* Michael Hammer and James Champy argue that the principles (like highly specialized divisions of work) that shaped the structure and management of business for hundreds of years should be retired. Instead the firm should emphasize combining tasks into integrated, unspecialized processes that are then carried out by committed employees.

Reengineering is achieved in several ways. Specialized jobs are combined into one so that formerly distinct jobs are integrated and compressed into enlarged, enriched ones.[30] A necessary correlate of combining jobs is that workers make more decisions, since each person's responsibilities are generally broader and deeper after reengineering; supervisory checks and controls are reduced and indeed committed employees largely control their own efforts. Finally, workers become collectively responsible for overall results rather than individually responsible for just their own tasks. As a result, their jobs change dramatically. "They share joint responsibility with their team members for performing the whole process, not just a small piece of it. They not only use a broader range of skills from day to day, they have to be thinking of a far greater picture."[31] Most importantly, "while not every member of the team will be doing exactly the same work . . . the lines between [the workers' jobs] blur." And to that extent reengineering also contributes to de-jobbing the enterprise.

The Future of Job Descriptions   Most firms today continue to utilize job descriptions and to rely on jobs as traditionally defined. However, it's clear that more and more firms are moving toward new organizational configurations, ones built around jobs that are broad and that may change every day. As one writer has said, "In such a situation people no longer take their cues from a job description or a supervisor's instructions. Signals come from the changing demands of the project. Workers learn to focus their individual efforts and collective resources on the work that needs doing, changing as that changes. Managers lose their 'jobs,' too. . . ."[32] The responsive organization feature below describes some practical HR implications.

HR and the Responsive Organization

Job Analysis, HR, and the De-Jobbed Company

Because job descriptions are (deservedly) so well ingrained in the way that most companies operate, it's unlikely that most firms could (or should) do without them, at least for now. But for the growing number of firms that are shifting to HR systems that don't use job descriptions, what replaces them?

In one firm—British Petroleum's exploration division—the need for flatter organizations and empowered employees inspired management to replace job descriptions with matrices listing skills and skill levels.[33] Senior management wanted to shift employees' attention from a job description/"that's not my job" mentality to one that would motivate employees to obtain the new skills they needed to accomplish their broader responsibilities. The solution was a skills matrix like that shown in Figure 3.13. Skills matrices were created for various jobs within two classes of employees, those on a management track, and those whose aims lay elsewhere (such as to stay in engineering). For each job or job family (such as drilling manager), a matrix was prepared. As in Figure 3.13, it identified (1) the basic skills needed for that job and (2) the minimum *level* of each skill required for that job or job family.

Such a matrix shifts employees' focus. The emphasis is no longer on a job description's listing of specific job duties. Instead the focus is on developing the new skills needed for the employees' broader, empowered, and often relatively undefined responsibilities.

The skills matrix approach has prompted other HR changes in BP's exploration division. For example, the matrices provide a constant reminder of what skills employees must improve, and the firm's new skill-based pay plan awards raises based on skills improvement. Similarly, performance appraisals now focus more on employee skills, and training emphasizes developing broad skills like leadership and planning—ones that are applicable across a wide range of responsibilities and jobs.

Broader HR issues are also involved when firms de-job. For one thing, ". . . you must find people who can work well without the cue system of job descriptions."[34] This puts a premium on hiring people with the skills and values to handle empowered jobs. As two reengineering experts put it:

> For multi-dimensional and changing jobs, companies don't need people to fill a slot, because the slot will be only roughly defined. Companies need people who can figure out what the job takes and do it, people who can create the slot that fits them. Moreover, the slot will keep changing.[35]

There's also a shift from training to education, in other words, from teaching employees the "how" of the job to increasing their insight and understanding regarding its "why." In a rapidly changing industrial environment the demands for flexibility and responsiveness mean that it's impossible to hire people ". . . who already know everything they're ever going to need to know. . . ."[36] Here continuing education over the course of the employees' organizational career becomes the norm.◆

The skills matrix appears as a grid. Included but not shown are descriptors for each level of each skill, beginning at the bottom (A) with the lowest level, and increasing with the highest level at the top. For instance, under technical expertise, level A might read, "Is acquiring basic knowledge and has awareness of the key skills," while level H might read, "Conducts and/or supervises complex tasks requiring advanced knowledge of key skills or a thorough working knowledge of a range of key skills."

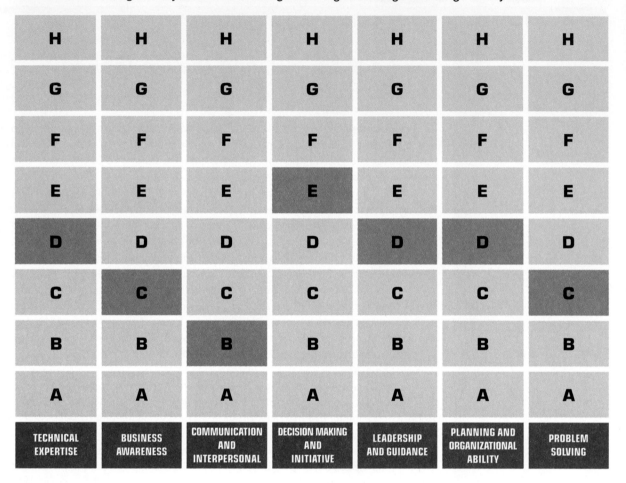

Figure 3.13
The Skills Matrix
The Darker Boxes Indicate the Minimum Level of Skill Required for the Job.

Chapter Review

Summary

1. Developing an organization structure results in jobs that have to be staffed. Job analysis is the procedure through which you find out (1) what the job entails and (2) what kinds of people should be hired for the job. It involves six steps: (1) Determine the use of the job analysis information, (2) collect background information, (3) select the positions to be analyzed, (4) collect job analysis data, (5) review information with participants, and (6) develop a job description and job specification.

2. There are five basic techniques one can use to gather job analysis data: interviews, direct observation, questionnaires, participant logs, and the U.S. Civil Service Procedure. These are good for developing job descriptions and specifications. The Department of Labor, functional job analysis, and PAQ approaches result in quantitative ratings of each job and are therefore useful for classifying jobs for pay purposes.

3. The job description should portray the work of the position so well that the duties are clear without reference to other job descriptions. Always ask, "Will the new employee understand the job if he or she reads the job description?"

4. The job specification takes the job description and answers the question, "What human traits and experience are necessary to do this job well?" It tells what kind of person to recruit and for what qualities that person should be tested. Job specifications are usually based on the educated guesses of managers; however, a more accurate statistical approach to developing job specifications can also be used.

5. Job analysis is in many ways the first personnel activity that affects commitment. Most people can't perform a job when they don't have the ability and skills to do the job. It is through job analysis that you determine what the job entails and what skills and abilities you should look for in job candidates.

6. Use the *Dictionary of Occupational Titles* to help write job descriptions. Find and reproduce the DOT descriptions that relate to the job you're describing. Then use those DOT descriptions to "anchor" your own description and particularly to suggest duties to be included.

7. De-jobbing is ultimately a product of the rapid changes taking place in business today. As firms try to speed *decision making* by taking steps like reengineering, individual jobs are becoming broader and much less specialized. Increasingly, firms don't want employees to feel limited by a specific set of responsibilities like those listed in a job description. As a result, more employees are deemphasizing detailed job descriptions, often substituting brief job summaries, perhaps combined with summaries of the skills required for the position.

Key Terms

job analysis	diary/logs	Department of Labor job
job description	position analysis	analysis
job specification	questionnaire (PAQ)	functional job analysis

Discussion Questions and Exercises

1. What items are typically included in the job description? What items are not shown?

2. What is job analysis? How can you make use of the information it provides?

3. We discussed several methods for collecting job analysis data—questionnaires, the position analysis questionnaire, and so on. Compare and contrast these methods, explaining what each is useful for and listing the pros and cons of each.

4. Describe the types of information typically found in a job specification.

5. Explain how you would conduct a job analysis.

6. Working individually or in groups, obtain copies of job descriptions for clerical positions at the college or university where you study, or the firm where you work. What types of information do they contain? Do they give you enough information to explain what the job involves and how to do it? How would you improve on the descriptions?

7. Working individually or in groups, use the job analysis questionnaire in this chapter to develop a job description for your professor in this class. Based on that, use your judgment to develop a job specification. Compare your conclusions with those of other students or groups. Were there any significant differences? What do you think accounted for the differences?

8. Working individually or in groups, obtain a copy of the DOT from your library. Choose any two positions and compare the jobs' DATA-PEOPLE-THINGS ratings. (These are the 4th, 5th, and 6th digits of the job's DOT number; ratings are explained at the end of the DOT). Do the ratings make sense based on what you know about the jobs? Why or why not?

9. Do you think companies can really do without detailed job descriptions? Why or why not?

10. Since the president's job in a firm is by nature broader than a factory worker's, is there less need for a job description for the president? Why or why not?

Application Exercises

RUNNING CASE: Carter Cleaning Company
The Job Description

Based on her review of the stores, Jennifer concluded that one of the first matters she had to attend to involved developing job descriptions for her store managers.

As Jennifer tells it, her lessons regarding job descriptions in her basic management and HR management courses were insufficient to fully convince her of the pivotal role job descriptions played in the smooth functioning of an enterprise. Many times during her first few weeks on the job, Jennifer found herself asking one of her store managers why he was violating what she knew to be recommended company policies and procedures. Repeatedly the answers were either "Because I didn't know it was my job" or "Because I didn't know that was the way we were supposed to do it." Jennifer knew that a job description, along with a set of standards and procedures that specified what was to be done and how to do it, would go a long way toward alleviating this problem.

In general, the store manager is responsible for directing all store activities in such a way that quality work is produced, customer relations and sales are maximized, and profitability is maintained through effective control of labor, supply, and energy costs. In accomplishing that general aim, a specific store manager's duties and responsibilities include quality control, store appearance and cleanliness, customer relations, bookkeeping and cash management, cost control and productivity, damage control, pricing, inventory control, spotting and cleaning, machine maintenance, employee safety, hazardous waste removal, human resource administration, and pest control.

The questions that Jennifer had to address follow.

Questions

1. What should be the format and final form of the store manager's job description?

2. Was it practical to specify standards and procedures in the body of the job description, or should these be kept separately?

3. How should Jennifer go about collecting the information required for the standards, procedures, and job description?

CASE INCIDENT: Hurricane Andrew

In August 1992 Hurricane Andrew hit South Florida and the Optima Air Filter Company. Many employees' homes were devastated and the firm found that it had to hire almost three completely new crews, one for each of its shifts. The problem was that the "old-timers" had known their jobs so well that no one had ever bothered to draw up job descriptions for them. When about 30 new employees began taking their posts, there was general confusion about what they should do and how they should do it.

The hurricane quickly became old news to the firm's out-of-state customers who wanted filters, not excuses. Phil Mann, the firm's president, was at his wits' end. He had about 30 new employees, 10 old-timers, and his original factory supervisor, Maybelline. He decided to meet with Linda Lowe, a consultant from the local university's business school who immediately had the old-timers fill out a job questionnaire that listed all their duties. Arguments ensued almost at once because both Phil and Maybelline thought the old-timers were exaggerating to make themselves look more important, while the old-timers insisted that the list faithfully reflected their duties. Meanwhile the customers clamored for their filters.

Questions

1. Should Phil and Linda ignore the old-timers' protests and write up the job descriptions as they see fit? Why? Why not? How would you go about resolving the differences?

2. How would you have conducted the job analysis?

 # Human Resource Management Simulation

One of the incidents in the simulation (incident A) involves an opportunity to conduct a job analysis. Although there are no particularly dangerous jobs in your operation, the Occupational Safety and Health Act of 1970 requires that a firm specify "elements of the job that endanger health, or are to be considered unsatisfactory or distasteful to the majority of the population." Providing a job description to employees is a good defense against possible legal actions. Because the firm does not have the personnel or in-house expertise to conduct such an analysis, you will need to decide which consultant should do the work. The proposals range from a complete organization-wide analysis to training your staff to do the analysis in-house. You may also decide that other programs should take precedence and delay this decision.

Video Case

Factory of the Future

The jobs in the Square D Company plant in this video are in many respects the opposite of the highly specialized jobs found in traditional factories. Workers at Square D, unlike their counterparts at traditional factories, operate in teams, in charge of their own "mini-factories," responsible for their own output and for keeping quality high. The changes have apparently been successful: Reject rates are down 75%, and employees make comments like "I think I'm somebody now."

Questions

1. Do you think Square D uses traditional job analysis in this factory? Why or why not?

2. Would a job description make sense for a Square D factory worker? Why or why not?

3. How do you think you'd have to change your job specifications if you moved from a traditional to a Square D-type factory job?

Source: ABC News, *Assembly Line Teams Are Better Trained and More Efficient,* "World News Tonight," February 24, 1993.

 ## Take It to the Net

We invite you to visit the Dessler page on the Prentice Hall Web site at:
http://www.prenhall.com/~dessler
for the monthly Dessler update and for this chapter's World Wide Web exercise.

Notes

1. For a good, recent discussion of job analysis, see James Clifford, "Job Analysis: Why Do It, and How Should It be Done?", *Public Personnel Management,* Vol. 23, no.2 (Summer 1994), pp. 321–340.
2. Ernest J. McCormick, "Job and Task Analysis," in Marvin D. Dunnette, ed., *Handbook of Industrial and Organizational Psychology* (Chicago: Rand McNally, 1976), pp. 651–696.
3. Richard Henderson, *Compensation Management: Rewarding Performance* (Englewood Cliffs, N.J.: Prentice Hall, 1994), pp. 139–150. See also Patrick W. Wright and Kenneth Wexley, "How to Choose the Kind of Job Analysis You Really Need," *Personnel,* Vol. 62, no. 5 (May 1985), pp. 51–55; C. J. Cranny and Michael E. Doherty, "Importance Ratings in Job Analysis: Note on the Misinterpretation of Factor Analyses," *Journal of Applied Psychology* (May 1988), pp. 320–322.
4. Ibid.
5. Wayne Cascio, *Applied Psychology in Personnel Management* (Reston, VA: Reston, 1978), p. 140.
6. The appendixes from Henderson, *Compensation Management,* pp. 148–152.
7. A complete explanation and definition of each of these seven attributes (knowledge, skills, abilities, etc.) can be found in U.S. Civil Service Commission, *Job Analysis* (Washington, DC: U.S. Government Printing Office, December 1976).
8. Note that the PAQ (and other quantitative techniques) can also be used for job evaluation, which is explained in Chapter 12.
9. Again we will see that *job evaluation* is the process through which jobs are compared to one another and their values determined. Although usually viewed as a job analysis technique, the PAQ is, in practice, actually as much or more of a job evaluation technique and could therefore be discussed in either this chapter or in Chapter 12. For a discussion of how to use PAQ for classifying jobs, see Edwin Cornelius III, Theodore Carron, and Marianne Collins, "Job Analysis Models and Job Classifications," *Personnel Psychology,* Vol. 32 (Winter 1979), pp. 693–708. See also Edwin Cornelius III, Frank Schmidt, and Theodore Carron, "Job Classification Approaches and the Implementation of Validity Generalization Results," *Personnel Psychology,* Vol. 37, no. 2 (Summer 1984), pp. 247–260.
10. Jack Smith and Milton Hakel, "Comparisons Among Data Sources, Response Bias, and Reliability and Validity of a Structured Job Analysis Questionnaire," *Personnel Psychology,* Vol. 32 (Winter 1979), pp. 677–692. See also Edwin Cornelius III, Angelo Denisi, and Allyn Blencoe, "Expert and Naive Raters Using the PAQ: Does It Matter?" *Personnel Psychology,* Vol. 37, no. 3 (Autumn 1984), pp. 453–464; Lee Friedman and Robert Harvey, "Can Raters with Reduced Job Description Information Provide Accurate Position Analysis Questionnaire (PAQ) Ratings?" *Personnel Psychology,* Vol. 34 (Winter 1986), pp. 779–789; and Robert J. Harvey et al., "Dimensionality of the Job Element Inventory, A Simplified Worker-Oriented Job Analysis Questionnaire," *Journal of Applied Psychology* (November 1988), pp. 639–646; Stephanie Butler and Robert Harvey, "A Comparison of Holistic Versus Decomposed Rating of Position

11. Analysis Questionnaire Work Dimensions," *Personnel Psychology* (Winter 1988), pp. 761–772.
11. This discussion is based on Howard Olson et al., "The Use of Functional Job Analysis in Establishing Performance Standards for Heavy Equipment Operators," *Personnel Psychology,* Vol. 34 (Summer 1981), pp. 351–364.
12. Regarding this discussion, see Henderson, *Compensation Management,* pp. 175–184.
13. James Evered, "How to Write a Good Job Description," *Supervisory Management* (April 1981), pp. 14–19; Roger J. Plachy, "Writing Job Descriptions That Get Results," *Personnel* (October 1987), pp. 56–58.
14. Ibid., p. 16.
15. This discussion is based on Ibid.
16. Ibid., p. 16.
17. Ibid., p. 17.
18. Ibid., p. 18.
19. Ernest Dale, *Organizations* (New York: American Management Association, 1967).
20. Deborah Kearney, *Reasonable Accommodations: Job Descriptions in the Age of ADA, OSHA, and Workers Comp* (New York: Van Nostrand Reinhold, 1994), p. 9.
21. Ibid. Unless otherwise noted, numbers 1 and 3 through 8 are based on or quoted from Kearney.
22. Michael Esposito, "There's More to Writing Job Descriptions Than Complying with the ADA," *Employment Relations Today* (Autumn 1992), p. 279.
23. The remainder of this chapter, except as noted, is based on Ernest J. McCormick and Joseph Tiffin, *Industrial Psychology* (Englewood Cliffs, NJ: Prentice Hall, 1974), pp. 56–61.
24. William Bridges, "The End of the Job," *Fortune,* September 19, 1994, p. 64.
25. For example, Charles Babbage listed six reasons for making jobs as specialized as possible: There is less time required for learning; there is less waste of material during the training period; there is less time lost in switching from task to task; proficiency increases with practice; hiring is made more efficient; and parts become uniform and interchangeable. Charles Babbage, on the economy of machinery and manufacturers (London: Charles Knight, 1832), pp. 169–176; reprinted in Joseph Litterer, *Organizations* (New York: John Wiley and Sons, 1969), pp. 73–75.
26. J. Richard Hackman and Greg Oldham, "Motivation Through the Design of Work: Test of a Theory," *Organizational Behavior and Human Performance,* Vol. 16, no. 2 (August 1976), pp. 250–279.
27. William H. Miller, "Chesebrough-Ponds At a Glance," *Industry Week,* October 19, 1992, pp. 14–15. For an interesting discussion of the need to move from a "it's not my job" mentality from the point of view of an employee, see Kathy Shaw, "It's Not in My Job Description," *CMA Magazine* (June 1994), p. 42.
28. Larry Hirschhorn and Thomas Gilmore, "The New Boundaries of the 'Boundaryless' Company," *Harvard Business Review* (May–June 1992), pp. 104–108. For another point of view, see George Stack, Jr. and Jill Black, "The Myth of the Horizontal Organization," *Canadian Business Review* (Winter 1994), pp. 28–31.

29. Michael Hammer and James Champy, *Reengineering the Corporation* (New York: Harper Business, 1993), p. 32.
30. Ibid., p. 51.
31. Ibid., p. 68.
32. William Bridges, "The End of the Job," p. 68.
33. Milan Moravec and Robert Tucker, "Job Descriptions for the 21st Century," *Personnel Journal* (June 1992), pp. 37–44.
34. William Bridges, "The End of the Job," p. 68.
35. Hammer and Champy, *Reengineering the Corporation,* p. 72.
36. Ibid.

Chapter 4
Personnel Planning and Recruiting

Chapter Outline

- ◆ **The Recruitment and Selection Process**
- ◆ **Employment Planning and Forecasting**
- ◆ **Recruiting Job Candidates**
- ◆ **Developing and Using Application Forms**

Behavioral Objectives

When you finish studying this chapter, you should be able to:

Explain the process of forecasting personnel requirements.

Discuss the pros and cons of eight methods used for recruiting job candidates.

Describe how to develop an application form.

Explain how to use application forms to predict job performance.

The Recruitment and Selection Process

The recruiting and selecting process can best be envisioned as a series of hurdles, illustrated in Figure 4.1. Specifically, recruiting and selecting require:

1. Doing employment planning and forecasting to determine the duties of the positions to be filled.
2. Building a pool of candidates for these jobs by recruiting internal or external candidates.
3. Having the applicants fill out application forms and perhaps undergo an initial screening interview.
4. Utilizing various selection techniques such as tests, background investigations, and physical exams to identify viable job candidates.
5. Sending to the supervisor responsible for the job one or more viable job candidates.
6. Having the candidate(s) go through one or more selection interviews with the supervisor and other relevant parties for the purpose of finally determining to which candidate(s) an offer should be made.

Recruiting and selecting is the subject of this and the next two chapters. In this chapter we'll focus on employment *planning and forecasting* (in other words, on how to determine what positions are to be filled) and on *recruiting* techniques. Chapter 5 focuses on *employee selection techniques* including tests, background checks, and physical exams. Finally, Chapter 6 is devoted to a discussion of the selection technique that is by far the most widely used, namely, interviewing job candidates.

Employment Planning and Forecasting

Employment planning is the process of formulating plans to fill future openings based on an analysis of the positions that are expected to be open and whether

Figure 4.1
Steps in Recruitment and Selection Process

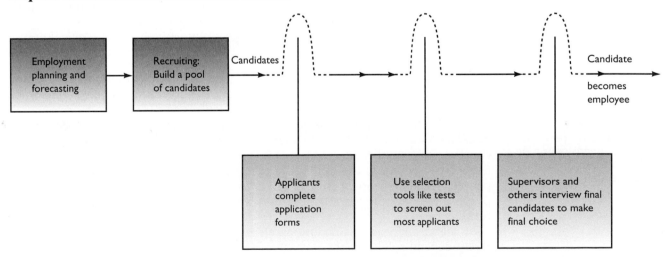

The recruitment and selection process is a series of hurdles aimed at selecting the best candidate for the job.

these will be filled by inside or outside candidates. *Employment planning,* therefore, refers to planning to fill any or all the firm's future positions, from maintenance clerk to CEO. However, we'll see in this chapter that most firms use the term *succession planning* to refer to the process of planning how the company's most important executive positions will be filled.

In any case, employment planning is best thought of as an integral part of the firm's strategic and HR planning processes. For example, plans to enter new businesses, to build new plants, or to reduce the level of activities all influence the number of and types of positions to be filled. At the same time decisions regarding how to fill these positions will have to be integrated with other aspects of the firm's HR plans, for instance, with plans for appraising and training current and new employees.

The fundamental employment planning decision will be whether projected positions will be filled internally or externally. In other words, should the projected open positions be filled by current employees? Or is the situation such that all or some of the openings must or should be filled by recruiting outside candidates?

Like any good plans, employment plans are built on premises—basic assumptions about the future. The purpose of *forecasting* is to develop these basic premises. If you are planning for *employment* requirements, you'll usually need three sets of forecasts: one for *personnel needs,* one for the *supply of inside candidates,* and one for the *supply of outside candidates.*

Factors in Forecasting Personnel Needs

Managers should consider several factors when forecasting personnel needs.[1] From a practical point of view, *the demand for your product or service* is paramount.[2] Thus, in a manufacturing firm, sales are projected first. Then the volume of production required to meet these sales requirements is determined. Finally, the staff needed to maintain this volume of output is estimated. In addition to production or sales demand, you will also have to consider several other factors:

1. *Projected turnover* (as a result of resignations or terminations).
2. *Quality and nature* of your employees (in relation to what you see as the changing needs of your organization).
3. *Decisions* to upgrade the quality of products or services or enter into new markets.
4. *Technological and administrative changes* resulting in increased productivity.
5. The *financial resources* available to your department.

Specific techniques for determining human resource requirements include trend analysis, ratio analysis, scatter plot analysis, and computerized forecasting.[3]

trend analysis
Study of a firm's past employment needs over a period of years to predict future needs.

Trend Analysis Trend analysis means studying your firm's employment levels over the last five years or so to predict future needs. For example, you might compute the number of employees in your firm at the end of each of the last five years, or perhaps the number in each subgroup (like salespeople, production people, secretarial, and administrative) at the end of each of those years. The purpose is to identify employment trends that you think might continue into the future.

Trend analysis is valuable as an initial estimate, but employment levels rarely depend solely on the passage of time. Other factors (like changes in sales volume and productivity) will also affect your future staffing needs.

ratio analysis
A forecasting technique for determining future staff needs by using ratios between sales volume and number of employees needed.

Ratio Analysis Another forecasting approach, **ratio analysis,** means making estimates based on the *ratio* between (1) some causal factor (like sales volume) and (2) number of employees required (for instance, number of salespeople). For example, suppose you find that a salesperson traditionally generates $500,000 in sales and that in each of the last two years you required ten salespeople to generate $5 million in sales. Also assume that your plans call for increasing your firm's sales to $8 million next year and to $10 million two years hence. Then, if the sales revenue–salespeople ratio remains the same, you would require six new salespeople next year (each of whom produces an extra $500,000 in sales). In the following year, you would need an additional four salespeople to generate the extra $2 million in sales (between next year's $8 million and the following year's $10 million in sales).

Ratio analysis can also be used to help forecast your other employee requirements. For example, you can compute a salesperson–secretary ratio and thereby determine how many new secretaries will be needed to support the extra sales staff.

Like trend analysis, ratio analysis assumes that productivity remains about the same—for instance, that each salesperson can't be motivated to produce much more than $500,000 in sales each. If sales productivity were to increase or decrease, then the ratio of sales to salespeople would change. A forecast based on historical ratios would then no longer be as accurate.

scatter plot
A graphical method used to help identify the relationship between two variables.

The Scatter Plot A **scatter plot** is another option. You can use scatter plots to determine whether two factors—a measure of business activity and your staffing levels—are related. If they are, then if you can forecast the measure of business activity, you should also be able to estimate your personnel requirements.

Here is an example.[4] A 500-bed hospital in Chicago expects to expand to 1,200 beds over the next five years. The director of nursing and the human resource director want to forecast the requirement for registered nurses. The human resource director therefore decides to determine the relationship between size of hospital (in terms of number of beds) and number of nurses required. She calls five similar hospitals of various sizes and gets the following figures:

Size of Hospital (Number of Beds)	Number of Registered Nurses
200	240
300	260
400	470
500	500
600	620
700	660
800	820
900	860

One way to determine the relationship between size of hospital and number of nurses is to draw a scatter plot as illustrated in Figure 4.2. *Hospital size* is shown on the horizontal axis. *Number of nurses* is shown on the vertical axis. If the two factors are related, then the points will tend to fall along a straight line, as they do here. If you then carefully draw in a line to minimize the distances between the line and each one of the plotted points, you will be able to estimate the number of nurses that will be needed for each given hospital size. Thus, for a 1,200-bed

Figure 4.2
Determining the Relationship Between Hospital Size and Number of Nurses

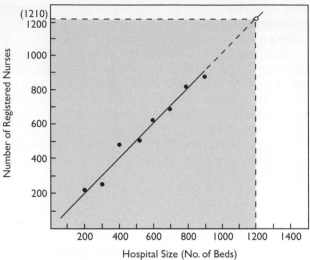

Note: After fitting the line, you can extrapolate—project—how many employees you'll need, given your projected volume.

hospital, the human resource director would assume she needs about 1,210 nurses.

Using Computers to Forecast Personnel Requirements Employers also use computerized systems to forecast personnel requirements. With such a system, a personnel specialist, working with line managers, compiles the information needed to develop a **computerized forecast** of personnel requirements.[5] Typical data needed include direct labor hours to produce one unit of product (a measure of productivity) and three sales projections—minimum, maximum, and probable—for the product line in question. Based on such data, a typical program generates figures on "average staff levels required to meet product demands," as well as separate forecasts for direct labor (such as assembly workers), indirect staff (such as secretaries), and exempt staff (such as executives).

With such a system, an employer can quickly translate estimates of projected productivity and sales levels into forecasts of personnel needs and can estimate the effects of various levels of productivity and sales on personnel requirements.[6]

Managerial Judgment Whichever forecasting approach you use, *managerial judgment* will play a big role. It's rare that any historical trend, ratio, or relationship will continue unchanged into the future. Judgment is thus needed to modify the forecast based on factors you believe will change in the future. Important factors that may modify your initial forecast of personnel requirements include the following:

1. *Decisions to upgrade the quality of products or services or enter into new markets.* These have implications for the nature of the employees you'll require. Ask, for instance, whether the skills of current employees fit with your organization's new products or services.

2. *Technological and administrative changes resulting in increased productivity.* Increased efficiency (in terms of output per hour) could reduce personnel needs. It might come about through installing new equipment or a new financial incentive plan, for instance.

computerized forecast
The determination of future staff needs by projecting a firm's sales, volume of production, and personnel required to maintain this volume of output, using computers and software packages.

3. *The financial resources available.* For example, a larger budget lets you hire more people and pay higher wages. Conversely, a projected budget crunch could mean fewer positions and lower salary offers.

Forecasting the Supply of Inside Candidates

The personnel demand forecast only provides half the staffing equation by answering the question: "How many employees will we need?" Next, supply must be forecast. However, before determining how many outside candidates to hire, you must forecast how many candidates for your projected job openings will come from within your organization from the existing ranks.

A qualifications inventory can facilitate forecasting the supply of inside candidates. **Qualifications inventories** contain summary data like each employee's performance record, educational background, and promotability, compiled either manually or in a computerized system.

qualifications inventories
Manual or computerized systematic records listing employees' education, career and development interests, languages, special skills, and so on to be used in forecasting inside candidates for promotion.

Manual Systems and Replacement Charts There are several types of manual systems used to keep track of employees' qualifications. In the *personnel inventory and development record* shown in Figure 4.3, information is compiled about each employee and then recorded on the inventory. The information includes education, company-sponsored courses taken, career and development interests, languages, and skills. Information like this can then be used to determine which current employees are available for promotion or transfer to projected open positions.

Some employers use **personnel replacement charts** (Figure 4.4) to keep track of inside candidates for their most important positions. These show the present performance and promotability for each potential replacement for important positions. As an alternative, you can develop a **position replacement card.** Here you make up a card for each position, showing possible replacements as well as present performance, promotion potential, and training required by each possible candidate.

personnel replacement charts
Company records showing present performance and promotability of inside candidates for the most important positions.

position replacement card
A card prepared for each position in a company to show possible replacement candidates and their qualifications.

Computerized Information Systems Qualifications inventories on hundreds or thousands of employees cannot be adequately maintained manually. Many firms computerize this information, and a number of packaged systems are available for accomplishing this task.[7]

In one such system, employees fill out a 12-page booklet in which they describe their background and experience. All this information is stored on disk. When a manager needs a qualified person to fill a position, he or she describes the position (for instance, in terms of the education and skills it entails) and then enters this information into the computer. After scanning its bank of possible candidates, the program presents the manager with a computer printout of qualified candidates.

According to one expert, the basic ingredients of a computerized human resource skills inventory should include the following:

Work experience codes: a list of work experience descriptors, titles, or codes describing jobs within the company so that the individual's present, previous, and desired jobs can be coded.

Product knowledge: the employee's level of familiarity with the employer's product lines or services as an indication of where the person might be transferred or promoted.

Industry experience: the person's industry experiences, since for certain positions knowledge of key related industries is very useful.

Figure 4.3
Personnel Inventory Form Appropriate for Manual Storage and Retrieval

PERSONNEL INVENTORY AND DEVELOPMENT RECORD			Date: month, year	
Department	Area or sub-department	Branch or section	Location	
Company service date (month, day, year)	Birthdate (month, day, year)	Marital status	Job title	

Education — Degree, year obtained, college, and major field of study

Grade school: 6 7 8 High school: 9 10 11 12 13
College: 1 2 3 4 5

Courses (company sponsored)

Type of course	Subject or course	Year	Type of course	Subject or course	Year

Career and development interests

Are you interested in an alternative type of work? Yes ☐ No ☐
Would you accept transfer to another division? Yes ☐ No ☐
Would you accept lateral moves for further development? Yes ☐ No ☐

If yes, specifically what type?   Comment on any qualifying circumstances

Photo

What type of training do you believe you require to:
A) Improve your skills and performance in your present position
B) Improve your experience and abilities for advancement.

Last name
First name
Middle name

What other assignments do you believe you are qualified to perform now?

Languages	Written		Spoken	
	☐	☐	☐	☐
	☐	☐	☐	☐

SS Number

Societies and organizations — Memberships in community organizations, etc., within last five years, indicate name of association and office held, if any

Skills

Type of skill	Certification, if any	Type of skill	Certification, if any

Other significant work experience, and/or military service. (Omit repetitive experiences)

	Location	From yr.	To yr.

Comments: Other significant experience, recreational activities, hobbies, interests, or personal data.

Formal education: the name of each postsecondary educational institution attended, the field of study, degree granted, and year granted.

Training courses: those taken or conducted by the employee and, possibly, training courses taught by outside agents like the American Management Association.

Foreign language skills: degree of proficiency in a foreign language other than the employee's native tongue.

Relocation limitations: the employee's willingness to relocate and the locales to which he or she would prefer to go.

Career interests: work experience codes to indicate what the employee would like to be doing for the employer in the future. Space can be provided for a brief pri-

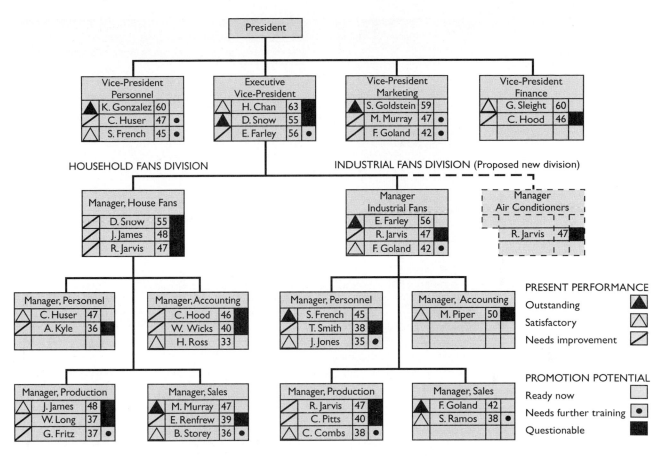

Figure 4.4
Management Personnel Replacement Chart

ority of choices, and a code should be included indicating whether the employee's main qualification for the work he or she wants to do is experience, knowledge, or interests.

Performance appraisals: updated periodically to indicate the employee's achievement on each dimension appraised (leadership ability, motivation, communication skills, and so on) along with a summary of the employee's strengths and deficiencies.[8]

The data elements in a human resources information system could number 100 or more. For example, one major vendor of a mainframe personnel/payroll package reportedly used by over 2,000 companies suggests the 140 elements shown in Table 4.1. Notice that these elements range from home address to driver's license number, employee weight, salary, sick leave used, skills, to veteran status.[9]

Skills are often included in these types of data banks. Including "training courses completed" might only show what the employee is trained to do, not what he or she has actually shown he or she can do. Including skills such as "remove boiler casings and doors" (number of times performed, date last performed, time spent) lets you use your computer to zero in on which employees are competent to accomplish the task that must be done. You can even include a skill level in the data bank, perhaps ranging from skill level 1 (can lead or instruct others), 2 (can perform the job with minimum supervision), 3 (has some experience: can assist experienced workers), to 4 (has not had opportunity to work on this job).[10]

TABLE 4.1 Typical Data Elements in a Human Resources Information System

Address (work)
Address (home)
Birthdate
Birthplace
Child support deductions
Citizenship
Claim pending (description)
Claim pending (outcome)
Claim pending (court)
Claim pending (date)
Date on current job
Department
Dependent (sex)
Dependent (number of)
Dependent (relationship)
Dependent (birthdate)
Dependent (name)
Discipline (appeal date)
Discipline (type of charge)
Discipline (appeal outcome)
Discipline (date of charge)
Discipline (outcome)
Discipline (hearing date)
Division
Driver's license (number)
Driver's license (state)
Driver's license (exp. date)
Education in progress (date)
Education in progress (type)
Educational degree (date)
Educational degree (type)
Educational minor (minor)
Educational level attained
Educational field (major)
EEO-1 code
Emergency contact (phone)
Emergency contact (name)
Emergency contact (relation)
Emergency contact (address)
Employee weight
Employee number
Employee code
Employee status
Employee height
Employee date of death
Federal job code
Full-time/part-time code

Garnishments
Grievance (type)
Grievance (outcome)
Grievance (filing date)
Handicap status
Health plan coverage
Health plan
  (no. dependents)
Injury date
Injury type
Job location
Job preference
Job position number
Job title
Job location
Leave of absence start date
Leave of absence end date
Leave of absence type
Life insurance coverage
Marital status
Marriage date
Medical exam (date)
Medical exam (restrictions)
Medical exam (blood type)
Medical exam (outcome)
Miscellaneous deductions
Name
Organizational property
Pay status
Pension plan membership
Performance rating
Performance increase ($)
Performance increase (%)
Phone number (work)
Phone number (home)
Prior service (term. date)
Prior service (hire date)
Prior service (term. reason)
Professional license (type)
Professional license (date)
Race
Rehire code
Religious preference
Salary points
Salary (previous)
Salary change date
Salary change reason

Salary change type
Salary
Salary range
Schools attended
Service date
Service branch
Service discharge type
Service ending rank
Service discharge date
Sex
Sick leave used
Sick leave available
Skill function (type)
Skill sub-function (type)
Skill (number of years)
Skill (proficiency level)
Skill (date last used)
Skill (location)
Skill (supervisory)
Social Security number
Spouse's employment
Spouse's date of death
Spouse's name
Spouse's birthdate
Spouse's sex
Spouse's social security
  number
Start date
Stock plan membership
Supervisor's name
Supervisor's work address
Supervisor's work phone
Supervisor's title
Termination date
Termination reason
Training schools attended
Training schools (date)
Training schools (field)
Training schools completed
Transfer date
Transfer reason
Union code
Union deductions
United Way deductions
Vacation leave available
Vacation leave used
Veteran status

Source: Donald Harris, "A Matter of Privacy: Managing Personal Data in Company Computers," *Personnel* (February 1987), p. 37.

The Matter of Privacy Several developments have intensified the HR manager's need to create better ways to control the personnel data stored in the organization's data banks. First, as you can see in Table 4.1, there is now a great deal of information about employees in most employers' data banks. Second, the expansion of end-user computing capabilities offers greater opportunities for more people to have access to these data.[11] Third, legislation such as the Federal Privacy Act of 1974 and the New York Personal Privacy Protection Act of 1985, gives some employees legal rights regarding who has access to information about their work history and job performance.

Balancing the employer's legitimate right to make this information available to those in the organization who need it with the employees' rights to privacy isn't easy. One approach is to use the access matrices incorporated in the software of many data base management systems. Basically, these matrices define the rights of users (specified by name, rank, or functional identification) to have various kinds of access (such as "read only" or "write only") to each data element contained in the data base. Thus, the computer programmers who are charged with the job of inputting data regarding employees might be authorized only to write information into the data base, while those in accounting are authorized to read a limited range of information such as the person's address, phone number, social security number, and pension status. The human resource director, on the other hand, might be authorized to both read and write all items when interacting with the data base.

Internal Sources of Candidates

Job posting can be an effective way of spreading the word about job opportunities to existing employees.

Although *recruiting* may bring to mind employment agencies and classified ads, current employees are often your largest source of recruits. Some surveys even indicated that up to 90% of all management positions are filled internally.[12]

Filling open positions with inside candidates has several advantages. Employees see that competence is rewarded and morale and performance may thus be enhanced. Having already been with your firm for some time, inside candidates may be more committed to company goals and less likely to leave. Promotion from within can boost employee commitment and provide managers a longer-term perspective when making business decisions. It may also be safer to promote employees from within, since you're likely to have a more accurate assessment of the person's skills than you would otherwise. Inside candidates may also require less orientation and training than outsiders.

Yet promotion from within can also backfire. Employees who apply for jobs and don't get them may become discontented; informing unsuccessful applicants as to why they were rejected and what remedial actions they might take to be more successful in the future is thus essential.[13] Similarly, many employers require managers to post job openings and interview all inside candidates. Yet the manager often knows ahead of time exactly whom he or she wants to hire, and requiring the person to interview a stream of unsuspecting inside candidates is therefore a waste of time for all concerned. Groups may also not be as satisfied when their new boss is appointed from within their own ranks as when he or she is a newcomer; sometimes, for instance, it is difficult for the newly chosen leader to shake off the reputation of being "one of the gang."[14]

Perhaps the biggest drawback, however, is inbreeding. When an entire management team has been brought up through the ranks, there may be a tendency to

Figure 4.5
Job Posting Form

Source: Bureau of National Affairs, Inc. *Recruiting and Selection Procedures* (Washington, DC, 1988), p. 35.

NO.____

POSTED: _____
CLOSING: _____

_____

There is a full-time position available for a _____ in the _____ Department. This position is/is not open to outside candidates.

PAY SCALE

	Minimum	Midpoint	Maximum
	$_____	$_____	$_____

or
SALARIED

DUTIES
See attached job description.

REQUIRED SKILLS AND ABILITIES
(Must possess all the following skills and abilities to be considered for this position.)
1. Demonstrated successful performance at past/present positions including:
   - ability to perform tasks in a complete and accurate manner
   - demonstrated timeliness and follow-through on duties and assignments
   - ability to work well with other people
   - ability to communicate effectively
   - reliability and good attendance
   - good organizational skills
   - problem solving attitude and approach
   - positive work attitude: enthusiastic, confident, outgoing, helpful, committed
2.

DESIRED SKILLS AND ABILITIES
(These skills and abilities will make a candidate more competitive.)

Application procedure FOR   EMPLOYEES is as follows:

1. Apply by phoning _____ , on ext.___ , by 3:00 p.m. _____

2. Ensure that a completed Internal Job Application and up-to-date resume/application is delivered to _____ by the same date.
Applicants will be pre-screened according to the above qualifications.
Selection will be made by the _____ .
    is an equal opportunity employer.
0255M/1

Copyright © 1988 by The Bureau of National Affairs, Inc. Washington, D.C. 20037
0361–7467/88/$0+.50

make decisions "by the book" and to maintain the status quo, when an innovative and new direction is needed. Balancing the benefits of morale and loyalty with the drawback of inbreeding is thus a challenge.

To be effective, promotion from within requires using job posting, personnel records, and skill banks.[15] **Job posting** means posting the open job and listing its attributes like qualifications, supervisor, working schedule, and pay rate (as in Figure 4.5). Some union contracts require job posting to ensure that union members get first choice of new and better positions. Yet job posting can also be a good practice even in nonunion firms, if it facilitates the transfer and promotion of

job posting
Posting notices of job openings on company bulletin boards is an effective recruiting method.

ELIGIBILITY

- All permanent employees who have completed their probationary period are eligible to use the open position listing policy in order to request consideration for a position that would constitute a growth opportunity.
- Employees who have been promoted or transferred, or who have changed jobs for any reason, must wait a six-month period before applying for a different position.

POLICY

- A list of open positions will be communicated to all employees in all facilities. Notices will include information on job title, salary grade, department, supervisor's name and title, location, brief description of the job content, qualifications, and instructions concerning whether or not candidates will be expected to demonstrate their skills during the interview process.
- Basic job qualifications and experience needed to fill the job will be listed on the sheet. Employees should consult with the human resource department if there are questions concerning the promotional opportunities associated with the job.
- Open position lists will remain on bulletin boards for five working days.
- Forms for use in requesting consideration for an open position may be obtained from the human resource department.
- The human resource department will review requests to substantiate the employee's qualifications for the position.
- The hiring manager will review requests for employees inside the company before going outside the company to fill the position.
- It is the responsibility of the employees to notify their managers of their intent to interview for an open position.
- The hiring manager makes the final decision when filling the position; however, the guidelines for filling any open position are based on the employees' ability, qualifications, experience, background, and the skills they possess that will allow them to carry out the job successfully. It is the responsibility of the hiring manager to notify the previous manager of the intent to hire the employee.
- Employees who are aware of a pending opening, and who will be on vacation when the opening occurs, may leave a request with the human resource department for consideration.
- It is the manager's responsibility to ensure that the human resource department has notified all internal applicants that they did or did not get the job before general announcement by the manager of the person who did get the job.
- "Blanket" applications will not be accepted. Employees should apply each time a position they are interested in becomes available.
- Since preselection often occurs, employees should be planning for their career growth by scheduling time with potential managers before posting, to become acquainted with them, and to secure developmental information to be used in acquiring appropriate skills for future consideration.
- There are occasions when jobs will not be listed. Two such examples might be (1) when a job can be filled best by natural progression or is a logical career path for an employee, and (2) when a job is created to provide a development opportunity for a specific high-performance employee.
- In keeping with this policy, managers are encouraged to work with employees in career development in order to assist them in pursuing upward movement in a particular career path or job ladder.

qualified inside candidates. (However, posting is often not used when promotion to a supervisory position is involved, since management often prefers to select personnel for promotion to management levels.)[16] *Personnel records* are also useful here. An examination of personnel records (including application forms) may uncover employees who are working in jobs below their educational or skill levels. It may also reveal persons who have potential for further training or those who already have the right background for the open jobs in question. Computerized systems discussed previously can help to ensure that qualified inside candidates are identified and considered for the opening. Some firms also develop *skill banks* that list current employees who have specific skills. For example, under "aerospace engineers," the names of all persons with this experience or training are listed. If you need an engineer in unit A, and the skill bank shows a person with those skills in unit B, that person may be approached about transferring to unit A, although he or she is not now using the aerospace skills.

One firm's job posting policies are presented in Figure 4.6. As you can see, important guiding policies include "All permanent employees . . . are eligible to use the open position listing policy . . . to request consideration for a position," and "A list of open positions will be communicated to all employees in all facilities."

Building Employee Commitment

Promotion from Within

Employees tend to be committed to firms that are committed to them. We'll see that two-way communications, guaranteed fair treatment, and job security are some of the things a firm's HR system can provide to show that the firm is indeed committed to its employees. But many employees will ultimately measure their firm's commitment by the degree to which they were able to achieve their career goals. We'll discuss promotion from within systems in more detail in Chapter 11 (Managing Careers). However, at this point it's useful to emphasize the fact that internal recruiting and promotion from within can be central to boosting employee commitment.

To build commitment, the promotion from within program should be comprehensive.[17] Certainly, firms often associated with committed employees—for example, Delta Airlines and Federal Express—have promotion from within *policies*. At Federal Express, for instance, "open positions are filled, whenever possible, by qualified candidates from within the existing work force."[18] But there's more to a successful promotion from within program than just a strong policy statement. As we'll see in Chapter 11, promotion from within is aided first by careful *employee selection*. As one Delta manager explained: "First of all, we hire for the future . . . the employment process favors applicants who have the potential for promotion." That helps explain how Chairman R.W. Allen climbed the ranks at Delta from an entry-level position to head of personnel and then to CEO and Chairman.

Effective promotion from within also depends on other HR actions. It depends on providing the *education and training* needed to help employees identify and develop their promotion potential. It also requires *career-oriented appraisals:* The supervisor and the employee are charged with linking the latter's past performance, career preferences, and developmental needs in a formal career plan. Finally, it requires a coordinated *system for accessing career records* and *posting job openings*, one that guarantees all eligible employees will be informed of openings and considered for them. For example, Federal Express has a job posting/career coordination system called JCATS (Job Change Applicant Tracking System). Announcements of new job openings via this electronic system usually take place each Friday. All employees applying for the position get numerical scores based on job performance and length of service. They are then advised as to whether they were chosen as candidates. Internal recruiting and promotion from within can thus be a force for creating employee commitment. However, a job posting policy alone will not do it.◆

Succession Planning   Forecasting the availability of inside or outside candidates is particularly important in succession planning. In early 1995, for instance, the business press was filled with reports that General Electric Chairman and CEO Jack Welsh had just had open heart surgery. While Mr. Welsh was able to resume his GE duties, many people inside and outside the firm naturally wanted to know whether GE's board of directors had adequate plans to find a successor in the event Welsh had to step down.

In a nutshell, succession planning refers to the plans a company makes to fill its most important executive positions. In practice, however, the process often involves a fairly complicated and integrated series of steps. For example, potential successors for top management might be routed through the top jobs at several key divisions as well as overseas, and they might be sent through the Harvard Business School's Advanced Management Program. As a result, a more comprehensive definition of succession planning is that it is the process of ensuring a suitable supply of successors for current and future senior or key jobs arising from business strategy, so that the careers of individuals can be planned and managed to optimize the organization's needs and the individuals' aspirations.[19]

Since succession planning requires balancing the organization's top-management needs with the potential and career aspirations of available candidates, it includes these activities:

Analysis of the demand for managers and professionals by company level, function, and skill.

Audit of existing executives and projection of likely future supply from internal and external sources.

Planning of individual career paths based on objective estimates of future needs and drawing on reliable performance appraisals and assessments of potential.

Career counseling undertaken in the context of a realistic understanding of the future needs of the firm, as well as those of the individual.

Accelerated promotions, with development targeted against the future needs of the business.

Performance-related training and development to prepare individuals for future roles as well as current responsibilities.

Planned strategic recruitment not only to fill short-term needs but also to provide people for development to meet future needs.

The actual activities by which openings are filled.[20]

Forecasting the Supply of Outside Candidates

If there are not enough inside candidates to fill anticipated openings, you will probably focus next on projecting supplies of outside candidates—those not currently employed by your organization. This may require forecasting *general economic* conditions, *local market* conditions, and *occupational market* conditions.

General Economic Conditions The first step is to forecast general economic conditions and the expected prevailing rate of unemployment. Usually, the lower the rate of unemployment, the lower the labor supply and the more difficult it will be to recruit personnel.

There is a wealth of published information you can use to develop economic forecasts. In December of each year, *Business Week* magazine presents its economic forecast for the following year; each week it presents a snapshot of the economy on its *outlook* page. *Fortune* magazine has a monthly forecast of the business outlook that is usually buttressed in its January issue with a forecast for the coming year. *Forbes* magazine has regular articles on both domestic and foreign business trends. Many banks, such as New York's Citibank, publish periodic analyses and forecasts of the economy. Each December the Prudential Insurance Company publishes an economic forecast for the coming year.

Several federal government agencies also provide economic forecasts. The U.S. Council of Economic Advisors prepares *Economic Indicators* each month showing the trend to date of various economic indicators. The regional branches of the Federal Reserve also publish economic reports monthly. The Federal Reserve Bank of St. Louis publishes a monthly summary that reports on various economic indicators.

Local Market Conditions Local labor market conditions are also important. For example, the build-up of computer and semiconductor programs resulted in relatively low unemployment recently in cities like Seattle, quite aside from general economic conditions in the country.

occupational market conditions
The Bureau of Labor Statistics of the U.S. Department of Labor publishes projections of labor supply and demand for various occupations, as do other agencies.

Occupational Market Conditions Finally, you may want to forecast the availability of potential job candidates in specific occupations (engineers, drill press operators, accountants, and so on) for which you will be recruiting. Recently, for instance, there has been an undersupply of computer systems specialists and nurses.

Forecasts for various occupations are available from many sources. For example, the Bureau of Labor Statistics of the U.S. Department of Labor publishes annual projections in the *Monthly Labor Review*. The National Science Foundation regularly forecasts labor market conditions in the science and technology fields. Other agencies providing occupational forecasts include the Public Health Service, the U.S. Employment Service, and the Office of Education.

Recruiting Job Candidates

Introduction

Once you have been authorized to fill a position, the next step is to develop an applicant pool, probably using internal recruiting and one or more of the recruitment sources described next. Recruiting is important, because the more applicants you have the more selective you can be in your hiring. If only two candidates apply for two openings, you may have little choice but to hire them. But if 10 or 20 applicants appear, then you can employ techniques like interviews and tests to screen out all but the best.

Some employers use a *recruiting yield pyramid* to calculate the number of applicants they must generate to hire the required number of new employees. In Figure 4.7, the company knows 50 new entry-level accountants must be hired next year. From experience, the firm also knows that the ratio of offers made to actual

**Figure 4.7
Recruiting Yield
Pyramid**

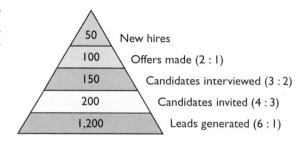

50 — New hires

100 — Offers made (2 : 1)

150 — Candidates interviewed (3 : 2)

200 — Candidates invited (4 : 3)

1,200 — Leads generated (6 : 1)

new hires is 2 to 1; about half the people to whom offers are made accept. Similarly, the firm knows that the ratio of candidates interviewed to offers made is 3 to 2, while the ratio of candidates invited for interviews to candidates actually interviewed has been 4 to 3. Finally, the firm knows that the ratio of new leads generated to candidates actually invited has been 6 to 1; in other words, of six leads that come in from the firm's advertising, college recruiting, and other recruiting efforts, one applicant in six typically is invited to come for an interview. Given these ratios, the firm knows it must generate 1,200 leads to be able to invite 200 viable candidates to its offices for interviews. The firm will then get to interview about 150 of those invited, and from these it will make 100 offers. Of those 100 offers, half (or 50 new CPAs) will be hired.

However, it's not just recruiting but *effective recruiting* that is important. For example, consider the results of a recent study of college recruiter effectiveness.[21] Subjects were 41 graduating students from four colleges (arts and sciences, engineering, industrial relations, and business) of a northeastern university. The students were questioned twice during their spring semester, once after they'd had their first round of interviews with employers, and once after their second round of interviews.

The quality of a firm's recruiting process had a big impact on what candidates thought of the firm. For example, when asked after the initial job interview why they thought a particular company might be a good fit, all 41 mentioned the nature of the job; however, 12 also mentioned the impression made by the recruiters themselves and 9 said the comments of friends and acquaintances affected their impressions. Unfortunately, the reverse was also true. When asked why they judged some firms as bad fits, 39 mentioned the nature of the job, but 23 said they'd been turned off by recruiters. For example, some were dressed sloppily; others were "barely literate"; some were rude; and some made offensively sexist comments. All these recruiters, needless to say, were ineffectual recruiters of their firms.

Recruiting efforts are more successful when the recruiters themselves are carefully chosen and trained. Here, an IRS recruiter participates in a job fair on the campus of Southwest Texas State University in San Marcos, Texas.

Line and staff cooperation in recruitment is essential. The HR manager who recruits and initially screens for the vacant job is seldom the one responsible for supervising its performance. He or she must therefore know exactly what the job entails, and this, in turn, means speaking with the supervisor involved. For example, the HR person might want to know something about the behavioral style of the supervisor and the members of the work group: Is it a tough group to get along with, for instance? He or she might also want to visit the work site and review the job description with the supervisor to ensure that the job has not changed since the description was written, and to obtain any additional insight into the skills and talents the new worker will need.

Advertising as a Source of Candidates

To use help wanted ads sucessfully, you need to address two issues: the media to be used and the ad's construction.[22] The selection of the best medium—be it the local paper, *The Wall Street Journal,* or a technical journal—depends on the type of positions for which you're recruiting. Your local newspaper is usually the best source of blue-collar help, clerical employees, and lower-level administrative employees. For specialized employees, you can advertise in trade and professional journals like the *American Psychologist, Sales Management, Chemical Engineering,* and *Electronics News.* In publications like *Travel Trade, Women's Wear Daily, American Banker, Hospital Administration,* and the *Chronicle of Higher Education,* you would most likely place your ads for professionals like bankers, hospital administrators, or educators. One drawback to this type of trade paper advertising is the long lead time that is usually required; there may be a month or more between insertion of the ad and publication of the journal or specialized paper, for instance. Yet ads remain good sources, and ads like Figure 4.8 continue to appear.

Help wanted ads in papers like *The Wall Street Journal* can be good sources of middle- or senior-management personnel. *The Wall Street Journal,* for instance, has several regional editions so that the entire country or the appropriate geographic area can be targeted for coverage.

Most firms use newspaper ads, but other media are used too. Table 4.2 summarizes when to use various media. For example, radio is best when multiple jobs are involved, such as staffing a new facility.

Principles of Help Wanted Advertising The construction of the ad is important. Experienced advertisers use a four-point guide called AIDA to construct their ads. First, you must attract *attention* to the ad. Figure 4.9 shows a page from one paper's classified section. Which ads attract attention? Note that closely printed ads are lost, while those with wide borders or a lot of empty space stand out. For the same reason, key positions are often advertised in separate display ads.

Develop *interest* in the job. As in Figure 4.10, interest may be created by the nature of the job itself, such as "you'll thrive on challenging work." Sometimes other aspects of the job, such as its location, can be used to create interest.

Create *desire* by amplifying the job's interest factors plus extras such as job satisfaction, career development, travel, or similar advantages. Write the ad with the target audience in mind. For example, nearby graduate schools appeal to engineers and professional people.

Finally, the ad should prompt *action.* In almost every ad you'll find a statement like "call today," "write today for more information," or "go to your nearest travel agent and sign up for the trip." The help wanted ad shown in Figure 4.11 is a good example of an action prompt.

The increased internationalization of the U.S. economy has created many opportunities for positions with multinational firms. Figure 4.12 provides an example of the use of ads for these broader opportunities.

Finally, while most employers know that discriminatory recruitment ads are generally illegal, questionable advertising still appears.[23] Therefore, it's important to remember that ads that are sex specific (calling for *man, woman, girl Friday,* and so forth) are questionable, as are sex-related gender terms like *yard man, repair man,* or ads implying a certain age (such as *student, recent grad,* or *retiree*). Similarly, terms like *bilingual required* or *Japanese* are also questionable. As we explained in Chapter 2, employers using ads like these may have to defend their rationale for limiting their search to the type of person identified in the ad.

Employment Agencies as a Source of Candidates

There are three basic types of employment agencies: (1) those operated by federal, state, or local governments; (2) those associated with nonprofit organizations; and (3) privately owned agencies.[24]

Public state employment service agencies exist in every state. They are aided and coordinated by the U.S. Department of Labor, which also maintains a nationwide computerized job bank to which all state employment offices are connected.

TABLE 4.2 Advantages and Disadvantages of Some Major Types of Media

TYPE OF MEDIUM	ADVANTAGES	DISADVANTAGES	WHEN TO USE
Newspapers	Short deadlines. Ad size flexibility. Circulation concentrated in specific geographic areas. Classified sections well organized for easy access by active job seekers.	Easy for prospects to ignore. Considerable competitive clutter. Circulation not specialized—you must pay for great amount of unwanted readers. Poor printing quality.	When you want to limit recruiting to a specific area. When sufficient numbers of prospects are clustered in a specific area. When enough prospects are reading help wanted ads to fill hiring needs.
Magazines	Specialized magazines reach pin-pointed occupation categories. Ad size flexibility. High-quality printing. Prestigious editorial environment. Long life—prospects keep magazines and reread them.	Wide geographic circulation—usually cannot be used to limit recruiting to specific area. Long lead time for ad placement.	When job is specialized. When time and geographic limitations are not of utmost importance. When involved in ongoing recruiting programs.
Radio and television	Difficult to ignore. Can reach prospects who are not actively looking for a job better than newspapers and magazines. Can be limited to specific geographic areas. Creatively flexible. Can dramatize employment story more effectively than printed ads. Little competitive recruitment clutter.	Only brief, uncomplicated messages are possible. Lack of permanence; prospect cannot refer back to it. (Repeated airings necessary to make impression.) Creation and production of commercials—particularly TV—can be time-consuming and costly. Lack of special-interest selectivity; paying for waste circulation.	In competitive situations when not enough prospects are reading your printed ads. When there are multiple job openings and there are enough prospects in specific geographic area. When a large impact is needed quickly. A "blitz" campaign can saturate an area in two weeks or less. Useful to call attention to printed ads.
"Point-of-purchase" (promotional materials at recruiting location)	Calls attention to employment story at a time when prospects can take some type of immediate action. Creative flexibility.	Limited usefulness; prospects must visit a recruiting location before it can be effective.	Posters, banners, brochures, audiovisual presentations at special events such as job fairs, open houses, conventions, as part of an employee referral program, at placement offices, or whenever prospects visit at organization facilities.

Source: Adapted from Bernard S. Hodes, "Planning for Recruitment Advertising: Part II," *Personnel Journal*, Vol. 28, no. 5 (June 1983), p. 499. Reprinted with the permission of *Personnel Journal*, Costa Mesa, CA. All rights reserved.

Using the computer-listed job information, an agency interviewer is better able to counsel job applicants concerning available jobs in their local and other geographical areas.

Although public agencies are a major source of blue-collar and white-collar workers, the experience of some employers with these agencies has been mixed. Applicants for unemployment insurance are required to register with these agen-

Figure 4.9
A Help Wanted Ad That Draws Attention

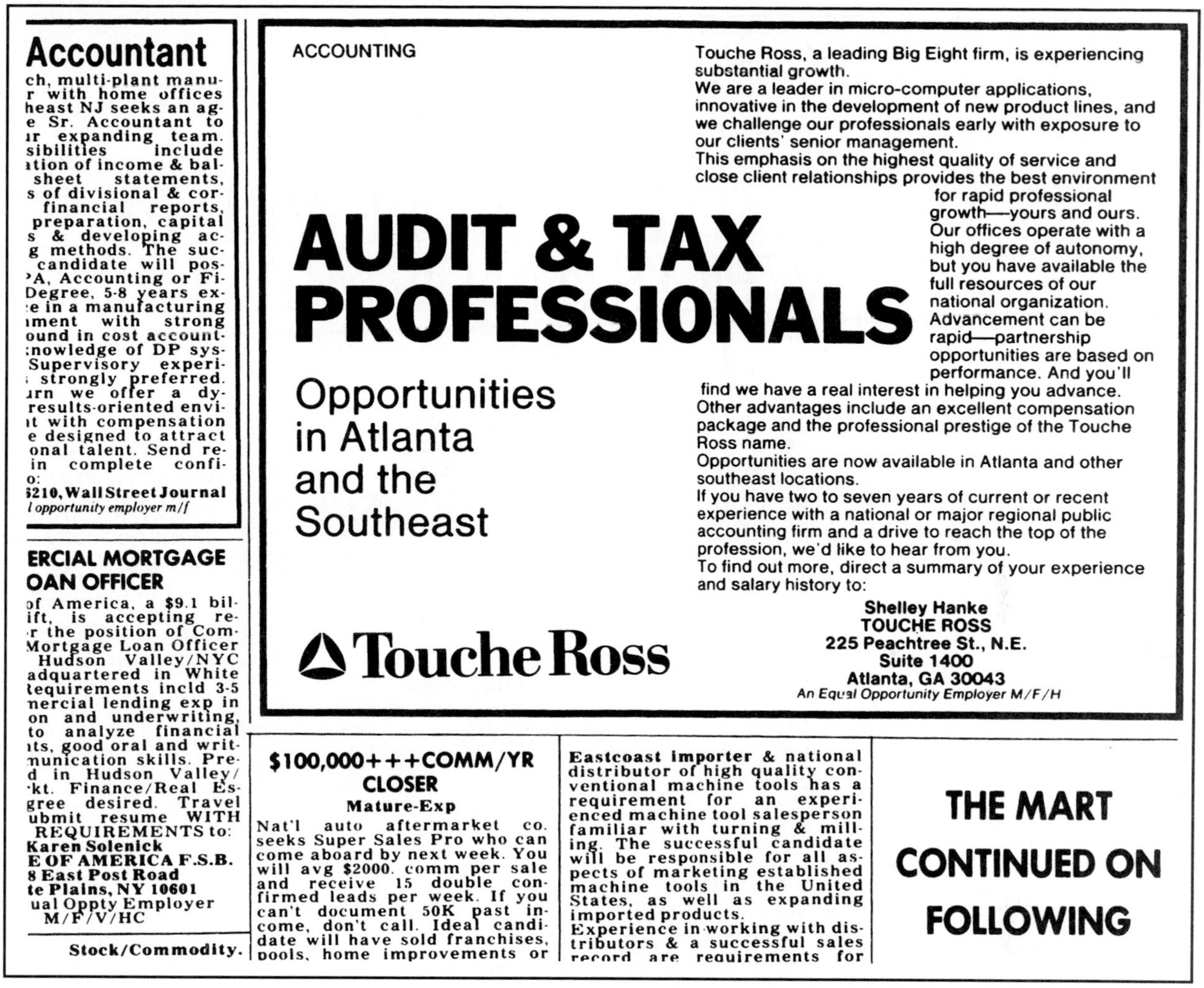

cies. They must make themselves available for job interviews to collect their unemployment payments. A fraction of these people are not interested in getting
back to work, so employers can end up with applicants who have little or no real
desire to obtain immediate employment.

Other employment agencies are associated with nonprofit organizations. For
example, most professional and technical societies have units that help their
members find jobs. Similarly, many public welfare agencies try to place people
who are in special categories, such as those who are physically disabled or are war
veterans.

Private employment agencies are important sources of clerical, white-collar,
and managerial personnel. Such agencies charge fees for each applicant they
place. These fees are usually set by state law and are posted in their offices.
Whether the employer or the candidate pays the fee is mostly determined by market conditions. However, the trend has been toward "fee-paid jobs" in which the
employer pays the fees. The assumption is that the most qualified candidates are
presently employed and would not be as willing to switch jobs if they had to pay
the fees themselves. Many private agencies now offer temporary help service and

Figure 4.10
A Help Wanted Ad That Creates Interest

Group Health Underwriters

WE NEED AN UNDERWRITER WHO'S AN OVERACHIEVER.

To keep pace with our rapidly expanding account base, we're looking for ambitious self starters to join the Employee Benefit Group in our Orinda office. The kind of pro's with proven records and super analytical skills.

If this sounds like you, consider joining The Travelers, a $46 billion insurance and financial services leader.

To qualify, you need at least 3 years of group health underwriting experience where you've gained a solid knowledge of employee benefits coverages. You must also have excellent communications and interpersonal skills.

In return, you'll thrive on challenging work in a dynamic environment. We've recently combined our New Business and Customer Relations Groups, creating a leaner, more aggressive force. As part of this new unit, you'll have broad exposure and career growth opportunities. Plus receive a highly competitive salary and benefits package.

So, if you're an overachiever, join The Travelers. And enjoy a career that's a cut above the rest.

Send your resume, with salary requirements, to: Sonia Mielnik, The Travelers Companies, 30-CR, SF426L1, One Tower Square, Hartford, CT 06183-7060.

TheTravelers
You're better off under the Umbrella.℠

Home Office: The Travelers Companies, Hartford, Connecticut.   An Equal Opportunity Employer.

provide secretarial, clerical, or semiskilled labor on a short term basis. These agencies can be useful in helping you cope with peak loads and fill in for vacationing employees; we'll return to such "temp" agencies below.

Some specific situations in which you might want to turn to an agency include the following:

We Can Take You Places.

Kaiser Permanente Medical Care Program is one of the largest Health Maintenance Organizations in the nation. We offer highly skilled professionals who are committed to those in need of quality medical care to consider these excellent opportunities and experience health care at its best.

We reward our people with competitive salaries, comprehensive benefits, educational programs and the ability to transfer between facilities without losing seniority. Kaiser Permanente is proud to be an equal opportunity employer.

Hayward

For these positions in our Hayward Medical Center please apply Monday-Thursday, 10am-1pm to **Personnel Department, 27400 Hesperian Blvd., Hayward, CA 94545** or call **Ellen Gutstadt at (415) 784-4258.**

Staff Nurses

ER: Nights & On-Call   **ICU/CCU:** Evenings & Nights
L&D: Nights   **Med/Surg:** Nights
ICN: All shifts available **Float:** All shifts available

Employee Health Service Nurse Practitioner: Requires 5 years of adult practitioner experience and a Master's degree.

Adult Nurse Practitioner: Requires 2 years of experience and a Master's degree.

OB Supervisor: A Bachelors degree, strong clinical and management skills combined with a clinical speciality are necessary to supervise our active tertiary, L&D, Gyn and perinatal units. RN licensure and 3 years of labor and delivery are required. MS degree preferred.

Advice Nurse: Two years of recent Med/Surg experience. Part-time and on-call positions available.

OR Nurses: Day and evening positions available with 6 months experience and a current CA RN license.

Night Shift Supervisor: To work 3 nights per week, Bachelors degree preferred.

We are also accepting applications for:
New Graduate Program:
Re-entry Program:

KAISER PERMANENTE
Medical Care Program

1. Your firm does not have its own HR department and is not geared to do recruiting and screening.
2. Your firm has found it difficult in the past to generate a pool of qualified applicants.
3. A particular opening must be filled quickly.

Figure 4.12
A Help Wanted Ad in
International
Management

INTERNATIONAL OPERATIONS MANAGEMENT TRAINEES
Tokyo, London, Zurich or Frankfurt

Salomon Brothers Inc, a major force in the international investment banking community, has excellent, entry level opportunities for hardworking, energetic individuals to join our International Operations Management Trainee Program. This program is designed to give candidates with little or no previous industry experience both product knowledge and operational management skills.

During this one year training program in our New York City headquarters, you will rotate through various operations areas and participate in a variety of special projects and assignments. The object is to develop a working knowledge of many areas through hands-on experience and participative observation. After your training is complete, you will be assigned to one of our Branch Offices in Japan, London, Zurich or Frankfort.

This position demands an independent thinker who is flexible and capable of demonstrating a high level of initiative. Your ability to develop a management perspective and demonstrate skill in performing many job functions will be important. Excellent communications skills and some fluency in Japanese, French, or German is essential. You must be able to relocate abroad.

We offer an excellent starting salary and a comprehensive benefits program, along with a unique opportunity for career growth. If you have a solid commitment to success and are ready for the challenge, send your resume, including salary history and a cover letter, in complete confidence to: **Management Trainee Recruiter, Salomon Brothers Inc, One New York Plaza, New York, N.Y. 10004.**
We are an Equal Opportunity Employer M/F

Salomon Brothers Inc

4. There is a perceived need to attract a greater number of minority or female applicants.
5. The recruitment effort is aimed at reaching individuals who are currently employed and who might feel more comfortable dealing with employment agencies rather than competing companies.

There are several other reasons to use an employment agency for some or all of your recruiting needs.[25] Employment agencies' promotional ads in *The Wall Street Journal* list advantages like "cut down on your interviews," "interview only the right people," and "have recruiting specialists save you time by finding, interviewing, and selecting only the most qualified candidates for your final hiring process."

Employment agencies are no panacea. For example, an employment agency prescreens applicants for your job, but this advantage can also backfire.[26] The employment agency's screening may let poor applicants bypass the preliminary stages of your own selection process. Unqualified applicants may thus go directly to the supervisors responsible for the hiring, who may in turn naively hire them. Such errors show up in high turnover and absenteeism rates, morale problems, and low quality and productivity. Similarly, potentially successful minority and non-minority applicants may be blocked from entering your applicant pool by improper testing and screening at the employment agency. To help avoid such problems, two experts suggest the following:

1. Give the agency an accurate and complete job description. The better the employment agency understands the job or jobs to be filled, the greater the likelihood that a reasonable pool of applicants will be generated.

2. Specify the devices or tools that the employment agency should use in screening potential applicants. Tests, application blanks, and interviews should be a proven part of the employer's selection process. At the very least, you should know which devices the agency uses and consider their relevance to the selection process. Of particular concern would be any subjective decision-making procedures used by the agency.

3. Where possible, periodically review data on accepted or rejected candidates. This will serve as a check on the screening process and provide valuable information if there is a legal challenge to the fairness of the selection process.

4. If feasible, develop a long-term relationship with one or two agencies. It may also be advantageous to designate one person to serve as the liaison between the employer and agency. Similarly, try to have a specific contact on the agency's staff to coordinate your recruiting needs.

There are several things you can do to select the best agency for your needs. Checking with other managers or HR people will reveal the agencies that have been the most effective at filling the sorts of positions you want to have filled. Another approach is to review seven or eight back issues of the Sunday classified ads in your library to find the agencies that consistently handle the positions you want. This will help narrow the field.

Once you've narrowed the field, here are some questions you should ask in order to decide which agency is best for your firm: What is the background of the agency's staff? What are the levels of their education and experience and their ages? Do they have the qualifications to understand the sorts of jobs for which you are recruiting? What is their reputation in the community and with the Better Business Bureau?

Contingent Workers and Temporary Help Agencies Many employers today are supplementing their permanent employee base by hiring contingent workers. Also defined as temporary workers, part-time workers, and just-in-time employees, the contingent work force is big and growing and is broadly defined as workers who don't have permanent jobs.[27]

Just how big is the contingent work force? One way to answer that is to note that in 1993, part-time workers (those employed for less than 35 hours per week) numbered 21 million, or about 17% of the U.S. labor force.[28] Slicing the numbers another way, in 1993 there were 1.7 million people working in the temporary help industry (for temporary help firms like Manpower, Inc. and Kelly Services), up from 732,000 in 1985. Temporary jobs represented 20% of all the new jobs created in the United States between 1991 and 1993.[29]

Contingent staffing owes its growing popularity to several factors. Historically, employers have always used "temps" to fill in for the days or weeks that permanent employees were out sick or on vacation. Increasingly, however, a desire for ever-higher productivity probably explains its growing popularity. In general, as one expert puts it, "Productivity is measured in terms of output per hour paid for," . . . and "if employees are paid only when they're working, as contingent workers are, overall productivity increases."[30] Employers also find that by tapping temporary help agencies, they can save the time and expense of personally recruiting and training new workers, as well as the expenses involved in personnel documentation (such as filing payroll taxes and maintaining absence records).[31] As a result, the contingent work force is no longer limited to clerical or maintenance staff: In one recent year almost 100,000 people found temporary work in engineering, science, or management support occupations, for instance.[32] In fact, growing numbers of firms use temporary workers such as engineers and other professionals to carry out engineering projects, to staff hospitals to meet fluctuating patient loads, and to serve as short-term chief financial officers, for instance.

The benefits of contingent staffing don't come without a price. While they may be more productive, and less expensive to recruit and train, contingent workers hired through temporary agencies generally cost employers 20% to 50% more than comparable permanent workers (per hour or per week), since the agencies themselves not only do the recruiting, screening, and paying but also earn a profit. One expert raises another concern: "People have a psychological reference point to their place of employment. Once you put them in the contingent category, you're saying they're expendable."[33] And one would assume that such expendable workers are less likely to exhibit the benefits of loyalty that many employers expect from their permanent workers. This problem is exacerbated by the fact that while "additional income" is the top reason individuals give for becoming temporary employees, the second most important reason is "as a way to get a full-time job." To the extent that a temp finds his or her hopes dashed, the ties that bind employer and employee are even more tenuous.[34]

In order to make such employment relationships as fruitful as possible, anyone recruiting temps should understand their main concerns. In one survey, six key concerns emerged:[35]

1. Temporary workers are discouraged by the dehumanizing and impersonal way that they are treated on the job.
2. Temporary workers feel insecure about their employment and are pessimistic about the future.
3. Temporary workers worry about their lack of insurance and pension benefits.
4. Temporary workers claim that employers fail to provide an accurate picture of their job assignments and in particular about whether temporary assignments are likely to become full-time positions.
5. Temporary workers feel underemployed, particularly those trying to return to the full-time labor market.
6. Temporary workers feel a generalized anger toward the corporate world and its values: Participants repeatedly expressed feelings of alienation and disenchantment.

Given such concerns, what can employers do to boost the likelihood that relationships with temporary workers will be mutually beneficial? Here are six guidelines:[36]

1. Provide honest information to both temporary agencies and temporary workers about the length of the job assignment.
2. Implement personnel policies that ensure fair and respectful treatment of temporary workers. (For example, in one instance claims of sexual harassment by an employer's supervisors were not addressed by the firm because the temps were not its legal employees. Nor were the claims addressed by the temporary agency because the perpetrators were not the agency's employees.)
3. Use independent contractors and permanent part-time employees to complement the conventional temporary agency work force. Especially where you re-

quire a highly skilled and committed work force, using permanent part-timers and independent contractors may provide a level of trained expertise and loyalty that exceeds that of employees from temporary agencies. These people are likely to be more familiar with your company's procedures and more committed to its goals than temporary workers.

4. Before hiring temporary workers, consider their potential impact on regular full-time employees. For example, any apparent exploitation or mistreatment of contingent workers may have a corrosive effect on permanent workers' morale.

5. Provide the necessary training and orientation for temporary workers. For example, one survey's comments included: "If you are expected to hit the ground running, that should be specified when requesting a temp from the agency"; "[Organizations] need to be more specific in their instructions to temps. Give them the [correct] tools and materials to do their jobs."

6. Beware of legal snares in your payroll decisions. In particular, the IRS has been paying special attention to jobs such as sales rep and janitor. Although such jobs are often contracted out, some employers may be categorizing their permanent workers incorrectly as independent contractors to avoid paying withholding taxes and social security taxes.[37] In other words, the employer should be careful not to use a contingent work force classification such as "independent contractor" as a means for illegally avoiding paying the taxes to which permanent employees are usually entitled.

Temporary Help Agencies   Given the increased use of contingent workers, it's not surprising that one survey reported over 84% of employers use such agencies, and their use is on the rise.[38]

The nature of the temporary-help relationship means the employer must address some special issues when dealing with this type of agency. Of course, putting time and effort into meeting with several and choosing the one that's best for you is important. But you must also ensure that basic policy and procedures are in place, including:[39]

Invoicing   Get a sample copy of the company's invoice. Make sure you understand the invoicing procedure and that it fits your company's needs.

Time Sheets   Also get a sample time sheet. With temps, the time sheet that is signed by the worker's supervisor is usually in effect an agreement to pay the agency's fees rather than simply a verification of hours worked.

Temp-to-Perm Policy   Specifically, what is the policy if the client wants to hire permanently one of the service's temps? Most services prefer to keep the temp on their payroll for a specific waiting period before moving the person to the client's payroll (at no extra cost).

Recruitment of and Benefits for Temp Employees   Find out how the temp service plans to recruit employees and what sorts of benefits it pays.

Inside Staff   Learn as much as you can about how the temp service's staff (such as the people who interview applicants) match skills to position requirements and place and dispatch the temp work force.

Dress Code   Clearly indicate the appropriate attire at each of your offices or plants.

Equal Employment Opportunity Statement   You should get a document from the temp service stating that it is not discriminating when filling temp orders.

Job Description Information   Set up a procedure whereby you can be reasonably sure that the temp service completely understands the nature of the job to be filled and the sort of person, in terms of skills and so forth, you want to fill it.

Executive Recruiters as a Source of Candidates

Executive recruiters (also known as *head hunters*) are special employment agencies retained by employers to seek out top-management talent for their clients. They fill jobs in the $40,000 and up category, although $50,000 is often the lower limit. The percentage of your firm's positions filled by these services might be small. However, these jobs would include your most crucial executive and technical positions. For executive positions, head hunters may be your *only* source. Their fees are always paid by the employer.

These firms can be very useful. They have many contacts and are especially adept at contacting qualified candidates who are employed and not actively looking to change jobs. They can also keep your firm's name confidential until late into the search process. The recruiter can save top management time by doing the preliminary work of advertising for the position and screening what could turn out to be hundreds of applicants. The recruiter's fee might actually turn out to be insignificant compared to the cost of the executive time saved.

But there are some pitfalls. As an employer, it is essential for you to explain completely what sort of candidate is required—and why. Some recruiters are also more salespeople than professionals. They may be more interested in persuading you to hire a candidate than in finding one who will really do the job. Recruiters also claim that what their clients *say* they want is often not really accurate. Therefore, be prepared for some in-depth dissecting of your request. In choosing a recruiter, one expert suggests following these guidelines:[40]

1. *Make sure the firm is capable of conducting a thorough search.* Under the code of the Association of Executive Recruiting Consultants, a head hunter cannot approach the executive talent of a former client for a vacancy with a new client for a period of two years after completing a search for the former client. Since former clients are off limits to the recruiter for a period of two years, the recruiter must make a search from a constantly diminishing market. Particularly for the largest executive recruiting firms, it could turn out to be very difficult to deliver a top-notch candidate, since the best potential candidates may already be working for the recruiter's former clients.

2. *Meet the individual who will be handling your assignment.* The person handling your search will determine the fate of the search. If this person hasn't the ability to seek out top candidates aggressively and sell them on your firm, it is unlikely you will get to see them. Beware of the fact that in wooing you as a new client, the search firm will send its best salesperson, someone with a record of successfully signing new clients. However, this is usually not the person who will be doing the actual search.

3. *Ask how much the search firm charges.* There are several things to keep in mind here. Search firm fees range from 25% to 35% of the guaranteed annual income of the position being filled. They are often payable one-third as a retainer at the outset, one-third at the end of 30 days, and one-third after 60 days, and they are not necessarily paid on a contingency basis only. Often a fee is payable whether or not the search is terminated for any reason. The out-of-pocket expenses are extra and could run to 10% to 20% of the fee itself, and sometimes more.

4. *Choose a recruiter you can trust.* This is essential because this person will find not only your firm's strengths, but its weaknesses too. It is therefore important that you find someone you can trust with what may be privileged information.

5. *Talk to some of their clients.* Finally, ask to be given the names of two or three companies for whom the search firm has recently completed assignments. Ask such questions as: Did the recruiter's appraisal of the candidate seem accurate? Did the firm really conduct a search, or was the job simply filled from

their files? And were time and care taken in developing the job specifications?[41]

As a job candidate, keep several things in mind when dealing with executive search firms. Most of these firms pay little heed to unsolicited résumés, preferring instead to ferret out their own candidates. Some firms have also been known to present an unpromising candidate to a client simply to make their other one or two proposed candidates look that much better. Some eager clients may also jump the gun, checking your references and undermining your present position prematurely. Also remember that executive recruiters and their clients are usually more impressed with candidates who are obviously "not looking" for a job, and that overeagerness to take the job can be a candidate's downfall.[42]

Small Business Applications

There comes a time in the life of most small businesses when it dawns on the owner that his or her managers are incapable of taking the company into the realm of expanded sales. A decision must then be made regarding what kinds of people to hire from outside and how this hiring should take place. Should the owner decide what type of person to hire and recruit this person himself or herself? Or should an outside expert be brought in to help with the search?

Using Executive Recruiters

The heads of most large firms often won't think twice about hiring executive search firms to conduct their search. However, small companies' owners (with their relatively limited funds) will hesitate before committing to a fee that could reach $20,000 to $30,000 (with expenses) for a $60,000 to $70,000 marketing manager. As a small business owner, however, you should keep in mind that this sort of thinking can be short-sighted when you consider what your options actually are.

Engaging in a search like this by yourself is not at all like looking for secretaries, supervisors, or data entry clerks. Recruiting lower-level employees can usually be accomplished easily by using the techniques described earlier, for instance, by placing ads, using relatively low-cost employment agencies, or even by placing help wanted signs in your front windows. However, executive recruiting is different, and if you haven't engaged in a search like this yourself, consider what you're doing carefully before you do it. When you are looking to hire a key executive to help you run your firm, chances are you are not going to find the person you want by placing ads or using most of the other traditional approaches. For one thing, the person you seek is probably already employed and is probably not reading the want ads. If he or she does happen to glance at the ads, chances are the person is happy enough not to take the effort to embark on a job search with you.

In other words, what you'll end up with is a drawer full of résumés of people who are, for one reason or another, out of work, or unhappy with their work, or unsuited for your job. It is then going to fall to you to try to find several gems in this group of résumés, and interview and assess these applicants yourself. This is hardly an attractive proposition unless you happen to be an expert at interviewing and checking backgrounds (and have nothing else to do).

There are thus two problems with conducting these kinds of executive searches yourself. First, as a nonexpert, you may not even know where to begin: You won't know where to place or how to write the ads; you won't know where to search, who to contact, or how to do the sort of job that needs to be done to interview people in order to screen out the laggards and misfits who may well appear on the surface to be viable candidates. You also won't know enough to really do the kind of background checking that a position at this level requires. Second, this process is going to be extremely time-consuming and will divert your attention from other duties. Many business owners find that when they consider the opportunity costs involved with doing their own searches, they are not saving any money at all. For example, the time they lose by having to do executive recruiting costs them X number of sales calls, so that their company actually comes out behind financially. Instead of being able to assess the chemistry between yourself and three carefully screened candidates from an executive recruiter, you'll find yourself plodding through résumés and interviews with perhaps 20 or 30 possible candidates. Often the question is not whether you can afford to use an executive recruiter, but whether you can afford not to.

In any event, if you do decide to do the job yourself, consider retaining the services of an industrial psychologist. He or she will be able to spend four or five hours assessing the problem-solving ability, personality, interests, and energy level of the two or three candidates in which you are most interested. Although you certainly don't want the psychologist to make the decision for you, the input can provide an additional perspective on the candidates.

Using the State Job Services

Smaller firms often find state job service offices quite useful for filling blue collar, clerical, and occasionally technical and managerial jobs. If you contact your local job service office, a representative/counselor will probably be sent to discuss your staffing needs. Short job descriptions keyed to the DOT may even be devised to use in recruiting efforts. Many of these job service offices are also linked with various governmental agencies that will arrange to subsidize the first three or four months of wages for certain (usually disadvantaged) groups of employees. The job service agencies are also a good source of information about prevailing wages for different classifications of jobs. In any event, if you're thinking of recruiting, it certainly pays to spend an hour or so discussing your needs with one of their counselors. ◆

College Recruiting as a Source of Candidates

Many promotable candidates are originally hired through college recruiting. This is therefore an important source of management trainees, as well as of professional and technical employees.

There are two main problems with on-campus recruiting. First, it is relatively expensive and time-consuming for the recruiters. Schedules must be set well in advance, company brochures printed, records of interviews kept, and much recruiting time spent on campus. Second, recruiters themselves are sometimes ineffective, or worse. Some recruiters are unprepared, show little interest in the candidate, and act superior. Many recruiters also don't effectively screen their student candidates. For example, students' physical attractiveness often outweighs other more valid traits and skills.[43] Some recruiters also tend to assign females to "female-type" jobs and males to "male-type" jobs.[44] Such findings underscore the need to train recruiters before sending them to the campus.[45]

You have two goals as a campus recruiter. Your main function is screening, which means determining whether a candidate is worthy of further consideration. Exactly which traits you look for will depend on your specific recruiting needs. However, the checklist presented in Figure 4.13 is typical. Traits to assess include motivation, communication skills, education, appearance, and attitude.[46]

**Figure 4.13
Campus Applicant
Interview Report**

Source: Adapted from
Joseph J. Famularo, *Handbook
of Personnel Forms, Records,
and Reports* (New York:
McGraw-Hill Book
Company, 1982), p. 70.

CAMPUS INTERVIEW REPORT

Name _____ Anticipated Graduation Date _____

Current Address _____
    If different than placement form

Position Applied For _____
_____

If Applicable (Use Comment Section if necessary)

        Drivers License   Yes _____ No _____

        Any special considerations affecting your availability for relocation?

_____

_____

        Are you willing to travel? _____ If so, what % of time _____
_____

EVALUATION	Outstanding	Above Average	Average	Below Average
Education: Courses relevant to job? Does performance in class indicate good potential for work?	_____	_____	_____	_____
Appearance: Was applicant neat and dressed appropriately?	_____	_____	_____	_____
Communication Skills: Was applicant mentally alert? Did he or she express ideas clearly?	_____	_____	_____	_____
Motivation: Does applicant have high energy level? Are his or her interests compatible with job?	_____	_____	_____	_____
Attitude: Did applicant appear to be pleasant, people-oriented?	_____	_____	_____	_____

COMMENTS: (Use back of sheet if necessary)

    _____

    _____

_____

Given Application   Yes _____ No _____ Received Transcript Release Authorization _____

Recommendations Invite _____ Reject _____

Interviewed by: _____ Date: _____

Campus _____

     While your main function is to find and screen good candidates, your other aim is to *attract* them to your firm. A sincere and informal attitude, respect for the applicant as an individual, and prompt follow-up letters can help you to sell the employer to the interviewee.

     Recruiters and schools must be chosen. As summarized in Table 4.3, employers choose college recruiters largely on the basis of who can do the best job of identifying good applicants and filling vacancies. Factors in selecting schools in

TABLE 4.3 Factors in Selecting College Recruiters

RECRUITING ASPECT	STRENGTH (1–7)
Identification of high-quality applicants	5.8
Professionalism of recruiters	5.6
Filling all vacancies	5.5
Generating the right number of applicants	5.5
High performance of new recruits	5.4
High retention of new recruits	5.3
High job acceptance rates	5.0
Administrative procedures	4.7
Turn-around times	4.5
Planning and goal setting	4.5
Meeting EEO/AA targets	4.4
Program evaluation	4.3
Cost control	4.2

Source: Reprinted with permission from the March 1987 issue of *Personnel Administrator*. Copyright 1987, The American Society for Personnel Administration, 606 North Washington Street, Alexandria, VA 22314.

which to recruit include the school's reputation and the performance of previous hires from it (see Table 4.4).

Good applicants are generally invited to the employer's office or plant for an on-site visit, and there are several ways to make sure this visit is fruitful.[47] The invitation letter should be warm and friendly but businesslike, and the person should be given a choice of dates to visit the company. Somebody should be assigned to meet the applicant and act as host, preferably meeting the person at the airport or at his or her hotel. A package describing the applicant's schedule as well as other information regarding the employer—such as annual reports and description of benefits—should be waiting for the applicant at the hotel. The interviews should be carefully planned and the schedule adhered to. Interruptions

TABLE 4.4 Factors in Selecting Schools in Which to Recruit

TOPIC	IMPORTANCE (1–7)
Reputation in critical skill areas	6.5
General school reputation	5.8
Performance of previous hires from the school	5.7
Location	5.1
Reputation of faculty in critical skill areas	5.1
Previous job offer and acceptance rates	4.6
Past practice	4.5
Number of potential recruits	4.5
Ability to meet EEO targets	4.3
Cost	3.9
Familiarity with faculty members	3.8
SAT or GRE scores	3.0
Alma mater of CEO or other executives	3.0

7 is high; 1 is low.
Source: Reprinted with permission from the March 1987 issue of *Personnel Administrator*. Copyright 1987, The American Society for Personnel Administration, 606 North Washington Street, Alexandria, VA 22314.

should be avoided; the candidate should have the undivided attention of each person with whom he or she interviews. Luncheon should be arranged at the plant or at a nearby restaurant or club, preferably hosted by one or more other recently hired graduates with whom the applicant may feel more at ease. An offer, if any, should be made as soon as possible, preferably at the time of the visit. If this is not possible, the candidate should be told when to expect a decision. If an offer is made, keep in mind that the applicant may have other offers too. Frequent follow-ups to "find out how the decision process is going" or to "ask if there are any other questions" may help to tilt the applicant in your favor.

Referrals and Walk-Ins as a Source of Candidates

Particularly for hourly workers, *walk-ins*—direct applications made at your office—are a major source of applicants.[48] Some organizations encourage such applicants by mounting "employee referrals" campaigns. Announcements of openings and requests for referrals are made in the organization's bulletin and posted on wall boards. Prizes are offered for referrals that culminate in hirings. This sort of campaign can cut recruiting costs by eliminating advertising and agency fees. It can also result in higher-quality candidates, since many people are reluctant to refer less qualified candidates. But the success of the campaign depends alot on your employees' morale.[49] And the campaign can backfire if an employee's referral is rejected and the employee becomes dissatisfied. Using referrals exclusively may also be discriminatory if most of your current employees are male or white.

Employee referral programs are popular. Of the firms responding to one survey, 40% said they use an employee referral system and hire about 15% of their employees through such referrals. A cash award for referring candidates who are hired is the most common referral incentive. Large firms reportedly spent about $34,000 annually on their referral programs (including cash payments for candidates), medium companies spent about $17,000, and small ones with fewer than 500 employees spent about $3,600. The cost per hire, however, was uniformly low, with average per hire expenses of only $388—far below the comparable cost of an employment service.[50]

Walk-ins are a major source of applicants. All walk-ins should be treated courteously and diplomatically, for the sake of both the employer's community reputation and the applicant's self-esteem. Many employers thus give every walk-in a brief interview with someone in the HR office, even if it is only to get information on the applicant "in case a position should open in the future." Good business practice also requires that all letters of inquiry from applicants be answered promptly and courteously.

Computerized Employee Data Bases

Employers increasingly use computerized résumé registries to find candidates. Several of these computerized data bases are now functioning, but the nature of one—Career Placement Registry, Inc. (CPR), of Alexandria, Virginia—illustrates how they work. CPR is not an employment agency but rather a company that compiles a data base of résumés from people who are looking for work. That data base is then available on-line to all businesses, service organizations, and government agencies that subscribe to DIALOG INFORMATION SERVICES, INC., a large computerized information network. (Companies that do not subscribe to DIALOG can have a résumé search done by CPR at a cost of about $50 for 12 CPR-registered résumés. Any employer that is aware of CPR can thus have access to its data base of résumés with or without subscribing to the DIALOG data base.)

The process is fairly simple. CPR compiles résumé data bases for both students and recent graduates and for experienced job seekers. Each applicant fills out data entry forms covering items such as name, address, career objectives (accounting, administration, advertising—52 in all), work experience, type of position desired, and educational background. Along with the "personal summary of qualifications," the form presents a fairly complete picture of each candidate's qualifications, occupational preferences, and desired salary range. The form is then returned to CPR along with a check for the registration fee: Students pay about $12 to register, while experienced job seekers pay $25 to $45, depending upon desired salary level. Résumés remain in the CPR data base for six months and are available to employers 24 hours a day, seven days a week. Candidates can also specify the geographic areas where they prefer to work.

This particular data base isn't too expensive to access. Employers get a manual explaining how to access it and can customize their search based on the skills and experience required, as well as preferred geographic areas. Employers pay no subscription fee—just the cost of being on-line with DIALOG (about $95 per hour) plus a print charge of $1 per résumé. This particular system is available to the approximately 50,000 employers that subscribe to DIALOG INFORMATION SERVICES, INC. (and through many university libraries.)[51]

Figure 4.14 summarizes one firm's experience using computerized employee data bases. *Inc.* magazine tested three services by performing two sample searches: "Restaurant supplier in Bozeman, Montana, seeks salesperson, two years' experience, willing to travel, for $25,000;" and "Atlanta benefits-management firm wants to hire female personnel director, five years' experience, with desktop-publishing skills, for $35,000." As you can see, the results were mixed. For the relatively easy-to-fill personnel director's position, all three data bases produced good candidates. For the relatively difficult salesperson's job, however, only one data base produced good candidates. Since one search can cost more than $500, an employer is well advised to determine ahead of time what others' experience with the data base has been for similar kinds of jobs.[52]

Recruiting a More Diverse Work Force

Recruiting a diverse work force is not just socially responsible, it's a necessity. As noted earlier, the composition of the U.S. work force is changing dramatically: The white labor force is projected to increase less than 15%, while the

Figure 4.14
Hiring Through Résumé Databases

COMPANY	SEARCH COST	RÉSUMÉS ON FILE	"SALESPERSON"	"PERSONNEL DIRECTOR"
kiNexus/AdEase 800-828-0422	$800 for one search $3,000 for five searches	175,000	6 résumés	7 résumés: all women, 4 good candidates (one with industry experience)
Job Bank USA 800-296-1872	$200 for two searches $495 for five searches	17,500	No responses ("No one will move to Bozeman for $25,000 a year.")	19 résumés: 11 women, 5 good candidates
SkillSearch 800-258-6641	$375 for intro search $3,000 for five searches	11,000	8 résumés: 3 good candidates	6 résumés: all women, all good candidates

black labor force will grow by nearly 29%, and the Hispanic labor force by more than 74% in the 1990s. Women will account for about 64% of the net increase in the labor force in these years. Related to this, about two-thirds of all single mothers are in the labor force today, as are almost 45% of mothers with children under three.

Therefore, smart employers have to actively recruit a more diverse work force. This means taking special steps to recruit older workers, minorities, and women. The Diversity Counts box on the following page describes one approach.

Older Workers as a Source of Candidates   Fewer 18- to 25-year-olds are entering the work force;[53] this has caused many employers to look into "harnessing America's gray power," either by encouraging retirement-age employees to stay with the company or by actively recruiting employees who are at or beyond retirement age.[54] Is it practical in terms of productivity to keep older workers on? The answer seems unequivocably to be "yes."[55] Age-related changes in physical ability, cognitive performance, and personality have little effect on worker's output except in the most physically demanding tasks.[56] Similarly, creative and intellectual achievements do not decline with age and absenteeism drops as age increases. Older workers also usually display more company loyalty than youthful workers, tend to be more satisfied with their jobs· and supervision, and can be trained or retrained as effectively as anyone.

Recruiting and attracting older workers involves any or all the sources described earlier (advertising, employment agencies, and so forth), but with one big difference. Recruiting and attracting older workers generally requires a comprehensive HR retiree effort before the recruiting begins. The aim is to make the company an attractive place in which the older worker can work. Specifically:

Examine your personnel policies. Check to make sure policies and procedures do not discourage recruitment of seniors or encourage valuable older people to leave. For example, policies like paying limited or no benefits to part-time workers, promoting early retirement, or offering no flexible work schedules will impede older worker recruitment and/or retention.

Develop flexible work options. These include part-time, shorter-than-30-hour workweeks, consulting or seasonal work, reduced hours with reduced pay, and flextime (building the workday around a core of required hours like 11 A.M. to 3 P.M. but otherwise letting workers come and go as they please). For example, at Wrigley Company, workers over 65 can progressively shorten their work schedules; another company uses "minishifts" to accommodate those interested in working less than full time.[57]

Create or redesign suitable jobs. At Xerox, unionized hourly workers over 55 with 15 years of service and those over 50 with 20 years of service can bid on jobs at lower stress and lower pay levels if they so desire.

Offer flexible benefit plans. Allowing employees to pick and choose among benefit options can be attractive to older as well as younger employees. For example, older employees often put more emphasis on longer vacations or on continued accrual of pension credits than do younger workers.

As one expert puts it,

To recruit older workers, the message must be tailored to their way of thinking. Appealing to job qualities they value will attract attention. These include flexible hours, flexible benefits, autonomy, opportunity to meet new friends, and working

Diversity Counts:
Recruiting Single Parents

About two-thirds of all single parents are in the work force today, and this group thus represents an important source of candidates.

Formulating an intelligent program for attracting single parents should begin with understanding the considerable problems that they often encounter in balancing work and family life.[62] In one recent survey, working single parents (the majority of whom were single mothers) stated that their work responsibilities interfered significantly with their family life. They described as a no-win situation the challenge of having to do a good job at work and being a good parent, and many expressed disappointment at feeling like failures in both endeavors. To quote from the survey's report,

many described falling into bed exhausted at midnight without even minimal time for themselves. They reported rushing through every activity and constantly feeling pressured to keep on going and do more. Vacations, which can be a time to rejuvenate, were often used for children's appointments or to handle unexpected emergencies. Also personal sick time or excused days off were often needed to care for sick children. As one mother noted, "I don't have enough sick days to get sick."[63]

The respondents generally viewed themselves as having ". . . less support, less personal time, more stress and greater difficulty balancing job and home life" than other working parents.[64] However, most were hesitant to dwell on their single-parent status at work for fear that such a disclosure would affect their jobs adversely. Thirty-five percent of the single mothers reported feeling that it was more difficult for them to achieve a proper work-family balance compared with 10% of the dual-earner mothers.[65] Some single mothers reported that they were treated differently than their male colleagues at work. For example, "When a single mother asks if she can go to her child's school play, she is seen as not committed to her job and often not allowed to go, while a male single parent is more often told 'Sure. It's just great that you are so interested in your children.'"[66]

Given such concerns, the first step in attracting (and keeping) single mothers is to make the workplace as "user friendly" for single mothers as is practical. Organizing regular, ongoing support groups and other forums at which single parents can share their concerns is a good way to provide the support that may be otherwise lacking. Furthermore, while many firms have instituted programs aimed at becoming more family friendly, these may not be extensive enough, particularly for single parents. For example, through *flextime* many employers already give employees a little flexibility (such as one-hour windows at the beginning or end of the day) around which to build their workdays. The problem is that "for some single mothers, this flexibility can help but it may not be sufficient to really make a difference in their ability to juggle work and family schedules."[67] In addition to increased flexibility employers can and should train their supervisors to have an increased awareness of and sensitivity to the sorts of challenges single parents face. As two researchers concluded:

Very often, the relationships which the single mother has with her supervisor and coworkers is a significant factor influencing whether the single-parent employee perceives the work environment to be supportive.[68]

For their part, single parents reentering the work force can turn to various agencies for support. For example, *displaced homemakers*—individuals who reenter the work force after a long period out of work, or who are forced to work due to hardship—can call the Displaced Homemakers Network (202-628-6767) for advice in obtaining training and placement.[69] Women entering or reentering the work force can also call Women Work! The National Network for Women's Employment in Washington, DC for referrals to local training programs and information about financial aid options, child support, and health insurance. The toll-free number is 1-800-235-2732.◆

with people their own age. You might also stress that you value their maturity and experience.[58]

Recruiting Minorities and Women   The same prescriptions that apply to recruiting older workers also apply to recruiting minorities and women. In other words, employers have to formulate comprehensive plans for attracting minorities and women, plans that may include reevaluating personnel policies, developing flexible work options, redesigning jobs, and offering flexible benefit plans. To paraphrase the expert quoted earlier, to recruit minorities and women employers must tailor their way of thinking and institute HR practices that make the firm attractive to them.

There are many specific things an employer can do to become more attractive to minorities. To the extent that many minority applicants may not meet the educational or experience standards for a job, many companies (including Aetna Life & Casualty) offer remedial training in basic arithmetic and writing.[59] Diversity data banks or nonspecialized minority-focused recruiting publications are another option. For example, Hispan Data provides recruiters at companies like McDonald's access to a computerized data bank; it costs a candidate $5.00 to be included.[60] Checking with your own minority employees can also be useful. For example, about 32% of job seekers of Hispanic origin cited "check with friends or relatives" as a strategy when looking for jobs.[61]

Some Other Recruiting Sources

More employers are also turning to relatively nontraditional sources of applicants.[70] For example, *moonlighters* have often been shunned by employers on the assumption that workers with full-time jobs at other firms might not have the required commitment to a second employer to do their jobs responsibly. Yet more employers are finding that moonlighters usually take second jobs because they must, and that their commitment to their second employer is thus high enough to do their jobs well. Advertising aimed at groups such as teachers, police officers, retail clerks, and firefighters can be a good source of such employees, particularly if you can provide flexible work hours. Other options include *retired* or *exiting military personnel* who often bring with them excellent skills. Testimonials from former military personnel who have joined your firm and ads with slogans such as "Join Our Team" can help attract these individuals. Disabled individuals are a most underused pool of labor. State rehabilitation agencies, Projects With Industry (write to the U.S. Department of Education, 330 C Street, S.W., Switzer Building, Washington, DC, 20202), and the U.S. Veterans' Administration can be helpful in identifying such candidates. The internet is another recruiting source (see page 155).

Recruiting Methods Used

The type of job generally determines what recruiting source is used. For managerial positions, 80% of the companies in one survey used newspaper ads, 75% used private employment agencies, and 65% relied on employee referrals. For professional and technical jobs, 75% used college recruiting, 75% also used ads in newspapers and technical journals, and 70% used private employment agencies. For recruiting sales personnel, 80% of the firms used newspaper ads, 75% used referrals, and 65% also used private employment agencies. For office and plant personnel, on the other hand, referrals and walk-ins were relied on by 90% of the firms, while 80% of the firms used newspaper ads and 70% used public employment agencies.[71]

CHAPTER 4 ◆ *Personnel Planning and Recruiting*   **153**

The Global Talent Search

As companies expand across national borders, they must increasingly tap overseas recruiting sources.[72] For example, Gillette International has an international graduate training program aimed at identifying and developing foreign nationals. Gillette subsidiaries overseas hire outstanding business students from top local universities. These foreign nationals are then trained for six months at the Gillette facility in their home countries. Some are selected to then spend 18 months being trained at the firm's Boston headquarters in areas such as finance and marketing. Those who pass muster are offered entry-level management positions at Gillette facilities in their home countries.

Coca-Cola also actively recruits foreign nationals. In addition to recruiting students abroad, it looks for foreign students studying in well-known international business programs like those at the University of South Carolina, UCLA, and the American Graduate School of International Management in Arizona. ◆

Developing and Using Application Forms

Purpose of Application Forms

application form
The form that provides information on education, prior work record, and skills.

Once you have a pool of applicants the selection process can begin, and for most employers the **application form** is the first step in this process. (Some firms first require a brief, prescreening interview.) The application form is a good way to quickly collect verifiable and therefore fairly accurate historical data from the candidate. It usually includes information about such areas as education, prior work history, and hobbies.

A filled-in form provides four types of information.[73] First, you can make judgments on substantive matters, such as "Does the applicant have the education and experience to do the job?" Second, you can draw conclusions about the applicant's previous progress and growth, a trait that is especially important for management candidates. Third, you can also draw tentative conclusions regarding the applicant's stability based on previous work record. (Here, however, you have to be careful not to assume that an unusual number of job changes necessarily reflects on the applicant's ability; for example, the person's last two employers may have had to lay off large numbers of employees.) Fourth, you may be able to use the data in the application to predict which candidates will succeed on the job and which will not, a point to which we return later.

Job application forms fall under the requirements of the Equal Opportunity Laws, and a number of questions both blunt and subtle are disallowed.

In practice, most organizations need several application forms. For technical and managerial personnel, for example, the form may require detailed answers to questions concerning the applicant's education and so on. The form for hourly factory workers might focus on the tools and equipment the applicant has used and the like.

Information Technology and HR
Recruiting on the Internet

Computers are playing a bigger and bigger role in helping employers recruit employees today. Computer applications range from recruiting on the Internet to automatically scanning and storing applicants' résumés.

A growing number of firms as well as many universities and the federal government are already recruiting using the Internet, the World Wide Web, and commercial on-line services like CompuServe.[1] For example, Winter, Wyman & Co., a Boston-based recruiting firm posts job descriptions on its World Wide Web page.[2] Similarly, Honeywell uses America On-Line's E-Span service to recruit for applicants for jobs such as UNIX Client/Server Applications Programmers, and the firm is considering creating a World Wide Web home page that would include employment listings. Another firm—American Contract Services—spends about $3,500 a year to run ads on the Internet, ads that "give us unlimited access, full descriptions of jobs, and no limit to how long the ad can appear." That compares to a typical two-column Sunday ad in a major city's newspaper which could cost between $1,500 and $2,000. Job hunters might use an Internet search aid like CareerMosaic to find jobs. For example, one such position-open ad was placed by a recruiting firm seeking a senior programmer for a position in California.[3]

For firms recruiting for employees who are not already on a service like Prodigy, America On-Line, or CompuServe, the Internet's On-Line Career Center is an alternative. As illustrated in Figure 4.15, corporate recruiters can use the career center to review résumés that have been deposited at the center and to place job openings by job title, key work, company name, and geographical region.

Employers are using information technology as an aid in recruiting in various other ways, too. For example, NEC Electronics, Inc., Unisys Corp., and LSI Logic Corp. have all hosted Internet-based "CyberFairs" to recruit for applicants.[4] The date and time of the fair, along with detailed job descriptions, are advertised in advance by the employers and by the firm organizing the CyberFairs, Hart Advertising network, an advertising and recruiting firm in Los Altos, California. This advertising is done via newspaper ads as well as via Hart's World Wide Web page. On the day of the fair, ". . . applicants log on and complete a prequalifying questionnaire before participating in a private on-line interview, during which candidates, recruiters and managers exchange typed messages on-line.[5]

Other firms like Cray Research, Inc., use their computers to process applicant résumés. Cray, for instance, receives about 200 résumés each week for positions in their four locations. Using special software these résumés are scanned into Cray's HR databases where its managers can have instant access to the 14,000 or so résumés in Cray's HR database system.[6]◆

1. See, for example, Elaine Appleton, "Recruiting on the Internet," *Datamation,* August, 1995, pp. 39–41.
2. *Ibid.,* p.39.
3. Alfred and Emily Glossbrenner, *Finding a Job on the Internet* (NY: McGraw-Hill, 1995), p. 163.
4. Julia King, "Job Networking," *Enterprise Networking,* Jan. 26, 1995.
5. *Ibid.*
6. Lura Romei, "Human Resource Management Systems Keep Computers Humming," *Managing Office Technology,* November 1994, p. 45.

Equal Opportunity and Application Forms

Employers should carefully review their application forms to ensure they comply with Equal Employment laws. Questions concerning race, religion, age, sex, or national origin are generally not illegal per se under federal laws, but are illegal under certain state laws. However, they are viewed with disfavor by the EEOC, and the burden of proof will always be on the employer to prove that the potentially

Figure 4.15
The Internet's Online
Career Center.

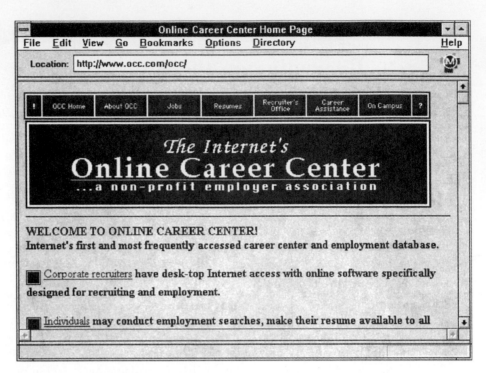

discriminatory items are both related to success or failure on the job and not unfairly discriminatory. For example, you generally can request photographs prior to employment and even ask such potentially discriminatory questions as, "Have you ever been arrested?" The problem is that an unsuccessful applicant might establish a prima facie case of discrimination by demonstrating that the item produces an adverse impact. The burden of proof would then shift to you to show that the item is a valid predictor of job performance and that it is applied fairly to all applicants—that, for instance, you check arrest records of all applicants, not just minority applicants.

Unfortunately, many employers' forms are highly questionable. A study of 50 actual application forms revealed 17 types of questions containing possible violations of federal regulations.[74] Many of the items should probably have been left out. These included questions regarding maiden name or name used previously, height and weight, age, religion, race or color, national origin, and sex. In addition, several more subtle types of potentially discriminatory questions often crept into the forms:

> *Education.* One common violation on many of the applications was a question on the dates of attendance and graduation from various schools—academic, vocational, or professional. This question may be illegal in that it may reflect the applicant's age.
>
> *Military background.* Questions concerning type of discharge (like those concerning arrest records) are usually considered unfairly discriminatory and unlawful.
>
> *Arrest records.* The courts have usually held that employers violate Title VII by disqualifying applicants from employment because of an arrest record. This item has an adverse impact on minorities and in most cases cannot be shown to be justified by business necessity.
>
> *Relatives.* Although legal for an applicant who is a minor, it is generally not acceptable to ask questions about an applicant's relatives when the applicant is an

adult because it can provide a window on the applicant's religion, race, or national origin. However, an employer can ask about any relatives who are currently employed by the employer.

Notify in case of emergency. It is generally legal to require the name, address, and phone number of a person who can be notified in case of emergency. However, asking the relationship of this person could indicate the applicant's marital status or lineage. In any event, information such as this can just as well be requested after the offer has been made and accepted.

Membership in organizations. Many forms ask the applicant to list memberships in clubs, organizations, or societies along with offices held. However, employers should add instructions not to include organizations that would reveal race, religion, physical handicaps, marital status, or ancestry. Those not adding such a clause may be indirectly asking for the applicant's race or religion, for instance, and would thus be guilty of making an unlawful inquiry.

Physical handicaps. It is usually illegal to require the listing of an applicant's physical handicaps, defects, or past illnesses unless the application blank specifically asks only for those that "may interfere with your job performance." Similarly, it is generally illegal to ask whether the applicant has ever received worker's compensation for previous injury or illness.

Marital status. In general, the application should not ask whether an applicant is single, married, divorced, separated, or living with anyone, or the names and ages of the applicant's spouse or children. Similarly, it may be shown to be discriminatory to ask a woman for her husband's occupation and then reject the woman because, say, her husband is in the military and therefore subject to frequent relocation.

Housing. Asking whether an applicant owns, rents, or leases a house may also be discriminatory. It can adversely affect minority groups and is difficult to justify on grounds of business necessity.

Figure 4.16 presents one employer's approach to collecting application form information.

Some employers require applicants to complete two separate forms. One form contains information deemed necessary for evaluating the person's future performance, information regarding, for instance, education and work history. The second (Figure 4.17) contains information compiled and used solely by the employer for its Equal Employment and Affirmative Action Reports. (These reports are required of most employers to monitor and demonstrate compliance with equal employment opportunity laws, and contains information about age, religion, national origin, and so forth.) The form in Figure 4.16 includes a cover letter that makes it clear that although the applicant must complete both forms, the information on the second is used solely for EEO reporting purposes and will not be used for screening applicants.

Using Application Forms to Predict Job Performance

Some firms use application forms to predict which candidates will be successful and which will not, in much the same way that employers use tests for screening. They do this by conducting statistical studies to find the relationship between (1) responses on the application form and (2) measures of success on the job. Some examples follow.

Using Application Forms to Predict Job Tenure One study was aimed at reducing turnover at a large insurance company. At the time of the study the company was experiencing a 48% turnover rate among its clerical personnel. This meant that for every two employees hired at the same time, there was about a 50–50 chance that one would not remain with the company 12 months or longer.

Figure 4.16
Example of Application Form

EMPLOYMENT APPLICATION

As an equal opportunity employer, the firm does not discriminate in hiring or in terms and conditions of employment because of an individual's race, creed, color, sex, age, religion, disability or natural origin. The firm only hires individuals authorized for employment in the United States.

_____ / _____ / _____
Date of Application

Position
Applying for: _____

Schedule   ( ) Full time   ( ) Temporary
Desired:
                  ( ) Part time

PERSONAL INFORMATION

Last Name	First Name	Middle Name	Are you authorized for employment in the U.S.? ( ) Yes ( ) No
Present Street Address	City	State	Zip	How long have you lived there? Yrs. Mo.
Previous Street Address	City	State	Zip	How long did you live there? Yrs. Mo.
Home Phone Number	Social Security Number	If you are under 18 years of age, state your age:	

EDUCATION

Type of School	Name and Location of School	Degree/Area of Study	Number of Years Attended	Graduated (Check One)
HIGH SCHOOL	Name / City State			Yes ☐ No ☐
JUNIOR COLLEGE	Name / City State			Yes ☐ No ☐
COLLEGE	Name / City State			Yes ☐ No ☐
GRADUATE SCHOOL	Name / City State			Yes ☐ No ☐
OTHER	Name / City State			Yes ☐ No ☐

ACADEMIC AND PROFESSIONAL ACTIVITIES AND ACHIEVEMENTS

Academic and Professional Activities and Achievements, Awards, Publications or Technical-Professional Societies. Indicate type or name. Exclude organizations which indicate race, creed, color, sex, age, religion, handicap or national origin of its members.	Date Awarded

SKILLS

Skills applicable to position applied for

PERSON TO CONTACT IN CASE OF EMERGENCY

This information is to facilitate contact in the event of an emergency and is not used in the selection process.

Full Name	Address	Phone	Relationship to you?
Place of Employment	Address	Phone	

15-10.22227 Rev. 5/92

GC 7520

158

Figure 4.16

(continued)

EMPLOYMENT HISTORY

List employment starting with your most recent position. Account for any time during this period that you were unemployed by stating the nature of your activities. If you have less than four places of employment, include personal references to be contacted. May we contact your present employer?
( ) Yes ( ) No

DATES	NAME AND ADDRESS OF EMPLOYER	POSITION HELD AND SUPERVISOR	LIST MAJOR DUTIES	WAGES	REASON FOR LEAVING
FROM: / MO. YR. TO: / MO. YR.	NAME ADDRESS PHONE	YOUR JOB TITLE SUPERVISOR		STARTING FINAL	
FROM: / MO. YR. TO: / MO. YR.	NAME ADDRESS PHONE	YOUR JOB TITLE SUPERVISOR		STARTING FINAL	
FROM: / MO. YR. TO: / MO. YR.	NAME ADDRESS PHONE	YOUR JOB TITLE SUPERVISOR		STARTING FINAL	
FROM: / MO. YR. TO: / MO. YR.	NAME ADDRESS PHONE	YOUR JOB TITLE SUPERVISOR		STARTING FINAL	

MISCELLANEOUS

Is there any additional information involving a change of your name or assumed name that will permit us to check your work record?
If yes, please explain.

Have you ever been employed by The Firm or any of its divisions or subsidiaries before? ☐ Yes ☐ No

If yes, Please indicate:	When	Where	Position

List Names of Friends or Relatives now employed by The Firm.

Have you ever been convicted of a crime? ☐ Yes ☐ No   If yes, please explain:

PLEASE READ THIS STATEMENT CAREFULLY

I hereby affirm that the information given by me on this application for employment is complete and accurate. I understand that any falsification or ommission will be immediate grounds for dismissal. I authorize a thorough investigation to be made in connection with this application concerning my character, general reputation, employment and education background, and criminal record, whichever may be applicable. I understand what this investigation may include and I hereby authorize the release of documents, and personal interviews with third parties, such as prior employers, family members, business associates, financial sources, friends, neighbors or others with whom I am acquainted. I further understand that I have the right to make a written request within a reasonable period of time for a complete and accurate disclosure of the nature and scope of the investigation.

It is understood that, as a condition of initial or continued employment, I agree to submit to such lawful examinations, medical, substance abuse, or other, as may be required by the compnay. The company will pay the reasonable cost of any such examination which may be required.

If I am hired, I agree that my employment and compensation can be terminated with or without cause and without notice, at any time, at the option of the firm or myself. I understand that no store manager or other representative of the firm other than a Vice-President, and in writing, has the authority to enter into any agreement for employment for any specified period of time, or to make any agreement contrary to the foregoing.

I have read and affirm as my own the above statements.

_____   _____
Signature   Date

APPLICANTS IN THE STATE OF MARYLAND ONLY

Under Maryland law an employer may not require or demand any applicant for employment or prospective employment or any employee to submit to or take a polygraph, lie detector or similar test or examination as a condition of employment or continued employment. Any employer who violates this provision is guilty of a misdemeanor and subject to a fine not to exceed $100.

_____   _____
Signature   Date

APPLICANTS IN THE STATE OF MASSACHUSETTS ONLY

It is unlawful in Massachusetts to require or administer a lie detector test as a condition of employment or continued employment. An employer who violates this law shall be subject to criminal penalties and civil liability.

_____   _____
Signature   Date

Figure 4.17
Equal Employment Opportunity Disclaimer Letter for Applicants

---

EQUAL OPPORTUNITY INFORMATION

The information on the reverse side of this form is requested as part of the affirmative action program and to provide statistical information in compliance with Federal and State regulations. Your response is strictly voluntary and will not result in any adverse treatment.

(reverse side of form)

EQUAL OPPORTUNITY INFORMATION

Date of Birth _____   Social Security Number _____

Racial/Ethnic Data:
☐ Black (Non-Hispanic)   ☐ Native American Indian or Alaskan   ☐ Asian/Pacific Islander

☐ Hispanic   ☐ White (Non-Hispanic)

Sex:
☐ Female   ☐ Male

Do you have any disabling or handicapping conditions: ☐ Yes   ☐ No   If yes, please describe: _____
_____

If a handicap has been identified, please describe any accommodations needed to assist you. _____
_____

Position(s) applied for:
_____   _____   _____
_____   _____   _____

This study was done as follows: The researcher obtained the application forms of about 160 clerical employees of the company from the firm's personnel files. The researcher then split the application forms into two categories: long-tenure and short-tenure employees. The researcher found that some responses on the application form were highly related to job tenure. The researcher was thereby able to use the company's application forms to predict which of the firm's new applicants would stay on the job and which would not.

The study helped the firm comply with its equal employment opportunity responsibilities. For example, some of the items on the application form (like marital status) could be viewed as potentially discriminatory. In this case the researcher was able to prove that these items did predict success or failure on the job (long tenure versus short tenure). There was thus a business necessity reason for asking them.[75] (Whether or not an employer would want to risk asking such "red-flag" questions is another matter.)

Using Application Forms to Predict Employee Theft   Employee theft and pilferage are serious problems that employers find difficult to deal with. Losses range up to $16 billion per year, but useful tests aimed at predicting stealing tend to be in-depth tests of personality and are difficult and time-consuming to administer and evaluate.

One solution is to use the application form to predict which applicants have a higher likelihood of stealing. One researcher carried out studies for both a mass merchandiser and a supermarket in Detroit. He found that responses to some application form items (like "does not own automobile" and "not living with parents") were highly related to whether or not the employee was subsequently caught stealing. The researcher was therefore able to identify potential thieves before they were hired (although, again, at the risk of asking "red-flag" questions).[76]

Chapter Review

Summary

1. Developing personnel plans requires three forecasts: one for *personnel requirements,* one for the *supply of outside candidates*, and one for the *supply of inside candidates*. To predict the need for personnel, first project the demand for the product or service. Next project the volume of production required to meet these estimates; finally, relate personnel needs to these production estimates.

2. Once personnel needs are projected, the next step is to build up a pool of qualified applicants. We discussed several sources of candidates, including internal sources (or promotion from within), advertising, employment agencies, executive recruiters, college recruiting, the internet, and referrals and walk-ins. Remember that it is unlawful to discriminate against any individual with respect to employment because of race, color, religion, sex, national origin, or age (unless religion, sex, or origin are bona fide occupational qualifications).

3. The initial selection screening in most organizations begins with an application form. Most managers use these just to obtain background data. However, you can use application form data to make *predictions* about the applicant's future performance. For example, application forms have been used to predict job tenure, job success, and employee theft.

4. Personnel planning and recruiting directly affect employee commitment because commitment depends on hiring employees who have the potential to develop. And the more qualified applicants you have, the higher your selection standards can be. Selection usually begins with effective testing and interviewing, to which we now turn.

Key Terms

trend analysis	personnel replacement charts	job posting
ratio analysis		occupational market conditions
scatter plot	position replacement cards	
computerized forecast		application form
qualifications inventories		

Discussion Questions and Exercises

1. Compare and contrast five sources of job candidates.

2. What types of information can an application form provide?

3. Discuss how equal employment laws apply to personnel planning and recruiting activities.

4. Working individually or in groups, develop an application form for the position supervisor of Data Processing Operations as described in the sample job description in Chapter 3. Compare the application forms produced by different individuals or groups: Are there any items that should be dropped due to EEO restrictions? Are there any items you would add to make your application form more complete?

5. Working individually or in groups, bring to class several classified and display ads from this Sunday's help wanted ads. Analyze the effectiveness of these ads using the guidelines discussed in this chapter.

6. Working individually or in groups, obtain a recent copy of the *Monthly Labor Review* or *Occupational Outlook Quarterly,* both published by the U.S. Bureau of Labor Statistics. Based on information in either of these publications, develop a forecast for the next five years of occupational market conditions for various occupations such as accountant, nurse, and engineer.

7. Working individually or in groups, visit your local office of your state employment agency. Come back to class prepared to discuss the following questions: What types of jobs seemed to be available through this agency, predominantly? To what extent do you think this particular agency would be a good source of professional, technical, and/or managerial applicants? What sort of paperwork are applicants to the state agency required to complete before their applications are processed by the agency? What other opinions did you form about the state agency?

8. Working individually or in groups, review help wanted ads placed over the last few Sundays by local employment agencies. Do some employment agencies seem to specialize in some types of jobs? If you were an HR manager seeking a relationship with an employment agency for each of the following types of jobs, which local agencies would you turn to first, based on their help wanted ad history: engineers; secretaries; data processing clerks; accountants; factory workers?

9. Working individually or in groups, interview an HR manager to determine the specific actions his or her company is taking to recruit a more diverse workforce. Back in class, compare the activities of the different employers.

Application Exercises

RUNNING CASE: Carter Cleaning Company
Getting Better Applicants

If you were to ask Jennifer and her father what the main problem was in running their firm, their answer would be quick and short: hiring good people. Originally begun as a string of coin-operated laundromats requiring virtually no skilled help, the chain grew to six stores, each heavily dependent on skilled managers, cleaner–spotters, and pressers. Employees generally have no more than a high school education (often less), and the market for them is very competitive. Over a typical weekend literally dozens of want ads for experienced pressers or cleaner–spotters can be found in area newspapers. All these people are usually paid around $7.00 per hour, and they change jobs frequently. Jennifer and her father are thus faced with the continuing task of recruiting and hiring qualified workers out of a pool of individuals they feel are almost nomadic in their propensity to move from area to area and job to job. Turnover in their stores (as in the stores of many of their competitors) often approaches 400%. "Don't talk to me about hu-

man resources planning and trend analysis," says Jennifer. "We're fighting an economic war and I'm happy just to be able to round up enough live applicants to be able to keep my trenches fully manned."

In light of this problem, Jennifer's father asked her to answer the following questions:

Questions

1. First, how would you recommend we go about reducing the turnover in our stores?

2. Provide a detailed list of recommendations concerning how we should go about increasing our pool of acceptable job applicants so we are no longer faced with the need of hiring almost anyone who walks in the door. (Your recommendations regarding the latter should include completely worded advertisements and recommendations regarding any other recruiting strategies you would suggest we use.)

CASE INCIDENT: Only Asians Wanted Here

It was a human resource manager's nightmare. IBM Japan Limited, IBM's Japanese subsidiary, seemed to have been recruiting in Japanese magazines in the United States in a discriminatory fashion. Although IBM Japan insists they never instructed their employment agency to screen out white people and black people in favor of Asians, it does seem that some discriminatory actions might have taken place.

The problem revolved around the employment agencies owned by a Japanese firm called Recruit. According to allegations made by Recruit USA's former staffers, Recruit USA had set up a fairly formal system to see that only Asians were hired for the IBM Japan jobs. According to one memo submitted by a former staffer to the EEOC, Recruit officials summarized the hiring policy as: "Foreigners, no good—IBM current rule . . . white people, black people—no, but second-generation Japanese or others of Asian descent o.k." Another Recruit agency in the United States allegedly set up a system of code words to discriminate against people it didn't want to hire. For example, if the job order said "see Adam," it meant the client only wanted a male employee. If the job order said "talk to Haruo," it meant the client only wanted a Japanese worker.

The whole story first broke when former Recruit employees took their allegation to the *San Francisco Chronicle*. Then the EEOC got involved and more allegations were unearthed. Japanese firms and other multinationals are therefore learning the truth of the old saying, "When in Rome, do as the Romans." But in this case it means that when you're doing business in a certain country, you'd better know and follow the laws of the land.

Questions

1. Do you think a client (in this case IBM Japan) should be held responsible for the actions of an independent employment agency that it hires? Why or why not?

2. Do you think it would be right for a company to discriminate in hiring people in the United States for work overseas, since it's not hiring them to work in the United States? Why or why not?

3. If you were the human resource manager of a company using an employment agency, how would you avoid the sort of discrimination problem described in this case?

 # Human Resource Management Simulation

Personnel planning and forecasting are key elements of the simulation. You will be furnished with the total number of operations/production employees needed each quarter and an estimate of how many employees may quit during the quarter. You will then need to hire and/or promote employees to fill jobs at all levels. If you do not hire enough people, the firm will need to schedule overtime work to fill production quotas and your team will be charged for this extra expense. Due to the nature of the work and lower-than-local wage rates, your organization has fairly high turnover when the simulation begins. Your team will need to discuss ways of decreasing this costly turnover rate.

Also one of the incidents (C) involves recruiting for temporary positions. Because temporary employees can be a good source of permanent employees, your decisions in this regard will be important.

Video Case

Nurse Shortage

Few jobs illustrate the importance of effective personnel planning and recruiting as does the job of nurse. In part because of an aging population and in part because of the increasing use of sophisticated medical technology, demand for nurses has outstripped supply by about 15% for a number of years. As a result, some hospitals are trying new tactics—such as giving nurses more autonomy and flexibility in scheduling—to make their jobs more attractive.

Questions

1. What do the employers in the video seem to be doing to plan for nurse shortages?

2. What are they doing to recruit nurses more effectively?

3. If you were the HR manager for a local hospital, what would you do to improve your hospital's nurse-recruiting efforts?

Source: ABC News, *Labor Market: Nurse Shortage,* "Business World," March 25, 1990.

Take It to the Net

We invite you to visit the Dessler page on the Prentice Hall Web site at:

http://www.prenhall.com/~dessler

for the monthly Dessler update and for this chapter's World Wide Web exercise.

Notes

1. Herbert G. Heneman, Jr., and George Seitzer, "Manpower Planning and Forecasting in the Firm: An Exploratory Probe," in Elmer Burack and James Walker, *Manpower Planning and Programming* (Boston: Allyn & Bacon, 1972), pp. 102–120; Sheldon Zedeck and Milton Blood, "Selection and Placement," from *Foundations of Behavioral Science Research in Organizations* (Monterey, CA: Brooks/Cole, 1974), in J. Richard Hackman, Edward Lawler III, and Lyman Porter, *Perspectives on Behavior in Organizations* (New York: McGraw-Hill, 1977), pp. 103–119. For a discussion of equal employment implications of work force planning, see James Ledvinka, "Technical Implications of Equal Employment Law for Manpower Planning," *Personnel Psychology,* Vol. 28 (Autumn 1975).

2. Roger Hawk, *The Recruitment Function* (New York: American Management Association, 1967). See also Paul Pakchar, "Effective Manpower Planning," *Personnel Journal,* Vol. 62, no. 10 (October 1983), pp. 826–830.

3. Richard B. Frantzreb, "Human Resource Planning: Forecasting Manpower Needs," *Personnel Journal,* Vol. 60, no. 11 (November 1981), pp. 850–857. See also John Gridley, "Who Will Be Where When? Forecast the Easy Way," *Personnel Journal,* Vol. 65 (May 1986), pp. 50–58.

4. Based on an idea in Elmer H. Burack and Robert D. Smith, *Personnel Management: A Human Resource Systems Approach* (St. Paul, MN: West, 1977), pp. 134–135. Reprinted by permission. Copyright 1977 by West Publishing Co. All rights reserved.

5. Glenn Bassett, "Elements of Manpower Forecasting and Scheduling," *Human Resource Management,* Vol. 12, no. 3 (Fall 1973), pp. 35–43, reprinted in Richard Peterson, Lane Tracy, and Allan Cabelly, *Systematic Management of Human Resources* (Reading, MA: Addison-Wesley, 1979), pp. 135–146.

6. For an example of a computerized system in use at Citibank, see Paul Sheiber, "A Simple Selection System Called 'Job Match,'" *Personnel Journal,* Vol. 58, no. 1 (January 1979), pp. 26–54.

7. For discussions of skill inventories, see, for example, John Lawrie, "Skill Inventories: Pack for the Future," *Personnel Journal* (March 1987), pp. 127–130; John Lawrie, "Skill Inventories: A Developmental Process," *Personnel Journal* (October 1987), pp. 108–110.

8. Alfred Walker, "Management Selection Systems That Meet the Challenge of the 80s," *Personnel Journal,* Vol. 60, no. 10 (October 1981), pp. 775–780.

9. Donald Harris, "A Matter of Privacy: Managing Personnel Data in Computers," *Personnel* (February 1987), pp. 34–39.

10. Amiel Sharon, "Skills Bank Tracks Talent, Not Training," *Personnel Journal* (June 1988), pp. 44–49.

11. This section is based on Harris, "A Matter of Privacy."

12. John Campbell and others, *Managerial Behavior, Performance, and Effectiveness* (New York: McGraw-Hill, 1970), p. 23. See also Allan Halcrow, "Recruitment by Any Other Name Is Turnover," *Personnel Journal,* Vol. 65 (August 1986), pp. 10–15.

13. David Dahl and Patrick Pinto, "Job Posting, an Industry Survey," *Personnel Journal,* Vol. 56, no. 1 (January 1977), pp. 40–41.

14. Jeffrey Daum, "Internal Promotion—Psychological Asset or Debit? A Study of the Effects of Leader Origin," *Organizational Behavior and Human Performance,* Vol. 13 (1975), pp. 404–413.

15. Arthur R. Pell, *Recruiting and Selecting Personnel* (New York: Regents, 1969), pp. 10–12.

16. Ibid., p. 11.

17. This is based on Gary Dessler, *Winning Commitment* (New York: McGraw-Hill Book Company, 1993).

18. Federal Express Employee Handbook, p. 28.

19. This is a modification of a definition found in Peter Wallum, "A Broader View of Succession Planning," *Personnel Management* (September 1993), p. 45.

20. Ibid., pp. 43–44.

21. Sara Rynes, Robert Breta, Jr., and Barry Gerhart, "The Importance of Recruitment in Job Choice: A Different Way of Looking," *Personnel Psychology,* Vol. 44, no. 3 (Autumn 1991), pp. 487–521.

22. Pell, *Recruiting and Selecting Personnel,* pp. 16–34. See also Barbara Hunger, "How to Choose a Recruitment Advertising Agency," *Personnel Journal,* Vol. 64, no. 12 (December

1985), pp. 60–62. For an excellent review of ads, see Margaret Magnus, *Personnel Journal,* Vols. 64 and 65, no. 8 (August 1985 and 1986), and Bob Martin, "Recruitment Ad Ventures," *Personnel Journal,* Vol. 66 (August 1987), pp. 46–63. For a discussion of how behavior can influence the initial attraction to an advertisement, see Tom Redman and Brian Mathews, "Advertising for Effective Managerial Recruitment," *Journal of General Management,* Vol. 18, no. 2 (Winter 1992), pp. 29–42.

23. John P. Kohl and David B. Stephens, "Wanted: Recruitment Advertising That Doesn't Discriminate," *Personnel* (February 1989), pp. 18–26. Age discrimination via inferred age preferences in media advertising in particular appears to be a continuing problem. See, for example, Ann McGoldrick and James Arrowsmith, "Recruitment Advertising: Discrimination on the Basis of Age," *Employee Relations,* Vol. 15, No. 5 (1993), pp. 54–65.

24. Pell, *Recruiting and Selecting Personnel,* pp. 34–42.

25. Stephen Rubenfeld and Michael Crino, "Are Employment Agencies Jeopardizing Your Selection Process?" *Personnel,* Vol. 58 (September–October 1981), pp. 70–77.

26. Ibid.

27. Allison Thomson, "The Contingent Work Force," *Occupational Outlook Quarterly* (Spring 1995), p. 45.

28. Ibid., p. 46.

29. Daniel C. Feldman, Helen Doerpinghaus, and William Turnley, "Managing Temporary Workers: A Permanent HRM Challenge," *Organizational Dynamics,* Vol. 23, no. 2 (Fall 1994), p. 49.

30. One Bureau of Labor statistics study suggests that temporary employees produce the equivalent of two or more hours of work per day than their permanent counterparts. For a discussion, see Shari Caudron, "Contingent Workforce Spurs HR Planning," *Personnel Journal* (July 1994), p. 54.

31. Thomson, "The Contingent Work Force," p. 47.

32. Ibid., p. 47.

33. Caudron, "Contingent Workforce Spurs HR Planning," p. 60.

34. Ibid., p.56.

35. Daniel Feldman et al., *Organizational Dynamics,* pp. 54–56.

36. Except as noted, the following are based on or quoted from Feldman et al., *Organizational Dynamics,* pp. 58–60.

37. Barbara Ettorre, "The Contingency Work Force Moves Mainstream," *Management Review,* p. 15.

38. Bureau of National Affairs, "Part-Time and Other Alternative Staffing Practices," *Bulletin to Management,* June 23, 1988, pp. 1–10.

39. This is based on or quoted from Nancy Howe, "Match Temp Services to Your Needs," *Personnel Journal* (March 1989), pp. 45–51.

40. John Wareham, *Secrets of a Corporate Headhunter* (New York: Playboy Press, 1981), pp. 213–225.

41. Pell, *Recruiting and Selecting Personnel,* pp. 56–63; David L. Chicci and Carl Knapp, "College Recruitment from Start to Finish," *Personnel Journal,* Vol. 59, no. 8 (August 1980), pp. 653–657.

42. Allen J. Cox, *Confessions of a Corporate Headhunter* (New York: Trident Press, 1973).

43. Robert Dipboye, Howard Fronkin, and Ken Wiback, "Relative Importance of Applicant Sex, Attractiveness, and Scholastic Standing in Evaluation of Job Applicant Résumés," *Journal of Applied Psychology,* Vol. 61 (1975), pp. 39–48. See also Laura M. Graves, "College Recruitment: Removing the Personal Bias from Selection Decisions," *Personnel* (March 1989), pp. 48–52.

44. Ibid., pp. 39–48. See also "A Measure of the HR Recruitment Function: The 1994 College Relations and Recruitment Survey," *Journal of Career Planning and Employment,* Vol. 55, No. 3 (Spring 1995), pp. 37–49.

45. Ibid. See also, "College Recruiting," in *Personnel* (May–June 1980). For a study of how applicant sex can impact recruiters' evaluations, see, for example, Laura Graves and Gary Powell, "The Affect of Sex Similarity on Recruiters' Evaluations of Actual Applicants: A Test of the Similarity-Attraction Paradigm," *Personnel Psychology,* Vol. 48, No. 1 (Spring 1995), pp. 85–98.

46. See, for example, Richard Becker, "Ten Common Mistakes in College Recruiting—or How to Try Without Really Succeeding," *Personnel,* Vol. 52, no. 2 (March–April 1975), pp. 19–28. See also Sara Rynes and John Boudreau, "College Recruiting in Large Organizations: Practice, Evaluation, and Research Implications," *Personnel Psychology,* Vol. 39 (Winter 1986), pp. 729–757.

47. Pell, *Recruiting and Selecting Personnel,* pp. 62–63.

48. Ibid.

49. Ibid., p. 13.

50. The study on employment referrals was published by Bernard Hodes Advertising, Dept. 100, 555 Madison Avenue, New York, N.Y. 10022. See also Allan Halcrow, "Employees Are Your Best Recruiters," *Personnel Journal* (November 1988), pp. 43–49. See also Andy Bargerstock and Hank Engel, "Six Ways to Boost Employee Referral Programs," *HR Magazine,* Vol. 39, No. 12 (December 1994), pp. 72ff.

51. For further information on this service, you can call CPR at 1-800-368-3093. Their complete address is Career Placement Registry, Inc., 302 Swann Avenue, Alexandria, VA 23301. See also Joyce Lain Kennedy, "The Job Search Goes Computer," *Journal of Career Planning and Employment,* Vol. 55, No. 1, November 1994, pp. 42ff.

52. Phaedra Hise, "Hiring Through Resume Databases," *Inc.,* Vol. 15, no. 5 (May 1993), p. 30.

53. Harold E. Johnson, "Older Workers Help Meet Employment Needs," *Personnel Journal* (May 1988), pp. 100–105.

54. This is based on Robert W. Goddard, "How to Harness America's Gray Power," *Personnel Journal* (May 1987), pp. 33–40.

55. Glenn McEvoy and Wayne Cascio, "Cumulative Evidence of the Relationship Between Employee Age and Job Performance," *Journal of Applied Psychology,* Vol. 74, no. 1 (February 1989), pp. 11–17.

56. Goddard, "How to Harness America's Gray Power," p. 33.

57. For this and other examples here, see Goddard, "How to Harness America's Gray Power."

58. *B & E Review* (July–September 1990), p. 7.

59. Elizabeth Blacharczyk, "Recruiters Challenged by Economy, Shortages," *HR News* (February 1990), p. B4. Diversity management programs may also make a firm more attractive to job candidates. See, for example, Margaret Williams and Talya Bauer, "The Effect of Managing Diversity Policy on Organizational Attractiveness," *Group & Organization Management,* Vol. 19, No. 3 (September 1994), pp. 295–308.

The Selection Process

Once you have a pool of completed application forms, the next step is to select the best person for the job. In most firms this means whittling down the applicant pool by using the screening tools explained in this chapter, including tests, assessment centers, and background and reference checks. The prospective supervisor can then interview a handful of viable candidates and decide who will be hired: We'll turn to interviewing next, in Chapter 6.[1]

Why the Selection Process is Important

Performance *Employee selection* is important for three reasons. First, your performance always depends in part on your subordinates. Employees who haven't the right skills or who are abrasive or obstructionist won't perform effectively, and your performance in turn will suffer.[2] The time to screen out undesirables is before they are in the door, not after.

Costs Second, effective screening is important because it's costly to recruit and hire employees. For example, one expert estimates that the total cost of hiring a manager who earns $60,000 a year is about $47,000, once search fees, interviewing time, reference checking, and travel and moving expenses are taken into consideration.[3] The cost of hiring nonexecutive employees, although not as high proportionally, is still high enough to warrant effective screening.

Legal Implications and Negligent Hiring Good selection is also important because of the legal implications of ineffective or incompetent selection. For one thing we saw in Chapter 2 that equal employment legislation, guidelines, and court decisions require you to systematically evaluate the effectiveness of your selection procedures to ensure that you are not unfairly discriminating against minorities, women, the elderly, or the handicapped. Second, courts are increasingly finding employers liable for damages when employees with criminal records or other problems take advantage of access to customer homes or other similar opportunities to commit crimes. Hiring workers with such backgrounds without proper safeguards is called *negligent hiring*.[4]

Several cases illustrate the problem. In one, *Ponticas* v. *K.M.S. Investments,* an apartment manager with a passkey entered a woman's apartment and assaulted her. Negligence by the owner and the operator of the apartment complex in not properly checking the apartment manager's background prior to hiring him was found to be the cause of the woman's personal injury. In another case, *Henley* v. *Prince Georges County,* an employee who turned out to have a criminal background murdered a young boy; management, aware of the man's prior murder conviction, was held liable.

Two experts argue that the recent increase in negligent hiring cases underscores the need for employers to carefully think through what the human requirements really are when conducting a job analysis.[5] Specifically, "Negligent hiring litigation points out that ability to do the job is interpreted beyond the type of information typically collected in a job analysis."[6] For example, "'nonrapist' is unlikely to appear as a required knowledge, skill, or ability in a job analysis of a repair person. Yet, it is that type of requirement that has been the focus of many negligent hiring suits."[7] On the other hand, it could be discriminatory to conclude that candidates with, say, conviction records are automatically not right for certain jobs. In other words, the fear of negligent hiring must be balanced with EEO concerns. Guidelines for protecting against negligent hiring claims include:[8]

Carefully scrutinize all information supplied by the applicant on his or her employment application. For example, look for unexplained gaps in employment.

Obtain the applicant's written authorization for references checks from prospective employees, and check former employers as references very carefully.

Save all records and information you obtain about the applicant during each stage of the selection process.

Reject applicants who make false statements of material facts in the application or who have records of conviction for offenses directly related and important to the positions in question.

Keep in mind the need to balance the applicants' privacy rights with others' "need to know," especially when damaging information is discovered.

Take immediate disciplinary action if problems develop.

Basic Testing Concepts

Validity

A test is basically a sample of a person's behavior, but some tests are more clearly representative of the behavior being sampled than others. A typing test, for example, clearly corresponds to some on-the-job behavior, in this case typing. At the other extreme, there may be no apparent relationship between the items on the test and the behavior. This is the case with projective personality tests, for example. In the *Thematic Apperception Test* illustrated in Figure 5.1, the person is asked to explain how he or she interprets the blurred picture. That interpretation is then used to draw conclusions about the person's personality and behavior. In such tests, it is much harder to "prove" that the tests are measuring what they are purported to measure—that they're *valid*.

test validity
The accuracy with which a test, interview, and so on measures what it purports to measure or fulfills the function it was designed to fill.

Test validity answers the question: "Does this test measure what it's supposed to measure?"[9] With respect to employee selection tests, the term *validity* often refers to evidence that the test is job related, in other words, that performance on the test is a *valid predictor* of subsequent performance on the job. A selection test must above all be valid since, without proof of its validity, there is no logical or legally permissible reason to continue using it to screen job applicants. In employment testing, there are two main ways to demonstrate a test's validity, *criterion validity* and *content validity*.[10]

Figure 5.1
Sample Picture from Thematic Apperception Test.
How do you interpret this picture?

criterion validity
A type of validity based on showing that scores on the test (*predictors*) are related to job performance (*criterion*).

Criterion Validity Demonstrating **criterion validity** means demonstrating that those who do well on the test also do well on the job, and that those who do poorly on the test do poorly on the job.[11] Thus, the test has validity to the extent that the people with higher test scores perform better on the job. In psychological measurement, a *predictor* is the measurement (in this case, the test score) that you are trying to relate to a *criterion*, like performance on the job. The term *criterion validity* comes from that terminology.

content validity
A test that is *content valid* is one in which the test contains a fair sample of the tasks and skills actually needed for the job in question.

Content Validity The **content validity** of a test is demonstrated by showing that the test constitutes a fair sample of the content of the job.[12] The basic procedure here is to identify job behaviors that are critical to performance and then randomly select a sample of those tasks and behaviors for the tests. A typing test used to hire a typist is an example. If the content of the typing test is a representative sample of the typist's job, then the test is probably content valid.

Demonstrating content validity sounds easier than it is in practice. Demonstrating that the tasks the person performs on the test are in fact a comprehensive and random sample of the tasks performed on the job, and demonstrating that the conditions under which the test is taken resemble the work situation, are not always easy. For many jobs, other evidence of a test's validity—such as its criterion validity—must therefore be demonstrated as well.

Reliability

A test has two important characteristics, *validity* and *reliability*. Validity is the more important characteristic because if you cannot ascertain what the test is measuring, it is of little use to you.

reliability
The characteristic which refers to the consistency of scores obtained by the same person when retested with the identical or equivalent tests.

Reliability is a test's second important characteristic and refers to its consistency. It is "the consistency of scores obtained by the same person when retested with the identical tests or with an equivalent form of a test."[13] A test's reliability is very important; if a person scored 90 on an intelligence test on a Monday and 130 when retested on Tuesday, you probably wouldn't have much faith in the test.

There are several ways to estimate a test's consistency or reliability. You could administer the same test to the same people at two different points in time, comparing their test scores at time 2 with their scores at time 1: This would be a *retest estimate*. Or you could administer a test and then administer what experts believe to be an equivalent test at a later date: This would be an *equivalent-form* estimate. The SAT exam is an example.

A test's *internal consistency* is another measure of its reliability. For example, suppose you have ten items on a test of vocational interests, which are supposed to measure in various ways the person's interest in working out of doors. You administer the test and then statistically analyze the degree to which responses to these ten items vary together. This would provide a measure of the internal reliability of the test and is referred to as an *internal comparison estimate*. Internal consistency is one reason you often find questions that apparently are repetitive on some test questionnaires.

Sources of Unreliability What could cause a test to be unreliable? Imagine for a moment that you are asked to take a test in, say, economics, and then you retake an equivalent test one month later. You find that your score changes dramatically.

There are at least four main *sources of error* that might explain this anomaly. First, the items may do a poor job of *sampling* the material; for example, test 1 focuses more on Chapters 1, 3, 5, and 7, while test 2 focuses more on Chapters 2, 4, 5, and 8. Further, one or more of the questions (items) may not do a good job of measuring what it is supposed to measure—such as your knowledge of, say, indifference curves. Second, there may be errors due to *chance response tendencies.* For example, the test itself is so boring or hard or inconsequential that you give up and start answering questions at random. (Highly personal questions on a psychological test might elicit the same response.) Third, there might be errors due to changes in the *testing conditions:* For instance, the room next month may be very noisy. And, finally, there could be *changes in the person* taking the test—in this case, you may have studied more, or forgotten more, or your mood may have changed. In any event you can see that many factors can affect a test's consistency, its *reliability.* (Reliability and validity are discussed in more detail in the appendix to this chapter.)

How to Validate a Test

Candidates for the position of data transcriber for the U.S. Census take a standardized test at the facility in Austin, Texas.

What makes a test like the Graduate Record Examination useful for college admissions directors? What makes a mechanical comprehension test useful for a manager trying to hire a machinist?

The answer to both questions is usually that people's scores on these tests have been shown to be *predictive* of how they perform. Thus, other things being equal, students who score high on the graduate admissions tests also do better in graduate school. Applicants who score higher on the mechanical comprehension test perform better as machinists.

In order for any selection test to be useful, an employer should be fairly sure that scores on the test are related in a predictable way to performance on the job. In other words, it is imperative that you *validate* the test before using it, by ensuring that test scores are a good *predictor* of some *criterion* like job performance. In other words, you must demonstrate the test's criterion validity, to use the phrase from earlier in this chapter. This *validation process* usually requires the expertise of an industrial psychologist and is coordinated by the HR department. Line management's role is to clearly describe the job and its requirements, so that the human requirements of the job and the job's performance standards are clear to the psychologist. This *validation process* consists of five steps.

Step 1. Analyze the Job Your first step is to analyze the job and write job descriptions and job specifications. Here specify the human traits and skills you believe are required for adequate job performance. For example, must an applicant be aggressive? Is shorthand required? Must the person be able to assemble small, detailed components? These requirements become your *predictors.* They are the human traits and skills you believe to be predictive of success on the job. In this first step, you also have to define what you mean by "success on the job," since it is this success for which you want predictors. The standards of success are called *criteria.* You could focus on *production-related criteria* (quantity, quality, and so on), *personnel data* (absenteeism, length of service, and so on), or *judgments* (of worker performance by persons like supervisors). For an assembler's job, predictors to be tested for might include manual dexterity and patience. Criteria that you would hope to predict with your test might include quantity produced per hour and number of rejects produced per hour.

Some employers make the mistake of carefully choosing predictors (such as manual dexterity) while virtually ignoring the question of which performance criteria are best. An illustrative study involved 212 employees of a gas utility company. In this study, the researchers found a significant relationship between the test battery that was used as a predictor and two performance criteria: supervisor ratings of performance and objective productivity indices. However, there was virtually no relationship between the same test battery and an objective quality index or employee self-ratings.[14]

Step 2. Choose Your Tests Next choose tests that you think measure the attributes (predictors) important for job success. This choice is usually based on experience, previous research, and "best guesses," and you usually won't start off with just one test. Instead you choose several tests, combining them into a *test battery* aimed at measuring a variety of possible predictors, such as aggressiveness, extroversion, and numerical ability. For the assembler's job, one test might be the Stromberg Dexterity Test illustrated in Figure 5.4. (See page 178.)

Step 3. Administer Test Next administer the selected test(s) to employees. You have two choices here. First, you can administer the tests to employees presently on the job. You then would compare their test scores with their *current* performance; this is called *concurrent validation*. Its main advantage is that data on performance are readily available. The disadvantage is that the current employees *may not be representative of new applicants* (who of course are really the ones for which you are interested in developing a screening test). Current employees have already received on-the-job training and have been screened by your existing selection techniques.[15]

Predictive validation is the more dependable way to validate a test. Here the test is administered to applicants before they are hired. Then these applicants are hired using only existing selection techniques, not the results of the new tests you are developing. After they have been on the job for some time, you measure their performance and compare it to their earlier tests. You can then determine whether their performance on the test could have been used to predict their subsequent job performance. In the case of our assembler's job, the ideal situation would be to administer the Stromberg Dexterity Test to all applicants. Then ignore the test results and hire assemblers as you usually do. Perhaps six months later, measure your new assemblers' performance (quantity produced per hour, number of rejects per hour) and compare this performance to their Stromberg test scores (see step 4).

Step 4. Relate Test Scores and Criteria The next step is to determine whether there is a significant relationship between scores (the predictor) and performance (the criterion). The usual way to do this is to determine the statistical relationship between (1) scores on the test and (2) performance through *correlation analysis,* which shows the degree of statistical relationship.

expectancy chart
A graph showing the relationship between test scores and job performance for a large group of people.

If performance on the test and on the job are correlated, you can develop an **expectancy chart**. This presents graphically the relationship between the test and job performance. To do this, split the employees into, say, five groups according to their test scores, with those scoring the highest fifth on the test, the second highest fifth, and so on. Then compute the percentage of high job performance *in each of these five test score groups* and present the data in an expectancy chart like that in Figure 5.2. This shows the likelihood of an employee's being rated a high performer if he or she scores in each of these five test score groups. Thus, a person scoring in the top fifth of the test has a 97% chance of being rated a high performer, while one scoring in the lowest fifth has only a 29% chance of being rated a high performer.[16]

Step 5. Cross-validation and Revalidation Before putting the test into use, you may want to check it by *cross-validating,* by again performing steps 3 and 4 on a new sample of employees. At a minimum, an expert should revalidate the test periodically.

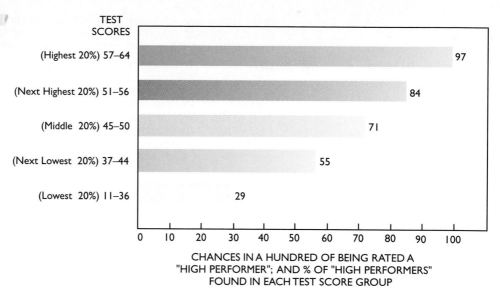

Figure 5.2
Expectancy Chart

Note: This expectancy chart shows the relation between scores made on the Minnesota Paper Form Board and rated success of junior drafts persons. Example: Those who score between 37 and 44 have a 55% chance of being rated above average and those scoring between 57 and 64 have a 97% chance.

TEST SCORES

(Highest 20%) 57–64   97
(Next Highest 20%) 51–56   84
(Middle 20%) 45–50   71
(Next Lowest 20%) 37–44   55
(Lowest 20%) 11–36   29

0 10 20 30 40 50 60 70 80 90 100

CHANCES IN A HUNDRED OF BEING RATED A
"HIGH PERFORMER"; AND % OF "HIGH PERFORMERS"
FOUND IN EACH TEST SCORE GROUP

The procedure you would use to demonstrate content validity differs from that used to demonstrate criterion validity as described in steps 1–5. Content validity tends to emphasize judgment. Here a careful job analysis is carried out to identify the work behaviors required. Then a sample of those behaviors is combined into a test that should then be content valid. A typing and shorthand test for a secretary would be an example. *The fact that the test is a comprehensive sample of actual, observable, on-the-job behaviors is what lends the test its content validity.* Criterion validity is determined through the five-step procedure previously described.

Testing Guidelines

Basic guidelines[17] for setting up a testing program include:[18]

1. *Use tests as supplements.* Do not use tests as your only selection technique; instead use them to supplement other techniques like interviews and background checks. Tests are not infallible. Even in the best of cases the test score usually accounts for only about 25% of the variation in the measure of performance. In addition, tests are often better at telling you which candidates will fail than which will succeed.

2. *Validate the tests in your organization.* Both *legal requirements* and *good testing practice* demand that the test be validated in your own organization. The fact that the same tests have been proven valid in similar organizations is *not* sufficient.

3. *Analyze all your current hiring and promotion standards.* Ask questions such as: "What proportion of minority and nonminority applicants are being rejected at each stage of the hiring process?" and "Why am I using this standard— what does it mean in terms of actual behavior on the job?" Remember that the burden of proof is always on you to prove that the predictor (such as intelligence) is related to success or failure on the job.

4. *Keep accurate records.* It is important to keep accurate records of why each applicant was rejected. For purposes of the Equal Employment Opportunity Commission, a general note such as "not sufficiently well qualified" would not be enough. As objectively as possible, state why the candidate was rejected. Remember that your reasons for rejecting the candidate may be subject to validation at a later date.

5. *Begin your validation program now.* If you don't currently use tests, or if you use tests that haven't been validated, begin your validation study now. Preferably

make this a predictive validation study: Administer the tests to applicants, hire the applicants without referring to the test scores, and at a later date correlate their test scores with their performance on the job.

6. *Use a certified psychologist.* The development, validation, and use of selection standards (including tests) generally require the assistance of a qualified psychologist. Most states require that persons who offer psychological services to the public be certified or licensed. Persons engaged in test validation often belong to the *American Psychological Association (APA)* and probably to *Division 14 (Division of Industrial and Organizational Psychology)* as well. Other qualified psychologists belong to the *Society for Industrial and Organizational Psychologists (SIOP)* but not to the APA. Most industrial and organizational psychologists hold a Ph.D. degree (the bachelor's degree is never sufficient). A potential consultant should be able to provide evidence of similar work and experience in the area of test validation. He or she should be familiar with the standards for psychological tests and the manual published by the APA. And the consultant should demonstrate familiarity with existing federal and state laws and regulations applicable to equal rights. The names of previous clients should be provided so you can verify references. Competent professionals generally will not make any claims for extraordinary results or guarantee certain, positive outcomes.

7. *Test conditions are important.* Administer your tests in areas that are reasonably private, quiet, well lighted, and ventilated, and make sure all applicants take the tests under the same test conditions. Once completed, test results should be held in the strictest confidence and be given only to individuals who have a legitimate need for the information and who also have the ability to understand and interpret the scores.

Ethical and Legal Questions in Testing

Equal Employment Opportunity Implications for Testing

We've seen that various federal and state laws bar discrimination with respect to race, color, age, religion, sex, disability, and national origin.[19] With respect to testing, these laws boil down to this: (1) You must be able to *prove* that your tests were related to success or failure on the job (validity), and (2) you must *prove* that your tests didn't unfairly discriminate against either minority or nonminority subgroups. The burden of proof rests with you; you are presumed "guilty" until proven innocent and must demonstrate the validity and selection fairness of the allegedly discriminatory item. Yet it appears that relatively few employers are validating their tests. The main reason for noncompliance is apparently that compliance can be an expensive inconvenience for the employer. For instance, you have to do a validation study, develop a good performance appraisal method, and do a thorough job analysis.

You can't avoid EEO laws by just not using tests. EEO guidelines and laws apply to any and all screening or selection devices, including interviews, applications, and references. In other words, the same burden of proving job relatedness falls on interviews and other techniques (including performance appraisals) that falls on tests. Thus, you could be asked to prove the validity and fairness of *any* screening or selection tool that has been shown to have an adverse impact on a protected group.[20] A detailed explanation of test unfairness is presented in the appendix to this chapter.

Your Alternatives Let's review where we are at this point. Assume that you've used a test and that a rejected minority candidate has demonstrated adverse impact to the satisfaction of a court. How might the person have done this? One way was to show that the selection rate for, say, the applicant's racial group was less than four-fifths that for the group with the highest selection rate. Thus, if 90% of white applicants passed the test but only 60% of blacks passed, then (since 60% is less than four-fifths of 90%) adverse impact exists.

You would then have three alternatives. One is to choose an alternative selection procedure that does not have an adverse impact. In other words, you could choose a different test or selection procedure that does not adversely impact minorities or women.[21]

The second alternative is to show that the test is valid, in other words, that it is a valid predictor of performance on the job. Ideally, you would do this by conducting your own validation study. Under certain circumstances you may also try to show the validity of the test by using information about the test's validity collected elsewhere.[22] In any event, the plaintiff would then have to prove that your explanation for using the test is inadequate.

A third alternative—in this case aimed at avoiding adverse impact rather than responding to it—is to monitor the selection test to see whether it has disparate impact. If so, you would then have to determine if the test is valid. In the absence of disparate rejection rates it's generally permissible to use selection devices that may not be valid or otherwise job related—but why would you want to?

Individual Rights of Test Takers and Test Security   Test takers have certain rights to privacy and information under the American Psychological Association's standard for educational and psychological tests.[23] They have the right to the confidentiality of the test results and the right to informed consent regarding the use of these results. Second, they have the right to expect that only people qualified to interpret the scores will have access to them or that sufficient information will accompany the scores to ensure their appropriate interpretation. Third, they have the right to expect that the test is equally fair to all test takers in the sense of being equally familiar. The tests, in other words, must be secure; no person taking the tests should have prior information concerning the questions or answers.[24]

The Issue of Privacy   In addition to the APA's standard, embedded in U.S. law are certain protections regarding an employee's rights to privacy.

At the federal level, there are few restrictions on an employer's right to disseminate information about employees either inside or outside the company. The U.S. Constitution does not expressly provide for the right to privacy, but certain U.S. Supreme Court decisions do protect individuals from intrusive governmental action in a variety of contexts.[25] For example, if you are a federal employee or (in many jurisdictions) a state or local government employee, there are limits on disclosure of personnel information to other individuals or agencies within or outside the agency.[26] Although not applicable to employees of private firms, the Federal Privacy Act illustrates the sorts of informational privacy issues legislatures are concerned about. The act (1) requires that an agency maintain only such information as is relevant and necessary to accomplish its purpose; (2) requires to the greatest extent practical that the information come directly from the individual; (3) establishes safeguards to ensure the security and confidentiality of records; and (4) gives federal employees the right to inspect personnel files and limits the disclosure of personnel information without an employee's consent.[27]

The common law of torts also provides limited protection against disclosing information about employees to people outside the company. The most well-known application here involves defamation (either libel or slander). If your employer or former employer discloses information that is false and defamatory and that causes you serious injury, you may be able to sue for defamation of character.[28]

Tests of Motor and Physical Abilities

There are many *motor abilities* you might want to measure. These include finger dexterity, manual dexterity, speed of arm movement, and reaction time. The Stromberg Dexterity Test as illustrated in Figure 5.4 is an example. It measures the speed and accuracy of simple judgment as well as the speed of finger, hand, and arm movements. Other tests include the *Crawford Small Parts Dexterity Test,* the *Minnesota Rate of Manipulation Test,* and the *Purdue Peg Board.*

Tests of *physical abilities* may also be required.[33] Physical abilities include static strength (lifting weights), dynamic strength (like pull-ups), body coordination (as in jumping rope), and stamina.[34]

Measuring Personality and Interests

A person's mental and physical abilities are seldom enough to explain his or her job performance. Other factors like the person's motivation and interpersonal skills are important too. Personality and interests inventories are sometimes used as predictors of such intangibles.

Personality tests can measure basic aspects of an applicant's personality, such as introversion, stability, and motivation. Many of these tests are *projective.*

**Figure 5.4
Minnesota Rate of
Manipulation Test
(top) and Stromberg
Dexterity Test
(bottom)**

Source: Educational Test Bureau and The Psychological Corporation.

Here an ambiguous stimulus like an ink blot or clouded picture is presented to the person taking the test. He or she is then asked to interpret or react to it. Since the pictures are ambiguous, the person's interpretation must come from within—be projected. He or she supposedly *projects* into the picture his or her own emotional attitudes about life. Thus, a security-oriented person might describe the woman in Figure 5.1 as "my mother worrying about what I'll do if I lose my job." Examples of personality tests (which are more properly called personality inventories) include the *Thematic Apperception Test,* the *Guilford-Zimmerman Temperament Survey,* and the *Minnesota Multiphasic Personality Inventory.* The Guilford-Zimmerman survey measures personality traits like emotional stability versus moodiness and friendliness versus criticalness. The Minnesota Multiphasic Personality Inventory taps traits like hypochondria and paranoia.

Personality tests—particularly the projective type—are the most difficult tests to evaluate and use. An expert must analyze the test taker's interpretations and reactions and infer from them his or her personality. The usefulness of such tests for selection then assumes you find a relationship between a measurable personality trait (like introversion) and success on the job.[35]

The difficulties notwithstanding, recent studies confirm that personality tests can help companies hire more effective workers. For example, industrial psychologists often talk in terms of the "Big Five" personality dimensions as they apply to personnel testing: extroversion, emotional stability, agreeableness, conscientiousness, and openness to experience.[36] One study focused on the extent to which these five personality dimensions predicted performance (for instance, in terms of job proficiency and training proficiency) for professionals, police officers, managers, sales workers, and skilled/semiskilled workers. Conscientiousness showed a consistent relationship with all job performance criteria for all the occupations. Extroversion was a valid predictor of performance for the two occupations that involved the most social interaction, namely managers and sales employees. Openness to experience and extroversion predicted training proficiency for all occupations.

A second study confirms the potential usefulness of personality tests in employee selection while underscoring the importance of careful job analysis. These researchers analyzed personnel testing studies and concluded that (under the right circumstances) the predictive power of a personality test can be quite high.[37] However, they also conclude that the full potential of using personality traits in personnel selection will be realized only when careful job analysis becomes the "standard practice for determining which traits are relevant to predicting performance on a given job, and when greater attention is directed to the selection of psychometrically sound and valid personality measures."[38] In summary, personality tests can be useful for helping employers predict which candidates will succeed on the job and which will not. However, your validation study must be carried out very carefully.

Interest inventories compare one's interests with those of people in various occupations. Thus, if a person takes the *Strong-Campbell Inventory,* he or she would receive a report comparing his or her interests to those of people already in occupations such as accounting, engineering, management, or medical technology.

Interest inventories have many uses. One example is in career planning, since a person will likely do better on jobs that involve activities in which he or she is interested. These tests can also be useful as selection tools. Clearly, if you can select people whose interests are roughly the same as those of successful incumbents in the jobs for which you are recruiting, it is more likely that the applicants will be successful on their new jobs.[39]

It is not just the fear of legal reprisal that can undermine a reference. Many supervisors don't want to diminish a former employee's chances for a job; others might prefer giving an incompetent employee good reviews if it will get rid of him or her. Even when checking references via the phone, therefore, you have to be careful to ask the right questions and try to judge whether the reference's answers are evasive and, if so, why.

HR managers don't seem to view reference letters as very useful. In one study, 12% replied that reference letters were "highly valuable," 43% call them "somewhat valuable," and 30% viewed them as having "little value," or (6%) "no value." Asked whether they preferred written or telephone references, 72% favored the telephone reference, since it allows a more candid assessment and provides a more interpersonal exchange. Not having a written record is also an appealing feature. In fact, reference letters ranked lowest—seventh out of seven—when rated by these human resource officers as selection tools. Ranked from top to bottom, these tools were, by the way, interview, application form, academic record, oral referral, aptitude and achievement tests, psychological tests, and finally, reference letters.[59]

Making Reference Checks More Productive   There are several things you can do to make your reference checking more productive.[60] One is to use a structured form as in Figure 5.8. The form helps ensure that you don't overlook important questions. Another suggestion is to use the references offered by the applicant as merely a source for other references who may know of the applicant's performance. Thus, you might ask each of the applicant's references, "Could you please give me the name of another person who might be familiar with the applicant's performance?" In that way, you begin getting information from references who may be more objective since they weren't referred directly by the applicant.

You might also conduct a thorough reference audit rather than just a reference check.[61] A reference audit requires contacting at least two superiors, two peers, and two subordinates from each job previously held by the candidate. You should thereby find that a reliable picture of the candidate is gradually formed. For example, you will find that the red flags raised by one or two colleagues are in fact problems that can be traced back through several previous jobs and employers. Of course, some employers do have policies that preclude employees (outside the human resources department) from providing reference information. And it is always risky to ask candidates to self-select the references. However, such audits can and probably will lead to a more accurate picture of your candidate than will the usual poking around that reference checks often involve.

Giving Employment References: Know the Law   There are also some caveats to follow when *supplying* employment references on former employees. Federal laws that affect references are the Privacy Act of 1974, the Fair Credit Reporting Act of 1970, the Family Education Rights and Privacy Act of 1974 (and Buckley Amendment of 1974), and the Freedom of Information Act of 1966. These laws give individuals in general and students (The Buckley amendment) the right to know the nature and substance of information in their credit files and files with government agencies, and (under the Privacy Act), to review records pertaining to them from any private business that contracts with a federal agency. It is therefore quite possible that your comments may be shown to the person you are describing. Also common law, and in particular the tort of defamation, applies to any information you supply. The communication is defamatory if it is false and tends to harm the reputation of another by lowering the person in the estimation of the community or by deterring other persons from associating or dealing with him or her.

Figure 5.8
Telephone or Personal Interview Form

Source: Adapted by permission of the publisher from *Book of Employment Forms,* American Management Association.

TELEPHONE OR PERSONAL INTERVIEW

☐ FORMER EMPLOYER
☐ CHARACTER REFERENCE

COMPANY _____ ADDRESS _____ PHONE _____

NAME OF PERSON
CONTACTED _____ POSITION
OR TITLE _____

1. I WISH TO VERIFY SOME FACTS GIVEN BY
   (MISS, MRS. MS.)
   MR. _____
   WHO IS APPLYING FOR EMPLOYMENT WITH OUR FIRM.
   WHAT WERE THE DATES OF HIS/HER EMPLOYMENT BY
   YOUR COMPANY?   FROM ____ 19 __ TO ____ 19 __

2. WHAT WAS THE NATURE OF HIS/HER JOB?   AT START _____

                                                AT LEAVING _____

3. HE/SHE STATES THAT HE/SHE WAS EARNING $ ____ PER ____
   WHEN HE/SHE LEFT. IS THAT CORRECT?   YES   NO $ _____

4. WHAT DID HIS/HER SUPERIORS THINK OF HIM/HER? _____

   WHAT DID HIS/HER SUBORDINATES THINK OF HIM/HER? _____

5. DID HE/SHE HAVE SUPERVISORY RESPONSIBILITY?   YES   NO _____

   (IF YES)HOW DID HE/SHE CARRY IT OUT? _____

6. HOW HARD DID HE/SHE WORK? _____

7. HOW DID HE/SHE GET ALONG WITH OTHERS? _____

8. HOW WAS HIS/HER ATTENDANCE RECORD?   PUNCTUALITY? _____

9. WHAT WERE HIS/HER REASONS FOR LEAVING? _____

10. WOULD YOU REHIRE HIM/HER? (IF NO) WHY?   YES   NO _____

11. DID HE/SHE HAVE ANY DOMESTIC, FINANCIAL OR
    PERSONAL TROUBLE WHICH INTERFERED WITH
    HIS/HER WORK?   YES   NO _____

12. DID HE/SHE DRINK OR GAMBLE TO EXCESS?   YES   NO _____

13. WHAT ARE HIS/HER STRONG POINTS? _____

14. WHAT ARE HIS/HER WEAK POINTS? _____

_____

REMARKS: _____

Suggested guidelines for defensible references are summarized in Figure 5.9. Guidelines include "Don't volunteer information," "Avoid vague statements," and "Do not answer trap questions such as 'Would you rehire this person?'" In practice many firms have a policy of not providing any information about former employees except for their dates of employment, last salary, and position titles.[62]

Being sued for defamation is increasingly a concern for employers. In one case, four employees were terminated for "gross insubordination" after disobeying a supervisor's order to review their expense account reports. In this Minnesota case (*Lewis* v. *Equitable Life Assurance*) the jury found that the employees' expense reports were actually honest. The employees argued for punitive damages under the tort of defamation. They argued that even though the employer did not publicize the defamatory matter to others, the employer should have known that the employees would have to release the (slanderous) reason for their firing when having to defend themselves to future employers. The court agreed and upheld jury awards totaling more than a million dollars to these employees. In other words, the employer may get sued if the employee is terminated for potentially defamatory reasons, even if the employer doesn't publicize the reason for the termination.[63]

Preemployment Information Services Computer data bases have made it easier to check background information about candidates. There was a time when the only source of background information was the information a candidate provided on the application form and (in some cases) what the employer could obtain through the use of private investigators. Today so-called preemployment information services use data bases to accumulate mounds of information about matters such as worker's compensation histories, credit histories, and conviction records. Employers are increasingly turning to these information services in order to make the right selection decision.

Figure 5.9
Guidelines for Defensible References

Source: Mary F. Cook, *Human Resources Director's Handbook* (Englewood Cliffs, NJ: Prentice Hall, 1984), p. 93.

1. Don't volunteer information. Respond only to specific company or institutional inquiries and requests. Before responding, telephone the inquirer to check on the validity of the request.
2. Direct all communication only to persons who have a specific interest in that information.
3. State in the message that the information you are providing is confidential and should be treated as such. Use qualifying statements such as "providing information that was requested"; "relating this information only because it was requested"; or "providing information that is to be used for professional purposes only." Sentences such as these imply that information was not presented for the purpose of hurting or damaging a person's reputation.
4. Obtain written consent from the employee or student, if possible.
5. Provide only reference data that relates and pertains to the job and job performance in question.
6. Avoid vague statements such as: "He was an average student"; "She was careless at times"; "He displayed an inability to work with others."
7. Document all released information. Use specific statements such as: "Mr. _____ received a grade of C—an average grade"; "Ms. _____ made an average of two bookkeeping errors each week"; or "This spring, four members of the work team wrote letters asking not to be placed on the shift with Mr. _____ ."
8. Clearly label all subjective statements based on personal opinions and feelings. Say "I believe . . ." whenever making a statement that is not fact.
9. When providing a negative or potentially negative statement, add the reason or reasons why, or specify the incidents that led you to this opinion.
10. Do not answer trap questions such as "Would you rehire this person?"
11. Avoid answering questions that are asked "off the record."

Yet there are two reasons to use caution with information about an applicant's criminal, credit, and worker's compensation histories.[64] First (as discussed in Chapter 2), various equal employment laws discourage or prohibit the use of such information in employee screening. For example, under the 1990 Americans with Disabilities Act (ADA), which became effective in July 1992, employers are prohibited from making preemployment inquiries into the existence, nature, or severity of a disability. As a result, a general request from an employer for information regarding a candidate's previous worker's compensation claims would likely be viewed as unlawful. Instead the employer would have to ask whether the candidate has the ability to perform a particular function on the job. Similarly, making employment decisions based on a person's arrest record would likely be viewed as unfairly discriminatory: some minorities suffer relatively high arrest rates, but an arrest does not mean that the person is guilty. On the other hand, use of conviction information for particular jobs (for instance, where security is involved) would be less problematical.

Similarly, several EEOC decisions held that employers violated Title VII by denying employment based on a poor credit rating. The EEOC held that a poor credit history should not, by itself, preclude a person from getting a job. Instead the question was whether a good credit history was required as a business necessity.

However, it's not just equal employment laws that suggest prudence in using background data: many states ban the use of such information as well. For example, Pennsylvania law provides that felony and misdemeanor convictions "may be considered by the employer only to the extent to which they relate to the applicant's suitability for employment in the position for which he has applied."[65] New York requires employers to notify an applicant before requesting a consumer report. It also requires the employer to obtain the written permission of the applicant before seeking a more extensive investigative report.[66] Under the Federal Fair Credit Reporting Act, employers that take adverse employment action based on a consumer report must follow two rules. First, the employer must advise the employee or candidate of the fact that he or she was turned down based on the consumer report and the name and address of the consumer reporting agency must be supplied. Second, the employer may not obtain a consumer report from a reporting agency under false pretenses.[67]

This being the case, even the apparently simple process of gathering background information about an applicant can develop into an explosive situation for an employer. A rejected applicant even somewhat familiar with the law could easily take an employer to court and win. Some suggestions for collecting background information thus include the following:

1. Check all applicable state laws.
2. Check beyond applicable state laws, and the impact of federal equal employment laws.
3. Remember the Federal Fair Credit Reporting Act.
4. Do not obtain information that will not be used.
5. Remember that using arrest information will be highly suspect.
6. Avoid blanket policies (such as "we hire no one with a record of worker's compensation claims").
7. Use information that is specific and job related.
8. Keep information confidential and up to date.
9. Never authorize an unreasonable investigation.[68]

hours in advance and the details of the investigation—including the date on which the cash was discovered missing and its amount.[71]

A third case underscores the importance of adhering to the Polygraph Protection Act's four standards.[72] In this case a doctor reported $200 missing from his hospital locker. The hospital questioned workers who had access to the locker room and searched their lockers. Each employee was told there might be a lie detector test and only one expressed reluctance. The hospital fired that employee based on its "strong suspicion" that he was the culprit. The employee then successfully sued the hospital under the Employee Polygraph Protection Act, showing that the employer hadn't, as required, proven that the loss was a loss to the business, since the theft from the doctor's locker didn't affect the "business of patient care." Furthermore, he showed that the hospital had failed to follow certain procedures under the act. The bottom line is that the polygraph can still be used by employers under limited conditions, but the act's four standards must be carefully followed.

The virtual elimination of the polygraph as a screening device has triggered a burgeoning market for other types of honesty testing devices; there is now a range of these from which to choose. Paper-and-pencil honesty tests are psychological tests designed to predict job applicants' proneness to dishonesty and other forms of counterproductivity.[73] Most of these tests measure attitudes regarding things like tolerance of others who steal, acceptance of rationalizations for theft, and admission of theft-related activities. Tests include the Phase II profile, the marketing rights to which were recently purchased by Wackenhut Corporation of Coral Gables, Florida, which provides security services to employers. Similar tests are published by London House, Incorporated, and Stanton Corporation.[74]

Several psychologists (including some speaking for the American Psychological Association) have expressed concerns about the proliferation of paper-and-pencil honesty tests.[75] Many of the supportive articles have been written by the test publishers themselves, they say. They also argue that additional independent peer review should be conducted before the validity of these devices is accepted.[76]

Even so, several recent studies support the validity of paper-and-pencil honesty tests. One study focused on 111 employees hired by a major retail convenience store chain to work at convenience store or gas station outlet counters.[77] "Shrinkage" was estimated to equal 3% of sales, and internal theft was believed to account for much of this. The researchers found that scores on an honesty test successfully predicted detected theft in this study, as measured by termination for theft.

Paper-and-pencil honesty testing may also help companies predict white-collar crime.[78] Subjects in one study included 329 federal prison inmates incarcerated for white-collar crime, and 344 individuals from several midwestern firms employed in white-collar positions. Three instruments were administered, including the California Psychological Inventory (a personality inventory), the Employment Inventory (a second personality inventory), and a biodata scale. The researchers concluded that " . . . there are large and measurable psychological differences between white-collar offenders and nonoffenders . . ." and that it was possible to construct a personality-based integrity test to differentiate between the two.[79]

Given all this, what can an employer do to detect dishonesty? One expert suggests the following steps:

Ask blunt questions.[80] Within the bounds of legality, you can ask very direct questions in the face-to-face interview. For example, says this expert, there is nothing wrong with asking the applicant: "Have you ever stolen anything from an employer?" Other questions to ask include: "Have you recently held jobs other than those listed on your application?" "Have you ever been fired or asked to leave a job?" "What reasons would past supervisors give if they were asked why they let you go?" "Have past employers ever disciplined you or warned you about absences or lateness?" "Is any information on your application misrepresented or falsified?"

Listen, rather than talk. Specifically, allow the applicant to do the talking so you can learn as much as possible about the person.

Ask for a credit check. Include a clause in your application form which gives you the right to conduct certain background checks on the applicant including credit checks and motor vehicle reports.

Check all references. Rigorously pursue employment and personal references.

Consider a paper-and-pencil test. Consider utilizing paper-and-pencil honesty tests and psychological tests as a part of your honesty screening program.

Test for drugs. Devise a drug testing program and give each applicant a copy of the policy.

Conduct searches. Establish a search-and-seizure policy. Give each applicant a copy of the policy and require each to return a signed copy. Basically, the policy should state that all lockers, desks, and similar property remain the property of the company and may be inspected routinely.

An Example of an Honesty Screening Program The Adolf Coors company scrapped polygraph testing of job applicants and substituted a three-step program. The steps include urinalysis, a paper-and-pencil honesty test, and a reference check. First, Coors uses an outside lab to conduct the urinalysis test. Next applicants take a Stanton Corporation paper-and-pencil survey of 83 questions on attitudes toward honesty and theft. The survey company provides Coors with a written report that categorizes applicants by levels of risk. For example, low-risk individuals are those who have never been involved in any extensive thefts, while marginal-risk applicants might be tempted to steal if they felt they wouldn't be caught. Finally, applicant references and background checks are performed by a company called Equifax Services. They involve contacting previous employers and educational institutions attended.[81]

A Caution There are several reasons to be cautious with any honesty testing program. First, as noted earlier, doubt has been expressed regarding how valid many (or most) paper-and-pencil honesty testing instruments are. Second, on purely humanitarian grounds, one could argue that a rejection (let alone an incorrect rejection) for dishonesty carries with it more stigma than does being rejected for, say, poor mechanical comprehension or even poor sociability. It's true that others may never know just why you rejected the candidate. However, the subject, having just taken and "failed" what may have been a fairly obvious "honesty test," may leave the premises feeling that his or her treatment was less than proper. Third, questions and tests in this area pose serious invasion-of-privacy issues, delving as they do into areas such as how you feel about stealing, or whether you have ever stolen anything. There are also more legal constraints to beware of. For instance, Massachusetts and Rhode Island both limit the use of paper-and-pencil honesty tests. Until more widespread evaluations are done, these tests should be used very cautiously and certainly only as supplements to other techniques like reference checking.

Graphology

The use of graphology (handwriting analysis) is based on the assumption that the writer's basic personality traits will be expressed in his or her handwriting.[82] Handwriting analysis thus has some resemblance to projective personality tests.

In graphology, the handwriting analyst studies an applicant's handwriting and signature in order to discover the person's needs, desires, and psychological makeup.[83] According to the graphologist, the writing in Figure 5.11 exemplifies "uneven pressure, poor rhythm, and uneven baselines." The variation of light and dark lines shows a "lack of control" and is "one strong indicator of the writer's inner disturbance."

While many scientists doubt the validity of handwriting analysis, some writers estimate that over 1,000 U.S. companies use handwriting analysis to assess applicants for certain strategic positions.[84] And the classified sections of international periodicals like the *Economist* still run ads from graphologists offering to aid in an employer's selection process.

Physical Examination

A medical examination is usually the next step in the selection process (although it may also take place after the new employee starts work).[85]

There are five main reasons for requiring preemployment medical exams. The exam can be used to determine that the applicant qualifies for the *physical requirements* of the position and to discover any *medical limitations* that should be taken into account in placing the applicant. The exam will also establish a *record and baseline* of the applicant's health for the purpose of future insurance or compensation claims. The examination can, by identifying health problems, also reduce *absenteeism and accidents* and, of course, detect *communicable diseases* that may be unknown to the applicant. The exam is usually performed by the employer's medical department in the largest organizations. Smaller employers retain the services of consulting physicians to perform such exams, which are almost always paid for by the employer. In any case remember that under the Americans with Disabilities Act, a person with a disability can't be rejected for the job if he or she is otherwise qualified and if the person could perform the job functions with reasonable accommodation. Under the ADA, a medical exam is permitted during the period between the job offer and commencement of work only if such exams are standard practice for all applications for that job category.[86]

Drug Screening

Drug abuse is a serious problem at work. Counselors at the Cocaine National Help Line polled callers of the 800-Cocaine hot line and found that 75% admitted to occasional cocaine use at work, 69% said that they regularly worked under the influence of a drug, and 25% recorded daily use at work. A study of long-distance

Figure 5.11
Handwriting Exhibit Used by Graphologist

Source: Reproduced with permission from Kathryn Sackhein, *Handwriting Analysis and the Employee Selection Process* (New York: Quorum Books, 1990), p. 45.

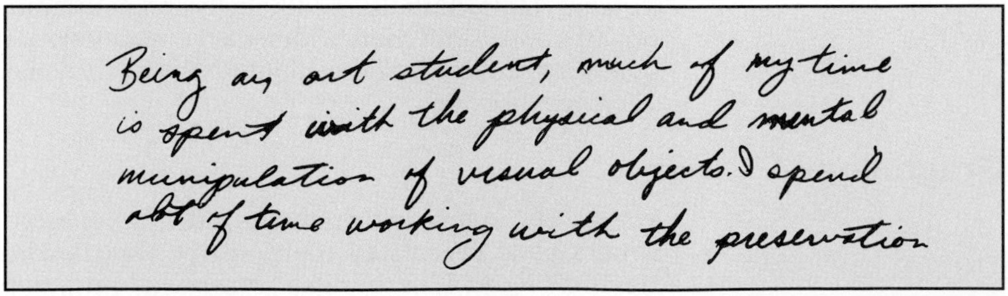

truck drivers found that over 62% reported using drugs at least occasionally.[87] The U.S. Chamber of Commerce estimates that employee drug and alcohol use costs U.S. employers over $60 billion each year in reduced productivity, increased accidents, increased sick benefits, and higher worker's compensation claims.[88]

More employers therefore conduct drug screenings. The most common practice is to test new applicants just before they are formally hired. Many firms also test current employees when there is a reason to believe the employee has been using drugs after a work accident, in the presence of obvious behavioral symptoms, or in the face of chronic lateness or high absenteeism. Some firms routinely administer drug tests on a random basis or periodic basis, while others require drug tests when an employee is transferred or promoted to a new position.[89]

Virtually all (96%) of employers that conduct such tests use urine sampling.[90] The preferred initial drug testing method is the immunoassay test. However, this test cannot differentiate between legal and illegal substances in the same chemical family. For example, popular over-the-counter pain killers like Advil and Nuprin can produce positive results for marijuana. Many firms therefore conduct the more expensive thin-layer chromotography method test to validate a positive immunoassay test. The highly personal nature of urine analysis has prompted an increasing number of employers to turn to another method, hair follicle testing. The method is called radioimmunoassay of hair (RIAH). It requires a small sample of hair, which is analyzed to detect prior ingestion of illicit drugs.[91]

Unfortunately, drug testing in general doesn't always correlate very closely with actual impairment levels.[92] While breathalizers and blood tests for alcohol like those given at the roadside to inebriated drivers do correlate closely with impairment levels, urine and blood tests for other drugs only indicate whether the drug residues are present: They cannot measure impairment or, for that matter, habituation or addiction.[93] Drug testing, therefore, raises several issues. Without strong evidence linking blood or urine drug levels to impairment, some argue that it is not justifiable on the grounds of boosting workplace safety.[94] Many argue that drug testing violates citizens' rights to privacy and due process and places employers in a position of considerable power. Many feel that the testing procedures themselves are degrading and intrusive. Others argue that one's use of drugs during leisure hours might be identified through workplace drug testing but have little or no relevance to the job itself.[95]

Drug testing also raises legal issues.[96] As one attorney has written, "It is not uncommon for employees to claim that drug tests violate their rights to privacy under common law or, in some states, a state statutory or constitutional provision."[97] Since it is less intrusive than urinalysis, hair follicle testing may seem a relatively safe procedure in such cases. Yet hair follicle testing can actually produce even more extensive personal information than urinalysis. For example, a three-inch hair segment will record six months of drug use. Furthermore, under certain conditions an employer is permitted to reveal private employee information including medical information such as drug test results. However, should drug testing information be promulgated recklessly, or in an unnecessary, unreasonable manner, the employer could be slapped with a suit for defamation.

Several federal laws have direct relevance for workplace drug testing. For example, under the Americans with Disabilities Act, a former drug user (one who no longer uses illegal drugs and successfully completed or is participating in a rehabilitation program) would probably be considered a qualified applicant with a disability.[98] Under the Drug Free Workplace Act of 1988, federal contractors must maintain a workplace free from illegal drugs. While this does not require contractors to conduct drug testing or rehabilitate their affected employees, many do. Effective January 1, 1995, new U.S. Department of Transportation workplace regulations went into effect. Firms with over 50 eligible employees in transportation industries must now conduct alcohol testing on workers with sensitive or safety-related jobs. These include mass transit workers, air traffic controllers, train crews, and school bus drivers.[99] Other laws, including the Federal Rehabilitation Act of 1973 and various state laws, give protection to rehabilitating drug users or to those who have a physical or mental addiction.[100]

What should you do when a job candidate tests positive? Most companies will not hire such candidates, and a few will immediately fire current employees whose tests results are positive.[101] For example, 120 of the 123 companies responding to the question, "If test results are positive, what action do you take?" indicated that applicants testing positive are not hired. Current employees have more legal recourse if dismissed and must therefore be told the reason for their dismissal if they are dismissed for a positive drug test.[102]

The Usefulness of Testing and Selection Devices

Just how useful is it for a firm to utilize testing and selection devices like those described previously? The evidence suggests that a well-designed program can improve performance and a firm's bottom line.

First, there is considerable anecdotal evidence. A typical selection program was implemented at Franciscan Health System of Dayton.[103] This firm, which operates two skilled-nursing care facilities and one acute care facility in Dayton, Ohio, faced several problems including turnover of 146% per year. This dramatic turnover, mostly occurring during the first six to eight months of employment, was in turn adversely impacting the company's productivity and quality of care.

Working with a consultant, the company devised a nursing assistant test battery. This consisted of three tests: an employment inventory aimed at identifying people who show conscientious work behaviors; a personality survey aimed at identifying candidates who are more people oriented and more likely to interact positively with others; and a job preferences inventory that looks for a match between actual job conditions and people's preferences for those job conditions.

The company reports that its testing program has been very successful. Turnover rates dropped to 71% annually one year after instituting the test battery, and to 51% within two years of its implementation. In total the company reports saving more than $300,000 annually due to reduced turnover and higher overall employee productivity among nursing assistants.[104]

Similarly, a research study found a significant positive relationship between organizations' use of five staffing practices and both annual profit and profit growth across all industries.[105] A random sample of 1,000 U.S. companies with 200 or more employees was drawn from *Dun's Business Rankings*. Questionnaires were mailed to the heads of the HR departments of the 1,000 firms, and 201 completed questionnaires were returned. Respondents were asked to indicate whether or not their firms used one or more of the following staffing practices: (1) follow-up studies of recruiting sources; (2) validation studies on the tests used in selection; (3) structured, standardized interviews; (4) intelligence tests for selection; and (5) weighted application blanks. As the researchers concluded, "Our finding of a positive relationship between the use of effective staffing practices and organizational profitability is encouraging, and may constitute some initial evidence of the ability of these practices to influence outcomes at the organizational level of analysis."[106]

The selection program's effectiveness of course depends on the validity of its components. Table 5.1 summarizes the results of one study of the validity of various selection devices. Tests with high face validity, such as tests of actual

TABLE 5.1 Validity of Various Selection Devices	
PREDICTOR	**VALIDITY**
Cognitive Ability and Special Aptitude	Moderate
Personality	Low
Interest	Low
Physical Ability	Moderate–High
Biographical Information	Moderate
Interviews	Low
Work Samples	High
Seniority	Low
Peer Evaluations	High
Reference Checks	Low
Academic Performance	Low
Self-Assessments	Moderate
Assessment Centers	High

Source: Neal Schmitt and Raymond Noe, "Personal Selection and Equal Employment Opportunity," in *International Review of Industrial and Organizational Psychology*, eds. Cary L. Cooper and Ivan T. Robertson. Copyright 1986 by John Wiley & Sons, Ltd. Reprinted by permission.

performance—work samples, peer evaluations, and assessment centers—rate highest. Indirect evaluations, such as psychological tests or academic performance, rate lower.

Tests with high face validity may also be more acceptable to job candidates. In one study the researchers found strong support for the relationship between face validity perceptions and organizational attractiveness.[107] In other words, candidates exposed to tests with higher face validity were more apt to view the employer as offering a more attractive place in which to work, while employers with selection procedures with low perceived face validity were more likely viewed by applicants as unfair and, hence, more likely to be targets for complaints and legal challenges.

Complying with the Immigration Law

Under the Immigration Reform and Control Act of 1986, employees hired in the United States have to prove they are eligible to be employed in the United States. A person does not have to be a U.S. citizen to be employed under this act. However, employers should ask a person who is about to be hired whether he or she is a U.S. citizen or an alien lawfully authorized to work in the United States. To comply with this law, the employers should follow the following procedures:[108]

1. Hire only citizens and aliens lawfully authorized to work in the United States.
2. Continue to advise all new job applicants of your policy to such effect.
3. Require all new employees to complete and sign the verification form designated by the Immigration and Naturalization Service (INS) to certify that they are eligible for employment.
4. Examine documentation presented by new employees, record information about the documents on the verification form, and sign the form.
5. Retain the form for three years or for one year past the employment of the individual, whichever is longer.
6. If requested, present the form for inspection by INS or Department of Labor Officers. No reporting is required.

There are two basic ways prospective employees can show their eligibility for employment. One is to show a document such as a U.S. passport or alien registration card with photograph that proves both the person's identity and employment eligibility. However, many prospective employees won't have either of these documents. Therefore, the other way to verify employment eligibility is to see a document that proves the person's identity, along with a document showing the person's employment eligibility, such as a work permit.

Employers cannot and should not use the so-called I-9 Employment Eligibility Verification form to discriminate in any way based on race or country of national origin. For example, the requirement to verify eligibility does not provide any basis to reject an applicant just because he or she is a foreigner, or not a U.S. citizen, or an alien residing in the United States, as long as that person can prove his or her identity and employment eligibility.

Small Business Applications

Testing

Just because a company is small doesn't mean it shouldn't engage in personnel testing. Quite the opposite: Hiring one or two mistakes may not be a big problem for a very large firm, but it could cause chaos in a small operation.

Although used by large firms in personnel testing, a number of tests are so easy to administer they are particularly good for smaller firms. One is the Wonderlic Personnel Test. This easy-to-use test measures general mental ability. In the form of a four-page booklet, it takes less than 15 minutes to administer. You first read the instructions and then time the candidate as he or she works through the 50 problems on the two inside sheets. The person's test can then be scored by totaling the number of correct answers. You compare the person's score to the minimum scores recommended for various occupations (Figure 5.12) to determine whether the person achieved the minimally acceptable score for the type of job in question.

A test like this can be useful for helping to identify people who are not up to the task of doing the job. However, you have to be careful not to misuse it. In the past, for instance, unnecessarily high cutoff scores were required by some employers for some jobs, a tactic which in effect unfairly discriminated against the members of certain minority groups. Similarly, it would probably not be either fair or wise to choose between two candidates who both exceeded the minimum score for a job by choosing the one with the higher score. Remember also that people of lower ability but higher motivation will often outperform those with higher ability but less motivation. Therefore, tests like the Wonderlic are only useful as supplements to a comprehensive screening program. The Wonderlic is available to employers, business owners, and human resource directors with or without previous training in personnel testing.[109]

The Predictive Index is another example of a test that is used by large companies but is equally valuable for small ones because of its ease of administration and interpretation. The index measures personality traits, drives, and behaviors that are work related—in particular, dominance (ranging from submissive to arrogant), extroversion (ranging from withdrawn to gregarious), patience (ranging from volatile to lethargic), and blame avoidance (ranging from sloppy to perfectionist). The Predictive Index test is a two-sided sheet on which candidates or current employees check off the words that best describe them (such as "helpful" or "persistent"). The test is then easily scored at your office with the use of a scoring template.

The Predictive Index provides valuable information about the candidate. For example, for a job that you know involves painstaking attention to details, you'd want to think twice about a candidate who rates toward the careless end of the range. For an exceedingly boring job, you'd no doubt lean toward the more patient candidates. Each candidate taking the Predictive Index will probably have his or her own unique pattern of responses. However, the Predictive Index program includes 15 standard patterns that are typical of many of the patterns you will see. For example, there is the "social interest" pattern, representing a person who is generally unselfish, congenial, persuasive, patient, and fairly unassuming. This is a person who'd be good with people and a good personnel interviewer, for instance.

Computerized testing programs like those described earlier in this chapter can be especially useful for small employers. For example, when hiring office help smaller employers typically depend on informal tests of typing and filing. A better way to proceed is to use a program like the Minnesota Clerical Assessment Battery published by Assessment Systems Corp. This program runs on a PC. It includes a typing test, proofreading test, filing test, business vocabulary test, business math test, and clerical knowledge test. It is therefore useful for evaluating the knowledge and skills of various office positions, including secretary, clerk-typist, bookkeeper, and filing clerk. Because it is computerized, administration and scoring are simplified and each test can be adapted to the particular position being applied for.[110]

Reference Checking Policies

The small business owner needs to be particularly careful about checking references and offering references on former employees. Checking references is important because, as noted earlier, while one or two hiring mistakes may not be disastrous for a very large firm, it could cause chaos in a small one. In fact, the most common employer mistake that leads to liability for negligent hiring is inadequately investigating an applicant's background.[111] Furthermore, the more frequently employers check references, the less likely they experience problems of absenteeism, tardiness, and poor work quality.[112] Therefore, it's important for small business owners to check backgrounds carefully.

It would also seem that small business owners should be more careful before volunteering reference information on former employees. As noted earlier in this chapter, suits claiming defamation are a growing employment menace; in fact, according to one survey published in the late 1980s, one-third of all slander and libel cases were brought by former employees against employers for statements made to prospective employers.[113] The more astonishing statistic is that the ex-employee-plaintiffs won in 77% of the cases, with average damages amounting to $166,094.[114]

What's particularly disturbing about findings like these is that small business owners seem to be more willing than large ones to volunteer information about former employees. In one survey, for instance, 90% of small businesses were "very" willing to offer such reference information, compared with only 20% of larger firms. Small firms were also relatively more willing than large firms to share information about employee arrests. (Remember that employment inquiries about an applicant's arrest record are illegal under Title VII of the Civil Rights Act, since the practice unfairly and adversely affects certain minority groups.)[115]

In any event, the evidence suggests that small business owners are much less cautious about the information they provide about former employees. Perhaps this reflects the absence of specialized HR staff. Whatever the cause, small business owners would do well to ensure that:

All employment references come from one person in the firm who is knowledgeable about the legal risks involving defamation.

Reference information is generally limited to the ex-employee's years of employment, wage or salary, job title, and superior at the time of termination.

References are based on facts and never on hearsay.

References are only provided based upon a signed and written request from an employer and a written request and release from liability from the former employee.

Verbal references are avoided.[116]◆

Figure 5.12
Minimum Scores on Wonderlic Personnel Test for Various Occupations

Source: Wonderlic Personnel Test Manual (Northfield, IL: E.F. Wonderlic & Associates, Inc., 1983), p. 6.

Position	No. of Questions Answered Correctly in 12 minutes
Administrator	30
Engineer	29
Accountant	28
Programmer	28
Supervisor/Manager	27
Management, Trainee	27
Field Repr. (Sales)	26
Salesman	26
Secretary	25
Accounting Clerk	25
Writer, News, etc.	25
Stenographer	24
Cashier	24
Bookkeeper	24
Foreman	24
Draftsman	23
Receptionist	23
Office, General	23
Lineman, Utility	22
Teller	22
Typist	21
Clerical	21
Key Punch Operator	20
Police, Patrolman	20
Skilled Trades	20
File Clerk	19
Maintenance	18
Telephone Operator	18
General Laborer	17
Factory, General	17
Labor, Skilled	17
Labor, Unskilled	16
Nurses Aide	15
Custodian	8

See the Tables presented in this Manual, "Test Scores by Position Applied For" and "Minimum Occupational Scores for The Wonderlic Personnel Test," for additional data on established scores.

Chapter Review

Summary

1. In this chapter we discussed several techniques for screening and selecting job candidates; the first was testing.

2. Test validity answers the question, "What does this test measure?" We discussed criterion validity and content validity. Criterion validity means demonstrating that those who do well on the test do well on the job; content validity is demonstrated by showing that the test constitutes a fair sample of the content of the job.

3. As used by psychologists, the term *reliability* always means consistency. One way to measure reliability is to administer the same (or equivalent) tests to the same people at two different points in time. Or you could focus on internal consistency, comparing the responses to roughly equivalent items on the same test.

4. There are many types of personnel tests in use, including intelligence tests, tests of physical skills, tests of achievement, aptitude tests, interest inventories, and personality tests.

5. For a selection test to be useful, scores should be predictably related to performance on the job; you must *validate* the test. This requires five steps: (a) analyze the job, (b) choose your tests, (c) administer the test, (d) relate test scores and criteria, and (e) cross-validate and revalidate the test.

6. Under equal rights legislation, an employer may have to be able to prove that his or her tests are predictive of success or failure on the job. This usually requires a predictive validation study, although other means of validation are often acceptable.

7. Some basic testing guidelines include (a) use tests as supplement to, (b) validate the tests for appropriate jobs, (c) analyze all current hiring and promotion standards, (d) beware of certain tests, (e) use a certified psychologist, and (f) maintain good test conditions.

8. The work sampling selection technique is based on "the assumption that the best indicator of future performance is past performance." Here you use the applicant's actual performance on the same (or very similar) job to predict his or her future job performance. The steps are (a) analyze applicant's previous work experience, (b) have experts list component tasks for job openings, (c) select crucial tasks as work sample measures, (d) break down these tasks into steps, (e) test the applicant, and (f) relate the applicant's work sample score to his or her performance on the job.

9. Management assessment centers are a third screening device and expose applicants to a series of real-life exercises. Performance is observed and assessed by experts, who then check their assessments by observing the participants when they are back at their jobs. Examples of "real-life" exercises include a simulated business game, an in-basket exercise, and group discussions.

10. Even though most people prefer not to give bad references, most companies still carry out some sort of reference check on their candidates. These can be useful in raising red flags, and structured questionnaires can improve the usefulness of the responses you receive.

11. Other selection tools we discussed include the polygraph, honesty tests, graphology, and the physical examination.

Key Terms

test validity	reliability	work sampling technique
criterion validity	expectancy chart	management assessment
content validity	work samples	centers

Discussion Questions and Exercises

1. Explain what is meant by reliability and validity. What is the difference between them? In what respects are they similar?

2. Explain how you would go about validating a test. How can this information be useful to a manager?

3. Write a short essay discussing some of the ethical and legal considerations in testing.

4. Explain why you think a certified psychologist who is specially trained in test construction should (or should not) always be used by a company developing a personnel test battery.

5. Explain how you would use work sampling for employee selection.

6. Working individually or in groups, develop a test for the Supervisor of Programming Operations for which a job description was presented in Chapter 3.

7. Working individually or in groups, contact the publisher of a standardized test such as the Scholastic Assessment Test and obtain from them written information regarding the test's validity and reliability. Present a short report in class discussing what the test is supposed to measure and the degree to which you think the test does what it is supposed to do, based on the reported validity and reliability scores.

8. Give some examples of how interest inventories could be used to improve employee selection. In doing so, suggest several examples of occupational interests that you believe might predict success in various occupations including college professor, accountant, and computer programmer.

9. Why is it important to conduct pre-employment background investigations? How would you go about doing so?

10. Explain how you would get around the problem of former employers being unwilling to give bad references on their former employees.

Application Exercises

RUNNING CASE: Carter Cleaning Company
Honesty Testing

Jennifer and her father have what the latter describes as an easy but hard job when it comes to screening job applicants. It is easy because for two important jobs—the people who actually do the pressing and those who do the cleaning–spotting—the applicants are easily screened with about 20 minutes of on-the-job testing. As with typists, as Jennifer points out, "applicants either know how to press clothes fast enough or how to use cleaning chemicals and machines, or they don't and we find out very quickly by just trying them out on the job."

On the other hand, applicant screening for the stores can also be frustratingly hard because of the nature of qualities that Jennifer would like to screen for. Two of the most critical problems facing her company are employee turnover and employee honesty. As mentioned previously, Jennifer and her father sorely need to implement practices that will reduce the rate of employee turnover. If there is a way to do this through employee testing and screening techniques, Jennifer would like to know about it because of the management time and money that are now being wasted by the never-ending need to recruit and hire new employees. Of even greater concern to Jennifer and her father is the need to institute new practices to screen out those employees who may be predisposed to steal from the company.

Employee theft is an enormous problem for the Carter Cleaning Centers, and one that is not just limited to employees who handle the cash. For example, the cleaner–spotter and/or the presser often open the store themselves without a manager present to get the day's work started, and it is not unusual to have one or more of these people steal supplies or "run a route." Running a route means that an employee canvasses his or her neighborhood to pick up people's clothes for cleaning and then secretly cleans and presses them in the Carter store, using the company's supplies, gas, and power. It would also not be unusual for an unsupervised person (or his or her supervisor, for that matter) to accept a one-hour rush order for cleaning or laundering, quickly clean and press the item, and return it to the customer for payment without making out a proper ticket for the item or posting the sale. The money, of course, goes into the person's pocket instead of into the cash register.

The more serious problem concerns the store manager and the counter workers who actually have to handle the cash. According to Jack Carter, "you would not believe the creativity employees use to get around the management controls we set up to cut down on employee theft." As one extreme example of this felonious creativity, Jack tells the following story: "To cut down on the amount of money my employees were stealing, I had a small sign painted and placed in front of all our cash registers. The sign said: "Your entire order free if we don't give you a cash register receipt when you pay. Call 962-0734." It was my intention with this sign to force all our cash–handling employees to place their receipts into the cash register where they would be recorded for my accountants. After all, if all the cash that comes in is recorded in the cash register, then we should have a much better handle on stealing in our stores,

right? Well, one of our managers found a diabolical way around this. I came into the store one night and noticed that the cash register that this particular manager was using just didn't look right although the sign was dutifully placed in front of it. It turned out that every afternoon at about 5:00 p.m. when the other employees left, this character would pull his own cash register out of a box that he hid underneath all our supplies. Customers coming in would notice the sign and of course the fact that he was meticulous in ringing up every sale. But unknown to them and to us, for about five months the sales that came in for about an hour every day went into his cash register, not mine. It took us that long to figure out where our cash for that store was going."

Questions

1. What would be the advantages and disadvantages to Jennifer's company of routinely administering honesty tests to all its employees?

2. Specifically, what other screening techniques could the company use to screen out theft-prone employees, and how exactly could these be used?

3. How should her company terminate employees caught stealing and what kind of procedure should be set up for handling reference calls about these employees when they go to other companies looking for jobs?

CASE INCIDENT: The Tough Screener

Everyone who knows Mark Rosen knows he is a very tough owner when it comes to screening applicants for jobs in his firm. His company, located in a large northeastern city, provides financial planning advice to wealthy clients and, related to that, sells insurance and sets up pension plans for individuals and businesses. His firm's clients range from professionals such as doctors and lawyers to business owners, who are fairly sophisticated in financial matters and very busy people. They expect accurate advice provided in a clear and expeditious manner. It is safe to say that Rosen's firm can be no better than its financial advisors.

Rosen has always been described as somewhat autocratic. The need to be very selective in whom he hires has led him to be extraordinarily careful about how he screens his job applicants. Some of his methods are probably beyond reproach. For example, he requires every applicant to provide

a list of names and phone numbers for at least five people the applicant worked with at each previous employer to be used as references. The resulting reference check is time-consuming but effective.

On the other hand, given recent legislation including the Civil Rights Act of 1991 and the Americans With Disabilities Act, some of his other "tough screening" methods could be problematical. Rosen requires that all applicants take a purported honesty test, which he found in the catalog of an office supply store. He also believes it is extremely important to check every viable applicant's credit history and worker's compensation history in order to screen out what he refers to as "potential undesirables." Unknown to his applicants, he runs a credit check on each of them and also retains the services of a firm that checks worker's compensation and driving violation histories.

Questions

1. What specific legal problems do you think Rosen can run into as a result of his firm's current screening methods? What steps would you suggest he take to eliminate these problems?

2. Given what you know about Rosen's business, write a two-page proposal describing an employee testing and selection program that you would recommend for his firm. Say a few words about the sorts of tests, if any, you would recommend and the application blank questions you would ask, as well as other methods including drug screening and reference checking.

 Human Resource Management Simulation

Employee selection is covered in the simulation with incident (D). You will be asked to choose one of four finalists for a supervisor's position. This is a hard decision because of the vast differences in education and experience of the candidates and because an element of affirmative action is also involved. Is it better to select the "perfect" candidate in terms of technical expertise, a candidate with better all-around education, or a candidate with more supervisory experience?

Video Case

Integrity Testing

How would like to take an employment selection test that asked questions about whether you love your father and whether you wish you were the gender you're not. While it may be surprising, those are apparently some of the selection questions asked of applicants by at least one big retailer, according to this video. As the video explains, more and more employers are using "integrity testing" to assess applicants' honesty, emotional stability, and religious convictions, and many people, of course, find this offensive.

Questions

1. Do you think tests like this may be valid predictors of success on some jobs? Why or why not?

2. Do you think it matters whether these tests are valid predictors? In other words, even if they are valid, should these tests be used? Why or why not?

3. If you wouldn't use such tests to try to measure integrity, how (if at all) would you assess an applicant's honesty, especially for a job (like cashier) that depends heavily on the employee's trustworthiness?

Source: ABC News, *Legalities of Integrity Testing,* "World News Tonight," September, 25, 1990.

Take It to the Net

We invite you to visit the Dessler page on the Prentice Hall Web site at:

http://www.prenhall.com/~dessler

for the monthly Dessler update and for this chapter's World Wide Web exercise.

Figure 5.14
Scatter Plot Showing Unrelated Criterion Scores and Predictor Scores.

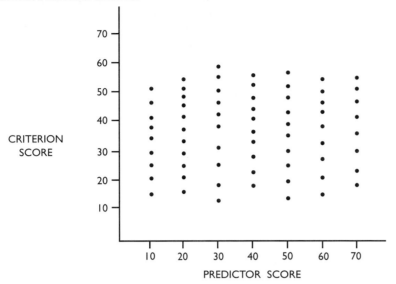

While inspection of the scatter plot provides an idea of the existence of a relationship between the predictor and criterion scores, the degree of the relationship is more precisely determined by the Pearson product moment correlation or the validity coefficient as it is called in the personnel selection context. In this example both predictor and criterion scores are assumed to be measured on interval scales. For other types of measurement in which scales are categorized, for example, when the criterion is simply a judgment that the employee meets a standard or does not meet the standard, (that is, a two-point scale), other kinds of validity coefficients such as phi or biserial may be computed.

The validity coefficient provides two kinds of important information. First, it indicates the *direction* of the relationship as positive or negative. A positive relationship, as in Figure 5.13, shows that as the predictor score increases so does the criterion score; a negative relationship exists when an increase in the predictor score is associated with a decrease in criterion score. Second, the size of the validity coefficient indicates the *degree* of relationship between predictor and criterion. Because it is a correlation, a validity coefficient may range from −1 through 0 to +1. The closer to +1 or −1 the stronger is the relationship. The validity coefficient is tested for its statistical significance to determine if its value is high enough to be considered different from zero and not just the result of a chance occurrence. If the validity coefficient is not statistically significant, the predictor should not be considered as valid for the criterion. In Figure 5.13 the validity coefficient is 0.40 for a sample of 50 employees. The statistical test for this correlation is given by the following formula:

$$t = \frac{r\sqrt{n-2}}{\sqrt{1-r^2}}$$

where r is the validity coefficient and n is the sample size from which it was computed. For this example, the conclusion is that a correlation of 0.40 has less than five chances in 100 of occurring by chance and, therefore, there probably is a true relation between the predictor score and the criterion score.

Appendix 5.1

Special Topics in Testing

Reliability

As discussed in the text, reliability is a characteristic of a test or of any measurement that describes its consistency. If the test or measure is free of random errors, then it will be consistent and reliable. For example, suppose we have a test that is a measure of mechanical aptitude and it is to be used to assess job applicants as part of a selection procedure. In measurement theory each individual is considered to possess a certain amount of mechanical aptitude, and this amount is a conceptual (theoretical) *true score* for that person. The test score for that person will include not only the true score, but also any other aspects of the testing situation that may cause the obtained score to vary from the true score. These other aspects are considered to be random and they therefore introduce an element of uncertainty as to what the true score is. In other words, we say the obtained score, X, is composed of two parts: (1) a true score, t, (2) a random error score, e, or $X = t + e$. Examples of sources of error that contribute to e include how the examinee felt at the time the test was taken (bad day/good day); variables in the environment such as noise, temperature, ventilation, lighting, and so on; and procedures for administering the test such as unclear instructions or improper timing. These and many other factors will in general cause the obtained score, X, to vary on repeated measurements of X for the same person even though the true score, t, does not change. From this it follows that the degree of agreement between X and t is an index of the reduction of random errors that affects the measurement. The correlation coefficient, rxt, which may assume any value from 0 to 1.00, is commonly used as a measure of reliability, where 0 means the scores on X are simply random numbers and 1.00 means the scores on X are free of random errors. It can be shown that the reliability coefficient, that is, the correlation between t and X, is equal to the percentage of the total variance in test scores that is true score variance, or $r_{xt} = \dfrac{\sigma_t^2}{\sigma_x^2}$.

Even though the true scores are not directly observable, the reliability coefficient can be estimated from the observed X scores by the methods presented on pages 170–171. Essentially each of the methods requires at least two measures from the same person on the same test. The correlation between the two measures yields an estimate of the test's reliability. It is important to note that the method used to estimate the reliability determines what sources of variance are treated as random error. For example, if the test is administered as equivalent forms (p. 170) in a single administration, sources of random error associated with the environment (temperature, noise, and so forth), the persons, and the passage of time (such as learning) are minimized if not eliminated. But at the same time, a *source* of error variance is introduced—for example, the difference in the item content or questions between the equivalent forms is treated as error.

The reliability coefficient, besides showing how consistent or dependable the obtained scores are, has another important application in that it can be used to estimate the amount of error contained in an observed score. A quantity, the standard error of measurement (SEM), can be computed by the following formula: SEM $= S_x = \sqrt{1 - r_{xx}}$ where S_x is the standard deviation of test scores in a group of testees and r_{xx} is the computed reliability coefficient (note: r_{xx} is an estimate of r_{xt}).

An obtained score plus or minus the SEM or a multiple of it can be used to determine a range of true scores for an individual. For example, in a group of testees, if the standard deviation of obtained test scores was 10 and the reliability of the test was 0.80, the SEM = $10\sqrt{1 - 0.80} = 4.47$. The true score for an individual who scores 35 is expected to lie between $X \pm 1.96$ SEM or in the range $26 - 44$ with 95% confidence. The computation assumes that true scores are normally distributed.

Validity

To express the degree of accuracy for a test, the most frequently used method is to compute the validity coefficient of the test for a criterion of interest. The validity coefficient is the correlation between the scores on the test (predictor) and the scores on the criterion for a group of employees. In a predictive validation method, over a period of time applicants are given the test and hired based on considerations other than the test scores obtained. These might be interviews, information on application blanks, reference checks, and even other tests. At a later time, for those applicants hired, criterion measures are obtained and the correlation between the test scores and the criterion is computed.

The first step in computing the validity coefficient is to display the predictor and criterion measures for each employee in a scatter plot as shown in Figure 5.13. Each point represents the intersection of a predictor score and criterion score for one individual. The circled point shows a person who scored 10 on the predictor at the time of application and 20 on the criterion when job performance was assessed by a supervisor. In this scatter plot it appears that *on average* those who scored higher on the predictor also scored higher on the criterion and vice versa. Note that for each predictor score there is a range of criterion scores. Compare Figure 5.13 to Figure 5.14 in which there does not appear to be any correspondence between predictor and criterion scores. Based on Figure 5.14 we would say that the *average* criterion score is the same for any predictor score, whether it is high or low.

Figure 5.13
Scatter Plot Showing Related Criterion and Predictor Scores.

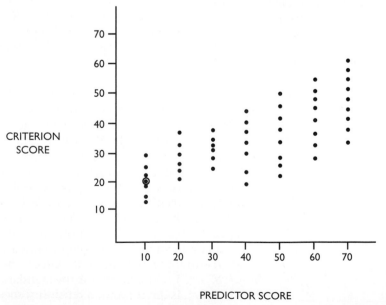

CRITERION SCORE

PREDICTOR SCORE

Aspects of the Quest for Validity

Unfortunately, things are not always so simple as they appear, and that is certainly the case when it comes to the matter of validating tests. The five-step process laid out earlier is a simple and practical one. However, you should also be aware of and consider certain matters that may complicate your quest to arrive at conclusions regarding the validity of the tests you might want to use.

First, there is the matter of which criterion to use. In brief, the so-called "criterion problem" revolves around " . . . whether different methods of measuring job performance, such as supervisor ratings, production output, and work samples, result in different validity results for the same test."[119] Basically, the problem here is that there are differences in the correlation coefficient when using different criteria. In other words, the same test could have one correlation coefficient when relating scores on a test to one criterion (perhaps using supervisor ratings), and a quite different coefficient when relating scores on a test to a second or other criteria (perhaps using production output). This obviously demands that care be taken in the choice of criteria. Consideration must also be given to analyzing the correlation between predictor and each criterion with the aim of determining why discrepancies may exist.

The second problem has been described in terms of disenchantment with the usual validity coefficient. This refers to the fact that in many cases basing a test's validity on a single correlation coefficient between predictor and criterion may be flawed for at least two reasons.[120] One is a "growing awareness that a single bivariate (two-variable) correlation is virtually uninterpretable."[121] For example, you know a correlation coefficient alone doesn't show cause and effect: Thus, to use an overworked example, a correlation between smoking and cancer (the tobacco industry would contend) doesn't necessarily prove that smoking leads to cancer; it may simply reflect that fact that other, unmeasured factors (like emotional stress) lead people to both smoke and get cancer. Thus, some psychologists question how much importance can be given to a single correlation coefficient—in this case, a validity coefficient that correlates test scores (predictor) and performance (criterion).

The other reason for disenchantment with the usual validity coefficient is the possible unreliability of the criterion itself. Specifically, a correlation (validity) coefficient may be deemed questionable because of an unreliable criterion (for instance, haphazard performance appraisal) or the fact that other criteria should have been used, or because of other related problems. (These problems are studied today under the topics of meta-analysis and validity generalization.) For example, the question can be raised as to how valid a validity coefficient is over the entire range of test scores or criterion. A test may do a good job of predicting performance for very high performers and so thereby produce a high-validity coefficient and an apparently valid test. But the point has been made that this apparent validity may not be generalizable to the lower range of test scores. For example, it may turn out that for some reason test scores correlate very highly for a certain range of performance (or for a certain range of test scores), but not nearly as well in other parts of the range.[122] In any event, the bottom line is that someone embarking on a validity study has to take more care than might be immediately apparent.[123]

Notes

1. For brief overviews of this process see, for example, Philip Schofield, "Improving the Candidate Job-Match," *Personnel Management*, Vol. 25, no. 2 (February 1993), p. 69, and Clive Fletcher, "Testing Times for the World of Psycho- metrics," *Personnel Management* (December 1993), pp. 46–50.

2. Frank Schmidt and others, "Impact of Valid Selection Procedures on Workforce Productivity," *Journal of Applied*

Figure 5.14
Scatter Plot Showing Unrelated Criterion Scores and Predictor Scores.

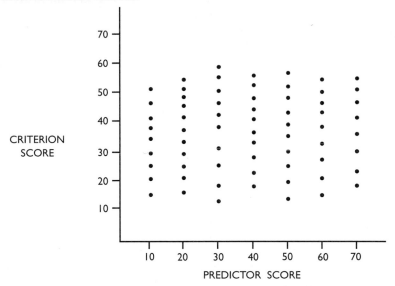

While inspection of the scatter plot provides an idea of the existence of a relationship between the predictor and criterion scores, the degree of the relationship is more precisely determined by the Pearson product moment correlation or the validity coefficient as it is called in the personnel selection context. In this example both predictor and criterion scores are assumed to be measured on interval scales. For other types of measurement in which scales are categorized, for example, when the criterion is simply a judgment that the employee meets a standard or does not meet the standard, (that is, a two-point scale), other kinds of validity coefficients such as phi or biserial may be computed.

The validity coefficient provides two kinds of important information. First, it indicates the *direction* of the relationship as positive or negative. A positive relationship, as in Figure 5.13, shows that as the predictor score increases so does the criterion score; a negative relationship exists when an increase in the predictor score is associated with a decrease in criterion score. Second, the size of the validity coefficient indicates the *degree* of relationship between predictor and criterion. Because it is a correlation, a validity coefficient may range from -1 through 0 to $+1$. The closer to $+1$ or -1 the stronger is the relationship. The validity coefficient is tested for its statistical significance to determine if its value is high enough to be considered different from zero and not just the result of a chance occurrence. If the validity coefficient is not statistically significant, the predictor should not be considered as valid for the criterion. In Figure 5.13 the validity coefficient is 0.40 for a sample of 50 employees. The statistical test for this correlation is given by the following formula:

$$t = \frac{r\sqrt{n-2}}{\sqrt{1-r^2}}$$

where r is the validity coefficient and n is the sample size from which it was computed. For this example, the conclusion is that a correlation of 0.40 has less than five chances in 100 of occurring by chance and, therefore, there probably is a true relation between the predictor score and the criterion score.

The validity coefficient can be interpreted as the percentage of improvement in criterion scores from selecting individuals by using the test compared to selecting them based on their criterion score. This means that if *all* applicants were hired and the best 50 were retained after criterion scores were obtained, a test with a validity coefficient of 0.40 would have selected employees that produced 40% of the criterion performance as the best 50. In other words, the efficiency of a selection instrument is directly and linearly related to its validity.

The Problem of Test Unfairness

A test might be valid when all applicants are considered but still discriminate unfairly against *subgroups* of applicants. Suppose a test is administered to 100 applicants, 60 of whom are white and 40 black. You find that for all 100 applicants the test is valid. But on closer examination, it turns out that 80% of the whites are selected, while only 20% of the blacks are selected. The fact that a lower proportion of blacks is selected could put the burden of proof on the employer to prove that blacks are not being unfairly discriminated against by the test. The employer could be required to validate the test separately for *both* blacks and whites.

Suppose the employer makes separate validation studies and finds the test is in fact valid for both blacks and whites. Then even though the test results in a larger proportion of rejects among blacks than whites, the test is, generally speaking, still legally acceptable. While it *does* "discriminate" between black and white candidates, it probably does not do so *unfairly* since it is valid in predicting performance for both groups.

It occasionally happens, however, that while a person's score on the test is a valid predictor of his or her performance on the job, members of one group consistently score better (or worse) than do members of another group and are, therefore, more likely to be hired. For example, assume an employer decides to hire applicants who will perform on the job in a "good" manner (equivalent to supervisor performance rating of 70–80). Further assume that the selection test is validated separately for whites and nonwhites and found to be valid for both. However, nonwhites who score 60 on the test tend to get "good" on-the-job performance ratings, while whites who score 80 on the test tend to get the "good" ratings.

If the employer decided to use the higher test score (80) as the cutoff score, then mostly whites would be hired, since relatively few nonwhites (for whom 60 was a high score) probably achieved scores as high as 80. (Perhaps nonwhites cannot read as well, for instance, and thus do more poorly, overall, than whites on the test, although once on the job the nonwhite who scores 60 will perform as well as the white who scores 80.)

Such a situation could be *unfairly discriminatory* to the nonwhites. Unfair discrimination exists when persons with equal probabilities of success on the job have unequal probabilities of being hired. In our case, a nonwhite who scores 60 and a white who scores 80 both have equal opportunities for being "good" performers. But since the employer chose to use the higher test score (80) as a cutoff, primarily whites, were hired, thus unfairly discriminating against those nonwhites *who had the same probability of performing in a "good" manner.*

There are two implications. First, employers should whenever feasible validate tests separately for both minorities and nonminorities, to ensure that the test is valid for both and to ascertain whether different cutoff scores for each group might be appropriate.[117] Second, an employer can generally use different cutoff

scores for each group (like 80 for whites and 60 for nonwhites) as long as each cut-off score corresponds to the same level of on-the-job performance (in our case "good").[118]

On the other hand, your study might show that the test is valid for both blacks and whites. Therefore, although there is adverse impact, the test passes the standards for a business necessity (job-relatedness) defense.

This is illustrated in Figure 5.15. Note that this test is valid for both groups together and also for the subgroups, since (while most minority candidates are rejected) they are "correctly" identified as probable unsuccessful performers.

Once subgroups are analyzed it can be seen that the test is valid for blacks and whites. Therefore, although there is adverse impact, the test passes the standard for business necessity.

Figure 5.15
Validation for Subgroups

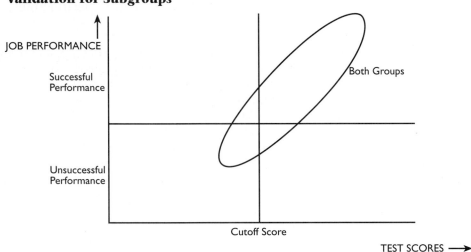

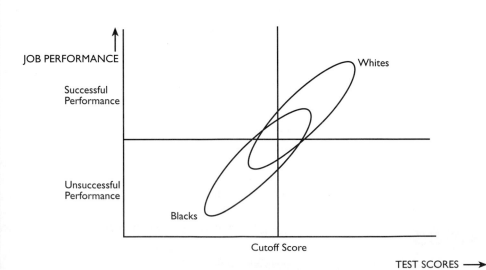

Once subgroups are analyzed it can be seen that the test is valid for blacks and whites. Therefore, although there is adverse impact, the test passes the standard for business necessity.

Aspects of the Quest for Validity

Unfortunately, things are not always so simple as they appear, and that is certainly the case when it comes to the matter of validating tests. The five-step process laid out earlier is a simple and practical one. However, you should also be aware of and consider certain matters that may complicate your quest to arrive at conclusions regarding the validity of the tests you might want to use.

First, there is the matter of which criterion to use. In brief, the so-called "criterion problem" revolves around " . . . whether different methods of measuring job performance, such as supervisor ratings, production output, and work samples, result in different validity results for the same test."[119] Basically, the problem here is that there are differences in the correlation coefficient when using different criteria. In other words, the same test could have one correlation coefficient when relating scores on a test to one criterion (perhaps using supervisor ratings), and a quite different coefficient when relating scores on a test to a second or other criteria (perhaps using production output). This obviously demands that care be taken in the choice of criteria. Consideration must also be given to analyzing the correlation between predictor and each criterion with the aim of determining why discrepancies may exist.

The second problem has been described in terms of disenchantment with the usual validity coefficient. This refers to the fact that in many cases basing a test's validity on a single correlation coefficient between predictor and criterion may be flawed for at least two reasons.[120] One is a "growing awareness that a single bivariate (two-variable) correlation is virtually uninterpretable."[121] For example, you know a correlation coefficient alone doesn't show cause and effect: Thus, to use an overworked example, a correlation between smoking and cancer (the tobacco industry would contend) doesn't necessarily prove that smoking leads to cancer; it may simply reflect that fact that other, unmeasured factors (like emotional stress) lead people to both smoke and get cancer. Thus, some psychologists question how much importance can be given to a single correlation coefficient—in this case, a validity coefficient that correlates test scores (predictor) and performance (criterion).

The other reason for disenchantment with the usual validity coefficient is the possible unreliability of the criterion itself. Specifically, a correlation (validity) coefficient may be deemed questionable because of an unreliable criterion (for instance, haphazard performance appraisal) or the fact that other criteria should have been used, or because of other related problems. (These problems are studied today under the topics of meta-analysis and validity generalization.) For example, the question can be raised as to how valid a validity coefficient is over the entire range of test scores or criterion. A test may do a good job of predicting performance for very high performers and so thereby produce a high-validity coefficient and an apparently valid test. But the point has been made that this apparent validity may not be generalizable to the lower range of test scores. For example, it may turn out that for some reason test scores correlate very highly for a certain range of performance (or for a certain range of test scores), but not nearly as well in other parts of the range.[122] In any event, the bottom line is that someone embarking on a validity study has to take more care than might be immediately apparent.[123]

Notes

1. For brief overviews of this process see, for example, Philip Schofield, "Improving the Candidate Job-Match," *Personnel Management,* Vol. 25, no. 2 (February 1993), p. 69, and Clive Fletcher, "Testing Times for the World of Psycho- metrics," *Personnel Management* (December 1993), pp. 46–50.
2. Frank Schmidt and others, "Impact of Valid Selection Procedures on Workforce Productivity," *Journal of Applied*

Psychology, Vol. 64 (December 1979), pp. 609–626. See also Robert M. Guion, "Changing Views for Personnel Selection Research," *Personnel Psychology,* Vol. 40, no. 2 (Summer 1987), pp. 199–213.

3. Robert E. Sibson, "The High Cost of Hiring," *Nation's Business* (February 1975), p. 85.

4. Bureau of National Affairs, *Bulletin to Management,* September 10, 1987, p. 295.

5. Ann Marie Ryan and Marja Lasek, "Negligent Hiring and Defamation: Areas of Liability Related to Pre-Employment Inquiries," *Personnel Psychology,* Vol. 44, no. 2 (Summer 1991), pp. 293–319.

6. Ibid., p. 302.

7. Ibid.

8. Steven Mitchell Sack, "Fifteen Steps to Protecting Against the Risk of Negligent Hiring Claims," *Employment Relations Today* (August 1993), pp. 313–320.

9. Leona Tyler, *Tests and Measurements* (Englewood Cliffs, NJ: Prentice Hall, 1971), p. 25. More technically, "validity refers to the degree of confidence one can have in inferences drawn from scores, considering the whole process by which the scores are obtained. Stated differently, validity refers to the confidence one has in the meaning attached to scores." (See Guion, "Changing Views for Personnel Selection Research," p. 208.)

10. Strictly speaking, a third way to demonstrate a test's validity is *construct validity.* A construct is a trait such as intelligence. Therefore, to take a simple example, if intelligence is important to the position of engineer, a test that measures intelligence would have construct validity for that position. To prove construct validity, an employer has to prove that the test actually measures the construct and that the construct is in turn required for the job. Federal agency guidelines make it difficult to prove construct validity, however, and as a result few employers use this approach as a means of satisfying the federal guidelines. See James Ledvinka, *Federal Regulation of Personnel and Human Resource Management* (Boston: Kent, 1982), p. 113.

11. Bureau of National Affairs, *Primer of Equal Employment Opportunity* (Washington, DC: BNA, 1978), p. 18. In practice, proving in court the criterion-related validity of paper-and-pencil tests has been difficult.

12. Ledvinka, *Federal Regulations,* p. 111.

13. Anne Anastasi, *Psychological Patterns* (New York: Macmillan, 1968), reprinted in W. Clay Hamner and Frank Schmidt, *Contemporary Problems in Personnel* (Chicago: St. Claire Press, 1974), pp. 102–109. Discussion of reliability based on Marvin Dunnette, *Personnel Selection and Placement* (Belmont, CA: Wadsworth Publishing Company, Inc., 1966), pp. 29–30.

14. Calvin Hoffman, Bary Nathan, and Lisa Holden, "A Comparison of Validation Criteria: Objective versus Subjective Performance Measures and Self- versus Supervisory Ratings," *Personnel Psychology,* Vol. 44 (1991), pp. 601–619.

15. Based on J. Tiffin and E. J. McCormick, *Industrial Psychology* (Englewood Cliffs, NJ: Prentice Hall, 1965), pp. 104–105; C. H. Lawshe and M. J. Balma, *Principles of Personnel Testing,* 2nd ed. (New York: McGraw-Hill, 1966).

16. Experts sometimes have to develop separate expectancy charts and cutting points for minorities and nonminorities if the validation studies indicate that high performers from either group (minority or nonminority) score lower (or higher) on the test. See our discussion of differential validity in the appendix to this chapter. For a good discussion of how to evaluate a selection test, see Raymond Berger and Donna Tucker, "How to Evaluate a Selection Test," *Personnel Journal,* Vol. 66, no. 6 (February 1987), pp. 88–91.

17. See, for example, Floyd L. Ruch, "The Impact on Employment Procedures of the Supreme Court Decision in the Duke Power Case," *Personnel Journal,* Vol. 50, no. 4 (October 1971), pp. 777–783; Hubert Field, Gerald Bagley, and Susan Bagley, "Employment Test Validation for Minority and Non-minority Production Workers," *Personnel Psychology,* Vol. 30, no. 1 (Spring 1977), pp. 37–46; Ledvinka, *Federal Regulations,* p. 110.

18. See Ruch, "The Impact on Employment Procedures," pp. 777–783, in Hamner and Schmidt, *Contemporary Problems in Personnel,* pp. 117–123; Dale Beach, *Personnel* (New York: Macmillan, 1970); Field, Bagley, and Bagley, "Employing Test Validation for Minority and Nonminority Production Workers," pp. 37–46; M. K. Distefano, Jr., Margaret Pryer, and Stella Craig, "Predictive Validity of General Ability Tests with Black and White Psychiatric Attendants," *Personnel Psychology,* Vol. 29, no. 2 (Summer 1976). Also see the Winter 1976 issue of *Personnel Psychology,* Vol. 2, no. 4. See also James Norborg, "A Warning Regarding the Simplified Approach to the Evaluation of Test Fairness and Employee Selection Procedures," *Personnel Psychology,* Vol. 37, no. 3 (Autumn 1984), pp. 483–486; Charles Johnson, Lawrence Messe, and William Crano, "Predicting Job Performance of Low Income Workers: The Work Opinion Questionnaire," *Personnel Psychology,* Vol. 37, no. 2 (Summer 1984), pp. 291–299; Frank Schmidt, Benjamin Ocasio, Joseph Hillery, and John Hunter, "Further Within-Setting Empirical Tests of the Situational Specificity Hypothesis in Personnel Selection," *Personnel Psychology,* Vol. 38, no. 3 (Autumn 1985), pp. 509–524.

19. Prentice Hall, "PH/ASPA Survey: Employee Testing Procedures—Where Are They Headed?" *Personnel Management: Policies and Practices,* April 22, 1975, described in James Ledvinka and Lyle Schoenfeldt, "Legal Developments in Employment Testing: Albemarle," *Personnel Psychology,* Vol. 31, no. 1 (Spring 1978), p. 9.

20. Ledvinka and Schoenfeldt, "Legal Developments," p. 9. See also Robert Wood and Helen Bearon, "Psychological Testing Free From Prejudice," *Personnel Management,* (December 1992), pp. 34–37, and Travis Gibbs and Matt Riggs, "Reducing Bias in Personnel Selection Decisions: Positive Effects of Attention to Irrelevant Information," *Psychological Reports,* Vol. 74, (1994), pp. 19-26. For a focus specifically on gender-based and sex role selection decisions, see Elissa Perry, Allison Davis-Blake, and Carol Kulik, "Explaining Gender-Based Selection Decisions: A Synthesis of Contextual and Cognitive Approaches," *Academy of Management Review,* Vol. 19, no. 4 (1994), pp. 786–820; and Mary B. McRae, "Influence of Sex Role Stereotypes on Personnel Decisions of Black Managers," *Journal of Applied Psychology,* Vol. 79, no. 2 (1994), pp. 306–309.

21. Ledvinka, *Federal Regulations,* p. 109.

22. Douglas Baker and David Terpstra, "Employee Selection: Must Every Job Test Be Validated?" *Personnel Journal,* Vol. 61 (August 1982), pp. 602–605.

23. This is based on Marilyn Quaintance, "Test Security: Foundations of Public Merit Systems," *Personnel Psychology,* Vol. 33, no. 1 (Spring 1980), pp. 25–32.

24. William Roskind, "DECO Versus NLRB, and the Consequences of Open Testing in Industry", *Personnel Psychology,* Vol. 33, no. 1 (Spring 1980), pp. 3–9; and James Ledvinka, Val Markos, and Robert Ladd, "Long-Range Impact of 'Fair Selection' Standards on Minority Employment," *Journal of Applied Psychology,* Vol. 67, no. 1 (February 1982), pp. 18–36.

25. Susan Mendelsohn and Katheryn Morrison, "The Right to Privacy at the Work Place," Part 1: "Employee Searchers," *Personnel* (July 1988), p. 20.

26. Wayne Outten and Noah A. Kinigstein, *The Rights of Employees* (New York: Bantam Books, 1984), pp. 53–54.

27. Mendelson and Morrisohn, "The Right to Privacy in the Work Place," p. 22.

28. Outten and Kinigstein, *The Rights of Employees,* pp. 54–55.

29. Ibid., p. 55.

30. *Kehr* v. *Consolidated Freightways of Delaware,* Docket No. 86–2126, July 15, 1987, U.S. Seventh Circuit Court of Appeals. Discussed in Commerce Clearing House, *Ideas and Trends,* October 16, 1987, p. 165.

31. For a discussion of these see Commerce Clearing House, *Ideas and Trends,* October 16, 1987, pp. 165–166.

32. Except as noted, this is based largely on Laurence Siegel and Irving Lane, *Personnel and Organizational Psychology* (Homewood, IL: Irwin, 1982), pp. 170–185. See also Tyler, *Tests and Measurements,* pp. 38–79, and Lawshe and Balma, *Principles of Personnel Testing,* pp. 83–160.

33. See, for example, Richard Reilly, Sheldon Zedeck, and Mary Tenopyr, "Validity and Fairness of Physical Ability Tests for Predicting Performance in Craft Jobs," *Journal of Applied Psychology,* Vol. 64, no. 3 (June 1970), pp. 262–274. See also Barten Daniel, "Strength and Endurance Testing," *Personnel Journal* (June 1987), pp. 112–122.

34. Results of meta-analyses in one recent study indicated that isometric strength tests were valid predictors of both supervisory ratings of physical performance and performance on work simulations. See Barry R. Blakley, Miguel Quinones, Marnie Swerdlin Crawford, and I. Ann Jago, "The Validity of Isometric Strength Tests," *Personnel Psychology,* Vol. 47 (1994), pp. 247–274.

35. If you read note 9, you will see that this approach calls for construct validation which, as was pointed out, is extremely difficult to demonstrate.

36. Murray R. Barrick and Michael K. Mount, "The Big Five Personality Dimensions and Job Performance: A Meta-Analysis," *Personnel Psychology,* Vol. 44, no. 1, Spring 1991, pp. 1–26. See also Mark Schmit and Ann Marie Ryan, "The Big Five in Personnel Selection: Factor Structure in Applicant and Non-Applicant Populations," *Journal of Applied Psychology,* Vol. 78, no. 6 (1993), pp. 966–974; Grant Marshal, et al., "The Five-Factor Model of Personality as a Framework for Personality-Health Research," *Journal of Personality and Social Psychology,* Vol. 67, no. 2 (1994), pp. 278–286. For a further discussion of the "big five" personality dimensions see, for example, Deniz Ones, Michael Mount, Murray Barrick, and John Hunter, "Personality and Job Performance: a Critique of the Tett, Jackson, and Rothstein (1991) Meta-Analysis," *Personnel Psychology,* Vol. 47, no. 1 (Spring 1994), pp. 147–172.

37. Robert Tett, Douglas Jackson, and Mitchell Rothstein, "Personality Measures as Predictors of Job Performance: A Meta-Analytic Review," *Personnel Psychology,* Vol. 44 (1991), p. 732.

38. Ibid.

39. For a study describing how matching (1) task and working condition preferences of applicants with (2) actual job and working conditions can be achieved, see Ronald Ash, Edward Levine, and Steven Edgell, "Study of a Matching Approach: The Impact of Ethnicity," *Journal of Applied Psychology,* Vol. 64, no. 1 (February 1979), pp. 35–41. For a discussion of how a standard clerical test can be used to screen applicants who will have to use video displays, see Edward Silver and Corwin Bennett, "Modification of the Minnesota Clerical Test to Predict Performance on Video Display Terminals," *Journal of Applied Psychology,* Vol. 72, no. 1 (February 1987), pp. 153–155.

40. Emma D. Dunnette and W. D. Borman, "Personnel Selection and Classification Systems," *Annual Review of Psychology,* Vol. 30 (1979), pp. 477–525, quoted in Siegel and Lane, *Personnel and Organizational Psychology,* pp. 182–183.

41. Paul Wernamont and John T. Campbell, "Signs, Samples, and Criteria," *Journal of Applied Psychology,* Vol. 52 (1968), pp. 372–376; James Campion, "Work Sampling for Personnel Selection," *Journal of Applied Psychology,* Vol. 56 (1972), pp. 40–44, reprinted in Hamner and Schmidt, *Contemporary Problems in Personnel,* pp. 168–180; Sidney Gael, Donald Grant, and Richard Ritchie, "Employment Test Validation for Minority and Nonminority Clerks with Work Sample Criteria," *Journal of Applied Psychology,* Vol. 60, no. 4 (August 1974); Frank Schmidt and others, "Job Sample vs. Paper and Pencil Trades and Technical Test: Adverse Impact and Examinee Attitudes," *Personnel Psychology,* Vol. 30, no. 7 (Summer 1977), pp. 187–198.

42. See, for example, George Burgnoli, James Campion, and Jeffrey Bisen, "Racial Bias in the Use of Work Samples for Personnel Selection," *Journal of Applied Psychology,* Vol. 64, no. 2 (April 1979), pp. 119–123.

43. Siegel and Lane, *Personnel and Organizational Psychology,* pp. 182–183.

44. Ann Howard, "An Assessment of Assessment Centers," *Academy of Management Journal,* Vol. 17 (1974), pp. 115–134; see also Louis Olivas, "Using Assessment Centers for Individual and Organizational Development," *Personnel,* Vol. 57 (May–June 1980), pp. 63–67.

45. *Development Dimensions, Inc., 1977-1978 Catalog.* (Pittsburgh: Development Dimensions Press, 1977), discussed in Wayne F. Cascio and Val Silbey, "Utility of the Assessment Center as a Selection Device," *Journal of Applied Psychology,* Vol. 64, no. 4 (April 1979), pp. 107–118.

46. See, for example, Larry Alexander, "An Exploratory Study of the Utilization of Assessment Center Results," *Academy of Management Journal,* Vol. 22, no. 1 (March 1970), pp. 152–157.

47. Steven Norton, "The Empirical and Content Validity of Assessment Centers Versus Traditional Methods of Predicting Management Success," *Academy of Management Review,* Vol. 20 (July 1977), pp. 442–453. Interestingly, a recent review concludes that assessment centers do predict managerial success, but after an extensive review, "we also assert that we do not know why they work." Richard Klimoski and Mary Brickner, "Why Do Assessment Centers Work? The Puzzle of Assessment Center Validity," *Personnel Psychology,* Vol. 40, no. 2 (Summer 1987), pp. 243–260.

48. John Hinrichs, "An Eight Year Follow-up of a Management Assessment Center," *Journal of Applied Psychology,* Vol. 63, no. 5 (October 1978), pp. 596 601.

49. For example, see Ahron Tziner, Simcha Ronen, and Dafna Hacohen, "A Four-Year Validation Study of an Assessment Center in a Financial Corporation," *Journal of Organizational Behavior,* Vol. 14 (1993), pp. 225–237; Leslie Joyce, Paul Thayer, and Samuel Pond, III, "Managerial Functions: An Alternative to Traditional Assessment Center Dimensions?" *Personnel Psychology,* Vol. 47 (1994), p. 109.

50. Cascio and Silbey, "Utility of the Assessment Center as a Selection Device." See also Paul R. Sackett, "Assessment Centers and Content Validity: Some Neglected Issues," *Personnel Psychology,* Vol. 40 (Spring 1987), pp. 13–26.

51. David Groce, "A Behavioral Consistency Approach to Decision Making in Employment Selection," *Personnel Psychology,* Vol. 34, no. 1 (Spring 1981), pp. 55–64.

52. For an alternative to assessment centers, see Donald Brush and Lyle Schoenfeldt, "Identifying Managerial Potential: An Alternative Assessment Center," *Personnel,* Vol. 57 (May–June 1980), pp. 72–73.

53. Philip Lowry, "Selection Methods: Comparison of Assessment Centers with Personnel Records Evaluations," *Public Personnel Management,* Vol. 23, no. 3 (Fall 1994), pp. 383–394.

54. Arthur Cosiegel, "The Miniature Job Training and Evaluation Approach: Traditional Findings," *Personnel Psychology,* Vol. 36, no. 1 (Spring 1983), pp. 41–56.

55. See, for example, George Beason and John Belt, "Verifying the Job Applicant's Background," *Personnel Administration* (November–December 1974), pp. 29–32; Bureau of National Affairs, "Selection Procedures and Personnel Records," *Personnel Policies Forum, No. 114* (September 1976), p. 4. See also Paul Sackett and Michael M. Harris, "Honesty Testing for Personnel Selection: A Review and Critique," *Personnel Psychology,* Vol. 37, no. 2 (Summer 1985), pp. 221–245.

56. Seymour Adler, "Verifying a Job Candidate's Background: The State of Pracatice in a Vital Human Resources Activity," *Review of Business,* Vol. 15, no. 2 (Winter 1993), pp. 3–8.

57. Ibid., p. 6.

58. For additional information, see Lawrence E. Dube, Jr., "Employment References and the Law," *Personnel Journal,* Vol. 65, no. 2 (February 1986), pp. 87–91. See also Mickey Veich, "Uncover the Resume Ruse," *Security Management* (October 1994), pp. 75–76.

50. Thomas von der Embse and Rodney Wyse, "Those Reference Letters: How Useful Are They?" *Personnel,* Vol. 62, no. 1 (January 1985), pp. 42–46.

60. Tiffin and McCormick, *Industrial Psychology,* pp. 78–79.

61. See Howard M. Fischer, "Select the Right Executive," *Personnel Journal* (April 1989), pp. 110–114.

62. James Bell, James Castagnera, and Jane Patterson Yong, "Employment References: Do You Know the Law?" *Personnel Journal,* Vol. 63, no. 2 (February 1984), pp. 32–36. In order to demonstrate defamation, several elements must be present: (a) the defamatory statement must have been communicated to another party; (b) the statement must be a false statement of fact; (c) injury to reputation must have occurred; and (d) the employer must not be protected under qualified or absolute privilege. For a discussion see Ryan and Lasek, "Negligent Hiring and Defamation," p. 307.

63. This is based on SKRSC Update, May–June 1985, Schachter, Kristoff, Ross, Sprague, and Curialle, California Street, San Francisco, CA.

64. This is based largely on Jeffrey M. Hahn, "Pre-Employment Information Services: Employers Beware?" *Employee Relations Law Journal,* Vol. 17, no. 1 (Summer 1991), pp. 45–69.

65. Ibid., p. 50.

66. Ibid., p. 53.

67. Ibid., p. 51.

68. Based in part on Ibid., pp. 64–66.

69. James Frierson, "New Polygraph Tests Limits," *Personnel Journal* (December 1988), pp. 84–89.

70. See Bureau of National Affairs, "Polygraph Law Parameters Outlined," *Bulletin to Management,* July 30, 1992, p. 234.

71. For additional detail on the legal aspects of polygraph testing, see Robert Faley, "Legal Issues Concerning Polygraph Testing in the Public Sector," *Public Personnel Management,* Vol. 19, no. 4 (Winter 1990) pp. 365–379.

72. This is based on "When Can Workers Refuse Lie Detector Tests?" *BNA Bulletin to Management,* March 9, 1995, p. 73, and is based on the case Lyle Z. Mercy Hospital Anderson, DCS Ohio, 1995, 10 IER cases 401.

73. John Jones and William Terris, "Post-Polygraph Selection Techniques," *Recruitment Today* (May–June 1989), pp. 25–31.

74. Norma Fritz, "In Focus: Honest Answers—Post Polygraph," *Personnel* (April 1989), p. 8.

75. Bureau of National Affairs, *Bulletin to Management,* September 10, 1987, p. 296.

76. See, for example, Kevin Murphy, "Detecting Infrequent Deception," *Journal of Applied Psychology,* Vol. 72, no. 4 (November 1987), pp. 611–614, for a discussion of the difficulty of using such tests to provide convincing evidence of deception.

77. John Bernardin and Donna Cooke, "Validity of an Honesty Test in Predicting Theft Among Convenience Store Employees," *Academy of Management Journal,* Vol. 36, no. 5 (1993), pp. 1097–1108.

78. The following is based on Judith Collins and Frank Schmidt, "Personality, Integrity, and White Collar Crime: A Construct Validity Study," *Personnel Psychology,* Vol. 46 (1993), pp. 295–311.

79. Ibid. For a description of another approach see, for example, Peter Bullard, "Pre-Employment Screening to Weed Out 'Bad Apples,'" *Nursing Homes* (June 1994), pp. 29–31.

80. These are based on Commerce Clearing House, *Ideas and Trends*, December 29, 1988, pp. 222–223. See also Bureau of National Affairs, "Divining Integrity Through Interview," *Bulletin to Management*, June 4, 1987, p. 184.

81. This example is based on Bureau of National Affairs, *Bulletin to Management*, February 26, 1987, p. 65.

82. See, for example, "Corporate Lie Detectors Under Fire," *Business Week*, January 13, 1973. For a discussion of how to improve the validity of the polygraph test, see Robert Forman and Clark McCauley, "Validity of a Positive Control Polygraph Test Using the Field to Practice Model," *Journal of Applied Psychology*, Vol. 71, no. 4 (November 1986), pp. 691–698.

83. Ulrich Sonnemann, *Handwriting Analysis as a Psychodiagnostic Tool* (New York: Grune & Stratton, 1950), pp. 144–145.

84. Jitendra Sharma and Harsh Vardham, "Graphology: What Handwriting Can Tell You About an Applicant," *Personnel*, Vol. 52, no. 2 (March–April 1975), pp. 57–63. Note that one recent empirical study resulted in the conclusion that "we find ourselves compelled to conclude that it is graphology, rather than just our small sample of graphologists, that is invalid." These researchers conclude that when graphology does seem to "work," it does so because the graphologist is reading a spontaneously written autobiography of the candidate and is thereby obtaining biographical information about the candidate from that essay. See Gershon Ben-Shakhar, Maya Bar-Hillel, Yoram Bilu, Edor Ben-Abba, and Anat Flug, "Can Graphology Predict Occupational Success? Two Empirical Studies and Some Methodological Ruminations," *Journal of Applied Psychology*, Vol. 71, no. 4 (November 1986), pp. 645–653.

85. Joseph Famularo, *Handbook of Modern Personnel Administration* (New York: McGraw-Hill, 1972), pp. 12–17, 18.

86. Mick Haus, "Pre-Employment Physicals and the ADA," *Safety and Health* (February 1992), pp. 64–65.

87. B. Guinn, "Job Satisfaction, Counterproductive Behavior, and Circumstantial Drug Use Among Long Distance Truckers," *The Journal of Psychoactive Drugs*, Vol. 15, no. 3 (1983), pp. 185–188; discussed in Scott MacDonald, Samantha Wells, and Richard Fry, "The Limitations of Drug Screening in the Workplace," *International Labor Review*, Vol. 132, no. 1 (1993), p. 99.

88. Ian Miners, Nick Nykodym, and Diane Samerdyke-Traband, "Put Drug Detection to the Test," *Personnel Journal*, Vol. 66, no. 8 (August 1987), pp. 191–197.

89. MacDonald, Wells, and Fry, "The Limitations of Drug Screening in the Workplace," p. 98. Not all agree that drug testing is worthwhile. See, for example, Mark Karper, Clifford Donn, and Marie Lyndaker, "Drug Testing in the Transportation Industry: The Maritime Case," *Employee Responsibilities and Rights*, Vol. 71, no. 3 (September 1994), pp. 219–233.

90. Eric Rolfe Greenberg, "Workplace Testing: Who's Testing Whom?" *Personnel* (May 1989), pp. 39–45.

91. Chris Berka and Courtney Poignand, "Hair Follicle Testing—An Alternative to Urinalysis for Drug Abuse Screening," *Employee Relations Today* (Winter 1991–1992), pp. 405–409.

92. MacDonald et al., "The Limitations of Drug Screening in the Workplace," pp. 102–104.

93. R.J. McCunney, "Drug Testing: Technical Complications of a Complex Social Issue," in *American Journal of Industrial Medicine*, Vol. 15, no. 5 (1989), pp. 589–600; discussed in MacDonald, "The Limitations of Drug Screening in the Workplace," p. 102.

94. MacDonald, "The Limitations of Drug Screening in the Workplace," p. 105.

95. For a discussion of this see MacDonald et al., "The Limitations of Drug Screening in the Workplace," pp. 105–106.

96. This is based on Ann M. O'Neill, "Legal Issues Presented by Hair Follicle Testing," *Employee Relations Today* (Winter 1991–1992), pp. 411–415.

97. Ibid., p. 411.

98. Ibid., p. 413.

99. Richard Lisko, "A Manager's Guide to Drug Testing," *Security Management*, Vol. 38, no. 8 (August 1994), p. 92.

100. For an additional perspective on drug testing as it applies to public agencies and unions see, for example, Nancy C. O'Neill, "Drug Testing in Public Agencies: Are Personnel Directors Doing Things Right?" *Public Personnel Management*, Vol. 19, no. 4 (Winter 1990), pp. 391–397; Michael H. LeRoy, "The Presence of Drug Testing in the Workplace and Union Member Attitudes," *Labor Studies Journal* (Fall 1991), pp. 33–42. For another approach see, for example, Darold Barnum and John Gleason, "The Credibility of Drug Tests: A Multi-Stage Bayesian Analysis," *Industrial and Labor Relations Review*, Vol. 47, no. 4 (July 1994), pp. 610–621.

101. Eric Rolfe Greenberg, "Workplace Testing: Results of a New AMA Survey," *Personnel* (April 1988), p. 40.

102. Michael A. McDaniel, "Does Pre-Employment Drug Use Predict on the Job Suitability?" *Personnel Psychology*, Vol. 41, no. 4 (Winter 1988), pp. 717–729.

103. This is based on Mark Thomas and Harry Brull, "Tests Improve Hiring Decisions at Franciscan," *Personnel Journal* (November 1993), pp. 89–92.

104. For another view see, for example, Raymond Berger and Donna Tucker, "Recruitment: How to Evaluate a Selection Test," *Personnel Journal New Product News* (March 1994), pp. 2 and 3.

105. David E. Terpstra and Elizabeth Rozell, "The Relationship of Staffing Practices to Organizational Level Measures of Performance," *Personnel Psychology*, Vol. 46 (1993), pp. 27–48.

106. Ibid., p. 42. See also Craig Russell, Adrienne Colella, and Philip Bobko, "Expanding the Context of Utility: The Strategic Impact of Personnel Selection," *Personnel Psychology*, Vol. 46 (1993), pp. 781–801.

107. James Smither, et al., "Applicant Reactions to Selection Procedures," *Personnel Psychology*, Vol. 46 (1993), pp. 49–75.

108. These are quoted from Commerce Clearing House, *Ideas and Trends*, May 1, 1987, pp. 70–71.

109. For information about ordering the Wonderlic, contact E. F. Wonderlic and Associates, Inc., 820 Frontage Rd., Northfield, IL 60093. Their phone number is 312/446-8900.

110. Reach Assessment Systems Corporation at 2233 University Ave., Suite 440, St. Paul, MN 55114, 612/647-9220.

111. See James Fenton, Jr. and Kay Lawrimore, "Employment Reference Checking, Firm Size, and Defamation Liabil-

ity," *Journal of Small Business Management* (October 1992), pp. 88–95.

112. Ibid., p. 88.

113. Ibid.

114. Scott Agnew, "Special Research—False Arrest, Libel and Slander," Jury Verdict Research, Inc., 1988, Solon, OH; referenced in Ibid., p. 88.

115. Ibid., p. 91.

116. These are based on or quoted from Fenton and Larrimore, "Employment Reference Checking," p. 94. Employers may have a "qualified privilege" for truthful references given in good faith with no malice, and truth is an absolute defense to defamation claims. However, as a practical matter, small business owners may not have the resources or time to devote to defending themselves against even baseless defamation claims.

117. David Robertson, "Update on Testing and Equal Opportunity," *Personnel Journal,* Vol. 56, no. 3 (March 1977), reprinted in Craig Schneier and Richard Beatty, *Personnel Administration Today* (Reading, MA: Addison–Wesley, 1978), p. 300. For a discussion of methods for setting cutoff scores see, for example, Richard E. Biddle, "How to Set Cutoff Scores for Knowledge Tests Used in Promotion, Training, Certification, and Licensing," *Public Personnel Management,* Vol. 22, no. 1 (Spring 1993), pp. 63–79.

118. Virginia R. Boehm, "Negro–White Differences in Validity of Employment and Training Selection Procedures: Summary of Research Evidence," *Journal of Applied Psychology,* Vol. 56 (1972), pp. 33–39, in Hamner and Schmidt, *Contemporary Problems in Personnel,* pp. 126–134. See also John Hunter and Frank Schmidt, "Differential and Single Group Validity of Employment Tests by Race: A Critical Analysis of Three Recent Studies," *Journal of Applied Psychology,* Vol. 63, no. 1 (1978), pp. 1–11. Note that the need for differential test scores is a separate problem from that of *differential validity.* Differential validity exists when the validity coefficients for two groups are significantly different in a statistical sense. Differential validity thus refers to the predictive capability of the test for each group. When a test is validated separately for two groups—say, white and nonwhite—it could thus turn out that (1) the test is *differentially valid* in that the validity coefficients (the correlation between test score and job performance) are different for the two groups, and/or (2) different cutoff scores are needed for each group, since us-ing the same cutoff score might be unfairly discriminatory to one group. In practice, differential validity is generally not a serious problem. Finally, also note that while the need for different cutoff scores is an important source of test unfairness, there are other ways to use a test unfairly. One could, for instance (to use an extreme example), give nonminority candidates the test answers ahead of time.

119. Barry R. Nathan and Ralph A. Alexander, "A Comparison of Criteria for Test Validation: A Meta-analytic Investigation," *Personnel Psychology,* Vol. 41, no. 3 (Autumn 1988), pp. 517–535.

120. Guion, "Changing Views for Personnel Selection Research," pp. 207–208.

121. Ibid., p. 207.

122. For a discussion, see David A. Waldman and Bruce J. Avolio, "Homogeneity of Test Validity," *Journal of Applied Psychology,* Vol. 74, no. 2 (April 1989), pp. 371–374.

123. For a discussion of how to evaluate psychological tests, see, for example, Robin Inwald, "How to Evaluate Psychological/Honesty Tests," *Personnel Journal* (May 1988), pp. 40–46. Dr. Inwald suggests a number of pointers, including beware of tests for which little or no validation research exists; beware of studies that are not based on the prediction model of validation; beware of studies that do not tell you how many people were incorrectly predicted to have job problems; beware of studies (or tests) that claim to successfully predict dangerous, violent, or nonviolent behavior or tendencies because violent behavior "cannot be predicted"; beware of studies that report significant correlations as their evidence of validity (since unusually high correlations would be questionable); beware of studies that use small numbers of participants to predict important job performance outcomes; beware of studies that have not been cross-validated; beware of claims that tests are valid for use with occupational groups for whom validation studies have not yet been conducted; beware of studies based on individuals filling out questionnaires or tests anonymously; beware of studies that have not used real job candidates as subjects for their validation efforts; and beware of tests whose validation studies have been designed, conducted, and published only by the test developer or publishing company without replication by other independent psychological agencies.

Chapter 6
Interviewing Candidates

Chapter Outline

- ◆ **Introduction: Basic Features of Interviews**
- ◆ **Interviewing Mistakes**
- ◆ **Designing and Conducting the Effective Interview**
- ◆ **Building Employee Commitment: A Total Selection Program**

Behavioral Objectives

When you finish studying this chapter, you should be able to:

Describe several basic types of interviews.

Explain the factors and problems that can undermine an interview's usefulness, and techniques for eliminating them.

List important "guidelines for interviewers."

Explain how to develop a structured or situational interview.

Discuss how to improve your performance as an interviewee.

Introduction: Basic Features of Interviews

An *interview* is a procedure designed to solicit information from a person's oral responses to oral inquiries; a *selection interview,* which we'll focus on in this chapter, is ". . . a selection procedure designed to predict future job performance on the basis of applicants' oral responses to oral inquiries."[1]

Since the interview is only one of several selection procedures, you could reasonably ask, "Why devote an entire chapter to this one selection tool?" The answer is that the interview is by far the most widely used personnel selection procedure. Estimates of the proportion of organizations using interviews for selection range from 70% for some types of interviews[2] to one study of 852 employers that found that 99% of them used interviews as a selection tool.[3] The point is that while not all companies use selection procedures like tests, assessment centers, and even reference checks, it would be highly unusual for a manager not to interview a prospective employee; interviewing is thus an indispensable management tool.

Types of Interviews

Interviews can be classified in four ways according to (1) degree of structure; (2) purpose; (3) content; and (4) the way the interview is administered. In turn, the seven main types of interviews used at work—structured, non-structured, situational, sequential, panel, stress, and appraisal—can each be classified in one or more of these four ways.

nondirective interview
An unstructured conversational-style interview. The interviewer pursues points of interest as they come up in response to questions.

The Structure of the Interview First, interviews can be classified according to the degree to which they are structured. In an **unstructured or nondirective type of interview,** you ask questions as they come to mind. There is generally no set format to follow, and the interview can take various directions. While questions can be specified in advance, they usually are not, and there is seldom a formalized guide for scoring the quality of each answer. Interviewees for the same job thus may or may not be asked the same or similar questions, and the interview's unstructured nature allows the interviewer to ask questions based on the candidate's last statements and to pursue points of interest as they develop.

directive interview
An interview following a set sequence of questions.

The interview can also be structured. In the classical **structured or directive interview,** the questions and acceptable responses are specified in advance and the responses are rated for appropriateness of content.[4] McMurry's *patterned interview* was one early example. Here the interviewer followed a printed form to ask a series of questions such as "What kind of a car do you own?" Comments printed beneath the questions (such as "Will he or she be able to use his or her car if necessary?") then guide the interviewer in evaluating the acceptability of the answers. Another question on the patterned interview form might be "How was the person's present job obtained?" The evaluative comment would then be "Has he or she shown self-reliance in getting his or her jobs?" In practice, however, not all structured interviews go so far as to specify acceptable answers. For example, Figure 6.1 shows a relatively structured interview guide that stops short of specifying the types of answers to watch for.

Structured and nonstructured interviews each have their pros and cons. With structured interviews all applicants are generally asked all required questions by all interviewers that they meet with, and structured interviews are generally more valid. Structured interviews can also help interviewers who may be less comfortable interviewing to ask questions and conduct useful interviews. On the other hand, structured interviews don't always leave the flexibility to pursue points of interest as they develop.

Figure 6.1
Structured Interview
Guide

APPLICANT INTERVIEW GUIDE

To the interviewer: This Applicant Interview Guide is intended to assist in employee selection and placement. If it is used for all applicants for a position, it will help you to compare them, and it will provide more objective information than you will obtain from unstructured interviews.

Because this is a general guide, all of the items may not apply in every instance. Skip those that are not applicable and add questions appropriate to the specific position. Space for additional questions will be found at the end of the form.

Federal law prohibits discrimination in employment on the basis of sex, race, color, national origin, religion, disability, and, in most instances, age. The laws of most states also ban some or all of the above types of discrimination in employment as well as discrimination based on marital status or ancestry. Interviewers should take care to avoid any questions that suggest that an employment decision will be made on the basis of any such factors.

Job Interest

Name _____ Position applied for _____

What do you think the job (position) involves? _____

Why do you want the job (position)? _____

Why are you qualified for it? _____

What would your salary requirements be? _____

What do you know about our company? _____

Why do you want to work for us? _____

Current Work Status

Are you now employed? _____ Yes _____ No. If not, how long have you been unemployed? _____

Why are you unemployed? _____

If you are working, why are you applying for this position? _____

When would you be available to start work with us? _____

Work Experience

(Start with the applicant's current or last position and work back. All periods of time should be accounted for. Go back at least 12 years, depending upon the applicant's age. Military service should be treated as a job.)

Current or last employer _____ Address _____

Dates of employment: from _____ to _____

Current or last job title _____

What are (were) your duties? _____

Have you held the same job throughout your employment with that company? _____ Yes _____ No. If not, describe the various jobs you have had with that employer, how long you held each of them, and the main duties of each. _____

What was your starting salary? _____ What are you earning now? _____ Comments _____

Name of your last or current supervisor _____

What did you like most about that job? _____

What did you like least about it? _____

Why are you thinking of leaving? _____

Why are you leaving right now? _____

Interviewer's comments or observations _____

(continued)

Figure 6.1
(continued)

What did you do before you took your last job? _____

    Where were you employed? _____

    Location _____ Job title _____

    Duties _____

    Did you hold the same job throughout your employment with that company? _____ Yes _____ No. If not, describe the jobs you held, when you held them and the duties of each. _____

    _____

    What was your starting salary? _____ What was your final salary? _____

    Name of your last supervisor _____

    May we contact that company? _____ Yes _____ No

    What did you like most about that job? _____

    What did you like least about that job? _____

    Why did you leave that job? _____

    Would you consider working there again? _____

    Interviewer: If there is any gap between the various periods of employment, the applicant should be asked about them. _____

    Interviewer's comments or observations _____

    _____

What did you do prior to the job with that company? _____

What other jobs or experience have you had? Describe them briefly and explain the general duties of each.

_____

Have you been unemployed at any time in the last five years? _____ Yes _____ No. What efforts did you make to find work? _____

What other experience or training do you have that would help qualify you for the job you applied for? Explain how and where you obtained this experience or training. _____

_____

Educational Background

What education or training do you have that would help you in the job for which you have applied? _____

_____

Describe any formal education you have had. (Interviewer may substitute technical training, if relevant.) _____

_____

Off-Job Activities

What do you do in your off-hours? ____ Part-time job ____ Athletics ____ Spectator sports ____ Clubs ____ Other

Please explain. _____

Interviewer's Specific Questions

Interviewer: Add any questions to the particular job for which you are interviewing, leaving space for brief answers. (Be careful to avoid questions which may be viewed as discriminatory.)

_____

_____

_____

Personal

Would you be willing to relocate? _____ Yes _____ No

Are you willing to travel? _____ Yes _____ No

(continued)

Figure 6.1
(continued)

What is the maximum amount of time you would consider traveling? _____

_____

Are you able to work overtime? _____

What about working on weekends? _____

Self-Assessment

What do you feel are your strong points? _____

_____

What do you feel are your weak points? _____

_____

Interviewer: Compare the applicant's responses with the information furnished on the application for employment.

Clear up any discrepancies. _____

_____

Before the applicant leaves, the interviewer should provide basic information about the organization and the job opening, if this has not already been done. The applicant should be given information on the work location, work hours, the wage or salary, type of remuneration (salary or salary plus bonuses, etc.), and other factors that may affect the applicant's interest in the job.

Interviewer's Impressions

Rate each characteristic from 1 to 4, with 1 being the highest rating and 4 being the lowest.

Personal Characteristics	1	2	3	4	Comments
Personal appearance					
Poise, manner					
Speech					
Cooperation with interviewer					
Job-related Characteristics					
Experience for this job					
Knowledge of job					
Interpersonal relationships					
Effectiveness					

Overall rating for job

1	2	3	4	5
___ Superior	___ Above Average	___ Average	___ Marginal	___ Unsatisfactory
	(well qualified)	(qualified)	(barely qualified)	

Comments or remarks _____

_____

_____

Interviewer _____ Date _____

Copyright 1992 The Dartnell Corporation, Chicago, IL. Adopted with permission.

stress interview
An interview in which the applicant is made uncomfortable by a series of often rude questions. This technique helps identify hypersensitive applicants and those with low or high stress tolerance.

The Purpose of the Interview Employee-related interviews can also be classified according to their purpose. Thus, as noted earlier, a *selection interview* is a type of interview designed to predict future job performance on the basis of applicants' oral responses to oral inquiries. A **stress interview** is a special type of selection interview in which the applicant is made uncomfortable by a series of sometimes rude questions. The aim of the stress interview is supposedly to help identify sensitive applicants and those with low or high stress tolerance.

In the typical stress interview, the applicant is made uncomfortable by being put on the defensive by a series of frank and often discourteous questions from the interviewer. The interviewer might first probe for weaknesses in the applicant's background, such as a job that the applicant left under questionable circumstances. Having identified these, the interviewer can then focus on them, hoping to get the candidate to lose his or her composure. Thus, a candidate for customer relations manager who obligingly mentions having had four jobs in the past two years might be told that frequent job changes reflect irresponsible and immature behavior. If the applicant then responds with a reasonable explanation of why the job changes were necessary, another topic might be pursued. On the other hand, if the formerly tranquil applicant reacts explosively with anger and disbelief, this might be taken as a symptom of low tolerance for stress.

The stress approach can be a good way to identify hypersensitive applicants who might be expected to overreact to mild criticism with anger and abuse. On the other hand, the stress interview's invasive and ethically questionable nature demands that the interviewer be both skilled in its use and sure that a thick skin and an ability to handle stress are really required for the job. This is definitely not an approach for amateur interrogators or for those without the skills to keep the interview under control.

appraisal interview
A discussion following a performance appraisal in which supervisor and employee discuss the employee's rating and possible remedial actions.

Interviews serve two more purposes in the employment context. An **appraisal interview** is a discussion following a performance appraisal in which supervisor and employee discuss the employee's rating and possible remedial actions. When an employee leaves a firm for any reason, an exit interview is often conducted. An *exit interview,* usually conducted by the HR department, aims at eliciting information about the job or related matters that might give the employer a better insight into what is right or wrong about the company. Many of the techniques explained in this chapter apply equally well to appraisal and exit interviews. However, a complete explanation of these interviews will be postponed until Chapters 16 and 17, respectively, so we can concentrate here on selection interviews.

The Content of the Interview   Interviews can also be classified according to the content of their questions. A **situational type of interview** is one in which the questions focus on the individual's ability to project what his or her behavior would be in a given situation.[5] For example, a candidate for a supervisor's position may be asked how he or she would respond to a subordinate coming to work late three days in a row. The interview can be both *structured and situational* with predetermined questions requiring the candidate to project what his or her behavior would be. In a structured situational interview the applicant could be evaluated, say, on his or her choice between letting the subordinate off with a warning versus suspending the subordinate for one week.

situational interview
A series of job-related questions which focuses on how the candidate would behave in a given situation.

job-related interview
A series of job-related questions which focuses on relevant past job-related behaviors.

Job-related interviews are those in which the interviewer attempts to assess the applicant's past behaviors for job-related information, but most questions are not considered situational. In other words, questions don't revolve around hypothetical situations or scenarios. Instead supposedly job-related questions (such as "Which courses did you like best in business school?") are asked in order to draw conclusions about, say, the candidate's ability to handle the financial aspects of the job to be filled.

The behavioral interview is gaining in popularity.[6] In a *behavioral interview* a situation is described and interviewees are asked how they have behaved *in the past* in such a situation.[7] Thus, while situational interviews ask interviewees to describe how they *would* react to a situation today or tomorrow, the behavioral interview asks interviewees to describe how they *did* react to situations in the past.[8]

Finally, *psychological interviews* are interviews conducted by a psychologist in which questions are intended to assess personal traits such as dependability.[9]

The interview may use situational, job-related, or behavioral questions and be either structured or unstructured. Psychological interviews generally have a significantly unstructured element.

Administering the Interview   Interviews can also be classified based on how they are administered: one-on-one or by a panel of interviewers; sequentially or all at once; and computerized or personally. For example, most interviews are administered *one-on-one*. As the name implies, two people meet alone and one interviews the other by seeking oral responses to oral inquiries. Most selection processes are sequential. In a *sequential interview* the applicant is interviewed by several persons in sequence before a selection decision is made. In an *unstructured sequential interview* each interviewer may look at the applicant from his or her own point of view, ask different questions, and form an independent opinion of the candidate. On the other hand, in a **structured sequential or serialized interview,** each interviewer rates the candidate on a standard evaluation form, and the ratings are compared before the hiring decision is made.[10]

The **panel interview** means the candidate is interviewed simultaneously by a group (or panel) of interviewers (rather than sequentially). The group structure has several advantages. A sequential interview often has candidates cover basically the same ground over and over again with each interviewer. The panel interview, on the other hand, allows each interviewer to pick up on the candidate's answers, much as reporters do in press conferences. This approach may elicit deeper and more meaningful responses than are normally produced by a series of one-on-one interviews. On the other hand, some candidates find panel interviews more stressful and they may actually inhibit responses. An even more stressful variant is the *mass interview.* In a mass interview several candidates are interviewed simultaneously by a panel. Here the panel poses a problem to be solved and then sits back and watches which candidate takes the lead in formulating an answer.

Increasingly, interviews aren't administered by people at all but are computerized. A *computerized selection interview* is one in which a job candidate's oral and/or computerized responses are obtained in response to computerized oral, visual, or written questions and/or situations. The basic idea is generally to present the applicant with a series of questions regarding his or her background, experience, education, skills, knowledge, and work attitudes—specific questions that relate to the job for which the person has applied.[11]

In a typical computerized interview the questions are presented in a multiple-choice format, one at a time, and the applicant is expected to respond to the questions on the computer screen by pressing a key corresponding to his or her desired response. For example, a sample interview question for a person applying for a job as a retail store clerk might be:[12]

How would your supervisor rate your customer service skills?

A. Outstanding
B. Above average
C. Average
D. Below average
E. Poor

Questions on a computerized interview like this come in rapid sequence and require concentration on the applicant's part.[13] The typical computerized inter-

serialized interview
An interview in which the applicant is interviewed sequentially by several persons and each rates the applicant on a standard form.

panel interview
An interview in which a group of interviewers questions the applicant.

The panel interview provides an effective way of allowing interviewers to follow up on each other's questions.

view then measures the response time to each question. A delay in answering certain questions such as "Can you be trusted?" can flag a potential problem.

Computer-aided interviews are generally used to reject totally unacceptable candidates and to select those who will move on to a face-to-face interview. For example, at Pic'n Pay stores, a chain of 915 self-service shoe stores headquartered in North Carolina, job applicants are given an 800 number to dial for the computerized interview and can take the interview at any touchtone phone. The Pic'n Pay interview involves 100 questions and lasts about ten minutes, with applicants pressing 1 for "yes" and 0 for "no." In Pic'n Pay's case, every applicant then gets a follow-up live telephone interview from one of six dedicated interviewers located at Pic'n Pay headquarters.

Computer-aided interviews can be very advantageous. Systems like those now on-line at Pic'n Pay and Great Western Bank of California substantially reduce the amount of time managers devote to inteviewing what often turn out to be unacceptable candidates.[14] Applicants are reportedly more honest with computers than they would be with people, presumably because computers are not judgmental.[15] The computer can also be sneaky: If an applicant takes longer than average to answer a question like, "Have you ever been caught stealing?" he or she may be summarily screened out or at least questioned more deeply in that area by a human interviewer. Several of the interpersonal interview problems we'll discuss later in this chapter, such as making a snap judgment about the interviewee based on his or her appearance, are also obviously avoided with this nonpersonal interviewing approach.[16] On the other hand, the mechanical nature of computer-aided interviews can leave applicants with the impression that the prospective employer is rather impersonal. A description of a relatively sophisticated actual computer-aided interview is presented in the Information Technology and HR box on page 224.

How Useful Are Interviews?

The ironic thing about interviews is that while they're used by virtually all employers, the statistical evidence regarding their validity is actually very mixed. Much of the earlier research gave selection interviews low marks in terms of reliability and validity.[18] However, recent studies indicate that the key to an interview's usefulness is the manner in which it is administered. Specifically, the following conclusions are warranted based on one recent study of interview validity:

> With respect to predicting job performance, situational interviews yield a higher mean validity than do job-related (or behavioral) interviews, which in turn yield a higher mean validity than do psychological interviews.[19]
>
> Structured interviews, regardless of content, are more valid than unstructured interviews for predicting job performance.[20]
>
> Both when they are structured and when they are unstructured, individual interviews are more valid than are panel interviews, in which multiple interviewers provide ratings in one setting.

In summary, structured situational interviews conducted one-on-one individually seem to be the most useful for predicting job performance. Unstructured interviews in general, psychological interviews, and panel interviews are somewhat less useful for predicting job performance.[21]

Interviewing and the Law: Employment Discrimination "Testers"

An interview is a selection procedure; interviewers must therefore avoid asking questions concerning, for instance, candidates' marital status, child care arrangements, ethnic background, and worker's compensation history.

Information Technology and HR
Computer Applications in Interviewing:
The Computer-Aided Interview

When Bonnie Dunn, 20 years old, tried out for a teller's job at Great Western Bank in Chatsworth, California, she faced a lineup of tough customers.[17]

One young woman sputtered contradictory instructions about depositing a check and then blew her top when the transaction wasn't handled fast enough. Another customer had an even shorter fuse. "You people are unbelievably slow," he said.

Both tough customers appeared on a computer screen, as part of a 20-minute automated job interview. Ms. Dunn was seated in front of a PC, responding via a color touch-screen and a microphone. She was tested on making change and sales skills, as well as keeping cool in tense situations.

When applicants sit down facing the computer at Great Western's bank branches, they hear it say, "Welcome to the interactive assessment aid." The computer doesn't understand what applicants say at that point, although it records their comments to be evaluated later. To begin the interview, applicants touch a label on the screen, eliciting an ominous foreword: "We'll be keeping track of how long it takes you and how many mistakes you make. Accuracy is more important than speed."

First, the computer tests the applicant on money skills, asking him or her to cash a check for $192.18, including at least three five-dollar bills and two dollars in quarters. Then, when an angry customer appears on the screen, candidates are expected to grab the microphone and mollify him. Later a bank official who listens to the recorded interviews gives applicants five points for maintaining a friendly tone of voice, plus up to 15 points for apologizing, promising to solve the customer's problem, and, taking a cue from the screen, suggesting that in the future he use the bank's deposit-only line.

The touchy young woman on the screen is tougher. Speaking rapidly, she says she wants to cash a $150 check, get $40 in cash, and put $65 in savings and the rest in checking. As an applicant struggles to sort that out, she quickly adds, "No, it has to be $50 in checking because I just wrote a check this morning." If the applicant then touches a label on the screen that says "?", the woman fumes, "How many times do I have to tell you?"

Great Western reports that its computer-aided interviewing system has been successful. Not only has it dramatically reduced the amount of useless interviewing managers have to do of unacceptable candidates, but candidates hired by the program were reportedly 26% less likely to quit or be fired within 90 days of hiring. (This is partly because the computer tells applicants what the job really involves, something a candidate might be reluctant to ask a person for fear of appearing negative.)◆

The increasing use of employment discrimination testers has made such care even more important. As defined by the EEOC, testers are "individuals who apply for employment which they do not intend to accept, for the sole purpose of uncovering unlawful discriminatory hiring practices."[22]

Although they're not really seeking employment, testers have legal standing, both with the courts and with the EEOC. As described in its "Policy Guidance on the Use of Testers in the Employment Selection Process," the EEOC takes the position that testers can file charges under Title VII and may be useful in unearthing employment discrimination.[23] Courts have also recognized the use of testers, even though their primary motive is not to seek jobs but to test for discrimination.[24] A case filed in 1991 illustrates the usual tester approach. A private, nonprofit civil rights advocacy group sent four university students—two white, two black—to an employment agency supposedly in pursuit of a job. Although the testers were given backgrounds and training to make them appear almost indistinguishable from each other in terms of qualifications, the white applicants and black applicants were allegedly treated quite differently. For example, both white applicants were given interviews and offered jobs, while the two black testers got neither interviews nor job offers.[25] A study by the Urban Institute suggests that such unequal treatment is "entrenched and widespread."[26]

An employer's best strategy is to be actively nondiscriminatory. However, a prudent employer will also take steps in planning the interview process and conducting the actual interviews to ensure that its interviewers avoid tester claims. Specifically:[27]

1. Caution interviewers that testers may be posing as applicants.
2. Train interviewers to make careful notes during and after the interview to substantiate the differences among applicants and to record responses to questions and other items of interest not on the applicant's résumé or application.
3. Try to avoid differences in the interviews themselves, perhaps through the use of an interview checklist.
4. If an applicant appears disinterested in the position, note specific signs of such "disinterest."
5. Consider using a point system for interviews. Assign applicants a certain number of points for relevant education, employment stability, work experience, and other criteria related to success on the job.
6. Have applicants execute a statement acknowledging that they are applying for the job out of a sincere interest in the job and for no other purpose. Signing that and later returning with a claim as a "tester" could constitute evidence of deceit if there is a lawsuit.
7. Remember that these testers often enter the employment process with phony résumés and fabricated qualifications, thus emphasizing the importance of carefully checking references.
8. Consider establishing an internal dispute resolution procedure that applicants and employees can turn to if they have an employment-related complaint against the firm. This can result in less expensive resolution than taking the matter to court.

Remember that you must comply with equal employment requirements. As explained in Chapter 3, *federal* equal employment laws generally do not prohibit interviewers from asking most questions. However, the EEOC does look with suspicion on certain inquiries such as marital status and child care.[28] This is one reason why using a structured interview form is particularly advisable, since it can be standardized and validated as a selection tool for EEOC purposes.[29]

Common Interviewing Mistakes

There are several common interviewing mistakes that undermine an interview's usefulness. We explain these next, since knowledge of the mistakes is the first step in avoiding them. In the following section we'll then discuss how to avoid the mistakes.

Snap Judgments

One of the most consistent findings in the interviewing literature is that interviewers tend to jump to conclusions—make snap judgments—about candidates during the first few minutes of the interview, or even before the interview begins based on test scores or résumé data. For example, one study showed that interviewers' access to candidates' test scores biased the interviewer's assessment of the candidate.[30] In another study the interviewer's evaluation of a candidate was only related to his or her decision about hiring the candidate for candidates with low passing scores on a selection test. For candidates with high passing scores on the test, evaluations of candidates in the interview were not related to interviewers' decisions.[31] Another researcher estimated that in 85% of the cases interviewers had made up their minds about candidates before the interview began on the basis of applicants' application forms and personal appearance.

Findings like these underscore that it's important for a candidate to start off on the right foot with the interviewer. Interviewers usually make up their minds about candidates during the first few minutes of the interview, and prolonging the interview past this point usually adds little to change their decisions.

Negative Emphasis

Jumping to conclusions is especially troublesome when the information the interviewer has about the candidate is negative. For example, in one study the researchers found that interviewers who previously received unfavorable reference letters about applicants gave the applicants less credit for past successes and held them more personally responsible for past failures after the inteview. Furthermore, the interviewers' final decisions to accept or reject applicants were always tied to what they expected of the applicants based on the references, quite aside from their interview performance.[32]

In other words, interviewers seem to have a consistent negative bias. They are generally more influenced by unfavorable than favorable information about the candidate. And their impressions are much more likely to change from favorable to unfavorable than from unfavorable to favorable. A common interviewing mistake is to make the interview itself mostly a search for negative information. In a sense, therefore, most interviews are probably loaded against the applicant. An applicant who is initially rated high could easily end up with a low rating, given the fact that unfavorable information tends to carry more weight in the interview. An interviewee who starts out with a poor rating will find it hard to overcome that first bad impression during the interview.[33]

Poor Knowledge of the Job

Interviewers who don't know precisely what the job entails and what sort of candidate is best suited for it usually make their decisions based on incorrect stereotypes about what a good applicant is. They then erroneously match interviewees with their incorrect stereotypes. On the other hand, interviewers who have a clear understanding of what the job entails hold interviews that are more useful. In one study, 30 professional interviewers were used.[34] Half were just given a brief description of the jobs for which they were recruiting. Specifically, they were told the "eight applicants here represented by their application blanks are applying for the position of secretary." In contrast, the other 15 interviewers were given much more explicit job information:

> The eight applicants . . . are applying for the position of executive secretary. The requirements are typing speed of 60 words per minute, stenography speed of 100 words per minute, dictaphone use and bilingual ability in either French, German, or Spanish. . . .

More job knowledge translated into better interviews. The 15 interviewers who had more job information generally agreed among themselves about each candidate's potential, while those without complete job information did not. The latter also did not discriminate as well among applicants and tended to give them all high ratings.

Pressure to Hire

Pressure to hire also undermines an interview's usefulness. In one study a group of managers was told to assume that they were behind in their recruiting quota. A second group was told that they were ahead of their quota. Those "behind" evaluated the same recruits much more highly than did those "ahead."[35]

Candidate-Order (Contrast) Error

candidate-order error
An error of judgment on the part of the interviewer due to interviewing one or more very good or very bad candidates just before the interview in question.

Candidate-order (or "contrast") error means that the order in which you see applicants affects how you rate them. In one study, managers were asked to evaluate a candidate who was "just average" after first evaluating several "unfavorable" candidates. The average candidate was evaluated more favorably than he might otherwise have been, since in contrast to the unfavorable candidates the average one looked better than he actually was. In some studies, only a small part of the applicant's rating was based on his or her actual potential. Most of the rating was based on the effect of having followed very favorable or unfavorable candidates.[36]

Influence of Nonverbal Behavior

Interviewers are also influenced by the applicant's nonverbal behavior. For example, several studies have shown that applicants who demonstrate greater amounts of eye contact, head moving, smiling, and other similar nonverbal behaviors are rated higher. In fact, these nonverbal behaviors often account for more than 80% of the applicant's rating.[37] In one study, 52 HR specialists reviewed videotaped job interviews in which the applicants' verbal content was identical. However, the interviewees' nonverbal behavior differed markedly. Those in one group had been instructed to exhibit minimal eye contact, a low energy level, and low voice modulation. The interviewees in a second group demonstrated the opposite behavior. Of the 26 personnel specialists who saw the high eye contact, high energy level candidate, 23 would have invited him or her for a second interview. None who saw the low eye contact, low energy level candidate would have recommended a second interview.[38] One implication is that an otherwise inferior candidate who is trained to "act right" in an interview will often be appraised more highly than will a more competent applicant without the right nonverbal interviewing skills.

An applicant's attractiveness and gender also play a role.[39] In one study, researchers found that whether attractiveness was a help or a hindrance to job applicants depended on the sex of the applicant and the nature of the job. Attractiveness was consistently an advantage for male applicants seeking white-collar jobs. Yet attractiveness was advantageous for female interviewees only when the job was nonmanagerial. When the position was managerial, there was a tendency for a woman's attractiveness to work against her in terms of recommendation for hiring and suggested starting salary. One explanation may be that interviewers tend to equate attractiveness with femininity. Thus, attractive ("more feminine") women are seen as less fit for "masculine-type" jobs like that of manager, quite aside from the women's actual qualifications or the talents actually needed for the job. The following Diversity Counts feature provides another example.

It will not surprise many women to hear that the way they dress can alter interviewers' selection decisions. In one study, 77 HR managers attending a conference evaluated videotapes of women interviewing for management positions. The women were dressed in one of four styles ranging from a light beige dress in a soft fabric (style 1) to a bright aqua suit with a short belted jacket (style 2) to a beige tailored suit with a blazer jacket (style 3) to "the most masculine" outfit, a dark navy, tailored suit and a white blouse with an angular collar (style 4). A comparison of the hiring recommendations associated with each style suggests that, up to a point, the more masculine the style, the more favorable the hiring recommendations were. Specifically, applicants received more favorable hiring recommendations as style masculinity increased from style 1 to style 3. However, applicants wearing style 4 (the most masculine style) were turned down. We might surmise the outfit was considered "too masculine" by the interviewers. The findings may not apply to every individual. However, for what it's worth, the researchers suggest that it might be better for women to risk dressing "too masculine" than "too feminine" when applying for management jobs.[40]◆

Telegraphing

Some interviewers are so anxious to fill a job that they help the applicant respond correctly to their questions by *telegraphing* the expected answer.[41] An obvious example might be a question like: "This job calls for handling a lot of stress. You can do that, can't you?"

The telegraphing isn't always so obvious. For example, interviewers' first impressions of candidates (from examining application blanks and test scores) tend to be positively linked to use of a more positive interview style and vocal style on the part of the interviewer. This can translate into sending subtle cues (like a smile) regarding what answer is being sought.[42]

Too Much/Too Little Talking

Too much or too little guidance on the interviewer's part is another common mistake. Some interviewers let the applicant dominate the interview to the point where too few substantive questions are pursued. At the other extreme some interviewers stifle the applicant by not giving the person sufficient time to answer questions.[43]

Playing District Attorney or Psychologist

Since the interviewer often plays the role of gatekeeper in determining whether or not the interviewee gets a job, there's sometimes a tendency for interviewers to misuse their power by playing district attorney or psychologist. For example, while it's smart to be alert for inconsistencies in applicants' responses, it's important to guard against turning the interview into a game of "gotcha" in which the interviewer derives pleasure from ferreting out and pouncing on interviewees' inconsistencies. Similarly, some interviewers play psychologist, probing for hidden meanings in everything the applicants say.[44]

Designing and Conducting the Effective Interview

Problems like those just addressed can be avoided by designing and conducting an effective interview, to which we now turn.

The Structured Interview

Since *structured situational interviews* are usually the most valid interviews for predicting job performance, conducting an effective interview ideally starts with designing a structured situational interview, a *series of hypothetical job-oriented questions with predetermined answers that are consistently asked of all applicants for a particular job*.[45] Usually a committee of persons familiar with the job develop situational and job-knowledge questions based on the actual job duties. They then reach consensus on what are and are not acceptable answers to these questions. The actual procedure consists of five steps as follows:[46]

Step 1. Job Analysis   First, write a description of the job in the form of a list of job duties, required knowledge, skills, abilities, and other worker qualifications.

Step 2. Evaluate the Job Duty Information   Next, rate each job duty on its importance to job success and on the amount of time required to perform it compared to other tasks. The aim here is to identify the main duties of the job.

Step 3. Develop Interview Questions   The employees who list and evaluate the job duties then develop interview questions. The interview questions are based on the listing of job duties with more interview questions generated for the more important duties.

A situational interview may actually contain situational, job-knowledge, and "willingness" questions (although the situational questions tend to be the most valid). *Situational questions* pose a hypothetical job situation, such as "What would you do if the machine suddenly began heating up?" *Job knowledge questions* assess knowledge essential to job performance that must be known before entering the job. These often deal with technical aspects of a job (such as "What is a ratchet wrench?"). *Willingness questions* gauge the applicant's willingness and motivation to work, to do repetitive physical work, to travel, to relocate, and so forth.

The rapport established with a job applicant not only puts the person at ease; it also reflects the company's attitude toward its public.

The employees who develop the questions then choose *critical incidents* for each question that reflect especially good or poor performance. For example, a situational question based on a critical incident that could be asked of a supervisor is as follows:

> *Your spouse and two teenage children are sick in bed with a cold. There are no relatives or friends available to look in on them. Your shift starts in three hours. What would you do in this situation?*

Step 4. Develop Benchmark Answers   Next develop answers and a five-point rating scale for each question, with specific answers developed for good (a 5 rating), marginal (a 3 rating), and poor (a 1 rating). For example, consider the preceding situational question where the spouse and children are sick. Each member of the team that developed the questions should write good, marginal, and poor answers based on "things you have actually heard said in an interview by people who subsequently were considered good, marginal, or poor as the case may be on the job." After a group discussion, consensus is reached on the answers to use as 5, 3, and 1 benchmarks for each scenario. Three benchmarks for the example question might be "I'd stay home—my spouse and family come first" (1); "I'd phone my supervisor and explain my situation" (3); and "since they only have colds, I'd come to work" (5).

Step 5. Appoint Interview Panel and Implement   These types of interviews are generally conducted by a panel, rather than sequentially. The panel should consist of three to six members, preferably the same employees who participated in writing the interviews and answers. Panel members may also be supervisors of the job to be filled, the job incumbent, peers, and HR representatives. The same interview members should be used to interview all candidates for the job.[47]

Before the interview, the job duties, questions, and benchmark answers are distributed to the panel members and reviewed. Next the panel interview is conducted usually in a quiet, comfortable, nonstressful atmosphere. Ideally, one member of the panel is designated to introduce the applicant to the panel and to ask all questions of all applicants in this and succeeding interviews to ensure consistency. However, all panel members record and rate the applicant's answers on the rating scale sheet by indicating where the candidate's answer to each question falls relative to the ideal poor, marginal or good answers. At the end of the interview, each applicant is directed to someone who explains the follow-up procedures and answers any questions the applicant has.[48]

Guidelines for Conducting an Interview

Whether or not you take the time to develop a structured situational panel-based interview, you can generally conduct the interview more effectively if you follow these guidelines:[49]

Plan the Interview   Begin by reviewing the candidate's application and résumé, and note any areas that are vague or that may indicate strengths or weaknesses. Review the job specification and plan to start the interview with a clear picture of the traits of an ideal candidate.

If possible, use a structured form. Interviews based on structured guides like those in Figures 6.1 (pages 218–220) and 6.2 usually result in the best interviews.[50] At a minimum, you should write out your questions prior to the interview.

The interview should take place in a private room where telephone calls are not accepted and interruptions can be minimized.

Also, plan to delay your decision. Interviewers often make snap judgments even before they see the candidate—on the basis of his or her application form, for instance—or during the first few minutes of the interview. Plan on keeping a record of the interview, and review this record after the interview. Make your decision then.[51]

Establish Rapport   The main reason for the interview is to find out about the applicant. To do this, start by putting the person at ease. Greet the candidate and start the interview by asking a noncontroversial question—perhaps about the weather or the traffic conditions that day. As a rule, all applicants—even unsolicited drop-ins—should receive friendly, courteous treatment, not only on humanitarian grounds but because your reputation is on the line.

Be aware of the applicant's status. For example, if you are interviewing someone who is unemployed, he or she may be exceptionally nervous and you may want to take additional steps to relax the person.[52]

Figure 6.2
Structured Interview Form for College Applicants

CANDIDATE RECORD

NAP 100 (10/77)

CANDIDATE NUMBER	NAME (LAST NAME FIRST)	COLLEGE NAME	COLLEGE CODE
U 921 (1-7)	(8-27)		(28-30)

INTERVIEWER NUMBER

0 (33-40)

INTERVIEWER NAME

SOURCE (41)	RACE (42)	SEX (43)	DEGREE (53)	AVERAGE (A = 4.0)	CLASS STANDING (58-59)
Campus ☐C	White ☐W	Male ☐M	Bachelors ☐B	Overall ___ (54-55)	Top 10% ☐10
Walk-In ☐W	Black ☐B	Female ☐F	Masters ☐M		Top 25% ☐25
Intern ☐I	Asian ☐A	Init.	Law ☐L		Top Half ☐50
Agency ☐A	Hispanic ☐H	Cont.	Majors	Acctg ___ (56-57)	Bottom Half ☐75
	Native Am. ☐NA	Date ___ (46-51)			

CAMPUS INTERVIEW EVALUATIONS

ATTITUDE – MOTIVATION – GOALS

POOR ☐   AVERAGE ☐   GOOD ☐   OUTSTANDING ☐

(POSITIVE, COOPERATIVE, ENERGETIC, MOTIVATED, SUCCESSFUL, GOAL-ORIENTED)
COMMENTS:

COMMUNICATIONS SKILLS-PERSONALITY-SALES ABILITY

POOR ☐   AVERAGE ☐   GOOD ☐   OUTSTANDING ☐

(ARTICULATE, LISTENS, ENTHUSIASTIC, LIKEABLE, POISED, TACTFUL, ACCEPTED, CONVINCING)
COMMENTS:

EXECUTIVE PRESENCE – DEAL WITH TOP PEOPLE

POOR ☐   AVERAGE ☐   GOOD ☐   OUTSTANDING ☐

(IMPRESSIVE, STANDS OUT, A WINNER, REMEMBERED, LEVELHEADED, AT EASE, AWARE)
COMMENTS:

INTELLECTUAL ABILITIES

POOR ☐   AVERAGE ☐   GOOD ☐   OUTSTANDING ☐

(INSIGHTFUL, CREATIVE, CURIOUS, IMAGINATIVE, UNDERSTANDS, REASONS, INTELLIGENT, SCHOLARLY)
COMMENTS:

JUDGMENT – DECISION MAKING ABILITY

POOR ☐   AVERAGE ☐   GOOD ☐   OUTSTANDING ☐

(MATURE, SEASONED, INDEPENDENT, COMMON SENSE, CERTAIN, DETERMINED, LOGICAL)
COMMENTS:

LEADERSHIP

POOR ☐   AVERAGE ☐   GOOD ☐   OUTSTANDING ☐

(SELF-CONFIDENT, TAKES CHARGE, EFFECTIVE, RESPECTED, MANAGEMENT MINDED, GRASPS AUTHORITY)
COMMENTS:

CAMPUS INTERVIEW SUMMARY

INVITE (Circle)	AREA OF INTEREST (Circle)	SEMESTER HRS.	OFFICES PREFERRED:	SUMMARY COMMENTS: _____
YES NO	AUDIT TAX	Acct'g. _____	No. 1	
DATE AVAILABLE	MCS ABC	Audit _____	No. 2	
	OTHER	Tax _____	No. 3	

Ask Questions   Try to follow your structured interview guide or the questions you wrote out ahead of time. A menu of questions to choose from (such as "What best qualifies you for the available position?") is presented in Figure 6.3.

Some suggestions for actually asking questions include: Avoid questions that can be answered "yes" or "no;" don't put words in the applicant's mouth or telegraph the desired answer, for instance, by nodding or smiling when the right an-

Figure 6.3
Interview Questions to Expect

Source: H. Lee Rust, *Job Search, The Complete Manual for Job Seekers* (New York, AMACOM, 1991), pp. 232–233.

1. Did you bring a résumé?
2. What salary do you expect to receive?
3. What was your salary in your last job?
4. Why do you want to change jobs or why did you leave your last job?
5. What do you identify as your most significant accomplishment in your last job?
6. How many hours do you normally work per week?
7. What did you like and dislike about your last job?
8. How did you get along with your superiors and subordinates?
9. Can you be demanding of your subordinates?
10. How would you evaluate the company you were with last?
11. What were its competitive strengths and weaknesses?
12. What best qualifies you for the available position?
13. How long will it take you to start making a significant contribution?
14. How do you feel about our company—its size, industry, and competitive position?
15. What interests you most about the available position?
16. How would you structure this job or organize your department?
17. What control or financial data would you want and why?
18. How would you establish your primary inside and outside lines of communication?
19. What would you like to tell me about yourself?
20. Were you a good student?
21. Have you kept up in your field? How?
22. What do you do in your spare time?
23. What are your career goals for the next five years?
24. What are your greatest strengths and weaknesses?
25. What is your job potential?
26. What steps are you taking to help achieve your goals?
27. Do you want to own your own business?
28. How long will you stay with us?
29. What did your father do? Your mother?
30. What do your brothers and sisters do?
31. Have you ever worked on a group project and, if so, what role did you play?
32. Do you participate in civic affairs?
33. What professional associations do you belong to?
34. What is your credit standing?
35. What are your personal likes and dislikes?
36. How do you spend a typical day?
37. Would you describe your family as a close one?
38. How aggressive are you?
39. What motivates you to work?
40. Is money a strong incentive for you?
41. Do you prefer line or staff work?
42. Would you rather work alone or in a team?
43. What do you look for when hiring people?
44. Have you ever fired anyone?
45. Can you get along with union members and their leaders?

(continued)

Figure 6.3
(continued)

> 46. What do you think of the current economic and political situation?
> 47. How will government policy affect our industry or your job?
> 48. Will you sign a noncompete agreement or employment contract?
> 49. Why should we hire you?
> 50. Do you want the job?

swer is given; don't interrogate the applicant as if the person is a criminal, and don't be patronizing, sarcastic, or inattentive; don't monopolize the interview by rambling, nor let the applicant dominate the interview so you can't ask all your questions; do ask open-ended questions; listen to the candidate to encourage him or her to express thoughts fully; and draw out the applicant's opinions and feelings by repeating the person's last comment as a question (such as "You didn't like your last job?").

When you ask for general statements of a candidate's accomplishments, also ask for examples.[53] Thus, if the candidate lists specific strengths or weaknesses, follow up with "What are specific examples that demonstrate each of your strengths?"

Close the Interview   Toward the close of the interview, leave time to answer any questions the candidate may have and, if appropriate, to advocate your firm to the candidate.

Try to end all interviews on a positive note. The applicant should be told whether there is an interest and, if so, what the next step will be. Similarly, rejections should be made diplomatically, for instance, with a statement like, "Although your background is impressive, there are other candidates whose experience is closer to our requirements." If the applicant is still being considered but a decision can't be reached at once, say this. If your policy is to inform candidates of their status in writing, do so within a few days of the interview.

Review the Interview   After the candidate leaves, review your interview notes, fill in the structured interview guide (if this was not done during the interview), and review the interview while it's fresh in your mind.

Remember that snap judgments and negative emphasis are two common interviewing mistakes: Reviewing the interview shortly after the candidate has left can help you minimize these two problems.

Small Business Applications

Many of the points discussed in this chapter can be combined into a practical interview procedure for a small business. Such a procedure is especially useful when time and resources are scarce, when HR specialists aren't available, and when a quick way to organize the interview process is required. The procedure consists of four steps as follows:[54]

1. Develop behavioral specifications for the job.
2. Determine what basic factors to probe for.
3. Use an interview plan.
4. Match the candidate to the job.

Develop Behavior Specifications

Even a small business can specify the kind of person who would be best for the job. A quick way to do so is to focus on four basic types of behaviors—*knowledge and experience, motivation, intellectual capacity, and personality,* and to ask the following questions:

Knowledge-Experience Factor   What must the candidate know to perform the job? What experience is absolutely necessary to perform the job?

Motivation Factor   What should the person like doing to enjoy this job? Is there anything the person should not dislike? Are there any essential goals or aspirations the person should have? Are there any unusual energy demands on the job? How critical is the person's drive and motivation?

Intellectual Factor   Are there any specific intellectual aptitudes required (mathematics, mechanical, and so on)? How complex are the problems to be solved? What must a person be able to demonstrate he or she can do intellectually? How should the person solve problems (cautiously, deductively, and so on)?

Personality Factor   What are the critical personality qualities needed for success on the job (ability to withstand boredom, decisiveness, stability, and so on)? How must the job incumbent handle stress, pressure, and criticism? What kind of interpersonal behavior is required in the job up the line, at peer level, down the line, and outside the firm with customers?

Specific Factors to Probe in the Interview

Next use a combination of open-ended questions like those in Figure 6.3 to probe the candidate's suitability for the job. For example:

Intellectual Factor   Here probe such things as complexity of tasks the person has performed, grades in school, test results (including scholastic aptitude tests, and so on), and how the person organizes his or her thoughts and communicates.

Motivation Factor   Probe such areas as the person's likes and dislikes (for each thing done, what he or she liked or disliked about it), the person's aspirations (including the validity of each goal in terms of the person's reasoning about why he or she chose it), and the person's energy level, perhaps by asking what he or she does on, say, a "typical Tuesday."

Personality Factor   Probe by looking for self-defeating patterns of behavior (aggressiveness, compulsive fidgeting, and so on) and by exploring the person's past interpersonal relationships. Here ask questions about the person's past interactions (working in a group at school, working with fraternity brothers or sorority sisters, leading the work team on the last job, and so on). Also try to judge the person's behavior in the interview itself—is the candidate personable? Shy? Outgoing?

Use an Interview Plan

You should also devise and use an interview plan to guide the interview. According to John Drake, significant areas to cover include the candidate's:[55]

> High school experiences
> College experiences
> Work experiences—summer, part-time
> Work experience—full-time (one by one)
> Goals and ambitions
> Reactions to the job you are interviewing for

Self-assessments (by the candidate of his or her strengths and weaknesses)

Military experiences

Present outside activities

Follow your plan, perhaps starting with an open-ended question for each topic, such as "Could you tell me about what you did when you were in high school?" Keep in mind that you are trying to elicit information about four main traits—intelligence, motivation, personality, and knowledge and experience. You can then accumulate the information as the person answers. Particular areas that you want to follow up on can usually be pursued by asking such questions as "Could you elaborate on that, please?"

Match Candidate to the Job

After following the interview plan and probing for the four factors, you should now be able to summarize the candidate's general strengths and limitations, and to draw conclusions about the person's intellectual capacity, knowledge/experience, motivation, and personality. You should then compare your conclusions to both the job description and the list of behavioral specifications developed earlier. This should provide a rational basis for matching the candidate to the job, one based on an analysis of the traits and aptitudes actually required. ◆

Building Employee Commitment

A Total Selection Program

Companies today need employees who are committed to their firms—employees who identify with the firm's values and goals and treat their firms like their own.[56] Therefore,

The commitment of Toyota U.S.A.'s team-member employees is a major part of the reason why the Camry consistently wins quality awards.

progressive companies like Toyota and Federal Express use what we might term value-based hiring practices. They don't just look at applicants' job-related skills. They try to get a sense of the person and his or her destiny and personal qualities and values. They identify common experiences and values that may flag the applicant's future fit with and success in the firm. They give their applicants realistic previews of what to expect. And, perhaps most important, they put enormous effort into combining interviews and other screening procedures like those covered in the previous chapter into *total selection programs* in order to find the best people. As Fujio Cho, president of Toyota Motor Manufacturing USA, put it:

You might be surprised, but our selection and hiring process is an exhaustive, painstaking system designed not to fill positions quickly, but to find the right people for those positions. What are we looking for? First, these people must be able to think for themselves . . . be problem solvers . . . and second, work in a team atmosphere. Simply put, we need strong minds, not strong backs. . . . We consider the selection of a team member as a long-term investment decision. Why go to the trouble of hiring a questionable employee only to have to fire him later?[57]

As summarized in Figure 6.4, Toyota's hiring process takes about 20 hours and six phases, spread over five or six days. The Kentucky Department of Employment Services conducts the initial pre-screening of Phase I. Here applicants fill out application forms summarizing their work experience and skills and view a video describing Toyota's work

Figure 6.4
Summary of Toyota Hiring Process
Based on Toyota Motor Manufacturing, USA Inc. documents.

THE PROCESS
Phase I   Orientation/Application

THE PROCESS

Phase I   Orientation/Application
Fill out an application and view a video of the Toyota work environment and selection system process (1 hour)

       Objective: To explain the job and collect information about work experiences and skills
       Conducted: Kentucky Department of Employment Services

Phase II   Technical Skills Assessment
Pencil/Paper tests
      General knowledge test (2 hours)
      Tool & die or general maintenance test (6 hours)[1]

       Objective: To assess technical knowledge and potential
       Conducted: Kentucky Department of Employment Services

Phase III   Interpersonal Skills Assessment
      Group and individual problem-solving activities (4 hours)
      Production assembly simulation (5 hours)[2]

       Objective: To assess interpersonal and decision-making skills
       Conducted: Toyota Motor Manufacturing

Phase IV   Toyota Assessment
Group interview and evaluation (1 hour)

       Objective: To discuss achievements and accomplishments
       Conducted: Toyota Motor Manufacturing

Phase V   Health Assessment
Physical exam and drug/alcohol tests (2½ hours)

       Objective: To determine physical fitness
       Conducted: Scott County General Hospital and University of Kentucky Medical Center

Phase VI   On-the-Job Observation
Observation and coaching on the job after being hired (6 months)

       Objective: To assess job performance and develop skills
       Conducted: Toyota Motor Manufacturing

[1]Skilled trades only
[2]Production only

environment and selection system. This takes about an hour and gives applicants a realistic preview of work at Toyota and of the hiring process's extensiveness. Many applicants simply drop out at this stage.

Phase II is aimed at assessing the applicant's technical knowledge and potential and in Toyota's case is also conducted by the Kentucky Department of Employment Services. Here applicants take the U.S. Employment Services' General Aptitude Test Battery (GATB), which helps identify problem-solving skills and learning potential, as well as occupational preferences. Skilled trades applicants (experienced mechanics, for example) also take a six-hour tool and die or general maintenance test. Kentucky Employment Services scores all tests and submits the files to Toyota. (Many state employment offices will arrange similar prescreening services for firms doing heavy recruiting in their areas, and many will also administer GATB tests for most firms in their areas.)

Toyota takes over the screening process in Phase III. The aim here is to assess applicants' interpersonal and decision-making skills. All applicants participate in four hours of group and individual problem-solving and discussion activities in the firm's assessment center. This is a separate location where applicants engage in exercises under the observation of Toyota screening experts.

The group discussion exercises help show how individual applicants interact with others in their group. In a typical exercise participants playing company employees constitute a team responsible for choosing new features for next year's car. Team members first individually rank 12 features based upon market appeal and then suggest one feature not included on the list. They must then come to a consensus on the best rank ordering.

The problem-solving exercises are usually administered individually and are aimed at assessing each applicant's problem-solving ability in terms of facets such as insight, flexibility, and creativity. In one typical exercise, an applicant is given a brief description of a production problem and is asked to formulate questions that will help him or her better understand the causes of the problem. The applicant then gets a chance to ask questions of a resource person, one with considerable information about the problem's cause. At the end of this question-and-answer period, the candidate fills out a form listing the problem's causes, recommended solutions, and the reasons for suggesting these solutions.

Also in Phase III, production line assembly candidates participate in a five-hour production assembly simulation. In one of these, candidates play the roles of the management and work force of a firm that makes electrical circuits. During a series of planning and manufacturing periods, the team must decide which circuits should be manufactured and how to effectively assign people, materials, and money to produce them.

A one-hour group interview constitutes Phase IV. Here groups of candidates discuss their accomplishments with Toyota interviewers. This phase helps give the Toyota assessors a more complete picture of what drives each candidate in terms of what each is proudest of and most interested in. Phase IV also gives Toyota another opportunity to watch its candidates interact with each other in groups. Those who successfully complete Phase IV (and are tentatively tapped as Toyota employees) then undergo two and a half hours of physical and drug/alcohol tests at area hospitals (Phase V). Finally, Phase VI involves closely monitoring, observing, and coaching the new employees on the job to assess their job performance and to develop their skills during their first six months at work.

What Toyota Is Looking for in Its Employees

Toyota's total selection process helps to select the kinds of workers management is looking for. The firm's HR chief has said that the first thing you have to do in designing a hiring process such as Toyota's "is to know what you want." Toyota is looking, first, for *interpersonal skills,* due to the firm's emphasis on team interaction.

Similarly, the whole thrust of Toyota's production process is to improve job processes through worker commitment to top quality, and so *reasoning* and *problem-solving skills* are also crucial human requirements. This emphasis on *kaizen*—on having the workers improve the system—helps explain Toyota's emphasis on hiring an intelligent, educated work force. The GATB and problem-solving simulations have in fact helped produce such a work force. "Those who did the best in their education did the best in the simulations," said one HR officer. All Toyota workers have at least a high school degree or equivalent, and many plant employees (including assemblers) are college educated.

Quality is one of Toyota's central values, and so the firm also seeks a history of *quality commitment* in the people it hires. This is one reason for the group interview that focuses on accomplishments. By asking candidates about what they are proudest of, Toyota gets a better insight into the person's values regarding quality and doing things right. This is very important in a firm devoted to having employees build quality into its cars each step of the way.

Toyota is also looking for employees who have an eagerness to learn, and a willingness to try it not only their way, but Toyota's way and the group's way. Toyota's production system is based on consensus decision making, job rotation, and flexible career paths, and these require open-minded, flexible team players, not dogmatists. Toyota's selection process and it's decision-making and problem-solving exercises help identify such people.

Basic Features of Toyota's Selection System

In summary, high-commitment firms like Toyota use total value-based hiring programs to select employees whose values are compatible with those of the firm. While firms do this in various ways, five common themes are apparent from the process at Toyota. First, value-based hiring requires that you've *clarified your firm's own values*. Whether it's excellence, *kaizen*/continuous improvement, integrity, or some other, value-based hiring begins with clarifying what those values are.

Second, high-commitment firms such as Toyota *commit the time and effort* for an exhaustive screening process. Eight to ten hours of interviewing even for entry-level employees is not unusual, and firms like Toyota will spend 20 hours or more with someone before deciding to hire. Many are rejected.

Third, the screening process does not just identify knowledge and technical skills. In addition, the candidates' *values and skills are matched with the needs of the firm*. Teamwork, *kaizen*, and flexibility are central values at Toyota, so problem-solving skills, interpersonal skills, and commitment to quality are crucial human requirements.

Fourth, value-based hiring always includes *realistic job previews*. High-commitment firms are certainly interested in "selling" good candidates. But it's more important to ensure that candidates know what working for the firm will be like, and even more important what sorts of values the firms cherish.

Finally, *self-selection* is an important screening practice at most of these firms. In some firms this just means realistic previews. At others, practices such as long probationary periods in entry-level jobs help screen out those who don't fit. And in firms like these the screening process itself demands a sacrifice of employees: the time and effort are always extensive. ◆

Chapter Review

Summary

1. There are several basic types of interviews: situational, nondirective, structured, sequential, panel, stress, and appraisal interviews. All interviews can be classified according to content, structure, purpose, and method of administration.

2. Several factors and problems can undermine the usefulness of an interview. These are making premature decisions, letting unfavorable information predominate, not knowing the requirements of the job, being under pressure to hire, not allowing for the candidate-order effect, and sending visual cues to telegraph enthusiasm.

3. The five steps in the interview include: plan, establish rapport, question the candidate, close the interview, and review the data.

4. Guidelines for interviewers include: Use a structured guide, know the requirements of the job, focus on traits you can more accurately evaluate (like motivation), let the interviewee do most of the talking, delay your decision until after the interview, and remember the EEOC requirements.

5. The steps in a structured or situational interview are: job analysis, evaluate the job duty information, develop interview questions with critical incidents, develop benchmark answers, appoint an interview committee, and implement.

6. As an interviewee, keep in mind that interviewers tend to make premature decisions and let unfavorable information predominate; your appearance and enthusiasm are important; you should get the interviewer to talk; it is important to prepare before walking in—get to know the job and the problems the interviewer wants solved; and you should stress your enthusiasm and motivation to work, and how your accomplishments match your interviewer's needs.

7. A quick procedure for conducting an interview is to develop behavioral specifications; determine the basic intellectual, motivation, personality, and experience factors to probe for; use an interview plan; and then match the individual to the job. The procedure is especially useful in small firms with HR groups, but can be used in large firms as well.

8. Value-based hiring can contribute to building employee commitment. It assumes that management has clarified the values it cherishes (such as quality at Toyota), spends adequate time in the selection process, and provides for realistic previews.

Key Terms

nondirective interview	appraisal interview	serialized interview
directive interview	situational interview	panel interview
stress interview	job-related interview	candidate-order error

Discussion Questions and Exercises

1. Explain the four basic ways in which interviews can be classified.

2. Briefly describe each of the following possible types of interviews: unstructured panel interviews; structured sequential interviews; job-related structured interviews.

3. For what sorts of jobs do you think computerized interviews are most appropriate? Why?

4. Give a short presentation entitled "How to be Effective as an Interviewee."

5. Why do you think ". . . situational interviews yield a higher mean validity than do job related or behavioral interviews, which in turn yield a higher mean validity than do psychological interviews?"

6. Similarly, how do you explain the fact that structured interviews, regardless of content, are more valid than unstructured interviews for predicting job performance?

7. Briefly discuss and give examples of at least five common interviewing mistakes. What recommendations would you give for avoiding these interviewing mistakes?

8. Working individually or in groups, develop a structured situational interview for hiring someone to teach a college-level course in human resource management.

9. Working individually or in groups, use the interview process described in this chapter's Small Business Applications feature to explain how you would interview a candidate for the job of President of the United States.

10. Explain why you think that it is (or is not) important to select candidates based on their values, as well as usual selection criteria such as skills and experience.

Application Exercises

RUNNING CASE: Carter Cleaning Company
The Better Interview

Like virtually all the other personnel management–related activities at Carter Cleaning Centers, the company currently has no organized approach to interviewing job candidates. Store managers, who do almost all the hiring, have a few of their own favorite questions that they ask. But in the absence of any guidance from top management, they all admit their interview performance leaves something to be desired. Similarly, Jack Carter himself is admittedly most comfortable dealing with what he calls the "nuts and bolts" machinery aspect of his business and has never felt particularly comfortable having to interview management or other job interviewees. Jennifer is sure that lack of formal interviewing practices, procedures, and training account for some of the employee turnover and theft problems. Therefore, she wants to do something to improve her company's batting average in this important area.

Questions

1. In general, what can Jennifer do to improve her employee interviewing practices? Should she develop interview forms that list questions for management and nonmanagement jobs, and if so what form should these take and what questions should be included?

2. Should she implement a training program for her managers, and if so, specifically what should be the content of such an interview training program? In other words, if she did decide to start training her management people to be better interviewers, what should she tell them and how should she tell it to them?

CASE INCIDENT: The Out-of-Control Interview

Maria Fernandez is a bright, popular, and well-informed mechanical engineer who graduated with an engineering degree from State University in June 1995. During the spring preceding her graduation she went out on many job interviews, most of which she thought were courteous and reasonably useful in giving both her and the prospective employer a good impression of where each of them stood on matters of importance to both of them. It was, therefore, with great anticipation that she looked forward to an interview with the one firm in which she most wanted to work, Apex Environmental. She had always had a strong interest in cleaning up the environment and firmly believed that the best use of her training and skills lay in working for a firm like Apex, where she thought she could have a successful career while making the world a better place.

The interview, however, was a disaster. Maria walked into a room in which five men, including the president of the company, two vice presidents, the marketing director, and another engineer began throwing questions at her that she felt were aimed primarily at tripping her up rather than finding out what she could offer through her engineering skills. The questions ranged from unnecessarily discourteous ("Why would you take a job as a waitress in college if you're such an intelligent person?") to irrelevant and sexist ("Are you planning on settling down and starting a family any time soon?"). Then, after the interview, she met with two of the gentlemen individually (including the president) and the discussions focused almost exclusively on her technical expertise. She thought that these later discussions went fairly well. However, given the apparent aimlessness and even mean-spiritedness of the panel interview, she was astonished when several days later she got a job offer from the firm.

The offer forced her to consider several matters. From her point of view the job itself was perfect—she liked what she would be doing, the industry, and the firm's location. And, in fact, the president had been quite courteous in subsequent discussions, as had been the other members of the management team. She was left wondering whether the panel interview had been intentionally tense to see how she'd stand up under pressure, and, if so, why they would do such a thing.

Questions

1. How would you explain the nature of the panel interview Maria had to endure? Specifically, do you think it reflected a well-thought-out interviewing strategy on the part of the firm or carelessness on the part of the firm's management? If it was carelessness, what would you do to improve the interview process at Apex Environmental?

2. Would you take the job offer if you were Maria? If you're not sure, is there any additional information that would help you make your decision, and if so, what is it?

3. The job of applications engineer for which Maria was applying requires: (1) excellent technical skills with respect to mechanical engineering; (2) a commitment to working in the area of pollution control; (3) the ability to deal well and confidently with customers who have engineering problems; (4) a willingness to travel worldwide; and (5) a very intelligent and well-balanced personality. What questions would you ask when interviewing applicants for the job?

 # Human Resource Management Simulation

You will notice in incident (D) that the candidates describe themselves very differently. How much weight should be placed on an interview? What if the candidate had a bad day before the interview?

Also, incident (B) involves job design. To what extent should the candidate be made aware of the detailed specifications of a job? Could such detail "turn off" a job candidate?

Video Case

Age Discrimination

As you'll learn in this video, the average age of the American work force is rising. But is seniority the advantage it once was? Hardly. Promotion based on seniority is very much a thing of the past. Also, younger, less qualified, and "lower cost" workers are often given positions at the expense of older workers. The personal trauma these older workers face is then compounded when they attempt to find new careers. As they try to start all over, they find that prospective employers' interview and selection processes are biased against them.

Questions

1. What are the questions you can and cannot ask if you are to avoid charges of age discrimination?

2. Why do you think age discrimination is the fastest growing area of EEOC charges?

3. As an HR manager for your employer, what would you tell manager/interviewers they should do with respect to their selection procedures to avoid charges of age discrimination?

4. Can you think of any conditions under which age might in fact be a valid predictor of performance on the job? What might they be?

Source: ABC News, *Age Discrimination in the Workplace,* "Business World," December 16, 1990.

 ## Take It to the Net

We invite you to visit the Dessler page on the Prentice Hall Web site at:
http://www.prenhall.com/~dessler

for the monthly Dessler update and for this chapter's World Wide Web exercise.

Appendix 6.1

Guidelines for Interviewees

Before you get into a position where you have to do interviewing, you will probably have to navigate some interviews yourself. Here are some hints for excelling in your interview.

The first thing to understand is that interviews are used primarily to help employers determine what you are like as a person.[58] In other words, information regarding how you get along with other people and your desire to work is of prime importance in the interview; your skills and technical expertise are usually best assessed through tests and a study of your educational and work history. Interviewers will look first for crisp, articulate answers. Specifically, whether you respond concisely, cooperate fully in answering questions, state personal opinions when relevant, and keep to the subject at hand are by far the most important elements in influencing the interviewer's decision.

There are seven things to do to get that extra edge in the interview.

1. *Preparation is essential.* Before the interview, learn all you can about the employer, the job, and the people doing the recruiting. At the library, look through business periodicals to find out what is happening in the employer's field. Who is the competition? How are they doing? Try to unearth the employer's problems. Be ready to explain why you think you would be able to solve such problems, citing some of your *specific accomplishments* to make your case.

2. *Uncover the interviewer's real needs.* Spend as little time as possible answering your interviewer's first questions and as much time as possible getting him or her to describe his or her needs. Determine what the person is looking to get accomplished, and the type of person he or she feels is needed. Use open-ended questions here such as: "Could you tell me more about that?"

3. *Relate yourself to the interviewer's needs.* Once you know the type of person your interviewer is looking for and the sorts of problems he or she wants solved, you are in a good position to describe your own accomplishments *in terms of the interviewer's needs*. Start by saying something like, "One of the problem areas you've said is important to you is similar to a problem I once faced." Then state the problem, describe your solution, and reveal the results.[59]

4. *Think before answering.*[60] Answering a question should be a three-step process: Pause—Think—Speak. *Pause* to make sure you understand what the interviewer is driving at, *think* about how to structure your answer, and then *speak*. In your answer, try to emphasize how hiring you will help the interviewer solve his or her problem.

5. *Remember that appearance and enthusiasm are important.* Appropriate clothing, good grooming, a firm handshake, and the appearance of controlled energy are important.

6. *Make a good first impression.* Remember that studies show that in most cases interviewers make up their minds about the applicant during the early minutes of the interview. A good first impression may turn to bad during the interview, but it is unlikely. Bad first impressions are almost impossible to overcome. One expert suggests paying attention to the following key interviewing considerations:

1. Appropriate clothing
2. Good grooming
3. A firm handshake
4. The appearance of controlled energy

Figure 6.5
Interview Questions to Ask

Source: H. Lee Rust, *Job Search, The Complete Manual for Job Seekers* (New York, AMACOM, 1991), pp. 234–235.

1. What is the first problem that needs attention of the person you hire?
2. What other problems need attention now?
3. What has been done about any of these to date?
4. How has this job been performed in the past?
5. Why is it now vacant?
6. Do you have a written job description for this position?
7. What are its major responsibilities?
8. What authority would I have? How would you define its scope?
9. What are the company's five-year sales and profit projections?
10. What needs to be done to reach these projections?
11. What are the company's major strengths and weaknesses?
12. What are its strengths and weaknesses in production?
13. What are its strengths and weaknesses in its products or its competitive position?
14. Whom do you identify as your major competitors?
15. What are their strengths and weaknesses?
16. How do you view the future for your industry?
17. Do you have any plans for new products or acquisitions?
18. Might this company be sold or acquired?
19. What is the company's current financial strength?
20. What can you tell me about the individual to whom I would report?
21. What can you tell me about other persons in key positions?
22. What can you tell me about the subordinates I would have?
23. How would you define your management philosophy?
24. Are employees afforded an opportunity for continuing education?
25. What are you looking for in the person who will fill this job?

5. Pertinent humor and readiness to smile
6. A genuine interest in the employer's operation and alert attention when the interviewer speaks
7. Pride in past performance
8. An understanding of the employer's needs and a desire to serve them
9. The display of sound ideas
10. Ability to take control when employers fall down on the interviewing job

Sample questions you can ask are presented in Figure 6.5. They include "Would you mind describing the job for me?" and "Could you tell me about the people who would be reporting to me?"

7. Remember that your *nonverbal behavior* may broadcast more about you than the verbal content of what you say. Here maintaining eye contact is very important. In addition, speak with enthusiasm, nod agreement, and remember to take a moment to frame your answer (pause, think, speak) so that you sound articulate and fluent.

Notes

1. Michael McDaniel, et al., "The Validity of Employment Interviews: A Comprehensive Review and Meta-analysis," *Journal of Applied Psychology,* Vol. 79, no. 4 (1994), p. 599.

2. R. L. Dipboye, *Selection Interviews: Process Perspectives* (Cincinnati: Southwestern Publishing Co., 1992).

3. L. Ulrich and D. Trumbo, "The Selection Interview Since 1949," *Psychological Bulletin,* Vol. 63 (1965), pp. 100–116, quoted in Michael McDaniel, et al., "The Validity of Employment Interviews," p. 599.

4. McDaniel, et al., "The Validity of Employment Interviews," p. 602.

5. Ibid., p. 601.

6. See, for example, T. Janz, "The Patterned Behavior Description Interview: The Best Profit of the Future in the Past," in eds. R. W. Eder and G. R. Ferris, *The Employment Interview: Theory, Research, and Practice* (Newbury Park, CA: Sage, 1989), pp. 158–168.

7. McDaniel, et al., "The Validity of Employment Interviews," p. 601.

8. See Philip Roth and Jeffrey McMillan, "The Behavior Description Interview," *The CPA Journal* (December 1993), pp. 76–79.

9. See A. M. Ryan and P. R. Sackett, "Exploratory Study of Individual Assessment Practices: Interrater Reliability and Judgments of Assessor Effectiveness," *Journal of Applied Psychology,* Vol. 74 (1989), pp. 568–579, cited in McDaniel, "The Validity of Employment Interviews," p. 601.

10. Arthur Pell, *Recruiting and Selecting Personnel* (New York: Regents, 1969), p. 119.

11. Douglas Rodgers, "Computer-Aided Interviewing Overcomes First Impressions," *Personnel Journal* (April 1987), pp. 148–152.

12. Ibid.

13. Gary Robins, "Dial-an-Interview," *Stores* (June 1994), pp. 34–35.

14. William Bulkeley, "Replaced by Technology: Job Interviews," *The Wall Street Journal,* August 22, 1994, pp. B1 and B7.

15. Ibid.

16. For additional information on computer-aided interviewing's benefits, see, for example, Christopher Martin and Denise Nagao, "Some Effects of Computerized Interviewing on Job Applicant Responses," *Journal of Applied Psychology,* Vol. 74, no. 1 (February 1989), pp. 72–80.

17. This is quoted from or paraphrased from William Bulkeley, "Replaced by Technology," pp. B1 and B7.

18. Neal Schmitt, "Social and Situational Determinants of Interview Decisions: Implications for the Employment Interview," *Personnel Psychology,* Vol. 29 (Spring 1976), pp. 79–101; Lynn Ulrich and Don Trumbo, "The Selection Interview Since 1949," *Psychological Bulletin,* Vol. 63 (1965), pp. 100–116. See, however, Frank Landy, "The Validity of the Interview in Police Officer Selection," *Journal of Applied Psychology,* Vol. 61 (1976), pp. 193–198. See also Vincent Loretto, "Effective Interviewing Is Based on More Than Intuition," *Personnel Journal,* Vol. 65 (December 1986), pp. 101–107; George Dreher et al., "The Role of the Traditional Research Design in Underestimating the Validity of the Employment Interview," *Personnel Psychology,* Vol. 41, no. 2 (Summer 1988), pp. 315–318; and M. M. Harris, "Reconsidering the Employment Interview: A Review of Recent Literature and Suggestions for Future Research," *Personnel Psychology,* Vol. 42, 1989, pp. 691–726.

19. This validity discussion and these findings are based on McDaniel, et al., "The Validity of the Employment Interview," pp. 607–610; the validities for situational, job-related, and psychological interviews were (.50), (.39), and (.29), respectively.

20. Mean validities were structured (.44) and unstructured (.33). The researchers note that in this case even the unstructured interviews were relatively structured suggesting that ". . .the validity of most unstructured interviews used in practice may be lower than the validity found in this study." Ibid., p. 609.

21. Reported mean validities were somewhat different when the criterion was training score rather than job performance.

22. This is based on John F. Wymer III and Deborah A. Sudbury, "Employment Discrimination 'Testers'—Will Your Hiring Practices 'Pass'?" *Employee Relations Law Journal,* Vol. 17, no. 4 (Spring 1992), pp. 623–633. Ibid., pp. 624–625.

23. Bureau of National Affairs, *Daily Labor Report,* December 5, 1990 at D-1.

24. See for example *Lea v. Cone Mills Corp.,* 438 F2d 86 (1971).

25. Wymer and Sudbury, "Employment Discrimination 'Testers,'" p. 629.

26. Urban Institute, *Opportunities Denied, Opportunities Diminished: Discrimination in Hiring.*

27. Adapted from Wymer and Sudbury, "Employment Discrimination 'Testers,'" pp. 631–632.

28. Frederic M. Jablin, "Use of Discrimination Questions in Screening Interviews," *Personnel Administrator,* Vol. 27, no. 3 (March 1982), pp. 41–44; also see Clifford M. Koen, Jr., "The Pre-employment Inquiry Guide," *Personnel Journal,* Vol. 59, no. 10 (October 1980), pp. 825–829.

29. Robert Dipboye, Richard Arvey, and David Terpstra, "Equal Employment and the Interview," *Personnel Journal,* Vol. 55 (October 1976).

30. McDaniel, et al., "The Validity of the Employment Interview," p. 608.

31. Anthony Dalessio and Todd Silverhart, "Combining Biodata Test and Interview Information: Predicting Decisions and Performance Criteria," *Personnel Psychology,* Vol. 47 (1994), p. 313.

32. S. W. Constantin, "An Investigation of Information Favorability in the Employment Interview," *Journal of Applied Psychology,* Vol. 61 (1976), pp. 743–749. It should be noted that a number of the studies discussed in this chapter involve having interviewers evaluate interviews based on written transcripts (rather than face to face) and that a study suggests that this procedure may not be equivalent to having interviewers interview applicants directly. See Charles Gorman, William Grover, and Michael Doherty, "Can We Learn Anything About Interviewing Real People from 'Interviews' of Paper People? A Study of the External Validity Paradigm," *Organizational Behavior and Human Per-*

formance, Vol. 22, no. 2 (October 1978), pp. 165–192. See also John Binning et al., "Effects of Pre-interview Impressions on Questioning Strategies in Same and Opposite Sex Employment Interviews," *Journal of Applied Psychology,* Vol. 73, no. 1 (February 1988), pp. 30–37; and Sebastiano Fisicaro, "A Reexamination of the Relation Between Halo Error and Accuracy," *Journal of Applied Psychology,* Vol. 73, no. 2 (May 1988), pp. 239–246.

33. David Tucker and Patricia Rowe, "Relationship Between Expectancy, Casual Attribution, and Final Hiring Decisions in the Employment Interview," *Journal of Applied Psychology,* Vol. 64, no. 1 (February 1979), pp. 27–34. See also Robert Dipboye, Gail Fontenelle, and Kathleen Garner, "Effect of Previewing the Application on Interview Process and Outcomes," *Journal of Applied Psychology,* Vol. 69, no. 1 (February 1984), pp. 118–128.

34. Don Langdale and Joseph Weitz, "Estimating the Influence of Job Information on Interviewer Agreement," *Journal of Applied Psychology,* Vol. 57 (1973), pp. 23–27; for a review of how to determine the human requirements of a job, see Anthony W. Simmons, "Selection Interviewing," *Employment Relations Today* (Winter 1991), pp. 305–309.

35. R. E. Carlson, "Selection Interview Decisions: The Effects of Interviewer Experience, Relative Quota Situation, and Applicant Sample on Interview Decisions," *Personnel Psychology,* Vol. 20 (1967), pp. 259–280.

36. R. E. Carlson, "Effects of Applicant Sample on Ratings of Valid Information in an Employment Setting," *Journal of Applied Psychology,* Vol. 54 (1970), pp. 217–222.

37. See Arvey and Campion, "The Employment Interview," p. 305.

38. T. V. McGovern and H. E. Tinsley, "Interviewer Evaluations of Interviewees' Nonverbal Behavior," *Journal of Vocational Behavior,* Vol. 13 (1978), pp. 163–171. See also Keith Rasmussen, Jr., "Nonverbal Behavior, Verbal Behavior, Resume Credentials, and Selection Interview Outcomes," *Journal of Applied Psychology,* Vol. 60, no. 4 (1984), pp. 551–556; Robert Gifford, Cheuk Fan Ng, and Margaret Wilkinson, "Nonverbal Cues in the Employment Interview: Links Between Applicant Qualities and Interviewer Judgments," *Journal of Applied Psychology,* Vol. 70, no. 4 (1985), pp. 729–736; Scott T. Fleischmann, "The Messages of Body Language in Job Interviews," *Employee Relations,* Vol. 18, no. 2 (Summer 1991), pp. 161–166.

39. Madelaine Heilman and Lewis Saruwatari, "When Beauty Is Beastly: The Effects of Appearance and Sex on Evaluation of Job Applicants for Managerial and Nonmanagerial Jobs," *Organizational Behavior and Human Performance,* Vol. 23 (June 1979), pp. 360–372. See also Tracy McDonald and Milton Hakel, "Effects of Applicant Race, Sex, Suitability, and Answers on Interviewers' Questioning Strategy and Ratings," *Personnel Psychology,* Vol. 38, no. 2 (Summer 1985), pp. 321–334. See also M. S. Singer and Christine Sewell, "Applicant Age and Selection Interview Decisions: Effect of Information Exposure on Age Discrimination in Personnel Selection," *Personnel Psychology,* Vol. 42, no. 1 (Spring 1989), pp. 135–154.

40. Sandra Forsythe, Mary Frances Drake, and Charles Cox, "Influence of Applicants' Dress on Interviewers' Selection Decisions," *Journal of Applied Psychology,* Vol. 70, no. 2 (1985), pp. 374–378.

41. Arthur Pell, "Nine Interviewing Pitfalls," *Managers* (January 1994), p. 29.

42. Thomas Dougherty, Daniel Turban, and John Callender, "Confirming First Impressions in the Employment Interview: A Field Study of Interviewer Behavior," *Journal of Applied Psychology,* Vol. 79, no. 5 (1994), p. 663.

43. See Pell, "Nine Interviewing Pitfalls," p. 29; Parth Sarathi, "Making Selection Interviews Effective," *Management and Labor Studies,* Vol. 18, no. 1 (1993), pp. 5–7.

44. Pell, "Nine Interviewing Pitfalls," p. 30.

45. This section based on Pursell, Campion, and Gaylord, "Structured Interviewing," and Latham et al., "The Situational Interview." See also Michael A. Campion, Elliott Pursell, and Barbara Brown, "Structured Interviewing," pp. 25–42, and Weekley and Gier, "Reliability and Validity of the Situational Interview," pp. 484–487.

46. See also Phillip Lowry, "The Structured Interview: An Alternative to the Assessment Center?" *Public Personnel Management,* Vol. 23, no. 2 (Summer 1994), pp. 201–215.

47. Pursell et al., "Structured Interviewing," p. 910.

48. From a speech by industrial psychologist Paul Green and contained in Bureau of National Affairs, *Bulletin to Management,* June 20, 1985, pp. 2–3.

49. Pell, *Recruiting and Selecting Personnel,* pp. 103–115.

50. Carlson, "Selection Interview Decisions," pp. 259–280.

51. William Tullar, Terry Mullins, and Sharon Caldwell, "Effects of Interview Length and Applicant Quality on Interview Decision Time," *Journal of Applied Psychology,* Vol. 64 (December 1979), pp. 669–674. See also McDonald and Hakel, "Effects of Applicants' Race, Sex, Suitability, and Answers," pp. 321–334.

52. Edwin Walley, "Successful Interviewing Techniques," *The CPA Journal* (September 1993), p. 70.

53. Pamela Kaul, "Interviewing Is Your Business," *Association Management* (November 1992), p. 29.

54. This is based on John Drake, *Interviewing for Managers: A Complete Guide to Employment Interviewing* (New York: AMACOM, 1982).

55. Ibid.

56. Based on Gary Dessler, *Winning Commitment* (New York: McGraw-Hill Book Company, 1993). Similarly, see Glenn Bassett, "From Job Fit to Cultural Compatibility: Evaluating Worker Skills and Temperament in the 90s," *Optimum, The Journal of Public Sector Management,* Vol. 25, no. 1 (Summer 1994), pp. 11-17.

57. Speech to the City Club, November 15, 1991, Cleveland, Ohio.

58. James Hollandsworth, Jr., and others, "Relative Contributions of Verbal, Articulative, and Nonverbal Communication to Employment Decisions in the Job Interview Setting," *Personnel Psychology,* Vol. 32 (Summer 1979), pp. 359–367. See also Sara Rynes and Howard Miller, "Recruiter and Job Influences on Candidates for Employment," *Journal of Applied Psychology,* Vol. 68, no. 1 (1983), pp. 147–154.

59. Richard Payne, *How to Get a Better Job Quickly* (New York: New American Library, 1979).

60. J. G. Hollandsworth, R. C. Ladinski, and J. H. Russel, "Use of Social Skills Training in the Treatment of Extreme Anxiety of Deficient Verbal Skills," *Journal of Applied Psychology,* Vol. 11 (1979), pp. 259–269.

Chapter 7

Orientation and Training

Chapter Outline

- ◆ **Orienting Employees**
- ◆ **The Training Process**
- ◆ **Training Needs Analysis**
- ◆ **Training Techniques**
- ◆ **Training for Special Purposes**
- ◆ **Evaluating the Training Effort**

Behavioral Objectives

When you finish studying this chapter, you should be able to:

Explain how to develop an orientation and socialization program.

Describe the basic training process.

Discuss at least two techniques used for assessing training needs.

Explain the pros and cons of at least five training techniques.

Describe how to evaluate the training effort.

Once employees have been recruited and selected, the next step is orientation and training. In this chapter we'll see that orienting and training employees means providing them with the information and skills they need to successfully perform their new jobs. We'll start with employee orientation.

Orienting Employees

employee orientation
A procedure for providing new employees with basic background information about the firm.

Employee orientation provides new employees with basic background information about the employer, information they need to perform their jobs satisfactorily, such as what the work hours are. Orientation is actually one component of the employer's new-employee socialization process. *Socialization* is the ongoing process of instilling in all employees the prevailing attitudes, standards, values, and patterns of behavior that are expected by the organization and its departments.[1]

The new employee's initial orientation, if handled correctly, helps him or her perform better by providing needed information about company rules and practices. It can also help reduce the new employee's first-day jitters and the **reality shock** he or she might otherwise experience (the discrepancy between what the new employee expected from his or her new job, and the realities of it).

reality shock
That state which results from the discrepancy between what the new employee expected from his or her new job, and the realities of it.

Orientation programs range from brief, informal introductions to lengthy, formal programs. In the latter, the new employee is usually given a handbook or printed materials that cover matters like working hours, performance reviews, getting on the payroll, and vacations, as well as a tour of the facilities. As illustrated in Figure 7.1, other information typically includes employee benefits, personnel policies, the employee's daily routine, company organization and operations, and safety measures and regulations.[2] Note that there is the real possibility that courts will find your employee handbook's contents represent a contract with the employee. Therefore, disclaimers should be included that make it clear that statements of company policies, benefits, and regulations do not constitute the terms and conditions of an employment contract either express or implied. Think twice before including statements in your handbook such as "No employee will be fired without just cause" or statements that imply or state that employees have tenure; they could be viewed as legal and binding commitments.

In this class for nurses' aides the supervisor continues orientation by explaining the exact nature of the job, introducing new colleagues, and familiarizing the new employees with their workplace.

The first part of the orientation is usually performed by the HR specialist, who explains such matters as working hours and vacation. The employee is then introduced to his or her new supervisor. The latter continues the orientation by explaining the exact nature of the job, introducing the person to his or her new colleagues, and familiarizing the new employee with the workplace. An example of a comprehensive orientation program is presented in the following box.

Building Employee Commitment

Orientation and Socialization

In many firms today orientation goes well beyond providing basic information about such aspects of the job as hours of work. More and more companies are finding that orientation can be used for other purposes, such as familiarizing new employees with the company's cherished goals and values. Orientation thus begins the process of synthesizing the employee's and the company's goals, one big step toward winning the employee's commitment to the firm.

Orientation (it is called "assimilation") at Toyota Motor Manufacturing USA is a case in point. While it covers traditional topics such as company benefits, it's mostly intended to socialize new employees, that is, to convert Toyota's new employees to the firm's ideology of quality, teamwork, personal development, open communication, and mutual respect. It lasts four days, as follows:

Day One. The first day begins at 6:30 a.m. with an overview of the program, a welcome to the company, and a discussion of the firm's organization structure and human resource department by the firm's vice president for human resources. The vice president devotes about an hour and a half to discussing Toyota history and culture, and about two hours to employee benefits. Another two hours are then spent discussing Toyota's policies about the importance of quality and teamwork.

Day Two. The second day starts with about two hours devoted to "communication training—the Toyota Motor Manufacturing way of listening." Here the importance of mutual respect, teamwork, and open communication is emphasized. The rest of the day is then devoted to general orientation issues. These include safety, environmental affairs, the Toyota production system, and the firm's library.

Day Three. This day also begins with two-and-a-half to three hours devoted to communication training, in this case "making requests and giving feedback." The rest of the day is spent covering matters such as Toyota's problem-solving methods, quality assurance, hazard communications, and safety.

Day Four. Teamwork is stressed in the morning session. Topics include teamwork training, Toyota's suggestion system, and the Toyota Team Member Activities Association. This session also covers what work teams are responsible for and how to work together as a team. The afternoon specifically covers fire prevention and fire extinguishers training.

Employees thus complete the four-day orientation/assimilation/socialization process having been steeped in—and it is hoped converted to—Toyota's ideology, in particular its mission of quality and its values of teamwork, *kaizen*/continuous improvement, and problem solving. That is a big step toward winning new employees' commitment to Toyota and its goals and values.◆

The Training Process

Introduction: Training and Responsiveness

training
The process of teaching new employees the basic skills they need to perform their jobs.

Training gives new or present employees the skills they need to perform their jobs. Training might thus mean showing a machinist how to operate his new machine, a new salesperson how to sell her firm's product, or a new supervisor how to interview and appraise employees. Whereas training focuses on skills needed to perform employees' current jobs, *employee and management development* (explained in Chapter 8) is training of a long-term nature. Its aim is to develop current or future employees for future jobs with the organization or to solve an organizational problem concerning, for instance, poor interdepartmental communication. The techniques used in both training and development are often the same, however, and the distinction between the two is always somewhat arbitrary.[3]

In fact, training's purposes are broader today than they have been in the past. Companies used to emphasize production process training—teaching the

Figure 7.1
Overview of Orientation Program

Source: *Handbook of Modern Personnel Administration* by Joseph Famularo. Copyright 1985, McGraw-Hill Book Company. Used with permission of McGraw-Hill, Inc.

Orientation Checklist
(Small southern manufacturing company)

HOURLY & SALARIED EMPLOYEE ORIENTATION GUIDE CHECKLIST
NOTE: ALL APPROPRIATE INFORMATION MUST BE DISCUSSED WITH EACH NEW EMPLOYEE

SUPERVISOR: This form is to be used as a guide for the orientation of new employees in your department.

In order to avoid duplication of instruction the information indicated below has been given to the employee by the Personnel Department.

PERSONNEL DEPARTMENT

EEO BOOKLET		ABSENCES - TARDINESS	
INSURANCE PROGRAM BOOKLET		VETERANS' RE-EMPLOYMENT RIGHTS & RESERVE STATUS	
SALARY CONTINUANCE INSURANCE BOOKLET		UNITED FUND	
SAFETY BOOKLET		VACATIONS	
PENSION PLAN BOOKLET		JURY DUTY	
EMPLOYEE HANDBOOK/LABOR AGREEMENT/RULES BOOKLET		SICK BENEFITS – A & S – LIMITATIONS, ETC.	
MATCHING GIFTS		LEAVE OF ABSENCE - MATERNITY - MEDICAL, ETC.	
EDUCATIONAL ASSISTANCE PROGRAM		SERVICE AWARDS	
PATENT AGREEMENT		VISITORS	
I.D. CARD		HOLIDAYS	
CREDIT UNION		FOOD SERVICES	
STOCK PURCHASE PLAN		FIRST AID & REQUIREMENTS OF REPORTING INJURY	
SAVINGS BOND PLAN		DIFFICULTIES, COMPLAINTS, DISCRIMINATION & GRIEVANCE PROCED.	
PROBATIONARY PERIOD		MILL TOUR	
PAY, SALARY, PROMOTIONS AND TRANSFERS		TERMINATION NOTICE AND PAY ESP. VACATION	
TRANSPORTATION		ALLOWANCE (VOLUNTARY RESIGNATION)	
TIME SHEET		INTRODUCTION TO GUARDS	
PERSONAL RECORDS		(OTHERS)	
BULLETIN BOARDS			
PERSONAL MAIL			
PARKING FACILITIES			

SIGNATURE OF EMPLOYEE:	WITNESS:	DATE

SUPERVISOR: The following is a check list of information necessary to orient the new employee to the job in your department. Please check off each point as you discuss it with the employee and return to the Personnel Department within three days following employee placement on the job:

INTRODUCTION TO FELLOW EMPLOYEES		HOURS OF WORK - OVERTIME - CALL IN PROCEDURES	
TOUR OF DEPARTMENT		REST, LUNCH PERIODS	
EXPLANATION OF NEW EMPLOYEES JOB, RESPONSIBILITIES AND PERFORMANCE EVALUATIONS		SUPPLY PROCEDURE	
		LINE OF AUTHORITY	
LAVATORY			
PHONE CALLS - PERSONAL/COMPANY			

SIGNATURE OF SUPERVISOR:	DATE

I have received a copy of the appropriate materials listed above and have had explained to me the information outlined. I understand this information concerning my employment with (Company name). Also, in case of voluntary separation (resignation) I understand the Company's policy, that in order to be eligible for any due vacation allowance, I must give my supervisor at least two weeks' notice in writing prior to my last day of work.

SIGNATURE OF EMPLOYEE:	WITNESS:	DATE

technical skills required to perform jobs, such as training assemblers to solder wires or teachers to devise lesson plans.[4] However, training and development programs and their objectives changed in the 1980s and 1990s. Employers had to adapt to rapid technological changes, improve product and service quality, and boost productivity to stay competitive.[5] Improving quality often requires remedial-education training, since quality-improvement programs assume employees can use critical thinking skills, produce charts and graphs, and analyze data.[6] Employees must also use or acquire skills in team building, decision making, and communication. Similarly, as firms became more technologically advanced, employees require training in technological and computer skills (such as desktop publishing and computer-aided design and manufacturing).[7] And as increased competition has put a premium on better service, employers have turned increasingly to customer-service training to provide employees with the tools and abilities they need to deal more effectively with customers, such as effective listening skills. All told, this shift from purely production-process training helps to explain why in one recent year an average production worker received 37 hours of training compared with only 31 hours in the previous year.[8]

More employers today are also taking advantage of the fact that training can strengthen employee commitment. Few things illustrate a firm's commitment to its employees more than continuing developmental opportunities to better themselves, and such commitment is usually reciprocated. This is one reason why high-commitment firms like Toyota provide about two weeks of training per year for all employees—about double the national average.

In summary, the expansion of training's role reflects the fact that "the game of economic competition has new rules."[9] In particular, it's no longer enough to just be efficient. Thriving today requires that the firm be fast and responsive. And it requires responding to customers' needs for quality, variety, customization, convenience, and timeliness. Meeting these new standards requires a work force that is more than just technically trained. It requires people who are capable of analyzing and solving job-related problems, working productively in teams, and "switching gears" and shifting from job to job as well.

Unfortunately, a "training gap" exists and may even be widening. While some companies—IBM, Xerox, Texas Instruments, and Motorola, for instance—devote 5% to 10% of their payroll dollars to training activities, the average training investment by U.S. firms (while large in dollar terms) is less than 2% of payroll.[10] Experts estimate that between 42% and 90% of U.S. workers need further training to get them up to speed.[11] In any case, training is moving to center stage as a means of improving employers' competitiveness.

The Five-Step Training and Development Process

We can conveniently think of a typical training or development program as consisting of five steps, as summarized in Figure 7.2. The purpose of the *needs analysis* step is to identify the specific job performance skills needed, to analyze the skills and needs of the prospective trainees, and to develop specific, measurable knowledge and performance objectives. (Here make sure that the performance deficiency is amenable to training rather than caused by, say, poor morale due to low salaries.) In the second, *instructional design* step, the actual content of the training program is compiled and produced including workbooks, exercises, and activities. Next there may be a third *validation* step in which the bugs are worked out of the training program by presenting it to a small representative audience. Fourth, the training program is *implemented,* using techniques like those discussed in this and the following chapter (such as on-the-job training and programmed learning).

Figure 7.2.
The Five Steps in the
Training and
Development Process.[1]

[1]These are adapted from Mary D. Carolan, "Today's Training Basics: Some New Golden Rules," *HR Focus* (April 1993), p. 18.

1. NEEDS ANALYSIS

- Identify specific job performance skills needed to improve performance and productivity.
- Analyze the audience to ensure that the program will be suited to their specific levels of education, experience, and skills, as well as their attitudes and personal motivations.
- Use research to develop specific measurable knowledge and performance objectives.

2. INSTRUCTIONAL DESIGN

- Gather instructional objectives, methods, media, description of and sequence of content, examples, exercises, and activities. Organize them into a curriculum that supports adult learning theory and provides a blueprint for program development.
- Make sure all materials, such as video scripts, leaders' guides, and participants' workbooks, complement each other, are written clearly, and blend into unified training geared directly to the stated learning objectives.
- Carefully and professionally handle all program elements—whether reproduced on paper, film, or tape—to guarantee quality and effectiveness.

3. VALIDATION

- Introduce and validate the training before a representative audience. Base final revisions on pilot results to ensure program effectiveness.

4. IMPLEMENTATION

- When applicable, boost success with a train-the-trainer workshop that focuses on presentation knowledge and skills in addition to training content.

5. EVALUATION AND FOLLOW-UP

- Assess program success according to:
  REACTION—Document the learners' immediate reactions to the training.
  LEARNING—Use feedback devices or pre- and posttests to measure what learners have actually learned.
  BEHAVIOR—Note supervisors' reactions to learners' performance following completion of the training. This is one way to measure the degree to which learners apply new skills and knowledge to their jobs.
  RESULTS—Determine the level of improvement in job performance and assess needed maintenance.

Fifth, there should be an *evaluation* and follow-up step in which the program's successes or failures are assessed.

Training and Learning

Training is essentially a learning process. To train employees, therefore, it is useful to know something about how people learn. Some suggestions based on learning theory follow.

First, it is easier for trainees to understand and remember material that is meaningful:[12]

1. At the start of training, provide the trainees with a bird's-eye view of the material to be presented. Knowing the overall picture facilitates learning.
2. Use a variety of familiar examples when presenting material.

3. Organize the material so that it is presented in a logical manner and in meaningful units.
4. Try to use terms and concepts that are already familiar to trainees.
5. Use as many visual aids as possible.

Second, make sure it is easy to transfer new skills and behaviors from the training site to the job site:[13]

1. Maximize the similarity between the training situation and the work situation.
2. Provide adequate training practice.
3. Label or identify each feature of the machine and/or step in the process.

Third, motivate the trainee:[14]

1. People learn best by doing. Try to provide as much realistic practice as possible.
2. Trainees learn best when correct responses are immediately reinforced, perhaps with a quick "well done."
3. Trainees learn best at their own pace. If possible, let trainees pace themselves.

Legal Aspects of Training

Under equal employment legislation several aspects of your training program must be assessed with an eye toward the program's impact on women and minorities.[15] For example, having relatively few women or minorities selected for the training program may require showing that the admissions procedures are valid—that they predict performance on the job for which the person is being trained.

Similarly, suppose completing the training program is a prerequisite for promotion. You should then be able to show that the training program itself has no adverse impact on women or minorities. In other words, members of protected groups should have as much chance of successfully completing the training as do white males. If they do not, the validity of the training requirements should be demonstrated. For example, it could turn out that the reading level of your training manuals is too high for many minority trainees, and that they are thus doing poorly in the program quite aside from their aptitude for the jobs for which they are being trained. The training program might then be found to be unfairly discriminatory.

Negligent training is another potential problem. *Negligent training* occurs when an employer fails to train adequately, and an employee subsequently harms a third party.[16] Courts will find the employer liable in cases of negligent training, particularly when the employer's business or service is oriented toward serving the public.[17] Precautions here include:

1. Confirm claims of skill and experience for all applicants.[18]
2. Reduce the risks of harm by extensively training employees who work with dangerous equipment, materials, or processes.
3. Ensure that the training includes procedures to protect third parties' health and safety (including that of other employees).
4. Evaluate the training activity to determine its effectiveness in reducing negligence risks.

Training Needs Analysis

The first step in training is to determine what training, if any, is required. Your main task in assessing the training needs of new employees is to determine what the job entails and to break it down into subtasks, each of which is then taught to the new employee. Assessing the training needs of current employees can be more complex, since you have the added task of deciding whether or not training is the solution. For example, performance may be down because the standards aren't clear or because the person isn't motivated.

task analysis
A detailed study of a job to identify the skills required so that an appropriate training program may be instituted.

performance analysis
Verifying that there is a performance deficiency and determining whether that deficiency should be rectified through training or through some other means (such as transferring the employee).

Task analysis and *performance analysis* are the two main techniques for identifying training needs. About 19% of employers reporting in one survey said they used **task analysis**—an analysis of the job's requirements—to determine the training required.[19] Task analysis is especially appropriate for determining the training needs of employees who are *new* to their jobs. **Performance analysis** appraises the performance of *current* employees to determine whether training could reduce performance problems like excess scrap or low output. Other techniques used to identify training needs include supervisors' reports, personnel records, management requests, observations, tests of job knowledge, and questionnaire surveys.[20]

Whichever technique is used—task analysis, performance analysis, or some other—employee input is essential. It's often true that no one knows as much about the job as the people actually doing it so that soliciting employee input is usually wise.[21]

Task Analysis: Assessing the Training Needs of New Employees

Task analysis is used for determining the training needs of employees who are new to their jobs. Particularly with lower-echelon workers, it is common to hire inexperienced personnel and train them.[22] Here your aim is to develop the skills and knowledge required for effective performance, and so the training is usually based on task analysis, a detailed study of the job to determine what specific skills—like soldering (in the case of an assembly worker) or interviewing (in the case of a supervisor)—are required.

The job description and job specification are helpful here. These list the specific duties and skills required on the job and become the basic reference point in determining the training required for performing the job.

Task Analysis Record Form   Some employers supplement the current job description and specification with a task analysis record form. This consolidates information regarding the job's required tasks and skills in a form that's especially helpful for determining training requirements. As illustrated in Table 7.1, a Task Analysis Record Form contains six types of information:

Column 1, Task List   Here the job's main tasks and subtasks are listed. For example, if one major task is "Operate paper cutter," subtasks 1.1 through 1.5 might include "Start motor," "Set cutting distance," "Place paper on cutting table," "Push paper up to cutter," and "Grasp safety release with left hand."

Column 2, How Often Performed   Here you indicate the *frequency* with which the task and subtasks are performed. For example, is it performed only once at the beginning of the shift, or many times, hour after hour?

Column 3, Quantity, Quality Standards   Here indicate the *standards of performance* for each task and subtask. These show the level to be attained by the trainee and should be as specific as possible. They should be expressed in measurable terms like "6 tolerance of 0.007 in.," "Twelve units per hour," or "Within two days of receiving the order," for instance.

TABLE 7.1 Task Analysis Record Form

TASK LIST	WHEN AND HOW OFTEN PERFORMED	QUANTITY AND QUALITY OF PERFORMANCE	CONDITIONS UNDER WHICH PERFORMED	SKILLS OR KNOWLEDGE REQUIRED	WHERE BEST LEARNED
1. Operate paper cutter	4 times per day		Noisy press room: distractions		
1.1 Start motor					
1.2 Set cutting distance		±tolerance of 0.007 in.		Read gauge	On the job
1.3 Place paper on cutting table		Must be completely even to prevent uneven cut		Lift paper correctly	"
1.4 Push paper up to cutter				Must be even	"
1.5 Grasp safety release with left hand		100% of time, for safety		Essential for safety	On the job but practice first with no distractions
1.6 Grasp cutter release with right hand				Must keep both hands on releases	"
1.7 Simultaneously pull safety release with left hand and cutter release with right hand					
1.8 Wait for cutter to retract		100% of time, for safety		"	"
1.9 Retract paper				Wait till cutter retracts	"
1.10 Shut off		100% of time, for safety			"
2. Operate printing press					
2.1 Start motor					
. . .					

Note: Task analysis record form showing some of tasks and subtasks performed by a printing press operator.

Column 4, Performance Conditions Here indicate the *conditions* under which the tasks and subtasks are to be performed. This is especially important if the conditions are crucial to the training—for example, where the person normally has to work under conditions of turmoil and stress (as in the case of an air traffic controller).

Column 5, Skills Required This is the heart of the task analysis form. Here you list the *skills* or *knowledge* required for each of the tasks and subtasks, specifying exactly what knowledge or skills you must teach the trainee. Thus, for the subtask "Set cutting distance" the person must be taught how to read the gauge.

Column 6, Where Best Learned Here you indicate whether the task is learned best *on* or *off the job.* Your decision is based on several considerations. Safety is one: For example, prospective jet pilots must learn something about the plane off the job in a simulator before actually getting behind the controls.

Performance Analysis: Determining the Training Needs of Current Employees

Performance analysis means verifying that there is a significant performance deficiency and determining whether that deficiency should be rectified through training or through some other means (such as transferring the employee). The first step is to appraise the employee's performance, since to improve it, you must first determine the person's current performance compared to what it should be. Examples of specific performance deficiencies follow:

> "I expect each salesperson to make ten new contracts per week, but John averages only six."
>
> "Other plants our size average no more than two serious accidents per month; we're averaging five."

Distinguishing between *can't do* and *won't do* problems is the heart of performance analysis. First, determine whether it's a *can't do* problem and, if so, its specific causes: The employees don't know what to do or what your standards are; there are obstacles in the system such as lack of tools or supplies; job aids are needed, such as color-coded wires that show assemblers which wire goes where; poor selection results in hiring people who haven't the skills to do the job; or training is inadequate. On the other hand, it might be a *won't do* problem. Here employees *could* do a good job if they wanted to. If so, the reward system might have to be changed, perhaps by installing an incentive system.

Setting Training Objectives

After training needs have been analyzed, concrete, measurable training objectives should be set. Training, development, or (more generally) *instructional objectives* are defined as ". . . a description of a performance you want learners to be able to exhibit before you consider them competent."[23] For example:

> *Given a tool kit and a service manual, the technical representative will be able to adjust the registration (black line along paper edges) on this Xerox duplicator within 20 minutes according to the specifications stated in the manual.*[24]

Objectives specify what the trainee should be able to accomplish after successfully completing the training program.[25] They thus provide a focus for the efforts of both the trainee and the trainer and a benchmark for evaluating the success of the training program.

Training Techniques

After you have determined the employees' training needs, set training objectives, and designed the program, the training program can be implemented. A description of the most popular training techniques follow.

On-The-Job Training

on-the-job training (OJT)
Training a person to learn a job while working at it.

On-the-job training (OJT) means having a person learn a job by actually performing it. Virtually every employee, from mailroom clerk to company president, gets some on-the-job training when he or she joins a firm. In many companies, OJT is the only type of training available. It usually involves assigning new employees to experienced workers or supervisors who then do the actual training.[26]

There are several types of on-the-job training. The most familiar is the coaching or understudy method. Here the employee is trained on the job by an experienced worker or the trainee's supervisor. At lower levels trainees may acquire skills for, say, running a machine by observing the supervisor. But this technique is also widely used at top-management levels. The position of assistant is often used to train and develop the company's future top managers, for instance. Job rotation, in which an employee (usually a management trainee) moves from job to job at planned intervals, is another OJT technique. Special assignments similarly give lower-level executives firsthand experience in working on actual problems.

Apprenticeship training is a structured process by which individuals become skilled workers through a combination of classroom instruction and on-the-job training.[27] It is widely used to train individuals for many occupations including electrician and plumber, and it is essentially the type of training new medical interns get during the several years they spend working in hospitals after graduation.

OJT has several advantages. It is relatively inexpensive; trainees learn while producing, and there is no need for expensive off-job facilities like classrooms or programmed learning devices. The method also facilitates learning since trainees learn by actually doing the job and get quick feedback about the correctness of their performance.

However, there are several trainer-related factors to keep in mind when designing OJT programs.[28] The trainers themselves should be carefully trained and given the necessary training materials. (Often, instead, an experienced worker is simply told to "go train John.") Experienced workers who are chosen as trainers should be thoroughly trained in the proper methods of instruction—in particular the principles of learning and perhaps the job instruction technique that we address next. A useful step-by-step job instruction approach for giving a new employee on-the-job training is as follows:

Step 1: Preparation of the Learner

1. Put the learner at ease—relieve the tension.
2. Explain why he or she is being taught.
3. Create interest, encourage questions, find out what the learner already knows about his or her job or other jobs.
4. Explain the why of the whole job and relate it to some job the worker already knows.

In a Textron assembly plant a newly hired employee receives on-the-job, in-depth training.

5. Place the learner as close to the normal working position as possible.

6. Familiarize the worker with the equipment, materials, tools, and trade terms.

Step 2: Presentation of the Operation

1. Explain quantity and quality requirements.

2. Go through the job at the normal work pace.

3. Go through the job at a slow pace several times, explaining each step. Between operations, explain the difficult parts, or those in which errors are likely to be made.

4. Again go through the job at a slow pace several times; explain the key points.

5. Have the learner explain the steps as you go through the job at a slow pace.

Step 3: Performance Tryout

1. Have the learner go through the job several times, slowly, explaining each step to you. Correct mistakes and, if necessary, do some of the complicated steps the first few times.

2. You, the trainer, run the job at the normal pace.

3. Have the learner do the job gradually building up skill and speed.

4. As soon as the learner demonstrates ability to do the job, let the work begin, but don't abandon him or her.

Step 4: Follow-Up

1. Designate to whom the learner should go for help if he or she needs it.

2. Gradually decrease supervision, checking work from time to time against quality and quantity standards.

3. Correct faulty work patterns that begin to creep into the work, and do it before they become a habit. Show why the learned method is superior.

4. Compliment good work; encourage the worker until he or she is able to meet the quality/quantity standards.

Job Instruction Training

job instruction training (JIT)
Listing of each job's basic tasks, along with key points in order to provide step-by-step training for employees.

Many jobs consist of a logical sequence of steps and are best taught step by step. This step-by-step process is called **job instruction training (JIT).** To begin, list all necessary steps in the job, each in its proper sequence. Alongside each step also list a corresponding "key point" (if any). The steps show *what* is to be done, while the key points show *how* it's to be done—and *why*. Here is an example of a job instruction training sheet for teaching a trainee how to operate a large motorized paper cutter.

Steps	*Key Points*
1. Start motor	None
2. Set cutting distance	Carefully read scale—to prevent wrong-sized cut
3. Place paper on cutting table	Make sure paper is even—to prevent uneven cut
4. Push paper up to cutter	Make sure paper is tight—to prevent uneven cut
5. Grasp safety release with left hand	Do not release left hand—to prevent hand from being caught in cutter
6. Grasp cutter release with right hand	Do not release right hand—to prevent hand from being caught in cutter
7. Simultaneously pull cutter and safety releases	Keep both hands on corresponding releases—to avoid hands being on cutting table

8. Wait for cutter to retract	Keep both hands on releases—to avoid having hands on cutting table
9. Retract paper	Make sure cutter is retracted; keep both hands away from releases
10. Shut off motor	None

Lectures

Lecturing has several advantages. It is a quick and simple way of providing knowledge to large groups of trainees, as when the sales force must be taught the special features of a new product. While written material like books and manuals could be used instead, they may involve considerable printing expense, and they don't permit the give and take of questioning that lectures do.

Some useful guidelines for presenting your lecture follow:[29]

Give your listeners signals to help them follow your ideas. For instance, if you have a list of items, start by saying something like "There are four reasons why the sales reports are necessary. . . . The first . . . the second . . . "

Don't start out on the wrong foot. For instance, don't open with an irrelevant joke or story or by saying something like, "I really don't know why I was asked to speak here today."

Keep your conclusions short. Just summarize your main point or points in one or two succinct sentences.

Be alert to your audience. Watch body language for negative signals like fidgeting and crossed arms.

Maintain eye contact with the trainees in the program. At a minimum you should look at each section of the audience during your presentation.

Make sure everyone in the room can hear. Use a mike or talk loudly enough so that you can be heard by people in the last row and if necessary repeat questions that you get from trainees from the front of the room before you answer.

Control your hands. Get in the habit of leaving them hanging naturally at your sides rather than letting them drift to your face, then your pockets, then your back, and so on. Putting your hands near your face can block your voice projection and also give the impression that you lack confidence in what you are saying.

Talk from notes rather than from a script. Write out clear, legible notes on large index cards and then use these as an outline rather than memorizing your whole presentation.

Eliminate bad habits. Beware of distracting your listeners by jiggling coins in your pocket or pulling on an earlobe.

Practice. If you have the time, make sure to rehearse under conditions similar to those under which you will actually give your presentation.

Audiovisual Techniques

Audiovisual techniques like films, closed-circuit television, audiotapes, and videotapes can be very effective and are widely used.[30] At Weyerhaeuser Company, for instance, portions of films like *Bridge on the River Kwai* have been used as a basis for discussing interpersonal relationships in the company's management school. The Ford Motor Company uses films in its dealer training sessions to simulate problems and sample reactions to various customer complaints.

Audiovisuals are more expensive than conventional lectures but offer some advantages. Consider using them in the following situations:

1. *When there is a need to illustrate how a certain sequence should be followed over time,* such as when teaching wire soldering or telephone repair. The stop action, instant reply, or fast- or slow-motion capabilities of audiovisuals can be useful.

2. *When there is a need to expose trainees to events not easily demonstrable in live lectures*, such as a visual tour of a factory or open-heart surgery.
3. *When the training is going to be used organizationwide* and it is too costly to move the trainers from place to place.

There are three options when it comes to video: You can buy an existing videotape or film; you can make your own; or you can have a production company produce the video for you. Dozens of businesses issue catalogs listing audiovisual programs on topics ranging from applicant interviewing to zoo management.

Teletraining Companies today are also experimenting with *teletraining*, through which a trainer in a central location can train groups of employees at remote locations via television hookups.[31] For example, AMP Incorporated uses satellites to train its engineers and technicians at 165 sites in the United States and 27 other countries. (The firm makes electrical and electronic connection devices.) To reduce costs for one training program, AMP supplied the program content. PBS affiliate WITF, Channel 33 of Harrisburg, Pennsylvania, supplied the equipment and expertise required to broadcast the training program to five AMP facilities in North America.[32]

Videoconferencing *Videoconferencing* is an increasingly popular way to train employees. It has been defined as ". . . a means of joining two or more distant groups using a combination of audio and visual equipment."[33] Videoconferencing allows people in one location to communicate live with people in another city or country or with groups in several other cities.[34] The communication links are established either by sending specially "compressed" audio and video signals over telephone lines or via satellite.

Given that videoconferencing is by nature visual, interactive, and remote, there are several things to keep in mind before getting up in front of the camera. Because the training is remote, it's particularly important to prepare a training guide ahead of time, specifically a manual the learners can use to keep track of the points that the trainer is making. A sampling of other hints would include:

Avoid bright, flashy jewelry or heavily patterned clothing.[35]

Arrive at least 20 minutes early.

Test all equipment you will be using.

Adjust lights (if necessary and if possible); put lighting in front of participants to avoid shadows.

Have all participants introduce themselves.

Avoid focusing just on one group at one remote site (if there are several) and avoid presenting just to the video camera and not to the in-house participants.

Project your voice and speak clearly; particularly if people at the remote site have a different native language, keep yours free of jargon and needlessly complex words.

Remember that excessive physical movement will cause distortion of the video image where compressed telephone transmission is being used.

Programmed Learning

programmed learning
A systematic method for teaching job skills involving presenting questions or facts, allowing the person to respond, and giving the learner immediate feedback on the accuracy of his or her answers.

Whether the programmed instruction device is a textbook or a computer, **programmed learning** consists of three functions:

1. Presenting questions, facts, or problems to the learner.
2. Allowing the person to respond.
3. Providing feedback on the accuracy of his or her answers.

A page from a programmed instruction book for learning calculus is presented in Figure 7.3. Note how facts and questions are presented. The learner can then respond, and the book gives feedback on the accuracy of his or her answers.

Figure 7.3
A Page from a Programmed Textbook

Source: Daniel Kleppner and Norman Ramsey, *Quick Calculus.* Copyright © 1985 by John Wiley & Sons, Inc. Reprinted by permission.

Sec. 2   Graphs

---

17   The most direct way to plot the graph of a function $y = f(x)$ is to make a table of reasonably spaced values of x and of the corresponding values of $y = f(x)$. Then each pair of values (x, y) can be represented by a point as in the previous frame. A graph of the function is obtained by connecting the points with a smooth curve. Of course, the points on the curve may be only approximate. If we want an accurate plot we just have to be very careful and use many points. (On the other hand, crude plots are pretty good for most purposes.)

Go to 18.

---

18   As an example, here is a plot of the function $y = 3x^2$. A table of values of x and y is shown and these points are indicated on the graph.

x	y
-3	27
-2	12
-1	3
0	0
1	3
2	12
3	27

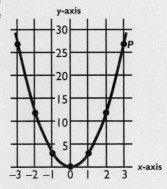

To test yourself, encircle below the pair of coordinates that corresponds to the point *P* indicated in the figure.

[(3,27) | (27,3) | none of these]

Check your answer. If correct, go on to 19. If incorrect study frame 16 once again and then go to 19.

The main advantage of programmed learning is that it reduces training time by about one-third.[36] In terms of the principles of learning listed earlier, programmed instruction can also facilitate learning since it lets trainees learn at their own pace, provides immediate feedback, and (from the learner's point of view) reduces the risk of error. On the other hand, trainees do not learn much more from programmed learning than they would from a traditional textbook. Therefore, the cost of developing the manuals and/or software for programmed instruction has to be weighed against the accelerated but not improved learning that should occur.

Vestibule or Simulated Training

vestibule or simulated training
Training employees on special off-the-job equipment, as in airplane pilot training, whereby training costs and hazards can be reduced.

Vestibule or **simulated training** is a technique in which trainees learn on the actual or simulated equipment they will use on the job but are actually trained off the job. Therefore, it aims to obtain the advantages of on-the-job training without actually putting the trainee on the job. Vestibule training is virtually a necessity when it is too costly or dangerous to train employees on the job. Putting new assembly-line workers right to work could slow production, for instance, and when safety is a concern—as with pilots—vestibule training may be the only practical alternative.

Vestibule training may just place in a separate room the equipment the trainees will actually be using on the job. However, it often involves the use of equipment simulators. In pilot training, for instance, the main advantages of flight simulators are as follows:[37]

Safety. Crews can practice hazardous flight maneuvers in a safe, controlled environment.

Learning efficiency. The absence of the conflicting air traffic and radio chatter that exists in real flight situations allows for total concentration on the business of learning how to fly the craft.

Money. The cost of flying a flight simulator is only a fraction of the cost of flying an aircraft. This includes savings on maintenance costs, pilot cost, fuel cost, and the cost of not having the aircraft in regular service.

Computer-Based Training

In computer-based training the trainee uses a computer-based system to interactively increase his or her knowledge or skills. While vestibule or simulated training doesn't necessarily have to rely on computerization, computer-based training almost always involves presenting trainees with computerized simulations and the use of multimedia including videotapes to help the trainee learn how to do the job.[38]

Consider two other examples of computer-assisted training. A computer-based training (CBT) program enables a major employer in the Pacific Northwest to do a better job of training personnel interviewers to conduct correct and legally defensible interviews.[39] Trainees start with a computer screen that shows the "applicant's" completed employment application, as well as information about the nature of the job. The trainee then begins a simulated interview by typing in questions, which are answered by a videotaped model acting as the applicant and whose responses to a multitude of questions have been programmed into the computer. Some items require follow-up questions, and as each question is answered the trainee records his or her evaluation of the applicant's answer and makes a decision about the person's suitability for the position. At the end of the session the computer tells the trainee where he or she went wrong (perhaps in asking discriminatory questions, for instance) and offers further instructional material to correct these mistakes.

Vestibule training simulates flight conditions at NASA headquarters.

As another example, Andersen Consulting uses a multimedia CBT program to dramatically reduce the six weeks of training most new consultants received before their first consulting assignments. The new system, known as the business practices course (BPC), is a self-paced, interactive computer-based training program.[40] The BPC consists of 15 modular computerized components that simulate a business situation the Andersen staff member might encounter in a consulting engagement at a hypothetical printing and book publishing company. Using audio and video clips stored on CD-ROM, the consultant-trainee interviews the company's personnel, receives phone calls, gets advice from senior Andersen consultants, reviews internal Andersen memos, and attends meetings with senior members of the client's management staff.[41] At the end of the computer-based program, the consultant-trainee delivers a presentation outlining the kinds of findings and recommendations that would normally be delivered to a client.

CBT programs can be very beneficial. Studies indicate that interactive technologies reduce learning time by an average of 50%.[42] They can also be very cost-effective once designed and produced: Federal Express reportedly expects to save more than $100 million by using an interactive system for employee training.[43] Other advantages include instructional consistency (computers, unlike human trainers, don't have good days and bad days), mastery of learning (if the trainee doesn't learn it, he or she generally can't move on to the next step in the CBT), increased retention, and increased trainee motivation (resulting from the responsive feedback of the CBT program).

Small Business Applications

Training

It does not pay to spend a lot of time hiring the best employees if the employees you hire aren't properly trained. In the book *Made in America,* a group of MIT researchers concluded, for instance, that superior training is one reason Japanese firms have often pulled ahead of U.S. firms within the same industries. Japanese firms will spend weeks in meticulous training programs developing their workers' expertise, while comparable U.S. firms often all but ignore the training process.

Because so much is riding on a relatively few employees, it is important that smaller firms carefully train their employees. The concepts and techniques explained in this chapter should enable you to do so. In addition, here is a practical procedure you can use to develop your training program.

Step 1. Set Training Objectives
First, write down your training objectives. For example, your objective might be to reduce scrap, or to get new employees up to speed within two weeks.

Step 2. Write a Detailed Job Description
A detailed job description is the heart of any training program. It should list the daily and periodic tasks of each job, along with a summary of the steps in each task. Thus, for the job presented in Table 7.1, a main task is "operate paper cutter." The press operator's job description should thus explain how the paper cutter should be operated, including steps such as start motor, set cutting distance, and place paper on cutting table. In other words, the job description should list what is to be done as well as how to do it.

Step 3. Develop an Abbreviated Task Analysis Record Form

For practical purposes, the small business owner can use an abbreviated Task Analysis Record Form containing just four columns. In the first, list *tasks* (including what is to be performed in terms of each of the main tasks, and the steps involved in each task). In column B, list *performance standards* (in terms of quantity, quality, accuracy, and so on). In column C, list *trainable skills* required, things the employee must know or do to perform the task. This column provides you with specific skills (such as "Keep both hands on releases") that you want to stress. In the fourth column, list *aptitudes required.* These are the human aptitudes (such as mechanical comprehension, tolerance for boredom, and so on) that the employee should have to be trainable for the task and for which the employee can be screened ahead of time.

Step 4. Develop A Job Instruction Sheet

Next develop a job instruction sheet for the job. As explained on page 257, a job instruction training sheet shows the steps in each task as well as key points for each.

Step 5. Prepare Training Program for the Job

You should now be ready to prepare all the final training documents and media for the job. Build the training manual for the job around the training sequence, listing steps in each job task and key points.

At a minimum, your training program should include the job description, abbreviated Task Analysis Record Form, and job instruction sheet, all collected in a trainer's manual. The latter should also contain a summary of the training program's objectives, the three forms mentioned earlier, and a listing of the trainable skills required. For the trainee, a separate manual might then consist of an introduction to the job, an explanation of how the job fits with other jobs in the plant or office, a job description, and a job instruction sheet.

You also have to make a decision regarding which media to use in your training program. A simple but effective on-the-job training program using current employees or supervisors as trainers requires only the materials we just described. However, it could turn out that the nature of the job or the number of trainees requires producing or purchasing special audio or visual tapes or films, a slide presentation, or more extensive printed materials.

Many smaller companies are saving on training expenses by entering into cooperative agreements with other firms in their geographic areas. For example, if a company's employees need generic courses (on topics like time management or computer skills, for instance) the firm can probably cut training costs by obtaining training time from an outside supplier as part of a cooperative employers group. Thus, if one firm has eight employees who need time management training and one down the street has a similar need, together they can hire a training supplier to teach a full class of 16 participants, thus sharing the trainer's costs.[44] ◆

Training For Special Purposes

Increasingly today training does more than just prepare employees to perform their jobs effectively. Training for special purposes—dealing with AIDS and adjusting to diversity, for instance—is required too. A sampling of such special-purpose training programs follows.

Literacy Training Techniques

Functional illiteracy is a serious problem for many employers. By some estimates there are 25 million American adults 17 years and older who are functional illiterates, either because they can't read at all or because they can only read up to a third- or fourth-grade level.[45] Yet as the U.S. economy shifts from goods to services, there is a corresponding need for workers who are more skilled, more literate, and better able to perform at least basic arithmetic skills.

Employers are responding to this problem in two main ways. First, companies are testing prospective employees' basic skills. Of the 1,005 companies that responded to an American Management Association (AMA) survey on workplace testing, for instance, 345 (34.3%) indicated they conduct basic skills testing.[46] In 89% of the responding companies, job applicants who are deficient in basic skills are refused employment. At about 3% of the other companies, current employees and candidates for promotion are tested (and often rejected) on their literacy scores.

The second response is to institute basic skills and literacy programs. According to the AMA survey, the areas in which remedial training is needed are mathematics, reading, and writing.

One simple approach is to have supervisors focus on basic skills by giving employees writing and speaking exercises. After the exercise has been completed, the supervisor can provide personal feedback.[47] One way to do this is to convert materials used in the employees' jobs into instructional tools. For example, if an employee needs to use a manual to find out how to replace a certain machine part, he or she should be taught how to use an index to locate the relevant section.[48] Another approach is to bring in outside professionals like teachers from a local high school or community college to institute, say, a remedial reading or writing program. Having employees attend adult education or high school evening classes is another option.

Another approach is to use an interactive video disk (IVD). This technique combines the drama of video with the power of microcomputers.[49] An example is Principles of Alphabet Literacy (PALS). It uses animated video and a computer-stored voice to enable nonreaders to associate sounds with letters and letters with words, and to use the words to create sentences.[50] A second IVD program is called SKILLPAC. This program, subtitled *English for Industry,* was designed mostly for nonnative English speakers. It combines video, audio, and computer technologies to teach language skills in the context of the specific workplace situation in which those skills will be used.[51]

AIDS Education

Many of the estimated 1 million Americans infected with the AIDS virus are in the work force, and this creates anxiety for many noninfected employees and a dilemma for their employers. On the one hand, infected individuals must be allowed to remain on their jobs, for both moral and legal reasons. On the other hand, the infected person's coworkers often require some type of training in order to reduce anxieties and maximize the chances that the employees will be able to work together effectively as a team.

Many firms therefore institute AIDS education programs. The program instituted in the Wellesley, Massachusetts office of Sun Life of Canada, a life insurance company, is typical.[52] Groups of 20 to 30 employees attended 90-minute seminars. In addition to providing detailed information about AIDS, the seminars offered a forum for discussion and questions. Management employees attended three-hour seminars in groups of 10 to 12 people. The seminars covered additional AIDS-related issues, including the need for confidentiality, the potential impact of discrimination laws, and the company's AIDS policy.

There was reportedly little resistance to holding or attending these seminars, in part because the reasons for them were widely communicated in the company's newsletters. Some management employees initially expressed skepticism about devoting so many hours to AIDS education, but after their sessions most reportedly felt differently. Based on pre- and postseminar questionnaires, the company believes that the seminars were useful in getting employees to learn the facts about AIDS, clearing up misconceptions, and helping to put the personal concerns of many employees to rest.

Training for International Business

As more firms find themselves competing in a global marketplace, they've increasingly had to implement special global training programs. The reasons for doing so range from avoiding lost business due to cultural insensitivity to improving job satisfaction and retention of overseas staff, to enabling a newly assigned employee to communicate with his or her colleagues abroad.[53]

Many global training programs are prepackaged. They are sold by vendors to employers who have to train one or more of their employees prior to overseas assignments. A sampling of the programs can help illustrate the wide range of programs available as well as what global training programs actually look like. Sample programs include:[54]

The Cultural Awareness Program: This is a one-day cultural awareness training program that looks at U.S. and cross-cultural values and assumptions concerning communication and identity issues.

Executive Etiquette for Global Transactions: This program prepares managers for conducting business globally by training them in the differing etiquette requirements in countries including Germany, Japan, Mexico, Russia, and Saudi Arabia.

Cross-Cultural Technology Transfer: This program shows trainees how cultural values affect one's perceptions of technology and technical learning.

International Protocol and Presentation: This shows trainees the correct way to handle people with tact and diplomacy in countries around the world.

Cross-Cultural Training and Orientation: Topics here include cross-cultural communication and business skills, practical approaches to managing culture shock and adjusting one's lifestyle, stress management, daily life in the host country, spouse's and family's concerns, area studies, and repatriation procedures.

Business Basics for the Foreign Executive: This covers negotiating cross-culturally, working with U.S. clients, making presentations, writing for U.S. business, and using the phone in the United States.

Language Programs: Various vendors supply language specialists whose services include translation, interpretation, cross-cultural training, and consulting on language-related needs.

Language Training: Training programs here provide language training delivered by certified instructors, usually determined by the learner's needs rather than by the requirements of a predetermined curriculum or textbook. Specific suggestions for conducting training programs abroad are presented in the Global HRM feature.

Training

As firms expand operations abroad, it becomes more important to train foreign nationals. For example, Gillette International brings foreign talent to its Boston headquarters for training in the techniques, policies, and values of the firm before they assumed new jobs in their home country.[55]

Training foreign nationals requires more than translating existing programs into other languages. Cultural differences influence both the applicability of training material and the reactions of trainees to the programs. Here are suggestions for conducting training programs abroad.[56]

1. Understand the taboos and turn-ons of the participants' culture. For example, in Japan, risk taking is by and large taboo. Therefore, you may find that you get no volunteers to participate in a training role-play exercise because doing so is taking a risk. Similarly, in the Middle East, role-plays are games for children, not for adults.

2. Critiquing other people in public is taboo in some Far Eastern cultures. For example, getting a volunteer to be an "observer" in a training discussion or role-play could be difficult because the role of the observer is often to critique the other participants' behavior.

3. Saving face and not putting people in embarrassing situations is important not just in the Far East. In Middle Eastern countries, and in East and West Africa and some European cultures including Spain and Italy, criticizing trainees or making them look foolish is not advisable. In fact, putting them in any activity in which their behavior will be discussed, debriefed, and/or criticized can create problems.

4. In some cultures you'll find it difficult to get feedback on your own effectiveness as a trainer. Even if you violate a taboo, the trainees may be reluctant to tell you so because to do so would be to criticize you and cause you to lose face.

5. Make sure to understand how the job you are training your trainees to do is viewed in their native culture. In the U.S., for instance, it's appropriate to tell the salespeople to write introductory letters to high-level executives to gain entry to their organizations. In Japan doing so would be highly unusual. Instead repeated personal visits to drop off business cards is often required.

6. Consider the effects of jet lag and diet changes. For example, while it may be 4:00 P.M. in Boston where you're doing your training, your French participants' body clocks may be set to a more tired 9:00 P.M. Similarly, Japanese participants may expect a rice meal, and all participants fresh from overseas would probably do better with mineral water than soda. ◆

Values Training

Many training programs today are aimed at educating employees about the firm's most cherished values and (it is hoped) convincing employees that these should be their values as well.

The orientation training programs at Saturn Corporation, similar to Toyota's, illustrate this. The first two days are devoted to discussions of benefits, safety and security, and the company's production process—just-in-time delivery, materials management, and so forth.[57] However, in the third and fourth days the focus shifts. The firm's top managers spend about an hour and a half discussing Saturn's values. Then all new employees get their copy of Saturn's "mission card." This allows the trainees and trainer to go through each of the Saturn values listed on the card—teamwork, trust and respect for the individual, and quality, for example—to illustrate its meaning. Short exercises are also used here. Thus, the new employees might be asked "If you saw a team member do this . . . what would you do?" Or, "If you saw a team member 'living' this value, what would you see?"

For their part, Saturn's supervisors get "converted" to Saturn's values in part through a special two-day leadership seminar called "Values and Beliefs." The program's basic aims are to familiarize supervisors with Saturn's core values and to illustrate how to translate them from words into actions. The first part, for instance, explains how values influence behavior and cautions managers to beware of any disparities between stated and operative values: "It's what you do, not what you say that sends the real signal to workers about what your department's operative values are," say the trainers. Thus, talking "trust" while insisting on time clocks may be a contradiction because the time clocks seem to say "We don't trust you." (There are no time clocks at Saturn.)

Succeeding sessions use lectures and exercises to explain and illustrate each of Saturn's basic values. Illustrations of core Saturn values such as "respecting people," "making our employees full partners," "building customer satisfaction through teamwork," and "putting quality in all we do" are presented here. The aim is to make believers of Saturn leaders through illustrating what these values mean.

Diversity Training

With an increasingly diverse work force, many more firms find they have to implement diversity training programs. As a personnel officer for one firm put it, "We're trying to create a better sensitivity among our supervisors about the issues and challenges women and minorities face in pursuing their careers."[58] Diversity training creates better cross-cultural sensitivity among supervisors and nonsupervisors with the aim of creating more harmonious working relationships among a firm's employees.

Diversity training is no panacea, and a poorly conceived program can backfire. Potential negative outcomes include ". . . the possibility of post-training participant discomfort, reinforcement of group stereotypes, perceived disenfranchisement or backlash by white males, and even lawsuits based on managers' exposure of stereotypical beliefs blurted out during 'awareness raising' sessions."[59]

Strictly speaking it's probably more accurate to talk about diversity-based training programs than about "diversity training." According to one survey of HR directors, specific training programs aimed at offsetting problems associated with a diverse work force included (from most used to least used): improving interpersonal skills; understanding/valuing cultural differences; improving technical skills; socializing employees into corporate culture; reducing stress; indoctrinating into U.S. work ethic; mentoring; improving English proficiency; improving basic math skills; improving bilingual skills for English-speaking employees.[60]

A supervisory training program at Kinney Shoe Corp. provides an example.[61] The firm conducts eight-hour seminars for Kinney Shoe executives and store managers. The program is called "Valuing Diversity." In part, the seminars are aimed at showing participants how their own upbringing affects the assumptions they make and their behavior. For example, the firm's studies indicated that managers responsible for hiring might make an assumption about an applicant's intelligence based on the person's accent and poor English-speaking skills. The manager might assume, in other words, that the person hasn't the skills to sell shoes, although he or she certainly could sell effectively. The program also shows how people from various cultures react differently to workplace situations. It does this by presenting a number of hypothetical situations. For example, one situation illustrates the fact that a Native American worker might be embarrassed by public praise from his or her supervisor.

Customer-Service Training

Today almost two-thirds of U.S. workers are in customer-service (rather than manufacturing) jobs, and more and more companies are finding it necessary to compete based on the quality of their service. It's no longer enough, for instance, to offer a clean room at a decent price when a customer checks into a Hilton. To stay competitive, employers like Hilton find they have to provide total customer service, from courteous bellhops to easy parking to speedy check-outs.

Many companies are therefore implementing customer-service training programs. The basic aim here is to train all employees to treat the company's customers in a courteous and hospitable manner. The saying "The customer is always right" is being emphasized by countless service companies today. However, putting the customer first requires employee customer-service training.

The customer-service training at Alamo Rent-a-Car is called the "Best Friends" program.[62] Carried out in the early 1990s, at a cost of millions of dollars, it introduced new customer-service policies and indoctrinated and retrained Alamo employees in the practices of excellent customer service.

"Best Friends" consisted of a five-day orientation/customer-service training program. First, employees were familiarized with Alamo's history, its growth and expansion, and the company's expectations regarding customer service and the firm's work ethics. The program then shifted to customer-service training. This included segments on the importance of exceptional customer service and how to define it, illustrative examples, and the specific employee skills needed to deliver such fine service.

In addition to these general sessions, Alamo employees received customer-service training related specifically to their jobs. For example, service agents got training on the firm's extensive car preparation test, which aims to ensure that customers get cars that are clean and running properly.

Early results suggest the training program has been successful. While other factors may have contributed to the improvements, sales complaints were down 15% from the year before training commenced. Similarly, rudeness complaints were down 50% from pretraining levels. The firm's business transactions jumped by 30% in one year.

Training for Teamwork and Empowerment

An increasing number of firms today use work teams and empowerment to improve their effectiveness. They adopt teamwork as a value and then organize work around close-knit work teams empowered to get their jobs done, which means they've been given the authorization and the ability to do their jobs. Both the team approach and worker empowerment are components of what many firms call worker involvement programs. **Worker involvement programs** aim to boost organizational effectiveness by getting employees to participate in the planning, organizing, and general managing of their jobs.

worker involvement programs
Programs that aim to boost organizational effectiveness by getting employees to participate in planning, organizing, and managing their jobs.

However, many firms find that teamwork doesn't just happen: Instead employees must be trained to be good team members. That is why firms like Toyota and Saturn spend considerable time training new employees to be good team members. You may recall, for instance, that Toyota devotes hours to training new employees to listen to each other and to cooperate. And throughout the training process, Toyota's dedication to teamwork is stressed. Short exercises are used to illustrate examples of good and bad teamwork and to mold new employees' attitudes regarding good teamwork.

Some firms use outdoor training such as Outward Bound programs to build teamwork.[63] Outdoor training usually involves taking a firm's management team out into rugged, mountainous terrain. There they learn team spirit and cooperation and the need to trust and rely on each other by overcoming physical obstacles. As one participant put it, "Every time I climbed over a rock, I needed someone's help."[64] An example of one activity is the "trust fall." Here an employee has to slowly lean back and fall backward from a height of, say, 10 feet into the waiting arms of five or ten team members. The idea is to build trust, and particularly trust in one's colleagues.

Not all employees are eager to participate in such activities. Firms such as Outward Bound have potential participants fill out extensive medical evaluations to make sure participants can safely engage in risky outdoor activities. Others feel that the outdoor activities are too contrived to be applicable back at work. However, they do illustrate the lengths to which employers will go to build teamwork.

Empowering employees (either individually or as teams) also almost always requires extensive training. It is rarely enough to just tell group members that they're "empowered" to do all the buying and selling and planning involved in producing, say, the auto component for which they are responsible. Instead extensive training is required to ensure they have the skills to do the job. Similarly, many companies today use work teams or special quality circles to analyze job-related problems and to come up with solutions. (A quality circle is a group of five to ten employees, often a work team, who meet for an hour or two each week during the work day to analyze a problem on their job and to develop solutions to it.) Therefore, much of the approximately 320 hours of training a new Saturn employee receives aims to develop the problem-solving and analysis skills required to help the work team be empowered—in this case, to analyze and solve problems. Training in how to use basic statistical analysis tools and basic accounting is an example.

Evaluating the Training Effort

After trainees complete their training (or perhaps at planned intervals during the training), the program should be evaluated to see how well its objectives have been met. Thus, if assemblers should be able to solder a junction in 30 seconds, or a Xerox technician repair a machine in 30 minutes, then the program's effectiveness should be measured based on whether these objectives are met. For example, are your trainees learning as *much* as they can? Are they learning as *fast* as they can? Is there a *better method* for training them? These are some of the questions you can answer by properly evaluating your training efforts.

Overall there is little doubt that training and development can be effective. For example, many companies that invested heavily in workplace training have substantially improved their positions. While it may not be just the training, Xerox retrained over 110,000 employees worldwide in the early 1980s and soon regained market share in its industry. General Motors is another firm that has used training to help recapture market share.[65] Formal studies of training programs also substantiate the potential positive impact of such programs. A study conducted in the early 1990s concluded that "firms that establish workplace education programs and reorganize work report noticeable improvements in their workers' abilities and the quality of their products."[66] Another study found that businesses that were operating below their expected labor productivity levels had significant increases in productivity growth after implementing new employee training programs.[67]

There are two basic issues to address when evaluating a training program. The first is the design of the evaluation study and, in particular, whether **controlled experimentation** will be used. The second is the *training effect to be measured*.

Controlled experimentation is the best method to use in evaluating a training program. In a controlled experiment, both a training group and a control group (that receives no training) are used. Data (for instance, on quantity of production or quality of soldered junctions) should be obtained both before and after the training effort in the group exposed to training and before and after a corresponding work period in the control group. In this way it is possible to determine the extent to which any change in performance in the training group resulted from the training itself rather than from some organizationwide change like a raise in pay; we assume the latter would have affected employees in both groups equally. In terms of current practices, however, one survey found that something less than half the companies responding attempted to obtain before-and-after measures from trainees; the number of organizations using control groups was

controlled experimentation
Formal methods for testing the effectiveness of a training program, preferably with before-and-after tests and a control group.

Figure 7.4
A Sample Outside Training Evaluation Form

Purpose: The following items assess the overall value of this training experience:
1. Did you find the quality of this program to be (select one):

_____	_____	_____	_____	_____
Poor	Fair	Average	Good	Outstanding

2. Do you feel that this program was worthwhile in terms of its cost and your time away from normal job duties?
   Yes _____   No _____   Undecided _____
3. Would you recommend this program to your peers?
   Yes _____   No _____   Undecided _____
4. Rate the program for the following qualities

	Poor				*Outstanding*
	1	2	3	4	5
a. Practical Value	_____	_____	_____	_____	_____
b. Thoroughness	_____	_____	_____	_____	_____
c. New ideas gained	_____	_____	_____	_____	_____
d. Helpful to self-development	_____	_____	_____	_____	_____
e. Relevance to your job	_____	_____	_____	_____	_____
f. Efficient use of time	_____	_____	_____	_____	_____
g. Maintaining your interest	_____	_____	_____	_____	_____
h. Clear, understandable	_____	_____	_____	_____	_____

Comments:
5. Check the degree to which the kinds of follow-up to this workshop listed here would be useful:

	Necessary	*Desirable*	*Unnecessary*
a. Talking with workshop members to share experiences in applying ideas	_____	_____	_____
b. Opportunity to consult with trainer if a problem arises	_____	_____	_____
c. Advanced workshop in this area	_____	_____	_____
d. Briefing for my superiors on what I've learned here	_____	_____	_____
e. Other	_____	_____	_____

negligible.[68] One expert suggests at least using an evaluation form like the one shown in Figure 7.4 to evaluate the training program.[69]

Training Effects to Measure

Four basic categories of training outcomes can be measured:

1. *Reaction.* First, evaluate trainees' reactions to the program. Did they like the program? Did they think it worthwhile?

2. *Learning.* Second, you can test the trainees to determine whether they learned the principles, skills, and facts they were supposed to learn.

3. *Behavior.* Next ask whether the trainees' behavior on the job changed because of the training program. For example, are employees in the store's complaint department more courteous toward disgruntled customers than previously?

4. *Results.* Last, but probably most importantly, ask: "What final results were achieved in terms of the training objectives previously set? Did the number of customer complaints about employees drop? Did the reject rate improve? Did scrappage cost decrease? Was turnover reduced? Are production quotas now being met?" and so forth. Improved results are, of course, especially important. The training program may succeed in terms of the reactions from trainees, increased learning, and even changes in behavior. But if the results are not achieved, then in the final analysis, the training has not achieved its goals. If so, the problem may lie in the training program. Remember, however, that the results may be inadequate because the problem was not amenable to training in the first place.

Chapter Review

Summary

1. In this chapter we focused on technical skills training for new employees and for present employees whose performance is deficient. For either, uncovering training requirements begins with analyzing the cause of the problem and determining the training that may be needed. Remember to ask whether it is a training problem or a more deep-rooted problem like poor selection or low wages.

2. The training process consists of five steps: needs analysis; instructional design; validation; implementation; evaluation.

3. Some principles of learning theory include: Make the material meaningful (by providing a bird's-eye view and familiar examples, organizing the material, splitting it into meaningful chunks, and using familiar terms and visual aids); make provision for transfer of training; and try to motivate your trainee.

4. *Job instruction training* is useful for training on jobs that consist of a logical sequence of steps. *Vestibule training* combines the advantages of on- and off-the-job training.

5. On-the-job training is a third basic training technique. It might take the form of the understudy method, job rotation, or special assignments and committees. In any case, it should have four steps: preparing the learner, presenting the operation (or nature of the job), doing performance tryouts, and following up. Other training methods include audiovisual techniques, lectures, and computer-assisted instruction.

6. In gauging the effectiveness of a training program there are four categories of outcomes you can measure: reaction, learning, behavior, and results. In some cases where training seems to have failed, it may be because training was not the appropriate solution.

Key Terms

employee orientation
reality shock
training
task analysis
performance analysis

on-the-job training (OJT)
job instruction training (JIT)
programmed learning

vestibule or simulated training
worker involvement programs
controlled experimentation

Discussion Questions and Exercises

1. "A well-thought-out orientation program is especially important for employees (like recent graduates) who have had little or no work experience." Explain why you agree or disagree with this statement.

2. You're the supervisor of a group of employees whose task it is to assemble tuning devices that go into radios. You find that quality is not what it should be and that many of your group's tuning devices have to be brought back and reworked; your own boss says that "You'd better start doing a better job of training your workers."
   a. What are some of the "staffing" factors that could be contributing to this problem?
   b. Explain how you would go about assessing whether it is in fact a training problem.

3. Explain how you would apply our principles of learning in developing a lecture, say, on orientation and training.

4. Pick out some task with which you are familiar—mowing the lawn, tuning a car—and develop a job instruction training sheet for it.

5. John Santos is an undergraduate business student majoring in accounting. He has just failed the first accounting course, Accounting 101, and is understandably up-

set. Explain how you would use performance analysis to identify what, if any, are Juan's training needs.

6. What are some typical on-the-job training techniques? What do you think are some of the main drawbacks of relying on informal on-the-job training for breaking new employees into their jobs?

7. You are to give a short lecture on the subject "Guidelines to Keep in Mind When Presenting a Lecture." Give a five or ten minute lecture on the subject making sure, of course, to follow the guidelines as enumerated in this chapter.

8. Working individually or in groups, you are to develop a short programmed learning program on the subject "Guidelines for Giving a More Effective Lecture." Use the example in Figure 7.3 and any other information you may have available to develop your programmed learning program.

9. This chapter points out that one reason for implementing special global training programs is the need to avoid business ". . . due to cultural insensitivity." What sort of cultural insensitivity do you think is referred to and how might that translate into lost business? What sort of training program would you recommend to avoid such cultural insensitivity?

10. This chapter presents several examples of how diversity training can backfire such as "the possibility of post-training participant discomfort." How serious do you think potential negative outcomes like these are and what would you do as an HR manager to avoid them?

Application Exercises

RUNNING CASE: Carter Cleaning Company
The New Training Program

At the present time the Carter Cleaning Centers have no formal orientation or training policies or procedures, and Jennifer believes this is one reason why the standards to which she and her father would like employees to adhere are generally not followed.

The Carters would prefer that certain practices and procedures be used in dealing with the customers at the front counters. For example, all customers should be greeted with what Jack refers to as a "big hello." Garments they drop off should immediately be inspected for any damage or unusual stains so these can be brought to the customer's attention, lest the customer later return to pick up the garment and erroneously blame the store. The garments are then supposed to be immediately placed together in a nylon sack to separate them from other customers' garments. The ticket also has to be carefully written up, with the customer's name and telephone number and the date precisely and clearly noted on all copies. The counterperson is also supposed to take the opportunity to try to sell the customer additional services such as waterproofing or simply notify the customer that "Now that people are doing their spring cleaning, we're having a special on drapery cleaning all this

month." Finally, as the customer leaves, the counterperson is supposed to make a courteous comment like "Have a nice day" or "Drive safely." Each of the other jobs in the stores—pressing, cleaning and spotting, periodically maintaining the coin laundry equipment, and so forth—similarly contain certain steps, procedures, and most important, standards the Carters would prefer to see upheld.

The company has also had other problems, Jennifer feels, because of a lack of adequate employee training and orientation. For example, two new employees became very upset last month when they discovered that they were not paid at the end of the week, on Friday, but instead were paid (as are all Carter employees) on the following Tuesday. The Carters use the extra two days in part to give them time to obtain everyone's hours and compute their pay. The other reason they do it, according to Jack, is that "frankly, when we stay a few days behind in paying employees it helps to ensure that they at least give us a few days' notice before quitting on us. While we are certainly obligated to pay them anything they earn, we find that psychologically they seem to be less likely to just walk out on us Friday evening and not show up Monday morning if they still haven't gotten their pay from the previous week. This way they at least give us a few days' notice so we can find a replacement."

Other matters that could be covered during an orientation, says Jennifer, include company policy regarding paid holidays, lateness and absences, health and hospitalization benefits (there are none, other than worker's compensation) and general matters like the maintenance of a clean and safe work area, personal appearance and cleanliness, time sheets, personal telephone calls and mail, company policies regarding matters like substance abuse, and eating or smoking on the job.

Jennifer believes that implementing orientation and training programs would help to ensure that employees know how to do their jobs the right way. And she and her father further believe that it is only when employees understand the right way to do their jobs that there is any hope their jobs will in fact

be accomplished the way the Carters want them to be accomplished.

Questions

1. Specifically what should the Carters cover in their new employee orientation program and how should they cover this information?

2. In the personnel management course Jennifer took, the book suggested using a task analysis record form to identify tasks performed by an employee. "Should we use a form like this for the counterperson's job, and if so, what would the filled-in form look like?"

3. Which specific training techniques should Jennifer use to train her pressers, her cleaner-spotters, her managers, and her counterpeople, and why?

CASE INCIDENT: Boeing's New Computer System

In 1990 the Boeing Commercial Airline Group in Seattle was about to install in its commercial spare parts department the largest computing system it had ever developed. The department sells spare parts to commercial airlines. The purpose of the new computer system was to automate many of the department's tasks, including inventory updates, customer inquiry responses, and pricing.

Boeing managers knew that installation of the new computer system would require extensive retraining of its employees. It would affect almost all of the 700 people in the spare parts department, and not just in terms of the technical aspects of using the new computer system. For one thing, the department's offices would become virtually paperless. And perhaps even more scary to the employees was the fact that they would have to spend much more of their day working at their computer terminals. In addition, interpersonal relationships would become more interdependent because each employee would be more reliant on information that others entered accurately onto the computer. Employees had to understand that suddenly they had many more "customers" relying on them—customers who, in fact, were other spare parts department employees.

As the training coordinator put it, "We realized that providing technical training alone wouldn't be enough to ensure a successful implementation." The new system's users would need tools to handle the

changes they would experience when the system came on-line. The training group wanted to make sure that it minimized the stress and confusion that implementation could potentially create. More to the point was that it wanted to make sure all the employees using the new system became "customer-oriented" in terms of providing the information their colleagues/customers in the spare parts department required.

Given the functional diversity of the group, Boeing knew a challenge lay ahead. Half of the group worked in a warehouse and was responsible for shipping, receiving, and storing parts. The other half worked in an office 30 miles away. Furthermore, it was a diverse group in terms of educational attainment.

In deciding the nature of the training program, Boeing had a variety of options from which to choose. Because there already was an entire in-house training department, one option was to have it do the training. On the other hand, preparing 700 people in a very short time might require the services of a consulting, training, and development firm geared to getting a program like this up and running. The training department also had to consider the specific types of training to be used, such as seminars, video instruction, lectures, or books. One San Francisco-based firm under consideration was well known for being able to quickly develop large-scale training programs that were generally based around seminars that utilized written and visual material, participative exercises, examples, and lectures.

However, before deciding whether the training program would be managed internally or by a consulting firm, Boeing knew that it had to be more clear about the actual training objectives. For instance, in addition to the purely technical aspects of the training, there was the need to make the employees who used the system more customer-oriented. Employee communication and assertiveness skills possibly had to be developed so that they could make their needs known if there was particular information they wanted from the system that was not being provided by the employees who would now input the data.

Questions

1. What sort of training do you think the spare parts department employees require?

2. How would you go about determining what the specific training objectives should be?

3. Do you think it's advisable for Boeing to go to an outside consulting firm to put together this program, or would you recommend handling it internally?

4. Whether done internally or through the consulting firm, explain how you would go about designing the necessary training program.

Source: This case incident is based on Steve Thieme, "Customer-Service Training Supports Work Systems," *Personnel Journal,* Vol. 72, no. 4 (1993), pp. 63–65.

 # Human Resource Management Simulation

You will have an opportunity in the simulation to budget an orientation program. Do you think it is worth the cost? To what extent does an effective orientation program help retain employees?

Training is also a key element in the simulation. You will need to decide whether you train those employees you promote. Although training costs for internal promotions and open-market hiring costs are relatively equal, the organization believes that supervisors and managers will be better prepared by the training program to assume managerial positions in the organization. Your team will need to wrestle with the decision of promoting (and training) from within or hiring qualified people from outside the organization. In addition, you will need to budget for technical and nontechnical types of training.

Incident (F) involves a budgetary decision concerning several training requests. As you make this decision, remember that almost all decisions involve setting a precedent. Whatever you decide to do, you may be asked to do it again in the future.

Video Case

Retraining in Cincinnati

With the dramatic restructuring of many industries, more and more companies—like the Cincinnati-based companies in this video—find they have to retrain their employees. These people either need to learn new jobs at their current company or need to prepare for new jobs and careers elsewhere. As this video emphasizes, being laid off can be an opportunity: Employees laid off by GE in Cincinnati, for instance, went on to successful careers in computers, advanced manufacturing, and horticulture.

Questions

1. Why do you think there's so much stress on "on-the-job training" in the Cincinnati area retraining programs?

2. What do you think accounts for the great success of the Cincinnati area training programs?

3. If you were assigned the task of developing a retraining program for workers in your company, what sorts of questions would you ask before recommending a program?

Source: ABC News, *Cincinnati Retraining Program,* "World News Tonight/American Agenda," April 15, 1993.

Take It to the Net

We invite you to visit the Dessler page on the Prentice Hall Web site at:
http://www.prenhall.com/~dessler

for the monthly Dessler update and for this chapter's WorldWideWeb exercise.

Notes

1. For a recent discussion of socialization see, for example, Georgia Chao et al., "Organizational Socialization: Its Content and Consequences," *Journal of Applied Psychology,* Vol. 79, no. 5 (1994), pp. 730–743.
2. Joseph Famularo, *Handbook of Modern Personnel Administration* (New York: McGraw-Hill, 1972), pp. 23.7–23.8. See also Ronald Smith, "Employee Orientation: Ten Steps to Success," *Personnel Journal,* Vol. 63, no. 12 (December 1984), pp. 46–49.
3. For a discussion of current types of and practices in job skills training, see Harley Frazis, Diane Helz, and Michael Horrigan, "Employer-Provided Training: Results from a New Survey," *Monthly Labor Review* (May 1995), p. 7.
4. See, for example, Carolyn Wiley, "Training for the 90s: How Leading Companies Focus on Quality Improvement, Technological Change, and Customer Service," *Employment Relations Today* (Spring 1993), p. 80.
5. See, for example, our discussion in Chapter One. Also see Ibid., p. 80.
6. The following is based on Ibid., pp. 81–82.
7. Harley Frazis, Diane Herz, and Michael Horrigan, "Employer-Provided Training: Results from a New Survey," *Monthly Labor Review* (May 1995), pp. 3–17.
8. Wiley, "Training for the 90s," p. 82.
9. This is based on Anthony F. Carnevale, "America and the New Economy," *Training and Development Journal,* Vol. 44, no. 11 (November 1990), pp. 31ff. See also Richard Saggers, "Training Climbs the Corporate Agenda," *Personnel Management,* Vol. 26, no.7 (July 1994), pp. 40–45.
10. Ibid.
11. Ibid.; "The Training Gap," *Training and Development Journal* (March 1991), p. 9. Terri Bergman, "Training: The Case for Increased Investment," *Employment Relations Today,* Vol. 21, no. 4 (Winter 1994), pp. 381–391.
12. Carnevale, based on Kenneth Wexley and Gary Yukl, *Organizational Behavior and Personnel Psychology* (Homewood, IL: Richard D. Irwin, 1977), pp. 289–295; E. J. McCormick and J. Tiffin, *Industrial Psychology* (Englewood Cliffs, NJ: Prentice-Hall, 1974), pp. 232–340.
13. Wexley and Yukl, *Organizational Behavior,* pp. 289–295.
14. R. E. Silverman, *Learning Theory Applied to Training* (Reading, MA: Addison-Wesley, 1970), Chapter 8; McCormick and Tiffin, *Industrial Psychology,* pp. 239–240.
15. This is based on Kenneth Wexley and Gary Latham, *Developing and Training Human Resources in Organizations* (Glenview, IL: Scott, Foresman, 1981), pp. 22–27. Note that these legal aspects apply equally to technical training and management development. See also Ron Zemke, "What Is Technical Training, Anyway?" *Training,* Vol. 23, no. 7 (July

1986), pp. 18–22. See also Bureau of National Affairs, "Sexual Harassment: Training Tips," *Fair Employment Practices,* June 25, 1987, p. 84.
16. Kenneth Sovereign, *Personnel Law* (Englewood Cliffs, NJ: Prentice-Hall, Inc., 1994), pp. 165–166.
17. Ibid., pp. 165–166; J. Fenton, William Ruud, and J. Kimbell, "Negligent Training Suits: A Recent Entry into the Corporate Employment Negligence Arena," *Labor Law Journal,* Vol. 42 (June 1991), p. 351.
18. These are based on Sovereign, *Personnel Law,* pp. 165–166.
19. Bureau of National Affairs, *Training Employees, Personnel Policies Forum, Survey 88* (Washington, DC: November 1965), p. 5. For further discussion of conducting a needs analysis, see Kenneth Nowack, "A True Training Needs Analysis," *Training and Development Journal* (April 1991), pp. 69–73.
20. B. M. Bass and J. A. Vaughan, "Assessing Training Needs," in Craig Schneier and Richard Beatty, *Personnel Administration Today* (Reading, MA: Addison-Wesley, 1978), p. 311. See also Ronald Ash and Edward Leving, "Job Applicant Training and Work Experience Evaluation: An Empirical Comparison of Four Methods," *Journal of Applied Psychology,* Vol. 70, no. 3 (1985), pp. 572–576; John Lawrie, "Break the Training Ritual," *Personnel Journal,* Vol. 67, no. 4 (April 1988), pp. 95–97; and Theodore Lewis and David Bjorkquist, "Needs Assessment—A Critical Reappraisal," *Performance Improvement Quarterly,* Vol. 5, no. 4 (1992), pp. 33–54.
21. See, for example, Gean Freeman, "Human Resources Planning—Training Needs Analysis," *Human Resources Planning,* Vol. 39, no. 3 (Fall 1993), pp. 32–34.
22. McCormick and Tiffin, *Industrial Psychology,* p. 245. See also James C. Georges, "The Hard Realities of Soft Skills Training," *Personnel Journal,* Vol. 68, no. 4 (April 1989), pp. 40–45; Robert H. Buckham, "Applying Role Analysis in the Workplace," *Personnel,* Vol. 64, no. 2 (February 1987), pp. 63–65; and J. Kevin Ford and Raymond Noe, "Self-Assessed Training Needs: The Effects of Attitudes Towards Training, Management Level, and Function," *Personnel Psychology,* Vol. 40, no. 1 (Spring 1987), pp. 39–54.
23. Richard Camp et al., *Toward a More Organizationally Effective Training Strategy and Practice* (Englewood Cliffs, NJ: Prentice Hall, 1986), p. 100.
24. J. P. Cicero, "Behavioral Objectives for Technical Training Systems," *Training and Development Journal,* Vol. 28 (1973), pp. 14–17. See also Larry D. Hales, "Training: A Product of Business Planning," *Training and Development Journal,* Vol. 40, no. 7 (July 1986), pp. 87–92, and Arnold H. Wensky and Robert Legendre, "Training Incentives," *Personnel Journal,* Vol. 68, no. 4 (April 1989), pp. 102–108.

25. I. L. Goldstein, *Training: Program Development and Evaluation* (Monterey, CA: Wadsworth, 1974). See also Stephen B. Wehrenberg, "Learning Contracts," *Personnel Journal,* Vol. 67, no. 9 (September 1988), pp. 100–103; Murray B. Heibert and Norman Smallwood, "Now for a Completely Different Look at Needs Analysis," *Training and Development Journal,* Vol. 41, no. 5 (May 1987), pp. 75–79; Erica Gordon Sorohan, "We Do; Therefore, We Learn," *Training & Development* (October 1993), pp. 47–55; Melvin LeBlanc, "Learning Objectives Key to Quality Safety," *Occupational Hazards* (January 1994), pp. 127–128.

26. Wexley and Latham, *Developing and Training,* p. 107.

27. Harley Frazis et al., "Employer-Provided Training: Results from a New Survey," p. 4.

28. Ibid., pp. 107–112. Four steps in on-the-job training based on William Berliner and William McLarney, *Management Practice and Training* (Homewood, IL: Irwin, 1974), pp. 442–443. See also Robert Sullivan and Donald Miklas, "On-the-Job Training That Works," *Training and Development Journal,* Vol. 39, no. 5 (May 1985), pp. 118–120, and Stephen B. Wehrenberg, "Supervisors as Trainers: The Long-Term Gains of OJT," *Personnel Journal,* Vol. 66, no. 4 (April 1987), pp. 48–51.

29. Donald F. Michalak and Edwin G. Yager, *Making the Training Process Work* (New York: Harper & Row, 1979), pp. 108–111. See also Richard Wiegand, "Can All Your Trainees Hear You?" *Training and Development Journal,* Vol. 41, no. 8 (August 1987), pp. 38–43.

30. Wexley and Latham, *Developing and Training,* pp. 131–133. See also Teri O. Grady and Mike Matthews," Video . . . Through the Eyes of the Trainee," *Training,* Vol. 24, no. 7 (July 1987), pp. 57–62. For a description of the use of computer-based multimedia training, see Erica Schroeder, "Training Takes Off, Using Multimedia," *PC Week,* August 29, 1994, pp. 33–34.

31. Mary Boone and Susan Schulman, "Teletraining: A High-Tech Alternative," *Personnel,* Vol. 62, no. 5 (May 1985), pp. 4–9. See also Ron Zemke, "The Rediscovery of Video Teleconferencing," *Training,* Vol. 23, no. 9 (September 1986), pp. 28–36; and Carol Haig, "Clinics Fill Training Niche," *Personnel Journal,* Vol. 66, no. 9 (September 1987), pp. 134–140.

32. Joseph Giusti, David Baker, and Peter Braybash, "Satellites Dish Out Global Training," *Personnel Journal* (June 1991), pp. 80–84.

33. Michael Emery and Margaret Schubert, "A Trainer's Guide to Videoconferencing," *Training* (June 1993), p. 60.

34. Ibid., p. 60.

35. These are based on or quoted from Emery and Schubert, "A Trainer's Guide to Videoconferencing," p. 61.

36. G. N. Nash, J. P. Muczyk, and F. L. Vettori, "The Role and Practical Effectiveness of Programmmed Instruction," *Personnel Psychology,* Vol. 24 (1971), pp. 397–418.

37. Wexley and Latham, *Developing and Training,* p. 141. See also Raymond Wlozkowski, "Simulation," *Training and Development Journal,* Vol. 39, no. 6 (June 1985), pp. 38–43.

38. See, for example, Tim Falconer, "No More Pencils, No More Books!" *Canadian Banker* (March/April 1994), pp. 21–25.

39. Ralph E. Ganger, "Training: Computer-Based Training Works," *Personnel Journal,* Vol. 73, no. 11 (November 1994), pp. 51–52. See also Anat Arkin, "Computing: The Future Means of Training?" *Personnel Management,* Vol. 26, No. 8 (August 1994), pp. 36–40.

40. This is based on Mickey Williamson, "High-Tech Training," *Byte* (December 1994), pp. 74–89.

41. Ibid., p. 75.

42. These are summarized in Rockley Miller, "New Training Looms," *Hotel and Motel Management,* April 4, 1994, pp. 26 and 30.

43. Ibid., p. 26.

44. Bob Filipczak, "Training Consortia: How They Work, How They Don't," *Training* (August 1994), pp. 51–57.

45. Harold W. McGraw, Jr., "Adult Functional Illiteracy: What to Do About It," *Personnel* (October 1987), p. 38; Catherine Petrini, "Literacy Programs Make the News," *Training and Development Journal* (February 1991), pp. 30–36.

46. This is based on Ellen Sherman, "Back to Basics to Improve Skills," *Personnel* (July 1989), pp. 22–26.

47. Ibid., p. 24.

48. Bureau of National Affairs, *Bulletin to Management,* December 17, 1987, p. 408.

49. Nancy Lynn Bernardon, "Let's Erase Illiteracy from the Workplace," *Personnel* (January 1989), pp. 29–32.

50. Ibid. The PALS course was developed by educator Dr. John Henry Martin.

51. Ibid., p. 32. SKILLPAC was created by the Center for Applied Linguistics and Dr. Arnold Packer, senior research fellow at the Hudson Institute in Indianapolis, Indiana.

52. Jeffrey Mello, "AIDS Education in the Work Place," *Training and Development Journal* (December 1990), pp. 65–70.

53. This is based on Sylvia Odenwald, "A Guide for Global Training," *Training and Development* (July 1993), pp. 22–31.

54. For a full description of these programs as well as the names of the vendors, see Ibid., pp. 24–27.

55. Jennifer Laabs, "The Global Talent Search," *Personnel Journal* (August 1991), pp. 38–42.

56. Pat McCarthy, "The Art of Training Abroad," *Training and Development Journal* (November 1990), pp. 13–18.

57. This is adapted from Gary Dessler, *Winning Commitment* (New York: McGraw-Hill, 1993), Chapter 7.

58. See Joyce Santora, "Kinney Shoes Steps Into Diversity," *Personnel Journal* (September 1991), p. 74.

59. Sara Rynes and Benson Rosen, "What Makes Diversity Programs Work?" *HR Magazine* (October 1994), p. 64. See also Thomas Diamante and Leo Giglio, "Managing a Diverse Workforce: Training as a Cultural Intervention Strategy," *Leadership & Organization Development Journal,* Vol. 15, No. 2 (1994), pp. 13–17.

60. Willie Hopkins, Karen Sterkel-Powell, and Shirley Hopkins, "Training Priorities for a Diverse Workforce," *Public Personnel Management,* Vol. 23, no. 3 (Fall 1994), p. 433.

61. This is based on Ibid., pp. 72–77.

62. Joyce Santora, "Alamo's Drive for Customer Service," *Personnel Journal* (April 1991), pp. 42–44.

63. This is based on Jennifer Laabs, "Team Training Goes Outdoors," *Personnel Journal* (June 1991), pp. 56–63.

64. Ibid., p. 56. See also Shari Caudron, "Teamwork Takes Work," *Personnel Journal,* Vol. 73, No. 2 (February 1994), pp. 41–49.

65. Carolyn Wiley, "Training for the 1990s," p. 79.

66. Laurie Bassi, "Upgrading the U.S. Workplace: Do Reorgani-

zation & Education Help?" *Monthly Labor Review* (May 1995), pp. 37–47.

67. Ann Bartel, "Productivity Gains from the Implementation of Employee Training Programs," *Industrial Relations,* Vol. 33, no. 4 (October 1994), pp. 411–425.

68. R. E. Catalano and D. L. Kirkpatrick, "Evaluating Training Programs—The State of the Art," *Training and Development Journal,* Vol. 22, no. 5 (May 1968), pp. 2–9. See also J. Kevin Ford and Steven Wroten, "Introducing New Methods for Conducting Training Evaluation and for Linking Training Evaluation to Program Redesign," *Personnel Psychology,* Vol. 37, no. 4 (Winter 1984), pp. 651–666. See also Basil Paquet et al., "The Bottom Line," *Training and Development Journal,* Vol. 41, no. 5 (May 1987), pp. 27–33.; Harold E. Fisher and Ronald Weinberg, "Make Training Accountable: Assess Its Impact," *Personnel Journal,* Vol. 67, no. 1 (January 1988), pp. 73–75; and Timothy Baldwin and J. Kevin Ford, "Transfer of Training: A Review and Directions for Future Research," *Personnel Psychology,* Vol. 41, no. 1 (Spring 1988), pp. 63–105. Anthony Montebello and Maurine Haga, "To Justify Training, Test, Test Again," *Personnel Journal,* Vol. 73, No. 1 (January 1994), pp. 83–87.

69. Donald Kirkpatrick, "Effective Supervisory Training and Development," Part 3: "Outside Programs," *Personnel,* Vol. 62, no. 2 (February 1985), pp. 39–42. See also James Bell and Deborah Kerr, "Measuring Training Results: Key to Managerial Commitment," *Training and Development Journal,* Vol. 41, no. 1 (January 1987), pp. 70–73. Among the reasons training might not pay off on the job are a mismatching of courses and trainee's needs, supervisory slip-ups (with supervisors signing up trainees and then forgetting to have them attend the sessions when the training session is actually given), and no help applying skills on the job. For a discussion, see Ruth Colvin Clark, "Nine Ways to Make Training Pay Off on the Job," *Training,* Vol. 23, no. 11 (November 1986), pp. 83–87. See also Herman Birnbrauer, "Troubleshooting Your Training Program," *Training and Development Journal,* Vol. 41, no 9 (September 1987), pp. 18–20; George Bickerstaffe, "Measuring the Gains from Training," *Personnel Management* (November 1993), pp. 48–51; Jim Spoor, "You Can Quantify Training Dollars and Program Value," *HR Focus* (May 1993), p. 3; Jack Trynor, "Is Training a Good Investment?" *Financial Analyst Journal* (September–October 1994), pp. 6–8; and Sarah Dolliver, "The Missing Link: Evaluating Training Programs," *Supervision* (November 1994), pp. 10–12.

Chapter 8
Developing Managers

Chapter Outline

- ◆ Nature & Purpose of Management Development
- ◆ Managerial On-the-Job Training
- ◆ Off-the-Job Management Development Techniques
- ◆ Using HR to Build a Responsive Learning Organization
- ◆ Executive Development: Key Factors for Success

Behavioral Objectives

When you finish studying this chapter, you should be able to:

Explain what management development is and why it is important.

Describe the main on-the-job development techniques and how they are used.

Discuss the main off-the-job development techniques.

Explain how to use HR techniques to develop the learning organization.

Nature and Purpose of Management Development

Management development is any attempt to improve managerial performance by imparting knowledge, changing attitudes, or increasing skills. It thus includes in-house programs like courses, coaching, and rotational assignments; professional programs like American Management Association Seminars; and university programs like executive MBA programs.[1] It is estimated that well over 1 million U.S. managers participate in management development programs yearly[2] for a cost to industry of several billion dollars a year.[3]

The ultimate aim of such development programs is, of course, to enhance the future performance of the organization itself. For this reason, the general management development process consists of (1) assessing the company's needs (for instance, to fill future executive openings, or to make the firm more responsive), (2) appraising the managers' performance, and then (3) developing the managers themselves.

Management development is important for several reasons. For one thing, promotion from within is a major source of management talent. One survey of 84 employers reports that about 90% of supervisors, 73% of middle-level managers, and 51% of executives were promoted from within; virtually all these managers, in turn, required some development to prepare them for their new jobs. Similarly, management development facilitates organizational continuity by preparing employees and current managers to smoothly assume higher-level positions. It also helps to socialize management trainees by developing in them the right values and attitudes for working in the firm.[4] And, it can foster organizational responsiveness by developing the skills that managers need to respond faster to change.

The Changing Nature of Management Development

Some management development programs are companywide and involve all or most new (or potential) management recruits. Thus, new college graduates may join Enormous Corp. and (with two dozen colleagues) become part of the companywide management development program. Here they may be rotated through a preprogrammed series of departmental assignments and educational experiences; the aims are identifying their management potential, and at providing the breadth of experience (in, say, production and finance) that will make the new managers more valuable in their first "real" assignment as group product leaders. Then superior candidates may be slotted onto a "fast track," a development program that prepares them more quickly to assume senior-level commands.

On the other hand, the management development program may be aimed at filling a specific position, such as CEO, perhaps with one of two potential candidates. When it is an executive position to be filled, the process is usually called **succession planning.** Succession planning refers to the process through which senior-level openings are planned for and eventually filled.

Such a succession program typically takes place in stages. First, an *organization projection* is made; here you anticipate your department's management needs based on factors like planned expansion or contraction. Next the HR department reviews its *management skills inventory* to identify the management talent now employed. These inventories, you may recall, contain data on things like educational and work experience, career preferences, and performance appraisals. Next management *replacement charts* are drawn. These summarize potential candidates for each of your management slots, as well as each person's development needs. As shown in Figure 8.1, the development needs for a future division vice president might include *job rotation* (to obtain more experience in the firm's finance and

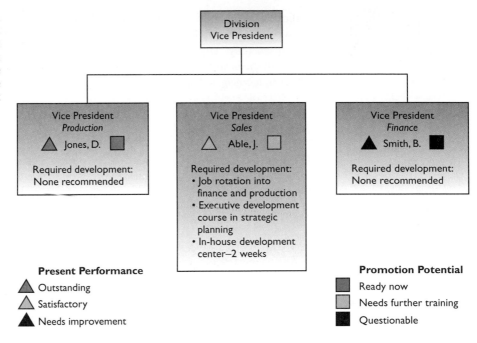

Figure 8.1
Management
Replacement Chart
Showing Development
Needs of Future
Divisional Vice
President

Division
Vice President

Vice President
Production

Jones, D.

Required development:
None recommended

Vice President
Sales

Able, J.

Required development:
• Job rotation into
  finance and production
• Executive development
  course in strategic
  planning
• In-house development
  center–2 weeks

Vice President
Finance

Smith, B.

Required development:
None recommended

Present Performance
△ Outstanding
△ Satisfactory
▲ Needs improvement

Promotion Potential
■ Ready now
■ Needs further training
■ Questionable

production divisions), *executive development programs* (to provide training in strategic planning), and assignment for two weeks to the employer's *in-house management development center.*[5]

HR and the Responsive Organization

The Responsive Manager

For the past few years management development's focus has been shifting from preparing managers to fill higher-level slots to preparing them to meet the challenges of managing in a fast-paced environment. Increasingly, therefore, the emphasis is on developing a manager's ability to learn and make decisions under conditions of rapid change.[6]

Two experts put it this way: "As decision makers take on increasing responsibility across their careers, their learning needs move from the arena of task learning to behavioral learning to conceptual or policy-level learning."[7] For example, today's corporate managers are under enormous pressure "to find the strategic opportunities their competitors have yet to find."[8] This means more emphasis on developing their conceptual ability to search for internal strategic opportunities to improve quality, service, and prices. Similarly, all managers—not just those to be posted overseas—have to be well schooled in global economics, foreign markets, and cross-cultural negotiating.[9] And to manage in flatter, more empowered organizations the leader must increasingly become a teacher, coach, and consultant rather than a "boss."[10]

This is causing a corresponding change in the techniques that are emphasized in management development programs. Historically on-the-job experiences, including on-the-job training, coaching, and rotational assignments, have been far and away the most popular management development techniques.[11] The problem is that these techniques tend to emphasize showing managers current procedures or (at best) getting them to think about how to "do what we're doing today a little better."[12] Today there's a shift toward development techniques that teach managers how to learn and how to develop the competencies they need to cope with change, such as sizing up foreign markets and searching for new strategic opportunities. Special *in-company executive development* programs, *action learning* and *lifelong learning*, are examples to be discussed later.[13]◆

Managerial On-the-Job Training

On-the-job training is one of the most popular development methods. Important techniques here include job rotation, the coaching/understudy approach, junior boards, and action learning.

Job Rotation

job rotation
A management training technique that involves moving a trainee from department to department to broaden his or her experience and identify strong and weak points.

Job rotation means moving management trainees from department to department to broaden their understanding of all parts of the business.[14] The trainee—often a recent college graduate—may spend several months in each department; this helps not only broaden his or her experience, but also discover the jobs he or she prefers. The person may just be an observer in each department but more commonly gets fully involved in its operations. The trainee thus learns the department's business by actually doing it, whether it involves sales, production, finance, or some other function.

Job rotation has several other advantages.[15] In addition to providing a well-rounded training experience for each person, it helps avoid stagnation through the constant introduction of new points of view in each department. It also tests the trainee and helps identify the person's strong and weak points. Periodic job changing can also improve interdepartmental cooperation; managers become more understanding of each other's problems, while rotation also widens the trainee's acquaintances among management.

Rotation does have disadvantages. It encourages generalization and tends to be more appropriate for developing general line managers than functional staff experts. You also have to be careful not to forget inadvertently a trainee at some deserted outpost.

There are several things you can do to improve a rotation program's success.[16] The program should be tailored to the needs and capabilities of the individual trainee and not be a standard sequence of steps that all trainees take. The trainee's interests, aptitudes, and career preferences should be considered, along with the employer's needs; the length of time the trainee stays in a job should then be determined by how fast he or she is learning. Furthermore, the managers to whom these people are assigned should themselves be specially trained to provide feedback and to monitor performance in an interested and competent way.

The Goodyear Tire and Rubber Company's training program for college graduates is a good example of job rotation.[17] Each trainee's program is tailored to match his or her experience, education, and vocational preference. Programs vary from 6 to 15 months, beginning with three weeks in an orientation program to make the trainees thoroughly acquainted with Goodyear. (Here they study the organization's structure, company objectives, and basic manufacturing processes and participate in informal meetings with top company officials.) After an additional month of factory orientation, trainees discuss their career interests with top-level managers and select up to six assignments in special departments, each of which will last about one month. (For example, a chemical engineering graduate might rotate through departments for fabric development, chemical materials development research, central process engineering, process development, and chemical production.) Trainees then select specific job assignments as the starting point of their careers.

Global HRM

Global Job Rotation and Management

As firms expand multinationally, *job rotation* is taking on a new meaning. At firms like Shell and British Petroleum (BP), rotating managers globally is a primary means through which the firms maintain their flexibility and responsiveness even as they grow to an enormous size.

The rationale for extensive global job rotation is summarized as follows by a Shell senior executive:

> The word summarizing today's business outlook is uncertainty, and the response must be flexibility. For a complex, international, multifunctional organization like the Shell group, the prerequisite for flexibility is a highly skilled, mobile, international body of staff.[18]

The advantage of global job rotation (rotating managers from, say, Sweden to New York, and from New York to Japan) is that it builds a network of informal ties—an information network—that ensures superior cross-border communication and mutual understanding as well as tight interunit coordination and control.

Improved communication and understanding stem from the personal relationships that are forged as managers work in the firm's various locations. These activities can also enhance organizational control. When employees from a firm's global locations are rotated or brought together at, say, the Harvard Business School or Europe's INSEAD for a management training program, the aim is more than just teaching basic skills. It is also to build a stronger identification with the company's culture and values. By creating shared values and a consistent view of the firm and its goals, management development activities like these can facilitate communication and ensure that through a sense of shared values and purpose the firm's policies are followed, even with a minimum reliance on more traditional forms of control.[19]◆

Coaching/Understudy Approach

In the *coaching/understudy approach,* the trainee works directly with the person he or she is to replace; the latter is in turn responsible for the trainee's coaching. Normally, the understudy relieves the executive of certain responsibilities, thereby giving the trainee a chance to learn the job.[20] This helps ensure that the employer will have trained managers to assume key positions when such positions are vacated due to retirement, promotions, transfers, or terminations. It also helps guarantee the long-run development of company-bred top managers.

To be effective, the executive has to be a good coach and mentor. Furthermore, this person's motivation to train the replacement will depend on the quality of the relationship between them. Some executives are also better at delegating responsibility, providing reinforcement, and communicating than are others; this also will affect the results.

Junior Boards

junior board
A method of providing middle-management trainees with experience in analyzing company problems by inviting them to sit on a junior board of directors and make recommendations on overall company policies.

Unlike job rotation, which aims to familiarize the trainees with the problems of each department, **junior boards** aim to give promising middle managers experience in analyzing overall company problems. The idea of a junior board (also called *multiple management*) is to give trainees top-level analysis and policymaking experience by having 10 to 12 trainees sit on a junior board of directors. The members of such boards come from various departments. They make recommendations regarding top-level issues like organization structure, executive compensation, and interdepartmental conflict to the official board of directors. This technique provides middle-management trainees with on-the-job training and experience in dealing with organizationwide problems.

Action Learning

action learning
A training technique by which management trainees are allowed to work full time analyzing and solving problems in other departments.

Action learning gives managers released time to work full time on projects, analyzing and solving problems in departments other than their own.[21] The trainees meet periodically with a four- or five-person project group, where their findings and progress are discussed and debated.

Action learning is similar to and grounded in other development methods. It is similar to the junior boards previously discussed except that trainees generally work full time on their projects, rather than analyzing a problem as a committee as they would on junior boards. It is also similar to giving a management trainee a special assignment or project. However, with action learning several trainees work together as a project group to compare notes and discuss each other's projects. Action learning often requires cooperation among several employers. For example, an employee from General Electric might be assigned to a government agency for a research project, while the agency might assign one of its managers to GE.

As an example, a CIGNA International Property and Casualty Corp. vice president spent four intensive weeks in an action learning group.[22] The group was assigned the problem of analyzing the strategies of one of the insurance company's business units over the previous three years. They were told not to formulate a new business strategy but to recommend whether the existing strategies required minor adjustments and whether they were being implemented incorrectly. The vice president's group consisted of 11 upper- and middle-management members from various CIGNA divisions with no one coming from the same division. Each of the four weeks was devoted to a different set of activities. In the first week the group received training from business professors as well as a briefing from the division staff that had the business problem. In the second week they split into four teams and traveled the country interviewing about 100 of the division's employees, distributors, and customers on a one-to-one basis. In the third week the group assimilated and analyzed the data, and in the fourth week they formulated recommendations and wrote a 40-plus-page paper. The group presented its recommendations to the president and executive staff of the troubled division at the end of the fourth week and fielded questions from the executives.[23]

The idea of developing managers this way has pros and cons. It gives trainees real experience with actual problems, and to that extent it can develop skills like problem analysis and planning. Furthermore, working with the others in the group, the trainees can and do find solutions to major problems. The main drawback is that in releasing trainees to work on outside projects, the employer loses, in a sense, the full-time services of a competent manager.

Off-the-Job Management Development Techniques

There are many techniques you can use to develop managers off the job, perhaps in a conference room at headquarters or off the premises entirely at a university or special seminar. These techniques are addressed next.

The Case Study Method

case study method
A development method in which the manager is presented with a written description of an organizational problem to diagnose and solve.

The **case study method** presents a trainee with a written description of an organizational problem. The person then analyzes the case in private, diagnoses the problem, and presents his or her findings and solutions in a discussion with other trainees.[24] The case method approach is aimed at giving trainees realistic experience in identifying and analyzing complex problems in an environment in which their progress can be subtly guided by a trained discussion leader. Through the class discussion of the case, trainees learn that there are usually many ways to approach and solve complex organizational problems. Trainees also learn that their solutions are often influenced by their own needs and values.

The case method ideally has five main features:[25] (1) the use of actual organizational problems; (2) the maximum possible involvement of participants in stating their views, inquiring into others' views, confronting different views, and making decisions; resulting in (3) a minimal degree of dependence on the faculty members; who, in turn, (4) hold the position that there are rarely any right or wrong answers, and that cases are incomplete and so is reality; and (5) who still strive to make the case method as engaging as possible through creation of appropriate levels of drama. As you can see, the instructor plays a crucial role.[26]

Problems to Avoid   Unfortunately, the case approach often falls far short of this mark.[27] In practice, faculty often dominate classroom discussions by asking students questions that they then themselves proceed to answer, through answering specific questions asked by students and through presenting statements of the facts about the case. Faculty also use "mystery to achieve mastery" by intentionally withholding information (for instance, regarding what the company actually did and what its competitors were doing at the time when the case was written) with the aim of maintaining control of the classroom discussion. In one study of the case method, Argyris found that there were inconsistencies between the approach that the faculty espoused and what they actually did. For example, (1) faculty said there are no right or wrong answers, yet some faculty members did take positions and give answers; (2) faculty said there are many different points of view possible; yet they seemed to select viewpoints and organize them in a way to suggest that they have a preferred route. Finally, few attempts were made by the faculty to relate the trainee's behavior in the classroom to their behavior back home.

There are several things you can do to make the case approach more effective. If possible, the cases should be actual cases from the trainees' own firms. This will help ensure that trainees understand the background of the case, as well as make it easier for trainees to transfer what they learn to their own jobs and situations. Argyris also contends that instructors have to guard against dominating the case analysis and make sure that they remain no more than a catalyst or coach. Finally, they must carefully prepare the case discussion and let the students discuss the case in small groups before class.[28]

Employees often talk today about the need to "shatter the glass ceiling"—the transparent but often impermeable barrier that many women face in trying to move up to the top management levels. The glass ceiling is not a real barrier, of course, but the practical net effect of various prejudices and lack of networking opportunities women face that together make it hard or impossible for women to move up to top management jobs.

While it certainly makes sense to shatter the glass ceiling for equity's sake there is research that suggests there may be an even better reason to do so and that is the distinct possibility that, as two researchers conclude, women may simply make better managers these days than do men.[1] Their basic point is that with the trend today toward high-involvement work teams, consensus decision making, and empowerment, the sorts of leadership styles that women already exhibit may be much more appropriate than are men's.

Their conclusion is, of course, based on the assumption that female managers' leadership styles are different than males, and based on their research that appears to be the case. Specifically, their findings indicate that women scored significantly higher than men on all measures of transformational leadership. Transformational leaders ". . . move followers to go beyond their self-interest to concerns for their group or organization. They help followers develop to higher levels of potential. Such leaders diagnose the needs of their followers and then elevate those needs to initiate and promote development. They align followers around a common purpose, mission, or vision. They provide a sense of purpose and future orientation . . ." The women more than did the men scored high on such traditional measures of transformational leadership as encouraging followers to question their old way of doing things or to break with the past, providing simplified emotional appeals to increase awareness and understanding of mutually desired goals, and providing learning opportunities to employees. On the other hand, male managers were more likely to be "transactional"-type leaders, basically by commending followers if they complied or disciplining them if they failed.

Why exactly the male and female managers differed on these leadership measures is not entirely clear. The researchers conclude that the more ". . . plausible explanation for the observed differences regarding transformational leadership ratings may lie in the tendencies of women to be more nurturing, interested in others, and more socially sensitive."[2] In any case, insofar as it may be such transformational leadership behaviors that are increasingly appropriate in organizations today, it could be that female managers have an edge in exhibiting the sorts of leadership style that ". . . comprises the most appropriate leadership behaviors to develop followers to achieve their highest levels of potential" today.[3] ◆

1. Bernard Bass and Bruce Avolio, "Shatter the Glass Ceiling: Women May Make Better Managers," *Human Resource Management*, Vol. 33, No. 4 (Winter 1994), pp. 549–560.
2. Ibid., p. 556.
3. Ibid., p. 558.

Management Games

management game
A development technique in which teams of managers compete with one another by making computerized decisions regarding realistic but simulated companies.

In a computerized **management game,** trainees are divided into five- or six-person companies, each of which has to compete with the other in a simulated marketplace. Each company sets a goal (such as "maximize sales") and is told it can make several decisions. For example, the group may be allowed to decide (1) how much to spend on advertising, (2) how much to produce, (3) how much inventory to maintain, and (4) how many of which product to produce. Usually the game itself compresses a two- or three-year period into days, weeks, or months. As in the real world, each company usually can't see what decisions the other firms have made, although these decisions do affect their own sales. For example, if a competitor decides to increase its advertising expenditures, that firm may end up increasing its sales at the expense of yours.[29]

Management games can be good development tools. People learn best by getting involved in the activity itself, and the games can be useful for gaining such involvement. Games are almost always interesting and exciting for the trainees because of their realism and competitiveness. They help trainees develop their problem-solving skills, as well as focus their attention on the need for planning rather than on just putting out fires. The companies also usually elect their own officers and develop their own divisions of work; the games can thus be useful for developing leadership skills and for fostering cooperation and teamwork.

Management games also have their drawbacks. One is that the game can be expensive to develop and implement. Games also usually force the decision makers to choose alternatives from a closed list (for instance, they might have choices of only three levels of production); in real life managers are more often rewarded for creating new, innovative alternatives. On the whole, though, trainees almost always react favorably to a well-run game, and it is a good technique for developing problem-solving and leadership skills.

Outside Seminars

Many organizations offer special seminars and conferences aimed at providing skill-building training for managers. The American Management Associations (AMA), for instance, provide thousands of courses in areas such as the following:

General management
Human resources
Sales and marketing
International management
Finance
Information systems and technology
Manufacturing and operations management
Purchasing, transportation, and physical distribution
Packaging
Research and technology management
General and administrative services
Insurance and employee benefits

The courses themselves range from "how to sharpen your business writing skills" to "strategic planning" and "assertiveness training for managers."[30] The outline of a typical course is presented in Figure 8.2; it is "advanced management techniques for experienced supervisors." As you can see, it is a two-and-a-half-day advanced course for first-line manufacturing supervisors with three to five years' experience who want to enhance their management skills. Topics covered include review of management and organization concepts, developing effective interpersonal skills, communication, motivation, and developing leadership skills. Many of the AMA courses can also be presented on site at the employer's place of business if ten or more employees are enrolled. Other organizations offering management development services include AMR International, Inc., the Conference Board, and Xerox Educational Systems.

Many of these programs offer *continuing education units (CEUs)* for course completion. Earning CEUs provides a recognized measure of educational accom-

Figure 8.2
**Content for a Typical
Middle-Management
American Management
Association Training
Program**

Source: American Management
Association

**4208Q/Advanced Management Techniques for Experienced Supervisors:
How to Work Effectively With People and Within the Organization**

Who Should Attend:
An advanced course for First-Line Manufacturing Supervisors with 3–5 years' experience who want to enhance their management skills. Especially useful for supervisors who have completed course #4271—The Management Course for New Manufacturing Supervisors, or course #4202—Productivity Improvement Methods and Techniques.

Key Topics:
- Review of management and organization concepts and how they relate to today's employees: planning, organizing, coordinating, controlling; authority, responsibility, accountability, reportability; dollar relationship to human resources utilization and lost time

- How to develop effective interpersonal skills: understanding behavior and personality; relating to people as individuals; self-awareness and opportunities to develop; how to positively affect attitudes and working relationships; team development; how to develop a warmer, more relaxed climate in dealing with people; how to come across firmly but fairly

- The communication workshop for supervisors: develop increased listening skills; writing and speaking clearly, concisely, and with more organization; how to use communication to reduce stress and fear; assertiveness in communication; how to sell your ideas to management

- The motivation workshop for supervisors: analyzing management style and its role in motivation; creating an environment where employees will work effectively; behavioral foundation for self-motivation; relating program content to actual problem situations

- Developing your leadership skills: how you are perceived by others; habits that reduce your leadership potential; applying course content to leadership development

Special Feature:
Examination of the supervisor's role—defining responsibilities, duties, authority, and the restriction of authority. **Discussions** on worker psychology—how the supervisor can effectively motivate, and the importance of communications. **Discussion** of various discipline techniques—when and where to use them and their effects on performance and morale. **Presentation** on reviewing employee performance with emphasis on improving their production and morale.

plishment, says the AMA, one that is today used by more than 1,000 colleges. CEUs generally can't be used to obtain degree-granting credit at most colleges or universities, but they do provide a record of the fact that the trainee participated in and completed a special conference or seminar.

University-Related Programs

Colleges and universities provide three types of management development activities. First, many schools provide *continuing education programs* in leadership, supervision, and the like. As with the AMA, these range from one- to four-day programs to executive development programs lasting one to four months.

The Advanced Management Program of the Graduate School of Business Administration at Harvard University is an example of one of these longer programs. As you can see in Figure 8.3, each class in this program consists of a group of experienced managers from all regions of the world. The program uses cases and lectures to provide top-level management talent with the latest management skills, as well as with practice in analyzing complex organizational problems. Similar programs include the Executive Program of the Graduate School of Business Administration at the University of California at Berkeley, the Management Development Seminar at the University of Chicago, and the Executive in Business

Figure 8.3
Ad for Harvard Executive Training Program

Administration Program of the Graduate School of Business at Columbia University. Most of these programs take the executives away from their jobs, putting them in university-run learning environments for their entire stay. The Columbia University program, for instance, is offered at Arden House in the Ramapo Mountains of New York.

Second, many colleges and universities also offer *individualized courses* in areas like business, management, and health care administration. Managers can take these as matriculated or nonmatriculated students to fill gaps in their backgrounds. Thus, a prospective division manager with a gap in experience with accounting controls might sign up for a two-course sequence in managerial accounting.

Finally, of course, many schools also offer *degree programs* such as the MBA or Executive MBA. The latter is a Master of Business Administration degree program geared especially to middle managers and above, who generally take their courses on weekends and proceed through the program with the same group of colleagues.

The Employer's Contribution   The employer usually plays a role in university-related programs.[31] First, many employers offer *tuition refunds* as an incentive for employees to develop job-related skills. Thus, engineers may be encouraged to enroll in technical courses aimed at keeping them abreast of changes in their field. Supervisors may be encouraged to enroll in programs to develop them for higher-level management jobs.

Employers are also increasingly granting technical and professional employees extended *sabbaticals*—periods of time off—for attending a college or university to pursue a higher degree or to upgrade skills. For example, Lucent Corporation has a program that includes a tuition refund and released time for up to one year of on-campus study. In addition, the company has a doctoral support program that permits tuition refund and released time for studies one day a week (and, for some, a full year's study on campus to meet residence requirements).

Some companies have experimented with offering selected employees in-house degree programs in cooperation with colleges and universities. Many also offer a variety of in-house lectures and seminars by university staff.

For example, Technicon, a high-tech medical instruments company, asked Pace University to offer an executive education program for its key middle managers. The theme of the 14-month program was successful management of high-tech businesses. The coursework covered topics ranging from finance to executive communication.[32]

Universities and corporations are also experimenting with video-linked classroom education. For example, the School of Business and Public Administration at California State University, Sacramento, and a Hewlett-Packard facility in Roseville, California, are video-linked. A video-link allows for classroom learning on campuses with simultaneous broadcasting to other locations via telephone communication lines.

Role Playing

role playing
A training technique in which trainees act out the parts of people in a realistic management situation.

The aim of **role playing** is to create a realistic situation and then have the trainees assume the parts (or roles) of specific persons in that situation.[33]

One such role from a famous role-playing exercise called the New Truck Dilemma is presented in Figure 8.4. When combined with the general instructions for the role-playing exercise, roles like these for all of the participants can trigger a spirited discussion among the role players, particularly when they all throw themselves into the roles. The idea of the exercise is to solve the problem at hand and thereby develop trainees' skills in areas like leadership and delegating.

> **Walt Marshall—Supervisor of Repair Crew**
>
> You are the head of a crew of telephone maintenance workers, each of whom drives a small service truck to and from the various jobs. Every so often you get a new truck to exchange for an old one, and you have the problem of deciding to which of your crew members you should give the new truck. Often there are hard feelings, since each seems to feel entitled to the new truck, so you have a tough time being fair. As a matter of fact, it usually turns out that whatever you decide is considered wrong by most of the crew. You now have to face the issue again because a new truck, a Chevrolet, has just been allocated to you for assignment.
>
> In order to handle this problem you have decided to put the decision up to the crew. You will tell them about the new truck and will put the problem in terms of what would be the fairest way to assign the truck. Do not take a position yourself, because you want to do what they think is most fair.

Role playing can be an enjoyable and inexpensive way to develop many new skills. With the New Truck Dilemma exercise, for instance, participants learn the importance of fairness in bringing about acceptance of resource allocation decisions. The role players can also give up their inhibitions and experiment with new ways of acting. For example, a supervisor could experiment with both a considerate and autocratic leadership style, whereas in the real world the person might not have this harmless way of experimenting. According to Maier, role playing also trains a person to be aware of and sensitive to the feelings of others.[34]

Role playing has some drawbacks. An exercise can take an hour or more to complete, only to be deemed a waste of time by participants if the instructor doesn't prepare a wrap-up explanation of what the participants were to learn. Some trainees also feel that role playing is childish, while others who may have had a bad experience with the technique are reluctant to participate at all. Knowing your audience and preparing a wrap-up are thus advisable.

Behavior Modeling

behavior modeling
A training technique in which trainees are first shown good management techniques in a film, are then asked to play roles in a simulated situation, and are then given feedback and praise by their supervisor.

Behavior modeling involves (1) showing trainees the right (or "model") way of doing something, (2) letting each person practice the right way to do it, and then (3) providing feedback regarding each trainee's performance.[35] It has been used, for example, to:

1. Train first-line supervisors to handle common supervisor-employee interactions better. This includes giving recognition, disciplining, introducing changes, and improving poor performance.
2. Train middle managers to better handle interpersonal situations, for example, performance problems and undesirable work habits.
3. Train employees and their supervisors to take and give criticism, ask and give help, and establish mutual trust and respect.

The basic behavior modeling procedure can be outlined as follows:

1. *Modeling.* First, trainees watch films or videotapes that show model persons behaving effectively in a problem situation. In other words, trainees are shown the right way to behave in a simulated but realistic situation. The film might thus show a supervisor effectively disciplining a subordinate, if teaching how to discipline is the aim of the training program.

2. *Role playing.* Next the trainees are given roles to play in a simulated situation; here they practice and rehearse the effective behaviors demonstrated by the models.

3. *Social reinforcement.* The trainer provides reinforcement in the form of praise and constructive feedback based on how the trainee performs in the role-playing situation.

4. *Transfer of training.* Finally, trainees are encouraged to apply their new skills when they are back on their jobs.

In-House Development Centers

in-house development centers
A company-based method for exposing prospective managers to realistic exercises to develop improved management skills.

Some employers have **in-house development centers.** These centers usually combine classroom learning (lectures and seminars, for instance) with other techniques like assessment centers, in-basket exercises, and role playing to help develop employees and other managers.

For example, the CBS's management school is set in country club surroundings in Old Westbury, New York.[36] Its basic aim is to give young managers firsthand experience at decision making.

At programs such as the CBS School for Management, teaching methods include the use of videotape and computer simulation.

To accomplish this, both the general management program (for upper-level managers) and the professional management programs (for entry-level managers) stress solving concrete business problems. The programs use various teaching methods but stress computerized case exercises. In one exercise, for instance, each student acts as a regional sales manager and has to make decisions regarding how to deal with a star saleswoman who wants to leave. As trainees make decisions (like whether or not to boost the saleswoman's salary to entice her to stay), the computer indicates the implications of the decision; thus, if she is paid more, others may also want that increase in pay. At the end of each day students get printouts evaluating their decisions with respect to setting goals, organizing work, managing time, and supervising subordinates.

Fortune magazine calls Crotonville, General Electric's Management Development Institute, the Harvard of the corporate America. The firm's 160-page catalog offers a wide array of management development courses. These range from entry-level programs in manufacturing and sales to a course for English majors called "Everything You Always Wanted to Know About Finance," as well as advanced management training.[37]

Organizational Development

organizational development (OD)
A method aimed at changing the attitudes, values, and beliefs of employees so that employees can improve the organization.

Organizational development (OD) is a method that is aimed at changing the attitudes, values, and beliefs of employees so that the employees themselves can identify and implement the technical changes such as reorganizations, redesigned facilities, and the like that are required, usually with the aid of an outside *change agent* or consultant.

Action research is the common denominator underlying most OD interventions. It includes (1) gathering data about the organization and its operations and attitudes, with an eye toward solving a particular problem (for example, conflict

Information Technology and HR
A Computerized Managerial Assessment and Development Program

There are a number of Computerized Management Assessment and Development programs that can facilitate an employer's development process. One particularly useful example of such a management development tool is called ACUMEN.[1]

ACUMEN is a sophisticated managerial assessment and development program. The Education Version of ACUMEN consists of three elements: instructions, a self-assessment, and an assessment report. After spending approximately 20 minutes interacting with ACUMEN's IBM-compatible program, you will receive a visual display or hard-output "management profile" that focuses on 12 basic management traits:

1. *Humanistic-helpful.* Measures your inclination to see the best in others, to encourage their growth and development, to be supportive.
2. *Affiliation.* Measures the degree of friendliness, sociability, and outgoing tendencies you are likely to exhibit.
3. *Approval.* Measures your need to seek others' approval and support in order to feel secure and worthwhile as a person.
4. *Conventional.* Measures your need to conform, follow the rules, and meet the expectations of those in authority.
5. *Dependence.* Measures your tendency to be compliant, passive, and dependent on others.
6. *Apprehension.* Measures your tendency to experience anxiety and self-blame.
7. *Oppositional.* Measures your tendency to take a critical, questioning, and somewhat cynical attitude.
8. *Power.* Measures your tendency to be authoritarian and controlling.
9. *Competition.* Measures your need to be seen as the best and, to some extent, to maintain a self-centered attitude.
10. *Perfectionism.* Measures your need to seek perfection, and your tendency to base your self-worth on your own performance.
11. *Achievement.* Measures your need to achieve and have an impact on things.
12. *Self-actualization.* Measures your level of self-esteem, interest in self-development, and general drive to learn about and experience life to the fullest extent.

When you complete the self-assessment, ACUMEN analyzes your responses and generates scores on the 12 scales. Each scale represents a particular attitude or thinking style. The way you think (your thinking style) affects:

◆ What you strive to achieve *(your goals).*
◆ Your effectiveness as a *leader.*
◆ How you relate to and *communicate* with other people.
◆ Whether you view *change* as positive or negative.
◆ How you respond to crises and *stress.*

The major aim of ACUMEN is to help you develop a fuller understanding and appreciation of how your own thinking styles and personal dispositions play a role in your productivity and management effectiveness. ACUMEN's analysis of your assessment responses, presented in graphic or textual form, provides this information.

When you view the graphic profile display, you will find that each scale's extension is of varying length. On the circular graph, some scales extend a long away from the center of the circle while other segments are relatively short. Similarly, scales on the bar graph will vary in length. The longer extensions indicate styles that are more prominent in your profile. By comparing the extensions, you will be able to find the thinking styles that have the most impact on your own behavior.

The text printout on each scale provides you with detailed assessment and development information for each scale. For example, you might find you have a high score on the humanistic-helpful scale. You're told here that you are likely to enjoy developing, helping, and teaching others, like to motivate others, and attempt to see the best in others. So far so good. However, on the oppositional scale your low score indicates a fairly accepting, agreeable type of person. Up to a point, these may be laudable traits for managers. But in terms of development, you should (the printout says) "beware of being too reticent about making critical comments" (which you will have to do as a manager). In summary, a computerized management tool like ACUMEN can be very valuable, both for assessing management aptitudes (say, for future promotability) and for providing detailed development advice for the trainee.◆

[1]ACUMEN is a trademark of Human Factors Advanced Technology Group. This box is from "What ACUMEN Is and How It Works," by HFATG.

between the sales and production departments); (2) feeding back these data to the parties (employees) involved; and then (3) having these parties team-plan solutions to the problems. In OD, the participants always get involved in gathering data about themselves and their organization, analyzing these data, and planning solutions based on these analyses.[38] OD efforts include survey feedback, sensitivity training, and team building.

survey feedback
A method that involves surveying employees' attitudes and providing feedback to department managers so that problems can be solved by the managers and employees.

Survey Feedback Survey feedback is a method that surveys employees' attitudes and provides feedback to department managers so that problems can be solved by the managers and employees. Attitude surveys such as the one in Figure 8.5 can be a useful OD technique. The results can be used to compare departments and to underscore dramatically the existence of some problem like low morale, and serve as a basis for discussion among employees for developing alternative solutions. Finally, results of attitude surveys can also be used to follow up on any change to see whether it has been successful in changing the participants' attitudes.

sensitivity training
A method for increasing employees' insights into their own behavior by candid discussions in groups led by special trainers.

Sensitivity Training Sensitivity training aims to increase participants' insights into their behavior and the behavior of others *by encouraging an open expression of feelings in the trainer-guided T-Group "laboratory."*[39] (The "T" is for training.) The assumption is that newly sensitized employees will then find it easier to work together amicably as a team. Sensitivity training seeks to accomplish its aim of increasing interpersonal sensitivity by requiring frank, candid discussions in the T-Group, discussions of participants' personal feelings, attitudes, and behavior. Participants are encouraged to inform each other truthfully of how their behavior is being seen and to interpret the kind of feelings it produces.[40] As a result, it is a controversial method surrounded by heated debate and is used much less today than in the past.[41]

team building
Improving the effectiveness of teams such as corporate officers and division directors through use of consultants, interviews, and team-building meetings.

Team Building Team building refers to a group of OD techniques aimed at improving the effectiveness of teams at work. And, in fact, the characteristic OD stress on action learning—on letting the trainees solve the problem—is perhaps most evident when the OD program is aimed at improving a team's effectiveness. Data concerning the team's performance are collected and then fed back to the members of the group. The participants examine, explain, and analyze the data and develop specific action plans or solutions for solving the team's problems.

The typical team-building program begins with the consultant interviewing each of the group members and the leader prior to the group meeting—asking them what their problems are, how they think the group functions, and what obstacles are in the way of the group's performing better.[42] (Or the consultant may interview the entire group at once, using open-ended questions such as: "What things do you see getting in the way of this group's being a better one?" Sometimes, an attitude survey is used to gather the basic background data for the meet-

Figure 8.5
Attitude Questionnaire of Texas Instruments, Inc.

This questionnaire is designed to help you give us your opinions quickly and easily. There are no "right" or "wrong" answers—it is your own, honest opinion that we want. Please do not sign your name.

DIRECTIONS:
Check ( ) one box for each statement to indicate whether you agree or disagree with it. If you cannot decide, mark the middle box.

EXAMPLE:

	Agree	?	Disagree
I would rather work in a large city than in a small town	2☐	1☐	0☐

	Agree	?	Disagree
1. The hours of work here are O.K.	2☐	1☐	0☐
2. I understand how my job relates to other jobs in my group	2☐	1☐	0☐
3. Working conditions in TI are better than in other companies	2☐	1☐	0☐
4. In my opinion, the pay here is lower than in other companies	2☐	1☐	0☐
5. I think TI is spending too much money in providing recreational programs	2☐	1☐	0☐
6. I understand what benefits are provided for TIers	2☐	1☐	0☐
7. The people I work with help each other when someone falls behind, or gets in a tight spot	2☐	1☐	0☐
8. My supervisor is too interested in her/his own success to care about the needs of other TIers	2☐	1☐	0☐
9. My supervisor is always breathing down our necks; he watches us too closely	2☐	1☐	0☐
10. My supervisor gives us credit and praise for work well done	2☐	1☐	0☐
11. I think badges should reflect rank as well as length of service	2☐	1☐	0☐
12. If I have a complaint to make, I feel free to talk to someone up-the-line	2☐	1☐	0☐
13. My supervisor sees that we are properly trained for our jobs	2☐	1☐	0☐
14. My supervisor sees that we have the things we need to do our jobs	2☐	1☐	0☐
15. Management is really trying to build the organization and make it successful	2☐	1☐	0☐
16. There is cooperation between my department and other departments we work with	2☐	1☐	0☐
17. I usually read most of Texins News	2☐	1☐	0☐
18. They encourage us to make suggestions for improvements here	2☐	1☐	0☐
19. I am often bothered by sudden speed-ups or unexpected slack periods in my work	2☐	1☐	0☐
20. Qualified TIers are usually overlooked when filling job openings	2☐	1☐	0☐
21. Compared with other TIers, we get very little attention from management	2☐	1☐	0☐
22. Sometimes I feel that my job counts for very little in TI	2☐	1☐	0☐
23. The longer you work for TI the more you feel you belong	2☐	1☐	0☐
24. I have a great deal of interest in TI and its future	2☐	1☐	0☐
25. I have little opportunity to use my abilities in TI	2☐	1☐	0☐

	Agree	?	Disagree
26. There are plenty of good jobs in TI for those who want to get ahead	2☐	1☐	0☐
27. I often feel worn out and tired on my job	2☐	1☐	0☐
28. They expect too much work from us around here	2☐	1☐	0☐
29. The company should provide more opportunities for employees to know each other	2☐	1☐	0☐
30. For my kind of job, working conditions are O.K.	2☐	1☐	0☐
31. I'm paid fairly compared with other TIers	2☐	1☐	0☐
32. Compared with other companies, TI benefits are good	2☐	1☐	0☐
33. A few people I work with think they run the place	2☐	1☐	0☐
34. The people I work with get along well together	2☐	1☐	0☐
35. My supervisor has always been fair in his/her dealings with me	2☐	1☐	0☐
36. My supervisor gets employees to work together as a team	2☐	1☐	0☐
37. I have confidence in the fairness and honesty of management	2☐	1☐	0☐
38. Management here is really interested in the welfare of TIers	2☐	1☐	0☐
39. Most of the higher-ups are friendly toward us	2☐	1☐	0☐
40. I work in a friendly environment	2☐	1☐	0☐
41. My supervisor lets us know what is expected of us	2☐	1☐	0☐
42. We don't receive enough information from top management	2☐	1☐	0☐
43. I know how my job fits in with other work in this organization	2☐	1☐	0☐
44. TI does a poor job of keeping us posted on the things we want to know about TI	2☐	1☐	0☐
45. I think TI informality is carried too far	2☐	1☐	0☐
46. You can get fired around here without much cause	2☐	1☐	0☐
47. I can be sure of my job as long as I do good work	2☐	1☐	0☐
48. I have plenty of freedom on the job to use my own judgment	2☐	1☐	0☐
49. My supervisor allows me reasonable leeway in making mistakes	2☐	1☐	0☐
50. I really feel part of this organization	2☐	1☐	0☐
51. The people who get promotions in TI usually deserve them	2☐	1☐	0☐
52. I can learn a great deal on my present job	2☐	1☐	0☐

(PLEASE CONTINUE ON REVERSE SIDE)

(continued)

Figure 8.5
(continued)

#	Statement	Agree	?	Disagree
53.	My job is often dull and monotonous	2☐	1☐	0☐
54.	There is too much pressure on my job	2☐	1☐	0☐
55.	I am required to spend too much time on the job	2☐	1☐	0☐
56.	I have the right equipment to do my work	2☐	1☐	0☐
57.	My pay is enough to live on comfortably	2☐	1☐	0☐
58.	I'm satisfied with the way employee benefits are handled here	2☐	1☐	0☐
59.	I wish I had more opportunity to socialize with my associates	2☐	1☐	0☐
60.	The people I work with are very friendly	2☐	1☐	0☐
61.	My supervisor welcomes our ideas even when they differ from her/his own	2☐	1☐	0☐
62.	My supervisor ought to be friendlier toward us	2☐	1☐	0☐
63.	My supervisor lives up to his promises	2☐	1☐	0☐
64.	We are kept well informed about TI's business prospects and standing with competitors	2☐	1☐	0☐
65.	Management ignores our suggestions and complaints	2☐	1☐	0☐
66.	My supervisor is not qualified for his/her job well	2☐	1☐	0☐
67.	My supervisor has the work well organized	2☐	1☐	0☐
68.	I have ample opportunity to see the end results of my work	2☐	1☐	0☐
69.	My supervisor has enough authority and backing to perform his job well	2☐	1☐	0☐
70.	I do not get enough instruction about how to do a job	2☐	1☐	0☐
71.	You can say what you think around here	2☐	1☐	0☐
72.	I know where I stand with my supervisor	2☐	1☐	0☐
73.	When terminations are necessary, they are handled fairly	2☐	1☐	0☐
74.	I am very much underpaid for the work I do	2☐	1☐	0☐

#	Statement	Agree	?	Disagree
75.	I'm really doing something worthwhile in my job	2☐	1☐	0☐
76.	I'm proud to work for TI	2☐	1☐	0☐
77.	Many TIers I know would like to see the union get in	2☐	1☐	0☐
78.	I received fair treatment in my last performance review	2☐	1☐	0☐
79.	During the past six months I have seriously considered getting a job elsewhere	2☐	1☐	0☐
80.	TI's problem-solving procedure is adequate for handling our problems and complaints	2☐	1☐	0☐
81.	I would recommend employment at TI to my friends	2☐	1☐	0☐
82.	My supervisor did a good job in discussing my last performance review with me	2☐	1☐	0☐
83.	My pay is the most important source of satisfaction from my job	2☐	1☐	0☐
84.	Favoritism is a problem in my area	2☐	1☐	0☐
85.	I have very few complaints about our lunch facilities	2☐	1☐	0☐
86.	Most people I know in this community have a good opinion of TI	2☐	1☐	0☐
87.	I usually read most of my division newspaper	2☐	1☐	0☐
88.	I can usually get hold of my supervisor when I need her/him	2☐	1☐	0☐
89.	Most TIers are placed in jobs that make good use of their abilities	2☐	1☐	0☐
90.	I receive adequate training for my needs	2☐	1☐	0☐
91.	I've gone as far as I can in TI			
92.	My job seems to be leading to the kind of future I want	2☐	1☐	0☐
93.	There is too much personal friction among people at my level in the company	2☐	1☐	0☐
94.	The amount of effort a person puts into his/her job is appreciated at TI	2☐	1☐	0☐
95.	Filling in this questionnaire is a good way to let management know what employees think	2☐	1☐	0☐
96.	I think some good will come out of filling in a questionnaire like this one	2☐	1☐	0☐

97. Please check on term which most nearly describes the kind of work you do: 1 ☐ Clerical or office 2 ☐ Production 3 ☐ Technical 4 ☐ Maintenance 5 ☐ Manufacturing 6 ☐ R & D 7 ☐ Engineering 8 ☐ Other

98. 1 ☐ Hourly 2 ☐ Salaried **99.** 1 ☐ Male 2 ☐ Female **100.** Do you supervise 3 or more TIers? 1 ☐ Yes 2 ☐ No

Name of your department:

Please write any comments or suggestions you care to make in the space below.

ings.) The consultant usually categorizes the interview data into themes and presents the themes to the group at the beginning of the meeting. They might include, for example, "Not enough time to get my job done," or "I can't get any cooperation around here." The themes are then ranked by the group in terms of their importance. The most important ones form the agenda for the meeting. The group examines and discusses the issues, examines the underlying causes of the problem, and begins work on a solution to the problems.

During one of these sessions it is likely that certain nonagenda items will emerge as a result of the participants' interaction. In discussing the theme "I can't get any cooperation around here," for instance, the group might uncover the fact that the manager is not providing enough direction. The manager might be allowing vacuums to develop that are leading to conflict and a breakdown of cooperation. These new items or problems, as well as the agenda items or themes, are generally pursued under the guidance of the consultant. Then steps are formulated to bring about the changes deemed desirable and a follow-up meeting is often scheduled. Here it is determined whether the steps have been implemented successfully.

Notice how the typical team-building intervention relies on the participants themselves doing the research: Information about the group's problems is obtained from the group; members of the group analyze and discuss the data in an atmosphere of cooperation; and, finally, the participants develop solutions or action steps for solving the problems that they themselves have identified.

Grid training is a formal approach to team building designed by Blake and Mouton.[43] As summarized in Table 8.1, Grid training is based on a device called the **managerial grid.** This represents different leadership styles, identifying specifically whether the leader is more concerned with people or with production.

The Grid program is aimed first at developing **"9,9" managers**—managers who are interested in getting results by being high on their concern both for production and for people; they want to get results through committed, cooperative subordinates, say Blake and Mouton. The Grid program assumes that possessing such a style makes it easier for you to work with your subordinates, superiors, and peers in analyzing group, intergroup, and organizational problems and developing action steps to solve these problems.

managerial grid
A matrix that represents different possible leadership styles.
"9,9" managers
A manager with this rating is highly concerned with people and with production.

Using HR to Build a Responsive Learning Organization

The former head of strategic planning at Royal Dutch Shell has said, "In the future, the only sustainable competitive advantage may be an organization's ability to learn faster than its competitors."[44] His statement underscores the fact that in a fast-changing world, the last thing a company needs is for new information—about competitors' actions, customers' preferences, or technological improve-

TABLE 8.1 Summary of Managerial Grid Leadership Styles		
TYPE OF LEADER AS RANKED ON GRID	CONCERN FOR PEOPLE	CONCERN FOR PRODUCTION
(1-1)	Low	Low
(1-9)	High	Low
(9-1)	Low	High
(9-9)	High	High

Anyone interested in seeing how companies use PC-based CD-ROM programs for developing managers need only stop by the lunch room at the Fred Meyer Discount Superstore in Tualatin, Oregon any lunch hour. It's likely they'd find one or more assistant managers tapping away at their PC touch-screens in the process of completing one of more than 200 CD-ROM interactive mini courses the firm provides on topics ranging from store policy and customer service procedures to specific features of the thousands of products on the superstore's shelves.[1] For example, assistant manager Holly Grady hopes that completing each course (which lasts 20 to 40 minutes each) will help her achieve promotions to and beyond store manager in the Fred Meyer organization, a firm with annual sales of over $3 billion.

The CD-ROM based training and development program has been in existence for about four years at the Fred Meyer company. At that time the firm decided to place PCs in each lunch room of its 133 stores in six northwestern states. Some of the CD-ROM training is simply mandatory for all employees to get updated on the specifics of their own jobs and of new products. Others like Ms. Grady use the development program to enhance their management skills as well as their opportunities for promotional advancement.

Training and development programs like the one in use at Fred Meyer are usually produced by specialist multimedia software houses like Graphic Media of Portland, Oregon. They produce not only custom-produced titles but also generic programs like a $999 package for teaching safety in the white collar workplace. Custom training and development programs like this can cost $60,000 to $100,000 per hour of production to produce. While that may be a big expense for a smaller firm, for larger organizations it might be minimal compared with the usual development program costs such as hiring professional trainers, and spending money on travel, food and lodging to bring employees together for training sessions. As Brandon Hall, editor and publisher of the Multimedia Training Newsletter in Sunnyville, California puts it, "Anyone who is involved in training more than 200 people needs to investigate or implement this technology."[2]◆

1. Charles Bermant, "For the Latest in Corporate Training, Try a CD-Rom," *The New York Times*, October 16, 1995, p. C5.
2. Ibid., p. 50.

ments—to be ignored by the company's managers, or lost in a bureaucratic sinkhole of nonactivity. For years, for instance, General Motors seemed oblivious to the competitive and technological advances of its foreign competitors; it finally awoke only when its board decided that too much market share had been lost. On the other hand, firms like Microsoft and General Electric are traditionally quick on their feet, "adept at translating new knowledge into new ways of behaving."[45]

HR's Role in Building Learning Organizations

Firms like GE have successfully made the leap into rebuilding themselves as learning organizations. A learning organization ". . . is an organization skilled at creating, acquiring, and transferring knowledge, and at modifying its behavior to reflect new knowledge and insights."[46] Learning organizations engage in five activities, which we'll discuss next: systematic problem solving; experimentation; learning from experience; learning from others; and transferring knowledge. HR can play a crucial role in each activity of building learning organizations.

HR and Systematic Problem Solving The learning organization depends on the scientific method rather than on guesswork for diagnosing problems. Employees and managers here don't make decisions based on assumptions; instead they insist on having data and using simple statistical tools to organize data and draw inferences.[47]

Training and development is crucial for fostering such systematic problem-solving skills. At Xerox, for instance, employees receive skill training in four areas. They are trained in using techniques like interviewing and surveying to generate ideas and collect information; to reach consensus by using special consensus-building techniques; to analyze and display data on special simple statistical charts; and to plan the actions they will take to solve the problem using special planning charts.

HR and Experimentation The learning organization also depends on *experimentation,* which means the systematic searching for and testing of new knowledge.[48] For example, Corning Glass continuously experiments with new formulations to increase yields and provide better grades of glass.[49] Steelmaker Allegheny Ludlam continually experiments with new rolling methods and improved technologies to raise productivity and reduce costs.[50]

HR is crucial for developing such an experimentation orientation on the part of employees and managers. For example, Chaparral Steel regularly sends its first-line supervisors on development trips around the globe to visit industry leaders and foster a better understanding of new work practices and technologies. GE sends manufacturing managers to Japan to study factory innovations. Both firms have training programs for building the skills required to perform and evaluate experiments, such as how to use statistical methods and design experiments. It's also HR's role to formulate incentive plans that ensure that employees who experiment with new processes or products aren't inadvertently punished for trying a new approach.

HR and Learning from Experience Learning organizations also have to "review their successes and failures, assess them systematically, and record the lessons in a form that employees find open and accessible."[51] (For example, several years ago Xerox studied its product development process to determine why the firm's new business initiatives often failed.[52])

Training and development plays an important role in facilitating such learning from past experience. For example, case studies and action learning can be used to study and illustrate what has previously been done correctly or incorrectly. Furthermore, companies can also enlist the help of faculty and students at local colleges or universities; they bring fresh perspectives and can view such case studies as opportunities to gain experience and increase their own learning.[53]

HR and Learning from Others A learning organization is also one that effectively learns from others. Sometimes, in other words, ". . . the most powerful insights come from looking outside one's immediate environment to gain a new perspective."[54]

Training and development plays a role in obtaining such expertise. For example, employees have to be trained to "cultivate the art of open, attentive listening"[55] in order to gain the fullest understanding of the other company's operations. Employees and managers also must be trained to *benchmark,* the process through which the best industry practices are uncovered, analyzed, adopted, and implemented.[56]

HR and Transferring Knowledge   Finally, learning organizations are adept at transferring knowledge, in other words, spreading knowledge quickly and efficiently throughout the organization.[57]

Training and development plays an important role in cultivating such expertise. For example, rotating assignments can be useful for transferring knowledge. The CEO of Time Life shifted the president of the company's music division (who had produced several years of rapid growth through innovative marketing) to the presidency of the book division where profits were flat.[58] As another example, in the late 1980s workers in one PPG glass plant were organized by the plant manager into small, self-managing teams with responsibility for work assignments. Several years later in an attempt to transfer the knowledge gained from this experience, the plant manager was promoted to director of human resources for the entire glass group. He then developed a training program for teaching first-level supervisors the behaviors they needed to manage employees in a participative, self-managing environment.[59]

In summary, learning organizations are skilled at creating, acquiring, and transferring knowledge, and at modifying their behavior to reflect new knowledge and insights. Learning organizations are built on a foundation of systematic problem solving, experimentation, learning from past experience, learning from others, and transferring knowledge. HR and particularly training and development play central roles in developing employees' and managers' skills and expertise in each of these areas.[60]

Providing Employees with Lifelong Learning

Employers can't build learning organizations just around managers. In today's downsized, flattened, high-tech, and empowered organizations, employers must also depend on their first-line employees—the team members building the Saturn cars, or the Microsoft programmers—to recognize new opportunities, identify problems, and react quickly with analyses and recommendations. As a result, the need has arisen for encouraging *lifelong learning,* in other words, for providing extensive continuing training from basic remedial skills to advanced decision-making techniques throughout employees' careers.

The experiences at one Canadian Honeywell manufacturing plant provide an example.[61] This plant called its lifelong learning program the Honeywell-Scarborough Learning for Life Initiative. It was ". . . a concerted effort to upgrade skill and education levels so that employees can meet workplace challenges with confidence."[62]

Honeywell's Lifelong Learning Initiative had several components. It began with adult basic education. Here the company, in partnership with the employees' union, offered courses in English as a second language, basic literacy, numeracy, and computer literacy.

Next the factory formed a partnership with a local community college. Through that partnership Honeywell provides college-level courses to all factory employees—hourly, professional, and managerial—giving them the opportunity to earn college diplomas and certificates.[63] This includes a 15-hour "skills for success" program designed to refresh adults in the study habits required to succeed academically. All courses take place at the factory immediately after work.

In addition, job-related training is provided for two hours every other week. These sessions focus on skills specifically important to the job, ". . . such as the principles of just-in-time inventory systems, team effectiveness, interpersonal communication skills, conflict resolution, problem solving and dealing with a diverse work force."[64]

Executive Development: Key Factors for Success

The idea that there are several key factors for an executive development program's success is illustrated by the results of a survey of executive development practices in 12 leading corporations.[65] This study found a surprisingly high degree of consensus among the 12 firms regarding the characteristics of effective and ineffective executive development processes. In particular, five major success criteria were listed by over 75% of the survey participants.

Five Key Factors for Success

These five key factors were as follows:

1. Extensive and visible involvement by the chief executive (CEO) is critical.

In all but one of the companies, extensive and visible involvement by the CEO was described as "essential" and the "single most important determinant" of success for the executive development program. This extensive involvement helped guarantee that the company's executive development process was consistent with the direction the CEO wanted the company to follow. It also lent the process a credibility unachievable in any other way.

2. Corporations with a successful executive development process have a clearly articulated and understood executive development policy and philosophy.

For example, 10 of the 12 companies surveyed listed four common objectives of their executive development processes: ensuring that qualified executives would be available to fill current and future assignments; serving as a major vehicle to perpetuate the organization's heritage and shape its culture by communicating its mission, beliefs, values, and management practices; preparing executives to respond to the complex business issues of the changing environment by providing managers with the experience, knowledge, and skills they need in future assignments; and developing a cadre of individuals prepared to assume senior-level general management responsibilities.

3. Successful executive development policies and strategies are directly linked to the corporation's business strategies, objectives, and challenges.

Nine of the 12 companies emphasized that their executive development policies and strategies were consciously linked to the company's business plans and objectives. For example, plans to expand overseas, diversify into new product lines, or consolidate manufacturing operations have implications for management/executive development activities. In the successful programs the development process was molded around the company's plans.

4. Successful executive development processes include three main elements: an annual succession planning process; planned on-the-job developmental assignments; and customized, internal, executive education programs supplemented by the selected use of university programs.

First, in all 12 companies succession plans were in place and were actively managed for key positions and individuals. Second, development needs were continually identified (based on these plans), and plans were developed and implemented to address these development needs. Third, a formal annual planning and review phase was in place to assess each candidate's progress and to review the company's replacement plans.

With respect to on-the-job development, "all the study participants agreed that it was the single most effective developmental tool available to organizations." The four types of on-the-job experience used most often were: assignment of people to membership on task forces assembled to address specific issues; job rotation experiences lasting from one to two years; overseas assignments; and temporary assignments of relatively short duration.

With respect to executive education, all the companies offered a mix of external university-type programs and customized internal programs. Some of the companies expressed concern about the prohibitive costs of the external programs, although virtually all sent selected employees to them.

5. Executive development is the responsibility of line management rather than of the HR function.

In all but one of the companies in this survey, the role of the HR department was seen as crucial but advisory. HR serves as a resource for line management regarding the development programs and activities to use and how to use them. However, the actual responsibility for achieving the goals of the executive development program—deciding who will fill future positions, or how to eliminate current managers' shortcomings, for instance—is line management's responsibility.

Executive Development in Global Companies

Selecting and developing executives to run the employer's overseas operations present management with a dilemma. One expert cites "an alarmingly high failure rate when executives are relocated overseas." This failure rate is usually caused by inappropriate selection and poor preplacement development.[66] Yet in an increasingly globalized economy, employers must develop managers for overseas assignments despite these difficulties.

A number of companies, including Dow, Colgate-Palmolive, and Ciba-Geigy, have developed and implemented international executive relocation programs that are successful. In addition to the general requirements for successful executive development programs previously listed, preparing and training executives for overseas assignments should also include the following considerations:

1. Choose international-assignment candidates whose educational backgrounds and experiences are appropriate for overseas assignments. As in most other endeavors, the best predictor of future performance is often a person's past performance. In this case the person who has already accumulated a track record of successfully adapting to foreign cultures (perhaps through overseas college studies and summer internships) will more likely succeed as an international transferee.

2. Choose those whose personalities and family situations can withstand the cultural changes they will encounter in their new environments. When many of these executives fail, it is not because these individuals couldn't adapt but because their spouses or children were unhappy in their new foreign setting. Thus, the person's family situation probably should have more influence on the assignment than it would in a domestic assignment.

3. Brief candidates fully and clearly on all relocation policies. Transferees should be given a realistic preview of what the assignment will entail, including the company's policies regarding matters such as moving expenses, salary differentials, and benefits such as paid schooling for the employees' children.

4. Give executives and their families comprehensive training in their new company's culture and language. At Dow Chemical, for instance, orientation begins with a briefing session, during which the transfer policy is explained in detail to the relocating executive. He or she is also given a briefing package compiled by the receiving area containing important information about local

matters, such as shopping and housing. In addition, an advisor, who is often the spouse of a recently returned expatriate, will visit the transferee and his or her spouse to explain what sort of emotional issues they are likely to face in the early stages of the move—such as feeling remote from relatives, for instance. The option of attending a two-week language and cultural orientation program offered by a school like Berlitz is also extended.

5. Provide all relocating executives with a mentor to monitor their overseas careers and help them secure appropriate jobs with the company when they repatriate. At Dow, for instance, this person is usually a high-level supervisor in the expatriate's functional area. The overseas assignee keeps his or her mentor up to date on his or her activities. Similarly, the mentor monitors the expatriate's career while he or she is overseas. Specifically, all job changes and compensation actions involving the expatriate must be reviewed with and supported by the mentor. This helps to avoid the problem of having expatriates feel "lost" overseas, particularly in terms of career progress.

6. Establish a repatriation program that helps returning executives and their families readjust to their professional and personal lives in their home country. At Dow, for instance, the head of the overseas assignee's department or division gives the transferee a letter stating that the foreign subsidiary guarantees that he or she will be able to return to a job at least at the same level as the one he or she is leaving. As much as a year in advance of the expatriate's scheduled return to headquarters, his or her new job is arranged by the person's mentor.[67]

Small Business Applications

The president of a smaller enterprise faces both unique advantages and disadvantages when it comes to developing employees for higher-level executive roles. On the negative side, this president has neither resources nor time to develop full-blown executive succession programs or to fund many outside programs like sending potential executives to the Harvard Business School. Yet at the same time the president of a smaller firm has the advantage of working more closely with and knowing more about each of his or her employees than does the CEO of a bigger, less personal firm.

A relative lack of resources notwithstanding, the smaller firm's president has few needs more important than that of developing senior managers. For most small firms with successful products, it is not a lack of financing that holds them back but a lack of management talent. This is so because all growing firms inevitably reach the point where the entrepreneur/owner can no longer solely make all the decisions. For the Dows and Mercks of the world, the question of succession planning and executive development is mostly a question of selecting the best of the lot and then developing them: There is usually an adequate supply of talent given these companies' enormous influx of new recruits. For the smaller company, the problem usually is not one of selecting the best of the lot. Instead it's making sure that key positions are filled and that the president will have the foresight to know when to surrender one set of reins over a part of the company's operations.

There are thus four main steps in the smaller company's executive development process:

Step 1. Problem Assessment
Particularly here the executive development process must begin with an assessment of the company's current problems and the owner's plans for the company's future. Obviously, if the owner/entrepreneur is satisfied with the current size of the firm and has no plans to retire in the near future, no additional management talent may be required.

On the other hand, if plans call for expansion, or current problems seem to be growing out of control, management development/succession planning might be the key. It often happens, for instance, that as a small company evolves from a mom-and-pop operation to a larger firm, the management system that adequately served the owner in the past is no longer effective. Problems arise as manufacturing orders that were previously profitable now incur overtime costs and excessive waste, and the informal order-writing process can no longer keep up with the volume of orders.

At this point the president must assess the problems in his or her firm. Begin with an analysis of the company's financial statements. For example, what is the trend of key financial ratios, such as the ratio of manufacturing costs to sales, or of sales overhead to sales? Are your profit margins level, or heading up or down? Are fixed costs remaining about the same, or heading up as a percentage of sales? Next analyze the organization function by function. In sales, is the backlog of orders growing? In manufacturing, are there inventory problems that require attention? In accounting, are you getting the accounting reports that you need and are the monthly and end-of-year reports produced in a timely fashion? Does the company have a personnel system in place such that as many personnel matters as possible—recruitment, testing, selection, training, and so forth—are routinized and carried out in an effective manner? The point is that the owner must assess the problems in his or her firm with an eye toward determining whether and when new management talent is required.

Step 2. Management Audit and Appraisal

One reason management selection and development are so important in small firms is that the "problems" assessed in step 1 are often just symptoms of inadequate management talent in smaller firms. It's simply not possible for the owner/entrepreneur to run a $5 million company the way he or she did when the company was one-tenth the size. Therefore, the lack of adequate management is a depressingly familiar cause for many of the problems in the small growing firm.

Use the problems found in step 1 as a starting point in conducting a management audit and appraisal of the people now helping you manage your firm. One simple and effective way to do this is by evaluating them on the traditional management functions of planning, organizing, staffing, leading, and controlling. For example, within their own areas of responsibility have they instituted plans, policies, and procedures that enable their activities to be carried out efficiently? Have they organized their activities in such a way that their subordinates have job descriptions and understand what their responsibilities are? In terms of staffing, have they selected competent employees; are their people adequately oriented and trained; and are the pay rates within their group viewed as fair and equitable? In terms of leadership, is the morale in their department satisfactory, and do their people seem to enjoy what they are doing? Are each person's interpersonal relations with other members of your team satisfactory? And in terms of control, has each person recommended and/or instituted a set of reports that provides both of you with the information you need to assess adequately how that department is doing?

Step 3. Analysis of Development Needs

Your next step is to determine whether any inadequacies uncovered in step 2 can be remedied via some type of development program. At one extreme, the person may not have the potential to grow beyond what he or she is now, and here development may serve no purpose. At the other extreme, the problems uncovered may just reflect a lack of knowledge. For example, sending your bookkeeper/accountant back to school for a course or two in management accounting could alleviate the problem. Another question to answer here is whether you (as the owner/entrepreneur) may be responsible for some of the problems yourself, and whether you should direct yourself to a management development program (or out of the firm altogether).

Step 4. Identify Replacement Needs
Your assessment may uncover a need to recruit and select new management talent. Here, as explained in Chapter 3, you should determine ahead of time the intellectual, personality, interpersonal, and experience criteria to be used. You should also map out an on-the-job development program that gives the person the breadth of experience he or she needs to perform the job.◆

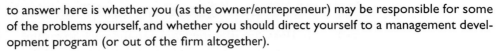

Chapter Review

Summary

1. Management development is aimed at preparing employees for future jobs with the organization, or at solving organizationwide problems concerning, for instance, inadequate interdepartmental communication.

2. On-the-job experience is by far the most popular form of management development. However, the preferred techniques differ by organizational level, with in-house programs being preferred for first-line supervisors and external conferences and seminars more widely used for top executives.

3. Managerial on-the-job training methods include job rotation, coaching, junior boards, and action learning. Basic off-the-job techniques include case studies, management games, outside seminars, university-related programs, role playing, behavior modeling, and in-house development centers.

4. HR can contribute to building the learning organization through its impact on: systematic problem solving, experimentation, learning from experience and from others, transferring knowledge, and providing employees with lifelong learning.

5. Organizational development (OD) is an approach to instituting change in which employees themselves play a major role in the change process by providing data, by obtaining feedback on problems, and by team-planning solutions. We described several OD methods including sensitivity training, Grid development, and survey feedback.

6. Grid programs and other intergroup team-building efforts aim at developing better problem solving and more cooperation at work through the *action research* process. Each work group analyzes work team problems and generates action plans for solving them. Then this same approach is used by special intergroup teams so that companywide problems are solved.

7. Successful development programs require CEO involvement, a clear development policy, linkage to plans, succession planning and development, and line responsibility.

Key Terms

management development
succession planning
job rotation
junior board
action learning
case study method
management game

role playing
behavior modeling
in-house development
  centers
organizational
  development (OD)

survey feedback
sensitivity training
team building
managerial grid
"9,9" managers

Discussion Questions and Exercises

1. How does the involvement approach to attitude surveys differ from simply administering surveys and returning the results to top management?
2. Compare and contrast three organizational development techniques.
3. Describe the pros and cons of five management development methods.
4. Discuss the key considerations in a typical small business management development program.
5. Do you think job rotation is a good method to use for developing management trainees? Why or why not?
6. Working individually or in groups, contact a provider of management development seminars such as the American Management Association. Obtain copies of their recent listings of seminar offerings. At what levels of managers do they aim their seminar offerings? What seems to be the most popular types of development programs? Why do you think that's the case?
7. Working individually or in groups, use the definition of a learning organization found in this chapter to discuss whether or not you think the college you are currently attending is (or is not) a learning organization? On what do you base your conclusion?
8. Working individually or in groups, develop a series of concrete examples to illustrate how a professor teaching human resource management could use at least eight of the management development techniques described in this chapter in teaching his or her HR course.

Application Exercises

RUNNING CASE: Carter Cleaning Company
Developing Managers

"Management development? Did you say management development? Jennifer, you're my daughter and I love you but I can't believe that with all the problems we're facing here—strong competition, softening economy, 400% turnover, employee theft, and supply and waste management cartage costs that are going through the roof—you actually want me to consider setting up some kind of a program that will turn that bunch of deadbeats that we have as managers into nice guys. I love you, Jenny, but please let's focus on the problems that we have to get solved today."

Actually, Jennifer was not altogether surprised with her father's reaction, but she did believe that her dad was being more than a little short-sighted. For example, she knew that some successful organizations, like Club Med, had a policy of rotating managers annually to help avoid their getting "stale," and she wondered whether such a program would make sense at Carter. She also felt that some type of simulations might help managers do a better job of dealing with their customers and subordinates, and she

further believed that periodic off-site meetings between her, her father, and the store managers might help to identify and solve problems with the stores. Outside seminars in areas like modern cleaning techniques might also help to boost the current store managers' interest and performance and, of course, there is also the possibility of scheduling potential managers (like a few of the current cleaner-spotters) for management development as well. The company really didn't have much money to spend on matters like this though, and Jennifer knew that to sell the idea to her father she would need a very concrete, tight set of recommendations.

Questions

1. Given a budget of $750, what type of management development program can Jennifer formulate for her current store managers? The proposal must include the specific activities (like job rotation) in which her managers should engage over the next four months.

2. Would it be worthwhile for the company to administer an attitude survey of all their employees? Jennifer knows she doesn't have a big company, but she is curious as to whether employees would anonymously express their concerns, their likes and dislikes, and perhaps even help identify problems like employee theft that they are encountering on their job. If the company does go ahead with the survey, what questions should they ask?

CASE INCIDENT: What We Need Around Here Is Better Human Relations

Hank called his three highest-ranking managers together for a surprise luncheon meeting. "Have lunch on United Mutual," said Hank, "I have an important topic I want to bring to your attention."

After Madeline, Raymond, and Allen ordered lunch, Hank launched into the agenda: "As office manager, I think we have to move into a rigorous human relations training and development program for our front-line supervisors. It's no longer a question of whether we should have a program, it's now a question of what kind and when."

Allen spoke out, "Okay, Hank, don't keep us in suspense any longer. What makes you think we need a human relations program?"

"Look at the problems we are facing: 25% turnover among the clerical and secretarial staffs; and productivity lower than the casualty insurance industry national standards. What better reasons could anybody have for properly training our supervisory staff?"

Madeline commented, "Hold on, Hank. Training may not be the answer. I think our high turnover and low productivity are caused by reasons beyond the control of supervision. Our wages are low and we expect our people to work in cramped, rather dismal office space."

Hank retorted, "Nonsense. A good supervisor can get workers to accept almost any working conditions. Training will fix that."

"Hank, I see another problem," said Allen. "Our supervisors are so overworked already that they will balk at training. If you hold the training on company time, they will say that they are falling behind in their work. If the training takes place after hours or on weekends, our supervisors will say that they are being taken advantage of."

"Nonsense," replied Hank. "Every supervisor realizes the importance of good human relations. Besides that, they will see it as a form of job enrichment."

"So long as we're having an open meeting, I'll give you my input," volunteered Raymond. "We are starting from the wrong end by having our first-line supervisors go through human relations training. It's our top management who needs the training the most. Unless they practice better human relations, you can't expect such behavior from our supervisors. How can you have a top management that is insensitive to people and a lower-level management that is sensitive? The system just won't work."

"What you say makes some sense," said Hank, "but I wouldn't go so far as to say top management is insensitive to people. Maybe we can talk some more about the human relations program after lunch."

Questions

1. What do you think Hank means by *human relations training?*

2. Should Hank go ahead with his plans for the human relations training and development program? Why or why not?

3. What do you think of Raymond's comment that top management should participate in human relations training first?

4. What is your opinion of Hank's statement that good leadership can compensate for poor working conditions?

5. If you were in Hank's situation, would you try to get top management to participate in a human relations training program?

6. What type of training and development activities would you recommend for first-line supervisors at United Mutual? How would you analyze the need for such a program?

7. What other factors could be causing the problems referred to by Hank?

Source: Andrew J. Dubrin, *Human Relations: A Job Oriented Approach,* pp. 343–44. © 1988. Reprinted by permission of Prentice Hall, Englewood Cliffs, NJ.

Human Resource Management Simulation

The training budget in the simulation includes training for promotions from within, as well as other types of managerial and supervisory training. In the simulation, sufficient training will reduce costs, increase productivity, lower turnover, decrease accidents, and increase moral. Clearly, training is important!

Video Case

Survival Training

While sending a group of employees into a redwood forest to climb trees may seem irrelevant to boosting productivity, this videocase shows that some field trips can in fact be very effective. The videocase emphasizes that far from being a frivolous game the survival training helps employees to overcome fear and to build self-esteem. For example, employees don't just get over their fear of heights. They also get over their fear of taking risks or even of losing their jobs. The survival training shown in the video also helps teach team members to support each other and to communicate.

Questions

1. Do you think it's realistic to believe that lessons learned in survival training can actually influence behavior back at the workplace? Why or why not?

2. How do you think survival training as a development technique compares with other development tools such as Harvard Executive courses? Under what conditions would you recommend a survival training program such as the one shown in the videocase?

3. Why did several of the companies emphasize that it's important to develop in employees the ability to overcome fear, build trust, and teach team members to support each other and to communicate, given the nature of jobs today?

Source: ABC News, *Survival Training for Employees,* "World News Tonight/American Agenda," July 22, 1993.

 # Take It to the Net

We invite you to visit the Dessler page on the Prentice Hall Web site at: http://www.prenhall.com/~dessler

for the monthly Dessler update and for this chapter's World Wide Web exercise.

Notes

1. Lester A. Digman, "Management Development: Needs and Practices," *Personnel,* Vol. 57 (July–August 1980), pp. 45–57. See also James Cureton, Alfred Newton, and Dennis Tesolowski, "Finding Out What Managers Need," *Training and Development Journal,* Vol. 40, no. 5 (May 1986), pp. 106–107, and results of a ten year survey show an increasingly important role for executive development in building and revitalizing corporate competitiveness. See Albert Vicere, Maria Taylor, and Virginia Freeman, "Executive Development in Major Corporations: A Ten-Year Study," *Journal of Management Development,* Vol. 13, No. 1 (1994), pp. 4–22.

2. William Kearney, "Management Development Programs Can Pay Off," *Business Horizons,* Vol. 18 (April 1975), pp. 81–88. See also Michael Hitt et al., "Human Capital and Strategic Competitiveness in the 1990s," *Journal of Management Development,* Vol. 13, no. 1 (1994), pp. 35–46.

3. According to a survey by Digman, the median percentage of executives receiving training during a typical year was 23%; middle managers, 38%; and first-line supervisors, 20%. See also Albert Vicere, Maria Taylor, and Virginia Freeman, "Executive Development in Major Corporations: A Ten-Year Study," *Journal of Management Development,* Vol. 13, no. 1 (1994), pp. 4–22.

4. "Trends in Corporate Education and Training," Report no. 870 (1986), The Conference Board, 845 Third Avenue, New York, NY 10022.

5. For discussions of the steps in succession planning see, for example, Kenneth Nowack, "The Secrets of Succession," *Training and Development* (November 1994), pp. 49–55, and Donald Brookes, "In Management Succession, Who Moves Up?" *Human Resources* (January/February 1995), pp. 11–13.

6. Robert Fulmer and Kenneth Graham, "A New Era of Management Education," *Journal of Management Development,* Vol. 12, no. 3 (1993), pp. 30–38.

7. Ibid., p. 33.

8. J. Conger, "The Brave New World of Leadership Training," *Organizational Dynamics,* Vol. 21, no. 3 (1993), p. 49.

9. Ibid., p. 51.

10. Ibid., p. 52.

11. Lise Saari et al., "A Survey of Management Training and Education Practices in U.S. Companies," *Personnel Psychology* (Winter 1988), pp. 731–743.

12. Fulmer and Graham, "A New Era of Management Education," p. 32.

13. Albert Vicere, et al., "Executive Development in Major Corporations," p. 18.

14. Dale Yoder et al., *Handbook of Personnel Management and Labor Relations* (New York: McGraw-Hill, 1958), pp. 10–27; for a recent review, see William Rothwell, H. C. Kazanas, and Darla Haines, "Issues and Practices in Management Job Rotation Programs as Perceived by HRD Professionals," *Performance Improvement Quarterly,* Vol. 5, no. 1 (1992), pp. 49–69.

15. Ibid. See also Jack Phillips, "Training Supervisors Outside the Classroom," *Training and Development Journal,* Vol. 40, no. 2 (February 1986), pp. 46–49.

16. Kenneth Wexley and Gary Latham, *Developing and Training Resources in Organizations* (Glenview, IL: Scott, Foresman, 1981), p. 118.

17. Ibid, pp. 118–119.

18. Quoted in Paul Evans, Yves Doz, and Andre Laurent, *Human Resource Management in International Firms* (New York: St. Martin's Press, 1990), p. 123.

19. Ibid.

20. Wexley and Latham, *Developing and Training Resources in Organizations,* p. 207.

21. This is based on Nancy Fox, "Action Learning Comes to Industry," *Harvard Business Review,* Vol. 56 (September–October, 1977), pp. 158–168.

22. This is based on Paul Froiland, "Action Learning: Taming Real Problems in Real Time," *Training* (January 1994), pp. 27–34.

23. For several other examples of action learning, see Barry Smith, "Building Managers from the Inside Out—Developing Managers Through Competency-Based Action Learning," *Journal of Management Development,* Vol. 12, no. 1 (1993), pp. 43–48; Thomas Downham, James Noel, and Albert Prendergast, "Executive Development," *Human Resource Management,* Vol. 31, nos. 1 and 2 (Spring/Summer 1992), pp. 95–107. See also Michael Gregory, "Accrediting Work-Based Learning: Action Learning, a Model for Empowerment," *Journal of Management Development,* Vol. 13, no. 4 (1994), pp. 41–52. Louise Keys, "Action Learning: Executive Development of Choice for the 1990s, *Journal of Management Development,* Vol. 13, no. 8 (1994), pp. 50–56.

24. Wexley and Latham, *Developing and Training Resources in Organizations,* p. 193.

25. Chris Argyris, "Some Limitations of the Case Method: Experiences in a Management Development Program," *Academy of Management Review,* Vol. 5, no. 2 (1980), pp. 291–298. For a discussion of the advantages of case studies over traditional methods, see, for example, Eugene Andrews and James Noel, "Adding Life to the Case Study," *Training and Development Journal,* Vol. 40, no. 2 (February 1986), pp. 28–33.

26. David Rogers, *Business Policy and Planning* (Englewood Cliffs, NJ: Prentice Hall, 1977), pp. 532–533.

27. Argyris, "Some Limitations of the Case Method," pp. 292–295.

28. Rogers, *Business Policy and Planning,* p. 533.

29. For a discussion of management games and also other noncomputerized training and development simulations, see Charlene Marmer Solomon, "Simulation Training Builds Teams Through Experience," *Personnel Journal* (June 1993), pp. 100–105; Kim Slack, "Training for the Real Thing," *Training and Development* (May 1993), pp. 79–89; Bruce Lierman, "How to Develop a Training Simulation," *Training and Development* (February 1994), pp. 50–52.

30. Mona Pintkowski, "Evaluating the Seminar Marketplace," *Training and Development Journal,* Vol. 40, no. 1 (January 1986), pp. 74–77.

31. Joseph Famularo, *Handbook of Modern Personnel Administration* (New York: McGraw-Hill, 1972), pp. 21.7–21.8. For an interesting discussion of how to design a management game that is both educational and stimulating, see Beverly Loy Taylor, "Around the World in 80 Questions," *Training and Development Journal,* Vol. 40, no. 3 (March 1986), pp. 67–70.

32. Lawrence G. Bridwell and Alvin B. Marcus, "Back to School—A High-Tech Company Sent Its Managers to Business School—to Learn "People" Skills," *Personnel Administrator,* Vol. 32, no. 3 (March 1987), pp. 86–91.

33. John Hinrichs, "Personnel Testing," in Marvin Dunnette, ed., *Handbook of Industrial and Organizational Psychology* (Chicago: Rand McNally, 1976), p. 855.

34. Norman Maier, Allen Solem, and Ayesha Maier, *The Role Play Technique* (San Diego, CA: University Associates, 1975), pp. 2–3. See also David Swink, "Role-Play Your Way to Learning," *Training and Development* (May 1993), pp. 91–97; Alan Test, "Why I Do Not Like to Role Play," *The American Salesman* (August 1994), pp. 7–20.

35. This section based on Allen Kraut, "Developing Managerial Skill via Modeling Techniques: Some Positive Research Findings—A Symposium," *Personnel Psychology,* Vol. 29, no. 3 (Autumn 1976), pp. 325–361.

36. "A Surprise CBS Morale Booster," *Business Week,* October 20, 1980, pp. 125–126. For a description of the experience of two other companies with in-house development centers see, for example, Thomas Patten, Jr., "The Corporate Learning Center: Two Companies' Experiences in Employment Development," *Employment Relations Today* (Winter 1993/94), pp. 411–418.

37. Thomas Stewart, "How GE Keeps Those Ideas Coming," *Fortune,* August 12, 1991, p. 43.

38. Mark Frohman, Marshall Sashkin, and Michael Kavanagh, "Action Research as Applied to Organization Development," *Organization and Administrative Science,* Vol. 7 (Spring–Summer 1976), pp. 129–142; Paul Sheibar, "The

and work later when it is heavy. The use of flextime seems to increase employees' receptiveness to changes in other procedures. It also tends to reduce the distinction between managers and workers and requires more delegation of authority by supervisors.

There are some disadvantages. Flextime is complicated to administer and may be impossible to implement where large groups of workers must work interdependently.[3] It also requires time clocks or other time records, which can be disadvantageous from the point of view of workers.

In any event, flextime seems to work. Surveys covering 445 employers (including drug companies, banks, electronics firms, and government agencies) indicate that the percentage of employees reporting flextime-driven productivity increases ranges from 5% or 10% in some firms to about 95% in one airline. On the whole, about 45% of employees involved in flextime programs report that the program has resulted in improved productivity.[4] The failure rate of flextime is also remarkably low, reportedly 8%, according to one study.[5]

Conditions for Success There are several ways to make a flextime program more successful.[6] First, management resistance—particularly at the supervisory level and particularly before the program is actually tried—has torpedoed several programs before they became operational, so supervisory indoctrination programs are important prerequisites to success. Second, flextime is usually more successful with clerical, professional, and managerial jobs, and less so with factory jobs (the nature of which tends to demand interdependence among workers). Third, experience indicates that the greater the flexibility of a flextime program, the greater the benefits the program can produce (although the disadvantages, of course, multiply as well). Fourth, the way the program is installed is important; a flextime project director to oversee all aspects of the program should be appointed, and frequent meetings should take place between supervisors and employees to allay their fears and clear up misunderstanding. A pilot study, say, in one department, is advisable.[7]

Flextime may be especially valuable for the employer when the group must share limited resources. For example, computer programmers often spend as much as two-thirds of their time waiting to make computer runs. As one researcher concludes, "because flextime expands the amount of time that the computer is available to the programmer, this allows its usage to be spread over more hours, and the time in queues to make runs and get output back is reduced."[8]

Three- and Four-Day Workweeks

four-day workweek
An arrangement that allows employees to work four ten-hour days instead of the more usual five eight-hour days.

A number of employers have also switched to a **four-day workweek**. Here employees work four ten-hour days instead of the more usual five eight-hour days.

Advantages Compressed workweek plans have been fairly successful as they have several advantages. Productivity seems to increase since there are fewer startups and shutdowns. Workers are more willing to work some evenings and Saturdays as part of these plans. According to one study, 80% of the firms on such plans reported that the plan "improves business results"; three-fifths said that production was up and almost two-fifths said that costs were down. Half the firms also reported higher profits. Even the four-day firms not reporting positive results reported that cost and profit factors at least remained the same. One study suggests that the four-day workweek is generally effective (in terms of reducing paid overtime, reducing absenteeism, and improving efficiency). Furthermore, workers also gain; there is a 20% reduction in commuter trips and an additional day off per week. Additional savings (for example, in child care expenses) may also occur.[9]

However, there has not been a lot of experience with shortened workweeks, and it is possible that the improvements are short-lived. In one study, for instance, four-day weeks resulted in greater employee satisfaction and productivity and less absenteeism when evaluated after 13 months, but these improvements were not found after 25 months.[10] A recent review of three-day, 38-hour workweeks concluded that compressed workweek schedules have significant positive and long-lasting effects on the organization if handled properly. Regardless of individual differences, those employees who had experienced the 3/38 schedule reacted favorably to it, particularly if they had participated in the decision to implement the new program and if their jobs had been enriched by the schedule change. Fatigue did not appear to be a problem in this survey.[11]

Disadvantages   There are also disadvantages, some of them potentially quite severe. Tardiness, for example, may become a problem. Of more concern is the fact that fatigue was cited by several firms as a principal drawback of the four-day workweek. (Note that fatigue was a main reason for adopting eight-hour days in the first place.)

Other Flexible Work Arrangements

job sharing
A concept that allows two or more people to share a single full-time job.

Employers are taking other steps to accommodate their employees' scheduling needs. **Job sharing** is a concept that allows two or more people to share a single full-time job. For example, two people may share a 40-hour-per-week job, with one working mornings and the other working afternoons. About 10% of the firms questioned in one survey indicated that they allow for job sharing.[12] *Work sharing* refers to a temporary reduction in work-hours by a group of employees during economic hard times as a way of preventing layoffs; thus 400 employees may all agree to work (and get paid for) only 35 hours per week in order to avoid having the firm lay off 30 workers. *Flexiplace,* in which employees are allowed or encouraged to work at home or in a satellite office closer to home, is another example of a flexible work arrangement that is becoming more popular today.

Telecommuting
A work arrangement in which employees work at remote locations, usually at home, using video displays, computers, and other telecommunications equipment to carry out their responsibilities.

Telecommuting is another option. Here employees work at home, usually with video displays, and use telephone lines to transmit letters, data, and completed work to the home office. For example, Best Western Hotels in Phoenix is using the residents of the Arizona Center for Women, a minimum-security prison, as an office staff. It is estimated that 7 million workers in the United States are telecommuting today in various jobs from lawyer to clerk to computer expert.[13]

Flexyears
A work arrangement under which employees can choose (at six-month intervals) the number of hours they want to work each month over the next year.

Still other employers, especially in Europe, are switching to a plan they call **flexyears.** Under this plan, employees can choose (at six-month intervals) the number of hours they want to work each month over the next year. A full-timer, for instance, might be able to work up to 173 hours a month. In a typical flexyear arrangement, an employee who wants to average 110 hours a month might work 150 hours in January (when the children are at school and the company needs extra help to cope with January sales). In February, the employee may work only 70 hours because he or she wants to, say, go skiing.[14]

Using Quality Circle Programs

A **quality circle** (QC) is a group of five to ten specially trained employees who meet for an hour once a week for the purpose of spotting and solving problems in their work area.[15] The circle is usually composed of a work group, people who work together to produce a specific component or service.

Steps in Establishing a Quality Circle

quality circle
A group of five to ten specially trained employees who meet on a regular basis to identify and solve problems in their work area.

HR usually plays a central role in establishing a QC program. The four steps in establishing and leading a quality circle are *planning, training, initiating,* and *operating.*

Planning the Circle The planning phase usually takes about one month and typically begins with a top-level executive making the decision to implement the quality circle (QC) technique. This leads to identifying and selecting a consultant who will assist top management in implementing the quality circles in the firm. However, in some cases an in-house *facilitator* will be identified and sent out for special circle methods training. The facilitator then returns to the firm and handles the tasks the consultant would otherwise have been responsible for.

One of the most important steps in the first phase is selecting the quality circle *steering committee*. The steering committee becomes the group that directs quality circle activities in the organization. The committee is usually multidisciplinary in that it draws on employees from functions such as production, human resources, quality control, training, marketing, engineering, finance, and the union. The success of the quality circle concept often hinges on how committed to the technique workers feel top management is. Therefore, the steering committee almost always has at least one or two top managers as members.

The steering committee has several responsibilities. Perhaps most important, its members should establish circle objectives in terms of the kinds of *bottom-line improvements* they would like to see. Yardsticks include reduced errors and enhanced quality, more effective teamwork, and increased attention to problem prevention. At the same time, the steering committee determines actions that are considered outside the charter of the circles—for instance, benefits and salaries, employment practices, policies on discharging employees, personalities, and grievances. The steering committee also chooses the in-house facilitator, the person who will be responsible for daily coordination of the firm's quality circle activities. In most cases the facilitator devotes full time to the quality circle tasks and is responsible for such specific duties as coordinating the activities of the circles, training leaders for each circle, attending circle meetings and providing expert advice and backup coordination, and maintaining records to reflect circle achievements.

Initial Training In the second phase, the facilitator and pilot project circle leaders meet (usually with the consultant) to be trained in basic QC philosophy, implementation, and operation. This training course typically takes four days and includes various activities. On the first day, for example, the consultant might meet with the leaders to discuss the nature and objectives of quality circles. On the remaining days, trainees use case studies to learn quality circle leadership techniques.

Initiating the Circles Initiating the pilot program's circles begins with department managers conducting quality circle familiarization meetings with employees, with the facilitator, circle leaders, and (ideally) an executive participating as speakers. Then circle leaders contact each employee to determine circle membership, which is voluntary, and the circles are constituted. The facilitator distributes manuals for circle leaders at this point; they contain an overview of the QC idea, as well as an explanation of data collection and problem-solving techniques.

The Circle in Operation Next each circle can turn to problem solving and analysis. In practice, this involves five steps: problem identification, problem selection, problem analysis, solution recommendations, and solution review by management.

Problem Identification   The problems identified by circle members are often mundane and may not be especially interesting to work groups outside the circle's work area. These problems might include how to keep the area cleaner, how to improve the work group's product quality, or how to speed up the packing of the work group's crates.

Problem Selection   Next members select the number-one problem they wish to focus on. Circle members are usually quite familiar with the impediments making it difficult for them to do their jobs. They are thus often in the best position to prioritize problems, although increasingly the choice is made by (or with the approval of) management.

Problem Analysis   In this next step, circle members collect and collate data relating to the problem and analyze them using data collection, analysis, and problem-solving techniques for which they are especially trained.

Notice that the group members, rather than outside experts or the group leader/supervisor, solve the problem. A big benefit of quality circles is the sense of satisfaction that members get from being involved in the actual problem analysis process. If they are prohibited from analyzing the problem by an inept leader, they will not only miss this sense of satisfaction but may actually resent (rather than be committed to) implementing the solution. Quality circles are as much a people-building opportunity as a quality-improving one. To derive all the benefits from a circle, the members themselves must thus be involved in the problem selection, analysis, and implementation.

Solution Recommendations   The group's solution is then presented to management by group members, with the aid of charts and graphs they prepare themselves. The presentation is usually oral rather than written and more often than not is voluntarily prepared by employees on their own time at break, lunch, and after work.

Solution Review and Decision by Management   Quality circles usually operate through the management chain of command. The presentation is made to the individual to whom the supervisor (frequently the circle leader) reports, not to the steering committee or to somebody on the executive level. Top managers may be present as observers.

According to one source, from 85% to 100% of circle suggestions are approved by the manager, often in the presentation meeting itself. Occasionally the manager will need verification of studies done and may even ask a staff person to assist in the verification. In those unusual instances when a manager must decline a recommendation, he or she is trained to explain why it was turned down, so as not to dampen the enthusiasm of the circle members.

There are several predictable problems that quality circles encounter which you should plan to avoid. One is the feeling on the part of the employees that this is "just another program," one that will probably evaporate once the initial excitement wears off. Gaining top management's commitment to quality circles is thus crucial for such a program's success. Some employees will complain that the circles are doomed because "management never pays attention to us anyway." Here again, the best solution is to underscore top management's commitment to the quality circle program. Selecting problems outside the circle's areas of expertise is another familiar problem, as when a production group decides to work on a shipping problem. Therefore, circle leaders should be trained to keep their members on track and to caution them

Members of a quality circle are responsible for identifying problems, then analyzing them and proposing solutions.

to focus on problems within their own areas—where they are the experts. Other area's problems can be handed over to those areas' circles or handed up the line where interdisciplinary teams can try to tackle them. Finally, some of the greatest resistance to the circles will come not from the employees but from the supervisors themselves, perhaps because they fear that the circles may undermine their traditional authority. This is another reason why top management's commitment is essential—to let supervisors know that the firm takes this program very seriously.

Making Quality Circles More Effective

Studies of quality circle effectiveness generally confirm that it is spotty at best.[16] Many of the so-called studies of QC effectiveness are actually anecdotal case studies. Here the researcher simply reports his or her observations regarding the effectiveness of quality circle programs based on perceived results and estimated dollar savings. In one such study, a company steering committee reported annualized savings of over $400,000 in one year, reflecting a three-to-one return on investment. Such results are impressive. However it's not possible to conclude from such studies that the quality circle program itself created the savings rather than, say, some parallel changes such as improvements in the firm's financial incentive plan.

Results of more careful experimental studies of quality circles generally indicate that the majority of such programs are successful but that many still are not. One study showed an initial improvement in attitudes, behaviors, and effectiveness but then a decline in each to the initial levels.[17] Results of one recent quality circle study are probably typical. The researcher concluded: "The fact that two of the four circles had actual cost savings ($9,600 and $11,280), none had noticeable quality improvements, all worked on job improvement issues, and three of the four were evaluated as successful by facilitators seems indicative of general quality circle performance."[18] Such spotty results, plus the cost of implementing their circles, prompted many firms to phase out their QC programs. Rather than throw the baby out with the bath water, though, many firms today are taking steps to make their QC programs more effective.

Toward More Effective Quality Circles Programs now in place at Northrop Corporation and at Honeywell Corporation illustrate some of the differences between traditional quality circles and second-generation employee participation teams. At Northrop the groups are no longer voluntary and now involve all workers on the shop floor. The groups are responsible for setting improvement targets and keeping reports on their progress, and they compete with other groups to achieve goals. At Honeywell Corporation (one of the pioneer users of QCs), the company has replaced about 700 of its traditional quality circles with about 1,000 work groups. These Honeywell groups are generally not voluntary and involve most shop-floor employees. And, in contrast to the bottom-up approach of quality circles, problems are often assigned to work groups by management.

Beyond tightening up the running of the teams themselves, other firms have found that instituting quality circles without making corresponding changes in management styles and company culture is futile. For example, one major banking company instituted quality circle teams to improve efficiency, communications, and team spirit.[19] However, when asked how they liked their quality circle program, participants reportedly used words such as "nuisance," "a joke," and "very unproductive" to describe circle meetings. Participants claimed there were no ideas generated during the sessions, that the sessions themselves were dull and boring, and that most felt a lack of emotional involvement. Most also claimed they really didn't understand what they were to do or accomplish with the quality circles. An investigation led to the conclusion that the bank's underlying culture was just not conducive to a participative quality circle program.

In a program like this, the bottom-up participation that management wants to encourage must be fostered by a fundamental change in philosophy from top management on down. In other words, managers must make it clear to everyone that they will listen to and act on employees' input, must create trust and confidence, and must show in concrete ways that they mean what they say about wanting employee input.

The bank began by changing some policies that contradicted such a philosophy. For example, the annual polygraph examinations (which were legal at the time) and the time clock were eliminated. An interdepartmental employee quality circle committee was instituted. This committee in turn established a two-way dialogue between management and workers through regularly scheduled meetings. The basic theme of these meetings was company profitability for survival; it was explained repeatedly that such profitability was the surest route to job security.

As a result of their experience, the consultants to this project suggest the following guidelines for introducing a QC program:

1. Level with the chief executive officer about the organization's current state of management and employee attitudes.
2. Allow the CEO and senior officials to be models for change in implementing constructive ideas.
3. If possible, make the program voluntary.
4. In the beginning, provide group members with solvable problems. Be prepared to change structures, policies, and procedures. Keep objectives simple.
5. Emphasize that these are not complaint sessions.
6. Communicate and educate every person in the organization about the program. Emphasize that group members need support.
7. Establish a climate of care and feedback.
8. Involve line managers and make them leaders of the groups whenever possible.
9. Provide additional training to complement quality circle training. Introduce the circles as an ongoing process of good supervision to the supervisors themselves.[20]

Total Quality Management Programs

Introduction

As the banking company's experience suggests, there is a lot more to implementing successful quality circle programs than organizing several groups and telling them to "go at it." At the bank, for instance, management philosophies and styles had to be changed, and a new company culture (without polygraphs and so on) had to be molded.

In fact, the most successful QC programs aren't run in isolation but are part of comprehensive companywide quality improvement programs: The teams' quality improvement projects are conducted within companywide plans and quality targets and goals; efforts are made to ensure the full support of middle managers; extensive training opportunities are provided; and the culture and reward systems are geared to encouraging employee involvement. Comprehensive

Information Technology and HR
Attitude Surveys

Despite downsizings, workers' overall job satisfaction actually improved from 1988 to 1994. Some reasons given were improved work flow, better cooperation between departments, and increased supervisors' fairness. Many firms today rely on attitude surveys to monitor how employees feel about working in their firms.

The use of employee attitude surveys has grown since 1944 when the National Industrial Conference Board "had difficulty finding fifty companies that had conducted opinion surveys."[2] Today most companies are aware of the need for employee anonymity, the impact of both the design of the questions and their sequence, and the importance of effective communication, including knowing the purpose of the survey before it's taken and getting feedback to the employees after it's completed. Computerization of surveys can provide anonymity, if there is no audit trail to the user, especially for short answers that are entered rather than written or typed on an identifiable machine.

Survey software packages are available that generate questions for a number of standard topics and can be customized by modifying existing questions or by adding questions. If the survey is computerized, then reports can be generated with ease to provide snapshots of a given period of time, trend analysis, and breakdowns according to various demographics. You may be interested in responses by age, sex, job categories, departments, divisions, functions, or geography.

The survey can be conducted by placing microcomputers in several locations convenient for employee use. Employees are advised where the computers will be, for how long, and when the data will be collected (for instance, daily at 5 P.M. for three weeks). The screen should not be viewable by supervisors or passersby. While there may be some risk that employees will take the survey more than once, there are comparable risks with other methods. (For example, who completes the survey mailed to the employee's home?)

Managers may be interested in knowing how they are perceived by their peers and subordinates. Packages are available that can be customized, which allow the manager to complete a self-assessment tool used to compare self-perceptions to the anonymous opinions of others. This comparison may assist in the development of a more effective manager.

Employees who are leaving the company are often asked their opinions during a formal or informal exit interview. Concerned about future references, employees often state innocuous reasons for leaving, reasons known to be acceptable to the company. However, if the exiting employees could respond to computer questions (such as, "If you could change some aspect of supervision, what would it be?" "If you could change some aspect of our benefits, what would it be?") and be assured that answers would not be looked at until several people had responded, more helpful information might be learned.◆

[1]BNA, *Bulletin to Management,* August 24, 1995, pp. 266–271.
[2]Martin Wright, "Helping Employees Speak Out About Their Jobs and the Workplace," *Personnel,* Vol. 63 (September 1986), p. 56.

quality improvement programs like this go by many names including total quality management (TQM), quality improvement process (QIP), and total quality control (TQC).[21] Regardless of labels, TQM is always a total corporate focus on meeting and often exceeding customers' expectations and significantly reducing the cost resulting from poor quality by shaping a new management system and corporate culture.[22,23]

Two major awards recognize companies that institute highly effective quality improvement programs. The Deming Prize, named after Dr. W. Edwards Deming and awarded by the Union of Japanese Scientists and Engineers, was the first such award. In 1987 Congress established the Malcolm Baldrige National Quality Award to promote quality awareness, recognize quality achievements of U.S. companies, and publicize successful quality strategies.[24] The award is considered by many in the United States to be the "Nobel Prize" for quality. Each year up to two companies can be chosen from three business categories—manufacturing, service, and small business—to receive the award. The 150 judges analyze information regarding such things as each applicant firm's leadership, human resources, quality assurance programs, and customer satisfaction. Firms winning the Baldrige Award have included Cadillac Motor Car Division, Federal Express Corp., and Motorola, Inc.

Miami-based Florida Power & Light Company (FPL), Florida's largest utility, was the first company outside Japan to win the Deming Prize. Awarded annually (and since 1986 outside Japan), the prize recognizes outstanding achievement in quality control management. The steps FPL took to win the award help to illustrate the activities involved in implementing comprehensive companywide total quality management programs, and the role of HR management in doing so.

Three Basic Features of FPL's Program

FPL's quality improvement program contains three main components or phases: policy deployment, quality improvement teams, and quality in daily work.

Policy Deployment In many quality programs, the employees identify problems to study without any coherent direction from top management regarding what the high-priority problems should be. Policy deployment is the process through which company management works together to focus resources on achieving customer satisfaction.

Policy deployment provides direction. At FPL the policy deployment process begins by determining what FPL customers actually want and then compiling these needs in a customer needs table. In other words, annual surveys are made of customer needs and these are then summarized and prioritized into five or six main categories. These needs drive the corporate agenda—the plans regarding where the company and the team should focus their efforts.

The point of the policy deployment process is to concentrate company resources on a few priority issues. Recently, for instance, the objectives emerging from the customer needs assessment included:

◆ Improve public confidence in safety programs.
◆ Reduce the number of complaints to the Florida Public Service Commission.
◆ Improve the reliability of electric service.
◆ Continue to emphasize safe, reliable, and efficient operation of nuclear plants.
◆ Strengthen fossil fuel plant reliability and availability.

Such objectives are then translated into more measurable terms, such as "increase fossil plant availability to about 95% of total time by 1994." Measurable objectives like these, which FPL refers to as *policies,* are then distributed to all FPL employees via their *Annual Guide to Corporate Excellence.* This publication folds out into a wall chart, and, as the company puts it, "Hung in offices throughout FPL, it reminds one and all to check whether their QI teams and daily work are contributing to the corporate vision."[25] It is through policy deployment that the measurable quality objectives (or policies) of FPL are deployed throughout the company, thus giving this process its name.

Quality Improvement Teams FPL uses four kinds of quality improvement teams or circles: functional teams, cross-functional teams, task teams, and lead teams. (In total, about 1,700 quality improvement teams operate at FPL.) *Functional teams* are composed of volunteers who typically work together as natural work units on a daily basis. They generally choose their own problems and meet one hour each week. The basic aim here is to involve first-line employees in improving their daily work activities so as to enhance the quality of their work life and to develop their skills. *Cross-functional teams* are ongoing teams that are formed to address problems that cut across organizational boundaries. *Task team* members are appointed from one or more departments to work on specific high-priority assigned problems. When the problem is solved, the task team is disbanded.

Finally, *lead teams* are headed by a vice president or other manager and serve as steering committees for all the teams that operate in their areas. It is the lead team, for instance, that decides how employees are assigned to serve on various teams, and establishes guidelines regarding frequency and duration of team meetings.

The basic customer-oriented policies (such as "improve reliability of service") emerging from the policy deployment process form the framework within which quality improvement teams focus their efforts. While the teams then generally select their own problem topics (called themes) to study, certain topics are off limits. These include the company's union agreement, absenteeism, pay, salaries, promotions, the apprenticeship program, and general safety rules produced by a joint safety committee.

Team members undergo extensive training, and this is one area in which the HR system has a major impact. One training program is called "team member training." In this two-day program employees are trained in special techniques, such as statistical quality control, and in group decision-making techniques such as brainstorming. Workbooks, case studies, and video presentations are used.

With about a thousand quality improvement recommendations presented per year, there is no shortage of examples of quality improvement team efforts. For example, one team discovered that it was bird droppings, not inclement weather, that caused some of FPL's high-voltage lines to short out fairly often.

Quality in Daily Work In addition to policy deployment and quality improvement teams, FPL encourages *quality in daily work* (QIDW). Individual employees are urged to identify their customers and their needs, keeping in mind that the customer may be external or internal (that is, within the company). The basic thrust of QIDW is to encourage individual employees to take a quality improvement approach to their work.

Human Resource Management and the Quality Improvement Effort

Lessons from FPL Based on FPL's experience, many HR actions can help to ensure a more effective total quality program. Some HR guidelines based on FPL's experience are as follows:

- Make sure all teams work within a policy—deployment process to ensure their efforts are consistent with the firm's goals.
- Do not institute quality circles as separate, parallel organization structures. Simply trying to superimpose quality circles outside the normal chain of command elicited resistance from supervisors, many of whom made comments like "I don't know what these people are doing—they're not helping me do my job."[26] The teams should, to the greatest extent possible, be composed of natural work units.

- Do not treat the quality improvement program as if it has an end. It is important to emphasize that a quality improvement program that is successful is really a systematic way of doing business, one that has no end.

- Recognize that training is essential. Quality improvement is successful largely because training continually upgrades the problem analysis and statistics skills of even first-line employees. This training is crucial both to provide the required analytical skills and also to emphasize the firm's commitment to the program.

- Give employees the skills they need to analyze and solve problems; then get them to analyze and solve the problem, and follow up on their suggestions. Whether or not the company achieves its quality goals is, although very important, almost secondary. The new culture that emerges is at the heart of the program.

- Do not focus exclusively on "boosting productivity" or assume that emphasizing quality means that productivity will necessarily fall. In fact, FPL and other companies have often found that as quality rises, so does productivity.

- Prioritize your needs. It is important to work on only a few needs at once: Do not dilute your resources.

- Recognize effort and encourage employees. A main benefit of this type of program is the sense of satisfaction it can foster in employees. This requires encouraging employees to identify and devise countermeasures against problems, and from giving them the tools and leeway required to get this job done. In fact, when FPL asked their employees what they wanted most, they didn't say "more money." They said they wanted their suggestions implemented and recognition from their supervisors.

- Reward individual and team efforts in a concrete manner, not necessarily just with money but with rewards like merchandise or pins.

- Remember that the first steps need to be taken by top management: "From the board of directors to every supervisor, management must adopt the principles and language of quality, follow the processes, set examples and guide others. A substantial commitment is necessary for employee education, and for awareness and recognition programs. These programs require reallocation of budgets and personnel, and will take time to produce results but will be worth it."[27]

HR's Role in Winning the Baldrige Award HR development and management plays a central role in meeting the criteria used for evaluating Malcolm Baldrige Quality Award applicants. As shown in Figure 9.1, Baldrige applicants are evaluated by a board of examiners consisting of quality experts. They evaluate seven basic areas: senior executive leadership (top management's symbolic commitment to quality); information and analysis (an adequate system for collecting statistical data on matters such as product or service quality); strategic quality planning (the adequacy of the firm's planning process and how key quality requirements are integrated into the firm's overall business planning process); management of quality (for example, rather than viewing design, production, and sales as separate entities, top firms usually recognize the integrated nature of their work so that the departments work together); quality and operational results (to show the firm is achieving continuous improvement in critical operational areas, such as in service quality levels); and customer focus and satisfaction (wherein the examiners look for objective, validated data regarding the applicant's success in satisfying the customer).

Finally, the applicant's *human resource development and management* is evaluated. Specifically, judges evaluate the firm's achievements with respect to developing and realizing the full potential of its employees to pursue the firm's quality and performance objectives. They also examine the firm's efforts to build and

Figure 9.1
Baldrige Award
Criteria Framework
Senior executive leadership is the "driver" of total quality management, with each of the other six elements, or Baldrige Categories, playing a crucial role.

Source: U.S. Department of Commerce, 1992.

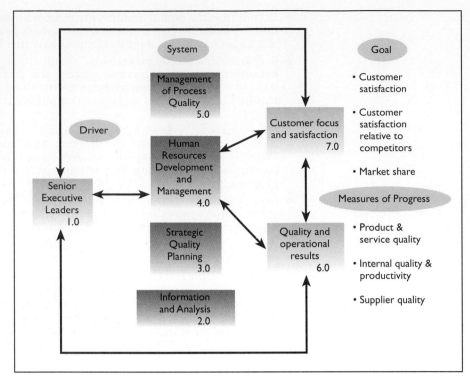

maintain an environment and culture for quality excellence, one conducive to full participation and personal and organizational growth.[28]

In practical terms, examiners focus in this category on the extent to which HR management and organizational behavior techniques (such as enrichment, empowerment, training, and career development) are used to fully tap each employee's potential. For example, employees should be trained to use problem-solving tools and group decision-making skills. The teams and employees should also have enriched and empowered jobs.

HR and ISO 9000   HR practices are also an integral part of companies' efforts to achieve ISO 9000 certification. ISO 9000 is the International Organization for Standardization's standard of quality management and quality assurance.[29] Certification usually requires a five-step process: ISO assessment (reviewing the company's quality systems and procedures); quality assurance and policy manual preparation (compiling the specific quality-oriented techniques and policies to be followed); training of employees in ISO 9000; documentation of work instructions (documenting each new work procedure, for instance); and registration audit (having the quality system reviewed by a special "registrar" who audits the company's quality efforts).

Employee training thus plays an important role in gaining ISO 9000 certification. For example, in one instance:

> *Perhaps the most serious problem was that even though a number of people were doing excellent work, they were simply unaware of the physical procedures they were following. Informal on-the-job training that was prevalent in the division was the culprit.[30]*

Training for ISO 9000 typically covers several things. Specifically, it covers the quality vocabulary associated with ISO 9000, the requirements of each section of the ISO 9000 standard, and the training systems quality assurance manuals.[31]

Creating Self-Directed Teams

The Nature of Self-Directed Teams

Individuals in most work teams such as this one at a paper mill have a high commitment to the group and its work goals, due in part to their shared experiences.

In the 1950s psychologist Rensis Likert formulated what would become the classic explanation of cohesive work teams for later generations of organizational experts.[32] First, he said that leadership and other processes of the organization should ensure that each employee will view the experience as one that builds and maintains his or her sense of personal worth and importance.[33] Furthermore, said Likert,

> *The most important source of satisfaction for this desire is the response we get from the people we are close to, in whom we are interested, and whose approval and support we are eager to have. The face-to-face groups with whom we spend the bulk of our time are, consequently, the most important to us. [Therefore,] management will make full use of the potential capacities of its human resources only when each person in an organization is a member of one or more effectively functioning work groups that have a high degree of group loyalty.*[34]

From a practical point of view, Likert might have added, employees probably tend to develop their first and perhaps most intense commitment to the people in their work groups and to their group's norms and ideals. To many people at work the company itself—what it is, where it's going, what its values are—is often little more than an abstraction. But the people with whom they work everyday—the door trim team at Saturn, the menswear group at the Penney's store, the securities group at Goldman Sachs—are real and worthy of their commitment. You can't let your teammates down.

For many firms the ideal situation, as Likert saw, is to organize work around small close-knit teams whose goals are high and whose aims are the same as the firm's. This is what more and more firms today are doing, firms such as Saturn, Toyota, Corning, and Texas Instruments. They and others like them are increasingly organizing the work around small self-contained teams, which are variously labeled self-managed teams, high-performance teams, autonomous work groups or, simply, superteams.[35] Whatever they're called, **self-directed teams** have much in common. Each team generally performs natural sets of interdependent tasks, such as all the steps needed to assemble a Saturn door. They all use consensus decision making to choose their own team members, solve job-related problems, design their own jobs, and schedule their own break time. And their jobs are always enriched in that they do many of the jobs formerly accomplished by supervisors, such as dealing with vendors and monitoring quality. Self-directed teams are also highly trained to solve problems, to design jobs, to interview candidates, and to understand financial reports. They are, therefore, generally *empowered:* They have the training and ability as well as the broad authority to get their jobs done.

self-directed teams
Highly trained work groups that use consensus decision making and broad authority to self-direct their activities.

Figure 9.3
Saturn RASI Card

Note: These cards are used to specify the level of involvement of each employee in each task.

RASI—Clarifies level of involvement; agree who owns the task, assign that person the "R". All other group members would assume A, S, or I positions depending on their role in relation to the task. Only one "R" can be assigned per task.

	Individual Roles and Responsibilities
R Responsibility	• Owns task (accountable and responsible) • Initiates action • Ensures the action is carried out • Performs tasks or delegates to appropriate others • Involves other team members appropriately
A Approval	• Approves or vetos the recommended action • Assures members are properly involved • Ensures resources are available for implementation • Sets parameters
S Support	• Provides support and resources • Shares knowledge and expertise • Questions and challenges • Offers options and input
I Inform	• Listens to assure understanding • Uses information • Keeps feedback loops open • Questions and expresses opinions

(FRONT)

SATURN
Meeting Effectiveness
Seven Key Steps
→

Before the Meeting
1. Identify RASI Attendance (Based on Meeting Type or Purpose)
2. Publish 4 Part Agenda
   1. Time Contract
   2. Agenda
   3. Meeting Type
   4. Expected Outcome(s)

Four Meeting Types
1. Presentation
2. Problem Solving
3. Status/Action
4. Decision

During the Meeting
3. Confirm RASI Roles of Attendees
4. Maintain Meeting Type
5. Achieve Expected Outcome(s)
6. Meet Time Contract
7. Assess Meeting Effectiveness

(BACK)

gives employees more challenging jobs to do, while empowering them gives them the skills, authority, and discretion they need to actually do them. "Enrich and empower" at work thus means doing three things: (1) enriching employees' jobs by changing the content of these jobs—letting employees plan their own work, control their own scrap, and obtain their own supplies, for instance; (2) giving them the training, tools, and support they need to enable them to do their new jobs; and (3) insisting that all managers follow through by actually letting the workers use their new, broader authority to do their jobs.

Saturn provides a good example. First, all production work here is accomplished by teams with enriched work assignments. This is evident from the 30 "work unit functions" for which all teams are responsible. A sampling of the 30 functions is presented in Figure 9.2. All teams are responsible for a broad range of functions, including "resolve their own conflicts; plan their own work; make their own job assignments; make selection decisions of new members; perform to their own budget; and obtain their own supplies." Saturn's documenting of the 30 functions clarifies the responsibilities of each team and helps legitimate the broad-based authority the teams are to exercise.

Second, team members get the skills and tools to do their jobs, since empowerment without ability is just a sham. (For example, workers can't use consensus decision making and make their own job assignments without the training and decision-making tools that will help them do so.) RASI cards are examples of the tools. As shown in Figure 9.3, RASI stands for Responsibility, Approval, Support, and Inform. Teams are trained to use the RASI process to specify the level of each person's involvement as they use consensus decision making to solve team problems and determine courses of action. Suppose a door installation team decides to look for new suppliers for an item. Individual roles and responsibilities will be assigned according to the RASI process: Mike and Tina might be responsible for initiating the action and ensuring it is carried out; Lynn and Karl must approve or veto the recommended action; and so on.

RASI process training is just part of the empowerment-producing training Saturn employees receive. New team members get at least 320 hours of training in their first year and at least 92 hours per year thereafter. And remember that at Saturn "training" doesn't just mean learning how to screw in bolts or position doors. Instead the emphasis is on broadening the employee and developing new skills, with the aim of making each person "all he or she can be." The emphasis is on learning new things and on broadening the person's horizons, for example, with problem-solving training.

Third, high-commitment firms make sure their managers actually let their people do their jobs as assigned. Team members have made comments like these:

> "You don't have anyone who is supervisor—you don't experience supervision—we are supervised very loosely, if at all."

> "We become responsible to the people (the team members) we work with everyday. What I do affects my coworkers; in other firms you're treated like children—here we're treated like adults."

> "In terms of budgeting, such as buying tools, we go through our own suppliers and choose the best and we know that in this way we'll affect the quality of the car."

> "If an issue comes up the work team handles it—all on our team must be agreeable or we don't leave the room until we're 100% committed, 70% comfortable."

> "We are responsible to make our jobs more cost-effective." ◆

Making Self-Directed Teams More Effective

There are several factors that contribute to successfully organizing self-directed teams. These include forming a commitment to the principle of teamwork, steeping employees in teamwork terminology and techniques, and fostering employee commitment by enriching and empowering the work and workers.

Three other teamwork success factors deserve emphasis. First, as summarized in Table 9.2, *insufficient training* is consistently listed as the single biggest barrier to effective self-directed teams. (We've seen that at firms such as Toyota, team-member training is extensive.) Such training usually emphasizes problem solving and communication skills. For example, 83% of responding companies with team training teach team members problem-solving skills. There is also an emphasis on training team members to communicate more effectively and to hold more effective meetings.[43]

Second, *communications* between top management and the teams should be free flowing so the teams can do their jobs. As one study of team-based programs concluded, "These results support the proposition . . . that employees believe that greater access to information about corporate operations is critical if they are to improve their effectiveness in decision making."[44] When asked what's the first

TABLE 9.2 Developing Self-directed Teams

BARRIERS TO SELF-DIRECTED TEAMS

Barriers	Percentage of Respondents That Mentioned Each
Insufficient training	54
Supervisor resistance	47
Incompatible systems	47
Lack of planning (implementation was too fast)	40
Lack of management support	31
Lack of union support	24

The results are from a 1990 survey by DDI, AQP, and *Industry Week.*

TYPES OF TEAM TRAINING

Type of Training	Percentage of Responding Companies That Offer Each
Problem solving	83
Meeting skills	65
Communication skills	62
Handling conflict	61
SDT (self-directed teams) roles and responsibilities	58
Quality tools and concepts	56
Evaluating team performance	39
Work flow and process analysis	36
Selecting team members	35
Presentation skills	35
Influencing others	29
Budgeting	14

The results are from a 1990 survey by DDI, AQP, and *Industry Week.*

Source: Richard Wellins and Jill George, "The Key to Self-directed Teams," *Training and Development Journal* (April 1991), p. 29.

thing to tell management to do in order to get employee commitment, one Saturn work team answered, "Tell them to listen."[45]

Firms that want to win their employees' commitment, therefore, tend to give their people extensive data on their operations' performance and prospects. At Saturn the employees consider this a matter of trust.[46] "They must trust you to do the job," says one assembler, "and they therefore trust you with a lot of confidential information, for instance, on the financials of our firm. They tell you 'here is the problem, what would you do about it?' "[47]

Saturn uses several channels to promulgate data. Managers send information continuously via the internal television network and financial documents, for instance. Furthermore, the chain of command is fairly flat so that the "point" people on the teams, including the team leaders, can quickly find the information and the resources they need. The firm also has "town hall" meetings once per month, with at least 500 to 700 people attending.

Making self-directed teams more effective also generally requires that HR refocus the firm's pay plans around *small-group incentives*.[48] A small-group incentive plan may be defined as ". . . a pay method designed to deliver a uniform award, based on the achievement of a single or multiple predetermined goal(s) to all members of a work group who share responsibility for work process and output."[49] For example, all the individual team members in a credit-processing team at IBM Credit might receive semiannual bonuses for the team's responding to all requests for credit approval within three days.[50]

Global HRM

Extending Participative Decision Making Abroad

While participative self-directed teams may be effective for a company in the United States, the firm can't necessarily export the approach overseas. There are deep and often irreconcilable cross-cultural differences in values and attitudes from country to country, so that management techniques that work in one country may actually backfire in another.

The findings of one recent study illustrate the problem very well.[51] The study examined how one U.S. multinational manufacturing company tried to implement participative decision making in its European subsidiaries, and how managers and employees in three European countries reacted to the company's efforts. Specifically, the study sought to ascertain how U.S. managers differ from their European counterparts regarding such issues as:

    what they think the ideal level of participation should be for their subordinates;

    how they view the benefits of increased participation;

    how much participation they feel their subordinates actually want; and

    how much participation they think their subordinates actually have.

The company was hoping to implement participative decision-making programs in Europe that were similar to ones that had been successful in the United States, but it got unexpected reactions from European managers and employees. For example, most Dutch managers felt that the prepackaged nature of U.S. efforts to improve participation by instituting work teams could actually hurt performance and motivation because the teams failed to take individual differences into account. Several Dutch managers ". . . stated that the type of programmatic, formalized efforts favored by the American parent would not allow managers to encourage participation in ways and at a pace that was consistent with their own styles or the needs of their subordinates."[52]

British managers had similar reservations about implementing the "American approach" to team-based participative management. Specifically, they were concerned that the program ignored individual differences in managerial styles and employee abilities. The British managers seemed threatened by the decision-making authority the new work teams would have.

Interestingly, most of the Spanish managers endorsed the idea of self-directed work teams and said they thought it could work in the Spanish plant. But the Spanish managers' stated beliefs were actually somewhat misleading: In fact, Spanish managers reported lower levels of participation among subordinates than did their Dutch and U.S. counterparts. In other words, the actual participation was lower—not higher—in the Spanish plants than elsewhere in Europe, although the managers were relatively enthusiastic about participative management.

Overall, the results showed that U.S. managers have different values and perspectives on employee participation than their counterparts in Britain, the Netherlands, and Spain. It also ". . . illustrates some of the problems that can occur from a human resource perspective when a company attempts to push American values toward participation in European subsidiaries." The company's efforts are often perceived by European managers as being heavy-handed and out of touch with local values.[53] As a result, even when the managers verbally support the parent's efforts, what they actually do may be quite different from what they agreed to. Therefore, before exporting an HR program like self-directed work teams, HR managers should try to accomplish three basic goals:[54]

1. If appropriate, build trust by communicating to local managers that previous corporate HR efforts may have reflected culturally specific beliefs that do not always fit local needs, and that the parent company is committed to developing synergistic policies.

2. Become more aware of the local cultural traditions that may affect attitudes toward participation in decision making.

3. Develop a working partnership with local HR executives to create blended strategies for employee participation that fit the local culture yet offer something of value to the corporation as a whole. In effect, this will require joint decision making between U.S. HR executives and their foreign counterparts. ◆

HR and Business Process Reengineering

What is *reengineering*?

Michael Hammer and James Champy, the fathers of reengineering, define it as "The fundamental rethinking and radical redesign of business processes to achieve dramatic improvements in critical, contemporary measures of performance, such as cost, quality, service, and speed."[55] One of business process reengineering's (BPR) basic assumptions is that the traditional way of organizing departments and processes around very specialized tasks is inherently duplicative, wasteful, and unresponsive to the firm's customers. In reengineering a company and its departments and processes, the reengineers, therefore, need to ask themselves: "Why do we do what we do?" and "Why do we do it the way we do?"

An Example One reengineering example took place at IBM Credit Corporation, the IBM unit that finances the computers, software, and services sold by IBM Corporation. As originally organized, the credit-checking and approval process took several weeks. (A process is a collection of activities with a clear customer goal. For example, the "credit checking" process is the sequence of activities which takes a credit request as its input and sees the request go through a sequence of steps until the approval or rejection goes to the customer). A salesperson would call in to get credit for a prospective customer. A sequence of steps was then carried out by individual workers, each of whom logged in the request, carted the request upstairs to the credit department, entered the information into a computer system, checked the credit, and dispatched it to the next link in the chain.

When the need for approving credit this sequence was assessed, IBM Credit made a monumental discovery. Specifically, if someone who got the financing request walked it through all the stages personally and at each stage did what needed to be done, the whole process took only 90 minutes rather than a week or more! Reengineering the process in this case involved substituting several generalists for all the specialists and letting a generalist do all the tasks for a request rather than having the process carried out like a relay race.[56]

The IBM example illustrates some of the basic characteristics of business process reengineering. In business process reengineering several *jobs are combined* into one so that an assembly-line process is replaced by generalists who carry out all the tasks themselves. Another reengineering characteristic is, therefore, that *workers make more decisions:* For example, each of the new generalists at IBM Credit had to be solely responsible for deciding on a potential client's creditworthiness. Related to this, *checks and controls are reduced,* and instead there's more emphasis on carefully selecting and training the new generalist. Reengineered processes also tend to take a *case manager approach* to dealing with customers, in that each customer ends up with a single point of contact when checking on the status of an order or request.[57]

HR's Role in Reengineering Processes

Two years after the concepts and techniques of reengineering were introduced, it was obvious that something was lacking. In their quest to focus on reorganizing the work and eliminating unneeded, duplicative operations, many companies bent on reengineering had neglected to simultaneously institute new HR practices; the firms had failed to win the commitment of their managers and employees to their new reengineered jobs.[58] We now understand that HR plays a crucial role in successfully implementing a reengineering. Following are some aspects of HR's role.

Building Commitment to Reengineering   Implementing reengineering successfully means winning employee commitment. As one expert says, "[Reengineering is] about an ongoing, never-ending commitment to doing things better."[59] Even the most brilliant reorganizations and organizational changes can be undermined by recalcitrant employees. Therefore, one key to reengineering is winning people's commitment to the changes and what those changes mean. HR, as we've seen, plays a big role in winning such commitment through HR practices like value-based hiring, building a sense of community, and installing effective two-way communications practices.

HR and Team Building   Business process reengineering generally results in reorganizing the work force from functional departments to process-oriented teams, such as teams of employees working together to process credit requests. As we see in this chapter, HR plays a central role in making self-directed teams more effective. For instance, HR provides the required training and ensures that communications between top management and the teams remain open and freely flowing.

Application Exercises

RUNNING CASE: Carter Cleaning Company
The Quality Circle Program

As a recent graduate and a person who keeps up with the business press, Jennifer is familiar with the benefits of programs such as quality circles and TQM.

Jack has actually installed a total quality program of sorts at Carter, and it has been in place for about five years. Jack holds employee meetings periodically, but particularly when there is a serious problem in a store—such as very poor-quality work or too many breakdowns—he contacts all the employees in that store and meets with them as soon as the store closes. Hourly employees get extra pay for these meetings, and they actually have been fairly useful in helping Jack to identify several problems.

Jennifer is now curious as to whether these employee meetings should be formalized and perhaps a formal quality circle program initiated.

Questions
1. Would you recommend a quality circle program to Jennifer? Why? Why not?
2. Given what you know about the supervision of these stores, would you recommend a management by objectives program for store managers? Why or why not?
3. Are new work arrangements such as flextime or four-day workweeks practical at Carter? Why?

CASE INCIDENT: Is the Honeymoon Over at Flat Rock?

It began in the 1980's with great promise: Mazda Motor Corp. was going to build an assembly plant in Flat Rock, Michigan—just outside Detroit—that would eventually provide thousands of high-paying and secure jobs. By 1990, however, conditions had seriously deteriorated and Mazda's honeymoon with Flat Rock seemed to have come to an end. Four top U.S. managers had quit the company since 1988, and Japanese executives had taken the senior posts. The company was on its fourth director of labor relations since hiring began in 1986. Unionized workers were boycotting Mazda's suggestion box, a cornerstone of Japanese-style management. Workers complained of job stress and increased injuries, and absenteeism was running approximately 10%, which was higher than in other Japanese plants in the United States. But let's start at the beginning, when Mazda began the task of staffing its new plant.

All job candidates applying at Flat Rock for assembly jobs went through a five-step screening process that was specifically designed to assess interpersonal skills, aptitude for teamwork, planning skills, and flexibility. This screening process encompassed a lot more than taking a paper-and-pencil test, enduring a few interviews, and providing references. At Mazda, applicants also had to perform tasks that simulated jobs that they might do on the actual factory floor. For example, applicants might bolt fenders onto a car or attach hoses in a simulated engine compartment. This helped Mazda's management to match workers' abilities with specific job requirements, and it also provided applicants with a realistic preview of what they were getting into.

For the initial work force, 10,000 of 100,000 candidates passed the five-step screening process. Of these, only 1,300 were hired. The cost of screening each one of these new employees was about $13,000 per worker.

But new hirees didn't just report to the factory floor and join a work team. First, they had to undergo detailed training. That started with a three-week hodgepodge of sessions in which they learned about interpersonal relations, charting quality, stimulating creativity, and the like. This was followed by three days devoted to learning Mazda's philosophy of increasing efficiency through continual improvement. After this basic training came job-specific training. Line workers, for example, spent five to seven more weeks picking up specific technical skills, then another three or four weeks being supervised on the assembly line.

Why did Mazda go to all this expense and effort? The company wanted literate, versatile employees who would accept the company's emphasis on teamwork, loyalty, efficiency, and quality. Moreover, it wanted to weed out any troublemakers. What

Mazda got was a work force better educated and nearly a generation younger than the old-line auto workers at most Big Three plants. Mazda also wanted smooth relations with its workers. So it invited the United Auto Workers to organize the plant's employees before operations began. What went wrong? How could all this preparatory work have resulted in a disgruntled work force? The following highlights a few of the causes.

The high turnover among U.S. managers created instability. U.S. managers complained about being left out of the information network. Major decisions were controlled by Mazda executives in Japan or local Japanese superiors. Each morning, for instance, U.S. managers got a "laundry list" from their Japanese "advisor" telling them just what they were supposed to do that day.

Workers' complaints were numerous. They said that the Japanese managers didn't listen to them. They criticized the company's policy for continuous improvement, claiming that this translated into a never-ending push to cut the number of worker-hours spent building each car. To support their argument, they pointed out that U.S. plants use 15% to 20% more workers to produce a similar number of cars. Workers said that even Mazda's team system, which is supposed to give employees more authority and flexibility, is a gimmick. Power was gradually taken away from team leaders; flexibility was a one-way street that management used to control workers; and the team system encouraged workers to pressure each other to keep up the rapid pace.

Japanese executives at Flat Rock responded by publicly lambasting workers for lacking dedication. As to high turnover in the management ranks, Japanese executives admit that Mazda's practice of making decisions by consensus often gives the appearance of keeping authority away from its U.S. executives. But Japanese executives can also claim that the U.S. workers have just not adapted to Mazda's way of doing business. In spite of worker complaints, management can proudly point to the fact that independent experts give Flat Rock's cars high marks for quality; every bit as high, in fact, as those built in Japan.

Questions

1. Contrast Mazda's selection and training process with those more typically used for manufacturing workers.

2. "Mazda's management doesn't understand the U.S. worker." Do you agree or disagree with this statement? Discuss.

3. What suggestions, if any, would you make to Flat Rock's top management regarding its employee practices that might reduce absenteeism, turnover, and improve employee job satisfaction?

Source: Stephen Robbins, *Organizational Behavior* (Englewood Cliffs, NJ: Prentice Hall, 1993), pp. 593–595. Based on W. J. Hampton, "How Does Japan Inc. Pick Its American Workers?," *Business Week*, October 3, 1988, pp. 84–88; G. A. Patterson, "Mazda-UAW's Michigan Honeymoon Is Over," *The Wall Street Journal*, April 17, 1990, p. B1; and J. J. Fucini and S. Fucini, *Working for the Japanese* (New York: Free Press, 1990).

Human Resource Management Simulation

Incident (B) addresses some of the topics involved in alternative work arrangements. Incident (H) involves the creation of self-directed teams. Does your team feel the organization is ready for some of these techniques, or should you wait until you have all your other problems ironed out?

Quality issues may be addressed through the quality-budget expenditure that you will be making each decision period. The quality of the goods produced or services rendered by your firm is listed on the report each period. An index has been established with a range from 100 (high quality) down to 0 (extremely low quality). Currently, the organization has a quality index of 50. This represents "average" quality. Although quality control is not normally the responsibilty of a human resource director, it is

incorporated in the simulation because it is closely related to such HR areas as grievances, training, and turnover. Currently, quality is checked at the end of the process (postprocess control). Various programs are provided in the simulation manual to address the quality issue in your organization.

Your team will also be given the opportunity to support an employee-participation program. Programs range from voluntary problem-solving groups to formal quality circle programs. To simplify the decision-making process, you must decide whether to budget $10,000 each quarter for a participation program. The budget includes funds for establishing and supervising these new programs as well as paying employees when they are attending meetings and not at their regular job.

Video Case

Meet Edwards Deming

In this videocase W. Edwards Deming emphasizes the value of building a quality product and explains how his Deming system can boost quality and thereby boost a company's success. You'll see that Deming puts worker commitment at the heart of his system, emphasizing the importance of "trusting and training your workers."

Questions

1. On the basis of the video, why do you think it makes sense for a company to boost the quality of its products?

2. What are some of the important elements of the Deming system?

3. Do you think using HR techniques to boost employee commitment is or would be an important part of a Deming-type approach to boosting quality? Why or why not?

Source: ABC News, *Person of the Week, R.E. Deming,* "World News Tonight," October 12, 1990.

Take It to the Net

We invite you to visit the Dessler page on the Prentice Hall Web site at:
http://www.prenhall.com/~dessler
for the monthly Dessler update, and for this chapter's World Wide Web exercise.

Notes

1. Donald Peterson, "Flexitime in the United States: The Lessons of Experience," *Personnel,* Vol. 57 (January–February 1980), pp. 21–37; *1987 AMS Flexible Work Survey* (Willow Grove, PA: Administrative Management Society, 1987); Commerce Clearing House, "ASPA/CCH Survey on Alternative Work Schedules," June 26, 1987; Bureau of National Affairs, "Flexible Work Schedules," *Bulletin to Management,* September 3, 1992, pp. 276–277.

2. Peterson, "Flexitime in the United States," p. 22.

3. Stanley Nollen, "Does Flexitime Improve Productivity?" *Harvard Business Review,* Vol. 56 (September–October 1977), pp. 12–22; Karen Kush and Linda Stroh, "Flextime: Myth or Reality?" *Business Horizons* (September–October 1994), pp. 51–55.

4. Ibid.

5. Stanley Nollen and Virginia Martin, *Alternative Work Schedules Part One: Flextime* (New York: AMACOM, 1978), p. 44.

6. Peterson, "Flexitime in the United States," pp. 29–31.

7. Another problem is that some employers let workers "bank" extra hours by working, say, 45 hours one week so they need work only 35 hours the next week. The problem is that in the 45-hour week the employees should, strictly speaking, be paid an overtime rate for the extra five hours worked. Some employers handle this problem by letting hours worked vary from day to day but requiring each week to be a 40-hour week. Others are experimenting with letting workers accumulate hours and be paid overtime if necessary. See J. C. Swart, "Flexitime's Debit and Credit Option," *Personnel Journal,* Vol. 58 (January–February 1979), pp. 10–12.

8. David Ralston, David Gustafson, and William Anthony, "Employees May Love Flextime, But What Does It Do to the Organization's Productivity?" *Journal of Applied Psychology,* Vol. 70, no. 2 (1985), pp. 272–279.

9. Herbert Northrup, "The Twelve Hour Shift in the North American Mini-steel Industry," *Journal of Labor Research,* Vol. 12, no. 3 (Summer 1991), pp. 261–278; Charlene Marner Solomon, "24-hour Employees," *Personnel Journal,* Vol. 70, no. 8 (August 1991), pp. 56ff.

10. Ibid. See also John Ivancevich and Herbert Lyon, "The Shortened Work Week: A Field Experiment," *Journal of Applied Psychology,* Vol. 62, no. 1 (1977), pp. 34–37.

11. Janina Latack and Lawrence Foster, "Implementation of Compressed Work Schedules: Participation and Job Redesign as Critical Factors for Employee Acceptance," *Personnel Psychology,* Vol. 38, no. 1 (Spring 1985), pp. 75–92. Interestingly, one way to determine how your employees will react to a 4/40 or flextime work schedule apparently is to ask them ahead of time. One study suggests that these will be the reactions that emerge three to six months after commencement of the program. See Randall B. Dunham, Jon L. Pierce, and Maria B. Castaneda, "Alternative Work Schedules: Two Field Quasi-Experiments," *Personnel Psychology,* Vol. 40, no. 2 (Summer 1987), pp. 215–242.

12. Commerce Clearing House, *Ideas and Trends,* February 26, 1982, p. 61; Charlene Marmer Solomon, "Job Sharing: One Job, Double Headache?" *Personnel Journal* (September 1994), pp. 88–96.

13. "These Top Executives Work Where They Play," *Business Week,* October 27, 1986, p. 132.

14. "After Flexible Hours, Now It's Flexiyear," *International Management* (March 1982), pp. 31–32.
15. This section based on Donald Dewar, *The Quality Circle Guide to Participation Management* (Englewood Cliffs, NJ: Prentice-Hall, 1980). See also James Thacker and Mitchel Fields, "Union Involvement in Quality-of-Work Life Efforts: A Longitudinal Investigation," *Personnel Psychology,* Vol. 40, no. 1 (Spring 1987), pp. 97–112. They conclude that unions' fears of QCs may be misplaced and that after quality-of-work-life involvement, "A majority of the rank and file members who perceived QWL—quality of work life—as successful gave equal credit for the success to both union and management. The rank and file members who perceived QWL as unsuccessful tended to blame management for the lack of success." See also Anat Rafaeli, "Quality Circles and Employee Attitudes," *Personnel Psychology,* Vol. 38 (Fall 1985), pp. 603–615; Mitchell Lee Marks, Edward Hackett, Philip Mirvis, and James Grady, Jr., "Employee Participation in a Quality Circle Program: Impact on Quality of Work Life, Productivity, and Absenteeism," *Journal of Applied Psychology,* Vol. 71, no. 1 (February 1986), pp. 61–69, and "Quality Circles: A New Generation," *BNA Bulletin to Management,* Vol. 38, no. 2 (January 1987), pp. 10–15. See also Preston C. Bottger and Philip Yetton, "Improving Group Performance by Training in Individual Problem Solving," *Journal of Applied Psychology,* Vol. 72, no. 4 (November 1987), pp. 651–657, and Murray R. Barrick and Ralph Alexander, "A Review of Quality Circle Efficacy and the Existence of Positive-Finding Bias," *Personnel Psychology,* Vol. 40, no. 3 (Autumn 1987), pp. 579–592.
16. This is based on Everett Adam, Jr., "Quality Circle Performance," *Journal of Management,* Vol. 17, no. 1 (1991), pp. 25–39.
17. R. W. Griffin, "Consequences of Quality Circles in an Industrial Setting: A Longitudinal Assessment," *Academy of Management Journal,* Vol. 31, no. 2 (1988), pp. 338–358; reported in Adam, "Quality Circle Performance," p. 27.
18. Adam, "Quality Circle Performance," p. 38.
19. Gopal Pati, Robert Salitore, and Saundra Brady, "What Went Wrong with Quality Circles?" *Personnel Journal* (December 1987), pp. 83–89.
20. Ibid., p. 86.
21. Thomas Berry, *Managing the Total Quality Transformation* (New York: McGraw-Hill, 1991), p. 1.
22. Ibid., p. xv.
23. These are adapted from ibid., pp. 53–54.
24. This is based on Shari Caudron, "How Xerox Won the Baldrige," *Personnel Journal* (April 1991), p. 100.
25. "Building a Quality Improvement Program at Florida Power & Light," *Target* (Fall 1988), p. 6.
26. Private conversation with Wayne Brunetti, Executive Vice President, Florida Power & Light Company.
27. "Building a Quality Improvement Program at Florida Power & Light," *Target* (Fall 1988), p. 8.
28. Joel E. Ross, *Total Quality Management: Text, Cases and Readings* (Delray Beach, FL: St. Lucie Press, 1993), p. 4.
29. Rob Murakami, "How to Implement ISO 9000," *CMA Magazine* (March 1994), p. 18.
30. Sidney Emmons, "ISO 9001 on a Shoestring," *Quality Progress* (May 1994), p. 50.
31. Rob Murakami, "How to Implement ISO 9000," p. 19.
32. The following is adapted from Gary Dessler, *Winning Commitment* (New York: McGraw-Hill, 1993), Chapter 5.
33. Rensis Likert, *New Patterns of Management* (New York: McGraw-Hill, 1961), p. 103.
34. Ibid., p. 104.
35. See, for example, Brian Dumaine, "Who Needs a Boss?" *Fortune,* May 7, 1990, p. 52; David Hames, "Productivity-Enhancing Work Innovations: Remedies for What Ails Hospitals?" *Hospital & Health Services Administration,* Vol. 36, no. 4 (Winter 1991), pp. 551–552; see also Shari Caudron, "Are Self-Directed Teams Right for Your Company?" *Personnel Journal* (December 1993), pp. 76–84.
36. John Hoerr, "Sharpening Minds for a Competitive Edge," *Business Week,* December 17, 1990, p. 72.
37. Toyota Motor Manufacturing, USA, Inc., Team Member Handbook, February 1988, p. 11.
38. This is based on internal company documents and is adapted from Dessler, *Winning Commitment,* Chapter 5.
39. *Toyota Topics* (June 1990), p. 8.
40. Dessler, *Winning Commitment,* Chapter 5, personal interview.
41. For a discussion see ibid., Chapters 2, 5, and 10. For other examples of empowerment, see Jane Pickard, "The Real Meaning of Empowerment," *Personnel Management* (November 1993), pp. 28–31.
42. This is based on ibid., Chapter 10.
43. See Richard Wellins and Jill George, "The Key to Self-Directed Teams," *Training and Development Journal* (April 1991), pp. 26–31.
44. Richard Majuka and Timothy Baldwin, "Team-Based Employee Involvement Programs: Effects of Design and Administration," *Personnel Psychology,* Vol. 44 (1991), p. 806.
45. Dessler, *Winning Commitment,* Chapter 4. For an additional insight on developing self-managing work teams see, for example, William Pasmore and Susan Malot, "Developing Self-Managing Work Teams: An Approach to Successful Integration," *Compensation and Benefits Review* (July–August 1994), pp. 15–23.
46. This is based on ibid.
47. Personal interview.
48. Sam Johnson, "Work Teams: What's Ahead in Work Design and Rewards Management," *Compensation & Benefits Review* (March–April 1993), pp. 35–41.
49. Ibid., p. 39.
50. For other insights into making self-directed teams more effective see, for example, Glenn Thompson and Paul Pearce, "The Team-Trust Game," *Training and Development* (May 1992), pp. 42, 43; Matthew Ferrero, "Self-Directed Work Teams Untax the IRS," *Personnel Journal* (July 1994), pp. 66–71; Katherine Romano, "Death of a Salesman," *American Management Association* (September 1994), pp. 10–16; and Mary Helen Yarborough, "Team Building: A New Direction for HR," *HR Focus* (July 1994), pp. 12, 13.
51. This is based on Dean McFarlin, Paul Sweeney, and John Cotton, "Attitudes Toward Employee Participation in Decision-making: A Comparison of European and American Managers in a United States Multinational Company," *Human Resource Management,* Vol. 31, no. 4 (Winter 1992), pp. 363–383.
52. Ibid., p. 371.
53. Ibid., p. 378.

Figure 10.7
(continued)

PROBLEM ANALYSIS— Determining pertinent data, differentiating significant from less significant facts, defining interrelationships, and arriving at sound practical solutions.		
DECISION-MAKING— Evaluating and selecting among alternative courses of action quickly and accurately.		
INTERPERSONAL RELATIONS—Effectiveness in relating to others at all organizational levels. Sensitive to the needs of others.		
COMMUNICATION— Ability to get ideas across in a clear and persuasive manner. Skilled in listening to and seeking clarification of other's point of view.		
EQUAL OPPORTUNITY— Supports and implements goals of affirmative action plan for minorities and females.		

(continued)

they think it fits best. Typically, a critical incident is retained if some percentage (usually 50% to 80%) of this second group assigns it to the same cluster as did the group in step 2.

4. *Scale the incidents.* This second group is generally asked to rate the behavior described in the incident as to how effectively or ineffectively it represents performance on the appropriate dimension (seven- or nine-point scales are typical).

5. *Develop final instrument.* A subset of the incidents (usually six or seven per cluster) is used as *behavioral anchors* for each dimension.

Example   Three researchers developed a BARS for grocery checkout clerks working in a large western grocery chain.[10] They collected a number of critical incidents and then clustered them into eight performance dimensions:

KNOWLEDGE AND JUDGMENT
CONSCIENTIOUSNESS

Figure 10.7
(continued)

Performance Factors/Skills	Performance Analysis & Examples	Improvement Plan
JOB KNOWLEDGE—An understanding of the functional components of own job as well as an awareness of work relationships with other areas. Knowledge of one's specialized and technical field of work.		
SAFETY AND HEALTH— Actively promotes and upholds the Corporation's Safety & Health principles. Initiates and works for realistic goals.		

SKILL IN HUMAN RELATIONS
SKILL IN OPERATION OF REGISTER
SKILL IN BAGGING
ORGANIZATIONAL ABILITY OF CHECKSTAND WORK
SKILL IN MONETARY TRANSACTIONS
OBSERVATIONAL ABILITY

They then developed a behaviorally anchored rating scale for one of these dimensions, "knowledge and judgment." Similar to Figure 10.8, it contained a scale (ranging from 1 to 9) for rating performance from "extremely poor" to "extremely good." Notice how the typical BARS is behaviorally anchored with specific critical incidents. Thus, in the supermarket example, there was a specific critical incident ("by knowing the price of items, this checker would be expected to look for mismarked and unmarked items"); this helped anchor or specify what was meant by "extremely good" performance. Similarly, there are other critical incident anchors along the performance scale.

Dealing with the Five Main Rating Scale Appraisal Problems

Five main problems can undermine appraisal tools such as graphic rating scales: unclear standards, halo effect, central tendency, leniency or strictness, and bias.

unclear performance standards
An appraisal scale that is too open to interpretation; instead include descriptive phrases that define each trait and what is meant by standards like "good" or "unsatisfactory."

Unclear Standards The problem of **unclear standards** is illustrated in Table 10.2. Although the graphic rating scale seems objective, it would probably result in unfair appraisals because the traits and degrees of merit are open to interpretation. For example, different supervisors would probably define "good" performance, "fair" performance, and so on differently. The same is true of traits such as "quality of work" or "creativity."

There are several ways to rectify this problem. The best way is to develop and include descriptive phrases that define each trait, as in Figure 10.3. There the form specified what was meant by "outstanding," "superior," and "good" quality of work. This specificity results in appraisals that are more consistent and more easily explained.

halo effect
In performance appraisal, the problem that occurs when a supervisor's rating of a subordinate on one trait biases the rating of that person on other traits.

Halo Effect The **halo effect** means that your rating of a subordinate on one trait (such as "gets along with others") biases the way you rate that person on other traits (such as "quantity of work"). This problem often occurs with employees who are especially friendly (or unfriendly) toward the supervisor. For example, an unfriendly employee will often be rated unsatisfactory for all traits rather than just for the trait "gets along well with others." Being aware of this problem is a major step toward avoiding it. Supervisory training can also alleviate the problem.[16]

central tendency
A tendency to rate all employees the same way, such as rating them all average.

Central Tendency Many supervisors have a **central tendency** when filling in rating scales. For example, if the rating scale ranges from 1 to 7, they tend to avoid the highs (6 and 7) and lows (1 and 2) and rate most of their people between 3 and 5. If you use a graphic rating scale, this central tendency could mean that all employees are simply rated "average." Such a restriction can distort the evaluations, making them less useful for promotion, salary, or counseling purposes. Ranking employees instead of using a graphic rating scale can avoid this central tendency problem because all employees must be ranked and thus can't all be rated average.

strictness/leniency
The problem that occurs when a supervisor has a tendency to rate all subordinates either high or low.

Leniency or Strictness Some supervisors tend to rate all their subordinates consistently high (or low), just as some instructors are notoriously high graders and others are not. This **strictness/leniency** problem is especially serious with graphic rating scales since supervisors aren't necessarily required to avoid giving all their employees high (or low) ratings. On the other hand, when you must rank subordinates, you are forced to distinguish between high and low performers.

TABLE 10.2 A Graphic Rating Scale with Unclear Standards

	EXCELLENT	GOOD	FAIR	POOR
Quality of work				
Quantity of work				
Creativity				
Integrity				

Note: For example, what exactly is meant by "good," "quantity of work," and so forth?

Thus, strictness/leniency is not a problem with the ranking or forced distribution approach.

In fact, if a graphic rating scale must be used, it may be a good idea to assume a distribution of performances—that, say, only about 10% of your people should be rated "excellent," 20% "good," and so forth. In other words, try to get a spread (unless, of course, you are sure all your people really do fall into just one or two categories).

bias
The tendency to allow individual differences such as age, race, and sex to affect the appraisal rates these employees receive.

Bias   Individual differences among ratees in terms of characteristics like age, race, and sex can affect their ratings, often quite apart from each ratee's actual performance.[17] In one study, for instance, researchers found a systematic tendency to evaluate older ratees (over 60 years of age) lower on "performance capacity" and "potential for development" than younger employees.[18] The ratee's race and sex can also affect the person's rating. However, here the **bias** is not necessarily consistently against minorities or women, as it seems to be in the case of older workers. In one study, high-performing females were often rated significantly higher than were high-performing males. Similarly, low-performing blacks were often rated significantly higher than were low-performing whites.[19]

An interesting picture of how age can distort evaluations emerges from a study of registered nurses. When the nurses were 30–39 years old, they and their supervisors each rated the nurses' performance virtually the same. In the 21–29 category, supervisors actually rated nurses higher than they rated themselves. However, for the 40–61 nurse age category, the supervisors rated nurses' performance lower than the nurses rated their own performance. The conclusion here may be that supervisors are tougher in appraising older subordinates. Specifically, they don't give them as much credit for their success, while attributing any low performance to their lack of ability.[20] A related problem is described in the Diversity Counts feature.

An employee's previous performance can also affect the evaluation of his or her current performance.[21] The actual error can take several forms. Sometimes the rater may systematically overestimate improvement by a poor worker or decline by a good worker, for instance. In some situations—especially when the change in behavior is more gradual—the rater may simply be insensitive to improvement or decline. In any case, it is important when rating performance to do so objectively. Try to block out the influence of factors such as previous performance, age, or race.

How to Avoid Appraisal Problems

There are at least three ways to minimize the impact of appraisal problems such as bias and central tendency. First, be sure to be familiar with the problems as just discussed. Understanding the problem can help you avoid it.

Second, choose the right appraisal tool. Each tool, such as the graphic rating scale or critical incident method, has its own advantages and disadvantages. For example, the ranking method avoids central tendency but can cause ill feelings when employees' performances are in fact all "high" (Table 10.3).

Third, training supervisors to eliminate rating errors such as halo, leniency, and central tendency can help them avoid these problems.[24] In a typical training program, raters are shown a video tape of jobs being performed and are asked to rate the worker. Ratings made by each participant are then placed on a flip chart and the various errors (such as leniency and halo) are explained. For example, if a trainee rated all criteria (such as quality, quantity, and so on) about the same, the trainer might explain that halo error had occurred. Typically, the trainer gives the

TABLE 10.3 Important Advantages and Disadvantages of Appraisal Tools

	ADVANTAGES	DISADVANTAGES
Graphic rating scales	Simple to use; provides a quantitative rating for each employee.	Standards may be unclear; halo effect, central tendency, leniency, bias can also be problems.
Alternation ranking	Simple to use (but not as simple as graphic rating scales). Avoids central tendency and other problems of rating scales.	Can cause disagreements among employees and may be unfair if all employees *are*, in fact, excellent.
Forced distribution method	End up with a predetermined number of people in each group.	Appraisal results depend on the adequacy of your original choice of cutoff points.
Critical incident method	Helps specify what is "right" and "wrong" about the employee's performance; forces supervisor to evaluate subordinates on an ongoing basis.	Difficult to rate or rank employees relative to one another.
Behaviorally anchored rating scale	Provides behavioral "anchors." BARS is very accurate.	Difficult to develop.
MBO	Tied to jointly agreed upon performance objectives.	Time-consuming.

correct rating and then illustrates the rating errors the participants made.[25] According to one study, computer-assisted appraisal training improved managers' ability to conduct performance appraisal discussions with their subordinates.[26]

Rater training is no panacea for reducing rating errors or improving appraisal accuracy. In practice, several factors including the extent to which pay is tied to performance ratings, union pressure, employee turnover, time constraints, and the need to justify ratings may be more important than training. This means that improving appraisal accuracy calls for not just training but also reducing outside factors such as union pressure and time constraints.[27]

Legal and Ethical Issues in Performance Appraisal

Appraisal and equal employment compliance are inseparable. Since passage of Title VII courts have addressed various issues (including promotion, layoff, and compensation decisions) in which performance appraisals play a significant role.[28] As summarized in Table 10.4, courts have often found that the inadequacies of the employer's appraisal system lay at the root of an illegal discriminatory action.[29]

An illustrative case covered layoff decisions. Here the court held that the firm had violated Title VII when it laid off several Hispanic-surnamed employees on the basis of poor performance ratings.[30] The court concluded that the practice was illegal because:

1. The appraisals were based on subjective supervisory observations.
2. The appraisals were not administered and scored in a standardized fashion.
3. Two of the three supervisory evaluators did not have daily contact with the employees being evaluated.

A recent study illustrates how bias can consciously or subconsciously influence the way one person appraises another. In this study researchers sought to determine the extent to which pregnancy is a source of bias in performance appraisals.[22] The subjects consisted of a sample of 220 undergraduate students between the ages of 17 and 43 attending a midwestern university.

Two video tapes were prepared of a woman participating in several employment exercises. Each video tape showed three five-minute scenarios in which this woman interacted with another woman. For example, she acted as a customer representative to deal with an irate customer, tried to sell a computer system to a potential customer, and dealt with a problem subordinate. In each case the performance level of the "employee" was designed to be average or slightly above average. The "employee" was the same in both video tapes and the video tapes were identical except for one difference: The first video tape was made in the "employee's" ninth month of pregnancy, while the second tape was made about five months later. The aim of the study was to investigate whether or not the "employee's" pregnancy influenced the performance appraisal rating she received for dealing with the irate customer, selling the computer system, and dealing with the problem subordinate. Several groups of student raters then watched either the "pregnant" or "not pregnant" tape. They then rated the "employee" on a five-point graphic rating scale for individual characteristics such as "ability to do the job," "dependability," and "physical mannerisms." For each characteristic the employee was rated from "very poor" (1) to "excellent" (5).

The results of this study suggest that pregnant women may face additional workplace discrimination above and beyond any gender bias that may already exist against women in general. Despite having been exposed to otherwise identical behavior by the same female "employee," the student raters of this study "with a remarkably high degree of consistency" assigned lower performance ratings to a pregnant woman as opposed to a nonpregnant one.[23] Furthermore, men raters seemed more susceptible to negative influence than did women. Given the fact that most employees still report to a male supervisor and that supervisory ratings are often the determinant of one's advancement, the researchers conclude that any bias which exists could make it even harder for women to have both children and careers. One implication is that raters must be forewarned of such problems and trained to use objectivity in rating subordinates. ◆

An important aspect of this case was that the court in effect accepted performance appraisals as selection tests. In other words, they concluded that the performance appraisal procedure used by the company had to comply with EEOC employee selection guidelines and that in this case it did not. While the appraisals *were* based on the "best judgments and opinions" of the appraisers, they were *not* based on any objective criteria that were supported by any record of validity.

Does this mean the performance appraisal development process should comply with the strict guidelines for developing any test? Today most assume this is not required.[31] For example, two writers argue that insisting on such validation can be "potentially damaging as it could eventually place the profession in a position it cannot satisfactorily defend.[32] However, do keep in mind that all the appraisal problems discussed above can undermine the legal defensibility of an appraisal.[33] To the extent that a supervisor unreasonably rates everyone toward the high (or low), allows the halo effect, practices personal bias, or relies solely on more recent events, courts have and will view the appraisal and subsequent personnel decision as indefensible.[34]

TABLE 10.4 Appraisal: A Summary of Court Cases and Significant Rulings

CASE	YEAR	COURT	PREVAILING PARTY	SIGNIFICANT RULING(S)
Griggs v. Duke Power Company	1971	Supreme	Employee	EEOC guidelines first endorsed. Adverse impact requires demonstration of job relatedness. Employer intent to discriminate irrelevant.
Marquez v. Omaha District Sales Office, Ford Division of the Ford Motor Company	1971	Appeals, 8th Circuit	Employee	Documentation necessary. Misuse of legal appraisal system may violate Title VII.
Rowe v. General Motors	1972	Appeals, 5th Circuit	Employee	Lack of appraiser training condemned. Subjective performance standards condemned. Communication of performance standards required.
Brito v. Zia Company	1973	Appeals, 10th Circuit	Employee	Performance appraisals are "employment tests." Adverse impact requires demonstration of validity of appraisal system. Objective performance standards should supplement subjective standards. Standardized administration and scoring of appraisals required.
Wade v. Mississippi Cooperative Extension Service	1974	District	Employee	Job analysis required. Appraisal on general traits condemned.
Albemarle Paper Company v. Moody	1975	Supreme	Employee	Appraisals as criteria must be job related. Endorsement of EEOC guidelines regarding criterion development.
Patterson v. American Tobacco Company	1978	Appeals, 4th Circuit	Employee	Job analysis necessary. Objective performance standards required.
Ramirez v. Hofheinz	1980	Appeals, 5th Circuit	Organization	Subjective performance standards supported. Past record of employer important.
Carpenter v. Stephen F. Austin State University	1983	Appeals, 5th Circuit	Employee	Updated analysis. Performance standards required to be demonstrably job related. Appraiser training required.
Chamberlain v. Bissel, Inc.	1982	District	Employee	Failure to warn of declining performance in evaluations
Grant v. C&P Telephone Co.	1984	District Court of DC	Organization	The plaintiff's work records were not only reviewed by upper-level personnel, he was warned repeatedly that termination was imminent if his work did not improve.
Nord v. U.S. Steel	1985	11th Circuit	Employee	The plaintiff successfully demonstrated that she had good performance appraisals before requesting a promotion. After request, her appraisals became negative, leading to her eventual termination.
John F. Winslow v. Federal Energy Regulatory Commission	1987	District	Employee	Employer's lack of documentation undermined employer's credibility.
Romei v. Shell Oil Co.	1991	New York Superior Court	Employee	Raises possibility that employer can be sued for libel for what is put in performance appraisal.

Sources: Based on Sami M. Abbasi, Kenneth W. Hollman, and Joe H. Murrey, Jr., "Employment at Will: An Eroding Concept in Employment Relationships," Labor Law Journal, Vol. 38, no. 1 (January 1987), pp. 26–27; Gerald Barrett and Mary Kernan, "Performance Appraisal and Terminations: A Review of Court Decisions Since Brito v. Zia with Implications for Personnel Practices," Personnel Psychology, Vol. 40, no. 3 (Autumn 1987), pp. 489–501; David Martin and Kathryn Bartol, "The Legal Ramifications of Performance Appraisal: An Update," Employee Relations Law Journal, Vol. 17, no. 2 (Autumn 1991), pp. 257–286.

Finally, remember that as in most human endeavors being legal doesn't always equal being ethical, yet ethics should be the bedrock of a performance appraisal. In fact most managers (and college students) understand that an appraiser or professor can "stick to the rules" and conduct a lawful review of one's performance but still fail to provide an honest assessment. As one commentator puts it:

> *The overall objective of high-ethics performance reviews should be to provide an honest assessment of performance and to mutually develop a plan to improve the individual's effectiveness. That requires that we tell people where they stand and that we be straight with them.*[35]

And, of course, it's exactly this type of honest and fruitful appraisal—not merely a legal one—that managers should shoot for. Guidelines for developing a legally defensible appraisal process include the following:[36]

1. Conduct a job analysis to ascertain characteristics (such as "timely project completion") required for successful job performance. Graphically:

$$\begin{array}{ccc} \text{Job} & & \text{Performance} & & \text{Performance} \\ \text{Analysis} & \rightarrow & \text{Standards} & \rightarrow & \text{Appraisal} \end{array}$$

2. Incorporate these characteristics into a rating instrument. (Note that while the professional literature recommends rating instruments that are tied to specific job behaviors, that is, BARS, the courts routinely accept less sophisticated approaches such as graphic rating scales.)

3. Make sure that definitive performance standards are provided to all raters and ratees.

4. Use clearly defined individual dimensions of job performance (like "quantity" or "quality") rather than undefined, global measures of job performance (like "overall performance").

5. When using graphic rating scales, avoid abstract trait names (for example, "loyalty," "honesty") unless they can be defined in terms of observable behaviors.

6. Employ subjective supervisory ratings (essays, for instance) as only one component of the overall appraisal process.

7. Train supervisors to use the rating instrument properly. Give instructions on how to apply performance appraisal standards ("outstanding," and so on) when making judgments. In six of ten cases decided against the employer, the plaintiffs were able to show that subjective standards had been applied unevenly to minority and majority employees.[37]

8. Allow appraisers substantial daily contact with the employee being evaluated.

9. Whenever possible, have more than one appraiser conduct the appraisal and conduct all such appraisals independently. This process can help to cancel out individual errors and biases.

10. Utilize formal appeal mechanisms and a review of ratings by upper-level personnel.

11. Document evaluations and reasons for any termination decision.

12. Where appropriate, provide corrective guidance to assist poor performers in improving their performance. Courts look favorably on this practice.

Who Should Do the Appraising?

Who should actually rate an employee's performance? Several options exist.

Appraisal by the Immediate Supervisor Supervisors' ratings still are the heart of most appraisal systems. Getting a supervisor's appraisal is relatively easy and also makes a great deal of sense. The supervisor should be—and usually is—in the best position to observe and evaluate his or her subordinate's performance and is responsible for that person's performance.

Using Peer Appraisals The appraisal of an employee by his or her peers can be effective in predicting future management success. From a study of military officers, for example, we know that peer ratings were quite accurate in predicting which officers would be promoted and which would not.[38] In another study that involved more than 200 industrial managers, peer ratings were similarly useful in predicting who would be promoted.[39] One potential problem is *logrolling*. Here all the peers simply get together to rate each other high.

With more firms using self-managing teams, peer or team appraisals are becoming more popular. At Digital Equipment Corporation, for example, an employee due for an appraisal chooses an appraisal chairperson each year. This person then selects one supervisor and three other peers to evaluate the employee's work.[40]

Rating Committees Many employers use rating committees to evaluate employees. These committees are usually composed of the employee's immediate supervisor and three or four other supervisors.

This food service supervisor is conducting a feedback session about his employee's performance during today's major banquet, not only to gain information about his performance but also to keep communications open and build employee commitment.

Using multiple raters can be advantageous. While there may be a discrepancy in the ratings made by individual supervisors, the composite ratings tend to be more reliable, fair, and valid.[41] Several raters can help cancel out problems like bias and the halo effect on the part of individual raters. Furthermore, when there *are* differences in raters' ratings, they usually stem from the fact that raters at different levels often observe different facets of an employee's performance; the appraisal ought to reflect these differences.[42] Even when a committee is not used, it is common to have the appraisal reviewed by the manager immediately above the one who makes the appraisal. This was found to be standard practice in 16 of 18 companies surveyed in one study.[43]

Self-ratings Employees' Self-ratings of performance are also sometimes used (usually in conjunction with supervisors' ratings). The basic problem with these is that employees usually rate themselves higher than they are rated by supervisors or peers.[44] In one study, for example, it was found that when asked to rate their own job performances, 40% of the employees in jobs of all types placed themselves in the top 10% ("one of the best"), while virtually all remaining employees rated themselves either in the top 25% ("well above average"), or at least in the top 50% ("above average"). Usually no more than 1% or 2% will place themselves in a below-average category, and then almost invariably in the top below-average category.

Supervisors requesting self-appraisals should know that their appraisals and the self-appraisals may accentuate appraiser-appraisee differences, and rigidify positions.[45] Furthermore, even if self-appraisals are not formally requested, each employee will enter the performance review meeting with his or her own self-appraisal in mind, and this will usually be higher than the supervisor's rating.

Appraisal by Subordinates More firms today let subordinates anonymously evaluate their supervisors' performance, a process many call *upward feedback*.[46] When conducted throughout the firm, the process helps top managers diagnose management styles, identify potential "people" problems, and take corrective action with individual managers as required. Such subordinate ratings are especially valuable when used for developmental rather than evaluative purposes.[47] Managers who receive feedback from subordinates who identify themselves view the upward appraisal process more positively than do manages who receive anonymous feedback; however, subordinates (not surprisingly) are more comfortable giving anonymous responses and those who have to identify themselves tend to provide inflated ratings.[48]

Federal Express uses an upward appraisal system called Survey Feedback Action (SFA). SFA has three phases. First, the survey itself (a standard, anonymous form) is given each year to every employee. It contains items designed to gather information about those things that help and hinder employees in their work environment. Sample items include: I can tell my manager what I think; my manager tells me what is expected; my manager listens to my concerns; my manager keeps me informed; upper management listens to ideas from my level; Fed Ex does a good job for our customers; in my environment we use safe work practices; and I am paid fairly for this kind of work. Results of the survey for a work group are then compiled and returned to the manager. To ensure anonymity the smaller units do *not* receive their own results. Instead their results are folded in with those of several other similar work units until a department of 20 or 25 people obtains the overall group's results.

A feedback session between the manager and his or her work group is the second phase. The session's goal is to identify specific concerns or problems, examine specific causes for these problems, and devise action plans to correct the problems. As a result, managers are trained to ask probing questions. For example, suppose a low-scoring survey item was, "I feel free to tell my manager what I think." Managers are trained to ask their groups questions such as "What constrains you?" (timing, specific behaviors); and "What do I do that makes you feel that I'm not interested?"

The feedback meeting should lead to a third, "action plan" phase. The plan itself is a list of actions that the manager will take to address employees' concerns and boost results. Managers thus get an action-planning worksheet containing four columns: (1) What is the concern? (2) What's your analysis? (3) What's the cause? (4) What should be done?

360-degree Feedback   Many firms have expanded the idea of upward feedback into what they call 360-degree feedback; here performance information is collected "all around" an employee, from his or her supervisors, subordinates, peers, and internal or external customers.[49] The feedback is generally used for training and development, rather than for pay increases.[50]

Most 360-degree feedback systems contain several common features. Appropriate parties—peers, supervisors, subordinates, and customers, for instance—complete survey questionnaires on an individual. The questionnaires can take many forms but often include supervisory skill items such as "returns phone calls promptly," "listens well," or, as at Fed Ex, "[my manager] keeps me informed."[51] Computerized systems then compile all this feedback into individualized reports that are prepared and presented to the person being rated. The ratees are often the only ones who get these completed reports. They then meet with their own supervisors and sometimes with their subordinates and share the informtion they feel is pertinent for the purpose of developing a self-improvement plan.[52]

The Appraisal Interview

Main Types of Interviews

appraisal interview
An interview in which the supervisor and subordinate review the appraisal and make plans to remedy deficiencies and reinforce strengths.

An appraisal typically culminates in an **appraisal interview.** This is an interview in which the supervisor and subordinate review the appraisal and make plans to remedy deficiencies and reinforce strengths. There are three basic types of appraisal interviews, each with its own objectives:[53]

Appraisal Interview Type	Appraisal Interview Objective
(1) Performance is satisfactory— Employee is promotable	(1) Make development plans
(2) Satisfactory—Not promotable	(2) Maintain performance
(3) Unsatisfactory—Correctable	(3) Plan correction

If the employee is unsatisfactory and the situation uncorrectable, there is usually no need for any appraisal interview because the person's performance is not correctable anyway. The person's poor performance is either tolerated for now, or he or she is dismissed.

Satisfactory—Promotable   Here the person's performance is satisfactory and there is a promotion ahead. This is the easiest of the three appraisal interviews. Your objective is to discuss the person's career plans and to develop a specific action plan for the educational and professional development the person needs to move to the next job.

Satisfactory—Not Promotable   This interview is for employees whose performance is satisfactory but for whom promotion is not possible. Perhaps there is no more room in the company. Some employees are also happy where they are and don't want a promotion.[54] Your objective here is not to improve or develop the person but to maintain satisfactory performance.

This is not easy. The best option is usually to find incentives that are important to the person and enough to maintain satisfactory performance. These might include extra time off, a small bonus, additional authority to handle a slightly enlarged job, and reinforcement, perhaps in the form of an occasional "Well done!"

Unsatisfactory—Correctable   When the person's performance is unsatisfactory but correctable, the interview objective is to lay out an action plan (as explained later) for correcting the unsatisfactory performance.

How to Prepare for the Appraisal Interview

There are three things to do in preparation for the interview.[55] First, assemble the data. Study the person's job description, compare the employee's performance to the standards, and review the files of the employee's previous appraisals. Next prepare the employee. Give your employees at least a week's notice to review their work, read over their job descriptions, analyze problems, and gather their questions and comments. Finally, choose the time and place. Find a mutually agreeable time for the interview and allow enough time for the entire interview. Interviews with lower-level personnel like clerical workers and maintenance staff should take no more than an hour. Appraising management employees often takes two or three hours. Be sure the interview is done in a private place where you won't be interrupted by phone calls or visitors.

How to Conduct the Interview

There are four things to keep in mind here:[56]

1. *Be direct and specific.* Talk in terms of objective work data. Use examples such as absences, tardiness, quality records, inspection reports, scrap or waste, orders processed, productivity records, material used or consumed, timeliness of tasks or projects, control or reduction of costs, numbers of errors, costs compared to budgets, customers' comments, product returns, order processing time, inventory level and accuracy, accident reports, and so on.

2. *Don't get personal.* Don't say "You're too slow in producing those reports." Instead try to compare the person's performance to a standard ("These reports should normally be done within ten days"). Similarly, don't compare the person's performance to that of other people ("He's quicker than you are").

3. *Encourage the person to talk.* Stop and listen to what the person is saying; ask open-ended questions such as "What do you think we can do to improve the situation?" Use a command such as "Go on" or "Tell me more." Restate the person's last point as a question, such as, "You don't think you can get the job done?"

4. *Don't tiptoe around.* Don't get personal, but do make sure the person leaves knowing specifically what he or she is doing right *and doing wrong.* Give specific examples; make sure the person understands; and get agreement before he or she leaves on how things will be improved, and by when. Develop an action plan showing steps and expected results as in Figure 10.10.

**Figure 10.10
Example of an Action
Plan**

ACTION PLAN

Date: May 18, 1997

For: John, Assistant Plant Manager

Problem: Parts inventory too high

Objective: Reduce plant parts inventory by 10% in June

Action Steps	When	Expected Results
Determine average monthly parts inventory	6/2	Established a base from which to measure progress
Review ordering quantities and parts usage	6/15	Identify overstock items
Ship excess parts to regional warehouse and scrap obsolete parts	6/20	Clear stock space
Set new ordering quantities for all parts	6/25	Avoid future overstocking
Check records to measure where we are now	7/1	See how close we are to objective

How to Handle a Defensive Subordinate Defenses are a very important and familiar aspect of our lives. When a person is accused of poor performance, the first reaction will sometimes be *denial*. By denying the fault, the person avoids having to question his or her own competence. Others react to criticism with *anger* and *aggression*. This helps them let off steam and postpones confronting the immediate problem until they are able to cope with it. Still others react to criticism by *retreating* into a shell.

In any event, understanding and dealing with defensiveness is an important appraisal skill. In his book *Effective Psychology for Managers,* psychologist Mortimer Feinberg suggests the following:

1. *Recognize that defensive behavior is normal.*
2. *Never attack a person's defenses.* Don't try to "explain someone to themselves" by saying things like, "You know the real reason you're using that excuse is that you can't bear to be blamed for anything." Instead try to concentrate on the act itself ("sales are down") rather than on the person ("you're not selling enough").
3. *Postpone action.* Sometimes it is best to do nothing at all. People frequently react to sudden threats by instinctively hiding behind their "masks." But, given sufficient time, a more rational reaction takes over.
4. *Recognize your own limitations.* Don't expect to be able to solve every problem that comes up, especially the human ones. More important, remember that a supervisor should not try to be a psychologist. Offering your people understanding is one thing; trying to deal with deep psychological problems is another matter entirely.

Argumentative behavior on the part of the manager during a performance appraisal meeting undermines the usefulness of the evaluation process.

How to Criticize a Subordinate When criticism is required, it should be done in a manner that lets the person maintain his or her dignity and sense of worth. Specifically, criticism should be done in private and should be done constructively. Provide examples of critical incidents and specific suggestions of what could be done and why. Avoid once-a-year "critical broadsides" by giving feedback on a daily basis, so that at the formal review there are no surprises. Never say the person is "always" wrong (since no one is ever "always" wrong or right). Finally, criticism should be objective and free of any personal biases on your part.

How to Ensure That the Appraisal Interview Leads to Improved Performance
You should clear up job-related problems and set improvement goals and a schedule for achieving them. In one study the researchers found that whether or not subordinates expressed satisfaction with their appraisal interview depended mostly on three factors: not feeling threatened during the interview; having an opportunity to present their ideas and feelings and to influence the course of the interview; and having a helpful and constructive supervisor conduct the interview.[57]

However, you don't just want subordinates to be satisfied with their appraisal interviews. Your main aim is to get them to improve their subsequent performance. Here researchers found that *clearing up job-related problems* with the appraisee and *setting measurable performance targets and a schedule for achieving them*—an action plan—were the actions that consistently led to improved performance.

How to Handle a Formal Written Warning There will be times when an employee's performance is so poor that a formal written warning is required. Such written warnings serve two purposes: (1) They may serve to shake your employee out of his or her bad habits, and (2) they can help you defend your rating of the employee both to your own boss and (if needed) to the courts. Thus, written warnings should identify the standards under which the employee is judged, make it clear that the employee was aware of the standard, specify any violation of the standard, and show the employee had an opportunity to correct his or her behavior.

Performance Appraisal in Practice

How do most employers actually appraise performance? A survey of current practice suggests the following:[58]

Almost all companies responding do have formal appraisal programs. About 93% of smaller organizations (those with fewer than 500 employees) have such programs. About 97% of large organizations have them.

Rating scales are by far the most widely used appraisal technique. About 62% of small organizations use rating scales, 20% use essays, and about 19% use MBO. Among large organizations, 51% use rating scales, just over 23% use essays, and about 17% use MBO.

However, those using ratings as the main appraisal technique typically also require narrative comments to justify ratings and to describe employee strengths and weaknesses and document development plans.[59] Those using essays as the main appraisal technique usually require an overall quantitative performance rating to facilitate employee comparisons for compensation decisions.

Ninety-two percent of appraisals are made by the employee's immediate supervisor. These appraisals are in turn reviewed by the appraiser's supervisor in 74% of the responding organizations.

Only about 7% of the organizations use self-appraisal in any part of the overall appraisal process.

Virtually all employees (99%) are informed of the results of their appraisals. Overall, about 77% are given a chance to respond with written comments on their appraisals.

In 69% of companies, appraisals are done annually.

Instructions are important: 82% of employers provide written instructions for appraisers, and 60% provide training.

The Role of Appraisals in Managing Performance

Appraisals serve several purposes including providing information upon which promotion and salary decisions are made. Ideally, however, appraisals should also serve a *managing performance* role, by providing a concrete basis for an analysis of an employee's work-related peformance and the steps that should be taken to maintain or change it. Therefore, we turn in this final section to a discussion of how appraisals can be done to better manage employee performance.

Should Appraisals Be Abolished?

Many experts feel that traditional appraisals don't help in managing performance and may actually backfire. They argue that most performance appraisal systems neither motivate employees nor guide their development.[60] Furthermore, ". . . they cause conflict between supervisors and subordinates and lead to dysfunctional behaviors."[61] The traits measured are often personal in nature and ". . . Who likes the idea of being evaluated on his or her: honesty, integrity, teamwork, compassion, cooperation [objectivity]. . . ?"[62]

Similarly, proponents of total quality management programs (including the late W. Edwards Deming) generally argue for eliminating performance appraisals.[63] They argue that the organization is a system of interrelated parts and that an employee's performance is more a function of factors like training, communication, tools, and supervision than of his or her own motivation.[64] They also argue that performance appraisals can have unanticipated consequences. Thus, employees might make themselves look better in terms of customer service by continually badgering customers to send in letters of support. Deming particularly argued against forced distribution appraisal systems because of their potential for undermining teamwork.[65]

Criticisms like these appear to be supported by surveys of how managers view appraisal systems. In one study of almost 300 managers from midwestern companies, 32% rated their performance appraisals as "very ineffective," while only 4% rated them "effective to a large extent."[66] Another survey of 181 manufacturing and service organizations concluded that 11% had stopped using annual appraisals, while another 25% planned to discontinue them within two years.[67] There's probably not much doubt that most appraisals are viewed with trepidation if not disdain.

Yet while these criticisms have merit, it's not practical to eliminate performance appraisals. Managers still need some way to review subordinates' work-related behavior. And, although Deming reportedly hated performance reviews, ". . . he really didn't offer any concrete solution to the problem or an alternative, other than just pay everybody at the same salary."[68] The solution instead is to create performance appraisal systems that make it possible to manage performance in today's team-oriented and quality-oriented environments. Creating more effective appraisals as described in this chapter is one way to do this. Others suggest also taking a TQM-based approach, to which we now turn.

TQM-Based Appraisals for Managing Performance

Total quality management (TQM) programs are organizationwide programs that integrate all functions and processes of the business such that all aspects of the business including design, planning, production, distribution, and field service are aimed at maximizing customer satisfaction through continuous improvements.[69] Deming said such programs are built on a number of principles, including: Cease dependence on inspection to achieve quality; aim for continuous improvement; institute extensive training on the job; drive out fear so that everyone may work effectively for the company; break down barriers between departments; eliminate work standards (quotas) on the factory floor; remove barriers that rob employees of their right to pride of workmanship (in particular, abolish the annual merit rating and all forms of management by objectives); and institute a vigorous program of education and self-improvement.[70]

TQM principles like these can be applied to designing TQM-based performance management systems. A *performance management system* can be defined as a performance appraisal system that does not force managers to give false or misleading measurements and instead facilitates open, job-related discussions between the supervisor and the employee.[71] The characteristics of such a TQM-based performance management system would include:

An appraisal scale that contains relatively few performance categories and avoids a forced distribution.[72]

Objective ways to measure results, avoiding subjective criteria such as teamwork and integrity.[73]

A determination about whether any performance deficiency is a result of (1) employee motivation, (2) inadequate training, or (3) factors (like poor supervision) that are outside the employee's control.

360-degree feedback from a number of different sources, not just supervisors but internal and possibly external "customers" of the employee as well.[74]

Adequate "samples" of work behavior—, "regular observations of their staff members' work behaviors and performance."[75]

An atmosphere of partnership and constructive advice.[76]

A thorough analysis of key external and internal customers' needs and expectations on which to base performance appraisal standards. (For example, if accurately completing the sales slip is important for the accounting department, then the retail sales clerk should be appraised in part on this dimension).

A form for implementing such a TQM-based performance management system is shown in Figure 10.11. As you can see, it consists of a performance contract specifying customer expectations and performance goals, as well as an internal customer feedback form.[77]

**Figure 10.11
Performance Contract
and Internal Customer
Feedback Forms**

Source: David Antonion, "Improving the Performance Management Process Before Discontinuing Performance Appraisals," *Compensation and Benefits Review* (May–June 1994), p. 33, 34.

PERFORMANCE CONTRACT

Within the next year, I understand that our organization's objectives are _____ _____

and that the goals of our department are _____ . I also understand that our work unit goals are _____ .

My key internal customers are _____ and their work needs and expectations are _____ .

To make my contribution toward attaining the goals stated above, I understand that I am expected to do the following:

My individual performance goals are _____ .

My goals for improving work methods (process) are _____ .

My goals for improving specific interpersonal work behaviors when I interact with the following _____ are _____ .

I believe these goals are acceptable and attainable. I also understand that I will be evaluated by multiple appraisal sources (supervisor, peers, internal, and, if appropriate, external customers).

Compensation for my work performance will be based on whether my performance was (1) outstanding, (2) fully competent, or (3) unsatisfactory. I understand that the following forms of compensation will be considered: (1) merit award for my individual performance goal attainment, (2) enhancement and utilization of my skills, (3) my work unit's or team's performance (gainsharing), and (4) our organization's performance (profit sharing).

_____   _____
Your signature   Supervisor's signature

(continued)

Figure 10.11
(continued)

INTERNAL CUSTOMER FEEDBACK

As an internal customer of (name)_____ , please give him/her feedback regarding his/her work performance and work behaviors. After you have completed this form, send it to _____ . Your reponses will be tabulated and then discussed with the individual.

To what extent did this individual meet your expectations of work quality in the areas you indicate as important:

	Exceeds	Meets	Doesn't Meet
1. Accuracy of the work you received			
2. Timeliness of the work you received			
3. Dependability of the work you received			
4. Sharing relevant information to help you do your work more efficiently			

In terms of your interactions with this person, please feel free to comment on any of the following:

1. The type of errors and the amount of rework

2. The nature of any work delays

3. Collaborative efforts to improve work or bussiness processes

4. Interpersonal work behaviors

Please list any *new* expectations that you have regarding the work you receive from this person.

Thank you for completing this feedback form. A follow-up interview with you may be established to discuss the feedback, and, if necessary, improvement goals and an action plan will be developed.

Chapter Review

Summary

1. People want and need feedback regarding how they are doing, and appraisal provides an opportunity for you to give them that feedback.
2. Before the appraisal, make sure to clarify the performance you expect so that the employee knows what he or she should be shooting for. Ask "What do I really expect this person to do?"

3. Performance appraisal tools include the graphic rating scale, alternation ranking method, forced distribution method, BARS, MBO, and critical incident method.

4. Appraisal problems to beware of include unclear standards, halo effect, central tendency, leniency or strictness problem, and bias.

5. Most subordinates probably want a specific explanation or examples regarding why they were appraised high or low, and for this, compiling a record of positive and negative critical incidents can be useful. Even if your firm requires that you summarize the appraisal in a form like a graphic rating scale, a list of critical incidents can be useful when the time comes to discuss the appraisal with your subordinate.

6. The subordinate should view the appraisal as a fair one, and in this regard there are four things to do: Evaluate his or her performance frequently; make sure you are familiar with the person's performance; make sure there is an agreement between you and your subordinate concerning his or her job duties; and finally, solicit the person's help when you formulate plans for eliminating performance weaknesses.

7. There are three types of appraisal interviews. When performance is unsatisfactory but correctable the objective is to lay out an action plan for correcting performance. For employees whose performance is satisfactory but for whom promotion is not possible the objective is to maintain satisfactory performance. Finally, the satisfactory—promotable interview has the main objective to discuss the person's career plans and to develop a specific action plan for the educational and professional development the person needs to move on to the next job.

8. To prepare for the appraisal interview, assemble the data, prepare the employee, and choose the time and place.

9. To bring about constructive change in your subordinate's behavior, get the person to talk in the interview. Try silence, use open-ended questions, state questions in terms of a problem, use a command question, use choice questions to try to understand the feelings underlying what the person is saying, and restate the person's last point as a question. On the other hand, don't do all the talking, don't use restrictive questions, don't be judgmental, don't give free advice, and don't get involved with name calling, ridicule, or sarcasm.

10. The best way to handle a defensive subordinate is to proceed very carefully. Specifically, recognize that defensive behavior is normal, never attack a person's defenses, postpone actions, and recognize your own limitations.

11. The most important thing you should aim to accomplish is to clear up job-related problems and set improvement goals and a schedule for achieving them.

12. Appraisals should also ideally serve a managing performance role by providing a concrete basis for an analysis of an employee's work-related performance. Creating more effective appraisals as described in this chapter is one way to accomplish this. Others suggest also taking a TQM-based approach. Characteristics of such an approach include: making the appraisal scale as broadly descriptive as possible so that it contains relatively few performance categories and avoids a forced distribution; measures results objectively; specifically identifies if the performance deficiency is a result of motivation, training, or factors outside the employee's control; uses 360 degree feedback; includes adequate samples of work behavior; addresses problems in an atmosphere of partnership and constructive advice; and bases performance standards on an analysis of key external and internal customers' needs and expectations.

Key Terms

graphic rating scale
alternation ranking
   method
paired comparison
   method
forced distribution
   method

critical incident method
behaviorally anchored
   rating scale (BARS)
management by
   objectives (MBO)
unclear performance
   standards

halo effect
central tendency
strictness/leniency
bias
appraisal interviews

Discussion Questions and Exercises

1. Discuss the pros and cons of at least four performance appraisal tools.
2. Working individually or in groups, develop a graphic rating scale for the following jobs: secretary, engineer, directory assistance operator.
3. Working individually or in groups, evaluate the rating scale in Figure 10.1. Discuss ways to improve it.
4. Explain how you would use the alternation ranking method, the paired comparison method, and the forced distribution method.
5. Working individually or in groups, develop, over the period of a week, a set of critical incidents covering the classroom performance of one of your instructors.
6. Explain in your own words how you would go about developing a behaviorally anchored rating scale.
7. Explain the problems to be avoided in appraising performance.
8. Discuss the pros and cons of using different potential raters to appraise a person's performance.
9. Explain the four types of appraisal interview objectives and how they affect the way you manage the interview.
10. Explain how to conduct an appraisal interview.
11. Answer the question: "How would you get the interviewee to talk during an appraisal interview?"

Application Exercises

RUNNING CASE: Carter Cleaning Company
The Performance Appraisal

After spending several weeks on the job, Jennifer was surprised to discover that her father had not formally evaluated any employee's performance for all the years that he had owned the business. Jack's position was that he had "a hundred higher-priority things to attend to," such as boosting sales and lowering costs, and, in any case, many employees didn't stick around long enough to be appraisable anyway. Furthermore, contended Jack, manual workers such as those doing the pressing and the cleaning did periodically get positive feedback in terms of praise from Jack for a job well done or criticism, also from Jack, if things did not look right during one of his swings through the stores. Similarly, Jack was never shy about telling his managers about store problems so that they, too, got some feedback on where they stood.

This informal feedback notwithstanding, Jennifer believes that a more formal appraisal approach is needed. She believes that there are criteria such as quality, quantity, attendance, and punctuality that should be evaluated periodically even if a worker is paid on piece rate. Furthermore, she feels quite strongly that the managers need to have a list of quality standards for matters such as store cleanliness, efficiency, safety, and adherence to budget on which they know they are to be formally evaluated.

Questions

1. Is Jennifer right about the need to evaluate the workers formally? The managers? Why or why not?
2. Develop a performance appraisal method for the workers and managers in each store.

CASE INCIDENT: Appraising the Secretaries at Sweetwater U

Rob Winchester, newly appointed vice president for administrative affairs at Sweetwater State University, faced a tough problem shortly after his university career began. Three weeks after he came on board in September, Sweetwater's president, Rob's boss, told Rob that one of his first tasks was to improve the appraisal system used to evaluate secretarial and clerical performance at Sweetwater U. Apparently, the main difficulty was that the performance appraisal was traditionally tied directly to salary increases given at the end of the year. So most administrators were less than accurate when they used the graphic rating forms that were the basis of the clerical staff evaluation. In fact, what usually happened was that each administrator simply rated his or her clerk or secretary as "excellent." This cleared the way for all support staff to receive a maximum pay increase every year.

But the current university budget simply did not include enough money to fund another "maximum" annual increase for every staffer. Furthermore, Sweetwater's president felt that the custom of providing invalid feedback to each secretary on his or her year's performance was not productive, so he had asked the new vice president to revise the system. In October, Rob sent a memo to all administrators telling them that in the future no more than half the secretaries reporting to any particular administrator could be appraised as "excellent." This move, in effect, forced each supervisor to begin ranking his or her secretaries for quality of performance. The vice president's memo met widespread resistance immediately—from administrators, who were afraid that many of their secretaries would begin leaving for more lucrative jobs in private industry, and from secretaries, who felt that the new system was unfair and reduced each secretary's chance of receiving a maximum salary increase. A handful of secretaries had begun quietly picketing outside the president's home on the university campus. The picketing, caustic remarks by disgruntled administrators, and rumors of an impending slowdown by the secretaries (there were about 250 on the campus) made Rob Winchester wonder whether he had made the right decision by setting up forced ranking. He knew, however, that there were a few performance appraisal experts in the School of Business, so he decided to set up an appointment with them to discuss the matter.

He met with them the next morning. He explained the situation as he had found it: The present appraisal system had been set up when the university first opened ten years earlier, and the appraisal form had been developed primarily by a committee of secretaries. Under that system, Sweetwater's administrators filled out forms similar to the one shown in Table 10.2. This once-a-year appraisal (in March) had run into problems almost immediately, since it was apparent from the start that administrators varied widely in their interpretations of job standards, as well as in how conscientiously they filled out the forms and supervised their secretaries. Moreover, at the end of the first year it became obvious to everyone that each secretary's salary increase was tied directly to the March appraisal. For example, those rated "excellent" received the maximum increases, those rated "good" received smaller increases, and those given neither rating received only the standard across-the-board cost-of-living increase. Since universities in general—and Sweetwater U in particular—have paid secretaries somewhat lower salaries than those prevailing in private industry, some secretaries left in a huff that first year. From that time on most administrators simply rated all secretaries excellent in order to reduce staff turnover, thus ensuring each a maximum increase. In the process, they also avoided the hard feelings aroused by the significant performance differences otherwise highlighted by administrators.

Two Sweetwater experts agreed to consider the problem, and in two weeks they came back to the vice president with the following recommendations. First, the form used to rate the secretaries was grossly insufficient. It was unclear what "excellent" or "quality of work" meant, for example. They recommended instead a form like that in Figure 10.3. In addition, they recommended that the vice president rescind his earlier memo and no longer attempt to force university administrators arbitrarily to rate at least half their secretaries as something less than excellent. The two consultants pointed out that this was, in fact, an unfair procedure since it was quite possible that any particular administrator might have staffers who were all or virtually all excellent—or conceivably, although less likely, all below standard. The experts said that the way to get all the administrators to take the appraisal process more seriously was to stop tying it to salary increases. In other words, they recommended that every administrator fill out a form like that in Figure 10.3 for each secretary at least once a year and then use this form as the basis of a counseling session. Salary increases would have to be made on some basis other than the performance appraisal, so that administrators would no longer hesitate to fill out the rating forms honestly.

Rob thanked the two experts and went back to his office to ponder their recommendations. Some of the recommendations (such as substituting the new rating form for the old) seemed to make sense. Nevertheless, he still had serious doubts as to the efficacy of any graphic rating form, particularly if he were to decide in favor of his original forced ranking approach. The experts' second recommendation—to stop tying the appraisals to automatic salary increases—made sense but raised at least one very practical problem: If salary increases were not to be based on performance appraisals, on what were they to be based? He began wondering whether the experts' recommendations weren't simply based on ivory tower theorizing.

Questions

1. Do you think that the experts' recommendations will be sufficient to get most of the administra-

tors to fill out the rating forms properly? Why? Why not? What additional actions (if any) do you think will be necessary?

2. Do you think that Vice President Winchester would be better off dropping graphic rating forms, substituting instead one of the other techniques we discussed in this chapter such as a ranking method?

3. What performance appraisal system would you develop for the secretaries if you were Rob Winchester? Defend your answer.

 # Human Resource Management Simulation

Your firm does not currently have a formal performance appraisal system. Some employees complain that the supervisors and managers give raises and perks to those they like and not necessarily to those who are most productive. Decreased turnover, increased morale, and higher productivity should result from a formal performance appraisal system.

In addition, incident (E) will provide several options for creating your own performance appraisal

program. An important aspect of your selection will be to answer the question "Who should do the appraising?" Your team should discuss the consequences of each alternative. You will also be required to select the type of rating scale you are going to use. Because your firm has never had a formal appraisal system, should you select one that is straightforward and simple, or a more complex scale that will do the job in the longer run?

Video Case

Back with a Vengeance

As this videocase emphasizes, conducting an effective appraisal interview is always important. However, an appraisal can have life-and-death implications when dealing with unstable employees, particularly those people who must be dismissed. In this case a terminated employee came back and shot and killed several managers who had been instrumental in the former employee's dismissal. The videocase shows that this person had a history as a troublemaker and that many clues regarding his unstable nature over many years had been ignored.

Questions

1. Could a company with an effective appraisal process have missed so many signals of instability over several years? Why or why not?

2. What safeguards would you build into your appraisal process to avoid missing such potentially tragic signs of instability and danger?

3. What would you do if confronted during an appraisal interview by someone who began making veiled threats regarding his or her use of firearms?

Source: ABC News, *Back With a Vengeance,* "20/20," April 16, 1993.

 ## Take It to the Net

We invite you to visit the Dessler page on the Prentice Hall Web site at:
http://www.prenhall.com/~dessler
for the monthly Dessler update, and for this chapter's World Wide Web exercise.

Notes

1. Kenneth Teel, "Performance Appraisal: Current Trends, Persistent Progress," *Personnel Journal* (April 1980), pp. 296–301. See also Christina Banks and Kevin Murphy, "Toward Narrowing the Research-Practice Gap in Performance Appraisals," *Personnel Psychology,* Vol. 38, no. 2 (Summer 1985), pp. 335–346. For a description of how to implement an improved performance appraisal system, see, for example, Ted Cocheu, "Performance Appraisal: A Case in Point," *Personnel Journal,* Vol. 65, no. 9 (September 1986), pp. 48–53; William H. Wagel, "Performance Appraisal with a Difference," *Personnel,* Vol. 64, no. 2 (February 1987), pp. 4–6; and Jeanette Cleveland et al., "Multiple Uses of Performance Appraisal: Prevalence and Correlates," *Journal of Applied Psychology,* Vol. 74, no. 1 (February 1989), pp. 130–135; Ian Carlton and Martyn Sloman, "Performance Appraisal in Practice," *Human Resource Management Journal,* Vol. 2, no. 3 (Spring 1992), pp. 80–94.

2. Teel, "Performance Appraisal," p. 301. For a good explanation of why sole reliance on appraisal by supervisors may not be a good idea, see Keki Bhote, "Boss Performance Appraisal: A Metric Whose Time Has Gone," *Employment Relations Today,* Vol. 21, No. 1 (Spring 1994), pp. 1–9.

3. Ibid. See also Martin Friedman, "Ten Steps to Objective Appraisals," *Personnel Journal,* Vol. 65, no. 6 (June 1986).

4. For a recent discussion see Gary English, "Tuning Up for Performance Management," *Training and Development Journal* (April 1991), pp. 56–60.

5. This is based on James Buford, Jr., Bettye Burkhalter, and Grover Jacobs, "Link Job Descriptions to Performance Appraisals," *Personnel Journal* (June 1988), pp. 132–140.

6. This is based on Commerce Clearing House, "Merck's New Performance Appraisal/Merit Pay System Is Based on Bell-Shaped Distribution," *Ideas and Trends,* May 17, 1989, pp. 88–90.

7. Commerce Clearing House Editorial Staff, "Performance Appraisal: What Three Companies Are Doing," Chicago, 1985. See also Richard Girard, "Are Performance Appraisals Passé?" *Personnel Journal,* Vol. 67, no. 8 (August 1988), pp. 89–90, which explains how companies can appraise performance using incidents instead of formal performance appraisals.

8. See, for example, Timothy Keaveny and Anthony McGann, "A Comparison of Behavioral Expectation Scales and Graphic Rating Scales," *Journal of Applied Psychology,* Vol. 60 (1975), pp. 695–703. See also John Ivancevich, "A Longitudinal Study of Behavioral Expectation Scales: Attitudes and Performance," *Journal of Applied Psychology* (April 1980), pp. 139–146.

9. Based on Donald Schwab, Herbert Heneman III, and Thomas DeCotiis, "Behaviorally Anchored Scales: A Review of the Literature," *Personnel Psychology,* Vol. 28 (1975), pp. 549–562. For a discussion, see also Uco Wiersma and Gary Latham, "The Practicality of Behavioral Observation Scales, Behavioral Expectations Scales, and Trait Scales," *Personnel Psychology,*" Vol. 30, no. 3 (Autumn 1986), pp. 619–628.

10. Lawrence Fogli, Charles Hulin, and Milton Blood, "Development of First Level Behavioral Job Criteria," *Journal of Applied Psychology,* Vol. 55 (1971), pp. 3–8. See also Terry Dickenson and Peter Fellinger, "A Comparison of the Behaviorally Anchored Rating and Fixed Standard Scale Formats," *Journal of Applied Psychology* (April 1980), pp. 147–154.

11. Keaveny and McGann, "A Comparison of Behavioral Expectation Scales," pp. 695–703; Schwab, Heneman, and DeCotiis, "Behaviorally Anchored Rating Scales"; and James Goodale and Ronald Burke, "Behaviorally Based Rating Scales Need Not Be Job Specific," *Journal of Applied Psychology,* Vol. 60 (June 1975).

12. Wayne Cascio and Enzo Valenzi, "Behaviorally Anchored Rating Scales: Effects of Education and Job Experience of Raters and Ratees," *Journal of Applied Psychology,* Vol. 62, no. 3 (1977), pp. 278–282. See also Gary P. Latham and Kenneth N. Wexley, "Behavioral Observation Scales for Performance Appraisal Purposes," *Personnel Psychology,* Vol. 30, no. 2 (Summer 1977), pp. 255–268; H. John Bernardin, Kenneth M. Alvares, and C. J. Cranny, "A Recomparison of Behavioral Expectation Scales to Summated Scales," *Journal of Applied Psychology,* Vol. 61, no. 5 (October 1976), p. 564; Frank E. Saal and Frank J. Landy, "The Mixed Standard Rating Scale: An Evaluation," *Organizational Behavior and Human Performance,* Vol. 18, no. 1 (February 1977), pp. 19–35; Frank J. Landy et al., "Behaviorally Anchored Scales for Rating the Performance of Police Officers," *Journal of Applied Psychology,* Vol. 61, no. 6 (December 1976), pp. 750–758; and Kevin R. Murphy and Joseph Constans, "Behavioral Anchors as a Source of Bias in Rating," *Journal of Applied Psychology,* Vol. 72, no. 4 (November 1987), pp. 573–577.

13. See Martin Levy, "Almost-Perfect Performance Appraisals," *Personnel Journal,* Vol. 68, no. 4 (April 1989), pp. 76–83, for a good example of how one company fine tuned its form for individual performance.

14. Edward C. Baig, "So You Hate Rating Your Workers?" *Business Week,* August 22, 1994, p. 14.

15. This is based on Peter H. Lewis, "A New Way to Rate Employee Performance More Effectively," *The New York Times,* December 19, 1993, p. 10. Employee Appraiser was developed by the Austin-Hayne Corporation of San Mateo, California.

16. Teel, "Performance Appraisal," pp. 297–298.

17. For a discussion of this see, for example, Wayne Cascio, *Applied Psychology in Personnel Management* (Reston, VA: Reston, 1978), pp. 337–341.

18. B. Rosen and T. H. Gerdee, "The Nature of Job Related Age Stereotypes," *Journal of Applied Psychology,* Vol. 61 (1976), pp. 180–183.

19. William J. Bigoness, "Effect of Applicant's Sex, Race and Performance on Employer's Performance Ratings: Some Additional Findings," *Journal of Applied Psychology,* Vol. 61 (February 1976). See also Duane Thompson and Toni Thompson, "Task-Based Performance Appraisal for Blue Collar Jobs: Evaluation of Race and Sex Effects," *Journal of Applied Psychology,* Vol. 70, no. 4 (1985), pp. 747–753.

20. Gerald Ferris, Valerie Yates, David Gilmore, and Kendrith Rowland, "The Influence of Subordinate Age on Performance Ratings and Casual Attributions," *Personnel Psychol-*

ogy, Vol. 38, no. 3 (Autumn 1985), pp. 545–557. As another example, see Gregory Dobbins and Jeanne Russell, "The Biasing Effects of Subordinate Likeableness on Leader's Responses to Poor Performers: A Laboratory and Field Study," *Personnel Psychology,* Vol. 39, no. 4 (Winter 1986), pp. 759–778. See also Michael E. Benedict and Edward Levine, "Delay and Distortion: Passive Influences on Performance Appraisal Effectiveness," *Journal of Applied Psychology,* Vol. 73, no. 3 (August 1988), pp. 507–514, and James Smither et al., "Effect of Prior Performance Information on Ratings of Present Performance: Contrast Versus Assimilation Revisited," *Journal of Applied Psychology,* Vol. 73, no. 3 (August 1988), pp. 487–496.

21. Kevin Murphy, William Balzer, Maura Lockhart, and Elaine Eisenman, "Effects of Previous Performance on Evaluations of Present Performance," *Journal of Applied Psychology,* Vol. 70, no. 1 (1985), pp. 72–84. See also Kevin Williams, Angelo DeNisi, Bruce Meglino, and Thomas Cafferty, "Initial Decisions and Subsequent Performance Ratings," *Journal of Applied Psychology,* Vol. 71, no. 2 (May 1986), pp. 189–195.

22. Jane Halpert, Midge Wilson, and Julia Hickman, "Pregnancy as a Source of Bias in Performance Appraisals," *Journal of Organizational Behavior,* Vol. 14 (1993), pp. 649–663.

23. Ibid., p. 655.

24. W. C. Borman, "Effects of Instruction to Avoid Halo Error in Reliability and Validity of Performance Evaluation Ratings," *Journal of Applied Psychology,* Vol. 65 (1975), pp. 556–560; Borman points out that since no control group (a group of managers who did not undergo training) was available, it is possible that the observed effects were not due to the short five-minute training experience. G. P. Latham, K. N. Wexley, and E. D. Pursell, "Training Managers to Minimize Rating Errors in the Observation of Behavior," *Journal of Applied Psychology,* Vol. 60 (1975), pp. 550–555; John Ivancevich, "Longitudinal Study of the Effects of Rater Training on Psychometric Error in Ratings," *Journal of Applied Psychology,* Vol. 64 (1979), pp. 502–508. For a related discussion, see, for example, Bryan Davis and Michael Mount, "Effectiveness of Performance Appraisal Training Using Computer Assistance Instruction and Behavior Modeling," *Personnel Psychology,* Vol. 37 (Fall 1984), pp. 439–452.

25. Walter Borman, "Format and Training Effects on Rating Accuracy and Rater Errors," *Journal of Applied Psychology,* Vol. 64 (August 1979), pp. 410–412, and Jerry Hedge and Michael Cavanagh, "Improving the Accuracy of Performance Evaluations: Comparison of Three Methods of Performance Appraiser Training," *Journal of Applied Psychology,* Vol. 73, no. 1 (February 1988), pp. 68–73.

26. Davis and Mount, "The Effectiveness of Performance Appraisal Training," pp. 439–452.

27. Dennis Warnke and Robert Billings, "Comparison of Training Methods for Improving the Psychometric Quality of Experimental and Administrative Performance Ratings," *Journal of Applied Psychology,* Vol. 64 (April 1979), pp. 124–131. See also Timothy Athey and Robert McIntyre, "Effect of Rater Training on Rater Accuracy: Levels of Processing Theory and Social Facilitation Theory Perspectives," *Journal of Applied Psychology,* Vol. 72, no. 4 (November 1987), pp. 567–572.

28. This is based primarily on Gary Lubben, Duane Tompason, and Charles Klasson, "Performance Appraisal: The Legal Implications of Title VII," *Personnel* (May–June 1980), pp. 11–21. See also Larry Axline, "Ethical Considerations of Performance Appraisals," *Management Review,* Vol. 83, No. 3 (March 1994), p. 62.

29. Shelley Burchett and Kenneth DeMeuse, "Performance Appraisal and the Law," *Personnel,* Vol. 62, no. 7 (July 1985), pp. 34–35.

30. See also Ian Carlson and Martyn Sloman, "Performance Appraisal in Practice," *Human Resource Management,* Vol. 2, no. 3 (Spring 1992), pp. 80–94.

31. See, for example, Caryn Beck-Dudley and Glenn McEvoy, "Performance Appraisals and Discrimination Suits: Do Courts Pay Attention To Validity?" *Employee Responsibilities and Rights,* Vol. 4, no. 2 (June 1991), pp. 149–163.

32. Gerarld Barrett and Mary Kernan, "Performance Appraisal and Terminations: A Review of Court Decisions Since *Brito v. Zia* with Implications for Personnel Practices," *Personnel Psychology,* Vol. 40, no. 3 (Autumn 1987), p. 499.

33. This is based on Kenneth L. Sovereign, *Personnel Law* (Englewood Cliffs, NJ: Prentice-Hall, 1994), pp. 113–114.

34. David Rosen, "Appraisals Can Make—or Break—Your Court Case," *Personnel Journal* (November 1992), pp. 113–118.

35. Larry Axline, "Ethical Considerations of Performance Appraisals," *Management Review* (March 1994), p. 62.

36. Wayne Cascio and H. John Bernardin, "Implications of Performance Appraisal Litigation for Personnel Decisions," *Personnel Psychology* (Summer 1981), pp. 211–212, and Barrett and Kernan, "Performance Appraisal and Terminations," pp. 489–504.

37. Barrett and Kernan, "Performance Appraisal and Terminations," p. 501.

38. R. G. Downey, F. F. Medland, and L. G. Yates, "Evaluation of a Peer Rating System for Predicting Subsequent Promotion of Senior Military Officers," *Journal of Applied Psychology,* Vol. 61 (April 1976), and Glenn McEvoy and Paul Buller, "User Acceptance of Peer Appraisals in an Industrial Setting," *Personnel Psychology,* Vol. 40, no. 4 (Winter 1987), pp. 785–798. See also Julie Barclay and Lynn Harland, "Peer Performance Appraisals: The Impact of Rater Competence, Rater Location, and Rating Correctability on Fairness Perceptions," *Group and Organization Management,* Vol. 20, No. 1 (March 1995), pp. 39–60.

39. Allan Kraut, "Prediction of Managerial Success by Peer and Training Staff Ratings," *Journal of Applied Psychology,* Vol. 60 (February 1975). See also Michael Mount, "Psychometric Properties of Subordinate Ratings of Managerial Performance," *Personnel Psychology,* Vol. 37, no. 4 (Winter 1984), pp. 687–702.

40. Carol Norman and Robert Zawacki, "Team Appraisals—Team Approach," *Personnel Journal* (September 1991), pp. 101–103.

41. Robert Libby and Robert Blashfield, "Performance of a Composite as a Function of the Number of Judges," *Organizational Behavior and Human Performance,* Vol. 21 (April 1978), pp. 121–129; Walter Borman, "Exploring Upper Limits of Reliability and Validity in Job Performance Ratings," *Journal of Applied Psychology,* Vol. 63 (April 1978), pp. 135–144; M. M. Harris and J. Schaubroeck, "A Meta-Analysis of Self-Supervisor, Self-Peer, and Peer-Supervisor Ratings," *Personnel Psychology,* Vol. 41 (1988), pp. 43–62.

42. Walter C. Borman, "The Rating of Individuals in Organizations: An Alternate Approach," *Organizational Behavior and Human Performance,* Vol. 12 (1974), pp. 105–124.

43. Teel, "Performance Appraisal," p. 301.

44. George Thornton III, "Psychometric Properties of Self-appraisal of Job Performance," *Personnel Psychology,* Vol. 33 (Summer 1980), p. 265; Cathy Anderson, Jack Warner, and Cassie Spencer, "Inflation Bias in Self-assessment Evaluations: Implications for Valid Employee Selection," *Journal of Applied Psychology,* Vol. 69, no. 4 (November 1984), pp. 574–580. See also Shaul Fox and Yossi Dinur, "Validity of Self-assessment: A Field Evaluation," *Personnel Psychology,* Vol. 41, no. 3 (Autumn 1988), pp. 581–592; and John W. Lawrie, "Your Performance: Appraise It Yourself!" *Personnel,* Vol. 66, no. 1 (January 1989), pp. 21–33, a good explanation of how self-appraisals can be used at work.

45. Herbert Myer, "Self-appraisal of Job Performance," *Personnel Psychology,* Vol. 33 (Summer 1980), pp. 291–293; Robert Holzbach, "Rater Bias in Performance Ratings: Superior, Self, and Peer Ratings," *Journal of Applied Psychology,* Vol. 63, no. 5 (October 1978), pp. 579–588. Herbert G. Heneman III, "Comparison of Self and Superior Ratings of Managerial Performance," *Journal of Applied Psychology,* Vol. 59 (1974), pp. 638–642; Richard J. Klimoski and Manuel London, "Role of the Rater in Performance Appraisal," *Journal of Applied Psychology,* Vol. 59 (1974), pp. 445–451; Hubert S. Field and William H. Holley, "Subordinates' Characteristics, Supervisors' Ratings, and Decisions to Discuss Appraisal Results," *Academy of Management Journal,* Vol. 20, no. 2 (1977), pp. 215–221. See also Robert Steel and Nestor Ovalle II, "Self-appraisal Based Upon Supervisory Feedback," *Personnel Psychology,* Vol. 37, no. 4 (Winter 1984), pp. 667–685. See also Gloria Shapiro and Gary Dessler, "Are Self-appraisals More Realistic Among Professionals or Nonprofessionals in Health Care?" *Public Personnel Management,* Vol. 14 (Fall 1985), pp. 285–291; James Russell and Dorothy Goode, "An Analysis of Managers' Reactions to Their Own Performance Appraisal Feedback," *Journal of Applied Psychology,* Vol. 73, no. 1 (February 1988), pp. 63–67; and Harris and Shaubroeck, "A Meta-Analysis of Self-Supervisor, Self-Peer, and Peer-Supervisor Ratings," pp. 43–62.

46. Manuel London and Arthur Wohlers, "Agreement Between Subordinate and Self-Ratings in Upward Feedback," *Personnel Psychology,* Vol. 44 (1991), pp. 375–390.

47. Ibid., p. 376.

48. David Antonioni, "The Effects of Feedback Accountability on Upward Appraisal Ratings," *Personnel Psychology,* Vol. 47 (1994), pp. 349–355.

49. Kenneth Nowack, "360-Degree Feedback: The Whole Story," *Training and Development* (January 1993), p. 69. For a description of some of the problems involved in implementing 360-degree feedback see Matthew Budman, "The Rating Game," *Across the Board,* Vol. 31, No. 2 (February 1994), pp. 35–38.

50. Catherine Romano, "Fear of Feedback," *Management Review* (December 1993), p. 39.

51. Ibid.

52. See, for instance, Gerry Rich, "Group Reviews—Are You Up To It?" *CMA Magazine* (March 1993), p. 5.

53. See also Jerald Greenberg, "Using Explanations to Manage Impressions of Performance Appraisal Fairness," *Employee Responsibilities and Rights,* Vol. 4, no. 1 (March 1991), pp. 51–60.

54. Johnson, *The Appraisal Interview Guide,* Chapter 9.

55. Judy Block, *Performance Appraisal on the Job: Making It Work* (New York: Executive Enterprises Publications, 1981), pp. 58–62. See also Terry Lowe, "Eight Ways to Ruin a Performance Review," *Personnel Journal,* Vol. 65, no. 1 (January 1986).

56. Block, *Performance Appraisal on the Job.*

57. Ronald Burke, William Weitzel, and Tamara Weis, "Characteristics of Effective Employee Performance Review and Development Interviews: Replication and Extension," *Personnel Psychology,* Vol. 31 (Winter 1978), pp. 903–919. See also Joane Pearce and Lyman Porter, "Employee Response to Formal Performance Appraisal Feedback," *Journal of Applied Psychology,* Vol. 71, no. 2 (May 1986), pp. 211–218.

58. Allan Locher and Kenneth Teel, "Appraisal Trends," *Personnel Journal* (September 1988), pp. 139–145. This paper describes a survey sent to 1,459 organizations belonging to the Personnel and Industrial Relations Association of Southern California; 324 companies responded.

59. Ibid., p. 140.

60. Edward E. Lawler, III, "Performance Management: The Next Generation," *Compensation and Benefits Review* (May–June 1994), p. 16.

61. Ibid., p. 16.

50. Dr. M. Michael Markowich, "Response: We Can Make Performance Appraisals Work," *Compensation and Benefits Review* (May–June 1995), p. 25.

63. See, for example, Greg Boudreaux, "Response: What TQM Says About Performance Appraisal," *Compensation and Benefits Review* (May–June 1994), pp. 20–24.

64. Ibid., p. 21.

65. See, for example, Lawler, "Performance Management: The Next Generation," p. 17.

66. David Antonioni, "Improve the Management Process Before Discontinuing Performance Appraisals," *Compensation and Benefits Review* (May–June 1994), p. 29.

67. Ibid.

68. Boudreaux, "Response: What TQM Says About Performance Appraisal," p. 23.

69. Based in part on Joel E. Ross, *Total Quality Management: Text, Cases and Readings* (Delray Beach, FL: Saint Lucie Press, 1993), p. 1.

70. Ibid., pp. 2–3, 35–36.

71. Boudreaux, "Response: What TQM Says About Performance Appraisal," p. 23.

72. Lawler, "Performance Management: The Next Generation," p. 17.

73. Markowich, "Response: We Can Make Performance Appraisals Work," p. 26.

74. Antonioni, "Improve the Management Process Before Discontinuing Performance Appraisals," p. 30.

75. Ibid.

76. Ibid.

77. See also Clive Fletcher, "Appraisal: An Idea Whose Time Has Gone?" *Personnel Management* (September 1993), pp. 34–37.

Chapter 11
Managing Careers

Chapter Outline

- ◆ **Introduction: HR and Career Management**
- ◆ **Factors That Affect Career Choices**
- ◆ **Career Management and the First Assignment**
- ◆ **Managing Promotions and Transfers**
- ◆ **Building Commitment: Helping Employees to Self-Actualize**

Behavioral Objectives

When you finish studying this chapter, you should be able to:

Discuss the factors that affect career choices.

Explain how you would make a new subordinate's first assignment more meaningful.

Discuss how to more effectively manage promotions and transfers.

List specific steps you could take to help employees to self-actualize.

Introduction: HR Career Management

Personnel activities like screening, training, and appraising serve two basic roles in organizations. First, their traditional role has been to staff the organization—to fill its positions with employees who have the requisite interests, abilities, and skills. Increasingly, however, these activities are taking on a second role of ensuring that the long-run interests of the employees are protected by the organization and that, in particular, the employee is encouraged to grow and realize his or her full potential. Referring to *staffing* or *personnel management* as *human resource management* reflects this second role. A basic assumption underlying this role is that the employer has an obligation to utilize its employees' abilities to the fullest and to give all employees a chance to grow and to realize their full potential and to develop successful careers.[1] One way this trend is manifesting itself is in the increased emphasis many firms are placing today on **career planning and development.**

career planning and development
The deliberate process through which a person becomes aware of personal career-related attributes and the lifelong series of stages that contribute to his or her career fulfillment.

Activities like personnel planning, screening, and training play a big role in the career development process. Personnel planning, for example, can be used not just to forecast open jobs but to identify potential internal candidates and the training they would need to fill these jobs. Similarly, an organization can use its periodic employee appraisals not just for salary decisions but for identifying the development needs of individual employees and ensuring that these needs are met. All the staffing activities, in other words, can be used to satisfy the needs of both the organization and the individual in such a way that they both gain: the organization from improved performance from a more committed work force and the employee from a richer, more challenging career.[2]

This is illustrated in Table 11.1. For example, performance appraisal's traditional focus has been on rating for the purpose of promotion, discipline, and rewards; using it to provide a career development focus means including development plans and individual goal setting. Similarly, HR planning tradition-

TABLE 11.1 HR: Traditional versus Career Development Focus

ACTIVITY	TRADITIONAL FOCUS	CAREER DEVELOP- MENT FOCUS
Human resource planning	Analyzes jobs, skills, tasks —present and future. Projects needs. Uses statistical data.	Adds information about individual interests, preferences, and the like to data. Provides career path information.
Training and development	Provides opportunities for learning skills, information, and attitudes related to job.	Adds individual growth orientation.
Performance appraisal	Rating and/or rewards.	Adds development plans and individual goal setting.
Recruiting and placement	Matching organization's needs with qualified individuals.	Matches individual and jobs based on a number of variables including employees' career interests.
Compensation and benefits	Rewards for time, productivity, talent, and so on.	Adds non-job-related activities to be rewarded, such as United Way leadership positions.

Source: Adapted from Fred L. Otte and Peggy G. Hutcheson, *Helping Employees Manage Careers* (Englewood Cliffs, NJ: Prentice-Hall, 1992), p. 10.

ally focuses on job analysis and satisfying the organization's staffing needs; adding a career development focus means including information about individual career interests and preferences as well as career path options.

Before proceeding, it would be useful to define some of the terms we'll be using throughout this chapter.[3] A *career* is a series of work-related positions, paid or unpaid, that help a person grow in job skills, success, and fulfillment. *Career development* is the lifelong series of activities (such as workshops) that contributes to a person's career exploration, establishment, success, and fulfillment. *Career planning* is the deliberate process through which someone becomes aware of personal skills, interests, knowledge, motivations, and other characteristics; acquires information about opportunities and choices; identifies career-related goals; and establishes action plans to attain specific goals.

Roles in Career Development

As summarized in Table 11.2, the individual, the manager, and the organization all have roles in the individual's career development. Ultimately it is the individual who must accept responsibility for his or her own career; assess interests, skills, and values; seek out career information and resources; and generally take those steps that must be taken to ensure a happy and fulfilling career. Within the organization the individual's manager plays a role, too. The manager should provide timely and objective performance feedback, offer developmental assignments and support, and participate in career development discussions, for instance. The manager acts as a coach, appraiser, advisor, and referral agent, for instance, listening to and clarifying the individual's career plans, giving feedback, generating career options, and linking the employee to organizational resources and career options (Table 11.3).

Finally, as we'll also see in this chapter, the employer plays a career development role. For example, it should provide career-oriented training and develop-

TABLE 11.2 Roles in Career Development
Individual
• Accept responsibility for your own career.
• Assess your interests, skills, and values.
• Seek out career information and resources.
• Establish goals and career plans.
• Utilize development opportunities.
• Talk with your manager about your career.
• Follow through on realistic career plans.
Manager
• Provide timely performance feedback.
• Provide developmental assignments and support.
• Participate in career development discussions.
• Support employee development plans.
Organization
• Communicate mission, policies, and procedures.
• Provide training and development opportunities.
• Provide career information and career programs.
• Offer a variety of career options.

Source: Fred L. Otte and Peggy G. Hutcheson, *Helping Employees Manage Careers* (Englewood Cliffs, NJ: Prentice-Hall, 1992), p. 56.

TABLE 11.3 Four Roles for Managers in Employee Development			
COACH	**APPRAISER**	**ADVISOR**	**REFERRAL AGENT**
Listens	Gives feedback	Generates options	Links employee
Clarifies	Clarifies standards	Helps set goals	to resources/people
Probes	Clarifies job	Recommends/advises	Consults on action
Defines concerns	responsibilities		plan

Source: Fred L. Otte and Peggy G. Hutcheson, *Helping Employees Manage Careers* (Englewood Cliffs, NJ: Prentice-Hall, 1992), p. 57.

ment opportunities, offer career information and career programs, and give employees a variety of career options. Ultimately, as we'll see, employers need not and should not provide such career-oriented activities purely out of altruism. Most employees will ultimately grade their employers on the extent to which the organization allowed them to excel and to become the people they believed they had the potential to become. And that will help determine their commitment to their employers and their overall job satisfaction.[4]

Factors That Affect Career Choices

The first step in planning a career for yourself or someone else is to learn as much as possible about the person's interests, aptitudes, and skills.

Identify the Person's Career Stage

career cycle
The stages through which a person's career evolves.

growth stage
The period from birth to age 14 during which the person develops a self-concept by identifying with and interacting with other people such as family, friends, and teachers.

Each person's career goes through stages, and the stage you are in will influence your knowledge of and preference for various occupations. The main stages of this **career cycle** follows.[5]

Growth Stage The **growth stage** lasts roughly from birth to age 14 and is a period during which the person develops a self-concept by identifying with and interacting with other people such as family, friends, and teachers. Toward the beginning of this period, role playing is important, and children experiment with different ways of acting; this helps them to form impressions of how other people react to different behaviors and contributes to their developing a unique self-concept or identity. Toward the end of this stage, the adolescent (who by this time has developed preliminary ideas about what his or her interests and abilities are) begins to think realistically about alternative occupations.

exploration stage
The period from around ages 15 to 24 during which a person seriously explores various occupational alternatives, attempting to match these alternatives with his or her interests and abilities.

Exploration Stage The **exploration stage** is the period (roughly from ages 15 to 24) during which a person seriously explores various occupational alternatives. The person attempts to match these alternatives with what he or she has learned about them and about his or her own interests and abilities from school, leisure activities, and work. Tentative broad occupational choices are usually made during the beginning of this period. Then toward the end of this period, a seemingly appropriate choice is made and the person tries out for a beginning job.

Probably the most important task the person has in this and the preceding stage is that of developing a realistic understanding of his or her abilities and talents. Similarly, the person must make sound educational decisions based on reliable sources of information about occupational alternatives.

establishment stage
The period, roughly from ages 24 to 44, that is the heart of most people's work lives.

Establishment Stage The **establishment stage** spans roughly ages 24 to 44 and is the heart of most people's work lives. During this period, it is hoped a suitable occupation is found and the person engages in those activities that help him or her earn a permanent place in it. Often and particularly in the professions, the person locks on to a chosen occupation early. But in most cases, this is a period during which the person is continually testing his or her capabilities and ambitions against those of the initial occupational choice.

trial substage
The period from about age 25 to 30 during which the person determines whether or not the chosen field is suitable and, if it is not, attempts to change it.
stabilization substage
The period, roughly from age 30 to 40, during which firm occupational goals are set and more explicit career planning is made to determine the sequence for accomplishing these goals.
midcareer crisis substage
The period occurring between the mid-thirties and mid-forties during which people often make a major reassessment of their progress relative to their original career ambitions and goals.
maintenance stage
The period from about ages 45 to 65 during which the person secures his or her place in the world of work.
decline stage
The period during which many people are faced with the prospect of having to accept reduced levels of power and responsibility.

The establishment stage is itself comprised of three substages. The **trial substage** lasts from about ages 25 to 30. During this period, the person determines whether or not the chosen field is suitable; if it is not, several changes might be attempted. (Jane Smith might have her heart set on a career in retailing, for example, but after several months of constant travel as a newly hired assistant buyer for a department store, she might decide that a less travel-oriented career such as one in market research is more in tune with her needs.) Roughly between the ages of 30 and 40, the person goes through a **stabilization substage.** Here firm occupational goals are set and the person does more explicit career planning to determine the sequence of promotions, job changes, and/or any educational activities that seem necessary for accomplishing these goals. Finally, somewhere between the mid-thirties and mid-forties, the person may enter the **midcareer crisis substage.** During this period, people often make a major reassessment of their progress relative to original ambitions and goals. They may find that they are not going to realize their dreams (such as being company president) or that, having been accomplished, their dreams are not all they were purported to be. Also during this period, people have to decide how important work and career are to be in their life. It is often during this midcareer substage that the person is faced for the first time with difficult choices between what he or she really wants, what really can be accomplished, and how much must be sacrificed to achieve it.

Maintenance Stage Between the ages of 45 to 65, many people simply slide from the stabilization substage into the **maintenance stage.** During this latter period, the person has typically created a place in the world of work and most efforts are now directed at maintaining that place.

Decline Stage As retirement age approaches, there is often a deceleration period in the **decline stage.** Here many people face the prospect of having to accept reduced levels of power and responsibility and learn to accept and develop new roles as mentor and confidante for those who are younger. There is then the more or less inevitable retirement, after which the person finds alternative uses for the time and effort formerly expended on his or her occupation.

Identify Occupational Orientation

Career-counseling expert John Holland says that a person's personality (including values, motives, and needs) is another important determinant of career choices. For example, a person with a strong social orientation might be attracted to careers that entail interpersonal rather than intellectual or physical activities and to occupations such as social work. Based on research with his Vocational Preference Test (VPT), Holland found six basic personality types or orientations.[6]

1. *Realistic orientation.* These people are attracted to occupations that involve physical activities requiring skill, strength, and coordination. Examples include forestry, farming, and agriculture.

2. *Investigative orientation.* Investigative people are attracted to careers that involve cognitive activities (thinking, organizing, understanding) rather than affective activities (feeling, acting, or interpersonal and emotional tasks). Examples include biologist, chemist, and college professor.

3. *Social orientation.* These people are attracted to careers that involve interpersonal rather than intellectual or physical activities. Examples include clinical psychology, foreign service, and social work.

4. *Conventional orientation.* A conventional orientation favors careers that involve structured, rule-regulated activities, as well as careers in which it is expected that the employee subordinate his or her personal needs to those of the organization. Examples include accountants and bankers.

5. *Enterprising orientation.* Verbal activities aimed at influencing others are attractive to enterprising personalities. Examples include managers, lawyers, and public relations executives.

6. *Artistic orientation.* People here are attracted to careers that involve self-expression, artistic creation, expression of emotions, and individualistic activities. Examples include artists, advertising executives, and musicians.

Most people have more than one orientation (they might be social, realistic, and investigative, for example), and Holland believes that the more similar or compatible these orientations are, the less internal conflict or indecision a person will face in making a career choice. To help illustrate this, Holland suggests placing each orientation in one corner of a hexagon, as in Figure 11.1. As you can see, the model has six corners, each of which represents one personal orientation (for example, enterprising). According to Holland's research, the closer two orientations are in this figure, the more compatible they are. Holland believes that if your number-one and number-two orientations fall side by side, you will have an easier time choosing a career. However, if your orientations turn out to be opposite (such as realistic and social), you may experience more indecision in making a career choice because your interests are driving you toward very different types of careers. In Table 11.4, we have summarized some of the occupations that have been found to be the best match for each of these six personal **occupational orientations.**

occupational orientation
The theory developed by John Holland that says there are six basic personal orientations that determine the sorts of careers to which people are drawn.

Figure 11.1
Choosing an Occupational Orientation

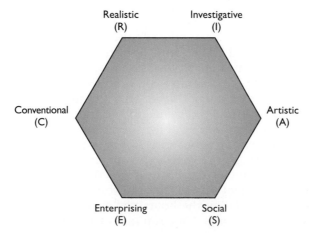

TABLE 11.4 Occupations Scoring High on Each Occupational Orientation Theme

REALISTIC	INVESTIGATIVE	ARTISTIC	SOCIAL	ENTERPRISING	CONVENTIONAL
Consider these occupations if you score *high* here:					
Agribusiness managers	Biologists	Advertising executives	Auto sales dealers	Agribusiness managers	Accountants
Carpenters	Chemists	Art teachers	Guidance counselors	Auto sales dealers	Auto sales dealers
Electricians	Engineers	Artists	Home economics teachers	Business education teachers	Bankers
Engineers	Geologists	Broadcasters	Mental health workers	Buyers	Bookkeepers
Farmers	Mathematicians	English teachers	Ministers	Chamber of Commerce executives	Business education teachers
Foresters	Medical technologists	Interior decorators	Physical education teachers	Funeral directors	Credit managers
Highway patrol officers	Physicians	Medical illustrators	Recreation leaders	Life insurance agents	Executive housekeepers
Horticultural workers	Physicists	Ministers	School administrators	Purchasing agents	Food service managers
Industrial arts teachers	Psychologists	Musicians	Social science teachers	Realtors	IRS agents
Military enlisted personnel	Research and development managers	Photographers	Social workers	Restaurant managers	Mathematics teachers
Military officers	Science teachers	Public relations directors	Special education teachers	Retail clerks	Military enlisted personnel
Vocational agricultural teachers	Sociologists	Reporters	YMCA/YWCA directors	Store managers	Secretaries

Note: for example, if you score high on "realistic," consider a career as a carpenter, engineer, farmer, and so on.

Source: Reproduced by special permission of the publisher, Consulting Psychologists Press, Inc., Palo Alto, CA 94306, from *Manual for the SVIV-SCII,* Fourth Edition, by Jo-Ida C. Hansen and David P. Campbell. © 1985 by the Board of Trustees of Leland Stanford Junior University.

Identify Skills

Successful performance depends not just on motivation but on ability too. You may have a conventional orientation, but whether you have the skills to be an accountant, banker, or credit manager will largely determine which specific occupation you ultimately choose. Therefore, you have to identify your skills—or those of your employees.

occupational skills
The skills needed to be successful in a particular occupation. According to the *Dictionary of Occupational Titles,* occupational skills break down into three groups depending on whether they emphasize data, people, or things.

An Exercise   One useful exercise for identifying **occupational skills** is to take a blank piece of paper and write the heading "The Most Enjoyable Occupational Tasks I Have Had." Then write a short essay that describes the tasks. Make sure to go into as much detail as you can about your duties and responsibilities and what it was about each task that you found enjoyable. (In writing your essay, by the way, notice that it's not necessarily the most enjoyable *job* you've had but the most enjoyable *task* you've had to perform; you may have had jobs that you really didn't like except for one of the specific duties or tasks in the job, which you really enjoyed.) Next, on other sheets of paper, do the same thing for two other tasks you have had. Now go through your three essays and *underline the skills that you mentioned the most often.* For example, did you enjoy putting together and coordinating the school play when you worked in the principal's office one year? Did you especially enjoy the hours you spent in the library doing research for your boss when you worked one summer as an office clerk?[7]

aptitudes
Inate abilities which include intelligence, numerical aptitude, mechanical comprehension, and manual dexterity, as well as talents such as artistic, theatrical, or musical ability that play an important role in career decisions.

Aptitudes and Special Talents   For career planning purposes, a person's **aptitudes** are usually measured with a test battery such as the general aptitude test battery (GATB). This instrument measures various aptitudes including intelligence and mathematical ability. Considerable work has been done to relate aptitudes, such as those measured by the GATB, to specific occupations. For example, the U.S. Department of Labor's *Dictionary of Occupational Titles* lists the nature and titles of hundreds of occupations, along with the aptitudes required for success in these occupations.[8]

Identify Career Anchors

Edgar Schein says that career planning is a continuing process of discovery—one in which a person slowly develops a clearer occupational self-concept in terms of what his or her talents, abilities, motives, needs, attitudes, and values are. Schein also says that as you learn more about yourself, it becomes apparent that you have a dominant career anchor, *a concern or value that you will not give up if a choice has to be made.* **Career anchors,** as their name implies, are the pivots around which a person's career swings; a person becomes conscious of them as a result of learning about his or her talents and abilities, motives and needs, and attitudes and values. Based on his research at the Massachusetts Institute of Technology, Schein believes that career anchors are difficult to predict ahead of time because they are evolutionary and a product of a process of discovery. Some people may never find out what their career anchors are until they have to make a major choice—such as whether to take the promotion to the headquarters staff or strike out on their own by starting a business. It is at this point that all the person's past work experiences, interests, aptitudes, and orientations converge into a meaningful pattern (or career anchor) that helps show what is personally the most important in driving the person's career choices. Based on his study of MIT graduates, Schein identified five career anchors.[9]

career anchors
A concern or value that you will not give up if a choice has to be made.

Technical/Functional Career Anchor   People who had a strong technical/functional career anchor tended to avoid decisions that would drive them toward general management. Instead they made decisions that would enable them to remain and grow in their chosen technical or functional fields.

Managerial Competence as a Career Anchor   Other people show a strong motivation to become managers and their career experience enabled them to believe that they had the skills and values required to rise to such general management positions. A management position of high responsibility is their ultimate goal. When pressed to explain why they believed they had the skills necessary to gain such positions, many in Schein's research sample answered that they were qualified for these jobs because of what they saw as their competencies in a combination of three areas: (1) analytical competence (ability to identify, analyze, and solve problems under conditions of incomplete information and uncertainty); (2) interpersonal competence (ability to influence, supervise, lead, manipulate, and control people at all levels); and (3) emotional competence (the capacity to be stimulated by emotional and interpersonal crises rather than exhausted or debilitated by them, and the capacity to bear high levels of responsibility without becoming paralyzed).

Creativity as a Career Anchor   Some of the graduates had gone on to become successful entrepreneurs. To Schein these people seemed to have a need "to build or create something that was entirely their own product—a product or process that bears their name, a company of their own, or a personal fortune that reflects their accomplishments." For example, one graduate had become a successful purchaser, restorer, and renter of townhouses in a large city; another had built a successful consulting firm.

Autonomy and Independence as Career Anchors   Some seemed driven by the need to be on their own, free of the dependence that can arise when a person elects to work in a large organization where promotions, transfers, and salary decisions make them subordinate to others. Many of these graduates also had a strong technical/functional orientation. However, instead of pursuing this orientation in an organization, they had decided to become consultants, working either alone or as part of a relatively small firm. Others had become professors of business, free-lance writers, and proprietors of a small retail business.

Security as a Career Anchor   A few of the graduates were mostly concerned with long-run career stability and job security. They seemed willing to do what was required to maintain job security, a decent income, and a stable future in the form of a good retirement program and benefits.

For those interested in *geographic security,* maintaining a stable, secure career in familiar surroundings was generally more important than was pursuing superior career choices, if choosing the latter meant injecting instability or insecurity into their lives by forcing them to pull up roots and move to another city. For others, security meant *organizational security.* They might today opt for government jobs, where tenure still tends to be a way of life. They were much more willing to let their employers decide what their careers should be.

Assessing Career Anchors   To help you identify career anchors, take a few sheets of blank paper and write out your answers to the following questions:[10]

1. What was your major area of concentration (if any) in high school? Why did you choose that area? How did you feel about it?
2. What is (or was) your major area of concentration in college? Why did you choose that area? How did you feel about it?
3. What was your first job after school? (Include military if relevant.) What were you looking for in your first job?
4. What were your ambitions or long-range goals when you started your career? Have they changed? When? Why?
5. What was your first major change of job or company? What were you looking for in your next job?
6. What was your next major change of job, company, or career? Why did you initiate or accept it? What were you looking for? (Do this for each of your major changes of job, company, or career.)
7. As you look back over your career, identify some times you have especially enjoyed. What was it about those times that you enjoyed?
8. As you look back, identify some times you have not especially enjoyed. What was it about those times you did not enjoy?
9. Have you ever refused a job move or promotion? Why?
10. Now review all your answers carefully, as well as the descriptions for the five career anchors (managerial competence, technical/functional, security, creativity, autonomy). Based on your answers to the questions, rate each of the anchors from 1 to 5; 1 equals low importance, 5 equals high importance.

Managerial competence _____
Technical/functional competence _____
Security _____ Creativity _____ Autonomy _____

What Do You Want to Do?

We have explained occupational orientations, skills, and career anchors and the role these play in choosing a career. But there is at least one more exercise you should try that can prove enlightening. Answer the question: "If you could have any kind of job, what would it be?" Invent your own job if need be, and don't worry about what you *can* do—just what you *want* to do.[11]

Identify High-Potential Occupations

Learning about yourself is only half the job of choosing an occupation. You also have to identify those occupations that are right (given your occupational orientations, skills, career anchors, and occupational preferences) as well as those that will be in high demand in the years to come.

Find Out About Occupations and Careers   Investigating occupations can take hours (or perhaps days or weeks) of library research. The *Dictionary of Occupational Titles* is the bible of the vocational field and lists detailed job descriptions for more than 20,000 occupations. The *Dictionary of Occupational Titles* provides a listing of the responsibilities, duties, and procedures for each job in the manual. Also listed for each job are the physical demands of the job, as well as individual working conditions, and (based on the judgment of experts) the interests, aptitudes, educational requirements, and vocational preparation required of those seeking each job. The *Occupational Outlook Handbook* gives an outline for about 700 occupations, including the prospects for the occupation and the major work, required training, earnings, and working conditions. There is also an *Occupational Outlook Handbook for College Graduates,* and the U.S. Employment Service publishes *Occupations in Demand,* a comprehensive listing of jobs most frequently requested of 2,500 job service offices around the country. *Occupations in Demand* provides information on local areas having large numbers of openings, industries requesting workers, pay ranges, and average number of openings available. It also lists jobs not requiring previous work experience.

Occupational Outlook Quarterly is published every three months and provides information about occupations that are most in demand. Another source is the *Encyclopedia of Careers and Vocational Guidance,* which provides descriptions of over 650 occupations. For information about federal jobs and filling out applications, try the U.S. Office of Personnel Management's *Handbook X118,* which gives detailed job descriptions for hundreds of government positions. The U.S. Office of Education, in conjunction with Harvard University, has developed a computerized career information system called the Guidance Information System (GIS). Using this computerized system, you provide input on your occupational preferences and skills. The system then suggests one or more feasible matching occupations.

There are two basic things you (or your employee) can and should do to improve the career decisions you make.[12] First, *take charge* of your own career by understanding that there are major decisions to be made, which require considerable personal planning and effort. In other words, you cannot leave your choices in the hands of others but must decide where you want to go in terms of a career and what job moves and education are required to get there.

Second, become an effective *diagnostician*. Determine (through career counseling, testing, self-diagnostic books, and so on) what your talents or values are and how these fit with the sorts of careers you are considering.[13] In other words, the key to career planning is self-insight—into what you want out of a career, into your talents and limitations, and into your values and how they will fit with the alternatives you are considering. As Schein points out: "Too many people never ask, much less attempt to answer, these kinds of questions. It was shocking to me when I conducted the interviews for the MIT panel study and discovered how many respondents said they had never in 10 years of their careers asked themselves the kinds of questions which I was asking just to fill in the details of their job history."[14]

Career Management Responsibilities of the Manager and the Employer

Career Management Guidelines

Along with the employee, the person's manager and employer both have career management responsibilities. Guidelines here include:

Avoid Reality Shock Perhaps at no other stage in the person's career is it more important for the employer to be career development-oriented than at the initial entry stage, when the person is recruited, hired, and given a first assignment and boss. For the employee this is a period during which he or she has to develop a sense of confidence, learn to get along with the first boss and with coworkers, learn how to accept responsibility, and, most important, gain an insight into his or her talents, needs, and values as they relate to initial career goals. For the new employee, in other words, this is (or should be) a period of *reality testing* during which his or her initial hopes and goals first confront the reality of organizational life and of the person's talents and needs.

For many first-time workers, this turns out to be a disastrous period, one in which their often naive expectations first confront the realities of organizational life. The young MBA or CPA, for example, might come to the first job seeking a challenging, exciting assignment in which to apply the new techniques learned in school and to prove his or her abilities and gain a promotion. In reality, however, the trainee is often turned off by being relegated to an unimportant low-risk job where he or she "can't cause any trouble while being tried out"; or by the harsh realities of interdepartmental conflict and politicking; or by a boss who is neither rewarded for nor trained in the unique mentoring tasks needed to properly supervise new employees.[15] **Reality shock** refers to the results of a period that may occur at the initial career entry when the new employee's high job expectations confront the reality of a boring, unchallenging job.

reality shock
Results of a period that may occur at the initial career entry when the new employee's high job expectations confront the reality of a boring, unchallenging job.

Provide Challenging Initial Jobs Most experts agree that one of the most important things you can do is provide new employees with challenging first jobs. In one study of young managers at AT&T, for example, the researchers found that the more challenging a person's job was in his or her first year with the company, the more effective and successful the person was even five or six years later.[16] Based on his own research, Hall contends that challenging initial jobs provide "one of the most powerful yet uncomplicated means of aiding the career development of new employees."[17] In most organizations, however, providing such jobs

Giving an employee responsibility for a major presentation to an important client is one way to front-load entry-level jobs with challenge and to foster employee commitment.

seems more the exception than the rule. In one survey of research and development organizations, for example, only 1 of 22 companies had a formal policy of giving challenging first assignments.[18] This imbalance, as one expert has pointed out, is an example of "glaring mismanagement" when one considers the effort and money invested in recruiting, hiring, and training new employees.[19]

Some firms "front-load" the job challenge by giving new employees considerable responsibility. At Saturn and Toyota even assembly workers are assigned at once to self-managing teams of highly skilled and motivated colleagues where they must quickly learn to be productive team members. At Goldman Sachs young professionals are expected to contribute at once and immediately find themselves on teams involved in challenging projects. As one manager there said:[20]

Even with fairly new employees, the partner in charge will usually not be the first one to speak when a project team meets with a client—often the newest member will; you take the responsibility and you're supported by the team. That's what attracts people to Goldman Sachs, the ability to make decisions early.

The merchandising manager trainee position at JC Penney's (their entry-level management position) is another good example. A trainee almost straight out of college might be assigned the job of supervising the jeans section in the menswear department. Fresh from college, in other words, he or she would be responsible (under the guidance of his or her manager) for the section's display, inventory management, customer service, and staffing. As one Penney's manager put it, "From my first day as a merchandising manager trainee—straight out of college—I was running the 'store within a store.' JC Penney gives you guidance as you go along but won't hold your hand. You're kind of 'bracketed' in what you can do but you're basically running your own little shop."[21]

The new merchandise manager trainees remain as trainees for about 12 months. During this time they are responsible for training themselves. To facilitate this process, they receive various training manuals, including "The Role of a First-Level Supervisor." This describes the trainee's responsibilities for activities including customer service, sales, gross profit, merchandising, visual merchandising, sales promotion, staffing, and time management. Each new trainee is also assigned a mentor—usually a merchandising manager or senior merchandising manager. The mentor provides guidance and weekly appraisals. The training program, however, is self-administered: Trainees are responsible for teaching themselves the merchandising job's details.

Trainees are appraised weekly by their mentors according to a schedule. At the end of week two, for instance, their personal selling skills are appraised. In week three their visual merchandising skills are evaluated, in week four their sales leadership, and so on.

At the end of eight weeks the trainees get an extensive appraisal. At this point trainees meet with three people—the store manager, merchandising manager, and senior merchandising manager—and has what one manager referred to as a "very frank, outgoing discussion." A typical comment might be, "You're going to have to be much more assertive if you want a successful career here." They "lay it on the table" as one executive said, telling the trainees where they stand, what progress is being made, and what development is required.

After six months trainees usually move into new assignments, where they assume more responsibility, often running larger departments. At the end of a year they're generally ready for promotion to merchandising manager.

Provide Realistic Job Previews in Recruiting   Providing recruits with realistic previews of what to expect once they begin working in the organization—ones that describe both the attractions and also possible pitfalls—can be an effective way of minimizing reality shock and improving their long-term performance. Schein points out that one of the biggest problems recruits and employers encounter during the crucial entry stage is getting accurate information in a "climate of mutual selling."[22] The recruiter (anxious to hook good candidates) and the candidate (anxious to present as favorable an impression as possible) often give and receive unrealistic information during the interview. The result is that the interviewer may not form a clear picture of the candidate's career goals, while at the same time the candidate forms an unrealistically favorable image of the organization.[23]

Realistic job previews can boost the survival rate among employees who are hired for relatively complex jobs like management trainee, salesperson, or life insurance agent.[24] They are also used successfully by firms such as Toyota and Saturn to show assembler recruits what their jobs will be like and how demanding the environments will be at these firms.

Be Demanding   There is often a "Pygmalion effect"[25] in the relationship between a new employee and his or her boss.[26] In other words, the more you expect and the more confident and supportive you are of your new employees, the better they will perform. Therefore, as two experts put it, "Don't assign a new employee to a 'dead wood,' undemanding, or unsupportive supervisor."[27] Instead choose specially trained, high-performing, supportive supervisors who can set high standards for new employees during their critical exploratory first year.

Provide Periodic Job Rotation and Job Pathing   The best way new employees can test themselves and crystallize their career anchors is to try out a variety of challenging jobs. By rotating to jobs in various specializations—from financial analysis to production to human resource, for example—the employee gets an opportunity to assess his or her aptitudes and preferences. At the same time, the organization gets a manger with a broader multifunctional view of the organization.[28] One extension of this is called *job pathing,* which means selecting carefully sequenced job assignments.[29]

Do Career-Oriented Performance Appraisals   Edgar Schein says that supervisors must understand that valid performance appraisal information is in the long run more important than protecting the short-term interests of one's immediate subordinates.[30] Therefore, he says, supervisors need concrete information regarding the employee's potential career path—information, in other words, about the nature of the future work for which he or she is appraising the subordinate, or which the subordinate desires.[31]

Provide Career Planning Workshops and Career Planning Workbooks   Employers also should take steps to increase their employees' involvement and expertise in planning and developing their own careers. One option here is to organize periodic career planning workshops. A *career planning workshop* has been defined as "a planned learning event in which participants are expected to be actively involved, completing career planning exercises and inventories and participating in career skills practice sessions."[32]

Figure 11.2 provides an illustrative agenda for a two-day career planning workshop. Such workshops usually contain a *self-assessment* activity in which individual employees actively analyze their own career interests, skills, and career

Figure 11.2
Sample Agenda—Two-Day Career Planning Workshop
Source: Fred L. Otte and Peggy G. Hutcheson, *Helping Employees Manage Careers* (Englewood Cliffs, NJ: Prentice-Hall, 1992), pp. 22–23.

Before the program—Two weeks prior to the workshop participants receive a letter confirming their participation in the program and package of work to be completed before coming to the workshop. The exercises in this package include skills inventory, values identification, life accomplishments inventory, and a reading describing career direction options.

Day 1

8:30–10:00 Introduction and Overview of Career Planning

Welcome and Introduction to Program

    Welcome by general manager
    Overview of agenda and outcomes
    Participant Introductions (Statements of
        expectations for the program)

Overview of Career Development

    Company's philosophy
    Why career planning is needed
    What career planning is and is not
    Career planning model

10:00–Noon Self-Assessment: Part 1

Individual Self-Assessment: Values

    Values card sort exercise
    Reconciling with values pre-work
    Introduce career planning summary work sheet

Individual Self-Assessment: Skills

    Motivated skills exercise
    Examining life accomplishments (synthesize)
        exercise with pre-work)
    Identifying accomplishment themes
    Preferred work skills (from pre-work inventory)
    Fill in career planning summary work sheet

1:00–3:30 Self Assessment: Part 2

Individual Self-Assessment: Career Anchors

    Career anchoring pattern exercise
    Small group discussions
    Fill in career planning summary work sheet

Individual Self-Assessment: Preferences

    What success means to me
    Skills, knowledge, personal qualities
    Fill in career planning summary work sheet

Individual Self-Assessment: Career Path Pattern

    Synthesize with direction options from pre-work
    Fill in career planning summary work sheet

3:30–4:30 Environmental Assessment

Information About the Company

Goals, growth areas, expectations, turnover, competition
    for jobs, skills for the future
Fill in career planning summary work sheet

Personal career profile

Reality test how you see self at this point by sharing in
    group

Day 2

8:30–10:00 Goal Setting

Warm-Up Exercise

Review of where we've been and where we're going

Setting goals—where do I want to be?

Creating an ideal future

Future skills and accomplishments
Desired lifestyle
Life and career goals

10:15–1:30 Environmental Assessment: Part 2

Career resources in the company

Introduce support services and hand out information

Marketing yourself—what it takes to achieve your goals
    here

Describe resource people who will be with the group for
    lunch and brainstorm questions/issues to be discussed

Lunch with resource people

Review lunch discussions

1:30–4:30 Developing career action plans

Making Career Decisions

Identifying long-range alternatives
Identifying short-range alternatives

Improving career decisions

Decision styles and ways to enhance them

Creating your career plan

Reconciling your goals with options
Next career steps
Development action plan
Contingency planning

Making It Happen—Making Commitments to Next Steps

Summary and Adjourn

anchors. There is then an *environmental assessment* phase in which relevant information about the company and its career options and staffing needs is presented. Finally, a career planning workshop typically concludes with goal setting and action planning in which the individual sets career goals and creates a career plan.

A career planning workbook may be distributed to employees either as part of a workshop or as an independent career planning aid. This is "a printed guide that directs its users through a series of assessment exercises, models, discussions, guidelines, and other information to support career planning."[33] It is usually self-paced, so that the employees can complete the exercises at their own pace. As in Table 11.5, the career planning workbook normally contains several career self-assessment exercises, as well as information about how to examine career options (such as where to find out more about specific occupations and careers). The workbook may also contain practical career-related information such as how to prepare a résumé. Finally, career planning workbooks usually contain guides for creating a career development action plan.

TABLE 11.5 Table of Contents for Short Career Planning Workbook

Chapter 1—Self-Assessment: Taking a Good Look at Yourself
  Introduction
  Accomplishments
  Common Themes
  Assessing Skill Strengths
  Knowledge
  Personal Traits
  Work-Related Values
  Summary
Chapter 2—Examining Career Directions
  Introduction
  Career Directions
  Job Information Resources
  Identifying Organizational and Job Realities
  Resources
  Summary
Chapter 3—Making the Most of a Career Development Discussion
  Introduction
  Preparing a Career Résumé
  Sample Career Résumé
  Preparing for the Career Development Discussion
  Suggestions for an Effective Career Development Discussion
  Summary
  Notes
Chapter 4—Preparing a Career Development Action Plan
  Introduction
  Examining Avenues for Development
  Evaluating Trade-offs
  Preparing a Career Development Strategy
  Afterword

Source: Fred L. Otte and Peggy G. Hutcheson, *Helping Employees Manage Careers* (Englewood Cliffs, NJ: Prentice-Hall, 1992), p. 147.

One of the thorniest problems a job hunter faces is the relative dearth of qualified advisors out there to help in the job search. As explained elsewhere, some employers have a policy of retaining outplacement specialists for the purpose of providing career counseling and job search help to the employees they lay off. However, such qualified outplacement specialists generally (though not always) deal exclusively with employer-paid assignments: You can't just walk into one and have them help you. Beyond this, the field of job search help runs the gamut from the generally qualified college career counseling centers, which can help you with your career choice, to the sometimes less-than-reputable "job search experts" who may charge an up-front fee of $2,000 or more and give you very little in return.

Some human resource managers, realizing the shortage of qualified help but not able to commit to the substantial fees that outplacement specialists often charge, provide computer-assisted programs to help discharged employees with their career and job search decisions. These computerized programs are generally also available to anyone who asks. They cost from $100 to $300.

One good example of such a computerized program is Career Navigator, for sale by outplacement specialist Drake Bean Morin, Inc., 100 Park Avenue, New York, New York 10017. The program contains both a comprehensive manual and a set of computer disks. It covers all the steps a job searcher would normally go through, from identifying career interests through sending thank-you letters after a job is obtained.

For example, section 2 ("Know Yourself") takes you step by step through a program in which you identify your interests, define your values, identify your accomplishments, and identify your skills. Here you'll not only be able to zero in on several ideal job preferences; you will also generate a list of accomplishment statements that will be useful for building your résumé and conducting interviews later in your job search.

Succeeding sections of the program take you step by step through the job search itself. By interacting with the computer you will learn how to use the telephone effectively, how to write effective letters (the program will actually print these out for you in the proper format), and how to interview effectively. The computerized program will help you create your résumé and will print it out for you (again in the proper format). And it will help you organize a job research campaign plan and give you a computerized printout of weekly action plans. It will even assess your weekly progress. It then gives you help in negotiating your offers, evaluating them, and even assessing the first three months on the new job. ◆

Provide Opportunities for Mentoring   Mentoring can be defined as "the use of an experienced individual [the mentor] to teach and train someone [the protégé] with less knowledge in a given area."[34] Through individualized attention "the mentor transfers needed information, feedback, and encouragement to the protégé . . ."[35] and in that way the opportunities for the protégé to optimize his or her career success are improved.

Organizational mentoring may be formal or informal. Informally, of course, middle- and senior-level managers will often voluntarily take up-and-coming employees under their wings not only to train them but to give career advice and to help them steer around political pitfalls.

However, many employers also establish formal mentoring programs. Here employers actively encourage mentoring relationships to take place and may in fact pair protégés with potential mentors. Training—perhaps in the form of instructional manuals—may be provided to facilitate the mentoring process and in particular to aid both mentor and protégé in understanding their respective responsibilities in the mentoring relationship.

Managing Promotions and Transfers

Making Promotion Decisions

Employers must decide on what basis to promote employees, and the way these decisions are made will affect the employees' motivation, performance, and commitment.

Decision 1: Is Seniority or Competence the Rule?   Probably the most important decision is whether promotion will be based on seniority or competence, or some combinations of the two. From the point of view of motivation, promotion based on competence is best. However, your ability to use competence as a sole criterion depends on several things, most notably whether or not your firm is unionized or governed by civil service requirements. Union agreements often contain a clause that emphasizes seniority in promotions, such as: "In the advancement of employees to higher paid jobs when ability, merit, and capacity are equal, employees with the highest seniority will be given preference."[36] Although this might seem to leave the door open for giving a person with less seniority but slightly better ability the inside track for a job, labor arbitrators have generally held that when clauses such as these are binding only *substantial differences in abilities can be taken into account.* In one case, for example, the arbitrator ruled that seniority should be disregarded only when an employee with less seniority stood "head and shoulders" above the employees with greater seniority.[37] Similarly, many organizations in the public sector are governed by civil service regulations that emphasize seniority rather than competence as the basis for promotion.[38]

Decision 2: How Is Competence Measured?   If promotion is to be based on competence, how will competence be defined and measured? Defining and measuring *past* performance is a fairly straightforward matter: The job is defined, standards are set, and one or more appraisal tools are used to record the employee's performance. But promotion also requires predicting the person's *potential;* thus, you must have a valid procedure for predicting a candidate's future performance.

Many employers simply use prior performance as a guide and extrapolate, or assume, that based on the person's prior performance he or she will perform well on the new job. This is the simplest procedure to use.

On the other hand, some employers use tests to evaluate promotable employees[39] and to identify those employees with executive potential.[40] Others use assessment centers to assess management potential.

Decision 3: Is the Process Formal or Informal?   Next and particularly if you decide to promote based on competence, you have to decide whether the promotion process will be formal or informal. Many employers still depend on an informal system. Here the availability and requirements of open positions are kept secret. Promotion decisions are then made by key managers from among employees they know personally and also from among those who, for one reason or another, have impressed them.[41] The problem is that when you don't make employees aware of the jobs that are available, the criteria for promotion, and how promotion decisions are made, the link between performance and promotion is cut. The effectiveness of promotion as a reward is thereby diminished.

Many employers therefore do establish formal, published promotion policies and procedures. Here employees are generally provided with a formal promotion policy statement that describes the criteria by which promotions are awarded. Formal systems often include a job-posting policy. This states that open positions and their requirements will be posted and circulated to all employees. As explained in Chapter 4, many employers also compile detailed information about the qualifications of employees, while others use work force replacement charts. Computerized information systems can be especially useful for maintaining qualifications inventories on hundred or thousands of employees. The net effect of such actions is twofold: (1) An employer ensures that all qualified employees are considered for openings; and (2) promotion becomes more closely linked with performance in the minds of employees.

Decision 4: Vertical, Horizontal, or Other? Finally, employers are increasingly having to deal with the question of how to "promote" employees in an era in which higher-level jobs are less available. On the one hand, layoffs due to mergers eliminated many of the higher-management positions that employees might normally aspire to, as has the flattening of most organization charts.[42] On the other hand, worker empowerment and a related emphasis on technological expertise have created cadres of highly trained professionals, technicians, and first-line workers who aspire to higher-level positions but find their upward movement blocked by a dearth of openings.

Several options are available here. Some firms, such as the exploration division of British Petroleum, have created two parallel career paths, one for managers and another for "individual contributors" such as engineers. In that way individual contributors, such as highly accomplished engineers, can move up to nonsupervisory but still more senior positions such as "senior engineer." These jobs have most of the perks and financial rewards attached to management-track positions at that level.[43]

Another option is to provide career development opportunities for an individual, either by moving the person horizontally or even within the same position he or she currently holds. Horizontally, for instance, a production employee might be moved to HR in order to give him or her an opportunity to develop new skills and test and challenge aptitudes. And, in a sense, "promotions" are possible even leaving the person in the same job: for example, some job enrichment is usually possible, and the firm can provide training that increases the opportunity for assuming increased responsibility.[44]

The accompanying Diversity Counts feature addresses the question of why women sometimes fail to get to the top of the corporate ladder when it comes to promotions.

Handling Transfers

Reasons for Transfers A transfer is a move from one job to another, usually with no change in salary or grade. Employees may seek transfers for personal enrichment, for more interesting jobs, for greater convenience—better hours, location of work, and so on—or for jobs offering greater possibilities for advancement.[52] Employers may transfer a worker in order to vacate a position where he or she is no longer needed, to fill one where he or she is needed, to retain a senior employee (bumping a less senior person when necessary), or more generally to find a better fit for the employee within the firm. Finally, many firms today are endeavoring to boost productivity by eliminating management layers. Transfers are thus increasingly a way to give employees who might have nowhere else to move in their

Diversity Counts

In Promotion and Career Management

There is no doubt that women still do not make it to the top of the career ladder in numbers that are in any way proportional to their numbers in U.S. industry. For example, while women constitute 40% of the work force, they hold less than 2% of the top-management positions.[45]

Many explanations have been put forth.[46] Blatant or subtle discrimination, including the belief that "women belong at home and are not committed to careers,"[47] inhibits many managers from taking women as seriously as men. The "old boy network" of informal friendships forged over lunch, at social events, at club meetings, and on the golf course is usually not open to women, although it's often here that promotional decisions are made. A woman who tries to act like "one of the boys" is often considered "too hard or too cold hearted," so that "women aspiring to executive positions have to stay within narrow bands of acceptable behavior where they may exhibit only certain traditional masculine and feminine qualities, and walking this fine line represents one of the most difficult tasks for executive women."[48] Unlike many men, women are often forced to make the "career versus family" decision, since the responsibilities of raising the children and managing the household still falls disproportionately on women. There may also be a dearth of women mentors, making it more difficult for women to find the role models and managerial mentors and protectors they need to help them guide their careers.

Women and their managers and employers can take a number of steps to enhance female employees' promotional and career prospects. Perhaps the most important task is to vigorously focus on taking the career interests of female employees seriously; in other words, the first step in stripping away the barriers that have impeded women's progress in the past is to accept that there have been and are problems that must be addressed.

Another step is instituting more flexible career tracks so that women who need to take off for several years to raise a family can return and resume their careers. Given the powerful role played by even subtle discrimination, employers also have to take exceptional care to ensure that in all aspects of promotion and career management—from HR and succession planning to performance appraisals, to carefully considering candidates for the company's jobs—the process is objective and not subject to hidden biases.

A recent study suggests other steps employers and managers can take. Career encouragement (encouraging female employees to take responsibility for their careers and to map out career plans) appears to increase women's training and development activities, which in turn enhances managerial advancement.[49] Training and development and career encouragement are increased and enhanced by self-confidence, so it is useful to take steps to enhance employees' career self-confidence.

Beyond that there are several things the employee herself can do, say several experts.[50]

Be able and capable: Learn and understand your business.

Be seen as able and capable: Do not let you abilities be discounted or ignored.

Find a mentor and engage in networking.

Train yourself beyond the job and increase your career assets so you will be available when a good job opportunity arises.

Know what you want and prepare to balance and prioritize your life.[51] ◆

firms opportunities for diversity of job assignment and, therefore, personal growth.

Effect on Family Life   Many firms have had policies of routinely transferring employees from locale to locale, either to give their employees more exposure to a wide range of jobs or to fill open positions with trained employees. Such easy-transfer policies have fallen into disfavor, however. This is partly because of the cost of relocating employees (paying moving expenses, buying back the employee's current home, and perhaps financing his or her next home, for instance) and partly because it was assumed that frequent transfers had a bad effect on an employee's family life.

One study suggests that the latter argument, at least, is without merit.[53] The study compared the experiences of "mobile" families who had moved on the average of once every two years with "stable" families who had lived in their communities for more than eight years. In general, the stable families were no more satisfied with their marriages and family life or children's well-being than were the mobile families. In fact, mobile men and women believed their lives to be more interesting and their capabilities greater than did stable men and women. Likewise, they were more satisfied with their family lives and marriage than were stable men and women.

However, mobility was associated with dissatisfaction with social relationships among men and women (for instance, in terms of opportunities to make friends at work and in the community). Developing new social relationships was cited as a problem for children of mobile parents, with missing old friends and making new friends a bigger problem for teenagers than for young children.

The major finding, however, was that there were few differences between mobile and stable families. Few families in the mobile group believed moving was easy. However, these families were as satisfied with all aspects of their lives (except social relationships) as were stable families. This study notwithstanding, there is no doubt that employees do resist geographical transfers more today than they did even a few years ago. In one study, for instance, "the proportion of top executives who were 'eager' or 'willing' to make a geographic move has dropped ten percentage points to 51.5% since 1979, while 45% described themselves as reluctant."[54]

Building Employee Commitment

Helping Employees to Self-Actualize

You will come to a point when you will ask whether you've achieved all you could have achieved, given your skills, your gifts, and your dreams for yourself, and if not then woe to the firm that prevented you from doing so.[55] Few needs are as strong as the need to fulfill your dreams, to become all you are capable of becoming. Firms that don't cater to this need lose their best employees or drift along with increasingly bitter, unhappy, and uncommitted ones. Psychologist Abraham Maslow said that the ultimate need is "the desire to become more and more what one is, to become anything that one is capable of becoming." Self-actualization, to Maslow, meant that what a man or woman *can* be, he or she *must* be. It refers to the desire for self-fulfillment, namely, to the tendency for the person to become actualized in what he or she is potentially."[56] An important key to winning employees' commitment is thus to help them self-actualize—to become all they can be.[57]

Ironically, many companies not only do not try to fulfill this need, they actively thwart it. As a healthy person matures and approaches adulthood, said Chris Argyris, he or she moves to a state of increased activity, independence, and stronger interests.[58] The person also becomes capable of behaving in a greater variety of ways and tends to have a much longer time perspective. And as he or she matures from the subordinate role of a child to an equal or superordinate role as an adult, the person also develops more awareness of and control over his or her actions. Often, said Argyris, the typical company with its short-cycle jobs, autocratic supervision, and relative dearth of growth opportunities thwarts these normal maturation changes by forcing employees into dependent, passive, and subordinate roles.

Not surprisingly, progressive firms such as Saturn and Federal Express do things differently. They all engage in practices that aim to ensure that all employees have every opportunity to actualize—to use all their skills and gifts at work, and become all they can be. Of course, actualizing doesn't have to mean just promotions or career success. Certainly, these are very important. But the crucial question is whether employees have that opportunity to develop and use all their skills and become—as Maslow would say—all they can be. Training employees to expand their skills and solve problems at work (as described in Chapters 7 and 8), enriching their jobs and empowering them to plan and inspect their own work (Chapter 9), and helping them continue their educations and grow (Chapters 7 and 8) are other ways to achieve this.

Examples of Career Management/Promotion-from-Within Programs

Yet, for many employees, "becoming all you can be" does include career progress. Many firms today, therefore, have comprehensive career management/promotion-from-within programs.

It is important to distinguish between promotion-from-within programs and policies. Many firms do have promotion-from-within *policies*. At JC Penney, "We believe in promotion from within whenever a unit's requirements and an associate's qualifications provide a suitable match. Promotions are based primarily on such factors as performance (including productivity), dependability, initiative, and availability."[59] At Federal Express "open positions are filled, whenever possible, by qualified candidates from within the existing workforce."[60] At IBM, "promotion is from within—and also based on merit."[61] At Delta Airlines, "Delta hires at entry-level, then trains and develops personnel to promote them to higher levels of responsibility."[62] At Toyota, where the team leader and group leader positions are stepping stones to all management positions in the plant, "it is TMM's philosophy to consider its current workforce when attempting to fill team leader and group leader job openings. [Furthermore] TMM is committed to filling open positions in the office classifications by promotions from within whenever possible. New hires are considered only after efforts to promote from within have been exhausted."[63]

However, there is more to a successful promotion-from-within *program* than a strong policy statement. At more progressive firms such as Federal Express, such a program contains five parts, consisting of a promotion-from-within policy (previously discussed); value-based hiring; developmental activities; career-oriented appraisals; and a coordinated system of career records and job postings.

Promotion-from-Within and Value-Based Hiring

Promotion-from-within is aided first by value-based hiring, which we explained in Chapter 6. As one Delta manager said: "First of all, we hire for the future. . . . The employment process favors applicants who have the potential for promotion for a good reason. Delta subscribes almost entirely to a promotion-from-within policy. Except for a handful of people with specialized skills, everyone is hired in at entry-level."[64] The story is similar at other progressive firms. Promotion-from-within assumes the people you hire have the potential to develop to the point where they're promotable. Hiring people who have promotion potential and values that are synchronous with those of the firm is thus a first step in any promotion-from-within program.

Developmental Activities

Next provide the educational and training resources needed to help employees identify and develop their promotion potential. At Ben & Jerry's, promotional development is encouraged with programs of career planning, company internships, and tuition assistance. Ben & Jerry's employees are encouraged to attend a sequence of eight four-hour career planning seminars, the aim of which is to help employees think about and plan their careers. Employees who have completed the seminars and want to learn about other jobs within the firm can then spend two or three days interning at another company job, on paid time. The firm offers up to 90% funding for tuition reimbursement for up to three courses per year. It also provides many classes, seminars, counseling and tutoring, both on company premises and off. These include community and college courses; business writing, taught by the Community Colleges of Vermont and including one-on-one tutoring; computer classes, in which employees can earn a certificate from Ben & Jerry's information services group; adult basic education tutoring and high school diploma program; management development counseling one-on-one, by invitation and request; professional development classes and seminars; and financial planning seminars and individual counseling.

Robert Holland, Ben & Jerry's CEO, believes that employees' development is an integral part of career management.

Ben & Jerry's is not alone. For example, IBM—even with its cutbacks—still has one of the most extensive training and education programs in industry. In its advanced education program IBM sponsors part-time or full-time advanced education programs at outside colleges and universities. "Consistent with IBM's goal to encourage individual career development," employees may also receive educational leaves of absence without pay after two years of satisfactory full-time employment, as part of IBM's educational leave of absence program.[65]

IBM's program is available to all employees on a voluntary basis. It is each employee's responsibility to decide what development is appropriate given his or her work interests and future goals. Managers are then charged with determining their employees' interest in participating in these programs and understanding the development needs of their employees. IBMers usually pursue their desired development activities with their own personal commitment of time and energy. But in doing so they're encouraged by the firm: "While participation in employee development planning is not, in itself, a guarantee of promotion, transfer or change in job, it can be helpful to you in setting your work goals and enhancing your capabilities."[66] The company's tuition refund plan also fully reimburses employees for the cost of tuition and other eligible education fees for approved courses and programs given by any accredited college, university, high school, business, or technical school.

The career development program at Saturn is similarly comprehensive. A career growth workshop uses vocational guidance tools (including a skills assessment disk and other career gap analysis tools) to help employees identify career-related skills and the development needs they require. This career growth workshop, according to one employee, "helps you assess yourself, and takes four to six hours. You use it for developing your own career potential. The career disk identifies your weaknesses and strengths: you assess yourself, and then your team assesses you."[67] Tuition reimbursement and other development aids are then available to help employees develop the skills they need to get ahead.

No career assessment, training, or education programs can guarantee an employee will be promoted, of course. Particularly in this era of consolidations, employees may well plateau, rising no higher at their own firms. However, the career programs are still valuable. These firms' educational assistance and development programs help guarantee that all employees have the opportunity to formulate realistic pictures of their career abilities, interests, and occupational options. They help ensure that all employees have an equal opportunity to make themselves promotable at their firms. These programs also make it easier for employees to choose and make lateral moves, ones that will let them broaden and challenge themselves, and, if needed, to compete for jobs at other firms. And, they provide a continuing opportunity for each employee to grow, by learning new subjects and meeting new academic challenges. Here is how one Saturn assembler summed it up:

> I'm an assembler now, and was a team leader for two-and-a-half years. My goal is to move into our people-systems [personnel] unit. I know things are tight now, but I know that the philosophy here is that the firm will look out for me—they want people to be all they can be. I know here I'll go as far as I can go; that's one reason I'm so committed to Saturn.[68]

Career-Oriented Appraisals

Career-oriented firms also stress career-oriented appraisals; they don't just assess past performance. Instead the supervisor and the employee are charged with linking the latter's past performance, career preferences, and developmental needs in a formal career plan.

JC Penney is a good example here. As illustrated in Figure 11.3, its Management Appraisal form requires both a "promotability recommendation" and "projections for associate development."

Here is how it works. Prior to the annual appraisal the associate and his or her manager review Penney's Management Career Grid (Figure 11.4). The grid itemizes all supervisory positions at JC Penney (grouped by operations jobs, merchandise jobs, personnel jobs, and general management jobs) and includes specific job titles such as "regional catalog sales manager," "cosmetic market coordinator," "regional training coordinator," and "project manager, public affairs." The firm also provides a "work activities scan sheet." This basically contains thumbnail job descriptions for all the grid's jobs.

The Management Career Grid also identifies typical promotional routes. As the instructions indicate: "When projecting the next assignment for a management associate, you should consider not only merchandise positions but also operations and personnel positions as well as general management positions."

Promotional projections can cross the four groups, as well as up one or two job levels. Thus, a senior merchandising manager might be projected for promotion to either assistant buyer or general merchandise manager. ("Assistant buyer" is classified as a general management job at Penney's since buying is done centrally. The potential general merchandise manager job is a merchandise group job, two levels above the person's current senior merchandising manager position.)

Career Records/Jobs Posting Systems

Finally, promotion-from-within requires career records/jobs posting systems. The basic purpose of such systems is to ensure that the career goals and skills of inside candidates are matched openly, fairly, and effectively with promotional opportunities. For example,

> Consider Goldman Sach's Internal Placement Center (IPC).[69] Its aim is to offer Goldman Sachs employees interested in pursuing career opportunities in different areas of the firm the resources to locate and apply for job openings. The IPC also makes it simpler for managers to consider qualified internal candidates when filling open positions, and furnishes managers with information about openings that could provide career development opportunities for their employees.[70]

The IPC process contains five steps. First, the hiring manager can choose to conduct an internal, external, or combined (internal and external) search, but "an internal or combined search is strongly encouraged."[71] Next the manager and recruiter fill out a job description form for the open position. The form includes job title, department and manager, a description of the position's responsibilities and duties, and a summary of qualifications required for the position. Third, listings of current job opportunities are posted in the Internal Placement Center and in the reception area on each floor. Fourth, any employee interested in applying for an open position submits an IPC application and current résumé to the Internal Placement Center.

Finally, the IPC coordinator and the recruiter assessing each applicant's qualifications. Within two weeks after submitting his or her application, the employee is informed by the IPC coordinator at his or her home address about the status of the application. (This is the case whether or not the employee is selected to be interviewed for a position.) Those chosen as candidates then start their interviews.

Federal Express has its own job postings/career coordination system called JCATS, for Job Change Applicant Tracking System. Announcements of new job openings via this electronic system usually take place every Friday. All employees posting for the position get numerical scores based on job performance and length of service and are then advised as to whether or not they were chosen as candidates.

At JC Penney, regional managers (who oversee several stores) and regional personnel managers get lists of promotable people from store managers. The regions and districts also keep their own career-related files on supervisory personnel, and there are an additional 4,000 files or so at the JC Penney corporate office. The four functional divisions (merchandising, operations, personnel, and general management) also have files.

The question of who gets what files is largely determined by each associate's chosen career path (as determined by the yearly appraisal). Thus, someone who aims to move from merchandising manager to assistant buyer would have a file set up in the general management offices.

JC Penney also has an employee data base on over 18,000 managers—where they're located, their appraisal codes, their chosen career routes, and so on. A senior executive reviews all recommendations for interregional or interdepartmental transfers. And the chief operating officer evaluates all the appraisals and career plans for all employees down through the director level. The result, says one of the firm's top personnel officers, is an ongoing dialogue between mangers and subordinates regarding their careers. They are always discussing—at least annually, usually a lot more often—what this person will be doing in the next 12 months, and what his or her career options are. And in turn the store manager is discussing the same thing regarding the individual with his or her own district manager. The emphasis is always on how to help this subordinate grow.[72]◆

Figure 11.3
Portion of JC Penney's Appraisal Form
Note: Career oriented appraisal.

Date & Initials Mo/year Follow Up		
9|10|95 GPT/HS		

Management Characteristics and Strategic Directions: Fill in letter for each using ratings below. See reverse for definitions.
Ratings: O = Outstanding G = Good S = Satisfactory ND = Needs Development TN = Too New to Rate or Not Applicable

I. Leadership _G_ II. Awareness _ND_ III. Sense of Urgency _ND_ IV. Judgement _G_ V. Planning & Organizing _G_ VI. Team Process Participation _G_ VII. Fashion Credibility _G_ VIII. EEO Management _G_

Additional Comments, Strengths and Opportunities Lee achieved very solid results in Men's -- nice sales, good team development and depth of lines. Shoes is a real opportunity for Lee. Many decisions must be made more quickly by Lee, using merchandise systems better.

OVERALL PERFORMANCE RATING [3] (See reverse for instructions)

Manager Signature	Date of Appraisal	Reviewer Signature	Date of Review	Associate Signature	Date of Appraisal	Is this associate willing to move residence? (Check One)
Garry D. Turner	4-15-96	Phil Adams	4-1-96	Lee Smith	4/15/96	[X] Yes [ ] Not Now

See Associate Career Gnd for Instructions

Promotability Recommendation: Enter letter here → [B]

A. This Year
D. Can grow with job
G. Recommend less responsibility

B. Second or third year
E. Recommend lateral transfer
H. Promotable this store

C. Fourth or fifth year
F. Is at responsibility level
I. Too New To Rate

High Potential: Check if this associate has exceptional growth potential. top 5% in drive and ability [ ]

Projections for Associate Development	Year 19 _97_		Year 19 ____	
	Position Title	Position Code/Volume	Position Title	Position Code/Volume
First Choice Projection	Sr.Merch.Mgr.	4300		
Alternate Projection				

DP. 2036 (Rev. 2/90) T.O.C. # 008-7427-1000

Retirement

Retirement for most employees is a bittersweet experience. For some it is the culmination of their careers, a time when they can relax and enjoy the fruits of their labor without worrying about the problems of work. For others, it is the retirement itself that is the trauma, as the once busy employee tries to cope with suddenly being "nonproductive" and with having the strange (and not entirely pleasant) experience of being home every day with nothing to do. For many retirees, in fact, maintaining a sense of identity and self-worth without a full-time job is the single most important task they'll face. And it's one that employers are increasingly trying to help their retirees cope with as a logical last step in the career management process.[73]

Retirement counseling on issues like Social Security and financial planning is becoming more important as conditions facing older workers become more complex.

Preretirement Counseling About 30% of the employers in one survey said they had formal preretirement programs aimed at easing the passage of their employees into retirement.[74] The most common preretirement counseling topics were:

Explanation of social security benefits (reported by 97% of those with preretirement education programs)

Leisure time (86%)

Finances and investment (84%)

Health (82%)

Living arrangements (59%)

Psychological adjustments (35%)

Second careers outside the company (31%)

Second careers inside the company (4%)

Among employers that did not have preretirement education programs, 64% believed that such programs were needed, and most of these said their firms had plans to develop them within two or three years.

Another important trend here is of granting part-time employment to employees as an alternative to outright retirement. Several recent surveys of blue- and white-collar employees showed that about half of all employees over age 55

Figure 11.4
Portion of JC Penney's Management Career Grid

Instructions and Use of Grid for Making Associate Projections of Development

1) Promotabilitiy - Enter the appropriate Promotability letter in the box provided. If the answer to Promotability Is D, F, or I, leave the "High Potential" and "Projections for Associate Development" sections blank.

2) High Potential - The High Potential box should be checked if this associate has exceptional growth potential — is within the top 5% in drive and ability. Please keep in mind that appraisal ratings and high potential ratings while related reflect two distinct judgments — performance in current assignment versus exceptional potential for growth. A "1" rated associate, is not necessarily high potential or vice versa.

FIELD MANAGEMENT

OPERATIONS		MERCHANDISE	
Position Title/Volume	Code	Position Title/Volume	Code
Regional Operations Manager	1002	Manager of Geographic Markets	1017
		Manager of Business Planning	1025
		District Manager	1121
		Store Manager 30+ D.S.	0109
		Entity Store Manager	0110
		Store Manager 22 - 30 D.S.	0108
		Store Manager 15 - 22 D.S.	0107
		Regional Business Planning Manager	1026
		Store Manager 10 - 15 D.S.	0106
		Store Manager Under 10 D.S.	0105
Regional Catalog Sales Center Manager	1150	Regional Merchandiser/Geographic Markets	1146
Regional Programs Manager	1100		
Regional Systems Manager	1027		
		Store Manager 5 - 10 S.L.	0104
Regional Catalog Sales Manager	1139	Business Planning Manager	**40( )0
District Operations Manager	2290	District Special Events & Publicity Manager	2800
District Operations/Personnel Manager	2310	Store Merchandise & Marketing Manager	4260
Regional Loss Prevention Manager	4804		
Operations Manager 30+ D.S.	1329	Store Manager 3 - 5 S.L.	0103
District Merchandise Systems Coordinator	2330	General Merchandising Manager 30+ D.S.	4299
D.L.D.C. Manager	3750	General Merchandising Manager 22 - 30 D.S.	4298
Operations Manager 25 - 30 D.S.	1328	Store Manager 1 - 3 S.L.	0102
		Regional Visual Merchandising Mgr - Geo. Mkts.	1085
		Regional Visual Merchandising Mgr - Metro Mkts.	1092
Regional Loss Prevention Representative	4805		
Regional Styling Salon Sales Manager	1109	General Merchandising Manager 15 - 22 D.S.	4297
Regional Maintenance Manager	1165	General Merchandising Manager 10 - 15 D.S.	4296
Regional Telecommunications Manager	1028	General Merchandising Manager under 10 D.S.	4295
District Loss Prevention Manager	5620	Store Manager under 1 S.L.	0101
		Multiple Unit D.L.D.C. Merchandiser	4450
Operations/Personnel Manager 10 - 25 D.S.	5356	D.L.D.C. Merchandiser	3760
D.L.D.C. Operations Manager	4930	District Merchandise Publicity Coordinator	5580
Systems Implementation & Training Manager	1130	Special Lines Market Coordinator	2340
Catalog Sales Center Manager	1010	District Visual Merchandising Manager	5630
Sales Support Manager	3210	Cosmetic Market Coordinator	0700
		Visual Merchandising Manager	4650
		Senior Merchandising Manager	4300
		Department Sales Manager	3460
		Shoe Department Manager	5590
		Cosmetic Manager	0710
(Functional Title) Manager	4980	Merchandising Manager	4310
		Fine Jewelry Manager	3360
		Multi Store Fine Jewelry Manager	4470
		Fine Jewelry Merchandiser	3370
		Shoe Department Merchandiser	5600
		Cosmetic Merchandiser	0720
		Merchandising Manager Trainee	4330

would like to continue working part-time after they retire, and some employers do build such options into their career management processes.

Chapter Review

Summary

1. The key to managing your career is gaining insight into what you want out of a career, into your talents and limitations, and into your values and how they fit with the alternatives you are considering.

2. The main stages in a person's career are: growth (roughly birth to age 14), exploration (roughly 15 to 24), establishment (roughly ages 24 to 44, the heart of most people's work lives), maintenance (45 to 65), and decline (preretirement). The establishment stage may consist of trial, stabilization, and midcareer crisis substages.

3. The first step in planning your career is to learn as much as you can about your own interest, aptitudes, and skills. Start by identifying your occupational orientation: realistic, investigative, social, conventional, enterprising, and artistic. Then identify your skills and rank them from high to low.

4. Next identify your career anchors: technical/functional, managerial, creativity, autonomy, and security. Then ask yourself what you want to do.

5. There are many sources you can turn to for learning about occupations and careers. These include the *Dictionary of Occupational Titles,* the *Occupational Outlook Handbook, Occupational Outlook Quarterly,* the *Encyclopedia of Careers and Vocational Guidance,* and the *Office of Personnel Management's Handbook X118.*

6. The supervisor plays an important role in the career management process. Important guidelines include: Avoid reality shock, be demanding, provide realistic job previews, conduct career-oriented performance appraisals, and encourage job rotation.

7. In making promotion decisions, you have to decide between seniority and competence, a formal or informal system, and ways to measure competence.

8. More firms today engage in practices aimed at helping employees "be all they can be," in other words, self-actualize. Training, job enrichment, and educational opportunities are examples. However, for many employees self-actualizing boils down to promotions and career progress. Many firms thus institute comprehensive career management/promotion-from-within programs.

9. Value-based hiring and developmental activities are two important components of such programs. Value-based hiring is important because promotion from within assumes you have employees who are promotable in the first place. Career developmental activities (including career assessment and planning) help employees identify their career interests and more intelligently plan career moves.

10. Career-oriented appraisals play a crucial role in managing careers. Here the supervisor and employee link the latter's past performance, career preferences, and developmental needs to develop an appropriate career plan.

11. Career records/job posting systems are also important. Maintaining career-related data on employees and then openly posting all jobs ensure that the career goals and skills of inside candidates are matched openly and fairly with promotional opportunities.

Key Terms

career planning and development	trial substage	occupational orientation
career cycle	stabilization substage	occupational skills
growth stage	midcareer crisis substage	aptitudes
exploration stage	maintenance stage	career anchors
establishment stage	decline stage	reality shock

Discussion Questions and Exercises

1. Briefly describe each of the stages in a typical career.
2. What is a career anchor? What are the main types of career anchors discussed in this chapter?
3. What are the main types of Holland occupational orientations discussed in this chapter?
4. Describe important sources of information you could use to learn about careers of interest to you.
5. Develop a résumé for yourself, using the guidelines presented in this chapter. (See the appendix.)
6. Write a one-page essay stating "Where I would like to be career-wise ten years from today."
7. Explain career-related factors to keep in mind when making the employee's first assignments.
8. Working individually or in groups, choose three occupations (such as management consultant, HR manager, or salesperson) and use some of the sources described in this chapter to make an assessment of the future demand for this occupation over the next ten years or so. Does this seem like a good occupation to pursue? Why or why not?
9. Working individually or in groups, choose several occupations such as programmer, lawyer, and accountant and identify as many job openings for these occupations on the Internet as you can. Do you think the Internet is a valuable job search source for these occupations? Why or why not?

Application Exercises

RUNNING CASE: Carter Cleaning Company
The Career Planning Program

Career planning has always been a pretty low-priority item for Carter Cleaning, since "just getting workers to come to work and then keeping them honest is enough of a problem," as Jack likes to say. Yet Jennifer thought it might not be a bad idea to give thought to what a career planning program might involve for Carter. A lot of their employees had been with them for years in dead-end jobs, and she frankly felt a little badly for them: "Perhaps we could help them gain a better perspective on what they want to do," she thought. And she definitely believed that the store management group needed better career direction if Carter Cleaning was to develop and grow.

Questions

1. What would be the advantages to Carter Cleaning of setting up such a career planning program?
2. Who should participate in the program? All employees? Selected employees?
3. Describe the program you would propose for injecting a career planning and development perspective into the Carter Cleaning Centers.

CASE INCIDENT: Reality Shock

Maria Blanco didn't know what to do. After graduating from Columbia University in 1995, she'd taken a job with a major New York talent agency, thinking she could pursue her first love, entertainment. The agency had a reputation for being like "family," but it turned out that it was like no family she'd ever known. The personnel director seemed to go out of his way to diminish the employee's importance by making comments like "If you want to leave, go ahead. I've got another one thousand applicants just like you."

She had spent her first year working in the mailroom and was now trying to figure out whether to leave for another big agency, find a small one, or change careers altogether. "This is not what I got an economics degree for," she thought. Now, in the summer of 1996, she was facing a very tight job market and hadn't been able to save a penny all year. All she knew was that she was miserable.

Questions

1. What would you do now if you were Maria? Why?

2. What could the talent agency have done to avoid problems like this?

 # Human Resource Management Simulation

Managing promotions is one of the principal decisions in the simulation. Do you promote from within or hire qualified people from outside the organization? While promoting from within increases morale, organizations also need "new blood" to bring new ideas and methods into the organization.

Incident (N) will give you some idea as to how hard certain promotion decisions are. The basic question raised is: "To what extent should a person's outside activities effect his or her ability to be promoted?"

Video Case

Too Old Too Soon

As this videocase shows, each year airline pilots and copilots who are entirely competent to fly planes are forced to retire. The Federal Aviation Administration's rationale behind mandatory retirement is that older pilots are not as safe as younger ones. The FAA's use of an eight-year-old study of private airplane pilots to substantiate mandatory retirement has created a great deal of controversy.

Questions

1. Consider other occupations where safety is a great concern—for example, bus driver, cab driver, and heavy equipment operator. Do you think jobs like those should be subject to mandatory retirement, too? Why or why not?

2. Do you think the FAA should make individual exceptions to the mandatory retirement rule? Why or why not?

3. Do you think it made sense for the FAA to base its mandatory retirement policy on the findings of an eight-year-old study of private plane pilots? Why or why not?

Source: ABC News, *Too Old Too Soon?* "20/20," June 28, 1991.

 # Take It to the Net

We invite you to visit the Dessler page on the Prentice Hall Web site at:
http://www.prenhall.com/~dessler
for the monthly Dessler update, and for this chapter's WorldWide Web exercise.

Appendix 11.1

Finding the Right Job

Helping You Get the Right Job

You have identified your occupational orientation, skills, and career anchors and have picked out the occupation you want and made plans for a career. And (if necessary) you have embarked on the required training. Your next step is to find a job that you want in the company and locale in which you want to work. Following are techniques for doing so.

Job Search Techniques

Do Your Own Research   Perhaps the most direct way of unearthing the job you want, where you want it, is to pick out the geographic area in which you want to work and find out all you can about the companies in that area that appeal to you, and the people you have to contact in those companies to get the job you want. Most public libraries have local directories. For example, the reference librarian in one Fairfax County, Virginia, library made the following suggestions for patrons seeking information about local businesses:

> *Industrial Directory of Virginia*
> *Industrial Directory of Fairfax County*
> *Principal Employers of the Washington Metro Area*
> *The Business Review of Washington*

Other general reference material you can use includes *Who's Who in Commerce and Industry, Who's Who in America, Who's Who in the East,* and *Poor's Register.* Using these guides, you can find the person in each organization who is ultimately responsible for hiring people in the position you seek.

Personal Contacts   According to one survey, the most popular way to seek job interviews is to rely on personal contacts such as friends and relatives.[75] For example, one Department of Labor study indicates that about 19% of managers got their jobs through friends and about 6% got them through relatives. Let as many responsible people as you can know that you are in the market for a job and specifically what kind of job you want. (Beware, though, if you are currently employed and don't want your job search getting back to your current boss; if that is the case, better just pick out two or three very close friends and tell them it is absolutely essential that they be discreet in looking for a job for you.)

No matter how close your friends or relatives are to you, by the way, you don't want to impose too much on them by shifting the burden of your job search to them. It is sometimes best just to ask them for the name of someone they think you should talk to in the kind of firm in which you'd like to work, and then do the digging yourself.

Answering Advertisements   Most experts agree that answering ads is a low-probability way to get a job, and it becomes increasingly less likely that you will get a job this way as the level of job increases. Answering ads, in other words, is fine for jobs that pay under $20,000 per year, but it's highly unlikely that as you move up in management you are going to get your job by simply answering classified ads. Nevertheless, good sources of classified ads for professionals and managers include *The New York Times, The Wall Street Journal,* and a separate *Wall Street Journal* listing of job openings.

In responding to ads, be sure to create the right impression with the materials you submit; check the typing, style, grammar, neatness, and so forth, and check your résumé to make sure it is geared to the job for which you are applying. In your cover letter, be sure to have a paragraph or so in which you specifically address why your background and accomplishments are appropriate to the job being advertised; you must respond clearly to the company's identified needs.[76]

Be very careful in replying to blind ads, however (those with just a post office box). Some executive search firms and companies will run ads even when no position exists just to gauge the market, and there is always the chance that you can be trapped into responding to your own firm.

Employment Agencies　　Agencies are especially good at placing people in jobs up to about $30,000 but they can be useful for higher-paying jobs as well. Their fees for professional and management jobs are usually paid by the employer. Assuming you know the job you want, review eight or so back issues of the Sunday classified ads in your library to identify the agencies that consistently handle the positions you want. Approach three or four initially, preferably in response to specific ads, and avoid signing any contract that gives an agency the exclusive right to place you.

Executive Recruiters　　Executive recruiters are retained by employers to seek out top talent for their clients, and their fees are always paid by the employer. They fill positions in the $40,000 and up category, although $50,000 is often the lower limit. They do not do career counseling, but if you know the job you want, it pays to contact a few. Send your résumé and a cover letter summarizing your job objective in precise terms, including job title and the size company you want, work-related accomplishments, current salary, and salary requirements. Firms are listed in the Yellow Pages under "Executive Search Consultants." However, beware, since some firms today call themselves executive search or career consultants but do no searches: They just charge a (often hefty) fee to help you manage your search. Remember that with a search firm you never pay a fee. A list of executive recruiters is also available from the Management Information Service of the American Management Association, 135 West 50th Street, New York, New York 11020.

Career Counselors　　Career counselors will not help you find a job per se; rather, they specialize in aptitude testing and career counseling. They are listed in the Yellow Pages under "Career Counseling" or "Vocational Guidance." Their services usually cost $300 or so and include psychological testing and interviews with an experienced career counselor. Check the firm's services, prices, and history as well as the credentials of the person you will be dealing with.

Executive Marketing Consultants　　Executive marketing consultants manage your job-hunting campaign. They generally are not recruiters and do not have jobs to fill. Depending on the services you choose, your cost will range from $400 to $5,000 or more. The process may involve months of weekly meetings. Services include résumé and letter writing, interview skill building, and developing a full job-hunting campaign. Before approaching a consultant, though, you should definitely do in-depth self-appraisal (as explained in this chapter) and read books like Richard Bolles's *The Quick Job Hunting Map* and *What Color Is Your Parachute?*

Then check out three or four of these firms (they are listed in the Yellow Pages under "Executive Search Consultants") by visiting each and asking: What exactly is your program? How much does each service cost? Are there any extra

Figure 11.5
Example of a Good Résumé

Source: Richard Payne, *How to Get a Better Job Quicker* (New York: Signet, 1988), pp. 80–81.

CONRAD D. STAPLETON
77 Pleasantapple Way
Coltsville, NY 10176
(914) 747-1012

CONFIDENTIAL

JOB OBJECTIVE:
: *Senior Production Manager* in a situation requiring extensive advertising and promotion experience.

PRESENT POSITION
: VALUE-PLUS DIVISION, INTERCONTINENTAL CORPORATION

1994–Present
: *Product Manager,* NEW PRODUCTS, LAUNDRYON SOAP and CARBOLENE CLEANER, reporting to Group Product Manager.

Recommended and obtained test market authorization, then managed all phases of development of THREE test brands, scheduled for introduction during Fall/Winter 1993. Combined first year national volume projects to $20 million, with advertising budget of $6 million. Concurrently developing several new products for 1994 test marketing.

Also responsible for two established brands: LAUNDRYON SOAP, a $7 million brand, and CARBOLENE CLEANER, a $4 million regional brand. Currently work with three advertising agencies on test and established brands.

1991–1993
: *Product Manager,* WEEKENDER PAINTS, a $6 million brand.

Developed and implemented a repositioning of this brand (including new copy and new package graphics) to counter a 10-year sales downtrend averaging 10% a year. Repositioning increased test market volume 16%, and national volume 8% the following year.

Later initiated development of new, more competitive copy than advertising used during repositioning. Test area sales increased 35%. National airing is scheduled for Fall 1991.

Developed plastic packaging that increased test market volume 10%.

Also developed and implemented profit improvement projects which increased net profit 33%.

1990
: *Product Manager,* SHINEZY CAR WASH, a $4 million brand.

Initiated and test marketed an improved aerosol formula and a liquid refill. Both were subsequently expanded nationally and increased brand volume 26%.

RICHARDS-DONALDS COMPANY

1989–1990
: *Assistant Product Manager,* reporting to Product Manager.

Concurrent responsibility on PAR and SHIPSHAPE detergents. Developed locally tailored annual promotion plans. These resulted in 30% sales increase on PAR and stabilization of SHIPSHAPE volume.

1988–1989
: *Product Merchandising Assistant*

Developed and implemented SUNSHINE SUDS annual promotion plan.

1987–1988
: Academic Leave of Absence to obtain MBA. See EDUCATION.

1985–1987
: *Account Manager,* Field Sales.

Account Manager for Shopper's Pal, the most difficult chain in Metropolitan Westchester. Achieved sales increase of 10% and distribution of all Lever products, introduced while I was on territory. Based on this performance was awarded Food'N Things Cooperatives, the second most difficult account, and achieved similar results.

(continued)

EDUCATION	READING SCHOOL, University of Maryland
	MBA in Marketing Management. Average grade 3.5 out of 4.0 Thesis: "The Distribution of Pet Supplies through Supermarkets," graded 4.0 out of 4.0. Courses included quantitative methods, finance, accounting and international business.
	ELTON COLLEGE, Kansas City, Missouri
	BA in Liberal Arts. Was one of 33, out of freshman class of 110, who completed four years of this academically rigorous program. Theses required each year. Judge in Student Court during senior year.

Figure 11.5 *(continued)*

costs, such as charges for printing and mailing résumés? What does the contract say? After what point will you get no rebate if you're unhappy with the services? Then review your notes, check the Better Business Bureau, and decide which of these firms (if any) is for you.

Writing Your Résumé

Your résumé is probably your most important selling document, one that can determine whether you "make the cut" and get offered a job interview. Here are some résumé pointers, as offered by employment counselor Richard Payne and other experts.[77] An example of a good résumé is presented in Figure 11.5.

Introductory Information   Start your résumé with your name, address, and telephone number. Using your office phone number, by the way, can indicate either that (1) your employer knows you are leaving or (2) you don't care whether he or she finds out. You're usually better off using your home phone number.

Job Objective   State your job objective next. This should summarize in one sentence the specific position you want, where you want to do it (type and size of company), and a special reason an employer might have for wanting you to fill the job. For example, "Production manager in a medium-size manufacturing company in a situation in which strong production scheduling and control experience would be valuable." Always try to put down the most senior title you know you can expect to secure, keeping in mind the specific job for which you are applying.

Job Scope   Indicate the scope of your responsibility in each of your previous jobs, starting with your most recent position. For each of your previous jobs, write a paragraph that shows job title, whom you reported to directly and indirectly, who reported to you, how many people reported to you, the operational and human resource budgets you controlled, and what your job entailed (in one sentence).

Your Accomplishments   Next (and this is very important) indicate your "worth" in each of the positions you held. This is the heart of your résumé. It shows for each of your previous jobs: (1) the concrete action you took and why you took it and (2) the specific result of your action—the "payoff." For example, "As production supervisor, I introduced a new process to replace costly hand soldering of component parts. The new process reduced assembly time per unit from 30 to 10 minutes and reduced labor costs by over 60%." Use several of these worth statements for each job.

Information Technology and HR
Finding A Job on the Internet

With more and more companies listing job openings on the Internet just about any serious job hunter should be using this valuable source.[1]

Here's just a sampling of how you can use the Internet to help you find a job. The On-Line Career Center, a non-profit employer association located in Ann Arbor, Michigan, lets job hunters submit their résumés at no charge and your résumé will remain on the system for 90 days. All expenses are paid by On-Line Career Center member employers, who are companies that pay an annual fee to post their job openings on the Center's Internet service. Corporate recruiters have desktop Internet access with on-line software specifically designed for recruiting and employment, while individuals may conduct employment searches and make their résumé available to all recruiters searching for applicants on the net.[2]

The Yahoo list at Stanford University is another way to discover job openings on the Internet. The Yahoo list at Stanford is a "list of lists" that helps you zero in on the Internet site that is of most use to you. In this case you can click on "business" and then on "employment." If you do,

you'll see a screen like the one in Figure 11.6. Following your search to other submenus might take you to a screen like the one in Figure 11.7, which shows career opportunities at Fidelity Investments.

Preparing your résumé for distribution on the Internet requires some special preparation, and you'll probably need a separate electronic version of your résumé. For one thing you'll probably need to save your electronic résumé "as a plain, pure, non-document mode, 7-bit ASCII text file."[3] You'll also have to set your left margin at zero but keep your right margin at 65. Also—unlike the typical paper résumé—you may want to start your electronic résumé with a list of key words; thus a freshly minted law school graduate interested in a particular specialty might list international intellectual property China as key words if that's the special area of expertise he or she wants to pursue. ◆

[1]Except as noted, this section is based on Alfred Glossbrenner and Emily Glossbrenner, *Finding a Job on the Internet* (NY: McGraw-Hill, 1995).
[2]Ibid., pp. 104–105.
[3]Ibid., p. 194.

Length   Keep your résumé to two pages or less and list education, military service (if any), and personal background (hobbies, interests, associations) on the last page.

Personal Data   Do not put personal data regarding age, marital status, or dependents on top of page one. If you must include it, do so at the end of the résumé, where it will be read after the employer has already formed an opinion of you.

Finally, two last points. First, do not produce a slipshod résumé: Avoid overcrowded pages, difficult-to-read copies, typographical errors, and other problems of this sort. Second, do not use a make-do résumé—one from ten years ago. Produce a new résumé for each job you are applying for, gearing your job objective and worth statements to the job you want.

Make Your Résumé Scannable   For many job applications it's important to write a scannable résumé, in other words, one that is electronically readable by a computer system. Many medium- and larger-size firms that do extensive recruiting and hiring now use software to quickly and automatically review large numbers of résumés, screening out those that don't seem to match (often based on the absence of certain key words that the employer is looking for).

Figure 11.6
The Yahoo List's
Business/Employment
screen.

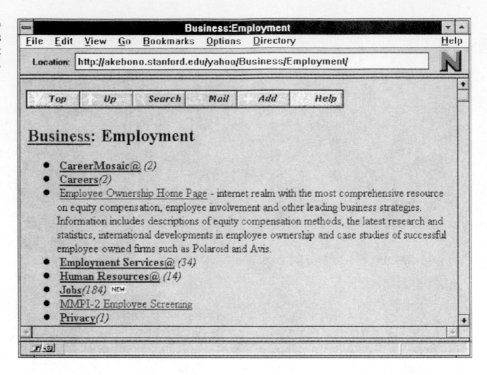

Figure 11.7
Career opportunities
with Fidelity
Investments.

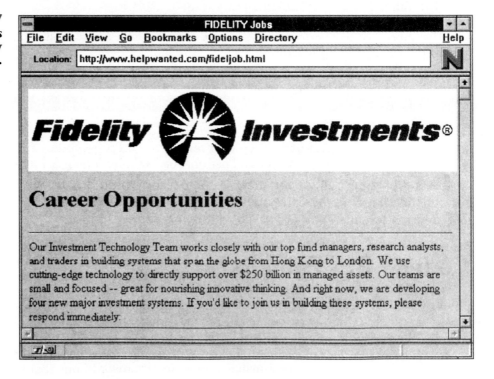

There are several guidelines to keep in mind for writing scannable résumés.[78] These can be summarized as follows:

Use type no smaller than 10 points and no larger than 14 points.

Do not use italicized type, and do not underline words.

Use type styles that work well for résumés and can be scanned as well as read, such as Helvetica, Futura, Optima, Times Roman, New Century Schoolbook, Courier, Univers, and Bookman.

Submit only high-resolution documents. Documents produced on a laser printer work best. Many photocopies and faxes are not clean enough for scanning.

Make sure to present your qualifications using powerful key words appropriate to the job or jobs for which you are applying. For example, trainers might use key words and phrases such as: *computer-based training, interactive video,* and *group facilitator.*

Handling the Interview

You have done all your homework and now the big day is almost here; you have an interview next week with the person who is responsible for hiring for the job you want. What do you have to do to excel in the interview? Here are some suggestions. (Also review interviewing in Chapter 6 at this point.)

Prepare, Prepare, Prepare   First, remember that preparation is essential. Before the interview, learn all you can about the employer, the job, and the people doing the recruiting. At the library, look through business periodicals to find out what is happening in the employer's field. Who is the competition? How are they doing?

Uncover the Interviewer's Needs   Spend as little time as possible answering your interviewer's first questions and as much time as possible getting the person to describe his or her needs: what the person is looking to get accomplished and the type of person needed. Use open-ended questions, such as "Could you tell me more about that?"

Relate Yourself to the Person's Needs   Once you have a handle on the type of person your interviewer is looking for and the sorts of problems he or she wants solved, you are in a good position to describe your own accomplishments in terms of the interviewer's needs. Start by saying something like, "One of the problem areas you've indicated is important to you is similar to a problem I once faced." Then state the problem, describe your solution, and reveal the results.

Think Before Answering   Recall from Chapter 6 that answering a question should be a three-step process: pause, think, speak. Pause to make sure you understand what the interviewer is driving at, think about how to structure your answer, and then speak. In your answer, try to emphasize how hiring you will help the interviewer solve his or her problem.

Make a Good Appearance and Show Enthusiasm   Appropriate clothing, good grooming, a firm handshake, and the appearance of controlled energy are important.

First Impressions Count   Studies of interviews show that in almost 80% of the cases, interviewers make up their minds about the applicant during the first few minutes of the interview. A good first impression may turn to bad during the interview, but it is unlikely. Bad first impressions are almost impossible to overcome.

Notes

1. J. Richard Hackman and J. Lloyd Suttle, *Improving Life at Work* (Santa Monica, CA: Goodyear, 1977); see also David Bowen and Edward Lawler, "Total Quality-Oriented Human Resources Management," *Organizational Dynamics,* Vol. 20, no. 4 (Spring 1992), pp. 29–41.

2. Hackman and Suttle, *Improving Life at Work,* p. 4. For a good discussion of how to maintain a career development process, see Beverly Kaye and Zandy Leibowitz, "Career Development: Don't Let It Fizzle," *HR Magazine* (September 1994), pp. 78–83. See also Robert Bolton and Jeffrey Gold, "Career Management: Matching the Needs of Individuals with the Needs of Organizations," *Personnel Review,* Vol. 23, No. 1 (1994), pp. 6–24.

3. These are quoted from Fred Otte and Peggy Hutcheson, *Helping Employees Manage Careers* (Englewood Cliffs, NJ: Prentice-Hall, 1992), pp. 5–6.

4. For example, one survey of "baby boomers" concluded that "allowed to excel" was the most frequently mentioned factor in overall job satisfaction in an extensive attitude survey of Canadian supervisors and middle managers between 30 and 45 years old. Judy Rogers, "Baby Boomers and Their Career Expectations," *Canadian Business Review* (Spring 1993), pp. 13–18.

5. Donald Super and others, *Vocational Development: A Framework for Research* (New York: Teachers College Press, 1957), and Edgar Schein, *Career Dynamics: Matching Individual and Organizational Needs* (Reading, MA: Addison-Wesley, 1978).

6. John Holland, *Making Vocational Choices: A Theory of Careers* (Englewood Cliffs, NJ: Prentice-Hall, 1973).

7. Richard Bolles, *The Quick Job Hunting Map* (Berkeley, CA: Ten Speed Press, 1979), pp. 5–6.

8. Ibid., p. 5.

9. Schein, *Career Dynamics,* pp. 128–129. For a recent description of how to apply career anchor theory in practice, see Thomas Barth, "Career Anchor Theory," *Review of Public Personnel Administration,* Vol. 13, no. 4 (1993), pp. 27–42.

10. Ibid., pp. 257–262.

11. This example is based on Richard Bolles, *The Three Boxes of Life* (Berkeley, CA: Ten Speed Press, 1976).

12. Schein, *Career Dynamics,* pp. 252–253.

13. For self-diagnosis books, see, for example, G. A. Ford and G. L. Lippitt, *A Life Planning Workbook* (Fairfax, VA: NTL Learning Resources, 1972).

14. Schein, *Career Dynamics,* p. 253.

15. Richard Bolles, *What Color Is Your Parachute?* (Berkeley, CA: Ten Speed Press, 1976), p. 86.

16. The Guidance Information System, Time Share Corporation, 630 Oakwood Avenue, West Hartford, CT 06110, described in Andrew Dubrin, *Human Relations: A Job-Oriented Approach* (Reston, VA: Reston, 1982), p. 358.

17. Gail Martin, "The Job Hunters Guide to the Library," *Occupational Outlook Quarterly* (Fall 1980), p. 10. See also Ronald Burke, "Career Development in a Professional Services Firm: On-the-Job Experinces and Continuous Learning," *Journal of Management Development,* Vol. 14, No. 1 (1995), pp. 25–33.

18. Robert Jameson, *The Professional Job Changing System* (Verona, NJ: Performance Dynamics, 1975).

19. Richard Payne, *How to Get a Better Job Quicker* (New York: New American Library, 1987).

20. Personal interview, March 1992.

21. Personal interview, March 1992.

22. Ibid.

23. Richard Reilly, Mary Tenopyr, and Steven Sperling, "The Effects of Job Previews on Job Acceptance and Survival Rates of Telephone Operator Candidates," *Journal of Applied Psychology,* Vol. 64 (1979).

24. Schein, *Career Dynamics,* p. 19.

25. J. Sterling Livingston, "Pygmalion in Management," *Harvard Business Review,* Vol. 48 (July–August 1969), pp. 81–89.

26. Joel Ross, *Managing Productivity* (Reston, VA: Reston, 1979).

27. Douglas Hall and Francine Hall, "What's New in Career Management?" *Organizational Dynamics,* Vol. 4 (Summer 1976).

28. H. G. Kaufman, *Obsolescence and Professional Career Development* (New York: AMACOM, 1974).

29. Hall and Hall, "What's New in Career Management?" p. 350.

30. See, for example, Terri Scandurg, "Mentorship and Career Mobility: An Empirical Investigation," *Journal of Organizational Behavior,* Vol. 13, no. 2 (March 1992), pp. 169–174.

31. Schein, *Career Dynamics,* p. 19. See also Robin Jacobs and Robert Bolton, "Career Analysis: The Missing Link in Managerial Assessment and Development," *Human Resource Management Journal,* Vol. 3, no. 2 (1994), pp. 55–62.

32. Otte and Hutcheson, *Helping Employees Manage Careers,* pp. 15–16.

33. Ibid., p. 143.

34. Timothy Newby and Ashlyn Heide, "The Value of Mentoring," *Performance Improvement Quarterly,* Vol. 5, no. 4 (1992), pp. 2–15.

35. Ibid., p. 2.

36. See for example, Daniel Quinn Mills, *Labor-Management Relations* (New York: McGraw-Hill, 1986), pp. 387–396.

37. James Healy, "The Factor of Ability in Labor Relations," in *Arbitration Today, Proceedings of the Eighth Annual Meeting of the National Academy of Arbitrators,* 1955, pp. 45–54, quoted in Pigors and Meyers, *Personnel Administration,* p. 283.

38. Charles Halaby, "Bureaucratic Promotion Criteria," *Administrative Science Quarterly,* Vol. 23 (September 1978), pp. 466–484.

39. Gary Dessler, *Winning Commitment* (New York: McGraw-Hill, 1993), pp. 144–149.

40. Ibid.

41. See Joseph Famularo, *Handbook of Modern Personnel Administration* (New York: McGraw-Hill, 1972), p. 17.

42. For a discussion, see Susan Schmidt, "The New Focus for Career Development Programs in Business and Industry," *Journal of Employment Counseling,* Vol. 31 (March 1994), pp. 22–28.

43. R. Tucker, M. Moravee, and K. Ideus, "Designing a Dual Career-Track System," *Training and Development,* Vol. 6 (1992), pp. 55–58; Schmidt, "The New Focus for Career Development," p. 26.

44. Schmidt, "The New Focus for Career Development," pp. 25–26.

45. Robert Marrujo and Brian Kleiner, "Why Women Fail to Get to the Top," *Equal Opportunities International,* Vol. 11, no. 4 (1992), pp. 1–5.
46. Unless otherwise noted this is based on ibid.
47. Ibid.
48. P. Watts, "Lending a Helping Hand," *Executive Female,* Vol. 12 (1989), pp. 38–40; quoted in ibid., p. 1.
49. Phyllis Tharenou, Shane Latimer, and Denise Conroy, "How Do You Make It to the Top? An Examination of Influences on Women's and Men's Managerial Advancement," *Academy of Management Journal,* Vol. 37, no. 4 (1994), pp. 899–931.
50. These are based on Marrujo and Kleiner, "Why Women Fail to Get to the Top," p. 3; and Ann Morrison, P. White, and Ellen Van Velsor, *Breaking the Glass Ceiling* (Reading, MA: Addison-Wesley Publishing Co., 1987).
51. See also Ronald Burke and Carol McKeen, "Supporting the Career Aspirations of Managerial and Professional Women," *Business and the Contemporary World* (Summer 1993), pp. 69–80.
52. See, for example, Richard Chanick, "Career Growth for Baby Boomers," *Personnel Journal,* Vol. 71, no. 1 (January 1992), pp. 40–46.
53. Ibid.
54. Commerce Clearing House, "Top Executives Are Growing Reluctant to Relocate," *Ideas and Trends,* December 10, 1982, p. 218.
55. This is based on Gary Dessler, *Winning Commitment* (New York: McGraw-Hill, 1993), Chapter 10.
56. Abraham Maslow, "A Theory of Human Motivation," *Psychological Review,* Vol. 50 (1943), pp. 370–396, reprinted in Michael Matteson and John Ivancevich, *Management Classics* (Santa Monica, CA: Goodyear Publishing Co., 1977), p. 336.
57. Ibid.
58. Chris Argyris, *Integrating the Individual and the Organization* (New York: John Wiley & Sons, 1964).
59. JC Penney Associate Handbook, p. 3. For many, success has been enlarged to include spiritual and emotional dimensions as well as traditional economic measures. See, for example, Fred Otte and William Kahnweiler, "Long-Range Career Planning During Turbulent Times," *Business Hori-*
zons, Vol. 38, No. 1 (January 1995), pp. 2–7.
60. Federal Express Employee Handbook, p. 28.
61. About Your Company, IBM Handbook, p. 17.
62. Delta Policies and Procedures Manual.
63. Toyota Team Member Handbook, p. 82.
64. Paulette O'Donnell speech, pp. 4–5.
65. *About Your Company,* IBM Handbook, p. 188.
66. Ibid., p. 188.
67. Personal interview, March 1992.
68. Personal interview, March 1992.
69. Goldman Sachs, "Internal Placement Center: Guidelines for Managers."
70. Ibid., p. 1.
71. Ibid.
72. Personal interview, March 1992.
73. Remember certain highly paid executives and employees receiving pensions of at least $25,000 a year at retirement can be forced to retire at 65, under federal law.
74. "Preretirement Education Programs," *Personnel,* Vol. 59 (May–June 1982), p. 47. Also see Daniel Halloran, "The Retirement Identity Crisis—and How to Beat It," *Personnel Journal,* Vol. 64 (May 1985), pp. 38–40 and Silvia Odenwald, "Pre-Retirement Training Gathers Steam," *Training and Development Journal,* Vol. 40, no. 2 (February 1986), pp. 62–63.
75. Jameson, *The Professional Job Changing System.* See also Kenneth McRae, "Career-Management Planning: A Boon to Managers and Employees," *Personnel,* Vol. 62, no. 5 (May 1985), pp. 56–60. See also John Wareham, "How to Make a Headhunter Call You," *Across the Board,* Vol. 32, No. 1 (January 1995), pp. 49–50.
76. The percentage of job seekers who look for work by placing or answering ads has almost doubled since 1970, according to data compiled by the Bureau of Labor Statistics. See Michelle Harrison Ports, "Trends in Job Search Methods, 1970–92," *Monthly Labor Review* (October 1993), pp. 63–67.
77. Payne, *How to Get a Better Job Quicker.* See also Larry Salters, "Résumé Writing for the 1990s," *Business and Economic Review,* Vol. 40, No. 3 (April 1994), pp. 11–18.
78. This is based on Erica Gordon Sorohan, "Electrifying a Job Search," *Training and Development* (October 1994), pp. 7–9.

Chapter 12
Establishing Pay Plans

Chapter Outline

- ◆ Basic Aspects of Compensation
- ◆ Basic Considerations in Determining Pay Rates
- ◆ Establishing Pay Rates
- ◆ Current Trends in Compensation
- ◆ Pricing Managerial and Professional Jobs
- ◆ Current Issues in Compensation Management

Behavioral Objectives

When you finish studying this chapter, you should be able to:

Discuss four basic factors determining pay rates.

Explain in detail each of the five basic steps in establishing pay rates.

Present the pros and cons of job evaluation.

Define comparable worth and explain its importance today.

Basic Aspects of Compensation

Compensation at Work

employee compensation
All forms of pay or rewards going to employees and arising from their employment.

Employee compensation refers to all forms of pay or rewards going to employees and arising from their employment,[1] and it has two main components. There are *direct financial payments* in the form of wages, salaries, incentives, commissions, and bonuses, and there are *indirect payments* in the form of financial benefits like employer-paid insurance and vacations.

In turn, there are essentially two ways to base direct financial payments to employees: on increments of time and on performance. Most employees are still paid mostly based on the time they put in on the job. For example, blue-collar workers are usually paid hourly or daily *wages;* this is often called *day work.* Some employees—managerial, professional, and usually secretarial and clerical—are *salaried.* They are compensated on the basis of a longer period of time (like a week, month, or year), rather than hourly or daily.

The second option is to pay for performance. *Piecework* is an example: it ties compensation directly to the amount of production (or number of "pieces") the worker produces, and is popular as an incentive pay plan. For instance, a worker's hourly wage is divided by the standard number of units he or she is expected to produce in one hour. Then for each unit produced over and above this standard, the worker is paid an incentive. Salespeople's commissions are another example of compensation tied to production (in this case, sales).

In this chapter we explain how to formulate plans for paying employees a fixed wage or salary; succeeding chapters cover financial incentives and bonuses and employee benefits.

Psychologists know that people have many needs, only some of which can be satisfied directly with money. Other needs—for achievement, affiliation, power, or self-actualization, for instance—also motivate behavior but can only be satisfied indirectly (if at all) by money.

Yet even with all our more modern motivation techniques (like job enrichment), there's no doubt that money is still the most important motivator. As two researchers put it:

> *Pay in one form or another is certainly one of the mainsprings of motivation in our society . . . . The most evangelical human relationist insists it is important, while protesting that other things are too (and are, perhaps in his view, nobler). It would be unnecessary to belabor the point if it were not for a tendency for money drives to slip out of focus in a miasma of other values and other practices. As it is, it must be repeated: Pay is the most important single motivator used in our organized society.*[2]

Basic Factors in Determining Pay Rates

Four basic factors influence the formulation of any pay plan: legal, union, policy, and equity factors.

Legal Considerations in Compensation

Numerous laws stipulate what employers can or must pay in terms of minimum wages, overtime rates, and benefits. These laws include:[3]

Davis-Bacon Act
A law passed in 1931 that sets wage rates for laborers employed by contractors working for the federal government.

Walsh-Healey Public Contract Act
A law enacted in 1936 that requires minimum-wage and working conditions for employees working on any government contract amounting to more than $10,000.

Fair Labor Standards Act
Congress passed this act in 1936 to provide for minimum wages, maximum hours, overtime pay, and child labor protection. The law has been amended many times and covers most employees.

1931 Davis-Bacon Act   The Davis-Bacon Act provides for the Secretary of Labor to set wage rates for laborers and mechanics employed by contractors working for the federal government. Amendments to the act provide for employee benefits and require contractors or subcontractors to make necessary payment for these benefits.

1936 Walsh-Healey Public Contract Act   The Walsh-Healey Public Contract Act sets basic labor standards for employees working on any government contract that amounts to more than $10,000. The law contains minimum wage, maximum hour, and safety and health provisions. Today it requires that time and a half be paid for work over 40 hours a week.

1938 Fair Labor Standards Act   The Fair Labor Standards Act, originally passed in 1938 and since amended many times, contains minimum wage, maximum hours, overtime pay, equal pay, record-keeping, and child labor provisions covering the majority of U.S. workers—virtually all those engaged in the production and/or sale of goods for interstate and foreign commerce. In addition, agricultural workers and those employed by certain larger retail and service companies are included.

One important provision governs overtime pay. It states that overtime must be paid at a rate of at least one and a half times normal pay for any hours worked over 40 in a workweek. Thus, if a worker covered by the act works 44 hours one week, he or she must be paid for 4 of those hours at a rate equal to one and a half times the hourly or weekly base rate the person would have earned for 40 hours. For example, if the person earns $5 an hour (or $200 for a 40-hour week), he or she would be paid at the rate of $7.50 per hour (5 times 1.5) for each of the 4 overtime hours worked, or a total of $30 extra. If the employee instead receives time off for the overtime hours, the number of hours granted off must also be computed at the one and a half time rate so that, for example, a person working 4 hours overtime would be granted 6 hours off in lieu of overtime pay.

The act also sets a minimum wage. This wage not only sets a floor or base wage for employees covered by the act; it also serves as an index that usually leads to increased wages for practically all workers whenever the minimum wage is raised. (The minimum wage in 1996 was $4.25 for the majority of those covered by the act.) The act also contains child labor provisions. These prohibit employing minors between 16 and 18 years of age in hazardous occupations such as mining and carefully restricts employment of those under 16.

Certain categories of employees are exempt from the act or certain provisions of the act, and particularly from the act's overtime provisions. An employee's exemption depends on the responsibilities, duties, and salary of the job. However, bona fide executive, administrative, and professional employees (like architects) are generally exempt from the minimum wage and overtime requirements of the act.[4]

Equal Pay Act of 1963
An amendment to the Fair Labor Standards Act designed to require equal pay for women doing the same work as men.

1963 Equal Pay Act   The Equal Pay Act, an amendment to the Fair Labor Standards Act, states that employees of one sex may not be paid wages at a rate lower than that paid to employees of the opposite sex for doing roughly equivalent work. Specifically, if the work requires equal skills, effort, and responsibility and is performed under similar working conditions, employees of both sexes must receive equal pay unless the differences in pay are based on a seniority system, a merit system, the quantity or quality of production, or "any factor other than sex." The act thus assumes that differences in pay may exist for men and women performing essentially the same jobs if those differences are based on such considerations as the quality or quantity of the person's work. Unfortunately, though, even today the average woman who works can still expect to earn only about 72 cents for each $1 earned by the average man who is working in the same occupation.[5] While it's down from the approximately 60 cents for each dollar earned by a man that prevailed throughout much of the post-World War II period, such a gap is still unacceptable.[6] The slight narrowing of the gap probably reflects several things, including changing values as well as convergence in men and women's schooling and work experience and declining wages in blue-collar (traditionally "men's") work.[7]

Civil Rights Act
This law makes it illegal to discriminate in employment because of race, color, religion, sex, or national origin.

Employee Retirement Income Security Act (ERISA)
The law that provides government protection of pensions for all employees with company pension plans. It also regulates vesting rights (employees who leave before retirement may claim compensation from the pension plan).

1964 Civil Rights Act Title VII of the **Civil Rights Act** is known as the Equal Employment Opportunity Act of 1964. It established the Equal Opportunity Employment Commission (EEOC). Title VII makes it an unlawful employment practice for an employer to discriminate against any individual with respect to hiring, compensation, terms, conditions, or privileges of employment because of *race, color, religion, sex,* or *national origin.*

1974 Employee Retirement Income Security Act (ERISA) The **Employee Retirement Income Security Act (ERISA)** in effect renegotiated every pension contract in the country. It provides for the creation of government-run employer-financed corporations to protect employees against their employer's pension plan failing. In addition, it set regulations regarding vesting rights. (Vesting refers to the equity or ownership the employees build up in their pension plan should their employment be terminated before retirement.) It also covers portability rights (the transfer of an employee's vested rights from one organization to another) and contains fiduciary standards to prevent dishonesty in the funding of pension plans.

The Tax Reform Act of 1986 The Tax Reform Act of 1986 represented the most extensive overhaul of the tax code in over 40 years.[8] It affected employee compensation in two ways. First, it reduced the number of individual tax rates to just three brackets—15%, 28%, and (today) a third bracket of 31%. Second, the act increased benefits coverage for rank-and-file employees while reducing tax-favored benefits that can be provided to highly paid employees.

Other Legislation Affecting Compensation Various other laws affect compensation decisions.[9] The *Age Discrimination in Employment Act of 1967 (ADEA)* originally prohibited discrimination in hiring individuals between 40 and 65 years old and applied to employers with 25 or more employees (and labor organizations with 25 or more members). ADEA protected workers with respect to compensation, terms, conditions, or privileges of employment. ADEA was amended effective January 1, 1987 to prohibit employers from requiring retirement at any age. The new law covers private employers with 20 or more employees, state and local governments, employment agencies that serve covered employers, and labor unions with 25 or more members.[10]

Each of the 50 states has its own worker's compensation laws, which today cover over 85 million workers. Among other things, the aim of these laws is to provide a prompt, sure, and reasonable income to victims of work-related accidents. The *Social Security Act of 1935* has been amended several times. It is aimed at protecting U.S. workers from total economic destitution in the event of termination of employment beyond their control. Employers and employees contribute equally to the benefits provided by this act. *This act also provided for unemployment compensation*—jobless benefits—for workers unemployed through no fault of their own for up to 26 weeks. (Social Security payments—payments to those who are disabled or retired, for instance—are discussed in Chapter 14.) The *federal wage garnishment law* limits the amount of an employee's earnings that can be garnished in any one week and protects the worker from discharge due to garnishment.

Union Influences on Compensation Decisions

Unions and labor relations laws also influence how pay plans are designed. The National Labor Relations Act of 1935 (or Wagner Act) and associated legislation and court decisions legitimatized the labor movement. It gave it legal protection and granted employees the right to organize, to bargain collectively, and to engage in concerted activities for the purpose of collective bargaining or other mutual aid or protection. Historically, the wage rate has been the main issue in collective bargaining. However, other issues including time off with pay, income security (for those in industries with periodic layoffs), cost-of-living adjustment, and various benefits like health care are also important.[11]

The National Labor Relations Board (NLRB) is the group created by the National Labor Relations Act to oversee employer practices and to ensure that employees receive their rights. It has made a series of rulings that underscores the need to involve union officials in developing the compensation package. For example, the employee's union must be given a written explanation of an employer's "wage curves"—the graph that relates jobs to pay rate. The union is also entitled to know the salary of each employee it is representing.[12]

Union Attitudes Toward Compensation Decisions   Several studies shed light on union attitudes toward compensation plans and on commonly held union fears.[13] Many union leaders fear that any system (like a time and motion study) used to evaluate the worth of a job can become a tool for management malpractice. They tend to feel that no one can judge the relative value of jobs better than the workers themselves. And they believe that management's usual method of using several compensable factors (like "degree of responsibility") to evaluate and rank the worth of jobs can be a manipulative device for restricting or lowering the pay of workers. One implication seems to be that the best way to gain the cooperation of union members in evaluating the worth of jobs is to get their active involvement in this process and in assigning fair rates of pay to these jobs. On the other hand, management has to ensure that its prerogatives—such as the right to use the appropriate job evaluation technique to assess the relative worth of jobs—are not surrendered.

Compensation Policies

An employer's compensation policies also influence the wages and benefits it pays, since these policies provide important compensation guidelines. One consideration is whether you want to be a leader or a follower regarding pay. For example, one hospital might have a policy of starting nurses at a wage at least 20% above the prevailing market wage. Other important policies include the basis for salary increases, promotion and demotion policies, overtime pay policy, and policies regarding probationary pay and leaves for military service, jury duty, and holidays. Compensation policies are usually written by the HR or compensation manager in conjunction with top management.[14]

Economists have proposed what they call segmented labor markets theories to emphasize that there are high- and low-wage employers.[15] Some employers choose to be leaders regarding pay and some followers, and as a result it's been noted that "A worker who moves from a low- to a high-wage employer within a U.S. city can usually increase his or her pay by over 50% with no change in job description."[16] Compensation policies have also been found to have measurable effects on workplace attitudes and behaviors.[17] Not surprisingly, workers receiving high wages are ". . . less likely to quit, are more satisfied with their pay, and report that they work harder than they have to."[18]

Equity and Its Impact on Pay Rates

The *need for equity* is a crucial factor in determining pay rates, specifically external equity and internal equity. Externally, pay must compare favorably with rates in other organizations or an employer will find it hard to attract and retain qualified employees. Pay rates must also be equitable internally: Each employee should view his or her pay as equitable given other pay rates in the organization. Some firms administer surveys to learn employees' perceptions and feelings about their compensation system. Questions typically addressed include "How satisfied are you with your pay?," "What criteria were used for your recent pay increase?," and "What factors do you believe are used when your pay is determined?"[19]

In practice, the process of establishing pay rates while ensuring external and internal equity takes five steps:

1. Conduct a *salary survey* of what other employers are paying for comparable jobs (to help ensure *external equity*).
2. Determine the worth of each job in your organization through *job evaluation* (to ensure *internal equity*).
3. Group similar jobs into *pay grades*.
4. Price each pay grade by using *wage curves*.
5. Fine tune pay rates.

Each of these steps is explained in the next section of this chapter.

Establishing Pay Rates

Step 1. Conduct the Salary Survey

salary survey
A survey aimed at determining prevailing wage rates. A good salary survey provides specific wage rates for specific jobs. Formal written questionnaire surveys are the most comprehensive, but telephone surveys and newspaper ads are also sources of information.

benchmark job
A job that is used to anchor the employer's pay scale and around which other jobs are arranged in order of relative worth.

Introduction Compensation or **salary surveys** play a central role in the pricing of jobs. Virtually every employer therefore conducts such surveys for pricing one or more jobs.[20]

An employer may use salary surveys in three ways. First, survey data are used to price **benchmark jobs** that are used to anchor the employer's pay scale and around which it's other jobs are then slotted based on their relative worth to the firm. (*Job evaluation,* explained next, is the technique used to determine the relative worth of each job.) Second, 20% or more of an employer's positions are usually priced directly in the marketplace, (rather than relative to the firm's benchmark jobs) based on a formal or informal survey of what comparable firms are paying for comparable jobs. Finally, surveys also collect data on *benefits* like insurance, sick leave, and vacation time and so provide a basis on which to make decisions regarding employee benefits.

There are many ways to conduct a salary survey. According to one British study, about 71% of the employers questioned rely to some extent on informal communication with other employers as a way of obtaining comparative salary information.[21] And 55% regularly review newspaper ads as a means of collecting comparative salary information, while 33% survey employment agencies to determine the wages for at least some of their jobs. About two-thirds of the firms also used commercial or professional surveys conducted by organizations like the American Management Association (or, in this case, its British counterparts). Finally, 22% of the firms also conducted formal questionnaire-type surveys with other employers.

Upward bias can be a problem regardless of the type of compensation survey.[22] While there's no scientific evidence to support the claim, at least one compensation expert argues that the way in which most surveys are constructed, interpreted, and used leads almost invariably to a situation in which firms set higher wages than they might otherwise. For example, "Companies like to compare themselves against well-regarded, high-paying, and high-performing companies," so that baseline salaries tend to be biased upward.[23] Similarly, "Companies that sponsor surveys often do so with an implicit (albeit unstated) objective: To show the company [is now] paying either competitively or somewhat below the market, so as to justify positive corrective action."[24] For these and similar reasons it's probably wise to review survey results with a skeptical eye and to acknowledge that upward bias may exist and perhaps should be adjusted for.

Formal and Informal Surveys by the Employer   Most employers rely heavily on formal or informal surveys of what other employers are paying.[25] Informal telephone surveys are good for collecting data on a relatively small number of easily identified and quickly recognized jobs, such as when a bank's human resource director wants to determine the salary at which a newly open cashier's job should be advertised. This informal phone technique is also good for checking discrepancies, such as when the human resource director wants to confirm whether some area banks are really paying tellers 10% more than his or her bank. Informal discussions among human resource specialists at professional conferences (like local meetings of the Society for Human Resource Management) are other occasions for informal salary surveys.

Perhaps 20% to 25% of employers use formal questionnaire surveys to collect compensation information from other employers. One page from such a survey is presented in Figure 12.1. It is part of a questionnaire that inquires about things like number of employees, overtime policies, starting salaries, and paid vacations. For a salary survey to be useful, it must be specific: most respondents in one study claimed that job categories were too broad or imprecise, for instance.[26]

Commercial, Professional, and Government Salary Surveys   Many employers also rely on surveys published by various commercial firms, professional associations, or government agencies. For example, the *Bureau of Labor Statistics (BLS)* annually conducts three types of surveys: (1) area wage surveys, (2) industry wage surveys, and (3) professional, administrative, technical, and clerical (PATC) surveys.

The BLS annually performs about 200 *area wage surveys*. These focus on clerical and manual occupations and provide pay data for a variety of jobs. An employer could use this information as an input in pricing jobs ranging from secretary to messenger to office clerk. Area wage surveys also provide data on weekly work schedules, paid holidays and vacation practices, and health insurance pension plans, as well as on shift operations and differentials.

Industry wage surveys provide data similar to that in the area wage surveys, but by industry rather than geographic area. They thus provide national pay data for workers in selected jobs for industries like building, trucking, and printing.

PATC surveys collect pay data on 80 occupational levels in the fields of accounting, legal services, personnel management, engineering, chemistry, buying,

**Figure 12.1
Compensation Survey**

Source: David Belcher and
Thomas Atchison,
Compensation Administration
(Englewood Cliffs, NJ:
Prentice Hall, 1987), pp.
112–113.

Name of organization participating in the survey:
Address: _____ Industry: _____
Code No.: _____ Date this form was completed: _____
Data furnished by: Name _____ Title _____

1. Briefly describe major products (or services) of your reporting unit: _____
_____
_____
_____
_____

2. Employment:
   Total number of employees in company, division, or plant for which survey data is reported:
   Hourly _____
   Nonexempt salaried _____
   Exempt salaried _____
   Total _____

3. General increase and structure adjustments:
   a. During the past twelve months, has your firm granted a general increase to employees in the following classifications?
   Hourly _____ No _____ Yes Amount or % _____ Date _____
   Nonexempt salaried _____ No _____ Yes Amount or % _____ Date _____
   Exempt salaried _____ No _____ Yes Amount or % _____ Date _____
   b. During the same period, did you have a structure adjustment?
   Hourly _____ No _____ Yes Amount or % _____ Date _____
   Nonexempt salaried _____ No _____ Yes Amount or % _____ Date _____
   Exempt salaried _____ No _____ Yes Amount or % _____ Date _____

4. Merit increases:
   a. Does your firm maintain a merit increase budget for granting pay increases during a time period?
   Hourly _____ No _____ Yes
   Nonexempt salaried _____ No _____ Yes
   Exempt salaried _____ No _____ Yes
   b. If no, what was the approximate salary increase for the last period?
   Hourly $ _____
   Nonexempt salaried $ _____
   Exempt salaried $ _____
   c. If yes (if you have a merit increase budget), it is:

	Merit	Promotion	Total
Hourly	_____ . ___ %	_____ . ___ %	_____ . ___ %
Nonexempt salaried	_____ . ___ %	_____ . ___ %	_____ . ___ %
Exempt salaried	_____ . ___ %	_____ . ___ %	_____ . ___ %

   d. What are the dates of your current budget year?
   From _____ to _____ , inclusive.

5. Union? _____ Yes _____ No
   If yes, list by name: _____
   _____
   _____
   _____

6. Cost of Living:
   Do you grant a cost-of-living allowance? _____ No _____ Yes
   If yes, what is the current amount and group involved? _____
   _____

7. Are any employee groups on automatic progression? _____ No _____ Yes
   If yes, groups, frequency, and amount: _____
   _____

8. Does your firm grant pay increases on an anniversary date or fixed calendar date(s)?

	Anniversary Date	Fixed Calendar	Date(s)
Hourly	_____	_____	_____
Nonexempt	_____	_____	_____
Exempt	_____	_____	_____

9. What is the frequency of your salary increases?

	Times per Year			
	1	2	3	Other
Hourly	____	____	____	_____
Nonexempt	____	____	____	_____
Exempt	____	____	____	_____

10. Any additional information that might help us interpret your pay data: _____
_____
_____
_____
_____

clerical supervisory, drafting, and clerical. They provide information about straight-time earnings (as in Table 12.1) as well as production bonuses, commissions, and cost-of-living increases.

The American Management Association of New York (AMA) conducts and furnishes executive, managerial, and professional compensation data as one of its services. For example, its *executive compensation service* provides about a dozen compensation reports on domestic executive positions as well as several foreign reports. The top-management report includes information from almost 4,000 firms covering about 31,000 executives in 75 top positions in 53 industries.[27] Listed are both salaries and bonuses earned by these executives. The AMA also publishes a middle-management report providing similar data on about 15,000 executives in 73 key jobs in about 650 firms. Its report on administrative and technical positions covers employee positions beneath middle management in about 600 companies. Its supervisory management compensation report surveys about 700 companies and 55 categories of first-line managers and staff supervisors.

The Administrative Management Society (AMS) conducts an annual survey of 13 clerical jobs, 7 data processing jobs, and various middle-management jobs in about 130 cities in the United States, Canada, and the West Indies (including many not covered by the BLS area wage surveys). The AMS surveys report data on salaries, length of workweeks, overtime, paid holidays, and the extent of union membership among survey participants for over 600,000 employees. They can provide a useful reference for employers making compensation decisions in the cities surveyed. Private consulting and/or executive recruiting companies like Hay Associates, Heidrick and Struggles, and Hewitt Associates annually publish data covering the compensation of top and middle management and members of boards of directors. Professional organizations like the Society for Human Resource Management and the Financial Executives Institute publish surveys of compensation practices among members of their associations.

For many firms, jobs are priced directly based on formal or informal salary surveys. In most cases, though, surveys are used to price benchmark jobs around which other jobs are then slotted based on their relative worth. Determining the relative worth of a job is the purpose of job evaluation, to which we now turn.

Step 2. Determine the Worth of Each Job: Job Evaluation

job evaluation
A systematic comparison done in order to determine the worth of one job relative to another.

Purpose of Job Evaluation   **Job evaluation** is aimed at determining a job's relative worth. It is a formal and systematic comparison of jobs to determine the worth of one job relative to another and eventually results in a wage or salary hierarchy. The basic procedure is to compare the *content of jobs* in relation to one another, for example, in terms of their effort, responsibility, and skills. Suppose you know (based on your salary survey and compensation policies) how to price key benchmark jobs and can use job evaluation to determine the relative worth of all the other jobs in your firm relative to these key jobs. Then you are well on your way to being able to equitably price all the jobs in your organization.

compensable factor
A fundamental, compensable element of a job, such as skills, effort, responsibility, and working conditions.

Compensable Factors   There are two basic approaches you could use for comparing several jobs. First, you could take a more intuitive approach. You might decide that one job is "more important" than another and not dig any deeper into why in terms of specific job-related factors.

As an alternative, you could compare the jobs by focusing on certain basic factors they have in common. In compensation management, these basic factors are called **compensable factors.** They are the factors that determine your defi-

TABLE 12.1 PATC Wage Survey

OKLAHOMA CITY, OKLAHOMA
Average Pay for Each Position, February 1993

Administrative, Clerical, Professional, and Technical Workers	Average Weekly Earnings
Accountants, Level II	$548
Accountants, Public, Level III	—
Attorneys, Level II	$911
Buyers/Contracting Specialists, Level I	531
Clerks, Accounting, Level II	318
Clerks, General, Level II	276
Clerks, Order, Level I	308
Computer Operators, Level II	353
Computer Programmers, Level II	532
Computer Systems Analysts, Level II	787
Drafters, Level II	424
Engineering Technicians, Level II	456
Engineers, Level II	719
Key Entry Operators, Level I	295
Personnel Assistants (Employment), Level II	—
Personnel Specialists, Level II	$514
Personnel Supervisors/Managers, Level II	—
Registered Nurses, Level II	—
Secretaries, Level III	$453
Switchboard Operators-Receptionists	279
Word Processors, Level II	352

Custodial, Maintenance, Material Movement, Powerplant, and Toolroom Workers	Average Hourly Earnings
Forklift Operators	$9.33
Genereal Maintenance Workers	8.55
Guards, Level I	6.22
Janitors	5.73
Maintenance Electricians	—
Maintenance Electronics Technicians, Level II	$16.14
Maintenance Machinists	13.14
Maintenance Mechanics, Machinery	13.19
Maintenance Mechanics, Motor Vehicle	12.89
Maintenance Pipefitters	—
Material Handling Laborers	$6.98
Order Fillers, Private Industry	8.53
Shipping/Receiving Clerks	—
Tool and Die Makers	17.25
Truckdrivers, Medium Truck	12.43
Warehouse Specialists	9.99

Source: Bureau of Labor Statistics. Adapted by the Bureau of National Affairs, Inc. 1994.

nition of job content, establish how the jobs compare to each other, and set the compensation paid for each job.

Some employers develop their own compensable factors. However, most use factors that have been popularized by packaged job evaluation systems or by federal legislation. For example, the Equal Pay Act focuses on four compensable factors—*skills, effort, responsibility,* and *working conditions.* As another example, the job evaluation method popularized by the Hay consulting firm focuses on three compensable factors: *know-how, problem solving,* and *accountability.*

The compensable factors you focus on depend on the job and the method of job evaluation to be used. For example, you might choose to include the compensable factor of decision making for a manager's job, which might be inappropriate for the job of assembler.

Identifying compensable factors plays a pivotal role in job evaluation. In job evaluation each job is usually compared with all comparable jobs *using the same compensable factors.* An employer thus evaluates the same elemental components for each job and is then better able to compare them—for example, in terms of the degree of skills, effort, responsibility, and working conditions present in each.[28]

Planning and Preparation for the Job Evaluation   Job evaluation is mostly a judgmental process, one that demands close cooperation between supervisors, personnel specialists, and the employees and their union representatives. The main steps involved include identifying the need for the program, getting cooperation, and then choosing an evaluation committee; the latter then carries out the actual job evaluation.[29]

Work stoppages may reflect employee dissatisfaction with pay plans and other forms of compensation such as benefits.

Identifying the need for job evaluation should not be difficult. For example, dissatisfaction reflected in high turnover, work stoppages, or arguments may result from the inequities of paying employees different rates for similar jobs.[30] Similarly, managers may express uneasiness with the current, informal way of assigning pay rates to jobs, accurately sensing that a more systematic means of assigning pay rates would be more equitable.

Next, since employees may fear that a systematic evaluation of their jobs may actually reduce their wage rates, *getting employee cooperation* for the evaluation is a second important step. You can tell employees that as a result of the impending job evaluation program, wage rate decisions will no longer be made just by management whim, that job evaluation will provide a mechanism for considering the complaints they have been expressing, and that no present employee's rate will be adversely affected as a result of the job evaluation.[31]

Next *choose a job evaluation committee,* and there are two reasons for doing so. First, the committee should bring to bear the points of view of several people who are familiar with the jobs in question, each of whom may have a different perspective regarding the nature of the jobs. Second, assuming the committee is composed at least partly of employees, the committee approach can help ensure greater acceptance by employees of the job evaluation results.

The composition of the committee can be important. The group usually consists of about five members, most of whom are employees. While management has the right to serve on such committees, its presence can be viewed with suspicion by employees and "it is probably best not to have managerial representatives involved in committee evaluation of nonmanagerial jobs . . . ."[32] However, an HR specialist can usually be justified on the grounds that he or she has a more impartial image than line managers and can provide expert assistance in the job evaluation. One method is to have this person serve in a nonvoting capacity.

Union representation is possible. In most cases, though, the union's position is that it is accepting job evaluation only as an initial decision technique and is reserving the right to appeal the actual job pricing decisions through grievance or bargaining channels.[33] Once appointed, each committee member should receive a manual explaining the job evaluation process and special instructions and training that explain how to conduct a job evaluation.

The evaluation committee performs three main functions. First, it usually identifies 10 or 15 key benchmark jobs. These will be the first jobs to be evaluated and will serve as the anchors or benchmarks against which the relative importance or value of all other jobs can be compared. Next, the committee may select compensable factors (although the human resource department will usually choose these as part of the process of determining the specific job evaluation technique to be used). Finally, the committee turns to its most important function—actually evaluating the worth of each job. For this, the committee will probably use one of the following job evaluation methods: the ranking method, the job classification method, the point method, or the factor comparison method.

Ranking Method of Job Evaluation   The simplest job evaluation method ranks each job relative to all other jobs, usually based on some overall factor like "job difficulty." There are several steps in the job **ranking method.**

1. *Obtain job information.* Job analysis is the first step. Job descriptions for each job are prepared and these are usually the basis on which the rankings are made. (Sometimes job specifications also are prepared, but the job ranking method usually ranks jobs according to "the whole job" rather than a number of compensable factors. Therefore, job specifications—which provide an indication of the demands of the job in terms of problem solving, decision making, and skills, for instance—are not quite as necessary with this method as they are for other job evaluation methods.)

2. *Select raters and jobs to be rated.* It is often not practical to make a single ranking of all jobs in an organization. The more usual procedure is to rank jobs by department or in "clusters" (such as factory workers, clerical workers). This eliminates the need for having to compare directly, say, factory jobs and clerical jobs.

3. *Select compensable factors.* In the ranking method, it is common to use just one factor (such as job difficulty) and to rank jobs on the basis of the whole job. Regardless of the number of factors you choose, it's advisable to explain the definition of the factor(s) to the evaluators carefully so that they evaluate the jobs consistently.

4. *Rank jobs.* Next the jobs are ranked. The simplest way is to give each rater a set of index cards, each of which contains a brief description of a job. These cards are then ranked from lowest to highest. Some managers use an "alternation ranking method" for making the procedure more accurate. Here you take the cards, first choosing the highest and the lowest, then the next highest and next lowest, and so forth until all the cards have been ranked. Since it is usually easier to choose extremes, this approach facilitates the ranking procedure. A job ranking is illustrated in Table 12.2. Jobs in this small health facility are ranked from maid up to office manager. The corresponding pay scales are shown on the right.

5. *Combine ratings.* Usually several raters rank the jobs independently. Then the rating committee (or employer) can simply average the rankings.

Pros and Cons   This is the simplest job evaluation method, as well as the easiest to explain. And it usually takes less time to accomplish than other methods.

Some of its drawbacks derive more from how it's used than from the method itself. For example, there's a tendency to rely too heavily on "guesstimates." Simi-

TABLE 12.2 Job Ranking by Olympia Health Care	
RANKING ORDER	**ANNUAL PAY SCALE**
1. Office manager	$28,000
2. Chief nurse	27,500
3. Bookkeeper	19,000
4. Nurse	17,500
5. Cook	16,000
6. Nurse's aide	13,500
7. Maid	10,500

After ranking, it becomes possible to slot additional jobs between those already ranked and to assign an appropriate wage rate.

larly, ranking provides no yardstick for measuring the value of one job relative to another. For example, job no. 4 may in fact be five times "more valuable" than job no. 5, but with the ranking system all you know is that one job ranks higher than the other. Ranking is usually more appropriate for small organizations that can't afford the time or expense of developing a more elaborate system.

classification (or grading) method
A method for categorizing jobs into groups.

classes
Dividing jobs into classes based on a set of rules for each class, such as amount of independent judgment, skill, physical effort, and so forth, required for each class of jobs. Classes usually contain similar jobs—such as all secretaries.

grades
A job classification system synonymous with class, although grades often contain *dissimilar* jobs, such as secretaries, mechanics, and firefighters. Grade descriptions are written based on compensable factors listed in classification systems, such as the federal classification system.

grade description
Written descriptions of the level of, say, responsibility and knowledge required by jobs in each grade. Similar jobs can then be combined into grades or classes.

Job Classification (or Grading) Evaluation Method Job **classification** is a simple, widely used method in which jobs are categorized into groups. The groups are called **classes** if they contain similar jobs, or **grades** if they contain jobs that are similar in difficulty but otherwise different. Thus, in the federal government's pay grade system, a "press secretary" and a "fire chief" might both be graded "GS–10" (GS stands for General Schedule). On the other hand, in its job class system, the State of Florida might classify all "secretary II's" in one class, all "maintenance engineers" in another, and so forth.

There are several ways to categorize jobs. One is to draw up *class descriptions* (the analogs of job descriptions) and place jobs into classes based on their correspondence to these descriptions. Another is to draw up a set of classifying rules for each class (for instance, how much independent judgment, skill, physical effort, and so on, does the class of jobs require?). Then the jobs are categorized according to these rules.

The usual procedure is to choose compensable factors and then develop class or grade descriptions that describe each class in terms of amount or level of compensable factor(s) in jobs. The federal classification system in the United States, for example, employs the following compensable factors: (1) difficulty and variety of work, (2) supervision received and exercised, (3) judgment exercised, (4) originality required, (5) nature and purpose of interpersonal work relationships, (6) responsibility, (7) experience, and (8) knowledge required. Based on these compensable factors, a **grade description** like that in Figure 12.2 is written. Then the evaluation committee reviews all job descriptions and slots each job into its appropriate class or grade; in the federal government system, for instance, the positions of automotive mechanic, welder, electrician, and machinist are classified as being in grade GS–10.

The job classification method has several advantages. The main one is that most employers usually end up classifying jobs anyway, regardless of the job evaluation method they use. They do this to avoid having to work with and price an unmanageable number of jobs; with the job classification method all jobs are already grouped into several classes. The disadvantages are that it is difficult to write

Figure 12.2
**Examples of Grade-
Level Definitions
in the Federal
Government**

Source: Douglass Bartley, *Job
Evaluation* (Reading, MA:
Addison-Wesley Publishing
Company, Inc., 1981), p. 36.

GRADE	DEFINITION
GS-1	Includes those classes of positions the duties of which are to perform, under immediate supervision, with little or no latitude for the exercise of independent judgment—
	(A) the simplest routine work in office, business, or fiscal operations; or
	(B) elementary work of a subordinate technical character in a professional, scientific, or technical field.
GS-2	Includes those classes of positions the duties of which are—
	(A) to perform, under immediate supervision, with limited latitude for the exercise of independent judgment, routine work in office, business, or fiscal operations, or comparable subordinate technical work of limited scope in a professional, scientific, or technical field, requiring some training or experience; or
	(B) to perform other work of equal importance, difficulty, and responsibility, and requiring comparable qualifications.
GS-3	Includes those classes of positions the duties of which are—
	(A) to perform, under immediate or general supervision, somewhat difficult and responsible work in office, business or fiscal operations, or comparable subordinate technical work of limited scope in a professional, scientific, or technical field, requiring in either case— (i) some training or experience; (ii) working knowledge of a special subject matter; or (iii) to some extent the exercise of independent judgment in accordance with well-established policies, procedures, and techniques; or (B) to perform other work of equal importance, difficulty, and responsibility, and requiring comparable qualifications.
GS-4	Includes those classes of positions the duties of which are—
	(A) to perform, under immediate or general supervision, moderately difficult and responsible work in office, business, or fiscal operations, or comparable subordinate technical work in a professional, scientific, or technical field, requiring in either case— (i) a moderate amount of training and minor supervisory or other experience;

the class or grade descriptions, and considerable judgment is required in applying them. Yet many employers (including the U.S. government) use this method with success. The government, in fact, has concluded that using more quantitative methods (like the two explained next) would cost much more than their additional accuracy warrants.[34]

point method
The job evaluation method in which a number of compensable factors are identified and then the degree to which each of these factors is present on the job is determined.

Point Method of Job Evaluation The **point method** is a more quantitative job evaluation technique. It involves identifying (1) several compensable factors, *each having several degrees,* as well as (2) the degree to which each of these factors is present in the job. Thus, assume that there are five degrees of responsibility an employer's jobs could contain. And assume a different number of points is assigned to each degree of each factor. Then, once the evaluation committee determines the degree to which each compensable factor (like "responsibility") is present in the job, the corresponding points for each factor can be added to arrive at a total point value for the job. The result is thus a quantitative point rating for each job. The point method is apparently the most widely used job evaluation method and is explained in detail in the appendix to this chapter.

factor comparison method
A widely used method of ranking jobs according to a variety of skill and difficulty factors, then adding up these rankings to arrive at an overall numerical rating for each given job.

Factor Comparison Job Evaluation Method The factor comparison method is also a quantitative technique and entails deciding which jobs have more of the chosen compensable factors. The method is actually a refinement of the ranking method. With the ranking method, you generally look at each job as an entity and rank the jobs on some overall factor like job difficulty. With the factor comparison method, you rank each job several times—once for each compensable factor you choose. For example, jobs might be ranked first in terms of the compensable factor "skill." Then they are ranked according to their "mental requirements," and so forth. Then these rankings are combined for each job into an overall numerical rating for the job. This too is a widely used method and is also explained in more detail in the appendix to this chapter.

Step 3. Group Similar Jobs into Pay Grades

pay grade
A pay grade is comprised of jobs of approximately equal difficulty.

Once a job evaluation method has been used to determine the relative worth of each job, the committee can turn to the task of assigning pay rates to each job, but it will usually want to first group jobs into pay grades. If the committee used the ranking, point, or factor comparison methods, it could assign pay rates to each individual job.[35] But for a larger employer such a pay plan would be difficult to administer, since there might be different pay rates for hundreds or even thousands of jobs. And even in smaller organizations there is a tendency to try to simplify wage and salary structures as much as possible. Therefore, the committee will probably want to group similar jobs (in terms of their ranking or number of points, for instance) into grades for pay purposes. Then, instead of having to deal with hundreds of pay rates, it might only have to focus on, say, 10 or 12.[36]

A pay grade is comprised of jobs of approximately equal difficulty or importance as determined by job evaluation. If the point method was used, the pay grade consists of jobs falling within a range of points. If the ranking plan was used, the grade consists of all jobs that fall within two or three ranks. If the classification system was used, then the jobs are already categorized into classes or grades. If the factor comparison method is used, the grade will consist of a specified range of pay rates, as explained in the appendix to this chapter. Ten to 16 grades per "job cluster" (a cluster is a logical grouping such as factory jobs, clerical jobs, and so on) are common.

Step 4. Price Each Pay Grade—Wage Curves

wage curve
Shows the relationship between the value of the job and the average wage paid for this job.

The next step is to assign pay rates to each of your pay grades. (Of course, if you chose not to slot jobs into pay grades, individual pay rates would have to be assigned to each individual job.) Assigning pay rates to each pay grade (or to each job) is usually accomplished with a wage curve.

The wage curve depicts graphically the pay rates currently being paid for jobs in each pay grade, relative to the points or rankings assigned to each job or grade by the job evaluation. An example of a wage curve is presented in Figure 12.3. Note that pay rates are shown on the vertical axis, while the pay grades (in terms of points) are shown along the horizontal axis. The purpose of the wage curve is to show the relationship between (1) the value of the job as determined by one of the job evaluation methods and (2) the current average pay rates for your grades.

Figure 12.3
Plotting a Wage Curve

Note: The average pay rate for jobs in each grade (Grade I, Grade II, Grade III, etc.) are plotted, and the wage curve fitted to the resulting points.

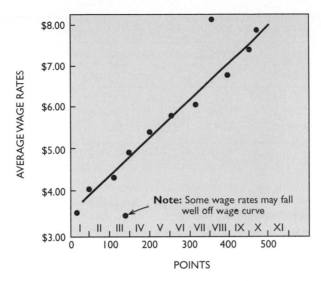

The pay rates on the graph are traditionally those now paid by the organization. If there is reason to believe that the present pay rates are substantially out of step with the prevailing market pay rates for these jobs, benchmark jobs within each pay grade are chosen and priced via a compensation survey. These new market-based pay rates are then plotted on the wage curve.

There are several steps in pricing jobs with a wage curve. First, *find the average pay for each pay grade,* since each of the pay grades consists of several jobs. Next *plot the pay rates* for each pay grade as was done in Figure 12.3. Then fit a line (called a *wage line*) through the points just plotted. This can be done either freehand or by using a statistical method. Finally, *price jobs.* Wages along the wage line are the target wages or salary rates for the jobs in each pay grade. If the current rates being paid for any of your jobs or grades fall well above or well below the wage line, that rate may be "out of line"; raises or a pay freeze for that job may be in order. Your next step, then, is to fine tune your pay rates.

Step 5. Fine Tune Pay Rates

Fine tuning involves correcting out-of-line rates and (usually) developing rate ranges.

rate ranges
A series of steps or levels within a pay grade, usually based upon years of service.

Developing Rate Ranges   Most employers do not just pay one rate for all jobs in a particular pay grade. Instead, they develop **rate ranges** for each grade so that there might, for instance, be ten levels or "steps" and ten corresponding pay rates within each pay grade. This approach is illustrated in Table 12.3, which shows the pay rates and steps for some of the federal government pay grades. As of the time of this pay schedule, for instance, employees in positions that were classified in grade GS–10 could be paid annual salaries between $24,011 and $31,211, depending on the level or step at which they were hired into the grade, the amount of time they were in the grade, and their merit increases (if any). Another way to depict the rate ranges for each grade is with a *wage structure,* as in Figure 12.4. The wage structure graphically depicts the range of pay rates (in this case, per hour) to be paid for each pay grade.

There are several benefits to using rate ranges for each pay grade. First, the employer can take a more flexible stance with respect to the labor market. For example, it makes it easier to attract experienced, higher-paid employees into a pay

TABLE 12.3 Federal Government Pay Schedule: Grades GS 8–GS 10

| | RATES AND STEPS WITHIN GRADE | | | | | | | | | |
GRADE	1	2	3	4	5	6	7	8	9	10
GS–8	19,740	20,398	21,056	21,714	22,372	23,030	23,688	24,346	25,004	25,662
GS–9	21,804	22,531	23,258	23,985	24,712	25,439	26,166	26,893	27,620	28,347
GS–10	24,011	24,811	25,611	26,411	27,211	28,011	28,811	29,611	30,411	31,211

Note: Federal grades range from GS–1 to top grade of GS–18 (annual rate of $84,157).
Source: The U.S. Office of Personnel Management.

grade where the starting salary for the lowest step may be too low to attract such experienced personnel. Rate ranges also allow you to provide for performance differences between employees within the same grade or between those with differing seniorities. As in Figure 12.4, most employers structure their rate ranges to overlap a bit so that an employee with more experience or seniority may earn more than an entry-level person in the next higher pay grade.

The rate range is usually built around the wage line or curve. One alternative is to arbitrarily decide on a maximum and minimum rate for each grade, such as 15% above and below the wage line. As an alternative, some employers allow the rate range for each grade to become wider for the higher pay ranges, re-

**Figure 12.4
Wage Structure**

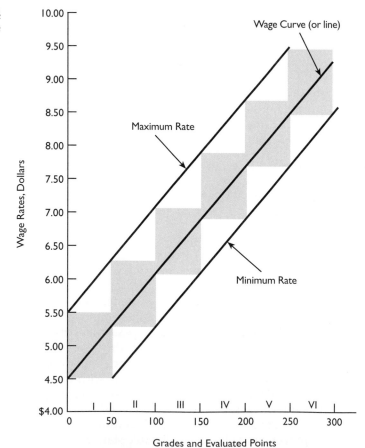

Note: This shows overlapping wage classes and maximum– minimum wage ranges.

flecting the greater demands and performance variability inherent in these more complex jobs.

Correcting Out-of-Line Rates The wage rate for a job may fall well off the wage line or well outside the rate range for its grade, as shown in Figure 12.3. *This means that the average pay for that job is currently too high or too low,* relative to other jobs in the firm. If a point falls well below the line, a pay raise for the job may be required. If the plot falls well above the wage line, pay cuts or a pay freeze may be required.

Underpaid employees should have their wages raised to the minimum of the rate range for their pay grade, assuming you want to retain the employees and have the funds. This can be done either immediately or in one or two steps.

Rates being paid to overpaid employees are often called *red circle, flagged,* or *overrates,* and there are several ways to cope with this problem. One is to freeze the rate paid to employees in this grade until general salary increases bring the other jobs into line with it. A second alternative is to transfer or promote some or all of the employees involved to jobs for which they can legitimately be paid their current pay rates. The third alternative is to freeze the rate for six months, during which time you try to transfer or promote the overpaid employees. If you cannot, then the rate at which these employees are paid is cut to the maximum in the pay range for their pay grade.

Current Trends in Compensation

Skill-Based Pay

Construction workers today are often compensated for their work through the method of skill-based pay, which originated with the guilds of the Middle Ages.

With skill-based pay, you are paid for the range, depth, and types of skills and knowledge you are capable of using rather than for the job you currently hold.[37] According to one expert, there are several key differences between skill-based pay (SBP) and job evaluation-driven job-based pay (JBP):[38]

1. *Competence testing.* With JBP, you receive the pay attached to your job regardless of whether or not you develop the competence needed to perform the job effectively. With SBP, your base pay is tied not to the job, but to your skills. You have to be certified as competent in the skills required by the job to get a pay increase.
2. *Effect of job change.* With JBP, your pay usually changes automatically when you switch jobs. With SBP that's not necessarily so. Before getting a pay raise, you must first demonstrate proficiency at the skills required by the new job.
3. *Seniority and other factors.* Pay in JBP systems is often tied to "time in grade" or seniority: In other words, the longer you're in the job, the more you get paid, regardless of how well you perform. SBP systems are based on skills, not seniority.
4. *Advancement opportunities.* Typically (but not always) there tend to be more opportunities for advancement with SBP plans than with JBP plans because of the companywide focus on skill building. A corollary to this is that SBP enhances organizational flexibility by making it easier for workers to move from job to job because their skills (and thus their pay) may be applicable to more jobs and thus more portable.

A skill-based pay plan was implemented at a General Mills manufacturing facility.[39] In this case, General Mills sought to boost the commitment and flexibility of its plant work force by implementing what it referred to as a high-involvement/high-performance work system, of which skill-based pay was one element. Other elements included egalitarian management practices such as having no reserved parking spaces for management and hiring employees who represented a close fit with the flexible, team-based organizational culture in the plant.

In this plant, the workers were paid based on their attained skill levels. There were basically four clusters (or "blocks") of jobs, corresponding to the four production areas: mixing, filling, packaging, and materials. Within each of these blocks workers could attain three levels of skill. Level 1 indicates limited ability, such as knowledge of basic facts and ability to perform simple tasks without direction.[40] Level 2 means the employee attained partial proficiency and could, for instance, apply technical principles on the job. Attaining Level 3 means the employee is fully competent in the area and could, for example, analyze and solve production problems. Each block or production area had a different average wage rate. There were, therefore, 12 pay levels (four blocks with three pay levels each) in the plant.

A new employee could start in any block, but always at Level 1. If after several weeks the employee was able to complete certification at the next higher skill level, his or her salary was correspondingly raised. Furthermore, employees were continually rotated from production area (or block) to production area. To be rotatable into a block, however, the employee had to achieve Level 2 performance within that skill block.

The system encouraged the learning of new skills. It also fostered flexibility by encouraging workers to learn multiple skills and willingly switch from block to block. The actual pricing of the 12 skill levels was accomplished in part by making the lowest of the 12 plant skill levels' wage rate equal to the average entry-level wage rate for similar jobs in the community. (Notice, therefore, that even with skill-based pay you still can't entirely escape evaluating jobs, market pricing them, and ranking them relative to one another in some fashion.)

Whether or not skill-based pay results in improved productivity is an open question. When used in conjunction with team-building and worker involvement and empowerment programs, it does appear to lead to higher quality as well as lower absenteeism rates and fewer accidents.[41] However, the findings in one firm, which are not conclusive, suggest that productivity was higher at its non-skill-based pay facility.[42]

HR and the Responsive Organization

Broadbanding

The trend today is for employers to reduce their salary grades and ranges from ten or more down to three to five, a process called *broadbanding.* Broadbanding means collapsing salary grades and ranges into just a few wide levels or "bands," each of which then contains a relatively wide range of jobs and salary levels. Thus, instead of having, say, ten salary grades each of which contains a salary range of, say, $15,000, the firm might collapse the ten grades into three broad bands, each with a set of jobs such that the difference between the lowest- and highest-paid jobs might be $40,000 or more. One survey found that almost one-third of the 3,400 employers responding said they had adopted a broadbanding approach or were considering doing so.[43]

Broadbanding's basic advantage is that it injects greater flexibility into employee compensation.[44] Broadbanding is especially sensible where firms flatten their hierarchies and organize around self-managing teams. The new, broad salary bands can include both supervisors and subordinates and can also facilitate moving employees slightly up or down along the pay scale without accompanying promotional raises or demotional pay cuts. For example, ". . . the employee who needs to spend time in a lower-level job to develop a certain skill set can receive higher-than-usual pay for the work, a circumstance considered impossible under traditional pay systems."[45]

Broadbanding also facilitates the sorts of less specialized, boundaryless jobs and organizations being embraced by many firms like General Electric. Less specialization and more participation in cross-departmental processes generally mean enlarged duties or capabilities and more possibilities for alternative career tracks; broader, more inclusive salary bands facilitate this. One expert argues that traditional quantitative evaluation plans actually reward unadaptability.[46] The argument here is that being slotted into a job that is highly routine as defined by a compensable factor such as "know-how" is unlikely to encourage job incumbents to think independently or be flexible. Instead, the tendency may be for workers to concentrate on the specific, routine jobs to which they are assigned and for which they are rewarded.

General Electric and Toyota are two employers who have broadbanded their pay scales. At Toyota there are only three plant job classifications: Division I includes all production team members; Division II includes all general maintenance team members; and Division III includes all tie and dye members. Similarly, General Electric, huge as it is, was able to restructure its entire pay plan into just five broad compensation bands.

Broadbanding a pay system involves several steps. First, as illustrated in Figure 12.5, the number of bands is decided upon and each is assigned a salary range. The bands usually have wide salary ranges and also overlap substantially. As a result, there's much more flexibility to move employees from job to job within bands and less need to "promote" them to new grades just to get them higher salaries.

The bands are then typically subdivided into either specific jobs (see Figure 12.6) or skill levels (see Figure 12.7). For example, a band may consist of a number of jobs each assigned a market value. More often, bands are subdivided into several skill levels. Recall that with this second approach, workers are not paid above market value just for doing a job well or for having seniority. Instead they must increase their competencies such as skills, knowledge, and abilities.[47] ◆

Figure 12.5
Setting Salary Ranges for Three Bands

Source: David Hofrichter, "Broadbanding: A 'Second Generation' Approach," *Compensation & Benefits Review,* Sept–Oct 1993, p. 56.

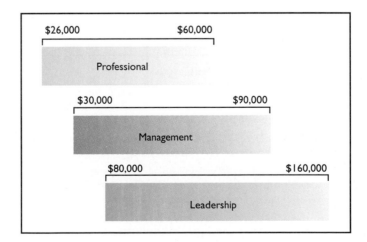

Information Technology and HR
Computerized Job Evaluations

As explained more fully in the appendix to this chapter, using a quantitative job evaluation plan such as the point plan can be a fairly time-consuming matter. This is so because accumulating the information about "how much" of each compensable factor the job contains has traditionally been done through an often tedious process in which evaluation committees debate the level of each compensable factor in a job. They then write down their consensus judgments and manually compute each job's point values.

According to one expert, CAJE—computer-aided job evaluation—can dramatically streamline this whole process.[1] Computer-aided job evaluation, she says, can simplify job analysis, help keep job descriptions up to date, increase evaluation objectivity, reduce the time spent in committee meetings, and ease the burden of system maintenance. CAJE "features electronic data entry, computerized checking of questionnaire responses and automated output—not only of job evaluations, but also of a variety of compensation reports."[2] Most CAJE systems have two main components.

There is a structured questionnaire. This contains items such as "enter total number of employees who report functionally to this position." Second, all CAJE systems are built around statistical models, which allow the computer program to price jobs more or less automatically based upon inputted information on such things as prices of benchmark jobs, current pay, and current pay grade midpoints.

Another expert points out that CAJE does not replace but enhances traditional evaluation systems.[3] He says that you still need a traditional job evaluation system to provide "the initial solid analysis of benchmark jobs"—in other words, to identify the relative worth of these benchmark jobs. Then CAJE "streamlines and speeds the job evaluation process for 'non-benchmark' jobs."[4]◆

[1]Sondra O'Neal, "CAJE: Computer-Aided Job Evaluation for the 1990s," *Compensation and Benefits Review* (November–December 1990), pp. 14–19.
[2]Ibid.
[3]Laurent Dufetel, "Job Evaluation: Still at the Frontier," *Compensation and Benefits Review* (July–August 1991), p. 64.
[4]Ibid.

Figure 12.6
Assigning Market Value

Source: David Hofrichter, "Broadbanding: A 'Second Generation' Approach," *Compensation & Benefits Review,* Sept–Oct 1993, pp. 56-57.

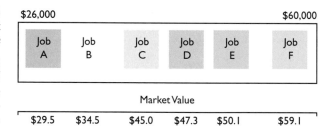

| $26,000 | | | | | $60,000 |
| Job A | Job B | Job C | Job D | Job E | Job F |

Market Value

| $29.5 | $34.5 | $45.0 | $47.3 | $50.1 | $59.1 |

Figure 12.7
Positioning Jobs within a Band

Source: David Hofrichter, "Broadbanding: A 'Second Generation' Approach," *Compensation & Benefits Review,* Sept–Oct 1993, pp. 56-57.

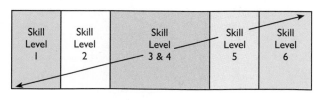

| Skill Level 1 | Skill Level 2 | Skill Level 3 & 4 | Skill Level 5 | Skill Level 6 |

Pay in Relation to Skills

Why Job Evaluation Plans Are Still Widely Used

Quantitative job evaluation systems such as the point and factor comparison plans are still used by 60% to 70% of all U.S. firms.[48] There are several reasons for this. Proponents argue that individual differences in skill attainment *can* be taken into consideration even when point-type plans are used, since most firms use salary ranges for groups of similar jobs. These salary ranges often reflect differences in the skills attained by, say, different people who may be working on the very same job.[49] Job evaluation advocates also argue that a job description is not necessarily a job restriction, since it's naive to "believe that employees automatically limit their behavior to what is written on a piece of paper."[50] Furthermore, they say, there's no reason why job evaluation needs to be limited to a specific job. Instead, one could theoretically evaluate the "job" of doing a whole project and from there ascertain the problem solving, accountability, and knowledge that a worker would need to do all the jobs involved in that project. Furthermore, neither skill-based pay nor market-based pay entirely eliminates the need for evaluating the worth of one job relative to others.

In the final analysis their relative ease of use and security are probably the major reasons for the continued widespread use of quantitative plans. Quantitative plans have also recently been facilitated by computerized packages, as explained in the accompanying Information Technology and HR box.

Building Employee Commitment

Compensation Management

Pay plans at well-known and progressive firms such as Saturn Corporation help illustrate the current trends in job evaluation and compensation management. As at the General Mills plant previously mentioned, the compensation plans at Saturn are elements in more comprehensive programs aimed at fostering employee commitment. These elements, as we've seen, include value-based hiring, career-oriented appraisals, and extensive employee involvement programs. Compensation therefore tends to reflect the trust with which these firms treat their employees, and the fact that employees are and should be treated as partners in the business.

The compensation policies at Saturn are typical.[51] Saturn's pay plan is built on four principles—salary, trust, few classifications, and pay-for-performance. All Saturn employees are salaried, and there are no time clocks in the facility. To report your hours you go to a keyboard and punch in the number of hours you worked. While there are some checks and balances, the process is basically an honor system. "What it comes down to," said one operating technician, "is a matter of trust."[52]

As at Toyota, there are also relatively few job classifications. Virtually all the assembly employees are classified as "operating technicians" as are all nonskilled trades members such as machinists. In addition, there are four additional classifications for skilled trades members.

Pay-for-performance is important, too. Under the reward system originally envisioned in the memorandum of agreement between Saturn and the UAW, about 20% of each employee's pay was to be "at risk." Specifically, each employee's base compensation was to equal 80% of straight-time wages of the average for comparable jobs rates in the U.S. automobile manufacturing industry. Over and above that, a reward system was to be developed that would be based on factors such as achievement of objective productivity targets, individual and work unit performance, quality bonuses, and eventually a "Saturn sharing formula" through which profits were to be shared above a specified level of return to Saturn. At a minimum, therefore, 20% of each person's pay was to be at risk, to be earned back if the individual and the company met their productivity goals. Then a profit-sharing formula was to kick in. A slower than expected startup at Saturn forced the firm to reduce the at-risk component to 5% and thus boost the "guaranteed" component of the pay. Under a modified skill-based approach, employees can earn that 5% back by meeting specified training goals (attending training sessions, improving their skills, and so on).

In summary, the trend in firms like Saturn is to

1. Offer packages of above-average pay combined with incentives and extensive benefits.
2. Build a compensation package that puts a significant portion of pay at risk.
3. Emphasize self-reporting of hours worked rather than devices like time clocks.
4. Build a pay plan that encourages employees to think of themselves as partners. This means that they should have a healthy share of the profits in good years and share in the downturn during bad times.
5. Provide a package of benefits that makes it clear employees are viewed as long-term investments. ◆

A Glimpse into the Future

The evolving practices in firms like Saturn provide us with a glimpse into the future of compensation management, and that future is now, as far as many firms are concerned. Here's what several compensation experts say we can expect.

First, with an increasing emphasis on flexibility and on empowering employees, "In the U.S. companies in the year 2000, most traditional job descriptions and hourly employee job classifications will be fed unceremoniously into the paper shredder."[53] Replacing them will be greater latitude for employees to evolve their responsibilities to meet customer needs as they see fit. And there will be an increasing emphasis on paying employees for their competencies rather than just for the job's responsibilities and activities. Measurement systems and rewards will increasingly emphasize paying for results.

Skill-based pay will actually be a return to the compensation methods of the far distant past. Under the apprentice systems that started with the guilds of the Middle Ages, apprentices had to demonstrate competence at their trade before becoming journeymen, and then masters. So when firms like General Mills condense dozens or hundreds of jobs into a few broad bands and then base pay differentials on skill levels, we're really returning, to some extent, to the past.[54]

One expert also suggests that as firms like IBM break themselves into small, specialized, and decentralized pieces, the concept of centrally determined compensation plans may become obsolete.[55] He says that at some point managers of decentralized units should get their own salary budgets and then "set pay levels for new hires, determine pay increases, decide when to give raises, and make all other decisions concerning cash compensation for the employees reporting to them."[56]

There will also be a growing emphasis on pay for improved results and on nontraditional pay (also called "alternative rewards"). As summarized in Figure 12.8, traditional pay plans based on job descriptions, job evaluations, and salary structures tend to focus, says this expert, on creating order, reinforcing the hierarchy, and directing behavior.[57] In the future (and, for many firms, now), the emphasis will shift from paying for the job to paying for the employee's contribution. Thus, the focus will shift from creating order and directing behavior to encouraging involvement and commitment, and to rewarding positive results. Nontraditional or alternative pay plans for doing this include competency

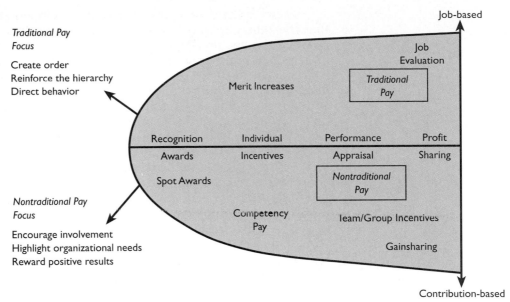

**Figure 12.8
Examples of
Traditional and
Nontraditional Pay**

Source: Sibson & Company, Inc. Reproduced in Charles Cumming, "Will Traditional Salary Administration Survive the Stampede to Alternative Rewards?" *Compensation and Benefits Review* (November–December 1992), p. 45.

Traditional Pay Focus

Create order
Reinforce the hierarchy
Direct behavior

Job-based

Job Evaluation

Traditional Pay

Merit Increases

Recognition Awards   Individual Incentives   Performance Appraisal   Profit Sharing

Spot Awards

Nontraditional Pay

Nontraditional Pay Focus

Encourage involvement
Highlight organizational needs
Reward positive results

Competency Pay

Team/Group Incentives

Gainsharing

Contribution-based

or skill-based pay and the sorts of spot awards, team incentives, and gainsharing we'll discuss in Chapter 13.

Pricing Managerial and Professional Jobs

Developing a compensation plan to pay executive, managerial, and professional employees is similar in many respects to developing a plan for any employees.[58] The basic aims of the plan are the same in that the goal is to attract good employees and maintain their commitment. Furthermore, the basic methods of job evaluation—classifying jobs, ranking them, or assigning points to them, for instance—are about as applicable to managerial and professional jobs as to production and clerical ones.

Yet for managerial and professional jobs, job evaluation provides only a partial answer to the question of how to pay these employees. Such jobs tend to emphasize nonquantifiable factors like judgment and problem solving more than do production and clerical jobs. There is also a tendency to pay managers and professionals based on ability—based on their performance or on what they can do—rather than on the basis of static job demands like working conditions. Developing compensation plans for managers and professionals, therefore, tends to be relatively complex, and job evaluation, while still important, usually plays a secondary role to nonsalary issues like bonuses, incentives, and benefits.

Compensating Managers

Basic Compensation Elements   There are five elements in a manager's compensation package: salary, benefits, short-term incentives, long-term incentives, and perquisites.[59]

The amount of salary managers are paid usually depends on the value of the person's work to the organization and how well the person is discharging his or her responsibilities. As with other jobs, the value of the person's work is usually determined through job analysis and salary surveys and the resulting fine tuning of salary levels.

Salary is the cornerstone of executive compensation: It is on this element that the others are layered, with benefits, incentives, and perquisites normally awarded in some proportion to the manager's base pay. *Benefits* (including time off with pay, health care, employee services, survivor's protection, and retirement coverage) are discussed in Chapter 14. *Short-term incentives* are designed to reward managers for attaining short-term (normally yearly) goals. *Long-term incentives* are aimed at rewarding the person for long-term performance (in terms of increased market share and the like). Incentives are discussed in Chapter 13. *Perquisites* (perks for short) begin where benefits leave off and are usually given to only a select few executives based on organizational level and (possibly) past performance. Perks include use of company cars, yachts, and executive dining rooms. These benefits are also covered in Chapter 14.

Executive compensation tends to emphasize performance incentives more than do other employees' pay plans, since organizational results are likely to reflect the contributions of executives more directly than those of lower-echelon employees. The heavy incentive component of executives' compensation can be illustrated with some examples of the highest-paid U.S. executives.[60] In 1995, for instance, the CEO of General Electric earned a salary of $2,000,000, a short term bonus of $3,250,000, and long-term compensation of $16,740,000. For the chairperson of Rockwell International, his salary component was $815,000 and the bonus was $2,000,000 for total compensation of $2,815,000. The chairperson of Coca Cola earned a salary of $1,680,000, a bonus of $3,200,000, and long-term compensation of $8,000,000 for a total of almost $13,000,000. In general, bonuses today equal 25% or more of a typical executive's base salary in many countries, including the United States, United Kingdom, France, and Germany.[61]

There is considerable disagreement regarding what determines executive pay and, therefore, whether top executives are worth what they are paid. At the lower-management levels (like first-line supervisor), there is no debate; supervisors' pay grades are usually set so that their median salaries are 10% to 25% above those of the highest-paid workers supervised. And many employers even pay supervisors for scheduled overtime, although the Fair Labor Standards Act does not require them to do so.[62]

It is at the top-management levels that questions regarding pay abound. The traditional wisdom is that a top manager's salary is closely tied to the size of the firm.[63] Yet two experts who tested this idea for the 148 highest-paid executives in the United States concluded that "the level of executive responsibility (as measured by total assets, total sales, total number of shares in the company, total value of the shares, and total corporate profits) is not an important variable in determining executive compensation."[64] Instead, say these experts, an executive's pay is mostly determined by the industry in which he or she works, and the "corporate power structure," since executives who also serve on their firms' boards of directors can heavily influence how they get paid.

Yet there is conflicting evidence. In one study, for instance, the researcher found that a statistical analysis of the total cash compensation of the chief executive officers of 129 companies showed that they were paid for both responsibility and performance. This researcher found that four compensable factors—company size, profitability, number of employees, and experience—accounted for 83% of the differences in pay. Therefore, it appears "that there are rational, acceptable, and abiding principles that govern the total cash compensation of top executives in manufacturing firms."[65]

In any case, shareholder activism is combining with congressional reform and other changes to tighten up the restrictions on what firms pay their top executives.[66] For example, the Securities and Exchange Commission voted in 1992 to approve final rules regarding executive compensation communications. The chief executive officer's pay is always to be disclosed as well as other officers' pay if their compensation (salary and bonus) exceeds $100,000. And for bankers, the Federal Deposit Insurance Act of 1991 contains a prohibition on excessive compensation. One result is that boards of directors must act responsibly in reviewing and setting executive pay. That, says one expert, includes determining the key performance requirements of the executive's job; assessing the appropriateness of the firm's current compensation practices; conducting a pay-for-performance survey; and testing shareholder acceptance of the board's pay proposals.[67]

The general trend today is to reduce the relative importance of base salary and boost the importance of short- and long-term executive incentives.[68] The main issue here is identifying the appropriate performance measures for each type of incentive and then determining how to link these to pay. Typical short-term measures of shareholder value include revenue growth and operating profit margin. Long-term shareholder value measures include rate of return above some predetermined base.

Managerial Job Evaluation Despite questions regarding the rationality of executive pay, job evaluation is still important in pricing executive and managerial jobs in most firms. According to one expert, "the basic approach used by most large companies to ensure some degree of equity among various divisions and departments is to classify all executive and management positions into a series of grades, to which a series of salary ranges is attached."[69]

As with nonmanagerial jobs, one alternative is to rank the executive and management positions in relation to each other, grouping those of equal value. However, the job classification and point evaluation methods are also used, with compensable factors like position scope, complexity, difficulty, and creative demands.

Compensating Professional Employees

Compensating nonsupervisory professional employees like engineers and scientists presents unique problems.[70] Analytical jobs put a heavy premium on creativity and problem solving, compensable factors not easily compared or measured. Furthermore, the professional's economic impact on the firm is often related only indirectly to the person's actual efforts; for example, the success of an engineer's invention depends on many factors, like how well it is produced and marketed.

The job evaluation methods we explained previously can be used for evaluating professional jobs.[71] The compensable factors here tend to focus on problem solving, creativity, job scope, and technical knowledge and expertise. Both the point method and factor comparison methods have been used, although the job classification method seems most popular. Here a series of grade descriptions are written, and each position is slotted into the grade having the most appropriate definition.

Yet, in practice, traditional methods of job evaluation are rarely used for professional jobs since "it is simply not possible to identify factors and degrees of factors which meaningfully differentiate among the values of professional work."[72] "Knowledge and the skill of applying it," as one expert notes, "are extremely difficult to quantify and measure."[73]

As a result, most employers use a market-pricing approach in evaluating professional jobs. They price professional jobs in the marketplace to the best of their ability to establish the values for benchmark jobs. These benchmark jobs and the employer's other professional jobs are then slotted into a salary structure. Specifically, each professional discipline (like mechanical engineering or electrical engineering) usually ends up having four to six grade levels, each of which requires a fairly broad salary range. This approach helps ensure that the employer remains competitive when bidding for professionals whose attainments vary widely and whose potential employers are literally found worldwide.[74]

Current Issues in Compensation Management

The Issue of Comparable Worth

comparable worth
The concept by which women who are usually paid less than men can claim that men in comparable rather than strictly equal jobs are paid more.

The Issue   Should women who are performing jobs *equal* to men's or just *comparable* to men's be paid the same as men? This is the basic issue in **comparable worth.**

Equal pay legislation in the United States and other industrialized countries has a history of debate over whether "equal" or "comparable" should be the standard for comparison when comparing men's and women's jobs.[75] For years, "equal" was the standard in the United States, though "comparable" was and is used in Canada and many European countries.[76] As a result of court rulings, though, some experts now believe that comparable worth may become the standard in the United States.[77]

The issue of comparable worth refers to the requirement to pay equal wages for jobs of comparable (rather than strictly equal) value to the employer. In a limited sense, this means jobs that while not equal *are at least quite similar,* such as assemblers on one line versus assemblers on a different assembly line. In its broadest sense, though, *comparable worth includes comparing quite dissimilar jobs,* such as nurses to fire truck mechanics or secretaries to electricians.[78]

The *Gunther* Supreme Court Case   *Gunther* v. *County of Washington* was a pivotal case. It involved Washington County, Oregon, prison matrons who claimed sex discrimination. In this case, the county had evaluated the men's jobs as having 5% more "job content" (based on a point evaluation system) than the women's jobs and paid the men 35% more.[79] The Supreme Court's decision for the female employees specifically stated that this was not a comparable worth case. However, prior to the *Gunther* case, wage discrimination claims based on sex had to be argued under the 1963 Equal Pay Act. The aggrieved employee thus had to show that the pay disparity existed in substantially equal jobs. In the *Gunther* case the Supreme Court held that a sex-based pay discrimination case could be argued under Title VII of the 1964 Civil Rights Act. Under the Civil Rights Act, it appeared it would be easier to compare men's and women's wages in comparable, rather than just equal, jobs.

Yet the issue is not clearcut. The Ninth Circuit Court of Appeals rejected the idea that paying wages based on prevailing market rates can in itself be evidence of intentional discrimination. The court, in *AFSCME* v. *State of Washington,* also ruled that nothing in Title VII was intended to "abrogate fundamental economic principles such as the laws of supply and demand or to prevent employers from competing in the labor market." Yet, as one law firm puts it, "until the U.S. Supreme Court rules on this issue, employers should continue to be cautious in initiating job evaluation studies and in perpetuating known wage disparities between male dominated and female dominated jobs, where the jobs are arguably of 'comparable value.'"[80] (The state of Washington subsequently agreed to pay

Diversity Counts
In Job Evaluation

Some experts have argued that job evaluation procedures like the point method are inherently unfair to women because they ignore or underestimate the skills associated with the types of jobs often held by women.[1] For example, one expert argues that many of the skills associated with doing jobs such as nursing and teaching go unrecognized because they ". . . mirror traditional duties within the home . . ." and are ignored because it's assumed that they need not be learned on the job or are somehow less important than skills that are based on on-the-job training.[2] As one commentator has noted:

What seems to have occurred is an assumption that because women often exercise such skills [cooking, cleaning, nursing, and sewing, to name a few] at home, they were somehow intrinsic to womanhood and did not need to be [learned] in the same way as typically male skills. Thus the definition of "skill" became molded by male perceptions of what was truly skillful, lower pay for women being the result.[3]

By this line of reasoning job evaluation procedures like the point method may have an inherent bias against women because they ignore the sorts of skills women may bring to the job, while crediting men for similar skills that need to be learned on the job. For example, while men "typically receive points for dirt and grease that they encounter on the job under a factor designated 'working conditions,' nurses, who deal with (vomit and blood) on a daily basis, receive no such points."[4] Similarly, male-dominated machinery-based factory jobs typically receive points for noise under the factor "working conditions." They may thus end up with higher evaluations than do (more female-oriented) clerical jobs, where the workers rarely get credit for concentrating and getting their jobs done amidst the distractions of phones and other interruptions.

Women may even suffer from the fact that much of the training on predominantly female jobs such as clerical jobs is "invisible." As one expert argues:

In contrast to many manufacturing and trade jobs which require a great deal of visible on-the-job training, skills such as typing and stenography are prerequisites for a [clerical] job, and must be learned outside of the employer's presence.[5]

Since these clerical skills may be more likely to go unrecognized, female dominated jobs (such as clerical jobs) and therefore women may not receive the points or for that matter the compensation that their skills would otherwise warrant.◆

[1]Jennifer Quinn, "Visibility and Value: The Role of Job Evaluation in Assuring Equal Pay for Women," *Law and Policy in International Business*, Vol. 25, No. 4 (Summer 1994), pp. 1403-1444.

[2]Ibid., p. 1411.

[3]Richard Townsend-Smith, "Sex Discrimination in Employment," *Law Practice & Policy*, Vol. 148 (1989), p. 15.

[4]Quinn, op cit., p. 1411.

[5]Ibid., p. 1412.

35,000 employees in female-dominated jobs almost $500 million in pay raises over seven years in settlement of this suit.)

Comparable Worth and Job Evaluation   The issue of comparable worth has important implications for an employer's job evaluation procedures. In virtually every comparable worth case that reached a court, the claim revolved around the use of the point method of job evaluation. Here each job is evaluated in terms of several factors (like effort, skill, and responsibility) and then assigned points based on the degree of each factor present in the job. As a result, point plans actually encourage assigning comparable worth ratings to different jobs. There are two sides to the problem. In the more familiar case, two positions such as Clerk-Typist IV and Junior Engineer might be evaluated as having the same number of points and, therefore, comparable worth. This would seem to imply that both jobs should be paid the same, although in practice market wage rates may be much higher for the male-dominated junior engineers than for the female-dominated clerk-typist.[81]

There is also the possibility of bias in the job evaluation plan itself. In particular, some traditional job evaluation point plans "tend to result in higher point totals for jobs traditionally held by males than for those traditionally held by females."[82] For example, the factor "supervisory responsibility" might heavily weight chain-of-command factors such as number of employees supervised and downplay the importance of functional authority or gaining the voluntary cooperation of other employees. The solution here is to rewrite the factor rules in job evaluation plans so as to give more weight to the sorts of activities that female-dominated positions frequently emphasize.[83]

Implications   Some argue that avoiding comparable worth problems doesn't mean quantitative job evaluation methods like point plans must be discarded, just used more wisely. For example, one approach is to stress prevailing market rates in pricing jobs, and then only use an evaluation method (like the point method) to slot in those jobs for which a market price is not readily available.[84] Another practical solution is to allow employers to price their jobs as they see fit, but to ensure that women have equal access to all jobs, as do men; the idea here is to eliminate the wage discrimination issue by eliminating sex-segregated jobs.[85] To avoid comparable worth problems, questions to ask include:

> Are your job duties and responsibilities clearly documented either by a job analysis questionnaire or a job description? Are they reviewed and updated annually?
>
> When was your pay system last reviewed? If more than three years have passed, serious inequities could exist.
>
> Do you have any circumstances where your system indicates that jobs are comparable, even in the marketplace, but you are paying those jobs occupied by females or minorities less than predominantly male and/or white jobs?
>
> When was the last time you statistically checked the effect of your pay system on females and minorities? Could it be that you have discrimination in fact though not in intent?
>
> Is your pay system clearly documented in a salary administration manual? If not, the credibility and defensibility of your pay practices are ripe for challenge.[86]
>
> Are you complying with state comparable work laws? Many states have passed their own comparable work laws, and states tend to broadly interpret laws that mandate equal pay for comparable work.[87] In some states, workers may collect substantial back pay and other damages by showing a wage disparity even when the comparable jobs seem substantially different on the surface.[88]

The Issue of Pay Secrecy

There are two opposing points of view with respect to the question of whether employees should know what other employees in the organization are being paid. The basic argument for "open pay" is that it improves employee motivation, and the thinking here is as follows: If employees believe that greater effort does not result in greater rewards, then, generally speaking, greater effort will not be forthcoming. On the other hand, if employees do see a direct relationship between effort and rewards, then greater effort will result. Proponents of open pay contend that workers who do not know each other's pay cannot easily assess how effort and rewards are related, or whether they are equitably paid, and as a result of this motivation tends to suffer. (They cannot, for example, say "Smith doesn't work hard and so is paid less than Jones, who does work hard.")

The opposing argument is that in practice there are usually real inequities in the pay scale, perhaps because of the need to hire someone "in a hurry," or because of the superior negotiating ability of a particular applicant. And even if the employee in a similar job who is being paid more actually deserves the higher salary because of his or her effort, skill, or experience, it's possible that lower-paid colleagues may convince themselves that they are underpaid relative to the higher-paid individual.

The research findings to this point are sketchy. One study found that managers' satisfaction with their pay increased following their firms' implementation of an open-pay policy.[89] A survey conducted by the Bureau of National Affairs found that fewer than half the firms responding gave employees access to salary schedules. Those not providing such information indicated, among other things, that "secrecy prevents much quibbling . . . ," "salary is a delicate matter . . . ," open pay "could well lead to unnecessary strain and dissatisfaction among managers . . . ," and "open systems too often create misunderstandings and petty complaints." The author of this study notes that "whether the inequities result from a growth situation or some other factor, it is clear that some inequities and openness are incompatible."[90] The implication for compensation management seems to be that a policy of open pay can, under the best of conditions, improve employees' satisfaction with their pay and possibly their effort as well. On the other hand, if conditions are not right—and especially if there are any lingering inequities in the employer's pay structure—moving to an open-pay policy is not advisable.

The Issues of Inflation and Salary Compression

Inflation and how to cope with it has been another important issue in compensation management.[91]

For example, *salary compression* means that longer-term employees' salaries are lower than those for workers entering the firm today, and it is a result of inflation. Its symptoms include (1) higher starting salaries, which compress current employees' salaries; and (2) unionized hourly pay increases that overtake supervisory and nonunion hourly rates.[92]

Dealing with salary compression is a tricky problem.[93] On the one hand, you don't want your long-termers to be treated unfairly or to become inordinately dissatisfied and possibly leave with their accumulated knowledge and expertise. On the other hand, mediocre performance or lack of assertiveness, rather than salary compression, may in many cases explain the low salaries.

In any case, there are several solutions.[94] As distasteful as it is to many employers to pay employees just for seniority, you can institute a program of providing raises based on longevity. These raises could be distributed in flat dollar amounts, or as a percentage of base pay, or as a combination of the two. Second, a much more aggressive merit pay program can be installed. This may at least help reduce the morale problems associated with pay compression, since employees know they have the potential for earning higher raises. Third, supervisors can be authorized to recommend "equity" adjustments for selected incumbents who are both highly valued by the organization and also viewed as unfairly victimized by pay compression.

Inflation has also put some pension plans in peril.[95] An executive who retired at the beginning of 1982 had lost over 50% of the purchasing power of a fixed-dollar company pension by today, for instance—a frightening state of affairs for retirees whose pensions are not indexed to inflation. While the rate of increase of consumer prices has recently slowed, some fear that inflation is only dormant and that rapid price increases will again occur.

Particularly in periods of high inflation, employers try to cope with inflation's impact in several ways. More employers grant across-the-board salary increases either in lieu of or in addition to performance-based merit increases. Others change their pension plans to index them to inflation so that the value of the pension payments increased along with the rise in the price of goods.[96] Others change the compensation mix to decrease the emphasis on taxable income like wages and salary and to substitute nontaxable benefits like flexible work hours, dental plans, day care centers, and group legal and auto insurance plans.[97]

Cost-of-living differentials can help employees cope with the high cost of living in cities such as Tokyo.

The cost-of-living adjustment (or COLA) clause is sometimes pushed by unions as another way to cope with inflation.[98] The COLA or escalator clause is designed to maintain the purchasing power of the wage rate and operates as follows. Specified increases in the Consumer Price Index trigger increases in the wage rate, with the magnitude of the increase depending on the negotiated COLA formula.[99] The most common formula provides a one-cent per hour wage adjustment for each 0.3% or 0.4% change in consumer prices.[100] Nonunion employees often then receive a similar adjustment. Periodically, the employer takes a portion of the dollar COLA adjustment and builds it into the employee's base salary, a procedure known as "baking in."[101] COLAs have become less of a concern to unions as inflation has moderated. The COLA clause was first adopted by the United Auto Workers and the General Motors Corporation in 1950; a study by the Bureau of Labor Statistics indicates that about 40% of the major union contracts negotiated recently (covering 6.5 million workers) contained COLA provisions, down from 58% and 9.3 million workers in 1980.[102]

In fact, General Motors Corporation is eliminating COLAs for its 125,000 salaried employees. It had previously instituted a pay-for-performance system and, pleased with the results, decided to expand it to all salaried workers. This move may signal the end, for now, of COLAs in UAW contracts.[103]

The Issue of Cost-of-Living Differentials

Cost-of-living differences between localities have escalated from occasional inconveniences to serious compensation problems. For example, a family of four might live in Atlanta for just over $39,000 per year while the same family's annual expenditures in Chicago or Los Angeles would be over $46,000.

Employers are using several methods to handle cost-of-living differentials. The main approach is to give the transferred person a nonrecurring payment, usually in a lump sum or perhaps spread over one to three years.[104] Other employers pay a differential for ongoing costs in addition to a one-time allocation. For example, one employer pays a differential of $6,000 per year to people earning $35,000 to $45,000 who are transferred from Atlanta to Minneapolis. The first $6,000 is a lump sum at the time of the move, and in the second year the employee gets another $6,000 in four quarterly increments. Employees already living in Minneapolis (or any other high-cost area) are given no adjustment.[105] Other companies simply increase the employee's base salary rate. They give the person an automatic raise equal to the amount by which living costs in the new locale exceed those in the old, in addition to any other promotion-based raise the employee may get.

Global HRM

The Issue of Compensating Expatriate Employees

The question of cost-of-living differentials has particular relevance to multinational firms. The annual cost of sending a U.S. expatriate manager from the United States to Europe varies widely according to the country. For example, it's estimated that the annual cost of keeping a U.S. expatriate in France might average $193,000, while in neighboring Germany the cost would be $246,000.[106]

Such wide discrepancies raise the issue of how multinational firms should compensate overseas employees. The issue is particularly important today, in part because of the growing need to staff overseas operations, and in part because of the increasing frequency with which managers and professionals are moved from country to country.

Two basic international compensation policies are popular: home-based and host-based policies.[107]

Under a home-based salary policy, an international transferee's base salary reflects his or her home country's salary structure. Additional allowances are then tacked on for cost-of-living differences and housing and schooling costs, for instance. This is a reasonable approach for short-term assignments and avoids the problem of having to change the employee's base salary every time he or she moves. However, it can result in some difficulty at the host office if, say, employees from several different countries at the same office are all being paid different base salaries for performing essentially the same tasks.

In the host-based plan the base salary for the international transferee is tied to the host country's salary structure. In other words, the manager from New York who is sent to France would have his or her base salary changed to the prevailing base salary for that position in France rather than keep his or her New York base salary. Of course, cost-of-living, housing, schooling, and other allowances are tacked on here as well. This approach can cause some consternation to our New York manager who might, for instance, see his or her base salary plummet with a transfer to Bangladesh. Conversely, he or she may face the problem of frequent salary fluctuations if he or she moves from country to country fairly often.

There's no one best way to deal with the international compensation problem. One compensation expert suggests a compromise, namely basing the person's new base salary on a percentage of home-country salary plus the higher of a percentage of (1) host-country salary or (2) the amount required in host-country currency to maintain a home-country standard of living in the host location.[108] A recent survey of multinational enterprises suggests that most set expatriates' salaries according to their home-country base pay.[109] Thus, a French manager assigned to Kiev by a U.S. multinational will generally have a base salary that reflects the salary structure in the manager's home country, in this case France. In addition there will be various allowances including cost-of-living, relocation, housing, education, and hardship allowances (the latter for countries with relatively poor quality of life such as China). The multinational employer will also usually pay any extra tax burdens resulting from taxes the manager is liable for over and above those he or she would have to pay in the manager's home country. As in the United States, about one-third of the expatriates' compensation package consists of benefits.◆

Small Business Applications

Developing a pay plan that is internally and externally equitable is as important in a small firm as in a large one. Paying wage rates that are too high for the area may be unnecessarily expensive, and paying less may guarantee poor-quality help and high turnover. Similarly, wage rates that are internally inequitable will reduce morale and cause the president to be badgered mercilessly by employees demanding raises "the same as Joe down the hall." The president who wants to concentrate on major issues like sales would thus do well to institute a rational pay plan as soon as possible.

Developing a Workable Pay Plan

The first step should be to conduct a wage survey. The basic methods for doing so were described earlier in this chapter, but in a smaller business you'll generally depend on less formal methods for collecting this information.

Three sources here can be especially useful. A careful perusal of the Sunday classified newspaper ads should yield useful information on wages offered for jobs similar to those you are trying to price. Second, your local Job Service office can be a wealth of information, compiling as it does extensive information on pay ranges and averages for many of the jobs listed in the *Dictionary of Occupational Titles*. (This is another reason for using job titles that are consistent with those in the DOT.) The Job Service office can provide information on wages within the local area served by that office, as well as on the geographic region served by the group of Job Service offices of which your office is one member. Finally, local employment agencies, always anxious to establish ties that could grow into business relationships, should be able to provide fairly good data regarding pay rates for different jobs.

Next, if you employ more than 20 employees or so, conduct at least a rudimentary job evaluation. For this, you will first require job descriptions, since these will be the source of data regarding the nature and worth of each job.

You will usually find it easier to split employees into three groups—managerial/professional, office/clerical, and plant personnel. For each of the three groups, determine the compensable factors to be evaluated and then rank or assign points to each job based on the job evaluation.

For each job or class of jobs (such as assemblers), you will want to create a pay range. The procedure for doing so was described earlier. However, in general, you should choose as the midpoint of your range the target salary as required by your job evaluation and then produce a range of about 30% around this average, broken into a total of five steps.

While it doesn't always work, you may find it useful to experiment with using the *Dictionary of Occupational Titles* data–people–things scores as a simple job evaluation method. As explained earlier (on page 93) the experts at the Department of Labor have produced data–people–things scores for each job in the *Dictionary of Occupational Titles*.

There are many situations in which these scores can be used for job evaluation purposes, although they are not designed to be so used. Assigning job evaluation ratings to jobs based on the data–people–things scores seems to work best when you're dealing with jobs that are fairly similar in many respects. It often works well in evaluating all manufacturing jobs in a company's plant, for instance. Here you may have a range of jobs such as textile loom fixer, production supervisor, weaver, production crew member, and fabricator. Strictly speaking, the data–people–things scores for each job reflect the degree to which each of these three factors is present in each job (for instance, the degree to which the job requires manipulating data, dealing with people, or dealing with things). These scores are listed in the dictionary for each job title. Therefore, it is simple for you to, say, add up the D–P–T numerical score for each job to see whether it produces for you what appears to be a logical hierarchy of jobs (in terms of their value to the company). Again, this approach is not for everyone, but it is so simple that it is worth a try. A weighting scheme could be included if you believed that one factor should be weighted more heavily than the others.

Compensation Policies

Compensation policies are important, too. For example, you have to have a policy on when and how raises are computed. Many small-business owners make the mistake of appraising employees on their anniversary date, a year after they are hired. The problem here is that the raise for one employee then becomes the standard for the next, as employees have time to compare notes over the space of several weeks or months. This produces a never-ending cycle of appraisals and posturing for ever-higher raises.

The better alternative is to have a policy of once-a-year raises during a standard one-week appraisal period, preferably about four weeks before the budget for next year must be produced. In this way, the administrative headache of conducting these appraisals and awarding raises is dealt with during a one (or two) week period. Furthermore, the total required raise money (which of course has to be computed in advance by the company president) is known more precisely when next year's budget is compiled. Other required compensation policies include amount of holiday and vacation pay (as explained in the next chapter), overtime pay policy, method of pay (weekly, biweekly, monthly), garnishments, and time card or sign-on sheet procedures.

Legal Issues

This chapter outlined a number of federal, state, and local laws to which small and large employers must adhere. Local and state laws will often cover companies not covered by the Fair Labor Standards Act, but the latter is actually quite comprehensive. It covers most employees of enterprises engaged in activities affecting interstate or foreign commerce. Retail and service companies are covered if their annual gross volume of business is not less than $362,500 a year and any other type of business is covered if its volume is not less than $250,000 a year.[110]

Misclassification of exempt employees is probably the biggest mistake made by smaller firms. As noted earlier, some employees are exempt from the overtime and/or minimum wage requirements of the FLSA. A common small-business mistake is to assume that putting employees on a yearly salary exempts them from the overtime provisions of the act. You cannot make those workers exempt simply by paying them a yearly salary, nor can you make them exempt by claiming they are "managers" because they spend some of their time supervising other employees. Strictly speaking, employees have to spend at least 50% of their time actually supervising other employees to be classified as executive, managerial, or supervisory employees. It is not enough that they spend 80% of their time doing the same work as the people they supervise, and only 20% of their time actually supervising.[111] Employees in administrative jobs ". . . directly related to management policies or general business operations . . ." and who are salaried and earning at least $250 a week may also be exempt: These might include, for instance, executive and administrative assistants such as executive assistant to the president or executive secretary, and staff members who act as advisory specialists such as personnel directors, controllers, and credit managers.[112]

There are other common wage-hour traps to avoid.[113] With respect to meal and break periods, an employee must generally be paid for meal periods unless the period is at least 20 minutes long, the employee is completely relieved of duties, and the employee can leave his or her work post. Also beware of how you handle compensatory time off. Many smaller employers believe they can have an employee work, say, 45 hours in one week, pay the person for 40 hours and give them compensatory time off of 5 hours in the following week. Under the law, this is not legal for two reasons. First, if there is to be compensatory time off, the employer must provide 1½ hours off for each overtime hour worked. Thus, if someone works 42 hours in one week, he or she should receive 3 hours of compensable time. Furthermore, you cannot manipulate the pay period, for instance, by generally paying for a pay period that ranges from Monday morning through Sunday night but then temporarily changing the pay period to Saturday morning through Friday night in order to accommodate the need to work extra hours on a weekend because of a rush job.[114] Great care also must be taken when it comes to paying for time recorded. For example, suppose employees are required to clock in. They consistently clock in 15 minutes early or get into the habit of not clocking out for lunch. Here it is possible that a wage and hour inspector may conclude that the employees were underpaid, since there is no record that they were clocked out for the period for which they were docked.

Also beware of how you use so-called independent contractors. Many small businesses hire management consultants or, say, part-time bookkeepers to keep their books and then classify these people as independent contractors. Independent contractors are, as their name implies, not employed by the firm and are thus not eligible for unemployment compensation, worker's compensation, or any other benefits accruing to the firm's employees. At first glance, this seems like a cost-effective way to run a firm, and to some extent it can be. However, care must be taken not to call people who are legitimately employees "independent contractors" just to get around paying them benefits. There are many factors that determine whether a person is in fact an independent contractor. For example, a worker who is required to comply with another person's instructions about when, where, and how he or she is to work is ordinarily considered an employee, not an independent contractor.[115]◆

Chapter Review

Summary

1. There are two bases on which to pay employees compensation: increments of time and volume of production. The former includes hourly or daily wages and salaries. Basing pay on volume of production ties compensation directly to the amount of production (or number of "pieces" the worker produces).

2. Establishing pay rates involves five steps: conduct salary survey, evaluate jobs, develop pay grades, use wage curves, and fine tune pay rates.

3. Job evaluation is aimed at determining the relative worth of a job. It compares jobs to one another based on their content, which is usually defined in terms of compensable factors like skills, effort, responsibility, and working conditions.

4. The ranking method of job evaluation has five steps: (a) obtain job information, (b) select clusters of jobs to be rated, (c) select compensable factors, (d) rank jobs, and (e) combine ratings (of several raters). This is a simple method to use, but there is a tendency to rely too heavily on guesstimates. The classification (or grading) method is a second qualitative approach that categorizes jobs based on a class description or classification rules for each class.

5. The point method of job evaluation requires identifying a number of compensable factors and then determining the degree to which each of these factors is present in the job.

6. The factor comparison method, as explained in the appendix, is a quantitative job evaluation technique that entails deciding which jobs have more of certain compensable factors than others.

7. Most managers group similar jobs into wage or pay grades for pay purposes. These are comprised of jobs of approximately equal difficulty or importance as determined by job evaluation.

8. The wage curve (or line) shows the average target wage for each pay grade (or job). It can help show you what the average wage for each grade should be, and whether any present wages or salaries are out of line. Developing a wage curve involves four steps: (a) find the average pay for each pay grade, (b) plot these wage rates for each pay grade, (c) draw the wage line, and (d) price jobs after plotting present wage rates.

9. Developing a compensation plan for executive, managerial, and professional personnel is complicated by the fact that factors like performance and creativity must take precedence over static factors like working conditions. Market rates, performance, and incentives and benefits thus play a much greater role than does job evaluation for these employees.

10. Broadbanding means collapsing salary grades and ranges into just a few wide levels or bands, each of which then contains a relatively wide range of jobs and salary levels.

11. Four main compensation issues discussed were comparable worth, pay secrecy, inflation, and cost-of-living differentials.

Key Terms

employee compensation
Davis-Bacon Act
Walsh-Healey Public
   Contract Act
Fair Labor Standards Act
Equal Pay Act of 1963
Civil Rights Act
Employee Retirement
   Income Security Act
   (ERISA)

salary survey
benchmark job
job evaluation
compensable factor
ranking method
classification (or grading)
   method
classes

grades
grade description
point method
factor comparison method
pay grade
wage curve
rate ranges
comparable worth

Discussion Questions and Exercises

1. What is the difference between exempt and nonexempt jobs?

2. Should the job evaluation depend on an appraisal of the jobholder's performance? Why? Why not?

3. What is the relationship between compensable factors and job specifications?

4. What are the pros and cons of the following methods of job evaluation: ranking, classification, factor comparison, point method?

5. In what respect is the factor comparison method similar to the ranking method? How do they differ?

6. Working individually or in groups, conduct salary surveys for the following positions: entry-level accountant, and entry-level chemical engineer. What sources did you use, and what conclusions did you reach? If you were the HR manager for a local engineering firm, what would you recommend that you pay for each job?

7. Working individually or in groups, use the BLS area wage surveys to determine local area earnings for the following positions: File Clerk I; Accounting Clerk II; Secretary V. How do the BLS figures compare with comparable jobs listed in your Sunday newspaper? What do you think accounts for any discrepancy?

8. Working individually or in groups, use the ranking method to evaluate the relative worth of the jobs listed in Question 7, above. (You may use the *Dictionary of Occupational Titles* as an aid.) To what extent do the local area earnings for these jobs correspond to your evaluations of the jobs?

9. What are the pros and cons of broadbanding, and would you recommend your current employer (or some other firm you're familiar with) use it? Why or why not?

10. It was recently reported in the news that the average pay for most university presidents ranged around $200,000 per year, but that a few earned closer to $500,000 per year. What would account for such a disparity in the pay of universities' chief executive officers?

Application Exercises

RUNNING CASE: Carter Cleaning Company
The New Pay Plan

Carter Cleaning Centers does not have a formal wage structure nor does it have rate ranges or use compensable factors. Wage rates are based mostly on those prevailing in the surrounding community and are tempered with an attempt on the part of Jack Carter to maintain some semblance of equity between what workers with different responsibilities in the stores are paid.

Needless to say, Carter does not make any formal surveys when determining what his company should pay. He peruses the want ads almost every day and conducts informal surveys among his friends in the local chapter of the laundry and cleaners trade association. While Jack has taken a "seat-of-the-pants" approach to paying employees, his salary schedule has been guided by several basic pay policies. While many of his colleagues adhere to a policy of paying absolutely minimum rates, Jack has always followed a policy of paying his employees about 10%

above what he feels are the prevailing rates, a policy that he believes reduces turnover while fostering employee loyalty. Of somewhat more concern to Jennifer is her father's policy of paying men about 20% more than women for the same job. Her father's explanation is, "They're stronger and can work harder for longer hours, and besides they all have families to support."

Questions
1. Is the company at the point where it should be setting up a formal salary structure complete with a job evaluation? Why?

2. Is Jack Carter's policy of paying 10% more than the prevailing rates a sound one, and how could that be determined?

3. Similarly, is Carter's male–female differential wise and if not, why not?

CASE STUDY: Job Evaluation for Bank Managers

The chairperson of the board of directors of the Second National Bank has proposed that all managerial positions be included in the bank's job evaluation plan. She has talked with executives in several large business organizations in which such a practice has been found entirely possible and helpful. She proposed this action to the board at its latest meeting. The president asked that no action be taken until she could discuss it with those who would be affected.

Most of the middle-management group appear to be opposed to such a procedure. The president, while trying to remain neutral, has expressed a fear that if salaries are fitted to job evaluation, she will lose her best people. Many department heads and assistants insist that their jobs simply can't be rated on the scale used for subordinate positions. Others argue that no individual or small group can possibly know what their jobs involve. It is also argued that the qualities for which managers are paid are so varied and intangible that no systematic comparison of jobs makes sense.

The HR manager and his staff are united in favoring the idea. The chairperson of the board, through the president, has asked the human resource department to prepare a statement in favor of the development, explaining what it would do and how it would be done.

Question

You have been assigned the responsibility for a first draft of this statement to be directed to the rest of the HR staff for discussion. What would your statement say?

Source: Dale Yoder and Paul D. Standohar, *Personnel Management & Industrial Relations* (Englewood Cliffs, NJ: Prentice Hall, 1982), p. 361.

 # Human Resource Management Simulation

The simulation requires your team to make decisions concerning the compensation for five levels of employees. Currently your firm is paying less than local comparable jobs and this is affecting your turnover and morale. However, budget constraints require that you plan ahead for any wage increases carefully. One key consideration is whether to give employees at all levels a small increase in a given decision period or to give a larger increase to one level at a time.

Video Case

Retirement Costs

For most employees today, especially younger ones, provisions for retirement pensions are becoming an increasingly important part of their overall compensation package. Why? Because, as this videocase shows, mobility from job to job and a strong desire on the part of employers to involve employees more heavily in planning their own retirement funds, have left retirement planning largely up to the employees. It's up to them to decide how and what proportion of their pay to divert to various pension options. Combine that with increased longevity and the need to plan on building a considerable nest egg prior to retirement and you can see why pension planning is a much more important part of compensation planning that it has ever been before.

Questions

1. Why can't recent college graduates depend only on Social Security benefits to get them through their retirement years?

2. In the videocase, John Ehrhardt says many employees are mishandling their pension planning. What does he mean by this, and what should be done about it?

3. Do you think it's generally a good idea to divert as much pay as possible from your salary into 401k savings plans as described in this videocase? Why or why not?

4. If you were looking for a job today, what do the contents of the videocase suggest about the sorts of questions you should ask your prospective employer regarding its compensation plan?

Source: Wall Street Journal Report, *Retirement Costs,* Show No. 676-3, September 5, 1992.

 ## Take It to the Net

We invite you to visit the Dessler page on the Prentice Hall Web site at:
http://www.prenhall.com/~dessler
for the monthly Dessler update, and for this chapter's World Wide Web exercise.

Appendix 12.1

Quantitative Job Evaluation Methods

The Factor Comparison Job Evaluation Method

The factor comparison technique is a *quantitative* job evaluation method. It has many variations and appears to be one of the most widely used, the most accurate, and the most complex job evaluation method.

It is actually a refinement of the ranking method and entails deciding which jobs have more of certain compensable factors than others. With the ranking method you generally look at each job as an entity and rank the jobs. With the factor comparison method you rank each job *several times—once for each compensable factor you choose.* For example, jobs might be ranked first in terms of the factor "skill." Then they are ranked according to their "mental requirements." Next they are ranked according to their "responsibility," and so forth. Then these rankings are combined for each job into an overall numerical rating for the job. Here are the required steps:

Step 1. Obtain Job Information This method requires a careful, complete job analysis. First, job descriptions are written. Then job specifications are developed, preferably in terms of the compensable factors the committee had decided to use. For the factor comparison method, these compensable factors are usually (1) mental requirements, (2) physical requirements, (3) skill requirements, (4) responsibility, and (5) working conditions. Typical definitions of each of these five factors are presented in Figure 12.9.

Step 2. Select Key Benchmark Jobs Next, 15 to 25 key jobs are selected by the job evaluation committee. These jobs will have to be representative benchmark jobs, acceptable reference points that represent the full range of jobs to be evaluated.

Step 3. Rank Key Jobs by Factors Here evaluators are asked to rank the key jobs on each of the five factors (mental requirements, physical requirements, skill requirements, responsibility, and working conditions). This ranking procedure is

	MENTAL REQUIREMENTS	PHYSICAL REQUIREMENTS	SKILL REQUIREMENTS	RESPONSIBILITY	WORKING CONDITIONS
Welder	1	4	1	1	2
Crane operator	3	1	3	4	4
Punch press operator	2	3	2	2	3
Security guard	4	2	4	3	1

TABLE 12.4 Ranking Key Jobs by Factors[1]

[1] 1 is high, 4 is low.

**Figure 12.9
Sample Definitions of
Five Factors Typically
Used in Factor
Comparison Method**

Source: Jay L. Otis and Richard
H. Leukart, *Job Evaluation: A
Basis for Sound Wage
Administration*, p. 181. ©1954,
renewed 1983. Reprinted by
permission of Prentice Hall,
Englewood Cliffs, NJ.

1. Mental Requirements
Either the possession of and/or the active application of the following:
A. (inherent) Mental traits, such an intelligence, memory, reasoning, facility in verbal expression, ability to get along with people and imagination.
B. (acquired) General education, such as grammar and arithmetic; or general information as to sports, world events, etc.
C. (acquired) Specialized knowledge such as chemistry, engineering, accounting, advertising, etc.

2. Skill
A. (acquired) Facility in muscular coordination, as in operating machines, repetitive movements, careful coordinations, dexterity, assembling, sorting, etc.
B. (acquired) Specific job knowledge necessary to the muscular coordination only; acquired by performance of the work and not to be confused with general education or specialized knowledge. It is very largely training in the interpretation of sensory impressions.

Examples
    (1) In operating an adding machine, the knowledge of *which key* to depress for a sub-total would be skill.
    (2) In automobile repair, the ability to determine the significance of a certain knock in the motor would be skill.
    (3) In hand-firing a boiler, the ability to determine from the appearance of the firebed how coal should be shoveled over the surface would be skill.

3. Physical Requirements
A. Physical effort, as sitting, standing, walking, climbing, pulling, lifting, etc.; both the amount exercised and the degree of the continuity should be taken into account.
B. Physical status, as age, height, weight, sex, strength and eyesight.

4. Responsibilities
A. For raw materials, processed materials, tools, equipment and property.
B. For money or negotiable securities.
C. For profits or loss, savings or methods' improvement.
D. For public contact.
E. For records.
F. For supervision.
    (1) Primarily the complexity of supervision *given* to subordinates; the number of subordinates is a secondary feature. Planning, direction, coordination, instruction, control and approval characterize this kind of supervision.
    (2) Also, the degree of supervision *received*. If Jobs A and B gave no supervision to subordinates, but A received much closer immediate supervision than B, then B would be entitled to a higher rating than A in the supervision factor.
       To summarize the four degrees of supervision:
          Highest degree—gives much—gets little
          High degree   —gives much—gets much
          Low degree   —gives none—gets little
          Lowest degree —gives none—gets much

5. Working Conditions
A. Environmental influences such as atmosphere, ventilation, illumination, noise, congestion, fellow workers, etc.
B. Hazards—from the work or its surroundings.
C. Hours.

based on job descriptions and job specifications. Each committee member usually makes this ranking individually, and then a meeting is held to develop a consensus on each job. The result of this process is a table, as in Table 12.4. This shows how each key job ranks on each of the five compensable factors.

Step 4. Distribute Wage Rates by Factors   This is where the factor comparison method gets a bit more complicated. In this step the committee members have to divide up the present wage now being paid for each key job, distributing it among the five compensable factors. They do this in accordance with their judgments about the importance to the job of each factor. For example, if the present wage for the job of common laborer is $4.26, our evaluators might distribute this wage as follows:

Mental requirements	$0.36
Physical requirements	$2.20
Skill requirements	$0.42
Responsibility	$0.28
Working conditions	$1.00
Total	$4.26

You make such a distribution for all key jobs.

Step 5. Rank Key Jobs According to Wages Assigned to Each Factor
Here you again rank each job, factor by factor, but the ranking is based on the wages assigned to each factor. As shown in Table 12.5, for example, for the "mental requirements" factor, the welder job ranks first, while the security guard job ranks last.

Each member of the committee first makes this distribution working independently. Then the committee meets and arrives at a consensus concerning the money to be assigned to each factor for each key job.

Step 6. Compare the Two Sets of Rankings to Screen Out Unusable Key Jobs   You now have two sets of rankings for each key job. One was your original ranking (from step 3). This shows how each job ranks on each of the five compensable factors. The second ranking reflects for each job the wages assigned to each factor. You can now draw up a table like the one in Table 12.6.

For each factor, this shows both rankings for each key job. On the left is the ranking from step 3. On the right is the ranking based on wages paid. For each factor, the ranking based on the amount of the factor (from step 3) should be about the same as the ranking based on the wages assigned to the job (step 5). If there's much of a discrepancy, it suggests that the key job might be a fluke, and from this point on, such jobs are no longer used as key jobs. (Many managers don't bother to screen out unusable key jobs. To simplify things, they skip our steps 5 and 6, going instead from step 4 to step 7; this is an acceptable alternative.)

Step 7. Construct the Job-Comparison Scale   Once you've identified the usable, true key jobs, the next step is to set up the job-comparison scale (Table 12.7). (Note that there's a separate column for each of the five comparable factors.) To develop it, you ll need the assigned wage table from step 4.

TABLE 12.5 Ranking Key Jobs by Wage Rates[1]

	HOURLY WAGE	MENTAL REQUIRE- MENTS	PHYSICAL REQUIRE- MENTS	SKILL REQUIRE- MENTS	RESPONSIBILITY	WORKING CONDITIONS
Welder	$9.80	4.00(1)	0.40(4)	3.00(1)	2.00(1)	0.40(2)
Crane operator	5.60	1.40(3)	2.00(1)	1.80(3)	0.20(4)	0.20(4)
Punch press operator	6.00	1.60(2)	1.30(3)	2.00(2)	0.80(2)	0.30(3)
Security guard	4.00	1.20(4)	1.40(2)	0.40(4)	0.40(3)	0.60(1)

[1] 1 is high, 4 is low.

TABLE 12.6 Comparison of Factor and Wage Rankings

	MENTAL REQUIRE- MENTS		PHYSICAL REQUIRE- MENTS		SKILL REQUIRE- MENTS		RESPONSIBILITY		WORKING CONDITIONS	
	A[1]	$[2]	A[1]	$[2]	A[1]	$[2]	A[1]	$[2]	A[1]	$[2]
Welder	1	1	4	4	1	1	1	1	2	2
Crane operator	3	3	1	1	3	3	4	4	4	4
Punch press operator	2	2	3	3	2	2	2	2	3	3
Security guard	4	4	2	2	4	4	3	3	1	1

[1]Amount of each factor based on step 3.
[2]Ratings based on distribution of wages to each factor from step 4.

For each of the factors for all key jobs, you write the job next to the appropriate wage rate. Thus, in the assigned wage table (Table 12.5), the welder job has $4.00 assigned to the factor "mental requirements." Therefore, on the job-comparison scale (Table 12.7) write "welder" in the "mental requirements" factor column, next to the "$4.00" row. Do the same for all factors for all key jobs.

Step 8. Use the Job-Comparison Scale Now all the other jobs to be evaluated can be slotted, factor by factor, into the job-comparison scale. For example, suppose you have a job of plater that you want to slot in. You decide where the "mental requirements" of the plater job would fit as compared with the "mental requirements" of all the other jobs listed. It might, for example, fit between punch press operator and inspector. Similarly, you would ask where the "physical requirements" of the plater's job fit as compared with the other jobs listed. Here you might find that it fits just below crane operator. You would do the same for each of the remaining three factors.

An Example Let us work through an example to clarify the factor comparison method. We'll just use four key jobs to simplify the presentation—you'd usually start with 15 to 25 key jobs.

Step 1. First, we do a job analysis.

Step 2. Here we select our four key jobs: welder, crane operator, punch press operator, and security guard.

Step 3. Based on the job descriptions and specifications, here we rank key jobs by factor, as in Table 12.4.

Step 4. Here we distribute wage rates by factor, as in Table 12.5.

Step 5. Then we rank our key jobs according to wage rates assigned to each key factor. These rankings are shown in parentheses in Table 12.5.

Step 6. Next compare your two sets of rankings. In each left-hand column (marked A) is the job's ranking from step 3 based on the amount of the compensable factor. In each right-hand column (marked $) is the job's ranking from step 5 based on the wage assigned to that factor, as in Table 12.6.

In this case, there are no differences between any of the pairs of A (amount) and $ (wage) rankings, so all our key jobs are usable. If there had been any differences (for example, between the A and $ rankings for the welder job's "mental requirements" factor) we would have dropped that job as a key job.

Step 7. Now we construct our job-comparison scale as in Table 12.7. For this, we use the wage distributions from step 4. For example, let us say that in steps 4 and 5 we assigned $4.00 to the "mental requirements" factor of the welder's job.

TABLE 12.7 Job (Factor) Comparison Scale

	MENTAL REQUIREMENTS	PHYSICAL REQUIREMENTS	SKILL REQUIREMENTS	RESPONSIBILITY	WORKING CONDITIONS
.20	....	....	....	Crane Operator	Crane Operator
.30	....	....	....	....	Punch Press Operator
.40	....	Welder	Sec. Guard	Sec. Guard	Welder
.50					
.60	....	....	....	....	Sec. Guard
.70					
.80				Punch Press Operator	
.90					
1.00					
1.10				(Plater)	
1.20	Sec. Guard				
1.30	....	Punch Press Operator			
1.40	Crane Operator	Sec. Guard	(Inspector)	(Plater)	
1.50	....	(Inspector)	....	....	
1.60	Punch Press Operator				
1.70	(Plater)				
1.80	....	....	Crane Operator	(Inspector)	
1.90					
2.00	....	Crane Operator..	Punch Press Operator	Welder	
2.20	....	(Plater)			
2.40	(Inspector)	....	....	....	(Plater)
2.60					
2.80					
3.00	....	....	Welder		
3.20					
3.40					
3.60					
3.80					
4.00	Welder				
4.20					
4.40					
4.60					
4.80					

Therefore, we now write "welder" on the $4.00 row under the "mental requirements" column as in Table 12.7.

Step 8. Now all our other jobs can be slotted, factor by factor, into our job-comparison scale. We do not distribute wages to each of the factors for our other jobs to do this. We just decide where, factor by factor, each of our other jobs should be slotted. We've done this for two other jobs in the factor comparison scale: They're shown in parentheses. Now we also know what the wages for these two jobs should be, and we can also do the same for all our jobs.

A Variation There are several variations to this basic factor comparison method. One converts the dollar values on the factor comparison chart (Table 12.7) to points. (You can do this by multiplying each of the dollar values by 100, for example.) The main advantage in making this change is that your system would no longer be "locked in" to your present wage rates. Instead, each of your jobs would be compared with one another, factor by factor, in terms of a more constant point system.

Pros and Cons We've presented the factor comparison method at some length because it is (in one form or another) a very widely used job evaluation method. Its wide use derives from several advantages: First, it is an accurate, systematic, quantifiable method for which detailed step-by-step instructions are available. Second, jobs are compared to other jobs to determine a relative value. Thus, in the job-comparison scale you not only see that the welder requires more mental ability than a plater; you also can determine about how much more mental ability is required—apparently about twice as much ($4.00 versus $1.70). (This type of calibration is not possible with the ranking or classification methods.) Third, this is also a fairly easy job evaluation system to explain to employees.

Complexity is probably the most serious disadvantage of the factor comparison method. While it is fairly easy to explain the factor comparison scale and its rationale to employees, it is difficult to show them how to build one. In addition, the use of the five factors is an outgrowth of the technique developed by its originators. However, using the same five factors for all organizations and for all jobs in an organization may not always be appropriate.

The Point Method of Job Evaluation

The point method is widely used. It requires identifying several compensable factors (like skills and responsibility), each with several degrees, and also the degree to which each of these factors is present in the job. A different number of points is usually assigned for each degree of each factor. So once you determine the degree to which each factor is present in the job, you need only add up the corresponding number of points for each factor and arrive at an overall point value for the job.[116] Here are the steps:

Step 1. Determine Clusters of Jobs to Be Evaluated Because jobs vary widely by department, you usually will not use one point-rating plan for all jobs in the organization. Therefore, the first step is usually to cluster jobs, for example, into shop jobs, clerical jobs, sales jobs, and so forth. Then the committee will generally develop a point plan for one group or cluster at a time.

Step 2. Collect Job Information This means performing a job analysis and writing job descriptions and job specifications.

Step 3. Select Compensable Factors Here select compensable factors, like education, physical requirements, or skills. Often each cluster of jobs may require its own compensable factors.

Step 4. Define Compensable Factors Next carefully define each compensable factor. This is done to ensure that the evaluation committee members each will apply the factors with consistency. Examples of definitions are presented in Figure 12.10. The definitions are often drawn up or obtained by the human resource specialist.

Figure 12.10
Example of One
Factor in a Point
Factor System

Source: Richard W. Beatty and
James R. Beatty, "Job
Evaluation," Ronald A. Berk
(Ed.) *Performance Assessment:*
Methods and Applications
(Baltimore: Johns Hopkins
University Press, 1986),
p. 322.

Example of One Factor in a Point Factor System (Complexity/Problem Solving)

The mental capacity required to perform the given job as expressed in resourcefulness in dealing with unfamiliar problems, interpretation of data, initiation of new ideas, complex data analysis, creative or developmental work.

Level	Point Value	Description of Characteristics and Measures
0	0	Seldom confronts problems not covered by job routine or organizational policy; analysis of data is negligible. *Benchmark:* General secretary, switchboard/receptionist.
1	40	Follows clearly prescribed standard practice and demonstrates straightforward application of readily understood rules and procedures. Analyzes noncomplicated data by established routine. *Benchmark:* Statistical clerk, billing clerk.
2	80	Frequently confronts problems not covered by job routine. Independent judgment exercised in making minor decisions where alternatives are limited and standard policies established. Analysis of standardized data for information of or use by others. *Benchmark:* Social worker, executive secretary.
3	120	Exercises independent judgment in making decisions involving nonroutine problems with general guidance only from higher supervision. Analyzes and evaluates data pertaining to nonroutine problems for solution in conjunction with others. *Benchmark:* Nurse, accountant, team leader.
4	160	Uses independent judgment in making decisions that are subject to review in the final stages only. Analyzes and solves nonroutine problems involving evaluation of a wide variety of data as a regular part of job duties. Makes decision involving procedures. *Benchmark:* Associate director, business manager, park services director.
5	200	Uses independent judgment in making decisions that are not subject to review. Regularly exercises developmental or creative abilities in policy development. *Benchmark:* Executive director.

Step 5. Define Factor Degrees   Next define each of several degrees for each factor so that raters may judge the amount or degree of a factor existing in a job. Thus, for the factor "complexity" you might choose to have six degrees, ranging from "job is repetitive" through "requires initiative." (Definitions for each degree are shown in Figure 12.10.) The number of degrees usually does not exceed five or six, and the actual number depends mostly on judgment. Thus, if all employees either work in a quiet, air-conditioned office or in a noisy, hot factory, then two degrees would probably suffice for the factor "working conditions." You need not have the same number of degrees for each factor, and you should limit degrees to the number necessary to distinguish among jobs.

Step 6. Determine Relative Values of Factors   The next step is to decide how much weight (or how many total points) to assign to each factor. This is important because for each cluster of jobs some factors are bound to be more important than others. Thus, for executives the "mental requirements" factor would carry far more weight than would "physical requirements." The opposite might be true of factory jobs.

   The next step is to determine the relative values or weights that should be assigned to each of the factors. Assigning factor weights is generally done by the evaluation committee. The committee members carefully study factor and degree definitions and then determine the relative value of the factors for the cluster of jobs under consideration. Here is one method for doing this:

First, assign a value of 100% to the highest-ranking factor. Then assign a value to the next highest factor as a percentage of its importance to the first factor, and so forth. For example,

Decision making	100%
Problem solving	85%
Knowledge	60%

Next sum up the total percentage (in this case 100% + 85% + 60% = 245%). Then convert this 245% to a 100% system as follows:

Decision making:	100 ÷ 245 = 40.82 =	40.8%
Problem solving:	85 ÷ 245 = 34.69 =	34.7%
Knowledge:	60 ÷ 245 = 24.49 =	24.5%
Totals		100.0%

Step 7. Assign Point Values to Factors and Degrees   In step 6 total weights were developed for each factor in percentage terms. Now assign points to each factor as in Table 12.8. For example, suppose it is decided to use a total number of 500 points in the point plan. Then since the factor "decision making" had a weight of 40.8%, it would be assigned a total of 40.8% × 500 = 204 points.

Thus, it was decided to assign 204 points to the decision-making factor. This automatically means that the highest degree for the decision-making factor would also carry 204 points. Then assign points to the other degrees for this factor, usually in equal amounts from the lowest to the highest degree. For example, divide 204 by the number of degrees (say, 5); this equals 40.8. Then the lowest degree here would carry about 41 points. The second degree would carry 41 plus 41, or 82 points. The third degree would carry 123 points. The fourth degree would carry 164 points. Finally, the fifth and highest degree would carry 204 points. Do this for each factor (as in Table 12.8).

Step 8. Write the Job Evaluation Manual   Developing a point plan like this usually culminates in a *point manual* or *job evaluation manual*. This simply consolidates the factor and degree definitions and point values into one convenient manual.

Step 9. Rate the Jobs   Once the manual is complete, the actual evaluations can begin. Raters (usually the committee) use the manual to evaluate jobs. Each job based on its job description and job specification is evaluated factor by factor to determine the number of points that should be assigned to it. First, committee members determine the degree (first degree, second degree, and so on) to which each factor is present in the job. Then they note the corresponding points (see

TABLE 12.8 Evaluation Points Assigned to Factors and Degrees

	FIRST-DEGREE POINTS	SECOND-DEGREE POINTS	THIRD-DEGREE POINTS	FOURTH-DEGREE POINTS	FIFTH-DEGREE POINTS
Decision making	41	82	123	164	204
Problem solving	35	70	105	140	174
Knowledge	24	48	72	96	123

Table 12.8) that were previously assigned to each of these degrees (in step 7). Finally, they add up the points for all factors, arriving at a total point value for the job. Raters generally start with rating key jobs and obtain consensus on these. Then they rate the rest of the jobs in the cluster.

"Packaged" Point Plans Developing a point plan of one's own can obviously be a time-consuming process. For this reason a number of groups (such as the National Electrical Manufacturer's Association and the National Trade Association) have developed standardized point plans. These have been used or adapted by thousands of organizations. They contain ready-made factor and degree definitions and point assignments for a wide range of jobs, and can often be used with little or no modification. One survey of U.S. companies found that 93% of those using a ready-made plan rated it successful.

Pros and Cons Point systems have their advantages, as their wide use suggests. This is a quantitative technique that is easily explained to and used by employees. On the other hand, it can be difficult to develop a point plan, and this is one reason many organizations have opted for ready-made plans. In fact, the availability of a number of ready-made plans probably accounts in part for the wide use of point plans in job evaluation.

Notes

1. Thomas Patten, Jr., *Pay: Employee Compensation and Incentive Plans* (New York: Free Press, 1977), p. 1. See also Jerry McAdams, "Why Reward Systems Fail," *Personnel Journal,* Vol. 67, no. 6 (June 1988), pp. 103–113; James Whitney, "Pay Concepts for the 1990s," Part I, *Compensation and Benefits Review,* Vol. 20, no. 2 (March–April 1988), pp. 33–44; and James Whitney, "Pay Concepts for the 1990s," Part II, *Compensation and Benefits Review,* Vol. 20, no. 3 (May–June 1988), pp. 45–50. See also "Aligning Work and Rewards: A Round Table Discussion," *Compensation and Benefits Review,* Vol. 26, No. 4 (July–August 1994), pp. 47–63 and Marlene Morganstern, "Compensation and the New Employment Relationship," *Compensation and Benefits Review,* Vol. 27, No. 2 (March 1995), pp. 37–44.
2. Orlando Behling and Chester Schriesheim, *Organizational Behavior* (Boston: Allyn & Bacon, 1976), p. 233.
3. Based partly on Richard Henderson, *Compensation Management* (Reston, VA: Reston, 1980).
4. A complete description of exemption requirements as found in U.S. Department of Labor, *Executive, Administrative, Professional & Outside Salesmen Exempted from the Fair Labor Standards Act* (Washington, DC: U.S. Government Printing Office, 1973).
5. Earl Mellor, "Weekly Earnings in 1985: A Look at More than 200 Occupations," *Monthly Labor Review,* Vol. 109, no. 9 (September 1986), pp. 27–34; Bureau of National Affairs, *Fair Employment Practices,* 1988, p. 27. See also John R. Hellenbeck et al., "Sex Differences in Occupational Choice, Pay, and Worth: A Supply-Side Approach to Understanding the Male-Female Wage Gap," *Personnel Psychology,* Vol. 40, no. 4 (Winter 1987), pp. 715–744.
6. Alison Wellington, "Changes in the Male/Female Wage Gap, 1976–85," *The Journal of Human Resources,* Vol. 28, no. 2 (1989), pp. 383–411, and June O'Neill and Solomon Polachek, "Why the Gender Gap in Wages Narrowed in the 1980s," *Journal of Labor Economics,* Vol. 11, no. 1 (1993), pp. 205–228.
7. O'Neill and Polachek, "Why the Gender Gap in Wages Narrowed in the 1980s."
8. Commerce Clearing House, *Ideas and Trends in Personnel,* October 31, 1986, pp. 169–171.
9. Henderson, *Compensation Management,* pp. 88–99.
10. Michael R. Carrell and Frank E. Kuzmits, "Amended ADEA's Effects on Human Resources Strategies Remain Dubious," *Personnel Journal,* Vol. 66, no. 5 (May 1987).
11. Henderson, *Compensation Management,* pp. 101–127.
12. Ibid., p. 115.
13. Edward Hay, "The Attitude of the American Federation of Labor on Job Evaluation," *Personnel Journal,* Vol. 26 (November 1947), pp. 163–169; Howard James, "Issues in Job Evaluation: The Union's View," *Personnel Journal,* Vol. 51 (September 1972), pp. 675–679; Henderson, *Compensation Management,* pp. 117–118; Harold Jones, "Union Views on Job Evaluations: 1971 vs. 1978," *Personnel Journal,* Vol. 58 (February 1979), pp. 80–85.
14. Joseph Famularo, *Handbook of Modern Personnel Administration* (New York: McGraw-Hill, 1972), pp. 27–29. See also Bruce Ellig, "Strategic Pay Planning," *Compensation and Benefits Review,* Vol. 19, no. 4 (July–August 1987), pp. 28–43; Thomas Robertson, "Fundamental Strategies for Wage and Salary Administration," *Personnel Journal,* Vol. 65, no. 11 (November 1986), pp. 120–132. One expert cautions against conducting salary surveys based on job title alone. He recommends job-content salary surveys that examine the content of jobs according to the size of each job so that, for instance, the work of the president of IBM and that of a small clone manufacturer would not be inadvertently compared. See Robert Sahl, "Job Content Salary Sur-

veys: Survey Design and Selection Features," *Compensation and Benefits Review* (May–June 1991), pp. 14–21.

15. See David I. Levine, "What Do Wages Buy?" *Administrative Science Quarterly,* Vol. 38 (1993), pp. 462–483.

16. Ibid., p. 462.

17. Ibid., pp. 462–465.

18. Ibid., p. 462.

19. Vicki Kaman and Jodie Barr, "Employee Attitude Surveys for Strategic Compensation Management," *Compensation and Benefits Review* (January–February 1991), pp. 52–65.

20. "Use of Wage Surveys," *BNA Policy and Practice Series* (Washington, DC: Bureau of National Affairs, 1976), pp. 313–314. In a recent survey of compensation professionals, uses of salary survey data were reported. The surveys were used most often to adjust the salary structure and ranges. Other uses included determining the merit budget, adjusting individual job rates, and maintaining pay leadership. D. W. Belcher, N. Bruce Ferris, and John O'Neill, "How Wage Surveys Are Being Used," *Compensation and Benefits Review* (September–October 1985), pp. 34–51. For further discussion, see, for example, Kent Romanoff, Ken Boehm, and Edward Benson, "Pay Equity: Internal and External Considerations," *Compensation and Benefits Review,* Vol. 18, no. 3 (May–June 1986), pp. 17–25.

21. Helen Murlis, "Making Sense of Salary Surveys," *Personnel Management,* Vol. 17 (January 1981), pp. 30–33. For an explanation of how market analysis can be used to ensure fair and competitive pay for all jobs in the organization, see, for example, Peter Olney, Jr., "Meeting the Challenge of Comparable Worth," Part 2, *Compensation and Benefits Review,* Vol. 19, no. 3 (May–June 1987), pp. 45–53.

22. This is based on Frederick W. Cook, "Compensation Surveys are Biased," *Compensation and Benefits Review* (September–October 1994), pp. 19–22.

23. Ibid., p. 19.

24. Ibid.

25. Henderson, *Compensation Management,* pp. 260–269.

26. Joan O'Brien and Robert Zawacki, "Salary Surveys: Are They Worth the Effort?" *Personnel,* Vol. 62, no. 10 (October 1985), pp. 70–74.

27. Patten, *Pay,* p. 177.

28. You may have noticed that job analysis as discussed in Chapter 3 can be a useful source of information on compensable factors, as well as on job descriptions and job specifications. For example, a quantitative job analysis technique like the position analysis questionnaire generates quantitative information on the degree to which the following five basic factors are present in each job: having decision making/communication/social responsibilities, performing skilled activities, being physically active, operating vehicles or equipment, and processing information. As a result, a job analysis technique like the PAQ is actually as (or some say, more) appropriate as a job evaluation technique in that jobs can be quantitatively compared to one another on those five dimensions and their relative worth thus ascertained. Another point worth noting is that you may find that a single set of compensable factors is not adequate for describing all your jobs. Many managers, therefore, divide their jobs into job clusters. For example, you might have a separate job cluster for factory workers, for clerical workers, and for managerial

personnel. Similarly, you would then probably have a somewhat different set of compensable factors for each job cluster.

29. A. N. Nash and F. J. Carroll, Jr., "Installation of a Job Evaluation Program," from *Management of Compensation* (Monterey, CA: Brooks/Cole, 1975), reprinted in Craig Schneier and Richard Beatty, *Personnel Administration Today: Readings and Commentary* (Reading, MA: Addison-Wesley, 1978), pp. 417–425; and Henderson, *Compensation Management,* pp. 231–239. According to one survey, about equal percentages of employers use individual interviews, employee questionnaires, or observations by personnel representatives to obtain the actual job evaluation information. See Mary Ellen Lo Bosco, "Job Analysis, Job Evaluation, and Job Classification," *Personnel,* Vol. 62, no. 5 (May 1985), pp. 70–75. See also Howard Risher, "Job Evaluation: Validity and Reliability," *Compensation and Benefits Review,* Vol. 21, no. 1 (January–February 1989), pp. 22–36; and David Hahn and Robert Dipboye, "Effects of Training and Information on the Accuracy and Reliability of Job Evaluations," *Journal of Applied Psychology,* Vol. 73, no. 2 (May 1988), pp. 146–153.

30. See, for example, Donald Petri, "Talking Pay Policy Pays Off," *Supervisory Management* (May 1979), pp. 2–13.

31. As explained later, the practice of red circling is used to delay downward adjustments in pay rates that are presently too high given the newly evaluated jobs. See also E. James Brennan, "Everything You Need to Know About Salary Ranges," *Personnel Journal,* Vol. 63, no. 3 (March 1984), pp. 10–17.

32. Nash and Carroll, "Installation of a Job Evaluation," p. 419.

33. Ibid.

34. C. F. Lutz, "Quantitative Job Evaluation in Local Government in the United States," *International Labor Review* (June 1969), pp. 607–619.

35. If you used the job classification method, then of course the jobs are already classified.

36. David Belcher, *Compensation Administration* (Englewood Cliffs, NJ: Prentice Hall, 1973), pp. 257–276.

37. Gerald Ledford, Jr., "Three Case Studies on Skill-Based Pay: An Overview," *Compensation and Benefits Review* (March–April 1991), pp. 11–23.

38. Ibid., p. 12. See also Kathryn Cofsky, "Critical Keys to Competency-Based Pay," *Compensation and Benefits Review* (November–December 1993), pp. 46–52.

39. Gerald Ledford, Jr., and Gary Bergel, "Skill-Based Pay Case Number 1: General Mills," *Compensation and Benefits Review,* (March–April 1991), pp. 24–38; see also Gerald Barrett, "Comparison of Skill-Based Pay with Traditional Job Evaluation Techniques," *Human Resource Management Review,* Vol. 1, no. 2 (Summer 1991), pp. 97–105. See also Barbara Dewey, "Changing to Skill-Based Pay: Disarming the Transition Land Mines," *Compensation and Benefits Review,* Vol. 26, No. 1 (January–February 1994), pp. 38–43.

40. This is based on Ledford and Bergel, "Skill-Based Pay Case Number 1," pp. 28–29.

41. Kevin Parent and Caroline Weber, "Case Study: Does Paying for Knowledge Pay Off?" *Compensation and Benefits Review* (September–October 1994), pp. 44–50, and Edward Lawler, III, Gerald Ledford, Jr., and Lei Chang, "Who Uses

Skill-Based Pay, and Why," *Compensation and Benefits Review* (March–April 1993), pp. 22–26.

42. Parent and Weber, "Case Study."

43. "Broadbanding of Pay Structures Gains Prominence," *Bulletin to Management, BNA Policy and Practice Series,* January 20, 1994, p. 17.

44. David Hofrichter, "Broadbanding: A 'Second Generation' Approach," *Compensation and Benefits Review* (September–October 1993), pp. 53–58. See also Gary Bergel, "Choosing the Right Pay Delivery System to Fit Banding," *Compensation and Benefits Review,* Vol. 26, No. 4 (July–August 1994), pp. 34–38.

45. Ibid., p. 55.

46. For example, see Sondra Emerson, "Job Evaluation: A Barrier to Excellence?" *Compensation and Benefits Review* (January–February 1991), pp. 39–51; Nan Weiner, "Job Evaluation Systems: A Critique," *Human Resource Management Review,* Vol. 1, no. 2 (Summer 1991), pp. 119–132.

47. Ibid., pp. 53 and 57.

48. Emerson, "Job Evaluation," p. 39.

49. This is based on Laurent Dufetel, "Job Evaluation: Still at the Frontier," *Compensation and Benefits Review* (July–August 1991), pp. 53–67.

50. Ibid. p. 54.

51. This is based on Gary Dessler, *Winning Commitment* (New York: McGraw-Hill, 1993), Chapter 9.

52. Personal interview.

53. Jude Rich, "Meeting the Global Challenge: A Measurement and Reward Program for the Future," *Compensation and Benefits Review* (July–August 1992), p. 27.

54. Ibid., p. 28.

55. A. W. Smith, Jr., "Structuralist Salary Management: A Modest Proposal," *Compensation and Benefits Review* (July–August 1992), pp. 22–25.

56. Ibid., p. 23.

57. Charles Cumming, "Will Traditional Salary Administration Survive the Stampede to Alternative Rewards?" *Compensation and Benefits Review* (November–December 1992), pp. 42–47.

58. Dale Yoder, *Personnel Management and Industrial Relations* (Englewood Cliffs, NJ: Prentice Hall, 1970), pp. 643–645; Famularo, *Handbook of Modern Personnel Administration,* pp. 32.1–32.6 and 30.1–30.8.

59. Bruce Ellig, *Executive Compensation—A Total Pay Perspective* (New York: McGraw-Hill, 1982), pp. 9–10. See also Bryan J. Brooks, "Trends in International Executive Compensation," *Personnel,* Vol. 64, no. 5 (May 1987), pp. 67–71 and Edwin Lewis, "New Approaches to Executive Pay," *Directors and Boards,* Vol. 18, No. 3 (Spring 1994), pp. 57–58.

60. "No Sign of Recession in Pay at the Top," *Business Week,* May 10, 1982, pp. 76–80. See also Peter D. Sherer, Donald Schwab, and Herbert Henneman, "Managerial Salary-Raise Decisions: A Policy-Capturing Approach," *Personnel Psychology,* Vol. 40, no. 1 (Spring 1987), pp. 27–38 and Ira Kay and Rodney Robinson, "Misguided Attacks on Executive Pay Hurt Shareholders," *Compensation and Benefits Review,* Vol. 26, No. 1 (January–February 1994), pp. 25–33.

61. "Executive Pay," *The Wall Street Journal,* April 11, 1996, pp. R16–R170.

62. Ernest C. Miller, "Setting Supervisors' Pay at Pay Differen-

tials," *Compensation Review,* Vol. 10 (Third Quarter 1978), pp. 13–16.

63. Nardash Agarwal, "Determinants of Executive Compensation," *Industrial Relations,* Vol. 20, no. 1 (Winter 1981), pp. 36–45. See also John A. Fossum and Mary Fitch, "The Effects of Individual and Contextual Attributes on the Sizes of Recommended Salary Increases," *Personnel Psychology,* Vol. 38, no. 3 (Autumn 1985), pp. 587–602.

64. Kenneth Foster, "Does Executive Pay Make Sense?" *Business Horizons* (September–October 1981), pp. 47–51.

65. Foster, "Does Executive Pay Make Sense?" p. 50.

66. This is based on William White, "Managing the Board Review of Executive Pay," *Compensation and Benefits Review* (November–December 1992), pp. 35–41.

67. Ibid., pp. 38–40; see also H. Anthony Hampson, "Tying CEO Pay to Performance: Compensation Committees Must Do Better," *The Business Quarterly,* Vol. 55, no. 4 (Spring 1991), pp. 18–22.

68. William White and Raymond Fife, "New Challenges for Executive Compensation in the 1990s," *Compensation and Benefits Review* (January–February 1993), pp. 27–35.

69. Famularo, *Handbook of Modern Personnel Administration,* pp. 32.1–32.6. See also Peter Sherer, et al., "Managerial Salary-Raise Decisions," pp. 27–38.

70. Famularo, *Handbook of Modern Personnel Administration,* pp. 30.1–30.15.

71. Ibid., pp. 30.1–30.5. See also Patric Moran, "Equitable Salary Administration in High-Tech Companies," *Compensation and Benefits Review,* Vol. 18, no. 5 (September–October 1986), pp. 31–40.

72. Robert Sibson, *Compensation* (New York: AMACOM, 1981), p. 194.

73. Ibid.

74. See also Bernisha Bridges, "The Role of Rewards in Motivating Scientific and Technical Personnel: Experience at Egland AFB," *National Productivity Review* (Summer 1993), pp. 337–348.

75. Helen Remick, "The Comparable Worth Controversy," *Public Personnel Management Journal* (Winter 1981), pp. 371–383.

76. Ibid., p. 377.

77. Ibid.

78. Ibid., p. 38; U.S. Department of Labor, *Perspectives on Working Women: A Data Book* (October 1980).

79. *County of Washington* v. *Gunther;* U.S. Supreme Court, No. 80–429 (June 8, 1981).

80. SKRSC Update, Schachter, Kristoff, Ross, Sprague, and Curiale, California Street, San Francisco, CA. (September–October 1985). For further information on comparable worth, see U.S. Commission of Civil Rights, *Comparable Worth: Issue for the 80's,* Vols. 1 and 2, June 6–7, 1984. See also Walter Fogel, "Intentional Sex-Based Pay Discrimination: Can It Be Proven?" *Labor Law Journal,* Vol. 27, no. 5 (May 1986), pp. 291–299.

81. See David Thomsen, "Compensation and Benefits—More on Comparable Worth," *Personnel Journal,* Vol. 60 (May 1981), pp. 348–349; Marvin Levine, "Comparable Worth in the 1980s: Will Collective Bargaining Supplant Legislative and Judicial Interpretations?" *Labor Law Journal,* Vol. 38, no. 6 (June 1987), pp. 323–335; Peter Olney, Jr., "Meeting the Challenge of Comparable Worth," Part II, *Compen-*

sation and Benefits Review, Vol. 19, no. 3 (May–June 1987), pp. 45–53; and Jennifer Quinn, "Visibility and Value: The Role of Job Evaluation in Assuring Equal Pay for Women," *Law and Public Policy in International Business,* Vol. 25, no. 4, (Summer 1994), pp. 1403–1444.

82. Mary Gray, "Pay Equity Through Job Evaluation: A Case Study," *Compensation and Benefits Review* (July–August 1992), p. 46.

83. Ibid., pp. 46–51.

84. Brinks, "The Comparable Worth Issue," p. 40.

85. Michael Carter, "Comparable Worth: An Idea Whose Time Has Come?" *Personnel Journal,* Vol. 60 (October 1981), p. 794; and Peter Olney, Jr., "Meeting the Challenge of Comparable Worth," Part I, *Compensation and Benefits Review,* Vol. 19, no. 2 (March–April 1987), pp. 34–44. See also Mary Virginia Moore and Yohannan Abraham, "Comparable Worth: Is It A Moot Issue? Part II: The Legal and Juridical Posture," *Public Personnel Management,* Vol. 23, No. 2 (Summer 1994), pp. 263–286.

86. Brinks, "The Comparable Worth Issue," p. 40.

87. James Coil, III and Charles Rice, "State Comparable Work Laws: Equal Pay for Unequal Work," *Employment Relations Today* (Autumn 1993), p. 333.

88. Ibid., p. 333. See also Paul Greenlaw and Robert D. Lee, Jr., "Three Decades of Experience with the Equal Pay Act," *Review of Public Personnel Administration,* Vol. 13, no. 4 (1993), pp. 43–58.

89. Charles M. Futrell, "Effects of Pay Disclosure on Satisfaction for Sales Managers: A Longitudinal Study," *Academy of Management Journal,* Vol. 21, no. 1 (March 1978), pp. 140–144.

90. Mary G. Miner, "Pay Policies: Secret or Open? and Why?" *Personnel Journal,* Vol. 53 (February 1974), reprinted in Richard Peterson, Lane Tracy, and Alan Cabelly, *Readings in Systematic Management in Human Resources* (Reading, MA: Addison-Wesley, 1979), pp. 233–239.

91. Margaret Yao, "Inflation Outruns Pay of Middle Managers, Increasing Frustration," *The Wall Street Journal,* June 9, 1981, p. 1. See also, "The Impact of Inflation on Wage and Salary Administration," *Personnel,* Vol. 58 (November–December 1981), p. 55.

92. This section based on or quoted from "The Impact of Inflation on Wage and Salary Administration," p. 55.

93. Wendell C. Lawther, "Ways to Monitor (and Solve) the Pay Compression Problem," *Personnel* (March 1989), pp. 84–87.

94. Ibid., p. 87.

95. Robert Dockson and Jack Vance, "Retirement in Peril: Inflation and the Executive Compensation Program," *California Management Review,* Vol. 24 (Summer 1981), pp. 87–94.

96. Ibid.

97. Joan Lindroth, "Inflation, Taxes, and Perks: How Compensation Is Changing," *Personnel Journal,* Vol. 60 (December 1981), pp. 934–940.

98. Clarence Deitch and David Dilts, "The COLA Clause: An Employer Bargaining Weapon?" *Personnel Journal,* Vol. 61 (March 1982), pp. 220–223.

99. Patten, *Pay,* p. 181.

100. Deitch and Dilts, "The COLA Clause," p. 221.

101. Patten, *Pay,* p. 182.

102. "Collective Bargaining in 1987," *Monthly Labor Review* (January 1987), p. 34.

103. *Dun's Business Monthly,* Vol. 129, no. 1 (January 1987), p. 18. See also, "End of an Era: COLA's on the Way Out," *Compensation and Benefits Review,* Vol. 18, no. 2 (March–April 1986), p. 4.

104. Rugus Runzheimer, Jr., "How Corporations Are Handling Cost of Living Differentials," *Business Horizons,* Vol. 23 (August 1980), p. 39.

105. Ibid., p. 39.

106. Jack Anderson, "Compensating Your Overseas Executives, Part II: Europe in 1992," *Compensation and Benefits Review* (July–August 1990), p. 28.

107. This is based on ibid., pp. 29–31.

108. Ibid., p. 31.

109. Richard Hodgetts and Fred Luthans, "U.S. Multinationals' Expatriates' Compensation Strategies," *Compensation and Benefits Review* (January–February, 1993), pp. 57–62.

110. Wayne Outten and Noah Kinigstein, *The Rights of Employees* (New York: Bantam Books, 1983), pp. 201–202.

111. Commerce Clearing House, "How to Avoid the Ten Most Common Wage-Hour Traps," *Ideas and Trends,* March 10, 1989, p. 43.

112. Arthur Silbergeld and Mark Tuvim, "Recent Cases Narrowly Construe Exemption from Overtime Provisions of Fair Labor Standards Act," *Employment Relations Today* (Summer 1994), pp. 241–250; see also Charles Fine, "Exempt or Not? Classification Can Mean Big Dollars," *Management Review* (July 1993), pp. 58–60. Also see Matthew Smith and Steven Winterbauer, "Overtime Compensation Under the FLSA: Pay Them Now or Pay Them Later," *Employee Relations Labor Journal,* Vol. 19, no. 1 (Summer 1993), pp. 23–51.

113. Ibid.

114. With more companies establishing all-salaried work forces, firms are seeking to erase, to as great an extent as possible, the distinction between exempt and nonexempt employees. As a result, there are some exceptions that permit fluctuating workweeks. See Christopher Martin and Jerry Newman, "The FLSA Overtime Provision: A New Controversy?" *Compensation and Benefits Review* (July–August 1991), pp. 60–63.

115. For a full discussion, see Peter Gold and Michael Esposito, "The Right to Control: Are Your Workers Independent Contractors or Employees?" *Compensation and Benefits Review* (July–August 1992), pp. 30–37.

116. For a discussion, see, for example, Roger Plachy, "The Point Factor Job Evaluation System: A Step-by-Step Guide, Part I," *Compensation and Benefits Review,* Vol. 19, no. 4 (July–August 1987), pp. 12–27; Roger Plachy, "The Case for Effective Point-Factor Job Evaluation, Viewpoint I," *Compensation and Benefits Review,* Vol. 19, no. 2 (March–April 1987), pp. 45–48; Roger Plachy, "The Point-Factor Job Evaluation System: A Step-by-Step Guide, Part II," *Compensation and Benefits Review,* Vol. 19, no. 5 (September–October 1987), pp. 9–24; and Alfred Candrilli and Ronald Armagast, "The Case for Effective Point-Factor Job Evaluation, Viewpoint II," *Compensation and Benefits Review,* Vol. 19, no. 2 (March–April 1987), pp. 49–54. See also Robert J. Sahl, "How to Install a Point-Factor Job Evaluation System," *Personnel,* Vol. 66, no. 3 (March 1989), pp. 38–42.

Chapter 13

Pay-for-Performance and Financial Incentives

Chapter Outline

- ◆ Money and Motivation: Background and Trends
- ◆ Incentives for Operations Employees
- ◆ Incentives for Mangers and Executives
- ◆ Incentives for Salespeople
- ◆ Incentives for Other Professionals
- ◆ Organization-wide Incentive Plans

Behavioral Objectives

When you finish studying this chapter, you should be able to:

Discuss how to use piecework, standard hour, and team or group incentive plans.

Discuss how to use short-term and long-term incentives for managers and executives.

List the pros and cons of salary plans and commission plans for salespeople.

Explain how an incentive plan might backfire and how to avoid such a problem.

Money and Motivation: Background and Trends

The use of financial incentives—financial rewards paid to workers whose production exceeds some predetermined standard—is not new, but was popularized by Frederick Taylor in the late 1800s. As a supervisory employee of the Midvale Steel Company, Taylor had become concerned with what he called "systematic soldiering"—the tendency of employees to work at the slowest pace possible and produce at the minimum acceptable level. What especially intrigued him was the fact that some of these same workers still had the energy to run home and work on their cabins, even after a hard 12-hour day. Taylor knew that if he could find some way to harness this energy during the workday, huge productivity gains would be achieved.

At this time, primitive piecework systems were already in use, but they were generally ineffective. Workers were paid a piece rate for each piece they produced, based on informally arrived at quotas. However, rate cutting by employers was flagrant, and the workers knew that if their earnings became excessive, their pay per piece would be cut. As a result, most workers produced just enough to earn a decent wage, but little enough so that their rate per piece would not be reduced.

fair day's work
Frederick Taylor's observation that haphazard setting of piecework requirements and wages by supervisors was not sufficient, and that careful study was needed to define acceptable production quotas for each job.

One of Taylor's great insights was in seeing the need for a standardized, acceptable view of a **fair day's work.** As he saw it, this fair day's work should depend not on the vague estimates of supervisors but on a careful, formal, scientific process of inspection and observation. It was this need to evaluate each job scientifically that led to the **scientific management** movement. In turn, scientific management gave way in the Depression-plagued 1930s to the human relations movement and its focus on satisfying workers' social—not just their financial—needs.

scientific management
The careful, scientific study of the job for the purpose of boosting productivity and job satisfaction.

Today's emphasis on quality-improvement teams and commitment-building programs is creating a renaissance for financial incentive or pay-for-performance plans. One expert estimates, for instance, that pay-for-performance (pay that puts some part of base salary at risk, or that pays individuals or teams based on their achieving quality or quantity goals) will rise to 15% to 20% of compensation for all U.S. employees over the next few years.[1] (Today it is estimated that such variable pay constitutes less than 5% of U.S. workers' compensation.)[2] Thus, traditional pay plans are giving way to skill-based plans, and to the sorts of spot awards, team incentives, and gainsharing plans discussed in this chapter.

There are sound competitive reasons for the growing emphasis on such performance-based compensation. For one thing, today's emphasis on cutting costs, restructuring, and boosting performance leads one logically to link pay and performance as Taylor did.

But the growing emphasis on pay-for-performance is also rooted in the trend toward quality-improvement teams and employee commitment programs. The entire thrust of such programs is to treat workers like partners and to get them to think of the business and its goals as their own. It is thus reasonable to pay them more like partners, too, by linking their pay more directly to performance.

Types of Incentive Plans

spot bonus
A spontaneous incentive awarded to individuals for accomplishments not readily measured by a standard.

There are several types of incentive plans.[3] *Individual incentive programs* give income over and above base salary to individual employees who meet a specific individual peformance standard.[4] **Spot bonuses** are awarded, generally to individual employees, for accomplishments that are not readily measured by a standard, such as "to recognize the long hours this employee put in last month," or "to recognize exemplary customer service this week."[5] *Group incentive programs* are like individual incentive plans but give pay over and above base salary to all team members when the group or team collectively meets a specified standard for performance, productivity, or other work-related behavior.[6] *Profit-sharing plans* are generally organizationwide incentive programs that provide employees with a share of the organization's profits in a specified period.[7] *Gainsharing programs* are organizationwide pay plans designed to reward employees for improvements in organizational productivity. As we'll see, gainsharing plans generally include employee suggestion systems and focus on reducing labor costs through employee suggestions and participation.[8] **Variable pay** refers to any plan that ties pay to productivity or to some other measure of the firm's profitability.

variable pay
Any plan that ties pay to productivity or profitability, usually as one-time lump payments.

For simplicity we will discuss these plans as follows: as incentives for operations employees; as incentives for managers and executives; as incentives for salespeople; as incentives primarily for white-collar and professional employees (merit pay); and as organizationwide incentives.

Incentives For Operations Employees

Piecework Plans

piecework
A system of pay based on the number of items processed by each individual worker in a unit of time, such as items per hour or items per day.

Several incentive plans are particularly well suited for use with operations employees, such as for those doing production work. **Piecework** is the oldest incentive plan and still the most commonly used. Earnings are tied directly to what the worker produces; the person is paid a *piece rate* for each unit he or she produces. Thus, if Tom Smith gets $0.40 apiece for stamping out door jambs, then he would make $40 for stamping out 100 a day and $80 for stamping out 200.

Developing a workable piece-rate plan requires both job evaluation and (usually) industrial engineering. Job evaluation enables you to assign an hourly wage rate to the job in question. But the crucial issue in piece-rate planning is the production standard, and this standard is usually developed by industrial engineers. Production standards are stated in terms of a standard number of minutes per unit or a standard number of units per hour. In Tom Smith's case, the job evaluation indicated that his door-jamb stamping job was worth $8 an hour. The industrial engineer determined that 20 jambs per hour was the standard production rate. Therefore, the piece rate (for each door jamb) was $8.00 divided by 20 = $0.40 per door jamb.

straight piecework plan
Under this pay system each worker receives a set payment for each piece produced or processed in a factory or shop.

guaranteed piecework plan
The minimum hourly wage plus an incentive for each piece produced above a set number of pieces per hour.

With a **straight piecework plan**, Tom Smith would be paid on the basis of the number of door jambs he produced; there would be no guaranteed minimum wage. However, after passage of the Fair Labor Standards Act, it became necessary for most employers to guarantee their workers a minimum wage. With a **guaranteed piecework plan**, Tom Smith would be paid $4.25 per hour (the minimum wage) whether or not he stamped out 13 door jambs per hour (at $0.40 each). But as an incentive he would also be paid at the piece rate of $0.40 for each unit he produced over 13.

Piecework generally implies straight piecework, a strict proportionality between results and rewards regardless of the level of output. Thus, in Smith's case, he continues to get $0.40 apiece for stamping out door jambs, even if he stamps out many more than planned, say, 500 per day. On the other hand, certain types of piecework incentive plans call for a sharing of productivity gains between worker and employer such that the worker does not receive full credit for all production above normal.[9]

Advantages and Disadvantages   Piecework incentive plans have several advantages. They are simple to calculate and easily understood by employees. Piece-rate plans appear equitable in principle, and their incentive value can be powerful since rewards are directly tied to performance.

Piecework also has some disadvantages. A main one is its somewhat unsavory reputation among many employees based on some employers' habits of arbitrarily raising production standards whenever they found their workers earning "excessive" wages. In addition, piece rates are stated in monetary terms (like $0.40 per piece). Thus, when a new job evaluation results in a new hourly wage rate, the piece rate must also be revised; this can be a big clerical chore. Another disadvantage is more subtle; since the piece rate is quoted on a per-piece basis, in workers' minds production standards become tied inseparably to the amount of money earned. When an attempt is made to revise production standards, it meets considerable worker resistance, even if the revision is fully justified.[10]

In fact, the industrial engineered specificity of piecework plans represents the seeds of piecework's biggest disadvantage these days. Piecework plans tend to be tailor-made for relatively specialized jobs in which employees do basically the same narrow tasks over and over again many times a day. This in turn fosters a certain rigidity: Employees become preoccupied with producing the number of units needed. They become less willing to concern themselves with meeting quality standards or switching from job to job (since doing so could reduce the person's productivity).[11] Employees tend to be trained to perform only a limited number of tasks. Similarly, attempts to introduce new technology or innovative processes may be more likely to fail, insofar as they require major adjustments to engineered standards and negotiations with employees. Equipment tends not to be as well maintained, since employees are focusing on maximizing each machine's output.

Problems such as these have led some firms to drop their piecework plans (as well as their standard hour plans, discussed next) and to substitute team-based incentive plans or programs such as gainsharing, which we will also discuss.

Standard Hour Plan

standard hour plan
A plan by which a worker is paid a basic hourly rate but is paid an extra percentage of his or her base rate for production exceeding the standard per hour or per day. Similar to piecework payment but based on a percent premium.

The **standard hour plan** is like the piece-rate plan, with one major difference. With a piece-rate plan the worker is paid a particular rate per each piece that he or she produces. With the standard hour plan the worker is rewarded by a *percent premium that equals the percent by which his or her performance exceeds the standard*. The plan assumes the worker has a guaranteed base rate.

As an example, suppose the base rate for Smith's job is $8 per hour. (The base rate may, but need not, equal the hourly rate determined by the job evaluation.) And again assume that the production standard for Smith's job is 20 units per hour, or 3 minutes per unit. Suppose that in one day (8 hours) Smith produces 200 door jambs. According to the production standard, this should have taken Smith 10 hours (200 divided by 20 per hour); instead it took him 8 hours. He produced at a rate 25% (40 divided by 160) higher than the standard rate. The standard rate would be 8 hours times 20 (units per hour) = 160: Smith actually produced 40 more, or 200. He will, therefore, be paid at a rate 25% above his base rate for the day. His base rate was $8 per hour times 8 hours equals $64. So he'll be paid 1.25 times 64 or $80.00 for the day.

The standard hour plan has most of the advantages of the piecework plan and is fairly simple to compute and easy to understand. But the incentive is expressed in units of time instead of in monetary terms (as it is with the piece-rate system). Therefore, there is less tendency on the part of workers to link their production standard with their pay. Furthermore, the clerical job of recomputing piece rates whenever hourly wage rates are reevaluated is avoided.[12]

Team or Group Incentive Plans

There are several ways to implement **team or group incentive plans.**[13] One is to set work standards for each member of the group and maintain a count of the output of each member. Members are then paid based on one of three formulas: (1) All members receive the pay earned by the highest producer, (2) all members receive the pay earned by the lowest producer, or (3) all members receive payment equal to the average pay earned by the group. The second approach is to set a production standard based on the final output of the group as a whole; all members then receive the same pay, based on the piece rate that exists for the group's job. The group incentive can be based on either the piece rate or standard hour plan, but the latter is somewhat more prevalent.

A third option is to choose a measurable definition of group performance or productivity that the group can control. You could, for instance, use broad criteria such as total labor-hours per final product: Piecework's engineered standards are thus not necessarily required here.[14]

There are several reasons to use team incentive plans. Sometimes several jobs are interrelated, as they are on project teams. Here one worker's performance reflects not only his or her own effort but that of coworkers as well; here team incentives make sense. Team plans also reinforce group planning and problem solving and help ensure collaboration.[15] In Japan, "the first rule is never reward only one individual." Instead, employees are rewarded as a group in order to reduce jealousy, make group members indebted to one another (as they would be to the group), and encourage a sense of cooperation.[16] There tends to be less bickering among group members over who has "tight" production standards and who has loose ones. Group incentive plans also facilitate on-the-job training, since each member of the group has an interest in getting new members trained as quickly as possible.[17]

A group incentive plan's chief disadvantage is that each worker's rewards are no longer based solely on his or her own efforts. To the extent that the person does not see his or her effort leading to the desired reward, a group plan may be less effective than an individual plan. In one study, however (in which the researchers arranged to pay the group based on the performance of its best member), the group incentive was as effective as an individual one in improving performance.[18]

Incentives for Managers and Executives

Most employers award their managers and executives a bonus or incentive because of the role managers play in determining divisional and corporate profitability.[19] One survey found, for instance, that about 90% of large companies pay managers and executives annual ("short-term") bonuses,[20] while another found that about 70% of small firms have such plans.[21] Similarly, long-term incentive plans (like stock options), which are intended to motivate and reward management for the corporation's long-term growth and prosperity, are used by over 50% of U.S. firms.[22] The widespread use of these bonuses may reflect the fact that they can and do pay for themselves by improving management and thus organizational performance.[23]

Short-Term Incentives: The Annual Bonus

annual bonus
Plans that are designed to motivate short-term performance of managers and are tied to company profitability.

Most firms have **annual bonus** plans aimed at motivating the short-term performance of their managers and executives. Unlike salaries, which rarely decline with reduced performance, short-term incentive bonuses can easily result in plus or minus adjustments of 25% or more in total pay.

There are three basic issues to be considered when awarding short-term incentives: eligibility, fund-size determination, and individual awards. *Eligibility* is usually decided in one of three ways. The first criterion is *key position*. Here a job-by-job review is conducted to identify the key jobs (typically only line jobs) that have measurable impact on profitability. The second approach to determining eligibilty is to set a *salary-level* cutoff point; all employees earning over that threshold amount are automatically eligible for consideration for short-term incentives. Finally, eligibility can be determined by *salary grade.* This is a refinement of the salary cutoff approach and assumes that all employees at a certain grade or above should be eligible for the short-term incentive program.[24] The simplest approach is just to use salary level as a cutoff.[25] As a rule, bonus eligibility begins somewhere around $40,000 to $50,000.[26]

The size of the bonus is usually greater for top-level executives. Thus, an executive earning $150,000 in salary may be able to earn another 80% of his or her salary as a bonus, while a manager in the same firm earning $80,000 can earn only another 30%. Similarly, a supervisor might be able to earn up to 15% of his or her base salary in bonuses. Average bonuses range from a low of 10% to a high of 80% or more: A typical company might establish a plan whereby executives could earn 45% of base salary, managers 25%, and supervisory personnel 12%.

How Much to Pay Out (Fund Size) Next a decision must be made regarding fund size—the total amount of bonus money that will be available—and there are several formulas to do this. Some companies use a *nondeductible formula.* Here a straight percentage (usually of the company's net income) is used to create the short-term incentive fund. Others use a *deductible formula* on the assumption that the short-term incentive fund should begin to accumulate only after the firm has met a specified level of earnings.

Jack Welch, CEO of General Electric, receives very high bonuses in addition to his regular compensation.

In practice, what proportion of profits is usually paid out as bonuses? There are no hard and fast rules, and some firms do not even have a formula for developing the bonus fund.[27] One alternative is to reserve a minimum amount of the profits, say, 10% for safeguarding stockholders' investments, and then to establish a fund for bonuses equal to, say, 20% of the corporate operating profit before taxes in excess of this base amount. Thus, if the operating profits were $100,000, then the management bonus fund might be 20% of $90,000 or $18,000.[28] Other illustrative formulas used for determining the executive bonus fund are as follows:

Ten percent of net income after deducting 5% of average capital invested in business.

Twelve and one-half percent of the amount by which net income exceeds 6% of stockholders' equity.

Twelve percent of net earnings after deducting 6% of net capital.[29]

Deciding Individual Awards The third issue is deciding the *individual awards* to be paid. Typically a target bonus is set for each eligible position and adjustments are then made for greater or less than targeted performance. A maximum amount, perhaps double the target bonus, may be set. Performance ratings are obtained for each manager and preliminary bonus estimates are computed. Estimates for the total amount of money to be spent on short-term incentives are thereby made and compared with the bonus fund available. If necessary, the individual estimates are then adjusted.

A related question is whether managers will receive bonuses based on individual performance, corporate performance, or both. Keep in mind that there is a difference between a profit-sharing plan and a true, individual incentive bonus. In a profit-sharing plan, each person gets a bonus based on the company's results, regardless of the person's actual effort. With a true individual incentive, it is the manager's individual effort and performance that are rewarded with a bonus.

Here, again, there are no hard and fast rules. Top-level executive bonuses are generally tied to overall corporate results (or divisional results if the executive is, say, the vice president of a major division). The assumption is that corporate results reflect the person's individual performance. But as one moves further down the chain of command, corporate profits become a less accurate gauge of a manager's contribution. For, say, supervisory personnel or the heads of functional departments, the person's performance is a more logical determinant of his or her bonus.

Many experts argue that in most organizations managerial and executive-level bonuses should be tied to both organizational and individual performance, and there are several ways to do this.[30] Perhaps the simplest is the *split-award method*, which breaks the bonus into two parts. Here the manager actually gets two separate bonuses, one based on his or her individual effort and one based on the organization's overall performance. Thus, a manager might be eligible for an individual performance bonus of up to $10,000 but receive an individual performance bonus of only $8,000 at the end of the year, based on his or her individual performance evaluation. In addition, though, the person might also receive a second bonus of $8,000 based on the company's profits for the year. Thus, even if there are no company profits, the high-performing manager would still get an individual performance bonus.

One drawback to this approach is that it pays too much to the marginal performer, who even if his or her own performance is mediocre, at least gets that second, company-based bonus. One way to get around this is to use the *multiplier method*. For example, a manager whose individual performance was "poor" might not even receive a company-performance-based bonus, on the assumption that the bonus should be a *product* of individual *and* corporate performance. When either is very poor, the product is zero.

Whichever approach is used, outstanding performers should never be paid less than their normal reward, regardless of organizational performance, and they should get substantially larger awards than do other managers. They are people the company cannot afford to lose, and their performance should always be adequately rewarded by the organization's incentive system. Conversely, marginal or below-average performers should never receive awards that are normal or average, and poor performers should be awarded nothing. The money saved on those people should be given to above-average performers.[31]

Long-Term Incentives

Long-term incentives are intended to motivate and reward top management for the firm's long-term growth and prosperity, and to inject a long-term perspective into the executives' decisions. If only short-term criteria were used, a manager

capital accumulation programs
Long-term incentives most often reserved for senior executives. Six popular plans include stock options, stock appreciation rights, performance achievement plans, restricted stock plans, phantom stock plans, and book value plans.

stock option
The right to purchase a stated number of shares of a company stock at today's price at some time in the future.

could, for instance, increase profitability by reducing plant maintenance; this tactic might, of course, catch up with the company over two or three years. Long-term incentives also are intended to encourage executives to stay with the company by giving them the opportunity to accumulate capital (like company stock) based on the firm's long-term success. Long-term incentives or **capital accumulation programs** are most often reserved for senior executives.[32]

There are six popular long-term incentive plans (for capital accumulation): stock options, stock appreciation rights, performance achievement plans, restricted stock plans, phantom stock plans, and book value plans.[33] The popularity of these plans changes over time due to economic conditions and trends, internal company financial pressures, changing attitudes toward long-term incentives and changes in tax law as well as other factors.[34,35]

Stock Options The **stock option** is perhaps the most popular long-term incentive. A stock option is the right to purchase a specific number of shares of company stock at a specific price during a period of time; the executive thus hopes to profit by exercising his or her option to buy the shares in the future but at today's price. The assumption is that the price of the stock will go up, rather than go down or stay the same. Unfortunately, this depends partly on considerations outside the executive's control, such as general economic conditions. Stock price is, of course, affected by the firm's profitability and growth, and to the extent the executive can affect these factors the stock option can be an incentive. However, in one survey it was found that over half the executives saw little or no relationship between their performance and the value of their stock options.[36]

A *book value plan* is one alternative to stock options. Here managers are permitted to purchase stock at current book value, a value anchored in the value of the company's assets. Executives can earn dividends on the stock they own, and as the company grows the book value of their shares may grow too. When these employees leave the company, they can sell the shares back to the company at the new higher book value.[37] The book value approach avoids the uncertainties of the stock market, emphasizing instead reasonable growth.

Other Plans There are several other popular long-term incentive plans. *Stock appreciation rights* (SARs) are usually combined with stock options; they permit the recipient either to exercise the option (by buying the stock) or to take any appreciation in the stock price in cash, stock, or some combination of these. A *performance achievement plan* awards shares of stock for the achievement of predetermined financial targets, such as profit or growth in earnings per share. With *restricted stock plans,* shares are usually awarded without cost to the executive but with certain restrictions that are specified in the Internal Revenue Code. For example, there is risk of forfeiture if an executive leaves the company before the specified time limit elapses. Finally, under *phantom stock plans* executives receive not shares but "units" that are similar to shares of company stock. Then at some future time they receive value (usually in cash) equal to the appreciation of the "phantom" stock they own.[38]

Whichever long-term plan is used, a main concern today is achieving a "better balance between the personal motives and financial incentives of executives and their fiduciary responsibility to shareholders."[39] The problem is that traditional executive incentives often don't build in any real risk for the executive, and so the executives' and the shareholders' interests could diverge. Often, for instance, options can be exercised with little or no cash outlay by the executive who then turns around and quickly sells his or her stock. There is, therefore, a growing emphasis on long-term executive incentives that build more executive risk into the formula.[40]

Performance Plans The need to tie executives' pay more clearly to the firm's performance while building in more risk has led many firms to institute *performance plans*. Performance plans "are plans whose payment or value is contingent on financial performance measured against objectives set at the start of a multi-year period."[41] For example, the executive may be granted so-called performance units. These grants are similar to annual bonuses but the measurement period is longer than a year. Thus, the executive might be able to achieve, say, a $100,000 grant, in units valued at $50 per unit, in proportion to his or her success in meeting the assigned financial goals.

Implementing Long-Term Incentives A study by consultants McKinsey and Company, Inc. suggests that giving managers stock options may be the simplest and wisest route as far as providing long-term incentives for top executives. In the McKinsey study about one-half the companies surveyed had stock options only, and about one-half had performance-based plans in which managers were given cash bonuses for long-term performance.

The results indicated that in most cases the return to shareholders of companies with long-term cash performance incentives did not differ significantly from that of companies that had only stock-based incentive plans (like stock options). This was so even though companies that paid cash bonuses had spent more to fund their incentive plans. Their most serious problem in awarding cash bonuses lay in identifying the proper performance measures. The survey concludes that successful long-term incentive plans should (1) use measures of performance that correlate with shareholder wealth creation (that is, return on equity and growth), not earnings-per-share growth; (2) establish valid target levels and communicate them clearly to participants; and (3) provide for target adjustment under certain well-defined circumstances (in other words, the performance standards can be modified if market conditions warrant it).[42]

Long-Term Incentives for Overseas Executives Developing effective long-term incentives for a firm's overseas operations presents some tricky problems, particularly with regard to taxation. For example, extending a U.S. stock option plan to local nationals in a firm's overseas operations could subject them to immediate taxation on the stocks, even though the shares could not be sold because of requirements built into the U.S.-based plan.[43]

The problem extends to U.S. executives stationed overseas. For example, it's not unusual for an executive to be taxed $40,000 on $140,000 of stock option income if he or she is based in the United States. However, if that person receives the same $140,000 stock option income while stationed overseas, he or she may be subject to both the $40,000 U.S. tax and a foreign income tax (depending on the country) of perhaps $94,000. Therefore, ignoring the overseas country's tax burden has the effect of either virtually eliminating the incentive value of the stock from the executive's point of view or dramatically boosting the cost of the stock to the company (assuming the company pays the foreign income tax). In any case, firms cannot assume that they can simply export their executives' incentive programs. Instead, they must adapt them to the circumstances by considering various factors including tax treatment, the regulatory environment, and foreign exchange controls.[44]

Incentives for Salespeople

Sales compensation plans have typically relied heavily on incentives (sales commissions), although this varies by industry. In the tobacco industry, for instance, salespeople are usually paid entirely via commissions, while in the transportation equipment industry salespeople tend to be paid a salary. However, the most prevalent approach is to use a combination of salary and commissions to compensate salespeople.[45]

The widespread use of incentives for salespeople is due to three factors: tradition, the unsupervised nature of most sales work, and the assumption that incentives are needed to motivate salespeople. The pros and cons of salary, commission, and combination plans follow.

Salary Plan

In a salary plan salespeople are paid a fixed salary, although there may be occasional incentives in the form of bonuses, sales contest prizes, and the like.[46]

There are several reasons to use straight salary. It works well when your main aim is prospecting (finding new clients) or when the salesperson is mostly involved in account servicing, such as developing and executing product training programs for a distributor's sales force or participating in national and local trade shows.[47] Jobs like these are often found in industries that sell technical products. This is one reason why the aerospace and transportation equipment industries have a relatively heavy emphasis on salary plans for their salespeople.

There are advantages to paying salespeople on a straight salary basis. Salespeople know in advance what their income will be, and the employer also has fixed, predictable sales force expenses. Straight salary makes it simple to switch territories or quotas or to reassign salespeople, and it can develop a high degree of loyalty among the sales staff. Commissions tend to shift the salesperson's emphasis to making the sale rather than to prospecting and cultivating long-term customers. A long-term perspective is encouraged by straight salary compensation.

The main disadvantage is that salary plans don't depend on results.[48] In fact, salaries are often tied to seniority rather than to performance, which can be demotivating to potentially high-performing salespeople who see seniority—not performance—being rewarded.

Commission Plan

Commission plans pay salespeople in direct proportion to their sales: they pay for results, and only for results.

The commission plan has several advantages. Salespeople have the greatest possible incentive, and there is a tendency to attract high-performing salespeople who see that effort will clearly lead to rewards. Sales costs are proportional to sales rather than fixed, and the company's selling investment is reduced. The commission basis is also easy to understand and compute.

But the commission plan too has drawbacks. Salespeople focus on making a sale and on high-volume items; cultivating dedicated customers and working to push hard-to-sell items may be neglected. Wide variances in income between salespeople may occur; this can lead to a feeling that the plan is inequitable. More serious is the fact that salespeople are encouraged to neglect nonselling duties like servicing small accounts. In addition, pay is often excessive in boom times and very low in recessions.

Combination Plan

Most companies pay their salespeople a combination of salary and commissions, and there is a sizable salary component in most such plans. The most frequent percentage split reported in one study was 80% base salary and 20% incentives. A close second was a 70/30 split, with a 60/40 split being the third most frequently reported arrangement.[49]

Combination plans provide some of the advantages of both straight salary and straight commission plans, and also some of their disadvantages. Salespeople have a floor to their earnings. Furthermore, the company can direct its salespeople's activities by detailing what services the salary component is being paid for, while the commission component provides a built-in incentive for superior performance.

However, the salary component is not tied to performance, and the employer is therefore trading away some incentive value. Combination plans also tend to become complicated, and misunderstandings can result. This might not be a problem with a simple "salary plus commission" plan, but most plans are not so simple. For example, there is a "commission plus drawing account" plan, where a salesperson is paid basically on commissions but can draw on future earnings to get through low sales periods. Similarly, in the "commission plus bonus" plan, salespeople are again paid primarily on the basis of commissions. However, they are also given a small bonus for directed activities like selling slow-moving items.

An example can help illustrate the complexities of the typical combination plan. In one company, for instance, the following three-step formula is applied:

Step 1: Sales volume up to $18,000 a month. Base salary plus 7% of gross profits plus 0.5% of gross sales.

Step 2: Sales volume from $18,000 to $25,000 a month. Base salary plus 9% of gross profits plus 0.5% of gross sales.

Step 3: Over $25,000 a month. Base salary plus 10% of gross profits plus 0.5% of gross sales.

In all cases, base salary is paid every two weeks, while the earned percentage of gross profits and gross sales is paid monthly.[50]

The sales force also may get various special awards.[51] At Oakite Company, for instance, several recognition awards are used to boost sales. For example, a President's Cup is awarded to the top division manager and there is a VIP Club for the top 10% of the sales force in total dollars sales. The VIP Club is well publicized within the firm and carries a lot of prestige. Other firms such as Airwick Industries award televisions and Lenox china as special sales awards.

Incentives for Other Professionals

Merit Pay as an Incentive

merit pay (merit raise)
Any salary increase awarded to an employee based on his or her individual performance.

Merit pay or a **merit raise** is any salary increase that is awarded to an employee based on his or her individual performance. It is different from a bonus in that it represents a continuing increment, whereas the bonus represents a one-time payment. Although the term *merit pay* can apply to the incentive raises given to any employees—exempt or nonexempt, office or factory, management or nonmanagement—the term is more often used with respect to white-collar employees and particularly professional, office, and clerical employees.

Merit pay has both advocates and detractors and is the subject of much debate.[52] Advocates argue that only pay or other rewards tied directly to performance can motivate improved performance. They contend that the effect of awarding pay raises across the board (without regard to individual performance) may actually detract from performance by showing employees they'll be rewarded the same regardless of how they perform.

On the other hand, merit pay detractors present good reasons why merit pay can backfire. One is that the usefulness of the merit pay plan depends on the validity of the performance appraisal system, since if performance appraisals are viewed as unfair, so too will the merit pay that is based on them.[53] Similarly, supervisors often tend to minimize differences in employee performance when computing merit raises. They give most employees about the same raise, either because of a reluctance to alienate some employees or because of a desire to give everyone a raise that will at least help them stay even with the cost of living. A third problem is that almost every employee thinks he or she is an above-average performer; being paid a below-average merit increase can thus be demoralizing.[54] However, while problems like these can undermine a merit pay plan, there seems little doubt that merit pay can and does improve performance. But you must make sure that the performance appraisals are carried out effectively.[55]

Merit Pay: Two New Options Traditional merit pay plans have two basic characteristics: (1) Merit increases are usually granted to employees at a designated time of the year in the form of a higher base salary (or *raise*), and (2) the merit raise is usually based exclusively on individual performance, although the overall level of company profits may affect the total sum available for merit raises.[56] Two adaptations of merit pay plans are becoming more popular today. One awards merit raises in one lump sum once a year. The other ties awards to both individual and organizational performance.

Lump-sum merit payments are attractive for several reasons. Traditional merit increases are cumulative, while some lump-sum merit raises are not. Since the employee's lump-sum merit raise (of, say 5% of his or her base salary) is awarded in one lump sum, the rise in payroll expenses can be significantly slowed. (Traditionally, someone with a salary of $20,000 per year might get a 5% increase. This moves the employee to a new base salary of $21,000. If the employee gets another 5% increase next year, then the new merit increase of 5% is tacked on not just to the $20,000 base salary but to the extra $1,000 the employee received last year.) Another advantage is that lump-sum merit raises can help contain benefit costs, since the level of benefit coverage is often tied to a person's current base pay. Lump-sum merit increases can also be more dramatic motivators than traditional merit pay raises. For example, a 5% lump-sum merit payment to our $20,000 employee is $1,000, as opposed to a traditional weekly increment of $19.25 for 52 weeks. Knowing that base salary levels are not being permanently affected by merit pay decisions can also give management more flexibility (say, in a particularly good year) to award somewhat higher lump-sum merit raises. However, before a firm surrenders the merit raise tool that's often used for raising base salaries, any substantial base salary inequities should be eliminated. That way, weaker performers' salaries are not frozen above higher performers' salaries. The timing of the merit increases may also become more important, since you must now consider the impact of the lump-sum payments on your firm's cash flow.

Another merit pay option is to award lump-sum merit pay based on both individual and organizational performance. A sample matrix for doing so is presented in Table 13.1. In this example the company's performance might be measured by rate of return or sales divided by payroll costs. Company performance is then weighted equally with the employee's performance as measured by his or her performance appraisal. Thus, an outstanding performer would still re-

TABLE 13.1 Lump-Sum Award Determination Matrix (an example)

THE EMPLOYEE'S PERFORMANCE (WEIGHT = .50)	THE ORGANIZATION'S PERFORMANCE (WEIGHT = 0.50)				
	Outstanding (1.00)	Excellent (0.80)	Commendable (0.60)	Marginal or Acceptable (0.40)	Unacceptable (0)
Outstanding (1.00)	1.00	0.90	0.80	0.70	0.50
Excellent (0.80)	0.90	0.80	0.70	0.60	0.40
Commendable (0.60)	0.80	0.70	0.60	0.50	0.30
Acceptable (0.00)	—	—	—	—	—
Unacceptable (0.00)	—	—	—	—	—

Source: John F. Sullivan, "The Future of Merit Pay Programs." *Compensation and Benefits Review* (May–June 1989), p. 29.

Instructions. To determine the dollar value of each employee's incentive award, (1) multiply the employee's annual, straight time wage or salary as of June 30 times his or her maximum incentive award and (2) multiply the resultant product times the appropriate percentage figure from this table. For example, if an employee had an annual salary of $20,000 on June 30 and a maximum incentive award of 7% and if her performance and the organization's performance were both "excellent," the employee's award would be $1,120: ($20,000 × 0.07 × 0.80 = $1,120).

ceive a lump-sum award even if the organization's performance were marginal. However, employees with unacceptable performance would receive no lump-sum awards even for a year in which the organization's performance was outstanding. The advantage of this approach is that it forces employees to focus on organizational goals like profitability and improved productivity. The drawback is that it can reduce the motivational value of the reward by reducing the impact of the employee's own performance on the reward.[57]

Incentives for Professional Employees

Professional employees are those whose work involves the application of learned knowledge to the solution of the employer's problems. They include lawyers, doctors, economists, and engineers. Professionals almost always reach their positions through prolonged periods of formal study.[58]

Pay decisions regarding professional employees involve unique problems. One is that for most professionals money has historically been somewhat less important as an incentive than it has been for other employees. This is true partly because professionals tend to be paid well anyway, and partly because they are already driven—by the desire to produce high-caliber work and receive recognition from colleagues.

However, that's not to say that professionals don't want financial incentives. For example, studies in industries like pharmaceuticals and aerospace consistently show that firms with the most productive research and development groups have incentive pay plans for their professionals, usually in the form of bonuses. However, professionals' bonuses tend to represent a relatively small portion of their total pay. The time cycle of the professionals' incentive plans also tends to be longer than a year, reflecting the long development time often spent in designing, developing, and marketing a new product.

**Figure 13.1
Vehicles Used to
Reward Key
Contributors**

Source: Michael F. Spratt and
Bernadette Steele, "Rewarding
Key Contributors,"
*Compensation and Benefits
Review* (July–August 1985),
p. 30.

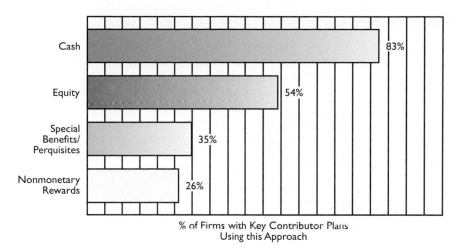

% of Firms with Key Contributor Plans
Using this Approach

There are also many nonsalary items professionals must have to do their best work. Not strictly incentives, these range from better equipment and facilities and a supportive management style to support for professional journal publications.

Rewarding Key Contributors

How do organizations typically reward their key contributors? According to a *Hay Executive and Key Contributor Compensation Survey* of high-technology firms, about 76% of the participants reported having some type of formal or informal key-contributor plan. As you can see in Figure 13.1, 83% of the firms with key-contributor programs used cash in a lump-sum payment to pay key contributors. About half these firms used some type of stock payment plan (stock options or stock grants). With respect to cash payments, maximum opportunities for individuals ranged from $5,000 to $30,000 (typically $5,000) for key personnel. Other recognition included nonmonetary rewards like automobiles, trips, and research funding, as well as sabbaticals, public recognition, freedom to choose projects, and "general work-life improvements."[59]

Customer Service Incentive Plans

Firms are also developing merit pay–type plans to reward employees for their contributions to customer service standards. One such program was instituted at the Aetna Life & Casualty Company.[60]

This plan had two components. The base pay program compensated employees based on their sustained overall performance. However, the customer service–based Star Performance Plan used one-time bonuses to reward employees for superior contributions, particularly in the area of customer service.[61] First, customer service standards were set. The employee had to exhibit knowledge of the customer and his or her needs, exhibit concern for others and their opinions, and be accessible to customers. Annual bonuses were then distributed to star performers from a fund that represented 2% of the firm's annual base salaries.

Organizationwide Incentive Plans

Many employers have incentive plans in which virtually all employees can participate. These include profit-sharing, employee stock ownership, and Scanlon plans.

Profit-Sharing Plans

profit-sharing plan
A plan whereby most employees share in the company's profits.

In a **profit-sharing plan**, most employees receive a share of the company's profits. Research on the effectiveness of such plans is sketchy. In one survey, about half the companies believed their profit-sharing plans had been beneficial,[62] but the benefits were not necessarily in terms of increased performance and motivation. Instead the plans may increase each worker's sense of commitment, participation, and partnership. They may also reduce turnover and encourage employee thrift.

There are several types of profit-sharing plans. In cash plans, the most popular, a percentage of profits (usually 15% to 20%) is distributed as profit shares at regular intervals. One example is the *Lincoln Incentive System,* which was first instituted at the Lincoln Electric Company of Ohio. In one version employees work on a guaranteed piecework basis, and total annual profits (less taxes, 6% dividends to stockholders, and a reserve for investment) are distributed each year among employees based on their merit rating.[63] The Lincoln plan also includes a suggestion system that pays individual workers rewards for savings resulting from suggestions. The plan has been quite successful.

Stephanie Kwolek, a DuPont scientist, received the company's highest award, the Lavoisier Medal for Technical Achievement, in recognition of her discoveries leading to the production of a new fiber called Kevlar.™

Profit sharing has perhaps reached its logical conclusion in Japan. Many employees there get a semiannual bonus that reflects the performance of the enterprise. The amount of this bonus is usually the equivalent of five to six months' salary for each employee.[64]

There are also *deferred profit-sharing plans*. Here a predetermined portion of profits is placed in each employee's account under the supervision of a trustee. There is a tax advantage to such plans, since income taxes are deferred, often until the employee retires and is taxed at a lower rate.

Employee Stock Ownership Plan (ESOP)

employee stock ownership plan (ESOP)
A corporation contributes shares of its own stock to a trust in which additional contributions are made annually. The trust distributes the stock to employees on retirement or separation from service.

Under the most basic form of **employee stock ownership plan (ESOP)**, a corporation contributes shares of its own stock—or cash to be used to purchase such stock—to a trust, one established to purchase shares of the firm's stock for employees.[65] These contributions are generally made annually in proportion to total employee compensation, with a limit of 15% of compensation. The trust holds the stock in individual employee accounts and distributes it to employees upon retirement or other separation from service (assuming the employee has worked long enough to earn ownership of the stock).

An employee stock ownership plan has several advantages. The corporation receives a tax deduction equal to the fair market value of the shares that are transferred to the trustee. Corporations can also claim an income tax deduction for dividends paid on ESOP-owned stock.[66] Employees are not taxed until they receive a distribution from the trust, usually at retirement when their tax rate is reduced. The Employee Retirement Income Security Act (ERISA) allows a firm to borrow against employee stock held in trust and then repay the loan in pretax rather than after-tax dollars, another tax incentive for using such plans.[67] The Deficit Reduction Act of 1984 and the Tax Reform Act of 1986 both included substantial tax advantages for ESOP formation, and ESOPs thereafter became a common vehicle for financing acquisitions. The Revenue Reconciliation Act of 1989 reduced several of the tax benefits associated with ESOPs, but the programs remain popular nevertheless.

Research suggests that ESOPs do encourage employees to develop a sense of ownership in and commitment to the firm.[68] They do so in part because they provide opportunities for increased financial incentives, create a new sense of ownership, and help to build teamwork.[69]

Scanlon Plan

Scanlon plan
An incentive plan developed in 1937 by Joseph Scanlon and designed to encourage cooperation, involvement, and sharing of benefits.

Few would argue with the fact that the most powerful way of ensuring commitment is to synchronize the organization's goals with those of its employees: to ensure in other words that the two sets of goals overlap, and that by pursuing his or her goals, the worker pursues the employer's goals as well. Many techniques have been proposed for obtaining this idyllic state, but few have been implemented as widely or successfully as the **Scanlon plan**, an incentive plan developed in 1937 by Joseph Scanlon, a United Steel Workers Union official.[70]

The Scanlon plan is remarkably progressive, considering that it was developed some 60 years ago. It contains many of the elements we associate with commitment-building programs and quality-improvement plans today. The Scanlon plan itself has been refined over the years by organizations such as Scanlon Plan Associates, a nonprofit support group for organizations that have Scanlon plans.

As currently implemented, Scanlon plans have the following basic features.[71] The first is the *philosophy of cooperation* on which it is based. This philosophy assumes that managers and workers have to rid themselves of the "us" and "them" attitudes that normally inhibit employees from developing a sense of ownership in the company. It substitutes instead a climate in which everyone cooperates because he or she understands that economic rewards are contingent on honest cooperation. A pervasive philosophy of cooperation must therefore exist in the firm for the plan to succeed.[72]

A second feature of the plan is what its practitioners refer to as *identity*. This means that to focus employee involvement, the company's mission or purpose must be clearly articulated and employees must fundamentally understand how the business operates in terms of customers, prices, and costs, for instance. *Competence* is a third basic feature. The program today, say three experts, "explicitly recognizes that a Scanlon Plan demands a high level of competence from employees at all levels."[73] The plan therefore assumes that hourly employees can competently perform their jobs as well as identify and implement improvements, and that supervisors have leadership skills for the participative management that is crucial to a Scanlon plan.

The Weirton, West Virginia steel plant has a successful ESOP in a highly competitive industry.

The fourth feature of the plan is the *involvement system*.[74] This takes the form of two levels of committees—the departmental level and the executive level. Productivity-improving suggestions are presented by employees to the appropriate departmental-level committees, which transmit the valuable ones to the executive-level committee. The latter then decides whether to implement the suggestion.

The fifth element of the plan is the *sharing of benefits formula*. Basically, the Scanlon plan assumes that employees should share directly in any extra profits resulting from their cost-cutting suggestions. If a suggestion is implemented and successful, all employees usually share in 75% of the savings. For example, assume that the normal monthly ratio of payroll costs to sales is 50%. (Thus, if sales are $600,000, payroll costs should be $300,000.) Assume suggestions are implemented and result in payroll costs of $250,000 in a month when sales were $550,000 and payroll costs should have been $275,000 (50% of sales). The saving attributable to these suggestions is $25,000 ($275,000 minus $250,000). Workers would typically share in 75% of this ($18,750) while $6,250 would go to the firm. In practice, a portion, usually one-quarter of the $18,750, is set aside for the months in which labor costs exceed the standard.

The Scanlon plan has been quite successful at reducing costs and fostering a sense of sharing and cooperation among employees. In one study, labor costs were cut by 10%, and grievances were cut in half after implementation of such a plan.[75]

Yet Scanlon plans do fail, and there are several conditions required for their success. They are usually more effective when there is a relatively small number of participants, generally fewer than 1,000. They are more successful when there are stable product lines and costs, since it is important that the labor costs/sales ratio remain fairly stable. Good supervision and healthy labor relations seem essential. And, of course, it is crucial that there be strong commitment to the plan on the part of management, particularly during the confusing phase-in period.[76]

Gainsharing Plans

gainsharing plan
An incentive plan that engages employees in a common effort to achieve productivity objectives and share the gains.

The Scanlon plan is actually an early version of what today is known as a **gainsharing plan**, an incentive plan that engages many or all employees in a common effort to achieve a company's productivity objectives; any resulting incremental cost-savings gains are shared among employees and the company.[77] In addition to the Scanlon plan, other popular types of gainsharing plans include the Rucker and Improshare plans.

The basic difference among these plans is in the formula used to determine employee bonuses.[78] The Scanlon formula divides payroll expenses by total sales. The Rucker formula uses sales value minus materials and supplies, all divided into payroll expenses. The Improshare plan creates production standards for each department. The Scanlon and Rucker plans include participative management systems using committees. Improshare does not include a participative management component but instead considers participation an outcome of the bonus plan. In a survey of 223 companies with gainsharing plans, 95 of the responding firms had custom-designed plans, while the rest used standardized plans like Scanlon, Rucker, or Improshare.[79]

Steps in Gainsharing Plan   There are eight basic steps in implementing a gainsharing plan.[80] *First,* establish general plan objectives. These might include boosting productivity or reinforcing teamwork, for instance.

Second, define specific performance measures. These usually include productivity measures such as labor or hours or cost per unit produced, loans processed per hour, or total cost per full-time employee. Possible financial measures include profits before interest and taxes, and return on net assets. The *third* step is formulating the funding formula, such as "payroll expenses divided by total sales." This creates the pot of dollars that is shared among participants. (In one study, by the way, an average of 46.7% of incremental gains was provided to employees, with the remainder staying with the company.)[81] *Fourth,* determine a method for dividing and distributing the employees' share of the gains among the employees themselves. Typical methods include equal percentage of pay or equal shares, although some plans also try to modify awards to a limited degree based on individual performance. *Fifth,* make the size of the payment meaningful to get participants' attention and motivate their behavior. One expert suggests a potential of 4% to 5% of pay and a 70% to 80% chance of achieving the plan's performance objectives as an effective combination. The *sixth* component is to choose the form of payment, which is usually cash but occasionally common stock or deferred cash. *Seventh,* decide how frequently bonuses are to be paid. This in turn depends on the performance measures used: Most financial performance measures tend to be computed annually, while labor productivity measures tend to be computed quarterly or monthly.

The *eighth* and last component is to develop the support or involvement system. The most commonly used systems for fostering a sense of employee involvement include steering committees, update meetings, suggestion systems, coordinators, problem-solving teams, department committees, training programs, newsletters, inside auditors, and outside auditors.

The financial aspects of a gainsharing program can be quite straightforward.[82] Assume a supplier wants to boost quality. Doing so would translate into fewer customer returns, less scrap and rework, and therefore higher profits. Historically, $1 million in output results in $20,000 (2%) scrap, returns, and rework. The company tells its employees that if next month's production results in only 1% scrap, returns, and rework, the 1% saved would be a gain, to be split 50/50 with the work force, less a small amount for reserve for months in which scrap exceeds 2%. Awards are posted monthly but allocated quarterly.[83]

Making the Plan Work   Several factors contribute to a gainsharing plan's successful implementation. While you may focus on just one goal (like quality), many firms use a "family of measures." For example, one firm chose seven variables (productivity, cost performance, product damage, customer complaints, shipping errors, safety, and attendance) and set specific goals for each (such as zero lost-time accidents, for safety). Then specific monthly bonuses were attached to each goal achieved.[84] Quality, customer service, productivity, and cost represent another familiar family of measures.[85]

Successful gainsharing programs have several other key ingredients, according to one expert.[86] Management must be committed to implementing and maintaining the gainsharing plan, since managers will have to set and maintain consistent team goals, foster an atmosphere conducive to team effort and cooperation, and reduce adversarial relationships between management and employees. The financial incentive component itself should be simple and should measure and reward performance with a specific set of measurable goals and a clear allocation formula. Employee involvement is required so that the employees who are actually doing the jobs are encouraged to suggest performance improvement ideas. And the partnership between management and employees, as they pursue common goals on which the gainsharing plan's success will depend, requires two-way communication rather than just goal setting and top-down directives.[87]

At-Risk Pay Plans

A growing number of firms including Saturn Corp., Toyota Motor Manufacturing, and Du Pont are implementing new organizationwide incentive plans. These are sometimes called variable pay plans but are essentially plans that put some portion of the employee's pay at risk, subject to the firm's meeting its financial goals.

The basic characteristic of all at-risk pay plans is that some portion of the employee's base salary is at risk. In the Du Pont plan, for instance, the employee's at-risk pay is a maximum of 6%. This means each employee's base pay will be 94% of his or her counterpart's salary in other (non-at-risk) Du Pont departments.[88] At Saturn, the at-risk component was initially designed to be about 20% but was recently cut back to 5% as discussed earlier. The at-risk approach is aimed in part at paying employees like partners. It is actually similar to much more extensive programs in Japan in which the at-risk portion might be 50% to 60% of a person's yearly pay. To the extent that at-risk pay is part of a more comprehensive program

availability of tools, and a hostile work force (or management) are just a few of the factors that impede performance. Motivation, in other words, is just one of the elements contributing to effective performance.

You get what you pay for. This fact cuts both ways. Psychologists are fond of saying that people often put their effort where they know they'll be rewarded, so a well-designed and functioning incentive plan can help to focus workers' attention on, say, cutting scrap or lowering costs. However, this can backfire. An incentive plan that rewards a group based on how many pieces they produce could lead to rushed production and lower quality. Awarding a plantwide incentive for reducing accidents may simply reduce the number of reported accidents.

"Pay is not a motivator."[94] Psychologist Frederick Herzberg makes the point that money only buys temporary compliance, and that as soon as the incentive is removed the "motivation" disappears too. He argues that too little money can create an atmosphere in which motivation won't take place. However, he says that adding more and more money won't boost motivation. Instead Herzberg says that employers should provide adequate financial rewards and then build other motivators like opportunities for achievement and psychological success into their jobs.

Rewards punish. Many view punishment and reward as two sides of the same coin. Reward has a potentially punitive effect in that, "Do this and you'll get that" is not really very different from "Do this or here's what will happen to you."[95]

Rewards rupture relationships. Incentive plans have the potential for reducing teamwork by encouraging individuals (or individual groups) to blindly pursue financial rewards for themselves. Some performance appraisal systems used for identifying incentive plan winners and losers may then exacerbate the situation, for instance, by forcing employees to be ranked.

Rewards can unduly restrict performance. One expert says that "Excellence pulls in one direction; rewards pull in another. Tell people that their income will depend on their productivity or performance rating, and they will focus on the numbers. Sometimes they will manipulate the schedule for completing tasks or even engage in patently unethical and illegal behavior."[96]

Rewards may undermine responsiveness. Since the employees' primary focus is on achieving some specific goal like cutting costs, any changes or extraneous distractions mean that achieving that goal will be harder. Incentive plans can, therefore, mediate against change and responsiveness.

Rewards undermine interest and motivation. There is considerable evidence that contingent financial rewards may actually undermine the intrinsic motivation that often results in optimal performance.[97] Two psychologists note, "The research has consistently shown that any contingent payment system tends to undermine intrinsic motivation."[98] The argument is that financial incentives undermine the feeling that the person is doing a good job voluntarily.

Potential pitfalls like these don't mean that financial incentive plans cannot be useful or should not be used. They do suggest, though, that such plans are more effective when implemented as part of a comprehensive management program aimed at bringing out the best in workers by tapping their commitment, self-discipline, and desire to do their jobs well. In general any incentive plan is more apt to succeed if implemented with management support, employee acceptance, and a supportive culture characterized by teamwork, trust, and involvement at all levels.[99] This probably helps to explain why some of the longest-lasting incentive plans, like the Scanlon and Rucker plans, depend heavily on two-way communications and employee involvement in addition to incentive pay. The employee commitment feature on page 492 presents an example of how one company did this.

Small Business Applications

Several other incentive-plan-improvement guidelines are especially relevant for the small business.

Adapt Incentives for Nonexempts to the Fair Labor Standards Act (FLSA)

Smaller firms without HR groups may be unaware that under the FLSA, only certain bonuses are excludable from overtime pay calculations.[100] Overtime rates must be paid to nonexempt employees based on their previous week's earnings, and unless the incentive bonuses are structured properly the amount of the bonus itself becomes part of the week's wages. It must then be included in base pay when computing any overtime that week.

Certain bonuses are excludable from overtime pay calculations. For example, Christmas and gift bonuses that are not based on employees' hours worked, or are paid pursuant to a contract, or are so substantial that employees don't consider them a part of their wages do not have to be included in overtime pay calculations. Similarly, purely discretionary bonuses in which the employer retains discretion over how much if anything will be paid are excludable.

The problem is that many other types of incentive pay definitely must be included in your calculations. Under the FLSA, bonuses to be included in overtime pay computations include those promised to newly hired employees, those provided in union contracts or other agreements, and those announced to induce employees to work more productively, steadily, rapidly, or efficiently or to induce them to remain with the company. Such bonuses would include individual and group production bonuses, bonuses for quality and accuracy of work, efficiency bonuses, attendance bonuses, length-of-service bonuses, and sales commissions.[101]

To see how incentive bonuses can affect overtime pay, consider the following example. Alison works 45 hours in a particular week at a straight-time rate of $5.00 an hour. In that week she also earns a production bonus of $18.00. Her new regular rate for that week becomes $45 \times \$5.00 = \$225.00 + \$18.00 = 243.00$, and $\$243.00$ divided by $45 = \$5.40$ per hour. Her new hourly rate is, therefore, $5.40 per hour for that week. Additional half-time pay ($2.70 per hour) is due her for the 5 hours overtime she worked as part of her 45 hours. Her total weekly pay for that week is, therefore, $\$243.00 + (5 \times 2.70) = \$256.50$.

The problem can be even more complicated with gainsharing and other productivity-related bonuses, since these are usually paid over intervals longer than a single pay period. Here determining the new regular rate for overtime pay calculations can be deferred until after the bonus is determined. However, at that point the bonus must be apportioned over the workweeks in which it was earned. This actually requires employers to go back and re-calculate overtime rates for all those weeks retroactively. This can be very time-consuming, as you can imagine.

According to one expert, an expeditious way of getting around this problem is to design your incentive bonuses as a percentage-of-wage bonus.[102] Basing the bonus awarded on a percentage of each employee's total pay—straight time and overtime for the period involved—protects the company from liability for any additional overtime pay under the FLSA. One way to do it is to design the incentive plan so that it generates a percentage that is applied to all wages. For example, each employee is paid a bonus equal to a predetermined percentage of his or her total wages. This percentage can be based on the number of weeks he or she is in the plan, or the person's level of participation, or some other criteria.

Consider the Current Business Stage of the Company

In designing the incentive plan, consider the firm's life-cycle stage.[103] Small companies experiencing rapid growth usually prefer a broader based profit-sharing plan to the more complicated individual incentive- or gainsharing-type plans. For one thing, profit-sharing plans tend to be simpler and less expensive to implement and require much less planning and administrative paperwork. Furthermore, small firms' employees tend to feel a more direct tie to the company's profitability than do those embedded in much larger firms. Similarly, companies in a survival or turnaround situation, or those threatened by takeover, may also opt for less complicated profit-sharing plans. That way top and middle managers can focus all their energies on the crisis rather than on the administrative effort required to implement gainsharing or individualized incentive plans.

Stress Productivity and Quality Measures If Possible

Remember that profitability is not always the same as productivity and that it is usually productivity and quality for which employees should be held accountable, not profitability. The reason is that productivity and quality are controllable, whereas profitability can be influenced by factors like competition and government regulations. As a result, unless it is a simple companywide profit-sharing plan that you are opting for, be careful to choose the productivity and/or quality standards carefully, focusing on measures that employees can actually control.

Get Employee Input in System Design

It is usually a mistake to implement an incentive plan without input from your employees. Therefore, many employers use a program design team composed of selected employees and supervisors. They work with the compensation specialist in the development of the plan, perhaps by explaining idiosyncrasies that need to be taken into consideration or by helping them understand the culture and attitudes in the plant. ◆

Building Employee Commitment

Example of a Total Compensation Program

Progressive firms like Federal Express aim to boost quality and productivity by using innovative incentive plans as part of their commitment-building programs.[104] At Federal Express, quarterly pay reviews and periodic national and local salary surveys are used to maintain salary ranges and pay schedules that are competitive. Internal equity is maintained through the use of job evaluation.

The result is a set of salary ranges such that salaries for each position tend to be equitable relative to other FedEx jobs. At the same time (thanks to the salary surveys), the base salaries are highly competitive as compared with similar jobs in the market. FedEx defines the market as "where we recruit" each pay group. The airline/air freight industry is the primary market for the FedEx pilot and maintenance groups, for instance. The pay rates of FedEx's direct competitors in the air freight industry are compared for the hourly pay group. The exempt salaried comparison market consists of major national companies, since these jobs are recruited nationally. Nonexempt salaried employees generally are hired locally. Therefore, the local market is surveyed for this pay group to determine FedEx's market position.

For virtually all FedEx positions, base salary alone probably makes pay competitive with market rates. However, there is also a heavy emphasis on pay-for-performance. As one manager put it, "We are convinced people want to see a relationship between performance and reward . . . I think people want to know that when they knock themselves out to reach their part of our 100% customer satisfaction goal, their efforts will not go unnoticed."[105] Federal Express, therefore, has as number of pay-for-performance programs.

Merit Program   All salaried employees receive merit salary increases based on their individual performance. Many hourly employees also now receive merit increases rather than automatic step progression increases to recognize individual performance. The performance appraisal process at Federal Express provides the vehicle for rating employees' performance and for "sharing that information for the individual's development and making pay increase recommendations based on sustained performance. It is [therefore] essential that performance appraisals are fair and accurately measure performance to ensure the integrity of the pay-for-performance principle."[106]

Pro Pay   Many hourly Federal Express employees can receive lump-sum merit bonuses once they reach the top of their pay range. Pro Pay is paid only if the employee has been at the top of his or her pay range for a specified period of time (normally six months) and only if he or she has had an above-average performance review.

Star/Superstar Program   Salaried employees with a specified performance rating may be nominated for a Star or Superstar lump-sum bonus. Stars represent up to the top 10% of performers in each division, while Superstars represent up to the top 1% of performers in each division.

Profit Sharing   Federal Express's profit-sharing plan distributes profits based on the overall profit levels of the corporation. The board of directors annually sets the amount paid, based on pretax profits. Payments to the plan can be in the form of stock, cash, or both and are usually made semiannually in June and December. The plan is designed to integrate with the firm's pension and savings plans to provide a comprehensive retirement program.

MBO/MIC and PBO/PIC Programs   These are individual incentive plans for managers and professionals. They were developed to provide management and many exempt employees the opportunity to receive financial rewards for helping attain corporate, departmental, and divisional objectives. The MIC and PIC programs (management incentive compensation and professional incentive compensation) generally reward achievement of divisional and corporate profit goals.[107] The MBO (or PBO) bonuses are tied to individual attainment of people, service, or profit-related goals. Thus, for a regional sales manager, a "people" goal could be an improvement in the person's leadership index score on the firm's annual feedback action survey.[108]

Bravo Zulu Voucher Program   The Bravo Zulu Voucher Program was established so managers could provide immediate rewards to employees for outstanding performance above and beyond the normal requirements of the job. (Bravo Zulu is a title borrowed from the U.S. Navy's semaphore signal for "well done.") Bravo Zulu vouchers can be in the form of a check or some other form of reward (such as dinner vouchers or theater tickets). It's estimated that more than 150,000 times a year a Federal Express manager presents an employee with one of these awards, which average about $50.[109]

dresses, blouses) per hour. Most of his pressers do not attain this ideal standard, though. In one instance, a presser named Walt was paid $6 per hour, and Jack noticed that regardless of the amount of work he had to do, Walt always ended up making about $200 at the end of the week. If it was a holiday week, for instance, and there were a lot of clothes to press, he might average 22 to 23 tops per hour (someone else did pants) and so he'd earn perhaps $210 to $220 and still finish up each day in time to leave by 3:00 p.m. so he could pick up his children at school. But when things were very slow in the store, his productivity would drop to perhaps 12 to 15 pieces an hour, so that at the end of the week he'd still end up earning close to $180 and in fact not go home much earlier than he did when it was busy.

Jack spoke with Walt several times, and while Walt always promised to try to do better, it gradually became apparent to Jack that Walt was simply going to earn his $200 per week no matter what. While Walt never told him so directly it dawned on Jack that Walt had a family to support and was not about to earn less than his "target" wage regardless of how busy or slow the store was. The problem was that the longer Walt kept pressing each day, the longer the steam boilers and compressors had to be kept on to power his machines, and the fuel charges alone ran close to $5 per hour. Jack clearly needed some way short of firing Walt to solve the problem, since the fuel bills were eating up his profits.

His solution was to tell Walt that instead of an hourly $6 wage he would henceforth pay him $0.25 per item pressed. That way, said Jack to himself, if Walt presses 25 items per hour at $0.25 he will in effect get a small raise. He'll get more items pressed per hour and will therefore be able to shut the machines down earlier.

On the whole, the experiment worked well. Walt generally presses 25 to 35 pieces per hour now. He gets to leave earlier, and with the small increase in pay he generally earns his target wage. Two problems have arisen, though. The quality of Walt's work dipped a bit, and his manager has to spend a minute or two each hour counting the number of pieces Walt pressed that hour. Otherwise Jack is fairly pleased with the results of his incentive plan and he's wondering whether to extend it to other employees and other stores.

Questions

1. Should this plan in its present form be extended to pressers in the other stores?

2. Should other employees be put on a similar plan? Why? Why not?

3. Is there another incentive plan you think would work better for the pressers?

4. A store manager's job is to keep total wages to no more than 30% of sales and to maintain the fuel bill and the supply bill at about 9% of sales each. Managers can also directly affect sales by ensuring courteous customer service and by ensuring that the work is done properly. What suggestions would you make to Jennifer and her father for an incentive plan for store managers?

CASE INCIDENT: Sales Quotas

The Superior Floor Covering Company has an incentive program for its salespeople. Incentive earnings are based on the amount of sales in relation to an assigned quota.

The quota is computed each year by management, taking into account the number and type of customers in each salesperson's territory and the previous year's sales records for the company and for its competitors. In the administration of this incentive program, the following problems have arisen. Suggest the solutions you would consider in eliminating these difficulties. Note also the parallels between the problems here and those involving blue-collar, manufacturing incentive plans.

Questions

1. Some of the best salespeople now have too many accounts in the area assigned to them. From the company's point of view, it would be advantageous to reduce the size of the districts covered by each of these representatives and to add several new salespeople who could give more thorough coverage. The outstanding salespeople resent this proposal, however, claiming that it would penalize them for their success.

2. The top-earning salespeople also complain that their base quotas increase each year, reflecting their previous success. This, too, they feel is discrimination against success.

3. Management believes that the company is not acquiring as many new accounts as it should. So-called missionary work, trying to induce a store that has not previously purchased Superior products to become a customer, takes more time and energy than selling old customers. Also the results of this missionary work may not show up for several years. The present incentive plan gives no credit for this type of work.

4. When business is booming within a salesperson's territory, he or she may receive high bonus earn-

ings even without great effort. When there is a great deal of unemployment in the territory or when competition decides to lower prices to penetrate this new market, his or her bonus earnings may decline even though sales efforts are at a maximum.

Source: George Strauss and Leonard R. Sayles, *Personnel: The Human Problems of Management,* 4th ed. (Englewood Cliffs, NJ: Prentice Hall, 1980), p. 636. Reprinted by permission.

 Human Resource Management Simulation

Incident G gives your team an opportunity to select a compensation plan for the firm. In making your selection, you may want to consider your organiza-

tion's short-term needs with the idea that you can develop a longer-range plan at a later date.

Video Case

Overpaid Executives

In this videocase you will see that the new standard for executive pay is pay-for-performance, and that an executive's "performance" is often evaluated on the basis of corporate profit. Unfortunately, as this videocase shows, shareholders in most corporations feel that CEOs are overpaid because their pay seemed to go up even though their performance went down. The problem is probably aggravated (as the videocase shows) by the fact that the gap between worker gains and CEO pay gains is disproportional. In other words, CEOs' pay rose about three times faster than did workers' pay during the previous few years.

Questions

1. Why was the chairman of Coca Cola in such a good position to defend his salary at the shareholders' meeting depicted in the videocase?

2. What are some of the measures of corporate performance to which executive pay-for-performance plans can be tied? What do you see as the pros and cons of each?

3. What would you say to those workers who argue that it's unfair that their salaries have gone up so little while CEO pay has skyrocketed?

Source: ABC News, *The U.S.'s Overpaid Executives,* "Nightline," April 17, 1992.

 Take It to the Net

We invite you to visit the Dessler page on the Prentice Hall Web site at:
http://www.prenhall.com/~dessler
for the monthly Dessler update, and for this chapter's WorldWide Web exercise.

Notes

1. Jude Rich, "Meeting the Global Challenge: A Measurement and Reward Program for the Future," *Compensation and Benefits Review* (July–August 1992), p. 27.

2. Ibid., p. 28.

3. Except as noted, this section is based on "Non-Traditional Incentive Pay Programs," *Personnel Policies Forum Survey,*

no. 148 (May 1991), The Bureau of National Affairs, Inc., Washington, D.C.

4. Ibid., p. 3.
5. Ibid., p. 9.
6. Ibid., p. 13.
7. Ibid., p. 19.
8. Ibid., p. 24.
9. Richard Henderson, *Compensation Management* (Reston, VA: Reston, 1979), p. 363. For a discussion of the increasing use of incentives for blue-collar employees, see, for example, Richard Henderson, "Contract Concessions: Is the Past Prologue?" *Compensation and Benefits Review,* Vol. 18, no. 5 (September–October 1986), pp. 17–30. See also A. J. Vogl, "Carrots, Sticks and Self-Deception," *Across-the-Board,* 3–1, No. 1 (January 1994), pp. 39–44.
10. David Belcher, *Compensation Administration* (Englewood Cliffs, NJ: Prentice Hall, 1973), p. 314.
11. For a discussion of these, see Thomas Wilson, "Is It Time to Eliminate the Piece Rate Incentive System?" *Compensation and Benefits Review* (March–April 1992), pp. 43–49.
12. Measured day work is a third type of individual incentive plan for production workers. See, for example, Mitchell Fein, "Let's Return to MDW for Incentives," *Industrial Engineering* (January 1979), pp. 34–37.
13. Henderson, *Compensation Management,* pp. 367–368. See also David Swinehart, "A Guide for More Productive Team Incentive Programs," *Personnel Journal,* Vol. 65, no. 7 (July 1986), Anne Saunier and Elizabeth Hawk, "Realizing the Potential of Teams through Team-based Rewards," *Compensation and Benefits Review* (July–August 1994), pp. 24–33 and Shari Caudron, "Tie Individual Pay to Team Success," *Personnel Journal,* Vol. 73, No. 10 (October 1994), pp. 40–46.
14. Another suggestion is as follows: equal payments to all members on the team; differential payments to team members based on their contributions to the team's performance; and differential payments determined by a ratio of each group member's base pay to the total base pay of the group. See Kathryn Bartol and Laura Hagmann, "Team-based Pay Plans: A Key to Effective Teamwork," *Compensation and Benefits Review* (November–December 1992), pp. 24–29.
15. James Nickel and Sandra O'Neal, "Small Group Incentives: Gainsharing in the Microcosm," *Compensation and Benefits Review* (March–April 1990), p. 24. See also Jane Pickard, "How Incentives Can Drive Teamworking," *Personnel Management* (September 1993), pp. 26–32, and Shari Caudron, "Tie Individual Pay to Team Success," *Personnel Journal* (October 1994), pp. 40–46.
16. Jon P. Alston, "Awarding Bonuses the Japanese Way," *Business Horizons,* Vol. 25 (September–October 1982), pp. 6–8.
17. See, for example, Peter Daly, "Selecting and Assigning a Group Incentive Plan," *Management Review* (December 1975), pp. 33–45. For an explanation of how to develop a successful group incentive program, see K. Dow Scott and Timothy Cotter, "The Team That Works Together Earns Together," *Personnel Journal,* Vol. 63 (March 1984), pp. 59–67.
18. Manuel London and Greg Oldham, "A Comparison of Group and Individual Incentive Plans," *Academy of Management Journal,* Vol. 20, no. 1 (1977), pp. 34–41. Note that the study was carried out under controlled conditions in a laboratory setting. See also Thomas Rollins, "Productivity-Based Group Incentive Plans: Powerful, But Use with Caution," *Compensation and Benefits Review,* Vol. 21, no. 3 (May–June 1989), pp. 39–50; discusses several popular group incentive plans, including gainsharing, and lists dos and don'ts for using them.
19. W. E. Reum and Sherry Reum, "Employee Stock Ownership Plans: Pluses and Minuses," *Harvard Business Review,* Vol. 55 (July–August 1976), pp. 133–143; Ralph Bavier, "Managerial Bonuses," *Industrial Management* (March–April 1978), pp. 1–5. See also James Thompson, L. Murphy Smith, and Alicia Murray, "Management Performance Incentives: Three Critical Issues," *Compensation and Benefits Review,* Vol. 18, no. 5 (September–October 1986), pp. 41–47.
20. Bureau of National Affairs, *Bulletin to Management,* January 6, 1983, p. 1.
21. James Brinks, "Executive Compensation: Crossroads of the 80s," *Personnel Administrator,* Vol. 26 (December 1981), p. 24.
22. "Long-Term Incentives: Trends and Approaches," *Personnel,* Vol. 57 (July–August 1982), pp. 60–61.
23. S. B. Prasod, "Top Management Compensation and Corporate Performance," *Academy of Management Journal* (September 1974), pp. 554–558; John Bouike, "Performance Bonus Plans: Boom for Managers and Stockholders," *Management Review* (November 1975), pp. 13, 18; "How Pay and Save Grows and Grows," *Forbes,* April 16, 1979, p. 113.
24. Bruce R. Ellig, "Incentive Plans: Short-Term Design Issues," *Compensation Review,* Vol. 16, no. 3 (Third Quarter 1984), pp. 26–36.
25. Bruce Ellig, *Executive Compensation—A Total Pay Perspective* (New York: McGraw-Hill, 1982), p. 187.
26. Ibid.
27. Ibid., p. 188.
28. See, for example, Bavier, "Managerial Bonuses," pp. 1–5. See also Charles Tharp, "Linking Annual Incentive Awards to Individual Performance," *Compensation and Benefits Review,* Vol. 17 (November–December 1985), pp. 38–43.
29. Ellig, *Executive Compensation,* p. 189.
30. F. Dean Hildebrand, Jr., "Individual Performance Incentives," *Compensation Review,* Vol. 10 (Third Quarter 1978), p. 32.
31. Ibid., pp. 28–33.
32. Edward Redling, "The 1981 Tax Act: Boom to Managerial Compensation," *Personnel,* Vol. 57 (March–April 1982), pp. 26–35.
33. The following based on ibid.
34. See both William M. Mercer Meidinger, Inc., "How Will Reform Tax Your Benefits?" *Personnel Journal,* Vol. 65, no. 12 (December 1986), pp. 49–63, and Jack H. Schechter, "The Tax Reform Act of 1986: Its Impact on Compensation and Benefits," *Compensation and Benefits Review,* Vol. 18, no. 6 (November–December 1986), pp. 11–24.
35. See also Paul Bradley, "Justify Executive Bonuses to the Board," *Personnel Journal* (September 1988), pp. 116–125, and his "Long-Term Incentives: International Executives Need Them Too," *Personnel* (August 1988), pp. 40–42.

36. Belcher, *Compensation Administration,* p. 548; Schechter, "The Tax Reform Act of 1986," p. 23. See also Rein Linney and Charles Marshall, "ISOs vs. NQSOs: The Choice Still Exists," *Compensation and Benefits Review,* Vol. 19, no. 1 (January–February 1987), pp. 13–25.

37. Basically, book value per share equals the firm's assets minus its prior (basically debt) liabilities, divided by the number of shares. See, for example, John Annas, "Facing Today's Compensation Uncertainties," *Personnel,* Vol. 33, no. 1 (January–February 1976).

38. Ray Stata and Modesto Maidique, "Bonus System for Balanced Strategy," *Harvard Business Review,* Vol. 59 (November–December 1980), pp. 156–163; Alfred Rappaport, "Executive Incentives Versus Corporate Growth," *Harvard Business Review,* Vol. 57 (July–August 1978), pp. 81–88. See also Crystal Graef, "Rendering Long-Term Incentives Less Risky for Executives," *Personnel,* Vol. 65, no. 9 (September 1988), pp. 80–84.

39. Ira Kay, "Beyond Stock Options: Emerging Practices in Executive Incentive Programs," *Compensation and Benefits Review* (November–December 1991), p. 19.

40. For a discussion see ibid., pp. 18–29.

41. Jeffrey Kanter and Matthew Ward, "Long-Term Incentives for Management, Part 4: Performance Plans," *Compensation and Benefits Review* (January–February 1990), p. 36.

42. Jude Rich and John Larson, "Why Some Long-Term Incentives Fail," *Compensation Review,* Vol. 16 (First Quarter 1984), pp. 26–37. See also Eric Marquardt, "Stock Option Grants: Is Timing Everything?" *Compensation and Benefits Review,* Vol. 20, no. 5 (September–October 1988), pp. 18–22.

43. Robert Klein, "Compensating Your Overseas Executives, Part 3: Exporting U.S. Stock Option Plans to Expatriates," *Compensation and Benefits Review* (January–February 1991), pp. 27–38.

44. For a discussion see ibid.

45. This section based primarily on John Steinbrink, "How to Pay Your Sales Force," *Harvard Business Review,* Vol. 57 (July–August 1978), pp. 111–122. See also John Tallitsch and John Moynahan, "Fine-Tuning Sales Compensation Programs," *Compensation and Benefits Review,* Vol. 26, No. 2 (March–April 1994), pp. 34–37.

46. Straight salary by itself is not, of course, an incentive compensation plan as we use the term in this chapter.

47. Steinbrink, "How to Pay," p. 112.

48. T. H. Patten, "Trends in Pay Practices for Salesmen," *Personnel,* Vol. 43 (January–February 1968), pp. 54–63. See also Catherine Romano, "Death of a Salesman," *Management Review,* Vol. 83, No. 9 (September 1994), pp. 10–16.

49. Steinbrink, "How to Pay," p. 115.

50. In the salary plus bonus plan, salespeople are paid a basic salary and are then paid a bonus for carrying out specified activities. For a discussion of how to develop a customer-focused sales compensation plan, see, for example, Mark Blessington, "Designing a Sales Strategy with the Customer in Mind," *Compensation and Benefits Review* (March–April 1992), pp. 30–41.

51. This is based on "Sales Incentives Get the Job Done," *Sales and Marketing Management,* September 14, 1981, pp. 67–120.

52. See, for example, Herbert Meyer, "The Pay for Performance Dilemma," *Organizational Dynamics* (Winter 1975), pp. 39–50; Thomas Patten, Jr., "Pay for Performance or Placation?" *Personnel Administrator,* Vol. 24 (September 1977), pp. 26–29; William Kearney, "Pay for Performance? Not Always," *MSU Business Topics* (Spring 1979), pp. 5–16. See also Hoyt Doyel and Janet Johnson, "Pay Increase Guidelines with Merit," *Personnel Journal,* Vol. 64 (June 1985), pp. 46–50.

53. Nathan Winstanley, "Are Merit Increases Really Effective?" *Personnel Administrator,* Vol. 27 (April 1982), pp. 37–41. See also William Seithel and Jeff Emans, "Calculating Merit Increases: A Structured Approach," *Personnel,* Vol. 60, no. 5 (June 1985), pp. 56–68.

54. James T. Brinks, "Is There Merit in Merit Increases?" *Personnel Administrator,* Vol. 25 (May 1980), p. 60. See also Dan Gilbert and Glenn Bassett, "Merit Pay Increases are a Mistake," *Compensation and Benefits Review,* Vol. 26, No. 2 (March–April 1994), pp. 20–25.

55. *Merit Pay: Fitting the Pieces Together* (Chicago: Commerce Clearing House, 1982).

56. Suzanne Minken, "Does Lump Sum Pay Merit Attention?" *Personnel Journal* (June 1988), pp. 77–83. Two experts suggest using neither straight merit pay nor lump-sum merit pay but rather tying the merit payment to the duration of the impact of the employee's work so that, for instance, the merit raise might last for two or three years. See Jerry Newman and Daniel Fisher, "Strategic Impact Merit Pay," *Compensation and Benefits Review* (July–August 1992), pp. 38–45.

57. John F. Sullivan, "The Future of Merit Pay Programs," *Compensation and Benefits Review* (May–June 1988), pp. 22–30.

58. This section based primarily on Robert Sibson, *Compensation* (New York: AMACOM, 1981), pp. 189–207.

59. Michael Sprat and Bernadette Steele, "Rewarding Key Contributors," *Compensation and Benefits Review,* Vol. 17 (July–August 1985), pp. 24–37.

60. Kyle Burns, "A Bonus Plan That Promotes Customer Service," *Compensation and Benefits Review* (September–October 1992), pp. 15–20.

61. See ibid., pp. 16–17.

62. Bert Metzger and Jerome Colletti, "Does Profit Sharing Pay?" (Evanston, IL: Profit Sharing Research Foundation, 1971), quoted in Belcher, *Compensation Administration,* p. 353. See also D. Keith Denton, "An Employee Ownership Program That Rebuilt Success," *Personnel Journal,* Vol. 66, no. 3 (March 1987), pp. 114–118 and Edward Shepard, "Profit Sharing and Productivity: Further Evidence from the Chemicals Industry," *Industrial Relations,* Vol. 33, No. 4 (October 1994), pp. 452–466.

63. Belcher, *Compensation Administration,* p. 351.

64. Mary O'Connor, "Employee Profit Sharing in Japan," *Personnel Journal,* Vol. 60 (August 1981), p. 614.

65. Based on Randy Swad, "Stock Ownership Plans: A New Employee Benefit," *Personnel Journal,* Vol. 60 (June 1981), pp. 453–455.

66. See James Brockardt and Robert Reilly, "Employee Stock Ownership Plans After the 1989 Tax Law: Valuation Issues," *Compensation and Benefits Review* (September–October 1990), pp. 29–36.

67. Donald Sullivan, "ESOPs," *California Management Review,* Vol. 20, no. 1 (Fall 1977), pp. 55–56. For a discussion of the effects of employee stock ownership on employee attitudes, see Katherine Klein, "Employee-Stock Ownership and Employee Attitudes: A Test of Three Models," *Journal of Applied Psychology,* Vol. 72, no. 2 (May 1987), pp. 319–331.

68. Everett Allen, Jr., Joseph Melone, and Jerry Rosenbloom, *Pension Planning* (Homewood, IL: Irwin, 1981), p. 316. Note that the Tax Reduction Act of 1975 has also led to the creation of the so-called TRAFOP. This is a regular employee stock ownership plan except that a portion of the investment tax credit that employers receive for investing in capital equipment can be invested in the employee stock ownership plan.

69. William Smith, Harold Lazarus, and Harold Murray Kalkstein, "Employee Stock Ownership Plans: Motivation and Morale Issues," *Compensation and Benefits Review* (September–October 1990), pp. 37–46.

70. Brian Moore and Timothy Ross, *The Scanlon Way to Improved Productivity: A Practical Guide* (New York: Wiley, 1978), p. 2.

71. These are based in part on Steven Markham, K. Dow Scott, and Walter Cox, Jr., "The Evolutionary Development of a Scanlon Plan," *Compensation and Benefits Review* (March–April 1992), pp. 50–56.

72. J. Kenneth White, "The Scanlon Plan: Causes and Correlates of Success," *Academy of Management Journal,* Vol. 22 (June 1979), pp. 292–312.

73. Markham et al., "The Evolutionary Development of a Scanlon Plan," p. 51.

74. Moore and Ross, *The Scanlon Way,* pp. 1–2.

75. George Sherman, "The Scanlon Plan: Its Capabilities for Productive Improvement," *Personnel Administrator* (July 1976).

76. White, "The Scanlon Plan," pp. 292–312. For a discussion of the Improshare plan, see Roger Kaufman, "The Effects of Improshare on Productivity," *Industrial and Labor Relations Review,* Vol. 45, no. 2 (1991), pp. 311–322.

77. Barry W. Thomas and Madeline Hess Olson, "Gainsharing: The Design Guarantees Success," *Personnel Journal* (May 1988), pp. 73–79. See also "Aligning Compensation with Quality," *Bulletin to Management, BNA Policy and Practice Series,* April 1, 1993, p. 97.

78. See Theresa A. Welbourne and Louis Gomez Mejia, "Gainsharing Revisited," *Compensation and Benefits Review* (July–August 1988), pp. 19–28.

79. Carla O'Dell and Jerry McAdams, *People, Performance, and Pay* (American Productivity Center and Carla O'Dell, 1987), p. 34.

80. Thomas and Olson, "Gainsharing," pp. 75–76. See also Thomas McGrath, "Gainsharing: Engineering the Human Factor of Productivity," *Industrial Engineering* (September 1993), pp. 61–63, and Paul Rossler and C. Patrick Koelling, "The Effect of Gainsharing on Business Performance at a Paper Mill," and *National Productivity Review* (Summer 1993), pp. 365–382.

81. O'Dell and McAdams, *People, Performance, and Pay,* p. 42.

82. This is paraphrased from Woodruff Imberman, "Boosting Plant Performance with Gainsharing," *Business Horizons,* (November–December 1992), p. 77.

83. For other examples, see Timothy Ross and Larry Hatcher, "Gainsharing Drives Quality Improvement," *Personnel Journal* (November 1992), pp. 81–89. See also Jerry McAdams, "Employee Involvement and Performance Reward Plans: Design, Implementation, and Results," *Compensation and Benefits Review,* Vol. 27, No. 2 (March 1995), pp. 45–55.

84. John Belcher, Jr., "Gainsharing and Variable Pay: The State of the Art," *Compensation and Benefits Review* (May–June 1994), pp. 50–60.

85. Robert Masternak, "Gainsharing Boosts Quality and Productivity at a B.F. Goodrich Plant," *National Productivity Review* (Spring 1993), pp. 225–238. See also Susan Hanlon, David Meyer, and Robert Taylor, "Consequences of Gainsharing: A Field Experiment Revisited," *Group & Organization Management,* Vol. 19, No. 1 (March 1994), pp. 87–111.

86. This is based on Thomas McGrath, "How Three Screw Machine Companies Are Tapping Human Productivity Through Gainsharing," *Employment Relations Today* (Winter 1993/94), pp. 437–446.

87. See, for example, Moore and Ross, *The Scanlon Way to Improved Productivity,* pp. 157–164; Ewing, "Gainsharing Plans," pp. 51–52. For a description of the implementation of a gainsharing plan in health care institutions, see Steven Markham et al., "Gainsharing Experiments in Health Care," *Compensation and Benefits Review* (March–April 1992), pp. 57–64. See also Dwight Willett, "Promoting Quality Through Compensation," *Business Quarterly* (Autumn 1993), pp. 107–111; and Robert Masternak, "Gainsharing: Overcoming Common Myths and Problems to Achieve Dramatic Results," *Employment Relations Today* (Winter 1993/94), pp. 425–436.

88. Robert McNutt, "Sharing Across the Board: Du Pont's Achievement Sharing Program," *Compensation and Benefits Review* (July–August 1990), pp. 17–24.

89. Belcher, *Compensation Administration,* pp. 309–310.

90. Robert Opsahl and Marvin Dunnette, "The Role of Financial Compensation in Industrial Motivation," *Psychological Bulletin,* Vol. 66 (1966), pp. 94–118.

91. See, for example, James Gutherie and Edward Cunningham, "Pay for Performance: The Quaker Oats Alternative," *Compensation and Benefits Review,* Vol. 24, no. 2 (March–April 1992), pp. 18–23.

92. Gary Yukl and Gary Latham, "Consequences of Reinforcement Schedules and Incentives Magnitudes for Employee Performance: Problems Encountered in an Industrial Setting," *Journal of Applied Psychology,* Vol. 60 (June 1975).

93. Louden and Deagan, *Wage Incentives,* p. 26.

94. The following five points are based on Alfie Kohn, "Why Incentive Plans Cannot Work," *Harvard Business Review* (September–October 1993), pp. 54–63.

95. Ibid., p. 58.

96. Ibid., p. 62.

97. Ibid.

98. Edward Deci and Richard Ryan, *Intrinsic Motivation and Self-Determination in Human Behavior* (New York: Plenum Press, 1985), quoted in ibid., p. 62.

99. Steven Gross and Jeffrey Bacher, "The New Variable Pay Programs: How Some Succeed, Why Some Don't," *Compensation and Benefits Review* (January–February 1993), pp. 55–56; see also George Milkovich and Carolyn

Milkovich, "Strengthening the Pay-Performance Relationship: The Research," *Compensation and Benefits Review* (November–December 1992), pp. 53–62; and Jay Schuster and Patricia Zingheim, "The New Variable Pay: Key Design Issues," *Compensation and Benefits Review* (March–April 1993), pp. 27–34.

100. This is based on William E. Buhl, "Keeping Incentives Simple for Nonexempt Employees," *Compensation and Benefits Review* (March–April 1989), pp. 14–19.

101. Ibid., pp. 15–16.

102. Ibid., pp. 17–18.

103. The following are based on Michael J. Cissell, "Designing Effective Reward Systems," *Compensation and Benefits Review* (November–December 1987), pp. 49–56.

104. The following is based on Gary Dessler, *Winning Commitment* (New York: McGraw-Hill Book Company, 1993), Chapter 9.

105. *Blueprints for Service Quality: The Federal Express Approach* (New York: AMA Membership Publication Division, 1991), pp. 31–32.

106. "Compensation at Federal Express," company document, P. 8.

107. Unless otherwise indicated the section on pay-for-performance is based on "Compensation at Federal Express," pp. 8–9.

108. *Blueprints for Service Quality,* p. 32.

109. *Blueprints for Service Quality,* pp. 34–35.

Chapter 14
Benefits and Services

Chapter Outline

- ◆ **Introduction**
- ◆ **Pay for Time Not Worked**
- ◆ **Insurance Benefits**
- ◆ **Retirement Benefits**
- ◆ **Employee Services Benefits**
- ◆ **Flexible Benefits Programs**

Behavioral Objectives

When you finish studying this chapter, you should be able to:

List and describe each of the basic benefits most employers might be expected to offer.

Explain how to reduce an employer's unemployment insurance bill.

Explain why the cost of insurance benefits is increasing and how employers can reduce these costs.

Discuss how to set up a flexible benefits program.

Introduction

benefits
Indirect financial payments given to employees. They may include health and life insurance, vacation, pension, education plans, and discounts on company products, for instance.

Benefits represent an important part of just about every employee's pay; they can be defined as all the indirect financial payments an employee receives for continuing his or her employment with the company.[1] Benefits are generally available to all a firm's employees and include such things as time off with pay, health and life insurance, and child care facilities.

Administering benefits today represents an increasingly specialized task. It demands expertise because workers are more financially sophisticated and demanding, and because federal legislation—concerning pregnancy benefits, for instance—requires that benefit plans comply with new laws.

Providing and administering benefits represents an increasingly expensive task, too. As you can see summarized in Figure 14.1, benefits as a percentage of payroll are about 41% today (compared to about 25.5% in 1961). That translates to around $15,000 in total annual benefits per employee or close to $7.00 per payroll hour. In terms of the costs of specific benefits, payments for time not worked (vacations, sick days, and so on) represent just over 10% of the average employer's payroll. Medical and related benefits (such as for health insurance) account for just over 11% of payroll. Legally required payments (such as for Social Security) represent about 9%, while retirement and savings plans and various other benefits account for the remaining benefit dollars. Most employees don't realize the market value and high cost to the employer of their benefits, so prudent employers list the benefits' true costs on each employee's pay stub.

Figure 14.1
Employee Benefits as a Percent of Payroll in 1993

Source: BNA Datagraph, *BNA Bulletin To Management,* Jan. 5, 1995, p. 4.

Total Annual Benefits Per Employee	
Mfg.	Non-Mfg.
$15,839	$14,476

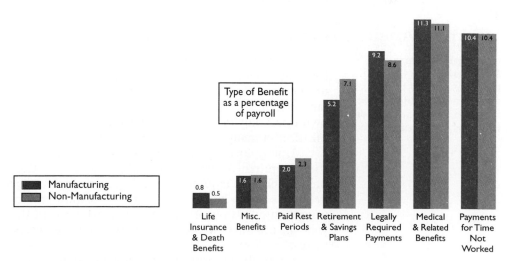

Source: U.S. Chamber of Commerce.

The Benefits Picture Today

A majority of companies in the United States today do offer at least some fringe benefits to their employees.[2] For example, about 92% of medium and larger firms and 69% of smaller firms provide health insurance. The use of supplemental health benefits is extensive too: Between 25% and 45% of companies (depending on size) provide vision care plan benefits; about 50% have a prescription drug plan; about 55% have some type of employee assistance programs; and about 40% of the companies provide health education/promotion/wellness programs.

Most firms also provide retirement/pension benefits. For example, 88% of large companies (those with 5,000 or more employees), 78% of medium-sized companies (500–4,999), and 73% of smaller companies (fewer than 500 employees) provide some type of plan.

There are many benefits and various ways to classify each. For example, Social Security is both a legally required employer payment and a contribution toward most employees' future retirement income. In the remainder of this chapter we will classify benefits as (1) pay for time not worked, (2) insurance benefits, (3) retirement benefits, and (4) services.

Pay for Time Not Worked

supplemental pay benefits
Benefits for time not worked such as unemployment insurance, vacation and holiday pay, and sick pay.

Supplemental pay benefits—in other words, pay for time not worked—are typically one of an employer's most expensive benefits because of the large amount of time off that many employees receive. Common time-off-with-pay periods include holidays, vacations, jury duty, funeral leave, military duty, sick leave, sabbatical leave, maternity leave, and unemployment insurance payments for laid-off or terminated employees. While some of these (such as unemployment insurance and maternity leave) can also be viewed as legally required benefits, the fact is that pay for time not worked is a substantial part of almost every employer's payroll bill. In this section we'll discuss some of the major time-off-with-pay elements, specifically: unemployment insurance (if the person is laid off); vacation and holiday pay; sick pay; severance pay (if the person is terminated); and supplemental unemployment benefits (which guarantee income if the plant is temporarily closed).

Unemployment Insurance

unemployment insurance
Provides weekly benefits if a person is unable to work through some fault other than his or her own.

All states have **unemployment insurance** or compensation acts. These provide for weekly benefits if a person is unable to work through some fault other than his or her own. The benefits derive from an *unemployment tax* on employers that can range from 0.1% to 5% of taxable payroll in most states. States each have their own unemployment laws; however, these all follow federal guidelines. Your organization's unemployment tax reflects its experience with personnel terminations.

Unemployment benefits are not meant for all dismissed employees, only those terminated through no fault of their own. Thus, strictly speaking, a worker fired for chronic lateness has no legitimate claim to benefits. But in practice many managers take a lackadaisical attitude toward protecting their employers against unwarranted claims. Therefore, employers spend thousands of dollars more per year on unemployment taxes than would be necessary if they protected themselves.

Carefully adhering to the procedures listed in Table 14.1 can help protect your employer. Determine whether you could answer yes to questions such as,

TABLE 14.1 An Unemployment Insurance Cost Control Survey

CAUSE—DO YOU . . .	YES	NO	SOME-TIMES	CAUSE—DO YOU	YES	NO	SOME-TIMES
Lateness				*Layoff*			
1. Tell employees whom to call when late	—	—	—	1. Hire employees with established "benefit year" if you anticipate layoffs	—	—	—
2. Keep documented history of lateness and warning notices	—	—	—	2. Keep employees on when the cost to replace them would more than offset paying their salary	—	—	—
3. Suspend chronically late employees before discharging them	—	—	—	3. Transfer empoloyees to different departments	—	—	—
Absenteeism				4. Have a flexible workweek that reflects high and low periods of productivity	—	—	—
1. Tell employees whom to call when absent	—	—	—	5. Temporarily lay off employees for one week during slack periods	—	—	—
2. Rule that three days' absence without calling in is reason for automatic discharge	—	—	—	6. Attempt to find temporary or part-time jobs for laid-off employees	—	—	—
3. Keep documented history of absence and warning notices	—	—	—	*Job Refusal*			
4. Request doctor's note on return to work	—	—	—	1. Issue a formal notice to employees collecting benefits to return to work	—	—	—
Illness				2. Require new employees to stipulate in writing their availability to work overtime, night shifts, etc.	—	—	—
1. Keep job open, if possible	—	—	—				
2. Offer leave of absence	—	—	—	*Not Qualified*			
3. Request doctor's note on return to work	—	—	—	1. Set probationary periods to evaluate new employees	—	—	—
Pregnancy				2. Conduct follow-up interviews one to two months after hire	—	—	—
1. Follow EEOC ruling, "no discharge"	—	—	—	*Deliberate Unsatisfactory Performance*			
2. Request doctor's note indicating how long employee may work	—	—	—	1. Document all instances, recording when and how employees did not meet job requirements	—	—	—
3. Change jobs within company when practical	—	—	—				
4. Offer maternity leave	—	—	—	2. Require supervisors to document the steps taken to remedy the situation	—	—	—
Leave of Absence				3. Require supervisors to document employee's refusal of advice and direction	—	—	—
1. Make written approval mandatory	—	—	—				
2. Stipulate date for return to work	—	—	—				
3. Offer position at end of leave	—	—	—				
Leave Job Voluntarily							
1. Conduct exit interview	—	—	—				
2. Obtain a signed resignation statement	—	—	—				
3. Mail job abandonment letter	—	—	—				
4. Mail job review questionnaire three to six months after separation	—	—	—				

(continued)

TABLE 14.1 —continued

CAUSE—DO YOU . . .	YES	NO	SOME-TIMES	CAUSE—DO YOU	YES	NO	SOME-TIMES
Violation of Company Rule				(c) successfully protests unwarranted claims and charges for unemployment benefits	—	—	—
1. Make sure all policies and rules of conduct are understood by all employees	—	—	—	(d) recommends appropriate tax remedies:			
2. Require all employees to sign a statement acknowledging acceptance of these rules	—	—	—	1. Verify the contribution rate assigned by the state	—	—	—
3. Meet with employee and fill out documented warning notice	—	—	—	2. Test for rate modification	—	—	—
4. Discharge at the time violation occurs, or suspend	—	—	—	3. Test for voluntary contribution and advisability of a joint account	—	—	—
Wrong Benefit Charges				4. Determine advantage of transfer of experience resulting from mergers, acquisition, or other corporate charges	—	—	—
1. Check state charge statement for							
(a) correct employee	—	—	—				
(b) correct benefit amount	—	—	—	*Communication*			
(c) correct period of liability	—	—	—	1. Hold periodic workshops with key personnel to review procedures and support effort to reduce turnover costs	—	—	—
Claim Handling							
1. Assign a claims supervisor or central office to process all separation information	—	—	—	2. Immediately investigate who or what is responsible for costly errors and why	—	—	—
2. Respond to state claim forms on time	—	—	—	*Management Reports*			
3. Use proper terminology on claim form and attach documented evidence regarding separation	—	—	—	1. Point to turnover problems as they occur by			
				(a) location	—	—	—
				(b) department	—	—	—
4. Attend hearings and appeal unwarranted claims	—	—	—	(c) classification of employee	—	—	—
5. Conduct availability checks and rehire employees collecting benefits	—	—	—	2. Evaluate the effectiveness of current policies and procedures used to			
				(a) recruit	—	—	—
Administration				(b) select	—	—	—
1. Have a staff member who knows unemployment insurance laws and who				(c) train	—	—	—
				(d) supervise	—	—	—
				(e) separate	—	—	—
(a) works with the personnel department to establish proper use of policies and procedures	—	—	—	3. Help create policies and procedures for			
				(a) less costly layoffs	—	—	—
(b) anticipates and reports costly turnover trends	—	—	—	(b) increased survival rate	—	—	—
				(c) retention of employees	—	—	—

Explanation: Each "no" or "sometimes" answer represents an area where you lack control; each "yes" is a strong point that acts to save you money.

Source: Reprinted from the January 1976 issue of *Personnel Administrator.* Copyright 1976, the American Society for Personnel Administration.

"Do you tell employees whom to call when they're late?" or "Do you have a rule that three days' absence without calling is reason for automatic discharge?" By establishing policies and rules in these areas, you will be able to show that an employee's termination was a result of the person's inadequate performance (rather than lack of work or some other cause beyond his or her control). Some additional guidelines for cutting unemployment insurance costs include:

Understand the unemployment insurance code. Many states annually publish updated employer's guides with names such as "Twenty-seven Ways to Avoid Losing Your Unemployment Appeal." You or someone on your staff should become an expert in understanding the unemployment insurance code in your state and how the system works.

Train managers and supervisors. Train managers and supervisors to use a checklist such as the one in Table 14.1. Don't let otherwise ineligible, dismissed employees successfully apply for unemployment compensation.

Conduct exit interviews. Routinely conducting exit interviews with everyone who leaves the organization can produce information useful for protesting unemployment claims.

Verify unemployment claims. Remember to check every unemployment claim against the individual's personnel file. Make sure to double-check the reasons the employee gives for why he or she left your employ.

File the protest against a former employee's claim on a timely basis. In most states you have ten days in which to protest a claim.

Know your local unemployment insurance official. Most unemployment officers appreciate cooperative employers and are historically understaffed and overworked. Taking a hostile, adversarial position may undermine your ability to get the benefit of their doubt on a claim you might otherwise have won.

Audit the annual benefit charges statement. Once a year you will receive a benefit charges statement regarding the status of your unemployment compensation account. Thoroughly audit this since errors such as inaccurate charges against your account may be included in it.[3]

Vacations and Holidays

The number of paid employee vacation days varies considerably from employer to employer. In the United States the average is about ten days per year.[4] Even within the same employer the number of vacation days will normally depend on how long the employee has worked at the firm. Thus, a typical vacation policy might call for:

1. One week after six months to one year of service;
2. Two weeks after 1 to 5 years of service;
3. Three weeks after 5 to 10 years of service;
4. Four weeks after 15 to 25 years of service; and
5. Five weeks after 25 years of service.[5]

The average number of annual vacation days is generally greater in industrialized countries outside the United States.[6] For example, compared with the average ten-day U.S. vacation, employees in Sweden and Austria can expect 30-day vacations, in France 25 days, and in the United Kingdom, Spain, Norway, Finland, and Belgium 20 to 25 days.

Several practical questions must be addressed in formulating an employer's vacation policies. For example, some vacation plans give the employee his or her regular base rate of pay while on vacation, while others provide for vacation pay based on average earnings (which may include overtime). Some but not all employers provide for accrued vacation time that is paid if an employee leaves before taking his or her vacation. Consideration must also be given to whether to penalize an employee who takes his or her annual vacation and then resigns before fully earning the vacation time he or she has already taken.

The number of paid holidays similarly varies considerably from employer to employer, from a minimum of about five to 13 or more. The most common paid holidays include New Year's Day, Memorial Day, Independence Day, Labor Day, Thanksgiving Day, and Christmas Day. Other common holidays include Martin Luther King, Jr., Day, Good Friday, President's Day (third Monday in February), Veteran's Day, the Friday after Thanksgiving, and the day before Christmas and the day before New Year's.[7]

A number of holiday pay policy issues must also be addressed. For example, many employers will not pay an employee for a holiday unless the employee has been at work the day before and the day after the holiday. Provisions must also be made for holidays that fall on a Saturday or Sunday: For example, employees are often given the following Monday off when the holiday falls on a Sunday, and Friday off when it falls on a Saturday. Most employers also provide for some pay premium—such as time and a half—when employees must work on a holiday.

Sick Leave

sick leave
Provides pay to an employee when he or she is out of work because of illness.

Sick leave provides pay to an employee when he or she is out of work because of illness. Most sick leave policies grant full pay for a specified number of permissible sick days—usually up to about 12 per year. The sick days are often accumulated at the rate of, say, one day per month of service.

Sick leave pay causes consternation for many employers. The problem is that while many employees use their sick days only when they are legitimately sick, others simply utilize their sick leave as extensions to their vacations, whether they are sick or not.

Employers have tried several tactics to eliminate or reduce the problem. Some now buy back unused sick leave at the end of the year by paying their employees a daily equivalent pay for each sick leave day not used. The drawback is that the policy can encourage legitimately sick employees to come to work despite their illness.[8] Others have experimented with holding monthly lotteries in which only employees with perfect monthly attendance are able to participate; those who participate are eligible to win a cash prize. Still others aggressively investigate all absences, for instance, by calling the absent employees at their homes when they are out sick.

Parental Leave and the Family and Medical Leave Act of 1993 Parental leave is a benefit whose time has come. About half of workers today are women, and 80% of them are expected to become pregnant at some time during their work lives.[9] Furthermore, many women and men today are heads of single-parent households. Partly as a response to this, the Family and Medical Leave Act of 1993 was signed into law by President Clinton. Among its provisions, which are summarized in Figure 14.2, the law stipulates that:

1. Private employers of 50 or more employees must provide eligible employees up to 12 weeks of unpaid leave for their own serious illness, the birth or adoption of a child, or the care of a seriously ill child, spouse, or parent.
2. Employers may require employees to take any unused paid sick leave or annual leave as part of the 12-week leave provided in the law.
3. Employees taking leave are entitled to receive health benefits while they are on unpaid leave under the same terms and conditions as when they were on the job.

**Figure 14.2
Family and Medical
Leave Act Poster**

YOUR RIGHTS

under the

FAMILY AND MEDICAL LEAVE ACT OF 1993

FMLA requires covered employers to provide up to 12 weeks of unpaid, job-protected leave to "eligible" employees for certain family and medical reasons. Employees are eligible if they have worked for a covered employer for at least one year, and for 1,250 hours over the previous 12 months, and if there are at least 50 employees within 75 miles.

REASONS FOR TAKING LEAVE: Unpaid leave must be granted for *any* of the following reasons:

► to care for the employee's child after birth, or placement for adoption or foster care;
► to care for the employee's spouse, son or daughter, or parent, who has a serious health condition; or
► for a serious health condition that makes the employee unable to perform the employee's job.

At the employee's or employer's option, certain kinds of *paid* leave may be substituted for unpaid leave.

ADVANCE NOTICE AND MEDICAL CERTIFICATION: The employee may be required to provide advance leave notice and medical certification. Taking of leave may be denied if requirements are not met.

► The employee ordinarily must provide 30 days advance notice when the leave is "foreseeable."
► An employer may require medical certification to support a request for leave because of a serious health condition, and may require second or third opinions (at the employer's expense) and a fitness for duty report to return to work.

JOB BENEFITS AND PROTECTION:

► For the duration of FMLA leave, the employer must maintain the employee's health coverage under any "group health plan."
► Upon return from FMLA leave, most employees must be restored to their original or equivalent positions with equivalent pay, benefits, and other employment terms.
► The use of FMLA leave cannot result in the loss of any employment benefit that accrued prior to the start of an employee's leave.

UNLAWFUL ACTS BY EMPLOYERS: FMLA makes it unlawful for any employer to:

► interfere with, restrain, or deny the exercise of any right provided under FMLA;
► discharge or discriminate against any person for opposing any practice made unlawful by FMLA or for involvement in any proceeding under or relating to FMLA.

ENFORCEMENT:

► The U.S. Department of Labor is authorized to investigate and resolve complaints of violations.
► An eligible employee may bring a civil action against an employer for violations.

FMLA does not affect any Federal or State law prohibiting discrimination, or supersede any State or local law or collective bargaining agreement which provides greater family or medical leave rights.

FOR ADDITIONAL INFORMATION: Contact the nearest office of the Wage and Hour Division, listed in most telephone directories under U.S. Government, Department of Labor.

U.S. Department of Labor, Employment Standards Administration
Wage and Hour Division, Washington, D.C. 20210

WH Publication 1420
June 1993

4. Employers must guarantee employees the right to return to their previous or equivalent position with no loss of benefits at the end of the leave; however, the law provides a limited exception from this provision to certain highly paid employees.

Having a clear procedure for any leave of absence (including one awarded under the Family and Medical Leave Act) is essential. An application form such as the one in Figure 14.3 should be the centerpiece of any such procedure. In gen-

Figure 14.3
Sample Application for Leave of Absence

BNA *Bulletin to Management,* September 30, 1993, p. 6.

Name _____ Date of Application _____

Location _____ Department _____

Type of Leave Requested (Check each that applies.)

[ ] Medical*   [ ] Educational
[ ] Family*   [ ] Other _____
[ ] Military

Start Date (first day of leave) _____ Return Date (date of return to work) ____

Absence is to be (check each that applies): [ ] unpaid
                                            [ ] fully paid
                                            [ ] partially paid (Please explain.)

                                            _____
                                            _____
                                            _____

Should vacation benefits be used?   [ ] No
                                           [ ] Yes (# of hours) ____

Reason for Requested Leave (Explain why leave is necessary.)

_____
_____
_____
_____
_____
_____
_____
_____
_____

*A medical certification is required for medical/family leaves of absence. The health care provider's certification must include:
◇ The date the health condition began;
◇ The expected duration of the condition;
◇ Appropriate medical facts necessary to verify leave requests;
◇ An estimate of the amount of time required to be off work; and
◇ If for a family member's serious health condition, a statement that the employee is needed to care for that family member.
Refer to the Family Leave of Absence Policy for further certification and reporting requirements.

Employee's Signature _____   Date _____

            I understand that if I do not return from my leave of absence at the expiration
            of this leave, unless an extension has been approved in advance, my
            employment may be terminated.

Supervisor's Signature _____   Date _____

eral, no employee should be given a leave until it's clear what the leave is for. If the leave is for medical or family reasons, medical certification should be obtained from the attending physician or medical practitioner. A form like this also places on record the employee's expected return date and the fact that without an authorized extension his or her employment may be terminated.

While leaves awarded under the Family and Medical Leave Act are generally unpaid, it is incorrect to assume that the leave is costless to the employer. For example, one study concluded that the costs associated with recruiting new temporary-replacement workers, training replacement workers, and compensating for the lower level of productivity of these workers could represent a substantial expense over and above what employers would normally pay their full-time employees.[10] An employer may also end up paying health insurance premiums for both the employee who is on leave and the person's temporary replacement.[11]

Severance Pay

severance pay
A one-time payment some employers provide when terminating an employee.

Some employers provide **severance pay**—a one-time payment—when terminating an employee. The payment may range from three or four days' wages to one or more years' salary. Other firms provide "bridge" severance pay by keeping employees (especially managers) on the payroll for several months till they've found a new job.

Such payments make sense on several grounds. It is a humanitarian gesture as well as good public relations. In addition, most managers expect employees to give them at least one or two weeks' notice if they plan to quit; it therefore seems appropriate to provide at least one or two weeks' severance pay if an employee is being terminated.

Plant closings and downsizings have put thousands of employees out of work, often with little or no notice or severance pay. Many states have been attempting to fight such closings, and a Supreme Court ruling (*Fort Halifax Packing Co.* v. *Coyne*, 1987) paved the way for states to cushion the economic impact of such closings. The Court ruled that states may force employers to provide severance pay to workers who lose their jobs because of plant closings. In the Fort Halifax case, laid-off packing company workers were paid amounts ranging from $490 to $8,680.[12] The Worker Adjustment and Retraining Notification ("plant closing") Act of 1989 requires covered employers to give employees 60 days' written notice of plant closures or mass layoffs.

Supplimental Unemployment Benefits

supplemental unemployment benefits
Provide for a "guaranteed annual income" in certain industries where employers must shut down to change machinery or due to reduced work. These benefits are paid by the company and supplement unemployment benefits.

In some industries (such as auto making), shutdowns to reduce inventories or change machinery are common, and in the past employees were laid off or furloughed and had to depend on unemployment insurance. **Supplemental unemployment benefits** are paid by the company and *supplement* unemployment benefits, thus enabling the workers to better maintain their standards of living. Supplemental benefits are becoming more prevalent in collective bargaining agreements. They provide benefits over and above state employment compensation for three contingencies: layoffs, reduced workweeks, and relocations. Such benefits are most popular in heavy manufacturing operations such as in the auto and steel industries. Here weekly or monthly plant shutdowns are normal, and some plan for guaranteeing minimum annual income is more appropriate.

Insurance Benefits

Worker's Compensation

worker's compensation
Provides income and medical benefits to work-related accident victims or their dependents regardless of fault.

Worker's compensation laws[13] are aimed at providing sure, prompt income and medical benefits to work-related accident victims or their dependents regardless of fault.[14] Every state has its own worker's compensation law. However, there has been continuing congressional interest in establishing minimum national standards for state compensation laws. This has provided an impetus for improving employers' job-related accident and illness benefits. Improvements have included expanded medical coverage, increased weekly benefits, and rehabilitation provisions.[15] Some states have their own insurance programs. However, most require employers to carry worker's compensation insurance with private state-approved insurance companies.

Worker's compensation benefits can be either monetary or medical. In the event of a worker's death or disablement, the person's dependents are paid a cash benefit based on prior earnings—usually one-half to two-thirds the worker's average weekly wage, per week of employment. In most states there is a set time limit—such as 500 weeks—for which benefits can be paid. If the injury causes a specific loss (such as an arm), the employee may receive additional benefits based on a statutory list of losses, even though he or she may return to work. In addition to these cash benefits, employers must furnish medical, surgical, and hospital services needed by the employee.

Although safety gear is always recommended, failure to wear it does not invalidate an employee's claim for benefits under worker's compensation laws.

For an injury or illness to be covered by worker's compensation, one must only prove that it arose while the employee was on the job. It does not matter that the employee may have been at fault; if he or she was on the job when the injury occurred, he or she is entitled to worker's compensation. For example, suppose all employees are instructed to wear safety goggles when working at their machines. One worker does not and is injured while on the job. The company must still provide worker's compensation benefits. The fact that the worker was at fault in no way waives his or her claim to benefits.

Worker's compensation is usually handled by state administrative commissions. However, neither the state nor the federal government contributes any funds for worker's compensation. Employers are responsible for insuring themselves or for arranging for the appropriate coverage through an insurance company.

The employment provisions of the Americans with Disabilities Act (ADA) influence how most employers handle worker's compensation cases. For one thing, ADA provisions generally prohibit employers from inquiring about an applicant's worker's compensation history, a practice that was widespread prior to the passage of the ADA. Furthermore, the ADA makes it more important that injured employees get back to work more quickly or are accommodated if their injury leads to a disability. Failing to let an employee who is on worker's compensation because of an injury return to work, or failing to accommodate him or her, could lead to litigation under ADA.[16]

Controlling Workers' Compensation Costs Minimizing the number of worker's compensation claims is an important goal for all employers. While the employer's insurance company usually pays the claims, the costs of the premiums depend on the number and amounts of claims that are paid. Minimizing such claims is thus important.

In practice, there are three main ways to reduce such claims. First, you can screen out accident-prone workers and also reduce accident-causing conditions in your facilities. Second, you can reduce the accidents and health problems that trigger these claims, by, for instance, instituting effective safety and health programs and complying with government standards on these matters.

Finally, you can institute rehabilitation programs for injured employees, since worker's compensation costs increase the longer an employee is unable to return to work. The objective is to institute corrective physical therapy programs (including exercise equipment; career counseling to guide injured employees into new, less strenuous jobs; and nursing assistance, for instance) so as to reintegrate recipients back into your work force.[17]

Life Insurance

group life insurance
Provides lower rates for the employer or employee and includes all employees, including new employees, regardless of health or physical condition.

Most employers provide **group life insurance** plans for their employees. As a group, employees can obtain lower rates than if they bought such insurance as individuals. And group plans usually contain a provision for including all employees—including new ones—regardless of health or physical condition.

In most cases the employer pays 100% of the base premium, which usually provides life insurance equal to about two years' salary. The employee then pays for any additional life insurance coverage. In some cases the cost of even the base premium is split 50:50 or 80:20 between the employer and employee, respectively. In general, there are three key personnel policy areas to be addressed: the benefits-paid schedule (benefits are usually tied to the annual earnings of the employee); supplemental benefits (continued life insurance coverage after retirement, and so on); and financing (the amount and percent that the employee contributes).[18]

Hospitalization, Medical, and Disability Insurance

Most employers—about 92% of medium and large firms and 69% of small firms—make available to their employees some type of hospitalization, medical, and disability insurance; along with life insurance, these benefits form the cornerstone of almost all benefit programs.[19] Hospitalization, health, and disability insurance is aimed at providing protection against hospitalization costs and loss of income arising from accidents or illness occurring from off-the-job causes. Many employers purchase such insurance from life insurance companies, casualty insurance companies, or Blue Cross (for hospital expenses) and Blue Shield (for physician expenses) organizations. Others contract directly with health maintenance organizations or preferred provider organizations, both of which are discussed later.

Most health insurance plans provide, at a minimum, basic hospitalization and surgical and medical insurance for all eligible employees as a group. As with life insurance, group rates are usually lower than individual rates and are generally available to all employees—including new ones—regardless of health or physical condition. Most basic plans pay for hospital room and board, surgery charges, and medical expenses (such as doctors' visits to the hospital). Some group plans also provide major medical coverage to meet high medical expenses that result from long-term or serious illnesses; with hospitalization costs rapidly rising this is an increasingly popular option. The employers' health and hospitalization plans must comply with the Americans with Disabilities Act.[20] For example, the employers' insurance policy shouldn't make distinctions on the basis of disability unless those distinctions are justified by recognized differences based on actuarial data or historic costs.[21]

Many employers are also sponsoring health-related insurance plans covering expenses like eye care and dental services. In fact, dental insurance plans have been one of the fastest-growing items over the past few years, with the number of persons in the United States with dental coverage growing to over 100 million today.[22] In most employer-sponsored dental plans, participants must pay a specified amount of deductible dental expenses (typically $25 or $50 each year) before the plan kicks in with benefits. In a majority of the cases the participants in such plans have premiums paid for entirely by their employers.[23]

Accidental death and dismemberment coverage is another option. This provides a fixed lump-sum benefit in addition to life insurance benefits when death is accidental. It also provides a range of benefits in case of accidental loss of limbs or sight. Other options provide payments for diagnostic visits to the doctor's office, vision care, hearing aid plans, payment for prescription drugs, and dental care plans. Employers must provide the same health care benefits to employees over the age of 65 that are provided to younger workers, even though the older workers are eligible for the federally funded Medicare health insurance plan.[24]

Disability insurance is aimed at providing income protection or compensation for loss of salary due to illness or accident. The disability payments usually begin when normal sick leave is used up and may continue to provide income to age 65 or beyond.[25] The disability benefits usually range from 50% to 75% of the employee's base pay if he or she is disabled.

Many employers offer membership in a **health maintenance organization (HMO)** as a hospital/medical option. The HMO itself is a medical organization consisting of several specialists (surgeons, psychiatrists, and so on) operating out of a community-based health care center. The HMO generally provides routine round-the-clock medical services at a specific site and usually stresses preventive medicine in a clinic-type arrangement to employees who pay a nominal fee. The HMO also receives a fixed annual fee per employee from the employer (or employer and employee), regardless of whether any service actually is provided.[26]

Preferred provider organizations (PPOs) have been defined as a cross between HMOs and the traditional doctor/patient arrangement: They are "groups of health care providers that contract with employers, insurance companies, or third-party payers to provide medical care services at a reduced fee."[27] Unlike an HMO with its relatively limited list of health care providers often concentrated in one health care center, PPOs let employees select providers (such as participating doctors) who agree to provide price discounts and submit to certain utilization controls, such as on the number of diagnostic tests that can be ordered.[28] Employees may obtain increased health cost savings and a wider choice of doctors than are typically available with an HMO. The doctors themselves benefit from the increased number of patients. HMOs and PPOs are compared in Figure 14.4.

Reducing Health Benefit Costs   The average cost per employee of health benefits has risen from about $1,700 in 1985 to over $3,900 today in some firms; giant firms like General Motors spend hundreds of millions of dollars per year just on health care benefits.[29] Caught between rising benefits costs and the belt tightening occurring in firms today, many managers now find controlling and reducing health care costs topping their to-do lists. As a result, many employers have been changing their medical plans to do the following.

1. Move away from 100% medical cost payments. In 1982, only about 30% of the surveyed companies required employees to pay a deductible on hospital expenses. By now, the percentage has more than doubled, with over 70% using a deductible.
2. Increase annual deductibles. In 1982, the average deductible was $100. Today, almost 40% of firms use a deductible of $150 or more.

health maintenance organization (HMO)
A prepaid health care system that generally provides routine round-the-clock medical services as well as preventive medicine in a clinic-type arrangement for employees, who pay a nominal fee in addition to the fixed annual fee the employer pays.

Preferred Provider Organizations (PPOs)
Groups of health care providers that contract with employers, insurance companies, or third-party payers to provide medical care services at a reduced fee.

Figure 14.4
How Health Insurance
Options Differ on Key
Dimensions

Source: George Milkovich and
Jerry Newman, *Compensation*
(Burr Ridge, IL: Irwin, 1993),
p. 444.

ISSUE	TRADITIONAL COVERAGE	HEALTH MAINTENANCE ORGANIZATION (HMO)	PREFERRED PROVIDER ORGANIZATION (PPO)
Who is eligible?	May live anywhere.	May be required to live in HMO–designated service area.	May live anywhere.
Who provides health care?	Doctor and health care facility of patient's choice.	Must use doctors and facilities designated by HMO.	May use doctors and facilities associated with PPO. If not, may pay additional copayment/deductible.
How much coverage on routine, preventative level?	Does not cover regular checkups and other preventative services. Diagnostic tests may be covered in part or full.	Covers regular checkups, diagnostic tests, other preventative services with low or no fee per visit.	Same as with HMO, if doctor and facility are on approved list. Copayments and deductibles are assessed at much higher rate for others not on list.
Hospital care	Covers doctors and hospital bills.	Covers doctors and hospital bills if HMO-approved hospital.	Covers doctors and hospitals if PPO–approved.

3. Reimburse less than 100% of hospital costs. In 1982, 67% of companies provided full reimbursement for hospital costs versus only 42% of companies in 1990.

4. Limit the annual out-of-pocket medical expenses an employee pays. Interestingly, the number of plans with a "stop-loss" amount, which limits the out-of-pocket expense an employee would have to pay during a year, has increased from 80% to 89% recently. In other words, while employers are asking employees to pay higher deductibles, they are giving employees more protection against catastrophic medical expenses.

5. Require medical contributions. Whereas only 31% of employers required employee contributions to their medical premiums in 1982, over 46% of plans require them today.[30]

6. Move to *managed care* programs. Managed care refers to the practice by which health maintenance organizations and the somewhat similar preferred provider organizations (PPOs) channel patients to the most cost-efficient providers of care, including physicians and hospitals.[31] Such a case management procedure—in which, for instance, a general practitioner serves as a gatekeeper and channels the patient to the appropriate specialist and/or hospital as needed—was cited as "very effective" by 69% of the employers in one survey that use it.[32]

7. Focus on health promotion and preventive health care. According to one survey, 56% of the firms were sponsoring drug and alcohol abuse programs; 31% were offering stop-smoking sessions; 45% were providing physical fitness classes; and 18% had exercise facilities on company premises. Many employers (70%) were training employees in first aid and CPR. Most were also increasing their communication efforts: 69% explain the problem of rising health care costs to employees and 54% offer tips about how to use company health benefits wisely.[33]

8. Provide incentives to encourage workers to live healthy lifestyles and seek preventive care. HealthTrust, Inc. has changed its health and hospitalization plan to include: a preventive-care program including mammograms, prostate exams, and well-baby care; a prenatal program called "Healthy Beginnings;" an employee assistance program for seeking help for emotional or substance abuse problems; a higher deductible ($1,000) for individuals injured when engaged in high-risk activities such as not wearing seatbelts when driving; and a voluntary wellness program that encourages participation by lowering premiums for employees and spouses who join.[34]

9. Form health care coalitions. In Minneapolis, the HR executives of several large, self-insured companies (they insure their employees themselves, rather than through an insurance company) pressured local health care providers to put more emphasis on the quality and cost-effectiveness of care. The main aim here was to cut back on the care delivered by expensive specialists, such as cardiologists and orthopedists, and to rely more on primary care physicians.[35] In Memphis, Tennessee, 11 self-insured employers including Federal Express and Holiday Inn formed a coalition to study health care costs, identify more efficient health care providers, and use their purchasing power to obtain discounts on health and hospital care prices.[36]

10. Reduce retirees' benefits. However, at some firms, such as the former Primerica, retirees argue that health insurance was part of the retirement benefits they were promised, and that cutting such benefits is unethical and possibly illegal.

Managing Health Care Costs: AIDS By now, the fatal nature of AIDS—Acquired Immune Deficiency Syndrome—is unfortunately well known to everyone.[37] However, in addition to the human suffering caused by AIDS, its potential impact on insurance companies and employers' insurance plans must be considered. The average estimated claims payout per AIDS case was about $68,000 in 1991, a considerable sum.[38]

The problem is that reining in these costs is hampered by several unique aspects of the AIDS disease. While at the present time it is always terminal, intensive medical intervention is usually necessary for only short periods of time. For most of the time, the need is more custodial and can often be as well administered at home or in nonhospital facilities as inside hospitals. While reduced costs are therefore possible with alternative treatment facilities, most employers' medical plans don't cover them. Such plans are thus self-defeating in requiring more expensive care where it is not needed.

There is also a constellation of psychological barriers that inhibit early diagnosis and more cost-effective treatment. Many AIDS sufferers are reluctant to discuss their illness with their employers for fear of losing their jobs and/or their insurance benefits. At the same time, the reactions of fearful coworkers to AIDS sufferers often further impede open discussions of the problem. The very nature of the disease also makes traditional cost-containment efforts virtually useless: Obtaining second surgical opinions, requiring outpatient surgery, and mandating psychiatric restrictions have little or no bearing in the treatment of AIDS, for instance.

Several insurance companies have concluded that the best way to control the cost of AIDS is to rethink the benefits plans with an eye toward providing required care in the least costly way. This often means treating the AIDS sufferer in his or her home and allowing the cost to be paid under the benefits plan (as is not usually allowed now). Thus, the emphasis will increasingly be on *individual case management* (ICM). Here a special ICM nurse will be assigned to the patient and an alternative treatment plan will be designed. The plan will be individualized, taking into consideration the patient's ability to care for himself or herself, the availability of others who are able to help in the person's treatment, and the age and condition of the patient. A case history can illustrate this:

> When the patient was admitted to the hospital, the insurance carrier's precertification office questioned him at length and determined that he was suffering from a late stage of mylobacterium intracellular, an opportunistic disease most commonly found among AIDS patients. After six weeks in the hospital, the patient was discharged to an intensive home care routine costing $390 per day. If he had remained in the hospital, the cost would have been $1,100 per day. The attempt at home care lasted only 12 days, at which time the patient's condition degenerated to a point where permanent hospitalization was necessary. Even this modest success with home care resulted in a savings to the plan of $8,520.[39]

In summary, steps recommended by one expert to help contain the health care benefits costs associated with AIDS are as follows:

> Medical plans should be expanded to provide coverage for outpatient services and alternate treatment facilities.
>
> Individual care management should be used to find the most appropriate type of care for each individual.
>
> Employers should not penalize or stigmatize those employees who admit they have AIDS.[40]

Mental Health Benefits It is estimated that employers spend just over 8% of their health plan dollars on mental health treatment.[41] These costs are rising quickly because of widespread drug and alcohol problems, an increase in the number of states (to 29 today) that require employers to offer a minimum package of mental health benefits, and the fact that other health care claims are higher for employees with high mental health claims.

For the employer, the bottom line is that the cost of mental health care benefits is substantial. One financial services firm in New York City found that its mental health benefits jumped 61% in one year, for instance.

The first step in slowing the rise in mental health benefits is for employers to identify whether and to what extent a funding problem exists. The New York financial services firm rejected the idea of placing across-the-board limits on mental health coverage. Instead it redesigned the mental health portion of its health benefits plan. The new plan emphasizes a utilization review to certify treatment, increased outpatient benefits, and a selected network of cost-efficient providers along with the provision of customized treatment plans in a negotiated provider network. The new program cut mental health benefit plan costs significantly while still providing needed benefits for company employees.[42]

Pregnancy Discrimination Act (PDA)
An amendment to Title VII of the Civil Rights Act that prohibits sex discrimination based on "pregnancy, childbirth, or related medical conditions." It requires employers to provide benefits—including sick leave and disability benefits and health and medical insurance—the same as for any employee not able to work because of disability.

The Pregnancy Discrimination Act The **Pregnancy Discrimination Act (PDA)** is aimed at prohibiting sex discrimination based on "pregnancy, childbirth, or related medical conditions."[43] Before enactment of this law in 1978, temporary disability benefits for pregnancies were generally paid in the form of either sick leave or disability insurance, if at all. However, while most employers provide temporary disability income to their employees for up to 26 weeks for most illnesses, those that provided benefits for pregnancy usually limited benefits to only six weeks for normal pregnancies. Many believed that the shorter duration of pregnancy benefits constituted discrimination based on sex, and it was this issue that the Pregnancy Discrimination Act was aimed at settling.

Specifically, the act requires employers to treat women affected by pregnancy, childbirth, or related medical conditions the same as any employees not

The Pregnancy Discrimination Act makes it illegal for an employer to discriminate against a pregnant woman with respect to benefits.

able to work, with respect to all benefits, including sick leave and disability benefits, and health and medical insurance. Thus, it is illegal for most employers to discriminate against women by providing benefits of lower amount or duration for pregnancy, childbirth, or related medical conditions. For example, if an employer provides up to 26 weeks of temporary disability income to employees for all illnesses, it is now required to provide up to 26 weeks for pregnancy and childbirth also rather than the more typical six weeks that prevailed before the act.

Interestingly, even some feminist groups argue against granting special pregnancy benefits to women. They say it mediates against equality in the workplace by seeking special treatment with regard to selected issues. Furthermore, they argue that special benefits for pregnancy would make women of childbearing age potentially more expensive employees and thus increase the likelihood they will be discriminated against, for instance, in hiring. It remains to be seen what the final disposition of this debate will be.

COBRA Requirements The ominously titled COBRA—Comprehensive Omnibus Budget Reconciliation Act—simply requires most private employers to make available to terminated or retired employees and their families continued health benefits for a period of time, generally 18 months. The former employee must pay for this coverage, if desired, as well as a small fee for administrative costs.

Care must be taken in administering COBRA, especially when it comes to informing employees of their COBRA rights. For one thing, you don't want a terminated or retired employee to get injured and then come back and claim that he or she didn't know that his or her insurance coverage could have been continued. Therefore, when a new employee first becomes eligible for your company's insurance plan, an explanation of COBRA rights should be received and acknowledged. More important, all employees separated from the company for any reason should sign a form acknowledging that they have received and understand their COBRA rights.

Retirement Benefits

Social Security

Social Security
Provides three types of benefits: retirement income at the age of 62 and thereafter; survivor's or death benefits payable to the employee's dependents regardless of age at time of death; and disability benefits payable to disabled employees and their dependents. These benefits are payable only if the employee is insured under the Social Security Act.

Many people assume that **Social Security** provides income only when they are old, but it actually provides three types of benefits. First are the familiar *retirement benefits*. These provide an income if you retire at age 62 or thereafter and are insured under the Social Security Act. Second, there are *survivor's or death benefits*. These provide monthly payments to your dependents regardless of your age at death, again assuming you were insured under the Social Security Act. Finally, there are *disability payments*. These provide monthly payments to you and your dependents if you become totally disabled for work and meet certain specified work requirements.[44] The Medicare program, which provides a wide range of health services to people 65 or over, is also administered through the Social Security system.

Social Security (technically, federal old age and survivor's insurance) is paid for by a tax on the employee's wages; employees and their employer share equally in this tax. If you are self-employed, you pay the entire sum less 2% of your self-employment income.

Pension Plans

pension plans
Plans that provide a fixed sum when employees reach a predetermined retirement age or when they can no longer work due to disability.

defined benefit pension plan
A plan that contains a formula for determining retirement benefits.

defined contribution plan
A plan in which the employer's contribution to employees' retirement or savings funds is specified.

deferred profit-sharing plan
A plan in which a certain amount of profits is credited to each employee's account, payable at retirement, termination, or death.

There are many types of **pension plans**.[45] For example, there are defined benefit pension plans and defined contribution benefit plans.[46] A **defined benefit pension plan** contains a formula for determining retirement benefits so that the actual benefits to be received are defined ahead of time. For example, the plan might include a formula that designates a dollar amount or a percentage of annual salary for predicting the individual's eventual pension. A **defined contribution plan** specifies what contribution the employer will make to a retirement or savings fund set up for the employee. The defined contribution plan does not define the eventual benefit amount, only the periodic contribution to the plan. In a defined benefit plan, the employee knows ahead of time what his or her retirement benefits will be upon retirement. With a defined contribution plan, the employee cannot be sure of his or her retirement benefits. Those benefits depend on both the amounts contributed to the fund and the retirement fund's investment earnings.

Under the 401(k) plan, based on Section 401(k) of the Internal Revenue Code, employees can have a portion of their compensation, which would otherwise be paid in cash, put into a company profit-sharing or stock bonus plan by the employer. This results in a pretax reduction in salary, so the employee isn't taxed on those set-aside dollars until after he or she retires (or removes the money from the pension fund). Some employers also match a portion of what the employee contributes to the 401(k) plan. One attraction of 401(k) is that employees may have a range of investment options for the 401(k) funds including mutual stock funds and bond funds.

There are several types of defined contribution plans.[47] In a savings and thrift plan (a 401(k) is one example), employees contribute a portion of their earnings to a fund; this contribution is usually matched in whole or in part by the employer. In **deferred profit-sharing plans**, employers typically contribute a portion of their profits to the pension fund, regardless of the level of employee contribution. An employee stock ownership plan (ESOP) is a qualified, tax-deductible stock bonus plan in which employers contribute stock to a trust for eventual use by employees.

The entire area of pension planning is complicated, partly because of the many federal laws governing pensions. For example, companies want to ensure that their pension contributions are qualified or tax deductible and must, therefore, adhere to the pertinent income tax codes. The Employee Retirement Income Security Act (ERISA) restricts what companies can, cannot, and must do in regard to pension plans (more on this in a moment). In unionized companies, the union must be allowed to participate in the administration of the pension plan under the Taft-Hartley Act.

While an employer usually must develop a pension plan to meet its own unique needs, there are several key policy issues to consider.[48]

Membership requirements. For example, what is the minimum age or minimum service at which employees become eligible for a pension?

Benefit formula. This usually ties the pension to the employee's final earnings, or an average of his or her last three or four years' earnings.

Retirement requirements. Although 65 is often considered a standard retirement age, federal law prohibits forced retirement of any competent employee. Yet most people opt for early retirement.[49] In companies such as General Motors, for example, only a small proportion of production and office workers retire as late as 65.[50] Partly due to union pressure and partly because early retirement helps open up jobs for younger employees, many employers now encourage early retirement. For example, some plans call for "30 and out." This permits an employee to retire after 30 years of continuous service, regardless of the person's age. In some cases, such as in the U.S. Army and among New York City employees, employees can retire with reduced pensions after 20 years of continuous service regardless of the employee's age.[51]

Funding. The question of how the plan is to be funded is another key issue. One aspect is whether the plan will be contributory or noncontributory. In the former, contributions to the pension funds are made by both employees and the employer. In a noncontributory fund—the prevailing type, by the way—only the employer contributes. Another aspect of this is that many pension plans are underfunded. Although under the Employee Retirement Income Security Act most pension plans are now guaranteed (as explained later), the fact of the matter is that an alarming number of employers' pension funds do not have adequate funds to cover expected pension benefits.[52]

Vesting. **Vesting** is another critical issue in pension planning. It refers to the money that the employer and employee have placed in the latter's pension fund that cannot be forfeited for any reason. The employees' contributions are always theirs and cannot be forfeited. However, until the passage of the Employee Retirement Income Security Act, the employer's contribution was not necessarily vested. Thus, suppose a person worked for a company for 30 years and the company then went out of business one year before he or she was to retire at age 65. Unless that employee's rights to the company's pension contributions were vested—by a union agreement or company policy, for instance—he or she might well not have a pension.[53]

vesting
Provision that money placed in a pension fund cannot be forfeited for any reason.

The Question of Portability Many employers today are redesigning their pension plans in order to make their pensions more "portable." For example, Duracel International, Inc. has redesigned and simplified its pension plan to make it easier for employees to take their retirement income when they leave and roll it over into a new employer's savings plan or IRA.[54]

Doing so represents a dramatic shift in pension planning for most employers. Traditionally, a main purpose of a pension was to "lock in" workers, to tie them to the company by giving them a substantial capital loss on their pensions should they leave before retirement age. For example, an employee who stayed with a company for 22 years might get only one-third the pension benefits that he or she would accrue by staying until the plan's 30-year requirement was met, which for many employees effectively locked them in for those last eight years.

There seems little doubt that pension coverage can and has reduced labor mobility for many firms.[55] The relationship between pension loss and employee mobility isn't necessarily a simple one. For instance, pensions that lock in employees may actually attract more stable workers in the first place, and at least one study has found that they do.[56] In other words, the lower quit rate for workers covered by such pensions may come not just from the lock-in nature of the pensions but from the fact that the employees attracted to firms that have such pensions may for other reasons be less predisposed to quit the firm and move on.

In any case, today's needs for flexible staffing and the realities of the ongoing corporate restructurings and downsizings are causing more employers to make their pension plans more portable. This is often facilitated by switching to defined contribution plans, since defined benefits plans are geared to what the person will receive upon retirement from the firm, although he or she may not see any prospects of staying with the firm until retirement. Other policy options that can reduce the loss of employees' pensions during job changes include: eliminating the requirement for a later age for receipt of initial benefits for workers who leave the firm before retirement; providing extra years of credit in defined benefit plans and extra contributions in defined contribution plans for laid-off workers; and no longer granting lower-percentage cost-of-living adjustments for retirees who have less service or who end employment before retirement.[57]

Pensions and the Law

Employee Retirement Income Security Act (ERISA)
Signed into law by President Ford in 1974 to require that pension rights be vested, and protected by a government agency, PBGC.

The **Employee Retirement Income Security Act (ERISA)** was signed into law in 1974.[58] ERISA was aimed at protecting the pensions of workers and in stimulating the growth of pension plans.

Before enactment of ERISA, pension plans often failed to deliver expected benefits to employees. Any number of reasons, such as business failure and inadequate funding, could result in employees losing their expected pensions and facing the prospect of being unable to retire.

Under ERISA, pension rights had to be vested under one of three formulas.[59]

100% vesting after 10 years of service (often referred to as *cliff vesting*).

25% vesting after 5 years, increasing 5% a year to 50% vesting after 10 years, and by 10% a year to 100% vesting after 15 years.

50% vesting after 5 years of service if the employee's age and years of service total 45 (or after 10 years of service if less), and increasing by 10% a year thereafter.

The Tax Reform Act of 1986 further tightened these vesting rules. As of today, participants in a pension plan must have a nonforfeitable right to 100% of their accrued benefits after five years of service. As an alternative, the employer may choose to phase in vesting over a period of three to seven years. Under the Tax Reform Act of 1986, an employer can require that an employee complete a period of no more than two years' service to the company before becoming eligible to participate in the plan. However, if you require more than one year of service, the plan must grant employees full and immediate vesting rights at the end of their required service.[60]

Pension Benefits Guarantee Corporation (PBGC)
Established under ERISA to ensure that pensions meet vesting obligations; also insures pensions should a plan terminate without sufficient funds to meet its vested obligations.

Among other things, the **Pension Benefits Guarantee Corporation (PBGC)** was established under ERISA to ensure that pensions meet vesting obligations; the PBGC also insures pensions should a plan terminate without sufficient funds to meet its vested obligations.[61]

Several factors are making some experts uncomfortable about the security of employees' pensions despite the existence of the Pension Benefit Guarantee Corp.[62] PBGC guarantees only defined benefit plans, not defined contribution plans. Furthermore, PBGC payments are not unlimited. It will pay an individual a pension of up to roughly $27,000 per year, for instance. This may seem like a lot, but it might not be to, say, an airline pilot who retired expecting a pension of $70,000 per year. Furthermore, according to the PBGC, more and more employers are terminating their defined benefit plans and replacing them with uninsured defined contribution plans. (Legislation is being considered to deal with this problem.)

Many companies are also eliminating their defined benefit plans and replacing them with annuities purchased from insurance companies. Most of the defined benefit plans were covered by the PBGC, but the annuities are not. The problem is that an increasing number of insurance firms are going bankrupt. This can leave the employees with worthless annuities and no pensions.

The problem of underfunded or unfunded pension plans also helped prompt the accounting profession's Financial Accounting Standards Board to introduce "Employers Accounting for Pensions," commonly known as FASB 87. This rule, which is one of a multitude of rules to which certified public accountants in the United States must adhere, mandates that:[63]

1. For both reported earnings and balance sheet calculations, accounting for defined benefits plans must estimate the size of the liability the employer is accumulating by using market interest rates. Since the cost of funding specific, defined benefits (of, say, $1,000 per month) 20 years from now will rise with an increase in market interest rates, this means that the reported liability to the employer will reflect more closely the plan's actual cost than it did previously.
2. The corporate balance sheet must include the unfunded liability of an underfunded pension plan.
3. If changes in the surplus of the plan (should the plan have a surplus) exceed 10% of its assets or liabilities, such changes must be reflected in the earnings statement in the form of operating earnings.

Note that FASB 87 does not apply to defined contribution plans. Unlike defined benefits plans, defined contribution plans do not guarantee how much money an employee will receive on retirement, but only what each party's contribution to the plan will be. The Omnibus Budget Reconciliation Act of 1987 lays out further rules regarding the funding of pension liabilities.[64] The net effect of these laws and accounting changes has been to prompt employers to move to defined contribution plans and to annuities.

Working Women and Retirement Benefits

Women will account for 64% of the growth of the work force in the 1990s. This increase has created pressure on the part of women and many women's groups to change three aspects of pension laws that they believe are discriminatory on the basis of sex:

The traditional rules regarding the accumulation of pension credits;

The limited right of a homemaker to her spouse's workplace pension; and

The gender-based actuarial tables used to calculate the rate at which accrued pensions are paid.

Changes have already been made. The Retirement Equity Act seeks to increase women's share of private-sector retirement benefits by changing some of ERISA's rules. For example, prior to the Retirement Equity Act, a woman who left her job to have a child before she was vested and remained at home until the child reached school age was likely to lose what credits she had previously amassed; she would have to start over again when she returned to work. Now a nonvested employee who leaves the employer's service and then comes back within five years can get credit for that earlier service, and employees who are absent from work because of pregnancy, childbirth, adoption, or infant care are protected against break-in-service penalties for a year. The act also lowers from 25 to 21 the maximum age that a private pension plan can require an employee to attain before he or she can participate in the plan. It allows women on maternity leave for up to five years to retain certain pension benefits and to require a spouse's written permission before a pension plan participant can waive survivor benefits. In a divorce settlement, the act also authorizes the court to award a person the right to part of the former spouse's pension as part of the benefit.[65]

Recent Trends

Retirement benefits are getting a new twist with so-called **golden offerings**—early retirement windows and other voluntary separation arrangements. These are aimed at avoiding dismissals by offering special retirement packages to long-term employees. According to one survey of a cross section of U.S. industries and locations, about one-third of companies offered such voluntary separation plans in the past few years, while another 9% were considering an offering.

Early Retirement Windows   Most of these plans take the form of **early retirement window** arrangements in which specific employees (often age 50+) are eligible to participate. The "window" represents the fact that the company opens up (for a limited time only) the chance for an employee to retire earlier than usual. The financial incentive is usually a combination of improved or liberalized pension benefits plus a cash payment. One expert concludes that early retirement has become the method of choice for reducing midmanagement and white-collar work forces, with about 13% of 362 employers surveyed providing such early retirement windows in one recent year.[66]

Other voluntary separation plans operate more like bonuses for leaving and may apply even to recent hires. The offerings are usually made regardless of age. The financial incentive is typically a cash payment that varies substantially by company but often is in the range of one week's pay per year of service. About one-third of those employees eligible to walk through the early retirement windows typically accept the offer, while about one-fourth of those offered other separation plans do likewise.[67]

Early retirement windows like these must be used with caution. The problem is that age discrimination is the fastest-growing type of discrimination claim today, and unless structured properly, early retirement programs can be challenged as de facto programs for forcing the discharge of older employees against their will.[68] While it is generally legal to use incentives like early retirement benefits to encourage individuals to choose early retirement, the employee's decision must be voluntary. In fact, in several cases individuals who were eligible for and elected early retirement later challenged their early retirement by claiming that their decision was not voluntary. In one case, for instance (*Paolillo* v. *Dresser Industries, Inc.*), employees were told on October 12 that they were eligible to retire under a "totally voluntary" early retirement program and that they must inform the company by October 18 to take advantage of this benefit. However, they were not informed of the details of the program (such as the amount of medical insurance and pension benefits for each individual employee) until October 15. This did not leave them much time, so that employees who had at first elected early retirement were able to subsequently sue, claiming coercion. The U.S. Court of Appeals for the Second Circuit (New York) agreed with their claim, arguing that an employee's decision to retire must be voluntary and without undue strain.[69]

Employers must exercise caution in encouraging employees to take early retirement. The waivers of future claims that they sign should meet EEOC guidelines. In particular, it must be knowing and voluntary, not provide for the release of prospective rights or claims, and not be an exchange for consideration that included benefits to which the employee was already entitled. It should give the employee ample opportunity to think over the agreement and seek advice from legal counsel.[70] The Older Workers' Benefit Protection Act (OWBPA), signed into law in 1990, imposes specific limitations on waivers that purport to release a terminating employee's potential claims against his or her employer based on age discrimination.[71]

Employee Services Benefits

While an employer's time off and insurance and retirement benefits account for the main part of its benefits costs, most employers also provide a range of services including personal services (such as counseling), job-related services (such as child care facilities), and executive perquisites (such as company cars and planes for its executives).

Personal Services Benefits

First, many companies provide service benefits in the form of personal services that most employees need at one time or another. These include credit unions, legal services, counseling, and social and recreational opportunities.

Credit Unions   Credit unions are usually separate businesses established with the assistance of the employer. Employees usually become members of a credit union by purchasing a share of the credit union's stock for $5 or $10. Members can then deposit savings that accrue interest at a rate determined by the credit union's board of directors. Perhaps more important to most employees, loan eligibility and the rate of interest paid on the loan are usually more favorable than those found in banks and finance companies.

Counseling Services   Employers are also providing a wider range of counseling services to employees. These include financial counseling (for example, in terms of how to overcome existing indebtedness problems); family counseling (for marital problems and so on); career counseling (in terms of analyzing one's aptitudes and deciding on a career); job placement counseling (for helping terminated or disenchanted employees find new jobs); and preretirement counseling (aimed at preparing retiring employees for what many find is the trauma of retiring). Many employers also make available to employees a full range of legal counseling through legal insurance plans.[72] In the open-panel legal plan, employees can choose their own attorney and then be reimbursed according to the fee schedule in the policy. In the closed-panel legal plan, employees are required to use one of a number of specified attorneys, who are paid directly by the insurance plan.

employee assistance program (EAP)
A formal employer program for providing employees with counseling and/or treatment programs for problems such as alcoholism, gambling, or stress.

Employee Assistance Programs (EAPs)   An **employee assistance plan (EAP)** is a formal employer program for providing employees with counseling and/or treatment programs for problems such as alcoholism, gambling, or stress. It is estimated that 50% to 75% of all employers with 3,000 or more employees now offer EAPs,[73] and there are four basic models in use today.[74] In the *in-house model* the entire assistance staff is employed by the company. In the *out-of-house model* the company contracts a vendor to provide employee assistance staff and services in its own offices, the company's offices, or a combination of both. In the *consortium model* several companies pool their resources to develop a collaborative EAP program. Finally, in the *affiliate model* a vendor already under contract to the employer subcontracts to a local professional rather than use its own salaried staff. This is usually to service employees in a client company location in which the EAP vendors do not have an office. Key ingredients for ensuring a successful EAP program include:[75]

Specify goals and philosophy. The short- and long-term goals expected to be achieved for both the employee and employer should be specified.

Develop a policy statement. Next a comprehensive EAP policy statement should be prepared. This should define the purpose of the program, employee eligibility, the roles and responsibility of various personnel in the organization, and procedures for taking advantage of the plan.

Ensure professional staffing. Give careful consideration to the professional and state licensing requirements as they apply to the people staffing these facilities. If necessary, retain the services of an experienced person to consult with you in drawing up job specifications for the required staff.

Maintain confidential record-keeping systems. Everyone involved with the EAP, including secretaries and support staff, must understand the importance of confidentiality. Furthermore, make sure files are locked, access is limited and monitored, and identifying information (which might otherwise find itself in an employee's computerized records) is kept to a minimum.

Provide supervisory training. While this needn't involve extensive training, supervisors should certainly understand the program's policies, procedures, and services as well as the company's policies regarding confidentiality. And perhaps more important, all supervisors should get some training regarding the outward symptoms of problems like alcoholism as well as how to encourage employees to use the services of the EAP.

Be aware of legal issues. For example, in most states counselors must disclose suspicions of child abuse to an appropriate state agency: Your in-house counselors thus put your company in the legal position of having to comply in such an instance. Three ways to safeguard your interests here include retaining legal advice on establishing your EAP, carefully screening the credentials of the staff you hire, and obtaining professional liability insurance for the EAP.

Other Personal Services Finally, some employers also provide various social and recreational opportunities for their employees, including company-sponsored athletic events, dance clubs, annual summer picnics, craft activities, and parties.[76] In practice, the benefits offered are limited only by your creativity in thinking up new benefits. One study of innovative benefits, for instance, found Canadian companies offering the following benefits, among others:

Lakefront vacations—the company owns lakeshore property and rents cottages and campsites to employees at low rates.

Weight loss program—several companies subsidize costs of weight loss workshops.

Adoption benefit—companies pay amounts of $500 to $1,500 per child for adoption costs.

Company country club—the company maintains a golf course, tennis courts, and football and baseball fields.

Cultural subsidy—the company will pay 33% of the cost of tickets to cultural activities such as theater, ballet, museum, and so on up to $100 per year per employee.

Lunch-and-learn program—interested employees can attend lunchtime talks on a variety of subjects, including stress management, weight control, computer literacy, fashion, and travel.

Home assistance—employees may use up to $1,500 of their annual profit-sharing award to save for a down payment on a house or to reduce their down payment, up to a maximum of $15,000.[77]

Job-Related Services Benefits

Job-related services aimed directly at helping employees perform their jobs, such as assistance in moving and day care centers, constitute a second group of services.

Subsidized Child Care   Today over 50% of all U.S. women with children under 6 years old are in the work force, up from 32% in 1970.[78] Subsidized day care is one increasingly popular benefit stemming directly from that trend.[79] Many employers simply investigate the day care facilities in their communities and recommend certain ones to interested employees. But more employers are setting up company-sponsored day care facilities themselves, both to attract young mothers to the payroll and to reduce absenteeism. Often (as at the Wang Laboratories day care facility in Lowell, Massachusetts), the center is a private tax-exempt venture run separately from but subsidized by the firm. Employees are charged $30 a week for a child's care, and about 75 children from 2 to 4 years old are now enrolled. Where successful, the day care facility is usually close to the workplace (often in the same building), and the employer provides 50% to 75% of the operating costs. To date, however, the publicity these programs have received exceeds their actual use, with most surveys showing fewer than 5% of employers providing subsidized day care.

Subsidizing day care facilities for children of employees has many benefits for the employer, including lower employee absenteeism.

A survey found that employers can gain considerably by instituting subsidized day care centers; increased ability to attract employees, lower absenteeism, improved morale, favorable publicity, and lower turnover are some of the benefits attributed to day care programs.[80] To make sure the program is worthwhile and that its costs do not get out of hand, however, good planning is needed. This often starts with a questionnaire to survey employees in order to answer such questions as: "What would you be willing to pay for care for one child in a child care center near work?" and "Have you missed work during the past six months because you needed to find new care arrangements?" To date the evidence regarding the actual effects of employer-sponsored child care on employee absenteeism, turnover, productivity, recruitment, or job satisfaction is positive, particularly with respect to reducing obstacles to coming to work and improving workers' attitudes.[81]

Elder Care   With the average age of the U.S. population rising, elder care is increasingly a concern for many employers and individuals. Elder care is designed to help employees who must help elderly parents or relatives who are not fully able to care for themselves.[82]

From the employer's point of view, elder care benefits are important for much the same reason as are child care benefits: The responsibility for caring for an aging relative can and will affect the employee's performance at work.[83] A number of employers are, therefore, instituting elder care benefits, including flexible hours, long-term care insurance coverage, and company-sponsored elder care centers.

The elder care program instituted by Aerospace Company helps to illustrate what a typical program involves. Utilizing a program kit made available by the American Association of Retired Persons (AARP), the company program had three parts.

1. A lunchtime elder care fair was held at which 31 community organizations involved with providing services to older people came to explain to employees the services that were available.

2. Next there were ten lunchtime information sessions for employees aimed at explaining various aspects of elder care, such as independent versus dependent living and housing, the aging process, and legal concerns of elder care.

3. Finally, the company also distributed AARP's publication entitled "Care Management Guide." This lists potential problems associated with elder care in a question-and-answer format.[84]

Subsidized Employee Transportation   Some employers also provide subsidized employee transportation.[85] In one such program, Seattle First National Bank negotiated separate contracts with a transit system to provide free year-round transportation to more than 3,000 of the bank's employees. At the other extreme, some employers just facilitate employee car pooling, perhaps by acting as the central clearing house to identify employees from the same geographic areas who work the same hours.

Food Services   Food services are provided in some form by many employers; they let employees purchase meals, snacks, or coffee, usually at relatively low prices. Most food operations are nonprofit, and, in fact, some firms provide food services below cost. The advantages to the employee are clear, and for the employer the service can ensure that employees do not drift away for long lunch hours. Even employers that do not provide full dining facilities generally make available food services such as coffee wagons or vending machines for the convenience of employees.

Educational Subsidies   Educational subsidies such as tuition refunds have long been a popular benefit for employees seeking to continue or complete their educations. Payments range from all tuition and expenses to some percentage of expenses to a flat fee per year of, say, $250 to $300. Some employers have experimented with providing in-house college programs, such as Master of Business Administration programs, in which college faculty teach courses on the employer's premises. Other in-house educational programs include remedial work in basic literacy and training for improved supervisory skills. As far as tuition reimbursement programs are concerned, one survey found that nearly all the 619 companies surveyed pay for courses directly related to an employee's present job. Most companies also reimburse non–job-related courses (such as a secretary taking an accounting class) that pertain to the company business (79%) and those that are part of a degree program (66%). Furthermore, about 14% of the employers pay for self-improvement classes, such as a foreign language, even though they are unrelated to company business or the employee's job.[86]

Executive Perquisites

Perquisites (perks, for short) are usually given to only a few top executives. Perks can range from the substantial to the almost insignificant. In addition to a $200,000 annual salary, for instance, the president of the United States has an expense account of $50,000 for household expenses and entertainment, $100,000 for travel, and free use of the White House and Camp David (not to mention a fleet of limousines, Air Force One, and various helicopters).[87] At the other extreme, perks may entail little more than the right to use the executive washroom.

A multitude of popular perks falls between these extremes. These include: management loans (which typically enable senior officers to use their stock options); salary guarantees (also known as *golden parachutes*), to protect executives even if their firms are the targets of acquisitions or mergers; financial counseling (to handle top executives' investment programs); and relocation benefits, often including subsidized mortgages, purchase of the executive's current house, and payment for the actual move.[88] A potpourri of other executive perks includes time off with pay (including sabbaticals and severance pay), outplacement assistance, company cars, chauffeured limousines, security systems, company planes and yachts, executive dining rooms, physical fitness programs, legal services, tax assistance, liberal expense accounts, club membership, season tickets, credit cards, and

Diversity Counts
In Building a Family-Friendly Benefits Package

More and more companies recognize that they need family-friendly benefits to successfully recruit and retain good employees and to maintain high productivity. In a nutshell, family-friendly benefits are benefits options that make it easier for parents of young children to be productive workers. Such benefits are increasingly mandatory in a decade in which about two-thirds of the new entrants into the work force will be women and in which about 60% of working men have working wives.[92] Many benefits already described in this chapter may in fact be considered family-friendly benefits options; a summary of family-friendly options includes:

1. *Building an on-site or near-site day care facility.* Some firms, such as a Hewlett-Packard electronics plant in Santa Rosa, California, have built such facilities. Construction costs can range from $500,000 to $1,000,000 and the center may need a steady supply of at least 75 children to be cost-effective. On the other hand, close proximity to the workplace makes such sites very popular with employees.

2. *Partially funding or subsidizing a near-site day care facility.* Doing so can avoid many of the costs, liabilities, and management problems of on-site centers while providing many of the advantages of a dedicated facility for the firm's employees.

3. *Providing a dependent care resource and referral service for employees.* With this very popular service employers pay a small per-employee fee ($9 to $30) to contract with a referral service that provides dependent care information to employees. The referral service might advise not just on child care but on elder care needs and services, too.

4. *Subsidizing dependent care costs of employees.* Some employers reimburse a percentage of employee dependent care costs, sometimes up to 100%, depending on the company.

5. *Providing, arranging for, or subsidizing temporary and emergency dependent care.* Breakdowns in child care arrangements represents one of the biggest reasons parents lose time from work.[93] Some employers therefore help employees by reimbursing them for child care expenses stemming from emergency or nonroutine events; some even provide all or partial payment to fund special activities such as summer camps for older children.

6. *Offering flextime, job sharing, and work-at-home arrangements.* Work arrangements discussed elsewhere in this book such as flexible work schedules can help reduce child care conflicts and make it easier for employees to do their jobs.

7. *Allowing use of employee leave days for care of sick children.* Many companies now allow extra days of paid sick leave for care of sick dependents. Others let employees use paid vacation time in small increments such as half-days to facilitate taking children to doctors' appointments or caring for sick dependents.

8. *Offering paid and/or extended leave for mothers and/or fathers after the arrival of a child.* Many employers are offering generous paid leave to mothers and fathers after the birth or adoption of a child, or for serious family medical problems, thus going beyond the strict requirements of the Family and Medical Leave Act.

9. *Allowing new mothers to phase back to work.* In addition to the paid and unpaid leave benefits, some companies let the new mother phase back to work, perhaps by working only partial days or partial weeks at first.[94]◆

children's education. As you can see, employers have many ways of making their hard-working executives' lives as pleasant as possible!

Indeed, this tendency continues in the face of growing populist sentiment and despite a decade of corporate downsizings, restructurings, and more restrictive tax laws.[89] Some of the most visible status perks such as executive apartments and suites are more rare as are company planes and full-time chauffeurs. However, two-thirds of companies still provide executives with personal or leased automobiles, over half provide supplemental life insurance, half set aside reserved parking spots, and half pay for executives' annual physical exams.[90] And more than 32% of surveyed companies now cover their CEO's spouse's travel expenses.[91]

Flexible Benefits Programs

flexible benefits program
Individualized plans allowed by employers to accommodate employee preferences for benefits.

"Variety is the spice of life," the saying goes. This applies very well to company benefits, since the benefits that one worker finds attractive may be unattractive to another. As a result, there is a trend toward **flexible benefits programs** that permit employees to develop individualized benefits packages for themselves by choosing the benefits options they prefer.

Employee Preferences for Various Benefits

Two researchers conducted a study that provides some insight into employee preferences for various benefits.[95] They mailed questionnaires listing seven possible benefit options to 400 employees of a midwestern public utility company. Completed questionnaires were received from 149 employees (about 38% of those surveyed). The seven benefit options were as follows:

1. A five-day workweek with shorter working days of 7 hours and 35 minutes.
2. A four-day workweek consisting of 9 hours and 30 minutes each day.
3. Ten Fridays off each year with full pay. This includes ten three-day weekends per year in addition to any three-day weekends previously scheduled.
4. Early retirement through accumulating ten days per year until retirement age. The retirement age will be 65 minus the number of accumulated days. Full pay will continue until age 65 is reached.
5. Additional vacation of two weeks per year with full pay, added to the present vacation.
6. A pension increase of $75 per month.
7. Family dental insurance fully paid for by the company.

Finally, employees were also asked to show their relative preference for a pay increase of 5% in addition to any general wage increase negotiated.

Results Two extra weeks of vacation was clearly the most preferred benefit, while the pay increase was second. Overall, the shorter workday was by far the least preferred benefit option.

But this is not the full story; the employee's age, marital status, and sex influenced his or her choice of benefits. For example, younger employees significantly favored the family dental plan over older employees. Younger employees also showed a greater preference for the four-day workweek. As might be expected, preference for the pension option increased significantly with employee age. Married workers showed more preference for the pension increase and for the family dental plan than did single workers. The preference for the family dental plan increased sharply as the number of dependents increased. In addition, the survey did not include health care benefits (which are a major concern to all employees today) as a benefit option.

Because employees do have different preferences for benefits, an increasing number of employers let employees individualize their benefits plans.[96]

The Cafeteria Approach

The terms *flexible benefits plan* and *cafeteria benefits plan* are generally used synonymously. Flexible benefits plans were initially called cafeteria plans because (as in a cafeteria) employees could spend their benefits allowances on a choice of benefits options. Over the years, *flexible* replaced *cafeteria,* although under the Internal Revenue Code regulations, the term *cafeteria* continues to be used.[97]

The idea is to allow the employee to put together his or her own benefit package, subject to two constraints. First, the employer must carefully limit total cost for each total benefits package. Second, each benefit plan must include certain nonoptional items. These include, for example, Social Security, worker's compensation, and unemployment insurance.

Subject to these two constraints, employees can pick and choose from the available options. Thus, a young parent might opt for the company's life and dental insurance plans, while an older employee opts for an improved pension plan. The list of possible options might include many of the benefits discussed in this chapter: vacations, insurance benefits, pension plans, educational services, and so on.

As an example, a flexible plan was instituted at IDS Financial Services, a Minneapolis-based American Express subsidiary. The 2,500 IDS employees covered by the plan automatically got core benefits including minimum life insurance, a number of vacation days based upon years of service, short-term disability that pays 100% of salary and gradually drops to 70% over time, long-term disability that begins after a 150-day absence, and an attendance bonus that is earned when no health-related time off is taken during the year. However, the company also contributed 5% of salary that the employee can use toward any one or a combination of three options: One choice is to put all or part of the 5% in a tax-deferred savings plan. (For the first 3% the employee puts in, the company will add another 2.5%). A second option is to take all or part of the 5% as cash. Option 3 is to put a portion of the entire credit toward extra benefits including medical coverage, life insurance, long-term disability, and vacation (employees can buy up to five days).[98]

Advantages and disadvantages of flexible benefit programs are summarized in Figure 14.5.[99] The flexibility is of course the main advantage. One problem is that implementing a cafeteria plan can involve substantial clerical and administrative costs. Each employee's benefits have to be carefully priced and periodically updated, and even a medium-sized firm would have to computerize the administration of its plan.[100] Although most employees favor flexible benefits, many don't like to spend time choosing among available options, and many choose the wrong ones. Various firms have developed computerized games such as one called "FlexSelect." This is a user-friendly interactive program for personal computers that helps employees make choices under a flexible benefits program.[101]

Flexible benefits plans are increasingly popular, so we may assume that the pros far outweigh the cons. One survey found that 27% of the firms responding had flexible benefits plans, with another 11% planning to add them.[102]

Computers and Benefits Administration

Whether it is a flexible benefits plan or some other, computers play an important role in benefits administration. For even a smaller company with 40 to 50 employees, the administrative problems of keeping track of the benefits status of each employee can be a time-consuming task as employees are hired and separated, and as they utilize or want to change their benefits. Even a fairly straight-

Figure 14.5
Advantages and Disadvantages of Flexible Benefit Programs

Source: Milkovich and Newman, *Compensation* (Burr Ridge, IL: Irwin, 1993), p. 405.

ADVANTAGES

1. Employees choose packages that best satisfy their unique needs.
2. Flexible benefits help firms meet the *changing* needs of a *changing* work force.
3. Increased involvement of employees and families improves understanding of benefits.
4. Flexible plans make introduction of new benefits less costly. The new option is added merely as one among a wide variety of elements from which to choose.
5. Cost containment—the organization sets the dollar maximum. Employee chooses within that constraint.

DISADVANTAGES

1. Employees make bad choices and find themselves not covered for predictable emergencies.
2. Administrative burdens and expenses increase.
3. Adverse selection—employees pick only benefits they will use. The subsequent high benefit utilization increases its cost.
4. Subject to nondiscrimination requirements in Section 125 of the Internal Revenue Code.

---

forward problem like keeping track of who is eligible for vacations and when becomes a chore when a lot of employees are involved. As a result, most companies at least make use of some sort of benefits spreadsheet (see the accompanying box) to facilitate tracking benefits. Others use packaged software to update information like vacation eligibility and to trigger, say, a memo to a supervisor when one of his or her subordinates is overdue for some time off.

Keeping Employees Informed   Computers are also being used to inform employees about their benefits and to answer routine questions that might otherwise go unasked or take up a human resource manager's time.[103] Such questions include: "In which option of the medical plan am I enrolled?" "Who are my designated beneficiaries for the life insurance plan?" "If I retire in two years, what will

Figure 14.6
Employee Benefits Menu

Source: Anthony J. Barra, "Employees Keep Informed with Interactive KIOSKs," *Personnel Journal* (October 1988), p. 46. Reprinted with permission.

Note: With "Benefits Window" employees use an interactive computer display to look up information about their benefits.

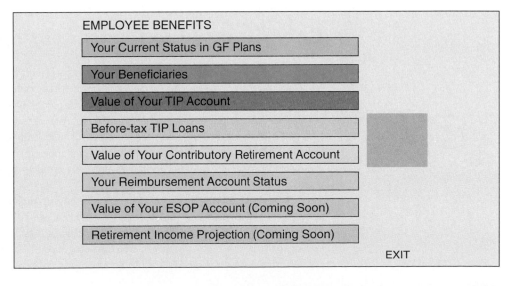

EMPLOYEE BENEFITS

Your Current Status in GF Plans

Your Beneficiaries

Value of Your TIP Account

Before-tax TIP Loans

Value of Your Contributory Retirement Account

Your Reimbursement Account Status

Value of Your ESOP Account (Coming Soon)

Retirement Income Projection (Coming Soon)

EXIT

Companies want to control benefits costs. One prerequisite is to be fully aware of how much the benefits offered are actually costing the company on an ongoing basis. A benefits spreadsheet will provide this information.

The spreadsheet should list the following, all in separate columns: each employee (by name or number), the job code (so you can compare benefits by job category in response to ERISA requirements); pay rate (annual, monthly, or hourly, since subsequent spreadsheet formulas will then calculate the appropriate rate for the benefit being considered); department (if you wish to compare departments or divisions); and each benefit. In order to accurately track your current liabilities for benefits accrued but not used, list separate columns for liability and use of these benefits.

For example, suppose you want a report on accrued vacations. In the liability column, calculate the accumulation minus use, times current hourly rate of pay. It is this column that will highlight how costly it is to allow employees to accumulate vacation or sick leave from year to year. If an employee accrues at a rate of $10 an hour now but does not use the vacation time until retirement, the cost of those hours could easily double or treble, as his or her pay rises.◆

be my monthly retirement income?" and "What is the current balance in my company savings plan?"

At General Foods Corporation employees use a computer system called Benefits Window, which gives employees the capability of easily looking up information about their benefits at centrally located interactive kiosks situated around the facilities. As illustrated in Figure 14.6, employees can key in their Social Security numbers and then identify such basic plan items as their beneficiaries, the value of their thrift investment plan (TIP) accounts, the value of their contributory retirement accounts, and the value of their ESOP accounts.

Small Business Applications

Benefits and Employee Leasing

Switching to an employee leasing arrangement can facilitate benefits management. Leasing firms arrange to have all the employer's employees transferred to the employee leasing firm's payroll. The employee leasing firm thus becomes the legal employer and handles all employee-related paperwork. This usually includes recruiting, hiring, paying tax liabilities (Social Security payments, unemployment insurance, and so on), as well as day-to-day details like performance appraisals (with the assistance of the on-site supervisor). However, it is with respect to benefits management that employee leasing is often most advantageous.

The most serious personnel problem many smaller employers face is getting insurance. Even group rates for life or health insurance can still be quite high when only 20 or 30 employees are involved. This is where employee leasing comes in. Remember that the leasing firm is the legal employer of your employees. Therefore, the employees are absorbed into a much larger insurable group, along with other employers' former employees. The bottom line is that the employee leasing company can often provide benefits smaller companies cannot obtain at anywhere near as favorable a cost if at all. A small-business owner may thereby be able to get insurance for its people that it couldn't otherwise afford. Furthermore, there will be some instances in which an employee leasing arrangement actually costs an employer virtually nothing. The leasing firm's fee may be more than outweighed by the reduced benefits cost to the employer, plus the in-house labor costs savings gained by letting the leasing company handle HRM.[104]

Employee leasing may sound too good to be true, and it often is. Many employers are understandably uncomfortable letting a third party become the legal employer of their employees (who literally have to be terminated by the employer and rehired by the leasing firm). There is also the matter of the somewhat erratic history of some employee leasing firms, a number of which have gone out of business after apparently growing successfully for several years. Such a business failure leaves the original employer with the need to hire back all its employees, and the problem of finding new insurance carriers to take on the job of insuring these "new" employees. The original insurance plan may have prevented the original insurer from cutting off services to the employer's employees. But if the health history of your employees has taken a turn for the worse, it may be hard to repurchase insurance at any price. Furthermore, Congress is continually tinkering with the tax code in such a way as to reduce the attractiveness of employee leasing's insurance benefits.

If you decide to use a leasing firm, there are several common-sense guidelines to follow. Of course, check the prospective leasing firm with your local Better Business Bureau. Get a full list of local clients so you can completely verify the leasing firm's references. Furthermore:[105]

Employee leasing is a relatively specialized field, given its legal and tax code ramifications. Therefore, work with a leasing firm that specializes in leasing rather than one that offers leasing as only part of its services.

Choose a financially stable and well-managed leasing firm. You should try to check the firm's capitalization and credit ratings. Also look at the number of years it has been in business.

Look for a firm that provides benefits at least as good as or better than those you now offer.

Make sure the firm pays its bills. If the leasing firm does not pay its insurance premiums on time, it could be a catastrophe for your firm. The leasing firm may be the legal entity responsible for the payments. However, from a practical point of view, it is your employees who will be left without insurance, and this will turn into a problem for your firm.

Finally, review the firm's policies. Remember that most leasing firms will not just administer your own firm's personnel policies. Instead they will institute their own personnel policies (regarding, for instance, performance appraisals, periodic reviews for raises, and so on). It is, therefore, important to ensure their personnel policies are consistent with yours and that any inconsistencies are worked out before the transition. ◆

Building Employee Commitment

Example of a Benefits Program

FedEx is a good example of how benefits can help foster high employee commitment.[106]

The firm's retirement benefits are exceptional. They actually consist of several plans to help the employee prepare for his or her retirement. The pension plan, profit-sharing plan, and employee stock ownership plan (as well as company-sponsored savings plans) combine to provide employees with a good income at retirement. The firm's pension plan alone provides employees with a fixed percentage of their salary. The normal retirement benefit payable at age 60 is 2% of the employee's final average pay times the employee's years of credited service (up to 25 years). This means that an employee's pension benefit at age 60 with 25 years of service with the company will be 50% of the person's final average pay. Final average pay is the average of the total compensation received during the highest-paid five consecutive years of the employee's last 15 years before retirement or disability. And that, according to the firm's head of personnel, means highest average total pay, including overtime and incentives.

All full-time permanent or part-time employees who have completed at least three consecutive months of employment with Federal Express can also participate in the firm's employee stock purchase plan. This lets them purchase Federal Express stock without commission through payroll deductions in an amount varying from 1% to a maximum of 10% of their total salary. These deductions accumulate for a designated period, at the end of which time Federal Express purchases the shares of stock for all participants.

There's more. The firm's tuition refund program lets any permanent employee with one year of continuous service receive financial reimbursement up to a maximum annual amount for his or her continuing education. Employees earn two weeks of vacation after one year with the firm, three weeks after five years, four weeks after ten years, and five weeks of vacation after twenty years with Federal Express.

But for some employees the best is last. Federal Express participates with other airlines that offer interline benefits in a discount travel program. Permanent employees who have completed a minimum of six months of continuous service are eligible to participate. And in a benefit that most employers would find hard to match, permanent employees are eligible to use FedEx's aircraft jump seats for free travel. Permanent employees may travel for personal or business purposes and make their arrangements through the jump seat reservations office in Memphis, which takes the request by phone and confirms it. There is also a computerized system called "Free Bird" that lets employees make the reservations themselves. Then they just have to be at the airport at least two hours prior to the flight, and away they go. ◆

Chapter Review

Summary

1. The financial *incentives* we discussed are usually paid to specific employees whose work is above standard. Employee *benefits*, on the other hand, are available to all employees based on their membership in the organization. We discussed four types of benefit plans: pay supplements, insurance, retirement benefits, and services.

2. Supplemental pay benefits provide pay for time not worked. They include unemployment insurance, vacation and holiday pay, severance pay, and supplemental unemployment benefits.

3. Insurance benefits are another type of employee benefit. Worker's compensation, for example, is aimed at ensuring prompt income and medical benefits to work accident victims or their dependents regardless of fault. Most employers also provide group life insurance and group hospitalization, accident, and disability insurance.

4. Two types of retirement benefits were discussed: Social Security and pensions. Social Security does not just cover retirement benefits but survivor's and disability benefits as well. There are three basic types of pension plans: group, deferred profit

sharing, and savings plans. One of the critical issues in pension planning is vesting the money that employer and employee have placed in the latter's pension fund, which cannot be forfeited for any reason. ERISA basically ensures that pension rights become vested and protected after a reasonable amount of time.

5. Most employers also provide benefits in the form of employee services. These include food services, recreational opportunities, legal advice, credit unions, and counseling.

6. Surveys suggest two conclusions regarding employees' preferences for benefits. First, time off (such as two extra weeks' vacation) seems to be the most preferred benefit. Second, the employee's age, marital status, and sex clearly influence his or her choice of benefits. (For example, younger employees were significantly more in favor of the family dental plan than were older employees.) This suggests the need for individualizing the organization's benefit plans.

7. The cafeteria approach allows the employee to put together his or her own benefit plan, subject to total cost limits and the inclusion of certain nonoptional items. Several firms have installed cafeteria plans; they require considerable planning and computer assistance.

Key Terms

benefits
supplemental pay benefits
unemployment insurance
sick leave
severance pay
supplemental unemployment benefits
worker's compensation
group life insurance
health maintenance organization (HMO)

Preferred Provider Organizations (PPOs)
Pregnancy Discrimination Act (PDA)
Social Security
pension plans
defined benefit pension plan
defined contribution plan
deferred profit-sharing plan

vesting
Employee Retirement Income Security Act (ERISA)
Pension Benefits Guarantee Corporation (PBGC)
golden offerings
early retirement window
employee assistance plan (EAP)
flexible benefits program

Discussion Questions and Exercises

1. You are applying for a job as a manager and are at the point of negotiating salary and benefits. What questions would you ask your prospective employer concerning benefits? Describe the benefits package you would try to negotiate for yourself.

2. Explain how you would go about minimizing your organization's unemployment insurance tax.

3. Explain how ERISA protects employees' pension rights.

4. In this chapter we presented findings concerning the preferences by age, marital status, and sex for various benefits. What are these findings and how would you make use of them if you were a human resource manager?

5. What is "portability"? Why do you think it is (or isn't) important to a recent college graduate?

6. Working individually or in groups, compile a list of the perks available to the following individuals: the head of your local airport; the president of your college or university; the president of a large company in your area. Do they all have certain perks in common? What do you think accounts for any differences?

7. Working individually or in groups, contact insurance companies that offer workers' compensation insurance and compile a list of their suggestions for reducing workers' compensation costs. What seem to be their main recommendations?

8. You are the HR consultant to a small business with about 40 employees. At the present time they offer only 5 days vacation, 5 paid holidays, and legally mandated benefits such as unemployment insurance payments. Develop a list of other benefits you believe they should offer, along with your reasons for suggesting them.

RUNNING CASE: Carter Cleaning Company
The New Benefit Plan

Carter Cleaning Centers has traditionally provided only legislatively required benefits for its employees. These include participation in the state's unemployment compensation program, Social Security, and worker's compensation (which is provided through the same insurance carrier that insures the stores for such hazards as theft and fire). The principals of the firm—Jack, Jennifer, and their families—have individual family-supplied health and life insurance.

At the present time, Jennifer can see several potential problems with the company's policies regarding benefits and services. First, she wants to do a study to determine whether similar companies' experiences with providing health and life insurance benefits suggest they enable these firms to reduce employee turnover and perhaps pay lower wages. Jennifer is also concerned with the fact that at the present time the company has no formal policy regarding vacations or paid days off or sick leave. Informally, at least, it is understood that employees get one week vacation after one year's work, but in the past the policy regarding paid vacations for days such as New Year's Day and Thanksgiving Day has been very inconsistent. Sometimes employees who had been on the job only two or three weeks were paid fully for one of these holidays, while at other times

employees who had been with the firm for six months or more had been paid for only half a day. Jennifer knows that this policy must be made more consistent.

She also wonders whether it would be advisable to establish some type of day care center for the employees' children. She knows that many of the employees' children either have no place to go during the day (they are preschoolers) or have no place to go after school, and she wonders whether a benefit such as day care would be in the best interests of the company.

Questions

1. Draw up a policy statement regarding vacations, sick leave, and paid days off for Carter Cleaning Centers.

2. What are the advantages and disadvantages to Carter Cleaning Centers of providing its employees with health, hospitalization, and life insurance programs?

3. How should Jennifer go about determining whether a day care center would be advisable for the company?

CASE INCIDENT: Sick Leave in Spring Valley

Slashes in federal aid to cities, a decline in the revenue from a 5% sales tax, and higher costs for everything from cleaning supplies to wages had brought hard times to Spring Valley. The combination of these factors made it seem impossible for Robert Donizetti, the city manager, and the budget committee of the city council to provide a balanced budget for the city.

Situated in a northwestern state, Spring Valley had a population of 12,000, a declining one that matched its declining revenue. In casting about for means to finance the small city's operations, Donizetti saw few opportunities for increasing revenue. In the past year one of the city's chief employers, the Acme Manufacturing Company, had been

forced to close its local factory, and all parts of the local economy had been affected by the national business recession. Hence, Donizetti went carefully over departmental budgets seeking ways to cut costs and eliminate waste.

One area in which Donizetti decided savings could be effected was through policy changes concerning sick leave. The city's work force consisted of only about 150 full-time employees, and figures in Donizetti's office showed that sick leave in the past six years averaged 7.34 days per year per employee. Not only was this costly in dollars in terms of Spring Valley's budget, but it also meant a loss of labor efficiency and productivity. Donizetti's statistics showed that female and older employees used more sick leave than males and younger workers. Donizetti prepared the following tables of sick leave averages by age and sex for the budget committee:

SICK LEAVE IN SPRING VALLEY BY SEX, 1990–1995

Year	Male	Female
1990	6.1	7.9
1991	5.9	7.7
1992	6.4	8.4
1993	6.3	8.7
1994	6.5	8.5
1995	6.8	8.9

SICK LEAVE IN SPRING VALLEY BY AGE, 1990–1995

Year	Under 30	Over 30
1990	5.1	6.8
1991	5.3	8.4
1992	5.7	8.1
1993	5.5	7.7
1994	5.8	8.3
1995	5.6	8.6

Spring Valley had not had many labor conflicts. Employee relations were handled through the human resource director, William Danforth, and the City Employees' Association, whose president was Jessica Blum. With respect to sick leave, the city had in recent years agreed to include in it family care, doctor appointments, and emergency time off for such events as funerals.

After a study of the problem, Donizetti recommended that the City Employees' Association and the human resource department together devise a sick leave incentive program to act as a deterrent to sick leave abuse, and as an equitable plan for the different uses of sick leave.

On June 6 the human resource department presented its proposal. Under its plan, employees would be reimbursed on February 1 of each year for 20% of the sick leave credits accumulated during the past year. An employee would have to have built up 45 sick leave days in order to draw cash payments, a move intended to reduce turnover in employment in the city.

The City Employees' Association made a counterproposal that included a choice by the employee to consider unused sick leave as vacation time or else to triple it and add it to retirement service. One hundred percent of unused days would be diverted to retirement.

The main point of contention at this stage concerned the percentage of sick leave credit for which an employee might be reimbursed. The city offered no alternative to the 20% yearly reimbursement, while the employees demanded that a 100% retirement-related incentive be adopted. After several fruitless attempts at negotiation, the two parties agreed to present the problem to a fact finder. His or her findings and suggestions for resolution of the issues would be used as a basis for further negotiations. The fact finder conducted private hearings with both parties and submitted a report on July 15.

Questions

1. Assume that you are the fact finder in the case. Analyze the sick leave problem in Spring Valley and propose a plan that is equitable to both parties.

2. If you were the city manager entrusted with pursuing the best interests of the city, which provisions in the proposal would you accept and which would you attempt to change?

3. Assume that you are the union negotiator. Which provisions would you accept and which would you attempt to change?

Source: Adapted from *Practicing Public Management: A Casebook* by C. Kenneth Meyer et al. Copyright © 1983 by St. Martin's Press, Inc., and used with permission of the publisher.

 Human Resource Management Simulation

Your organization offers meager fringe benefits to its employees. These benefits are currently 11% of wages and include Social Security tax (FICA); unemployment insurance; a low-benefit, high-deductible health care plan; and worker's compensation insurance. Your team will need to assess your firm's fringe benefits and decide what new benefits are needed. Although your budget constraints will make large improvements impossible, do not let this keep you from making progress toward a better benefit program for your employees. A cafeteria plan is also available.

Video Case

Workers' Compensation: Overcompensating?

This videocase highlights the problems many employers are having in keeping up with the sharp rise in workers' compensation costs and in benefits costs overall. As business owner Dennis Maroney says in the videocase, his firm's workers' compensation costs quadrupled in just about three years—from over $100,000 in 1991 to over $400,000 in 1993. Maroney and the others in this videocase argue that much of this increase stems from the greater number of workers filing claims not only for things like slips and falls, but for work-related stress, too.

Questions

1. The videocase questions whether workers should be asked to foot some of the bill for their work-related medical expenses. Discuss whether or not you think this is a good idea and why you take that position.

2. The videocase seems to suggest that recessions and layoffs may contribute to the number of workers' comp claims filed. Do you think that may be a valid observation, and, if so, why would that be the case?

3. If you were the HR manager for your company, what steps would you recommend to reduce your employer's workers' compensation claims?

4. Based on what you saw in the videocase, how would you recommend reining in the rapid rise in workers' compensation premiums?

Source: Wall Street Journal Report, *Overcompensating?* Show No. 519-3, September 5, 1992.

Take It to the Net

We invite you to visit the Dessler page on the Prentice Hall Web site at:
http://www.prenhall.com/~dessler
for the monthly Dessler update, and for this chapter's World Wide Web exercise.

Notes

1. Based on Frederick Hills, Thomas Bergmann, and Vida Scarpello, *Compensation Decision Making* (Fort Worth: The Dryden Press, 1994), p. 424. See also L. Kate Beatty, "Pay and Benefits Break Away from Tradition," *HR Magazine,* Vol. 39, No. 11 (November 1994), pp. 63–68.
2. Morton Grossman and Margaret Magnus, "The Boom in Benefits," *Personnel Journal* (November 1988), pp. 51–59; "Employee Benefits in Smaller Firms," Bureau of National Affairs, *Bulletin to Management,* June 27, 1991, pp. 196–197.
3. This is based on Bonnie De Clark, "Cutting Unemployment Insurance Costs," *Personnel Journal,* Vol. 62 (November 1983), pp. 868–870.
4. K. Matthes, "In Pursuit of Leisure: Employees Want More Time Off," *HR Focus,* no. 7 (1992).
5. Richard Henderson, *Compensation Management* (Englewood Cliffs: Prentice-Hall, 1994), p. 556.
6. Matthes, "In Pursuit of Leisure."
7. Henderson, *Compensation Management,* p. 555.
8. Miriam Rothman, "Can Alternatives to Sick Pay Plans Reduce Absenteeism?" *Personnel Journal,* Vol. 60 (October 1981), pp. 788–791; Richard Bunning, "A Prescription for Sick Leave," *Personnel Journal,* Vol. 67, no. 8 (August 1988), pp. 44–49.
9. This is based on Margaret Meiers, "Parental Leave and the Bottom Line," *Personnel Journal* (September 1988), pp. 108–115.
10. Dawn Gunch, "The Family Leave Act: A Financial Burden?" *Personnel Journal* (September 1993), p. 49.
11. See, for example, Kirk Maldonado, "Questions and Answers Regarding the Family and Medical Leave Act of 1993," *Benefits Law Journal,* Vol. 7, no. 1 (Spring 1994), pp. 73–87. See also Edward Lee Isler, Peter Turza, and John Seeley, "Impact of the Family and Medical Leave Act on Employee Benefits," *Benefits Law Journal,* Vol. 7, no. 3 (Autumn 1994), pp. 271–289.

12. *San Francisco Chronicle,* June 2, 1987, p. 10.
13. Joseph Famularo, *Handbook of Modern Personnel Administration* (New York: McGraw-Hill, 1972), pp. 51–62.
14. Richard Henderson, *Compensation Management* (Reston, VA: Reston, 1979), p. 250. For an explanation of how to reduce worker's compensation costs, see Betty Strigel Bialk, "Cutting Worker's Compensation Costs," *Personnel Journal,* Vol. 66, no. 7 (July 1987), pp. 95–97.
15. Henderson, *Compensation Management,* p. 90. Also see Bureau of National Affairs, "Worker's Compensation Total Disability Benefits by State," (1989), pp. 172–173, for a list showing worker's compensation by state.
16. "Worker's Compensation and ADA," *BNA Bulletin to Management,* August 6, 1992, p. 248.
17. See, for example, Bialk, "Cutting Workers' Compensation Costs," pp. 95–97.
18. Robert E. Sibson, *Wages and Salaries: A Handbook for Line Managers* (New York: American Management Association, 1967), p. 235.
19. "Employee Benefits in Small Firms," *Bureau of National Affairs Bulletin to Management,* June 27, 1991, pp. 196–197.
20. Richard Gisonny and Michael Langan, "EEOC Provides Guidance on Application of ADA on Health Plans," *Benefits Law Journal,* Vol. 6, no. 3 (Autumn 1993), pp. 461–467.
21. Johnathan Mook, "The ADA and Employee Benefits: A Regulatory and Litigation Update," *Benefits Law Journal,* Vol. 7, no. 4 (Winter 1994–95), pp. 407–429.
22. Rita Jain, "Employer-Sponsored Dental Insurance Eases the Pain," *Monthly Labor Review* (October 1988), p. 18. "Employee Benefits," *Commerce Clearing House Ideas and Trends in Personnel,* January 23, 1991, pp. 9–11.
23. Ibid., p. 23.
24. Bureau of National Affairs, *Bulletin to Management,* December 23, 1982, p. 1; "TEFRA—The Tax Equity and Fiscal Responsibility Act of 1982," *Personnel,* Vol. 59 (November–December 1982), p. 43.
25. A.N. Nash and S.J. Carroll, Jr., "Supplemental Compensation," in *Perspectives on Personnel: Human Resource Management,* in Herbert Heneman III and Donald Schwab, eds. (Homewood, IL: Irwin, 1978), p. 223.
26. Thomas Snodeker and Michael Kuhns, "HMOs: Regulations, Problems, and Outlook," *Personnel Journal,* Vol. 60 (August 1981), pp. 629–631.
27. Frederick Hills, Thomas Bergmann, and Vida Scarpello, *Compensation Decision Making* (Fort Worth: The Dryden Press, 1994), p. 137.
28. George Milkovich and Jerry Newman, *Compensation* (Burr Ridge, IL: Irwin, 1993), p. 445.
29. "Health Care Costs Continue to Climb," *BNA Bulletin to Management,* February 6, 1992, p. 33.
30. Hewitt Associates, "Health Care Costs Becoming Shared Responsibility," *News and Information,* June 21, 1984. See also, *Health Care Cost Containment* (New York: William Mercer-Meidinger, 1984), as discussed in *Compensation Review* (Fourth Quarter 1984), pp. 8–9; and Thomas Paine, "Outlook for Compensation and Benefits: 1986 and Beyond," Hewitt Associates, October 30, 1985. See also John Parkington, "The Trade-off Approach to Benefits Cost Containment: A Strategy to Increase Employee Satisfaction," *Compensation and Benefits Review,* Vol. 19, no. 1

(January–February 1987), pp. 26–35; Hewitt Associates, "Employer-Sponsored Medical Plans Designed to Make Employees Better Health Care Consumers, Study Says," *News and Information,* July 28, 1989 (100 Half Day Road, Lincolnshire, IL 60015); Janet Norwood, "Measuring the Cost and Incidence of Employee Benefits," *Monthly Labor Review,* Vol. 111, no. 8 (August 1988), pp. 3–8; Robert C. Penzkover, "Health Incentives at Quaker Oats," *Personnel Journal,* Vol. 68, no. 3 (March 1989), pp. 114–118; Anne Skagen, "Managing Health Care Costs," Part III, "Focus on Case Management," *Compensation and Benefits Review,* Vol. 20, no. 6 (November–December 1988), pp. 56–63; Hewitt Associates, *News and Information,* February 6, 1990, and "Health Care Cost Sharing: Coating the Pill," *BNA Bulletin to Management,* March 10, 1994, p. 73; and "Requiring Employers to Share Health Care Costs Results in Lower Use of All Health Care Services . . .", *BNA Bulletin to Management,* March 10, 1994, p. 79.
31. Robert Jenkins, "The Strengths and Scope of Managed Health Care Today," *Employment Relations Today* (Spring 1992), pp. 43–50.
32. "Managing Health Care Costs," *BNA Bulletin to Management,* August 27, 1992, p. 272.
33. Hewitt Associates, "Employers Trim Future Health Care Costs by Keeping Employees 'Well,'" *News and Information,* June 7, 1984; and Morton Grossman and Margaret Magnus, "The Boom in Benefits," *Personnel Journal* (November 1988), pp. 51–55. See also "Could Wellness Programs Thrive?" *Personnel,* Vol. 65, no. 3 (March 1988), pp. 6–7, lists specific examples of wellness programs now in place. See also Marjorie Blanchard, "Wellness Programs," *Personnel Journal,* Vol. 68, no. 5 (May 1989), pp. 30–31, for examples of wellness program benefits, and BNA, "Benefit Cost Containment Trend Continues," 1989, p. 2, for examples of how companies are proceeding.
34. Don Bohl, "Company Bets That Wellness Incentives Plus Preventive Care Will Contain Health Care Costs," *Compensation and Benefits Review* (July–August 1993), pp. 20–23.
35. Shari Caudron, "Teaming up to Cut Health-Care Costs," *Personnel Journal* (September 1993), p. 104. See also "Fraudulent Health Plans Targeted," *BNA Bulletin to Management,* April 14, 1994, p. 120.
36. Ibid., p. 107. See also Ann Knoll, "Top Ten Mistakes Made in Employee Health Benefit Plans," *Compensation and Benefits Review* (January–February 1994), pp. 54–58.
37. The following is based on Michael Gomez, "Managing Health Care Costs," Part I, "The Dilemma of AIDS," *Compensation and Benefits Review* (September–October 1988), pp. 23–31; and Nancy Breuer, "AIDS Issues Haven't Gone Away," *Personnel Journal,* Vol. 71, no. 1 (January 1992), pp. 47–49. See also Kato Keeton, "AIDS Related Attitudes Among Government Employees: Implications for Training Programs," *Review of Public Personnel Administration* (Spring 1993), pp. 65–80.
38. "AIDS Insurance Costs Examined," *BNA Bulletin to Management,* July 23, 1992, p. 226.
39. Quoted from Gomez, "Managing Health Care Costs," p. 28.
40. Ibid., p. 31.
41. This is based on Thomas C. Billet, "Managing Health Care

Cost," Part II, "Coping with Mental Health," *Compensation and Benefits Review* (September–October 1988), pp. 32–36.

42. Ibid., pp. 35–36.

43. This is based on Paul Greenlaw and Diana Foderaro, "Some Practical Implications of the Pregnancy Discrimination Act," *Personnel Journal*, Vol. 58 (October 1979), pp. 677–681. See also Commerce Clearing House, "Supreme Court Says Giving Women Pregnancy Leave Is Lawful Even in the Case Where Men Receive No Disability Leave Whatever," *Ideas and Trends in Personnel*, January 23, 1987, pp. 9–10.

44. Jerome B. Cohen and Arthur Hanson, *Personnel Finance* (Homewood, IL: Irwin, 1964), pp. 312–320. See also BNA, January 14, 1988, pp. 12–13. This article explains changes in the Social Security law and presents an exhibit showing how to estimate your Social Security benefits.

45. See, for example, Henderson, *Compensation Management*, pp. 289–290; Famularo, *Handbook*, pp. 37.1–37.9.

46. Avy Graham, "How Has Vesting Changed Since Passage of Employee Retirement Income Security Act?" *Monthly Labor Review* (August 1988), pp. 20–25.

47. Ibid., p. 20.

48. Sibson, *Wages and Salaries*, p. 234. For an explanation of how to minimize employee benefits litigation related to pension and health benefits claims, see Thomas Piskorski, "Minimizing Employee Benefits Litigation Through Effective Claims Administration Procedures," *Employee Relations Law Journal*, Vol. 20., no. 3 (Winter 1994/95), pp. 421–431.

49. For a discussion of demographic trends with specific reference to average age of employees, see, for example, D. Quinn Mills, "Human Resources in the 1980's," *Harvard Business Review*, Vol. 58 (July–August 1979), pp. 154–163.

50. *The Economist*, August 5, 1978, p. 57.

51. For a discussion of the pros and cons of early retirement, see, for example, Jeffrey Sonnenfelt, "Dealing with the Aging Workforce," *Harvard Business Review*, Vol. 57 (November–December 1978), pp. 81–92.

52. A.F. Ehrbar, "Those Pension Plans Are Even Weaker Than You Think," *Fortune*, Vol. 94, no. 5 (November 1977), pp. 104–107, discussed in H. Chruden and A. Sherman, Jr. *Personnel Management* (Cincinnati: South-Western 1980), pp. 500–501. See also Carroll Roarty, "How Merabank Lowered Pension Costs Without Lowering Morale," *Personnel Journal*, Vol. 66, no. 11 (November 1987), pp. 64–71, which relates how this bank changed its profit-sharing and pension plans and saved money without sacrificing morale.

53. See Irwin Tepper, "Risk vs. Return in Pension Fund Investment," *Harvard Business Review*, Vol. 56 (March–April 1977), pp. 100–107, and William Rupert, "ERISA: Compliance May Be Easier Than You Expect and Pay Unexpected Dividends," *Personnel Journal*, Vol. 55 (April 1976). For a discussion of a recent survey regarding retirement planning and the challenges that employers face in planning retirement policy for the year 2000, see Diane Filipowski, "Retirement Planning in the Year 2000," *Personnel Journal* (July 1993), p. 34.

54. Kathleen Murray, "How HR Is Making Pensions Portable," *Personnel Journal* (July 1993), pp. 36–46.

55. Steven Allen, Robert Clark, and Ann McDermed, "Pensions, Bonding, and Lifetime Jobs," *The Journal of Human Resources*, Vol. 28, no. 3 (Summer 1993), pp. 463–481.

56. Ibid.

57. Murray, "How HR Is Making Pensions Portable," p. 43.

58. Robert Paul, "The Impact of Pension Reform on American Business," *Sloan Management Review*, Vol. 18 (Fall 1976), pp. 59–71. See also John M. Walbridge, Jr., "The Next Hurdle for Benefits Manager: Section 89," *Compensation and Benefits Review*, Vol. 20, no. 6 (November–December 1988), pp. 22–35.

59. Henderson, *Compensation Management*, p. 292. Actually, ERISA applies not just to pensions but to various other benefits including retiree medical benefits as well. For a discussion, see Michael Langan, "ERISA After Twenty Years: Past, Present, and Future," *Benefits Law Journal*, Vol. 7, no. 3 (Autumn 1994), pp. 255–270.

60. Bureau of National Affairs, "Tax Reform Act: Major Changes in Store for Compensation Programs," *Bulletin to Management*, October 9, 1986, p. 1.

61. In fact, unfunded pension liabilities of American firms have continued to grow. "Pension Survey: Unfunded Liabilities Continue to Grow," *Business Week*, August 25, 1980, pp. 94–97. See also James Benson and Barbara Suzaki, "After Tax Reform," Part III, "Planning Executive Benefits," *Compensation and Benefits Review*, Vol. 20, no. 2 (March–April 1988), pp. 45–57; and BNA, "Post-Retirement Benefits Impact of FASB New Accounting Rule," February 23, 1989, p. 57.

62. For a discussion see Milton Zall, "Understanding the Risks to Pension Benefits," *Personnel Journal* (January 1992), pp. 62–69.

63. Robert Arnott and Peter Bernstein, "The Right Way to Manage Your Pension Fund," *Harvard Business Review* (January–February 1988), pp. 95–102. See also *401(k): Cash or Deferred Arrangements*, Coopers & Lybrand (USA), 1991.

64. A task force of consultants from William A. Mercer-Meidinger Hansen, Inc. "The Omnibus Budget Reconciliation Act of 1987: What It Means to Pensions and Employee Benefits," *Compensation and Benefits Review* (March–April 1988), pp. 14–32.

65. Judith Mazo, "Another Compliance Challenge for Employers: The Retirement Equity Act," *Personnel*, Vol. 62, no. 2 (February 1985), pp. 43–49. See also Deborah Nikkel, "HIRS Implementation: A Systematic Approach," *Personnel*, Vol. 62, no. 2 (February 1985), pp. 66–69. See also Jack Schechter, "The Impact of Tax Reform on Employee Benefits: A Half Time Report," *Personnel*, Vol. 65, no. 1 (January 1988), pp. 46–51.

66. "Trends," *BNA Bulletin to Management*, May 7, 1992, p. 143.

67. "Plan Design and Experience in Early Retirement Windows and in Other Voluntary Separation Plans," prepared by the staff of Hewitt Associates, 1986. See also Eugene Seibert and Jo Anne Seibert, "Retirement Windows," *Personnel Journal*, Vol. 68, no. 5 (May 1989), pp. 30–31, examples of wellness program benefits.

68. Marco Colosi, Philip Rosen, and Sara Herrin, "Is Your Early Retirement Package Courting Disaster?" *Personnel Journal* (August 1988), pp. 59–67.

69. *Paolillo v. Dresser Industries*, 821F.2d81 (2d cir. 1987).
70. See also Eugene Seibert and Jo Anne Seibert, "Look into Window Alternatives," *Personnel Journal* (May 1989), pp. 80–87.
71. Arthur Silbergeld, "Release Agreements Must Comply with the Older Workers' Benefit Protection Act," *Employment Relations Today* (Winter 1992/93), pp. 457–460.
72. See Henderson, *Compensation Management*, pp. 336–339. See also Lewis Burger, "Group Legal Service Plans: A Benefit Whose Time Has Come," *Compensation and Benefits Review*, Vol. 18, no. 4 (July–August 1986), pp. 28–34.
73. Richard T. Hellan, "Employee Assistance: An EAP Update: A Perspective for the '80s," *Personnel Journal*, Vol. 65, no. 6 (1986), p. 51.
74. See Dale Masi and Seymour Friedland, "EAP Actions & Options," *Personnel Journal* (June 1988), pp. 61–67.
75. Based on ibid. See also Harry Turk, "Questions—and Answers: Avoiding Liability for EAP Services," *Employment Relations Today* (Spring 1992), pp. 111–114.
76. "Employee Benefit Costs," Bureau of National Affairs, *Bulletin to Management*, January 16, 1992, pp. 12–14.
77. The Research Staff of Hewitt Associates, *Innovative Benefits*, Hewitt Associates, 160 Bloor Street East, Toronto, Ontario.
78. Jennifer S. MacLeod, "Meeting the Needs of Today's Working Parents," *Employment Relations Today*, Vol. 13, no. 2 (Summer 1986), p. 127. See also Susan Velleman, "A Benefit to Meet Changing Needs: Child-Care Assistance," *Compensation and Benefits Review*, Vol. 19, no. 3 (May–June 1987), pp. 54–58; and June O'Neill, "A Flexible Work Force: Opportunities for Women," *Journal of Labor Relations*, Vol. 13, no. 1 (Winter 1992), pp. 67–72.
79. *Dun's Review* (July 1981), p. 49. See also Velleman, "A Benefit to Meet Changing Needs," pp. 54–62; Bureau of National Affairs, "Child Care Benefits Offered by Employers," *Bulletin to Management*, March 17, 1988, pp. 84–85. For a discussion of other employer child care options and the costs and problems of implementing them, see Caroline Eichman and Barbara Reisman, "How Small Employers Are Benefitting from Offering Child Care Assistance," *Employment Relations Today* (Spring 1992), pp. 51–62.
80. "Employers and Child Care: Establishing Services Through the Workplace," Women's Bureau, U.S. Department of Labor, Washington, D.C., 1982. See also BNA, "Special Survey on Child Care Assistance Programs," *Bulletin to Management*, March 26, 1987. Donald J. Peterson and Douglas Massengill, "Child Care Programs Benefit Employers, Too," *Personnel*, Vol. 65, no. 5 (May 1988), pp. 58–62; and Toni A. Campbell and David E. Campbell, "Employers and Child Care," *Personnel Journal*, Vol. 67, no. 4 (April 1988), pp. 84–87.
81. Lorri Johnson, "Effectiveness of an Employee-Sponsored Child Care Center," *Applied H.R.M. Research*, Vol. 2, no. 1 (Summer 1991), pp. 38–67.
82. Commerce Clearing House, "As the Population Ages, There Is Growing Interest in Adding Elder Care to the Benefits Package," *Ideas and Trends*, August 21, 1987, pp. 129–131.
83. Kelli Earhart, R. Dennis Middlemist, and Willie Hopkins, "Elder Care: An Emerging Employee Assistance Issue," *Employee Assistance Quarterly*, Vol. 8, no. 3 (1993), pp. 1–10.
84. For another example, see "Elder Care: A Maturing Benefit," *BNA Bulletin to Management*, February 20, 1992, pp. 50, 55.
85. Mary Zippo, "Subsidized Employee Transportation: A Three Way Benefit," *Personnel*, Vol. 57 (May–June 1980), pp. 40–41.
86. Hewitt Associates, *Survey of Educational Reimbursement Programs*, 1984.
87. Bruce Ellig, *Executive Compensation—A Total Pay Perspective* (New York: McGraw-Hill, 1982), p. 141.
88. Lindroth, "Inflation, Taxes, and Perks," p. 939.
89. Matthew Budman, "The Persistence of Perks," *Across the Board* (February 1994), pp. 44–46.
90. Ibid., p. 44.
91. Ibid., p. 45.
92. This is based on Shirley Hand and Robert Zawacki, "Family-Friendly Benefits: More Than a Frill," *HR Magazine* (October 1994), pp. 79–84.
93. Caroline Eichman, "Surveys Reveal Needs for Work/Family Benefits—By Both Employees and Employers," *Employment Relations Today* (Winter 1992/93), pp. 389–395.
94. For a further discussion see, for example, Douglas Hall and Victoria Parker, "The Role of Workplace Flexibility in Managing Diversity," *Organizational Dynamics*, Vol. 22, no. 1 (1993), pp. 5–18.
95. J. Brad Chapman and Robert Ottermann, "Employee Preference for Various Compensation and Fringe Benefit Options" (Berea, OH: ASPA Foundation, 1975). See also, William White and James Becker, "Increasing the Motivational Impact of Employee Benefits," *Personnel* (January–February 1980), pp. 32–37; and Barney Olmsted and Suzanne Smith, "Flex for Success!" *Personnel*, Vol. 66, no. 6 (June 1989), pp. 50–55.
96. Ibid.; Albert Cole, "Flexible Benefits Are a Key to Better Employee Relations," *Personnel Journal* (January 1983), pp. 49–53. See also, Lance Tane, "Guidelines to Successful Flex Plans: Four Companies' Experiences," *Compensation and Benefits Review*, Vol. 17 (July–August 1985), pp. 38–45; Peter Stonebraker, "A Three-Tier Plan for Cafeteria Benefits," *Personnel Journal*, Vol. 63, no. 12 (December 1984), pp. 50–53; Commerce Clearing House, "Flexible Benefits: Will They Work for You?" Chicago, 1983; and George F. Dreher, Ronald A. Ash, and Robert D. Bretz, "Benefit Coverage and Employee Cost: Critical Factors in Explaining Compensation Satisfaction," *Personnel Psychology*, Vol. 41, no. 2 (Summer 1988), pp. 237–254; and Melissa Barringer and Olivia Mitchell, "Workers' Preferences Among Company-Provided Health Insurance Plans," *Industrial and Labor Relations Review*, Vol. 48, no. 1 (October 1994), pp. 141–152.
97. Henderson, *Compensation Management*, p. 568.
98. Barbara Anne Soloman, "The Change to 'Flexible': No Easy Task," *Personnel*, Vol. 62, no. 5 (May 1985), pp. 10–12. Note that flexible benefits plans are not the same as flexible spending accounts. A flexible spending account is a benefit offered by an employer whereby it allows the employee to pay for certain expenses with pretax dollars; this essentially means that the employee gets a tax deduction for these expenses even before filing a tax return. For a discussion, see "Flexible Spending Ac-

Figure 15.1
Percent of Employees Participating in Selected Employee Benefit Plans

Adapted from William J. Wiatrowski, "Employee Benefits for Union and Nonunion Workers," *Monthly Labor Review*, February 1994, p. 35.

*Difference significant at 95%.

Benefit	Percent	
	Union	Nonunion
Paid leave		
Holidays	95	91
Lunch	10	7
Funeral leave	86	78
Military	59	52
Sick leave	55	71
Unpaid leave		
Maternity	41	36
Paternity	33	23
Insurance plans		
Sickness and accident	71	36
Wholly employer financed	60	25
Long-term disability	28	44
Wholly employer financed	26	33
Partly employer financed	2	11
Medical care	91	81
Individual		
Wholly employer financed	63	34
Partly employer financed	28	47
Family		
Wholly employer financed	52	18
Partly employer financed	39	63
Dental care	70	57
Individual		
Wholly employer financed	56	29
Partly employer financed	15	28
Family		
Wholly employer financed	49	19
Partly employer financed	21	38
Life insurance		
Wholly employer financed	86	78
Retirement income plans		
All retirement	90	74
Defined benefit pension	86	50
Wholly employer financed	81	48
Partly employer financed	5	2
Defined contribution	33	52
Savings and thrift	16	33

The table title: Percent of Employees Participating in Selected Employee Benefit Plans, Unions versus Nonunion; Full-Time Employees in Medium and Large Private Establishments, 1991* correlation between job satisfaction and voting for union representation in one study. Notice that dissatisfaction with issues such as job security and wages was most strongly correlated with a vote for the union, while the employees' satisfaction with factors such as supervisor and type of work was less so.[8]

The author of this study contends that dissatisfaction alone will not automatically lead to unionization. First, she says, dissatisfied employees must believe they are without the ability to influence a change in the conditions causing the dissatisfaction. Then a large enough group of employees would have to believe it could improve things through collective action. Thus, dissatisfied employees who believe the union will be instrumental in achieving their goals present a potent combination.[9] Indeed, union instrumentality—the workers' belief that the union can successfully get the improvements the worker seeks—is consistently a predictor of pro-union voting.[10]

As stated earlier, the urge to unionize often boils down to the belief on the workers' part that it is only through unity that they can get their fair share of the pie and also protect themselves from the arbitrary whims of management. Here is how one writer describes the reasons behind the early unionization of automobile workers:

> *In the years to come, economic issues would make the headlines when union and management met in negotiations. But in the early years the rate of pay was not the major complaint of the autoworkers. . . . Specifically, the principal grievances of the autoworkers were the speed-up of production and the lack of any kind of job security. As production tapered off, the order in which workers were laid off was determined largely by the whim of foremen and other supervisors. The system encouraged workers to curry favor by doing personal chores for supervisory employees—by bringing them gifts or outright bribes. The same applied to recalls as production was resumed. The worker had no way of knowing when he would be laid off, and had no assurance when, or whether, he would be recalled. . . . Generally, what the workers revolted against was the lack of human dignity and individuality,*

Figure 15.2
Early Auto Plant Working Conditions
Note: In addition to the back-breaking work required in the early auto plants, health hazards were an ever-present danger. Lighting was poor, dust often filled the air, and unguarded moving belts led to many injuries.

Source: Warner Pflug, *The UAW in Pictures* (Detroit: Wayne State University Press, 1971), p. 14.

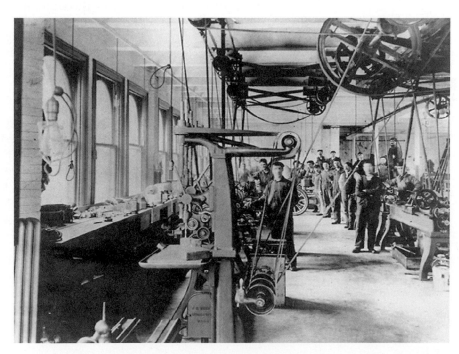

and a working relationship that was massively impersonal, cold, and nonhuman. They wanted to be treated like human beings—not like faceless clockcard numbers.[11] [See Figure 15.2 for a picture of early auto plant working conditions.][12]

What Do Unions Want?
What Are Their Aims?

closed shop
A form of union security in which the company can hire only union members. This was outlawed in 1947 but still exists in some industries (such as printing).

union shop
A form of union security in which the company can hire nonunion people but they must join the union after a prescribed period of time and pay dues. (If they do not, they can be fired.)

agency shop
A form of union security in which employees who do not belong to the union must still pay union dues on the assumption that union efforts benefit all workers.

open shop
Perhaps the least attractive type of union security from the union's point of view, the workers decide whether or not to join the union; and those who join must pay dues.

We can generalize by saying that unions have two sets of aims, one for *union security* and one for *improved wages, hours, working conditions,* and *benefits* for their members.

Union Security   First and probably foremost, unions seek to establish security for themselves. They fight hard for the right to represent a firm's workers and to be the *exclusive* bargaining agent for all employees in the unit. (As such, they negotiate contracts for all employees *including* those not members of the union.) Five types of union security are possible.

1. **Closed shop.**[13] The company can hire only union members. This was outlawed in 1947 but still exists in some industries (such as printing).
2. **Union shop.** The company can hire nonunion people but they must join the union after a prescribed period of time and pay dues. (If not, they can be fired.)
3. **Agency shop.** Employees who do not belong to the union still must pay union dues on the assumption that the union's efforts benefit *all* the workers.
4. **Open shop.** It is up to the workers whether or not they join the union—those who do not, do not pay dues.
5. Maintenance of membership arrangement. Employees do not have to belong to the union. However, *union members* employed by the firm *must* maintain membership in the union for the contract period.

Improved Wages, Hours, and Benefits for Members   Once their security is assured, unions fight to better the lot of their members—to improve their wages, hours, and working conditions, for example. The typical labor agreement also gives the union a role in other HR activities, including recruiting, selecting, compensating, promoting, training, and discharging employees.

The AFL-CIO

What It Is   The American Federation of Labor and Congress of Industrial Organizations (AFL-CIO) is a voluntary federation of about 100 national and international labor unions in the United States. It was formed by the merger of the AFL and CIO in 1955, with the AFL's George Meany as its first president. For many people, it has become synonymous with the word *union* in the U.S.

There are about 2.5 million workers who belong to unions that are not affiliated with the AFL-CIO. Of these workers, about one half belong to the largest independent union, the United Auto Workers (about 1 million members).[14] The formerly independent Teamsters union, with about 2 million members, rejoined the AFL-CIO in 1987.

The Structure of the AFL-CIO   There are three layers in the structure of the AFL-CIO (and other U.S. unions). First, there is the *local* union. This is the union the worker joins and to which he or she pays dues. It is also usually the local union that signs the collective bargaining agreement determining the wages and working conditions. The local is in turn a single chapter in the *national* union. For example, if you were a typesetter in Detroit, you would belong to the local union there, but the local union is one of hundreds of local chapters of the International Typographical Union with headquarters in Colorado Springs.

The third layer in the structure is the *national federation,* in this case, the AFL-CIO. This federation is composed of about 100 national and international unions, which in turn comprise more than 60,000 local unions.

Most people tend to think of the AFL-CIO as the most important part of the labor movement, but it is not. The AFL-CIO itself really has little power, except what it is allowed to exercise by its constituent national unions. Thus, the president of the teachers' union wields more power in that capacity than in his capacity as a vice president of the AFL-CIO. Yet as a practical matter, the AFL-CIO does act as a spokesperson for labor, and its president, Lane Kirkland, has accumulated political clout far in excess of a figurehead president.

Unions and the Law

Background

Until about 1930 there were no special labor laws. Employers were not required to engage in collective bargaining with employees and were virtually unrestrained in their behavior toward unions: The use of spies, blacklists, and the firing of agitators were widespread. "Yellow dog" contracts, whereby management could require nonunion membership as a condition for employment, were widely enforced. Most union weapons—even strikes—were illegal.

This one-sided situation lasted from the Revolution to the Great Depression (around 1930). Since then, in response to changing public attitudes, values, and economic conditions, labor law has gone through three clear changes: from "strong encouragement" of unions, to "modified encouragement coupled with regulation," and finally to "detailed regulation of internal union affairs."[15]

Period of Strong Encouragement: The Norris-LaGuardia Act (1932) and the National Labor Relations or Wagner Act (1935)

Norris-LaGuardia Act
This law marked the beginning of the era of strong encouragement of unions and guaranteed to each employee the right to bargain collectively "free from interference, restraint, or coercion."
National Labor Relations Board (NLRB)
The agency created by the Wagner Act to investigate unfair labor practice charges and to provide for secret-ballot elections and majority rule in determining whether or not a firm's employees want a union.

The **Norris-LaGuardia Act** set the stage for a new era in which union activity was encouraged. It guaranteed to each employee the right to bargain collectively "free from interference, restraint, or coercion." It declared yellow dog contracts unenforceable. And it limited the courts' abilities to issue injunctions for activities such as peaceful picketing and payment of strike benefits.[16]

Yet this act did little to restrain employers from fighting labor organizations by whatever means they could muster. Therefore, the National Labor Relations (or Wagner) Act was passed in 1935 to add teeth to the Norris-LaGuardia Act. It did this by (1) banning certain unfair labor practices; (2) providing for secret-ballot elections and majority rule for determining whether a firm's employees were to unionize; and (3) creating the **National Labor Relations Board (NLRB)** for enforcing these two provisions.

Unfair Employer Labor Practices The **Wagner Act** deemed "statutory wrongs" (but not crimes) five unfair labor practices used by employers:

1. It is unfair for employers to "interfere with, restrain, or coerce employees" in exercising their legally sanctioned right of self-organization.

National Labor Relations (or Wagner) Act

This law banned certain types of unfair labor practices and provided for secret-ballot elections and majority rule for determining whether or not a firm's employees want to unionize.

2. It is an unfair practice for company representatives to dominate or interfere with either the formation or the administration of labor unions. Among other management actions found to be unfair under practices 1 and 2 are bribing employees, using company spy systems, moving a business to avoid unionization, and blacklisting union sympathizers.

3. Companies are prohibited from discriminating in any way against employees for their legal union activities.

4. Employers are forbidden to discharge or discriminate against employees simply because the latter file unfair practice charges against the company.

5. Finally, it is an unfair labor practice for employers to refuse to bargain collectively with their employees' duly chosen representatives.

An unfair labor practice charge is filed (see Figure 15.3) with the National Labor Relations Board. The board then investigates the charge and determines if formal action should be taken. Possible actions include dismissal of the complaint, request for an injunction against the employer, or an order that the employer cease and desist.

From 1935 to 1947 Union membership increased quickly after passage of the Wagner Act in 1935. Other factors such as an improving economy and aggressive union leadership contributed to this as well. But by the mid-1940s the tide had begun to turn. Largely because of a series of massive postwar strikes, public policy began to shift against what many viewed as the union excesses of the times. The stage was set for passage of the Taft-Hartley Act of 1947.

Period of Modified Encouragement Coupled With Regulation: The Taft-Hartley Act (1947)

Taft-Hartley Act

Also known as the Labor Management Relations Act, this law prohibited union unfair labor practices and enumerated the rights of employees as union members. It also enumerated the rights of employers.

The **Taft-Hartley** (or Labor Management Relations) **Act** reflected the public's less enthusiastic attitudes toward unions. It amended the National Labor Relations (Wagner) Act with provisions aimed at limiting unions in four ways: (1) by prohibiting unfair union labor practices, (2) by enumerating the rights of employees as union members, (3) by enumerating the rights of employers, and (4) by allowing the president of the United States to temporarily bar national emergency strikes.

Unfair Union Labor Practices The Taft-Hartley Act enumerated several labor practices that unions were prohibited from engaging in:

1. First, unions were banned from restraining or coercing employees from exercising their guaranteed bargaining rights. For example, some specific union actions the courts have held illegal under this provision include stating to an antiunion employee that he or she will lose his or her job once the union gains recognition; issuing patently false statements during union organizing campaigns; and making threats of reprisal against employees subpoenaed to testify against the union at NLRB hearings.

2. It is also an unfair labor practice for a union to cause an employer to discriminate in any way against an employee in order to encourage or discourage his or her membership in a union. In other words, the union cannot try to force an employer to fire a worker because he or she doesn't attend union meetings, opposes union policies, or refuses to join a union. There is one exception to this. Where a closed or union shop prevails (and union membership is therefore a prerequisite to employment), the union may demand discharge for a worker who fails to pay his or her initiation fees and dues.

**Figure 15.3
NLRB Form 501: Filing
an Unfair Labor
Practice Charge**

FORM EXEMPT UNDER
44 U.S.C. 3512

FORM NLRB 501
(2 81)

UNITED STATES OF AMERICA
NATIONAL LABOR RELATIONS BOARD
CHARGE AGAINST EMPLOYER

INSTRUCTIONS: File an original and 4 copies of this charge with NLRB Regional Director for the region in which the alleged unfair labor practice occurred or is occurring.	**DO NOT WRITE IN THIS SPACE**	
	CASE NO.	DATE FILED

1. EMPLOYER AGAINST WHOM CHARGE IS BROUGHT

a. NAME OF EMPLOYER	b. NUMBER OF WORKERS EMPLOYED	
c. ADDRESS OF ESTABLISHMENT *(street and number, city, State, and ZIP code)*	d. EMPLOYER REPRESEN-TATIVE TO CONTACT	e. PHONE NO.
f. TYPE OF ESTABLISHMENT *(factory, mine, wholesaler, etc.)*	g. IDENTIFY PRINCIPAL PRODUCT OR SERVICE	

h. THE ABOVE-NAMED EMPLOYER HAS ENGAGED IN AND IS ENGAGING IN UNFAIR LABOR PRACTICES WITHIN THE MEANING OF SECTION 8(a), SUBSECTIONS (1) AND ——————————————— OF THE NATIONAL
(list subsections)
LABOR RELATIONS ACT, AND THESE UNFAIR LABOR PRACTICES ARE UNFAIR LABOR PRACTICES AFFECTING COMMERCE WITHIN THE MEANING OF THE ACT.

2. BASIS OF THE CHARGE *(be specific as to facts, names, addresses, plants involved, dates, places, etc.)*

BY THE ABOVE AND OTHER ACTS, THE ABOVE-NAMED EMPLOYER HAS INTERFERED WITH, RESTRAINED, AND COERCED EMPLOYEES IN THE EXERCISE OF THE RIGHTS GUARANTEED IN SECTION 7 OF THE ACT.

3. FULL NAME OF PARTY FILING CHARGE *(if labor organization, give full name, including local name and number)*

4a. ADDRESS *(street and number, city, State, and ZIP code)*	4b. TELEPHONE NO.

5. FULL NAME OF NATIONAL OR INTERNATIONAL LABOR ORGANIZATION OF WHICH IT IS AN AFFILIATE OR CONSTITUENT UNIT *(to be filled in when charge is filed by a labor organization)*

6. DECLARATION

I declare that I have read the above charge and that the statements therein are true to the best of my knowledge and belief.

By ————————————————————   ————————————————————
   (signature of representative or person filing charge)   (title, if any)

Address ————————————   ————————————   ————————
                              (telephone number)   (date)

WILLFULLY FALSE STATEMENTS ON THIS CHARGE CAN BE PUNISHED BY FINE AND IMPRISONMENT
(U.S. CODE, TITLE 18, SECTION 1001)

3. It is an unfair labor practice for a union to refuse to bargain in good faith with the employer about wages, hours, and other employment conditions. Certain strikes and boycotts are also considered unfair union labor practices.

4. It is an unfair labor practice for a union to engage in "featherbedding." (Here an employer is required to pay an employee for services not performed.)

Rights of Employees The Taft-Hartley Act also protected the rights of employees against their unions. For example, many people felt that compulsory unionism violated the basic U.S. right of freedom of association. New right-to-work laws sprang up in 19 states (mainly in the South and Southwest). These outlawed labor contracts that made union membership a condition for keeping one's job. In New York, for example, many printing firms have union shops. There you can't work as a press operator unless you belong to a printers' union. In Florida such union shops—except those covered by the Railway Labor Act—are illegal. There printing shops typically employ both union and nonunion press operators. This provision also allowed an employee to present grievances directly to the employer (without going through the union) and required the employee's authorization before union dues could be subtracted from his or her paycheck.

Rights of Employers The Taft-Hartley Act also explicitly gave employers certain rights. First, it gave them full freedom to express their views concerning union organization. For example, you can as a manager tell your employees that in your opinion unions are worthless, dangerous to the economy, and immoral. You can even, generally speaking, hint that unionization and subsequent high-wage demands might result in the permanent closing of the plant but not its relocation. Employers can set forth the union's record in regard to violence and corruption, if appropriate, and can play upon the racial prejudices of workers by describing the union's philosophy toward integration. In fact, your only major restraint is that you must avoid threats, promises, coercion, and direct interference with workers who are trying to reach a decision. There can be no threat of reprisal or force or promise of benefit.[17]

The employer (1) cannot meet with employees on company time within 24 hours of an election or (2) suggest to employees that they vote against the union while they are at home or in the employer's office, although he or she can do so while in their work area or where they normally gather.

National Emergency Strikes The Taft-Hartley Act also allows the U.S. president to intervene in **national emergency strikes.** These are strikes (for example, on the part of steel firm employees) that might "imperil the national health and safety." The president may appoint a board of inquiry and, based on its report, apply for an injunction restraining the strike for 60 days. If no settlement is reached during that time, the injunction can be extended for another 20 days. During this last period, employees are polled in a secret ballot to ascertain their willingness to accept the employer's last offer.

Period of Detailed Regulation of Internal Union Affairs: The Landrum-Griffin Act (1959)

Landrum-Griffin Act
The law aimed at protecting union members from possible wrongdoing on the part of their unions.

In the 1950s, Senate investigations revealed unsavory practices on the part of some unions, and the result was the **Landrum-Griffin Act** (officially, the Labor Management Reporting and Disclosure Act). An overriding aim of this act was to protect union members from possible wrongdoing on the part of their unions. It also was an amendment to the National Labor Relations (Wagner) Act.

First, this law contains a bill of rights for union members. Among other things, this provides for certain rights in the nomination of candidates for union office. It also affirms a member's right to sue his or her union and ensures that no member can be fined or suspended without due process, which includes a list of specific charges, time to prepare defense, and a fair hearing.

This act also laid out rules regarding union elections. For example, national and international unions must elect officers at least once every five years, using some type of secret-ballot mechanism. And it regulates the kind of person who can serve as a union officer. For example, persons convicted of felonies (bribery, murder, and so on) are barred from holding union officer positions for a period of five years after conviction.

The Senate investigators also discovered flagrant examples of employer wrongdoing. Union agents had been bribed, and so-called "labor relations consultants" had been used to buy off union officers, for example. Such bribery had been a federal crime starting with the passage of the Taft-Hartley Act. But the Landrum-Griffin Act greatly expanded the list of unlawful employer actions. For example, companies can no longer pay their own employees to entice them not to join the union. The act also requires reports from unions and employers, covering such practices as the use of labor relations consultants.

Labor Law Today

The question of whether the courts and the NLRB are contributing to a more encouraging or discouraging climate for unions today is not entirely clear-cut.

On the one hand, some NLRB decisions favor unions. In one case known as the *Jean Country* case, a union and a shopping center took their case to the NLRB. The question was whether the union could picket a store (Jean Country) on private property in a shopping mall. Under the old rule that dated back to 1986, the NLRB would balance the union's right to engage in labor activity with the property owner's right to decide how the property should be used. It would then decide whose rights prevailed in that instance. Technicalities aside, in this case the NLRB basically modified its rule, thus making it easier for unions to show why their rights should prevail.[18]

On the other hand, many important recent NLRB and court decisions have gone against unions, and this could have the effect of weakening workers' union rights. For example, in one decision[19] the NLRB made it harder for workers adversely affected by outrageous violations to take legal action. It required that they seek administrative redress instead. In another decision,[20] the NLRB held it would no longer evaluate the impact of misleading employer campaign statements upon worker free choice in a union representation election.[21]

The Supreme Court's decision in *TWA* v. *Independent Federation of Flight Attendants* is an instance of a court's ruling strengthening management's hand. For the first time, the Supreme Court held that management can announce it will continue to operate during a strike, "and that employees in the bargaining unit who wish to work during the strike will be considered the permanent holders of any new jobs they fill, assuming they want to stay in those jobs."[22] Strikers who want to return to their previous jobs must wait for an opening to occur, said the Court. This may prove discouraging to union members considering a walkout, given the employer's right to also bring in outside replacements. In a 1992 case reminiscent of the *Jean Country* case, the Supreme Court held that union organizers do not have the right to trespass on private property to get their message to employees. As long as the employees are not inaccessible—as they would be if they lived on company property, for instance—the court said nonemployee union organizers would have to stay off the employer's property.[23] This means, said one NLRB member, that in the future unions will have to show "extreme difficulty" in reaching employees in order to gain access to private property.[24] The pendulum today seems to have swung a bit more toward discouragement of union activities. Clinton administration actions may change this.

Global HRM

Unions Go Global

Any company that thinks it can avoid the pressures of unionization by sending manufacturing and jobs abroad is sorely mistaken.[25] Today, as we've seen, all businesses are becoming increasingly globalized, and regional trade treaties like NAFTA will undoubtedly increase the amount of business more firms do abroad. This fact is not lost on unions, some of which are already directly and indirectly expanding their influence abroad.

Here are just a few examples:

U.S. unions are helping Mexican unions to organize, especially U.S.-owned factories. For example, the United Electrical Workers is subsidizing organizers at Mexico plants of the General Electric company.

When the Campbell Soup Company threatened to move some operations to Mexico, the Farm Labor Organizing Committee, a midwestern union, discouraged the move by helping its Mexican counterpart win a stronger contract, one that would have cost Campbell Soup higher wages if it made the move.

In 1991, Diamond Walnut Growers began permanently replacing striking employees. Their union, the International Brotherhood of Teamsters, gained the support of European unions and environmentalists who are running a European boycott that is hurting Diamond Walnut's exports.

U.S. unions gain several things by forming such alliances. By helping workers, (for example, in Mexico) unionize, they of course help to raise the living standards of local workers. In addition, they help to discourage corporate flight from the United States in search of low wages, and they help to solidify their own U.S. positions with the added leverage they get from having unions abroad to help them fight their corporate campaigns.◆

The Union Drive and Election

It is through the union drive and election that a union tries to be recognized to represent employees.[26] This process has five basic steps: (1) initial contact, (2) authorization cards, (3) hearing, (4) campaign, and (5) the election.

Step 1. Initial Contact

During the *initial contact* stage, the union determines the employees' interest in organizing, and an organizing committee is established.

The initiative for the first contact between the employees and the union may come from the employees, from a union already representing other employees of the firm, or from a union representing workers elsewhere. Sometimes a union effort starts with a disgruntled employee contacting the local union to learn how to organize his or her place of work. Sometimes, though, the campaign starts when a union decides it wants to expand to representing other employees in the firm or when the company looks like an easy one to organize. In any case, there is an initial contact between a union representative and a few employees.

Once an employer becomes a target, a union official usually assigns a representative to assess employee interest. The representative visits the firm to determine whether enough employees are interested to make a union campaign worthwhile. He or she also identifies employees who would make good leaders in the organizing campaign and calls them together to create an organizing committee. The objective here is to "educate the committee about the benefits of forming a union, the law and procedures involved in forming a local union, and the issues management is likely to raise during a campaign."[27]

The union must follow certain guidelines when it starts contacting employees. The law allows union organizers to solicit employees for membership as long as it doesn't endanger the performance or safety of the employees. Therefore, much of the contact often takes place off the job, for example, at home or at eating places near work. Organizers can also safely contact employees on company grounds during off hours (such as lunch or break time). Under some conditions, union representatives may solicit employees at their work stations, but this is rare. Yet, in practice, there will be much informal organizing going on at the workplace as employees debate the merits of organizing. In any case, this initial contact stage may be deceptively quiet. In some instances the first inkling management has of a union campaign is the distribution or posting of a handbill soliciting union membership.

Labor Relations Consultants   Labor relations consultants are increasingly having an impact on the unionization process, with both management and unions now being supplemented by trained outside advisors. These advisors may be law firms, researchers, psychologists, labor relations specialists, or public relations firms. In any case, their role is to provide advice and related services to both management and unions, not only when a vote is anticipated (although this is when most of them are used) but at other times as well. For the employer, the consultant's services may range from ensuring that the firm properly fills out routine forms, to managing the whole union campaign. Unions, on the other hand, may use public relations firms to improve their image or specialists to manage corporate campaigns aimed at pressuring the firm's shareholders and creditors into influencing management to agree to the union's demands.

An important element in organizing union drives is handing out literature to employees at the plant gate.

The use by management of consultants (who are often referred to disparagingly by unions as "union busters") has apparently grown tremendously over the past 25 years. A study by the AFL-CIO's Department of Organization and Field Services concluded, for example, that management consultants were involved in 85% of the elections they surveyed and that the consultant "ran the show" for the employers 72% of the time.[28] The widespread use of such consultants—only some of whom are actually lawyers—has raised the question of whether these consultants have advised their clients to engage in activities that are illegal or questionable under various labor laws. One tactic, for instance, is to delay the union vote with lengthy hearings at the NLRB. The longer the delay in the vote, it is argued, the more time the employer has to drill antiunion propaganda into the employees. During these delays employees who are not antiunion can be eliminated and the bargaining unit can

Information Technology and HR
Computers Assist Both Labor and Management

Both sides of labor-management relations may benefit from the use of computers. Management may track grievances to see where and on what subjects training is needed. Labor may find that computers provide new ways to assist members.

Management is able to track trends in grievances within any given time period for the whole company, a division or department, or a particular supervisor or group of supervisors. For example, the researcher might hypothesize that supervisors with less than one year of experience in their positions might generate more grievances than experienced supervisors. If this proves to be true, then either new supervisors should be trained before starting in the position or should be offered frequent training sessions during their first year. However, research might prove that in some departments, this hypothesis is not true. Thus, if there are a number of grievances from a large department, an investigation might reveal the need for (1) managerial training, probably defined by the subject of the grievances, (2) better communication on a topic (such as the importance of following safety rules), or (3) the development of a process that allows more input from employees before instituting new policies. Grievance topics may be coded for easy computer tracking and may incorporate more than one code.

Labor, too, can benefit from computerization. With the demographic changes in the workplace, labor is searching for new ways to meet the needs of its members and potential members. For example, computer-based networks nationwide would help to adjust the unemployment caused by having skills in one location and jobs in another. As Hallett suggests, unions could become "the single best source of information, training, standards, and individuals [with] specific skills and talents."[1] With the support of international unions, locals could be linked effectively and relatively inexpensively using telephone lines to provide this source of information, thus assuring their members a degree of job security.

For both management and labor, it is in the area of computerized costing that technology currently offers the best potential. As one expert put it

"Access to computer data banks has significantly shortened our research time prior to negotiations. And the application of software spreadsheets has made contract cost analysis a much easier and more accurate process. In the future of collective bargaining, more development of comptuter skills is a necessity."[2]

Computers are increasingly a necessity once negotiations start. For instance, as negotiators quickly review their demands, computerized spreadsheets let both sides estimate how the changes may impact their costs. Thus, the costs of, say, an additional holiday can be quickly estimated. ◆

[1]Geffrey J. Hallet, "Unions in Our Future?" *Personnel Administration,* Vol. 31, no. 4 (April 1986), pp. 40–94.
[2]Michael Carrell and Christina Heavrin, *Labor Relations and Collective Bargaining* (Englewood Cliffs: Prentice Hall, 1995), p. 340.

be packed with promanagement employees.[29] Other consultants are accused of advising employers to lie to the NLRB, for example, by backdating memoranda in order to convince the board that the wage increase being offered was decided months before the campaign ever began.[30] The ethics of the matter aside, any employers using such consultants are required to report their use.

Step 2. Obtaining Authorization Cards

In order for the union to petition the NLRB for the right to hold an election, it must show that a sizable number of employees may be interested in being organized. The next step is thus for union organizers to try to get the employees to sign

authorization cards
In order to petition for a union election, the union must show that at least 30% of employees may be interested in being unionized. Employees indicate this interest by signing authorization cards.

authorization cards. Thirty percent of the eligible employees in an appropriate bargaining unit must sign before an election can be petitioned.

During this stage, both union and management typically use various forms of propaganda. The union claims it can improve working conditions, raise wages, increase benefits, and generally get the workers better deals. Management need not be silent; it can attack the union on ethical and moral grounds and cite the cost of union membership, for example. Management can also explain its track record, express facts and opinions, and explain the law applicable to organizing campaigns and the meaning of the duty to bargain in good faith (if the union should win the election) to its employees. However, neither side can threaten, bribe, or coerce employees, and an employer may not make promises of benefit to employees or make unilateral changes in terms and conditions of employment that were not planned to be implemented prior to the onset of union organizing activity.

What Management Can Do   There are several steps management can take with respect to the authorization cards themselves. For example, the NLRB has ruled that "an employer may lawfully inform employees of their right to revoke their authorization cards, even when employees have not solicited such information." The employer can also distribute pamphlets which explain just how employees can revoke their cards.[31] However, management can go no further than explaining to employees the procedure for card revocation and furnishing resignation language. Any type of material assistance such as postage or stationery is prohibited. The employer also cannot check to determine which employees have actually revoked their authorization cards.

What can you do about educating employees who have not yet decided whether to sign their cards? Above all, it is an unfair labor practice to tell employees that they cannot sign a card or to give them the impression that it is against their best interests to do so. What you can do is explain the legal and practical consequences of signing or not signing. For example, management can prepare its supervisors to be able to explain what the card authorizes the union to do. This is important because most cards don't just authorize the union to petition an election. For example, the authorization card in Figure 15.4 actually does three things: It lets the union seek a representation election (it can be used as evidence that 30% of your employees have an interest in organizing); it designates the union as a bargaining representative in all employment matters; and it states the employee has applied for membership in the union and will be subject to union rules and bylaws. The latter is especially important; the union, for instance, may force the employee to picket and fine any member who does not comply with union instructions. Explaining the serious legal and practical implications of signing the card can thus be an effective management weapon.

Second, do not look through signed authorization cards if confronted with them by union representatives. Doing so could be construed as an unfair labor practice by the NLRB, which could view it as spying on those who signed. It could also later form the basis of a charge alleging discrimination due to union activity if someone who signed a card is subsequently disciplined. Examining signed cards could also give rise to a claim that the union should be recognized as the employees' bargaining representative without an election: The union could claim the employer no longer has a good faith doubt that a majority of the employees signed cards authorizing the union to represent them, since it saw the cards.

During this stage, unions can picket the company, subject to three constraints: (1) The union must file a petition for an election within 30 days after the start of picketing; (2) the firm cannot already be lawfully recognizing another

can even attack the union on ethical and moral grounds, while insisting that employees will not be as well off and may lose freedom. But neither side can threaten, bribe, or coerce employees.

Step 5. The Election

Finally the election can be held within 30 to 60 days after the NLRB issues its Decision and Direction of Election. The election is by secret ballot and the NLRB provides the ballots (see Figure 15.7), voting booth, and ballot box and counts the votes and certifies the results of the election.

The union becomes the employees' representative if it wins the election, and winning means getting a majority of the votes *cast, not* a majority of the workers in the bargaining unit. (It is also important to keep in mind that when an employer commits an unfair labor practice, a "no union" election may be reversed. As representatives of their employer, supervisors must therefore be very careful not to commit such "unfair" practices.)

How to Lose an NLRB Election

Of the 3,600 or so collective bargaining elections held recently, about half were lost by companies.[33] Yet according to a study by the University Research Center, many of these elections should probably not have been lost. According to expert Matthew Goodfellow, there is no sure way an employer can win an election. However, there are five sure ways an employer could lose one.

Figure 15.7
Sample NLRB Ballot

UNITED STATES OF AMERICA
National Labor Relations Board

OFFICIAL SECRET BALLOT

FOR CERTAIN EMPLOYEES OF

_____

Do you wish to be represented for purposes of collective bargaining by —

_____

MARK AN "S" IN THE SQUARE OF YOUR CHOICE

YES   NO

☐   ☐

DO NOT SIGN THIS BALLOT. Fold and drop in ballot box.
If you spoil this ballot return it to the Board Agent for a new one.

Reason 1. Asleep at the Switch   In 68% of the companies studied (those that lost to the union) executives were caught unaware, not having paid attention to symptoms of low employee morale. In these companies turnover and absenteeism had increased, productivity was erratic, and safety was poor. Grievance procedures were rarely used. When the first reports of authorization cards being distributed began trickling back to top managers, they usually responded with a knee-jerk reaction.

A barrage of one-way communications ensued in which top management bombarded workers with letters describing how the company was "one big family" and calling for a "team effort." As Goodfellow observes,

> *Yet the best strategy is to not be caught asleep in the first place:*

> *Overall, prudence dictates that management spend time and effort even when the atmosphere is calm testing the temperature of employee sentiments and finding ways to remove irritants. Doing that cuts down on the possibility that an election will ever take place. . . .*

Reason 2. Appointing a Committee   Of the losing companies, 36% formed a committee to manage the campaign. According to the expert, there are three problems in doing so:

1. Promptness is of the essence in an election situation, and committees are notorious for slow deliberation.
2. Most of the members of such a committee are neophytes so far as an NLRB situation is concerned. Their views therefore are mostly reflections of wishful thinking rather than experience.
3. A committee's decision is usually a homogenized decision, with everyone seeking to compromise on differences. The result is often close to the most conservative opinion—but not necessarily the most knowledgeable or most effective one.

This expert suggests instead giving full responsibility to a single decisive executive. This person should in turn be assisted by a human resource director and a consultant/advisor with broad experience in labor relations.

Reason 3. Concentrating on Money and Benefits   In 54% of the elections studied, the company lost because top management concentrated on the "wrong" issues: money and benefits. As this expert puts it:

> *Employees may want more money, but quite often if they feel the company treats them fairly, decently, and honestly, they are satisfied with reasonable, competitive rates and benefits. It is only when they feel ignored, uncared for, and disregarded that money becomes a major issue to express their dissatisfaction.*

Reason 4. Industry Blind Spots   The researcher found that in some industries employees felt more ignored and disregarded than in others. For example, in industries that are highly automated (such as paper manufacturing and automotive), there was some tendency for executives to regard hourly employees as "just cogs in the machinery," although this is changing today as firms such as Chrysler implement more quality-improvement programs. Here (as in reason 3) the solution is to begin paying more serious attention to the needs and attitudes of employees.

Reason 5. Delegating Too Much to Divisions or Branches   For companies with plants scattered around the country, unionization of one or more plants tends to lead to unionization of others. Organizing several of the plants gives the union a wedge in the form of a contract that can be used to tempt other plants' workers. Indeed, in the United States, United Kingdom, and several other countries the tendency is for increased decentralization and ". . . widespread reports of a shift to the plant level away from the company-wide agreements."[34]

Part of the solution here is to keep the first four "reasons" in mind and thereby keep those first few plants from being organized. Beyond that, firms with multiplant operations should not abdicate all decisions concerning personnel and industrial relations to plant managers. Effectively dealing with unionization—taking the "pulse" of the workers' attitudes, knowing what is bothering them, reacting appropriately when the union first appears, and so on—generally requires strong centralized guidance from the main office and its human resource staff.

The Supervisor's Role

Supervisors must be knowledgable about what they can and can't do to legally hamper organizing activities, lest they commit unfair labor practices. Such practices could (1) cause a new election to be held after your company has won a previous election, or (2) cause your company to forfeit the second election and go directly to contract negotiation. (In one case a plant superintendent reacted to a union's initial organizing attempt by prohibiting distribution of union literature in the plant's lunchroom. Since solicitation of off-duty workers in nonwork areas is generally legal, the company subsequently allowed the union to post union literature on the company's bulletin board and to distribute union literature in nonworking areas inside the plant. However, the NLRB still ruled that the initial act of prohibiting distribution of the literature was an unfair labor practice, one that was not "made right" by the company's subsequent efforts. The NLRB used the superintendent's action as one reason for invalidating an election that the company had won.[35]) To avoid such problems, employers should have rules governing distribution of literature and solicitation of workers and train supervisors in how to apply them.[36]

Rules Regarding Literature and Solicitation There are a number of steps an employer can take to legally restrict union organizing activity.[37]

> Nonemployees can always be barred from soliciting employees during their work time—that is, when the employee is on duty and not on a break. Thus, if the company cafeteria is open to whomever is on the premises, union organizers can solicit off-duty employees who are in the cafeteria but not the cafeteria workers (such as cooks) who are not on a break.

> Employers can usually stop employees from soliciting other employees for any purpose if one or both employees are on paid-duty time and not on a break.

> Most employers (not including retail stores, shopping centers, and certain other employers) can bar nonemployees from the building's interiors and work areas as a right of private property owners. In certain cases, nonemployees can also be barred from exterior private property areas such as parking lots—if there is a business reason (such as safety) and the reason is not just to interfere with union organizers.

> Employees can be denied access to interior or exterior areas that only if the employer can show that the rule is required for reasons of production, safety, or discipline. (However, in general, off-duty employees cannot be considered to have the same status as nonemployees. They therefore cannot be prohibited from remaining on the premises or returning to the premises unless this prohibition is also required for reasons of production, safety, or discipline.)

Such restrictions are only valid if they are not imposed in a discriminatory manner. For example, if employees are permitted to collect money for wedding, shower, and baby gifts, to sell Avon products or Tupperware, or to engage in other solicitation during their working time, the employer will not be able to lawfully prohibit them from union soliciting during work time. To do so would discriminate on the basis of union activity, which is an unfair labor practice. Here are two examples of specific rules aimed at limiting union organizing activity:

> "Solicitation of employees on company property during working time interferes with the efficient operation of our business. Nonemployees are not permitted to solicit employees on company property for any purpose. Except in break areas where both employees are on break or off the clock, no employee may solicit another employee during working time for any purpose."

> "Distribution of literature on company property not only creates a litter problem but also distracts us from our work. Nonemployees are not allowed to distribute literature on company property. Except in the performance of his or her job, an employee may not distribute literature unless both the distributor and the recipient are off the clock or on authorized break in a break area or off company premises. Special exceptions to these rules may be made by the company for especially worthwhile causes such as United Way, but written permission must first be obtained and the solicitation will be permitted only during break periods."[38]

Finally, remember that there are many more ways to commit unfair labor practices than just keeping union organizers off your private property. For example, one employer decided to have a cookout and paid day off two days before a union representation election. The NLRB held that this was too much of a coincidence and represented coercive conduct. The union had lost the first vote but won the second vote as a result.[39]

Guidelines for Employers Wishing to Stay Union-Free

In addition to establishing rules and training supervisors in their application, you can use several additional guidelines for preserving a union-free workplace including:

1. *Practice preventive employee relations.* Fair discipline policies, open worker management communications, and fair salaries, wages, and benefits can contribute to preserving a union-free workplace.

2. *Recognize the importance of location.* Unions have traditionally been weaker in the South and Southwest than in the North, Northeast, or Far West, for instance.

3. *Seek early detection.* Detect union organizing activity as early as possible, and remember that your best source is probably first-line supervisors. They should be trained to look for changes in employee behavior. In addition, you should look for direct signs of union activity such as posters, buttons, and authorization cards.

4. *Do not volunteer.* Obviously, never voluntarily recognize a union without a secret election supervised by the NLRB.

5. *Beware of the authorization cards.* As previously explained, authorization cards must be handled correctly. When confronted by the union submitting authorization cards, get another manager in as a witness and do not touch the cards (or, worse, count or examine them in any way). When the organizer leaves, call your lawyer.

6. *Present your case.* Again, present your case to your employees forcefully and relentlessly. Executives' speeches to employees during working hours, informal meetings in the dining areas, and informational letters are all good tools.

Information Technology and HR
Estimating Offers Costs with Computers

Management students, whether they ultimately work for management or labor, are usually introduced to gaming—computer simulations that answer what-if questions. Sometimes the simulations are complex strategies; sometimes they are as basic as looking at cash flow projections. These concepts may be applied to labor management negotiations. When labor suggests a 5% wage increase the first year, followed by 3% in each of the next two years, management counters with 3, 3, 5, understanding that their proposal will cost less over the course of the three years. However, costing out other benefits may not be as easily understood. Therefore, programs that rapidly calculate the direct and indirect cost of benefits offer the opportunity for more knowledgable bargaining.[1]

To quickly calculate the costs of offers or counteroffers, a simple table based on the percent of (1) each step in salary ranges, or (2) each employee's annual pay, or (3) a particular benefit can be created. For example, if each wage step is 4% higher than the one below, and the first step of each grade equals the middle step of the previous grade, simply changing the first grade's first step in the table of the wage plan will update it. Then by linking this table to the rate each employee is paid (keyed to that table), the new total cost is available. If an employee is paid at the rate of step 4, grade 3, a cell address next to that employee's name tells the company what is budgeted for that employee. If that employee has worked an average of 100 hours overtime each of the last three years, a formula would be placed next to the employee's name that includes the cell address plus the hourly rate (if the wage plan is not in hourly figures) times 100 (to represent the 100 hours).

If one side suggests that the benefits package should be raised by 7% to include so many dollars for child care, the negotiator should have available the number of employees who have expressed an interest in this benefit and how many children are involved as well as a range of possible costs of child care in the area. By combining this information with the current percentage of payroll assigned to benefit costs, it will be clear whether or not the 7% is a realistic figure of probable costs. The negotiator might be willing to give 5% and, with data of probable use and cost figured in, be able to negotiate a wording of the benefit that will better control costs, keeping them within the intended range.

Computers, then, help to prepare the negotiator for the bargaining sessions and could possibly shorten the time spent bargaining. If bargaining is done off-site, portable or laptop computers with 30- or 40-megabyte memories provide support.◆

[1]M. Steven Potash, "A Scientific Approach to Bargaining," *ABA Journal* (January 1986), p. 58.

12. Be sure as you make each bargaining move that you know its *relationship* to all other moves.
13. Measure each move against your *objectives*.
14. Pay close attention to the *wording* of every clause negotiated; words and phrases are often a source of grievances.
15. Remember that collective bargaining negotiations are, by their nature, part of a *compromise* process. There is no such thing as having all the pie.
16. Learn to *understand* people and their personalities.
17. Consider the impact of present negotiations on those in *future years*.

There are also several things negotiators can do to foster the trust on which many successful negotiations are based. Trust, to paraphrase one expert, means that "I trust you when I expect you to cooperate and not exploit me."[55] Trust-building behaviors include:

Show willingness to trust. Give indications of your own growing propensity to trust by not exploiting any moves made by the other negotiator and then by sending signals of your own intention to trust because of the benefits that might accrue to your own side from doing so.

Check understanding. Check the understanding of the other negotiator that the trusting signals are being correctly interpreted.

Reinforce the other party's willingness to trust. Continue to progressively work toward increasing the preparedness of the other negotiator to offer trust rather than be exploitive.

Indicate the adverse consequences of a failure to respond. Finally, and only if all the previous moves have failed to generate a willingness to offer trust, send signals as to the adverse consequences of trust being offered and not reciprocated.[56]

Impasses, Mediation, and Strikes[57]

Impasse Defined   In collective bargaining, an impasse occurs when the parties are not able to move further toward settlement. An impasse usually occurs because one party is demanding more than the other will offer. Sometimes an impasse can be resolved through a third party, a disinterested person such as a mediator or arbitrator. If the impasse is not resolved in this way, a work stoppage, or *strike,* may be called by the union to bring pressure to bear on management.[58]

Third-Party Involvement   Three types of third-party interventions are used to overcome an impasse: mediation, fact-finding, and arbitration. With **mediation** a neutral third party tries to assist the principals in reaching agreement. The mediator usually holds meetings with each party to determine where each stands regarding its position, and then this information is used to find common ground for further bargaining. The mediator is always a go-between. As such, he or she communicates assessments of the likelihood of a strike, the possible settlement packages available, and the like. The mediator does not have the authority to fix a position or make a concession.

In certain situations as in a national emergency dispute where the president of the United States determines that it would be a national emergency for a strike to occur, a *fact-finder* may be appointed. A fact-finder is a neutral party who studies the issues in a dispute and makes a public recommendation of what a reasonable settlement ought to be.[59] For example, presidential emergency fact-finding boards have successfully resolved impasses in certain critical transportation disputes.

Arbitration is the most definitive type of third-party intervention, since the arbitrator often has the power to determine and dictate the settlement terms. Unlike mediation and fact-finding, arbitration can guarantee a solution to an impasse. With binding arbitration, both parties are committed to accepting the arbitrator's award. With nonbinding arbitration, they are not. Arbitration may also be voluntary or compulsory (in other words, imposed by a government agency). In the United States, voluntary binding arbitration is the most prevalent.

Strikes   A strike is a withdrawal of labor, and there are four main types of strikes. An economic strike results from a failure to agree on the terms of a contract—from an impasse, in other words. Unfair labor practice strikes, on the other hand, are aimed at protesting illegal conduct by the employer. A **wildcat strike** is an unauthorized strike occurring during the term of a contract. A **sympathy strike** occurs when one union strikes in support of the strike of another.[60] Picketing is one of the first activities occurring during a strike. The purpose of picketing is to

mediation
Intervention in which a neutral third party tries to assist the principals in reaching agreement.

arbitration
The most definitive type of third-party intervention, in which the arbitrator usually has the power to determine and dictate the settlement terms.

wildcat strike
An unauthorized strike occurring during the term of a contract.
sympathy strike
A strike that takes place when one union strikes in support of the strike of another.

A strike, like the major league baseball strike of 1994, is an extreme response to failure to reach an agreement between labor and management.

inform the public about the existence of the labor dispute and often to encourage others to refrain from doing business with the struck employer.

Employers can make several responses when they become the object of a strike. One is to *shut down* the affected area and thus halt their operations until the strike is over. A second alternative is to *contract out* work during the duration of the strike in order to blunt the effects of the strike on the employer. A third alternative is for the employer to *continue operations,* perhaps using supervisors and other nonstriking workers to fill in for the striking workers. A fourth alternative is the *hiring of replacements* for the strikers. In an economic strike, such replacements can be deemed permanent and would not have to be let go to make room for strikers who decided to return to work. If the strike were an unfair labor practice strike, the strikers would be entitled to return to their jobs upon making an unconditional offer to do so. Major work stoppages involving a thousand or more workers have dropped significantly over the past ten years or so, from about 140 in 1981 to about 40 in 1991.[61]

Preparing for the Strike   When a strike is imminent, plans must be made to deal with it. For example, two experts say that when a strike is imminent or already under way, following these guidelines can minimize confusion.[62]

◆ Pay all striking employees what they are owed on the first day of the strike.

◆ Secure the facility. Supervisors should be on the alert for strangers on the property and access should be controlled. The company should consider hiring guards to protect replacements coming to and from work, and to watch and control the picketers, if necessary.

◆ Notify all customers. You may decide not to notify customers but to respond to inquiries only. A standard official response to all customers should be prepared and should be merely informative.

◆ Contact all suppliers and other persons with whom you do business who will have to cross the picket line. Establish alternative methods of obtaining supplies.

◆ Make arrangements for overnight stays in the facility and for delivered meals in case the occasion warrants such action.

◆ Notify the local unemployment office of your need for replacement workers.

◆ Photograph the facility before, during, and after picketing. If necessary, install videotape equipment and a long-distance microphone to monitor picket line misconduct.

◆ Record any and all facts concerning strikers' demeanor and activities and such incidents as violence, threats, mass pickets, property damage, or problems. Record police response to any request for assistance.

◆ Gather the following evidence: number of pickets and their names; time, date, and location of picketing; wording on every sign carried by pickets; and descriptions of picket cars and license numbers.

Other Alternatives   Management and labor each have other weapons they can use to try to break an impasse and achieve their aims. The union, for example, may resort to a corporate campaign. A corporate campaign is an organized effort by the union that exerts pressure on the corporation by pressuring the company's other unions, shareholders, directors, customers, creditors, and government agencies, often directly. Thus, individual members of the board of directors might be shocked by picketing of their homes, political figures might be pressured to agree to union demands, and the company's banks might become targets of a union member **boycott.**[63]

boycott
The combined refusal by employees and other interested parties to buy or use the employer's products.

Inside games are another union tactic, one often used in conjunction with corporate campaigns. Inside games can be defined as union efforts to convince employees to impede or to disrupt production, for example, by slowing the work pace, refusing to work overtime, filing mass charges with government agencies, refusing to do work without receiving detailed instructions from supervisors or management even though such instruction has not previously been required, and engaging in other disruptive activities such as castigating management and sick outs.[64] While the employees are at work and being paid, they are essentially "on strike"; inside games can be viewed as essentially de facto strikes—albeit "strikes" in which the employees are being supported by the company, which continues to pay them. Thus in one inside game at Caterpillar's Aurora, Illinois plant, United Auto Workers' grievances in the final stage before arbitration rose from 22 to 336. The effect, of course, was to clog the grievance procedure and tie up workers and management in unproductive endeavors on company time.[65]

For their part, employers can try to break an impasse with lockouts. A **lockout** is a refusal by the employer to provide opportunities to work. The employees are (sometimes literally) locked out and prohibited from doing their jobs (and thus from getting paid).

lockout
A refusal by the employer to provide opportunities to work.

A lockout is not generally viewed as an unfair labor practice by the NLRB. For example, if your product is a perishable one (such as vegetables), then a lockout may be a legitimate tactic to neutralize or decrease union power. A lockout is viewed as an unfair labor practice by the NLRB only when the employer acts for a prohibited purpose. It is not a prohibited purpose to try to bring about a settlement of negotiations on terms favorable to the employer. Lockouts today are not widely used, though; employers are usually reluctant to cease operations when employees are willing to continue working (even though there may be an impasse at the bargaining table).[66] However, in 1994, baseball players went on strike and the owners threatened a lockout; the players then returned to work.

The Contract Agreement Itself

The actual contract agreement may be 20 or 30 pages long or longer. It may contain just general declarations of policy or a detailed specification of rules and procedures. The tendency today is toward the longer, more detailed contract. This is largely a result of the increased number of items the agreements have been covering.

The main sections of a typical contract cover subjects such as these:

1. Management rights
2. Union security and automatic payroll dues deduction
3. Grievance procedures
4. Arbitration of grievances
5. Disciplinary procedures
6. Compensation rates
7. Hours of work and overtime
8. Benefits: vacations, holidays, insurance, pensions
9. Health and safety provisions
10. Employee security seniority provisions
11. Contract expiration date

Changes to Expect After Being Unionized

Unionization will have profound effects on the organization. Professor Dale Beach says there are five basic areas in which the union's impact will be felt.[67] Unionization will restrict management's freedom of action; it will result in union pressure for uniformity of treatment of all employees; it will require improved human resources policies and practices; it will require one spokesperson to be used for the employees; and it will lead to centralization of labor relations decision making.

Perhaps the most obvious impact of unionization is that it restricts management's freedom of action. Decisions such as who gets laid off when business slows, who gets to work overtime, and who gets a raise will now be subject to a union challenge, for example.

Partly because of the prospect of such challenges and partly because the union contract contains written provisions regarding pay, benefits, promotion, and the like, unionization also leads to a systematizing, centralizing, and sophistication of the employer's human resource policies, procedures, and rules. Standardized employee appraisal procedures may be introduced, for example.

Contract Administration: Grievances

The Important Role of Contract Administration

Hammering out a labor agreement is not the last step in collective bargaining; in some respects, it is just the beginning. No labor contract can ever be so complete that it covers all contingencies and answers all questions. For example, suppose the contract says you can only discharge an employee for "just cause." You subsequently discharge someone for speaking back to you in harsh terms. Was it within your rights to discharge this person? Was speaking back to you harshly "just cause"?

grievance
Any factor involving wages, hours, or conditions of employment that is used as a complaint against the employer.

Problems like this are usually handled and settled through the labor contract's **grievance** procedure. This procedure provides an orderly system whereby employer and union determine whether or not the contract has been violated.[68] It is the vehicle for administering the contract on a day-to-day basis. Through this grievance process, various clauses are interpreted and given meaning and the contract is transformed into a "living organism." Remember, though, that this day-to-day collective bargaining involves interpretation only; it usually does not involve negotiating new terms or altering existing ones.[69]

What Are the Sources of Grievances?

From a practical point of view, it is probably easier to list those items that don't precipitate grievances than to list the ones that do. Just about any factor involving wages, hours, or conditions of employment has and will be used as the basis of a grievance.

However, certain grievances are more serious than others since they are usually more difficult to settle. Discipline cases and seniority problems including promotions, transfers, and layoffs would top this list. Others would include grievances growing out of job evaluations and work assignments, overtime, vacations, incentive plans, and holidays.[70] Here are five actual examples of grievances as presented by Reed Richardson:[71]

Absenteeism. An employer fired an employee for excessive absences. The employee filed a grievance stating that there had been no previous warnings or discipline related to excessive absences.

Insubordination. An employee on two occasions refused to obey a supervisor's order to meet with him unless a union representative was present at the meeting. As a result, the employee was discharged and subsequently filed a grievance protesting discharge.

Overtime. Sunday overtime work was discontinued after a department was split. Employees affected filed a grievance protesting loss of the overtime work.

Plant rules. The plant had a posted rule barring employees from eating or drinking during unscheduled breaks. The employees filed a grievance claiming the rule was arbitrary.

Seniority. A junior employee was hired to fill the position of a laid-off senior employee. The senior employee filed a grievance protesting the action.

Always Ask: What Is the Real Problem? A grievance is often just a symptom of an underlying problem. For example, an employee's concern for his or her security may prompt a grievance over a transfer, work assignment, or promotion. Sometimes bad relationships between supervisors and subordinates are to blame: This is often the cause of grievances over "fair treatment," for example. Organizational factors such as automated jobs or ambiguous job descriptions that frustrate or aggravate employees also cause grievances. Union activism is another cause; for example, the union may solicit grievances from workers to underscore ineffective supervision. Problem employees are yet another cause of grievances. These are individuals, who, by their nature, are negative, dissatisfied, and grievance prone.[72] *Disciplinary measures*—a major source of grievances—and *dismissal*—a frequent result of disciplinary measures—are explained in Chapter 16.

The Grievance Procedure

Most collective bargaining contracts contain a very specific grievance procedure. This specifies the various steps in the procedure, time limits associated with each step, and specific rules such as "all charges of contract violation must be reduced to writing." Virtually every labor agreement signed today contains a grievance procedure clause. (Nonunionized employers need such procedures, too; we'll discuss this in the following chapter.)

Union grievance procedures differ from firm to firm. Some contain simple two-step procedures. Here the grievant, union representative, and company representative first meet to discuss the grievance. If a satisfactory solution is not found, the grievance is brought before an independent third-person arbitrator, who hears the case, writes it up, and makes a decision.

At the other extreme, the grievance procedure may contain six or more steps. The first step might be for the grievant and shop steward to meet informally with the grievant's supervisor to try to find a solution. If one is not found, a formal grievance is filed and a meeting scheduled among the employee, shop steward, and the supervisor's boss. The next steps involve the grievant and union representatives meeting with higher- and higher-level managers. Finally, if top management and the union cannot reach agreement, the grievance may go to arbitration.

Guidelines for Handling Grievances

Developing the Proper Environment The best way to handle a grievance is to develop a work environment in which grievances don't occur in the first place.[73] Constructive grievance handling depends first on your ability to recognize, diagnose, and correct the causes of potential employee dissatisfaction (causes such as unfair appraisals, inequitable wages, or poor communications) before they become formal grievances.

Some Guidelines: Do's and Don'ts[74] As a manager, your behavior in handling grievances is crucial. You are on the firing line and must, therefore, steer a course between treating employees fairly and maintaining management's rights and prerogatives. Walter Baer has developed a list of do's and don'ts as useful guides in handling grievances.[75] Some of the most critical ones are presented next:

Do

> Investigate and handle each and every case as though it may eventually result in an arbitration hearing.
>
> Talk with the employee about his or her grievance; give the person a good and full hearing.
>
> Require the union to identify specific contractual provisions allegedly violated.
>
> Comply with the contractual time limits of the company for handling the grievance.
>
> Visit the work area of the grievance.
>
> Determine whether there were any witnesses.
>
> Examine the grievant's personnel record.
>
> Fully examine prior grievance records.
>
> Treat the union representative as your equal.
>
> Hold your grievance discussions privately.
>
> Fully inform your own supervisor of grievance matters.

Don't

> Discuss the case with the union steward alone—the grievant should definitely be there.
>
> Make arrangements with individual employees that are inconsistent with the labor agreement.
>
> Hold back the remedy if the company is wrong.
>
> Admit to the binding effect of a past practice.
>
> Relinquish to the union your rights as a manager.
>
> Settle grievances on the basis of what is "fair." Instead, stick to the labor agreement, which should be your only standard.
>
> Bargain over items not covered by the contract.
>
> Treat as subject to arbitration claims demanding the discipline or discharge of managers.
>
> Give long written grievance answers.
>
> Trade a grievance settlement for a grievance withdrawal (or try to make up for a bad decision in one grievance by bending over backward in another).
>
> Deny grievances on the premise that your "hands have been tied by management."
>
> Agree to informal amendments in the contract.

Diversity Counts
Gender Differences in Disputes and Dispute Resolution

One of the reasons for grievance processes is that problems and disputes in the workplace are normal and probably unavoidable.[1] As explained elsewhere in this chapter, disputes commonly arise over issues such as work assignments, work schedules, and discipline; once such disputes arise, it is usual for them to be addressed. They may be addressed formally (such as through union-negotiated grievance procedures) or informally, such as in face-to-face conversations.

Given the likelihood that you will find yourself engaged in some type of workplace dispute, the results of one recent study regarding gender differences in disputes and dispute resolution provide some useful food for thought. The study focused on male and female clerical workers' disputes over tasks and interpersonal treatment and involved 34 in-depth interviews with 23 women and 11 men clerical workers in both unionized and non-unionized firms.[2] The researchers draw three conclusions from their study.

First, there are gender differences in the origins of workplace problems and disputes. At least with these workers in these companies ". . . women workers displayed more sensitivity to problems associated with interpersonal relations in the workplace than men, more often voicing workplace disputes concerning personality conflicts."[3] On the other hand, the men clerical workers were relatively less likely to express concerns over personality conflicts in the workplace.[4]

Second, more women generally described how difficult it was to resolve personality conflicts through formalized channels (including grievance procedures). The reason, apparently, is that the sorts of personality conflicts sensed by the female clerical workers rarely ". . . escalate to a point that they can be labeled or proven as harassment."[5] Instead they were more subtle occurrences that "eat away at women workers" to use the researchers' phrase.[6] As a result, women were much less likely to use formal dispute resolution procedures for eliminating interpersonal conflicts, but instead were much more likely to request lateral transfers to solve problems in the workplace. In turn such lateral transfers may reduce a woman's likelihood of receiving a raise or getting more training, since her average tenure on a job will tend to be lower than a man (who either discounts the interpersonal conflict or tries to solve it through some formal or informal procedure).

A third conclusion is that, given the above, workplace dispute resolution procedures may actually constrain women's abilities to succeed at work. For example suppose it is true that formal dispute resolution procedures such as grievance processes are unlikely to be useful forums for addressing simple interpersonal conflicts. Then women may be at a disadvantage when it comes to solving an interpersonal conflict that they may be relatively attuned to. One implication is that more formal and informal procedures should be built into an employer's dispute resolution processes in order to give both women and men a better opportunity to air interpersonal disputes and get on with their work.◆

[1] This feature is based on Patricia Gwartney-Gibbs and Denise Lach, "Gender Differences in Clerical Workers' Disputes over Tasks, Interpersonal Treatment, and Emotion," *Human Relations*, Vol. 46, No. 6 (1994), pp. 611–639.
[2] Ibid., p. 615.
[3] Ibid., p. 633.
[4] Ibid., p. 634.
[5] Ibid., p. 634.
[6] Ibid., p. 634.

The Future of Unionism

Unions Fall on Hard Times

The 1970s and 1980s were hard times for unions, and during those years their rolls dropped steeply. About 22% of the nonfarm U.S. work force belonged to unions in 1975. By 1992 that figure had dropped to about 16%. This slide actually began in the early 1950s. By then most easily organized workers in industries like mining, transportation, and manufacturing had already unionized.

Several factors contributed to the decline in union membership. Traditionally, unions have appealed mostly to blue-collar workers, and the proportion of blue-collar jobs has been decreasing as service-sector and white-collar service jobs have increased. Furthermore, several economic factors, including intense international competition, outdated equipment and factories, mismanagement, new technology, and government regulation, have hit those industries (like mining and manufacturing) that have traditionally been unionized. The effect of all this has been the permanent layoff of hundreds of thousands of union members, the permanent closing of company plants, the relocation of companies to nonunion settings (either in the United States or overseas), and mergers and acquisitions that have eliminated union jobs and affected collective bargaining agreements. Other changes, including the deregulation of trucking, airlines, and communications, have helped to erode union membership as well.[76]

Furthermore, the various EEO, safety, and similar laws described elsewhere in this book now provide the sort of protection that up to a few years ago only unions could provide. Foremost on the list are those court decisions (discussed elsewhere in this book) that erode the employment-at-will doctrine and make it more difficult for employers in many states to fire employees without just cause. On this and many other fronts, employee rights regarding job security, privacy, occupational safety, equal employment opportunities, pension vesting, and pay policies are now provided by law. To that extent, the role formerly played by unions has been reduced.[77]

Double-breasting is another way that companies are putting unions under more pressure. This term refers to a tactic whereby employers avoid their obligations under union contracts by establishing and running nonunion companies to which they may transfer union work. The NLRB permits this under certain circumstances. It is, for instance, a common practice in the construction industry.

Figure 15.9
Union's Formula for a Turnaround

Among the campaign proposals of the AFL-CIO ticket led by John Sweeney:

- **ORGANIZING:** Create a separate AFL-CIO organizing department.

- **POLITICS:** Create a training center to develop campaign organizers, campaign managers and candidates. Create a policy center to develop new approaches to economic and public policy.

- **CORPORATE CAMPAIGNS:** Create a Strategic Campaign Fund that could provide grants to unions 'in important and difficult contract fights.'

- **STRIKES:** Create a support team to help in long-running strikes.

- **PENSIONS:** Create a clearinghouse to manage a database of union pension-fund investments to support unions in corporate-governance campaigns.

- **OTHER:** Expand AFL-CIO Executive Council from 33 to 45 vice presidents and bar individuals over 70 from running for top AFL-CIO offices.

Beyond these factors, technology will influence unionization. Computer systems and other modern technologies may reduce labor demand, for instance. Electronic work (like processing credit card claims) is highly portable compared with factory work. Modern office work—and its workers—can thus be shifted almost literally at the touch of a button from one state to another, and even overseas.[78]

In a major test for unions, workers at Nissan Motor Manufacturing Corp., U.S.A., in Smyrna, Tennessee, rejected the United Auto Workers in the first union vote at a U.S. auto plant wholly owned by a Japanese firm.[79] After a bitter, 18-month union organizing campaign, workers voted more than two to one against UAW representation in 1989, apparently because pay, job security, and management practices were already so favorable at the plant.

What's Next for Unions?

Does all this mean we no longer need unions? Probably not. But it does mean a change in the way unions operate and the role they see for themselves.

First, unions are increasingly going after a "piece of the pie" in terms of ownership and control of corporations. As a United Steelworkers Union president put it, "We are not going to sit around and allow management to louse things up like they did in the past."[80] Today, over 8 million workers own a piece of their employers through employee stock ownership plans. Recall that these ESOPs are basically pension plans through which a company's employees accumulate shares of their company's stock. As a result, nonmanagement employees now sit on boards of directors at more than 300 firms in their role as representatives of the firm's employee stock ownership plans.

Second, unions are becoming both more aggressive and more sophisticated in the way they present themselves to the public. The AFL-CIO has a program to train a thousand unionists in the fundamentals of how to come across well on television, for instance. Unions are also entering into more cooperative pacts with employers, for instance, working with them in developing team-based employee participation programs: See the Building Employee Commitment feature below.

During the last ten years or so, the major union effort has been aimed at organizing white-collar workers. Service-oriented industries such as insurance, banking, retail trade, and government are now being organized by unions. More than 10% of white-collar workers have already become unionized. The number is increasing rapidly, particularly among professionals, many of whom work in the public sector.[81] And the new team elected in 1995 to head the AFL-CIO promises much more aggressive organizing efforts. New President John Sweeney's "Formula for a Turnaround" is summarized in Figure 15.9.

Building Employee Commitment

The quality circles and total quality management programs discussed elsewhere in this book are a two-edged sword as far as unions are concerned. On the one hand, they can be the basis for building better communications and for boosting union management harmony. On the other hand, they may undercut union security by building relationships between workers and management that make unions obsolete. Unions are therefore a bit schizophrenic when it comes to the subject of commitment-building participation programs.

Based on the research, at least, worker participation programs don't seem to be the threat union leaders fear they may be. One study, for instance, found few differences between how quality programs' participants and nonparticipants viewed the performance of their unions.[82] Another researcher found that quality program participants were actually more involved in and satisfied with the union than were nonparticipants.[83]

Perhaps the critical issue is whether or not the union is asked to help develop and implement the total quality program. For example, one study concluded that union officers were much less likely to view the quality program negatively when they were involved in its design and implementation.[84] Similarly, in another study, the researchers found that "union members who participated in [such] programs were less likely than nonparticipants to view [them] as a threat to the union, and also remained more loyal to the union."[85]◆

Are Employee Participation Programs Unfair Labor Practices?

The proliferation of employee participation programs—quality circles, quality improvement programs, quality of work life teams, and so on—has added urgency to a question that's been debated in labor relations circles for over 50 years: Are employee participation programs like these "sham unions" and therefore illegal under the National Labor Relations Act? At the present time, they are "subject to serious legal challenge under the National Labor Relations Act (NLRA)"[86] for unfair labor practices.

To understand the problem, it's useful to know that a principal goal of the National Labor Relations (or Wagner) Act was to outlaw so-called sham unions. Two years before passage of the NLRA, the National Recovery Act of 1933 tried to give employees the right to organize and bargain collectively. This in turn triggered an enormous increase in sham unions that were actually company-supported organizations aimed at keeping legitimate unions out. As Senator Robert Wagner explained then, "at the present time genuine collective bargaining is being thwarted immeasurably by the proliferation of company unions."[87] These sham unions were one of the principal factors motivating Senator Wagner to sponsor the 1935 National Labor Relations Act.

The problem is that, because of the way the NLRA is written and frequently interpreted, participative programs such as quality circles and quality-improvement teams could be viewed as sham unions. In part, this is so because the NLRA defines a *labor organization* as

> *Any organization of any kind, or any agency or employee representation committee or plan, in which employees participate and which exists for the purpose, in whole or in part, of dealing with employers concerning grievances, labor disputes, wages, rates of pay, hours of employment, or conditions of work.*[88]

Whether or not an employer's participation program will be viewed as an impermissible labor organization revolves around two main criteria. One is dominance. If the employer formulates the idea for the committees; creates them; controls the development of their constitution or governing rules; maintains control over the committees' functions; controls the internal management of the program; controls or participates in the program's meetings; or allows the committees to meet on its premises and use its supplies while paying employees for time spent in committee meetings, the organizations could be considered impermissibly dominated by the employer. The NLRB has often taken the position that even potential domination is impermissible. Courts, though, have often taken the position that actual domination had to be shown before a violation could be established.[89]

The participation committee's actual role is the second consideration. If the committees focus exclusively on issues such as quality and productivity improvement, they may be more likely to be viewed by the courts as outside the purview of the National Labor Relations Act. On the other hand, if the committees become involved in union-type matters such as wages, working conditions, and hours of work, they may be more likely to be viewed as basically unions. Thus, in the *Electromation Corp.* case decided in 1992 by the NLRB, the firm set up action committees to advise management regarding matters such as absenteeism/infractions, pay progression, and the attendance bonus plan. When a teamsters local lost a certification election at this firm, the union filed an unfair labor practice suit with the NLRB. It claimed, in part, that the action committees were unlawfully dominated labor organizations. The NLRB decided in favor of the union but did not really clarify when and under what conditions participation programs might be acceptable. The matter continues to move through the courts.

Toward "Safe" Participation Programs   For now, two experts urge employers to take prudent steps to avoid having their employee participation programs viewed as sham unions.[90]

1. If you want to establish participation programs, involve employees in the formation of these programs to the greatest extent practical.
2. Continually emphasize to employees that the committees exist for the *exclusive purpose* of addressing such issues as quality and productivity. Stress that they are not intended to be vehicles for dealing with management on items that are generally viewed as mandatory bargaining items between unions and management, such as pay and working conditions.
3. Of course, make sure you don't try to set up such committees at the same time union organizing activities are beginning in your facility.
4. Fill the committees with volunteers rather than elected employee representatives. Also rotate membership frequently to ensure broad employee participation.
5. Participate in the day-to-day activities of the committees as little as possible. Avoid even the suspicion of unlawful interference in or, worse, the perception of domination.

At Corning the union plays a major role in its team-based production program's success. Union and management signed a joint philosophical statement that they called "a partnership in the workplace." It articulates six "essential values" including "recognition of the rights of workers to participate in decisions that affect their working lives."[91] As part of its new role, the union has a hand in the content and administration of all the firm's training programs, and work redesign committees (which include shop floor workers) work on restructuring their jobs. What we may be moving toward, proposes one expert, is an era in which union-management relations are more similar to what they've traditionally been in countries like Germany and Japan, where both the workers and their unions have considerable input in how their firms are run.[92]

At other firms, new types of labor contracts called modern operating agreements (MOA) are being signed to formalize these new, more cooperative union management arrangements. Unlike traditional union agreements, MOAs "are designed to give hourly workers a greater say in how their jobs are performed. The agreements establish work teams, decentralize decision making, include union representatives on key plant operating committees, reduce the number of job classifications, and use a pay-for-knowledge system that links employees' wage rates to the number of different operations they can perform."[93] Increasingly, in other words, the labor agreements of tomorrow will probably reflect employers growing awareness of the need to do what it takes to win their employees' commitment.

Unfortunately, the outlook, while bright, is not entirely cloudless. For example, inside-games advocates are generally not just out to disrupt the company. Instead, they also push for the elimination of all cooperative labor-management activities, (such as quality control programs), and all cooperation on community work like United Way fund raising or other charitable endeavors. The claim is that workers must choose sides, and that working with management in any manner reduces the propensity for workers to join in solidarity actions and, therefore, to participate in corporate campaign and inside-game activities.[94] Indeed, union literature describing inside games is often couched in emotionally charged rhetoric, with references to how to "hurt the company," use "guerrilla tactics," and "mobilize the [union] membership into a fighting force."[95] So, all things considered, it is possible but by no means a sure bet that the next few years will see a period of relative union-management partnership and harmony.

Chapter Review

Summary

1. Union membership has been alternately growing and shrinking since as early as 1790. A major milestone was the creation in 1886 of the American Federation of Labor by Samuel Gompers. Most recently the trend in unionization has been toward organizing white-collar workers, particularly since the proportion of blue-collar workers has been declining. In any case, we saw that while wages and benefits are important factors in unionization, workers are also seeking fair, humane, and equitable treatment.

2. In addition to improved wages and working conditions, unions seek security when organizing. We discussed five possible arrangements, including the closed shop, the union shop, the agency shop, the open shop, and maintenance of membership.

3. The AFL-CIO is a national federation comprised of 109 national and international unions. It can exercise only that power it is allowed to exercise by its constituent national unions.

4. During the period of strong encouragement of unions, the Norris-LaGuardia Act and the Wagner Act were passed; these marked a shift in labor law from repression to strong encouragement of union activity. They did this by banning certain types of unfair labor practices, by providing for secret-ballot elections, and by creating the National Labor Relations Board.

5. The Taft-Hartley Act reflected the period of modified encouragement coupled with regulation. It enumerated the rights of employees with respect to their unions, enumerated the rights of employers, and allowed the U.S. president to temporarily bar national emergency strikes. Among other things, it also enumerated certain union unfair labor practices. For example, it banned unions from restraining or coercing employees from exercising their guaranteed bargaining rights. And employers were explicitly given the right to express their views concerning union organization.

6. The Landrum-Griffin Act reflected the period of detailed regulation of internal union affairs. It grew out of discoveries of wrongdoing on the part of both management and union leadership and contained a bill of rights for union members. (For example, it affirms a member's right to sue his or her union.)

7. There are four steps in a union drive and election: the initial contact, obtaining authorization cards, holding a hearing with the NLRB, and the election itself. Remember that the union need only win a majority of the votes *cast, not* a majority of the workers in the bargaining unit.

8. There are five surefire ways to lose an NLRB election: be caught sleeping at the switch, form a committee, emphasize money and benefits, have an industry blind spot, and delegate too much to divisions. Supervisors should be trained regarding how to administer the employer's union literature and solicitation rules.

9. Bargaining collectively in good faith is the next step if and when the union wins the election. Good faith means that both parties communicate and negotiate, and that proposals are matched with counterproposals. We discussed the structure of the negotiating teams and their preparations. We also discussed the actual bargaining sessions and the distinction between mandatory, voluntary, and illegal bargaining items. We also listed some hints on bargaining, including do not hurry, be prepared, find out why, and be a good listener.

10. An impasse occurs when the parties aren't able to move further toward settlement. Third-party involvement—namely, arbitration, fact-finding, or mediation—is one alternative. Sometimes, though, a strike occurs. Preparing for the strike involves such steps as securing the facility, notifying all customers, and photographing the facility. Boycotts and lockouts are two other anti-impasse weapons sometimes used by labor and management.

11. Grievance handling has been called day-to-day collective bargaining. It involves the continuing interpretation of the collective bargaining agreement but usually not its renegotiation.

12. When just about any management action might lead to a grievance, the most serious actions involve discipline cases, seniority problems, actions growing out of a job evaluation and work assignments, and overtime and benefits. But remember that a grievance is often just a symptom; always try to find the underlying problem.

13. Most agreements contain a carefully worded grievance procedure. It may be a two-step procedure or (at the other extreme) involve six or more steps. In any case, the steps usually involve meetings between higher- and higher-echelon managers until (if agreement isn't reached) the grievance goes to arbitration. Grievance handling is as important in nonunion organizations as in those that are unionized.

Key Terms

closed shop
union shop
agency shop
open shop
Norris-LaGuardia Act
National Labor Relations Board (NLRB)
Wagner Act
Taft-Hartley Act
national emergency strikes

Landrum-Griffin Act
authorization cards
bargaining unit
collective bargaining
good faith bargaining
voluntary bargaining items
illegal bargaining items
mandatory bargaining items

mediation
arbitration
wildcat strike
sympathy strike
boycott
lockout
grievance

Discussion Questions and Exercises

1. Explain the structure and purpose of the AFL-CIO.
2. Discuss five sure ways to lose an NLRB election.
3. Describe important tactics you would expect the union to use during the union drive and election.
4. Briefly explain why labor law has gone through a cycle of repression and encouragement.
5. Explain in detail each step in a union drive and election.
6. Discuss what you, as a supervisor, should keep in mind about how to prepare for union contract negotiations.

7. What is meant by good faith bargaining? When is bargaining not in good faith?

8. You are the president of a small firm of 30 employees. While you are not unionized, you would like to have an appeals process that would serve a purpose similar to that of a grievance procedure. Working individually or in groups, prepare a presentation describing what this appeals process might entail.

9. Define impasse, mediation, and strike, and explain the techniques that are used to overcome an impasse.

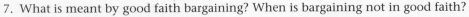

Application Exercises

RUNNING CASE: Carter Cleaning Company
The Grievance

On visiting one of Carter Cleaning Company's stores, Jennifer was surprised to be taken aside by a long-term Carter employee, who met her as she was parking her car. "Murray (the store manager) told me I was suspended for two days without pay because I came in late last Thursday," said George. "I'm really upset, but around here the store manager's word seems to be law, and it sometimes seems like the only way anyone can file a grievance is by meeting you or your father like this in the parking lot." Jennifer was very disturbed by this revelation and promised the employee she would look into it and discuss the situation with her father. In the car heading back to headquarters she began mulling over what Carter Cleaning Company's alternatives might be.

Questions

1. Do you think it is important for Carter Cleaning Company to have a formal grievance process? Why or why not?

2. Based on what you know about the Carter Cleaning Company, outline the steps in what you think the ideal grievance process would be for this company.

3. In addition to the grievance process, can you think of anything else that Carter Cleaning Company might do to make sure that grievances and gripes like this one get expressed and also get heard by top management?

CASE INCIDENT: Disciplinary Action

Facts The employee, a union shop steward, was on her regularly scheduled day off at home. She was called by her supervisor and told to talk to three union members and instruct them to attend a work function called a "Quest for Quality Interaction Committee" meeting. The Quest for Quality program was a high priority with the employer for improving patient care at the facility and was part of a corporate program. The union had objected to the implementation of the Quest for Quality program and had taken a position that employees could attend the program if their jobs were threatened, but they should do so under protest and then file a grievance afterward.

On the day in question, the union shop steward, in a three-way conversation with the three employees, told them that she would not order them to attend the Quest for Quality meeting, although she

had been asked by her supervisor to instruct them to go to the meeting. The supervisor who had called the union shop steward had herself refused to order the employees to attend the meeting, but relied on the union shop steward to issue the order to the employees. When the union shop steward failed to order the employees to attend the meeting, the employer suspended the union shop steward for two weeks. She grieved the two-week suspension.

The union position was that the company had no authority to discipline the union shop steward on her day off for failure to give what it termed a management direction to perform the specific job function of attending a mandatory corporate meeting. The union pointed out that it was unfair that the employer refused to order the employees directly to attend the meeting but then expected the union shop steward to do so. The union argued that while it is not unusual to call upon a union shop steward for assistance in problem solving, the company had no right to demand that he or she replace supervisors or management in giving orders and then discipline the union official for refusing to do so.

The company position was that the opposition of the union to the Quest for Quality meetings put the employees in a position of being unable to attend the meetings without direction from the union shop steward; that the union shop steward was given a job assignment of directing the employees to attend the meeting; and that failure to follow that job assignment was insubordination and just cause for her suspension.

Nonetheless, the union contended that the arbitrator must examine the nature of the order when deciding whether the insubordination was grounds for discipline. As to the nature of the order in this case, the employer had to demonstrate that the order was directly related to the job classification and work assignment of the employee disciplined. The refusal

to obey such an order must be shown to pose a real challenge to supervisory authority. The employee did not dispute the fact that she failed to follow the orders given to her by her supervisor, but pointed out that she was not on duty at the time and that the task being given to her was not because of her job with the company but because of her status as a union shop steward.

Questions

1. As the arbitrator, do you think the employer had just cause to discipline the employee?

2. If the union's opposition to the Quest for Quality program encouraged the employees not to participate, why shouldn't the union be held responsible for directing the employees to attend?

Adapted from *Cheltenham Nursing and Rehabilitation Center,* 89 LA 361 (1987); in Michael Carrell and Christina Heavrin, *Labor Relations and Collective Bargaining* (Englewood Cliffs, NJ: Prentice-Hall, 1995), pp. 100–101.

 # Human Resource Management Simulation

There is always a possibility that your firm will become organized by a labor union. Danger signals include low morale, lower than average wages and/or benefits, and a high accident rate. You will have an opportunity to discuss unionization and several approaches to it in incident L.

Video Case

Shrinking Unions

This videocase introduces John Sweeney, the AFL-CIO's newly elected president. You'll see that Mr. Sweeney campaigned as a risk-taker and champion of change, one who says he will pump life back into the organized labor movement. He plans to do this by aggressively targeting the fastest-growing segments of the nation's work force, namely women, minorities, and the service industry.

Questions

1. Why do union organizers say they want to focus first on organizing women, minorities and the service industry?

2. Correspondent Consuelo Mack makes the point that it's going to be relatively difficult for them to organize workers in the private sector "where market forces and global competition have proven to be formidable foes." Do you think she's right? Why or why not?

3. Do you think what organizer Richard Bensinger says in the case ("we organize around anger") is true? What do you think he means by that statement, and why do you think he's right or wrong?

4. If you were the HR manager in a company employing many women and minorities, what steps would you take to limit the effectiveness of the organizing efforts of Mr. Sweeney and his associates?

Source: Wall Street Journal Report, *Shrinking Unions,* Show No. 683-2, October 28, 1995.

Take It to the Net

We invite you to visit the Dessler page on the Prentice Hall Web site at:
http://www.prenhall.com/~dessler
for the monthly Dessler update, and for this chapter's WorldWide Web exercise.

Notes

1. "Union Membership and Earnings," *BNA Bulletin to Management,* March 2, 1995, pp. 68–69.
2. "Union Membership in 1991," *BNA Bulletin to Management,* March 5, 1992, pp. 68–69. Ibid.
3. "Beyond Unions: A Revolution in Employee Rights Is in the Making," *Business Week,* July 8, 1985, p. 72; Bureau of National Affairs, "Union Membership in 1988," *Bulletin to Management,* April 13, 1989. See also Timothy Koeller, "Union Activity and the Decline in American Trade Union Membership," *Journal of Labor Research,* Vol. 15, no. 1 (Winter 1994), pp. 19–32.
4. From the Bureau of Labor Statistics, discussed in "Union Wages," *BNA Bulletin to Management,* April 2, 1992, pp. 100–101; see also *BNA Bulletin to Management,* "Union Membership and Earnings," March 2, 1995, p. 69.
5. William Wiatrowski, "Employee Benefits for Union and Nonunion Workers," *Monthly Labor Review* (February 1994), pp. 34–36.
6. Ibid., p. 35.
7. W. Clay Hamner and Frank Schmidt, "Work Attitude as Predictors of Unionization Activity," *Journal of Applied Psychology,* Vol. 63, no. 4 (1978), pp. 415–421. See also Amos Okafor, "White Collar Unionization: Why and What to Do," *Personnel,* Vol. 62, no. 8 (August 1985), pp. 17–20. See also Michael E. Gordon and Angelo DeNisi, "A Re-Examination of the Relationship Between Union Membership and Job Satisfaction," *Industrial and Labor Relations Review,* Vol. 48, no. 2 (January 1995), pp. 222–236.
8. Jeanne Brett, "Why Employees Want Unions," *Organizational Dynamics* (Spring 1980), and John Fossum, *Labor Relations* (Dallas, TX: Business Publications, 1982), p. 4.
9. Clive Fullager and Julian Barling, "A Longitudinal Test of a Model of the Antecedents and Consequences of Union Loyalty," *Journal of Applied Psychology,* Vol. 74, no. 2 (April 1989), pp. 213–227. Adrienne Eaton, Michael Gordon and Jeffrey Keefe, "The Impact of Quality of Work Life Programs and Grievance Systems Effectiveness on Union Commitment," *Individual and Labor Relations Review,* Vol. 45, no. 3 (April 1992), pp. 591–604.
10. See, for example, Satish Deshpande, "A Meta-Analysis of Some Determinants of Union Voting Intent," *Relations Industrielles,* Vol. 47, no. 2 (1992), pp. 334–341; and Hugh Hindman and Charles Smith, "Correlates of Union Membership and Joining Intentions in a Unit of Federal Employees," *Journal of Labor Research.* Vol. 14, no. 4 (Fall 1993), pp. 439–454. See also Lee Graf et al., "Profiles of Those Who Support Collective Bargaining in Institutions of Higher Learning and Why: An Empirical Examination," *Journal of Collective Negotiations,* Vol. 23, no. 2 (1994), pp. 151–162.
11. Warner Pflug, *The UAW in Pictures* (Detroit: Wayne State University Press, 1971), pp. 11–12.
12. See also M. Gordon and others, "Commitment to the Union: Development of a Measure and an Examination of Its Correlates," *Journal of Applied Psychology* (August 1980), pp. 474–499. For an interesting discussion of this, see Bert Klandermans, "Perceived Cost and Benefits of Participation in Union Action," *Personnel Psychology,* Vol. 39, no. 2 (Summer 1986), pp. 379–398.
13. These are based on Richard Hodgetts, *Introduction to Business* (Reading, MA: Addison-Wesley, 1977), pp. 213–214.
14. "Boardroom Reports," The Conference Board, New York, December 15, 1976, p. 6. See also "Perspectives on Employment," Research Bulletin #194, 1986, The Conference Board, 845 Third Avenue, New York, N.Y. 10020.
15. The following material is based on Arthur Sloane and Fred Witney, *Labor Relations,* (Englewood Cliffs, NJ.: Prentice-Hall, 1977), p. 137.
16. Ibid., p. 106.
17. Ibid., p. 121.
18. Commerce Clearing House. This is based on "NLRB Announces New Rule on When Unions Can Picket Stores in Malls," *Ideas and Trends,* November 2, 1988, pp. 181–184. Jean Country and Brook Shopping Centers, Inc., as nominee for Dollar Land Syndicate (Retail and Wholesale Employees Union, Local 305, AFL-CIO), 291 NLRB No. 4, Sept. 27, 1988. It should be noted that the NLRB held that in balancing the interests involved, it was essential to consider whether those seeking to exercise the right to organize on private property had reasonable alternative means of doing so without trespassing on the owner's property. Previously, the NLRB had held it must sometimes refrain from considering that issue in determining whether such organizational rights could be exercised under a balancing test. In a 1992 case, *Lechmere, Inc.* v. *NLRB,* "the court has been asked to decide whether an operator of a chain of New England retail stores committed an unfair labor practice when it prevented non-employee union organizers from distributing union literature on a company property." The issue again raises the question—first raised by the Supreme Court 35 years ago in *NLRB* v. *Babcok & Wilcox*—as to whether union organizers can be banned from company premises when they can easily contact employees "through the usual channels" of communication. On January 27, 1992, the Supreme Court decided in favor of the employer in this case. For a discussion of this, see Craig Hukill, "Labor and the Supreme Court: Significant Issues of 1991–92," *Monthly Labor Review* (January 1992), p. 35.
19. Clear Pine Moldings.
20. Midland National Life Insurance Company.

21. This is based on "Taft Act Losing Teeth," a summary of a speech by Professor Charles Craver of the George Washington University. National Law Center, in Bureau of National Affairs, *Bulletin to Management*, March 16, 1989, p. 88.

22. Commerce Clearing House, "Supreme Court Ruling Gives Management Greater Power to Fill Jobs During a Strike," *Ideas and Trends*, March 23, 1989, p. 46.

23. *Lechmere Inc.* v. *National Labor Relations Board*, U.S. S. Ct., No. 90-970, 1/27/92.

24. "Difficulties Foreseen for Union Organizing Efforts," *BNA Bulletin to Management*, February 13, 1992, p. 42.

25. This is based on David Moberg, "Like Business, Unions Must Go Global," *The New York Times*, December 19, 1993, p. 13.

26. See William J. Glueck, "Labor Relations and the Supervisor," in M. Jean Newport, *Supervisory Management: Tools and Techniques* (St. Paul, MN: West, 1976), pp. 207–234. See also "Big Labor Tries the Soft Sell," *Business Week*, October 13, 1986, p. 126.

27. William Fulmer, "Step by Step Through a Union Election," *Harvard Business Review*, Vol. 60 (July–August 1981), pp. 94–102. For an interesting description of contract negotiations see Peter Cramton and Joseph Tracy, "The Determinants of U.S. Labor Disputes," *Journal of Labor Economics*, Vol. 12, no. 2 (April 1994), pp. 180–209.

28. *Labor Relations Consultants: Issues, Trends, Controversies* (Rockville, MD: Bureau of National Affairs, 1985), p. 7.

29. Ibid., p. 71.

30. Ibid., p. 72.

31. Commerce Clearing House, "More on Management's Pre-election Campaign Strategy," *Ideas and Trends in Personnel*, August 20, 1982, pp. 158–159.

32. Fulmer, "Step by Step," p. 94. See also "An Employer May Rebut Union Misrepresentations," Bureau of National Affairs, *Bulletin to Management*, January 16, 1986, p. 17.

33. This section is based on Matthew Goodfellow, "How to Lose an NLRB Election," *Personnel Administrator*, Vol. 23 (September 1976), pp. 40–44. Union win loss ratio based on "Union Win Loss Ratio Stable in '88," Bureau of National Affairs, *Bulletin to Management*, April 20, 1989, p. 121.

34. Harry Katz, "The Decentralization of Collective Bargaining: A Literature Review and Comparative Analysis," *Industrial and Labor Relations Review*, Vol. 47, no. 1 (October 1993), p. 11.

35. Frederick Sullivan, "Limiting Union Organizing Activity Through Supervisors," *Personnel*, Vol. 55 (July–August 1978), pp. 55–65. Richard Peterson, Thomas Lee, and Barbara Finnegan, "Strategies and Tactics in Union Organizing Campaigns," *Industrial Relations*, Vol. 31, no. 2 (Spring 1992), pp. 370–381. See also Alan Story, "Employer Speech, Union Representation Elections, and the First Amendment," *Berkeley Journal of Employment and Labor Law*, Vol. 16, no. 2 (1995), pp. 356–457.

36. Ibid., p. 60.

37. Ibid., pp. 62–65.

38. Ibid., pp. 64–65. The appropriateness of these sample rules may be affected by factors unique to an employer's operation, and they should therefore be reviewed by the employer's attorney before implementation.

39. B&D Plastics Inc. 302 NLRB No. 33, 1991, 137 LRRM 1039; discussed in "No Such Things as a Quote Free Lunch," *BNA Bulletin to Management*, May 23, 1991, pp. 153–154.

40. Charles Wentz, Jr., "Preserving a Union-Free Workplace," *Personnel* (October 1987), pp. 68–72.

41. Francis T. Coleman, "Once a Union, Not Always a Union," *Personnel Journal*, Vol. 64, no. 3 (March 1985), p. 42. See total article, pp. 42–45, for an excellent discussion of the benefits of decertification for both employers and workers. See also "Decertification: Fulfilling Unions' Destiny?" *Personnel Journal*, Vol. 66 (June 1987), pp. 144–148. "Union Election Win Rate Decreases," *BNA Bulletin to Management*, November 10, 1994, pp. 356–357.

42. "Union Election Win Rate Decreases," *BNA Bulletin to Management*, November 10, 1994, pp. 356–357.

43. William Fulmer, "When Employees Want to Oust Their Union," *Harvard Business Review*, Vol. 56 (March–April 1978), pp. 163–170; Coleman, "Once a Union, Not Always a Union," pp. 42–45. See also "Decertification: Fulfilling Unions Destiny?" pp. 144–148.

44. Fulmer, "When Employees Want to Oust Their Union," p. 167. See also David Meyer and Trevor Bain, "Union Decertification Election Outcomes: Bargaining Unit Characteristics and Union Resources," *Journal of Labor Research*, Vol. 15, no. 2 (Spring 1994), pp. 117–136.

45. *The Economist*, November 17, 1979, p. 50.

46. See also William Fulmer and Tamara Gilman, "Why Do Workers Vote for Union Decertification?" *Personnel*, Vol. 58 (March–April 1981), pp. 28–35, and Shane Premeaux et al., "Managing Tomorrow's Unionized Workers," *Personnel* (July 1989), pp. 61–64, for a discussion of some important differences (in preferred management styles) between unionized and nonunionized employees.

47. Dale Yoder, *Personnel Management* (Englewood Cliffs, NJ: Prentice Hall, 1972), p. 486. See also Michael Ballot, *Labor-Management Relations in a Changing Environment* (New York: John Wiley and Sons, 1992), pp. 169–425.

48. Quoted in Reed Richardson, *Collective Bargaining by Objectives* (Englewood Cliffs, NJ: Prentice Hall, 1977), p. 150; adapted from Charles Morris, ed., *The Developing Labor Law* (Washington, DC: Bureau of National Affairs, 1971), pp. 271–310.

49. John Fossum, *Labor Relations*, pp. 246–250.

50. Boulwareism is the name given to a strategy, now generally held in disfavor, by which the company, based on an exhaustive study of what it thought its employees wanted, made but one offer at the bargaining table and then refused to bargain any further unless convinced by the union on the basis of new facts that its original position was wrong. The NLRB subsequently found that the practice of offering the same settlement to all units, insisting that certain parts of the package could not differ among agreements and communicating to the employees about how negotiations were going amounted to an illegal pattern. Fossum, *Labor Relations*, p. 267. See also William Cooke, Aneil Mishra, Gretchen Spreitzer, and Mary Tschirhart, "The Determinants of NLRB Decision-Making Revisited," *Industrial and Labor Relations Review*, Vol. 48, no. 2 (January 1995), pp. 237–257.

51. Commerce Clearing House, "Drug Testing/Court Rulings," *Ideas and Trends*, January 25, 1988, p. 16.

52. Bargaining items based on Richardson, *Collective Bargaining*, pp. 113–115; bargaining stages based on William Glueck, "Labor Relations and the Supervisor," in M. Gene

Newport, *Supervisory Management* (St. Paul, MN: West, 1976), pp. 207–234.

53. See also Yoder, *Personnel Management,* pp. 517–518.

54. Richardson, *Collective Bargaining,* p. 150.

55. R.E. Fells, "Developing Trust in Negotiation," *Employee Relations,* Vol. 15, no. 1 (1993), p. 35.

56. Ibid., pp. 40–41.

57. Fossum, *Labor Relations,* pp. 298–322.

58. Although considerable research has been done on the subject, it's not clear what sorts of situations precipitate impasses. At times, however, it seems that the prospect of having the impasse taken to an arbitrator actually "chills" the negotiation process. Specifically, if neither the union nor the management negotiators want to make the tough political decision to make the tough choices, they might consciously or unconsciously opt to declare an impasse knowing that the arbitrator will then have to take the heat. See Linda Babcock and Craig Olson, "The Causes of Impasses in Labor Disputes," *Industrial Relations,* Vol. 31, no. 2 (Spring 1992), pp. 348–360.

59. Fossum, *Labor Relations,* p. 312. See also Thomas Watkins, "Assessing Arbitrator Competence," *Arbitration Journal,* Vol. 47, no. 2 (June 1992), pp. 43–48.

60. Ibid., p. 317.

61. "Work Stoppages," *BNA Bulletin to Management,* March 19, 1992, pp. 84–85.

62. Stephen Cabot and Gerald Cureton, "Labor Disputes and Strikes: Be Prepared," *Personnel Journal,* Vol. 60 (February 1981), pp. 121–126. See also Brenda Sunoo, "Managing Strikes, Minimizing Loss," *Personnel Journal,* Vol. 74, no. 1 (January 1995), pp. 50ff.

63. For a discussion see Herbert Northrup, "Union Corporate Campaigns and Inside Games as a Strike Form," *Employee Relations Law Journal,* Vol. 19, no. 4 (Spring 1994), pp. 507–549.

64. Ibid., p. 513.

65. Ibid., p. 518.

66. For a discussion of the cost of a strike, see Woodruff Imberman, "Strikes Cost More Than You Think," *Harvard Business Review,* Vol. 57 (May–June 1979), pp. 133–138. The NLRB held in 1986 in Harter Equipment, Inc., 280 NLRB No. 71, that an employer could lawfully hire temporary replacements during the course of a lockout, in the absence of proof of specific antiunion motivation, in order to bring economic pressure to bear upon a union to support a legitimate bargaining position.

67. Dale Beach, *Personnel* (New York: Macmillan, 1975), pp. 117–119.

68. Arthur A. Sloane and Fred Witney, *Labor Relations,* 5th ed. (Englewood Cliffs, NJ: Prentice Hall, 1977), pp. 229–231.

69. Richardson, *Collective Bargaining,* p. 184.

70. Lester Bittel, *What Every Supervisor Should Know* (New York: McGraw-Hill, 1974), p. 308, based on a study of 1,000 grievances made by the American Arbitration Association.

71. Richardson, *Collective Bargaining.*

72. J. Brad Chapman, "Constructive Grievance Handling," in M. Gene Newport, *Supervisory Management* (St. Paul: West Publishing Co., 1976), pp. 253–274. For a discussion of the impact of supervisory behavior on grievance initiation, see Brian Bemmels, "The Determinants of Grievance Initia-

tion," *Industrial and Labor Relations Review,* Vol. 47, no. 2 (January 1994), pp. 285–301.

73. See, for example, Clyde Summers, "Protecting All Employees Against Unjust Dismissal," *Harvard Business Review,* Vol. 58 (January–February 1980), pp. 132–139; and George Bohlander and Harold White, "Building Bridges: Non-Union Employee Grievance Systems," *Personnel* (July 1988), pp. 62–66.

74. Newport, *Supervisory Management,* p. 273, for an excellent checklist.

75. For a full discussion of these and others, see Walter Baer, *Grievance Handling: 101 Guides for Supervisors* (New York: American Management Association, 1970). For an interesting discussion of major league baseball's grievance arbitration system, see Glenn Wong, "Major League Baseball's Grievance Arbitration System: A Comparison with Nonsport Industry," *Labor Law Journal,* Vol. 38, no. 2 (February 1987), pp. 84–99.

76. "AFL-CIO Launching New Strategy to Win Over Nonunion Workers," *Compensation and Benefits Review,* Vol. 18, no. 5 (September–October 1986), p. 8; Shane R. Premeaux, R. Wayne Moody, and Art Bethke, "Decertification: Fulfilling Unions' 'Destiny'?" *Personnel Journal,* Vol. 66, no. 6 (June 1987), p. 144; and Peter A. Susser, "The Labor Impact of Deregulation," *Employment Relations Today,* Vol. 13, no. 2 (Summer 1986), pp. 117–123.

77. "Beyond Unions," pp. 72–77.

78. Dennis Chamot, "Unions Need to Confront the Results of New Technology," *Monthly Labor Review* (August 1987), p. 45.

79. Bureau of National Affairs, "Union 'No' at Nissan," *Bulletin to Management,* August 10, 1989, pp. 249–250.

80. "The Battle for Corporate Control," *Business Week,* May 18, 1987, p. 107.

81. Sar Levitan and Frank Gallo, "Collective Bargaining and Private Sector Employment," *Monthly Labor Review* (September 1989), pp. 24–33; Charles Craver, "The American Labor Movement in the Year 2000," *Business Horizons* (November–December 1993), pp. 64–69; and Barbara Ettorre, "Will Unions Survive?" *Management Review* (August 1993), pp. 9–15.

82. Thomas Kochan, Harry Katz, and Nancy Mower, *Worker Participation and American Unions: Threat or Opportunity* (Kalamazoo, MI: W.E. Upjohn, 1984).

83. Nil Verma, "Employee Involvement Programs: Do They Alter Worker Affinity Towards Unions?" Proceedings of the 39th Annual Meetings (New Orleans, December 1986) (Madison, WI: Industrial Relations Research Association, 1987), pp. 306–312.

84. Adrienne Eaton, "The Extent and Determinants of Local Union Control of Participative Programs," *Industrial and Labor Relations Review,* Vol. 43, no. 5 (1990), pp. 604–620.

85. Adrienne Eaton, Michael Gordon, and Jeffrey Keefe, "The Impact of Quality of Work Life Programs and Grievance System Effectiveness on Union Commitment," *Industrial and Labor Relations Review,* Vol. 45, no. 3 (April 1992), p. 591. See also Keith Knauss and Michael Matuszak, "An Anti-Union Corporate Culture and Quality Improvement Programs," *Labor Studies Journal,* Vol. 19, no. 3 (Fall 1994), pp. 21–39.

86. This is based on Kenneth Jenero and Christopher Lyons, "Employee Participation Programs: Prudent or Prohib-

ited?" *Employee Relations Law Journal*, Vol. 17, no. 4 (Spring 1992), pp. 535–566. See also Edward Cohen-Rosenthal and Cynthia Burton, "Improving Organizational Quality by Forging the Best Union-Management Relationship," *National Productivity Review*, Vol 13, no. 2 (Spring 1994), pp. 215–31.

87. 78 Congressional Records 4229, 4230 (1934).

88. Jenero and Lyons, "Employee Participation Programs," p. 539.

89. See ibid., p. 551, for instance.

90. These are based on ibid., pp. 564–565. See also "Fallout from Electromation," *BNA Bulletin to Management*, March 4, 1993, p. 65; and Bob Smith, "Employee Committee or Labor Union?" *Management Review*.

91. For a discussion of this, see John Hoerr, "What Should Unions Do?" *Harvard Business Review* (May–June 1991), pp. 30–45. See also Roy Marshall, "The Future Role of Government in Industrial Relations," *Industrial Relations*, Vol. 31, no. 1 (Winter 1992), pp. 31–49.

92. Ibid., pp. 42–43; for an additional view on this topic, see David Blanchflower and Richard Freeman, "Unionism in the United States and Other Advanced OECD Countries," *Industrial Relations*, Vol. 31, no. 1 (Winter 1992), pp. 56–79.

93. "New Agreements Improve Labor Relations," *Bulletin to Management*, September 5, 1991, p. 279; and Joseph D. Reid, "Future Unions," *Industrial Relations*, Vol. 31, no. 1 (Winter 1992), pp. 122–136. For another view see George Bohlander and Marshall Campbell, "Forging a Labor-Management Partnership: The Magna Copper Experience," *Labor Studies Journal*, Vol. 18, no. 4 (Winter 1994), pp. 3–20.

94. Northrup, "Union Corporate Campaigns and Inside Games as a Strike Form," pp. 519–520.

95. Ibid., pp. 519–520. Joseph Mosca and Steven Pressman, "Unions in the 21st Century," *Public Personnel Management*, Vol. 24, No. 2 (Summer 1995), pp. 159–166.

Communications activities including in-house television centers, frequent roundtable discussions, and in-house newsletters that provide continuing opportunities for the firm to let all employees be updated on important matters regarding the firm.

Saturn uses several **top-down programs** to get data to all employees. "The communication is excellent," says one assembler. "We get information continuously via the internal television network, and from financial documents." "And the hierarchy is pretty flat here," says another, "so the point people on the teams, including the team leaders, can quickly find the information and the resources that you need." One union leader says, "We have 'town hall' meetings once per month and usually have at least 500 to 700 people attending. That plus the broadcasts usually make sure that everyone's knowledge base is up—you better know the facts if you want to work here."

Toyota's management similarly works hard to share what it knows with every team member. There are twice-a-day five-minute team information meetings at job sites, where employees get the latest news about the plant. There's also a television in each work-site break area. The television runs continuously presenting plantwide information from the in-house Toyota broadcasting center. There are quarterly "roundtable" discussions between top management and selected nonsupervisory staff, as well as the in-house newsletter. The hotline described earlier in this chapter is another channel of top-down information in that it gives management a chance to answer publicly any anonymous (or nonanonymous) questions team members might have. The firm's president is often in the plant, fielding questions, providing performance information, and ensuring that all in the company are "aware of Toyota's goals and where we are heading."

Guaranteed Fair Treatment and Employee Discipline

Guaranteed Fair Treatment Programs at Work

guaranteed fair treatment
Employer programs that are aimed at ensuring that all employees are treated fairly, generally by providing formalized, well-documented, and highly publicized vehicles through which employees can appeal any eligible issues.

The potential for grievances and discontent is always present. Just about any factor involving wages, hours, or conditions of employment has and will be used as the basis of a grievance in most firms. Discipline cases and seniority problems (including promotions, transfers, and layoffs) would probably top the list. Others would include grievances growing out of job evaluations and work assignments, overtime, vacations, incentive plans, and holidays.

Whatever the source of grievances, many firms today (and virtually all unionized ones) give employees channels through which to air grievances. A grievance procedure helps to ensure that every employee's grievance is heard and treated fairly, and unionized firms do not hold a monopoly on such fair treatment. Even in nonunionized firms, formal grievance procedures can help ensure that labor-management peace prevails.

Programs such as Federal Express's Guaranteed Fair Treatment go beyond most grievance procedures: (1) Special, easily available forms make filing the grievance easy; (2) employees are encouraged to use the system; and (3) the highest levels of top management are routinely involved in reviewing complaints. As their employee handbook says:

> *Perhaps the cornerstone of Federal Express' 'people' philosophy is the guaranteed fair treatment procedure (GFTP). This policy affirms your right to appeal any eligible issue through this process of systematic review by progressively higher levels of management. Although the outcome is not assured to be in your favor, your right to participate within the guidelines of the procedure is guaranteed. At Federal Express, where we have a 'people-first' philosophy, you have a right to discuss your complaints with management without fear of retaliation.*[6]

The net effect is twofold: Complaints don't get a chance to accumulate; and all managers think twice before doing anything unfair, since their actions will likely be brought to their bosses' attention. In fact, each Tuesday morning, a group of five Federal Express executives gathers to review and rule on employee complaints and grievances filed through the program. They include CEO Fred Smith, Chief Operating Officer James Barksdale, the firm's chief HR officer, and two other senior vice presidents.[7]

Eligible Concerns GFTP is available to all permanent FedEx employees. It covers all concerns regarding matters such as job promotion and discipline affecting the individual complainant. As the firm's handbook points out, "If for any reason you are a recipient of discipline, you will have access to the GFTP."[8]

Steps The FedEx guaranteed fair treatment procedure contains three steps. In step one, *management review,* the complainant submits a written complaint to a member of management (manager, senior manager, or managing director) within

Employee commitment at Federal Express has been fostered by CEO Fred Smith's people-first values.

seven calendar days of the occurrence of the eligible issue. Then the manager, senior manager, and managing director of the employee's group review all relevant information; hold a telephone conference and/or meeting with the complainant; make a decision to either uphold, modify, or overturn management's action; and communicate their decision in writing to the complainant and the department's personnel representative. All this occurs within ten calendar days of receipt of the complaint.

In step two, *officer complaint,* the complainant submits a written complaint to an officer (vice president or senior vice president) of the division within seven calendar days of the step one decision. The vice president and senior vice president then review all relevant information; conduct an additional investigation, when necessary; make a decision to either uphold, overturn, or modify management's action, or initiate a board of review; and communicate their decision in writing to the complainant with copies to the department's personnel representative and the complainant's management. As in step one, the step two review generally occurs within ten calendar days of receipt of the complaint.

Finally, in step three, *executive appeals review,* the complainant submits a written complaint within seven calendar days of the step two decision to the employee relations department. This department then investigates and prepares a GFTP case file for the appeals board executive review. The appeals board—CEO Smith, COO Barksdale, the chief personnel officer, and three senior vice presidents—then reviews all relevant information; makes a decision to either uphold, overturn, or initiate a board of review or to take other appropriate action; and generally does this within 14 calendar days of receipt of the complaint. Barring the formation of a separate board of review, the appeals board's decision is final.

A five-member board of review is used when there is a question of fact regarding the complaint.[9] Two members are chosen by the complaining employee from a list of names submitted by the board chair. Three are selected by the board chair from a list of names submitted by the employee. Board chairpersons are chosen from the ranks of management at the director level or above.

Documentation Packets of forms in folders entitled "Guaranteed Fair Treatment Procedure," available from the personnel department, are used to file GFTP-registered complaints. They include a fact sheet listing the complainant's name and work history; a GFTP tracking sheet to keep track of the complaint at each step; and instructions and space for management's rationale (for instance, in terms of applicable policies and procedures), a write-up from the personnel department, and places for key documents (termination letters, and so on). There is also space for back-up material including witness statements, medical statements, and training records. These packets are widely available.

open-door program
IBM's fair treatment program, which gives every IBM employee the right to appeal the actions of his or her supervisor by taking the concern to successively higher levels of management.

IBM has a similar fair treatment program called **open-door.** It gives every employee the right to appeal his or her supervisor's actions. Employees are told to first discuss the problem with their immediate manager, their manager's manager, their personnel manager, or their branch or site manager. If that doesn't solve the problem, they are instructed to go to their unit's senior manager. Programs like IBM's haven't the structure and formality of FedEx's guaranteed fair treatment program. However, they do help ensure that healthy communication occurs regarding disciplinary matters and that employees' voices are heard.

Fairness in Disciplining

discipline
A procedure that corrects or punishes a subordinate because a rule or procedure has been violated.

The purpose of **discipline** is to encourage employees to behave sensibly at work, where being sensible is defined as adhering to rules and regulations. In an organization, rules and regulations serve about the same purpose that laws do in society; discipline is called for when one of these rules or regulations is violated.[10] A fair and just discipline process is based on three foundations: *rules and regulations; a system of progressive penalties;* and *an appeals process.*

A set of clear *rules and regulations* is the first foundation. These rules address things like theft, destruction of company property, drinking on the job, and insubordination. Examples of rules include:

> Poor performance is not acceptable. Each employee is expected to perform his or her work properly and efficiently and to meet established standards of quality.
>
> Liquor and drugs do not mix with work. The use of either during working hours and reporting for work under the influence of either are both strictly prohibited.
>
> The vending of anything in the plant without authorization is not allowed, nor is gambling in any form permitted.

The purpose of these rules is to inform employees ahead of time as to what is and is not acceptable behavior. Employees must be told, preferably in writing, what is not permitted. This is usually done during the employee's orientation. The rules and regulations are usually listed in the employee orientation handbook.

A *system of progressive penalties* is a second foundation of effective disciplining. Penalties may range from oral warnings to written warnings to suspension from the job to discharge. The severity of the penalty is usually a function of the type of offense and the number of times the offense has occurred. For example, most companies issue warnings for the first unexcused lateness. However, for a fourth offense, discharge is the more usual disciplinary action.

Finally, there should be an *appeals process* as part of the disciplinary process; this helps to ensure that discipline is meted out fairly and equitably. Programs like FedEx's Guaranteed Fair Treatment and IBM's open-door program help ensure their employees a real appeals process.[11]

Discipline Guidelines

Since arbitration may be a step in the discipline process (particularly in unionized firms), employers should ensure that their disciplinary actions will be viewed as fair by an independent arbitrator. Based on past disciplinary cases, here are guidelines that arbitrators may use when deciding whether there was just cause for the disciplinary action:

Make sure the evidence supports the charge of employee wrongdoing. In one study, "the employer's evidence did not support the charge of employee wrongdoing" was the reason arbitrators gave most frequently for reinstating discharged employees or for reducing disciplinary suspensions. Other sample arbitrator statements included, for example, "The evidence was not persuasive against the employee."[12]

Ensure that the employees' due process rights are protected. Arbitrators normally reverse discharges and suspensions that are imposed in a manner that violates basic notions of fairness or employee due process procedures.[13] Typical due process and procedural errors committed by employers include failing to follow established progressive discipline procedures, denying the employee an opportunity to tell his or her side of the story, lacking probable cause to discipline the employee; and not providing the employee a formal charge of wrongdoing.[14]

The discipline should be in line with the way management usually responds to similar incidents. In one case the employer's rule stated that "leaving the plant without permission during working hours" made the worker subject to immediate discharge. A worker did leave the plant and was thus discharged. The arbitrator later found that employees frequently left the plant while they were clocked in and openly went into town for personal matters. Since the rule was not consistently applied in the past, the arbitrator ruled that the worker was wrongfully discharged.[15]

The employee should be adequately warned of the consequences of his or her alleged misconduct. The person should be told of any undesirable behavior that is noted and the consequences that may result if the employee chooses not to change that behavior.

The rule that allegedly was violated should be "reasonably related" to the efficient and safe operation of the particular work environment. Employees, in other words, are usually allowed by arbitrators to question the reason behind any rule or order.

Management must adequately investigate the matter before administering discipline. Furthermore, the investigation must be fair and objective.

The investigation should produce substantial evidence of misconduct.

Applicable rules, orders, or penalties should be applied evenhandedly and without discrimination.

The penalty should be reasonably related to the misconduct and to the employee's past history. In other words, each employee should be judged on the basis of his or her personal work record; only then should the appropriate discipline be imposed.[16]

Right to counsel. All union employees have the right to bring help when they are called in for an interview that they reasonably believe might result in disciplinary action. Typically, unionized employees may bring a union representative, and nonunion employees—who should be told of their rights—may bring a coworker. Note that this is a legal right of employees according to the National Labor Relations Board.[17]

Other sensible disciplining guidelines include:

Don't rob your subordinate of his or her dignity.[18] Discipline your subordinate in private (unless he or she requests counsel) and avoid entrapment. That is, don't deliberately rig a situation that causes the employee to require disciplining.

Remember that the burden of proof is on you. In our society, a person is always considered innocent until proven guilty.

Get the facts. Don't base your decision on hearsay evidence or on your "general impression."

Don't act while angry. Very few people can be objective and sensible when they are angry.

Discipline Without Punishment

Traditional discipline has two major potential flaws. First, although fairness guidelines like those previously mentioned can take the edge off this, no one ever feels good about being punished. Yet that is what discipline is: An employee does something wrong and is punished. There may, therefore, be residual bad feelings among all involved. A second shortcoming is that, as the saying goes, "a person convinced against his or her will is of the same opinion still." In other words, forcing your rules on employees may gain their short-term compliance but not their active cooperation when you are not on hand to enforce the rules.

Discipline without punishment (or nonpunitive discipline) is aimed at avoiding these disciplinary problems. This is accomplished by gaining the employees' acceptance of your rules and by reducing the punitive nature of the discipline itself.

Here is an example. Assume there has been a breach of discipline (such as disregarding safety rules) or unsatisfactory work performance (such as carelessness in handling materials). In such a case, the following steps would constitute a typical nonpunitive approach to discipline.[19]

Step 1: First, issue an oral reminder. As a supervisor, your goal here is to get the employee to agree to solve the problem. You will meet privately with the employee and (instead of warning him or her of possible disciplinary sanctions) remind the person of (1) the reason for the rule and (2) the fact that he or she has a responsibility to meet performance standards. Keep a written record of the incident in a separate working file in your desk rather than in the employee's personnel file.

Step 2: Should another incident arise within six weeks, issue the employee a formal written reminder, a copy of which is placed in the personnel file. In addition, privately hold a second discussion with the employee, again without any threats. As in step 1, the aim is to discuss the need for the rule and to obtain the employee's acceptance of the need to act responsibly at work. Make sure the person understands the rule and your explanation for why improvement is required, and express your confidence in the person's ability to act responsibly at work. Should another such incident occur in the next six weeks, a follow-up meeting might be held. Here reiterate the need to act responsibly and investigate the possibility that the person is ill-suited to or bored with the job. Usually, though, the next step after the written reminder would be a paid one-day leave (step 3).

Step 3: The next step is a paid one-day "decision-making leave." If another incident occurs after the written warning in the next six weeks or so, the employee is told to take a one-day leave with pay to stay home and consider whether or not the job is right for him or her and whether or not the person wants to abide by the company's rules. The fact that the person is paid for the day is a final expression of the company's hope that the employee can and will act responsibly with respect to following the rules. When the employee returns to work, he or she meets with you and gives you a decision regarding whether or not the rules will be followed. At that point (assuming a positive response), you again explain your confidence in the employee and, if necessary, work out a brief action plan to help the person change his or her behavior.

Step 4: If no further incidents occur in the next year or so, the one-day paid suspension would be purged from the person's file. If the behavior repeats itself, dismissal (see later discussion) would be required.

The process must of course be changed in exceptional circumstances. Criminal behavior or in-plant fighting might be grounds for immediate dismissal, for instance. And if several incidents occurred at very close intervals, step 2—the written warning—might be skipped.

Diversity Counts
Guaranteed Fair Treatment: *"Comparing males and females in a discipline situation."*

Watching a movie like "King Arthur" may lead you to the conclusion that chivalry in general and a protective attitude toward women in particular is a well-established value in many societies, but that may not be the case.[1] Not only is chivalry not necessarily a prevailing value, but there is even a competing hypothesis in the research literature. What several researchers call "The Evil Woman Thesis" certainly doesn't argue that women are evil. Instead it ". . . argues that women who commit offenses violate stereotypic assumptions about the proper behavior of women. These women will be penalized for their inappropriate sex role behavior in addition to their other offenses."[2]

In other words, the unfortunately titled "Evil Woman Thesis" argues that when a woman doesn't act the way other men and women think she should act, they tend to overreact and treat her more harshly than they might if the alleged misdeed was done by a man.

While such a thesis might seem ridiculous on its face, the results of at least one careful study seem to indicate that it may in fact have considerable validity. In this study, 360 graduate and undergraduate university business school students in a southern city (split about 50–50 between men and women) were asked to review a labor arbitration case. The case involved two employees, one male and one female, with similar work records and tenure with their employers. Both were discharged for violation of company rules related to alcohol and drugs. The case portrays one worker's behavior as a more serious breach of company rules: the more culpable worker (a male in half the cases and a female in the other half) had brought the intoxicant to the work setting.

The male and female decision-maker/students were asked to express their agreement with two alternative approaches to arbitrating the dispute that arose when the culpable employee was discharged. The researchers assumed that only the male decision-maker students might come down more harshly on the culpable employee when that employee was a woman, and they were therefore surprised at their results.

In their study, they found evidence of a bias against the culpable woman employee by both the male and female students making the decisions about how to discipline the worker. In other words, the female workers in the labor case clearly received harsher treatment from the student decision-makers. And, again, at least in this study, it wasn't just the male student decision-makers that prescribed harsher penalties for the woman culpable employee. As the researchers conclude, "note that women, as decision-makers, appear to be as willing as men to impose harsher discipline on women than upon men."[3] In most respects, including the willingness to fire the culpable worker, it was the woman worker who could expect the harsher treatment, not the man.

In this study, student decision-makers were asked to come to some conclusions regarding discipline based on what they read in the case, so there is no way to conclude based solely on this study that the findings would necessarily apply in real world settings or under different conditions. However, the results of this study certainly provide food for thought regarding the fact that women just might be treated more harshly than men in a discipline situation.

1. This is based on Sandra Hartman, et al. "Males and Females in a Discipline Situation: Exploratory Research on Completing Hypotheses," *Journal of Managerial Issues,* Vol. 6, No. 1 (Spring 1994), pgs. 64–68.

2. Ibid, pg. 57.

3. Ibid, pg. 64.

Nonpunitive discipline can be effective. Employees seem to welcome the less punitive aspects and don't seem to abuse the system by misbehaving to get a day off with pay. Grievances, sick leave usage, and disciplinary incidents all seem to drop in firms using these new procedures. However, there will still be times when dismissals will be required.

Electronic Trespassing and Employee Privacy

Electronic searches of employees have become quite widespread. In one recent survey 22% of employers reported engaging in electronic employee searches, including searches of employees' electronic work files, electronic mail files, and voicemail messages.[20] Most employers said they hadn't engaged in a regular pattern of searches but admitted to engaging in such searches between one and five times in the preceding two years, either to verify wrongdoing or to monitor performance.[21]

Electronic eavesdropping is not without risks. While no federal law covers all aspects of an employee's right to privacy in the workplace, some specific federal and state laws do apply. In one case, for instance, the owners of a liquor store used an extension phone in their home next door to monitor and record employees' calls from work during a three-month period, recording more than 22 hours of conversations. They picked up not only one illicit deal by one employee but also several steamy phone calls between that employee and a customer. A court subsequently found that the employers had gone too far by listening in longer than necessary for their investigation (and by informing the employee's spouse), and they were therefore liable for the employee's legal expenses plus a sizable cash settlement.[22] Another potential pitfall is discovering, while electronically eavesdropping, that a worker has AIDS or, say, takes antidepressants: Penalizing the employee might violate the Americans with Disabilities Act.[23]

Experts recommend establishing an electronic eavesdropping policy as a way to avoid potential problems. Issues to be addressed include:[24]

Offensive messages. Prohibit the use of E-mail in ways that may be disruptive, offensive to others, or harmful to morale.

Personal messages. Ban E-mail use to solicit or proselytize others for commercial ventures, religious or political causes, outside organizations, or other non-job-related solicitations.

Access. Employees are not to attempt to gain access to other employees' E-mail files without permission, but management's rights to enter an employee's E-mail files for business purposes are reserved.

Business use. The purpose of the firm's electronic message systems is to facilitate transmittal of business-related information within the organization exclusively.

Passwords. All computer pass codes and other pass codes must be available to the company, which may access them at any time.

Search authorization. Where appropriate, obtain authorizations from employees allowing the company to inspect their personal possessions and property, including E-mail and other electronic message systems on company premises. Inform employees that searches may be conducted without advance notice, and that anyone who does not consent to inspection may be subject to discipline.

Managing Dismissals

dismissal
Involuntary termination of an employee's employment with the firm.

Dismissal is the most drastic disciplinary step you can take toward an employee and one that must be taken with deliberate care.[25] Specifically, the dismissal should be *just* in that *sufficient cause* exists for it. Furthermore, the dismissal should occur only after *all reasonable steps* to rehabilitate or salvage the employee have failed. However, there are undoubtedly times when dismissal is required, and in these instances it should be carried out forthrightly.[26]

Grounds for Dismissal

There are four bases for dismissal: unsatisfactory performance; misconduct; lack of qualifications for the job; and changed requirements of (or elimination of) the job. *Unsatisfactory performance* may be defined as a persistent failure to perform assigned duties or to meet prescribed standards on the job.[27] Specific reasons here include excessive absenteeism, tardiness, a persistent failure to meet normal job requirements, or an adverse attitude toward the company, supervisor, or fellow employees. *Misconduct* can be defined as deliberate and willful violation of the employer's rules and may include stealing, rowdyism, and insubordination. *Lack of qualifications* for the job is defined as an employee's incapability of doing the assigned work although the person is diligent. Since the employee in this case may be trying to do the job, it is especially important that every effort be made to salvage him or her. *Changed requirements of the job* may be defined as an employee's incapability of doing the work assigned after the nature of the job has been changed. Similarly, an employee may have to be dismissed when his or her job is eliminated. Here again, the employee may be industrious, so every effort should be made to retrain or transfer this person, if possible.

Insubordination, a form of misconduct, is sometimes the grounds for dismissal, although it may be relatively difficult to prove. Stealing, chronic tardiness, and poor-quality work are fairly concrete grounds for dismissal, while insubordination is sometimes harder to translate into words. To that end, it may be useful to remember that some acts are or should be considered insubordinate whenever and wherever they occur. These include:

insubordination
Willful disregard or disobedience of the boss's authority or legitimate orders; criticizing the boss in public.

1. Direct disregard of the boss's authority. At sea, this is called mutiny.
2. Flat out disobedience of, or refusal to obey, the boss's orders—particularly in front of others.
3. Deliberate defiance of clearly stated company policies, rules, regulations, and procedures.
4. Public criticism of the boss. Contradicting or arguing with him or her is also negative and inappropriate.
5. Blatant disregard of the boss's reasonable instructions.
6. Contemptuous display of disrespect; making insolent comments, for example; and, more important, portraying these feelings in the attitude shown while on the job.
7. Disregard for the chain of command, shown by going around the immediate supervisor or manager with a complaint, suggestion, or political maneuver. Although the employee may be right, that may not be enough to save him or her from the charges of insubordination.
8. Participation in (or leadership of) an effort to undermine and remove the boss from power. If the effort doesn't work (and it seldom does), those involved will be "dead in the water."[28]

As in most human endeavors, it is dangerous to take the position that any of these acts should always lead to dismissal. Even at sea (as the movie *The Caine Mutiny* illustrates), there may be extenuating circumstances for the apparent insubordination. Cases like these should therefore be reviewed by the supervisor's boss. At least having insubordination accepted as a handicap under the Americans with Disabilities Act doesn't seem to be a risk. In one case that astonished many observers, an employee of General Electric (GE) brought suit against the firm under a Vermont state law prohibiting discrimination against the handicapped.[29]

When this employee got a new supervisor who started enforcing the company's rules, the employee claimed that the company knew he suffered from a disability, namely "an emotional condition that is characterized by feelings of inferiority and unacceptability" that made him unable to follow orders. He also claimed that his other "handicap" was his inability to get along with his new supervisor. The judge agreed with the company that GE did not have to make reasonable accommodation by transferring him to another supervisor since "the ability to follow the orders of superiors is an essential function of any position . . . [so] employees who are insubordinate are not otherwise qualified for the position."[30]

Termination at Will

termination at will
The idea, based in law, that the employment relationship can be terminated at will by either the employer or the employee for any reason.

For more than 100 years the prevailing rule in the United States has been that without an employment contract, the employment relationship can be **terminated at will** by either the employer or the employee. In other words, the employee could resign for any reason, at will, and the employer could similarly dismiss an employee for any reason, at will. Today, however, dismissed employees are increasingly taking their cases to court, and in many states employers are finding that they no longer have a blanket right to fire. Instead federal laws and various state court rulings increasingly limit management's right to dismiss employees at will.

Consider an example. You're fired for no apparent reason and given two weeks' pay and two hours to leave the firm. You've worked for this company for almost three years with consistently good reviews. Your job, you know, was not dissolved. Instead you were replaced by someone with less seniority and experience—and at lower pay. You ask your supervisor why you were fired, and he says he just can't tell you. What legal recourse do you have?

Increasingly today the answer to this question depends on the state where you work.[31] The United States is currently one of the few remaining industrialized countries without federal legislation addressing management's right to dismiss employees at will. And in only three states—Michigan, Pennsylvania, and Wisconsin—has legislation been introduced that would erode the at-will rule. Yet today, despite this dearth of laws, discharged employees are turning to their state courts for relief—and winning their cases.

In 20 states—California, Connecticut, Idaho, Illinois, Indiana, Kansas, Maryland, Massachusetts, Michigan, Missouri, Montana, New Hampshire, New Jersey, New York, Oregon, Pennsylvania, Texas, Virginia, Washington, and West Virginia—courts have ruled that there are public policy exceptions to the common law doctrine that employees may be discharged for any reason an employer chooses. They have held, for instance, that it is against public policy for an employer to fire an employee because the person refused to give false testimony in court to protect the employer or to sell a drug that the employee knew was tainted.

In 13 states—California, Connecticut, Idaho, Louisiana, Maine, Massachusetts, Michigan, Montana, Nebraska, New Hampshire, North Carolina, Oklahoma, and Washington—courts have taken the position that company manuals or handbooks (or even employment interviews) may constitute implied contracts to which an employer is legally bound. In Idaho, for instance, the state Supreme Court ruled in *Jackson* v. *Minidoka Irrigation* that the employee handbook was an enforceable employment contract with respect to discharge hearing, retirement benefits, and vacation pay.

Courts in 7 states—Florida, Illinois, Minnesota, Missouri, North Dakota, South Carolina, and Washington—have granted limited exceptions to the at-will doctrine for other reasons. In Florida, for instance (where the employment at-will rule is still strictly adhered to) a court in *Chatelier* v. *Robertson* found for the employee, who had transferred his business to his employer in exchange for lifetime employment but was subsequently fired.

Of course, employees may also be protected by various federal laws. The Civil Rights Act and state fair employment laws prohibit employers from discharging employees because of their age, race, sex, religion, or national origin. Under federal law, for instance, if the employee is over 40 and is replaced by someone younger—even if that person is also over 40—the dismissed employee may have a basis for an age discrimination charge. As another example, employees who report safety violations at their place of work are generally protected from discharge by the Occupational Safety and Health Act.

Avoiding Wrongful Discharge Suits

wrongful discharge
An employee dismissal that does not comply with the law or does not comply with the contractual arrangement stated or implied by the firm via its employment application forms, employee manuals, or other promises.

With the increased likelihood that terminated employees can and will sue for **wrongful discharge**, it behooves employers to protect themselves against wrongful discharge suits. The time to do that is before mistakes have been made and suits have been filed. Here is what one expert recommends to avoid wrongful discharge suits.

- Have applicants sign the *employment application* and make sure it contains a clearly worded statement that employment is for no fixed term and that the employer can terminate at any time. In addition, the statement should inform the job candidate that "nothing on this application can be changed."

- Review your *employee manual* to look for and delete statements that could prejudice your defense in a wrongful discharge case. For example, delete any reference to the fact that "employees can be terminated only for just cause" (unless you really mean that). Also consider not outlining progressive discipline procedures in the manual since you may be obligated to stick with the rules and follow the steps exactly or be sued for failing to do so. Similarly, references to probationary periods or permanent employment may be unwise since they imply a permanence you may not really mean to imply. Never limit the right to discharge or list specific reasons for discharge.[32] Always add a sentence or paragraph that reserves for the employer the right to make changes to the handbook in the future, and always include a waiver statement in the front of the handbook that asserts the company hires only at will.[33] An acknowledgment form like the one in Figure 16.1 can be useful in underscoring the fact that the handbook is not a contract and that employment-at-will remains in force.[34]

- Make sure that no one in a position of authority makes *promises* you do not intend to keep, such as by saying "If you do your job here, you can't get fired."

- Have clear written rules listing infractions that may require *discipline* and *discharge,* and then make sure to adhere to the rules. Generally, employees must be given an opportunity to correct unacceptable behavior, and you should be careful not to single out any one person.

- If a rule is broken, get the worker's side of the story in front of witnesses, and preferably get it signed. Then make sure to *check out* the story, getting both sides of the issue.

- Be sure that employees are evaluated at least annually. If an employee is showing evidence of incompetence, give that person a warning and provide a chance to improve. All evaluations should be put in writing and signed by the employee.[35]

- Keep careful records of all actions such as employee evaluations, warnings or notices, memos outlining how improvement should be accomplished, and so on. Keep all efforts at counseling or discipline confidential to avoid defamation charges.[36]

Figure 16–1
TJP Inc. Employee
Handbook
Acknowledgment
Form

TJP INC. EMPLOYEE HANDBOOK ACKNOWLEDGMENT FORM

This employee handbook has been given to _____

on (date) _____

by _____ (title) _____

Employee's effective starting date _____

Employee's pay period _____

Employee's hours and workweek are _____

Welcome to TJP Inc. Below are a list of your benefits with their effective date:

Benefit	**Effective Date**
Hospitalization _____	_____
Life insurance _____	_____
Retirement _____	_____
Vacation _____	_____
Sick leave _____	_____
Holidays _____	_____
Personal days _____	_____
Bereavement _____	_____
Worker's compensation _____	_____
Social Security _____	_____
Your first performance appraisal will be on _____	_____

I understand that my employee handbook is for informational purposes only and that I am to read and refer to the employee handbook for information on employment work rules and company policies. TJP Inc. may modify, revoke, suspend or terminate any and all policies, rules, procedures and benefits at any time without prior notice to company employees. This handbook and its statements do not create a contract between TJP Inc. and its employees. This handbook and its statements do not affect in any way the employment-at-will relationship between TJP Inc. and its employees.

(Employee's signature) _____

(Date) _____

- ◆ Make sure that the company's policy about probationary periods is clear and that employees cannot infer that once they are past the probationary period their jobs are "safe."[37]
- ◆ Remember that there are a number of public policy issues often used by the courts to protect employees from arbitrary discharge. In the past, in various jurisdictions, these have included whistleblowing, garnishment for anyone's indebtedness, complaining or testifying about equal pay or wage/hour law violations, and filing a worker's compensation claim.[38]
- ◆ Before taking any irreversible steps, *review* the person's personnel file. For example, long-seniority employees may merit more opportunities to correct their actions than newly hired workers.
- ◆ Finally, consider *"buying out"* a wrongful discharge claim with settlement pay. Do not stand in the way of a terminated employee's future employment, since a person with a new job is less likely to bring a lawsuit against the former employer than someone who remains unemployed.[39]

♦ In addition:

Don't discharge anyone who is about to vest in employee benefits.

Don't discharge a female employee just before maternity leave.

Don't "constructively discharge" employees by placing them in a lower paying job in hopes of a resignation.

Don't try to induce employees to waive existing rights in exchange for gaining other rights.

Don't deviate from internal complaint resolution guidelines and procedures.

Don't oversell promises of job security in handbooks or oral discussions.[40]

Dismissal Procedures

In the event of a dismissal, these additional steps should be followed:

Hold warning discussions before taking any final action. An employee must be made aware that he or she is not performing satisfactorily.

Get written confirmation of the final warning.

Prepare a checklist of all property that should be accounted for, including computer disks and manuals.

Change security codes and locks previously used by discharged individuals.

If the dismissal involves large numbers of employees (say, 25 or more), prepare and secure approval for a news release.

Always prepare for the possibility that the discharged individual may act irrationally or even violently, either immediately or in weeks to come.

Decide beforehand how you are going to tell other employees about this person's dismissal. An informal departmental meeting of those directly involved with this person is usually sufficient.

Consider having your attorney create an employee release. Such releases are obtained from employees who have asserted claims or who are the subject of employment actions such as discharges and layoffs. They release the employer from claims by giving the employee something of value—"consideration" in legal terms.[41] State laws vary and determine what can and cannot be included in such releases. However, in general any such release should include: (1) a general release of the employee's claims; (2) a covenant not to sue the employer; and (3) an indemnification and payback provision relating to breaches of the release and convenant-not-to-sue provisions.[42]

The Termination Interview   Dismissing an employee is one of the most difficult tasks you'll face at work.[43] The dismissed employee, even if warned many times in the past, will often still react with total disbelief or even violence. Guidelines for the **termination interview** itself are as follows:

termination interview
The interview in which an employee is informed of the fact that he or she has been dismissed.

Step 1   Plan the interview carefully. According to experts at Hay Associates, this means:

Schedule the meeting on a day early in the week.

Make sure the employee keeps the appointment time.

Never inform an employee over the phone.

Allow ten minutes as sufficient time for notification in the interview.

Avoid Fridays, preholidays, and vacation times when possible.

Use a neutral site, never your own office.

Have employee agreements, human resources file, and release announcement (internal and external) prepared in advance.

Be available at a time after notification after the interview in case questions or problems arise.

Have phone numbers ready for medical or security emergencies.

Step 2 Get to the point. Do not beat around the bush by talking about the weather or making other small talk. As soon as the employee enters your office, give the person a moment to get comfortable and then inform him or her of your decision.

Step 3 Describe the situation. Briefly, in three or four sentences, explain why the person is being let go. For instance, "Production in your area is down four percent, and we are continuing to have quality problems. We have talked about these problems several times in the past three months and the solutions are not being followed through. We have to make a change."[44] Remember to describe the situation rather than attacking the employee personally by saying things like "Your production is just not up to par." Also emphasize that the decision is final and irrevocable; other in-house positions were explored, management at all levels concurs, and all relevant factors—performance, workload, and so on—were considered. Don't take more than 10 to 15 minutes for the interview.

Step 4 Listen. It is important to continue the interview until the person appears to be talking freely and reasonably calmly about the reasons for his or her termination and the support package (including severance pay) he or she is to receive.

Figure 16.2
Behavioral Reaction to Termination and Suggested Response
Source: Hay Associates, Philadelphia, Pa. 19103

Hostile and angry	Defensive and bargaining	Formal and procedural (lawsuit?)	Stoic	Crying/ sobbing
Hurt Anger Disappointment Relief	Guilt Fear Uncertainty Disbelief	Vengeful Suppressed Controlled	Shock Disbelief Numbness	Sadness Grief Worry
• Summarize what you have heard in a tentative style: "It sounds as if you are pretty angry about this." • Avoid confronting the anger or becoming defensive. • Remain objective; stick to the facts and give the employee helpful information.	• Let the employee know you realize this is a difficult time for him or her as well as for yourself. • Don't get involved in any bargaining discussions. • Offer reassurance about the future and connect this to the counseling process.	• Allow the employee freedom to ask any questions as long as they pertain to his or her own case. • Try to avoid side issues and discussion of "political" motivations. • Keep the tone formal. This is a good way to lead into the role the career counselor will play.	• Communicate to the employee that you recognize his or her shock and say the details can be handled later if the employee prefers. • Ask if there are any specific questions for the moment. If not, tell the employee about the career counselor and make the introduction.	• Allow the person an opportunity to cry if that occurs. Just offer some tissues. • Avoid inane comments such as "What are you crying about, it's not that important." • When the person regains composure, press on with the facts and explain the counseling process.

Do not get into arguments; instead, actively listen and get the person to talk by using open-ended questions, restating his or her last comment, and using silence and a nod of your head. Use the Behavioral Reaction Chart (Figure 16.2) to gauge the person's reaction and to decide how best to proceed.

Step 5 Next carefully review all elements of the severance package. Describe severance payments, benefits, access to office support people, and the way references will be handled. However, under no conditions should any promises or benefits beyond those already in the support package be implied. Do not promise to "look into" something and get back to the subordinate at a later date. This will simply complicate the termination process. The termination should be complete when the person leaves your office.

Step 6 Identify the next step. The terminated employee may be disoriented and unsure what to do next. Explain where the employee should go upon leaving the interview. Remind the person whom to contact at the company regarding questions about the support package or references.

outplacement counseling
A systematic process by which a terminated person is trained and counseled in the techniques of self-appraisal and securing a new position.

Outplacement Counseling[45] **Outplacement counseling** is a systematic process by which a terminated person is trained and counseled in the techniques of conducting a self-appraisal and securing a new job that is appropriate to his or her needs and talents.[46] As the term is generally used, *outplacement* does not mean the employer takes responsibility for placing the terminated person in a new job. Instead it is a counseling service whose purpose is to provide the person with advice, instructions, and a sounding board to help formulate career goals and successfully execute a job search. Outplacement counseling thus might more accurately (but more ponderously) be called "career counseling and job search skills for terminated employees." The counseling itself is done either by the employer's in-house specialist or by outside consultants. The outplacement counseling is considered part of the terminated employee's support or severance package.

Outplacement counseling is usually conducted by outplacement firms such as Drake Beam Moran Inc., and Right Associates Inc. Middle- and upper-level managers who are let go will typically have office space and secretarial services they can use at local offices of such firms, in addition to the counseling services.

Exit Interviews Many employers conduct final exit interviews with employees who are leaving the firm. These are usually conducted by the HR department. They aim at eliciting information about the job or related matters that might give the employer a better insight into what is right—or wrong—about the company. The assumption, of course, is that since the employee is leaving, he or she will be candid.

That the person will be candid is debatable. The person might have his or her own ax to grind, for instance, and could use the exit interview to try to retaliate against former foes. Or the person might simply not want to cause trouble that might come back to haunt him or her when in need of references for a new job.

Based on one survey, the quality of information you can expect to get from exit interviews is questionable. The researchers found that at the time of separation, 38% of those leaving blamed "salary and benefits," while only 4% blamed "supervision." Followed up 18 months later, however, 24% blamed supervision and only 12% blamed salary and benefits. Getting to the real problem during the exit interview may thus require some heavy digging.[47]

Managing Separations: Layoff and Retirement

Introduction

Nondisciplinary separations are a fact of life in organizations and can be initiated by either employer or employee. For the employer, reduced sales or profits may require layoffs or downsizings, for instance, while employees may terminate their own employment to retire or to seek better jobs.

The Plant Closing Law   Until recently there were no federal laws requiring notification of employees when an employer decided to close its facility. However, in 1989 the Worker Adjustment and Retraining Notification Act (popularly known as the **plant closing law**) became effective. The law requires employers of 100 or more employees to give 60 days' notice before closing a facility or starting a layoff *of 50 people or more*. The law does not prevent the employer from closing down, nor does it require saving jobs. The act simply gives employees time to seek other work or retraining by giving them advance notice of the shutdown.

    Not all plant closings and layoffs are covered by the law, although many are. Employers are responsible for giving notice to employees who will (or who reasonably may be expected to) experience a covered "employment loss." Employment losses include terminations (other than discharges for cause, voluntary departures, or retirement), layoffs exceeding six months, and reductions of more than 50% in employees' work hours during each month of any six-month period. Generally speaking, workers who are reassigned or transferred to certain employer-sponsored programs or who are given an opportunity to transfer or relocate to another employer location within a reasonable commuting distance need not be notified. While there are exceptions to the law, the penalty for failing to give notice is fairly severe: one day's pay and benefits to each employee for each day's notice that should have been given, up to 60 days.

    The law is not entirely clear about how the notice to employees must be worded. However, if you write a letter to the individual employees to be laid off, a paragraph toward the end of the letter that might suit the purpose would be as follows:

> *Please consider this letter to be your official notice, as required by the federal plant closing law, that your current position with the company will end 60 days from today because of a (layoff or closing) that is now projected to take place on (date). After that day your employment with the company will be terminated, and you will no longer be carried on our payroll records or be covered by any company benefit programs. Any questions concerning the plant closing law or this notice will be answered in the HR office.*[48]

plant closing law
The Worker Adjustment and Retraining Notification Act, which requires notifying employees in the event an employer decides to close its facility.

As more U.S. firms relocate their manufacturing plants to foreign countries in order to minimize costs, workers in San Antonio, Texas protest the signing of any free trade agreements, which they think encourage such actions.

Managing Layoffs

layoff
A situation in which there is a temporary shortage of work and employees are told there is no work for them but that management intends to recall them when work is again available.

A **layoff,** in which workers are sent home for a time, is a situation in which three conditions are present: (1) There is no work available for the employees; (2) management expects the no-work situation to be temporary and probably short term; and (3) management intends to recall the employees when work is again available.[49] A layoff is therefore not a termination, which is a permanent severing of the employment relationship. However, some employers do use the term *layoff* as a euphemism for discharge or termination.

bumping/layoff procedures
Detailed procedures that determine who will be laid off if no work is available; generally allow employees to use their seniority to remain on the job.

Bumping/Layoff Procedures   Employers who encounter frequent business slow-downs and layoffs often have detailed procedures that allow employees to use their seniority to remain on the job. Most such procedures have these features in common:[50]

1. For the most part, seniority is the ultimate determinant of who will work.
2. Seniority can give way to merit or ability, but usually only when none of the senior employees is qualified for a particular job.
3. Seniority is usually based on the date the employee joined the organization, not the date he or she took a particular job.
4. Because seniority is usually companywide, an employee in one job is usually allowed to bump or displace an employee in another job provided the more senior employee is able to do the job in question without further training.

Alternatives to Layoffs   Many employers today recognize the enormous investments they have in recruiting, screening, and training their employees and in winning their commitment and loyalty. As a result, many employers are more hesitant to lay off employees at the first signs of business decline. Instead they are using new approaches to either blunt the effects of the layoff or eliminate the layoffs entirely.

voluntary reduction in pay plan
An alternative to layoffs in which all employees agree to reductions in pay to keep everyone working.

voluntary time off
An alternative to layoffs in which some employees agree to take time off to reduce the employer's payroll and avoid the need for a layoff.

rings of defense
An alternative layoff plan in which temporary supplemental employees are hired with the understanding that they may be laid off at any time.

There are several alternatives to layoff. With the **voluntary reduction in pay plan**, all employees agree to reductions in pay in order to keep everyone working. Other employers arrange to have all or most of their employees accumulate their vacation time and to concentrate their vacations during slow periods. Temporary help thus does not have to be hired for vacationing employees during peak periods, and employment automatically falls off when business declines. Other employees agree to take **voluntary time off**, which again has the effect of reducing the employer's payroll and avoiding the need for a layoff. Control Data Corporation avoids layoffs with what it calls its **rings of defense** approach. Temporary supplemental employees are hired with the understanding that their work is of a temporary nature and they may be laid off at any time or fired. Then when layoffs come, the first ring of defense is the cadre of supplemental workers.[51]

Adjusting to Downsizings and Mergers

downsizings
Refers to the process of reducing, usually dramatically, the number of people employed by the firm.

Downsizing—reducing, usually dramatically, the number of people employed by the firm—is used by more and more employers.[52] About half the firms surveyed by the American Management Association in one recent year were downsizing their firms and most planned on continuing the cuts the following year.[53]

Although it's not clear why, most firms don't find that their operating earnings improve after major staff cuts are made. In one survey, for instance, only 43% of the surveyed firms that had downsized in the past ten years saw operating earnings increase.[54] There are probably many ways to explain this anomaly but declining employee morale as a result of downsizing is one plausible candidate. Therefore, firms that are downsizing must also give attention to the employees not dismissed. Certainly those "downsized-out" should be treated fairly. But it is around those you retain that the business will be built.

Dealing with the Survivors Immediately After the Downsizing   You will face one of two situations immediately following downsizing.[55] First, you may anticipate no further reductions, and you can assure your people of that. However, remember not to promise that no further reductions will occur unless you are sure you will keep the promise.

The second situation is more difficult because here you know that more reductions will probably take place. The best you can do is to be honest with those remaining, explaining that while future downsizings will probably occur, they will be informed of these reductions as soon as possible. You may well experience a transitory drop in productivity and increased attrition, but the alternative is being dishonest with all the people involved.

Specific Steps to Take A postdownsizing program instituted at Duracell, Inc. illustrates the steps involved in a well-conceived program. After several months of planning, the program began with a series of *announcement activities*.[56] These included a full staff meeting at the facility, followed by a program in which every employee was informed individually of his or her status with the firm. In addition, each survivor received a description of the support services and assistance being made available to those leaving Duracell. This helped reduce the survivors' concern about their friends and former colleagues.

Next there was an *immediate follow-up* phase during the first few days after the announcement. Here survivors were split into groups that included the senior management of the facility. At these sessions, employees were encouraged to discuss how they felt about the layoffs and to express their concerns and feelings about their future with the company and the future of the facility as a team.

A mechanism for providing *long-term support* was also built into the program. Key management was encouraged to meet with the remaining staff frequently and informally in order to provide them ongoing support in an open-door atmosphere. Finally, there was a follow-up meeting with the survivors about two months after the downsizing to make sure all concerns had been aired and addressed.[57]

Rebuilding employee commitment can be a key to a successful downsizing. And, as one experienced chief executive recently put it, "If companies are committed to building positive attitudes in their employees, they must actively and explicitly institute programs to achieve this during the downsizing process. This means that instead of a pure plan for cost reduction, the restructuring strategy must be broadened to achieve the additional goal of lighting a new fire of employee enthusiasm."[58]

As in any commitment-building program, communication is always crucial. In a downsizing program at the Diner's Club subsidiary of Citicorp, for instance, attitude surveys in conjunction with an opening up of top-down communications were used by management to inform and become better informed about what was happening in their subsidiary.[59] In this case the surveys helped management to know that the new postdownsizing push for customer service was unsettling to those employees who had little direct customer contact and who therefore felt disenfranchised from the main thrust of the firm's changes.[60] As at Citicorp, downsizings usually occur in conjunction with other realignments in employees' responsibilities; unless all employees are committed to the firm's new direction and to their new roles, the downsizing is unlikely to produce the hoped-for benefits.[61]

Handling the Merger/Acquisition In terms of dismissals and downsizings, mergers or acquisitions are usually one-sided: In many mergers, in other words, one company essentially acquires the other, and it is often the employees of the latter who find themselves out looking for new jobs.

In such a situation the employees in the acquired firm will be hypersensitive to mistreatment of their colleagues. It thus behooves you to take care that those let go are treated with courtesy. Seeing your former colleagues fired is bad enough for morale. Seeing them fired under conditions that look like bullying rubs salt in the wound and poisons the relationship for years to come. As a rule, therefore,[62]

> Avoid the appearance of power and domination.
>
> Avoid win/lose behavior.
>
> Remain businesslike and professional in all dealings.
>
> Maintain as positive a feeling about the acquired company as possible.
>
> Remember that the degree to which your organization treats the acquired group with care and dignity will affect the confidence, productivity, and commitment of those remaining.

Building Employee Commitment

Lifetime Employment Without Guarantees

lifetime employment without guarantees
Refers to a commitment on the part of firms like Toyota and Saturn to do all that is reasonably possible to avoid layoffs and non-performance-based dismissals while recognizing that ultimately the employment relationship must be at will.

kio Kitano, CEO of Toyota S.A., combines Japan's time employment concept th the realities of the U.S. tomobile industry.

Job security and employee commitment go hand-in-hand. For one thing, the cost involved in value-based hiring and in extensively training, empowering, and actualizing employees presumes the firm is committed to keeping them around. That is why Toyota USA's president has said, "At Toyota we hire people who we hope will stick around for 30 or 40 years or the remainder of their working years. So we always try to remember that hiring a 30-year employee who will earn $30,000 to $40,000 a year is really a million dollar plus decision for us."[63] Furthermore, commitment is a two-way street: Employees are committed to companies that are committed to them, and few things express an employer's commitment like the goal of lifetime employment. It is an ultimate manifestation of the fact that the firm's destiny is inextricably intertwined with that of its staff. That's why firms like Toyota, Saturn, and Federal Express follow a policy that one could call lifetime employment without guarantees.

Take Toyota. On the one hand, the firm's documents and managers' comments continually refer to lifetime employment. The team member handbook, for instance, states it this way:

> Lifetime employment is our goal—the ultimate result of you and the company working together to ensure TMM's success. We believe that job security is fundamental to the development of motivated employees. We also know that career employees have a significant stake in the company's success. If TMM is profitable, your job will be secure and you will receive a fair salary over the course of your career. We feel we have hired the best to make up our Toyota team. Job security demands that you must do everything possible to maximize the efficiency of the company in order to maintain its competitive edge in the marketplace. We count on you to help us search for a better way . . . to obtain success . . . job security at TMM.[64]

But in reality, there are no guarantees. For example, the team member handbook also prominently displays the usual employment-at-will disclaimer found in virtually all company handbooks these days:

> All employment relationships at TMM will be "employment-at-will" arrangements. This means that either the team member or TMM may terminate the employment relationships at any time and for any reason. No contract, implied or otherwise, will be considered to exist between TMM and any TMM team member.[65]

Yet Toyota employees are convinced—probably for good reason—that their jobs are secure as long as they do them. As one body shop team member said, "They always say they'd never lay someone off. In lean times, we'd be kept on to make the process more efficient."[66]

That kind of confidence is probably not misplaced. While the plant hasn't been in operation long enough to test the no-layoff policy, Toyota USA's president publicly takes the position that the firm would in fact redeploy, not dismiss, its people if times got tough:

> At TMM we have not yet reached the point of making adjustments in production. However, should adjustments become necessary, TMM would use it as an opportunity for further training of our team members, as we call our employees. Team members would use this time to work on their *kaizen* ideas [continual improvement], which they have been too busy to pursue when production is in full swing.[67]

As previously mentioned, firms like Toyota take several steps to help ensure that employment is indeed "for keeps": temporary, part-time employees provide the slack that helps these firms downsize without laying off permanent employees; as much as 10% to 20% of compensation is at risk and drops when sales or profits plummet; and, perhaps most important, these firms' high commitment usually lets them stay "lean and mean" and thus more efficient and flexible than their competitors.◆

Retirement

retirement
The point at which a person gives up one's work, usually between the ages of 60 to 65, but increasingly earlier today due to firms' early retirement incentive plans.

Retirement for most employees is bittersweet. For some it is the culmination of their careers, a time when they can relax and enjoy the fruits of their labor without worrying about the problems of work. For others, it is the retirement itself that is the trauma, as the once busy employee tries to cope with suddenly being "nonproductive" and with the strange (and not entirely pleasant) experience of being home every day with nothing to do. For many retirees, in fact, maintaining a sense of identity and self-worth without a full-time job is the single most important task they'll face. And it's one that employers are increasingly trying to help their retirees cope with as a logical last step in the career management process.[68]

preretirement counseling
Counseling provided to employees who are about to retire, which covers matters such as benefits advice, second careers, and so on.

Preretirement Counseling   About 30% of the employers in one survey said they had formal **preretirement counseling** aimed at easing the passage of their employees into retirement.[69] The most common preretirement practices were:

Explanation of Social Security benefits (reported by 97% of those with preretirement education programs)

Leisure-time counseling (86%)

Financial and investment counseling (84%)

Health counseling (82%)

Psychological counseling (35%)

Counseling for second careers outside the company (31%)

Counseling for second careers inside the company (4%)

Among employers that did not have preretirement education programs, 64% believed that such programs were needed, and most of these said their firms had plans to develop them within two or three years.

Another important trend here is that of granting part-time employment to employees as an alternative to outright retirement. Several recent surveys of blue- and white-collar employees showed that about half of all employees over age 55 would like to continue working part-time after they retire.[70]

Chapter Review

Summary

1. Managers of more progressive firms know that commitment is built on trust, and that trust requires floods of two-way communications. Firms like this therefore set up programs such as Guaranteed Fair Treatment, Speak Up!, opinion surveying, and Top-Down for keeping employees informed.

2. Firms give employees vehicles through which to speak their minds. For example, IBM's Speak Up! and Toyota's hotline provide employees with anonymous channels through which they can express concerns to top management.

3. Firms such as IBM and Federal Express also engage in periodic anonymous opinion surveys. These provide standardized channels through which management can take the pulse of employee attitudes. Top-down programs, including roundtable discussions, in-house television broadcasts, and top managers continuously mingling with the rank-and-file, are techniques firms use to ensure healthy top-down communications.

4. Guaranteed Fair Treatment programs, such as the one at Federal Express, help to ensure that grievances are handled fairly and openly. Steps include management review, officer complaint, and executive appeals review.

5. A fair and just discipline process is based on three prerequisites: rules and regulations, a system of progressive penalties, and an appeals process. We listed a number of discipline guidelines, including that discipline should be in line with the way management usually responds to similar incidents; that management must adequately investigate the matter before administering discipline; and that managers should not rob a subordinate of his or her dignity.

6. We discussed a new approach to discipline called discipline without punishment. Its basic aim is to gain an employee's acceptance of the rules by reducing the punitive nature of the discipline itself. In particular, employees are given a paid day off to consider their infraction before more punitive disciplinary steps are taken.

7. Managing dismissals is an important part of any supervisor's job. Among the reasons for dismissal are unsatisfactory performance, misconduct, lack of qualifications, changed job requirements, and insubordination. In dismissing one or more employees, however, remember that termination at will as a policy has been weakened by exceptions in many states. Furthermore, great care should be taken to avoid wrongful discharge suits. For example, delete statements from your employee manual that could prejudice your defense, have clear written rules regarding discipline and discharge, and don't constructively discharge employees by placing them in a lower-paying job in hopes of a resignation.

8. Dismissing an employee is always difficult and the termination interview should be handled properly. Specifically, plan the interview carefully (for instance, early in the week), get to the point, describe the situation, and then listen until the person has expressed his or her feelings. Then discuss the severance package and identify the next step.

9. Nondisciplinary separations such as layoffs and retirements occur all the time. The plant closing law (the Worker Adjustment and Retraining Notification Act) sets down requirements to be followed with regard to official notice before operations with 50 or more people are to be closed down.

10. Many firms today seek alternatives to layoffs. These include voluntary reduction in pay plans, voluntary time off, and the rings of defense approach, which involves using temporary, part-time employees who are let go in adverse times.

11. Job security and employee commitment go hand in hand. That's why firms like Toyota, Saturn, and Federal Express emphasize what might be called lifetime employment without guarantees. On the one hand, these firms do all they can to ensure job security and in return they expect their employees to commit themselves

to the firm and its goals. Yet even in these firms, employment at will is the rule. This means that either the employee or the firm may terminate the employment relationship at any time and for any reason.

12. Disciplinary actions are one big source of grievances. Discipline should be based on rules, adhere to a system of progressive penalties, and permit an appeals process. Other fairness guidelines include the fact that the discipline should be in line with the way management usually responds to similar incidents. Other important gudelines include emphasize rules, remember that the burden of proof is on you, and don't fail to get the facts.

Key Terms

speak up! programs	termination at will	voluntary reduction in
opinion surveys	wrongful discharge	pay plan
top-down programs	termination interview	voluntary time off
guaranteed fair	outplacement counseling	rings of defense
treatment	plant closing law	downsizings
open-door program	layoff	lifetime employment
discipline	bumping/layoff	without guarantees
dismissal	procedures	retirement
insubordination		preretirement counseling

Discussion Questions and Exercises

1. Explain the role of communications and guaranteed fair treatment in fostering employee commitment.

2. Describe specific techniques you would use to foster top-down communication in an organization.

3. Describe the similarities and differences between a program such as Federal Express's guaranteed fair treatment program and a typical union grievance procedure.

4. Explain how you would ensure fairness in disciplining, discussing particularly the prerequisites to disciplining, disciplining guidelines, and the new "discipline without punishment" approach.

5. Why is it important in what some consider our highly litigious society to manage dismissals properly?

6. What are the techniques you would use as alternatives to layoffs? What do such alternatives have to do with what we refer to as lifetime employment without guarantees? Why do you think alternatives like these are important, given industry's need today for highly committed employees?

7. Working individually or in groups, interview managers or administrators at your employer or at this college in order to determine the extent to which the employer or college builds two-way communications, and the specific types of programs (such as Speak-Up programs) that are used. Do the managers think they are effective? What do the employees (or faculty members) think of the programs if they are in use at the employer or college?

8. Working individually or in groups, obtain copies of the student handbook for this college and determine to what extent there is a formal process through which students can air grievances. Do you think the process should be an effective one? Based on your contacts with other students, has it been an effective grievance process?

9. Working individually or in groups, determine the nature of the academic discipline process in this college. Do you think it is an effective one? Based on what you read in Chapter 16, would you recommend any modification of the student discipline process?

Application Exercises

RUNNING CASE: Carter Cleaning Company
Guaranteeing Fair Treatment

Being in the laundry and cleaning business, the Carters have always felt strongly about not allowing employees to smoke, eat, or drink in their stores. Jennifer was therefore surprised to walk into a store and find two employees eating lunch at the front counter. There was a large pizza in its box, and the two of them were sipping colas and eating slices of pizza and submarine sandwiches off paper plates. Not only did it look messy, but there were also grease and soda spills on the counter and the store smelled from onions and pepperoni, even with the four-foot-wide exhaust fan pulling air out through the roof. In addition to being a turnoff to customers, the mess on the counter increased the possibility that a customer's order might actually become soiled in the store.

While this was a serious matter, neither Jennifer nor her father felt that what the counter people were doing was grounds for immediate dismissal, partly because the store manager had apparently condoned their actions. The problem was they didn't know what to do. It seemed to them that the matter called for more than just a warning but less than dismissal.

Questions

1. Should a disciplinary system be established at Carter's Cleaning Centers?

2. If so, what should it cover, and how would you suggest they deal with the errant counter people?

CASE INCIDENT: Job Insecurity at IBM

For over 50 years IBM was known for its policy of job security. Throughout all those years, it had never laid off any employees, even as the company was going through wrenching changes. For example, in the late 1970s and 1980s, IBM had to close down its punch card manufacturing plants and division, but the thousands of employees who worked in those plants were simply given an opportunity to move to comparable jobs in other IBM divisions.

Unfortunately, IBM's full-employment policy is evaporating, and fast. As IBM's computer industry market share dropped throughout the 1980s, both its sales revenue and profits began to erode. By 1991 it had become apparent that a drastic restructuring was needed. The firm therefore accelerated its downsizing efforts, instituting various early retirement and incentive plans aimed at getting employees voluntarily to leave IBM. Various imaginative schemes were introduced, including spinning off certain operations to groups of employees who then quit IBM while becoming independent consultants, doing tasks very similar to those they used to do while employees of IBM. By 1992, however, at least 40,000 more employees still had to be trimmed, and by 1993 it had be-

come apparent that IBM's cherished full employment policy had to be discarded. For the first time, IBM began laying off employees, and eventually tens of thousands more employees were let go, beginning with about 300 employees of the firm's Armonk, New York headquarters.

Questions

1. What do you think accounts for the fact that a company like IBM can have high commitment but still lose market share, sales, and profitability? In other words, why do you think employee commitment did not translate into corporate success as well as it might have at IBM?

2. What sorts of steps do you think IBM could have taken in order to continue to avoid layoffs? If you don't think any such steps were feasible, explain why.

3. Given IBM's experience with its full employment policy, what do you think are the implications for other companies thinking of instituting full employment policies of their own?

Human Resource Management Simulation

Two incidents in the simulation pertain to this chapter. Incident K requires your team to make a decision concerning which, if any, outplacement services you offer to an employee that you are discharging. Remember that whatever you do, you are setting a precedent for future cases. Furthermore, keep in mind that you are making a strong statement to your employees about fairness when you make decisions about outplacement.

Incident M concerns the actions you will take in disciplining an employee. There are two ways to look at this incident—one from the viewpoint of the company (the bottom line and precedent), and the other from the viewpoint of the employee. You may want to role play each side to reach your decision.

Video Case

Big Brother at Work

This videocase discusses the fact that employers are using a growing array of surveillance devices to spy on their employees, and that this has privacy advocates up in arms. The videocase shows, for instance, that about 60 employees at the Boston Sheraton Hotel were stunned to learn that management was secretly taping them during off hours in the men's dressing room. They're now suing Sheraton for invasion of privacy. Yet the videocase also shows that, according to the American Civil Liberties Union, the Bill of Rights does not apply to private corporations—only to government. So, to a large extent, as Betsy Stark says in the videocase, ". . . anything you do on company time or company equipment belongs to the company."

Questions

1. Do you think it's necessary for companies to use devices such as hidden cameras and micro-

phones to secretly watch and listen to employees in order to reduce employee theft and similar problems? Why or why not?

2. The videocase emphasizes that some companies use surveillance equipment not just for security purposes but to track employee productivity. Do you think this is an advisable step for employers to take? Why or why not?

3. It appears that there may be a question of "reasonableness" when it comes to using surveillance equipment on employees. If so, what are some examples of situations under which you think it would be reasonable to use surveillance equipment on your employees?

Source: Wall Street Journal Report, *Big Brother at Work,* Show No. 658-2, May 6, 1995.

Take It to the Net

We invite you to visit the Dessler page on the Prentice Hall Web site at:
http://www.prenhall.com/~dessler
for the monthly Dessler update, and for this chapter's WorldWideWeb exercise.

Notes

1. Anne B. Fisher, "Morale Crisis," *Fortune,* November 18, 1991, p. 70.
2. This is based on Allan Farnham, "The Trust Gap," *Fortune,* December 4, 1989, p. 57.
3. *Think Magazine,* Vol. 55, no. 6 (1989).
4. Toyota Motor Manufacturing, U.S.A., Inc., *Team Member Handbook* (February 1988), pp. 52–53.
5. *All About Your Company, IBM Employee Handbook,* p. 184. The section on building employee commitment and the material on Speak Up! top down, and related programs is

based on Gary Dessler, *Winning Commitment* (New York: McGraw-Hill, 1993), pp. 37–51.

6. *The Federal Express Employee Handbook,* August 7, 1989, p. 89.

7. *Blueprints for Service Quality: The Federal Express Approach, AMA Management Briefing* (New York: AMA Membership Publications Division, 1991), p. 42.

8. Ibid. p. 89.

9. Ibid. p. 45.

10. Lester Bittel, *What Every Supervisor Should Know* (New York: McGraw-Hill, 1974), p. 308; based on a study by the American Arbitration Association of 1,000 grievances. For a study of the variables influencing disciplinary action, see, for example, Wanda Trahan and Dirk Steiner, "Factors Affecting Supervisors' Use of Disciplinary Action Following Poor Performance," *Journal of Organizational Behavior,* Vol. 15, No. 2 (March 1994), pp. 129-139.

11. Commerce Clearing House, *Personnel Practices/Communications* (Chicago: CCH, 1982), pp. 2351–2352.

12. For an example of a peer review appeals process see, for example, Dawn Anfuso, "Coors Taps Employee Judgement," *Personnel Journal* (February 1994), pp. 50–59.

13. George Bohlander, "Why Arbitrators Overturn Managers in Employee Suspension and Discharge Cases," *Journal of Collective Negotiations,* Vol. 23, no. 1 (1994), pp. 76–77.

14. Ibid., p. 82.

15. Ibid. See also Ahmad Karim, "Arbitrator Considerations in Modifying Discharge Decisions in the Public Sector," *Journal of Collective Negotiations,* Vol. 22, no. 3 (1993), pp. 245–251, and Joseph Martocchio and Timothy Judge, "When we don't see eye to eye: Discrepancies Between Supervisors and Subordinates in Absence Disciplinary Decisions." *Journal of Management,* Vol. 21, No. 2 (1995), pp. 251–278.

16. Commerce Clearing House, *Ideas and Trends in Personnel,* April 8, 1982, p. 88. See also Brian Klaas and Daniel Feldman, "The Impact of Appeal Systems Structure on Disciplinary Actions," *Personnel Psychology,* Vol. 47 (1994), pp. 91–108.

17. Commerce Clearing House, "One Thing Unions Offer Is "Fair Discipline—But Management Can Offer That Too," *Ideas and Trends in Personnel,* September 3, 1982, p. 168. See also Brian Klass and Daniel Feldman, "The Impact of Appeal System Structure on Disciplinary Decisions," *Personnel Psychology,* Vol. 47, No. 1 (Srping, 1994), pp. 91–108.

18. Commerce Clearing House, "Non-union Employees, NLRB Rules, Have the Right to Help During Questioning by Management," *Ideas and Trends in Personnel,* August 6, 1982, p. 151.

19. These are based on George Odiorne, *How Managers Make Things Happen* (Englewood Cliffs, NJ: Prentice Hall, 1961), pp. 132–143; see also Bittel, *What Every Supervisor Should Know,* pp. 285–298. See also Cynthia Fukami and David Hopkins, "The Role of Situational Factors in Disciplinary Judgments," *Journal of Organizational Behavior,* Vol. 14, No. 7 (December, 1993), pp. 665–676.

20. Nonpunitive discipline discussions based on David Campbell et al., "Discipline Without Punishment—At Last," *Harvard Business Review* (July–August 1985), pp. 162–178; and Gene Milbourn, Jr., "The Case Against Employee Punishment," *Management Solutions* (November 1986), pp. 40–45.

Mark Sherman and Al Lucia, "Positive Discipline and Labor Arbitration," *Arbitration Journal,* Vol. 47, no. 2 (June 1992), pp. 56–58; Michael Moore, Victor Nichol, and Patrick McHugh, "No-Fault Programs: A Way to Cut Absenteeism," *Employment Relations Today* (Winter 1992/93), pp. 425–432; and "'Positive Discipline' Replaces Punishment," *BNA Bulletin to Management,* April 27, 1995, p. 136.

21. "Searching Employees Electronically," *BNA Bulletin to Management,* June 3, 1993, p. 169.

22. Ibid.

23. Deborah Jacobs, "Are You Guilty of Electronic Trespassing?" *Management Review* (April 1994), pp. 21–25.

24. Ibid., p. 22.

25. These are based on "E-Mail Raises Privacy Questions," *BNA Bulletin to Management,* February 25, 1993, p. 64.

26. Joseph Famularo, *Handbook of Modern Personnel Administration* (New York, McGraw-Hill, 1972), pp. 65.3–65.5.

27. Ibid.

28. Ibid., pp. 65.4–65.5.

29. From a press release dated August 6, 1987. The Goodrich & Sherwood Company, 521 Fifth Avenue, New York, NY 10017. Reprinted in Commerce Clearing House, *Ideas and Trends,* October 2, 1987, p. 157.

30. Milton Bordwin, "Is Insubordination a New Disability?" *Management Review* (October 1994), pp. 33–37.

31. Ibid., p. 34.

32. Bureau of National Affairs, *The Employment-at-Will Issue* (Washington, DC: BNA, 1982). See also Emily Joiner, "Erosion of the Employment at Will Doctrine," *Personnel,* Vol. 61, no. 5 (September–October 1984), pp. 12–18; Harvey Steinberg, "Where Law and Personnel Practice Collide: The At Will Employment Crossroad," *Personnel,* Vol. 62, no. 6 (June 1985), pp. 37–43.

33. See Teresa Brady, "Employee Handbooks: Contracts or Empty Promises?" *Management Review* (June 1993), pp. 33–35.

34. Ibid., p. 35.

35. Note, however, that under recent court rulings at least one U.S. Court of Appeals (for the Seventh Circuit) has held that employee handbooks distributed to long-term employees before employers began amending their handbooks to contain "no contract" and "at-will employment" disclaimers may still be viewed by the court as contracts with these employees. The case was *Robinson* v. *Ada S. McKinley Community Services,* Inc., 19F.3d 359 (7th Cir. 1994); see Kenneth Jenero, "Employers Beware: You May Be Bound by the Terms of Your Old Employee Handbooks," *Employee Relations Law Journal,* Vol. 20, no. 2 (Autumn 1994), pp. 299–312.

36. Robert Paul and James Townsend, "Wrongful Termination: Balancing Employer and Employee Rights—A Summary with Recommendations," *Employee Responsibilities and Rights Journal,* Vol. 6, no. 1 (1993), pp. 69–82. Wrongful termination is particularly a problem when the employee is a "whistle-blower." See for example Rosalia Costa-Clarke, "The Cost Implications of Terminating Whistle-Blowers," *Employment Relations Today,* Vol. 21, No. 4 (Winter 1994), pp. 447–454.

37. Ibid., p. 81.

38. Ibid.

39. Ibid., p. 74.

40. Based on a speech by Peter Panken and presented in BNA, *Bulletin to Management,* June 20, 1985, pp. 11–12.

41. Based on comments by attorney Richard Curiale in BNA, *Bulletin to Management,* November 17, 1983, p. 8. See also BNA, *Bulletin to Management,* May 18, 1989, p. 154; averting wrongful discharge litigation, specific guidelines. Also see Commerce Clearing House, "How to Discharge: Some Guidelines," *Ideas and Trends in Personnel,* January 11, 1988, p. 4. Except as noted, this section was based on Miriam Rothman, "Employee Termination, I: A Four-Step Procedure," *Personnel* (February 1989), pp. 31–35; and Steven Jesseph, "Employee Termination, II: Some Do's and Don'ts," *Personnel* (February 1989), pp. 36–38. For a good checklist see author Silbergeld, "Avoiding Wrongful Termination Claims: A Checklist for Employers," *Employment Relations Today,* Vol. 20, No. 4 (Winter, 1993), pp. 447–454.

42. See James Coil, III and Charles Rice, "Three Steps to Creating Effective Employee Releases," *Employment Relations Today* (Spring 1994), pp. 91–94. Wrongful termination is a problem for managerial employees as well. See, for example, Clinton Longenecker and Frederick Post, "The Management Termination Trap," *Business Horizons,* Vol. 37, No. 3 (May–June, 1994), pp. 71–79.

43. Based on ibid., p. 92.

44. William J. Morin and Lyle York, *Outplacement Techniques* (New York: AMACOM, 1982), pp. 101–131; and F. Leigh Branham, "How to Evaluate Executive Outplacement Services," *Personnel Journal,* Vol. 62 (April 1983), pp. 323–326; Sylvia Milne, "The Termination Interview," *Canadian Manager* (Spring 1994), pp. 15–16.

45. Morin and York, *Outplacement Techniques,* p. 117. See also Sonny Weide, "When You Terminate An Employee," *Employment Relations Today* (August 1994), pp. 287–293.

46. Commerce Clearing House, *Ideas and Trends in Personnel,* July 9, 1982, pp. 132–146.

47. Ibid., p. 132.

48. Joseph Zarandona and Michael Camuso, "A Study of Exit Interviews: Does the Last Word Count?" *Personnel,* Vol. 62, no. 3 (March 1985), pp. 47–48.

49. Quoted from Commerce Clearing House, *Ideas and Trends,* August 9, 1988, p. 133; see also Bureau of National Affairs, "Plant Closing Notification Rules: A Compliance Guide," *Bulletin to Management,* May 18, 1989. See also Nancy Ryan, "Complying with the Worker Adjustment and Retraining Notification Act (WARNACT)," *Employee Relations Law Journal,* Vol. 18, no. 1 (Summer 1993), pp. 169–176.

50. Commerce Clearing House, *Personnel Practices/Communications,* p. 1402.

51. Ibid., p. 1410.

52. Commerce Clearing House, *Ideas and Trends in Personnel,* July 9, 1982, p. 131; Robert Tomasko, "Downsizing: Layoffs and Alternatives to Layoffs," *Compensation and Benefits Review,* Vol. 23, no. 4 (July–August 1991), pp. 19–32.

53. See Eric Greenberg, "Upswing in Downsizings to Continue," *Management Review* (February 1993), p. 5.

54. Ibid.

55. Ibid.

56. This is based on Steven Jesseph, "Employee Termination, II: Some Do's and Don'ts," *Personnel* (February 1989), pp. 36–38. See also Michael Miller and Cherylon Robinson, "Managing the Disappointment of Job Termination: Outplacement as a cooling-out devise," *The Journal of Applied Behavioral Science,* Vol. 30, No. 1 (March, 1994), pp. 5–21.

57. Les Feldman, "Duracell's First Aid for Downsizing Survivors," *Personnel Journal* (August 1989), p. 94.

58. Ibid. See also Daniel Feldman and Carrie Leana, "Managing Layoffs in the 90s," *B&E Review* (January–March 1993), pp. 3–13.

59. James Emshoff, "How to Increase Employee Loyalty While You Downsize," *Business Horizons* (March–April 1994), pp. 49–57.

60. Ibid., pp. 52–53.

61. Ibid., p. 54.

62. Ibid. See also Robert Ford and Pamela Perrewé, "After the Layoff: Closing the Barn Door Before All the Horses Are Gone," *Business Horizons* (July–August 1993), pp. 34–40.

63. These are based on Dan Kleinman, "Witness to a Merger," *Personnel Journal* (November 1988), pp. 64–67.

64. Alex Warren, speech to the City Club, Cleveland, Ohio, November 15, 1991, p. 7.

65. Team Member Handbook, Toyota Motor Manufacturing, U.S.A., February 1988, p. 102.

66. Ibid., p. 103.

67. Personal interview, March 1992.

68. Fujio Cho, "Employee Motivation by Applying the Toyota Promotion System," speech to the Asian Business Club of Harvard Business School, March 4, 1991, p. 2.

69. Remember that certain highly paid executives and employees who will receive pensions of at least $25,000 a year at retirement can be forced to retire at 65, under federal law.

70. "Preretirement Education Programs," *Personnel,* Vol. 59 (May–June 1982), p. 47. For a discussion of why it is important for retiring employees to promote aspects of their lives aside from their careers, see Daniel Halloran, "The Retirement Identity Crisis—and How to Beat It," *Personnel Journal,* Vol. 64 (May 1985), pp. 38–40. For an example of a program aimed at training preretirees to prepare for the financial aspects of their retirement, see, for example, Silvia Odenwald, "Pre-Retirement Training Gathers Steam," *Training and Development Journal,* Vol. 40, no. 2 (February 1986), pp. 62–63; "Pay Policies," Bureau of National Affairs, *Bulletin to Management,* March 29, 1990, p. 103.

Chapter 17
Employee Safety and Health

Chapter Outline

- ♦ Why Employee Safety and Health are Important
- ♦ Basic Facts About Occupational Safety Law
- ♦ The Supervisor's Role in Safety
- ♦ What Causes Accidents?
- ♦ How to Prevent Accidents
- ♦ Employee Health: Problems and Remedies

Behavioral Objectives

When you finish studying this chapter, you should be able to:

Discuss OSHA and how it operates.

Describe the supervisor's role in safety.

Explain in detail three basic causes of accidents.

Explain in detail how to prevent accidents at work.

Discuss major health problems at work and how to remedy them.

Why Employee Safety and Health Are Important

Safety and accident prevention concerns managers for several reasons, one of which is that the work-related accidents figures are staggering. For example, in a recent year there were more than 6,200 deaths and over 6.5 million injuries resulting from accidents at work—that's over eight cases per 100 full-time workers in 1993. And many safety experts feel that such figures seriously underestimate the actual number of injuries.[1]

But figures like these don't tell the full story. They don't reflect the human suffering incurred by the injured workers and their families or the economic costs incurred by employers—costs that averaged over $23,000 per serious accident in the early 1990s.[2] Nor do they reflect the legal implications. The owners of a Hamlet, North Carolina food processing plant were sued and imprisoned because exit doors were bolted when a tragic fire occurred in 1992; in 1991 a federal jury found a construction contractor guilty of federal criminal charges for violating OSHA regulations after three of his employees were killed in a sewage tunnel explosion;[3] and in 1992 a company president charged with making false statements to OSHA got a sentence of 8 to 14 months in jail.[4]

Basic Facts About Occupational Safety Law

Purpose

Occupational Safety and Health Act
The law passed by Congress in 1970 "to assure so far as possible every working man and woman in the nation safe and healthful working conditions and to preserve our human resources."

Occupational Safety and Health Administration (OSHA)
The agency created within the Department of Labor to set safety and health standards for almost all workers in the United States.

The **Occupational Safety and Health Act**[5] was passed by Congress in 1970 "to assure so far as possible every working man and woman in the nation safe and healthful working conditions and to preserve our human resources." The only employers not covered by the act are self-employed persons, farms in which only immediate members of the employer's family are employed, and certain workplaces that are already protected by other federal agencies or under other statutes. Federal agencies are covered by the act, although provisions of the act usually don't apply to state and local governments in their role as employers.

Under the act's provisions, the **Occupational Safety and Health Administration (OSHA)** was created within the Department of Labor. OSHA's basic purpose is to administer the act, and to set and enforce the safety and health standards that apply to almost all workers in the United States. The standards are enforced through the Department of Labor; OSHA has inspectors working out of branch offices throughout the country to ensure compliance.

OSHA Standards

OSHA operates under the "general" standard that each employer:

shall furnish to each of his [or her] employees employment and a place of employment which are free from recognized hazards that are causing or are likely to cause death or serious physical harm to his [or her] employees.

To carry out this basic mission, OSHA is responsible for promulgating legally enforceable standards. These are contained in five volumes covering general industry standards, maritime standards, construction standards, other regulations and procedures, and a field operations manual.

Figure 17.1
OSHA Standards
Example

Source: General Industry Standards and Interpretations, U.S. Department of Labor, OSHA (Volume 1: Revised 1989, Section 1910.28(b) (15)), p. 67.

Guardrails not less than 2″ × 4″ or the equivalent and not less than 36″ or more than 42″ high, with a midrail, when required, of a 1″ × 4″ lumber or equivalent, and toeboards, shall be installed at all open sides on all scaffolds more than 10 feet above the ground or floor. Toeboards shall be a minimum of 4″ in height. Wire mesh shall be installed in accordance with paragraph (a) (17) of this section.

The standards are very complete and seem to cover just about every conceivable hazard in great detail. For example, a small part of the standard governing handrails for scaffolds is presented in Figure 17.1. OSHA regulations list not just standards but also hazard communication and training. For example, OSHA's Hazard Communication Standard requires employers to establish hazard communication programs to inform employees about potential chemical hazards. Hazards have to be communicated through training programs, container labels, and particularly materials safety data sheets (known as MSDS), which list the nature of treatment for exposure to hazardous substances.

OSHA Recordkeeping Procedures

Under OSHA, employers with 11 or more employees must maintain records of occupational injuries and illnesses. (Employers having ten or fewer employees are exempt from recordkeeping unless they are selected to participate in the annual statistical survey carried out by the Bureau of Labor Statistics.)

Both occupational injuries and occupational illnesses must be reported. An occupational illness is any abnormal condition or disorder caused by exposure to environmental factors associated with employment. Included here are acute and chronic illnesses that may be caused by inhalation, absorption, ingestion, or direct contact with toxic substances or harmful agents. As summarized in Figure 17.2, all occupational illnesses must be reported.[6] Similarly, most occupational injuries also must be reported, specifically those injuries that result in medical treatment (other than first aid), loss of consciousness, restriction of work (one or more lost workdays), restriction of motion, or transfer to another job.[7] If an on-the-job accident occurs that results in the death of an employee or in the hospitalization of five or more employees, all employers, regardless of size, must report the accident in detail to the nearest OSHA office. A form used to report occupational injuries or illness is shown in Figure 17.3.

OSHA's recordkeeping requirements are broader than they might at first appear because of its expansive definition of occupational injuries and illnesses.[8] Examples of recordable conditions include: food poisoning suffered by an employee after eating in the employer's cafeteria; colds compounded by drafty work areas; and ankle sprains that occur during voluntary participation in a company softball game at a picnic the employee was required to attend.[9] Given OSHA's "recent ambitious pursuit of record-keeping violations during investigations," it behooves employers to fastidiously record injuries or illnesses incurred at work.

Inspections and Citations

OSHA standards are enforced through inspections and (if necessary) citations. Originally every employer covered by the act was subject to inspection by OSHA compliance officers, who were authorized to "enter without delay and at reasonable times any factory, plant, establishment . . . where work was performed . . . ," and to "inspect and investigate during regular working hours, and at other

**Figure 17.2
What Accidents Must
Be Reported Under the
Occupational Safety
and Health Act (OSHA)**

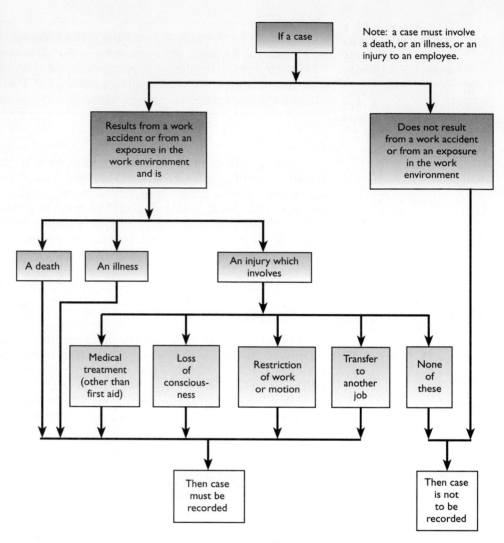

reasonable times, . . . any such place of employment and all pertinent conditions, structures, machines, . . . and to question privately any such employer, owner, operator, agent or employee."[10] Today OSHA may not conduct warrantless inspections without an employer's consent. It may, however, inspect after acquiring a judicially authorized search warrant or its equivalent.[11]

Inspection Priorities OSHA has a list of inspection priorities. Imminent danger situations get top priority. These are conditions in which it is likely a danger exists that can immediately cause death or serious physical harm. Second priority is given to catastrophes, fatalities, and accidents that have already occurred. (Such situations must be reported to OSHA within 48 hours.) Third priority is given to valid employee complaints of alleged violation of standards. Next in priority are periodic special-emphasis inspections aimed at high-hazard industries, occupations, or substances. Finally, random inspections and reinspections generally have last priority. Most inspections result from employee complaints.

OSHA no longer follows up every employee complaint with an inspection. The focus now is on high-priority problems.[12] Under its priority system, OSHA conducts an inspection within 24 hours when a complaint indicates an immedi-

Figure 17.3
Form Used to Record Occupational Injuries and Illnesses

OSHA No. 101
Case or File No. _____

Form approved
OMB No. 44R 1453

Supplementary Record of Occupational Injuries and Illnesses

EMPLOYER

1. Name _____
2. Mail address _____
   (No. and street)   (City or town)   (State)
3. Location, if different from mail address _____

INJURED OR ILL EMPLOYEE

4. Name _____ Social Security No. _____
   (First name)   (Middle name)   (Last name)
5. Home address _____
   (No. and street)   (City or town)   (State)
6. Age _____ 7. Sex: Male _____ Female _____ (Check one)
8. Occupation_____
   (Enter regular job title, *not* the specific activity he/she was performing at time of injury.)
9. Department_____
   (Enter name of department or division in which the injured person is regularly employed, even
   though he/she may have been temporarily working in another department at the time of injury.)

THE ACCIDENT OR EXPOSURE TO OCCUPATIONAL ILLNESS

10. Place of accident or exposure _____
    (No. and street)   (City or town)   (State)
    If accident or exposure occurred on employer's premises, give address of plant or establishment in
    which it occurred. Do not indicate department or division within the plant or establishment. If accident
    occurred outside employer's premises at an identifiable address, give that address. If it occurred on a
    public highway or at any other place which cannot be identified by number and street, please provide
    place references locating the place of injury as accurately as possible.
11. Was place of accident or exposure on employer's premises? _____(Yes or No)
12. What was the employee doing when injured? _____
    (Be specific. If he/she was using tools or equipment or handling
    _____
    material, name them and tell what he/she was doing with them.)
    _____
13. How did the accident occur?_____
    (Describe fully the events which resulted in the injury or occupational illness. Tell what
    _____
    happend and how it happened. Name any objects or substances involved and tell how they were involved. Give
    _____
    full details on all factors which led or contributed to the accident. Use separate sheet for additional space.)

OCCUPATIONAL INJURY OR OCCUPATIONAL ILLNESS

14. Describe the injury or illness in detail and indicate the part of body affected. _____
    (e.g.: amputation of right index finger
    _____
    at second joint; fracture of ribs; lead poisoning; dermatitis of left hand, etc.)
15. Name the object or substance which directly injured the employee. (For example, the machine or thing
    he/she struck against or which struck him/her; the vapor or poison inhaled or swallowed; the chemical or
    radiation which irritated the skin; or in cases of strains, hernias, etc., the thing he/she was lifting, pulling,
    etc.)
    _____
    _____
16. Date of injury or initial diagnosis of occupational illness_____
    (Date)
17. Did employee die? _____ (Yes or No)

OTHER

18. Name and address of physician _____
19. If hospitalized, name and address of hospital _____

_____
Date of report _____ Prepared by _____
Official position _____

many employees had yet to experience an injury from unsafe performance, so this "punishment" was also missing.

The Safety Program   The safety program stressed positive reinforcement and training. A reasonable goal (in terms of observed incidents performed safely) was set and communicated to workers to ensure that they knew what was expected of them in terms of good performance. Next came a training phase. Here employees were presented with safety information during a 30-minute training session. Employees were shown pairs of slides (35mm transparencies) depicting scenes that were staged in the plant. In one transparency, for example, the wrapping supervisor was shown climbing over a conveyor; the parallel slide illustrated the supervisor walking around the conveyor. After viewing an unsafe act, employees were asked to describe what was wrong ("What's unsafe here?"). Then, once the problem had been aired, the same incident was again shown performed in a safe manner and the safe-conduct rule was explicitly stated ("Go around, not over or under, conveyors").

At the conclusion of the training phase, the employees were shown a graph with their pretraining safety record (in terms of observed incidents performed safely) plotted. They were encouraged to consider increasing their performance to the new safety goal for the following reasons: for their own protection; to decrease costs for the company; and to help the plant get out of last place in the safety ranking of the parent company. Then the graph and a list of safety rules (do's and don'ts) were posted in a conspicuous place in the work area.

Reinforcement and Safety   The graph played a central role in the study's final, "positive reinforcement" phase. Whenever observers walked through the plant collecting safety data, they posted on the graph the percentage of incidents they had seen performed safely by the group as a whole, thus providing the workers with feedback on their safety performance. Workers could then compare their current safety performance with both their previous performance and their assigned goal. In addition, supervisors praised workers when they performed selected incidents safely. Safety in the plant subsequently improved markedly.[56]

Reducing Unsafe Acts Through Top-Management Commitment

One of the most consistent findings in the literature is that successful factory programs require a strong management commitment to safety.[57] This commitment manifests itself in top management's being personally involved in safety activities on a routine basis; giving safety matters high priority in company meetings and production scheduling; giving the company safety officer high rank and status; and including safety training in new workers' training.

Summary: How to Reduce Accidents

1. Check for and *remove unsafe conditions;* use a checklist like the one presented in the appendix to the chapter. If the hazard cannot be removed, guard against it (for instance, with guardrails) or if necessary use personal protective equipment such as goggles or safety shoes.
2. Through *selection,* try to screen out employees who might be accident prone for the job in question (but remember the requirements of the Americans with Disabilities Act).
3. Establish a *safety policy* emphasizing that the firm will do everything practical to eliminate or reduce accidents and injuries and emphasizing the importance of accident and injury prevention at your firm.

4. Set specific *loss control goals*. Analyze the number of accidents and safety incidents and then set specific safety goals to be achieved, for instance, in terms of frequency of lost-time injuries per number of full-time employees.[58]

5. Encourage and *train your employees* to be safety conscious; show them that top management and all supervisors are serious about safety.

6. Enforce *safety rules*.

7. Conduct *safety and health inspections* regularly. Also investigate all accidents and "near misses" and have a system in place for letting employees notify management about hazardous conditions.[59]

Controlling Worker's Compensation Costs

Worker's compensation costs have soared, with the average claim costing $34,000 in 1990, twice the average of a claim in 1980.[60] While these costs are generally paid by the employer's insurance carrier, the insurance premiums themselves are proportional to the firm's worker's compensation experience rate. Thus, the more worker's compensation claims a firm has, the more the firm will pay in insurance premiums.

There are several factors in reducing worker's compensation claims:

Before the accident. The appropriate time to begin "controlling" worker's compensation claims is before the accident happens, not after. This involves taking all the steps previously summarized. For example, remove unsafe conditions, screen out employees who might be accident prone for the job in question (remembering the ADA, however), and establish a safety policy and loss control goals.

After the accident. The occupational injury or illness can obviously be a traumatic event for the employee, and the way the employer handles it can influence the injured worker's reaction to it. The employee is going to have specific needs and specific questions, such as where to go for medical help and whether he or she will be paid for any time off. It is usually at this point that the employee decides whether to retain a worker's compensation attorney to plead his or her case. Employers are therefore admonished to provide first aid and make sure the worker gets quick medical attention; make it clear that you are interested in the injured worker and his or her fears and questions; document the accident; file any required accident reports; and encourage a speedy return to work.[61]

Facilitate the employee's return to work. According to one discussion of managing worker's compensation costs:

Perhaps the most important and effective thing an employer can do to reduce costs is to develop an aggressive return-to-work program, including making light-duty work available. Surely the best solution to the current workers' compensation crisis, for both the employer and the employee, is for the worker to become a productive member of the company again instead of a helpless victim living on benefits.[62]

HR and the Responsive Organization

Employee Safety and Health

Corporate downsizings and reengineering aren't necessarily incompatible with improved worker safety, although that might at first seem the case.[63] Downsizing, for instance, strips away several of the lynch pins around which employee safety is normally built. For example, consider the downsizing program of Du Pont Canada. The program removed more than half the levels in manufacturing management and reduced the bureaucracy by shifting more decision-making responsibility down to the nonsupervisory employees themselves. Productivity and profit levels rose, but so did loss-work injuries, which had suddenly taken an ominous upward turn.

Many of the supervisors blamed the eroding safety results on self-management. There were fewer supervisors, and those remaining had to manage more employees and manage differently—acting more like coaches in order to build commitment and teamwork. As a result the supervisors were spending less time on the shop floor and putting less time into safety, partly on the assumption that the self-managed teams should be managing their own safety programs.

Within a year Du Pont Canada had taken steps to turn the safety situation around. In the changeover to self-managed teams, authority and accountability for safety (as well as for some other matters) had unintentionally become blurred.[64] Du Pont Canada's top management responded to this by reemphasizing that each person is responsible for his or her own safety and that supervisors and managers are directly responsible for those who work for them, including their safety. And (at the risk of appearing to rescind some of the team's self-management authority) top management reemphasized that violations of safety rules would not be tolerated and that discipline would be reemphasized to ensure that safety rules were followed. In this way, as one Du Pont Canada executive later put it:

> Without giving up on self-management, or adding back supervision, people in the company went back to considering safety as an integral part of the job. It became accepted that to be truly world-competitive meant being excellent on all fronts. There was not a significant increase in the use of discipline for safety violations. Reemphasizing the priority of safety seemed to be enough.[65] ◆

Employee Health: Problems and Remedies[66]

A number of health-related substances and problems can undermine employee performance at work. These include alcoholism, stress, asbestos, video displays, AIDS, and workplace violence.

Alcoholism and Substance Abuse

Alcoholism is a serious and widespread disease.[67] Fifty percent of alcoholics are women, 25% are white-collar workers, 45% are professional/managerial personnel, 37% are high school graduates, and 50% have completed or attended college. Most are members of households. Some experts estimate that as many as 50% of all "problem employees" in industry are actually alcoholics. In one auto assembly plant, 48.6% of the grievances filed over the course of one year were alcohol related.[68] In the United States alone, substance abusers cost employers about $30 billion annually in lost production and account for 40% of all industrial fatalities.

The effects of alcoholism on the worker and the work are severe.[69] Both the quality and quantity of the work decline sharply. A form of "on-the-job absenteeism" occurs as efficiency declines. The alcoholic's on-the-job accidents do not appear to increase significantly, apparently because he or she becomes much more cautious (but his or her effectiveness suffers as well). However, the *off-the-job* accident rate is three to four times higher than for nonalcoholics. Contrary to popular opinion, turnover among alcoholics is not unusually high. The morale of other workers is affected as they have to do the work of their alcoholic peer.

Recognizing the alcoholic on the job is another problem. The early symptoms such as tardiness can be similar to those of other problems and thus hard to classify. The supervisor is not a psychiatrist, and without specialized training, identifying—and dealing with—the alcoholic is difficult.

A chart showing observable behavior patterns that indicate alcohol-related problems is presented in Table 17.1. As you can see, alcohol-related problems range from tardiness in the earliest stages of alcohol abuse to prolonged unpredictable absences in its later stages.[70]

Traditional Techniques Used to Deal with These Problems   The four traditional techniques for dealing with these problems are disciplining, discharge, in-house counseling, and referral to an outside agency. Discipline short of discharge is used more often with alcoholics than for dealing with drug problems or emotional illness. Discharge is frequently used to deal with alcoholism and drug problems; it is almost never used in the case of serious emotional illness.[71]

In-house counseling, one example of an employee assistance program, is used often in dealing with alcoholics and those with emotional disorders. In most cases the counseling is offered by the HR department or the employer's medical staff. Immediate supervisors with special training also provide counseling in many instances.

Many companies use outside agencies such as Alcoholics Anonymous, psychiatrists, and clinics to deal with the problems of alcoholism and emotional illness. Outside agencies are used less often in the case of drug problems.

Trice[72] suggests a number of specific actions managers can take to deal with employee alcoholism—actions that all involve supervisory training or company policy. He says supervisors should be trained to identify the alcoholic and the problem he or she creates. Employers should also establish a company policy that recognizes alcoholism as a health problem and places it within the firm's health plan.

The use of drugs, especially in the workplace, is a growing concern for U.S. companies and has led to increased numbers of alcohol and drug abuse counseling programs.

Workplace Substance Abuse and the Law   Because of the seriousness of the problem and the passage of a new federal law, most employers are taking additional steps to deal with alcohol and substance abuse on the job. The federal Drug-Free Workplace Act of 1988 requires employers with federal government contracts or grants to ensure a drug-free workplace by taking (and certifying that they have taken) a number of steps. Specifically, to be eligible for contract awards or grants, employers must agree to:

Publish a policy prohibiting the unlawful manufacture, distribution, dispensing, possession, or use of controlled substances in the workplace.

Establish a drug-free awareness program that informs employees about the dangers of workplace drug abuse.

Inform employees that they are required, as a condition of employment, not only to abide by the employer's policy but also to report any criminal convictions for drug-related activities in the workplace.

Notify the federal contracting or granting agency of any criminal convictions of employees for illegal drug activity in the workplace.

Take appropriate personnel action against any employee convicted of a criminal drug offense.

Make a "good faith" effort to maintain a drug-free workplace by complying with the law's requirements.[73]

New U.S. Department of Transportation rules expanding drug testing in the transportation industry went into effect in 1995.[74] These rules require random breath alcohol tests as well as preemployment, postaccident, reasonable

numbers are just the tip of the iceberg. For example, while 29 U.S. Postal Service supervisors and colleagues were slain by disgruntled postal workers in the last ten years, there were also 422 assaults by postal employees on their coworkers in 1990, 403 in 1991, 396 in 1992, and about 350 in 1993.[106]

Of course, employees themselves are not always the perpetrators. In a survey of nearly 600 full-time workers nationwide, 68% of violent attacks were attributed to clients, patients, and other strangers.[107] Coworkers accounted for about 20% of the attacks, and an employer or boss about 7%. Yet the fact remains that nearly 2.2 million workers were victims of physical attacks in the workplace last year, and it's estimated that 25% of workers were either attacked, harassed, or threatened during the year ending in July 1993.[108] Violence against employees has therefore become a deadly serious safety problem at work.[109]

Employers should eliminate such violence on humanitarian grounds, but there are legal reasons to do so as well. Employers may be found liable for the violent acts of their employees.[110] For example, an employer may be sued directly by the victim of an employee's violent act on the basis that the employer negligently hired or negligently retained someone who the employer should reasonably have known could cause the violent act. And even if the employee was not negligently hired or retained, employers may still in general be liable for employees' violent acts when the employees' actions were performed within the scope of employment.

Reducing Incidents of Workplace Violence   There are several concrete steps employers can take to reduce the incidence of workplace violence. These include instituting improved security arrangements, improving employee screening, training for violence reduction, and enhancing attention to retaining employees.

Heightened Security Measures   Heightened security measures are an employer's first line of defense against workplace violence, whether that violence derives from coworkers, customers, or outsiders. NIOSH suggests these sensible precautions for reducing the risk of workplace violence:[111] improve external lighting; use drop safes to minimize cash on hand and post signs noting that only a limited amount of cash is on hand; install silent alarms and surveillance cameras; increase the number of staff on duty; provide staff training in conflict resolution and nonviolent response; and close establishments during high-risk hours late at night and early in the morning.[112]

Improved Employee Screening   With about 30% of workplace attacks committed by coworkers, screening out potentially explosive internal and external applicants is the employer's next line of defense. At a minimum this means instituting a sound preemployment investigation. Obtain a detailed employment application and solicit an applicant's employment history, education background, and references.[113] A personal interview, personnel testing, and a review and verification of all information provided should also be included. Sample interview questions to ask might include, for instance, "What frustrates you?" and "Who was your worst supervisor and why?"[114]

Certain background circumstances should provide a red flag indicating the need for a more in-depth background investigation of the applicant. This investigation should help screen out potentially violent employees and provide a record that everything that could have been done was done to screen out the violent employee. Red flags include:[115]

An unexplained gap in employment.

Incomplete or false information on the résumé or application.

A negative, unfavorable, or false reference.

Prior insubordinate or violent behavior on the job.

A criminal history involving harassing or violent behavior.

A prior termination for cause with a suspicious (or no) explanation.

A history of depression or significant psychiatric problems.

A history of drug or alcohol abuse.

Strong indications of instability in the individual's work or personal life as indicated, for example, by frequent job changes or geographic moves.

Lost licenses or accreditations.[116]

Workplace Violence Training Enhanced security and screening should be supplemented with workplace violence training. Firms such as Excellence in Training Corp. offer video training programs that explain what workplace violence is, identify its causes and signs, and offer tips on how to prevent it and what to do when it occurs.[117] Supervisors can also be trained to identify the types of multiple clues that typically preceed violent incidents. Common signs include:[118]

Verbal threats. Individuals often talk about what they may do. An employee might say, "Bad things are going to happen to so-and-so," or "That propane tank in the back could blow up easily."

Physical actions. Troubled employees may try to intimidate others, gain access to places where they do not belong, or flash a concealed weapon in the workplace to test reactions.

Frustration. Most cases do not involve a panicked individual; a more likely scenario would involve an employee who has a frustrated sense of entitlement to a promotion, for example.

Obsession. An employee may hold a grudge against a coworker or supervisor, and some cases stem from romantic interest.[119]

Enhanced Attention to Retaining Employees Employers can also enhance their procedures for evaluating which employees should or should not be retained. Particularly given the potential liability of retaining employees who subsequently commit violent acts, circumstances to beware of in deciding whether or not to retain employees include:[120]

An act of violence on or off the job.

Erratic behavior evidencing a loss of perception or awareness of actions.

Overly defensive, obsessive, or paranoid tendencies.

Overly confrontational or antisocial behavior.

Sexually aggressive behavior.

Isolationist or loner tendencies.

Insubordinate behavior with a suggestion of violence.

Tendency to overreact to criticism.

Exaggerated interest in war, guns, violence, mass murders, catastrophes, and so on.

The commission of a serious breach of security.

Possession of weapons, guns, knives, or like items at the workplace.

Violation of privacy rights of others such as searching desks or stalking.

Chronic complaining and the raising of frequent, unreasonable grievances.

A retributory or get-even attitude.

Other Commonsense Steps to Take Beyond these actions, there are a number of other commonsense steps an employer can take. While they should always be taken in any organization, we repeat them here for their relevance: Reduce un-

Diversity Counts

In Occupational Safety and Health

While there are more fatal occupational injuries to men than to women, the proportion of women who are victims of assault is much higher. Of all women who die on the job, 39% are the victims of assault, for instance, whereas only 18% of males who died at work were murdered. Violence against women in the workplace is therefore a particularly serious problem.[126]

Fatal workplace violence against women has three main sources. Of all females murdered at work, over three-fourths were victims of random criminal violence carried out by an assailant unknown to the victim, as might occur during a robbery. The remaining criminal acts were carried out either by coworkers or by family members or previous friends or acquaintances.

There's nothing "typical" about workplace violence, but research sheds some light on the typical female victim (who, remember, is often the victim of random violence). The typical female assault victim is a white female (79%), in her early thirties (mean age approximately 31), working as a salesperson (31%) in a convenience store (46%), and is shot by an unknown assailant (88%) about 11:00 p.m.[127]

While workplace violence data would be tragic under any circumstances, these "typical" figures are particularly disconcerting. As one expert notes, jobs that involve serving the public, such as convenience-store employee, fast-food server, or retail store cashier are exactly the sorts of jobs that are easily filled by women, since they offer flexible hours, require minimal training, and allow women to raise children and work their way through school.[128] It is therefore particularly ". . . shocking to think that women carry the horrible risk of being murdered while working at the very job they need to survive."[129]

It would seem that concrete security improvements including better lighting, cash drop-boxes, and similar steps are especially pertinent if such violent acts against women are to be reduced. Some firms, such as Abbott Laboratories in the Chicago area, have taken additional steps including implementing a task force on workplace violence, training supervisors to identify which employees may be violent, and establishing an employee assistance program to which a new workplace violence prevention team refers potentially violent employees.[130]

necessary job stress; avoid affronts to employees' dignity (such as public condemnations); solicit and promptly address grievances; and institute employee assistance programs.[121]

Dealing with Angry Employees What do you do when confronted by an angry, potentially explosive employee? Here are some suggestions:[122]

Make eye contact.

Stop what you are doing and give your full attention.

Speak in a calm voice and create a relaxed environment.

Be open and honest.

Let the person have his or her say.

Ask for specific examples of what the person is upset about.

Be careful to define the problem.

Ask open-ended questions and explore all sides of the issue.

Legal Constraints on Reducing Workplace Violence As sensible as it is to try to screen out potentially violent employees, doing so incurs the risk of liability and lawsuits. Most states have policies that encourage the employment and rehabilitation of ex-offenders; some states therefore limit the use of criminal records in hiring decisions.[123] For example, except in certain limited instances, Article 23-A of the New York Corrections Law makes it unlawful to discriminate against job applicants on the basis of their prior criminal convictions. Similarly, Title VII of the Civil Rights Act of 1964 has been interpreted by the courts as restricting employers from making employment decisions based on arrest records, since doing so may unfairly discriminate against minority groups. Aside from federal law, most states prohibit discrimination based on arrest records under any circumstances, and on prior convictions unless a direct relationship exists between the prior conviction and the job, or the employment of the individual presents an unreasonable risk to people or property.[124] And profiling employees could end up merely describing a mental impairment and run afoul of the Americans with Disabilities Act.[125] Eliminating workplace violence while safely navigating the legal shoals is, therefore, a tricky business.

Chapter Review

Summary

1. The area of safety and accident prevention is of concern to managers at least partly because of the staggering number of deaths and accidents occurring at work. There are three reasons for safety programs: moral, legal, and economic.

2. The purpose of OSHA is to ensure every working person a safe and healthful workplace. OSHA standards are very complete and detailed and are enforced through a system of workplace inspections. OSHA inspectors can issue citations and recommend penalties to their area directors.

3. Supervisors play a key role in monitoring workers for safety. Workers in turn have a responsibility to act safely. A commitment to safety on the part of top management that is filtered down through the management ranks is an important aspect of any safety program.

4. There are three basic causes of accidents: chance occurrences, unsafe conditions, and unsafe acts on the part of employees. In addition, three other work-related factors (the job itself, the work schedule, and the psychological climate) also contribute to accidents.

5. Unsafe acts on the part of employees are a second basic cause of accidents. Such acts are to some extent the result of certain behavior tendencies on the part of employees, and these tendencies are possibly the result of certain personal characteristics.

6. Most experts doubt that there are accident-prone people who have accidents regardless of the job. Instead the consensus seems to be that the person who is accident prone in one job may not be on a different job. For example, vision is related to accident frequency for drivers and machine operators but might not be for other workers, such as accountants.

7. There are several approaches to preventing accidents. One is to reduce unsafe conditions. The other approach is to reduce unsafe acts—for example, through selection and placement, training, positive reinforcement, propaganda, and top-management commitment.

8. Alcoholism, drug addiction, stress, and emotional illness are four important and growing health problems among employees. Alcoholism is a particularly serious problem and one that can drastically lower the effectiveness of your organization. Techniques including disciplining, discharge, in-house counseling, and referrals to an outside agency are used to deal with these problems.

him, too. He has a terrible temper, which he loses about once a month. When this happens, everyone tries to get out of his way.

Jesse is now 53 years old. He's happy with the Bien Works. He likes the town and wouldn't move. Bien is like his own firm, since he's isolated geographically from Hartley. Since Bien makes more money for Hartley than his budget calls for, it lets Jesse alone. He has lower turnover than expected. Absenteeism is also low. His safety record is about average. All in all, Hartley and Jesse are happy with the Bien Works.

Except for OSHA. For some reason, the OSHA inspector came around Bien often. The local inspector was James Munsey. In April, he came to Bien when Jesse was at a meeting at Hartley. He determined that the buffing manufacturing was producing unsafe gases. As is his right, he shut the plant down that day. Jesse flew back and modified the gas filters. James passed the filters, and Bien started production again.

In May, James came back and shut the plant again when Jesse was at a Rotary meeting. Again, the filters were cleaned and modified. This time Jesse was really angry. After the plant was reopened and James gone, Jesse held a meeting of all employees. At the meeting, he said: "Look, this OSHA guy is killing us. This is an old works. We can't afford to be shut down. At my recent meeting at corporate headquarters, I tried to make the case that we needed a new building here. The sharp pencil boys pointed out that we are profitable now but not if we have to build a new plant. The industry is overcrowded, and Hartley will close this plant rather than spend money on it. If we get shut down or have to buy a lot of antipollution garbage, they could shut us down. That OSHA guy is the enemy—just like a traffic cop. We've got to pull together, or we could all sink together."

The employees had never seen Jesse so angry before, and they feared for their jobs now more than ever. There was a lot of unemployment in the area.

Questions

1. What do you think of Jesse's approach to safety?
2. What changes, if any, would you recommend? Explain why.

Source: William F. Glueck and George Stevens, *Cases and Exercises in Personnel/Human Resources Management,* 3rd ed. (Plano, TX: Business Publications, 1983), pp. 145–146. Copyright 1983, Business Publications, Inc. Reprinted by permission.

 # Human Resource Management Simulation

One of the problems facing the HR director of your firm is an accident rate higher than it should be. Some of the causes of this are a higher-than-average turnover rate, a less-than-satisfactory morale level, and a lack of any type of accident prevention or safety program. The accident rate for the organization (as measured by employee-days lost per 1 million employee-hours) is 494. The simulation allows you to start and maintain a safety program for your firm. Your accident rate will be printed on your quarterly status report and you can monitor your progress.

Incident J also allows your team to emphasize safety if you want to budget for it. Incident I gives your team an opportunity to consider various health, assistance, and wellness issues.

Video Case
Fetal Protection Policy at Work

This video presents the legal case of several women who were denied factory jobs at Johnson Controls, the nation's largest maker of lead car batteries. The case went all the way to the Supreme Court, which ruled against the company's fetal protection policies. These policies barred women from being given jobs that might be dangerous to an unborn baby. As the video case shows, all the justices agreed that a policy to hire only women who were unable to have children was a violation of sex discrimination laws.

Questions

1. Why exactly was the company policy ruled to be a violation of federal sex discrimination laws?

2. Legalities aside, do you think the company was right or wrong to try to prevent women who were able to have children from getting jobs in the factory? Why or why not?

3. Johnson Controls claimed to be trying to avoid causing deformities in unborn children. Do you feel the company's HR department and safety engineers could have devised safety techniques other than the outright banning of women who might bear children to protect against this threat? How exactly might they do this?

Source: ABC News, *SC Rejects Barring Women From Hazardous Jobs,* "World News Tonight," March 20, 1991.

Take It to the Net

We invite you to visit the Dessler page on the Prentice Hall Web site at:

http://www.prenhall.com/~dessler

for the monthly Dessler update, and for this chapter's World Wide Web exercise.

Self-inspection Checklists

General

	OK	ACTION NEEDED
1. Is the required OSHA workplace poster displayed in your place of business as required where all employees are likely to see it?	☐	☐
2. Are you aware of the requirement to report all workplace fatalities and any serious accidents (where 5 or more are hospitalized) to a federal or state OSHA office within 48 hours?	☐	☐
3. Are workplace injury and illness records being kept as required by OSHA?	☐	☐
4. Are you aware that the OSHA annual summary of workplace injuries and illnesses must be posted by February 1 and must remain posted until March 1?	☐	☐
5. Are you aware that employers with 10 or fewer employees are exempt from the OSHA record-keeping requirements, unless they are part of an official BLS or state survey and have received specific instructions to keep records?	☐	☐
6. Have you demonstrated an active interest in safety and health matters by defining a policy for your business and communicating it to all employees?	☐	☐
7. Do you have a safety committee or group that allows participation of employees in safety and health activities?	☐	☐
8. Does the safety committee or group meet regularly and report, in writing, its activities?	☐	☐
9. Do you provide safety and health training for all employees requiring such training, and is it documented?	☐	☐
10. Is one person clearly in charge of safety and health activities?	☐	☐
11. Do all employees know what to do in emergencies?	☐	☐
12. Are emergency telephone numbers posted?	☐	☐
13. Do you have a procedure for handling employee complaints regarding safety and health?	☐	☐

Develop Your Own Checklist.

These Are Only Sample Questions.

Source: OSHA Handbook for Small Business.

Workplace

ELECTRICAL WIRING, FIXTURES AND CONTROLS

Develop Your Own Checklist.

These Are Only Sample Questions.

	OK	ACTION NEEDED
1. Are your workplace electricians familiar with the requirements of the National Electrical Code (NEC)?	☐	☐
2. Do you specify compliance with the NEC for all contract electrical work?	☐	☐
3. If you have electrical installations in hazardous dust or vapor areas, do they meet the NEC for hazardous locations?	☐	☐
4. Are all electrical cords strung so they do not hang on pipes, nails, hooks, etc.?	☐	☐
5. Is all conduit, BX cable, etc., properly attached to all supports and tightly connected to junction and outlet boxes?	☐	☐
6. Is there no evidence of fraying on any electrical cords?	☐	☐
7. Are rubber cords kept free of grease, oil and chemicals?	☐	☐
8. Are metallic cable and conduit systems properly grounded?	☐	☐
9. Are portable electric tools and appliances grounded or double insulated?	☐	☐
10. Are all ground connections clean and tight?	☐	☐
11. Are fuses and circuit breakers the right type and size for the load on each circuit?	☐	☐
12. Are all fuses free of "jumping" with pennies or metal strips?	☐	☐
13. Do switches show evidence of overheating?	☐	☐
14. Are switches mounted in clean, tightly closed metal boxes?	☐	☐
15. Are all electrical switches marked to show their purpose?	☐	☐
16. Are motors clean and kept free of excessive grease and oil?	☐	☐
17. Are motors properly maintained and provided with adequate overcurrent protection?	☐	☐
18. Are bearings in good condition?	☐	☐
19. Are portable lights equipped with proper guards?	☐	☐

	OK	ACTION NEEDED
20. Are all lamps kept free of combustible material?	☐	☐
21. Is your electrical system checked periodically by someone competent in the NEC?	☐	☐

EXITS AND ACCESS

	OK	ACTION NEEDED
1. Are all exits visible and unobstructed?	☐	☐
2. Are all exits marked with a readily visible sign that is properly illuminated?	☐	☐
3. Are there sufficient exits to ensure prompt escape in case of emergency?	☐	☐
4. Are areas with limited occupancy posted and is access/egress controlled to persons specifically authorized to be in those areas?	☐	☐
5. Do you take special precautions to protect employees during construction and repair operations?	☐	☐

FIRE PROTECTION

	OK	ACTION NEEDED
1. Are portable fire extinguishers provided in adequate number and type?	☐	☐
2. Are fire extinguishers inspected monthly for general condition and operability and noted on the inspection tag?	☐	☐
3. Are fire extinguishers recharged regularly and properly noted on the inspection tag?	☐	☐
4. Are fire extinguishers mounted in readily accessible locations?	☐	☐
5. If you have interior standpipes and valves, are these inspected regularly?	☐	☐
6. If you have a fire alarm system, is it tested at least annually?	☐	☐
7. Are plant employees periodically instructed in the use of extinguishers and fire protection procedures?	☐	☐
8. If you have outside private fire hydrants, were they flushed within the last year and placed on a regular maintenance schedule?	☐	☐
9. Are fire doors and shutters in good operating condition?	☐	☐

Develop Your Own Checklist.

These Are Only Sample Questions.

	OK	ACTION NEEDED
Are they unobstructed and protected against obstruction?	☐	☐
10. Are fusible links in place?	☐	☐
11. Is your local fire department well acquainted with your plant, location and specific hazards?	☐	☐
12. Automatic Sprinklers:		
Are water control valves, air and water pressures checked weekly?	☐	☐
Are control valves locked open?	☐	☐
Is maintenance of the system assigned to responsible persons or a sprinkler contractor?	☐	☐
Are sprinkler heads protected by metal guards where exposed to mechanical damage?	☐	☐
Is proper minimum clearance maintained around sprinkler heads?	☐	☐

Develop Your Own Checklist.

These Are Only Sample Questions.

HOUSEKEEPING AND GENERAL WORK ENVIRONMENT

	OK	ACTION NEEDED
1. Is smoking permitted in designated "safe areas" only?	☐	☐
2. Are NO SMOKING signs prominently posted in areas containing combustibles and flammables?	☐	☐
3. Are covered metal waste cans used for oily and paint soaked waste?	☐	☐
Are they emptied at least daily?	☐	☐
4. Are paint spray booths, dip tanks, etc., and their exhaust ducts cleaned regularly?	☐	☐
5. Are stand mats, platforms or similar protection provided to protect employees from wet floors in wet processes?	☐	☐
6. Are waste receptacles provided, and are they emptied regularly?	☐	☐
7. Do your toilet facilities meet the requirements of applicable sanitary codes?	☐	☐
8. Are washing facilities provided?	☐	☐
9. Are all areas of your business adequately illuminated?	☐	☐
10. Are floor load capacities posted in second floors, lofts, storage areas, etc.?	☐	☐
11. Are floor openings provided with toe boards and railings or a floor hole cover?	☐	☐

	OK	ACTION NEEDED
12. Are stairways in good condition with standard railings provided for every flight having four or more risers?	☐	☐
13. Are portable wood ladders and metal ladders adequate for their purpose, in good condition and provided with secure footing?	☐	☐
14. If you have fixed ladders, are they adequate, and are they in good condition and equipped with side rails or cages or special safety climbing devices, if required?	☐	☐
15. For Loading Docks: Are dockplates kept in serviceable condition and secured to prevent slipping?	☐	☐
Do you have means to prevent car or truck movement when dockplates are in place?	☐	☐

MACHINES AND EQUIPMENT

	OK	ACTION NEEDED
1. Are all machines or operations that expose operators or other employees to rotating parts, pinch points, flying chips, particles or sparks adequately guarded?	☐	☐
2. Are mechanical power transmission belts and pinch points guarded?	☐	☐
3. Is exposed power shafting less than 7 feet from the floor guarded?	☐	☐
4. Are hand tools and other equipment regularly inspected for safe condition?	☐	☐
5. Is compressed air used for cleaning reduced to less than 30 psi?	☐	☐
6. Are power saws and similar equipment provided with safety guards?	☐	☐
7. Are grinding wheel tool rests set to within ⅛ inch or less of the wheel?	☐	☐
8. Is there any system for inspecting small hand tools for burred ends, cracked handles, etc.?	☐	☐
9. Are compressed gas cylinders examined regularly for obvious signs of defects, deep rusting or leakage?	☐	☐
10. Is care used in handling and storing cylinders and valves to prevent damage?	☐	☐
11. Are all air receivers periodically examined, including the safety valves?	☐	☐

Develop Your Own Checklist.

These Are Only Sample Questions.

	OK	ACTION NEEDED	
12. Are safety valves tested regularly and frequently?	☐	☐	**Develop Your Own Checklist.**
13. Is there sufficient clearance from stoves, furnaces, etc., for stock, woodwork, or other combustible materials?	☐	☐	
14. Is there clearance of at least 4 feet in front of heating equipment involving open flames, such as gas radiant heaters, and fronts of firing doors of stoves, furnaces, etc.?	☐	☐	**These Are Only Sample Questions.**
15. Are all oil and gas fired devices equipped with flame failure controls that will prevent flow of fuel if pilots or main burners are not working?	☐	☐	
16. Is there at least a 2-inch clearance between chimney brickwork and all woodwork or other combustible materials?	☐	☐	
17. For Welding or Flame Cutting Operations: Are only authorized, trained personnel permitted to use such equipment?	☐	☐	
Have operators been given a copy of operating instructions and asked to follow them?	☐	☐	
Are welding gas cylinders stored so they are not subjected to damage?	☐	☐	
Are valve protection caps in place on all cylinders not connected for use?	☐	☐	
Are all combustible materials near the operator covered with protective shields or otherwise protected?	☐	☐	
Is a fire extinguisher provided at the welding site?	☐	☐	
Do operators have the proper protective clothing and equipment?	☐	☐	

MATERIALS

	OK	ACTION NEEDED
1. Are approved safety cans or other acceptable containers used for handling and dispensing flammable liquids?	☐	☐
2. Are all flammable liquids that are kept inside buildings stored in proper storage containers or cabinets?	☐	☐
3. Do you meet OSHA standards for all spray painting or dip tank operations using combustible liquids?	☐	☐
4. Are oxidizing chemicals stored in areas separate from all organic material except shipping bags?	☐	☐
5. Do you have an enforced NO SMOKING rule in areas for storage and use of hazardous materials?	☐	☐
6. Are NO SMOKING signs posted where needed?	☐	☐

	OK	ACTION NEEDED

7. Is ventilation equipment provided for removal of air contaminants from operations such as production grinding, buffing, spray painting and/or vapor degreasing, and is it operating properly? ☐ ☐

8. Are protective measures in effect for operations involved with X-rays or other radiation? ☐ ☐

9. For Lift Truck Operations:
   Are only trained personnel allowed to operate forklift trucks? ☐ ☐

   Is overhead protection provided on high lift rider trucks? ☐ ☐

10. For Toxic Materials:
    Are all materials used in your plant checked for toxic qualities? ☐ ☐

    Have appropriate control procedures such as ventilation systems, enclosed operations, safe handling practices, proper personal protective equipment (e.g., respirators, glasses or goggles, gloves, etc.) been instituted for toxic materials? ☐ ☐

EMPLOYEE PROTECTION

	OK	ACTION NEEDED

1. Is there a hospital, clinic or infirmary for medical care near your business? ☐ ☐

2. If medical and first-aid facilities are not nearby, do you have one or more employees trained in first aid? ☐ ☐

3. Are your first-aid supplies adequate for the type of potential injuries in your workplace? ☐ ☐

4. Are there quick water flush facilities available where employees are exposed to corrosive materials? ☐ ☐

5. Are hard hats provided and worn where any danger of falling objects exists? ☐ ☐

6. Are protective goggles or glasses provided and worn where there is any danger of flying particles or splashing of corrosive materials? ☐ ☐

7. Are protective gloves, aprons, shields or other means provided for protection from sharp, hot or corrosive materials? ☐ ☐

8. Are approved respirators provided for regular or emergency use where needed? ☐ ☐

9. Is all protective equipment maintained in a sanitary condition and readily available for use? ☐ ☐

Develop Your Own Checklist.

These Are Only Sample Questions.

10. Where special equipment is needed for electrical workers, is it available? ☐ ☐

11. When lunches are eaten on the premises, are they eaten in areas where there is no exposure to toxic materials, and not in toilet facility areas? ☐ ☐

12. Is protection against the effects of occupational noise exposure provided when the sound levels exceed those shown in Table G-16 of the OSHA noise standard? ☐ ☐

Develop Your Own Checklist.

These Are Only Sample Questions.

Notes

1. "Workplace Fatalities," *BNA Bulletin to Management,* September 1, 1994, pp. 276–277; "Occupational Injuries and Illnesses," *BNA Bulletin to Management,* January 12, 1995, pp. 12–13.
2. *Workers' Compensation Manual for Managers and Supervisors* (Chicago: Commerce Clearing House, Inc., 1992), p. 12. See also Guy Toscano and Janice Windau, "The Changing Character of Fatal Work Injuries," *Monthly Labor Review,* Vol. 117, No. 10 (October, 1994), pp. 17–28.
3. *U.S.* v. *S.A. Healy Company,* DC E Wis, No. 90-CR-123, 2/20/91.
4. *U.S.* v. *Mickey,* DC N Ohio, 1-92-CR-0380, 12/4/92.
5. Much of this is based on "All About OSHA" (revised), U.S. Department of Labor, Occupational Safety and Health Administration (Washington, DC, 1980).
6. Bureau of National Affairs, "OSHA Hazard Communication Standard Enforcement," *Bulletin to Management,* February 23, 1989, p. 13.
7. "What Every Employer Needs to Know About OSHA Record Keeping," U.S. Department of Labor, Bureau of Labor Statistics (Washington, DC, 1978), report 412–3, p. 3.
8. Brian Jackson and Jeffrey Myers, "Just When You Thought You Were Safe: OSHA Record-Keeping Violations," *Management Review* (May 1994), pp. 62–63.
9. Ibid., p. 62.
10. "All About OSHA," p. 18.
11. "Supreme Court Says OSHA Inspectors Need Warrants," *Engineering News Record,* June 1, 1978, pp 9–10. W. Scott Railton, "OSHA Gets Tough on Business," *Management Review,* Vol. 80, no. 12 (December 1991), pp. 28–29.
12. Michael Verespej, "OSHA Revamps Its Inspection Policies," *Industry Week,* September 17, 1979, pp. 19–20. See also Horace E. Johns, "OSHA's Impact," *Personnel Journal,* Vol. 67, no. 11 (November 1988), pp. 102–107.
13. This section is based on "All About OSHA," pp. 23–25. See also Robert Sand, "OSHA Access to Privileged Materials: Criminal Prosecutions; Damages for Fear of Cancer," *Employee Relations Law Journal,* Vol. 19, no. 1 (Summer 1993), pp. 151–157.
14. "OSHA: Reforms and Penalties," *BNA Bulletin to Management,* January 28, 1993, p. 25.
15. Bureau of National Affairs, "OSHA Instruction on Penalties," *Bulletin to Management,* February 7, 1991, p. 33; Commerce Clearing House, "OSHA Will Begin Higher Fines March 1st," *Ideas and Trends in Personnel,* January 23, 1991, p. 14; John Bruening, "OSHRC on the Comeback Trail," *Occupational Hazards* (January 1991), pp. 33–36. OSHA is also stressing record-keeping violations. See for example, Brian Jackson and Jeffrey Myers, "Just When You Thought You Were Safe: OSHA Record-Keeping Violations," *Management Review,* Vol. 83, No. 5 (May, 1994), pp. 62–63.
16. Roger Jacobs, "Employee Resistance to OSHA Standards: Toward a More Reasonable Approach," *Labor Law Journal* (April 1979), pp. 219–230. See also Charles Chadd, "Managing OSHA Compliance: The Human Resources Issues," *Employee Relations Law Journal,* Vol. 20, No. 1 (Summer, 1994), pp. 101–113.
17. Ibid., p. 220.
18. Charles Chadd, "Managing OSHA Compliance: The Human Resources Issues," *Employee Relations Law Journal,* no. 4 (Summer 1994), p. 106.
19. These are based on ibid., pp. 227–230.
20. Michael Verespej, "Has OSHA Improved?" *Industry Week,* August 4, 1980, p. 50.
21. "What Every Employer Needs to Know About OSHA Record Keeping."
22. Willie Hammer, *Occupational Safety Management and Engineering,* 3rd ed. (Englewood Cliffs, NJ: Prentice Hall, 1985), pp. 62–63.
23. See Stephen Yohay, "Comprehensive OSHA Reform a Serious Prospect," *Employee Relations Law Journal,* Vol. 17, no. 4 (Spring 1992), pp. 661–672.
24. Ibid., p. 662.
25. This is based on Robert Scherer, Daniel Kaufman, and M. Fall Anina, "Complaint Resolution by OSHA in Small and Large Manufacturing Firms," *Journal of Small Business Management* (January 1993), pp. 73–83. See also Robert Sand, "Pragmatic Suggestions for Negotiating Reductions in OSHA Citations," *Employee Relations Law Journal,* Vol. 20, No. 1, Summer, 1994, pp. 153–159.
26. Ibid., p. 79.

27. Ibid. Note that although penalty reductions were about twice as large in large firms, the amount of total penalties paid by large and small firms differed as well, amounting to $566 for small firms, and $1,209 for large firms.
28. Lester Bittel, *What Every Supervisor Should Know* (New York: McGraw-Hill, 1974), p. 25. For an example of an effective safety training program, see Michael Pennacchia, "Interactive Training Sets the Pace," *Safety and Health,* Vol. 135, no. 1 (January 1987), pp. 24–27, and Philip Poynter and David Stevens, "How to Secure an Effective Health and Safety Program at Work," *Professional Safety,* Vol. 32, no. 1 (January 1987), pp. 32–41. Appointing a safety committee can also be useful. See for example, Neville Tompkins, "Getting the Best Help from your Safety Committee," *H R Magazine,* Vol. 40, No. 4 (April 1995), p. 76.
29. David S. Thelan, Donna Ledgerwood, and Charles F. Walters, "Health and Safety in the Workplace: A New Challenge for Business Schools," *Personnel Administrator,* Vol. 30, no. 10 (October 1985), p. 44.
30. Hammer, *Occupational Safety Management and Engineering.*
31. "A Safety Committee Man's Guide," Aetna Life and Casualty Insurance Company, Catalog 872684.
32. Ibid., pp. 17–21. OSHA has identified ten major causes of accidents: inadequate training, inability to do the job, lack of job understanding, improper tools and equipment, poor-quality materials, poor maintenance, poor work environment, incorrect shop routing, tight work schedules, and overly tight schedules. See Myron Peskin and Frances McGrath, "Industrial Safety: Who is Responsible and Who Benefits," *Business Horizons,* Vol. 35, no. 3 (May–June 1992), pp. 66–70. See also Daniel Webb, "Why Safety Programs Fail," *Management Review,* Vol. 83, No. 2 (February, 1994), pp. 51–54.
33. Willard Kerr, "Complementary Theories of Safety Psychology," in Edwin Fleishman and Alan Bass, *Industrial Psychology* (Homewood, IL: Dorsey Press, 1974), pp. 493–500. See also Alan Fowler, "How to Make the Workplace Safer," *People Management,* Vol. 1, No. 2 (January, 1995), pp. 38–39.
34. List of unsafe acts from "A Safety Committee Man's Guide," Aetna Life and Casualty Insurance Company.
35. A.G. Arbous and J.E. Kerrich, "The Phenomenon of Accident Proneness," *Industrial Medicine and Surgery,* Vol. 22 (1953), pp. 141–148, reprinted in Fleishman and Bass, *Industrial Psychology,* p. 485.
36. Ernest McCormick and Joseph Tiffin, *Industrial Psychology* (Englewood Cliffs, NJ: Prentice Hall, 1974), pp. 522–523; Norman Maier, *Psychology and Industrial Organization* (Boston: Houghton-Mifflin, 1965), pp. 458–462; Milton Blum and James Nayler, *Industrial Psychology* (New York: Harper & Row, 1968), pp. 519–531. For example, David DeJoy, "Attributional Processes and Hazard Control Management in Industry," *Journal of Safety Research,* Vol. 16 (Summer 1985), pp. 61–71.
37. McCormick and Tiffin, *Industrial Psychology,* p. 523.
38. John Miner and J. Frank Brewer, "Management of Ineffective Performance," in Marvin Dunnette, ed., *Handbook of Industrial and Organizational Psychology* (Chicago: Rand McNally, 1976), pp. 995–1031; McCormick and Tiffin, *Industrial Psychology,* pp. 524–525. Younger employees prob-

ably have more accidents also, at least in part because they fail to perceive specific situations as being as risky as do older employees. See, for example, Peter Finn and Barry Bragg, "Perceptions of the Risk of an Accident by Young and Older Drivers," *Accident Analysis and Prevention,* Vol. 18, no. 4 (August 1986). See also Olivia Mitchell, "The Relation of Age to Workplace Injuries," *Monthly Labor Review,* Vol. 111, no. 7 (July 1988), pp. 8–13.
39. Blum and Nayler, *Industrial Psychology,* p. 522.
40. Miner and Brewer, "Management of Ineffective Performance," in Dunnette, ed., *Handbook of Industrial and Organizational Psychology,* pp. 1004–1005.
41. Maier, *Psychology and Industrial Organization,* pp. 463–467; McCormick and Tiffin, *Industrial Psychology,* pp. 533–536; and Blum and Nayler, *Industrial Psychology,* pp. 525–527.
42. D. Wechsler, "Test for Taxicab Drivers," *Journal of Personnel Research,* Vol. 5 (1926), pp. 24–30, quoted in Maier, *Psychology and Industrial Organization,* p. 64. See also Leo DeBobes, "Psychological Factors in Accident Prevention," *Personnel Journal,* Vol. 65 (January 1986). See also Curtiss Hansen, "A Causal Model of the Relationship Among Accidents, Biodata Personality, and Cognitive Factors," *Journal of Applied Psychology,* Vol 74, no. 1 (February 1989), pp. 81–90.
43. Maier, *Psychology and Industrial Organization,* p. 463.
44. S.E. Wirt and H.E. Leedkee, "Skillful Eyes Prevent Accidents," Annual Newsletter, National Safety Council, Industrial Nursing Section (November 1945), pp. 10–12, quoted in Maier, *Psychology and Industrial Organization,* p. 466.
45. Gerald Borofsky, Michelle Bielema, and James Hoffman, "Accidents, Turnover, and Use of a Pre-employment Screening Interview," *Psychological Reports* (1993), pp. 1067–1076.
46. Ibid., p. 1069.
47. Ibid., p. 1072.
48. Judy D. Olian, "Genetic Screening for Employment Purposes," *Personnel Psychology,* Vol. 37, no. 3 (Autumn 1984), pp. 423–438.
49. Maier, *Psychology and Industrial Organization,* p. 464.
50. *Workers' Compensation Manual for Managers and Supervisors,* pp. 22–23.
51. S. Laner and R. J. Sell, "An Experiment on the Effect of Specially Designed Safety Posters," *Occupational Psychology,* Vol. 34 (1960), pp. 153–169, in McCormick and Tiffin, *Industrial Psychology,* p. 536.
52. McCormick and Tiffin, *Industrial Psychology,* p. 537. A group of international experts met in Belgium in 1986 and concluded that a successful safety poster must be simple and specific and reinforce safe behavior rather than negative behavior. See "What Makes an Effective Safety Poster," *National Safety and Health News,* Vol. 134, no. 6 (December 1986), pp. 32–34.
53. David Gunsch, "Employees Exercise to Prevent Injuries," *Personnel Journal* (July 1993), pp. 58–62.
54. OSHA has published two useful training manuals: *Training Requirements of OSHA Standards* (February 1976) and *Teaching Safety and Health in the Work Place,* U.S. Department of Labor, Occupational Safety and Health Administration (1976); J. Surry, "Industrial Accident Research: Human Engineering Approach" (Toronto: University of

Toronto, Department of Industrial Engineering, June 1968), Chapter 4, quoted in McCormick and Tiffin, *Industrial Psychology,* p. 534. For an example of a very successful incentive program aimed at boosting safety at Campbell Soup Company, see Frederick Wahl, Jr., "Soups on for Safety," *National Safety and Health News,* Vol. 134, no. 6 (December 1986), pp. 49–53. For a discussion of how employee involvement can impact job re-design and employee safety, see Douglas May and Catherine Schwoerer, "Employee Health by Design: Using Employee Involvement Teams in Ergonomics Job Redesign," *Personnel Psychology,* Vol. 47, No. 4 (Winter, 1994), pp. 861–876.

55. Judi Komaki, Kenneth Barwick, and Lawrence Scott, "A Behavioral Approach to Occupational Safety: Pinpointing and Reinforcing Safe Performance in a Food Manufacturing Plant," *Journal of Applied Psychology,* Vol. 63 (August 1978), pp. 434–445. See also Robert Reber, Jerry Wallin, and David Duhon, "Preventing Occupational Injuries Through Performance Management," *Public Personnel Management,* Vol. 22, no. 2 (Summer 1993), pp. 301–311, Anat Arkin, "Incentives to Work Safely," *Personnel Management,* Vol. 26, No. 9 (September 1994), pp. 48–52, and Peter Makin and Valerie Sutherland, "Reducing Accidents Using a Behavioral Approach," *Leadership & Organizational Development Journal,* Vol. 15, No. 5 (1994), pp. 5–10.

56. Judi Komaki, Arlene Heinzmann, and Lorealie Lawson, "Effect of Training and Feedback: Component Analysis of a Behavioral Safety Program," *Journal of Applied Psychology,* Vol. 65 (June 1980), pp. 261–270. See also Jorma Sari, "When Does Behavior Modification Prevent Accidents?" *Leadership & Organizational Development Journal,* Vol. 15, No. 5 (1994), pp. 11–15.

57. Dove Zohar, "Safety Climate in Industrial Organization: Theoretical and Implied Implications," *Journal of Applied Psychology,* Vol. 65 (February 1980), p. 97. For a discussion of the importance of getting employees involved in managing their own safety program, see John Lutness, "Self-managed Safety Program Gets Workers Involved," *Safety and Health,* Vol. 135, no. 4 (April 1987), pp. 42–45. See also Frederick Streff, Michael Kalsher and E. Scott Geller, "Developing Efficient Workplace Safety Programs: Observations of Response Co-Variations," *Journal of Organizational Behavior Management,* Vol. 13, No. 2 (1993), pp. 3–14.

58. *Workers' Compensation Manual for Managers and Supervisors,* p. 24. James Frierson, "An Analysis of ADA Provisions on Denying Employment Because of a Risk of Future Injury," *Employee Relations Law Journal,* Vol. 17, no. 4 (Spring 1992), pp. 603–622.

59. Bureau of National Affairs, "Workplace Safety: Improving Management Practices," *Bulletin to Management,* February 9, 1989, pp. 42 and 47; see also Marlene Morgenstern, "Workers' Compensation: Managing Costs," *Compensation and Benefits Review* (September–October 1992), pp. 30–38. See also Linda Johnson, "Preventing Injuries: The Big Payoff," *Personnel Journal* (April 1994), pp. 61–64; and David Webb, "The Bathtub Effect: Why Safety Programs Fail," *Management Review* (February 1994), pp. 51–54.

60. *Workers' Compensation Manual for Managers and Supervisors,* p. 10.

61. See, for example, ibid., pp. 36–39.

62. Ibid., p. 51.

63. This is based on J. M. Stewart, "The Multi-Ball Juggler," *Business Quarterly* (Summer 1993), pp. 33–39.

64. Ibid., p. 38.

65. Ibid., p. 37.

66. This section based largely on Miner and Brewer, "Management of Ineffective Performance," pp. 1005–1023.

67. James Schreir, "Survey Supports Perceptions: Work-Site Drug Use Is on the Rise," *Personnel Journal* (October 1987), pp. 114–118. Pallassana Balgopal, "Combating Alcoholism in Industries: Implications for Occupational Social Work," *Management and Labor Studies,* Vol. 17, no. 1 (January 1992), pp. 33–42. For a review of the background factors possibly leading to drug abuse, see for example, Richard Clayton et al., "Risk and Protective Factors: A Brief Review," *Drugs & Society, a Journal of Contemporary Issues,* Vol. 8, No. 3–4 (1995), pp. 7–14.

68. Gopal Pati and John Adkins, Jr., "The Employer's Role in Alcoholism Assistance," *Personnel Journal,* Vol. 62, no. 7 (July 1983), pp. 568–572. For a discussion of how the work environment can encourage drug dealing, see Richard Lyles, "Should the Next Drug Bust Be in Your Company?" *Personnel Journal,* Vol. 63 (October 1984), pp. 46–49.

69. Harrison Trice, "Alcoholism and the Work World," *Sloan Management Review,* no. 2 (Fall 1970), pp. 67–75, reprinted in W. Clay Hamner and Frank Schmidt, *Contemporary Problems in Personnel,* rev. ed., (Chicago: St. Clair Press, 1977), pp. 496–502. Note also that dependence on ordinary substances can be as devastating as hard drug problems. See, for example, Peter Minetos, "Are You Addicted to Legal Drugs?" *Safety and Health,* Vol. 136, no. 2 (August 1987), pp. 46–49. For a discussion of substance abuse in the small business see, for example, Harry Lasher and John Grashof, "Substance Abuse in Small Business: Business Owner Perceptions and Reactions," *Journal of Small Business Management* (January 1993), pp. 63–72.

70. Pati and Adkins, "Employer's Role in Alcoholism Assistance." See also Commerce Clearing House, "How Should Employers Respond to Indications an Employee May Have an Alcohol or Drug Problem?" *Ideas and Trends,* April 6, 1989, pp. 53–57.

71. Based on Miner and Brewer, "Management of Ineffective Performance." The survey was conducted jointly by the American Society for Personnel Administration and the Bureau of National Affairs. The results were based on an analysis of the questionnaire data made by Professors Miner and Brewer, who acknowledge the assistance of John B. Schappi, associate editor of the Bureau of National Affairs, and Mary Green Miner, director of *BNA Surveys,* in making this information available.

72. Trice, "Alcoholism and the Work World." See also Larry A. Pace and Stanley J. Smits, "Substance Abuse: A Proactive Approach," *Personnel Journal,* Vol. 68, no. 4 (April 1989), pp. 84–90, and Commerce Clearing House, "Typical Behavior Changes in an Employee with a Drinking Problem," *Ideas and Trends,* April 6, 1989, p. 56.

73. This is quoted from Bureau of National Affairs, "Drug-Free Workplace: New Federal Requirements," *Bulletin to Management,* February 9, 1989, pp. 1–4. Note that the Drug-Free Workplace Act does not mandate or mention testing employees for illegal drug use.

74. January 1, 1995 for employers with 50 or more safety-sensitive workers; January 1, 1996 for smaller employers. "Alcohol Misuse Prevention Programs: Department of Transportation Final Rules," *BNA Bulletin to Management,* March 24, 1994, pp. 1–8.

75. From Henry Balevic, "Drug Abuse in the Workplace" (Personnel Services, Inc., 2303 W. Meadowview Road, Greensboro, NC 27407), reprinted in Bureau of National Affairs, *Bulletin to Management,* August 29, 1985, p. 72. Stanley Smits and Larry Pace, "Workplace Substance Abuse: Establish Policies," *Personnel Journal* (May 1989), pp. 88–93.

76. Bureau of National Affairs, *Bulletin to Management,* December 19, 1985, p. 200. Based on a speech by San Francisco attorneys Victor Schacter and Robert Kristoff. See also Alfred Klein, "Employees Under the Influence—Outside the Law?" *Personnel Journal,* Vol. 65, no. 9 (September 1986), pp. 56–58; Martin Aron, "Drug Testing: The Employer's Dilemma," *Labor Law Journal,* Vol. 38, no. 3 (March 1987), pp. 157–165; Bureau of National Affairs, "Drug Testing 'To Do' List," *Bulletin to Management,* August 10, 1989, p. 250.

77. This is based on Terry Beehr and John Newman, "Organizational Stress, Employer Health, and Organizational Effectiveness: A Factor Analysis, Model, and Literature Review," *Personnel Psychology,* Vol. 31 (Winter 1978), pp. 665–699. See also Stephan Motowizlo, John Packard, and Michael Manning, "Occupational Stress: Its Causes and Consequences for Job Performance," *Journal of Applied Psychology,* Vol. 71, no. 4 (November 1986), pp. 618–629.

78. Eric Sundstrom, et al., "Office Noise, Satisfaction, and Performance," *Environment and Behavior,* Vol. 26, no. 2 (March 1994), pp. 195–222.

79. Andre DuBrin, *Human Relations: A Job Oriented Approach* (Reston, VA: Reston, 1978), pp. 66–67.

80. John Newman and Terry Beehr, "Personal and Organizational Strategies for Handling Job Stress: A Review of Research and Opinion," *Personnel Psychology* (Spring 1979), pp. 1–43. See also Bureau of National Affairs, "Work Place Stress: How to Curb Claims," *Bulletin to Management,* April 14, 1988, p. 120.

81. Karl Albrecht, *Stress and the Manager* (Englewood Cliffs, NJ: Spectrum, 1979). For a discussion of the related symptoms of depression see James Krohe, Jr., "An Epidemic of Depression?" *Across-the-Board* (September 1994), pp. 23–27. See also James Krohe, "An Epidemic of Depression?" *Across the Board,* Vol. 31, No. 8 (September, 1994), pp. 23–27.

82. Michael Leiter, David Clark, and Josette Durup, "Distinct Models of Burnout and Commitment Among Men and Women in the Military," *Journal of Applied Behavioral Science,* Vol. 30, no. 1 (March 1994), pp. 63–64.

83. "Solutions to Workplace Stress," *BNA Bulletin to Management,* February 11, 1993, p. 48. See also Christopher Bachler, "Workers Take Leave of Job Stress," *Personnel Journal,* Vol. 74, No. 1 (January, 1995) p. 38.

84. Pascale Carayon, "Stressful Jobs and Non-Stressful Jobs: A Cluster Analysis of Office Jobs," *Ergonomics,* Vol. 37, no. 2 (1994), pp. 311–323.

85. Ibid.

86. Ibid., pp. 319–320.

87. Herbert Freudenberger, *Burn-Out* (Toronto: Bantam Books, 1980). See also Susan Jackson, Richard Schwab, and Randall Schuler, "Toward an Understanding of the Burnout Phenomenon," *Journal of Applied Psychology,* Vol. 71, no. 4 (November 1986), pp. 630–640, and James R. Redeker and Jonathan Seagal, "Profits Low? Your Employees May Be High!" *Personnel,* Vol. 66, no. 6 (June 1989), pp. 72–76. See also Cary Cherniss, "Long Term Consequences of Burnout: An Exploratory Study," *Journal of Organizational Behavior,* Vol. 13, no. 1 (January 1992), pp. 1–11; and Raymond Lee and Blake Ashforth, "A Further Examination of Managerial Burnout: Toward an Integrated Model," *Journal of Organizational Behavior,* Vol. 14 (1993), pp. 3–20.

88. This is based on Philip Voluck and Herbert Abramson, "How to Avoid Stress-Related Disability Claims," *Personnel Journal* (May 1987), pp. 95–98.

89. For a discussion, see ibid., p. 96.

90. See, for example, Michael Smith and others, "An Investigation of Health Complaints and Job Stress in Video Display Operations," *Human Factors* (August 1981), pp. 387–400; see also Bureau of National Affairs, "How to Protect Workers from Reproductive Hazards," *Fair Employment Practices,* July 23, 1987, pp. 89–90. See also Commerce Clearing House, "Suffolk County New York Passes Law Covering Employers with Twenty Terminals or More Regarding VDT Regulation," *Ideas and Trends* (1988), p. 48.

91. Bureau of National Affairs, "No Link Found Between VDTs and Miscarriages," *Bulletin to Management,* March 21, 1991, p. 81.

92. J.A. Savage, "Are Computer Terminals Zapping Workers' Health?" *Business and Society Review* (1994).

93. Bureau of National Affairs, "Solutions to VDT Viewing Problems," *Bulletin to Management,* November 5, 1987, pp. 356–357.

94. Bureau of National Affairs, "AIDS and the Workplace: Issues, Advice, and Answers," *Bulletin to Management,* November 14, 1985, pp. 1–6. See also David Ritter and Ronald Turner, "AIDS: Employer Concerns and Options," *Labor Law Journal,* Vol. 38, no. 2 (February 1987), pp. 67–83; and Bureau of National Affairs, "How Employers Are Responding to AIDS in the Workplace," *Fair Employment Practices,* February 18, 1988, pp. 21–22. For a complete guide to services and information regarding "The Work Place and AIDS," see *Personnel Journal,* Vol. 66, no. 10 (October 1987), pp. 65–80. See also William H. Wager, "AIDS: Setting Policy, Educating Employees at Bank of America," *Personnel,* Vol. 65, no. 8 (August 1988), pp. 4–10. See also Margaret Magnus, "AIDS: Fear and Ignorance," *Personnel Journal,* Vol. 67, no. 2 (February 1988), pp. 28–32, for poll regarding major workplace comments associated with AIDS. See also "AIDS/HIV in the Workplace: A Fact Sheet for Employees," *BNA Bulletin to Management,* October 6, 1994.

95. Commerce Clearing House, "The Wells Fargo AIDS Policy," *Ideas and Trends,* April 5, 1988, pp. 52–53.

96. Quoted or paraphrased from Michael Esposito and Jeffrey Myers, "Managing AIDS in the Workplace," *Employee Relations Law Journal,* Vol. 19, no. 1 (Summer 1993), p. 68.

97. Marco Colossi, "Do Employees Have the Right to Smoke?" *Personnel Journal* (April 1988), pp. 72–79.

98. Bureau of National Affairs, "Where There's Smoke There's Risk," *Bulletin to Management,* January 30, 1992, pp. 26 and 31.

99. Daniel Warner, "'We Do Not Hire Smokers': May Employers Discriminate Against Smokers?" *Employee Responsibilities and Rights Journal,* Vol. 7, no. 2 (1994), p. 129.

100. Commerce Clearing House, "State Laws Regulating Smoking," *Ideas and Trends,* January 9, 1987, pp. 4–5.

101. Jim Collison, "Workplace Smoking Policies: Sixteen Questions and Answers," *Personnel Journal* (April 1988), p. 81. See also Daniel Warner, "We Do Not Hire Smokers: May Employers Discriminate Against Smokers?" *Employee Responsibilities and Rights,* Vol. 7, No. 2 (June, 1994), pp. 129–140.

102. Daniel Warner, "We Do Not Hire Smokers," p. 138.

103. Bureau of National Affairs, "Smoking Bans on the Rise," *Bulletin to Management,* March 16, 1989, p. 82.

104. Gus Toscano and Janice Windau, "The Changing Character of Fatal Work Injuries," *Monthly Labor Review* (October 1994), pp. 17–28.

105. Ibid., p. 17.

106. Based on Louis DiLorenzo and Darren Carroll, "The Growing Menace: Violence in the Workplace," *New York State Bar Journal* (January 1995), p. 24.

107. "Workplace Violence: Sources and Solutions," *BNA Bulletin to Management,* November 4, 1993, p. 345.

108. Ibid., p. 345.

109. See also Pamela Johnson and Juile Indvik, "Workplace Violence: An Issue of the 90s," *Public Personnel Management,* Vol. 23, no. 4 (Winter 1994), pp. 515–523.

110. Alfred Feliu, "Workplace Violence and the Duty of Care: The Scope of an Employer's Obligation to Protect Against the Violent Employee," *Employee Relations Law Journal,* Vol. 20, no. 3 (Winter 1994/95), pp. 381–406.

111. "Workplace Violence: Sources and Solutions," *BNA Bulletin to Management,* November 4, 1993, p. 345.

112. Ibid.

113. Feliu, "Workplace Violence and the Duty of Care," p. 395.

114. Dawn Anfuso, "Workplace Violence," *Personnel Journal* (October 1994), pp. 66–77.

115. Feliu, "Workplace Violence and the Duty of Care," p. 395.

116. Quoted from Feliu, "Workplace Violence and the Duty of Care," p. 395.

117. Anfuso, "Workplace Violence," p. 71. Excellence in Training Corp. is in Des Moines, Iowa.

118. "Preventing Workplace Violence," *BNA Bulletin to Management,* June 10, 1993, p. 177. See also Jenny McCune, "Companies Grapple with Workplace Violence," *Management Review,* Vol. 83, No. 3 (March 1994), pp. 52–57.

119. Quoted or paraphrased from ibid., p. 177 and based on recommendations from Chris Hatcher.

120. Feliu, "Workplace Violence and the Duty of Care," pp. 401–402.

121. See, for example, Feliu, "Workplace Violence and the Duty of Care," p. 402.

122. Donna Rosato, "New Industry Helps Managers Fight Violence," *USA Today,* August 8, 1995, p. 1.

123. Louis DiLorenzo and Darren Carroll, "The Growing Menace: Violence in the Workplace," *New York State Bar Journal* (January 1995), p. 25.

124. Quoted from Feliu, "Workplace Violence and the Duty of Care," p. 393.

125. DiLorenzo and Carroll, "The Growing Menace," p. 27.

126. This is based on Beverly Younger, "Violence Against Women in the Workplace," *Employee Assistance Quarterly,* Vol. 9, no. 3/4 (1994), pp. 113–133.

127. Ibid., p. 120.

128. Ibid., p. 121.

129. Ibid.

130. Ibid., pp. 129–130.

ment refers to operations in one country that are controlled by entities in a foreign country. This might mean building new facilities in another country, as Toyota did when it built its Camry manufacturing plant in Georgetown, Kentucky. Or it might mean that the firm acquires property or operations in a foreign country, as when Matsushita bought (and subsequently was forced to divest itself of) control of Rockefeller Center in New York City. Strictly speaking, a foreign direct investment means acquiring control by owning more than 50% of the operation. But in practice, it is possible for any firm (including a foreign firm) to gain effective control by owning less. In any event, a foreign direct investment turns a firm into a multinational enterprise. A *multinational enterprise* is one that controls operations in more than one country.

Joint ventures and wholly-owned subsidiaries are two examples of foreign direct investments. A *joint venture* is defined as "the participation of two or more companies jointly in an enterprise in which each party contributes assets, owns the entity to some degree, and shares risk."[5] In contrast, a *wholly-owned subsidiary* is owned 100% by the foreign firm. Thus, in the United States today, Toyota Motor Manufacturing, Inc. and its facility in Georgetown, Kentucky make up a wholly-owned subsidiary of Toyota Motor Corporation, which is based in Japan. A joint venture, a wholly-owned subsidiary, or simply the need to staff one or more company offices abroad requires a considerable international effort by a company's HR managers, as we'll see.

Companies obviously differ in their degree of international involvement. An *international business* is any firm that engages in international trade or investment.[6] *International trade* refers to the export or import of goods or services to consumers in another country. Similarly, *international investment* refers to the investment of resources in business activities outside a firm's home country.

The multinational corporation is one type of international business enterprise. A *multinational corporation* (MNC) can be defined as "an internationally integrated production system over which equity based control is exercised by a parent corporation that is owned and managed essentially by the nationals of the country in which it is [situated]."[7] (Equity based control means the parent owns a large share of the foreign operation). In other words, the multinational corporation operates manufacturing and marketing facilities in several countries; these operations are coordinated by a parent firm, whose owners are mostly based in the firm's home country.

Firms like General Electric and ITT have long been multinational corporations, but marketing expert Theodore Levitt contends that the MNC's reign as the preeminent international trade vehicle is nearing its end. It is being replaced, he says, by a new type of international enterprise he calls the global corporation. Whereas the multinational corporation operates in a number of countries and adjusts its products and practices to each, the *global corporation* operates as if the entire world (or major regions of it) were a single entity. They sell essentially the same things in the same way everywhere, much as Sony sells a standardized product such as Walkman throughout the world with components that may be made or designed in different countries.[8]

HR and International Business

Consistent with these international business options, international HR management takes several forms. First, it can mean formulating and implementing HR policies and activities in the home-office headquarters of multinational companies like Coca-Cola and IBM.[9] HR responsibilities include selecting, training, and transferring parent-company personnel abroad, and formulating HR policies for the firm as a whole and for its foreign operations. Some firms just apply parent-country HR policies to subsidiaries abroad, but most adapt their home-office HR practices to those common in the host countries, as we'll see.

Conducting HR activities in the foreign subsidiary of an MNC is a second form of international HRM. For example, Sumitomo Bank and Sony must conduct HR operations in their U.S. subsidiaries.[10] Again, local HR practices are often based on the parent firm's HR policies, albeit fine tuned for local-country practices and legal constraints.

International HR management is important in smaller firms, too. For example, Apex Engineering may have only $4 million in sales and sell abroad exclusively by exporting through sales agents in Europe. What kinds of international HR decisions would its managers have to make? There are many examples. Someone may have to be sent abroad to help train the independent European sales agents; international HR policies will then have to be created to provide guidelines for paying these home-office employees' travel and living expenses and possibly for posting them abroad for several months. And, as European sales rise, a decision may have to be made to hire one or more engineers in the home office who are fluent in the language of one or more European countries.

How Intercountry Differences Affect HRM

To a large extent, companies operating only within the borders of the United States have the luxury of dealing with a relatively limited set of economic, cultural, and legal variables. Notwithstanding the range from liberal to conservative,

While vacationers like these in Luxembourg are legally entitled to five weeks' holiday, standards vary widely even within Europe.

for instance, the United States is basically a capitalist competitive society. And while a multitude of cultural and ethnic backgrounds are represented in the U.S. work force, various shared values (such as an appreciation for democracy) help to blur the otherwise sharp cultural differences. While the different states and municipalities certainly have their own laws affecting HRM, a basic legal framework as laid down by federal law also helps to produce a fairly predictable set of legal guidelines regarding matters such as employment discrimination, labor relations, and safety and health.

A company operating multiple units abroad is generally not blessed with such relative homogeneity. For example, minimum legally mandated holidays may range from none in the United Kingdom to five weeks per year in Luxembourg. And while there are no formal requirements for employee participation in Italy, employee representatives on boards of directors are required in companies with more than 30 employees in Denmark. The point is that the management of the HR function in multinational companies is complicated enormously by the need to adapt personnel policies and procedures to the differences among countries in which each subsidiary is based. The following are some intercountry differences that demand such adaptation.[11]

Cultural Factors Wide-ranging cultural differences from country to country demand corresponding differences in personnel practices among a company's foreign subsidiaries. We might generalize, for instance, that the cultural norms of the Far East and the importance there of the patriarchal system will mold the typical Japanese worker's view of his or her relationship to an employer as well as influence how that person works. Japanese workers have often come to expect lifetime employment in return for their loyalty, for instance. And incentive plans in Japan tend to focus on the work group, while in the West the more usual prescription is still to focus on individual worker incentives.[12] Similarly, in a recent study of about 330 managers from Hong Kong, the People's Republic of China, and the United States, U.S. managers tended to be most concerned with getting the job done while Chinese managers were most concerned with maintaining a harmonious environment; Hong Kong managers fell between these two extremes.[13]

A well-known study by Professor Geert Hofstede underscores other international cultural differences. Hofstede says societies differ first in *power distance,* in other words, the extent to which the less powerful members of institutions accept and expect that power will be distributed unequally.[14] He concluded that the institutionalization of such an inequality was higher in some countries (such as Mexico) than in others (such as Sweden).

His findings identified several other cultural differences. *Individualism versus collectivism* refers to the degree to which ties between individuals are normally loose rather than close. In more individualistic countries, "all members are expected to look after themselves and their immediate families."[15] Individualistic countries include Australia and the United States. Collectivist countries include Indonesia and Pakistan. *Masculinity versus femininity* refers, said Hofstede, to the extent to which society values assertiveness ("masculinity") versus caring (what he called "femininity"). Japan and Austria ranked high in masculinity; Denmark and Chile ranked low.

Such intracountry cultural differences have several HR implications. First, they suggest the need for adapting HR practices such as testing and pay plans to local cultural norms. They also suggest that HR staff in a foreign subsidiary is best drawn from host-country citizens. A high degree of sensitivity and empathy for the cultural and attitudinal demands of coworkers is always important when selecting employees to staff overseas operations. However, such sensitivity is especially important when the job is HRM and the work involves "human" jobs like interviewing, testing, orienting, training, counseling, and (if need be) terminating. As one expert puts it, "An HR staff that shares the employee's cultural background is more likely to be sensitive to the employee's needs and expectations in the work place—and is thus more likely to manage the company successfully."[16]

Economic Factors Differences in economic systems among countries also translate into intercountry differences in HR practices. In free enterprise systems, for instance, the need for efficiency tends to favor HR policies that value productivity, efficient workers, and staff cutting where market forces dictate. Moving along the scale toward more socialist systems, HR practices tend to shift toward preventing unemployment, even at the expense of sacrificing efficiency.

Labor Cost Factors Differences in labor costs may also produce differences in HR practices. High labor costs can require a focus on efficiency, for instance, and on HR practices (like pay-for-performance) aimed at improving employee performance.

Intercountry differences in labor costs are substantial. For example, hourly compensation costs in U.S. dollars for production workers in manufacturing recently ranged from $2.65 in Mexico and $4.31 in Hong Kong to $16.79 in the United States and a high of $25.56 in Germany. Other illustrative rates were: Italy, $15.97; France, $16.31; Singapore, $5.38; Japan, $19.20; and Canada, $16.36.[17]

There are other comparative labor costs to consider. For example, wide gaps exist in hours worked. Thus, Portuguese workers average about 1,980 hours of work annually, while German workers average 1,648 hours. Employees in Europe generally receive four weeks of vacation as compared with just over two weeks in the

United States. And several European countries including the United Kingdom and Germany require substantial severance pay to departing employees, usually equal to at least two year's service in the United Kingdom and one year in Germany.[18]

Industrial Relations Factors Industrial relations, and specifically the relationship between the worker, the union, and the employer, vary dramatically from country to country and have an enormous impact on HR management practices. In Germany, for instance, *codetermination* is the rule. Here employees have the legal right to a voice in setting company policies. In this and several other countries workers elect their own representatives to the supervisory board of the employer, and there is also a vice president for labor at the top-management level.[19] On the other hand, in many other countries the state interferes little in the relations between employers and unions. In the United States, for instance, HR policies on most matters such as wages and benefits are set not by the state but by the employer, or by the employer in negotiations with its labor unions. In Germany, on the other hand, the various laws on codetermination including the Works Constitution Act (1972), the Co-Determination Act (1976), and the ECSC Co-Determination Act (1951) largely determine the nature of HR policies in many German firms.

The European Community (EC)[20] In 1992 the 12 separate countries of the European community (EC) were unified into a common market for goods, services, capital, and even labor. Generally speaking, tariffs for goods moving across borders from one EC country to another disappeared, and employees (with some exceptions) find it easier to move relatively freely between jobs in various EC countries.

However, differences remain. Figure 18.1 summarizes recent employment practices and policies among EC countries. Thus, many countries have minimum wages while others do not, and maximum hours permitted in the workday and workweek vary from no maximum in the United Kingdom to 48 per week in Greece and Italy. Other differences are apparent in matters like minimum annual holidays, minimum notice to be given by employer, termination formalities, and employee participation.

The impact of the European Union will be to gradually reduce these sorts of differences. Social legislation and examinations by the union's European Parliament and it's administrative European Commission are slowly reducing some. However, even if all the differences summarized in the figure are eventually eliminated, HR practices will still differ from country to country; cultural differences will require that, no doubt. Even into the near future, in other words, and even just within Europe, managing human resources multinationally will present tricky problems for HR managers.

In Summary: The Impact of Intercountry Differences on HR HR managers must consider the potential impact of intercountry differences on HR operations conducted globally. For example, differences in culture, economic systems, labor costs, and legal and industrial relations systems complicate the task of training employees who will have to work together. Such intercountry differences also mean there will be corresponding differences in management styles and practices from country to country, and such differences ". . . may strain relations between headquarters and subsidiary personnel or make a manager less effective when working abroad than at home."[21] International assignments thus run a relatively high risk of failing unless special steps are taken to select, train, and compensate international assignees.

Figure 18.1
Current Employment Practices and Policies Among EC Countries

Source: Sedel, Rae, "Europe 1992: HR Implications of the European Unification," *Personnel*, October 1989, p. 22. (reprinted with the permission of the publisher from *Personnel Today*, April 4, 1989).

Country	Employment Formalities	Minimum Pay	Max. Hours (Including overtime)	Minimum Annual Holiday	Minimum Notice to Be Given by Employer	Termination Formalities	Employee Participation
Belgium	Certain terms must be in writing.	Yes	8 per day; 40 per week	4 weeks.	Workers: 14–28 days. Others: 3 months for up to 5 years' service + 3 mos. for every 5 years' service. Higher paid employees' notice period agreed on when notice given or decided by Court.	Can terminate without notice for gross misconduct (but this does not include all instances of incompetence). Redundancy payments.	Work councils.
Denmark	Contracts usually oral.	No, but must conform to one of 2 compulsory wage systems.	Depends on collective agreement.	2½ days per month.	Workers depends on collective agreement. Others: 1–6 months.	Can terminate without notice for gross misconduct; unfair dismissal and redundancy payments.	Employee representatives on board of directors where there are more than 30 employees.
France	Contracts in writing. Collective agreements may be generally binding.	Yes	10 per day. 39 per week.	2½ days per month (includes 5 Saturdays).	1 month after 6 months' service; 2 months after 2 years' service.	Unfair dismissal. Redundancy payments. Authorization of redundancies required.	Employee and union representatives. Works councils.
Germany	Fixed-term agreements restricted; collective agreements may be generally binding.	No, but if a collective agreement, this must make provision.	8 per day. 48 per week.	18 days.	Workers: 2 weeks to 3 months. Others: 6 weeks to 6 months from end of calendar-year quarter.	Unfair dismissal. Prior consultation on redundancies or dismissals with works council and in some cases the labor authorities.	Works councils.
Greece	No substantial formalities.	Yes	48 per week.	4 weeks (after 1 year's employment).	Workers: none. Others: 1 month to 2 years.	Severance payments of 5–52 days' pay for workers or 1–24 months' pay for other employees. If notice given, only ½ payable.	Employee committees.

Ireland	Employees may require employers to supply written statements of terms of employment.	No	No generally applicable statutory maximum.	3 weeks.	1–8 weeks.	Unfair dismissal. Redundancy payments.	No formal requirements.
Italy	Contracts in writing, National collective agreements.	Collective agreement.	48 per week. 8 per day.	Collective agreement.	Collective agreement.	Severance payments, Can dismiss only for redundancy or good cause.	No formal requirements.
Luxembourg	Written contracts must be provided. Agreements may be binding on a sector.	Yes	40 per week, 8 per day.	25 working days (5 days' holiday equals one week).	4 weeks to 6 months, depending on category of worker and length of service.	Severance payments, 1–12 months. Prior notification of redundancy and redundancy payments.	Employees' representatives. Joint works councils. Employee directors.
The Netherlands	No substantial formalities.	Yes	48 per week. 8½ per day. 5½ days per week.	4 weeks.	Interval of payment (usually 2 weeks or 1 month) or a period of up to 13 weeks (26 weeks for older employees) based on length of service, whichever is longer.	Authorization of labor office usually required to dismiss with notice. May need to go to the Court; either procedure can take several months.	Works council in undertakings with 35 or more employees.
Portugal	Fixed-term contracts must be in writing.	Yes	Office workers: 42 hours per week. Others: 48 per week; 8 per day.	Not less than 21 days nor more than 30 days.	Redundancy-notice period fixed when conditions of redundancy established.	Can dismiss only for "just cause" or redundancy. Prior notification of redundancies.	Workers' commissions and registered trade unions.
Spain	No substantial formalities.	Yes	40 per week. 9 per day	2½ days per month.	1 month after 1 year's service, 3 months after 2 years.	Only for specified causes. Dismissal for other causes: compensation to 45 days pay per year of service.	Employee delegates and committees, employee directors.
United Kingdom	Written statement of terms of employment.	No	No	No	1–13 weeks.	Unfair dismissal. Redundancy payments. Prior notification of redundancies.	No formal requirements.

Improving International Assignments Through Selection

Why International Assignments Fail

It has been estimated that 20% to 25% of all overseas assignments fail, where failure is defined as the premature return of employees to the United States or the inability of expatriates to achieve their business goals.[22] The exact number of failures is understandably difficult to quantify. However, one survey of U.S., European, and Japanese multinationals concluded that three-quarters of U.S. multinational companies experience expatriate assignment failure rates of 10% or more.[23] European and Japanese multinationals reported lower failure rates, with only about one-sixth of Japanese multinationals and 3% of European multinationals reporting more than a 10% expatriate recall rate.

The reasons reported for expatriate failure differed between the U.S., European, and Japanese multinationals.[24] For U.S. multinationals, the reasons in descending order of importance were inability of spouse to adjust, managers' inability to adjust, other family problems, managers' personal or emotional immaturity, and inability to cope with larger overseas responsibility. Managers of European firms emphasized only the inability of the manager's spouse to adjust as an explanation for the expatriates failed assignment. Japanese firms emphasized (in descending order) inability to cope with larger overseas responsibility, difficulties with new assignment, personal or emotional problems, lack of technical competence, and finally, inability of spouse to adjust.

These findings underscore a truism regarding selection for international assignments, namely, that it's usually not inadequate technical competence but family and personal problems that undermine the international assignee. As one expert puts it:

> The selection process is fundamentally flawed. . . . Expatriate assignments rarely fail because the person cannot accommodate to the technical demands of the job. The expatriate selections are made by line managers based on technical competence. They fail because of family and personal issues and lack of cultural skills that haven't been part of the process.[25]

International Staffing: Sources of Managers

There are several ways to classify international managers. *Locals* are citizens of the countries where they are working. *Expatriates* are noncitizens of the countries in which they are working.[26] *Home-country nationals* are the citizens of the country in which the multinational company's headquarters is based.[27] *Third-country nationals* are citizens of a country other than the parent or the host country—for example, a British executive working in a Tokyo subsidiary of a U.S. multinational bank.[28]

Expatriates represent a minority of managers. Thus, "most managerial positions are filled by locals rather than expatriates in both headquarters or foreign subsidiary operations."[29]

There are several reasons to rely on local, host-country management talent for filling the foreign subsidiary's management ranks. Many people simply prefer not working in a foreign country, and in general the cost of using expatriates is far greater than the cost of using local management talent.[30] The MNC may be viewed locally as a "better citizen" if it uses local management talent, and indeed some governments actually press for the "nativization" of local management.[31] There may also be a fear that expatriates, knowing they're posted to the foreign subsidiary for only a few years, may overemphasize short-term projects rather than focus on perhaps more necessary long-term tasks.[32]

There are also several reasons for using expatriates—either home-country or third-country nationals—for staffing subsidiaries. The major reason is reportedly technical competence: In other words, employers can't find local candidates with the required technical qualifications.[33] Multinationals also increasingly view a successful stint abroad as a required step in developing top managers. For instance, the head of General Electric's Asia-Pacific region was transferred back to a top executive position of vice chairman at GE in 1995. Control is another important reason. Multinationals sometimes assign home-country nationals from their headquarters staffs abroad on the assumption that these managers are more steeped in the firm's policies and culture and more likely to unquestioningly implement headquarters' instructions.

International Staffing Policy

Multinational firms' top executives are often classified as either ethnocentric, polycentric, or geocentric.[34] In an ethnocentric corporation, ". . . the prevailing attitude is that home country attitudes, management style, knowledge, evaluation criteria, and managers are superior to anything the host country might have to offer."[35] In the polycentric corporation, "there is a conscious belief that only host country managers can ever really understand the culture and behavior of the host country market; therefore, the foreign subsidiary should be managed by local people."[36] Geocentrism, rarely seen, assumes that management candidates must be searched for on a global basis, on the assumption that the best manager for any specific position anywhere on the globe may be found in any of the countries in which the firm operates.

These three multinational attitudes translate into three international staffing policies. An ethnocentric staffing policy is one in which all key management positions are filled by parent-country nationals.[37] At Royal Dutch Shell, for instance, virtually all financial controllers around the world are Dutch nationals. Reasons given for ethnocentric staffing policies include lack of qualified host-country senior management talent, a desire to maintain a unified corporate culture and tighter control, and the desire to transfer the parent firm's core competencies (for instance, a specialized manufacturing skill) to a foreign subsidiary more expeditiously.[38]

A polycentric-oriented firm would staff foreign subsidiaries with host-country nationals and its home-office headquarters with parent-country nationals. This may reduce the local cultural misunderstandings that expatriate managers may exhibit. It will also almost undoubtedly be less expensive. One expert estimates that an expatriate executive can cost a firm up to three times as much as a domestic executive because of transfer expenses and other expenses such as schooling for children, annual home leave, and the need to pay income taxes in two countries.[39]

A geocentric staffing policy "seeks the best people for key jobs throughout the organization, regardless of nationality."[40] This may allow the global firm to use its human resources more efficiently by transferring the best person to the open job, wherever he or she may be. It can also help build a stronger and more consistent culture and set of values among the entire global management team. Team members here are continually interacting and networking with each other as they move from assignment to assignment around the globe and participate in global development activities.

Selecting International Managers

There are common traits that managers to be assigned domestically and overseas will obviously share. Wherever a person is to be posted, he or she will need the technical knowledge and skills to do the job and the intelligence and people skills to be a successful manager, for instance.[41]

However, as discussed earlier in this chapter, foreign assignments make demands on expatriate assignees that are different from what the manager would face if simply assigned to a management post in his or her home country. There is the need to cope with a work force and management colleagues whose cultural inclinations may be drastically different from one's own, and the considerable stress that being alone in a foreign land can bring to bear on the single manager. And, of course, if spouse and children will share the assignment, there are the complexities and pressures that the family will have to confront, from learning a new language, to shopping in strange surroundings, to finding new friends and attending new schools.

Selecting managers for expatriate assignments, therefore, means screening them for traits that predict success in adapting to what may be dramatically new environments. A list of such expatriate selection traits would include:[42]

Adaptability and flexibility: ability to adapt to new circumstances and situations and to respond flexibly to different and often novel ideas and viewpoints.[43]

Cultural toughness: the ability to succeed in an alien culture.

Self-orientation: self-esteem, self-confidence, and mental well-being.

Others orientation: the ability to interact effectively with host-country nationals and more generally to develop long-lasting friendships.[44]

Perceptual ability: the ability to understand why people behave as they do and to empathize with them.

Family adaptability: the ability of the manager's spouse and children to adapt to and be happy in the foreign environment.

A recent study identified five factors perceived by international assignees to contribute to success in a foreign assignment. They were job knowledge and motivation, relational skills, flexibility/adaptability, extracultural openness, and family situation. (Some of the specific items that constitute each of these five factors are presented in Figure 18.2).[45] In this study 338 international assignees from many countries and organizations completed questionnaires; they were asked to indicate which of various listed managerial traits were important for the success of managers on foreign assignment. Various reported items including managerial ability, organizational ability, administrative skills, and creativity were then statistically combined into a single "job knowledge and motivation" factor. Respect, courtesy and tact, display of respect, and kindness were some of the items comprising the "relational skills" factor. "Flexibility/adaptability" included such items as resourcefulness, ability to deal with stress, flexibility, and emotional stability. "Extracultural openness" included variety of outside interests, interest in foreign countries, and openness. Finally, several items including adaptability of spouse and family, spouse's positive opinion, willingness of spouse to live abroad, and stable marriage comprise the "family situation" factor.[46]

The five factors were not equally important in the foreign assignee's success, according to the responding managers. As the researchers conclude, "Family situation was generally found to be the most important factor, a finding consistent with other research on international assignments and transfers."[47] Therefore, while all

Source: Adapted from Arthur Winfred Jr. and Winston Bennett, Jr., "The International Assignee: The Relative Importance of Factors Perceived to Contribute to Success,"*Personnel Psychology,* Vol. 48 (1995), pp. 106-107.

I) **Job Knowledge and Motivation**
   Managerial ability
   Organizational ability
   Imagination
   Creativity
   Administrative skills
   Alertness
   Responsibility
   Industriousness
   Initiative & energy
   High motivation
   Frankness
   Belief in mission & job
   Perseverance
II) **Relational Skills**
   Respect
   Courtesy & tact
   Display of respect
   Kindness
   Empathy
   Nonjudgmentalness
   IntegrityConfidence

III) **Flexibility/Adaptability**
   Resourcefulness
   Ability to deal with stress
   Flexibility
   Emotional stability
   Willingness to change
   Tolerance for ambiguity
   Adaptability
   Independence
   Dependability
   Political sensitivity
   Positive self-image
IV) **Extra-Cultural Openness**
   Variety of outside interests
   Interest in foreign cultures
   Openness
   Knowledge of local language(s)
   Outgoingness & extraversion
   Overseas experience
V) **Family Situation**
   Adaptability of spouse & family
   Spouse's positive opinion
   Willingness of spouse to live abroad
   Stable marriage

five factors were perceived as important to the foreign assignee's success, the company that ignores the candidate's family situation does so at its peril.

Adaptability Screening This being the case, *adaptability screening* is generally recommended as an integral part of the expatriate screening process. Generally conducted by a professional psychologist or psychiatrist, adaptability screening aims to assess the family's probable success in handling the foreign transfer and to alert the couple to personal issues (such as the impact on children) the foreign move may involve.[48]

Past experience is often the best predictor of future success. Companies like Colgate-Palmolive, therefore, look for overseas candidates whose work and non-work experience, education, and language skills already demonstrate a commitment to and facility in living and working with different cultures.[49] Even several successful summers spent traveling overseas or participating in foreign student programs would seem to provide some concrete basis for believing that the potential transferee can accomplish the required adaptation when he or she arrives overseas.

Realistic previews at this point are also crucial. Again, both the potential assignee and his or her family require all the information you can provide on the problems to expect in the new job (such as mandatory private schooling for the children) as well as any information obtainable about the cultural benefits, problems, and idiosyncrasies of the country in question. International human resource managers speak about avoiding culture shock in much the same way as we discussed using realistic previews to avoid reality shock among new employees. In any case, the rule here is to spell it out ahead of time, as firms like Ciba-Geigy do for their international transferees.[50]

There are also paper-and-pencil tests that can be used to more effectively select employees for overseas assignments. Generally speaking, of course, any such test should be company specific and validated as a tool for placing candidates overseas. However, experts have developed and validated general-purpose tests that focus on the aptitudes and personality characteristics of successful overseas

Diversity Counts

Sending Women Managers Abroad

While the number and proportion of women managers working domestically has climbed fairly quickly in the past few years, the same apparently can't be said about sending women managers abroad. One recent estimate states that women filled only about 6% of the overseas international management positions at major companies, for instance, compared with about 37% of domestic U.S. management positions.[1]

This raises the interesting question of why more firms don't send more women managers abroad, and the answer seems to come down to several erroneous assumptions regarding sending women managers overseas. One myth is that women are reluctant to transfer overseas and/or simply do not want to be international managers. International management expert Nancy Adler points out that this myth seems to be based in part on research that has shown that when men are assigned overseas and are accompanied by their non-working spouses, the wife's inability to adjust is a major reason that the assignments fail. However, findings like these certainly do not necessarily extend to working career women. For example, surveys of more than one thousand MBAs revealed no significant difference between female and male MBAs in pursuing international careers. In fact, "more than 4 out of 5 MBAs—both women and men—wanted international assignment at some time during their career."[2] Yet the erroneous myth that women don't want to serve overseas remains a problem: In one series of interviews most women said that they found that it had never occurred to their employers to consider women for overseas posts.[3]

The fact that dual-career marriages make sending female managers abroad impossible is a second erroneous assumption limiting women managers' access to positions abroad. For example, in one survey, more than three-fourths of the HR executives sighted dual-career marriages as a reason for not sending women managers abroad, yet responses of women international managers in a separate interview indicated that dual-career couples' career problems can indeed be ironed out.[4]

Perhaps the most persistent impediment to sending women managers abroad is the assumption that they would face so much foreign prejudice that they could not succeed if sent. The assumption here is that foreigners in general (and foreign men in particular) in many societies are so unduly prejudiced against women managers that the latter could not do their jobs effectively. Yet, here also, the evidence belies the assumption: In one survey, all the women managers (97%) reported that their international assignments were successful.[5] Even in a historically patriarchal society like Hong Kong's, another study found that ". . . problems associated with their gender in conjunction with that specific cultural environment did not materialize and did not engender any significant impediment to [the women managers'] effective managerial performance in ways that might have been anticipated."[6] In other words, here too, as these researchers conclude, "the excuse used by some companies for not sending women on overseas assignments—that local values are antithetical to such female participation—appeared to be unfounded."[7]

1. Nancy Adler, "Women Managers in a Global Economy," *Training & Development,* April 1994, pg. 31.
2. Ibid., p. 32.
3. Ibid., p. 32.
4. Ibid., p. 32.
5. Ibid., p. 32–33.
6. R.I. Westwood and S.M. Leung, "International Studies of Management & Organization," Vol. 24, No. 3, p. 81.
7. Ibid., p. 81.

candidates. The Overseas Assignment Inventory is one such assessment tool. Based on 12 years of research with more than 7,000 candidates, the test's publisher contends that it is useful in identifying characteristics and attitudes such candidates should have.[51]

Training and Maintaining International Employees

Painstaking screening is just the first step in ensuring the foreign assignee's success. The employee may then require special training, and in addition international HR policies must be formulated for compensating the firm's overseas managers and maintaining healthy labor relations.

Orienting and Training Employees for International Assignments

When it comes to providing the orientation and training required for success overseas, the practices of most U.S. firms reflect more form than substance. One consultant says that despite many companies' claims, there is generally little or no systematic selection and training for assignments overseas. One relevant survey concluded that a sample of company presidents and chairpersons agreed that international business was growing in importance and required employees firmly grounded in the economics and practices of foreign countries. However, few of their companies actually provided such overseas-oriented training to their employees.[52]

Orientation and training for international assignments can help employees (and their families) avoid "culture shock" and better adjust to their new surroundings.

What sort of special training do overseas candidates need? One firm specializing in such programs prescribes a four-step approach.[53] Level 1 training focuses on the impact of cultural differences, and on raising trainees' awareness of such differences and their impact on business outcomes. Level 2 focuses on attitudes and aims at getting participants to understand how attitudes (both negative and positive) are formed and how they influence behavior. (For example, unfavorable stereotypes may subconsciously influence how a new manager responds to and treats his or her new foreign subordinates.) Finally, Level 3 training provides factual knowledge about the target country, while Level 4 provides skill building in areas like language and adjustment and adaptation skills. (Additional guidelines for developing international executives—such as "Brief candidates fully and clearly on all relocation policies," and "Provide all relocating executives with a mentor to monitor their overseas careers and help them secure appropriate jobs with the company when they repatriate"—were discussed in Chapter 8.)

Beyond these special training practices there is also the need for more traditional training and development of overseas employees. At IBM, for instance, such development includes using a series of rotating assignments that permits overseas IBM managers to grow professionally. At the same time, IBM and other major firms have established management development centers around the world where executives can come to hone their skills. Beyond that, classroom programs (such as those at the London Business School, or at INSEAD in Fountainebleu, France) provide overseas executives the sorts of opportunities to hone their functional skills that similar programs stateside do for their U.S.-based colleagues.

In addition to honing functional skills, international management development often aims to foster improved control of global operations by building a unifying corporate culture. The assumption here is that the firm should bring together managers from its far-flung subsidiaries and steep them for a week or two in the firm's cherished values and current strategy and policies. The managers should then be more likely to consistently adhere to these values, policies, and aims once they return to their assignments abroad.

International Compensation

The whole area of international compensation management presents some tricky problems. On the one hand, there is a certain logic in maintaining companywide pay scales and policies so that, for instance, divisional marketing directors throughout the world are all paid within the same narrow range. This reduces the risk of perceived inequities and dramatically simplifies the job of keeping track of disparate country-by-country wage rates.

Yet not adapting pay scales to local markets can present an HR manager with more problems than it solves. The fact is that it can be enormously more expensive to live in some countries (like Japan) than others (like Greece); if these cost-of-living differences aren't considered, it may be almost impossible to get managers to take "high-cost" assignments.

However, the answer is usually not just to pay, say, marketing directors more in one country than in another. For one thing, you could thereby elicit resistance when telling a marketing director in Tokyo who's earning $3,000 per week to move to your division in Spain, where his or her pay for the same job (cost of living notwithstanding) will drop by half. One way to handle the problem is to pay a similar base salary companywide and then add on various allowances according to individual market conditions.[54]

Determining equitable wage rates in many countries is no simple matter. We've seen that there is a wealth of "packaged" compensation survey data already available in the United States, but such data are not so easy to come by overseas. As a result, "one of the greatest difficulties in managing total compensation on a multinational level is establishing a consistent compensation measure between countries that builds credibility both at home and abroad."[55]

Some multinational companies deal with this problem for local managers by conducting their own annual compensation surveys. For example, Kraft conducts an annual study of total compensation in Belgium, Germany, Italy, Spain, and the United Kingdom. Kraft tries to maintain a fairly constant sample group of study participants (companies) in its survey. It then focuses on the total compensation paid to each of ten senior management positions held by local nationals in these firms. The survey covers all forms of compensation including cash, short- and long-term incentives, retirement plans, medical benefits, and perquisites.[56] Kraft then uses these data to establish a competitive value for each element of pay. This information in turn becomes the input for annual salary increases and proposed changes in the benefit package.

The most common approach to formulating expatriate pay is to equalize purchasing power across countries, a technique known as the balance sheet approach.[57] The basic idea is that each expatriate should enjoy the same standard of living he or she would have had at home. With the balance sheet approach, four main home-country groups of expenses—income taxes, housing, goods and services, and reserve—are the focus of attention. The employer estimates what each of these four expenses is for the expatriate's home country and also what each is expected to be in the expatriate's host country. Any differences—such as additional income taxes or housing expenses—are then paid by the employer.

The European Community unites 12 countries with many common bonds and many differences.

CAMBIO — WECHSEL —
EXCHANGE — CHANGE
SCENIC TRAVEL 28 05 1993

		N
DOLLARO USA	1431 1431	O
DOLLARO CANADESE	1100 1100	—
STERLINA INGLESE £2231 £2231		C
FRANCO FRANCESE	260 260	O
MARCO TEDESCO·D·M	882 882	M
FRANCO SVIZZERO	980 980	M
SCELLINO AUST	124 124	I
FIORINO OLANDESE	781 781	S
CORONA DANESE	225 225	S
CORONA SVEDESE	190 190	I
FRANCO BELGA	42 42	O
PESETA SPAGN	11 11	N
CORONA NORVEGESE	205 205	
MARCO FNL	255 255	
YEN GIAPPONESE	12·5 12·5	

FREE OF CHARGE
SANS COMMISSION

In practice this usually boils down to building the expatriate's total compensation around five or six separate components. For example, *base salary* will normally be in the same range as the manager's home-country salary. In addition, however, there might be an overseas or foreign service premium. This is paid as a percentage of the executive's base salary,[58] in part to compensate the manager for the cultural and physical adjustments he or she will have to make. There may also be several allowances, including a housing allowance and an education allowance for the expatriate's children. Income taxes represent another area of concern. In many cases a U.S. manager posted abroad may have to pay not only U.S. taxes but income taxes to the country to which he or she is posted, too.

One international compensation trend awards long-term incentive pay to overseas managers. While it may not seem particularly logical, many U.S. multinationals only permit the top managers at corporate headquarters to participate in long-term incentive programs like stock option plans.[59] Equally problematical is the fact that many of the multinationals that do offer overseas managers long-term incentives (32 of 40 in one survey) use only overall corporate performance criteria when awarding incentive pay. Since the performance of the company's stock on a U.S. stock market may have little relevance to, say, a manager in a German subsidiary, the incentive value of such a reward is highly suspect. This is particularly so in that, as one expert writes, "regardless of size, a foreign subsidiary's influence on its parent company's stock price (in U.S. dollars) is more likely to result from exchange rate movements than from management action."[60]

The answer here, more multinationals are finding, is to formulate new long-term incentives specifically for overseas executives. More and more U.S. multinationals are thus devising performance-based long-term incentive plans that are tied more closely to performance at the subsidiary level. These can help build a sense of ownership among key local managers while providing the financial incentives needed to attract and keep the people you need overseas.

Performance Appraisal of International Managers

Several things complicate the task of appraising an expatriate's performance.[61] For one thing, the question of who actually appraises the expatriate is a crucial issue. Obviously local management must have some input in the appraisal, but the appraisals may then be distorted by cultural differences. Thus, a U.S. expatriate manager in India may be evaluated somewhat negatively by his host-country bosses who find his use of participative decision making inappropriate in their culture. On the other hand, home-office managers may be so geographically distanced from the expatriate that they can't provide valid appraisals because they're not fully aware of the situation the manager actually faces. This can be problematical: The expatriate may be measured by objective criteria such as profits and market share, but local events such as political instability may undermine the manager's performance while remaining "invisible" to home-office staff.[62]

Two experts make five suggestions for improving the expatriate appraisal process:

1. Stipulate the assignment's difficulty level. For example, being an expatriate manager in China is generally considered more difficult than working in England, and the appraisal should take such difficulty-level differences into account.
2. Weight the evaluation more toward the on-site manager's appraisal than toward the home-site manager's distant perceptions of the employee's performance.

10. What do you think accounts for the fact that worker participation has a long and relatively extensive history in Europe? How do you think this relatively extensive participation affects the labor relations process?

11. As an HR manager, what program would you establish to reduce repatriation problems of returning expatriates?

Application Exercises

RUNNING CASE: Carter Cleaning Company Going Abroad

With Jennifer gradually taking the reigns of Carter Cleaning Company, Jack decided to take his first long vacation in years and go to Mexico for a month in January, 1996. What he found surprised him: While he spent much of the time basking in the sun in Acapulco, he also spent considerable time in Mexico City and was surprised at the dearth of cleaning stores, particularly considering the amount of air pollution in the area. Traveling north he passed through Juarez, Mexico and was similarly surprised at the relatively few cleaning stores he found there. As he drove back into Texas, and back towards home, he began to think about whether the NAFTA Agreement might not be enough of a boost to the Mexican economy to actually make it advisable to consider expanding his chain of stores into Mexico.

Quite aside from the possible economic benefits, he had liked what he saw in the lifestyle in Mexico and was also attracted by the idea of possibly facing the sort of exciting challenge he faced twenty years ago when he started Carter Cleaning in the U.S.: "I guess entrepreneurship is in my blood," is the way he put it.

As he drove home to have dinner with Jennifer, he began to formulate the questions he would have to ask before deciding whether or not to expand abroad.

Questions

1. Assuming they began by opening just one or two stores in Mexico, what do you see as the main HR-related challenges he and Jennifer would have to address?

2. How would you go about choosing a manager for your new store if you were Jack or Jennifer? For instance, would you hire someone locally or send someone from one of your existing stores? Why?

3. The cost of living in Mexico is substantially below that of the Southeastern United States where Carter is now located: How would you go about developing a pay plan for your new manager if you decided to send an expatriate to Mexico?

4. Present a detailed explanation of the factors you would look for in your candidate for expatriate manager to run the stores in Mexico.

Video Case

Self-Directed Work Teams

By focusing on self-directed work teams at Rockwell, this videocase helps to summarize a number of the concepts and techniques in this book. As you'll see in this video, self-directed work teams of ten to fifteen workers decide their schedules and monitor their own quality—and Rockwell's products are widely acclaimed for their quality. Interestingly, self-directed work teams apparently don't just boost quality: The number of workers at Rockwell declined over the period depicted in this case by about 800 workers at this plant even while missile production and quality both rose.

Questions

1. What compensation program is credited for employees' making their own decision to close the plant for two weeks when there was an insufficient order backlog?

2. Why is it unusual for a company like Rockwell to use the HR methods it is using?

3. What impact do Rockwell programs such as self-directed work teams appear to have on the commitment of Rockwell workers?

4. In what way does a program built around self-directed work teams require a comprehensive HR approach (one that includes recruitment and selection, for instance)? Please be specific.

Source: ABC News, *Self-Directed Work Teams,* "Business World," March 10, 1991.

Take It to the Net

We invite you to visit the Dessler page on the Prentice Hall Web site at:
http://www.prenhall.com/~dessler
for the monthly Dessler update, and for this chapter's World Wide Web exercise.

Appendix 18-1

A Final Word: Toward an HR Philosophy, and Auditing the HRM Function

Toward a Philosophy of HR Management

The Need for a Philosophy

In Chapter 1 we said that people's actions are always based in part on the assumptions they make, and that this is especially true in regard to human resource management. The basic assumptions you make about people—Can they be trusted? Do they dislike work? Can they be creative? Why do they act as they do?—comprise your philosophy of HR. And the people you hire, the training you provide, your leadership style all reflect (for better or worse) this basic philosophy.

Yet throughout this book we have emphasized the "nuts and bolts" of HR management by focusing on the concepts and techniques all managers need to carry out their personnel-related tasks. It is, therefore, easy to lose sight of the fact that these techniques, while important, cannot be administered effectively without a unifying philosophy. To repeat, it is this philosophy or vision that helps guide you in deciding the people to hire, the training to provide, and how to motivate employees.

For more and more employers, the essence of the difference between personnel management and human resource management is indeed a philosophical one; it revolves around the latter's emphasis on improving the employees' quality of work life, which means finding out how employees can better satisfy their important personal needs by working in the organization. In practice, this means providing employees with fair and equitable treatment, an opportunity for each employee to use his or her skills to the utmost and to self-actualize, open and trusting communications, an opportunity to take an active role in making important job-related decisions, adequate and fair compensation, and a safe and healthy work environment. Such actions can translate into improved commitment. However, this emphasis on satisfying employees' important personal needs at work goes beyond mere techniques. Building commitment not only depends on techniques but also on your basic values and assumptions about people. Thus, a Theory Y leader who believes the best about his or her subordinates will probably treat them in a way that enhances their commitment. In an organization with the opposite assumptions, you can be sure that lower commitment will prevail as the manager tries to closely monitor and control each worker's actions.

Every personnel decision you make affects your employees' quality of work life and commitment in some way. Thus, selection should emphasize placing the right person on the right job, where the person can have a more satisfying, actualizing experience. Similarly, an equitable grievance procedure will help protect employee rights and dignity and, therefore, contribute to the quality of work life of your employees. Every personnel action you take, in other words, affects your employees' commitment, and your actions will in turn reflect your basic assumptions about people. It is when your personnel actions are geared not just to satisfying your organization's staffing needs but also to satisfying your employees' needs to grow and to self-actualize that your personnel management system can be properly referred to as a human resource management system.

Building Employee Commitment

A Recap

Many employers translate such an HRM philosophy into practices that win their employees' commitment. Commitment-building HRM practices that we described in this book include the following:

Establish people-first values. As one manager said, "You start the process of boosting employee commitment by making sure you know how you and your top managers really feel about people." In other words, you must be willing to commit to the idea that your employees are your most important assets and that they can be trusted, treated with respect, involved in making on-the-job decisions, and encouraged to grow and reach their full potential. Then put those values in writing, hire and promote into management people who have people-first values from the start, and translate your people-first values into actions every day.

Guarantee fair treatment. Establish a "super" grievance procedure that guarantees fair treatment of all employees in all grievance and disciplinary matters. Boost upward and downward communications with Speak Up! programs. Institute multiple, formal, easy-to-use channels that employees can use to express concerns and gripes and to get answers to matters that concern them. Also use periodic opinion surveys such as survey-feedback-action, and use every opportunity to tell employees what's going on in your organization.

Use value-based hiring. The time to start building commitment is before—not after—employees are hired. High-commitment firms are thus very careful about whom they hire. Start by clarifying your firm's own values and ideology so they can be part of the screening process. Then make your screening process exhaustive, for instance, by designing screening tools like structured interviews to help select applicants based, in part, on their values. Recruit actively, so those who are hired see that many were rejected and that they are part of an elite. Go on to provide candid, realistic previews of what working at your firm will be like. Remember that self-selection is important—for instance, use long probationary periods or a long, exhaustive screening process that requires some "sacrifice" on the part of employees.

Provide for employee security. Practice lifetime employment without guarantees. While specifying that all employment relationships will be employment-at-will arrangements, emphasize your commitment to lifetime employment without guarantees with statements such as: "Stable employment and continual improvement of the well-being of our team members are essential and can be obtained through the smooth, steady growth of our company." Company practices that facilitate employee security include using a compensation plan that places much of each employee's salary at risk, hiring large numbers of temporary or part-time employees, and cross-training employees to wear "several hats."

Assess the rewards package. Build a pay plan that encourages employees to think of themselves as partners. This means employees should have a healthy share of the profits in good years and share in the downturn during bad times. Therefore, put a significant portion of pay at risk. Institute stock ownership plans that encourage employees to see they have a significant investment in your firm. Emphasize self-reporting of hours worked rather than devices like time clocks.

Actualize employees. High-commitment firms engage in actualizing practices that aim to ensure that all employees have every opportunity to use all their skills and gifts at work and become all they can be. Commit to actualizing, front-load new employees' jobs with challenge, enrich workers' jobs and empower them, and institute comprehensive promotion-from-within/ career progress programs.

Practices like these serve a dual role in organizations. They create a work environment that helps ensure that employees can use their aptitudes and skills to the fullest and satisfy their important personal needs by working in the organization. At the same time they can help an employer win the commitment of its employees by creating a situation in which the employees' and employer's goals become one. Then (it is hoped), employees do their jobs not just because they have to do them but because they want to do them—they do their jobs as if they own the company. And in an era that requires high levels of worker flexibility, creativity, quality, and initiative, committed employees are a firm's best competitive edge.[71]◆

Auditing the HR Function

Designing an HR system is not enough. Effectively implementing it is another.

Several suggestions have been made for ways to assess how a firm's HR department is actually doing. One approach is to use accounting and statistical techniques to calculate the cost of human resources, such as the dollar investment in human assets resulting from training. In this way the bottom-line contribution of HR can be quantitatively assessed.[72] For an employer with the wherewithal to conduct such a program, it may well be worth considering. A second, less rigorous, but still effective approach follows.

The HR Review

At a minimum, an HR review should be conducted, aimed at tapping top managers' opinions regarding how effective HR has been. Such a review should contain two parts: what should be, and what is.[73]

The question "what should be" refers to the HRM department's broad aims and involves two things. It should start, first, with a very broad philosophy or vision statement. This might envision HR as being "recognized as an excellent resource rather than a bureaucratic entity, a business-oriented function, and the conscience of the company," for example. This vision might also enumerate the characteristics of the HR staff, for instance, as "being experts in their areas of responsibility, demonstrating a commitment to excellence, and being creative, analytical problem solvers." The vision statement should thus set the tone for HR.

Second, this broad vision gets more focus with an HRM mission statement. This describes what the mission of the department should be, for instance, "to contribute to the achievement of the company's business objectives by assisting the organization in making effective and efficient use of employee resources and, at the same time, assisting employees at all levels in creating for themselves satisfying and rewarding work lives."[74]

Next the HR review's focus shifts to an evaluation of "what is." This part of the evaluation consists of six steps and requires input from the corporate HR staff, division heads, divisional HR heads, and those other experts (like the benefits administrator) who report directly to the head of corporate HR. The issues to be addressed are as follows:

1. *What are the HR functions?* Here those providing input (division heads and so forth) give their opinions about what they think HR's functions should be. The list can be extensive, ranging from EEO enforcement and health benefits management to employee relations management, recruitment and selection, training, and even community relations management. The important point here is to crystallize what HR and its main "clients" believe are HR's functions.

2. *How important are these functions?* The participants then rate each of these functions on a ten-point scale of importance, ranging from low (1–3) to medium (4–7) to high (8–10). This provides an estimate of how important each of the 15 or 20 identified HRM functions are in the views of HRM executives and of their clients (like division managers).

3. *How well is each of the functions performed?* Next have the same participants evaluate how well each of these HR functions is actually being performed. You may find, for example, that four functions—say, employee benefits,

compensation, employee relations, and recruiting—receive "high" ratings from more than half the raters. Other functions may get "medium" or "low" ratings.

4. *What needs improvement?* The next step is to determine which of the functions rated most important are not being well performed. Functions (like "labor relations") that are assessed as highly important but evaluated as low in terms of performance will require the quickest attention. To formalize the comparison of importance and performance ratings, have the participants compare the median importance and performance ratings for each of the 15 to 20 functions identified in step 1.

   The discussions at this stage will help identify the HR functions in which the department has to improve its performance. They should help to pinpoint specific problems that contributed to the low performance ratings and help provide recommendations for improving performance.

5. *How effectively does the corporate HR function use resources?* This next step consists of checks to determine whether the HR budget is being allocated and spent in a way that's consistent with the functions HR should be stressing. First, make an estimate of where the HR dollars are being spent—for instance, on recruiting, EEO compliance, compensation management, and so on. Questions to ask here are: "Is expense allocation consistent with the perceived importance and performance of each of the HR functions?" and "Should any dollars be diverted to low-performing functions to improve their effectiveness?"

6. *How can HR become most effective?* This final step is aimed at allowing you one last, broader view of the areas that need improvement and how they should be improved. For example, at this step it may be apparent that a large divisionally organized company needs to strengthen divisional and on-site HRM staffs so that responsibilities for certain HR functions can be moved closer to the user.

Notes

1. "The Gross National Product," *Occupational Outlook Quarterly* (Fall 1989), U.S. Department of Labor; see also Ellen Brandt, "Global HR," *Personnel Journal* (March 1991), pp. 38–44; and Charlene Marmer Solomon, "HR Heads into the Global Age," *Personnel Journal* (October 1993), pp. 76–77, and Gary Florkowski and Randal Schuller, "Auditing Human Resource Management in the Global Environment," International Journal of *Human Resource Management,*" Vol. 5, No. 4 (December 1994), pp. 827–851.

2. Gary Dessler, *Managing Organizations in an Era of Change* (Ft. Worth, TX: Dryden, 1995), Chapter 2.

3. See, for example, John Daniels and Lee Radebaugh, *International Business* (Reading, MA: Addison-Wesley, 1994), p. 544.

4. Dessler, *Managing Organizations in an Era of Change,* pp. 45–46.

5. Katherine Rudie Harrigan, "Joint Ventures and Global Strategies," *Columbia Journal of World Business,* Vol. 19 (Summer 1984), pp. 7–16; Michael Czinkota et al., *International Business* (Ft. Worth, TX: Dryden Press, 1992), p. 278.

6. Charles Hill, *International Business* (Burr Ridge, IL: Irwin, 1994), p. 4.

7. Richard Robinson, *Internationalization of Business: An Introduction* (Hindsdale, IL: Dryden, 1984), pp. 271–272.

8. Theodore Levitt, "The Globalization of Markets," *Harvard Business Review* (May–June 1983), pp. 92–102.

9. For a discussion, see Dennis Briscoe, *International Human Resource Management* (Englewood Cliffs, NJ: Prentice Hall, 1995), pp. 6–8.

10. Ibid., p. 6.

11. These are based on Eduard Gaugler, "HR Management: An International Comparison," *Personnel* (August 1988), pp. 24–30. See also Yasuol Kuwahara, "New Developments in Human Resource Management in Japan," *Asia Pacific Journal of Human Resources,* Vol. 31, no. 2 (1993), pp. 3–11; and Charlene Marmer Solomon, "How Does Your Global Talent Measure Up," *Personnel Journal* (October 1994), pp. 96–108.

12. For a discussion of this, see ibid., p. 26; see also George Palmer, "Transferred to Tokyo—A Guide to Etiquette in the Land of the Rising Sun," *Multinational Business,* no. 4 (1990/1991), pp. 36–44.

13. David Ralston, Priscilla Elsass, David Gustafson, Fannie Cheung, and Robert Terpstra, "Eastern Values: A Comparison of Managers in the United States, Hong Kong, and the People's Republic of China," *Journal of Applied Psychology,* Vol. 71, no. 5 (1992), pp. 664–671.

14. Geert Hofstede, "Cultural Dimensions in People Management," in Vladimir Pucik, Noel Tishy, and Carole Barnett (Eds.), *Globalizing Management* (New York: John Wiley & Sons, Inc., 1992), p. 143.

15. Ibid.

16. Gaugler, "HR Management," p. 27. See also Simcha Ronen and Oded Shenkar, "Using Employee Attitudes to Establish MNC Regional Divisions," *Personnel* (August 1988), pp. 32–39.

17. "Labor Costs in Manufacturing by Nation," *BNA Bulletin to Management,* August 4, 1994, pp. 244–245.

18. "Comparing Employment Practices," *BNA Bulletin to Management,* April 22, 1993, p. 1.

19. This is discussed in Gaugler, "HR Management," p. 28.

20. This is based on Rae Sedel, "Europe 1992: HR Implications of the European Unification," *Personnel* (October 1989), pp. 19–24. See also Chris Brewster and Ariane Hegewish, "A Continent of Diversity," *Personnel Management* (January 1993), pp. 36–39.

21. Daniels and Radebaugh, *International Business,* p. 764.

22. Charlene Marmer Solomon, "Success Abroad Depends on More than Job Skills," *Personnel Journal* (April 1994), p. 51.

23. R. L. Tung, "Selection and Training Procedures of U.S., European, and Japanese Multinationals," *California Management Review,* Vol. 25 (1982), pp. 51–71.

24. Discussed in Charles Hill, *International Business,* pp. 511–515.

25. Michael Schell, quoted in Charlene Marmer Solomon, "Success Abroad Depends on More than Job Skills," p. 52.

26. Daniels and Radebaugh, *International Business,* p. 767.

27. Arvind Phatak, *International Dimensions of Management* (Boston: PWS-Kent, 1989), pp. 106–107.

28. Ibid., p. 106.

29. Daniels and Radebaugh, *International Business,* p. 767.

30. Ibid., p. 768; Phatak, *International Dimensions of Management,* p. 106.

31. Phatak, *International Dimensions of Management,* p. 108.

32. Daniels and Radebaugh, *International Business,* p. 769.

33. Ibid., p. 769; Phatak, *International Dimensions of Management,* p. 106.

34. Howard Perlmutter, "The Torturous Evolution of the Multinational Corporation," *Columbia Journal of World Business,* Vol. 3, no. 1 (January–February 1969), pp. 11–14, discussed in Phatak, *International Dimensions of Management,* p. 129.

35. Phatak, *International Dimensions of Management,* p. 129.

36. Ibid.

37. Hill, *International Business,* p. 507.

38. Ibid., pp. 507–510.

39. Ibid., p. 509.

40. Ibid.

41. Phatak, *International Dimensions of Management,* p. 113; and Charlene Marmer Solomon, "Staff Selection Impacts Global Success," *Personnel Journal* (January 1994), pp. 88–101. For another view, see Anne Harzing, "The Persistent Myth of High Expatriate Failure Rates," *International Journal of Human Resource Management,* Vol. 6, No. 2 (May 1995), pp. 457–474.

42. These are based on Hill, *International Business,* pp. 513–516; Phatak, *International Dimensions of Management,* pp. 113–116; Daniels and Radebaugh, *International Business,* pp. 770–776; and Michael Czinkota, Pietra Rivoli, and Ilkka Ronkainen, *International Business* (Ft. Worth, TX: Dryden, 1992), pp. 514–516.

43. Phatak, *International Dimensions of Management,* p. 114.

44. Several of these are based on M. Mendenhall and G. Oddou, "The Dimensions of Expatriate Acculturation: A Review," *Academy of Management Review,"* Vol. 10 (1985), pp. 39–47.

45. Winfred Arthur, Jr. and Winston Bennett, Jr., "The International Assignee: The Relative Importance of Factors Perceived to Contribute to Success," *Personnel Psychology,* Vol. 48 (1995), pp. 99–114; table on pp. 106–107. See also Davison and Betty Punnett, "International Assignments: Is There a Role for Gender and Race in Decisions?" *International Journal of Human Resource Management,* Vol. 6, No. 2 (May 1995), pp. 411–441.

46. Ibid., pp. 105–108.

47. Ibid., p. 110.

48. Phatak, *International Dimension of Management,* p. 119.

49. See, for example, Blocklyn, "Developing the International Executive," p. 45.

50. Ibid., p. 45.

51. Discussed in Madelyn Callahan, "Preparing the New Global Manager," *Training and Development Journal* (March 1989), p. 30. The publisher of the inventory is the New York consulting firm Moran, Stahl & Boyer; see also Jennifer Laabs, "The Global Talent Search," *Personnel Journal* (August 1991), pp. 38–44 for a discussion of how firms such as Coca-Cola recruit and develop international managers, and T.S. Chan, "Developing International Managers: A Partnership Approach," *Journal of Management Development,* Vol. 13, No. 3 (1994), pp. 38–46.

52. Callahan, "Preparing the New Global Manager," pp. 29–30. See also Charlene Marmer Solomon, "Global Operations Demand that HR Rethink Diversity," *Personnel Journal* (July 1994), pp. 40–50.

53. This is based on ibid., p. 30. See also Daniel Feldman, "Repatriate Moves as Career Transitions," *Human Resource Management Review,* Vol. 1, no. 3 (Fall 1991), pp. 163–178; and John Yanouzas and Sotos Boukis, "Transporting Management Training into Poland: Some Surprises and Disappointments," *Journal of Management Development,* Vol. 12, no. 1 (1993), pp. 64–71. See also Jennifer Laabs, "How Gilette Grooms Global Talent," *Personnel Journal* (August 1993), pp. 64–76, and Charlene Marmer Solomon, "Transplanting Corporate Cultures Globally," *Personnel Journal* (October 1993), pp. 78–88.

54. James Stoner and R. Edward Freeman, *Management,* 4th ed. (Englewood Cliffs, NJ: Prentice Hall, 1989), p. 783. See also John Cartland, "Reward Policies in a Global Corporation," *Business Quarterly* (Autumn 1993), pp. 93–96; and Laura Mazur, "Europay,"*Across-the-Board* (January 1995), pp. 40–43.

55. Hewitt Associates, "On Compensation," (May 1989), p. 1 (Hewitt Associates, 86–87 East Via De Ventura, Scottsdale, Arizona 85258).

56. Hewitt Associates, "On Compensation," p. 2.

57. Hill, *International Business,* pp. 519-520.

58. Phatak, *International Dimensions of Management,* p. 134.

59. This is based on Brian Brooks, "Long-Term Incentives: International Executives Need Them, Too," *Personnel* (August 1988), pp. 40–42. See also James Ward and Mark Blumenthal, "Localization: A Study in Cost Containment," *Innovations in International Compensation,* Vol. 17, no. 4

(November, 1991), pp. 3–4. See also Laura Mazur, "Europay," *Across the Board,* Vol. 32, No. 1 (January 1995), pp. 40–43.

60. Brooks, "Long-Term Incentives," p. 41.

61. Except as noted, this is based on Gary Addou and Mark Mendenhall, "Expatriate Performance Appraisal: Problems and Solutions," in Mark Mendenhall and Gary Addou, *International Human Resource Management* (Boston: PWS-Kent Publishing Co., 1991), pp. 364–374.

62. Ibid., p. 366. See also Maddy Janssens, "Evaluating International Managers' Performance: Parent Company Standards as Control Mechanism," *The International Journal of Human Resource Management,* Vol. 5, no. 4 (December 1994), pp. 853–873.

63. Robert Sauer and Keith Voelker, *Labor Relations: Structure and Process* (New York: Macmillan, 1993), pp. 510–525.

64. Ibid., p. 516. See also Marino Regini, "Human Resource Management and Industrial Relations in European Companies," *The International Journal of Human Resource Management,* Vol. 4, no. 3 (September 1993), pp. 555–568.

65. Quoted from ibid., p. 519.

66. Definition based on Dennis Briscoe, *International Human Resource Management,* p. 65. See also Linda Stroh, "Predicting Turnover Among Repatriates: Can Organizations Affect Retention Rates?" *International Journal of Human Resource Management,* Vol. 6, No. 2 (May 1995), pp. 443–456.

67. Phatak, *International Dimensions of Management,* p. 124. See also Reyer Swaak, "Today's Expatriate Families: Dual Careers and Other Obstacles," *Compensation and Benefits Review,* Vol. 27, No. 3 (May 1995), pp. 21–26.

68. These are based on Briscoe, *International Human Resource Management,* p. 66; Phatak, *International Dimensions of Management,* p. 124; and Daniels and Radebaugh, *International Business,* p. 772.

69. Briscoe, *International Human Resource Management,* p. 66.

70. Phatak, *International Dimensions of Management,* p. 126.

71. For a discussion of employees as a competitive advantage see, for example, Peg Anthony and Lincoln Norton, "Link HR to Corporate Strategy." *Personnel Journal,* April 1991, pp. 75-86. Several studies suggest that personnel policies do tend to cluster, indicating that HR policies flow in a consistent manner from a firm's strategy. In one study six policy areas—job design, promotions, recruiting, training, grievance procedures, and communication clustered into "high-commitment" versus "rigid, formalized" HR systems. In a second study, Arthur found that HR systems in a steel mill could be categorized as emphasizing either cost reduction or employee commitment. Personal correspondence with Professor Casey Ichniowski, Graduate School of Business Administration, Columbia University, Uris 713, New York, NY 10027, April 1990; Jeffrey Arthur, "The Link Between Business Strategy and Industrial Relations Systems," *Industrial and Labor Relations Review,* Vol. 45, no. 3 (April 1992), pp. 488–506.

72. For a recent discussion along these lines, see Joel Lapointe and Jo Ann Verdin, "How to Calculate the Cost of Human Resources," *Personnel Journal* (January 1988), pp. 34–45.

73. This is based on Bruce R. Ellig, "Improving Effectiveness Through and HR Review," *Personnel* (June 1989), pp. 56–64.

74. Ibid., p. 57.

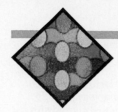

Index
Name and Organization

Note: Key terms are boldface.

A

Abbasi, Sami M., 364
Abbott Laboratories, 652
Adkins, John I., Jr., 638
Adler, Nancy, 682
Administrative Management Society (AMS), 428
Adolf Coors, 193
Aerospace Company, 526
Aetna Life and Casualty Company, 64, 153, 483
AFL-CIO, 544, 548–49, 555, 579, 626
Airwick Industries, 480
Alamo Rent-a-Car, 268
Albrecht, Karl, 641
Alcoa Aluminum, 12, 688
Allegheny Ludlam, 299
Allen, R.W., 130
American Airlines, 23, 60
American Association of Retired Persons, 526
American Contract Services, 155
American Express, 530
American Federation of Labor, 544
American Federation of Labor and Congress of Industrial Organizations (AFL-CIO), 544, 548–49, 555, 579, 626
American Management Association (AMA), 264, 287, 288, 426, 428
American Psychological Association (APA), 38, 174, 175, 192
American Telephone & Telegraph Company (AT&T), 13, 15, 109, 182, 392
America on-Line, 155
AMP Incorporated, 259
AMR International, Inc., 287
Andersen Consulting, 262
Antonion, David, 373
Apex Engineering, 673
Apple, 11, 21
Aramco, 46
Argyris, Chris, 285, 402
Arthur Andersen, 23
Asea Brown Boveri (ABB), 11, 16, 17
Assessment Systems Corp., 199
Association of Executive Recruiting Consultants, 144
Atchison, Thomas, 427
Austin-Hayne, 359
Avolio, Bruce, 286
Avontos, 359

B

Babbage, Charles, 108
Baer, Walter, 576
Bakke, Allen, 69
Barksdale, James, 595
Barnevik, Percy, 16
Barra, Anthony J., 531
Barrett, Gerald, 364

Bartley, Douglas, 88, 433
Bartol, Kathryn, 364
Bass, Bernard, 286
Baxter Healthcare Corporation, 66
Beach, Dale, 574
Beatty, James R., 464
Beatty, Richard W., 464
Belcher, David, 427
Ben & Jerry's, 403
Berlitz, 303
Bermant, Charles, 298
Best Western Hotels, 315
Blake, Robert R., 297
Blue Cross/Blue Shield, 513
Boeing Commercial Airline Group, 274–75
Bolles, Richard, 412
Borman, Walter C., 356
Boureslan, Ali, 46
Braniff Airlines, 13
Brett, Jeanne M., 545
British Petroleum (BP), 111, 283, 399
Buford, James, Jr., 347
Burger, Warren Earl, 43, 58
Burger King, 20
Burkhalter, Bettye, 347
Bush, George, 46, 49
Byham, William C., 182

C

Cadillac Motor Car Division, 321
California State University School of Business and Public Administration, 290
Campbell, David P., 388
Campbell Soup Company, 554
Career Placement Registry, Inc. (CPR), 149–50
Carnegie Mellon University, 10
Carrell, Michael R., 585
Caterpillar, 573
CBS School for Management, 292
Champy, James, 110, 312, 332, 334
Chaparral Steel, 299
Chesebrough-Ponds USA, 110
Cho, Fujio, 235
Chrysler Corporation, 563
Ciba-Geigy, 302, 681
CIGNA International Property and Casualty Corp., 284
Citibank, 132, 671
Citicorp, 17, 610
Clinton, Bill, 508, 554
Cobb, Douglas Ford, 489
Coca-Cola, 154, 672
Colgate-Palmolive Company, 24–25, 302, 681
Columbia University, 290
CompuServe, 155
Conference Board, 287
Control Data Corporation, 609
Cook, Mary F., 129, 188
Corning, Inc., 325, 326, 581
Corning Glass, 299
Cray Research, Inc., 155

Crispen, Patrick, 271
Crocker National Corporation, 23
Crotonville, 292

D

Delta Airlines, 15, 37, 130, 402–3
Deming, W. Edwards, 321, 372
DHL, 23
DIALOG INFORMATION SERVICES, INC., 149, 150
Diamond Walnut Growers, 554
Digital Equipment Corporation, 366
Diner's Club, 610
Displaced Homemakers Network, 152
Division 14 (Division of Industrial and Organizational Psychology), 174
Domino's Pizza, 20
Dow Chemical, 302–3, 687
Drake, John, 234
Drake Bean Morin, Inc., 397, 607
Drucker, Peter, 12, 15
Dubrin, Andrew J., 307
Dufetel, Laurent, 440
DuPont, 484, 487, 627
Du Pont Canada, 635–36
Duracel International, Inc., 520, 610

E

Eastern, 13
Equifax Services, 193
Excellence in Training Corp., 651

F

Famularo, Joseph, 147, 249, 352
Farm Labor Organizing Committee, 554
Federal Express Corp., 18–19, 22, 23, 24, 130, 131, 235, 321, 367, 402, 405, 492–94, 516, 533–34, 591, 593, 594–95, 596, 611
Federal Reserve Bank of St. Louis, 132
Feinberg, Mortimer, 370
Fidelity Investments, 135, 416
Filipczak, Bob, 271
Financial Executives Institutes, 428
Fine, Sidney A., 98
Fleishman, Edwin A., 183
Florida Power & Light Company (FPL), 321–23
Ford Motor Company, 11, 258
Franciscan Health System of Dayton, 196
Fred Meyer Discount Superstore, 298
Freudenberger, Herbert, 642
Frito-Lay, 19
Fucini, J.J., 337
Fucini, S., 337

G

General Electric Company, 15, 109, 131, 284, 292, 298, 299, 439, 475, 554, 601–2, 672, 679

S

Sackhein, Kathryn, 194
Safety, Inc., 648
Salomon Brothers Inc., 140
Saturn Corporation, 15, 21, 24, 29–30,
    266–67, 268, 300, 325, 327–29, 331, 393,
    394, 402, 404, 441–42, 487, 591, 593, 594,
    611
Sayles, Leonard R., 497
Scanlon, Joseph, 485
Scanlon Plan Associates, 485
Schein, Edgar H., 389–92, 394
Schmitt, Neal, 183, 197
Seattle First National Bank, 527
Sedel, Rae, 676
Shell, 283
Smith, Adam, 108
Smith, Fred, 18, 595
Society for Human Resource Management,
    428
Society for Industrial and Organizational
    Psychologists (SIOP), 174
Sony Corporation, 672, 673
Spratt, Michael F., 483
Standohar, Paul D., 457
Stanford University, 415
Stanton Corporation, 192, 193
State Farm Insurance Companies, 34
Steelcase Office Furniture Company, 591
Steele, Bernadette, 483
Stevens, George, 656
Strauss, George, 497
Stromberg Company, 16
Sullivan, John F., 482
Sumitomo Bank, 673
Sun Life of Canada, 264
Swart, J. Carroll, 649
Sweeney, John, 579

T

Tandy Corporation, 25
Target, 10
Taylor, Frederick Winslow, 108, 471
Teamsters Union, 548, 554
Technicon, 290
Texas Instruments Company, 250, 295–96,
    325
Thieme, Steve, 275
Thomas, Clarence, 38
Tiffin, Joseph, 630
Time Life, 300
Touche Ross, 137
Townsend-Smith, Richard, 447
Toyota Motor Corporation, 672
Toyota Motor Manufacturing USA, 11, 18, 21,
    24, 235–38, 248, 266, 268, 325, 326, 330,
    393, 394, 402, 439, 441, 487, 592, 594,
    611–12, 671, 672
Travelers Companies, The, 138
Trice, Harrison, 637

U

Unilever United States, Inc., 110
Union Carbide, 687
Union of Japanese Scientists and Engineers,
    321
Unisys Corp., 155
United Airlines, 23, 56
United Auto Workers, 441, 450, 548, 573,
    579
United Electrical Workers, 554
U.S. Chamber of Commerce, 195
United Steelworkers Union, 485, 579
United Technologies, 444
University of California at Berkeley, 288
University of Chicago, 288

UPS, 23
Urban Institute, 225
US Air, 23

V

Verser, Gertrude Casselman, 291
Vincze, Julian W., 19
Volvo, 21

W

Wackenhut Corporation, 193
Wagner, Robert, 580
Wal-Mart, 20, 21
Walters, Barbara, 76
Waltz, Dennis, 326
Wang Laboratories, 526
Weber, Brian, 69
Welch, Jack, 15, 131, 475
Wellins, Richard, 330
Wells Fargo, 23
Westwood, R.I., 682
Weyerhaeuser Company, 258
Winter, Wyman & Co., 155
WITF, Channel 33 of Harrisburg, 259
World Wide Web, 155
Wright, Gail J., 61
Wright, Martin, 320
Wrigley Company, 151

X

Xerox Corporation, 151, 250, 299
Xerox Educational Systems, 287

Y

Yoder, Dale, 457

Subject

legal issues in, 421–24, 453–54
line vs. staff responsibilities in, 7
of managers, 443–45
of overseas employees, 451
policies, 421, 424–25, 453
of professional employees, 445–46
Title VII and, 59
traditional vs. career development focus in, 383
unemployment, 423–24
union influences on decisions on, 424
Compensation managers, 5
Competence
as career anchor, 389
core competencies, 21
promotion based on, 398
Scanlon Plan and demands for, 485
Competence testing, 437
Competition, global, 11
Competition Scale, 293
Competitive advantage, 20–21
Competitive intelligence, 23
Competitive strategy, 19–20
Competitors, new, 14
Comprehensive Occupational Safety and Health Reform Act (1991), 626
Comprehensive Omnibus Budget Reconciliation Act (COBRA) of 1985, 518
Compression, salary, 449–50
Compulsory arbitration, 65–66
Computer-aided design/computer-aided manufacturing systems, 10
Computer-based training (CBT), 261–62
Computer-interactive performance test, 183
Computerized attitude surveys, 320
Computerized employee data bases, 149–50
Computerized forecast, 122
Computerized information systems, 123–26
Computerized job bank, Department of Labor, 135–36
Computerized job evaluation, 440
Computerized Management Assessment and Development Programs, 293–94
Computerized management game, 286–87
Computerized performance appraisal, 359
Computerized selection interview, 222–23, 224
Computerized testing programs, 199
Computers. *See also* Information technology
benefits administration and, 530–32
estimating offers costs with, 570
in labor relations, 556
to monitor safety, 648
Computing, distributed, 10–11
Concession, 567
Conciliation proceedings, 61–62, 64
Concurrent validation, 172
Conditions, bargaining, 567
Conditions, working. *See* Working conditions
Conferences, fact-finding, 64
Confidential record-keeping system, 525
Consent decrees, 48
Consent election, 558
Consistency, internal, 170
Consortium employee assistance programs, 524
Constitutional amendments, 34
Construct validity, 211n10
Consultants
decertification elections and, 566
executive marketing, 412–14
labor relations, 555–56
Contacts, personal, 411
Content validity, 170, 173
Contingent workers, 12, 141–43

Continuing education programs, 288
Continuing education units (CEUs), 287–88
Contract(s)
labor, administration of, 574–77
pension, 423
performance, 373–74
"yellow dog," 549
Contracting out work, 572
Contractors
federal, 36, 37
independent, 454
Contrast error, 227
Contributors, key, 483
Control
functional, 5
as managerial function, 2
worker, 579
Controlled experimentation, 270
Conventional orientation, 387
Conventional Scale, 293
Conviction records, 59
Cooperation
creative, 4
employee, 430
philosophy of (Scanlon plan), 485
union-management, 579
Coordination, 632
Coordinative function of personnel manager, 5
Core competencies, 21
Corporate campaign, 572–73
Corporate culture, 318–19, 683–84
Corporation
global, 672
multinational (MNC), 672
Correlation analysis, 172
Cost containment/reduction
AIDS and, 516–17
controlling workers' compensation, 512–13, 635
in health benefits, 514–16
labor and, 4
Cost leadership, 21
Cost-of-living adjustment (COLA), 450
Cost-of-living differentials, 450–51
Costs
labor, 4, 674–75
of selection process, 168
Counseling
career, 412, 524, 688
computerized career and job search, 397
family, 524
financial, 524, 527
in-house, 637
job placement, 524
outplacement, 607
preretirement, 406–8, 524, 612
Counseling services, 524
Counteroffers in collective bargaining, computer estimates of costs of, 570
Country club, company, 525
Court of Appeals, Second Circuit, 56
Court rulings, decline of unions and. *See also* Supreme Court
Coworkers, hostile environment created by, 39–40
Crawford Small Parts Dexterity Test, 178
Creativity as career anchor, 389–90
Credit check, 193
Credit unions, 524
Crime, white-collar, 192
Criteria (standards of success), 171
Criterion problem, 210
Criterion score, 206, 207–8
Criterion validity, 170, 173

Critical incident-based situational question, 229
Critical incident method, 351, 362
Critical incidents, 353–54
Cross-Cultural Technology Transfer, 265
Cross-Cultural Training and Orientation, 265
Cross-functional teams, 322
Cross-validation, 172 73
Cultural Awareness Programs, 265
Cultural subsidy, 525
Cultural toughness, 680
Culture
company, 318–19, 683–84
international differences in, 673–74, 683
training abroad and, 266
Customer service incentive plans, 483
Customer-service training, 268
CyberFairs, 155

D

Data bases, employee, 149–50
Davis-Bacon Act (1931), 422
Day care facility, on-site or near-site, 528
Day-to-day collective bargaining, 574
Day work, 421
Death benefits, 518
Decertification elections, 566
Decision making, participative, 331–32
Decision-making leave, 598
Decisions
career-related. *See* Career management
promotion, 398–99
Decline stage of career cycle, 386
Deductible formula, 475
Defamation, 175–76, 185, 186, 188, 195, 213n62, 215n116
Defense, rings of, 609
Defensiveness, 370
Deferred profit-sharing plan, 484, 519
Deficit Reduction Act (1984), 484
Defined benefit pension plan, 519
Defined contribution plan, 519, 522
Degree of a factor, 463, 464
Degree programs, 290
De-jobbing, trend toward, 109–12
Demands, 567, 568
Deming Prize, 321
Denial, 370
Denmark, 676
Dental plans, 513–14, 529
Department of Labor job analysis, 93–96, 97
Dependence Scale, 293
Dependent care, 528
Deregulation, 13, 578
Development, 4, 123, 124. *See also* Career management; Management development; Training
executive, 301–5
needs, analysis of, 304–5
promotional, 403–4
Diary/log, 91
Dictionary of Occupational Titles (DOL), 98, 100, 101, 103–4, 106, 107, 389, 391, 452
Differential validity, 215n118
Differentiation strategy, 21
Dignity of subordinates, 597
Dilatory tactics, 567
Direct financial payments, 421
Directive interview, 217–20, 223
Disability claims, stress-related, 643
Disability insurance, 37, 513–18
Disability payments, 518

Information systems, 123–26
Information technology, 10–11
    appraisal statistics, 489
    attitude surveys, 320
    career counseling and, 397
    CD-ROM-based management development
        programs, 298
    computer-aided interview, 222–23, 224
    computerized job evaluations, 440
    computerized managerial assessment and
        development program, 293–94
    computerized performance appraisal, 359
    estimating offers costs with computers, 570
    human resource methods and influence of,
        312
    Internet and
        finding career on, 415, 416
        recruiting on, 155, 156, 415, 416
        training via, 271
    in job analysis and staffing, 95
    labor relations and, 556
    in testing, 183
    utilization analysis, 63
In-house counseling, 637
In-house employee assistance programs, 524
**In-house management development
    centers,** 281, 292
"Innovator" role of personnel manager, 5
Inside games, 573
Inspections, safety and health, 635
    OSHA, 621–24, 626–27
    self-inspection checklists, 658–65
Instructional objectives, 255. *See also* Training
Insubordination, 575, 601
Insurance, unemployment, 136–37, 504–7
Insurance benefits, 512–18, 532–33
    hospitalization, medical, and disability,
        513–18
    life, 513
    workers' compensation, 512–13
Intellectual capacity, 234
Intelligence, competitive, 23
Intelligence (IQ) tests, 177
Interactive video disk (IVD), 264
Interest inventories, 179
Internal comparison estimate, 170
Internal consistency, 170
Internal Revenue Code, 477, 519, 530
International assignments, 678–83
International Association of Firefighters v. *The
    City of Cleveland,* 70
International business, 670–97
    compensation management and, 451,
        684–85
    defined, 672
    equal employment opportunity abroad, 46,
        48–49
    growth of, 671
    inter-country differences in human
        resources management, 673–77
    internationalization, 671–77
    labor relations and, 686–87
    orienting for, 683–84
    participative decision making abroad,
        331–32
    performance appraisal and, 685–86
    recruiting sources for overseas employees,
        154
    repatriation and, 687–88
    selection for international assignments,
        678–83
    training for, 265–66, 683–84
    types of, 671–72
International executive, 302–3, 478
International investment, 672

International Protocol and Presentation, 265
International staffing policy, 679
International trade, 672
Internet
    finding job on, 415, 416
    recruiting on, 155, 156, 415, 416
    training via, 271
Interpersonal competence, 389
Interviews, 86–90, 181, 197
    appraisal, 221, 368–71
    closing, 233
    computer-aided, 222–23, 224
    direct observation in conjunction with, 90
    exit, 221, 507, 607
    legal issues, 223–25
    questions, 229, 231–33, 234, 243
    reviewing, 233
    selection, 197, 217–45
        common mistakes in, 225–28
        effective, 229–33
        guidelines, 230–33
        interviewee guidelines, 242–43, 417
        small business application, 233–35
        steps in, 229–30
        types of, 217–23, 229–30
    termination, 605–7
    validity, 223
Intrinsic motivation, 490
Invasion-of-privacy suits, 175–76
Inventory(ies)
    interest, 179
    personnel, 123, 124
    qualifications, 123–26
    skills, 123–25
        computerized, 95
        management, 280
Investigations, background, 184–89
Investigative orientation, 387
Investment
    foreign direct, 671–72
    international, 672
Invoicing, 143
Involvement system (Scanlon plan), 485
Ireland, 677
ISO 9000 certification, 324–25
Italy, 677

J

Jackson v. *Minidoka Irrigation,* 602
Japan, 673–74
Jean Country case, 553
Jitters, first-day, 247
Job(s)
    benchmark, 425, 440, 445–46, 458
    changed requirements of, 601
    defined, 108
    defining, for performance appraisal, 343,
        344–45
    de-jobbing, trend toward, 109–12
    effect of job change, skill–based pay and,
        437
    "fee-paid," 137
    finding right, 411–17
    matching candidate to, 235
    unsafe, 628–30
Job analysis, 2, 82–117, 467n28
    defined, 83
    equal employment opportunity and, 86
    in factor comparison method, 458
    information for, 86–96
        Department of Labor (DOL) procedure,
            93–96, 97
        functional job analysis approach, 96, 98
        interviews, 86–90

observation, 90
participant diary/logs, 91
position analysis questionnaire (PAQ),
    93, 94
questionnaires, 87, 88–89, 90, 103, 104
U.S. Civil Service procedure for
    collecting, 91– 92
information technology in, 95
in "jobless" world, 108–12
in point method of job evaluation, 463
ranking method and, 431
small business application, 103–5
steps in, 84–86
structured interview and, 229
uses of, 83–84
validation process and, 171–72
Job analysts, 5
Job classification (or grading) evaluation
    method, 432–33, 445
Job clusters, 467n28
Job-comparison scale, 460–62
Job context, 83
Job description, 83, 85, 96–106, 253, 343,
    467n28
    authority, 100
    defined, 83
    future of, 110–11
    guidelines, 101–2
    job identification, 97–99
    job summary, 99–100
    in point method of job evaluation, 463
    relationships statement, 100
    responsibilities and duties, 100
    small business applications, 103–5
    standards of performance, 101
    temporary employees and, 143
    training and, 262
    working conditions and physical
        environment, 101
Job enlargement, 108
Job enrichment, 109, 327–29
Job evaluation, 116n9, 425, 492
    alternatives to, 437–39
    bias in, 447
    classification (or grading) evaluation
        method of, 432–33, 445
    comparable worth and, 447–48
    compensable factors in, 424, 428–30, 432,
        433, 444, 445, 463, 467n28
    computerized, 440
    factor comparison method, 434, 445,
        458–63
    managerial, 445
    manual for, 465
    pay rates establishment and, 428–34,
        452–53, 458–66
    planning and preparing for, 430–31
    point method of, 433–34, 445, 447,
        463–66
    purpose of, 428
    ranking method of, 431–32
    reasons for use of, 441
Job functions, essential, 102
Job instruction sheet (training sequence
    form), 263
Job instruction training (JIT), 257–58
Job knowledge
    expatriate selection and, 680, 681
    interviewer mistakes and, 226–27
    questions on, 229
Job pathing, 394
Job performance
    application forms to predict, 157–61
    conditions, 254
    employee selection and, 168

Job performance *(cont.)*
  improving, 4
  personality tests and, 179
  standards of, 83, 101, 173, 253, 360,
    488–89
  unsatisfactory, 601
Job placement counseling, 524
Job posting, 128–30, 131, 405
Job previews, realistic, 238, 394, 681
Job-related interviews, 221
Job-related service benefits, 525–27
Job-related training, 300
Job rotation, 108–9, 256, 280–83, 394
Job satisfaction, union representation and,
    545–47
Job search, 397, 411–14
Job Service agencies, state, 146, 452
Job sharing, 315, 528
Job specialization, 108, 116*n*25
Job specifications, 85–86, 96, 107–8, 253,
    467*n*28
  behavioral, 234
  defined, 83
  in point method of job evaluation, 463
Job stress, 640–42, 643
Job tenure, 158–60
John F. Winslow v. *Federal Energy Regulatory
    Commission,* 364
Johnson v. *Mayor and City Council of Baltimore,*
    55
Johnson v. *Transportation Agency, Santa Clara
    County,* 70
Joint venture, 672
Judgment
  job specifications based on, 107
  managerial, 122–23
  snap, in interviews, 225–26, 233
Junior boards, 284
Just-in-time employees. *See* Contingent
    workers

K

"Kaizen" production process, 238, 248
Kentucky Department of Employment
    Services, 237
Key contributors, rewarding, 483
Know-how as compensable factor, 430
Knowledge, 234
  task analysis of required, 255
  transferring, 300
Knowledge work, 12–13

L

Labor area, population of, 63
Laboratory, T-group, 294
Labor costs, 4, 674–75
Labor force, 9–10
Labor force. *See* Work force diversity
Labor law, 549–54
Labor Management Relations Act of 1947
    (Taft-Hartley Act), 519, 550–52
Labor-Management Reporting and Disclosure
    Act (Landrum-Griffin Act of 1959),
    552–53
Labor markets
  defining relevant, 53
  local conditions, 132
Labor movement, 544–49
Labor needs, planning, 2
Labor relations, 543–89. *See also* Unions
  collective bargaining process, 566–74
  computer applications in, 556
  consultants on, 555–56
  contract administration, 574–77

grievances, 574–77
international, 675, 686–87
laws on, 13
line vs. staff responsibilities in, 8
specialists on, 5
Lakefront vacations, 525
Landrum-Griffin Act (1959), 552–53
Language programs, 265
Language skills, 124
Language training, 265
Law(s), 13. *See also* Equal employment
    opportunity legislation; Legal issues;
    Supreme Court; *specific laws*
  common, 186
  immigration, 197–98
  labor, 549–54
  occupational safety, 13, 620–27
  on parental leave, 508–11
  wage garnishment, 424
  workers' compensation, 423
Layoffs, 362–63, 578, 608–9
Lead (element), 643
Leaderless group discussion, 181, 182
Leadership
  cost, 21
  Federal Express leadership evaluation
    program, 18–19
  as managerial function, 2
  managerial grid, 297
  styles, gender and, 286
  transactional-type, 286
  transformational, 286
Lead teams, 322
Learning
  action, 282, 284
  from experience, 299
  lifelong, 282, 300
  from others, 299
  principles of, 251–52
  programmed, 260–61
Learning organization, responsive, 297–300
Leasing, employee, 532–33
Leave
  of absence, 510–11
  decision-making, 598
  parental, 508–11, 528
  sick, 508–11
Lechmere, Inc. v. *NLRB,* 586*n*18
Lectures, training, 258
Legal issues
  AIDS at work, 37
  in background investigations and reference
    checks, 185
  in compensation, 421–24, 453–54
  in dealing with substance abuse, 639–40
  in employment references, 186–88
  interviewing and, 223–25
  in pay rates, 453–54
  in performance appraisal, 362–65
  safety programs, 620
  in selection, 168–69
  in testing, 174–76
    drug testing, 195–96
  in training, 252
  workplace violence and, 652–53
Legislation. *See* Law(s)
Leniency in performance appraisals, 360–61
Letters of reference, 186
Lewis v. *Equitable Life Assurance,* 188
Liability for negligent hiring, 168–69
Licensing, 671
Life-cycle stage of business, 492
Life insurance, 513
Lifelong learning, 282, 300
Lifetime employment without guarantees,
    611–12, 693

Lincoln Incentive System, 484
Line function of personnel manager, 4
Line management, 133, 302
Line manager, 3–8
  human resource management
    responsibilities, 4
Literacy training, 264
Literature, union, 564–65
Loans, management, 527
Local employment agencies, 452
Local equal employment opportunity
    legislation, 51, 52
Local labor market conditions, 131, 132
Local 28 Sheet Metal Workers v. *EEOC,* 69
Lockouts, 573, 588*n*66
Logs, job analysis and, 91
Long-term incentive program, 444,
    476–78
  for overseas managers, 685
Loss control goals, 635
Lump-sum merit raises, 481–82
Lunch-and-learn program, 525
Luxembourg, 677

M

McDonnell-Douglas Test, 53–54
Machines, information on, 83
Made in America, 262
Magazine advertisement, 134, 136
Maintenance stage of career cycle, 386
Major medical coverage, 513
Malcolm Baldrige National Quality Award,
    321
  criteria framework, 323–24
Managed care programs, 515
Management. *See also* Career management;
    Executives; Management development;
    Manager(s); Personnel management
  audit, 304
  bargaining preparation, 568
  cooperation with union, 579
  individual case (ICM), 516–17
  information technology in, 293–94
  loans, 527
  multiple, 284
  participative, 485
  quality circle and, 317–18
  resistance to flextime, 314
  scientific, 471
  traits, 293
Management assessment centers,
    181–84
Management by objectives (MBO), 357,
    362
Management development, 2, 279–310
  building responsive learning organization,
    297–300
  CD-ROMs and, 298
  computerized, 293–94
  defined, 280
  executive development, 281, 301–5
  nature and purpose of, 280–82
  new management practices, 13–17
  off-the-job techniques, 285–97
  on-the-job training, 282–84
  for responsive manager, 281–82
  in smaller organization, 303–5
  training contrasted with, 248
Management Development Seminar
    (University of Chicago), 288
Management games, 181, 182, 286–87
Management process, 2
Management review of written complaint,
    595
Management skills inventory, 280